Baseball Prospectus
2002

Jeff Bower
Clay Davenport
Jeff Hildebrand
Gary Huckabay
Rany Jazayerli
Chris Kahrl
Keith Law
Mat Olkin
Dave Pease
Joe Sheehan
Greg Spira
Michael Wolverton
Keith Woolner
Derek Zumsteg

Brassey's Sports

Brassey's

WASHINGTON, D.C.

ISBN 1-57488-428-X

Printed in the United States of America on acid-free paper that meets the American National Standards Institute Z39-48 Standard.

Brassey's, Inc.
22841 Quicksilver Drive
Dulles, Virginia 20166

Designed by Pen & Palette Unlimited

First Edition

10 9 8 7 6 5 4 3 2 1

Contents

Fungoes

Foreword

by Gary Huckabay

Welcome to *Baseball Prospectus 2002.* Thanks for choosing to spend some of your hard-earned money and even more valuable time on this book.

If you're familiar with previous *BP* annuals, you're probably familiar with what's inside. We've made a few small changes, primarily at your request, and we've tried to hang on to what you've told us you like. You will find more special-interest articles at the back of the book, and we've trimmed a couple of the more marginal players from team chapters where possible—call it our riff on contraction. The book is still heavy enough to use to clobber someone.

If this is your first purchase of a *Baseball Prospectus* annual, thanks for taking the leap! The basic goal behind what we're doing is to evaluate players with a minimum of external influences. The stats you see in the book aren't the actual stats of the players. Instead, they're a translation of each player's actual performance level into what that performance level would look like in a neutral ballpark in the majors. For more details on how this works and why we do it, check out Clay Davenport's explanation on page 1. The basic idea is that different environments can radically affect raw stats. A guy who hit .300 with 20 home runs in Dodger Stadium had a considerably better year than a guy who hit .300 with 20 home runs at Lancaster in the California League. All we're trying to do with these translations is put everyone's performance in context.

Some of this book can appear a bit intimidating. It's not meant to be. The basic concepts are pretty simple, and we try to focus on the implications and importance of the numbers, rather than just the numbers themselves. The essays that accompany the team chapters are often split between a post mortem of the previous season, and a look ahead at what's likely to occur in 2002 and beyond. Our prognostications are often subject to significant and hilarious error, but hopefully, even where we end up being a fair distance from reality, you'll find the material entertaining and thought-provoking. If you want to tell us how wrong we are ahead of time, and possibly be included in our annual "blooper reel" at the Web site, go to *www.baseballprospectus.com,* and send us an e-mail. Our butts are on the line, so why not add yours to the row?

When we started *Baseball Prospectus* in 1995, we took a certain pride in being outsiders. We weren't in the baseball industry, and we didn't really talk to anyone in the industry. This provided a high level of objectivity (or so we hoped), and it formed the base for the analysis and writing in this book and on our Web site. More than one of us chided other writers and columnists for being too close to people in the game to make the hard choices and write criticial pieces. As time has passed, we've pretty much lost that mantle, if we ever really had it in the first place. This book would be vastly different, and probably wouldn't be possible, if it weren't for the assistance of people in every front office in Major League Baseball and in the front offices of at least 30 minor league teams. We want to take this opportunity to thank everyone who took some of their valuable time to talk with people from *BP*. Thanks!

In addition, we want to thank the literally thousands of readers who have spread the word to their friends, league mates, spouses, and family pets. Our growth has been almost unmanageable, and it's entirely due to our readers and the generous support of people in the "mainstream" media around the country. We do appreciate the opportunity to discuss baseball in every forum, and it's been a tremendous amount of fun to meet and talk with people around the country. We thank all of you for your support. Every e-mail that comes in is read, and, occasionally, the person sending the e-mail is absorbed into *BP*.

This book is dedicated to the victims and families of the attacks in New York, Virginia, and Pennsylvania on September 11, 2001. I'm writing this in the very first few hours of 2002. 2001 was a miserable year for many, and we hope this book finds you doing better in 2002, with good health, generous spirit, and friends and family abundant in your life. We want 2002 to be a time of reborn optimism in every endeavor, no matter how trivial or profound.

This project is the result of the work of a few very dedicated baseball fans with very patient significant others, and we're honored to share our love of this awe-inspiring game with you. This book is no substitute for actually playing or watching a live baseball game, so if it's sunny outside, put the book down, make a couple of phone calls, grab a glove, a bat, and a bucket of balls, and go outside. The book will be here when you get back, and the household chores can wait. We appreciate your patronage, but we're realistic about the value of any book compared to dirt-and-grass baseball.

Go on. You'll feel better.

Gary Huckabay
Clayton, California
January 1, 2002

Davenport Translations

by Clay Davenport

> i got a baseball prospecus book of your with richard hidalgo on the cover. as i was thumbing through it, I started noticeing strange mistakes like in the case of ken griffey jr, and you have him down for 61 hr in 98. absolute bull #!@&. look on any baseball card and it will prove you wrong. the hero sammy sosa, you have him down for 64 hr in 1998, but he had 66, 63 in 1999, and 53 in 2000. all you stats contadict those. once again your stats are BULL &%#$!

We get letters like this from time to time, generally from people who haven't troubled themselves to read page one. Since you're reading this, we can assume that we won't get a similar letter from you, because you will understand the following:

This is not a baseball encyclopedia.

There are dozens of books available that have the players' real statistics in them. They're published by *Baseball America* and *The Sporting News* and STATS Inc. and Total Sports and Neft & Cohen, not to mention all the fantasy baseball magazines. They're on our shelves, and they can easily be on yours. Those books show you what the player did. Our book shows you what the player's performance was actually worth.

We are baseball analysts.

Baseball statistics are just numbers, but to anyone who has followed baseball enough, they are capable of telling more stories than a Southern politician. Like the politician's tales, though, not all of the stories are true. If a political story is part fact and part, er, exaggeration, a baseball stat is part player skill and part lie. How do baseball statistics lie?

- **With the offensive baseline.** To win, it doesn't matter how many runs a team scores; it only matters that they score more than their opponent. Other stats work the same way: what counts for a player is how much better he is than the league average. Different leagues have different baselines: the Carolina League hit .247 and averaged 4.0 runs per game, while the California League hit .264 and averaged 5.0 runs per game. Hitters look better in California, pitchers look better in Carolina, but it's just looks—the average player in the two leagues is really almost exactly the same. Our natural tendency is to apply one standard ("a .300 hitter") without considering the context of the performance.
- **With the ballpark.** Some parks are easier places to hit, and some are harder (when they're all easy, you have a hitters' league, like the pre-1998 Pacific Coast League, and the easy park looks average). Having a major-league team in Denver, one mile above sea level, has made people aware of this; the effect is far more important there than anywhere else in the majors. Still, there are other major-league stadia, such as The Ballpark in Arlington and Safeco Field in Seattle, where this effect makes a significant difference, one which is often ignored.

  This is also true in the minor leagues in places like Asheville, Myrtle Beach, El Paso, Tacoma, Lancaster, and New Orleans, where the parks are as big an influence within their own leagues as Coors Field is in the National League.
- **With the competition.** This one we know and often exaggerate. The majors are better than Triple-A, which is better than Double-A, and so on down to the complex leagues in Florida and Arizona. Players who hit .340 in A–ball cannot be expected to do the same in the majors, especially if they are old for their league.
- **With the wrong stats.** Although it is still working its way through the establishment, statistical knowledge in baseball has grown significantly in recent years. There are far better ways to measure player performance than batting average, home runs, and RBI.

Our job is to strip out the lies. What you see in this book are spin-free statistics, held to major-league standards.

We call them Translated stats, or Translations, or Davenport Translations, or DTs, depending on our mood. They are not, strictly speaking, a measure of what a player "could have done" in the majors or "should have done" or "will do"; they are a re-scaled measure of what he actually did, with the assumption that the biases affected him in an average way. If a hitter fails to take advantage of Coors Field, his stats will be marked down, because if he stays the same in a ballpark where everyone else gets better, he is now worse, relative to everyone else. Relativity is what the DTs are all about.

The first step in the DT process is to measure a player's overall performance. For a hitter, we use Equivalent Average, or EqA. This is one of those "better than batting average" statistics I just mentioned. If you take two teams in the same league at random, the chance that the team with the better batting average scored more runs is only about 50-50. The chance that the team with the better EqA scored more runs, though, is about 90%. That is because EqA not only uses the information contained in batting average (hits and at-bats), but also doubles, triples, home runs, walks, stolen bases, times caught stealing, and times hit by pitch. No published statistic that we have seen does a better job at estimating team run scoring over all of baseball history than does EqA, certainly not Linear Weights, Runs Created, or on-base-plus-slugging.

Equivalent Average has one other feature that makes it very useful for this book: it closely approximates the scale of batting average. This makes it easy for people who do not work with EqA on a daily basis to understand, at a glance, whether a given EqA is good or bad. The league-average EqA is always, by definition, .260. An EqA of .300 signifies a very good hitter—Eddie Murray and Eric Davis had career EqAs of .300. The best career mark is held by Babe Ruth at .375, not so far off from Ty Cobb's .366 lifetime batting average. The best single-season EqA now belongs to Barry Bonds, thanks to his staggering .427 in 2001. Again, that's close to the best single-season BA mark, whether you use Hugh Duffy's 1894 (.440), Nap Lajoie's 1901 (.426), or Rogers Hornsby's 1924 (.424). We won't go into EqA much further here; there is more info online at *http://www.baseballprospectus.com.*

Once you have calculated the player's EqA, including adjustments for league offensive level and home park, you have to adjust it for the quality of opposition. An average Triple-A player will see his EqA drop by about 14% upon moving to the majors. The difference between Double-A and the majors is about 20%; players in high-A leagues drop about 26%, low-A leagues about 30%, and the short-season leagues about 36%. An average hitter in the Pioneer League, with a .260 EqA there, would only be expected to hit for a .166 EqA in the majors; to be an average major-league hitter, he'd need to hit .406 in the Pioneer League.

It really does work all the way down: Rick Ankiel, with a major-league career EqA of .202, hit .316 in the Appalachian League last year. Apply a 36% penalty and you get . . . .202.

The final step in the Translations process is to produce a new statistical line for the player. This new statistical line has to have the following properties:

- It is normalized to a standard league, with a .270 batting average, .340 on-base percentage, and .440 slugging average.
- The translated stats must produce an Equivalent Average equal to the adjusted EqA calculated above for the player.
- The player's hit rate, walk rate, double rate, triple rate, home-run rate, and stolen-base rate, relative to the new standards, must be maintained as nearly as possible with his rates relative to his original league.

The last requirement is the killer; it simply isn't possible to maintain all of those rates simultaneously in all cases. As an example, if you tried to translate Babe Ruth's 1920 season—when his home-run rate was 13 times the league average—to a modern league, you get 250 home runs, but at the same time, his relative batting average calls for only 200 hits. The system recognizes that compromises must be made, that ratios cannot be perfect. The aberrations can be minimized, mathematically, and that is what the Translations program does: it finds the solution that produces the right EqA while minimizing the error in the various ratios.

Pitchers' statistics are calculated similarly. First, we go through a process of turning the pitching statistics into an equivalent batting line. We make it a point to note how much the pitcher's expected run total differs from his actual run total; we'll put that info back in after the Translation. Then the statistics are translated, with two changes from hitters. First, of course, they're translated in the opposite direction, so that the batting statistics look better as one moves up through organized baseball. Second, the adjustment is about one-third smaller, since a pitcher can expect better defensive support in the majors than he got in the minors. Once the translations are done, we simply rework them back into a pitching line.

Then there's the matter of fielding. The DTs list a fielding rating for a player's primary and, in some cases, secondary position. The system used is explained in detail beginning on page 4.

Section 1: Reading a Hitter's DT

Adam Dunn OF Bats L Age 22

YEAR	TEAM	LGE	AB	H	DB	TP	HR	BB	SO	R	RBI	SB	CS	OUT	BA	OBP	SLG	EQA	EQR	DEFENSE
1999	Rockford	Mid	318	75	13	1	7	29	70	39	27	10	6	249	.236	.309	.349	.225	30	64-LF -8
2000	Dayton	Mid	442	97	17	1	12	69	112	68	51	12	4	349	.219	.332	.344	.237	48	115-LF -6
2001	Chattang	Sou	144	42	5	0	10	19	30	24	24	4	2	104	.292	.380	.535	.297	25	39-LF -1
2001	Louisvil	Int	215	66	9	0	19	36	47	41	49	4	1	150	.307	.414	.614	.329	46	54-LF 0
2001	Cincnnti	NL	245	67	18	1	20	36	63	56	45	4	2	180	.273	.373	.600	.308	47	63-RF 2
2002	*Cincnnti*	*NL*	*534*	*154*	*25*	*1*	*36*	*84*	*135*	*105*	*90*	*12*	*5*	*385*	*.288*	*.385*	*.541*	*.302*	*96*	

The first line of all translations includes the player's name, his primary 2001 position(s), his batting handedness, and his age on July 1, 2002.

Translated statistics are provided for the 1999–2001 seasons and are all translated to the same scale. The average player on this scale has the line shown in Table 1.

Table 1. Average Player 1999–2001 Season

YEAR	TEAM	LGE	AB	H	DB	TP	HR	BB	SO	R	RBI	SB	CS	OUT	BA	OBP	SLG	EQA	EQR	DEFENSE	
2001	Anywhere	All	500	135	27	3	18	49	85	72	68	9	4	374	.270	.340	.440	.260	64	150-OF	0

Runs and runs batted in are computed by comparing the player's actual runs scored and runs batted in with his original equivalent runs, and assuming he would maintain the same relation with his adjusted equivalent runs.

The projection for the 2002 season is from the Wilton projection system, which combines a prognostic model (extrapolating from past performance, adding normal growth and decline patterns) with an analog approach (searching the database for players with similar batting profiles, and assuming future development similar to the comparisons). The numbers have been re-translated from the standard scale to the expected offensive environment of the park shown. However, the model does not attempt to guess major-league playing time. It estimates total playing time, based on the player's age and history, and produces a statistical line as if the player were going to receive all his playing time in the major leagues.

The fielding numbers show games played, position, and runs above average for that position. "Games played" in this case is the estimate of full nine-inning games played. Outfielders will show a specific position (left, right, center) if more than 50% of their playing time came there; otherwise, they will show as "OF." Even if one position is listed, though, the rating still includes performance at other outfield spots.

Section 2: Reading a Pitcher's DT

C.C. Sabathia — Throws L — Age 21

YEAR	TEAM	LGE	IP	H	ER	HR	BB	K	ERA	W	L	H/9	HR/9	BB/9	K/9	KW	PERA	STUFF
1999	MahngVal	NYP	18.0	16	10	0	16	13	5.00	1	1	8.0	0.0	8.0	6.5	0.4	3.14	8
1999	Columbus	SAL	15.0	15	9	2	7	10	5.40	1	1	9.0	1.2	4.2	6.0	0.7	1.40	19
1999	Kinston	Car	31.0	35	26	6	21	17	7.55	1	2	10.2	1.7	6.1	4.9	0.4	8.07	-7
2000	Kinston	Car	55.0	56	35	9	26	41	5.73	2	4	9.2	1.5	4.3	6.7	0.8	4.94	17
2000	Akron	Eas	88.7	87	53	10	51	65	5.38	4	6	8.8	1.0	5.2	6.6	0.6	4.72	15
2001	Clevelnd	AL	179.3	160	88	17	90	163	4.42	10	10	8.0	0.9	4.5	8.2	0.9	4.16	27

The first line of the pitcher DTs contains the same information as the batter DTs, except that it shows how he throws instead of how he bats.

The standard line for the pitcher DTs is shown in Table 2.

KW is the normalized strikeout-to-walk ratio. An average pitcher, in translation, has six strikeouts and three walks per nine innings, a ratio of 2.00, which is reported in the KW column as 1.0.

PERA is Peripheral ERA: the ERA you would expect from the pitcher given his other statistics. While there are pitchers whose ERA and PERA consistently differ in one direction or the other, in two out of three cases this difference seems to indicate nothing but luck. A pitcher whose actual ERA is considerably better than his PERA is likely to get worse in the future.

The Stuff statistic gives a quick evaluation of the pitcher's ability to start in the majors, with ten being an average major league score and zero being about the bottom of the majors. The stat is described more thoroughly in its own article on page 11.

Table 2. Standard Pitcher

YEAR	TEAM	LGE	IP	H	ER	HR	BB	K	ERA	W	L	H/9	HR/9	BB/9	K/9	KW	PERA	STUFF
2001	Anywhere	All	150.0	150	75	17	50	100	4.50	8	8	9.0	1.0	3.0	6.0	1.0	4.50	10

Fielding Translations

by Clay Davenport

Measuring defensive performance is one of the most contentious issues in sabermetrics. The problem is that fielding, especially good fielding, doesn't show up on the scoreboard clearly.

No one can argue that somebody is a great pitcher or a great hitter simply based on how good he looks hitting or pitching; the results are there for everyone to see. Good fielding, though, is far more subtle; while it results in fewer runs allowed, we tend to give all of the credit to the pitcher. Evaluating defense requires that we sort out the contributions of eight other players from the performance of the pitcher.

Defense is a team concept in baseball to a much greater extent than offense is. You can isolate a hitter's performance from that of the rest of the team: what other hitters in the lineup do has a fairly small impact on a player's statistical line, and that impact is mostly seen in a few categories such as runs scored, runs batted in, sacrifices, and intentional walks. Fielding stats, though, are heavily influenced by the other players on the team, especially the pitchers. It simply isn't possible to write a program that assesses how Derek Jeter did in the field last year unless it assesses the Yankees as a whole. This team dependence also makes evaluating defense hideously complicated; it isn't possible to give a brief description or avoid some of the uglier math.

We at *Baseball Prospectus* are quite proud of the fielding system we've used for the past three years. We think it solves many of the problems present in other methods of evaluating defense: it appears to handle aging appropriately—for example, players seem to struggle in the field as rookies, and then improve; old middle infielders struggle as they get older—and it handles position shifts the way one would expect. We are pleased to find that many of its features anticipate "discoveries" made by Bill James in his Win Shares system, as introduced in last year's *New Bill James Historical Baseball Abstract.* At the same time, we are dismayed that he presents his work as new and revolutionary, when in fact he's retracing some steps.

Like other systems for evaluating defensive performance, ours works on the basis of comparing the number of plays a fielder actually made to what a league-average fielder would have made in his place. Finding what the average fielder in the league did is easy; finding what that fielder would have done is the central problem and is where you have to look at the rest of the team. When rating hitters, there is really only one team-wide adjustment that we use: the park factor. For rating fielders, we need five. One is the park factor; the others are:

- **Balls in play.** A ball that is not put into play cannot be fielded; any ball put in play that is not turned into an out is a defensive failure. Those concepts seem straightforward, but other defensive metrics have failed to address one or both of them. Team strikeouts matter; the more the team has, the fewer opportunities the defense has, and the less important the defense becomes. Errors are universally recognized as defensive failures, but non-home-run hits are failures by the defense as well.
- **Ground balls and fly balls.** The opportunities for any individual fielder depend on the pitching staff's tendencies. The ratio of infield assists to outfield putouts is a strong indicator of the staff's overall tendency, although it's not perfect: if a team has a strong quality gap between the infield and outfield, that can push the ratio in favor of the better fielders and cause us to downgrade them in error. A second useful statistic is the pitcher's invidivual chances per inning, strikeout-adjusted. Ground-ball pitchers get more chances, fly-ball pitchers fewer chances, and their pitching tendency is a larger influence on this figure than their own fielding skills.
- **Left/right balance of the pitching staff.** Opportunities can often be weighted to one side of the diamond or the other. This is largely a function of pitcher handedness: a team with more innings thrown by left-handers will generally face more right-handed hitters, which generally leads to more balls being hit to shortstop, third base, and left field. We use the number of innings pitched by left- and right-handed pitchers on the team, and we assess them separately for their expected ball-in-play impact. (For example, a left-handed strikeout pitcher won't have as much impact on third-base opportunities as a left-handed control pitcher.) We also look at the ratio of plays made on the left side (shortstop, third base, and left field when available) to the ratio of plays made on the right side (second base, first base, right field).
- **Men on first base.** Most defensive systems reward double plays more than any other defensive event. Ours is no exception. You cannot estimate how many double plays a team should have turned, however, unless you

Table 1. 2001 American League

	IP	H	HR	BB	HBP	SO	E	R
Total	20114	20842	2483	7269	937	14474	1589	11013
Pitch	???	???	2483	7269	937	14474	0	???
Field	???	???	0	0	0	0	1589	???

first know how many men were on first base to be doubled. Double plays are not the only area affected, though: the number of men on first also counts in trying to figure how many infield assists go to second base and how many go to first base.

The first thing we do is define an overall value for the team; the sum of the individual ratings will match the team's when we are done. There are some things—walks, strikeouts, hit-by-pitch, home runs—that are almost entirely the responsibility of the pitcher. There are other things—errors—that are totally the responsibility of the fielder. The rest are shared values, although not necessarily shared equally.

What we can do is deconstruct the total league (and team) statistics into component parts, as seen in Table 1.

Spaces marked "???" are values we don't really know; they depend on how we share the balls in play between the pitchers and fielders. An educated guess is that the share is about 70% fielding, 30% pitching. Why 70/30, and not 50/50 or 20/80? I don't know; I can't tell you for certain that 70/30 is more accurate than some other ratio, or that the ratio doesn't change dramatically with time or level of play. To some extent, it is an arbitrary choice; however, I do know that:

- Voros McCracken's work on pitchers and hits allowed suggests that the pitcher has little control (he says "none," I disagree) over how many hits he allows, after you control for his strikeout rate. You simply wouldn't get a result like that if the split were 50/50. McCracken's work is strong evidence that the weight leans strongly towards the fielders.
- A 70/30 split has the result of evening the valuation of pitchers over time. Most methods for rating pitchers have trouble with pitchers of the 1880s, when they would often throw 500 innings in a season. These systems would have you believe that pitchers of that era were the most valuable commodity in history, because those systems treat all innings the same and credit them to the pitcher. The defense was far more important in the 1880s than it is today; the pitcher, until 1885 restricted to underhand deliveries, had far less control over the outcome of the pitcher-batter matchup, and doesn't deserve the same credit for them. Assigning more responsibility to the fielders effectively reduces the responsibility we assign to pitchers; somewhere around the 70/30 ratio is the point at which the top pitchers in all eras appear nearly equal in value.

Back to the chart. We assign 70% of the non-homer hits to the fielders and 30% to the pitchers. We can also take the strikeouts out of the innings pitched and give 30% of the IP to the pitchers and 70% to the fielders. Remembering to add the home runs and strikeouts back into the pitcher numbers, we have Table 2.

From this point, we can do an EqA analysis of each part, using a modified EqA formula that employs pitching statistics rather than batting stats (you could, of course, convert the pitching lines into batting lines, estimating at-bats, doubles, and triples, which I do within the program; to keep the examples from swallowing this entire book, I won't do so here).

The pitching portion has a raw EqA of:

$$[2H+3HR+1.5(BB+HBP)]/(3\times IP+H+BB+HBP)$$

or .8508; the fielding portion is the same, except that each error counts the same as a hit, giving us .5897.

The way EqA works, runs go up as double the difference in ratio: since the ratio of pitcher's EqA to fielder's EqA is 1.44—44% higher—that implies that the pitcher's responsibility for runs, per plate appearance, is 88% higher than the responsibility of the fielders. The pitcher's share of all runs, then, is:

Table 2. 2001 American League

	IP	H	HR	BB	HBP	SO	E	R
Total	20114	20842	2483	7269	937	14474	1589	11013
Pitch	8604	7991	2483	7269	937	14474	0	???
Field	11510	12851	0	0	0	0	1589	???

Table 3. 2001 American League

	IP	H	HR	BB	HBP	SO	E	R
Total	20114	20842	2483	7269	937	14474	1589	11013
Pitch	8604	7991	2483	7269	937	14474	0	6798
Field	11510	12851	0	0	0	0	1589	4215

Table 4. 2001 New York Yankees

	IP	H	HR	BB	HBP	SO	E	R
Total	1442	1429	158	465	55	1266	109	713
Pitch	728	539	158	465	55	1266	0	403
Field	714	890	0	0	0	0	109	310

$$(1.88 \times \text{pitcher PA}) / (1.88 \times \text{pitcher PA} + \text{field PA})$$

or 62%. So the last two columns are shown in Table 3.

Now, all of that work we did for the league needs to be repeated for the teams. Taking the 2001 Yankees and skipping through to the end, we get Table 4.

Going back to the league averages, you would expect pitchers with 728 pitcher innings, working with a .982 park factor, to have allowed 565 runs. Yankees pitchers were 162 runs better than that. Likewise, the fielders should have been expected to give up 261 runs; we rate them 49 runs below average. Yankee pitchers succeeded last year in spite of well-below-average defensive support. Keep that last number in mind: at the end of the process, the individual Yankees ratings must total −49.

Add all of the individual RAA figures together. When we do all of this for the Yankees of 2001, we get a total of −65 RAR for the individuals; the team expected fielding total was 310 runs, the team expectation was −49, or 359. The team numbers currently add up to 375.

To get back down, we'll take the ratio of current runs to desired runs—375/359, or 1.045. Then we go back through each player, multiply his rate by 1.045, and recalculate his RAA, which should then add up to the right figure.

For historical perspective, an analysis of the 1884 Providence Grays would produce something like Table 5.

The expected pitching runs for the Grays in their .963 park would be 180, making their pitching +81, thanks mostly to Old Hoss Radbourn. Their expected fielding runs would be 452, meaning they were an incredible +163 on defense. The fielding was given responsibility for 72% of league runs, compared to just 38% in 2001. No team today could reach +160 runs, just as no pitcher could throw 600 innings, because the game is different.

Bill James scores Radbourn's season at 89 Win Shares, the best of all time, and 60% more than Babe Ruth accumulated in his best season. I rated it as 11.2 wins above replacement, which is still a spectacular season—13th all-time—but not better than Ruth's best. Radbourn's season might not have even been the best in his league, in fact: Pud Galvin wasn't all that far behind him, and Galvin got much less support from his defense than Radbourn.

Fielding analysis would have been easier if several statistics had been better designed at the beginning. None is more outrageous, in retrospect, than "games." Whether a fielder played the entire game or was a defensive replacement in the ninth inning, he was credited with one game, so

Table 5. 1884 National League and 1884 Providence Grays

1884 National League

	IP	H	HR	BB	HBP	SO	E	R
Total	8047	8074	321	1821	—	4348	3953	5028
Pitch	3429	2647	321	1821	—	4348	0	1397
Field	4618	5427	0	0	0	0	3953	3631

1884 Providence Grays

	IP	H	HR	BB	HBP	SO	E	R
Total	1035	825	26	172	—	639	398	388
Pitch	460	266	26	172	—	639	0	99
Field	575	559	0	0	—	0	398	289

we have to estimate how many "real" games he played. Plate appearances are the primary tool for making this estimate, but there is also information to be gleaned by looking at the sum of team games played and the sum of an individual fielder's games at different positions. We usually end up with a best guess, and occasionally we end up with a really bad estimate, especially with outfielders. Knowing whether a fly chaser played left, right, or center—another oversight by Henry Chadwick and his compatriots—makes for substantial improvements. We have that data for recent seasons and for the minor leagues, and it is used in the book.

Let's take a look at each position, first examining the Fielding Translations, then taking a peek at how the system rates the best of all-time, as compared to *Total Baseball VII*. Note that our numbers have been normalized to "average" fielding conditions over time, in the same way that offensive numbers are adjusted for a high-offense or low-offense era. Without that adjustment, half of the players in the lists would be from the 1800s.

First Base

The central problem with first basemen is sorting out their unassisted putouts (for which we want to give them full credit) from their assisted ones (which, nine times out of ten, we don't). To do that, we make some assumptions:

- With no men on base, all assists go to first base.
- With a man on first base, pitchers and second basemen go to first half the time and to second half the time.
- With a man on first base, shortstops and third basemen will go to second base three-quarters of the time.

Those aren't exactly the right ratios, but they're reasonable approximations, according to the Retrosheet data, at least within our time. So we get, using team fielding stats:

Team assists to first =

$$TA1 = (2b\ A + P\ A) \times (1 - .5 \times MO1) + (3B\ A + SS\ A) \times (1 - .75 \times MO1)$$

League assists to first =

LA1 = use the same formula with league totals.

Then we look back at the individual to get:

Individual unassisted putouts =

$$IUPO = PO - (G'/TmG) \times TA1$$

$$DeltaPO = IUPO - (G'/LgG) \times (LgPO - LA1) \times FBAdj$$

In these, G' refers to a player's estimated full games played at first base. TmG and LgG are team and league games played; MO1 is the team's man-on-first percentage. FBAdj is the total adjustment to opportunities that came from the ball-in-play, ground-ball /fly-ball, and left/right adjustments.

Assists and errors are easier, because they don't have to go through the putout analysis; those are:

$$DeltaA = A - (G'/LgG) \times FBAdj \times LgA$$

$$DeltaE = (G'/LgG) \times FBAdj \times LgE - E$$

The player's total rating is based on our estimate that he (DeltaPO+DeltaA+DeltaE) plays above average. A rating for the position is found by the normal number of plays per game:

$$Norm = (LgA + LgE + LgPO - LA1)/LgG$$

$$Rate1B = (Norm + (Sum\ of\ Deltas)/G')/Norm$$

$$RAA1B = (Rate1B - 1) \times Norm \times G' \times .7$$

Table 6. Top Ten Defensive First Basemen

Total Baseball	*Baseball Prospectus*
Keith Hernandez, 150	Keith Hernandez, 174
Fred Tenney, 128	Pete O'Brien, 146
Vic Power, 124	Vic Power, 144
Bill Buckner, 121	Fred Tenney, 126
George Sisler, 89	John Olerud, 115
Mark Grace, 85	Norm Cash, 103
Eric Karros, 84	Don Mattingly, 91
Jeff Bagwell, 81	Roger Connor, 89
Sid Bream, 76	Ed Konetchy, 89
Darrell Evans, 76	Mark Grace, 82

The lists in Table 6 have four out of ten players in common. No one in the 1980s actually believed Bill Buckner was a good first baseman; he rates highly in *Total Baseball* because he literally always threw to the pitcher and never took ground balls to the bag himself. Those missing putouts show up in the Prospectus system, and he rates at +6.

Middle Infield

Middle infielders have to be evaluated together, because about a third of the putouts they record are really optional plays that either one could have made, mostly pop-ups and covering the bag on stolen-base attempts. Who actually gets the opportunity varies by team; while most teams tend to split them, if one of the infielders has the stature of, say, a Cal Ripken, he may get a disproportionate share of the putouts. We don't want to overrate him based on that.

The format is the same as with first basemen: we evaluate how many of each type of play we would expect from each player and compare that to how many he actually made. We again need to account for how many of their putouts are assisted and how many are coming from other positions. You also want to watch for the bonus assists that come from double plays started by someone else and not go overboard with the credit you give for the DP.

Modify team putouts for second base and shortstop (average actual PO with a league-average split of PO between the two):

$$2B\ PO' = [2B\ PO + (SS\ PO + 2B\ PO)/(1 + LgSSPO/Lg2BPO)]/2$$

$$SS\ PO' = 2B\ PO + SS\ PO + 2B\ PO'$$

Team assists to second base =

$$TA2 = (3b\ A + SS\ A) \times (.75 \times MO1) + .5 \times (C\ A)$$

League assists to second base =

LA2 = the same.

Individually:

$$Delta\ DP = DP - G' \times SBAdj \times MO1 \times LgDP / LgG / LgMO1$$

Individual unassisted putouts =

$$IUPO = PO' - (G'/TmG) \times TA2 - DeltaDP$$

$$DeltaPO = IUPO - (G'/LgG) \times (LgPO - LA2) \times SBAdj$$

$$DeltaA = A - DelDP - G' \times SBAdj \times LgA/LgG$$

$$DeltaE = G' \times SBAdj \times LgG - E$$

$$Norm = [(LgPO - LA2) + LgA + LgE + LgDP]/LgG$$

$$Rate = [Norm + (Sum\ of\ Deltas)/G']/Norm$$

$$RAA2B = (Rate - 1) \times Norm \times G' \times .7$$

All of the formulae for shortstops are the same as for second basemen, except that:

$$SA2 = (P\ A + 1B\ A + 2B\ A) \times .5 \times MO1 + .5 \times (C\ A)$$

Table 7. Top Ten Defensive Second Basemen

Total Baseball	*Baseball Prospectus*
Nap Lajoie, 368	Bill Mazeroski, 284
Bill Mazeroski, 363	Bid McPhee, 229
Bid McPhee, 319	Nap Lajoie, 187
Fred Pfeffer, 259	Bobby Grich, 167
Glenn Hubbard, 229	Bobby Lowe, 151
Bobby Doerr, 180	Glenn Hubbard, 145
Joe Gerhardt, 160	Ryne Sandberg, 141
Lou Bierbauer, 157	Frankie Frisch, 122
Bobby Knoop, 150	Johnny Evers, 118
Ski Melillo, 148	Bobby Doerr, 118

Five players appear on both lists in Table 7. Notice that while a second baseman is the best overall defender in both systems, in the Prospectus system he isn't so far removed from the rest of the positions. Bobby Grich and Ryne Sandberg have 13 Gold Gloves between them; there is little question that Frankie Frisch and Johnny Evers would have been likely recipients as well.

Table 8. Top Ten Defensive Shortstops

Total Baseball	*Baseball Prospectus*
Bill Dahlen, 304	Ozzie Smith, 265
Jack Glasscock, 245	Joe Tinker, 259
Ozzie Smith, 242	Mark Belanger, 239
Joe Tinker, 216	Roy McMillan, 209
Dave Bancroft, 198	Marty Marion, 197
George Davis, 192	Dal Maxvill, 189
George McBride, 174	Everett Scott, 177
Rabbit Maranville, 173	Bill Dahlen, 168
Mickey Doolan, 168	Jack Glasscock, 160
Mark Belanger, 164	Germany Smith, 160

In Table 8, it's hard to find fault with ranking Ozzie Smith #1, while Everett Scott and Marty Marion also strike me as great additions. I would have liked to have seen Rabbit Maranville on the *BP* list, but he only came in at 135.

Third Base

Third base is really simple, because putouts are almost always unassisted and are so heavily dependent on the foul territory available for pop-up catching that they give you very little information. We had been dividing them by eight to reduce their impact; James simply cut to the chase and disregarded them altogether for rating third basemen. Tip your cap to him for that one.

$$Delta\ DP = DP - G' \times TBAdj \times MO1 \times LgDP/LgG/LgMO1$$

$$Delta\ A = A - G' \times TBAdj \times LgA/LgG$$

$$Delta\ PO = (PO - G' \times TBAdj \times LgPO/LgG)/8$$

$$Delta\ E = G' \times TBAdj \times LgE / LgG - E$$

$$Norm = (LgPO + LgA + LgE + LgDP)/LgG$$

Seven out of ten show up on both lists in Table 9; on the *BP* list, Gary Gaetti, Tim Wallach, and Robin Ventura knock off Aurelio Rodriguez, Lave Cross, and Ron Santo—thirteen Gold Gloves against six and one guy who played way too early for them. Take the system that puts Brooks Robinson where he belongs.

Table 9. Top Ten Defensive Third Basemen

Total Baseball	*Baseball Prospectus*
Mike Schmidt, 265	Brooks Robinson, 255
Clete Boyer, 201	Mike Schmidt, 229
Buddy Bell, 199	Tim Wallach, 177
Aurelio Rodriguez, 184	Clete Boyer, 173
Terry Pendleton, 181	Buddy Bell, 171
Brooks Robinson, 152	Jimmy Collins, 165
Lave Cross, 137	Gary Gaetti, 165
Jimmy Collins, 136	Terry Pendleton, 159
Graig Nettles, 136	Graig Nettles, 149
Ron Santo, 135	Robin Ventura, 132

Table 10. Top Ten Defensive Outfielders

Total Baseball	*Baseball Prospectus*
Tris Speaker, 248	Willie Mays, 241
Richie Ashburn, 227	Tris Speaker, 229
Max Carey, 201	Richie Ashburn, 200
Willie Mays, 184	Curt Flood, 177
Roberto Clemente, 173	Paul Blair, 170
Barry Bonds, 169	Gary Maddox, 155
Rickey Henderson, 154	Willie Davis, 132
Carl Yastrzemski, 143	Amos Otis, 124
Garry Maddox, 142	Dom DiMaggio, 121
Kirby Puckett, 139	Devon White, 120

Outfield

The outfield poses a set of problems all its own. The worst one is that the outfield really consists of three positions which have been jumbled together as one by the record keepers, and we are not entirely satisfied with our efforts at teasing them apart again.

Of course, with recent players, including the minor-league players in this book, we have the left/right/center breakdown and use it. When we don't have the breakdown, we use chances per game, compared to the other players on the team, to break players into center field and corner outfield positions. A "game adjustment" multiplier is applied to the player's outfield games to reflect the advantage a center fielder has—and the disadvantage a corner player has—for putouts; for this book, it is:

$$\text{Gadj} = (.85 \times \text{LF G} + 1.2 \times \text{CF G} + .95 \times \text{RF G})/\text{OF G}$$

The values are flexible, according to the data of the leagues. These are typical.

Outfield numbers then follow like those of the infielders:

$$\text{Delta PO} = \text{PO} - \text{G}' \times \text{Gadj} \times \text{OFadj} \times \text{LgPO}/\text{LgG}/3$$

$$\text{Delta A} = \text{A} - \text{G} \times \text{OFadj} \times \text{MO1} \times \text{LgA}/\text{LgG}/\text{LgMO1}/3$$

$$\text{Delta E} = \text{G}' \times \text{OFAdj} \times \text{MO1} \times \text{LgE}/\text{LgG}/\text{LgMO1}/3 - \text{E}$$

$$\text{Delta DP} = \text{DP} - \text{G}' \times \text{OFadj} \times \text{MO1} \times \text{LgDP}/\text{LgG}/\text{LgMO1}/3$$

$$\text{Norm} = (\text{LgPO} + 3 \times \text{LgA} + \text{LgE} + \text{LgDP})/\text{LgG}/3$$

We've included men-on-first adjustments in the outfield-assist and double-play ratings for obvious reasons. The reason for including the error rating is that most outfield errors are committed to benefit runners who are already on first base, either the single-plus-error variety, allowing the batter to advance, or on attempts to throw out advancing base runners. Opportunities for such errors are increased by having men on base.

There is no comparison between the two lists in Table 10. There is no way that even a good left fielder is worth as much as a good center fielder, and the TB list has three left fielders.

If you're curious, Andruw Jones is already up to 112.

Catchers

Catchers pose unique problems to the analyst. As with first basemen, a relevant statistic, putouts, is buried within a mass of strikeouts, as are, regrettably, some of the assists. Fortunately, as with third basemen, the putouts are so dependent upon park configuration that I don't believe they are of much value. One of a catcher's responsibilities—throwing out base stealers—is an elective play, and you can't catch them if they don't go. Other presumed strengths—calling a game, framing pitches—are almost totally outside the domain of regular statistics. As Keith Woolner demonstrated in *Baseball Prospectus 1999*, catcher ERA is a statistic with little value; the variation between good and bad catchers is no larger than the variation between seasons for a single player. I'm going to ignore it, at whatever risk.

Within the book, at least, we do have access to stolen-base and caught-stealing totals by catcher, so the rating process focuses almost entirely on those, on non-CS assists, errors, and passed balls.

$$\text{Delta SB} = \text{G}' \times \text{MO1} \times \text{LgSB}/\text{LgG}/\text{LgMO1} - \text{SB}$$

$$\text{Delta CS} = \text{CS} - \text{G}' \times \text{MO1} \times \text{LgCS}/\text{LgG}/\text{LgMO1}$$

$$\text{Delta A} = (\text{A} - \text{CS}) - \text{G}' \times \text{MO1} \times (\text{LgA} - \text{LgCS})/\text{LgG}/\text{LgMO1}$$

$$\text{Delta E} = \text{G}' \times \text{MO1} \times (\text{LgPB} + \text{LgE})/\text{LgG}/\text{LgMO1} - \text{PB} - \text{E}$$

$$\text{Norm} = (\text{LgA} + \text{LgSB} + \text{LgE} + \text{LgPB})/\text{LgG}$$

Just three players are common to both lists in Table 11. The *BP* top ten won 28 Gold Gloves among them; every player on the list who played in the Gold Glove era won at least two.

Table 11. Top Ten Defensive Catchers

Total Baseball	*Baseball Prospectus*
Pop Snyder, 151	Gary Carter, 184
Jim Hegan, 150	Johnny Bench, 167
Lou Criger, 133	Ray Schalk, 136
Bill Killefer, 131	Jim Sundberg, 131
Tony Pena, 120	Johnny Edwards, 125
Bill Bergen, 119	Yogi Berra, 122
Charlie O'Brien, 110	Al Lopez, 115
Chief Zimmer, 105	Lance Parrish, 107
Osse Schreckengost, 98	Lou Criger, 103
Jim Sundberg, 98	Tony Pena, 98

Pitchers

Don't rate them. Their chances depend as much on how many ground balls they induce as anything else.

Stuff Rating

by Clay Davenport

A new feature in this year's pitching Translations is a rating called, simply enough, "Stuff." It is an attempt to evaluate a pitcher's performance for evidence of his pitching ability, both now and with a natural amount of growth figured in. It is a tool whose primary use is to do for pitchers what the original Major League Equivalencies, and later the DTs, did for hitters—identify the real prospects.

The Stuff rating is not a direct measure of a pitcher's stuff in the way that *Baseball America* would use the term. Rather, it's the statistical consequences of his pitching ability. To an extent, these statistical consequences are already used to produce the Peripheral ERA statistics. However, the Stuff rating is intended to do more than just predict the number of runs a pitcher allows; it's designed to assess his fitness to pitch in the majors for an extended period of time.

The Stuff rating is designed to be used with translated statistics, since these have already accounted for league offensive levels and the competitive distance between a pitcher's league and the major leagues. It is set up so that an average major-league starter will score as a ten, and the lowest level of major-league ability will score a zero. The formula is:

$$\text{Stuff} = (6 \times K/9) - [1.333 \times (ERA + PERA)] - (5 \times HR/9) - (3 \times BB/9)$$

For an average pitcher, the DTs define rates for the stats as K/9: 6.00, ERA: 4.50, PERA: 4.50, HR/9: 1.00, and BB/9: 3.00.

Striking out hitters is the most important thing a prospect, or even a major-league pitcher, can do. Strikeouts represent a pitcher's ability to get outs for himself, without the aid of his teammates. Several lines of recent work, most notably by Voros McCracken, indicate that the strikeout rate is the primary factor in determining how many hits a pitcher will allow. It appears that it also establishes a baseline for a given pitcher, and that an erosion in his strikeout rate will normally be accompanied by a decline in his overall pitching effectiveness.

However, strikeouts do not tell a pitcher's entire story. An outstanding pitcher will also have some semblance of control, will not be prone to the gopher ball, and will not allow opponents to score. The multipliers on each component are not derived from any theory but were chosen simply because they fit the data I had better than any alternatives I could find—the Stuff score is an empirical, not a theoretical, value.

There are two other important adjustments to the formula, one that can reduce the rating and one that can enhance it. A pitcher is expected to go six innings per appearance; for every inning he averages below six, he will be penalized three points. On the other hand, the strikeout and walk rates, and also the peripheral ERA, are age-adjusted; that's a built-in assumption that strikeout rates will increase up to about age 26, and walk rates will decline after age 22.

For every year since 1992, I rated every pitcher in my database based on his previous two years of play. I eliminated any pitcher who had 1) pitched 50 or more major-league innings in that time, 2) pitched in 25 or more major-league games, 3) pitched fewer than 20 innings in the most recent year, or 4) had fewer than 50 (games + 3 × games started) pitched. The first two requirements generally eliminated players who were no longer rookies, while the latter ensured a reasonable sample size. I spent a lot of time wrestling with formulas to penalize pitchers who made only five starts before I decided that it just wasn't worthwhile to rate pitchers with so little experience.

There is a clear, strong, linear relationship between a pitcher's two-year Stuff score and his chance of making it to the major leagues. There is an even stronger, and exponential, relationship between a pitcher's Stuff score and his chance of having a substantial major-league career, defined as accumulating either 100 or 300 major-league innings.

Figure 1 is the basis for this claim. It charts all the pitchers who were entered on my lists for the 1993–94, 1994–95,

Figure 1. The percentage of all players from 1993–97 who pitched at least one inning, 100 innings, or 300 innings in the majors through 2001, based on five-point ranges of Stuff.

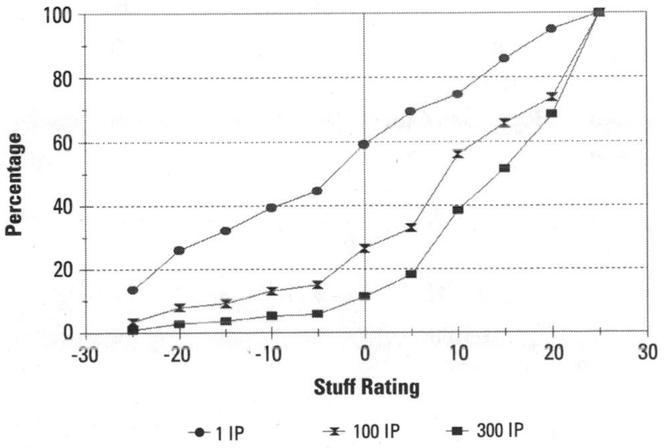

1995–96, and 1996–97 two-year blocks, with their career innings pitched through the 2001 season. It certainly is not a complete history, as quite a few pitchers in here may move up to 100- or 300-inning status in the future, but it does give a good idea about what can be expected from a given pitcher or group of pitchers in the next five or so years. That's enough time to make the tool quite useful in fantasy leagues that permit you to pick up minor leaguers and keep them for the future. Of particular note:

- Pitchers with a Stuff score of 20 or better have a 75% chance of a major-league career of at least 300 innings (a "lasting" career).
- Pitchers with Stuff scores below zero have less than a 10% chance of a lasting major-league career; most of the ones who do reach 300 innings have been converted to relief.
- The chances of making the major leagues drops by 1.6 percentage points per point of Stuff, with a near-100% chance at 25 or better. A pitcher with a 0 Stuff rating has a 60% ($100-25\times1.6$) chance of making the majors.
- The chance of a lasting career, in contrast, drops by about 7% per point. The same zero-Stuff pitcher may have a 60% chance of pitching in the majors, but only about a 16% ($100\times.93^{25}$) chance of sticking around for a 300-inning career.

One thing to keep in mind is that the system is designed primarily to evaluate and rate starting pitchers. Relievers with outstanding stats will show up on the lists—Armando Benitez topped the lists in 1994–95—but the penalties built in to weed out minor-league relievers (who can rarely be considered good prospects and who in fact rarely make the majors) tend to do a very thorough job of eliminating them from high consideration. In addition, most major-league relief pitchers were minor-league starters, and I have yet to find any statistical relationship that will translate starting performance with relieving performance.

One of the persistent myths about performance analysts is that we reject scouting opinions out of hand, looking only at statistics. This isn't the case; it is just that, if the stats and the scouts disagree, we tend to believe the stats more. What follows, though, is purely statistical: we're going to compare the Stuff ratings for a given year, without any subjective input whatsoever, to the list of top pitching prospects compiled by *Baseball America* for the same year.

There are three separate comparisons to be made within a given year. The first is to compare the top tens in each list. Table 1 lists the Stuff top ten for the 1990–91 seasons, the 10 highest-rated pitching prospects from the 1992 *Baseball America* Top 100, and their career accomplishments through 2001.

Four of the ten pitchers (Pedro Martinez, Roger Salkeld, Arthur Rhodes, and Lance Dickson) appear on both lists. We would much rather have had Denny Neagle (who didn't make the *BA* Top 100) and Pat Mahomes instead of Frank Rodriguez, Todd Van Poppel, and Mark Wohlers. The Stuff list turned out to be distinctly superior to the *Baseball America* list, although results for the 1990s are pretty even, as shown in Table 2.

The second way to do this is to look at the whole list, not just the top ten. *Baseball America* normally had about 40 pitchers on its lists, and the second halves of those lists generally did better than the Stuff ratings. That's not a surprise. The Stuff top ten generally consists of pitchers who scored in the high teens and above, pitchers who had a 70%+ chance of success. Get down to the 40th- or 45th-best pitcher, and we're down to Stuff scores of 7 or 8, figures that suggest only a 25–30% chance of long-term success. It does not surprise me that intelligent scouting—something *BA* reflects—can

Table 1. Top 10 Pitching Prospects, 1990–91

Baseball America

Name	W	SV	IP
1. Brien Taylor	0	0	0
2. Todd Van Poppel	30	3	671
3. Roger Salkeld	10	0	189
4. Arthur Rhodes	56	12	760
5. Frank Rodriguez	29	5	654
6. Pedro Martinez	132	3	1693
7. Mark Wohlers	36	112	482
8. Kurt Miller	2	0	81
9. Tyrone Hill	0	0	0
10. Lance Dickson	0	0	14
Total	295	135	4543

Stuff

Name	W	SV	IP
Pedro Martinez	132	3	1693
Sam Militello	4	0	69
Lance Dickson	0	0	14
Scott Taylor	1	0	26
Denny Neagle	114	3	1691
Roger Salkeld	10	0	189
Arthur Rhodes	56	12	760
Salomon Torres	11	0	284
Pat Mahomes	41	5	654
Rick Huisman	2	1	39
Total	371	24	5418

Table 2. Top 10 Pitching Prospects, 1990–91 through 1999–2000

	Baseball America			Stuff			Better?
	W	SV	IP	W	SV	IP	
1990–91	295	135	4543	371	24	5418	Stuff
1991–92	205	13	3692	398	8	6456	Stuff
1992–93	276	44	4686	336	218	5872	Stuff
1993–94	257	303	4387	321	162	5975	Stuff
1994–95	370	146	5893	314	4	5700	*BA*
1995–96	288	10	4558	205	1	3725	*BA*
1996–97	192	24	3368	195	3	3430	Even
1997–98	129	7	2346	118	19	2210	*BA*
1998–99	100	1	1543	69	35	1112	*BA*
1999–00	47	0	542	49	0	625	Stuff
Net	2159	683	35558	2376	474	40523	Stuff

boost the success rate from, say, 25% to 40%, which is more than enough to explain their domination of Table 3, which includes all pitchers named in *BA*'s Top 100 versus an equal number from the Stuff lists.

Another reason for *BA*'s dominance is the inclusion of pitchers who did not meet the criteria to be on the Stuff list, usually pitchers who had been taken in the most recent draft. In the top-ten list in Table 1, Brien Taylor, Tyrone Hill, and Frank Rodriguez were such pitchers, albeit not successful ones, but Shawn Estes, Troy Percival, Joey Hamilton, Allen Watson, and Justin Thompson were also on *BA*'s 1992 Top 100 list, without having made 13 starts in the minors. Counting pitchers I disqualified—such as Chan Ho Park and Billy Wagner in 1994, Dustin Hermanson, Livan Hernandez, Matt Morris, and Kerry Wood in 1996—gives the *BA* list a powerful advantage.

Removing that advantage by disqualifying those pitchers from *BA*'s list and dropping an equal number of pitchers from the Stuff lists doesn't remove the *BA* advantage, but it cuts the gap in wins from 500 to 200 and reduces the edge in innings from more than 6,000 to less than 3,000.

So what does this have to do with your fantasy team? Take a look at Table 4, which lists the top 50 pitchers in Stuff.

Table 3. Top 100 Pitching Prospects, 1990–91 through 1999–2000

	Baseball America			Stuff			Better?
	W	SV	IP	W	SV	IP	
1990-91	1132	687	19535	1188	181	19809	*BA*
1991-92	1070	624	18504	1066	149	18828	*BA*
1992-93	1068	646	19317	1107	280	20215	*BA*
1993-94	1034	626	18048	965	233	17229	*BA*
1994-95	1069	462	18447	827	325	15036	*BA*
1995-96	716	141	12936	652	121	12263	*BA*
1996-97	532	41	9808	521	31	9743	*BA*
1997-98	438	150	7612	323	44	5514	*BA*
1998-99	316	38	5263	215	40	3967	*BA*
1999-00	85	0	1231	100	0	1763	*BA*
Net	7460	3415	130701	6964	1404	124367	*BA*

Table 4. 2001–2001 Minor League Stuff Top 50

1. Josh Beckett, Marlins
2. Nick Neugebauer, Brewers
3. John Stephens, Orioles
4. Jake Peavy, Padres
5. Tim Spooneybarger, Braves
6. Carlos Zambrano, Cubs
7. Joaquin Benoit, Rangers
8. Justin Duchscherer, Rangers
9. Juan Cruz, Cubs
10. Carlos Hernandez, Astros
11. Jose Valverde, Diamondbacks
12. Adam Johnson, Twins
13. Eric Cyr, Padres
14. Sean Douglass, Orioles
15. Colby Lewis, Rangers
16. Kurt Ainsworth, Giants
17. Dennis Tankersley, Padres
18. Joey Nation, Cubs
19. Jon Rauch, White Sox
20. Jose Mieses, Brewers
21. Brandon Claussen, Yankees
22. Seung Song, Red Sox
23. Rafael Soriano, Mariners
24. Erik Bedard, Orioles
25. Clint Nageotte, Mariners
26. Beltran Perez, Diamondbacks
27. Aquilino Lopez, Mariners
28. Bobby Bradley, Pirates
29. Jason Jennings, Rockies
30. Adrian Hernandez, Yankees
31. Francisco Rodriguez, Angels
32. Casey Fossum, Red Sox
33. Billy Traber, Mets
34. Mario Ramos, A's
35. Grant Roberts, Mets
36. Jimmy Gobble, Royals
37. Derrick Van Dusen, Mariners
38. Josh Hall, Reds
39. Runelvys Hernandez, Royals
40. Ryan Vogelsong, Pirates
41. Craig Anderson, Mariners
42. Chris Capuano, Diamondbacks
43. Jeremy Lambert, Cardinals
44. Chad Harville, A's
45. Brad Lidge, Astros
46. Jeff Heaverlo, Mariners
47. Corey Thurman, Royals
48. Mike Meyers, Cubs
49. Adam Wainwright, Braves
50. Chris Narveson, Cardinals

Note: The Mariners' Ryan Anderson, who did not pitch in 2001, would certainly make this list based on his 2000 season alone.

Anaheim Angels

Let's get the fun rumors out of the way first. The Angels, passing hands from Disney to John Henry after the Marlins are folded, will add Ryan Dempster, Josh Beckett, and A.J. Burnett to their current pitching staff. Turning all of their resources to scouting and developing some affordable hitters, the Halos embark on a Braves-style dynasty fueled by their awesome young rotation. Henry receives plaudits as the savior of competitive baseball in Orange County, the Angels are reclassified as a large-market team, and the Dodgers glare jealously across the Basin's urban sprawl as legions of new Angels fans flock to Edison International Field. The Rally Monkey gets a series on the Disney Channel, while somewhere in the ether, the Singing Cowboy bursts into joyful song.

We hate to play the Grinch, but back in the real world, the consolidated might of Major League Baseball's owners has consistently managed to derail its own best-laid plans. There's no reason to believe the same thing won't happen here. Contraction's bark is loud, but its bite isn't vicious. The Angels will begin 2002 as they ended 2001: unlucky enough to play in the same division as the two best organizations in baseball, and reluctantly owned and operated by the Mouse. There's nothing the Angels can do about the former, while the latter is a cautionary tale for corporate ownership of baseball franchises.

Disney Inc. has a massive investment in the city of Anaheim. The company believes that professional sports is an important component of the atmosphere and the national perception of Anaheim, so it was a natural fit to take over the Angels when Gene Autry was ready to sell in 1995. It's that relationship with Anaheim that has caused President Tony Tavares to repeatedly say that Disney is not interested in folding the Angels, and that the company won't allow the team to move somewhere else. Rumors that Disney was so disheartened with its foray into baseball that it would be willing to contract the club appear to have been just that.

In retrospect, the first signs of trouble were pretty easy to see. After Disney acquired the Angels, the marketing machine shifted into high gear, with the assumption that what worked for a string of $100-million movies, a cruise line, and numerous theme parks would work just as well for a baseball team. The company has put a lot of work into promoting a family-friendly image—Disney is the enthusiastic owner of family.com, after all—and immediately set about improving the local baseball scene. Anaheim Stadium was turned over to Walt Disney Imagineering, which supervised its conversion from a multi-purpose stadium to a baseball-only facility. The two-year project gave the stadium a complete face-lift, combining the nostalgic features that HOK Sports Facilities Group has been building into new stadiums for a decade with the flash and glitz of a theme park. Special family-sized seating areas offered good views of the terraced bullpens, and wider walkways and concourses funneled patrons to a "youth oriented interactive game area." Energy provider Edison International bought the naming rights to the remodeled park. With the new ownership, change was in the air for a historically mediocre Angels club.

Angels Prospectus

2001 record: 75–87; Third place, AL West

Pythagenport W/L: 77–85

Runs scored: 691 (12th in AL)

Runs allowed: 730 (fourth in AL)

Team EqA: .249 (11th in AL)

2001 batters age: 27.9 (tied for third-youngest in AL)

2001 pitchers age: 28.1 (tied for sixth-youngest in AL)

Ballpark: Edison International Field; slight hitters' park; Park Factor of 1.029

2001: Got pitching from sources young and old, while their offense fell off a cliff.

2002: More of the same: good on the mound, not as good at the plate.

Disney, an entertainment company first and foremost, jumped on the synergy bandwagon in the 1990s. As a Disney property, the Angels were heavily involved in interesting and unusual projects. The team's image and identity were front and center in the Disney film *Angels in the Outfield.* The team's distinctive halo logo was replaced with a winged cartoonish thing, again consistent with the strategy of branding the Angels as a Disney product. The hope was that a benevolent confluence of consumer attention would win additional Angels fans from among the Disney faithful and convince existing Angels fans to start watching the Disney Channel. The sports teams would give family vacations in Anaheim additional depth: Tired of Disneyland? Catch an Angels or Mighty Ducks game! We play lots of cartoons on the scoreboard, and there are plenty of things for the kids to do.

Over the last two decades, in the wake of the live-action debacle *The Black Hole,* Disney entertainment has been obsessed with presentation and packaging. The product itself has grown increasingly formulaic: Take a disadvantaged hero/heroine with a heart of gold, add one seemingly unobtainable love interest, sprinkle in one or two animal or inanimate-object sidekicks with a penchant for cracking wise, squeeze one unrepentantly-evil-villain-with-sniveling-henchmen, grate a random number of musical cuts by washed-up pop artists, mix well, and bake at 450 degrees. The formula makes scads of money for the company. Perhaps the uninitiated would maintain that a visit to a Six Flags park is better than a visit to Disneyland, because the coasters plummet further and go faster, but Disney is selling the cartoon characters and the "It's A Small World" diorama, not the ride itself. Many Americans have grown up with Disney and have in their blood a love for its offerings. In the nineties, Disney had the Midas touch.

The company has had a lot of trouble turning its baseball team to gold, though, and the strenuous marketing effort probably has a lot to do with that struggle. The *Major League* movie series didn't turn anyone into an Indians fan, so it isn't surprising that *Angels in the Outfield* had about the same effect. A new stadium is a nice thing, but people only need to see it once, no matter how many gewgaws you've packed inside it; every major-league team relies in large part on the repeat visitors, and they are the ones who generally won't respond to facilities. Ask an Angels fan what Disney has changed since it took over the Angels, and he'll tell you about the stadium, the logo, and the Rally Monkey before he gets to anything related to the team itself.

It's a classic case of too much sizzle and not enough steak. What baseball teams need to sell is a winning team; what Disney has tried to do is put a mediocre team in a big shiny box with the Disney logo on it, and fans aren't buying. In fact, it's certainly possible that the people the Angels are wooing look at the last six years and conclude that the team is spending time and effort on the wrong things entirely. People making that decision will spend their entertainment budget somewhere else—like Knott's Berry Farm.

On the field, the Angels did a better job in 2001 than most people expected them to do. Yes, the club shut it down early, going 2-16 following the resumption of play after September 11, but that's not too surprising when you consider that the Athletics and the Mariners were lapping the field in the American League, leaving the Halos without much to play for. Prior to that, the team was 73-71 and playing about that well. Despite getting dusted both overall and in head-to-head play by the A's and the M's, the Angels played .500 ball.

The offense was a major disappointment, thanks to a confluence of bad luck. First baseman Mo Vaughn suffered a ruptured biceps in March and missed all of the 2001 season. Tim Salmon, the long-time Angels right fielder coming off perhaps his best season, had injury problems of his own, never got on track, and posted the worst year of his career. Darin Erstad suffered virtually the same fate, and a year after putting it all together is back to being a talented cipher. The lack of depth in the minors killed this team down the stretch—Orlando Palmeiro was the team's top DH, and he hit like a shortstop. A bad one.

It didn't have to be this bad, but the Angels released designated hitter Jose Canseco before the start of the season, unhappy with what they saw in spring training. Canseco was incredulous, thinking he was supposed to have been tuning up his swing for the regular season rather than trying to hit jacks off Double-A pitchers. When he finally caught on with the White Sox, he hit major-league pitching about as well as he hits guys in bars. The Angels could have used a .366 OBP and a .477 SLG in their lineup.

The Angels subsequently brought in Glenallen Hill to fill the spot, but after he struggled through 66 at-bats and a strained oblique that knocked him out for more than a month, the Angels cut him, too. Maybe the club knows something we don't, but if we have a guy who hit .351/.569 over the last three years, we give him a little bit longer to fight through it. Salmon and Erstad could bounce back this year, which would give the offense a needed shot in the arm.

The Angels have the makings of a good pitching staff. Manager Mike Scioscia handled his young charges very gently for the second straight season. Scant months after filtering Ken Hill and Tim Belcher out of their system, the Angels pitching staff was solidly above-average. Led by homegrown starters Jarrod Washburn, Ramon Ortiz, and Scott Schoeneweis, the regular rotation made all but 13 starts, providing durability and consistency to a team that sorely needed it. Ismael Valdes and Pat Rapp contributed as the other two starters. Replacing them with Kevin Appier and Aaron Sele will be an improvement.

The Angels liberally used one of the best and cheapest bullpens in the game in 2001, and it responded with good work. Scioscia isn't much for the situational reliever, so the best pitchers in the Angels pen work multiple innings and chew up space between the starters and closer Troy Percival. The Angels have some useful-looking arms in the minors, and they appear to have correctly ascertained the difference between the value of a starter and that of a reliever and are setting up their usage patterns accordingly.

We spent most of last year's essay castigating the Angels for their pathetic minor-league system, and not much has changed in that respect. The Angels may have the worst position-player prospects of any major-league organization, even with the presence of a couple of outfielders at Salt Lake who could help out if the offense is another horror show in 2002. Minor-league veteran Jose Fernandez, the best hitter in the system, was waived after the season and went to the Cubs. Last year's first-round pick Casey Kotchman might have the best bat remaining, and he's about a year removed from his senior prom. General Manager Bill Stoneman has spent resources on pitching, but it's too early to tell if prospects like Joe Torres and Chris Bootcheck will make any noise for the team.

If everything that broke wrong for the Angels in 2001 breaks right in 2002, and if the pitching staff continues its good work, this team could surprise people. Of course, even if that happens, they'll have to make it past the Mariners and Athletics.

The longer-term prospects for this team are uncertain, given the aging lineup and the dearth of impact players in the minors. This is where something as simple as a Dominican scouting operation could begin to pay dividends. If the Mouse has any money left over after building Disney's California Adventure, the company might want to throw a few dollars in that direction.

We've written at length about the danger of a deep-pocketed media company coming up with a business plan that involves throwing money around like Sir Elton John to sign the top free agents, to build a great farm system, and to cherry-pick the best people from front offices around the league all in the name of creating a dynasty that makes the Yankees look like, well, the Angels. But when corporate owners are more concerned with ensuring that the uniforms are the most family-friendly shade of periwinkle than with the vanilla status quo of the team's scouting and player development, such a turnabout looks like a remote possibility.

HITTERS (BA: .270, OBP: .340, SLG: .440, EqA: .260)

Alfredo Amezaga SS Bats R Age 24

YEAR	TEAM	LGE	AB	H	DB	TP	HR	BB	SO	R	RBI	SB	CS	OUT	BA	OBP	SLG	EQA	EQR	DEFENSE
1999	Boise	Nwn	202	45	4	2	1	12	34	25	14	5	2	159	.223	.272	.277	.193	13	40-2B -4 10-SS -1
2000	Lk Elsin	Cal	429	103	12	3	3	40	71	55	31	33	13	339	.240	.308	.303	.219	38	90-2B -1 14-SS 3
2001	Arkansas	Tex	288	77	9	4	3	18	55	39	16	15	10	221	.267	.315	.358	.228	27	70-SS 0
2001	SaltLake	PCL	197	41	5	2	1	13	41	22	12	7	4	161	.208	.264	.269	.187	12	49-SS -5
2002	*Anaheim*	*AL*	*455*	*124*	*14*	*5*	*5*	*38*	*90*	*71*	*40*	*28*	*14*	*344*	*.273*	*.329*	*.358*	*.239*	*48*	

Amezaga made strides with the bat at Arkansas, so the Angels betrayed their desperation by moving him to the PCL. Most players can't handle that kind of itinerary, especially if they're suspect to begin with like Amezaga. There's talk about him displacing either David Eckstein or Adam Kennedy, although it's not clear what the impetus for that would be.

Garret Anderson LF Bats L Age 30

YEAR	TEAM	LGE	AB	H	DB	TP	HR	BB	SO	R	RBI	SB	CS	OUT	BA	OBP	SLG	EQA	EQR	DEFENSE
1999	Anaheim	AL	616	192	35	2	23	28	71	87	79	3	4	428	.312	.342	.487	.270	81	153-CF 12
2000	Anaheim	AL	644	188	40	3	37	16	77	89	113	7	6	463	.292	.309	.536	.268	86	140-CF 2
2001	Anaheim	AL	672	202	35	2	32	30	86	88	128	12	7	477	.301	.330	.501	.270	90	148-LF 6
2002	*Anaheim*	*AL*	*594*	*178*	*33*	*2*	*26*	*36*	*77*	*85*	*86*	*8*	*5*	*421*	*.300*	*.340*	*.493*	*.276*	*84*	

As a supporting player on a team with some offensive talent, or as a center fielder, Anderson has value. The problem is one of perception: major media outlets around the country were calling Anderson the Angels' 2001 MVP, an insane proposition for a corner outfielder who put up a .314 OBP while playing on the same team as Troy Glaus. Anderson is a good defensive center fielder with pop on a team that doesn't need that.

Larry Barnes 1B Bats L Age 27

YEAR	TEAM	LGE	AB	H	DB	TP	HR	BB	SO	R	RBI	SB	CS	OUT	BA	OBP	SLG	EQA	EQR	DEFENSE
1999	Erie	Eas	499	124	19	6	16	34	99	57	74	9	2	377	.248	.300	.407	.237	51	121-1B 4
2000	Edmonton	PCL	395	90	21	7	6	37	78	44	41	2	4	309	.228	.294	.362	.220	35	93-1B -2
2001	SaltLake	PCL	395	98	18	5	14	27	82	62	56	5	1	298	.248	.297	.425	.239	42	81-1B -3
2001	Anaheim	AL	40	5	0	0	1	1	8	2	2	0	0	35	.125	.146	.200	.119	1	
2002	*Anaheim*	*AL*	*451*	*115*	*22*	*6*	*15*	*50*	*96*	*61*	*66*	*5*	*2*	*338*	*.255*	*.329*	*.430*	*.257*	*57*	

With Mo Vaughn down for the season, the Angels were shallower than a Backstreet Boys CD at first base and designated hitter. Barnes got two shots at some playing time and wasn't able to capitalize on them. He'll never be a productive major-league hitter; he's overmatched in Double-A, to be honest.

Jeff DaVanon RF Bats B Age 28

YEAR	TEAM	LGE	AB	H	DB	TP	HR	BB	SO	R	RBI	SB	CS	OUT	BA	OBP	SLG	EQA	EQR	DEFENSE
1999	Midland	Tex	369	101	23	6	8	40	70	62	41	11	6	274	.274	.349	.434	.262	48	86-RF -2
1999	Edmonton	PCL	129	36	5	2	5	17	25	26	14	8	3	96	.279	.366	.465	.279	20	33-RF 5
2001	SaltLake	PCL	251	67	14	5	8	28	52	36	36	7	2	186	.267	.345	.458	.268	35	64-RF 0
2001	Anaheim	AL	88	18	3	1	5	11	25	8	9	1	3	73	.205	.293	.432	.231	9	21-RF 0
2002	*Anaheim*	*AL*	*408*	*106*	*21*	*7*	*14*	*50*	*94*	*72*	*48*	*6*	*4*	*306*	*.260*	*.341*	*.449*	*.266*	*56*	

DaVanon is the best-hitting outfielder the Angels have in their system. He doesn't really do anything well enough to hold down a regular major-league job, but he'll provide some depth at the position and push a Triple-A team towards a title. Who can really tell the difference between Ballatore and Dom Perignon, anyway?

Gary DiSarcina SS Bats R Age 34

YEAR	TEAM	LGE	AB	H	DB	TP	HR	BB	SO	R	RBI	SB	CS	OUT	BA	OBP	SLG	EQA	EQR	DEFENSE
1999	Anaheim	AL	270	65	8	1	1	13	28	32	29	2	2	207	.241	.280	.289	.195	17	81-SS 4
2000	Anaheim	AL	37	15	1	0	1	1	3	5	10	0	1	23	.405	.436	.514	.308	6	12-SS 2
2002	*Anaheim*	*AL*	*220*	*55*	*6*	*1*	*2*	*14*	*23*	*24*	*28*	*1*	*2*	*167*	*.250*	*.295*	*.314*	*.203*	*15*	

With the passing of the 2001 season, an all-too-large salary albatross drops off the Angels' neck as DiSarcina heads into free agency. A torn shoulder tendon ended up costing him all of 2001, and the market for shortstops who can't throw is pretty tight. Even in his prime, DiSarcina was an incredibly overrated player.

David Eckstein SS Bats R Age 27

YEAR	TEAM	LGE	AB	H	DB	TP	HR	BB	SO	R	RBI	SB	CS	OUT	BA	OBP	SLG	EQA	EQR	DEFENSE
1999	Trenton	Eas	495	138	22	3	5	69	48	87	42	19	9	366	.279	.383	.366	.263	65	125-2B 6
2000	Pawtuckt	Int	426	100	9	0	4	51	44	67	30	9	7	333	.235	.338	.284	.222	39	112-2B 8
2001	Anaheim	AL	582	178	26	2	5	46	52	85	43	27	4	408	.306	.372	.383	.266	74	116-SS 3 12-2B 0
2002	*Anaheim*	*AL*	*504*	*142*	*20*	*2*	*9*	*57*	*49*	*88*	*45*	*18*	*8*	*370*	*.282*	*.355*	*.383*	*.257*	*62*	

The savior of the infield in 2001, Eckstein made a successful switch from second base to shortstop and stabilized the leadoff spot in the order. He was an astute pickup by the Angels as a minor-league free agent in 2000. Eckstein will be an acceptable shortstop as long as he continues to handle the position defensively, which frees the team to fix other problems.

Darin Erstad CF Bats L Age 28

YEAR	TEAM	LGE	AB	H	DB	TP	HR	BB	SO	R	RBI	SB	CS	OUT	BA	OBP	SLG	EQA	EQR	DEFENSE
1999	Anaheim	AL	582	153	22	5	14	41	89	82	52	12	7	436	.263	.312	.390	.235	59	75-1B 2 69-LF 17
2000	Anaheim	AL	666	241	38	6	26	55	72	115	95	28	9	434	.362	.411	.554	.317	123	136-LF 16
2001	Anaheim	AL	631	172	34	1	11	65	98	93	66	22	11	470	.273	.348	.382	.250	73	146-CF 14
2002	*Anaheim*	*AL*	*576*	*166*	*29*	*3*	*16*	*59*	*86*	*92*	*60*	*20*	*8*	*418*	*.288*	*.354*	*.432*	*.270*	*79*	

He's starting to look like vintage Howard Johnson, alternating good years and bad ones. Erstad followed up his career-year 2000 with a below-average performance last year, one that owed a lot to strained ligaments in his right knee. Erstad is a great defensive center fielder, and unless there's something about playing the position that gums up his works offensively, he's wasted anywhere else. A free agent after the season, he's likely to be elsewhere by the trade deadline.

Jorge Fabregas C Bats L Age 32

YEAR	TEAM	LGE	AB	H	DB	TP	HR	BB	SO	R	RBI	SB	CS	OUT	BA	OBP	SLG	EQA	EQR	DEFENSE
1999	Florida	NL	225	48	11	2	3	23	25	20	21	0	0	177	.213	.292	.320	.211	18	68-C 8
2000	Omaha	PCL	129	29	4	1	1	9	9	7	15	1	1	101	.225	.275	.295	.196	9	22-C -1
2000	KansasCy	AL	140	39	2	0	4	7	10	12	17	1	0	101	.279	.313	.379	.233	13	38-C 2
2001	Anaheim	AL	148	35	5	2	2	3	13	10	16	0	0	113	.236	.252	.338	.196	10	43-C 2
2002	*Anaheim*	*AL*	*231*	*52*	*7*	*2*	*4*	*19*	*21*	*17*	*23*	*1*	*0*	*179*	*.225*	*.284*	*.325*	*.205*	*17*	

It would be cool to be a fan of a league in which a few teams stack their starting eight with great, durable players and populate their benches with guys like Fabregas. Rather than gloves, the scrubs would get pom-poms, and instead of taking BP, they would work on nifty public displays of disrespect for the opposition. Fabregas can't hit, but he stands a good chance of incorporating the Nestea Plunge, a mannequin, some soft-shoe, and a Mariners uniform into an insulting skit that will keep the Big Ed crowds in stitches. The Angels think so too; he'll be back in 2002.

Jose Fernandez 3B Bats R Age 27

YEAR	TEAM	LGE	AB	H	DB	TP	HR	BB	SO	R	RBI	SB	CS	OUT	BA	OBP	SLG	EQA	EQR	DEFENSE
1999	Ottawa	Int	464	117	24	2	12	24	128	60	55	11	6	353	.252	.294	.390	.228	44	110-3B -6 10-1B 0
2000	Indianap	Int	470	127	34	3	10	41	91	63	59	8	3	346	.270	.335	.419	.253	56	116-3B 5
2001	SaltLake	PCL	441	128	23	1	24	49	83	77	87	8	6	318	.290	.371	.510	.288	71	110-3B 4
2001	Anaheim	AL	25	2	2	0	0	2	9	1	0	0	1	24	.080	.148	.160	.107	0	
2002	*ChiCubs*	*NL*	*421*	*121*	*25*	*2*	*19*	*46*	*94*	*70*	*68*	*11*	*6*	*306*	*.287*	*.358*	*.492*	*.281*	*64*	

Fernandez was the Angels' Minor League Player of the Year after making a run at the PCL Triple Crown at Salt Lake. In early October he underwent surgery on the hamate bone in his hand, and the Cubs snarfed him up off waivers the next day. Considering Fernandez was far and away the best hitter the Angels had in their high minors, it's saying something that he won't be missed.

Benji Gil IF Bats R Age 29

YEAR	TEAM	LGE	AB	H	DB	TP	HR	BB	SO	R	RBI	SB	CS	OUT	BA	OBP	SLG	EQA	EQR	DEFENSE
1999	Calgary	PCL	400	94	19	1	13	22	92	54	46	13	4	310	.235	.283	.385	.225	37	102-SS -15
2000	Anaheim	AL	299	73	15	1	6	27	52	27	22	10	7	233	.244	.317	.361	.230	30	81-SS -2
2001	Anaheim	AL	260	80	15	4	9	15	49	35	40	2	4	184	.308	.345	.500	.272	36	42-SS -6 16-2B 1
2002	*Anaheim*	*AL*	*357*	*96*	*19*	*3*	*12*	*31*	*72*	*47*	*43*	*8*	*6*	*267*	*.269*	*.327*	*.440*	*.257*	*44*	

The Pod Person left Gil early: he hit his last home run of the season on July 18. His option was picked up for 2002, but he's not likely to get this much playing time again. That projection looks pretty optimistic.

Troy Glaus 3B Bats R Age 25

YEAR	TEAM	LGE	AB	H	DB	TP	HR	BB	SO	R	RBI	SB	CS	OUT	BA	OBP	SLG	EQA	EQR	DEFENSE
1999	Anaheim	AL	547	135	26	0	32	66	126	84	79	5	1	413	.247	.334	.470	.265	75	149-3B 6
2000	Anaheim	AL	554	160	30	1	50	104	143	114	98	14	12	406	.289	.403	.617	.319	117	151-3B 6
2001	Anaheim	AL	589	157	36	2	46	109	137	107	114	9	3	435	.267	.385	.569	.307	114	156-3B -3
2002	*Anaheim*	*AL*	*540*	*159*	*26*	*1*	*43*	*99*	*136*	*106*	*97*	*10*	*5*	*386*	*.294*	*.404*	*.585*	*.322*	*114*	

Glaus didn't destroy the league the way he did in 2000. He still turned in an excellent season and is the state-of-the-art third baseman in the American League, pending the return of Eric Chavez's walks. It'll be tremendous fun watching Glaus and Chavez over the next few years. Imagine what the AL shortstop situation would look like if those two guys hadn't been moved 45 feet to the right.

Jeff Guiel OF Bats L Age 28

YEAR	TEAM	LGE	AB	H	DB	TP	HR	BB	SO	R	RBI	SB	CS	OUT	BA	OBP	SLG	EQA	EQR	DEFENSE
1999	Erie	Eas	177	40	6	2	5	25	33	26	18	2	2	139	.226	.326	.367	.236	19	46-LF 0
2000	Erie	Eas	414	92	18	2	14	37	100	43	44	1	3	325	.222	.295	.377	.224	39	35-LF 1 23-1B -1
2001	Arkansas	Tex	179	49	9	1	10	17	52	26	26	2	1	131	.274	.343	.503	.276	26	15-RF -1
2001	SaltLake	PCL	219	61	9	1	8	15	35	29	27	2	0	158	.279	.327	.438	.255	26	44-RF -1
2002	*Anaheim*	*AL*	*397*	*104*	*20*	*2*	*16*	*40*	*94*	*56*	*49*	*3*	*2*	*295*	*.262*	*.330*	*.443*	*.260*	*51*	

Jeff Guiel and his older brother Aaron are truly from the same mold: both lefties, both mediocre defensive outfielders with no glaring weaknesses at the plate. Neither player is likely to make it to the majors for anything more than a cup of coffee, but long after they've retired they'll still smoke the softball at Guiel family reunions.

Nathan Haynes CF Bats L Age 22

YEAR	TEAM	LGE	AB	H	DB	TP	HR	BB	SO	R	RBI	SB	CS	OUT	BA	OBP	SLG	EQA	EQR	DEFENSE
1999	Visalia	Cal	144	34	5	0	1	11	27	17	9	6	5	115	.236	.297	.292	.204	11	34-CF -2
1999	Lk Elsin	Cal	109	28	5	2	1	8	19	12	9	5	3	84	.257	.310	.367	.229	11	26-CF -1
2000	Erie	Eas	459	100	13	2	6	24	110	42	33	24	14	373	.218	.265	.294	.195	31	112-CF -11
2001	Arkansas	Tex	320	86	10	3	4	26	66	38	18	22	11	245	.269	.327	.356	.235	33	71-CF 5
2002	*Anaheim*	*AL*	*418*	*109*	*15*	*3*	*8*	*36*	*95*	*57*	*33*	*24*	*10*	*319*	*.261*	*.319*	*.368*	*.239*	*45*	

Haynes hasn't made much progress since being the centerpiece of the 1999 Randy Velarde trade, and the Angels are anxious to see some signs that he's ready to contribute at the major-league level or bring value in a trade. Haynes has always been raw; he's in the wrong organization for molding his tools into skills.

Adam Kennedy 2B Bats L Age 26

YEAR	TEAM	LGE	AB	H	DB	TP	HR	BB	SO	R	RBI	SB	CS	OUT	BA	OBP	SLG	EQA	EQR	DEFENSE
1999	Memphis	PCL	361	105	19	3	8	24	33	54	49	15	5	261	.291	.340	.427	.259	44	51-2B -10 19-SS -2
1999	St Louis	NL	103	26	11	1	1	1	7	12	16	0	1	78	.252	.273	.408	.220	9	26-2B -4
2000	Anaheim	AL	595	162	34	11	10	21	64	79	70	22	9	442	.272	.301	.417	.239	62	146-2B 4
2001	Anaheim	AL	478	137	25	3	7	29	61	50	42	11	8	349	.287	.338	.395	.246	53	124-2B 0
2002	*Anaheim*	*AL*	*540*	*153*	*30*	*6*	*10*	*34*	*66*	*72*	*68*	*17*	*9*	*396*	*.283*	*.326*	*.417*	*.251*	*63*	

Kennedy has paid lip service to avoiding outs but hasn't shown any improvement in doing so. Another Angel stuck in neutral, he's essentially the same player he was in 1999: enough power to be intriguing, but otherwise replaceable. Players this young shouldn't be known quantities.

Casey Kotchman 1B Bats L Age 19

YEAR	TEAM	LGE	AB	H	DB	TP	HR	BB	SO	R	RBI	SB	CS	OUT	BA	OBP	SLG	EQA	EQR	DEFENSE
2001	Provo	Pio	21	7	2	0	0	1	0	3	4	0	0	14	.333	.364	.429	.266	3	
2002	*Anaheim*	*AL*	*72*	*24*	*7*	*0*	*0*	*4*	*0*	*8*	*8*	*0*	*0*	*48*	*.333*	*.368*	*.431*	*.273*	*9*	

The 13th pick in the 2001 draft is a first baseman with a potent bat and a reputation for a slick glove. Kotchman is about as projectable as a prep player can be, hitting for good average and power in high school with a 32/2 walk-to-strikeout ratio in his senior year. He was shut down early in his first pro season with a mysterious hand injury that bears watching.

Ben Molina C Bats R Age 27

YEAR	TEAM	LGE	AB	H	DB	TP	HR	BB	SO	R	RBI	SB	CS	OUT	BA	OBP	SLG	EQA	EQR	DEFENSE
1999	Edmonton	PCL	237	59	9	0	7	12	16	22	33	1	1	180	.249	.297	.376	.224	21	53-C 5
1999	Anaheim	AL	101	27	3	0	2	5	5	8	11	0	1	75	.267	.313	.356	.224	9	30-C 1
2000	Anaheim	AL	470	136	19	2	15	18	29	57	69	1	0	334	.289	.324	.434	.251	53	125-C 6
2001	Anaheim	AL	317	85	6	0	8	17	43	31	42	0	1	233	.268	.318	.363	.230	29	85-C 2
2002	*Anaheim*	*AL*	*399*	*110*	*13*	*1*	*14*	*27*	*42*	*43*	*59*	*1*	*1*	*290*	*.276*	*.322*	*.419*	*.249*	*45*	

Another in the parade of Angels hitters with high batting averages and limited secondary skills, Molina regressed in his second year as a starter. He's a reliable defensive catcher who isn't going to get much better with the bat. He'll be the starter in Anaheim in 2002.

Jose Molina C Bats R Age 27

YEAR	TEAM	LGE	AB	H	DB	TP	HR	BB	SO	R	RBI	SB	CS	OUT	BA	OBP	SLG	EQA	EQR	DEFENSE
1999	Iowa	PCL	238	56	10	1	3	17	49	20	21	0	1	183	.235	.294	.324	.210	19	67-C -2
2000	Iowa	PCL	248	53	4	0	2	18	59	18	14	1	3	198	.214	.267	.254	.180	14	71-C 2
2001	SaltLake	PCL	208	53	8	1	4	13	44	23	24	1	1	156	.255	.303	.361	.223	18	61-C -1
2001	Anaheim	AL	45	16	1	0	3	3	8	9	5	0	0	29	.356	.396	.578	.315	8	14-C 3
2002	*Anaheim*	*AL*	*279*	*72*	*10*	*1*	*6*	*25*	*65*	*28*	*28*	*1*	*1*	*208*	*.258*	*.319*	*.366*	*.234*	*27*	

Ben's little brother is a similar player to him, but not as good at the plate, and with a stronger arm behind it. Los Dos Molinas behind the dish is a neat trick, and there are bigger stiffs around the league in reserve spots. Jose will have to compete with Fabregas for a roster spot and is unlikely to win the battle.

Jose Nieves IF Bats R Age 27

YEAR	TEAM	LGE	AB	H	DB	TP	HR	BB	SO	R	RBI	SB	CS	OUT	BA	OBP	SLG	EQA	EQR	DEFENSE
1999	Iowa	PCL	388	93	20	2	9	20	59	44	46	9	6	301	.240	.282	.371	.218	33	95-SS -7
1999	ChiCubs	NL	182	45	8	1	2	6	23	15	17	0	2	139	.247	.286	.335	.207	14	49-SS 1
2000	ChiCubs	NL	200	43	6	3	5	8	39	17	23	1	1	158	.215	.245	.350	.197	14	28-3B 2 15-SS -5
2001	SaltLake	PCL	251	71	12	3	8	8	33	40	28	7	5	185	.283	.310	.450	.248	28	45-2B -4 12-SS 0
2001	Anaheim	AL	53	14	3	1	2	2	17	5	4	0	1	40	.264	.310	.472	.248	6	
2002	*Anaheim*	*AL*	*448*	*113*	*21*	*5*	*15*	*27*	*77*	*55*	*59*	*7*	*8*	*342*	*.252*	*.295*	*.422*	*.236*	*46*	

The Angels felt good enough about their bullpen and bad enough about their middle infeld to deal Mike Fyhrie for Nieves in spring training. Nieves was called up and sent down three separate times, with a trip to the DL in there somewhere. A year later, it's still not clear what the point of picking him up was.

Mike O'Keefe LF Bats L Age 24

YEAR	TEAM	LGE	AB	H	DB	TP	HR	BB	SO	R	RBI	SB	CS	OUT	BA	OBP	SLG	EQA	EQR	DEFENSE
1999	Boise	Nwn	263	58	10	0	4	31	48	27	32	2	1	206	.221	.308	.304	.214	22	66-LF -5
2000	CedarRpd	Mid	393	70	11	1	9	40	80	41	30	3	3	326	.178	.261	.280	.189	25	105-LF -9
2001	R Cucmng	Cal	416	112	17	3	11	31	78	53	63	11	2	306	.269	.321	.404	.246	46	88-LF -8
2002	*Anaheim*	*AL*	*396*	*103*	*18*	*2*	*13*	*42*	*81*	*56*	*63*	*9*	*2*	*295*	*.260*	*.331*	*.414*	*.256*	*49*	

The Anaheim system has really started to resemble a factory outlet for mediocre outfielders. O'Keefe took a step forward last year, but as a 23-year-old in high-A ball, that's par for the course. His reckless defensive style puts himself and others at risk.

Orlando Palmeiro LF Bats L Age 33

YEAR	TEAM	LGE	AB	H	DB	TP	HR	BB	SO	R	RBI	SB	CS	OUT	BA	OBP	SLG	EQA	EQR	DEFENSE
1999	Anaheim	AL	314	90	13	1	1	36	26	45	22	5	5	229	.287	.370	.344	.248	35	76-LF 0
2000	Anaheim	AL	239	74	15	3	1	35	18	36	25	4	1	166	.310	.402	.410	.282	35	55-LF 0
2001	Anaheim	AL	230	59	11	1	2	26	21	30	23	5	7	178	.257	.338	.339	.230	23	47-OF -6
2002	*Anaheim*	*AL*	*277*	*73*	*13*	*2*	*2*	*40*	*24*	*40*	*23*	*5*	*5*	*209*	*.264*	*.356*	*.347*	*.246*	*31*	

Despite the trouble the Angels had with their lineup, Palmeiro was still protected from left-handers and ended up with about the same amount of playing time in 2001 as he'd had in 2000. Palmeiro saw a lot of action as a designated hitter and batted ninth most of the time. Think about that one for a minute.

Robb Quinlan 1B Bats R Age 25

YEAR	TEAM	LGE	AB	H	DB	TP	HR	BB	SO	R	RBI	SB	CS	OUT	BA	OBP	SLG	EQA	EQR	DEFENSE
1999	Boise	Nwn	292	65	9	1	5	17	60	26	37	2	2	229	.223	.269	.312	.197	20	64-3B -5
2000	Lk Elsin	Cal	489	128	29	2	4	42	83	57	56	3	2	363	.262	.321	.354	.230	46	111-1B 1 13-RF -2
2001	Arkansas	Tex	499	128	28	4	12	44	85	68	61	0	3	374	.257	.320	.401	.240	53	111-1B 5
2002	*Anaheim*	*AL*	*446*	*123*	*23*	*3*	*9*	*45*	*82*	*55*	*66*	*1*	*2*	*325*	*.276*	*.342*	*.401*	*.254*	*53*	

Quinlan has made some strides with the bat, but he's way too old to be of much use to a major-league team. He's good enough to sub for Larry Barnes without missing a beat, though, and should move on to Salt Lake in 2002. There's no word on why he and Nen are hoarding b's.

John Raburn IF Bats B Age 23

YEAR	TEAM	LGE	AB	H	DB	TP	HR	BB	SO	R	RBI	SB	CS	OUT	BA	OBP	SLG	EQA	EQR	DEFENSE
2000	Boise	Nwn	293	56	9	2	0	33	78	29	20	12	3	240	.191	.275	.235	.189	19	33-SS -5 21-3B -1
2001	CedarRpd	Mid	250	64	2	1	0	47	47	37	9	18	6	192	.256	.378	.272	.244	28	49-2B -12 13-SS -3
2002	*Anaheim*	*AL*	*303*	*78*	*8*	*2*	*1*	*44*	*69*	*36*	*23*	*16*	*4*	*229*	*.257*	*.352*	*.307*	*.242*	*33*	

The best player on the Cedar Rapids team before suffering a season-ending injury to his left thumb on June 26, Raburn was one of only two Kernels to make the Midwest League All-Star team. He's an intriguing prospect in an organization virtually devoid of them; keep an eye on him this year.

Tim Salmon RF Bats R Age 33

YEAR	TEAM	LGE	AB	H	DB	TP	HR	BB	SO	R	RBI	SB	CS	OUT	BA	OBP	SLG	EQA	EQR	DEFENSE
1999	Anaheim	AL	349	96	24	2	18	59	72	59	67	4	1	254	.275	.380	.510	.294	59	89-RF 2
2000	Anaheim	AL	559	167	35	1	36	97	122	104	93	0	2	394	.299	.408	.558	.314	109	119-RF 0
2001	Anaheim	AL	476	115	20	0	20	98	105	66	52	8	3	364	.242	.378	.410	.272	70	119-RF 0
2002	*Anaheim*	*AL*	*514*	*130*	*24*	*1*	*28*	*109*	*120*	*84*	*83*	*6*	*2*	*386*	*.253*	*.384*	*.467*	*.291*	*88*	

Trying to hit the ground running after surgeries on his right foot and left shoulder in 2000, Salmon plainly wasn't right all season. He hit better after a stint on the DL in July with a shoulder strain. Salmon has always been brittle, and most of the decline in his production in 2001 appears to have been injury-related. The extension he signed last spring runs through 2005, so a return to form by Salmon is a must for the Angels.

Brian Specht SS Bats B Age 21

YEAR	TEAM	LGE	AB	H	DB	TP	HR	BB	SO	R	RBI	SB	CS	OUT	BA	OBP	SLG	EQA	EQR	DEFENSE			
2000	Lk Elsin	Cal	341	76	20	2	2	34	81	47	23	11	7	272	.223	.296	.311	.211	28	88-SS	-9		
2001	R Cucmng	Cal	268	55	11	3	5	18	75	32	21	10	3	216	.205	.259	.325	.202	20	63-SS	-11		
2001	Arkansas	Tex	157	37	7	1	2	10	32	11	12	1	1	121	.236	.284	.331	.208	12	43-SS	-6		
2002	*Anaheim*	*AL*	*403*	*95*	*20*	*3*	*7*	*43*	*106*	*52*	*38*	*12*	*5*	*313*	*.236*	*.309*	*.352*	*.229*	*39*				

Specht was a hot high-school shortstop whom Anaheim drafted and signed in 1999. He's been moved up quickly, not really making any headway at the plate but not losing ground either. The organization is going to have to solve his poor defensive instincts to get away with playing him at shortstop in the majors; the rest of his defensive game is fair.

Scott Spiezio UT Bats B Age 29

YEAR	TEAM	LGE	AB	H	DB	TP	HR	BB	SO	R	RBI	SB	CS	OUT	BA	OBP	SLG	EQA	EQR	DEFENSE			
1999	Vancouvr	PCL	105	38	6	1	5	12	15	22	22	0	0	67	.362	.434	.581	.332	21	24-2B	2		
1999	Oakland	AL	246	63	18	0	11	27	32	31	35	0	0	183	.256	.334	.463	.263	32	34-2B	6	23-3B	-6
2000	Anaheim	AL	294	73	10	2	18	37	49	45	47	1	2	223	.248	.338	.480	.267	41	19-1B	-5	11-3B	-1
2001	Anaheim	AL	457	130	30	4	14	36	56	61	55	5	2	329	.284	.342	.460	.266	60	89-1B	15	12-LF	-1
2002	*Anaheim*	*AL*	*424*	*116*	*24*	*3*	*17*	*46*	*59*	*60*	*60*	*3*	*2*	*310*	*.274*	*.345*	*.465*	*.272*	*60*				

Spiezio's versatility and power make him a nice player to have, and he helped take a little bit of the sting out of losing Mo Vaughn for the season—not much of it, mind you, but at least he kept Larry Barnes at bay. He'd have more value if Scioscia let him play more infield.

Mo Vaughn 1B Bats L Age 34

YEAR	TEAM	LGE	AB	H	DB	TP	HR	BB	SO	R	RBI	SB	CS	OUT	BA	OBP	SLG	EQA	EQR	DEFENSE	
1999	Anaheim	AL	520	151	19	0	35	48	112	62	106	0	0	369	.290	.361	.529	.289	83	67-1B	-3
2000	Anaheim	AL	607	170	26	0	39	72	159	90	114	2	0	437	.280	.370	.516	.291	99	143-1B	-14
2002	*NY Mets*	*NL*	*474*	*124*	*17*	*0*	*28*	*63*	*128*	*60*	*84*	*1*	*0*	*350*	*.262*	*.348*	*.475*	*.280*	*72*		

A ruptured left biceps led to Vaughn missing all of 2001. Taking his age, weight, and general conditioning into account, the safe bet is to expect nothing more than the mediocre play he's given the Angels so far. Compared to the bodies they were dragging out there in 2001, of course, he'll be a tremendous help.

Shawn Wooten C/1B Bats R Age 29

YEAR	TEAM	LGE	AB	H	DB	TP	HR	BB	SO	R	RBI	SB	CS	OUT	BA	OBP	SLG	EQA	EQR	DEFENSE			
1999	Erie	Eas	519	130	20	1	15	36	102	56	66	2	1	390	.250	.306	.380	.230	50	124-3B	8		
2000	Erie	Eas	192	49	9	1	8	12	31	25	26	3	1	144	.255	.303	.438	.244	21	38-C	1		
2000	Edmonton	PCL	247	78	17	2	9	13	37	34	31	0	0	169	.316	.355	.510	.283	36	47-C	0		
2001	Anaheim	AL	221	72	7	1	9	6	36	25	33	2	0	149	.326	.350	.489	.277	30	18-C	1	16-1B	-3
2002	*Anaheim*	*AL*	*453*	*132*	*20*	*2*	*20*	*33*	*79*	*60*	*68*	*2*	*0*	*321*	*.291*	*.340*	*.477*	*.273*	*63*				

Wooten had a heck of a season, backing up Ben Molina at catcher and helping out at first base. He's a free swinger who makes good contact; at a corner, that can easily be a liability, but as a catcher, he could turn in a couple of pretty good seasons. The last time the Angels had an offensively oriented catcher/infielder this interesting, they traded him for Andy Sheets (Phil Nevin). As the Topps All-Rookie team catcher, he'll have a cool little gold cup in the corner of his baseball card in 2002.

PITCHERS (ERA: 4.50, H/9: 9.0, HR/9: 1.0, BB/9: 3.0, K/9: 6.0, KW: 2.0, PERA: 4.50)

Chris Bootcheck Throws R Age 23

YEAR	TEAM	LGE	IP	H	ER	HR	BB	K	ERA	W	L	H/9	HR/9	BB/9	K/9	KW	PERA	STUFF
2001	R Cucmng	Cal	84.7	100	66	21	29	45	7.02	3	6	10.6	2.2	3.1	4.8	0.8	6.01	-5
2001	Arkansas	Tex	36.3	41	22	5	13	15	5.45	2	2	10.2	1.2	3.2	3.7	0.6	7.40	-6

A tall, skinny right-hander who was the Angels' second first-round pick in 2000, Bootcheck needs another good pitch before he can start dominating batters. He's got a middling curve and has been known to screw around with a change-up; either pitch could significantly help his cause. Unless he starts strong, he'll spend next year in the Arkansas rotation.

Toby Borland   Throws R   Age 33

YEAR	TEAM	LGE	IP	H	ER	HR	BB	K	ERA	W	L	H/9	HR/9	BB/9	K/9	KW	PERA	STUFF
1999	Edmonton	PCL	28.3	30	26	6	27	23	8.26	1	2	9.5	1.9	8.6	7.3	0.4	8.26	-39
2000	Erie	Eas	12.7	12	6	0	9	7	4.26	1	0	8.5	0.0	6.4	5.0	0.4	7.58	-29
2001	SaltLake	PCL	71.3	62	30	2	37	58	3.79	5	3	7.8	0.3	4.7	7.3	0.8	3.19	-1

Borland has been passed around like Big Mouth Billy Bass at a gift exchange. That's not really surprising, given his terrible control. He kept the ball down and did well at Salt Lake in 2001. This is the type of pitcher every pitching coach wants a chance to save.

Brian Cooper   Throws R   Age 27

YEAR	TEAM	LGE	IP	H	ER	HR	BB	K	ERA	W	L	H/9	HR/9	BB/9	K/9	KW	PERA	STUFF
1999	Erie	Eas	154.0	169	89	27	33	89	5.20	7	10	9.9	1.6	1.9	5.2	1.3	4.16	1
1999	Edmonton	PCL	32.3	28	10	0	11	23	2.78	3	1	7.8	0.0	3.1	6.4	1.0	4.70	19
1999	Anaheim	AL	26.7	27	16	3	15	15	5.40	1	2	9.1	1.0	5.1	5.1	0.5	4.10	-2
2000	Edmonton	PCL	65.0	80	52	16	19	26	7.20	2	5	11.1	2.2	2.6	3.6	0.7	7.87	-25
2000	Anaheim	AL	89.3	104	60	15	29	36	6.04	4	6	10.5	1.5	2.9	3.6	0.6	5.65	-10
2001	SaltLake	PCL	166.7	195	124	31	74	69	6.70	6	13	10.5	1.7	4.0	3.7	0.5	5.37	-19
2001	Anaheim	AL	12.7	14	7	2	4	7	4.97	0	1	9.9	1.4	2.8	5.0	0.9	2.94	-8

Cooper is a tease, a pitcher with a good strikeout-to-walk ratio who loses it for extended periods and looks terrible. He looked quite good in his short stint with the Angels last year and was acceptable at Salt Lake. Another full season with the Stingers will do him good after the monthly trips he made through the system early in his career.

Brendan Donnelly   Throws R   Age 30

YEAR	TEAM	LGE	IP	H	ER	HR	BB	K	ERA	W	L	H/9	HR/9	BB/9	K/9	KW	PERA	STUFF
1999	Durham	Int	61.3	60	28	6	19	44	4.11	4	3	8.8	0.9	2.8	6.5	1.2	3.60	-3
2000	Syracuse	Int	43.7	47	33	7	29	25	6.80	2	3	9.7	1.4	6.0	5.2	0.4	8.03	-37
2000	Iowa	PCL	18.3	21	14	4	6	10	6.87	1	1	10.3	2.0	2.9	4.9	0.8	11.35	-34
2001	Arkansas	Tex	27.7	27	18	4	18	22	5.86	1	2	8.8	1.3	5.9	7.2	0.6	3.48	-21
2001	SaltLake	PCL	41.0	40	18	5	10	32	3.95	3	2	8.8	1.1	2.2	7.0	1.6	2.52	0

A road-weary Donnelly—he'd pitched for five teams in the previous two seasons—signed with the Angels prior to last season. He pitched so well he was added to the 40-man roster in October. Even if he repeats his career-best performance, he'll need some luck to see action with the Angels in 2002.

Radhames Dykhoff   Throws L   Age 27

YEAR	TEAM	LGE	IP	H	ER	HR	BB	K	ERA	W	L	H/9	HR/9	BB/9	K/9	KW	PERA	STUFF
1999	Rochestr	Int	78.3	85	49	12	31	44	5.63	4	5	9.8	1.4	3.6	5.1	0.7	4.55	-14
2000	Binghmtn	Eas	23.7	24	14	4	10	19	5.32	1	2	9.1	1.5	3.8	7.2	0.9	3.03	-11
2000	Norfolk	Int	39.3	40	27	7	23	32	6.18	1	3	9.2	1.6	5.3	7.3	0.7	6.37	-20
2001	Arkansas	Tex	80.3	91	55	8	48	22	6.16	3	6	10.2	0.9	5.4	2.5	0.2	7.20	-41

Dykhoff is a career minor leaguer who serves up lots of hittable pitches. He's behind Mark Lukasiewicz, and in the wrong organization. For a team sporting great flycatchers, such as this year's Twins, he could be a useful spare part. For the Angels, he's a contender for Coolest Name of the Year award.

Steve Green   Throws R   Age 24

YEAR	TEAM	LGE	IP	H	ER	HR	BB	K	ERA	W	L	H/9	HR/9	BB/9	K/9	KW	PERA	STUFF
1999	Lk Elsin	Cal	122.3	135	72	16	41	54	5.30	6	8	9.9	1.2	3.0	4.0	0.7	5.89	0
1999	Erie	Eas	39.0	41	25	6	19	23	5.77	2	2	9.5	1.4	4.4	5.3	0.6	5.87	5
2000	Erie	Eas	77.7	82	49	12	36	48	5.68	3	6	9.5	1.4	4.2	5.6	0.7	4.15	6
2000	Edmonton	PCL	45.0	49	29	5	26	19	5.80	2	3	9.8	1.0	5.2	3.8	0.4	6.95	-10
2001	SaltLake	PCL	58.7	59	24	3	15	28	3.68	4	3	9.1	0.5	2.3	4.3	0.9	4.27	7

(Steve Green *continued*)

Green took a step forward with Salt Lake in 2001 and was called up for an emergency start in Anaheim, which went well. Having piqued the Angels' interest, he tore a muscle in his forearm and was shut down for the season. He'll be rehabbing for part of 2002 as well and won't be a factor.

Shigetoshi Hasegawa Throws R Age 33

YEAR	TEAM	LGE	IP	H	ER	HR	BB	K	ERA	W	L	H/9	HR/9	BB/9	K/9	KW	PERA	STUFF
1999	Anaheim	AL	77.3	84	48	12	28	44	5.59	4	5	9.8	1.4	3.3	5.1	0.8	4.43	-13
2000	Anaheim	AL	98.0	99	48	9	31	58	4.41	6	5	9.1	0.8	2.8	5.3	0.9	3.35	-4
2001	Anaheim	AL	56.0	54	25	5	19	39	4.02	3	3	8.7	0.8	3.1	6.3	1.0	4.04	0

One of the American League's most reliable relievers, Hasegawa hit the DL in June with a partial tear in his rotator cuff. He responded well to treatment and finished up the season strong. His peripherals all look good, so he's recommended for 2002.

Mike Holtz Throws L Age 29

YEAR	TEAM	LGE	IP	H	ER	HR	BB	K	ERA	W	L	H/9	HR/9	BB/9	K/9	KW	PERA	STUFF
1999	Edmonton	PCL	26.3	25	16	5	13	26	5.47	1	2	8.5	1.7	4.4	8.9	1.0	2.38	-2
1999	Anaheim	AL	23.7	23	13	3	13	17	4.94	1	2	8.7	1.1	4.9	6.5	0.7	6.80	-13
2000	Anaheim	AL	42.0	36	17	3	15	40	3.64	3	2	7.7	0.6	3.2	8.6	1.3	4.73	11
2001	Anaheim	AL	39.3	36	18	5	14	36	4.12	2	2	8.2	1.1	3.2	8.2	1.3	5.22	5

Holtz was the top left-hander in the Angels' pen until the middle of May, when he hit the DL with an inflamed throwing elbow. Holtz and his Frisbee curve were back at the end of the month just in time to experience this extreme usage pattern: in his final 49 appearances, he pitched a total of 25 2/3 innings. Signed by Oakland to a two-year contract.

John Lackey Throws R Age 23

YEAR	TEAM	LGE	IP	H	ER	HR	BB	K	ERA	W	L	H/9	HR/9	BB/9	K/9	KW	PERA	STUFF
1999	Boise	Nwn	81.0	91	66	14	56	40	7.33	2	7	10.1	1.6	6.2	4.4	0.4	7.26	-8
2000	CedarRpd	Mid	27.7	30	13	2	6	12	4.23	2	1	9.8	0.7	2.0	3.9	1.0	2.82	9
2000	Lk Elsin	Cal	96.3	112	71	18	42	44	6.63	3	8	10.5	1.7	3.9	4.1	0.5	5.91	-5
2000	Erie	Eas	57.0	63	33	10	9	31	5.21	3	3	9.9	1.6	1.4	4.9	1.7	3.88	12
2001	Arkansas	Tex	121.0	132	69	18	34	64	5.13	6	7	9.8	1.3	2.5	4.8	0.9	4.64	5
2001	SaltLake	PCL	61.3	64	30	5	18	30	4.40	4	3	9.4	0.7	2.6	4.4	0.8	6.40	4

The Angels' top pitching prospect did a good job in 2001. Lackey has pitched a whopping 363 innings over the last two seasons while moving through five levels. His performances at Arkansas and Salt Lake were essentially similar, ERA differences aside. If he's able to survive the workload, he'll be a good major-league pitcher.

Al Levine Throws R Age 34

YEAR	TEAM	LGE	IP	H	ER	HR	BB	K	ERA	W	L	H/9	HR/9	BB/9	K/9	KW	PERA	STUFF
1999	Anaheim	AL	81.7	90	48	11	24	37	5.29	4	5	9.9	1.2	2.6	4.1	0.8	3.57	-14
2000	Anaheim	AL	96.0	102	53	9	40	42	4.97	5	6	9.6	0.8	3.8	3.9	0.5	3.44	-15
2001	Anaheim	AL	75.0	77	38	6	27	38	4.56	4	4	9.2	0.7	3.2	4.6	0.7	2.66	-10

One of the best relievers nobody has ever heard of had another fine season in 2001. Levine wasn't as good at erasing inherited runners in 2001 as he had been in 2000, but that's a minor complaint. He's a late bloomer who could improve again this season.

Mark Lukasiewicz Throws L Age 29

YEAR	TEAM	LGE	IP	H	ER	HR	BB	K	ERA	W	L	H/9	HR/9	BB/9	K/9	KW	PERA	STUFF
1999	Syracuse	Int	98.0	115	80	24	43	55	7.35	3	8	10.6	2.2	3.9	5.1	0.6	5.62	-28
2000	Syracuse	Int	40.0	40	32	9	27	39	7.20	1	3	9.0	2.0	6.1	8.8	0.7	4.15	-16
2001	SaltLake	PCL	26.0	25	12	5	3	26	4.15	2	1	8.7	1.7	1.0	9.0	4.3	1.56	13
2001	Anaheim	AL	22.3	22	15	5	9	24	6.04	1	1	8.9	2.0	3.6	9.7	1.3	6.13	5

Looking for some left-handed help after the bullpen was used very heavily to open the season, the Angels called up Lukasiewicz, who had been off to a good start at Salt Lake. He was filler material with the big club, surrendering lots of big flies. Given the depth of the Angels' pen, he'll be scrapping for a job in 2002.

Bart Miadich — Throws R — Age 26

YEAR	TEAM	LGE	IP	H	ER	HR	BB	K	ERA	W	L	H/9	HR/9	BB/9	K/9	KW	PERA	STUFF
1999	High Des	Cal	103.7	118	73	16	50	45	6.34	4	8	10.2	1.4	4.3	3.9	0.4	6.86	-20
1999	El Paso	Tex	24.0	28	16	4	8	11	6.00	1	2	10.5	1.5	3.0	4.1	0.7	9.73	-25
2000	Erie	Eas	37.7	38	24	4	25	24	5.73	2	2	9.1	1.0	6.0	5.7	0.5	4.33	-22
2000	Edmonton	PCL	22.7	24	14	4	9	15	5.56	1	2	9.5	1.6	3.6	6.0	0.8	5.60	-10
2001	SaltLake	PCL	55.3	51	31	5	37	46	5.04	3	3	8.3	0.8	6.0	7.5	0.6	3.21	-11
2001	Anaheim	AL	9.3	8	7	2	8	10	6.75	0	1	7.7	1.9	7.7	9.6	0.6	4.02	-4

Since being converted to relief, Miadich has been effective. He had an excellent season closing for Salt Lake, and in two short stints for the Angels he didn't embarrass himself. He'll be looking for a full-time job with the big club in 2002. The Angels' willingness to assemble a no-name bullpen is one of the few things the organization has done well of late.

Ramon Ortiz — Throws R — Age 26

YEAR	TEAM	LGE	IP	H	ER	HR	BB	K	ERA	W	L	H/9	HR/9	BB/9	K/9	KW	PERA	STUFF
1999	Erie	Eas	97.7	107	66	17	42	58	6.08	4	7	9.9	1.6	3.9	5.3	0.7	3.71	1
1999	Edmonton	PCL	53.0	50	27	7	20	48	4.58	3	3	8.5	1.2	3.4	8.2	1.2	4.02	25
1999	Anaheim	AL	50.3	47	25	6	21	44	4.47	3	3	8.4	1.1	3.8	7.9	1.0	5.49	19
2000	Anaheim	AL	108.0	111	63	15	45	72	5.25	5	7	9.3	1.3	3.8	6.0	0.8	4.62	7
2000	Edmonton	PCL	86.7	85	45	9	36	59	4.67	5	5	8.8	0.9	3.7	6.1	0.8	4.78	8
2001	Anaheim	AL	214.3	219	109	23	72	128	4.58	12	12	9.2	1.0	3.0	5.4	0.9	4.39	6

Last year was another solidly above-average season for Ortiz, who didn't miss a turn in 2001. He had his bouts with flakiness, and the popular comparisons to Pedro Martinez are premature, but he's a very solid building block for the next good Angels team. The sharpening of his control is a good sign.

Troy Percival — Throws R — Age 32

YEAR	TEAM	LGE	IP	H	ER	HR	BB	K	ERA	W	L	H/9	HR/9	BB/9	K/9	KW	PERA	STUFF
1999	Anaheim	AL	54.3	48	25	8	18	57	4.14	3	3	8.0	1.3	3.0	9.4	1.6	3.19	16
2000	Anaheim	AL	50.0	45	25	6	25	49	4.50	3	3	8.1	1.1	4.5	8.8	1.0	4.02	7
2001	Anaheim	AL	57.3	42	16	3	17	68	2.51	5	1	6.6	0.5	2.7	10.7	2.0	2.65	31

Anaheim's career saves leader rebounded from a middling 2000 to post some great numbers in 2001. Percival will be back for 2002 but has made lots of noise about being knifed in the back by Angels management during the negotiations for a long-term deal, so he may be somewhere else in 2003. That's probably not a bad thing for the Angels, considering his age and the team's bullpen depth.

Lou Pote — Throws R — Age 30

YEAR	TEAM	LGE	IP	H	ER	HR	BB	K	ERA	W	L	H/9	HR/9	BB/9	K/9	KW	PERA	STUFF
1999	Edmonton	PCL	154.3	169	91	23	48	79	5.31	7	10	9.9	1.3	2.8	4.6	0.8	4.96	-6
1999	Anaheim	AL	28.7	26	11	1	10	20	3.45	2	1	8.2	0.3	3.1	6.3	1.0	2.33	5
2000	Edmonton	PCL	30.3	30	16	3	15	20	4.75	1	2	8.9	0.9	4.5	5.9	0.7	4.29	-16
2000	Anaheim	AL	53.0	47	19	3	14	44	3.23	4	2	8.0	0.5	2.4	7.5	1.6	3.41	13
2001	Anaheim	AL	88.7	87	44	10	30	63	4.47	5	5	8.8	1.0	3.0	6.4	1.0	3.80	1

Pote started the year as a multi-inning reliever in the Shigetoshi Hasegawa mold, going two innings or longer in more than half of his appearances. He even snuck in an emergency start, beating the Yankees on August 6. He's the Scott Williamson-style setup man in 2002.

Pat Rapp — Throws R — Age 34

YEAR	TEAM	LGE	IP	H	ER	HR	BB	K	ERA	W	L	H/9	HR/9	BB/9	K/9	KW	PERA	STUFF
1999	Boston	AL	149.0	148	72	11	58	89	4.35	9	8	8.9	0.7	3.5	5.4	0.8	4.04	1
2000	Baltimor	AL	184.0	186	91	16	68	105	4.45	10	10	9.1	0.8	3.3	5.1	0.8	5.65	2
2001	Anaheim	AL	169.0	181	96	18	68	78	5.11	8	11	9.6	1.0	3.6	4.2	0.6	4.54	-5

We thought he was finished, but Rapp refused to disappear quietly, signing a one-year deal and pitching his way into regular work before a bruised forearm knocked him from the rotation in September. He's not a bad gamble as a short-term signing for a team that can stomach the risk of the bad Rapp showing.

Scott Schoeneweis Throws L Age 28

YEAR	TEAM	LGE	IP	H	ER	HR	BB	K	ERA	W	L	H/9	HR/9	BB/9	K/9	KW	PERA	STUFF
1999	Edmonton	PCL	40.7	46	27	7	14	19	5.98	2	3	10.2	1.5	3.1	4.2	0.7	9.21	-25
1999	Anaheim	AL	41.7	43	19	3	12	22	4.10	3	2	9.3	0.6	2.6	4.8	0.9	5.21	-9
2000	Anaheim	AL	172.7	186	92	18	55	77	4.80	9	10	9.7	0.9	2.9	4.0	0.7	4.91	-2
2001	Anaheim	AL	211.0	223	109	19	73	99	4.65	11	12	9.5	0.8	3.1	4.2	0.7	4.78	0

Schoeneweis repeated his pattern of starting the season strong (posting a 2.91 ERA in April) and slowly reverting to the mean over the rest of the year. He was steady and kept the Angels in games, which is saying something considering their offensive woes. Finesse guys with the kind of strikeout-to-walk ratio that Schoeneweis sports are always in danger of cratering.

Scot Shields Throws R Age 26

YEAR	TEAM	LGE	IP	H	ER	HR	BB	K	ERA	W	L	H/9	HR/9	BB/9	K/9	KW	PERA	STUFF
1999	Lk Elsin	Cal	107.0	102	46	2	48	60	3.87	7	5	8.6	0.2	4.0	5.0	0.6	3.95	0
1999	Erie	Eas	70.3	74	46	14	27	55	5.89	3	5	9.5	1.8	3.5	7.0	1.0	3.46	12
2000	Edmonton	PCL	165.0	162	93	20	81	120	5.07	8	10	8.8	1.1	4.4	6.5	0.7	6.07	5
2001	SaltLake	PCL	132.3	155	94	29	40	66	6.39	5	10	10.5	2.0	2.7	4.5	0.8	5.78	-13
2001	Anaheim	AL	10.7	10	5	0	7	7	4.22	1	0	8.4	0.0	5.9	5.9	0.5	0.73	-2

Shields sharpened his control at Salt Lake, but his situation is similar to that of Schoeneweis: he's a control artist, minus the advantage of being left-handed, and his mistakes get casually cuffed around, Peter McNeely-style.

Derrick Turnbow Throws R Age 24

YEAR	TEAM	LGE	IP	H	ER	HR	BB	K	ERA	W	L	H/9	HR/9	BB/9	K/9	KW	PERA	STUFF
1999	Piedmont	SAL	154.0	167	98	20	72	76	5.73	6	11	9.8	1.2	4.2	4.4	0.5	5.10	0
2000	Anaheim	AL	37.7	39	29	6	29	25	6.93	1	3	9.3	1.4	6.9	6.0	0.4	4.12	-13
2001	Arkansas	Tex	14.0	13	6	0	6	7	3.86	1	1	8.4	0.0	3.9	4.5	0.6	3.20	2

The former Rule 5 draft pick missed most of what was to be a very promising season, breaking his right ulna during his follow-through. Obviously, a broken bone is bad enough, but when a pitcher suffers an injury like this while pitching, you have to wonder if this is another Tony Saunders case.

Ismael Valdes Throws R Age 28

YEAR	TEAM	LGE	IP	H	ER	HR	BB	K	ERA	W	L	H/9	HR/9	BB/9	K/9	KW	PERA	STUFF
1999	LosAngls	NL	205.7	217	110	31	49	129	4.81	11	12	9.5	1.4	2.1	5.6	1.3	4.19	8
2000	ChiCubs	NL	66.7	76	48	15	22	40	6.48	2	5	10.3	2.0	3.0	5.4	0.9	4.93	-3
2000	LosAngls	NL	43.7	45	21	5	11	26	4.33	3	2	9.3	1.0	2.3	5.4	1.2	6.35	1
2001	Anaheim	AL	168.0	174	84	18	48	95	4.50	10	9	9.3	1.0	2.6	5.1	1.0	4.03	6

Valdes's continuing injury problems are keeping him from the big contract. None of his hand or shoulder problems last year were worrisome in the long term, but they look enough like a pattern that it would be crazy to make an extended commitment to him. When he was healthy, he was very good; he'll help some team in 2002.

Jarrod Washburn Throws L Age 27

YEAR	TEAM	LGE	IP	H	ER	HR	BB	K	ERA	W	L	H/9	HR/9	BB/9	K/9	KW	PERA	STUFF
1999	Edmonton	PCL	57.7	57	28	7	18	40	4.37	3	3	8.9	1.1	2.8	6.2	1.1	4.50	9
1999	Anaheim	AL	62.7	62	30	5	22	39	4.31	4	3	8.9	0.7	3.2	5.6	0.9	4.42	3
2000	Edmonton	PCL	32.0	34	17	3	14	14	4.78	2	2	9.6	0.8	3.9	3.9	0.5	3.99	-8
2000	Anaheim	AL	78.3	85	51	14	30	49	5.86	3	6	9.8	1.6	3.4	5.6	0.8	3.36	3
2001	Anaheim	AL	195.3	200	96	23	51	120	4.42	11	11	9.2	1.1	2.3	5.5	1.2	3.70	9

Washburn cemented his position as the low-wattage ace of the Angels with another good season. The lefty uses his fastball-slider combo to keep hitters off balance, and he changes speeds well. His workloads have been reasonable and he's pitched especially well on the road. Look for more of the same in 2002.

Ben Weber   Throws R   Age 32

YEAR	TEAM	LGE	IP	H	ER	HR	BB	K	ERA	W	L	H/9	HR/9	BB/9	K/9	KW	PERA	STUFF
1999	Fresno	PCL	85.0	87	43	7	33	45	4.55	4	5	9.2	0.7	3.5	4.8	0.7	3.62	-15
2000	Fresno	PCL	77.0	79	39	9	21	47	4.56	4	5	9.2	1.1	2.5	5.5	1.1	3.61	-8
2000	San Fran	NL	10.3	10	4	0	3	5	3.48	1	0	8.7	0.0	2.6	4.4	0.8	14.45	-21
2000	Anaheim	AL	14.3	14	4	0	2	8	2.51	2	0	8.8	0.0	1.3	5.0	2.0	3.04	5
2001	Anaheim	AL	69.0	68	32	4	30	38	4.17	4	4	8.9	0.5	3.9	5.0	0.6	3.30	-8

After a disappointing debut in San Francisco, Weber proved last season that he belongs in the majors. Prior to breaking his ankle in September, Weber was good for one plus innings and was the Angels' most extreme ground-ball pitcher. If he hits the weights and the andro hard this winter, he'll be a strong contender to play Master Chief Ogre in *Revenge of the Nerds VII: Saving Private Booger.*

Matt Wise   Throws R   Age 26

YEAR	TEAM	LGE	IP	H	ER	HR	BB	K	ERA	W	L	H/9	HR/9	BB/9	K/9	KW	PERA	STUFF
1999	Erie	Eas	98.0	108	56	14	25	49	5.14	5	6	9.9	1.3	2.3	4.5	1.0	4.87	1
2000	Edmonton	PCL	124.0	130	58	12	26	63	4.21	7	7	9.4	0.9	1.9	4.6	1.2	3.77	6
2000	Anaheim	AL	37.7	41	22	6	11	20	5.26	2	2	9.8	1.4	2.6	4.8	0.9	4.59	-1
2001	SaltLake	PCL	122.7	136	71	23	22	70	5.21	6	8	10.0	1.7	1.6	5.1	1.6	6.07	-3
2001	Anaheim	AL	49.7	49	29	10	17	48	5.26	3	3	8.9	1.8	3.1	8.7	1.4	4.41	16

The Angels called up Wise to cover for Ismael Valdes, and he didn't do a bad job. He's ready to eat innings at the bottom of the rotation now, and he'll be in the mix for a spot in 2002. Wise is plenty young enough to benefit from a full season in Salt Lake to work on his location.

Baltimore Orioles

Last year, baseball fans got to say good-bye to some truly great players. Mark McGwire's departure was frustrating in that we didn't really get one last cheer, but we had all year to applaud Tony Gwynn one final time. The way Yankees fans sent off Paul O'Neill was one of the highlights of a great World Series, and Tim Raines may have ended his career by fulfilling his dream of playing with his son.

Amidst all that, it's Cal Ripken's retirement that means the most.

Ripken's overdue decision to leave does not impact the Orioles on the field. Frankly, there were few spectacles more desperate than the adulation showered on the gray ghost for cleanly fielding a two-hopper hit right at him in his final weeks on the diamond. But more than just saying good-bye to a favorite player, Orioles fans were forlornly making their break with a happier past, because Ripken was the last physical connection to two decades of glory. The Iron Man's departure cuts the Orioles' last cord to their days as the best organization in the game. As an active link to the Orioles of Earl Weaver and the Robinsons, of Jim Palmer and Mike Flanagan and Rick Dempsey, Ripken meant something.

Orioles Prospectus

2001 record: 63–98; Fourth place, AL East

Pythagenport W/L: 66–96

Runs scored: 687 (13th in AL)

Runs allowed: 829 (tenth in AL)

Team EqA: .247 (12th in AL)

2001 batters age: 30.3 (fourth-oldest in AL)

2001 pitchers age: 27.2 (fifth-youngest in AL)

Ballpark: Oriole Park at Camden Yards; moderate pitchers' park; Park Factor of .963

2001: Old, boring, unimpressive, and expensive. Nice park, though.

2002: They're still lost, desperately in need of a complete management overhaul.

Ripken's retirement was compelling and the farewells so agonizing because of the persistent awareness of what the Orioles used to be. Whether you look back to the winning traditions of Jack Dunn's Orioles in the International League before the Second World War, or whether you prefer to start with the great American League teams of 1964–83, Baltimore baseball set the standard of how to build a winning ball club. This wasn't the home of romantic failure, like Boston, or of hopeless drudgery, like Cleveland. For more than 20 years, the Orioles ruled the roost while the Yankees crawled through the oblivion of corporate ownership.

You'll find echoes of the ideas of Earl Weaver and Harry Dalton and Paul Richards within the operating philosophies of successful big-league organizations today. A side benefit was that the success of the Oriole Way created a fan base that understood better than most about how to build a winner. And for a generation raised on Earl Weaver's writings on the subject of managing, the Oriole Way created fans who expected to win.

Now, what was once described as baseball's perfect franchise—by the Yankees' Graig Nettles, of all people—is now little more than a way station for mediocrities (or worse) on the field and in the front office. You won't find the Oriole Way anywhere within Peter Angelos's Orioles. If you tried to draw a distinction between the past and the present, you could not come up with two organizations more dissimilar than the Weaver Orioles and the Angelos Orioles. Twenty or 30 years ago, the Orioles appreciated that you could get talent on the cheap to supplement a great core. They were the best in the game at it, up until the point that the team was purchased by a crazy old lawyer, one or two crazy old lawyer/owners ago.

The last five years have been demoralizing, as a 90-win team under Davey Johnson slipped to a 77-win team under Ray Miller to a 65-win team under Mike Hargrove. General managers and various front-office apparatchiks continue to come and go, while the franchise declines further into bad-joke/Devil Rays territory.

The seeds of the problems that plague the organization today were planted during the brief successes of the mid-1990s, as a farm system that still hasn't really recovered from the departure of Harry Dalton after 1971 continues to sputter. The Orioles finally seemed to recognize, in the middle of 2000, that they had problems at every level of the organization. As a result, they began trying to convert their collection of mostly adequate major leaguers into anything that might help the Orioles within the next decade, a process that General Manager Syd Thrift managed to blow. The deadline deals brought in a number of surgery cases but nothing resembling a good major-league regular in the making. Thrift advanced the modest claim that the deals of 2000 would be a success if "two pitchers pitched in the major leagues and two of these position players contribute to a winning major-league team." You could broadly interpret goals such as "pitching in the major leagues" (how well?) and "contributing to a winner" (how much, and will that winner be the Orioles?), but the ghastly reality is that the players in question probably won't fulfill Thrift's goals at all.

Thrift's status as GM is a major stumbling block for any progress. This is the man who mistook Howard Stern's producer for an Orioles pitching prospect. Thrift's attempts at ducking responsibility for acquiring vinegar of Lesli Brea's vintage degenerated into his trying to make fun of beat writers for spelling Brea's name incorrectly. He initially forgot to put Ed Rogers on the 40-man roster and subsequently claimed that he was just trying to keep his underlings on their toes.

The Orioles' commitment to youth, at least in the last two years, has been merely cosmetic. This past season was supposed to be when things would finally be a little different, when the Orioles would finally try to make some commitments to youth. Indeed, desperate to say anything that might inspire confidence, they even refried the White Sox' recent "The Kids Can Play" marketing campaign, highlighting their young players.

Unfortunately, advertising requires some kernel of truth if it's going to be believable. A Maryland chicken rancher might fire up a marketing campaign touting "The Bountiful Breasts of Delmarva," and while some people might think that's just the latest John Waters movie, just about everyone is going to be disappointed. A marketing campaign touting Ryan Kohlmeier or Jerry Hairston Jr. or Chris Richard could just as easily have promoted the new guy on the groundskeeping crew for all any of them will have to do with the next good Orioles team. There are few things easier for an organization to dig up than a first baseman, a relief pitcher, and a second baseman. Worse yet, Hairston and Richard are not young kids, they're guys in the middle of their careers, and Kohlmeier has already been lost on waivers.

In part, the problem of launching a viable Orioles youth movement is that there isn't a whole lot of talent to work with, and this has led to the return to another problem the organization faced in the '70s: affiliate Rochester is openly griping about the lousy collection of talent with which it's been stuck. The Orioles' long-term affiliation with Rochester might be threatened if the organization doesn't show a modicum of interest in securing some minor-league free agents to crank out an International League contender, if nothing else.

There's not even an element of historical chic to make these losers lovable. There's nothing that makes you pity them. The Orioles haven't earned anyone's pity, although they do deserve your contempt. They are the creation of a management team whose primary experience is in the crucial areas of political infighting, survival, and toadying. Most of the team's players have already had meaningful careers on other teams in other cities. Jeff Conine is the original Mr. Marlin. Tony Batista was Miguel Tejada's older-brother figure coming up in the A's chain five years ago. Pat Hentgen is long removed from his days as a Blue Jays star. If Marty Cordova's heyday wasn't last year with the Indians, it was six years ago in Minnesota.

In a situation as bleak as this, is there reason for hope? Surprisingly enough, yes. First, like Spain when it financed its bid for dominance in Europe with American silver during the 16th and 17th centuries, the Angelos family commands financial resources that transcend its normal revenue streams. Peter Angelos's fee of nearly a billion dollars for working on Maryland's tobacco settlement gives him seed money. If he plows some small fraction of it into the franchise, it might yield handsome results. Then again, making financial commitments has never been the organization's problem. The problem has been one of identifying and hiring talent, especially front-office talent, and then having the self-control to sit back and let the professionals do their jobs. Confusing professionalism with talent is also an issue: the Orioles need to understand that there is a significant difference between hiring J.P. Ricciardi and hiring Syd Thrift.

One productive way for Angelos to use his cash is to buy out the staffers who need to be replaced so that a new breed of management, reflecting contemporary innovations in organizational philosophy, can be hired. Innovation isn't easy, especially when there is an organizational culture in place that coddles incompetence and actively discourages thinking. In this, Syd Thrift's enfeebled Orioles resemble the Orioles of the mid-1970s, before Jerold Hoffberger finally sold the team to Edward Bennett Williams. For all intents and purposes, the organization's player-development program had been adrift since Harry Dalton's departure in 1971.

What happened immediately after Dalton was replaced provides a cautionary tale for any organization in transition. At the time, the Orioles brought in some young guys with ideas of their own who failed to connect with the Dalton people who had remained with the Orioles. The old gang then turned around and sabotaged the organization by focusing on their antagonisms with the new guys and whining about the good old days, instead of doing their jobs.

If Peter Angelos really wants to be an activist owner who actually helps his franchise, he's going to have to take an interest in who he has working for him, and he needs to begin by dumping the anachronisms. For starters, he'll need a general manager who can completely reverse the way the team spends money. Thrift's lack of vision and meager accomplishments make him an easy target; personnel decisions elsewhere in the organization won't be so cut and dried. Scouting Director Tony DeMacio's background with the Braves' organization (where his main claim to fame was scouting Tom Glavine) seems to indicate a bias towards pitching and tools players, and his three drafts have generally supported that conclusion. There are some exceptions, most notably Larry Bigbie, but the initial results have been mixed. Still, this is the Orioles, and "mixed" is improvement. Unvortunately, the Orioles are still far too quick to quit on players such as Calvin Pickering and Jayson Werth, and they're too reluctant in accepting pitchers such as Josh Towers and John Stephens who impress scoreboards more than radar guns.

If DeMacio's drafts are going to make any kind of difference in the years to come, the Orioles need to have a GM in place who can exploit the available talent that floats through waivers, the Rule 5 draft, and minor-league free agency. Even under Thrift's punch-drunk rule, the team made a start in the right direction by nabbing Jay Gibbons, but the failure to claim or acquire catchers such as Ramon Castro or Bobby Estalella last summer was inexcusable.

Because of their relative wealth, the Orioles can follow the lead of the Reds, who in recent years have signed up adequate veterans for the twin goals of 1) stocking a roster or temporarily filling lineup slots and 2) flipping those players to contenders during the July trading frenzy. Signing players such as Cordova or Segui doesn't fit that bill on a couple of levels. First, giving such players three- or four-year deals makes them a little less attractive to other teams. Second, they're both bad risks, because Segui isn't going to provide the kind of first-base power most contenders want, and Cordova is a DH with a miserable multiyear history.

Angelos also needs to invest his money in the acquisition of big-ticket free agents. The Orioles need to control their past habit of spending for spending's sake and use their money to bring in the kind of talent they really need, whether it's a third baseman like Scott Rolen or Adrian Beltre (allowing the O's to put Tony Batista at shortstop) or a center fielder or a catcher. If Thrift's poor track record is a deterrent to quality free agents, that only creates greater incentive to remove him.

More hope for the future comes from the Orioles' decision to move the fences back and make Camden Yards a safer haven for pitchers. Developing pitchers is the most difficult element of a player-development program, recent successes in Oakland and Houston notwithstanding. By making it easier for their young pitchers to succeed, the Orioles will ease the pressure on their staff, make their pitchers better-looking commodities in trade, and force themselves to place a premium on developing and acquiring offensive talent. As playbooks go, it's worked well for the Athletics for almost 30 years, and it worked for the Orioles in Memorial Stadium. As a way of getting back to the original Oriole Way, it might be a little overt, but if this team is going to rise any higher than a dogfight for fourth place, it's a start.

HITTERS (BA: .270, OBP: .340, SLG: .440, EqA: .260)

Brady Anderson RF Bats L Age 38

YEAR	TEAM	LGE	AB	H	DB	TP	HR	BB	SO	R	RBI	SB	CS	OUT	BA	OBP	SLG	EQA	EQR	DEFENSE	
1999	Baltimor	AL	561	170	29	5	27	91	92	110	83	35	7	398	.303	.419	.517	.316	111	136-CF	0
2000	Baltimor	AL	503	136	20	0	23	87	91	88	51	17	10	377	.270	.387	.447	.281	79	122-CF	-2
2001	Baltimor	AL	433	100	13	3	10	62	67	55	51	11	5	338	.231	.335	.344	.237	46	109-RF	0
2002	*Clevelnd*	*AL*	*481*	*109*	*20*	*2*	*16*	*84*	*83*	*72*	*49*	*17*	*6*	*378*	*.227*	*.342*	*.376*	*.247*	*58*		

Q: Who were the last five players to hit worse than Anderson's .202 in more than his 430 at-bats?

A:

1. Rob Deer, 1991	.179	448
2. Mark McGwire, 1991	.201	483
3. Bob Boone, 1984	.202	450
4. Brooks Robinson, 1975	.201	482
5. Jim Sundberg, 1975	.199	472

Orioles' leadoff batters hit .192 in 2001, 39 points less than the second-worst team in the majors. Three out of five times, that hitter was Anderson, who didn't get his average above the Mendoza Line until the season's final weekend. In one of the winter's more enlightened moves, he was released by the Orioles to clear space on the 40-man roster. Anderson was subsequently signed by the Indians to a wacky year-plus-two-option-years contract, a move that marks an ugly starting point in the education of Mark Shapiro.

Tony Batista 3B/SS Bats R Age 28

YEAR	TEAM	LGE	AB	H	DB	TP	HR	BB	SO	R	RBI	SB	CS	OUT	BA	OBP	SLG	EQA	EQR	DEFENSE			
1999	Arizona	NL	144	36	5	0	5	14	16	16	20	2	0	108	.250	.325	.389	.244	16	43-SS	7		
1999	Toronto	AL	373	110	23	1	28	18	69	60	78	2	0	263	.295	.333	.587	.292	60	96-SS	13		
2000	Toronto	AL	616	165	32	2	42	28	106	93	109	5	4	455	.268	.306	.531	.267	83	154-3B	13		
2001	Toronto	AL	270	58	12	1	14	15	57	31	46	0	1	213	.215	.264	.422	.223	25	72-3B	-3		
2001	Baltimor	AL	310	88	17	5	14	21	41	45	45	5	1	223	.284	.329	.506	.273	43	26-3B	1	20-SS	5
2002	*Baltimor*	*AL*	*539*	*144*	*29*	*3*	*28*	*38*	*96*	*75*	*89*	*5*	*2*	*397*	*.267*	*.315*	*.488*	*.269*	*75*				

When in doubt, tell the kids that Santa does live in the Great White North, and his name is Gord Ash. If it wasn't for the Blue Jays handing over Batista and Gibbons for nothing, the Orioles wouldn't have gotten much free talent last year. Batista was the subject of one of the better moves the Orioles tried all season, when they moved him back to shortstop once it became clear that Brian Roberts's fielding problems weren't going away. Batista played as well there as he usually does—that is, better than most baseball people think he does—and his hitting improved. With Bordick back, Batista will have to return to third base in 2002.

Larry Bigbie OF Bats L Age 24

YEAR	TEAM	LGE	AB	H	DB	TP	HR	BB	SO	R	RBI	SB	CS	OUT	BA	OBP	SLG	EQA	EQR	DEFENSE	
1999	Delmarva	SAL	174	38	8	1	1	22	44	13	18	1	1	137	.218	.306	.283	.210	14	32-LF	1
2000	Frederck	Car	207	51	5	0	3	16	34	26	22	4	2	158	.246	.300	.314	.212	16	53-RF	-1
2000	Bowie	Eas	114	25	5	0	0	8	29	9	4	2	0	89	.219	.270	.263	.190	7	30-LF	1
2001	Bowie	Eas	272	70	11	2	7	35	53	36	28	7	5	207	.257	.342	.390	.248	32	68-RF	-3
2001	Baltimor	AL	132	33	4	0	3	18	36	16	12	4	1	100	.250	.340	.348	.242	14	31-OF	-1
2001	Rochestr	Int	43	13	3	0	1	3	7	5	3	1	1	31	.302	.348	.442	.259	5	10-LF	1
2002	*Baltimor*	*AL*	*415*	*110*	*15*	*2*	*10*	*50*	*94*	*46*	*54*	*6*	*2*	*307*	*.265*	*.344*	*.383*	*.257*	*51*		

Bigbie was called up to Baltimore on three separate occasions last year, and after a dismal start (a .155 EqA in the first call-up), he hit almost exactly as well as he had in the minors. After spending the winter working out, he doubled his isolated power without sacrificing singles, walks, or strikeouts. That's significant improvement, almost enough to make comparisons to Andy Van Slyke a little less silly. Bigbie should spend most of 2002 at Rochester, but he looks like a guy who will build a useful career.

Mike Bordick SS Bats R Age 36

YEAR	TEAM	LGE	AB	H	DB	TP	HR	BB	SO	R	RBI	SB	CS	OUT	BA	OBP	SLG	EQA	EQR	DEFENSE	
1999	Baltimor	AL	630	184	39	7	11	48	90	94	77	14	4	450	.292	.346	.429	.261	79	154-SS	23
2000	Baltimor	AL	390	122	22	1	18	29	62	70	59	6	6	274	.313	.362	.513	.283	58	96-SS	-6
2000	NY Mets	NL	195	52	6	0	5	12	26	18	22	3	1	144	.267	.315	.374	.234	19	51-SS	-4
2001	Baltimor	AL	231	64	11	0	9	18	31	35	34	9	4	170	.277	.341	.442	.262	30	56-SS	-2
2002	*Baltimor*	*AL*	*504*	*134*	*22*	*2*	*14*	*43*	*76*	*70*	*61*	*10*	*6*	*376*	*.266*	*.324*	*.401*	*.250*	*59*		

According to the front-office spin, Bordick's injury was the reason for the Orioles' dismal season. As if. He separated his shoulder in June when he was taken out on a potential double play, then he tore his labrum while playing on a rehab assignment in August. He's expected to be ready for spring; you should probably expect reduced arm strength, at least in the first half of the season.

Ivanon Coffie 3B Bats L Age 25

YEAR	TEAM	LGE	AB	H	DB	TP	HR	BB	SO	R	RBI	SB	CS	OUT	BA	OBP	SLG	EQA	EQR	DEFENSE			
1999	Frederck	Car	283	68	13	2	9	19	62	26	37	4	3	218	.240	.293	.396	.228	27	52-3B	-1	12-SS	-7
1999	Bowie	Eas	199	34	7	2	3	14	46	17	19	1	1	166	.171	.227	.271	.172	10	48-3B	-1		
2000	Bowie	Eas	346	82	18	2	8	27	55	41	34	1	3	267	.237	.297	.370	.222	31	73-SS	-8		
2000	Rochestr	Int	78	17	1	1	0	2	21	4	9	0	0	61	.218	.245	.256	.172	4				
2000	Baltimor	AL	60	14	5	1	0	4	10	6	6	1	0	46	.233	.293	.350	.221	5	12-3B	2		
2001	Rochestr	Int	208	54	7	1	8	15	43	32	33	3	0	154	.260	.311	.418	.245	23	16-3B	-1	12-1B	-4
2002	*ChiCubs*	*NL*	*399*	*102*	*18*	*3*	*11*	*36*	*85*	*47*	*53*	*5*	*1*	*298*	*.256*	*.317*	*.398*	*.243*	*43*				

(Ivanon Coffie *continued*)

Coffie entered spring training as a potential utility man in Baltimore. After missing three months with a broken finger, he was restricted to playing first base and DH. He's been traded to the Cubs, where he shouldn't push past either Augie Ojeda or Mark Bellhorn. Frankly, if he can't back up the middle infield, he's pretty much useless.

Jeff Conine 1B/3B Bats R Age 36

YEAR	TEAM	LGE	AB	H	DB	TP	HR	BB	SO	R	RBI	SB	CS	OUT	BA	OBP	SLG	EQA	EQR	DEFENSE	
1999	Baltimor	AL	444	136	30	1	15	25	35	54	76	0	3	311	.306	.347	.480	.270	59	91-1B -6	10-LF 0
2000	Baltimor	AL	408	123	21	2	14	31	47	53	46	4	3	288	.301	.354	.466	.271	55	38-3B 2	37-1B 4
2001	Baltimor	AL	530	181	25	2	16	67	65	82	105	11	9	358	.342	.419	.487	.302	90	79-1B -3	36-LF 3
2002	*Baltimor*	*AL*	*471*	*135*	*21*	*2*	*15*	*55*	*57*	*60*	*67*	*6*	*6*	*342*	*.287*	*.361*	*.435*	*.274*	*67*		

Conine was voted the Most Valuable Oriole by the Baltimore press, which is sort of like being voted the biggest rock star in Oglala by the local high school. However, the writers got this one right; Conine was worth 3.3 wins more than a replacement player, and that was tops on this team. He was the worst best player in the majors, nosing under Elmer Dessens in Cincinnati and Fred McGriff in Tampa Bay.

Rick Elder 1B/OF Bats L Age 22

YEAR	TEAM	LGE	AB	H	DB	TP	HR	BB	SO	R	RBI	SB	CS	OUT	BA	OBP	SLG	EQA	EQR	DEFENSE	
1999	Bluefld	App	158	33	6	1	4	16	64	16	16	1	0	125	.209	.285	.335	.213	13	23-1B -6	
2000	Delmarva	SAL	51	4	0	0	1	6	19	3	5	0	1	48	.078	.175	.137	.117	1	10-1B -1	
2001	Delmarva	SAL	410	85	16	3	11	48	138	52	46	3	1	326	.207	.292	.341	.217	36	48-1B -11	43-LF -1
2002	*Baltimor*	*AL*	*406*	*91*	*16*	*3*	*12*	*54*	*149*	*55*	*58*	*3*	*1*	*316*	*.224*	*.315*	*.367*	*.239*	*44*		

Elder started the season like a house on fire, but he burned out faster than "Afroman": he hit .344/.450/.677 in April and .221/.326/.384 after that. For the third straight year, he finished the season on the DL, this time after colliding with an outfield fence. This is the Orioles, so he's called a prospect.

Brook Fordyce C Bats R Age 32

YEAR	TEAM	LGE	AB	H	DB	TP	HR	BB	SO	R	RBI	SB	CS	OUT	BA	OBP	SLG	EQA	EQR	DEFENSE
1999	ChiSox	AL	331	102	24	1	10	18	42	36	48	2	0	229	.308	.349	.477	.273	45	90-C -2
2000	ChiSox	AL	124	34	8	1	5	5	20	18	20	0	0	90	.274	.313	.476	.257	15	37-C 3
2000	Baltimor	AL	177	60	11	0	10	8	24	23	28	0	0	117	.339	.375	.571	.304	30	48-C -7
2001	Baltimor	AL	293	67	13	0	8	23	48	33	22	1	2	228	.229	.290	.355	.217	25	88-C -11
2002	*Baltimor*	*AL*	*320*	*81*	*14*	*1*	*12*	*25*	*53*	*33*	*40*	*1*	*1*	*240*	*.253*	*.307*	*.416*	*.246*	*36*	

It's one thing to dump a free agent you don't think you can sign, as the O's did with Charles Johnson. However, you don't have to keep whatever you get in the trade. Doing so leads to signing mediocrities such as Fordyce for too long (three years) and too much money ($7.25 million). Granted, even we never thought he'd be this bad, with no offensive or defensive value. Signing a non-star, 30-year-old catcher to a three-year deal is inexcusably dumb.

Jay Gibbons LF/1B Bats L Age 25

YEAR	TEAM	LGE	AB	H	DB	TP	HR	BB	SO	R	RBI	SB	CS	OUT	BA	OBP	SLG	EQA	EQR	DEFENSE	
1999	Hagerstn	SAL	300	70	15	1	9	22	59	36	42	1	0	230	.233	.287	.380	.223	27	22-1B -3	
1999	Dunedin	Fla	213	53	9	0	7	18	43	24	26	1	1	161	.249	.307	.390	.233	21	54-1B -1	
2000	Tennesse	Sou	485	135	27	1	17	46	66	73	60	2	1	351	.278	.347	.443	.264	63	95-1B -13	10-LF -1
2001	Baltimor	AL	226	58	9	0	17	18	34	30	39	0	1	169	.257	.320	.522	.269	32	28-LF 2	
2002	*Baltimor*	*AL*	*442*	*119*	*20*	*1*	*23*	*46*	*72*	*64*	*70*	*1*	*1*	*324*	*.269*	*.338*	*.475*	*.275*	*64*		

Gibbons was a good acquisition in the 2000 Rule 5 draft, even though the Orioles already had first base covered three times over, which forced Gibbons to spend time in left field and as the DH. His season ended when he broke a bone in his wrist while swinging a bat, an injury followed by lingering soreness when he tried to rush back to play winter ball. Gibbons has promise, but when you factor in the injury, lingering concerns about it, and Thrift's compulsion to avoid trying anything that might work, Gibbons is probably staring at quality time in Rochester this summer.

Geronimo Gil C Bats R Age 26

YEAR	TEAM	LGE	AB	H	DB	TP	HR	BB	SO	R	RBI	SB	CS	OUT	BA	OBP	SLG	EQA	EQR	DEFENSE	
1999	SanAnton	Tex	350	88	16	1	13	38	60	37	46	1	0	262	.251	.327	.414	.249	40	72-C -3	22-RF -1
2000	SanAnton	Tex	356	90	16	1	9	22	65	34	44	2	1	267	.253	.303	.379	.229	33	75-C 3	12-RF -1
2001	LasVegas	PCL	276	71	9	0	8	15	51	32	32	0	1	206	.257	.299	.377	.225	25	62-C 3	12-1B 2
2001	Rochestr	Int	82	21	5	1	2	1	21	7	13	0	0	61	.256	.271	.415	.224	7	23-C -3	
2001	Baltimor	AL	59	19	2	0	0	5	6	3	6	0	0	40	.322	.390	.356	.261	7	17-C -1	
2002	*Baltimor*	*AL*	*392*	*100*	*16*	*1*	*12*	*32*	*76*	*39*	*50*	*1*	*1*	*293*	*.255*	*.311*	*.393*	*.242*	*42*		

Along with Kris Foster, Gil was brought in for Mike Trombley 35 seconds before the trading deadline. He's the latest version of the slick-fielding Henry Blanco-type who doesn't hit much. The real tragedy is that those two months between Rochester and Baltimore made him the best catcher in the entire organization in 2001. (For instant depression, see Werth, Jayson.) Gil should earn most of playing time behind the plate, regardless of the team's contractual commitment to Fordyce.

Jerry Hairston 2B Bats R Age 26

YEAR	TEAM	LGE	AB	H	DB	TP	HR	BB	SO	R	RBI	SB	CS	OUT	BA	OBP	SLG	EQA	EQR	DEFENSE	
1999	Rochestr	Int	412	112	21	4	6	24	47	53	40	14	9	309	.272	.333	.386	.243	45	87-2B -4	17-SS -2
1999	Baltimor	AL	175	50	14	1	4	9	21	26	17	8	4	129	.286	.330	.446	.257	22	50-2B 5	
2000	Rochestr	Int	203	56	13	1	4	25	31	39	19	5	3	150	.276	.366	.409	.264	27	52-2B 2	
2000	Baltimor	AL	180	48	4	0	6	19	19	26	19	8	6	138	.267	.357	.389	.253	22	49-2B 9	
2001	Baltimor	AL	535	138	28	5	10	47	63	68	52	27	12	409	.258	.329	.385	.244	60	153-2B 8	
2002	*Baltimor*	*AL*	*487*	*129*	*23*	*3*	*13*	*55*	*61*	*76*	*50*	*21*	*11*	*369*	*.265*	*.339*	*.405*	*.259*	*63*		

Hairston has a real chance to be this year's AL Gold Glove winner, now that Roberto Alomar is a Met. Unfortunately, his bat has been stagnant since 1998, and his aggressive baserunning is worth more in rotisserie than in baseball. It's not just the barely break-even stolen-base rate; Hairston was only six-for-ten trying to advance a base on fly-ball outs. You might expect that kind of dopiness on the Royals, but the Orioles can't afford it.

Willie Harris 2B/CF Bats L Age 24

YEAR	TEAM	LGE	AB	H	DB	TP	HR	BB	SO	R	RBI	SB	CS	OUT	BA	OBP	SLG	EQA	EQR	DEFENSE	
1999	Delmarva	SAL	279	58	11	1	1	15	43	28	21	8	7	228	.208	.249	.265	.178	15	63-2B -4	
2000	Delmarva	SAL	500	108	23	5	5	63	95	72	41	16	11	403	.216	.308	.312	.217	44	107-2B -12	19-CF 1
2001	Bowie	Eas	538	147	24	3	7	42	69	70	42	37	12	403	.273	.329	.368	.243	58	90-2B -5	41-CF 2
2002	*Baltimor*	*AL*	*502*	*131*	*20*	*4*	*8*	*55*	*81*	*79*	*52*	*29*	*11*	*382*	*.261*	*.334*	*.365*	*.250*	*60*		

On a team that plays six first basemen regularly, a guy like Harris is pretty valuable as a pinch runner and defensive replacement. The downside is that guys like him are at their most useful in close games, the kind that the Orioles don't often play. Harris is fun to watch and works his butt off, and I've heard three different people compare him to Tony Phillips. His defense at second base has gotten mixed reviews, and the Orioles keep changing their mind about where he's going to play, but with Hairston's utility up in the air, second base makes the most sense.

Mike Kinkade UT Bats R Age 29

YEAR	TEAM	LGE	AB	H	DB	TP	HR	BB	SO	R	RBI	SB	CS	OUT	BA	OBP	SLG	EQA	EQR	DEFENSE	
1999	Norfolk	Int	311	90	17	2	6	16	29	44	41	5	1	222	.289	.332	.415	.251	35	34-3B 0	13-C -1
1999	NY Mets	NL	46	9	2	1	2	3	8	3	6	1	0	37	.196	.274	.413	.230	5		
2000	Binghmtn	Eas	316	98	19	2	8	26	40	50	48	12	5	223	.310	.372	.459	.279	46	64-C 2	13-3B -2
2000	Rochestr	Int	56	19	4	0	1	9	11	9	9	0	1	38	.339	.438	.464	.303	10		
2001	Baltimor	AL	161	48	3	0	5	15	27	20	17	2	1	114	.298	.366	.410	.264	20	25-LF -2	
2002	*Baltimor*	*AL*	*357*	*106*	*17*	*2*	*12*	*36*	*55*	*53*	*52*	*3*	*1*	*252*	*.297*	*.361*	*.457*	*.282*	*53*		

Kinkade is a pure hitter who isn't quite good enough with the bat to be a regular big-league DH. He's been tried all over the field without much success, but if you ask, he'll catch or play the infield and outfield corners. If this team didn't already have a small army of right-handed hitters lodged in the infield and outfield corners, he'd be a useful spare part. On the Orioles, he rots.

Jose Leon 3B Bats R Age 25

YEAR	TEAM	LGE	AB	H	DB	TP	HR	BB	SO	R	RBI	SB	CS	OUT	BA	OBP	SLG	EQA	EQR	DEFENSE
1999	Arkansas	Tex	337	69	12	0	14	19	118	29	40	2	2	270	.205	.255	.365	.206	26	71-3B -2
2000	Arkansas	Tex	298	71	13	2	11	9	66	31	30	1	1	228	.238	.267	.406	.220	26	46-3B -4 18-1B -4
2000	Bowie	Eas	69	16	1	0	1	2	13	5	5	3	1	55	.232	.266	.290	.194	5	16-3B 1
2001	Bowie	Eas	98	31	7	1	3	7	20	16	17	1	1	68	.316	.365	.500	.283	14	23-3B -5
2001	Rochestr	Int	420	113	18	3	12	26	89	53	50	6	3	310	.269	.316	.412	.242	45	104-3B 6
2002	*Baltimor*	*AL*	*452*	*121*	*19*	*2*	*18*	*34*	*108*	*51*	*58*	*7*	*3*	*334*	*.268*	*.319*	*.438*	*.258*	*57*	

Leon is probably the best part of the package the Orioles received in exchange for Mike Timlin. Well, he's the part that's still standing, anyway. The Orioles like his glove work, because of his strong arm, and he does come in well on bunts. Unfortunately, he isn't as much of a prospect as Willis Otanez was, and his plate discipline has been AWOL for years.

Fernando Lunar C Bats R Age 25

YEAR	TEAM	LGE	AB	H	DB	TP	HR	BB	SO	R	RBI	SB	CS	OUT	BA	OBP	SLG	EQA	EQR	DEFENSE
1999	Greenvil	Sou	342	65	12	1	2	6	65	25	25	0	1	278	.190	.219	.249	.161	14	90-C 0
2000	Greenvil	Sou	104	17	2	0	0	6	15	5	3	0	0	87	.163	.209	.183	.140	3	30-C 8
2000	Atlanta	NL	55	10	2	0	0	2	14	5	5	0	2	47	.182	.245	.218	.158	2	18-C -1
2000	Bowie	Eas	81	21	6	1	0	4	8	10	6	0	0	60	.259	.308	.358	.225	7	21-C 3
2001	Baltimor	AL	168	46	7	0	0	8	28	9	17	0	0	122	.274	.316	.315	.217	13	46-C 2
2002	*Baltimor*	*AL*	*272*	*64*	*9*	*1*	*2*	*16*	*49*	*24*	*23*	*0*	*0*	*208*	*.235*	*.278*	*.298*	*.194*	*17*	

Lunar needs to consider an illegal stance, because he's a lot better behind the plate than he is next to it. He's managed to hit his weight (190) in just two of his 11 stops since 1995, both times coming since his escape from Atlanta. Assuming the Orioles learn nothing by the start of the season about the silliness of carrying three catchers, Lunar will be on the roster out of a ludicrously inflated sense of his value.

Luis Matos CF Bats R Age 23

YEAR	TEAM	LGE	AB	H	DB	TP	HR	BB	SO	R	RBI	SB	CS	OUT	BA	OBP	SLG	EQA	EQR	DEFENSE
1999	Frederck	Car	278	71	10	1	6	13	35	29	30	15	5	212	.255	.291	.363	.224	25	65-CF -1
1999	Bowie	Eas	286	61	10	1	7	9	39	33	28	9	4	229	.213	.239	.329	.192	19	66-CF -1
2000	Bowie	Eas	183	44	7	3	2	13	24	20	25	9	6	145	.240	.301	.344	.220	16	48-CF -1
2000	Baltimor	AL	182	44	7	3	1	10	26	21	17	14	5	142	.242	.293	.330	.220	16	57-CF 8
2001	Bowie	Eas	47	13	3	0	1	5	7	5	7	0	1	35	.277	.353	.404	.250	5	
2001	Baltimor	AL	99	23	7	0	5	11	26	17	13	7	0	76	.232	.314	.455	.264	14	26-CF 1
2002	*Baltimor*	*AL*	*463*	*121*	*20*	*3*	*13*	*40*	*83*	*61*	*58*	*18*	*4*	*346*	*.261*	*.320*	*.402*	*.254*	*56*	

Matos separated his left shoulder sliding into third base during an exhibition game in March, costing him his slim chance of making the team out of spring training. A quality center fielder with a great arm, he could benefit from more Triple-A experience. He should get a shot by August, and while he's not a great prospect, he can be a decent regular on a team carrying heavy hitters in the outfield corners.

Darnell McDonald OF Bats R Age 23

YEAR	TEAM	LGE	AB	H	DB	TP	HR	BB	SO	R	RBI	SB	CS	OUT	BA	OBP	SLG	EQA	EQR	DEFENSE
1999	Frederck	Car	522	119	20	3	5	42	92	61	54	14	6	409	.228	.289	.307	.208	40	108-RF -8
2000	Bowie	Eas	463	101	11	3	6	21	90	48	34	8	3	365	.218	.256	.294	.190	29	104-RF -10
2001	Bowie	Eas	119	30	6	1	2	9	27	14	17	2	2	91	.252	.308	.370	.227	11	30-LF -1
2001	Rochestr	Int	395	91	17	2	2	29	69	36	33	11	8	312	.230	.284	.299	.201	28	101-CF 1
2002	*Baltimor*	*AL*	*483*	*119*	*19*	*3*	*8*	*41*	*96*	*60*	*53*	*12*	*7*	*371*	*.246*	*.305*	*.348*	*.227*	*46*	

When you're a former #1 draft pick who cost almost $2 million to sign away from college football, you get promoted even when there is no clear reason why, just because it's time for you to move up. Don Buford claims it takes high-school draftees as many as four or five years to develop, and McDonald has already put in five. He gets talked up for his power and speed potential, even though neither quality has surfaced on the diamond very often.

Melvin Mora — CF/SS — Bats R — Age 30

YEAR	TEAM	LGE	AB	H	DB	TP	HR	BB	SO	R	RBI	SB	CS	OUT	BA	OBP	SLG	EQA	EQR	DEFENSE
1999	Norfolk	Int	304	85	15	1	7	34	51	45	29	13	7	226	.280	.362	.405	.261	39	48-SS -11 28-CF -1
2000	NY Mets	NL	218	58	14	2	6	15	44	34	30	6	3	163	.266	.318	.431	.249	25	37-SS -3 16-CF -3
2000	Baltimor	AL	199	60	11	3	2	14	28	25	17	5	9	148	.302	.360	.417	.252	24	52-SS 0
2001	Baltimor	AL	439	123	20	0	12	43	79	53	56	11	5	321	.280	.358	.408	.261	56	79-CF 4 40-SS 5
2002	*Baltimor*	*AL*	*396*	*110*	*19*	*2*	*12*	*45*	*74*	*60*	*44*	*8*	*4*	*290*	*.278*	*.351*	*.427*	*.270*	*55*	

Before the All-Star break he was probably the Orioles' best player, getting his EqA up as high as .301. He faded badly before suffering a season-ending elbow injury in early September. Did he wear down from playing every day or from caring for the quintuplets his wife had in July?

Ntema Ndungidi — LF — Bats L — Age 23

YEAR	TEAM	LGE	AB	H	DB	TP	HR	BB	SO	R	RBI	SB	CS	OUT	BA	OBP	SLG	EQA	EQR	DEFENSE
1999	Delmarva	SAL	232	37	7	1	0	36	57	23	18	9	2	197	.159	.276	.198	.183	14	52-LF -6
1999	Frederck	Car	200	45	8	2	0	29	43	31	13	2	1	156	.225	.328	.285	.219	18	54-LF -3
2000	Frederck	Car	327	78	12	2	9	44	84	41	44	8	4	253	.239	.331	.370	.241	36	82-LF -8
2000	Bowie	Eas	139	29	4	0	3	20	34	14	11	1	1	111	.209	.316	.302	.217	12	36-LF -3
2001	Bowie	Eas	347	67	13	1	3	33	88	31	32	2	3	283	.193	.267	.262	.186	21	62-LF -8
2002	*Seattle*	*AL*	*432*	*99*	*14*	*2*	*9*	*57*	*114*	*57*	*50*	*7*	*4*	*337*	*.229*	*.319*	*.333*	*.233*	*44*	

Ndungidi's apparent nervous breakdown in the 2000 Arizona Fall League was widely reported. What has gone unnoticed is that his game hasn't recovered. He came to camp heavy and never really lost the weight, sapping his speed. His power evaporated, his walk rate dropped, and his already bad defense got even worse. At this point, he should probably be stricken from prospect lists. Nabbed in the minor league portion of the Rule 5 draft by the Mariners.

Tim Raines — LF/PH — Bats B — Age 42

YEAR	TEAM	LGE	AB	H	DB	TP	HR	BB	SO	R	RBI	SB	CS	OUT	BA	OBP	SLG	EQA	EQR	DEFENSE
1999	Oakland	AL	134	31	3	0	5	25	15	20	18	4	1	104	.231	.352	.366	.252	17	30-LF 0
2001	Montreal	NL	78	25	7	1	0	17	5	13	4	1	0	53	.321	.442	.436	.308	14	16-LF -3
2001	Baltimor	AL	11	3	0	0	1	6	0	2	4	3	0	8	.273	.529	.545	.393	4	
2002	*Baltimor*	*AL*	*137*	*30*	*6*	*1*	*3*	*31*	*13*	*20*	*11*	*2*	*0*	*107*	*.219*	*.363*	*.343*	*.260*	*18*	

Rock fulfilled his wish of playing with his son, thanks to the efforts of the Expos', not Orioles', front office. He's really playing just for the love of the game at this point, as he isn't within spitting distance of any milestones or records. Shame on Pat Gillick and Bob Watson for making room for somebody like Pat Borders on Team USA in 2000, but not for Raines.

Tim Raines Jr. — CF — Bats B — Age 22

YEAR	TEAM	LGE	AB	H	DB	TP	HR	BB	SO	R	RBI	SB	CS	OUT	BA	OBP	SLG	EQA	EQR	DEFENSE
1999	Delmarva	SAL	438	87	21	4	1	52	137	52	34	23	11	361	.199	.286	.272	.201	33	115-CF -5
2000	Frederck	Car	474	102	18	2	2	48	107	62	29	43	15	387	.215	.296	.274	.210	39	124-CF -3
2001	Frederck	Car	89	20	3	1	2	10	23	12	10	9	3	72	.225	.303	.348	.231	9	19-CF 0
2001	Bowie	Eas	263	68	13	1	3	30	58	39	26	19	7	202	.259	.338	.350	.242	29	65-CF 1
2001	Rochestr	Int	135	34	4	1	2	10	28	18	12	9	3	104	.252	.303	.341	.226	13	31-CF -4
2001	Baltimor	AL	23	5	2	0	0	3	7	6	1	3	0	18	.217	.308	.304	.238	2	
2002	*Baltimor*	*AL*	*508*	*120*	*22*	*3*	*6*	*62*	*128*	*70*	*46*	*27*	*7*	*395*	*.236*	*.319*	*.327*	*.235*	*53*	

Little Rock is a solid prospect, but he's definitely not his father, who stole 71 major-league bases when he was 21, Junior's age last year. A natural righty who has been switch-hitting only since turning pro, he made dramatic improvements hitting from the left side in 2001, and he needs to continue improving if he's going to be more than just a runner. He has the range for center field, but not the arm. Raines is going to need another year in the minors; a good one will have him up permanently by the end of the summer. He's more likeable as a prospect than that projection indicates.

Keith Reed RF Bats R Age 23

YEAR	TEAM	LGE	AB	H	DB	TP	HR	BB	SO	R	RBI	SB	CS	OUT	BA	OBP	SLG	EQA	EQR	DEFENSE
1999	Delmarva	SAL	248	51	11	1	3	16	56	26	17	1	1	198	.206	.257	.294	.189	15	54-RF -8
2000	Delmarva	SAL	277	65	9	1	8	17	60	29	39	9	4	215	.235	.284	.361	.219	24	65-RF -1
2000	Frederck	Car	249	51	6	1	7	14	59	26	24	5	1	199	.205	.252	.321	.197	17	60-RF -6
2001	Frederck	Car	274	64	8	0	7	12	57	24	24	6	4	214	.234	.267	.339	.204	20	67-RF -6
2001	Bowie	Eas	68	15	1	0	1	6	10	6	7	2	1	54	.221	.284	.279	.198	5	18-CF 1
2001	Rochestr	Int	75	22	6	1	2	5	13	11	10	1	1	54	.293	.338	.480	.266	10	16-RF -4
2002	*Baltimor*	*AL*	*472*	*111*	*16*	*2*	*14*	*33*	*104*	*57*	*48*	*7*	*3*	*364*	*.235*	*.285*	*.367*	*.224*	*43*	

Reed is the Orioles prospect over whom scouts drool now that Darnell McDonald has proven to be such a bust. Scouting Director Tony DiMacio is infatuated with the idea that he's going to bring in the best talent from the Northeast, and Reed is his biggest prize, often referred to as the next Joe Carter. The dubious taste of that comparison aside, Reed's performance so far has been uninspiring, considerably less than what you'd expect from a 22-year-old future major leaguer. Any excitement generated by his Rochester performance was ruined by a disastrous outing in the Arizona Fall League, after which he was left off of the 40-man roster and ignored in the Rule 5 draft.

Chris Richard RF/1B Bats L Age 28

YEAR	TEAM	LGE	AB	H	DB	TP	HR	BB	SO	R	RBI	SB	CS	OUT	BA	OBP	SLG	EQA	EQR	DEFENSE	
1999	Arkansas	Tex	444	113	20	2	21	33	78	59	67	5	5	336	.255	.314	.450	.249	52	124-1B 0	
2000	Memphis	PCL	377	98	15	0	16	40	68	52	62	7	3	282	.260	.336	.427	.256	47	82-RF 4	11-1B 0
2000	Baltimor	AL	199	57	15	2	14	13	33	38	36	7	5	148	.286	.343	.593	.291	34	51-1B -5	
2001	Baltimor	AL	487	141	33	3	18	47	86	80	67	9	10	356	.290	.359	.480	.274	70	96-RF 2	16-1B 0
2002	*Baltimor*	*AL*	*510*	*140*	*30*	*2*	*21*	*57*	*94*	*75*	*75*	*6*	*6*	*376*	*.275*	*.347*	*.465*	*.275*	*75*		

Listed as a right fielder, he actually played 36 games in center field, the first time he'd ever played there as a pro. Amazingly, he acquitted himself rather well for a career first baseman. He led the team in home runs with 15; you have to go six deep on the Orioles to catch Barry Bonds. Richard will miss the entire first half, and probably most of the year, with a torn rotator cuff. That creates an opportunity for guys such as Gibbons, Bigbie, and Matos to acquire jobs in camp.

Cal Ripken 3B Bats R Age 41

YEAR	TEAM	LGE	AB	H	DB	TP	HR	BB	SO	R	RBI	SB	CS	OUT	BA	OBP	SLG	EQA	EQR	DEFENSE
1999	Baltimor	AL	331	118	23	0	21	10	27	51	58	0	1	214	.356	.380	.616	.316	60	71-3B -4
2000	Baltimor	AL	309	83	15	0	17	19	33	43	57	0	0	226	.269	.317	.482	.260	39	73-3B 6
2001	Baltimor	AL	480	125	13	0	17	28	54	47	74	0	2	357	.260	.303	.394	.231	46	111-3B 4

Ripken is almost certainly the best shortstop in baseball history, although he falls behind Honus Wagner if you make no allowances for changes in the game since the turn of the century. Clay Davenport has been messing with a stat he calls Wins Above Replacement Position (WARP), which combines batting and fielding. Here are the top ten seasons for the game's best four shortstops, in WARP×10:

Honus Wagner	118	108	107	104	104	101	90	80	79	77
Cal Ripken	118	108	94	72	68	66	63	61	53	41
Arky Vaughan	102	85	85	80	74	54	50	50	46	39
Alex Rodriguez	109	100	92	70	60	41				

Vaughan beats Ripken by small margins in their fourth- and fifth-best seasons and loses the other eight spots. Rodriguez cannot yet cover any rank against Ripken. If Bill James wants to rate Vaughan higher he can, but we're sticking with Cal.

Brian Roberts SS/2B Bats B Age 24

YEAR	TEAM	LGE	AB	H	DB	TP	HR	BB	SO	R	RBI	SB	CS	OUT	BA	OBP	SLG	EQA	EQR	DEFENSE
1999	Delmarva	SAL	176	34	8	1	0	19	44	14	15	8	3	146	.193	.273	.250	.191	12	46-SS 5
2000	Frederck	Car	170	42	6	2	0	19	24	20	12	6	7	135	.247	.324	.306	.216	15	42-SS -7
2001	Bowie	Eas	83	22	3	0	2	8	12	10	7	7	0	61	.265	.334	.373	.256	10	18-2B 1
2001	Rochestr	Int	165	43	4	1	1	27	20	15	12	19	3	125	.261	.365	.315	.256	21	44-SS -12
2001	Baltimor	AL	275	76	14	3	2	14	31	46	18	12	3	202	.276	.311	.371	.234	27	48-SS -6
2002	*Baltimor*	*AL*	*493*	*128*	*19*	*4*	*5*	*54*	*69*	*54*	*53*	*16*	*6*	*371*	*.260*	*.333*	*.345*	*.242*	*53*	

In the organizational tradition of David Lamb and Jesse Garcia, Roberts has been praised for his fielding, so his performance in 2001 was a disappointment. He was coming off of elbow surgery in 2000, and his throwing was erratic. Nine of his 14 major-league errors at shortstop were on throws—not that a stiff-backed David Segui helped much. Roberts hit well for his first two months, but once teams saw him again, his bat disappeared like a teenager's allowance. If his defense doesn't recover, he has no future beyond the International League.

Ed Rogers SS Bats R Age 20

YEAR	TEAM	LGE	AB	H	DB	TP	HR	BB	SO	R	RBI	SB	CS	OUT	BA	OBP	SLG	EQA	EQR	DEFENSE
2000	Delmarva	SAL	340	76	10	3	4	14	67	31	29	13	5	269	.224	.254	.306	.194	22	80-SS -14
2000	Bowie	Eas	49	12	2	0	1	3	15	3	6	1	1	38	.245	.288	.347	.213	4	12-SS -2
2001	Bowie	Eas	192	36	8	1	0	7	39	10	12	7	2	158	.188	.220	.240	.165	9	53-SS -1
2001	Frederck	Car	299	69	16	2	7	13	47	32	33	11	4	234	.231	.270	.368	.216	25	73-SS -8
2002	*Baltimor*	*AL*	*461*	*110*	*20*	*3*	*9*	*28*	*91*	*49*	*47*	*19*	*6*	*357*	*.239*	*.282*	*.354*	*.222*	*41*	

Having compared Rogers to Derek Jeter and Nomar Garciaparra, the Orioles bought their own hype and started him at Double-A Bowie. He was overmatched, then he got back on track at Frederick. It's not completely out of the question that Rogers could develop into the stud the scouts hyped. At his age, Jeter and Cristian Guzman were hitting .206 and .179, respectively, in the Sally League, while Miguel Tejada was hitting .196 in the Northwestern.

David Segui 1B Bats L Age 35

YEAR	TEAM	LGE	AB	H	DB	TP	HR	BB	SO	R	RBI	SB	CS	OUT	BA	OBP	SLG	EQA	EQR	DEFENSE
1999	Seattle	AL	342	103	22	3	10	28	38	43	38	1	2	241	.301	.356	.471	.272	47	85-1B 1
1999	Toronto	AL	94	30	3	0	6	7	15	14	13	0	0	64	.319	.366	.543	.295	15	
2000	Texas	AL	345	118	26	1	12	29	45	49	54	0	1	228	.342	.393	.528	.302	57	38-1B 1
2000	Clevelnd	AL	219	73	8	0	10	17	29	38	45	0	0	146	.333	.384	.507	.294	34	34-1B 4
2001	Baltimor	AL	296	97	18	1	12	51	53	53	50	1	1	200	.328	.431	.517	.317	56	61-1B -10
2002	*Baltimor*	*AL*	*456*	*140*	*24*	*2*	*18*	*60*	*72*	*66*	*61*	*1*	*1*	*317*	*.307*	*.388*	*.487*	*.300*	*78*	

Segui was the team's best hitter when he was healthy. That wasn't often, thanks to a hamstring pull, spiked hand, knee injury, inner ear infection, and another knee injury. Despite Segui's .317 EqA, he was a bad signing—with three more years and $21 million more to go—because the Orioles already had Conine, Richard, Gibbons, and Kinkade available to play first base.

PITCHERS (ERA: 4.50, H/9: 9.0, HR/9: 1.0, BB/9: 3.0, K/9: 6.0, KW: 2.0, PERA: 4.50)

John Bale Throws L Age 28

YEAR	TEAM	LGE	IP	H	ER	HR	BB	K	ERA	W	L	H/9	HR/9	BB/9	K/9	KW	PERA	STUFF
1999	Knoxvill	Sou	64.3	64	36	12	19	55	5.04	3	4	9.0	1.7	2.7	7.7	1.4	5.59	-8
1999	Syracuse	Int	21.0	22	12	1	11	7	5.14	1	1	9.4	0.4	4.7	3.0	0.3	5.74	-24
2000	Syracuse	Int	78.3	75	41	5	45	52	4.71	4	5	8.6	0.6	5.2	6.0	0.6	4.47	-8
2001	Rochestr	Int	32.3	28	10	1	6	28	2.78	3	1	7.8	0.3	1.7	7.8	2.3	3.01	19
2001	Baltimor	AL	25.3	23	14	2	16	20	4.97	1	2	8.2	0.7	5.7	7.1	0.6	4.51	-2

The record book says Bale started seven games in Rochester, but that's just because the team was desperate for a warm body; he is a reliever. Bale was primarily used in long relief for anywhere from two to four innings, although he was called on to be a one-out lefty on a few occasions. He certainly pitched well enough to earn a spot in the 2002 pen; he'll never pitch well enough to justify trading Jayson Werth for him.

Rick Bauer Throws R Age 25

YEAR	TEAM	LGE	IP	H	ER	HR	BB	K	ERA	W	L	H/9	HR/9	BB/9	K/9	KW	PERA	STUFF
1999	Frederck	Car	149.3	180	123	36	62	69	7.41	5	12	10.8	2.2	3.7	4.2	0.6	6.60	-12
2000	Frederck	Car	19.0	21	12	2	7	8	5.68	1	1	9.9	0.9	3.3	3.8	0.6	9.07	-13
2000	Bowie	Eas	132.0	157	98	29	43	61	6.68	5	10	10.7	2.0	2.9	4.2	0.7	7.38	-14
2001	Bowie	Eas	55.3	69	43	13	14	20	6.99	2	4	11.2	2.1	2.3	3.3	0.7	5.71	-18
2001	Rochestr	Int	114.7	120	59	13	33	66	4.63	6	7	9.4	1.0	2.6	5.2	1.0	5.92	4
2001	Baltimor	AL	32.7	38	22	7	9	15	6.06	1	3	10.5	1.9	2.5	4.1	0.8	5.73	-7

(Rick Bauer *continued*)

In the Orioles organization last year, if you could make it to Rochester and pitch a good game—just one—then you could get yourself called up to the bigs. Bauer went 10-4 for a dull 60-84 Rochester team, easily the best season in his career, and he was rewarded with a half-dozen Baltimore starts. As a result, he threw 207 innings, 55 more than he's ever thrown in one year, which makes him an injury risk in 2002.

Steve Bechler **Throws R** **Age 22**

YEAR	TEAM	LGE	IP	H	ER	HR	BB	K	ERA	W	L	H/9	HR/9	BB/9	K/9	KW	PERA	STUFF
1999	Delmarva	SAL	148.0	167	108	25	79	71	6.57	5	11	10.2	1.5	4.8	4.3	0.4	5.80	0
2000	Frederck	Car	161.0	195	135	42	63	81	7.55	5	13	10.9	2.3	3.5	4.5	0.6	7.10	-2
2001	Frederck	Car	81.7	85	41	7	30	41	4.52	4	5	9.4	0.8	3.3	4.5	0.7	3.80	7
2001	Bowie	Eas	71.0	87	59	21	19	38	7.48	2	6	11.0	2.7	2.4	4.8	1.0	4.48	1
2001	Rochestr	Int	8.0	13	15	5	6	5	16.88	0	1	14.6	5.6	6.8	5.6	0.4	19.60	-47

Bechler is a big, strong kid who's been the organization's minor-league workhorse; his 80 starts over the past three years is more than anyone in the organization except Sidney Ponson and Jason Johnson. He mixes a knuckle-curve with mid-90s heat but leaves both in the middle of the plate way too often. His two starts for Rochester should be ignored; one came after he'd travelled all day and hadn't slept or eaten in 24 hours. You can guess the results. And no, that does *not* build character.

Erik Bedard **Throws L** **Age 23**

YEAR	TEAM	LGE	IP	H	ER	HR	BB	K	ERA	W	L	H/9	HR/9	BB/9	K/9	KW	PERA	STUFF
2000	Delmarva	SAL	112.0	107	49	5	45	68	3.94	7	5	8.6	0.4	3.6	5.5	0.8	5.65	5
2001	Frederck	Car	92.3	88	45	10	36	72	4.39	5	5	8.6	1.0	3.5	7.0	1.0	3.85	18

A big-time prospect whose name people don't yet know, Bedard came from a Canadian high school with no baseball team. He then had to walk on to a community college team, so he is quite inexperienced for his age. He allowed just 27 runs in 17 starts, with 13 of those runs coming in back-to-back disasters. His pitches have a lot of movement, breaking in on and destroying left-handed hitters. He missed six weeks with tendinitis, then pitched well at Frederick and in the Arizona Fall League.

Lesli Brea **Throws R** **Age ???**

YEAR	TEAM	LGE	IP	H	ER	HR	BB	K	ERA	W	L	H/9	HR/9	BB/9	K/9	KW	PERA	STUFF
1999	St Lucie	Fla	117.7	113	75	10	93	81	5.74	5	8	8.6	0.8	7.1	6.2	0.4	6.60	-15
2000	Binghmtn	Eas	90.3	101	81	19	73	55	8.07	2	8	10.1	1.9	7.3	5.5	0.4	6.07	-26
2000	Rochestr	Int	21.0	24	14	4	8	11	6.00	1	1	10.3	1.7	3.4	4.7	0.7	9.20	-14
2000	Baltimor	AL	10.0	10	7	1	8	5	6.30	0	1	9.0	0.9	7.2	4.5	0.3	9.61	-31
2001	Rochestr	Int	84.3	80	45	9	45	67	4.80	4	5	8.5	1.0	4.8	7.2	0.7	6.17	-13

No one really knows how old Brea is. He's in our database as 27, which is just the midpoint of all of the guesses. Officially, he'll be 23 this year, because that's what the Orioles believed when they got him. Regardless, the fact is that even though his pitches look good to scouts, they also look good to hitters.

Sean Douglass **Throws R** **Age 23**

YEAR	TEAM	LGE	IP	H	ER	HR	BB	K	ERA	W	L	H/9	HR/9	BB/9	K/9	KW	PERA	STUFF
1999	Frederck	Car	97.7	110	67	18	38	52	6.17	4	7	10.1	1.7	3.5	4.8	0.7	5.57	4
2000	Bowie	Eas	157.3	177	107	29	58	86	6.12	6	11	10.1	1.7	3.3	4.9	0.7	5.05	4
2001	Rochestr	Int	165.0	160	83	17	69	120	4.53	9	9	8.7	0.9	3.8	6.5	0.9	4.97	17
2001	Baltimor	AL	21.0	20	12	3	10	16	5.14	1	1	8.6	1.3	4.3	6.9	0.8	5.08	11

Douglass owns one of the most consistent performance records you'll see from any pitcher, with some improvements added in 2001 courtesy of an improved curve. There's no flash, no ten-strikeout games, no low-hitters, just a steady string of sinkers pounded into the dirt, six or seven innings at a time, with three or four runs allowed. Douglass is a big guy who could turn into an innings-eater in the majors, a fourth-starter type. He's a better bet to work out than Josh Towers or Willis Roberts.

Scott Erickson **Throws R** **Age 34**

YEAR	TEAM	LGE	IP	H	ER	HR	BB	K	ERA	W	L	H/9	HR/9	BB/9	K/9	KW	PERA	STUFF
1999	Baltimor	AL	233.0	250	127	24	83	105	4.91	12	14	9.7	0.9	3.2	4.1	0.6	4.39	-2
2000	Baltimor	AL	100.3	112	61	12	39	41	5.47	4	7	10.0	1.1	3.5	3.7	0.5	6.87	-10

Erickson underwent ligament-replacement surgery in August 2000. He wanted to come back in 2001, but there was clearly no point in rushing him. He was throwing all of his pitches regularly by last August and September, quite capable of going 80 to 100 pitches in the bullpen. Many pitchers, most of them younger, have returned from such surgery with no ill effects; the pre-injury Erickson would be a major plus to this team, just for the innings he'd eat and the value he'd have at the trading deadline.

Juan Figueroa Throws R Age 23

YEAR	TEAM	LGE	IP	H	ER	HR	BB	K	ERA	W	L	H/9	HR/9	BB/9	K/9	KW	PERA	STUFF
1999	Burlingt	Mid	114.0	116	67	16	49	80	5.29	5	8	9.2	1.3	3.9	6.3	0.8	4.56	18
1999	WnstnSlm	Car	60.0	62	29	4	21	29	4.35	4	3	9.3	0.6	3.2	4.3	0.7	9.30	2
2000	WnstnSlm	Car	55.0	55	24	7	9	38	3.93	3	3	9.0	1.1	1.5	6.2	2.1	6.66	18
2000	Birmnghm	Sou	56.0	60	34	7	24	28	5.46	2	4	9.6	1.1	3.9	4.5	0.6	5.43	1
2000	Bowie	Eas	42.0	41	25	5	22	31	5.36	2	3	8.8	1.1	4.7	6.6	0.7	6.32	13
2001	Bowie	Eas	101.3	123	76	21	33	34	6.75	3	8	10.9	1.9	2.9	3.0	0.5	7.25	-15
2001	Frederck	Car	39.7	40	12	0	4	14	2.72	3	1	9.1	0.0	0.9	3.2	1.8	2.77	8

In addition to the contributions of Brook Fordyce, this is what Charles Johnson brought. Considering the lousy track record of the Orioles' player-development team, they would have been better off with the draft picks a free-agent Johnson would have returned rather than counting on their ability to identify other organizations' talent. Figueroa's velocity was down, his ERA was up, and he found himself back in A ball. Pitchers with 35 Double-A starts who go back to A–ball aren't prospects.

Kris Foster Throws R Age 27

YEAR	TEAM	LGE	IP	H	ER	HR	BB	K	ERA	W	L	H/9	HR/9	BB/9	K/9	KW	PERA	STUFF
1999	Vero Bch	Fla	14.0	15	8	3	3	8	5.14	1	1	9.6	1.9	1.9	5.1	1.3	4.27	-19
1999	SanAnton	Tex	51.3	51	31	5	32	34	5.44	2	4	8.9	0.9	5.6	6.0	0.5	5.46	-19
2001	Jacksnvl	Sou	15.3	14	6	2	3	16	3.52	1	1	8.2	1.2	1.8	9.4	2.7	1.48	13
2001	LasVegas	PCL	22.3	21	7	0	5	11	2.82	1	1	8.5	0.0	2.0	4.4	1.1	6.07	-11
2001	Rochestr	Int	10.3	10	7	1	8	7	6.10	0	1	8.7	0.9	7.0	6.1	0.4	9.23	-33
2001	Baltimor	AL	10.0	9	6	1	8	8	5.40	0	1	8.1	0.9	7.2	7.2	0.5	3.44	-8

Foster came over from the Dodgers in the Mike Trombley trade. He hits triple digits on the gun, even after surgery in 2000 to clear out his shoulder. Control has always been an issue. Foster has tinkered with a slider, discarded his curve, and reworked his delivery a couple of times. He doesn't change speeds at all, so unless he gets a little more intentional about his wildness, he's not likely to succeed.

Buddy Groom Throws L Age 36

YEAR	TEAM	LGE	IP	H	ER	HR	BB	K	ERA	W	L	H/9	HR/9	BB/9	K/9	KW	PERA	STUFF
1999	Oakland	AL	48.3	44	17	1	15	32	3.17	3	2	8.2	0.2	2.8	6.0	1.1	4.95	0
2000	Baltimor	AL	62.0	59	25	4	17	44	3.63	4	3	8.6	0.6	2.5	6.4	1.3	4.91	1
2001	Baltimor	AL	68.0	62	22	4	9	51	2.91	6	2	8.2	0.5	1.2	6.8	2.8	3.65	10

Most Games Pitched Over Six Consecutive Years

1.	Kent Tekulve	1978–83	469
2.	Mike Myers	1996–2001	463
3.	Robb Nen	1996–2001	445
4.	Buddy Groom	1996–2001	441
5.	Mike Marshall	1971–76	440
6.	Mitch Williams	1986–91	436
7.	Duane Ward	1988–93	434
8.	Eddie Guardodo	1996–2001	431
9.	Jeff Shaw	1996–2001	430
10.	Mike Stanton	1996–2001	430

Four of the second ten (Turk Wendell, Bob Wickman, Roberto Hernandez, and Jose Mesa) also made the list in the last six years. It's a golden age for the gripping drama of the managerial waddle to the mound and the call to the bullpen, so Groom deserves to be remembered as one of the kings of his day.

Beau Hale **Throws R** **Age 23**

YEAR	TEAM	LGE	IP	H	ER	HR	BB	K	ERA	W	L	H/9	HR/9	BB/9	K/9	KW	PERA	STUFF
2001	Frederck	Car	33.7	34	14	2	6	17	3.74	2	2	9.1	0.5	1.6	4.5	1.4	3.23	12
2001	Bowie	Eas	62.7	73	43	12	19	26	6.18	2	5	10.5	1.7	2.7	3.7	0.7	7.22	-10

Hale had a promising debut and a disappointing finish. The organization's first-round pick in 2000 out of the University of Texas, Hale justified his draft position quickly, starting his career by dominating high-A hitters. Moving up to Bowie, he suffered tendinitis, his velocity dropped, and he got hammered. Hale relies almost entirely on his low-90s heat and a power slider, with little in the way of off-speed stuff. Without the fastball, he was in trouble. It's too soon to say he has to be a reliever; he needs to regroup this year.

Pat Hentgen **Throws R** **Age 33**

YEAR	TEAM	LGE	IP	H	ER	HR	BB	K	ERA	W	L	H/9	HR/9	BB/9	K/9	KW	PERA	STUFF
1999	Toronto	AL	205.7	218	110	28	54	117	4.81	11	12	9.5	1.2	2.4	5.1	1.1	4.37	4
2000	St Louis	NL	196.7	206	107	21	73	105	4.90	10	12	9.4	1.0	3.3	4.8	0.7	4.47	1
2001	Baltimor	AL	59.3	62	31	7	18	31	4.70	3	4	9.4	1.1	2.7	4.7	0.9	3.45	3

Initially, Hentgen was told he had "elbow tendinitis." When it didn't get better, he was told it was a "sprained elbow." While he was rehabbing that, he blew out the elbow completely and had to have Tommy John surgery in August. He'll spend this year (his second on a two-year deal) taking Scott Erickson's place in the "Pay for No Play" club, an Orioles specialty.

Jason Johnson **Throws R** **Age 28**

YEAR	TEAM	LGE	IP	H	ER	HR	BB	K	ERA	W	L	H/9	HR/9	BB/9	K/9	KW	PERA	STUFF
1999	Rochestr	Int	42.7	43	31	7	29	34	6.54	2	3	9.1	1.5	6.1	7.2	0.6	4.15	-6
1999	Baltimor	AL	117.3	121	65	14	46	70	4.99	6	7	9.3	1.1	3.5	5.4	0.8	5.11	0
2000	Rochestr	Int	51.3	46	22	3	23	42	3.86	3	3	8.1	0.5	4.0	7.4	0.9	2.33	15
2000	Baltimor	AL	111.0	116	71	18	50	78	5.76	5	7	9.4	1.5	4.1	6.3	0.8	6.94	-3
2001	Baltimor	AL	195.0	208	114	26	73	108	5.26	9	13	9.6	1.2	3.4	5.0	0.7	4.78	0

Why did Johnson have his best season? First, he's a fly-ball pitcher, and prior to the season the Orioles moved the Camden Yards fences back six to 20 feet, depending on the direction. The result? Johnson's home-run rate at home last year was just .87 per nine innings, compared to 1.74 on the road. That's a drop from 2000, when it was 1.91 at home and 1.61 on the road. Why did he collapse after August 1? His last nine starts were against the Blue Jays, Red Sox, A's, and Yankees.

Jorge Julio **Throws R** **Age 23**

YEAR	TEAM	LGE	IP	H	ER	HR	BB	K	ERA	W	L	H/9	HR/9	BB/9	K/9	KW	PERA	STUFF
1999	Jupiter	Fla	115.0	124	65	13	41	54	5.09	6	7	9.7	1.0	3.2	4.2	0.7	6.29	0
2000	Jupiter	Fla	83.3	88	51	10	42	44	5.51	4	5	9.5	1.1	4.5	4.8	0.5	9.02	-10
2001	Rochestr	Int	43.3	41	23	5	21	37	4.78	2	3	8.5	1.0	4.4	7.7	0.9	6.37	6
2001	Baltimor	AL	23.3	21	10	2	9	21	3.86	2	1	8.1	0.8	3.5	8.1	1.2	5.25	13

Coming over from the Expos in exchange for Ryan Minor, Julio pitched exclusively out of the bullpen for the first time in his career. He throws hard and is best suited to just letting it rip for an inning or two, without worrying about pacing himself. Untouchable in 12 innings at Bowie, he struggled a little in first looks at higher levels. He'll eventually enter the closer picture in Baltimore.

Ryan Kohlmeier **Throws R** **Age 25**

YEAR	TEAM	LGE	IP	H	ER	HR	BB	K	ERA	W	L	H/9	HR/9	BB/9	K/9	KW	PERA	STUFF
1999	Bowie	Eas	58.3	60	44	14	29	55	6.79	2	4	9.3	2.2	4.5	8.5	0.9	3.77	4
2000	Rochestr	Int	45.0	41	20	5	15	41	4.00	3	2	8.2	1.0	3.0	8.2	1.4	2.84	14
2000	Baltimor	AL	28.0	27	12	1	12	17	3.86	2	1	8.7	0.3	3.9	5.5	0.7	2.69	-1
2001	Baltimor	AL	41.3	49	37	12	18	28	8.06	1	4	10.7	2.6	3.9	6.1	0.8	6.97	-20
2001	Rochestr	Int	40.0	43	21	5	9	21	4.72	2	2	9.7	1.1	2.0	4.7	1.2	3.80	-4

Touted as a prospect by an organization unfamiliar with having any, Kohlmeier notched saves in 13 of 14 opportunities in 2000 in the shakiest of fashions. In 2001, he was even shakier and lost the closer's job in May. He's an extreme fly-ball pitcher, but he was hit so hard, especially by lefties, that even moving the fences back couldn't help him. He was claimed on waivers by the White Sox after the season. That might just be another Syd Thrift boner, or it could be that potentially adequate relievers aren't valuable commodities.

Calvin Maduro Throws R Age 27

YEAR	TEAM	LGE	IP	H	ER	HR	BB	K	ERA	W	L	H/9	HR/9	BB/9	K/9	KW	PERA	STUFF
1999	Rochestr	Int	173.0	170	98	20	59	115	5.10	8	11	9.3	1.4	3.1	6.0	1.0	4.64	6
2000	Baltimor	AL	24.3	28	22	7	13	18	8.14	1	2	10.4	2.6	4.8	6.7	0.7	8.44	-22
2001	Rochestr	Int	63.7	73	48	13	28	33	6.79	2	5	10.3	1.8	4.0	4.7	0.6	6.37	-18
2001	Baltimor	AL	91.0	95	49	9	34	49	4.85	5	5	9.4	0.9	3.4	4.8	0.7	4.04	-2

Maduro was one of the Orioles' Aruban wunderkinds who never really panned out, in part because he had the misfortune of being traded to the Phillies in 1996. Coming back from a sprained elbow last year, he moved into the rotation almost by default and pitched well against a brutal closing schedule, logging eight quality starts in a dozen chances. Throughout his career, Maduro has consistently pitched much worse from the stretch. He should hang on in Triple-A as a sixth starter, waiting for somebody to break down.

Jose Mercedes Throws R Age 31

YEAR	TEAM	LGE	IP	H	ER	HR	BB	K	ERA	W	L	H/9	HR/9	BB/9	K/9	KW	PERA	STUFF
1999	LasVegas	PCL	91.3	106	59	17	23	38	5.81	4	6	10.4	1.7	2.3	3.7	0.8	5.86	-13
1999	Calgary	PCL	26.7	30	12	2	4	9	4.05	2	1	10.1	0.7	1.4	3.0	1.1	4.20	-2
1999	Norfolk	Int	33.0	35	17	2	12	14	4.64	2	2	9.5	0.5	3.3	3.8	0.6	4.51	-8
2000	Baltimor	AL	147.0	155	76	13	52	69	4.65	8	8	9.5	0.8	3.2	4.2	0.7	3.83	-5
2001	Baltimor	AL	195.7	198	94	19	60	117	4.32	11	11	9.1	0.9	2.8	5.4	1.0	5.84	4

There are reasons to believe that Mercedes pitched better last year, when he went 8-17 with a 5.82 ERA, than he did in 2000, when he was 14-7 with a 4.02 ERA. He struck out more batters, walked fewer, and didn't really give up more home runs. What was different was that in 2000 he pitched better with men on than with the bases empty (.249 EqA vs. .286), and in 2001 it was the other way around (.284 vs. .265). That's the difference between allowing 16 fewer runs than expected and 25 more than expected, and a lot of that can just be a difference in luck.

Mike Paradis Throws R Age 24

YEAR	TEAM	LGE	IP	H	ER	HR	BB	K	ERA	W	L	H/9	HR/9	BB/9	K/9	KW	PERA	STUFF
2000	Delmarva	SAL	96.0	108	73	13	65	40	6.84	3	8	10.1	1.2	6.1	3.8	0.3	7.43	-19
2000	Frederck	Car	48.3	51	27	2	28	18	5.03	2	3	9.5	0.4	5.2	3.4	0.3	6.48	-10
2001	Bowie	Eas	140.7	155	99	20	82	68	6.33	5	11	9.9	1.3	5.2	4.4	0.4	8.46	-16

Scouts insist that Paradis's arm is good enough for him pitch in the majors, but that he just doesn't have enough command. Last time we checked, command was a pretty important part of the job description, and while his walk rates are consistent with the scouts' assessment, his strikeout rates are not. He's a first-round pick who throws in the low 90s, so unless he embarks on a six-state killing spree, he'll get an opportunity.

Chad Paronto Throws R Age 26

YEAR	TEAM	LGE	IP	H	ER	HR	BB	K	ERA	W	L	H/9	HR/9	BB/9	K/9	KW	PERA	STUFF
1999	Frederck	Car	72.3	88	59	16	32	28	7.34	2	6	10.9	2.0	4.0	3.5	0.4	8.14	-25
1999	Bowie	Eas	45.7	50	33	5	34	18	6.50	2	3	9.9	1.0	6.7	3.5	0.3	10.18	-35
2000	Bowie	Eas	42.7	45	24	4	19	20	5.06	2	3	9.5	0.8	4.0	4.2	0.5	4.69	-7
2000	Rochestr	Int	36.0	42	26	6	15	15	6.50	1	3	10.5	1.5	3.8	3.8	0.5	7.12	-24
2001	Rochestr	Int	43.0	46	34	7	31	27	7.12	1	4	9.6	1.5	6.5	5.7	0.4	7.46	-36
2001	Baltimor	AL	28.3	31	18	5	10	15	5.72	1	2	9.8	1.6	3.2	4.8	0.8	7.64	-21

Paronto made a partial move to the bullpen in 2000, and in 2001 he stayed there. It didn't help, as he continued his taterrific ways. He's big, he throws hard, and he's another one of the Orioles' favored projects from the Northeast. Paronto will either get a lot of player-development people fired, or he'll contribute to the ongoing malaise choking the life out of the organization. Claimed on waivers by the Indians, where he'll break hearts in Buffalo.

John Parrish — Throws L — Age 24

YEAR	TEAM	LGE	IP	H	ER	HR	BB	K	ERA	W	L	H/9	HR/9	BB/9	K/9	KW	PERA	STUFF
1999	Frederck	Car	36.0	39	25	8	13	26	6.25	1	3	9.8	2.0	3.3	6.5	1.0	5.25	12
1999	Bowie	Eas	54.3	57	39	6	43	30	6.46	2	4	9.4	1.0	7.1	5.0	0.3	5.17	-6
2000	Rochestr	Int	101.0	100	59	12	54	74	5.26	5	6	8.9	1.1	4.8	6.6	0.7	4.92	13
2000	Baltimor	AL	37.7	38	27	5	29	28	6.45	1	3	9.1	1.2	6.9	6.7	0.5	6.93	-1
2001	Rochestr	Int	130.7	127	68	14	57	97	4.68	7	8	8.7	1.0	3.9	6.7	0.9	5.23	11
2001	Baltimor	AL	22.0	23	18	5	16	19	7.36	1	1	9.4	2.0	6.5	7.8	0.6	6.64	-9

Parrish's on-field performance is likely to be tarnished by off-field problems related to a DUI arrest last November, which would be a shame. He's been a successful starter throughout his minor-league career, although the Orioles naturally couldn't resist trying him in relief. He doesn't throw hard, at least not anywhere but on the Camden Yards gun that had Doug Jones throwing in the high 80s, and his command comes and goes. Parrish has had flashes of success, and he's a lefty, so he'll get more second chances than John Travolta as long he tackles his off-field problems.

Sidney Ponson — Throws R — Age 25

YEAR	TEAM	LGE	IP	H	ER	HR	BB	K	ERA	W	L	H/9	HR/9	BB/9	K/9	KW	PERA	STUFF
1999	Baltimor	AL	212.7	232	125	31	67	111	5.29	10	14	9.8	1.3	2.8	4.7	0.8	4.47	4
2000	Baltimor	AL	225.3	227	112	26	68	151	4.47	13	12	9.1	1.0	2.7	6.0	1.1	4.43	14
2001	Baltimor	AL	143.7	154	77	20	35	80	4.82	7	9	9.6	1.3	2.2	5.0	1.1	5.16	5

The injury bug bit Ponson last season, after three years of concern over his workload. Tendinitis set into his elbow in April, and despite a stay on the DL, he never completely healed, complaining of stiffness in the joint throughout the season. Between permanent concerns about his conditioning and the legitimate worry that there's more bad news to come (legit considering what happened with the injuries to Hentgen and Matt Riley), no sane team will be trading for him.

Matt Riley — Throws L — Age 22

YEAR	TEAM	LGE	IP	H	ER	HR	BB	K	ERA	W	L	H/9	HR/9	BB/9	K/9	KW	PERA	STUFF
1999	Frederck	Car	47.0	51	31	10	15	34	5.94	2	3	9.8	1.9	2.9	6.5	1.1	4.17	20
1999	Bowie	Eas	124.3	126	69	19	42	92	4.99	6	8	9.1	1.4	3.0	6.7	1.1	4.33	24
1999	Baltimor	AL	12.0	15	14	4	11	6	10.50	0	1	11.3	3.0	8.3	4.5	0.3	6.51	-27
2000	Bowie	Eas	73.3	81	63	16	52	48	7.73	2	6	9.9	2.0	6.4	5.9	0.5	7.77	-3

Two years ago, Riley was one of the hottest pitching prospects in baseball and one of the zaniest. Now he's 18 months removed from Tommy John surgery after the organization misdiagnosed his elbow problems, and a year of rehab has allegedly forced him to mature. He's hoping to make as much of a recovery as Kerry Wood did. His velocity should be fine; it's his command and his curveball about which we can't be sure. Riley might be ready for the majors in time for the second half.

Luis Rivera — Throws R — Age 24

YEAR	TEAM	LGE	IP	H	ER	HR	BB	K	ERA	W	L	H/9	HR/9	BB/9	K/9	KW	PERA	STUFF
1999	Myrtle B	Car	63.3	61	31	6	25	47	4.41	4	3	8.7	0.9	3.6	6.7	0.9	4.74	8
2000	Richmond	Int	23.7	27	19	4	17	10	7.23	1	2	10.3	1.5	6.5	3.8	0.3	8.16	-26
2000	Rochestr	Int	9.0	9	4	0	5	3	4.00	1	0	9.0	0.0	5.0	3.0	0.3	5.92	-16

The heralded prospect from the B.J. Surhoff trade, Rivera missed all of 2001 with a torn labrum after missing most of 2000 with a sore elbow and shoulder tendinitis, half of 1999 with blisters, and half of 1998 with a sore back. Yet Syd Thrift claims he had no concerns about Rivera when he traded for him? Labrum tears come in such a variety of grades that it's impossible to know how well Rivera will recover and whether he'll still have that high-90s moving fastball. This could easily be the last time he shows up in the book.

Willis Roberts — Throws R — Age 27

YEAR	TEAM	LGE	IP	H	ER	HR	BB	K	ERA	W	L	H/9	HR/9	BB/9	K/9	KW	PERA	STUFF
1999	Toledo	Int	96.3	106	66	11	58	40	6.17	4	7	9.9	1.0	5.4	3.7	0.3	6.62	-25
2000	Chattang	Sou	33.7	32	14	0	16	16	3.74	2	2	8.6	0.0	4.3	4.3	0.5	5.08	-4
2000	Louisvil	Int	123.7	148	100	26	60	49	7.28	4	10	10.8	1.9	4.4	3.6	0.4	6.60	-29
2001	Baltimor	AL	136.7	136	69	14	52	90	4.54	7	8	9.0	0.9	3.4	5.9	0.9	4.88	-1

In signing Roberts as a minor-league free agent, the Orioles were taking the same flyer they had in signing Mercedes a year before, picking up a pitcher who had performed well in the Dominican Winter League. After three months in the rotation, Roberts was converted to closer for the final two months. Although he started out well in the role, he was only six of ten in save opportunities, just like Kohlmeier was last year. Having just scraped the egg off of its collective face in the wake of Kohlmeier's spontaneous combustion, the organization is not excited about letting Roberts close in 2002, so he could find himself in almost any role.

B.J. Ryan **Throws L** **Age 26**

YEAR	TEAM	LGE	IP	H	ER	HR	BB	K	ERA	W	L	H/9	HR/9	BB/9	K/9	KW	PERA	STUFF
1999	Chattang	Sou	41.3	37	17	1	18	31	3.70	3	2	8.1	0.2	3.9	6.8	0.9	3.10	3
1999	Rochestr	Int	13.3	11	6	2	4	16	4.05	1	0	7.4	1.4	2.7	10.8	2.0	2.40	30
1999	Baltimor	AL	18.0	10	4	0	10	28	2.00	2	0	5.0	0.0	5.0	14.0	1.4	2.61	54
2000	Rochestr	Int	24.7	25	15	5	9	23	5.47	1	2	9.1	1.8	3.3	8.4	1.3	5.19	3
2000	Baltimor	AL	42.3	39	25	6	25	41	5.31	2	3	8.3	1.3	5.3	8.7	0.8	5.34	3
2001	Baltimor	AL	53.7	47	27	6	29	51	4.53	3	3	7.9	1.0	4.9	8.6	0.9	5.03	3

A tall sidearming left-hander with a herky-jerky motion, Ryan murders left-handed hitters with low-90s heat and a late-breaking slider. After Ryan's tough first half, Hargrove started using him for very short stints; he went longer than one inning just twice after mid-July. The change helped him, as he gave up only three runs in his final 18 innings over 30 appearances. He's a good second southpaw ready to grow into the job of primary situational lefty.

Rich Stahl **Throws L** **Age 21**

YEAR	TEAM	LGE	IP	H	ER	HR	BB	K	ERA	W	L	H/9	HR/9	BB/9	K/9	KW	PERA	STUFF
2000	Delmarva	SAL	92.7	97	61	8	65	43	5.92	4	6	9.4	0.8	6.3	4.2	0.3	6.90	-7
2001	Delmarva	SAL	30.3	36	28	7	21	16	8.31	1	2	10.7	2.1	6.2	4.7	0.4	6.41	-7
2001	Frederck	Car	31.0	32	19	2	20	14	5.52	1	2	9.3	0.6	5.8	4.1	0.3	5.31	-2

According to most sources, Stahl is the Orioles' top pitching prospect. Injuries have prevented him from pitching a full season, although neither injury (back, bone spur) is the kind about which to worry. A more significant source of concern is Stahl's inability to match his league's average strikeout rate, 95-mph fastball or not. He draws comparisons to Randy Johnson because of his height (6′7″), but the parallel doesn't work on any other level. If a Leakey digs him up in 30,000 years, Stahl might be identified as a member of another species; he has the longest thigh bones you'll see on a hominid.

John Stephens **Throws R** **Age 22**

YEAR	TEAM	LGE	IP	H	ER	HR	BB	K	ERA	W	L	H/9	HR/9	BB/9	K/9	KW	PERA	STUFF
1999	Delmarva	SAL	169.3	172	85	21	49	111	4.52	9	10	9.1	1.1	2.6	5.9	1.1	5.64	19
2000	Frederck	Car	120.7	122	52	11	24	71	3.88	7	6	9.1	0.8	1.8	5.3	1.5	4.48	18
2001	Bowie	Eas	123.7	123	57	15	27	85	4.15	8	6	9.0	1.1	2.0	6.2	1.6	2.77	23
2001	Rochestr	Int	58.0	55	28	6	21	47	4.34	3	3	8.5	0.9	3.3	7.3	1.1	5.46	25

A freak neck injury suffered while he was fielding his position left Stephens with shoulder damage from which he's never recovered. (Most scouts stop here.) His fastball may only reach 85 mph. (The rest of the scouts stop here.) That said, the young Australian has been better than most pitchers who throw 95. He started in Bowie, came up to Rochester for five games, and then went back down to Bowie. In his last 40 innings in Double-A, he allowed one run, 17 hits, and fanned 45 batters. He followed that by going back up to Rochester for four games, tossing 28 innings with a 3.21 ERA and a 32-to-6 strikeout-to-walk ratio. Stephens's great control, excellent curve and circle change, and intelligence should be enough to get him taken seriously, especially in this organization. He's a better prospect than the next guy.

Josh Towers **Throws R** **Age 25**

YEAR	TEAM	LGE	IP	H	ER	HR	BB	K	ERA	W	L	H/9	HR/9	BB/9	K/9	KW	PERA	STUFF
1999	Bowie	Eas	186.7	222	120	37	26	75	5.79	8	13	10.7	1.8	1.3	3.6	1.4	4.68	0
2000	Rochestr	Int	150.3	160	73	21	20	86	4.37	9	8	9.6	1.3	1.2	5.1	2.2	4.03	12
2001	Rochestr	Int	41.0	42	17	3	9	20	3.73	3	2	9.2	0.7	2.0	4.4	1.1	4.67	5
2001	Baltimor	AL	144.0	163	74	20	15	55	4.63	8	8	10.2	1.3	0.9	3.4	1.8	4.53	0

(Josh Towers *continued*)

Like Stephens, Towers worked his way up the ladder without an ounce of respect from scouts. As you might expect from a guy who has walked 109 men in his entire six-year pro career, control and a no-fear attitude carried him to the majors. He ran through the league in June, but from July 1 onward his ERA was 6.12, and he struggled away from Camden Yards' new spaciousness. He'll have to make an adjustment or two if he's going to beat the Quadruple-A rap.

John Wasdin **Throws R** **Age 29**

YEAR	TEAM	LGE	IP	H	ER	HR	BB	K	ERA	W	L	H/9	HR/9	BB/9	K/9	KW	PERA	STUFF
1999	Pawtuckt	Int	28.0	26	10	1	8	20	3.21	2	1	8.4	0.3	2.6	6.4	1.3	2.88	16
1999	Boston	AL	72.7	74	37	12	15	56	4.58	4	4	9.2	1.5	1.9	6.9	1.9	3.87	4
2000	Boston	AL	46.3	46	24	7	12	36	4.66	2	3	8.9	1.4	2.3	7.0	1.5	4.15	3
2000	Colorado	NL	38.3	37	17	5	7	31	3.99	2	2	8.7	1.2	1.6	7.3	2.2	4.16	11
2001	Colorado	NL	24.7	28	17	5	7	14	6.20	1	2	10.2	1.8	2.6	5.1	1.0	5.51	-15
2001	Rochestr	Int	21.7	24	14	4	6	14	5.82	1	1	10.0	1.7	2.5	5.8	1.2	5.12	-7
2001	Baltimor	AL	53.0	47	20	4	15	45	3.40	4	2	8.0	0.7	2.5	7.6	1.5	4.32	12

The Orioles picked up Wasdin after the Rockies released him. For the most part, they used him in long relief, to mop up in losses. He was a lot better in that role (2.84 ERA when pitching more than two innings) than in short relief (6.00 in outings of two innings or less). As an innings-eater on a team with a weak rotation, Wasdin has value. The Orioles didn't get it, trading him to the Phillies for Chris Brock.

Boston Red Sox

Identifying great players who have already demonstrated their greatness is easy. Signing them is easy, too, if your team has the money. And if money is no object, you can build a tremendous core for your roster to form the foundation of a championship ballclub. The problem for the Red Sox and their embattled GM, Dan Duquette, is that a core of four or five of these players won't even get you to the playoffs unless everything breaks your way. In 2001, nothing broke the Red Sox's way.

> **Red Sox Prospectus**
>
> **2001 record:** 82–79; Second place, AL East
>
> **Pythagenport W/L:** 83–79
>
> **Runs scored:** 772 (seventh in AL)
>
> **Runs allowed:** 745 (fifth in AL)
>
> **Team EqA:** .259 (seventh in AL)
>
> **2001 batters age:** 29.9 (tied for fifth-oldest in AL)
>
> **2001 pitchers age:** 30.8 (oldest in AL)
>
> **Ballpark:** Fenway Park; slight hitters' park; Park Factor of 1.023
>
> **2001:** Injuries to two of the best players in baseball doomed them.
>
> **2002:** They stand to improve just through better health, and should challenge the Yankees for the division title.

Duquette's mandate has always been clear: anything less than a world championship is a disappointment to a Red Sox Nation that has waited 83 years for one. To that end, he went out and acquired what is unquestionably the core of a championship club. He selected Nomar Garciaparra in the first round of his first draft, then signed the shortstop to a prescient five-year deal after Garciaparra's Rookie of the Year debut. He traded two prospects to the Expos for Pedro Martinez, then the reigning Cy Young Award winner, and signed him to what was at the time the largest contract in baseball history. He traded two modest prospects to Houston for emerging star Carl Everett and signed him to a three-year deal. And last winter, he signed Manny Ramirez, among the game's top offensive forces, to what was at the time the second-biggest contract in the game's history. That core, surrounded even with average players, would get just about any team to the playoffs.

Two things knocked the Red Sox off the path to the 2001 playoffs. The first problem, as everyone knows, was injuries. Garciaparra's nagging wrist injury resulted in surgery that cost him the first four months of the 2001 season. Pedro Martinez suffered a slight labrum tear in his pitching shoulder that kept him out from mid-June to mid-August. Catcher Jason Varitek, in the midst of his best season yet, broke his elbow in June and missed the rest of the campaign. Carl Everett suffered a few injuries, not least of which was the bruised ego and broken reputation that had him on the Acela out of Boston by season's end.

The other problem that ruined the Red Sox season has received less scrutiny. Despite having the highest Opening Day payroll of any team in baseball, the team's roster beyond its stars was horrible. Good players were overpaid. Bad players ate up valuable space on the 25- and 40-man rosters and often cost more than the good players. The farm system, briefly rated among the game's best in the mid- to late 1990s, dried up almost completely, providing no support whatsoever to the big club in a season when that support was desperately needed. This roster situation was the culmination of a go-for-broke effort that started with the team's playoff run in 1998 and that has left the team in progressively worse shape each year.

The Sox are in their current predicament in large part due to Duquette, long an outspoken advocate of building through the farm system, developing a pattern of trading prospects for veterans. Some trades have pretty clearly panned out, such as dealing Tony Armas Jr. and Carl Pavano for Pedro Martinez, but many more have not. Dealing Chris Reitsma and the now-injured John Curtice for Dante Bichette was a fiasco; Bichette was lousy with the stick in 2001 and ran his mouth most of the season, while Reitsma will probably be one of the Reds' top three starters in 2002. Throwing Justin Duchscherer away last year for Doug Mirabelli just weeks after Ramon Castro passed unclaimed through waivers was inexcusable. Last summer's deal for Ugueth Urbina cost the Sox a fifth starter in Tomo Ohka and a top left-handed pitching prospect in Rich Rundles.

Perhaps no trade exemplifies Duquette's recent win-now attitude better than his July 2000 deal for Ed Sprague. Overreacting to the team's hole at third base, Duquette traded for Sprague, two years removed from his last extended period of usefulness at the plate and carrying his career-long love/hate relationship with his glove. Acquiring Sprague was, in and of itself, a bad idea. But in exchange for Sprague, Duquette gave up not one but two prospects, one of whom, Dennis Tankersley, is now one of the top ten pitching prospects in baseball. Sprague, meanwhile, didn't hit in Boston, still couldn't field, and was released a few weeks after he came to the Red Sox.

These deals and ones like them, combined with the expansion draft and the normal attrition of prospects as they climb the minor-league ladder, have left the Red Sox at a severe disadvantage compared to their immediate rival, the Yankees, and also to the rising AL contenders in Oakland, Seattle, and Chicago. The Red Sox had two serious prospects above A–ball in 2001 in Casey Fossum and Freddy Sanchez, and neither is likely to contribute much to the parent club before 2003. While other teams could either call on their player-development system to fill small gaps in the majors or to provide trade bait for needed veterans, the Sox had to play 2001 with essentially the same roster with which they started the season.

Duquette's other shift in philosophy has hurt the Sox both financially and on the field. When Duquette first came to the Red Sox, he worked to find free talent. An active GM can fill most bench and middle-relief spots with minimum-salary players obtained via waivers, the Rule 5 draft, and minor-league free agency. With a little luck, the effort will yield a starting hitter or two and perhaps a fourth or fifth starter.

In Duquette's first few years, he nabbed several players via these methods, and the dividends were substantial. Troy O'Leary was an early waiver claim. Brian Daubach was signed as a minor-league free agent, as was Rich Garces.

More recently, Duquette has been less aggressive in acquiring cheap talent, which has restricted the team's ability to compete for top players in the same way that the lack of tradeable prospects has. In 1999, the Sox signed O'Leary to a four-year deal for more than $4 million per year, flying directly in the face of the replaceable-talent theory. If you found one Troy O'Leary out there on waivers, the odds are that you will find another when you need one. You take an O'Leary, get three years out of him, and non-tender him as soon as he's eligible for arbitration.

Instead of looking at free talent sources, the Red Sox have been opting to bring in highly paid veterans to surround their stars. Dante Bichette took home $7 million this year to be a DH who hits like a second baseman. Mike Lansing, whose contract came over as part of the price of acquiring Rolando Arrojo, earned $6.25 million this year and was kept on the roster all season even though he could barely out-hit Rey Ordonez. Bret Saberhagen earned $4.5 million to make two starts before he called it quits. And the Sox paid more than $11 million to five middle relievers, only one of whom was appreciably better than the minimum-salary pitching one might find with a modicum of effort.

All of this wasted money would be irrelevant if the Sox were winning. The Boston Red Sox are incredibly profitable, even though they're not a well-run business. Should they win the World Series, the resulting profits and the increase in the business's value would be enormous. With the team on the block and a sale expected by the time this book hits shelves, the pressure on the team and on Duquette in particular to win in 2001 was even higher than it had been in previous years. So having the biggest payroll in baseball was not a problem.

However, the reckless spending cost the Red Sox a great deal in terms of missed opportunities. The custodians of the majority-owning Yawkey Trust were not willing to authorize a payroll above the $110 million at which the team started the season. Had the Sox not acquired Bichette's abysmal contract in 2000 and not committed $9 million to Saberhagen and Rod Beck, they would have had another $16 million to add to the $4.5 million they spent on Hideo Nomo—enough to pay Mike Mussina, Mike Hampton, or just about any player they might have wanted—and that only scratches the surface of the impact of the Sox's misguided financial commitments.

So while it's convenient to write off the disappointing 2001 season as the result of injuries and bad luck, the year could easily have been different had Duquette continued to follow the philosophy that allowed him to build successful teams in 1995, 1998, and 1999. With money and roster spots wasted on players who contributed little or nothing to the team, the Sox were fortunate to stay close as long as they did.

Not that Boston's upper management ever considered their own culpability when making their late August decision to fire manager Jimy Williams. Williams was hardly the ideal manager; among his flaws was his refusal to give Trot Nixon any experience against left-handers, a decision that stunted the young hitter's growth against righties as well. But Williams's record in the win column was nearly beyond reproach. He kept the doubly shorthanded Sox within striking distance of the Yankees until the day he was fired, after which new manager/former pitching coach Joe Kerrigan presided over a meltdown that culminated in a backbreaking three-game sweep at the hands of the dreaded Yankees.

The timing of the Williams firing was its most curious aspect. Williams and Duquette had been engaging in a very public battle of wills for years, dating back at least to Williams's bizarre decision to give the ineffective Steve Avery the one extra start in 1999 that triggered his $5 million option for the following season. They fought over Nixon. They fought over Israel Alcantara, who Williams refused to play and who Duquette refused to send back to the minors. They sniped at each other endlessly in the press. None of this would have mattered a whit had the team won a championship, of course, but in the blame game that played out during the subpar 2000 and 2001 seasons, the criticism flowed downward and buried Williams.

The silver lining for Red Sox fans is that many of the mistakes that flattened the Olde Towne Team in 2001 are gone. Saberhagen, O'Leary, Bichette, Lansing, Beck, and John Valentin are among 11 members of the 2001 Red Sox who became free agents after the season, wiping a total of more than $40 million in salaries off of the books. Garciaparra and Varitek are expected to be healthy for 2002, and the prognosis for Pedro Martinez is cautiously optimistic, although even a partially torn labrum can end a pitcher's season without notice.

The Sox have enough talent on the major-league roster to contend in the weak AL East. The Yankees are old and have thinned their farm system almost as badly as the Red Sox have, and the Three Stooges behind them are in no shape to compete in the short term. But it's going to take a substantial change in philosophy and a willingness to break with the mistakes of the recent past for the Sox to get the playoff lottery ticket that might bring Red Sox fans the World Series victory they so richly deserve.

HITTERS (BA: .270, OBP: .340, SLG: .440, EqA: .260)

Israel Alcantara LF Bats R Age 29

YEAR	TEAM	LGE	AB	H	DB	TP	HR	BB	SO	R	RBI	SB	CS	OUT	BA	OBP	SLG	EQA	EQR	DEFENSE
1999	Trenton	Eas	297	78	17	1	16	19	78	39	46	3	2	221	.263	.312	.488	.259	38	50-LF 3 10-1B -1
1999	Pawtuckt	Int	81	21	3	0	7	7	27	11	18	0	0	60	.259	.335	.556	.284	13	13-LF -1
2000	Pawtuckt	Int	300	87	12	1	26	20	82	53	64	2	1	214	.290	.341	.597	.295	51	46-RF -2
2000	Boston	AL	45	13	2	0	4	2	6	9	7	0	0	32	.289	.319	.600	.288	7	
2001	Pawtuckt	Int	459	130	18	1	34	55	99	76	83	8	2	331	.283	.364	.549	.296	79	61-RF 5
2001	Boston	AL	38	11	1	0	0	3	11	3	3	1	0	27	.289	.341	.316	.234	4	
2002	*Boston*	*AL*	*447*	*127*	*18*	*1*	*32*	*53*	*110*	*72*	*82*	*8*	*2*	*322*	*.284*	*.360*	*.544*	*.295*	*76*	

He may have blown his shot. Although his antagonist was fired in late August, Alcantara hadn't hit at all since The Kick, and observers said his head was clearly not right after the brouhaha that surrounded the incident. He's the new Felix "Sucker Punch" Martinez, although unlike Martinez, Izzy can contribute something to a baseball team—his bat. Given the chance, Alcantara should produce, but chances will be scarce now.

Dante Bichette DH Bats R Age 38

YEAR	TEAM	LGE	AB	H	DB	TP	HR	BB	SO	R	RBI	SB	CS	OUT	BA	OBP	SLG	EQA	EQR	DEFENSE
1999	Colorado	NL	578	153	31	1	31	45	78	90	111	4	5	430	.265	.320	.483	.260	74	137-LF -8
2000	Cincnnti	NL	462	134	24	2	16	35	63	64	71	5	2	330	.290	.345	.455	.266	60	108-RF 0
2000	Boston	AL	113	33	3	0	8	7	19	12	14	0	0	80	.292	.333	.531	.278	16	
2001	Boston	AL	391	118	28	1	14	22	66	48	51	2	2	275	.302	.343	.486	.271	52	50-LF -6
2002	*Boston*	*AL*	*502*	*125*	*27*	*1*	*22*	*41*	*82*	*68*	*77*	*4*	*3*	*380*	*.249*	*.306*	*.438*	*.245*	*57*	

Bichette has the highest mouth/production ratio in baseball, and that's saying something. He cried and whined through a well-deserved benching in April, got his full-time job back, and proceeded to stink up the joint so badly that the lawyers in Newton and Wellesley were preparing Clean Air Act lawsuits. He doesn't hit enough to DH and never has. Some GM will be dumb enough to ignore the Coors Field effect and sign Bichette; just hope it's not for your favorite team.

Tony Blanco 3B Bats R Age 20

YEAR	TEAM	LGE	AB	H	DB	TP	HR	BB	SO	R	RBI	SB	CS	OUT	BA	OBP	SLG	EQA	EQR	DEFENSE
2000	Lowell	NYP	29	4	0	0	0	1	14	1	0	1	0	25	.138	.177	.138	.123	1	
2001	Augusta	SAL	380	83	17	1	11	14	83	34	47	1	0	297	.218	.251	.355	.202	27	47-3B -11
2002	*Boston*	*AL*	*382*	*93*	*19*	*1*	*16*	*23*	*92*	*37*	*45*	*2*	*0*	*289*	*.243*	*.286*	*.424*	*.234*	*38*	

Blanco's tools had observers touting him before he made it out of short-season ball, but a shoulder injury and a total lack of plate discipline led to a very disappointing full-season debut in 2001. He's very susceptible to the pitch low and away; that weakness contributed to his 17 ground-ball double plays. He had to DH much of the season due to the injury, then underwent shoulder surgery in late August, so 2002 will be a somewhat more accurate test of his tools.

Morgan Burkhart 1B Bats B Age 30

YEAR	TEAM	LGE	AB	H	DB	TP	HR	BB	SO	R	RBI	SB	CS	OUT	BA	OBP	SLG	EQA	EQR	DEFENSE	
1999	Sarasota	Fla	248	71	9	0	16	27	37	38	42	3	1	178	.286	.363	.516	.288	39	57-1B -1	
1999	Trenton	Eas	244	52	11	1	10	23	43	33	33	2	0	192	.213	.296	.389	.231	25	24-1B -3	
2000	Pawtuckt	Int	357	86	14	1	21	60	87	53	67	0	0	271	.241	.365	.462	.276	54	60-1B 4	14-LF -1
2000	Boston	AL	72	21	4	0	4	16	22	16	17	0	0	51	.292	.446	.514	.323	15		
2001	Pawtuckt	Int	421	109	15	1	24	64	105	62	59	1	0	312	.259	.364	.470	.278	64	96-1B 2	
2001	Boston	AL	33	6	2	0	1	1	10	4	4	0	0	27	.182	.206	.333	.178	2		
2002	*Boston*	*AL*	*457*	*122*	*18*	*1*	*25*	*69*	*114*	*71*	*75*	*2*	*0*	*335*	*.267*	*.363*	*.475*	*.281*	*70*		

Signing Burkhart was a great gamble for the Sox, but ultimately one that didn't pay off. He can hit enough to play first base, barely, but can't field the position at all, and he doesn't hit enough to be a DH. The financial outlay and roster spot burned on this gamble were insignificant to the Sox, who have plenty of money and a lousy farm system. Burkhart is expected to spend 2002 in Japan.

Brian Daubach 1B Bats L Age 30

YEAR	TEAM	LGE	AB	H	DB	TP	HR	BB	SO	R	RBI	SB	CS	OUT	BA	OBP	SLG	EQA	EQR	DEFENSE	
1999	Boston	AL	378	114	35	3	22	32	81	61	71	0	1	265	.302	.360	.585	.300	65	54-1B -2	
2000	Boston	AL	492	126	32	2	22	38	114	53	73	1	1	367	.256	.317	.463	.255	61	77-1B -2	
2001	Boston	AL	408	113	27	3	25	54	93	58	75	1	0	295	.277	.367	.542	.294	69	100-1B 0	12-RF -1
2002	*Boston*	*AL*	*465*	*127*	*31*	*3*	*25*	*58*	*112*	*64*	*77*	*1*	*1*	*339*	*.273*	*.354*	*.514*	*.284*	*73*		

Daubach's consistent counting stats mask some variances in his output, with 2001 ranking in between his previous two seasons. Daubach was one of Duquette's smartest signings. Obtained for nothing as a former replacement player with a Quadruple-A label, Daubach has outproduced Tino Martinez over the last three years for about $15 million less. However, just as they found him in the pile of first baseman, the Sox should now go back to the pile to find another one like him rather than go to arbitration.

Juan Diaz 1B Bats R Age 26

YEAR	TEAM	LGE	AB	H	DB	TP	HR	BB	SO	R	RBI	SB	CS	OUT	BA	OBP	SLG	EQA	EQR	DEFENSE
1999	SanAnton	Tex	257	69	14	1	8	20	80	34	41	0	0	188	.268	.326	.424	.250	29	61-1B -5
2000	Sarasota	Fla	52	12	3	0	3	2	17	5	8	0	0	40	.231	.266	.462	.234	5	14-1B 0
2000	Trenton	Eas	200	56	9	1	14	7	58	29	39	0	0	144	.280	.304	.545	.270	27	35-1B -5
2000	Pawtuckt	Int	43	11	0	0	6	5	9	10	14	1	0	32	.256	.333	.674	.310	9	10-1B 0
2001	Pawtuckt	Int	281	73	12	1	19	17	79	43	47	0	0	208	.260	.311	.512	.265	38	36-1B -8
2002	*Boston*	*AL*	*282*	*77*	*14*	*1*	*17*	*23*	*85*	*43*	*56*	*0*	*0*	*205*	*.273*	*.328*	*.511*	*.273*	*40*	

Diaz nearly ate himself out of baseball last winter while Red Sox Nation was demanding his installation as the team's 2001 first baseman. He didn't start his season in earnest until June, after which he showed the same package he showed before an ankle injury ended his 2000 season: tremendous power dampened by a total lack of plate discipline. Slider away, fastball in, slider away, sit down. His cup of coffee will be bitter.

Carl Everett CF Bats B Age 31

YEAR	TEAM	LGE	AB	H	DB	TP	HR	BB	SO	R	RBI	SB	CS	OUT	BA	OBP	SLG	EQA	EQR	DEFENSE
1999	Houston	NL	467	151	31	3	26	45	87	83	104	23	7	323	.323	.396	.570	.314	89	121-CF -3
2000	Boston	AL	490	150	32	4	35	46	99	79	103	11	4	344	.306	.375	.602	.310	92	121-CF -3
2001	Boston	AL	409	111	24	4	16	29	90	64	61	8	2	300	.271	.334	.467	.266	55	90-CF -7
2002	*Texas*	*AL*	*478*	*144*	*29*	*4*	*26*	*47*	*104*	*78*	*95*	*14*	*4*	*338*	*.301*	*.364*	*.542*	*.292*	*78*	

The armchair psychologist's dream. The radio talk-show host's dream. Or both. Everett might be misunderstood, or he might be schizophrenic, but either way, he's not showing any signs that he's improving, and he's not producing at the plate, which is the real problem. If you're hitting .300/.400/.550, no one cares if you question whether dinosaurs existed. Everett was traded to the Rangers for pennies on the dollar and should be a huge bargain for them.

Luis Garcia 1B Bats R Age 23

YEAR	TEAM	LGE	AB	H	DB	TP	HR	BB	SO	R	RBI	SB	CS	OUT	BA	OBP	SLG	EQA	EQR	DEFENSE
2000	Augusta	SAL	509	105	17	3	14	34	120	52	49	4	1	405	.206	.257	.334	.200	36	115-1B -4
2001	Sarasota	Fla	272	69	9	0	10	12	65	29	31	1	1	204	.254	.286	.397	.225	25	54-1B -2
2001	Trenton	Eas	237	66	16	1	11	25	66	31	38	0	1	172	.278	.347	.494	.274	34	57-1B -5
2002	*St Louis*	*NL*	*477*	*129*	*23*	*2*	*17*	*42*	*128*	*61*	*61*	*3*	*1*	*349*	*.270*	*.328*	*.434*	*.255*	*58*	

Garcia is the prospect that Juan Diaz is supposed to be. A former pitcher, Garcia has a fluid power swing—the ball just flies off his bat—but he also has shown more than adequate plate discipline. Traded to the Cardinals for Dustin Hermanson, he could be a cheap, above-average solution at first base by mid-2002.

Nomar Garciaparra SS Bats R Age 28

YEAR	TEAM	LGE	AB	H	DB	TP	HR	BB	SO	R	RBI	SB	CS	OUT	BA	OBP	SLG	EQA	EQR	DEFENSE
1999	Boston	AL	525	193	41	4	29	45	34	101	102	13	3	335	.368	.425	.627	.338	111	131-SS 0
2000	Boston	AL	519	197	51	3	22	54	44	100	91	5	2	324	.380	.440	.617	.342	111	133-SS -4
2001	Boston	AL	83	25	4	0	4	7	8	14	8	0	1	59	.301	.361	.494	.277	12	21-SS 0
2002	*Boston*	*AL*	*431*	*156*	*34*	*2*	*21*	*50*	*37*	*83*	*74*	*8*	*2*	*277*	*.362*	*.428*	*.596*	*.336*	*90*	

If you're looking for someone to blame for the compost pile that was the Red Sox's 2001 season, here are two culprits: Garciaparra and team doctor/part-owner Arthur Pappas. Neither man had the good sense to realize in October 2000 that Garciaparra should have wrist surgery immediately, to avoid his missing three or four months of the regular season recovering from it. Former Bruin forward Jason Allison had a similar injury and remarked that it took him more than a year to get back to full strength; the Sox and Garciaparra wasted five months with their Russian-roulette strategy. It backfired. Nomar played in 21 games, didn't look like himself at the plate, and shut it down for the year. He should be 100 percent or close to it in 2002, but the Sox need to learn a lesson from the episode or they'll face the same problem again.

Scott Hatteberg C Bats B Age 32

YEAR	TEAM	LGE	AB	H	DB	TP	HR	BB	SO	R	RBI	SB	CS	OUT	BA	OBP	SLG	EQA	EQR	DEFENSE
1999	Pawtuckt	Int	35	6	2	0	0	3	6	3	4	0	0	29	.171	.237	.229	.165	2	
1999	Boston	AL	81	23	3	0	2	17	12	12	12	0	0	58	.284	.414	.395	.284	12	19-C -3
2000	Boston	AL	232	63	11	0	10	36	34	20	36	0	1	170	.272	.369	.448	.274	33	43-C -11
2001	Boston	AL	277	72	12	0	6	34	22	35	28	1	1	206	.260	.347	.368	.246	31	64-C -23
2002	*Oakland*	*AL*	*264*	*65*	*10*	*1*	*7*	*40*	*29*	*29*	*36*	*0*	*1*	*200*	*.246*	*.345*	*.371*	*.251*	*32*	

He got his big chance, and he blew it. Hatteberg is usually more than acceptable at the plate, but he did nothing with the whimper-stick in 2001, and at 32, he's not likely to get another shot. He should be entering Joe Oliver territory—minor-league deals, non-roster invitations to spring training, cups of coffee—where you get things on the basis of your experience, not your potential production. Maybe he and Oliver got to chat when the latter had another sip with Boston in September.

Shea Hillenbrand 3B Bats R Age 26

YEAR	TEAM	LGE	AB	H	DB	TP	HR	BB	SO	R	RBI	SB	CS	OUT	BA	OBP	SLG	EQA	EQR	DEFENSE
1999	Trenton	Eas	285	67	8	0	7	0	27	33	29	4	4	222	.235	.260	.337	.199	20	50-C -12
2000	Trenton	Eas	533	155	27	2	11	12	40	64	63	2	2	380	.291	.312	.411	.239	53	65-1B 5 35-3B -4
2001	Boston	AL	468	130	19	2	14	15	53	55	51	2	4	342	.278	.308	.417	.238	47	118-3B -5
2002	*Boston*	*AL*	*458*	*131*	*22*	*1*	*14*	*22*	*48*	*66*	*59*	*4*	*3*	*330*	*.286*	*.319*	*.430*	*.248*	*51*	

April: .343/.356/.515. Everything after: .241/.274/.363. Once word got around that Hillenbrand would swing at curveballs in the dirt, he got very little to hit the rest of the way. Outside of a three-walk day versus the Phillies (including one intentional walk), he drew seven unintentional walks in 390 plate appearances after May 1. He's also a butcher at third base and in three years has made no progress with his plate discipline. Hillenbrand plays hard but is a total waste of the Red Sox' time.

Rontrez Johnson CF Bats R Age 25

YEAR	TEAM	LGE	AB	H	DB	TP	HR	BB	SO	R	RBI	SB	CS	OUT	BA	OBP	SLG	EQA	EQR	DEFENSE
1999	Sarasota	Fla	502	119	22	2	7	55	71	69	41	10	9	392	.237	.317	.331	.223	46	132-CF -7
2000	Trenton	Eas	534	128	18	1	6	42	75	66	42	20	14	420	.240	.299	.311	.211	43	133-CF 5
2001	Trenton	Eas	261	67	12	1	8	21	39	41	26	12	5	199	.257	.324	.402	.246	30	72-CF -6
2001	Pawtuckt	Int	189	54	15	2	4	10	32	30	20	6	3	138	.286	.337	.450	.261	24	40-CF -3
2002	*Boston*	*AL*	*507*	*137*	*27*	*2*	*11*	*46*	*79*	*81*	*50*	*20*	*12*	*382*	*.270*	*.331*	*.396*	*.246*	*57*	

Johnson is the kind of fifth outfielder most teams would like to have and is proof that a good bench doesn't have to cost good money. He plays a solid defensive center field and hits line drives with a little bit of power. He doesn't walk enough to hold a full-time job or even to warrant regular playing time, but he should draw interest this winter as a minor-league free agent.

Mike Lansing SS/2B Bats R Age 34

YEAR	TEAM	LGE	AB	H	DB	TP	HR	BB	SO	R	RBI	SB	CS	OUT	BA	OBP	SLG	EQA	EQR	DEFENSE
1999	Colorado	NL	142	39	7	0	4	5	20	21	13	2	0	103	.275	.304	.408	.238	14	35-2B 1
2000	Colorado	NL	358	80	12	5	9	26	45	52	38	7	2	280	.223	.276	.360	.216	30	86-2B -11
2000	Boston	AL	139	29	4	0	0	5	23	10	13	0	0	110	.209	.236	.237	.164	6	35-2B 0
2001	Boston	AL	352	93	18	0	11	23	43	48	37	3	3	262	.264	.311	.409	.238	36	69-SS -8 26-2B -2
2002	*Boston*	*AL*	*403*	*95*	*16*	*2*	*10*	*34*	*55*	*57*	*36*	*7*	*3*	*311*	*.236*	*.295*	*.360*	*.220*	*35*	

Lansing deserves a lot of credit for stepping in as the semiregular shortstop in Garciaparra's absence, but even the position switch couldn't make his offensive ineptitude excusable. For the second year in a row, Lansing couldn't even muster a .300 OBP, and he probably should have been cut before spring training. He has nothing to offer a major-league team, so he will probably play 120 games for the Devil Rays or Royals in 2002.

Darren Lewis OF Bats R Age 34

YEAR	TEAM	LGE	AB	H	DB	TP	HR	BB	SO	R	RBI	SB	CS	OUT	BA	OBP	SLG	EQA	EQR	DEFENSE
1999	Boston	AL	467	116	16	6	2	41	46	62	39	15	10	361	.248	.315	.321	.220	41	130-CF 2
2000	Boston	AL	268	66	7	0	4	19	30	41	17	10	6	208	.246	.304	.317	.215	22	68-OF 1
2001	Boston	AL	164	48	10	1	1	9	22	19	12	4	5	121	.293	.338	.384	.239	17	46-OF 4
2002	*ChiCubs*	*NL*	*364*	*86*	*12*	*2*	*4*	*36*	*46*	*50*	*27*	*14*	*10*	*288*	*.236*	*.305*	*.313*	*.212*	*30*	

This is a colossal waste of a roster spot. Lewis's only apparent ability is in the field, and even that has been called into question as observers noticed that he tends to stick to easy plays to avoid making errors. He's a lousy base-stealer and has never hit. Yet Jimy Williams always found ways to put his 0-for-4 in the lineup, often as a platoon mate for Trot Nixon. The Sox don't have a strong enough lineup to carry weak links on their bench.

James Lofton SS Bats B Age 28

YEAR	TEAM	LGE	AB	H	DB	TP	HR	BB	SO	R	RBI	SB	CS	OUT	BA	OBP	SLG	EQA	EQR	DEFENSE
1999	Tri-Cit	Wst	342	69	9	1	1	7	50	29	23	9	7	279	.202	.218	.243	.160	14	
2000	Tri-Cit	Wst	383	86	13	2	4	13	65	33	26	18	9	305	.225	.250	.300	.191	24	
2001	Sonoma	Wst	52	7	2	0	0	4	14	5	1	0	0	45	.135	.202	.173	.137	2	
2001	Trenton	Eas	114	32	4	0	5	9	22	19	10	2	1	83	.281	.336	.447	.260	14	12-SS -1
2001	Pawtuckt	Int	153	46	6	0	6	10	27	18	12	2	3	110	.301	.344	.458	.261	19	37-SS 3
2001	Boston	AL	26	6	1	0	0	1	3	1	1	2	1	21	.231	.259	.269	.188	2	
2002	*Boston*	*AL*	*364*	*86*	*13*	*1*	*7*	*23*	*69*	*42*	*33*	*11*	*6*	*284*	*.236*	*.282*	*.335*	*.206*	*27*	

After washing out of the Reds' system, Lofton rejuvenated his career by playing with the Western League's Tri-City Posse in 2000. The Sox signed him, and Lofton became a small singles machine, showing a little speed, a little pop, and a good glove at shortstop—in other words, almost everything Lou Merloni doesn't have, but with the same "scrappy" sheen. Lofton could walk a little more, but that's a quibble if he can play short and hit .280–.290. He's a minor-league free agent.

Steve Lomasney C Bats R Age 24

YEAR	TEAM	LGE	AB	H	DB	TP	HR	BB	SO	R	RBI	SB	CS	OUT	BA	OBP	SLG	EQA	EQR	DEFENSE	
1999	Sarasota	Fla	192	42	7	0	6	19	64	25	19	3	1	151	.219	.301	.349	.223	18	43-C 0	
1999	Trenton	Eas	155	34	5	0	9	25	44	19	23	4	3	124	.219	.347	.426	.259	21	46-C -4	
2000	Trenton	Eas	237	52	13	1	7	19	83	25	21	3	4	189	.219	.297	.371	.223	22	60-C -10	
2001	Trenton	Eas	215	49	11	1	9	21	74	22	25	0	1	167	.228	.302	.414	.236	23	51-C -5	
2001	Pawtuckt	Int	64	18	3	0	2	4	19	10	9	2	0	46	.281	.330	.422	.256	8	17-C -6	
2002	*Boston*	*AL*	*381*	*95*	*18*	*1*	*15*	*40*	*135*	*48*	*46*	*2*	*2*	*288*	*.240*	*.321*	*.420*	*.247*	*44*		

Saturday Night Live, back when it was funny, ran a great skit with Chevy Chase called "Those Unlucky Andersons." Various maladies would befall the family—their winning lottery ticket went through the wash; the cat got stuck in the freezer—and Chase's uniform remedy was, "Put some butter on that." The sketch was a rare bird in that the gag got funnier as the sketch went on. When Mrs. Anderson puts her hand to her eye and leans over, Chase asks, "Did you lose a contact?" and she responds, "No, my whole eye!"

Well, Steve Lomasney is an honorary Anderson, for two reasons. One is that he has suffered a number of freak injuries—such as a foul ball breaking his nose—that have negatively affected his development. The other is that this year's injury nearly cost him his eye: He was hit in the face by a ball during batting practice, and the result was reminiscent of Bryce Florie's injury the year before. Lomasney's eye was saved, but the long-term damage to his vision is not yet known, and his career is on hold. We wish him the best.

Lou Merloni SS Bats R Age 31

YEAR	TEAM	LGE	AB	H	DB	TP	HR	BB	SO	R	RBI	SB	CS	OUT	BA	OBP	SLG	EQA	EQR	DEFENSE	
1999	Pawtuckt	Int	229	59	12	1	6	25	36	38	29	1	1	171	.258	.348	.397	.253	27	28-SS -3	26-3B 3
1999	Boston	AL	125	33	5	0	2	7	14	18	14	0	0	92	.264	.312	.352	.225	11	19-SS -2	
2000	Boston	AL	127	42	11	2	0	2	19	10	17	1	0	85	.331	.346	.449	.265	15	34-3B -2	
2001	Boston	AL	146	41	8	0	4	7	27	22	14	2	1	106	.281	.324	.418	.247	16	36-SS 2	
2001	Pawtuckt	Int	197	50	8	0	5	15	34	29	20	2	0	147	.254	.317	.371	.235	20	29-SS -6	18-2B -1
2002	*Boston*	*AL*	*314*	*88*	*15*	*1*	*8*	*29*	*54*	*47*	*37*	*2*	*1*	*227*	*.280*	*.341*	*.411*	*.254*	*37*		

If Merloni was from New York or Fargo or Johannesburg, he wouldn't have seen the light of Fenway. Merloni has very little to contribute to a major-league club, just a gallon of scrappiness and a first name fans like to shout. He doesn't walk, he has no power, and he is not a good fielder. If Garciaparra is even sort of healthy, he'll be on the field. If he's not, Merloni is not an adequate replacement.

Doug Mirabelli C Bats R Age 31

YEAR	TEAM	LGE	AB	H	DB	TP	HR	BB	SO	R	RBI	SB	CS	OUT	BA	OBP	SLG	EQA	EQR	DEFENSE	
1999	Fresno	PCL	313	85	18	1	11	40	51	48	39	6	2	230	.272	.355	.441	.268	43	62-C 0	18-1B 3
1999	San Fran	NL	88	23	3	0	2	8	23	10	11	0	0	65	.261	.330	.364	.237	9	23-C 3	
2000	San Fran	NL	234	57	11	2	6	33	52	23	28	1	0	177	.244	.341	.385	.249	27	65-C 0	
2001	Texas	AL	49	6	2	0	2	10	18	4	3	0	0	43	.122	.271	.286	.198	4	14-C 5	
2001	Boston	AL	141	40	7	0	10	18	31	17	27	0	0	101	.284	.377	.546	.299	25	41-C -3	
2002	*Boston*	*AL*	*328*	*84*	*16*	*1*	*14*	*47*	*79*	*44*	*44*	*2*	*1*	*245*	*.256*	*.349*	*.439*	*.266*	*45*		

Mirabelli was an offensive star for the Sox, but that obscured two important facts. One is that he's never hit like this before, so we're probably looking at a small-sample fluke. The other is that the Sox gave up Justin Duchscherer, a real pitching prospect, for a mediocre backup catcher after passing up all sorts of free catching talent available on waivers or through free agency, such as Ramon Castro, Sal Fasano, Tom Wilson, and Creighton Gubanich. Pitching prospects are scarce. Backup catchers with pop aren't.

Trot Nixon RF Bats L Age 28

YEAR	TEAM	LGE	AB	H	DB	TP	HR	BB	SO	R	RBI	SB	CS	OUT	BA	OBP	SLG	EQA	EQR	DEFENSE
1999	Boston	AL	377	105	22	5	16	49	66	66	51	3	1	273	.279	.365	.491	.283	58	105-RF -8
2000	Boston	AL	421	119	26	8	13	58	75	63	58	8	1	303	.283	.372	.475	.284	65	105-RF 0
2001	Boston	AL	536	160	32	4	30	81	98	107	93	6	4	380	.299	.396	.541	.305	98	140-RF -11
2002	*Boston*	*AL*	*474*	*141*	*32*	*5*	*25*	*80*	*90*	*91*	*75*	*6*	*2*	*335*	*.297*	*.399*	*.544*	*.311*	*90*	

(Trot Nixon *continued*)

The bright spot in Boston's 2001 season was almost totally obscured by the light-sucking effects of the general meltdown, but Nixon's age-27 season had him finally arriving as a major-league hitter. Playing every day helped, and Nixon can still take another step up if he learns from the new experience against lefties and starts to hit them for more than a 604 OPS. He still has some room to grow and should make an All-Star team or two in the next few years.

Troy O'Leary LF Bats L Age 32

YEAR	TEAM	LGE	AB	H	DB	TP	HR	BB	SO	R	RBI	SB	CS	OUT	BA	OBP	SLG	EQA	EQR	DEFENSE			
1999	Boston	AL	591	171	36	4	30	50	80	83	101	1	2	422	.289	.348	.516	.280	88	155-LF	2		
2000	Boston	AL	509	137	29	4	14	38	67	65	68	0	2	374	.269	.322	.424	.247	57	129-LF	1		
2001	Boston	AL	341	87	17	5	15	26	63	54	52	1	3	257	.255	.315	.466	.253	41	86-LF	-1		
2002	*Boston*	*AL*	*493*	*136*	*26*	*4*	*22*	*46*	*82*	*69*	*78*	*1*	*3*	*360*	*.276*	*.338*	*.479*	*.268*	*67*				

O'Leary is the biggest lesson of Duquette's GM career, one it's not entirely clear that he learned. O'Leary was a smart waiver snag and gave the Red Sox several good years at no money, but the Sox then signed him to a four-year, $14.8-million Pompeii deal that Vesuviused all over them by the time the first year was done. The lesson: If you get a guy like this for free, then you can get another guy just like him for free.

Jose Offerman 2B Bats B Age 33

YEAR	TEAM	LGE	AB	H	DB	TP	HR	BB	SO	R	RBI	SB	CS	OUT	BA	OBP	SLG	EQA	EQR	DEFENSE			
1999	Boston	AL	578	173	36	11	9	90	69	103	67	17	12	417	.299	.395	.446	.284	89	125-2B	-9		
2000	Boston	AL	446	116	13	3	10	64	62	70	40	0	8	338	.260	.354	.370	.244	50	75-2B	-5	31-1B	1
2001	Boston	AL	525	147	24	3	10	63	84	81	51	5	2	380	.280	.358	.394	.257	64	87-2B	-8	38-1B	3
2002	*Boston*	*AL*	*496*	*131*	*21*	*4*	*10*	*76*	*77*	*77*	*47*	*6*	*9*	*373*	*.264*	*.362*	*.383*	*.254*	*61*				

Three years into a four-year deal, Offerman has become one of Duquette's biggest flops in a most embarrassing way. Offerman was signed because of his high OBPs, the importance of which is still not appreciated by many fans and members of the media. He posted a .391 OBP in his first year in Boston, the fourth time in five years he'd been at .384 or better, but his patience has almost completely disappeared. He desperately needs to be traded.

Calvin Pickering 1B Bats L Age 25

YEAR	TEAM	LGE	AB	H	DB	TP	HR	BB	SO	R	RBI	SB	CS	OUT	BA	OBP	SLG	EQA	EQR	DEFENSE	
1999	Rochestr	Int	373	99	14	0	15	50	93	53	53	1	3	277	.265	.365	.424	.265	50	96-1B	-8
1999	Baltimor	AL	40	6	1	0	1	11	14	4	5	0	0	34	.150	.333	.250	.218	4		
2000	Rochestr	Int	200	42	8	0	6	31	69	18	27	2	2	160	.210	.318	.340	.227	20	56-1B	-3
2001	Rochestr	Int	471	128	17	0	22	61	138	60	95	0	1	344	.272	.363	.448	.272	66	68-1B	-7
2001	Boston	AL	50	15	1	0	3	8	11	4	7	0	0	35	.300	.397	.500	.298	9	11-1B	-1
2002	*Boston*	*AL*	*484*	*138*	*16*	*0*	*25*	*73*	*148*	*67*	*86*	*1*	*2*	*348*	*.285*	*.379*	*.473*	*.285*	*76*		

Heavy P came into town almost unnoticed, or at least as unnoticed as any nearly-300-pound man can be. Pickering was a great waiver claim for Boston: They need a first baseman with some power, and Pickering has that and the willingness to take a walk. He might fan 175 times in the process, but if the Sox decide to move Brian Daubach now that he's arbitration-eligible, Pickering would be a fine replacement.

Manny Ramirez LF Bats R Age 30

YEAR	TEAM	LGE	AB	H	DB	TP	HR	BB	SO	R	RBI	SB	CS	OUT	BA	OBP	SLG	EQA	EQR	DEFENSE	
1999	Clevelnd	AL	512	174	34	3	45	90	115	128	158	2	4	342	.340	.449	.682	.354	127	130-RF	-2
2000	Clevelnd	AL	427	152	31	2	39	79	103	87	114	1	1	276	.356	.460	.712	.366	112	80-RF	-8
2001	Boston	AL	531	171	33	2	45	83	127	100	130	0	1	361	.322	.419	.646	.336	118	55-LF	-1
2002	*Boston*	*AL*	*493*	*162*	*32*	*2*	*39*	*83*	*122*	*104*	*130*	*1*	*2*	*333*	*.329*	*.425*	*.639*	*.340*	*112*		

After an MVP-level start to the season, Ramirez tailed off badly after May and never found his groove again. Nagging hamstring problems cropped up, and various reports indicated that he was upset by the discord and malaise in the clubhouse. A winning season would likely cure that very quickly, and there's no reason to expect Manny not to return to his early-2001 form. The Sox will need him to do so if they expect to catch the Yanks.

Freddy Sanchez SS Bats R Age 24

YEAR	TEAM	LGE	AB	H	DB	TP	HR	BB	SO	R	RBI	SB	CS	OUT	BA	OBP	SLG	EQA	EQR	DEFENSE
2000	Lowell	NYP	136	30	8	1	1	4	19	16	9	1	2	108	.221	.249	.316	.188	8	32-SS 0
2000	Augusta	SAL	112	27	5	0	0	8	20	12	10	2	0	85	.241	.294	.286	.205	8	30-SS -1
2001	Sarasota	Fla	286	81	17	2	1	15	32	32	17	3	2	207	.283	.321	.367	.232	27	66-SS -5
2001	Trenton	Eas	182	53	10	0	4	9	20	22	18	2	1	130	.291	.329	.412	.247	20	41-SS -6
2002	*Boston*	*AL*	*472*	*138*	*27*	*2*	*5*	*33*	*60*	*57*	*47*	*6*	*3*	*337*	*.292*	*.339*	*.390*	*.247*	*51*	

Sanchez flew through the system on high batting averages and great defense at shortstop, winning raves for his tools. He is probably headed for third base, although depending on how he develops, it might make more sense to move Garciaparra's arm over there. This is all based on the assumption that Sanchez' singles-hitting ways will continue despite his suspect batting eye, which is not guaranteed. Still, his tools alone make him a prospect.

Angel Santos 2B Bats B Age 22

YEAR	TEAM	LGE	AB	H	DB	TP	HR	BB	SO	R	RBI	SB	CS	OUT	BA	OBP	SLG	EQA	EQR	DEFENSE
1999	Augusta	SAL	487	104	21	1	10	45	93	57	37	12	7	390	.214	.283	.322	.209	39	45-SS -2 42-2B -3
2000	Trenton	Eas	281	66	15	1	3	24	62	26	26	12	6	221	.235	.298	.327	.216	24	79-2B 0
2001	Trenton	Eas	525	129	21	0	14	49	103	66	47	19	7	403	.246	.313	.366	.233	53	126-2B -17
2002	*Boston*	*AL*	*501*	*126*	*23*	*1*	*13*	*53*	*108*	*61*	*48*	*8*	*4*	*379*	*.251*	*.323*	*.370*	*.230*	*53*	

A dark horse for the Sox' second-base job in 2002, Santos probably is best suited for a utility role right now. The Sox made yet another organizational blunder by failing to push Santos until August, choosing instead to waste another year on the now-departed Jim Chamblee. Santos showed some growth as a Double-A repeater; he probably needs a year of Triple-A and some work on shortening his swing before he can kick Offerman to the curb.

Dernell Stenson LF Bats L Age 24

YEAR	TEAM	LGE	AB	H	DB	TP	HR	BB	SO	R	RBI	SB	CS	OUT	BA	OBP	SLG	EQA	EQR	DEFENSE
1999	Pawtuckt	Int	440	111	24	2	15	45	112	53	66	1	1	330	.252	.328	.418	.249	51	111-1B -19
2000	Pawtuckt	Int	383	98	11	0	21	38	97	54	62	0	0	285	.256	.328	.449	.257	48	65-1B -4 21-LF -1
2001	Pawtuckt	Int	469	108	14	1	16	42	107	52	66	0	0	361	.230	.295	.367	.223	42	114-LF -8
2002	*Boston*	*AL*	*441*	*117*	*18*	*0*	*20*	*46*	*110*	*57*	*70*	*0*	*0*	*324*	*.265*	*.335*	*.442*	*.260*	*56*	

Stenson is just 23, yet he's a Triple-A veteran coming off of his worst year yet in the pros. Stenson showed very little enthusiasm for the game last year; some blamed that on the death of his father early in the season, but the organization's total disinterest in him can't be helping. He plays a passable left field, though he would probably benefit offensively from a return to first base. He has a big upside if he leaves the organization.

Chris Stynes 3B/2B Bats R Age 29

YEAR	TEAM	LGE	AB	H	DB	TP	HR	BB	SO	R	RBI	SB	CS	OUT	BA	OBP	SLG	EQA	EQR	DEFENSE
1999	Cincnnti	NL	113	26	1	0	2	11	12	17	13	4	2	89	.230	.298	.292	.208	9	22-2B 0
2000	Cincnnti	NL	381	125	22	1	12	26	50	68	38	5	2	258	.328	.374	.486	.285	56	69-3B 1
2001	Boston	AL	361	106	19	2	9	22	48	55	34	3	6	261	.294	.338	.432	.252	42	41-3B -6 40-2B 1
2002	*ChiCubs*	*NL*	*364*	*109*	*17*	*1*	*12*	*33*	*51*	*68*	*53*	*6*	*5*	*260*	*.299*	*.358*	*.451*	*.270*	*49*	

Acquired from the Reds to be the Sox' 2001 third baseman—a questionable idea at best—Stynes got hurt in spring training and lost the job to Shea Hillenbrand. He finally received a more or less full-time role in July, and given regular playing time, went .259/.299/.363 after the All-Star break. Stynes is a singles hitter who doesn't walk and has no power, and as such, he should never see another full-time job.

John Valentin 3B/SS Bats R Age 35

YEAR	TEAM	LGE	AB	H	DB	TP	HR	BB	SO	R	RBI	SB	CS	OUT	BA	OBP	SLG	EQA	EQR	DEFENSE
1999	Boston	AL	447	117	27	1	13	36	60	57	69	0	1	331	.262	.322	.414	.245	49	109-3B 7
2000	Boston	AL	35	9	2	0	2	1	4	6	3	0	1	27	.257	.278	.486	.236	4	
2001	Pawtuckt	Int	37	9	0	0	2	8	4	7	4	0	0	28	.243	.378	.405	.270	5	
2001	Boston	AL	60	13	0	0	2	9	7	8	6	0	0	47	.217	.326	.317	.226	6	15-SS 0
2002	*Boston*	*AL*	*329*	*77*	*18*	*1*	*10*	*43*	*44*	*47*	*37*	*0*	*1*	*253*	*.234*	*.323*	*.386*	*.239*	*35*	

(John Valentin *continued*)

He's probably done. It's a shame Valentin suffered so many injuries over the last few years, because at one point, he was an All-Star, one of the most underrated players in baseball. He embarrassed himself by whining about being bumped off shortstop in 1997 and never had the season at the plate to put that memory behind him. The Sox can't wait on him any longer, unfortunately.

Jason Varitek C Bats L Age 30

YEAR	TEAM	LGE	AB	H	DB	TP	HR	BB	SO	R	RBI	SB	CS	OUT	BA	OBP	SLG	EQA	EQR	DEFENSE
1999	Boston	AL	479	133	37	2	22	42	75	69	75	1	2	348	.278	.338	.501	.272	67	131-C -12
2000	Boston	AL	444	113	28	1	12	54	74	53	64	1	1	332	.255	.343	.403	.253	53	119-C -9
2001	Boston	AL	174	53	11	1	8	22	30	20	26	0	0	121	.305	.385	.517	.297	29	50-C -2
2002	*Boston*	*AL*	*394*	*111*	*25*	*1*	*14*	*50*	*68*	*51*	*57*	*1*	*1*	*284*	*.282*	*.363*	*.457*	*.275*	*56*	

Varitek's broken elbow was a cruel addition to the injury brigade, and one that hurt about as much as Garciaparra's injury did. Varitek was off to a great start, one that had him in the top tier of AL catchers, when he went down, and despite the plethora of free catching talent available in 2001, the Sox ended up giving most of the playing time to Scott Hatteberg, who couldn't hit the windshield if the bus stopped short. Varitek is expected to be 100 percent by spring training, and both he and the Sox need a big season from him.

Quilvio Veras 2B Bats B Age 31

YEAR	TEAM	LGE	AB	H	DB	TP	HR	BB	SO	R	RBI	SB	CS	OUT	BA	OBP	SLG	EQA	EQR	DEFENSE
1999	San Dieg	NL	481	137	26	2	6	60	81	92	40	25	17	361	.285	.366	.385	.256	60	117-2B 4
2000	Atlanta	NL	300	91	8	0	7	47	46	53	37	24	13	222	.303	.405	.400	.278	45	79-2B -4
2001	Atlanta	NL	259	69	15	2	3	23	44	41	26	7	4	194	.266	.339	.375	.243	28	66-2B 0
2002	*Boston*	*AL*	*428*	*122*	*19*	*2*	*7*	*57*	*75*	*77*	*41*	*22*	*15*	*321*	*.285*	*.369*	*.388*	*.259*	*55*	

Could Veras really be done? It seems unlikely; he posted a .278 EqA in 2000, and his loss of speed in 2001 could just be a result of a longer-than-usual recovery time from the torn ACL he suffered in July of 2000. Veras is, at best, Luis Castillo—a second baseman with some walks and little power, but whose value largely depends on how many plink hits fall in for singles. He's certainly worth a chance.

Kevin Youkilis 3B Bats R Age 23

YEAR	TEAM	LGE	AB	H	DB	TP	HR	BB	SO	R	RBI	SB	CS	OUT	BA	OBP	SLG	EQA	EQR	DEFENSE
2001	Lowell	NYP	206	46	11	1	2	51	33	37	18	2	2	162	.223	.383	.316	.252	26	58-3B 4
2002	*Boston*	*AL*	*250*	*59*	*14*	*1*	*3*	*50*	*43*	*32*	*22*	*3*	*2*	*193*	*.236*	*.363*	*.336*	*.248*	*29*	

Barry Bonds led all of baseball with a .515 OBP; Youkilis was second at .504. He led the entire Boston farm system with 73 walks, despite playing just 64 games. He doesn't have the speed most managers like at the top of the lineup, but then again, that's a dumb criterion, and Boston has never been a running team anyway. He could outwalk Shea Hillenbrand right now in a fair fight.

PITCHERS (ERA: 4.50, H/9: 9.0, HR/9: 1.0, BB/9: 3.0, K/9: 6.0, KW: 2.0, PERA: 4.50)

Rolando Arrojo Throws R Age 33

YEAR	TEAM	LGE	IP	H	ER	HR	BB	K	ERA	W	L	H/9	HR/9	BB/9	K/9	KW	PERA	STUFF
1999	TampaBay	AL	148.3	149	79	20	50	106	4.79	7	9	9.0	1.2	3.0	6.4	1.1	4.59	10
2000	Colorado	NL	108.0	107	53	11	38	71	4.42	6	6	8.9	0.9	3.2	5.9	0.9	4.91	6
2000	Boston	AL	70.7	73	35	9	18	44	4.46	4	4	9.3	1.1	2.3	5.6	1.2	4.26	7
2001	Boston	AL	102.3	96	43	7	33	74	3.78	6	5	8.4	0.6	2.9	6.5	1.1	3.45	7

Written off in mid-May as an expensive bust—the Sox took on Mike Lansing's contract as part of the deal to get Arrojo in July 2000—Arrojo jumped into Pedro Martinez's spot in the rotation and was the team's second-best starter for his nine outings, with six quality starts and a superb 1.5 Support-Neutral Wins Above Replacement. Unfortunately, he went down with a sore shoulder in August and wasn't the same when he returned. There's some upside here.

Brad Baker   Throws R   Age 21

YEAR	TEAM	LGE	IP	H	ER	HR	BB	K	ERA	W	L	H/9	HR/9	BB/9	K/9	KW	PERA	STUFF
2000	Augusta	SAL	137.7	140	72	8	70	66	4.71	7	8	9.2	0.5	4.6	4.3	0.5	5.42	2
2001	Sarasota	Fla	123.0	135	88	19	72	64	6.44	5	9	9.9	1.4	5.3	4.7	0.4	7.69	-5

Baker cruised through the first two months of his first season in high-A ball, then had a three-start stretch in which 16 runs in 12 1/3 innings blew his ERA all to hell. He was inconsistent the rest of the season, and while there's been no report of an injury yet, this is certainly the pattern of a pitcher with arm trouble. Even if that's not the case, Baker shouldn't get the obligatory promotion to Double-A; baseball isn't public school, after all.

Willie Banks   Throws R   Age 33

YEAR	TEAM	LGE	IP	H	ER	HR	BB	K	ERA	W	L	H/9	HR/9	BB/9	K/9	KW	PERA	STUFF
2000	Norfolk	Int	51.3	60	37	7	27	15	6.49	2	4	10.5	1.2	4.7	2.6	0.3	6.62	-28
2001	Syracuse	Int	148.0	155	86	17	67	82	5.23	7	9	9.4	1.0	4.1	5.0	0.6	4.67	-6
2001	Boston	AL	10.0	8	3	0	4	10	2.70	1	0	7.2	0.0	3.6	9.0	1.3	3.02	23

Perhaps the ace of the 2001 Ken Phelps All-Stars, Banks sliced through Triple-A last year with his funky deliveries and huge arsenal of variations on his pitches, earning a cup of coffee in September during which he pitched well. There's little doubt he could be a league-average pitcher in the majors; if the Sox discard Banks this offseason, they'll do a lot worse than him in their fifth starter slot.

Rod Beck   Throws R   Age 33

YEAR	TEAM	LGE	IP	H	ER	HR	BB	K	ERA	W	L	H/9	HR/9	BB/9	K/9	KW	PERA	STUFF
1999	ChiCubs	NL	32.0	37	20	5	11	12	5.63	2	2	10.4	1.4	3.1	3.4	0.5	7.06	-28
1999	Boston	AL	13.7	11	4	0	4	12	2.63	1	1	7.2	0.0	2.6	7.9	1.5	1.62	19
2000	Boston	AL	41.0	35	13	2	10	35	2.85	4	1	7.7	0.4	2.2	7.7	1.8	2.73	15
2001	Boston	AL	80.3	82	46	14	27	60	5.15	4	5	9.2	1.6	3.0	6.7	1.1	4.21	-3

Beck was having an adequate season for the second straight year when his pitches started to drift back up in the zone, resulting in copious souvenirs for the college students in Fenway's $300 bleacher seats. A late-season exam revealed that Beck had shredded the ligament in his pitching elbow and will need Tommy John surgery, ending his tenure with the Sox and, in all likelihood, his pitching career.

Frank Castillo   Throws R   Age 33

YEAR	TEAM	LGE	IP	H	ER	HR	BB	K	ERA	W	L	H/9	HR/9	BB/9	K/9	KW	PERA	STUFF
1999	Nashvill	PCL	123.0	136	74	19	37	60	5.41	6	8	10.0	1.4	2.7	4.4	0.8	5.95	-8
2000	Toronto	AL	134.3	130	65	15	46	103	4.35	8	7	8.7	1.0	3.1	6.9	1.1	3.08	15
2001	Boston	AL	139.0	139	62	13	33	85	4.01	8	7	9.0	0.8	2.1	5.5	1.3	4.26	9

The Sox got exactly what they wanted out of Castillo and then some. He threw 136 2/3 innings of above-average baseball. He ranked third on the team in Support-Neutral Wins Above Replacement, behind Martinez and Nomo. He was good when he was healthy, and he was healthy as often as he was in 2000. Jimy Williams and Joe Kerrigan kept him on a short leash, so he should be good for at least another 20 starts in 2002. Another great bargain for Duquette.

David Cone   Throws R   Age 39

YEAR	TEAM	LGE	IP	H	ER	HR	BB	K	ERA	W	L	H/9	HR/9	BB/9	K/9	KW	PERA	STUFF
1999	NY Yanks	AL	193.7	173	86	19	75	175	4.00	12	10	8.0	0.9	3.5	8.1	1.2	3.43	24
2000	NY Yanks	AL	167.0	168	92	22	67	119	4.96	9	10	9.1	1.2	3.6	6.4	0.9	6.17	4
2001	Boston	AL	142.3	137	70	15	54	109	4.43	8	8	8.7	0.9	3.4	6.9	1.0	4.41	12

It was a better season than 2000, but it was still the second-worst of his career. Cone had enough life on his pitches in 2001 to be a league-average pitcher, but his days as anything more than that appear to be over. He might try to pull one more year out of his elbow in an attempt to reach 200 wins (he's seven short), but he's at the point where a bad month will lead to retirement.

Paxton Crawford Throws R Age 24

YEAR	TEAM	LGE	IP	H	ER	HR	BB	K	ERA	W	L	H/9	HR/9	BB/9	K/9	KW	PERA	STUFF
1999	Trenton	Eas	160.0	171	89	18	59	78	5.01	8	10	9.6	1.0	3.3	4.4	0.7	5.23	4
2000	Trenton	Eas	53.3	51	20	5	6	39	3.38	4	2	8.6	0.8	1.0	6.6	3.3	4.06	25
2000	Pawtuckt	Int	58.3	59	31	7	21	40	4.78	3	3	9.1	1.1	3.2	6.2	1.0	4.82	13
2000	Boston	AL	29.0	27	10	0	11	17	3.10	2	1	8.4	0.0	3.4	5.3	0.8	3.84	10
2001	Boston	AL	38.0	37	17	3	12	24	4.03	2	2	8.8	0.7	2.8	5.7	1.0	4.27	9
2001	Pawtuckt	Int	32.0	37	20	5	8	12	5.63	2	2	10.4	1.4	2.3	3.4	0.8	6.53	-10

Many Red Sox fans saw Crawford as the solution to the team's perceived pitching problem, which was on its face an absurd load to put on the shoulders of a pitcher who took three years to escape Double-A. A back problem nearly wiped out Crawford's entire 2001 season, anyway. When he pitched, he was ineffective, and he spent some time experimenting with a new grip on his change-up to help him avoid blisters. He's a long shot to contribute in 2002.

Chris Elmore Throws L Age 25

YEAR	TEAM	LGE	IP	H	ER	HR	BB	K	ERA	W	L	H/9	HR/9	BB/9	K/9	KW	PERA	STUFF
2000	Lowell	NYP	68.3	70	27	0	20	20	3.56	5	3	9.2	0.0	2.6	2.6	0.5	4.38	-8
2001	Sarasota	Fla	59.7	63	27	3	17	20	4.07	4	3	9.5	0.5	2.6	3.0	0.6	6.14	-19
2001	Trenton	Eas	77.3	83	41	7	27	33	4.77	4	5	9.7	0.8	3.1	3.8	0.6	5.69	-8

Remember the name. Elmore has come quickly because, despite a mid-80s fastball, he has gotten good results all the way through Double-A. He has great control, works inside and out well, murders lefties, and is effective enough against righties that he should move beyond a lefty specialist role in time. That is, if the Sox don't stick him in that role in 2001 and arrest his development.

Casey Fossum Throws L Age 24

YEAR	TEAM	LGE	IP	H	ER	HR	BB	K	ERA	W	L	H/9	HR/9	BB/9	K/9	KW	PERA	STUFF
2000	Sarasota	Fla	151.0	155	76	17	44	90	4.53	8	9	9.2	1.0	2.6	5.4	1.0	5.64	7
2001	Trenton	Eas	117.0	110	48	8	37	82	3.69	8	5	8.5	0.6	2.8	6.3	1.1	4.85	15
2001	Boston	AL	44.7	45	23	4	19	25	4.63	2	3	9.1	0.8	3.8	5.0	0.7	4.75	-2

Bring on the new Messiah. Now that Paxton Crawford is no longer the answer to the Sox' perceived pitching problems, Fossum assumes the mantle as the great hope of Red Sox Nation. He has a hard, 12-to-6 curve that dazzled minor-league hitters, but his debut as a major-league starter resulted in a 5.97 ERA with poor peripherals in seven outings. A half-year in Triple-A would do him a world of good.

Franklin Francisco Throws R Age 22

YEAR	TEAM	LGE	IP	H	ER	HR	BB	K	ERA	W	L	H/9	HR/9	BB/9	K/9	KW	PERA	STUFF
2001	Augusta	SAL	62.7	61	40	7	42	46	5.74	3	4	8.8	1.0	6.0	6.6	0.5	5.09	-4

Francisco came out of nowhere this year to blow away the Sally League with a 97-mph fastball and a menacing mound presence. Observers compared him physically to Armando Benitez, and he's pretty close to Benitez on the gun. The Sox are trying to bring him along as a reliever unless he develops an effective breaking pitch. While they're thinking "closer," remember that even Benitez took years to seize that title in the majors.

Rich Garces Throws R Age 31

YEAR	TEAM	LGE	IP	H	ER	HR	BB	K	ERA	W	L	H/9	HR/9	BB/9	K/9	KW	PERA	STUFF
1999	Pawtuckt	Int	26.3	30	20	6	11	17	6.84	1	2	10.3	2.1	3.8	5.8	0.8	3.77	-23
1999	Boston	AL	38.7	33	13	1	15	33	3.03	3	1	7.7	0.2	3.5	7.7	1.1	1.68	14
2000	Boston	AL	75.3	66	27	6	19	68	3.23	5	3	7.9	0.7	2.3	8.1	1.8	2.78	15
2001	Boston	AL	65.7	62	30	5	24	49	4.11	4	3	8.5	0.7	3.3	6.7	1.0	3.86	1

He just keeps right on rolling—out to the mound and through opposing hitters. Garces says he plans to slim down to about 230 pounds to induce the Sox to give him a long-term deal. While such deals for relievers tend to be bad moves, Garces has been extremely effective for three straight seasons, and the weight loss should help him stay healthy; a September meltdown added a run and a half to his ERA. He'd even make a fine closer.

Eric Glaser — Throws R — Age 24

YEAR	TEAM	LGE	IP	H	ER	HR	BB	K	ERA	W	L	H/9	HR/9	BB/9	K/9	KW	PERA	STUFF
1999	Lowell	NYP	73.7	88	64	19	35	39	7.82	2	6	10.8	2.3	4.3	4.8	0.6	6.24	-7
2000	Augusta	SAL	114.0	144	110	37	45	60	8.68	3	10	11.4	2.9	3.6	4.7	0.7	5.71	-19
2001	Sarasota	Fla	84.0	95	59	16	34	45	6.32	3	6	10.2	1.7	3.6	4.8	0.7	4.27	-19

Considered the least promising of Augusta's 2000 trio of starting pitching prospects, Glaser had the best season of the three and is the only one likely to start 2002 in Double-A. Jerome Gamble missed the entire season (save three outings) due to injuries, and Brad Baker was inconsistent. The Sox have pigeonholed Glaser in the swingman role because he doesn't throw that hard, but anyone with his track record should be in the rotation until he shows he can't handle it.

Josh Hancock — Throws R — Age 24

YEAR	TEAM	LGE	IP	H	ER	HR	BB	K	ERA	W	L	H/9	HR/9	BB/9	K/9	KW	PERA	STUFF
1999	Augusta	SAL	141.3	166	104	25	62	54	6.62	5	11	10.6	1.6	3.9	3.4	0.4	7.23	-12
2000	Sarasota	Fla	147.0	167	91	22	46	60	5.57	6	10	10.2	1.3	2.8	3.7	0.7	7.34	-8
2001	Trenton	Eas	133.7	136	68	12	49	75	4.58	7	8	9.2	0.8	3.3	5.0	0.8	5.58	2

Mild sleeper. Hancock saw his stock rise over the course of the summer as his stuff improved, including a hard-dropping curve and a low-90s fastball, and as he gained stamina, pitching more regularly into the seventh inning without a drop in velocity. He absolutely needs a year of Triple-A to consolidate these gains, but with the Sox' upper minors very thin in the pitching department, he could get a call-up this summer.

Sun-Woo Kim — Throws R — Age 24

YEAR	TEAM	LGE	IP	H	ER	HR	BB	K	ERA	W	L	H/9	HR/9	BB/9	K/9	KW	PERA	STUFF
1999	Trenton	Eas	152.0	162	87	23	44	92	5.15	7	10	9.6	1.4	2.6	5.4	1.0	6.08	10
2000	Pawtuckt	Int	145.0	149	77	21	40	98	4.78	8	8	9.2	1.3	2.5	6.1	1.2	6.74	11
2001	Pawtuckt	Int	90.3	93	50	13	30	61	4.98	4	6	9.3	1.3	3.0	6.1	1.0	6.22	5
2001	Boston	AL	46.3	44	19	1	20	26	3.69	3	2	8.5	0.2	3.9	5.1	0.6	5.24	-3

Kim has great stuff and a questionable track record marked by inconsistency and long bouts of total ineffectiveness. He leaves the ball up and gets very rattled with men on, habits that could be fixed if the Sox still had, say, a top-notch major-league pitching coach. A return to Triple-A would probably do more harm than good; Kim could really use a year in a major-league bullpen, Earl Weaver-style, to get his feet wet.

Mike Kusiewicz — Throws L — Age 25

YEAR	TEAM	LGE	IP	H	ER	HR	BB	K	ERA	W	L	H/9	HR/9	BB/9	K/9	KW	PERA	STUFF
2000	Tennesse	Sou	152.0	171	102	25	62	74	6.04	6	11	10.1	1.5	3.7	4.4	0.6	5.96	-7
2001	Trenton	Eas	88.0	90	45	10	27	54	4.60	5	5	9.2	1.0	2.8	5.5	1.0	5.77	-1
2001	Pawtuckt	Int	38.3	39	20	4	14	23	4.70	2	2	9.2	0.9	3.3	5.4	0.8	6.57	-1

A former Rockies prospect who missed nearly two years with elbow injuries resulting from overuse in 1997, Kusiewicz spent a year and a half in the Blue Jays' system before the Sox grabbed him. Kusiewicz relies on the good movement he has on most of his pitches, eschewing the plain fastball for a mixture of cutters, sliders, and curves. He had a reverse platoon split this year, due to the way his fastball moves away from right-handed hitters. He's the kind of pitcher every team should be taking chances on.

Mauricio Lara — Throws L — Age 23

YEAR	TEAM	LGE	IP	H	ER	HR	BB	K	ERA	W	L	H/9	HR/9	BB/9	K/9	KW	PERA	STUFF
2000	Lowell	NYP	84.3	81	30	0	26	41	3.20	6	3	8.6	0.0	2.8	4.4	0.8	3.58	11
2000	Augusta	SAL	30.3	33	22	5	17	17	6.53	1	2	9.8	1.5	5.0	5.0	0.5	4.42	-13
2001	Augusta	SAL	109.3	119	60	12	35	47	4.94	5	7	9.8	1.0	2.9	3.9	0.7	6.05	-4

He has been passed by Seung Song on the depth charts but is still a very good prospect. Lara has a good fastball and curve and an improving change-up, but he didn't have very good command early in the season, probably as a result of back problems that cost him a few starts. The Sox have been putting an emphasis on developing very young pitchers from outside the U.S., with Lara, Seung Song, and Rene Miniel the early gems.

Sang-Hoon Lee Throws L Age 31

YEAR	TEAM	LGE	IP	H	ER	HR	BB	K	ERA	W	L	H/9	HR/9	BB/9	K/9	KW	PERA	STUFF
2000	Pawtuckt	Int	68.0	64	32	7	26	55	4.24	4	4	8.5	0.9	3.4	7.3	1.1	3.38	-2
2000	Boston	AL	11.3	12	7	2	4	6	5.56	0	1	9.5	1.6	3.2	4.8	0.8	2.54	-13
2001	Pawtuckt	Int	50.3	62	47	16	20	30	8.40	1	5	11.1	2.9	3.6	5.4	0.8	7.08	-37

He fell apart in the second half after a reasonable start to the season. Lee's fastball has been less than advertised in terms of velocity and movement, and coaches have not had any success in getting him to keep the ball down, leading to Paw-taterrific results. His two-year deal ran out after the 2001 season, and while the Sox weren't expected to bring him back, you can bet that someone will take a chance on him.

Derek Lowe Throws R Age 29

YEAR	TEAM	LGE	IP	H	ER	HR	BB	K	ERA	W	L	H/9	HR/9	BB/9	K/9	KW	PERA	STUFF
1999	Boston	AL	106.3	98	37	6	21	79	3.13	8	4	8.3	0.5	1.8	6.7	1.9	2.43	11
2000	Boston	AL	95.3	84	31	5	18	78	2.93	8	3	7.9	0.5	1.7	7.4	2.2	2.19	15
2001	Boston	AL	98.3	89	37	6	28	78	3.39	7	4	8.1	0.5	2.6	7.1	1.4	3.44	9

Lowe pitched most of 2001 like a man with elbow pain. His curve wasn't sharp, his sinker didn't sink, and everything was up in the zone. The Sox moved him to the rotation, and he fared extremely well in three starts . . . against the Devil Rays, Orioles, and Tigers, three of the AL's four worst offenses. If Lowe is healthy, he'll make a fine starter, but his starting stint in 2001 shouldn't give anyone false hope.

Anastacio Martinez Throws R Age 21

YEAR	TEAM	LGE	IP	H	ER	HR	BB	K	ERA	W	L	H/9	HR/9	BB/9	K/9	KW	PERA	STUFF
1999	Lowell	NYP	52.7	63	42	11	24	20	7.18	2	4	10.8	1.9	4.1	3.4	0.4	9.31	-13
1999	Augusta	SAL	39.0	52	47	14	24	18	10.85	1	3	12.0	3.2	5.5	4.2	0.4	11.83	-23
2000	Augusta	SAL	122.0	138	89	20	64	56	6.57	4	10	10.2	1.5	4.7	4.1	0.4	7.38	-5
2001	Sarasota	Fla	139.3	158	95	28	44	77	6.14	5	10	10.2	1.8	2.8	5.0	0.9	5.70	6

This Martinez is a young fireballer who emerged in 2001 after a mediocre debut in Augusta. He showed improved velocity (clocked at 94 in an August start) and control, filling the gap created by Jerome Gamble's injury. However, his perceived status as a "workhorse" took its toll, as his ERA after July 1 was 4.27. The Sox have had a serious run of injuries to starting pitching prospects of late, and while to some degree that's the nature of the beast, it's also a potential sign that your front office needs to be checked for signs of Dallas Green Disease.

Pedro Martinez Throws R Age 30

YEAR	TEAM	LGE	IP	H	ER	HR	BB	K	ERA	W	L	H/9	HR/9	BB/9	K/9	KW	PERA	STUFF
1999	Boston	AL	222.3	144	40	8	31	310	1.62	22	3	5.8	0.3	1.3	12.5	5.0	1.99	65
2000	Boston	AL	212.3	150	48	15	26	281	2.03	20	4	6.4	0.6	1.1	11.9	5.4	1.50	60
2001	Boston	AL	119.3	82	26	5	24	155	1.96	11	2	6.2	0.4	1.8	11.7	3.2	2.29	57

This Martinez was en route to another Cy Young season, perhaps one with a playoff run at the end of it, when he went down with shoulder soreness that was eventually diagnosed as a partially torn labrum. The brave faces of Fenway are saying that an off-season of rest will solve the problem, but they said the same thing about Garciaparra's wrist last October. Without a healthy Pedro Martinez, the Sox have little chance of contention.

Allen McDill Throws L Age 30

YEAR	TEAM	LGE	IP	H	ER	HR	BB	K	ERA	W	L	H/9	HR/9	BB/9	K/9	KW	PERA	STUFF
1999	Oklahoma	PCL	47.7	50	29	7	20	31	5.48	2	3	9.4	1.3	3.8	5.9	0.8	4.57	-18
2000	Memphis	PCL	25.7	23	14	1	18	20	4.91	1	2	8.1	0.4	6.3	7.0	0.6	5.48	-16
2000	Toledo	Int	20.0	19	7	0	8	11	3.15	1	1	8.6	0.0	3.6	4.9	0.7	2.24	-8
2001	Pawtuckt	Int	69.3	71	38	10	24	49	4.93	4	4	9.2	1.3	3.1	6.4	1.0	4.32	-10
2001	Boston	AL	15.0	13	7	2	7	15	4.20	1	1	7.8	1.2	4.2	9.0	1.1	4.95	8

McDill is a great one-out lefty who should never, ever be allowed to face a right-handed hitter unless his team has a seven-run lead. Between Pawtucket and Boston, lefties were 14-for-89 off McDill with one homer, one double, and three walks. The Sox still took all year to decide to recall him, even as the team wasted time and money on Pete Schourek, Bill Pulsipher, and Ned Flanders. For the minimum salary, McDill can fit the bill.

Rene Miniel — Throws R — Age 21

YEAR	TEAM	LGE	IP	H	ER	HR	BB	K	ERA	W	L	H/9	HR/9	BB/9	K/9	KW	PERA	STUFF
2001	Augusta	SAL	118.3	115	52	2	54	58	3.95	7	6	8.7	0.2	4.1	4.4	0.5	5.57	3

He started the season in the Augusta bullpen and ended it as the league's best pitcher, dropping his ERA by more than four runs between May 15 and the end of the season and pitching seven no-hit innings in one start before he was removed after hitting his pitch limit of 80. He runs his fastball into the mid 90s, has good movement on all of his pitches, and changes speeds well. He won't be relieving again anytime soon.

Greg Montalbano — Throws L — Age 24

YEAR	TEAM	LGE	IP	H	ER	HR	BB	K	ERA	W	L	H/9	HR/9	BB/9	K/9	KW	PERA	STUFF
2000	Lowell	NYP	9.3	8	4	0	5	7	3.86	1	0	7.7	0.0	4.8	6.8	0.7	4.19	15
2001	Sarasota	Fla	80.0	105	85	29	32	42	9.56	2	7	11.8	3.3	3.6	4.7	0.7	5.33	-23
2001	Trenton	Eas	47.0	55	39	12	19	28	7.47	1	4	10.5	2.3	3.6	5.4	0.7	6.33	-10

He looks like a star in the making, although he's at least a year and a half away. Montalbano has very good stuff, with a late-breaking fastball and a change-up that has improved markedly, and he has great poise on the mound. He needs experience, and for that, he has to stay healthy, something he's had trouble with so far. To their credit, the Sox have recently done well in teaching young pitchers new pitches, particularly off-speed pitches, and Montalbano could be the first fruit of that endeavor.

Hideo Nomo — Throws R — Age 33

YEAR	TEAM	LGE	IP	H	ER	HR	BB	K	ERA	W	L	H/9	HR/9	BB/9	K/9	KW	PERA	STUFF
1999	Milwauke	NL	179.0	174	94	25	65	145	4.73	10	10	8.7	1.3	3.3	7.3	1.1	4.46	15
2000	Detroit	AL	196.3	183	98	27	73	179	4.49	11	11	8.4	1.2	3.3	8.2	1.2	4.10	21
2001	Boston	AL	200.7	173	95	24	91	209	4.26	12	10	7.8	1.1	4.1	9.4	1.1	4.29	27

Nomo was the perfect free agent for Boston this year. The Sox missed out on Mike Mussina, the year's only premier pitching free agent willing to pitch in the AL, so rather than throw money at Kevin Appier or Denny Neagle, they went bargain hunting and landed the eventual AL strikeout leader. That said, Nomo was a fool to turn down the Sox' three-year offer; the team is better off hitting the bargain bins again than overpaying for three more years of this.

Bret Saberhagen — Throws R — Age 38

YEAR	TEAM	LGE	IP	H	ER	HR	BB	K	ERA	W	L	H/9	HR/9	BB/9	K/9	KW	PERA	STUFF
1999	Boston	AL	122.7	119	43	10	9	80	3.15	9	5	8.7	0.7	0.7	5.9	4.4	2.74	19
2001	Boston	AL	16.0	17	8	3	0	10	4.50	1	1	9.6	1.7	0.0	5.6	-1.0	5.93	8

Saberhagen will never be fully appreciated by those who look only at his career totals. His tenure in baseball was one of great volatility, even greater than that witnessed by the average starting pitcher. Great starters are usually marked by their consistency, but Sabes was as inconsistent as a great pitcher can be, racking up good years interspersed with incredible ones in 1985, 1987, 1991, 1994, and, remarkably, 1999. Had his health not abandoned him in 1992, he would have been a worthwhile Hall of Fame candidate, but skill is only part of the Hall equation.

Seung Song — Throws R — Age 22

YEAR	TEAM	LGE	IP	H	ER	HR	BB	K	ERA	W	L	H/9	HR/9	BB/9	K/9	KW	PERA	STUFF
2000	Lowell	NYP	73.3	70	31	4	25	46	3.80	5	3	8.6	0.5	3.1	5.6	0.9	4.94	17
2001	Augusta	SAL	71.3	73	37	7	25	40	4.67	4	4	9.2	0.9	3.2	5.0	0.8	4.43	7
2001	Sarasota	Fla	45.3	41	19	2	20	35	3.77	3	2	8.1	0.4	4.0	6.9	0.9	2.73	25

The main knock against Song before the season was that his change-up was weak. He went to spring training, spent the entire time working on his change-up, and mastered it to the point where he could use it as another out pitch next to his 93-mph tailing fastball. Song has the whole package: three good pitches, great control, poise, pitching smarts, and health. And, unlike most of the Sox recent Asian pitchers, he has some command of English. He's their best prospect from any country.

Ugueth Urbina **Throws R** **Age 28**

YEAR	TEAM	LGE	IP	H	ER	HR	BB	K	ERA	W	L	H/9	HR/9	BB/9	K/9	KW	PERA	STUFF
1999	Montreal	NL	77.0	59	27	6	30	90	3.16	6	3	6.9	0.7	3.5	10.5	1.5	3.78	24
2000	Montreal	NL	14.0	10	4	1	4	20	2.57	2	0	6.4	0.6	2.6	12.9	2.5	3.70	42
2001	Montreal	NL	45.3	41	23	7	19	46	4.57	2	3	8.1	1.4	3.8	9.1	1.2	4.46	9
2001	Boston	AL	21.3	14	4	1	3	30	1.69	2	0	5.9	0.4	1.3	12.7	5.0	2.02	50

Acquiring Urbina was an understandable overreaction, but an overreaction nonetheless. Derek Lowe blew several early saves, including two against the Yankees that, had they been converted, would have put the Sox in first place in late August. However, the Sox' main problem was that they weren't scoring enough runs, so handing two pitching prospects to Montréal for Urbina was a bad move. Handing him about $9 million in arbitration will be a worse one, especially with plenty of other good relievers in the pen.

Rolando Viera **Throws L** **Age 28**

YEAR	TEAM	LGE	IP	H	ER	HR	BB	K	ERA	W	L	H/9	HR/9	BB/9	K/9	KW	PERA	STUFF
2001	Sarasota	Fla	11.0	16	18	6	8	6	14.73	0	1	13.1	4.9	6.5	4.9	0.4	9.78	-84

The Sox used a seventh-round draft pick on Viera, a probably-27-year-old left-handed reliever from Cuba who doesn't have a whole lot of upside. He didn't impress scouts in his brief time in Sarasota or in the Arizona Fall League, because even though he throws from a variety of arm angles, it's mostly mediocre stuff. Viera might end up a lefty specialist in a major-league bullpen; if that's what you get from a seventh-round draft pick, is it success?

Tim Wakefield **Throws R** **Age 35**

YEAR	TEAM	LGE	IP	H	ER	HR	BB	K	ERA	W	L	H/9	HR/9	BB/9	K/9	KW	PERA	STUFF
1999	Boston	AL	144.3	142	76	16	60	103	4.74	8	8	8.9	1.0	3.7	6.4	0.9	5.03	0
2000	Boston	AL	161.7	173	97	26	53	101	5.40	7	11	9.6	1.4	3.0	5.6	1.0	4.98	-4
2001	Boston	AL	172.3	155	73	12	69	141	3.81	11	8	8.1	0.6	3.6	7.4	1.0	4.03	13

Wakefield belonged on the All-Star team after a first half that put him among the AL's top three pitchers, but he hit the skids in July and never recovered his early-season form. Wakefield still led the Sox in Adjusted Runs Prevented and was an above-average starter on the whole. Given regular work, he has usually been effective to very effective, which would seem to indicate that he should be placed in the rotation and left there. Jimy was never able to do that; perhaps the new manager will.

Chicago White Sox

In the seven seasons in which MLB has crowned an American League Central champion, the Cleveland Indians have claimed the honor six times, the Chicago White Sox once. No one else has ever won the division.

By the end of this decade, the White Sox will hold the record for most AL Central titles, and it's entirely possible that the Tigers, Royals, and Twins will still have their collective goose egg. This Sox team is poised for a run of success in the American League Central that's going to do wonders for movie-ticket sales in Detroit, Kansas City, and Cleveland.

White Sox Prospectus

2001 record: 83–79; Third place, AL Central

Pythagenport W/L: 81–81

Runs scored: 798 (sixth in AL)

Runs allowed: 795 (eighth in AL)

Team EqA: .263 (sixth in AL)

2001 batters age: 28.6 (seventh-oldest in AL)

2001 pitchers age: 26.0 (youngest in AL)

Ballpark: Comiskey Park; moderate hitters' park; Park Factor of 1.026

2001: Nailed by the Plexiglass Principle and the loss of Frank Thomas for the season.

2002: The AL Central favorite has the best young core in the league, bar none.

It's hard to not be excited about baseball on Chicago's South Side. Sure, the Cubs get more publicity, and they deserve credit for their revamped player-development system, their 88-win season in 2001, and their pretty good right fielder. But the team in town with the brightest future plays in Comiskey Park. The young lineup the Cubs are developing? The White Sox already have theirs in place. The crop of system-developed pitchers coming into Wrigley Field? The Sox rotation for 2002 will feature four starters they can call their own and a fifth who was acquired for two farm products.

If you're a fan of the Sox, one of the fun things about the success you're about to witness is the players for whom you'll be cheering. For better or for worse, many fans like rooting for a team comprised of players who came up through their team's system. Certainly, teams built from within are lionized by a media that has never quite gotten its hands around the idea that there's nothing wrong with baseball players changing teams in mid-career.

Assuming the Sox do what's best by making catcher Mark Johnson and third baseman Joe Crede full-time players, they will field a lineup that, save Jose Valentin, consists entirely of guys who have had all their major-league success with the White Sox. Not all of them are drafted-and-developed guys, but the ones who aren't are players such as Paul Konerko, who never had a job until he came to Chicago. It's one thing for a team such as the 2001 Twins, who went into last season not trying to compete, to make a claim like that. It's quite another for a division favorite to look at its roster and say the same.

The White Sox have done a much better job filling roster spots from within than they have by going into the trade and free-agent markets. Prior to the 2001 season, new Sox GM Kenny Williams showed a damaging preference for mediocre veterans, signing Sandy Alomar to catch and making trades for Royce Clayton and David Wells. All of these moves flopped: Alomar and Wells missed most of the season with injuries, while Clayton hit .263/.315/.393 and forced the Sox to spend the season jerking around their real starting shortstop, Jose Valentin. Even a minor pickup such as reliever Antonio Osuna was a disaster, as the right-hander missed the season with a torn labrum.

This winter, Williams's affection for veterans popped up again when he traded two of the Sox' prized arms—Kip Wells and Josh Fogg—along with journeyman Sean Lowe to the Pirates to acquire right-hander Todd Ritchie. Since signing with the Bucs as a minor-league free agent three years ago, Ritchie has established himself as a mid-rotation innings muncher with a pronounced platoon split. He'll be more expensive than the pitchers the Sox gave up because he has more service time, but it's not likely that he'll pitch that much better than, say, Kip Wells will. The only thing the Sox gained in the deal was experience, making the trade a near-perfect match for the Mike Sirotka/David Wells and Aaron Myette/Royce Clayton exchanges that threw up all over the Sox last year.

It doesn't appear that Williams learned any lessons from his first forays into the trade market, which doesn't bode well as the Sox move from building a team to making it into a contender. If Williams is determined to trade some of the young talent at his disposal, he'd be better served to bring in what the team really needs: a long-term solution at catcher, a successor to Ray Durham at second base, and a left fielder who bats left-handed and can mash. Acquiring Ritchie didn't help the White Sox nearly as much as adding Carlos Lee and another arm to the trade to get Brian Giles would have. Williams should also be looking at the Marlins' Cliff Floyd, the Blue Jays' Jose Cruz, and the Diamondbacks' Erubiel Durazo.

Continued vigilance by Williams will be important, because as optimistic as we are about the White Sox, the team is not perfect, particularly at the plate. The Sox don't walk as much as you'd like to see, meaning they need to hit .280 or .290 as a team to put enough runners on base to have a championship-caliber offense. This was one of the biggest differences between the division winners of 2000 and the 83-79 team in 2001. Two seasons ago, the Sox batted .288, leading the AL in BA and runs scored. Last season, they slipped to .268 at the plate and to sixth in runs. (Caveat: the league BA dropped nine points, so the falloff isn't as bad as it looks.) The 22-point drop in OBP was a near-match for the drop in batting average; they weren't trading hits for walks.

A healthy Frank Thomas in the DH slot will have a significant effect on the team OBP. Replacing the veteran mistakes of 2001 with walk-positive younger players such as Mark Johnson and Joe Crede won't hurt, and both Paul Konerko and Magglio Ordonez showed increased walk rates relative to the league last season. It's not unrealistic to think that the 2002 White Sox could have the best offense in the league.

The other thing Williams will need to watch is how much the team's lineup lists to the right side. Johnson taking over behind the plate would help, but the return of Frank Thomas will cut into Jeff Liefer's playing time, and Liefer was one of the few sources of left-handed power the Sox had last year. Top prospect Joe Borchard is likely to be in Chicago sometime this season, and his opportunities will come at the expense of Chris Singleton. The Jeff Bagwell/Craig Biggio Astros of the post-strike era, with a lineup loaded with right-handed hitters, offer an example of the perils of ignoring balance. They've suffered, both in pennant races and postseasons, against teams capable of neutralizing good right-handed hitting.

The solution most likely lies in left field, where Carlos Lee lumbers. Lee, a converted third baseman, is an awkward outfielder and the type of hitter—good average, good power, low walks—that the Sox have hanging from the rafters. Whether it's trading Lee to create space for Liefer, or using him as part of a package to get the type of hitter mentioned above, it's clear that Lee's lineup spot is the key to better balance for the White Sox.

As the Sox begin to run off division titles, watch for the media's treatment of the team to change. The franchise shares the third-biggest city in baseball with the Cubs, giving the Sox effectively the 15th-biggest market of any team in the game, according to Mike Jones's research (you can see all of Jones's work on the Web at *home.nycap.rr.com/nickandaj/marketsize.html*). Despite this, the Sox have found themselves lumped with the small-market crowd in the never-ending debate about who can and cannot compete.

That the Sox are not a small-market team should be obvious. The mischaracterization stems from a few factors. First, attendance at New Comiskey hasn't been very impressive, in part because of a deal the Sox have with the state that provides an incentive for them to keep ticket prices sky-high. Second, Jerry Reinsdorf takes a back seat only to Bud Selig among baseball's hand-wringers, and he plays up the notion that his team just isn't capable of supporting a high payroll. This image was reinforced by 1997's "white flag" trade; while that deal laid the groundwork for 2000's division title and the good things still to come, the notion of the Sox as penurious non-contenders was cemented.

Should the Sox have the level of success we expect them to have, their revenues will rise. As the young players they develop perform well and accumulate service time, the Sox payroll will rise. Without moving, without building a new park, without sparking a mini-baby boom in the Chi-town area, the Sox will find themselves dubbed a large-market team.

The lesson isn't that it's silly to call a Chicago team "small market." The lesson is that the relationship between payroll and success is not simple. Spending money doesn't cause winning so much as winning causes you to spend money, in part because revenues grow to support the expenditures and because successful baseball players become expensive.

It happened in Cleveland, where the Indians had one of the lowest payrolls in baseball at the start of their run, then watched it rise as they racked up division titles, pennants, and sellouts. The Sox are at the start of that cycle now, with a young core of inexpensive talent. That core will win, and it will make more money in 2006 than it does in 2002.

It's just another way in which the White Sox of the '00s will resemble the Indians of the '90s.

HITTERS (BA: .270, OBP: .340, SLG: .440, EqA: .260)

Sandy Alomar Jr. C Bats R Age 36

YEAR	TEAM	LGE	AB	H	DB	TP	HR	BB	SO	R	RBI	SB	CS	OUT	BA	OBP	SLG	EQA	EQR	DEFENSE
1999	Clevelnd	AL	136	42	9	0	8	3	20	18	26	0	1	95	.309	.324	.551	.277	19	35-C -6
2000	Clevelnd	AL	353	104	16	2	7	12	36	42	40	2	2	251	.295	.325	.411	.244	37	88-C -7
2001	ChiSox	AL	220	57	7	1	5	13	15	18	22	1	2	165	.259	.305	.368	.225	20	62-C 1
2002	*ChiSox*	*AL*	*321*	*83*	*13*	*2*	*9*	*22*	*30*	*38*	*40*	*1*	*2*	*240*	*.259*	*.308*	*.390*	*.233*	*32*	

Alomar was neither very good nor very healthy, and he was therefore the symbol for everything the White Sox did wrong in the winter following their 2000 division title. Signing him to a two-year, $5.4-million contract was a waste of money. For the six or seven weeks he's healthy in 2002, he'll make a decent backup for Mark Johnson.

Harold Baines DH Bats L Age 43

YEAR	TEAM	LGE	AB	H	DB	TP	HR	BB	SO	R	RBI	SB	CS	OUT	BA	OBP	SLG	EQA	EQR	DEFENSE
1999	Baltimor	AL	343	116	18	1	25	40	33	58	80	1	2	229	.338	.407	.615	.325	69	
1999	Clevelnd	AL	84	24	2	0	1	10	9	5	16	0	0	60	.286	.362	.345	.246	9	
2000	Baltimor	AL	221	62	7	0	11	27	34	24	30	0	0	159	.281	.359	.462	.273	31	
2000	ChiSox	AL	61	14	2	0	2	6	10	3	10	0	0	47	.230	.299	.361	.223	6	
2001	ChiSox	AL	84	13	1	0	0	8	14	3	7	0	0	71	.155	.228	.167	.146	3	
2002	*ChiSox*	*AL*	*313*	*66*	*7*	*0*	*10*	*43*	*47*	*27*	*40*	*0*	*1*	*248*	*.211*	*.306*	*.329*	*.217*	*27*	

It's over. As much as Harold Baines might want to keep going, as good a person as he is, as good a player as he was, he has nothing left to give. He can't even stay healthy as a DH, which is a pretty good sign that his body has had it. At this writing he hasn't retired, and as long as the Devil Rays are around, there's always a chance.

Joe Borchard CF Bats B Age 23

YEAR	TEAM	LGE	AB	H	DB	TP	HR	BB	SO	R	RBI	SB	CS	OUT	BA	OBP	SLG	EQA	EQR	DEFENSE
2000	WnstnSlm	Car	53	13	0	0	2	5	9	5	5	0	0	40	.245	.321	.358	.232	5	13-RF 0
2000	Birmnghm	Sou	23	5	0	1	0	2	8	3	3	0	0	18	.217	.280	.304	.201	2	
2001	Birmnghm	Sou	531	141	20	1	23	54	155	83	82	3	3	393	.266	.339	.437	.258	66	133-CF -2
2002	*ChiSox*	*AL*	*470*	*136*	*19*	*1*	*21*	*57*	*142*	*68*	*68*	*2*	*2*	*336*	*.289*	*.366*	*.468*	*.280*	*70*	

The only thing standing between Joe Borchard and ridiculous amounts of money is a small improvement in his strike-zone judgment. Even without that, he's ready to join the White Sox lineup and is on the short list for AL Rookie of the Year. The potential problem is position: Borchard doesn't have the speed you'd like to see in a center fielder, and the Sox are set at the outfield corners.

The AL Central has one heck of a crop of good, young center fielders. Torii Hunter has the best range in baseball and good power. Carlos Beltran can hit, run, and throw, and he was perhaps the best center fielder in the league last year. The Indians turn center over to Milton Bradley this year; after years of promise, he should put up a .275 EqA with good defense. Even the Tigers have Andres Torres, who runs like the wind and has shown some plate discipline in the minors.

Jose Canseco DH, dammit! Bats R Age 37

YEAR	TEAM	LGE	AB	H	DB	TP	HR	BB	SO	R	RBI	SB	CS	OUT	BA	OBP	SLG	EQA	EQR	DEFENSE
1999	TampaBay	AL	426	124	17	1	36	54	119	75	94	3	0	302	.291	.379	.589	.310	81	
2000	TampaBay	AL	215	57	10	0	11	39	57	29	30	2	0	158	.265	.388	.465	.289	35	
2000	NY Yanks	AL	110	28	4	0	6	22	33	16	18	0	0	82	.255	.379	.455	.281	17	
2001	ChiSox	AL	256	69	8	0	17	47	65	49	50	2	1	188	.270	.384	.500	.293	44	
2002	*ChiSox*	*AL*	*354*	*83*	*12*	*0*	*22*	*62*	*100*	*53*	*58*	*2*	*1*	*272*	*.234*	*.349*	*.455*	*.270*	*52*	

Remember the movie *Working Girl* from the '80s? Somewhere in that film, vastly underrated comedic talent Joan Cusack says, "Sometimes I dress up in my underwear and sing. It doesn't make me Madonna."

That's Jose Canseco. He can put on a glove and spikes and stand between the second baseman and the bleachers, but it doesn't make him an outfielder. He's a designated hitter, and a pretty good one. If the Twins had kept Matt Lawton and signed Canseco last year, they might have ended up in the AL playoffs instead of in oblivion.

Royce Clayton SS Bats R Age 32

YEAR	TEAM	LGE	AB	H	DB	TP	HR	BB	SO	R	RBI	SB	CS	OUT	BA	OBP	SLG	EQA	EQR	DEFENSE
1999	Texas	AL	460	134	21	5	15	34	88	67	50	7	6	332	.291	.345	.457	.264	59	128-SS -7
2000	Texas	AL	509	124	19	5	15	36	81	66	51	11	8	393	.244	.298	.389	.229	49	141-SS -4
2001	ChiSox	AL	433	120	21	4	10	35	62	65	62	9	8	321	.277	.334	.413	.248	49	121-SS 13
2002	*ChiSox*	*AL*	*476*	*121*	*22*	*4*	*16*	*45*	*78*	*68*	*52*	*8*	*7*	*362*	*.254*	*.319*	*.418*	*.246*	*54*	

Know any people who can't resist a bargain? "Ooh, there's a '30% Off' sale at Useless Crap'R'Us!" They buy things just because the price is right, irrespective of whether they need or want the items. It's the thrill of the buy, of getting something at less than cost.

That's how Kenny Williams ended up with Royce Clayton. The price was a couple of B–/C+ arms, because the Rangers had just signed Alex Rodriguez. Of course, the Sox didn't need a shortstop—Jose Valentin had just re-upped for three seasons—and even if they had needed one, they certainly didn't need Royce Clayton. Clayton was terrible in the first half, helping bury the Sox. His big second half helped them get over .500, but on the whole, he was the shortstop equivalent of a set of hand-stitched leg warmers going for $4.99 a pair.

Joe Crede 3B Bats R Age 24

YEAR	TEAM	LGE	AB	H	DB	TP	HR	BB	SO	R	RBI	SB	CS	OUT	BA	OBP	SLG	EQA	EQR	DEFENSE
1999	Birmnghm	Sou	294	65	12	1	3	15	48	30	32	1	4	233	.221	.260	.299	.188	18	72-3B -6
2000	Birmnghm	Sou	554	156	22	0	22	41	110	76	83	2	3	401	.282	.340	.440	.258	68	135-3B -10
2001	Charlott	Int	468	123	24	1	18	44	81	64	62	2	1	346	.263	.332	.434	.255	57	122-3B 3
2001	ChiSox	AL	50	12	1	1	0	3	10	3	7	1	0	38	.240	.293	.300	.209	4	14-3B -3
2002	*ChiSox*	*AL*	*514*	*148*	*23*	*1*	*24*	*47*	*99*	*82*	*95*	*2*	*2*	*368*	*.288*	*.348*	*.477*	*.274*	*72*	

The Sox have been very conservative with Crede, giving him a season and a half at Double-A and leaving him at Triple-A for all of 2001. He looks ready to take over in Chicago, especially with the glove, but the presence of Clayton and Jose Valentin complicates the matter. A lousy spring cost him a shot at a major-league job last year, and the same thing could happen in 2002.

Chad Durham CF Bats R Age 24

YEAR	TEAM	LGE	AB	H	DB	TP	HR	BB	SO	R	RBI	SB	CS	OUT	BA	OBP	SLG	EQA	EQR	DEFENSE
1999	Bristol	App	277	57	6	1	0	17	49	25	18	18	8	228	.206	.255	.235	.180	16	67-CF 0
2000	Burlingt	Mid	527	117	11	4	1	27	94	50	23	28	13	422	.222	.261	.264	.187	32	127-CF -10
2001	WnstnSlm	Car	546	121	13	3	2	36	92	46	32	32	15	439	.222	.271	.267	.193	36	132-CF -1
2002	*ChiSox*	*AL*	*541*	*133*	*15*	*3*	*3*	*40*	*99*	*58*	*38*	*34*	*16*	*423*	*.246*	*.298*	*.301*	*.208*	*42*	

Similar in build to his older brother, Chad Durham has led his league in stolen bases for three straight seasons. He hasn't shown any of the rest of Ray's skill set, however, and at best projects as a sixth outfielder and pinch runner. How the Sox treat Chad Durham this year will be a clue as to whether they intend to keep Ray beyond 2002.

Ray Durham 2B Bats B Age 30

YEAR	TEAM	LGE	AB	H	DB	TP	HR	BB	SO	R	RBI	SB	CS	OUT	BA	OBP	SLG	EQA	EQR	DEFENSE
1999	ChiSox	AL	606	184	30	8	14	67	92	106	58	33	11	433	.304	.376	.449	.280	90	147-2B -3
2000	ChiSox	AL	607	172	34	9	18	68	92	115	71	25	14	449	.283	.362	.458	.273	87	145-2B 3
2001	ChiSox	AL	611	171	43	10	22	67	95	109	67	21	11	451	.280	.354	.491	.277	91	147-2B 3
2002	*ChiSox*	*AL*	*549*	*155*	*33*	*8*	*18*	*71*	*89*	*101*	*59*	*20*	*10*	*404*	*.282*	*.365*	*.470*	*.280*	*84*	

Ray Durham is an absurdly consistent player. While other second basemen get hurt all the time, Durham has played in at least 150 games in every full season of his career and has never been on the disabled list. He now has four straight years of at least a .270 EqA and is as complete an offensive player as you'll find. Give the Sox credit for not moving him to center field last year.

Tony Graffanino IF Bats R Age 30

YEAR	TEAM	LGE	AB	H	DB	TP	HR	BB	SO	R	RBI	SB	CS	OUT	BA	OBP	SLG	EQA	EQR	DEFENSE			
1999	Durham	Int	345	100	21	5	8	30	43	54	48	12	8	253	.290	.351	.449	.265	46	84-2B	2		
1999	TampaBay	AL	129	42	10	4	2	8	19	20	18	3	2	89	.326	.369	.512	.287	20	17-2B	3	16-SS	-2
2000	TampaBay	AL	20	6	1	0	0	1	2	4	1	0	0	14	.300	.365	.350	.248	2				
2000	ChiSox	AL	146	40	5	1	2	19	22	24	15	7	4	110	.274	.362	.363	.251	17	16-SS	5	15-2B	2
2001	ChiSox	AL	145	46	8	0	3	17	25	25	16	4	1	100	.317	.392	.434	.284	21	21-3B	-1	15-2B	3
2002	*ChiSox*	*AL*	*379*	*113*	*20*	*3*	*9*	*47*	*61*	*65*	*48*	*8*	*4*	*270*	*.298*	*.376*	*.438*	*.278*	*55*				

A bad year at a bad time has doomed Graffanino to utility status, but he's making the best of it. He didn't hit in 1998, when the Braves had openings in the middle infield and gave him 189 at-bats. Since then, he's posted major-league OBPs of .364, .363, and .370, establishing himself as one of the best utility infielders in the game. He's a big part of what should be a very good Sox bench in 2002.

Timothy Hummel 2B/SS Bats R Age 23

YEAR	TEAM	LGE	AB	H	DB	TP	HR	BB	SO	R	RBI	SB	CS	OUT	BA	OBP	SLG	EQA	EQR	DEFENSE			
2000	Burlingt	Mid	148	37	5	1	1	13	22	15	14	4	2	113	.250	.312	.318	.219	13	33-SS	-3		
2000	WnstnSlm	Car	101	28	2	0	2	9	12	12	7	1	1	74	.277	.342	.356	.239	10	25-3B	-3		
2001	Birmnghm	Sou	509	140	30	4	8	49	68	74	54	10	3	399	.285	.330	.389	.240	56	92-2B	-9	35-SS	-6
2002	*ChiSox*	*AL*	*486*	*135*	*23*	*4*	*10*	*49*	*66*	*61*	*52*	*8*	*3*	*354*	*.278*	*.344*	*.403*	*.256*	*58*				

Hummel, a second-round pick in 2000, is a comparable player to Ray Durham but without Durham's excellent speed. A shortstop at Old Dominion, he's now a so-so second baseman who some people think will eventually move to third base. That would cloud his career prospects in this organization; leaving him at second base would give the Sox options if they can't or won't re-sign Durham at the end of the 2002 season.

Jeff Inglin DH/LF Bats R Age 26

YEAR	TEAM	LGE	AB	H	DB	TP	HR	BB	SO	R	RBI	SB	CS	OUT	BA	OBP	SLG	EQA	EQR	DEFENSE	
1999	Birmnghm	Sou	439	113	22	3	12	43	63	49	48	12	2	328	.257	.329	.403	.249	51	99-LF	-4
1999	Charlott	Int	39	7	0	0	3	3	8	7	7	0	1	33	.179	.251	.410	.210	3		
2000	Birmnghm	Sou	255	69	11	2	5	26	43	39	35	3	1	187	.271	.343	.388	.249	29	15-LF	0
2000	Charlott	Int	146	41	6	1	5	10	17	17	27	2	0	105	.281	.334	.438	.259	18	36-LF	0
2001	Charlott	Int	485	125	22	4	23	42	95	63	69	2	3	363	.258	.322	.462	.256	60	56-LF	-3
2002	*ChiSox*	*AL*	*436*	*115*	*22*	*3*	*13*	*46*	*82*	*56*	*57*	*6*	*2*	*323*	*.264*	*.334*	*.417*	*.255*	*53*		

The Sox signed Jose Canseco rather than call up Inglin last year, so you know they're excited about him. He's like a lot of Quadruple-A hitters: capable of helping a team in the right situation but limited enough that the right situation is pretty narrowly defined. He's under six feet tall, which doesn't help his case. He needs a new organization.

Mark Johnson C Bats L Age 26

YEAR	TEAM	LGE	AB	H	DB	TP	HR	BB	SO	R	RBI	SB	CS	OUT	BA	OBP	SLG	EQA	EQR	DEFENSE	
1999	ChiSox	AL	205	49	9	0	5	34	51	26	16	3	1	157	.239	.352	.356	.247	24	66-C	0
2000	ChiSox	AL	211	49	8	0	4	25	35	27	23	3	2	164	.232	.317	.327	.223	19	69-C	5
2001	Charlott	Int	199	51	4	2	4	27	31	24	23	2	1	149	.256	.345	.357	.243	22	47-C	-7
2001	ChiSox	AL	173	45	5	1	6	24	27	22	19	2	1	129	.260	.355	.405	.259	22	55-C	3
2002	*ChiSox*	*AL*	*350*	*88*	*12*	*2*	*11*	*52*	*61*	*48*	*37*	*5*	*2*	*264*	*.251*	*.348*	*.391*	*.255*	*43*		

Johnson has been the Sox' best option for catcher since the middle of the 1999 season. Despite this, they've messed around with Sandy Alomar, Josh Paul, and Brook Fordyce while shuttling Johnson between Illinois and North Carolina. Feh. He was the semi-regular in the second half of 2001; if he can get 350-400 at-bats in 2002, the Sox will get back to the top of the division. Good arm.

Paul Konerko — 1B — Bats R — Age 26

YEAR	TEAM	LGE	AB	H	DB	TP	HR	BB	SO	R	RBI	SB	CS	OUT	BA	OBP	SLG	EQA	EQR	DEFENSE
1999	ChiSox	AL	509	155	32	4	25	40	60	71	79	1	0	354	.305	.357	.530	.288	79	91-1B 3
2000	ChiSox	AL	518	158	27	1	23	41	63	80	94	1	0	360	.305	.368	.494	.285	78	120-1B 3
2001	ChiSox	AL	582	172	28	0	37	57	77	97	104	1	0	410	.296	.365	.534	.292	95	142-1B -3
2002	*ChiSox*	*AL*	*520*	*161*	*27*	*1*	*32*	*56*	*70*	*83*	*94*	*1*	*0*	*359*	*.310*	*.377*	*.550*	*.304*	*91*	

While the overall value of his 2001 season was about the same as his 2000 season, Konerko increased his power and his walk rate relative to the league, both good developmental signs. The AL has so many great first basemen that Konerko gets lost in the shuffle, but he's been a good hitter for three seasons and is still just 26 years old. Jeff Bagwell is a good comp for Konerko, and he had a massive power spike at 26, slugging .750 in the Astrodome in 1994.

Carlos Lee — LF — Bats R — Age 26

YEAR	TEAM	LGE	AB	H	DB	TP	HR	BB	SO	R	RBI	SB	CS	OUT	BA	OBP	SLG	EQA	EQR	DEFENSE
1999	Charlott	Int	93	30	3	0	4	6	13	13	17	1	1	64	.323	.368	.484	.280	13	13-3B -3
1999	ChiSox	AL	490	148	33	2	17	8	63	66	82	4	2	344	.302	.318	.482	.260	59	97-LF -4
2000	ChiSox	AL	567	174	30	2	25	31	83	104	88	13	4	397	.307	.346	.499	.278	81	138-LF 4
2001	ChiSox	AL	558	158	34	3	26	40	73	79	87	15	8	408	.283	.336	.495	.271	78	123-LF 0
2002	*ChiSox*	*AL*	*554*	*167*	*31*	*2*	*26*	*44*	*78*	*92*	*96*	*15*	*5*	*392*	*.301*	*.353*	*.505*	*.285*	*85*	

Lee shares a lot of similarities with Konerko. They're both right-handed hitters who hit .290 with good power and who walk a bit less than you'd like. Lee doesn't manage the strike zone as well as Konerko, so he doesn't get ahead in the count as often, which is all the difference between them.

Jeff Liefer — LF/1B — Bats L — Age 27

YEAR	TEAM	LGE	AB	H	DB	TP	HR	BB	SO	R	RBI	SB	CS	OUT	BA	OBP	SLG	EQA	EQR	DEFENSE	
1999	Charlott	Int	169	52	14	1	7	17	24	29	26	1	1	118	.308	.373	.527	.293	27	25-1B 3	16-LF -2
1999	ChiSox	AL	113	30	7	1	0	6	25	8	14	2	0	83	.265	.303	.345	.223	10	13-LF 0	12-1B 2
2000	Charlott	Int	447	117	21	1	29	44	105	66	77	2	3	333	.262	.330	.508	.270	63	61-1B 4	16-LF -1
2001	Charlott	Int	121	33	5	0	6	14	38	21	20	2	1	89	.273	.361	.463	.274	18	28-1B 4	
2001	ChiSox	AL	254	68	11	0	20	21	60	38	41	0	1	187	.268	.327	.547	.278	38	29-LF -1	12-1B -2
2002	*ChiSox*	*AL*	*430*	*120*	*21*	*1*	*27*	*50*	*110*	*65*	*77*	*4*	*2*	*312*	*.279*	*.354*	*.521*	*.287*	*69*		

Liefer is in the wrong place at the wrong time. With Frank Thomas returning and neither Carlos Lee nor Paul Konerko in need of being platooned, there aren't going to be any at-bats for him in Chicago. He's ready to play John Lowenstein to someone's Gary Roenicke; he just needs to find a manager with Earl Weaver's sensibilities.

Miguel Olivo — C — Bats R — Age 23

YEAR	TEAM	LGE	AB	H	DB	TP	HR	BB	SO	R	RBI	SB	CS	OUT	BA	OBP	SLG	EQA	EQR	DEFENSE
1999	Modesto	Cal	241	58	10	3	6	13	61	30	25	2	3	186	.241	.282	.382	.219	21	62-C -6
2000	Modesto	Cal	229	54	11	2	4	7	54	28	23	2	1	176	.236	.262	.354	.205	17	50-C -2
2000	Midland	Tex	59	12	0	0	1	3	15	5	6	0	0	47	.203	.242	.254	.171	3	13-C -4
2001	Birmnghm	Sou	325	78	17	1	12	29	61	39	46	4	2	249	.240	.310	.409	.240	35	90-C -7
2002	*ChiSox*	*AL*	*343*	*90*	*19*	*2*	*11*	*30*	*75*	*50*	*42*	*3*	*2*	*255*	*.262*	*.322*	*.426*	*.250*	*40*	

Olivo came over from the A's for Chad Bradford in what looked like a great trade for both teams. 2001 was a lost season, though: he regressed defensively, didn't hit, and questions about his attitude persisted. He bounced back to have a great season in the Arizona Fall League and should get at least a cup of coffee in Chicago this year.

Magglio Ordonez — RF — Bats R — Age 28

YEAR	TEAM	LGE	AB	H	DB	TP	HR	BB	SO	R	RBI	SB	CS	OUT	BA	OBP	SLG	EQA	EQR	DEFENSE
1999	ChiSox	AL	619	192	33	3	32	41	56	98	115	12	6	433	.310	.354	.528	.286	95	145-RF 0
2000	ChiSox	AL	580	186	34	3	33	53	56	98	120	18	4	398	.321	.380	.560	.306	103	140-RF -4
2001	ChiSox	AL	594	191	34	1	36	73	60	102	119	24	8	411	.322	.399	.564	.313	113	142-RF -7
2002	*ChiSox*	*AL*	*552*	*176*	*33*	*2*	*33*	*66*	*57*	*99*	*111*	*18*	*6*	*382*	*.319*	*.392*	*.565*	*.314*	*105*	

He looked like he was going to be a Kirby Puckett type—really good even without walking much—but he's now improved his walk rate for two seasons running. Ordonez's great bat speed, with power to all fields, makes him a fun hitter to watch. At less than $8 million per year through age 30, he's one of the biggest bargains in baseball.

With Ordonez, Konerko, Lee, and Frank Thomas, the White Sox have what may be the best lineup core in baseball. The 2002 American League MVP could easily be determined by the order in which these guys bat: Konerko or Lee, hitting behind Thomas, Ordonez, and Ray Durham, could drive in 165 runs.

Josh Paul C Bats R Age 27

YEAR	TEAM	LGE	AB	H	DB	TP	HR	BB	SO	R	RBI	SB	CS	OUT	BA	OBP	SLG	EQA	EQR	DEFENSE
1999	Birmnghm	Sou	323	80	16	2	3	20	69	37	32	4	4	247	.248	.297	.337	.215	26	83-C 0
2000	Charlott	Int	169	38	3	1	4	10	37	25	17	5	2	133	.225	.275	.325	.206	13	47-C -1
2000	ChiSox	AL	70	20	3	2	1	5	15	15	7	1	0	50	.286	.342	.429	.260	9	21-C 2
2001	ChiSox	AL	139	38	7	0	5	14	22	21	20	6	2	103	.273	.340	.432	.261	18	45-C -6
2001	Charlott	Int	76	20	3	0	4	6	17	11	13	0	0	56	.263	.317	.461	.255	9	17-C 0
2002	*ChiSox*	*AL*	*286*	*75*	*13*	*2*	*9*	*28*	*59*	*48*	*37*	*8*	*3*	*214*	*.262*	*.328*	*.416*	*.253*	*34*	

Paul is an organizational favorite who isn't the player Mark Johnson is, but he gets treated better because he was a #1 pick and a local boy. What you see is what you get: his offense is BA-driven, and his defense isn't horrible. He will make a decent backup catcher well into the 2010s, with roster value because he runs well for a catcher and is willing to play third base in an emergency.

Herb Perry 3B Bats R Age 32

YEAR	TEAM	LGE	AB	H	DB	TP	HR	BB	SO	R	RBI	SB	CS	OUT	BA	OBP	SLG	EQA	EQR	DEFENSE
1999	Durham	Int	103	30	5	0	5	4	20	17	17	0	0	73	.291	.327	.485	.265	13	
1999	TampaBay	AL	208	55	9	1	7	14	37	29	32	0	0	153	.264	.337	.418	.253	25	41-3B 0
2000	TampaBay	AL	28	6	1	0	0	2	6	2	1	0	0	22	.214	.267	.250	.181	2	
2000	ChiSox	AL	380	120	28	1	13	17	60	66	59	4	1	261	.316	.360	.497	.283	55	99-3B 5
2001	ChiSox	AL	285	78	21	1	8	24	48	41	34	2	2	209	.274	.341	.439	.259	36	58-3B -3
2002	*Texas*	*AL*	*369*	*104*	*20*	*1*	*14*	*33*	*65*	*59*	*55*	*2*	*1*	*266*	*.282*	*.341*	*.455*	*.261*	*46*	

Hawk Harrelson is as irritating as a Tabasco enema, but "The Milkman"—his moniker for Perry, because "he delivers"—really is a cool nickname. Perry delivered a lot less in 2001, though, as he struggled to stay healthy following his surprise performance in 2000. Bumped out of Chicago by Joe Crede, Perry was traded to the Rangers, with whom he'll be a good bench player and backup for Mike Lamb and Carlos Pena.

Julio Ramirez CF Bats R Age 24

YEAR	TEAM	LGE	AB	H	DB	TP	HR	BB	SO	R	RBI	SB	CS	OUT	BA	OBP	SLG	EQA	EQR	DEFENSE
1999	Portland	Eas	571	132	26	6	11	26	151	65	49	40	12	450	.231	.266	.356	.216	49	137-CF 3
2000	Calgary	PCL	343	75	15	2	5	15	83	32	36	13	10	278	.219	.256	.318	.194	23	90-CF -4
2001	ChiSox	AL	37	4	0	0	0	2	13	2	1	2	0	33	.108	.154	.108	.111	1	15-CF 3
2001	Charlott	Int	320	66	9	1	8	20	74	34	24	12	5	260	.206	.256	.316	.197	22	88-CF -1
2002	*ChiSox*	*AL*	*532*	*117*	*18*	*3*	*15*	*40*	*140*	*60*	*53*	*27*	*11*	*425*	*.220*	*.274*	*.350*	*.213*	*44*	

Kenny Williams made his share of mistakes, but he also made some moves that looked good but didn't work. Trading Jeff Abbott for Julio Ramirez was one of them. Abbott had no spot on a team bulging with right-handed-hitting corner outfielders, and getting a high-upside center fielder seemed like a good idea. Ramirez was brutal in a platoon role, although in fairness he didn't get an extended trial. He'll reemerge as a fourth outfielder; don't expect him to hold a regular job unless he completely overhauls his approach at the plate.

Liu Rodriguez IF Bats B Age 25

YEAR	TEAM	LGE	AB	H	DB	TP	HR	BB	SO	R	RBI	SB	CS	OUT	BA	OBP	SLG	EQA	EQR	DEFENSE	
1999	Birmnghm	Sou	247	64	10	1	2	15	36	34	28	3	2	185	.259	.306	.332	.218	20	36-2B -5	21-SS 3
1999	ChiSox	AL	92	23	2	2	1	11	10	8	12	0	0	69	.250	.347	.348	.241	10	13-2B 0	11-SS -3
2000	Charlott	Int	398	101	18	2	4	45	38	39	40	2	6	303	.254	.338	.339	.231	39	75-2B 2	45-SS -4
2001	Charlott	Int	448	123	20	0	1	40	56	51	35	6	4	329	.275	.337	.326	.230	42	92-2B -6	19-SS -3
2002	*ChiSox*	*AL*	*400*	*111*	*19*	*1*	*3*	*43*	*50*	*50*	*45*	*6*	*4*	*293*	*.278*	*.348*	*.352*	*.242*	*42*		

(Liu Rodriguez *continued*)

The Sox not only have depth in real prospects, they have a seemingly endless supply of good bench players. Rodriguez would be an asset as a fifth infielder who can handle both up-the-middle spots, pinch-run, and reach base from both sides of the plate. He's blocked by Tony Graffanino, a better offensive player who can't handle shortstop as well as Rodriguez does.

Aaron Rowand OF Bats R Age 24

YEAR	TEAM	LGE	AB	H	DB	TP	HR	BB	SO	R	RBI	SB	CS	OUT	BA	OBP	SLG	EQA	EQR	DEFENSE
1999	WnstnSlm	Car	520	123	27	2	18	21	94	71	61	8	7	404	.237	.275	.400	.222	47	99-RF -5
2000	Birmnghm	Sou	549	135	21	4	19	25	116	71	86	14	5	419	.246	.288	.403	.230	53	138-RF 8
2001	Charlott	Int	331	92	18	0	17	21	43	50	45	7	2	241	.278	.332	.486	.269	45	79-RF -2
2001	ChiSox	AL	123	38	4	0	5	16	24	22	22	5	1	86	.309	.401	.463	.296	20	40-OF 5
2002	*ChiSox*	*AL*	*489*	*143*	*24*	*2*	*22*	*38*	*89*	*82*	*76*	*14*	*4*	*350*	*.292*	*.343*	*.485*	*.276*	*70*	

Rowand is getting squeezed, with two good corner outfielders ahead of him and Joe Borchard coming up hard behind him. The pressure might have been good for Rowand, as he showed much improved plate discipline in 2001 and played very well in September with the Sox. Spring training will be huge: if he can establish himself as at least a platoon center fielder, he should have a career. If he tanks, Borchard will pass him, and Rowand could easily end up on the Chad Mottola career path.

Chris Singleton CF Bats L Age 29

YEAR	TEAM	LGE	AB	H	DB	TP	HR	BB	SO	R	RBI	SB	CS	OUT	BA	OBP	SLG	EQA	EQR	DEFENSE
1999	ChiSox	AL	493	152	33	6	18	17	40	71	70	19	5	346	.308	.333	.509	.276	69	127-CF 14
2000	ChiSox	AL	508	132	22	5	12	29	75	80	60	22	8	384	.260	.301	.394	.235	51	145-CF 10
2001	ChiSox	AL	392	121	20	5	8	22	53	58	46	10	12	283	.309	.347	.446	.258	48	121-CF 7
2002	*ChiSox*	*AL*	*449*	*131*	*24*	*5*	*13*	*32*	*61*	*65*	*57*	*13*	*9*	*327*	*.292*	*.339*	*.454*	*.263*	*58*	

Another player who should be part of a good Sox bench this year, Singleton is a very good center fielder, hits enough to be an asset off the bench—even against lefties—and can step into the lineup without killing the team. He'll make a great caddy for Borchard, able to play against tough righties and come in for defense in the late innings.

Frank Thomas DH/1B Bats R Age 34

YEAR	TEAM	LGE	AB	H	DB	TP	HR	BB	SO	R	RBI	SB	CS	OUT	BA	OBP	SLG	EQA	EQR	DEFENSE
1999	ChiSox	AL	479	151	28	0	19	82	58	72	78	3	3	331	.315	.423	.493	.308	87	48-1B -6
2000	ChiSox	AL	570	191	37	0	46	104	83	109	137	1	3	382	.335	.442	.642	.344	133	30-1B 0
2001	ChiSox	AL	68	16	4	0	4	10	10	9	10	0	0	52	.235	.333	.471	.265	9	
2002	*ChiSox*	*AL*	*454*	*138*	*24*	*0*	*28*	*86*	*66*	*73*	*85*	*1*	*2*	*318*	*.304*	*.415*	*.542*	*.317*	*90*	

Frank Thomas has had one good year in the last four, and while his two MVPs and career 1000 OPS should still make him a Hall-of-Famer, players whose careers die out swiftly sometimes struggle with the voters. Thomas has 348 home runs and 1,193 RBI, unimpressive totals for a Hall of Fame first baseman. Yes, he should come back and add to those totals, but didn't we all think the same of Dale Murphy at one point?

Jose Valentin 3B/SS/CF Bats B Age 32

YEAR	TEAM	LGE	AB	H	DB	TP	HR	BB	SO	R	RBI	SB	CS	OUT	BA	OBP	SLG	EQA	EQR	DEFENSE
1999	Milwauke	NL	257	58	8	5	10	44	48	43	36	2	2	201	.226	.343	.412	.255	33	75-SS -12
2000	ChiSox	AL	563	158	35	6	27	52	93	103	89	19	2	407	.281	.346	.508	.282	86	139-SS 0
2001	ChiSox	AL	438	118	21	2	31	52	98	78	71	8	7	327	.269	.350	.539	.284	70	59-3B -5 39-SS 0
2002	*ChiSox*	*AL*	*520*	*135*	*26*	*5*	*27*	*65*	*109*	*96*	*78*	*13*	*6*	*391*	*.260*	*.342*	*.485*	*.274*	*77*	

Mishandled badly by the White Sox last year, Valentin still put up a performance, when healthy, that made his $5 million salary look like a bargain. The experiment with him in center field is over, leaving him to bounce between third base and shortstop. Joe Crede is better than Royce Clayton, so hopefully Valentin can return to being the best non-trinity shortstop in the AL. He's vastly underrated.

Mario Valenzuela OF Bats R Age 25

YEAR	TEAM	LGE	AB	H	DB	TP	HR	BB	SO	R	RBI	SB	CS	OUT	BA	OBP	SLG	EQA	EQR	DEFENSE
1999	Burlingt	Mid	476	117	20	3	7	25	84	56	42	6	4	363	.246	.287	.345	.213	38	117-LF -6
2000	WnstnSlm	Car	539	120	19	1	18	41	111	68	62	6	2	421	.223	.279	.362	.216	46	138-RF -5
2001	Birmnghm	Sou	348	92	15	2	10	15	60	45	44	3	4	260	.264	.297	.405	.230	33	88-LF 1
2001	Charlott	Int	176	44	5	1	9	9	31	18	23	2	0	132	.250	.289	.443	.241	19	46-RF -3
2002	*ChiSox*	*AL*	*525*	*142*	*24*	*2*	*19*	*40*	*102*	*78*	*67*	*8*	*3*	*386*	*.270*	*.322*	*.432*	*.253*	*62*	

Grade-C prospect who has the same problem as Rowand and Leifer and Inglin and Jeff Abbott: no place to play. Valenzuela is even worse off, because he's the same type of player as Rowand, but clearly inferior. He will eventually get his six-year rights and reach the major leagues as a fifth outfielder.

PITCHERS (ERA: 4.50, H/9: 9.0, HR/9: 1.0, BB/9: 3.0, K/9: 6.0, KW: 2.0, PERA: 4.50)

Lorenzo Barcelo Throws R Age 24

YEAR	TEAM	LGE	IP	H	ER	HR	BB	K	ERA	W	L	H/9	HR/9	BB/9	K/9	KW	PERA	STUFF
1999	Birmnghm	Sou	19.0	18	7	0	6	10	3.32	1	1	8.5	0.0	2.8	4.7	0.8	4.13	12
2000	Charlott	Int	100.0	118	69	24	16	52	6.21	4	7	10.6	2.2	1.4	4.7	1.6	4.79	4
2000	ChiSox	AL	38.3	38	17	4	7	26	3.99	2	2	8.9	0.9	1.6	6.1	1.9	3.23	8
2001	ChiSox	AL	22.3	21	9	1	8	14	3.63	1	1	8.5	0.4	3.2	5.6	0.9	4.99	0

He looks like a hell of a pitcher when he's out there, but he can't stay healthy. Barcelo had Tommy John surgery in 1999, came back from that, then missed most of last year after shoulder surgery. He's expected back for spring training, and his career numbers (.302 opponent OBP, better than two-to-one strikeout-to-walk ratio) mean you have to treat him as a serious prospect.

Rocky Biddle Throws R Age 26

YEAR	TEAM	LGE	IP	H	ER	HR	BB	K	ERA	W	L	H/9	HR/9	BB/9	K/9	KW	PERA	STUFF
2000	Birmnghm	Sou	143.0	158	92	21	62	70	5.79	6	10	9.9	1.3	3.9	4.4	0.6	5.88	-11
2000	ChiSox	AL	24.0	29	16	4	7	7	6.00	1	2	10.9	1.5	2.6	2.6	0.5	8.17	-18
2001	ChiSox	AL	132.0	135	70	14	49	81	4.77	7	8	9.2	1.0	3.3	5.5	0.8	5.45	0

Does this sounds familiar? Rocky Biddle had Tommy John surgery in 1999, came back from it, then had shoulder surgery in 2001 and is expected to be back for spring training. Biddle should have opened the 2001 season at Charlotte, but the Sox had some injuries, and he had some major-league experience, so he drew the short straw. Despite some terrible stretches, he stayed in the majors all year, probably to his detriment.

Mark Buehrle Throws L Age 23

YEAR	TEAM	LGE	IP	H	ER	HR	BB	K	ERA	W	L	H/9	HR/9	BB/9	K/9	KW	PERA	STUFF
1999	Burlingt	Mid	100.3	111	56	16	18	52	5.02	5	6	10.0	1.4	1.6	4.7	1.4	5.12	6
2000	Birmnghm	Sou	111.0	124	58	15	17	45	4.70	6	6	10.1	1.2	1.4	3.6	1.3	3.77	5
2000	ChiSox	AL	53.7	52	23	4	16	37	3.86	3	3	8.7	0.7	2.7	6.2	1.2	3.90	8
2001	ChiSox	AL	213.7	220	99	22	46	120	4.17	13	11	9.3	0.9	1.9	5.1	1.3	3.24	13

The gap between Buehrle's DT-ERA and his DT-PERA is nearly a full run, which is about as large a gap as you'll see for a full major-league season. This is normally an indicator that a pitcher will improve his numbers the following year. Because Buehrle was a bit over his head last year—particularly in terms of hits allowed—it's likely that he'll regress this season. He will only be a disappointment to people expecting a repeat of last year, though. Buehrle has a tremendous pickoff move, as good as Andy Pettitte's.

Cal Eldred Throws R Age 34

YEAR	TEAM	LGE	IP	H	ER	HR	BB	K	ERA	W	L	H/9	HR/9	BB/9	K/9	KW	PERA	STUFF
1999	Milwauke	NL	85.7	95	62	18	39	54	6.51	3	7	10.0	1.9	4.1	5.7	0.7	7.49	-12
2000	ChiSox	AL	114.0	104	53	10	48	96	4.18	7	6	8.2	0.8	3.8	7.6	1.0	4.04	17
2001	ChiSox	AL	7.7	8	4	1	3	6	4.70	0	1	9.4	1.2	3.5	7.0	1.0	12.10	-5

In his *New Historical Baseball Abstract,* Bill James revives his "Decade in a Box" feature, a section in which he provides all kinds of information—some serious, some fun—about each ten-year stretch from 1870 through today. One of the humorous notations is, "Could I Try This Career Over?" a phrase placed next to names like Ken Brett and Bob Cerv, players who had ability, but who never lived up to the potential they showed in their early 20s.

Cal Eldred might like to try his career over. He's all but retired as this book is being written, and he seems content with the idea. In 1992, a 24-year-old Eldred just missed pitching a forgettable Brewers team to the AL East title, making 14 starts in which he threw 100 innings and posted a 1.79 ERA. Rookie manager Phil Garner worked Eldred into the ground, including one stretch of 387 pitches in three starts over 12 days, capped by a 143-pitch outing. Eldred was never as effective a pitcher after that. He would never again have an ERA under 4.00 (save a four-start season in 1995), and he would spend most of the next nine years either injured, rehabbing an injury, or waiting for the next injury.

Cal Eldred—and pitchers like him whose paths to fame and fortune ended before they began—are a good reason to not begrudge baseball players the money they make. Their careers are short, they subject their talent to considerable risk, they can suffer tremendous pain, and when they're no longer of use to their employers, they're discarded.

Alan Embree Throws L Age 32

YEAR	TEAM	LGE	IP	H	ER	HR	BB	K	ERA	W	L	H/9	HR/9	BB/9	K/9	KW	PERA	STUFF
1999	San Fran	NL	56.0	52	26	6	22	48	4.18	3	3	8.4	1.0	3.5	7.7	1.1	3.25	5
2000	San Fran	NL	62.3	59	26	4	21	44	3.75	4	3	8.5	0.6	3.0	6.4	1.0	5.04	0
2001	San Fran	NL	22.7	25	17	6	9	20	6.75	1	2	9.9	2.4	3.6	7.9	1.1	12.62	-16
2001	ChiSox	AL	34.0	33	17	6	7	32	4.50	2	2	8.7	1.6	1.9	8.5	2.3	4.98	9

Embree is a hard thrower who continues to be used in a specialist role, despite all evidence pointing to his being ill-suited for it. It took Mike Remlinger a long time to find his niche; Embree has a fair amount in common with Remlinger and could still end up with a career. Signed by the Padres, where he'll get turned around.

Josh Fogg Throws R Age 25

YEAR	TEAM	LGE	IP	H	ER	HR	BB	K	ERA	W	L	H/9	HR/9	BB/9	K/9	KW	PERA	STUFF
1999	WnstnSlm	Car	103.7	102	46	6	38	61	3.99	7	5	8.9	0.5	3.3	5.3	0.8	4.94	10
1999	Birmnghm	Sou	56.7	66	40	12	18	28	6.35	2	4	10.5	1.9	2.9	4.4	0.8	6.95	-5
2000	Birmnghm	Sou	193.3	201	86	13	47	87	4.00	12	9	9.4	0.6	2.2	4.1	0.9	4.46	4
2001	Charlott	Int	115.3	132	81	25	35	66	6.32	4	9	10.3	2.0	2.7	5.2	0.9	6.04	-13
2001	ChiSox	AL	13.7	9	3	0	3	16	1.98	2	0	5.9	0.0	2.0	10.5	2.7	1.82	39

Fogg's strong cup of coffee after rosters expanded helped raise his profile and get him out of the Land of Never-Ending Pitching Prospects. He was traded to the Pirates in the Todd Ritchie deal. A closer in college, he's done a little bit of everything as a pro, getting by with command rather than heat. He'll be in the Bucs' rotation mix this spring; in the long term, he should be a good setup man.

Keith Foulke Throws R Age 29

YEAR	TEAM	LGE	IP	H	ER	HR	BB	K	ERA	W	L	H/9	HR/9	BB/9	K/9	KW	PERA	STUFF
1999	ChiSox	AL	103.7	81	31	10	18	122	2.69	9	3	7.0	0.9	1.6	10.6	3.4	2.02	34
2000	ChiSox	AL	87.0	73	29	8	18	90	3.00	7	3	7.6	0.8	1.9	9.3	2.5	2.61	24
2001	ChiSox	AL	79.0	66	24	3	21	71	2.73	7	2	7.5	0.3	2.4	8.1	1.7	2.09	18

You think he looks at Derek Lowe and wonders? Lowe, like Foulke, used to be a starter before being moved to the closer role, and like Foulke, was not a fire-breathing closer in the classic mold. Unlike Foulke, though, Lowe had a poor 2001 season and is now moving back to the rotation. Foulke has expressed a desire to be a starter, so maybe the solution is just to suck for a few weeks this summer. His big new contract pretty much means he'll be a reliever for the rest of his career.

Jon Garland   Throws R   Age 22

YEAR	TEAM	LGE	IP	H	ER	HR	BB	K	ERA	W	L	H/9	HR/9	BB/9	K/9	KW	PERA	STUFF
1999	WnstnSlm	Car	116.0	128	68	14	43	49	5.28	5	8	9.9	1.1	3.3	3.8	0.6	5.33	2
1999	Birmnghm	Sou	38.7	43	26	6	18	19	6.05	1	3	10.0	1.4	4.2	4.4	0.5	5.82	1
2000	Charlott	Int	104.7	103	42	4	31	53	3.61	7	5	8.9	0.3	2.7	4.6	0.9	2.42	16
2000	ChiSox	AL	73.3	76	42	9	33	42	5.15	3	5	9.3	1.1	4.1	5.2	0.6	5.85	3
2001	Charlott	Int	33.3	32	14	1	12	20	3.78	2	2	8.6	0.3	3.2	5.4	0.8	2.97	18
2001	ChiSox	AL	110.0	127	72	14	52	58	5.49	5	8	9.7	1.1	4.0	4.4	0.6	4.07	-5

Sometimes, the best deals are the ones you don't make. In December, the Sox were apparently set to send Garland to Anaheim for Darin Erstad, who can be a free agent after 2002 and has sucked rocks in two of the last three seasons. Garland is the young pitcher on the Sox with the most upside. He's pencilled into the 2002 rotation, but his command is shaky enough that he'd be better served starting the year in long relief. If he's a starter in April, he won't get through the season in the majors. Long term, he'll be fine.

Matt Ginter   Throws R   Age 24

YEAR	TEAM	LGE	IP	H	ER	HR	BB	K	ERA	W	L	H/9	HR/9	BB/9	K/9	KW	PERA	STUFF
1999	Burlingt	Mid	39.0	44	29	6	21	17	6.69	1	3	10.2	1.4	4.8	3.9	0.4	5.16	-12
2000	Birmnghm	Sou	174.7	179	82	11	61	84	4.23	10	9	9.2	0.6	3.1	4.3	0.7	4.85	5
2000	ChiSox	AL	11.0	14	13	4	6	6	10.64	0	1	11.5	3.3	4.9	4.9	0.5	11.16	-35
2001	Charlott	Int	74.7	70	31	4	27	52	3.74	5	3	8.4	0.5	3.3	6.3	1.0	3.34	10
2001	ChiSox	AL	39.0	38	16	2	13	23	3.69	2	2	8.8	0.5	3.0	5.3	0.9	4.67	0

With Bill Simas out for the year and Bobby Howry just looking like it, Ginter opened an opportunity for himself as Keith Foulke's setup man. He was moved to the pen just last summer, and his strikeout rate picked up. Ginter has a fastball/slider combination, with no real third pitch, so he's in the bullpen to stay. The Sox are going to have an excellent pen this year.

Gary Glover   Throws R   Age 25

YEAR	TEAM	LGE	IP	H	ER	HR	BB	K	ERA	W	L	H/9	HR/9	BB/9	K/9	KW	PERA	STUFF
1999	Knoxvill	Sou	84.0	82	38	7	27	54	4.07	6	4	8.8	0.8	2.9	5.8	1.0	4.20	15
1999	Syracuse	Int	81.0	85	48	11	33	46	5.33	4	5	9.4	1.2	3.7	5.1	0.7	5.40	4
2000	Syracuse	Int	170.3	182	100	25	60	101	5.28	8	11	9.6	1.3	3.2	5.3	0.8	5.58	4
2001	Charlott	Int	34.0	35	15	4	6	21	3.97	2	2	9.3	1.1	1.6	5.6	1.8	2.13	15
2001	ChiSox	AL	99.7	105	56	14	30	60	5.06	5	6	9.5	1.3	2.7	5.4	1.0	4.91	-5

Stolen from the Blue Jays for Scott Eyre, Glover gave the White Sox good innings in the swing-man role, stepping in for starts as various old guys were injured, traded, or ineffective, while filling Sean Lowe's place as the long man when Lowe was starting. He doesn't have much upside but is a safe choice for the 90 or so low-leverage innings every staff has to assign to someone.

Matt Guerrier   Throws R   Age 23

YEAR	TEAM	LGE	IP	H	ER	HR	BB	K	ERA	W	L	H/9	HR/9	BB/9	K/9	KW	PERA	STUFF
1999	Bristol	App	24.7	25	16	2	18	16	5.84	1	2	9.1	0.7	6.6	5.8	0.4	3.78	-7
2000	WnstnSlm	Car	33.7	31	12	0	13	21	3.21	3	1	8.3	0.0	3.5	5.6	0.8	4.33	1
2000	Birmnghm	Sou	22.0	22	12	2	12	13	4.91	1	1	9.0	0.8	4.9	5.3	0.5	4.68	-7
2001	Birmnghm	Sou	92.3	100	55	13	35	47	5.36	4	6	9.7	1.3	3.4	4.6	0.7	5.18	1
2001	Charlott	Int	78.3	86	42	9	20	33	4.83	4	5	9.9	1.0	2.3	3.8	0.8	3.97	3

Minor-league closers usually fade into oblivion. Guerrier, who saved 26 games in 2000, was moved to the rotation and pitched well at two levels, then continued to impress people in the Arizona Fall League. His development was a factor in the trade of Kip Wells and the near-deal of Jon Garland. He'll be in camp in March and with the Sox by mid-June. Health is a concern; he wasn't abused last year, but he'd never thrown anything close to 200 innings before, either.

Bobby Howry Throws R Age 28

YEAR	TEAM	LGE	IP	H	ER	HR	BB	K	ERA	W	L	H/9	HR/9	BB/9	K/9	KW	PERA	STUFF
1999	ChiSox	AL	69.3	56	29	7	32	79	3.76	5	3	7.3	0.9	4.2	10.3	1.2	3.82	19
2000	ChiSox	AL	69.3	62	28	5	24	59	3.63	5	3	8.0	0.6	3.1	7.7	1.2	2.72	10
2001	ChiSox	AL	82.0	80	41	10	29	61	4.50	5	4	8.8	1.1	3.2	6.7	1.1	4.20	-1

He never said a word, but Howry wasn't the same in 2001 following off-season shoulder surgery. The Sox aren't worried, having given him a two-year contract in midsummer. Being locked in at $1.5 million a year makes Howry great trade bait, especially given the ChiSox' ridiculous pitching depth. There's a ton of teams for which he could rack up saves.

Sean Lowe Throws R Age 31

YEAR	TEAM	LGE	IP	H	ER	HR	BB	K	ERA	W	L	H/9	HR/9	BB/9	K/9	KW	PERA	STUFF
1999	ChiSox	AL	96.0	95	48	9	38	61	4.50	6	5	8.9	0.8	3.6	5.7	0.8	3.10	-4
2000	ChiSox	AL	74.0	73	40	9	32	53	4.86	4	4	8.9	1.1	3.9	6.4	0.8	4.93	-5
2001	ChiSox	AL	127.0	130	57	11	30	68	4.04	8	6	9.2	0.8	2.1	4.8	1.1	3.49	0

For the third year in a row, Lowe was a savior for the Sox. He threw mop-up relief, set up Foulke on occasion, and made six starts to boot. He has been much more effective in the long-relief role, throwing ground ball after ground ball. Traded to the Pirates in the Todd Ritchie deal, Lowe could end up with just about any job, but he would help them most in the bullpen.

Gary Majewski Throws R Age 22

YEAR	TEAM	LGE	IP	H	ER	HR	BB	K	ERA	W	L	H/9	HR/9	BB/9	K/9	KW	PERA	STUFF
1999	Bristol	App	75.7	81	52	9	47	38	6.19	3	5	9.6	1.1	5.6	4.5	0.4	4.78	2
2000	Burlingt	Mid	122.7	129	86	19	76	79	6.31	5	9	9.5	1.4	5.6	5.8	0.5	4.53	9
2000	WnstnSlm	Car	36.0	38	20	2	19	14	5.00	2	2	9.5	0.5	4.8	3.5	0.4	6.55	-2
2001	Vero Bch	Fla	78.3	100	75	21	41	26	8.62	2	7	11.5	2.4	4.7	3.0	0.3	8.59	-32
2001	WnstnSlm	Car	42.0	48	27	7	13	18	5.79	2	3	10.3	1.5	2.8	3.9	0.7	4.54	-4

The Ron Hassey Award winner in 2001, Majewski was traded to the Dodgers in the Antonio Osuna deal, then returned to the Sox in the James Baldwin trade. He had to be thrilled, as he was pitching horribly for Vero Beach, then picked up where he'd left off upon returning to the Carolina League. He's a few years away, and he appears here mostly because he was involved in two trades for major leaguers last year. The stuff future closers are made of.

Corwin Malone Throws L Age 21

YEAR	TEAM	LGE	IP	H	ER	HR	BB	K	ERA	W	L	H/9	HR/9	BB/9	K/9	KW	PERA	STUFF
2000	Burlingt	Mid	72.0	74	57	9	67	47	7.13	2	6	9.3	1.1	8.4	5.9	0.4	8.35	-13
2001	Kannapls	SAL	108.3	105	55	5	62	61	4.57	6	6	8.7	0.4	5.2	5.1	0.5	3.58	11
2001	WnstnSlm	Car	34.7	34	16	2	13	22	4.15	2	2	8.8	0.5	3.4	5.7	0.8	3.55	19
2001	Birmnghm	Sou	16.0	17	13	3	13	13	7.31	1	1	9.6	1.7	7.3	7.3	0.5	3.15	13

Two things stand out about Malone's season: the sudden improvement in his command, and the way in which his performance remained constant as he moved through the system—look at the PERA column. While he has shot towards the top of a number of prospect lists, let's remember that he's thrown only about 50 innings above the Sally League. He bears a physical resemblance to Arthur Rhodes; in a few years, their careers will start to look alike as well.

Onan Masaoka Throws L Age 24

YEAR	TEAM	LGE	IP	H	ER	HR	BB	K	ERA	W	L	H/9	HR/9	BB/9	K/9	KW	PERA	STUFF
1999	LosAngls	NL	65.3	62	38	8	39	55	5.23	3	4	8.5	1.1	5.4	7.6	0.7	4.35	5
2000	Albuquer	PCL	36.3	36	24	1	34	18	5.94	1	3	8.9	0.2	8.4	4.5	0.3	3.59	-17
2000	LosAngls	NL	27.3	24	12	2	12	24	3.95	2	1	7.9	0.7	4.0	7.9	1.0	3.89	12
2001	LasVegas	PCL	75.7	79	44	10	32	43	5.23	3	5	9.4	1.2	3.8	5.1	0.7	5.83	-9
2001	Charlott	Int	14.3	13	7	3	6	17	4.40	1	1	8.2	1.9	3.8	10.7	1.4	5.33	19

The Dodgers never recognized what they had in Masaoka, jerking him from role to role for the last four years. He has too much ability to be restricted to a specialist role and too little to make him stand out as a starter. Why are teams willing to let right-handed relievers be two-inning setup men, but they won't give left-handers with the same skill set a comparable chance? Masaoka is eventually going to have some good years; with a couple of breaks, he could have Mike Stanton's career, and earnings to match.

Antonio Osuna — Throws R — Age 29

YEAR	TEAM	LGE	IP	H	ER	HR	BB	K	ERA	W	L	H/9	HR/9	BB/9	K/9	KW	PERA	STUFF
1999	San Bern	Cal	20.3	18	7	0	8	13	3.10	1	1	8.0	0.0	3.5	5.8	0.8	3.77	-9
2000	LosAngls	NL	67.3	60	31	6	29	62	4.14	4	3	8.0	0.8	3.9	8.3	1.1	3.90	9
2001	ChiSox	AL	5.0	6	6	3	2	6	10.80	0	1	10.8	5.4	3.6	10.8	1.5	18.76	-27

And now, "Torn Labrums on Parade." Bachelor #1 is a right-handed reliever who came over from the Dodgers to add to the bullpen depth of the Sox. Five innings into the season, he visited Dr. Lewis Yocum and never came back. Staying healthy is an ability, the same as throwing a slider or painting the corners. Osuna doesn't appear to possess it, so he may never get back to his 1998 level.

Jim Parque — Throws L — Age 27

YEAR	TEAM	LGE	IP	H	ER	HR	BB	K	ERA	W	L	H/9	HR/9	BB/9	K/9	KW	PERA	STUFF
1999	ChiSox	AL	185.0	189	96	20	66	110	4.67	10	11	9.2	1.0	3.2	5.4	0.8	4.87	5
2000	ChiSox	AL	194.7	198	93	18	58	110	4.30	12	10	9.2	0.8	2.7	5.1	0.9	4.16	6
2001	ChiSox	AL	29.3	34	21	6	10	14	6.44	1	2	10.4	1.8	3.1	4.3	0.7	7.49	-12

Bachelor #2 is a smallish left-hander who was trying to figure out where his fastball had gone when he was diagnosed with his own torn labrum. Parque wasn't overpowering when he was healthy, so it may take some time before he's effective again. He'll be good for a while beginning in 2004. Until then, pass.

Jon Rauch — Throws R — Age 23

YEAR	TEAM	LGE	IP	H	ER	HR	BB	K	ERA	W	L	H/9	HR/9	BB/9	K/9	KW	PERA	STUFF
1999	Bristol	App	59.3	67	38	9	20	28	5.76	3	4	10.2	1.4	3.0	4.2	0.7	8.37	-7
2000	WnstnSlm	Car	108.0	117	71	22	36	73	5.92	4	8	9.8	1.8	3.0	6.1	1.0	5.14	11
2000	Birmnghm	Sou	52.0	51	26	7	16	42	4.50	3	3	8.8	1.2	2.8	7.3	1.3	3.89	27
2001	Charlott	Int	26.7	33	26	10	8	21	8.78	1	2	11.1	3.4	2.7	7.1	1.3	6.99	3

A year ago, Bachelor #3 was atop or near the top of every major prospect list. A lousy month at Charlotte raised red flags, and he didn't pitch again in 2001. Rauch is coming back slowly; he won't be ready for spring training, and given his already slender resume above A ball, it's hard to imagine him having an impact with the Sox before 2004.

Advances in reconstructive elbow surgery have made us less worried about pitchers forced to undergo the well-known Tommy John procedure. Unfortunately, there's been less success in repairing shoulder damage, so a torn labrum is now about the worst thing that can happen to a pitcher, short of being traded to the Rockies. Osuna, Parque, and Rauch are all in for a long road back, and there's a chance that none of the three will be effective again.

Ken Vining — Throws L — Age 27

YEAR	TEAM	LGE	IP	H	ER	HR	BB	K	ERA	W	L	H/9	HR/9	BB/9	K/9	KW	PERA	STUFF
1999	Birmnghm	Sou	13.7	15	11	2	10	5	7.24	1	1	9.9	1.3	6.6	3.3	0.3	15.94	-50
2000	Birmnghm	Sou	44.0	46	25	4	21	23	5.11	2	3	9.4	0.8	4.3	4.7	0.5	7.99	-31
2001	Charlott	Int	44.3	41	22	3	24	32	4.47	3	2	8.3	0.6	4.9	6.5	0.7	2.40	-9
2001	ChiSox	AL	8.3	11	10	3	7	3	10.80	0	1	11.9	3.2	7.6	3.2	0.2	16.86	-71

As good as Kelly Wunsch was in 2000, remember that for roles like lefty one-out guy (LOOGY) there's always someone else. Vining was briefly someone else for the Sox in 2001, and with his fastball/curve combination will get lots of chances to be someone else for a variety of teams.

David Wells — Throws L — Age 39

YEAR	TEAM	LGE	IP	H	ER	HR	BB	K	ERA	W	L	H/9	HR/9	BB/9	K/9	KW	PERA	STUFF
1999	Toronto	AL	239.3	238	108	28	52	167	4.06	15	12	8.9	1.1	2.0	6.3	1.6	4.30	15
2000	Toronto	AL	245.0	237	88	20	25	164	3.23	18	9	8.7	0.7	0.9	6.0	3.3	3.67	20
2001	ChiSox	AL	106.0	111	49	11	20	56	4.16	6	6	9.4	0.9	1.7	4.8	1.4	4.41	7

Wells's weight finally reached the point where it ruined a season for him, contributing to back problems that eventually required surgery. He's apparently healthy and down about 20 pounds, impressive enough for the Yankees to give him a two-year contract. He's 39, still overweight, and has back problems. Wells is not likely to be both effective and healthy; which of the two he's more likely to be is something we won't know until March.

Kip Wells   Throws R   Age 25

YEAR	TEAM	LGE	IP	H	ER	HR	BB	K	ERA	W	L	H/9	HR/9	BB/9	K/9	KW	PERA	STUFF
1999	WnstnSlm	Car	85.7	86	46	8	39	53	4.83	5	5	9.0	0.8	4.1	5.6	0.7	5.28	6
1999	Birmnghm	Sou	64.7	69	40	7	31	31	5.57	3	4	9.6	1.0	4.3	4.3	0.5	3.53	0
1999	ChiSox	AL	36.7	33	14	2	13	29	3.44	3	1	8.1	0.5	3.2	7.1	1.1	3.63	23
2000	ChiSox	AL	107.3	109	60	13	47	70	5.03	5	7	9.1	1.1	3.9	5.9	0.7	5.71	4
2000	Charlott	Int	62.0	71	45	12	26	32	6.53	2	5	10.3	1.7	3.8	4.6	0.6	5.50	-7
2001	Charlott	Int	26.0	25	13	3	9	18	4.50	2	1	8.7	1.0	3.1	6.2	1.0	4.43	10
2001	ChiSox	AL	139.3	136	69	13	58	94	4.46	8	7	8.8	0.8	3.7	6.1	0.8	4.84	2

The Sox probably put too much on Wells following his great September 1999 performance, starting him in the majors in 2000 despite his having very little experience above A-ball. One of our favorite sayings—"There's no such thing as a pitching prospect"—is mostly about injuries, but never underestimate the ability of an organization to mess up the rare healthy one. Last year, Wells worked his way back into the rotation, but after some second-half beatings, found himself in the bullpen and a near-constant state of flux mechanically. The Pirates did a great job of buying low; Wells could be their #1 starter by the All-Star break.

Brian West   Throws R   Age 21

YEAR	TEAM	LGE	IP	H	ER	HR	BB	K	ERA	W	L	H/9	HR/9	BB/9	K/9	KW	PERA	STUFF
1999	Bristol	App	18.3	28	32	9	18	7	15.71	0	2	13.7	4.4	8.8	3.4	0.2	14.97	-54
2000	Burlingt	Mid	148.7	157	83	7	81	52	5.02	8	9	9.5	0.4	4.9	3.1	0.3	6.31	-3
2001	WnstnSlm	Car	170.0	191	121	25	94	75	6.41	6	13	10.1	1.3	5.0	4.0	0.4	5.78	-3

Most football players-turned-baseball players are toolsy outfield prospects. This one is a 6′4″ rock of a man who throws hard, although his performance belies that. He had just 130 strikeouts in the Carolina League. He's raw, at least two years from turning into anything useful, but notable for his size and his fastball.

Danny Wright   Throws R   Age 24

YEAR	TEAM	LGE	IP	H	ER	HR	BB	K	ERA	W	L	H/9	HR/9	BB/9	K/9	KW	PERA	STUFF
1999	Bristol	App	17.0	19	13	2	11	8	6.88	1	1	10.1	1.1	5.8	4.2	0.4	4.79	-21
2000	WnstnSlm	Car	134.7	140	70	9	57	60	4.68	7	8	9.4	0.6	3.8	4.0	0.5	5.82	-1
2000	Birmnghm	Sou	39.0	42	28	5	24	21	6.46	1	3	9.7	1.2	5.5	4.8	0.4	4.19	-1
2001	Birmnghm	Sou	128.0	127	60	10	47	78	4.22	7	7	8.9	0.7	3.3	5.5	0.8	5.11	8
2001	ChiSox	AL	68.3	76	49	11	37	34	6.45	3	5	10.0	1.4	4.9	4.5	0.5	5.48	-9

The Sox have had a lot of unreliable pitchers at the major-league level the past few seasons, which is the main reason guys like Danny Wright have found themselves discovering that yes, there are direct flights from Birmingham to Chicago. The other reason is that the Sox have a 737 full of pitching prospects, and they all have to pitch somewhere. Sometimes, somewhere is Comiskey Park. Wright, a fastball/curveball pitcher, needs time at Triple-A to work on his control and a third pitch.

Kelly Wunsch   Throws L   Age 29

YEAR	TEAM	LGE	IP	H	ER	HR	BB	K	ERA	W	L	H/9	HR/9	BB/9	K/9	KW	PERA	STUFF
1999	Huntsvil	Sou	48.7	49	23	2	27	21	2.65	2	3	9.1	.4	5.0	3.9	.4	4.25	-23
1999	Louisvil	Int	43.7	49	23	5	15	14	4.67	2	3	10.1	1.0	3.1	2.9	.5	4.74	-26
2000	ChiSox	AL	61.0	54	22	3	24	51	2.37	4	3	8.0	.4	3.5	7.5	1.1	3.25	8
2001	ChiSox	AL	22.0	23	12	4	9	15	6.11	1	1	9.4	1.6	3.7	6.1	.8	4.91	-14

Relief pitchers are fungible. Wunsch was great in 2000, but when he needed rotator-cuff surgery last summer, there were plenty of candidates to take over his role. That the options the White Sox tried weren't all that effective doesn't make Wunsch more valuable than any other LOOGY. He's supposed to be healthy in the spring and will have first dibs on his old job.

Cleveland Indians

The magnitude of a Juan Gonzalez contract—or any other high-dollar free agent—is not a realistic acquisition for the Cleveland Indians.

— Mark Shapiro, new Indians general manager (Source: ESPN.com)

The Cleveland Indians were sixth in the major leagues in operating revenue in 2001.

Very clearly, the lineage of Albert Belle, Manny Ramirez, Juan Gonzalez is over.

— Shapiro (Source: ESPN.com)

The Cleveland Indians were fourth in the major leagues in attendance in 2001.

Bucking for commissioner, Mark?

Throughout the post-strike era—when the notions that market size determined payroll and payroll determined success somehow became a key part of baseball's marketing strategy—the Cleveland Indians were the shining example of how a franchise in one of the game's smallest markets could build and sustain a contending team. The Tribe developed young players, gave them the opportunity to succeed, and committed to them with long-term contracts that represented a rare thing in management-player relations: a win/win opportunity.

The turnaround was pretty amazing. After all, it wasn't long ago that the Indians were the standard for bad baseball, a status that was cemented by their portrayal as the ultimate sad sacks in the 1990 movie *Major League*. That film looks dated today, as the only resemblance between the Jim Thome Tribe and the Charlie Sheen team is the catcher played by Tom Berenger, who spends most of the movie creaking around like a slightly more mobile Sandy Alomar. Just a few years after the film, the Indians embarked on the greatest run in franchise history, winning six division titles in seven years, reaching two World Series, and coming tantalizingly close, in 1997, to their first championship since 1948. A laughingstock had become a dynasty, thanks to a new mallpark and the success of John Hart's player-retention strategy.

Indians Prospectus

2001 record: 91-71; First place, AL Central; Lost to Mariners in Division Series 3-2

Pythagenport W/L: 88-75

Runs scored: 897 (second in AL)

Runs allowed: 821 (ninth in AL)

Team EqA: .272 (tied for second in AL)

2001 batters age: 31.2 (second-oldest in AL)

2001 pitchers age: 28.1 (tied for sixth-youngest in AL)

Ballpark: Jacobs Field; moderate hitters' park; Park Factor of 1.026

2001: The last gasp of a mini-dynasty that always seemed one pitcher short.

2002: Breaking out the sackcloth and ashes; don't buy the financial whining, but their days as the division's big dog are over.

Now, with Hart in Texas and only Thome and some bit players remaining from the teams that made it cool to be an Indians fan, the new administration is pulling out the sackcloth and ashes, desperate to lower expectations. The Indians are falling all over themselves to emphasize the small size of their market, using it as an excuse for not retaining their best players.

Cleveland is a medium market—the 18th-largest in baseball, according to Mike Jones's market-size estimates—and there are some warning signs that the steady rise in ticket prices has begun to impact attendance at Jacobs Field. But we have seven years of evidence that says that Cleveland can and will support a successful team. The Indians brought in $162 million last season, and there's no way a team bringing in that kind of dough can't compete for top talent in the marketplace. They may choose not to—and it's clear the Indians are doing just that—but they certainly are able to.

The Indians are a great example of just how stupid the owners' revenue-sharing plan, enacted in the wake of the 1994 strike, really is. As the Indians succeeded, as they grew their revenues through on-field performance and marketing, they were forced to subsidize teams from much larger markets who weren't doing those things. Last year the Indians, in the 18th-largest market in baseball, paid $13.2 million into the revenue-sharing pool. The Anaheim Angels and Philadelphia Phillies, playing in the fifth- and sixth-largest markets, collected more than $21 million from this pool. Why? Because the Indians made a lot of money, and the two large-market teams didn't invest in their product.

The system penalizes the Indians for setting aside their so-called disadvantages and working to maximize their revenues, a process that includes investing in the product by sustaining a competitive payroll. No sensible plan would penalize a team for success, yet the 1995 revenue-sharing plan created a bizarre system of incentives that does just that, while rewarding apathy and encouraging the reprehensible behavior of people such as Carl Pohlad and Claude Brochu.

No well-conceived revenue-sharing plan would penalize a team in a market the size of Cleveland. A system in which the Indians pay money to the Phillies is laughable on its face. If the problem is that certain markets are too small to generate sufficient revenues, then fixing the problem requires that money flow from large-market teams to small-market ones, *regardless of the actual revenues being generated in those markets*. The teams in New York and Chicago and Philadelphia and Boston have an advantage because of the size of those cities and the potential revenues available to them? Fine. Set up a revenue-sharing system based on market size. A system based on actual revenue or, worse still, payroll, is merely going to exact a higher toll on those teams that decline to go the Pohlad route and instead work like hell to build, develop, and promote the local nine, teams such as the Indians, Cardinals, Rockies, and A's.

This is all the more reason to respect what the Indians have accomplished, because their success was being undermined by MLB's Rube Goldberg system. Perhaps that same system is also the reason for the Indians' recent behavior. If revenue sharing is a function of payroll and not market size, and if there's a chance you've maximized your revenues, why not reduce payroll, especially if you're not seeing all the additional revenue that an investment in payroll should bring?

That's a generous rationalization for the Indians' activities over the winter. Frankly, it assumes a greater understanding of baseball economics than we've seen from any front office. More likely, the Indians are just spending money badly.

It's one thing to say that you cannot, or will not, pay players such as Juan Gonzalez or Roberto Alomar. It's another thing entirely to then dole out multiyear contracts to Bob Wickman and Ricky Gutierrez. That's exactly what the Indians did, however, making themselves a lesser baseball team without dramatically lowering their payroll. The Indians of the John Hart Era spent their money on players in their 20s, players they developed who had significant upside and carried some risk. The Indians of the Mark Shapiro Era are spending their money on players in their 30s who at best will repeat their recent performances and who are almost certain to decline throughout the lives of their contracts.

Essentially, this winter's Indians looked a lot like the Royals did the past few years, claiming they can't afford a $10-million player while spending $12 million on an assortment of lousy ones. It's a terrible strategy, perhaps the fastest way for a team to go from division champ to oblivion. The moves look even worse when you consider that the rest of baseball is going in the opposite direction, shunning mid-level players such as Wickman and Gutierrez while taking chances on players shorter on service time and longer on potential.

The 2002 Indians are going to be an old team, one of the oldest in baseball. Of the projected regulars, only Russ Branyan and Milton Bradley will be on the right side of 27. The infield of Thome, Gutierrez, Omar Vizquel, and Travis Fryman will have an average age of 32.8, while Brady Anderson and Ellis Burks, teammates on the 1988 Red Sox, will form two-thirds of the outfield on some days. Matt Lawton, acquired for Alomar, is thought of as young, but he's already 30.

The pitching staff will be younger than the regulars, but beyond Bartolo Colon, little is certain. C.C. Sabathia had a good rookie season, but he's just 21 and comes with the standard caveats about younger pitchers. Charlie Manuel did an excellent job with him in 2001 and will again be on the spot. He'll have to show patience with Sabathia's inevitable struggles and fight the urge to overwork him when he pitches well. Sabathia is not a rookie, but a 21-year-old arm is still a developing one.

At the other end of the wild-left-hander career spectrum, Chuck Finley is the nominal #3 starter, having given the Indians two subpar seasons to date. He's not likely to be a factor for the Tribe: if he's healthy, he'll be attractive to any number of contenders in the trade market.

The back of the Tribe rotation has been a major problem for the past few years. The team has been guilty of hoping for the best in the interminable comebacks of Jaret Wright and Charles Nagy, and they have been rewarded with ineffective pitching on the rare occasions either has been healthy. The Indians used nine starting pitchers in 2001 and 13 in 2000, and the revolving door hasn't been good for the team or for the pitchers involved. If they do nothing else in spring training, the Indians have to decide who from among their stable of B−/C+ arms will be their #4 and #5 starters, and stand by that decision.

The Indians' primary problem right now is player development. Years of drafting low and giving up compensation picks have left their system dry, with virtually no serious position-player prospects and just a couple of pitchers garnering attention. The Roberto Alomar deal with the Mets was an attempt to correct this, but the main prospects acquired by the Indians—Alex Escobar and Billy Traber—were merely the best in the Mets' system, a thin one. Escobar hasn't been able to stay healthy, while Traber has only one season as a professional under his belt. They'll look good in this organization, flaws and all.

It's not too late for the Tribe to forget trying to play the middle, concede the next two seasons to the White Sox, and work on getting young talent into the system by any means possible. The Sox have already passed the Indians, and the Twins will be better than them by 2003. The longer the Indians try to get by with mediocre, expensive veterans, the harder they make the inevitable rebuilding process. Among current Indians, only Branyan, Bradley, and some pitchers will be part of a good team come the middle of the decade. Everyone else with value needs to be swapped, preferably to teams with better talent to offer than the Mets had.

Conceding the next two seasons is not going to go over well in a city that's become accustomed to success. You sell it by being honest, pointing back ten years to a team that wasn't paying the going rate for service time, that developed its own talent, that brought pride back to the city by the Cuyahoga.

The Indians have a new front office. They'd do well to learn from the experience of the old one.

HITTERS (BA: .270, OBP: .340, SLG: .440, EqA: .260)

Roberto Alomar 2B Bats B Age 34

YEAR	TEAM	LGE	AB	H	DB	TP	HR	BB	SO	R	RBI	SB	CS	OUT	BA	OBP	SLG	EQA	EQR	DEFENSE
1999	Clevelnd	AL	553	182	40	3	25	93	84	133	115	35	6	377	.329	.431	.548	.328	116	145-2B 3
2000	Clevelnd	AL	600	188	37	2	20	57	72	106	84	40	4	416	.313	.379	.482	.294	98	148-2B -6
2001	Clevelnd	AL	577	204	35	12	23	82	61	119	105	28	7	379	.354	.437	.575	.334	122	148-2B -3
2002	*NY Mets*	*NL*	*522*	*158*	*30*	*5*	*17*	*77*	*65*	*105*	*85*	*32*	*5*	*369*	*.303*	*.392*	*.477*	*.305*	*95*	

Alomar probably became a Hall-of-Famer with his 2001 performance, which could have won an MVP Award in many years. Even though his defense is more reputation than reality, he is as complete a player as any in the last 20 years. Gold Gloves aside, he's probably underrated in the big picture. A big season in New York could change that.

Josh Bard C Bats B Age 24

YEAR	TEAM	LGE	AB	H	DB	TP	HR	BB	SO	R	RBI	SB	CS	OUT	BA	OBP	SLG	EQA	EQR	DEFENSE
2000	Salem VA	Car	317	76	6	0	4	22	33	32	20	2	1	242	.240	.290	.297	.203	22	89-C -6
2000	ColSprin	PCL	17	3	0	0	0	0	2	0	1	0	0	14	.176	.176	.176	.120	0	
2001	Carolina	Sou	127	29	7	0	2	15	23	12	21	0	1	99	.228	.312	.331	.220	11	35-C 0
2001	MahngVal	NYP	46	9	0	0	2	4	2	4	5	0	1	38	.196	.266	.326	.196	3	
2001	Akron	Eas	199	51	7	0	4	14	26	24	23	0	0	148	.256	.309	.352	.224	18	40-C -1
2002	*Clevelnd*	*AL*	*406*	*107*	*11*	*0*	*11*	*37*	*54*	*45*	*44*	*1*	*0*	*299*	*.264*	*.325*	*.372*	*.234*	*40*	

Part of the booty acquired from the Rockies for Jacob Cruz, Bard is primarily noted as a defensive catcher with a good arm. He has hit for a reasonable average and has shown some doubles power while maintaining decent strikeout-to-walk ratios. Unlike most of the prospects we highlight, Bard isn't a high-upside guy. As a switch-hitter who can throw, though, he's going to make the majors, and he is going to be around for a while.

Milton Bradley CF Bats B Age 24

YEAR	TEAM	LGE	AB	H	DB	TP	HR	BB	SO	R	RBI	SB	CS	OUT	BA	OBP	SLG	EQA	EQR	DEFENSE
1999	Harrisbg	Eas	347	97	19	3	9	23	61	48	36	8	7	257	.280	.327	.429	.249	40	74-CF -5
2000	Ottawa	Int	344	96	15	1	6	38	55	51	25	8	12	260	.279	.352	.381	.244	38	87-CF 2
2000	Montreal	NL	155	34	8	1	2	12	29	19	14	2	1	122	.219	.279	.323	.206	12	38-CF 1
2001	Montreal	NL	220	50	16	3	1	18	53	19	19	7	4	174	.227	.288	.341	.215	19	63-CF 4
2001	Ottawa	Int	139	37	6	2	2	22	28	20	13	11	1	103	.266	.372	.381	.272	20	34-CF 1
2001	Buffalo	Int	116	28	2	0	5	18	29	17	14	7	2	90	.241	.343	.388	.255	15	27-CF -1
2002	*Clevelnd*	*AL*	*461*	*131*	*28*	*3*	*11*	*60*	*99*	*71*	*47*	*8*	*8*	*338*	*.284*	*.367*	*.430*	*.265*	*61*	

Bradley is emerging from the shadow of questions about his attitude while taking significant steps forward as a hitter. Getting him comfortable enough to carry his impressive Triple-A plate discipline (79 unintentional walks in 592 at-bats) to the majors (35 UIBB in 392 AB) is going to be the key. With Kenny Lofton gone, Bradley should be the Indians' starting center fielder for the next five years, Alex Escobar be damned.

Russell Branyan 3B/LF Bats L Age 26

YEAR	TEAM	LGE	AB	H	DB	TP	HR	BB	SO	R	RBI	SB	CS	OUT	BA	OBP	SLG	EQA	EQR	DEFENSE			
1999	Buffalo	Int	398	79	11	1	25	43	176	43	54	6	3	322	.198	.282	.420	.232	42	104-3B	-3		
1999	Clevelnd	AL	38	8	3	0	1	3	17	4	6	0	0	30	.211	.284	.368	.219	3				
2000	Buffalo	Int	231	54	7	1	19	24	91	41	51	1	1	178	.234	.310	.519	.265	32	35-3B	-2	19-LF	0
2000	Clevelnd	AL	191	46	8	2	16	20	67	31	36	0	0	145	.241	.326	.555	.280	30	32-LF	-3		
2001	Clevelnd	AL	315	77	15	2	22	39	114	51	56	1	1	239	.244	.332	.514	.273	47	59-3B	-5	23-LF	-1
2002	*Clevelnd*	*AL*	*382*	*95*	*16*	*2*	*27*	*51*	*153*	*56*	*67*	*2*	*1*	*288*	*.249*	*.337*	*.513*	*.275*	*57*				

One of the reasons an extreme player, such as Branyan, has difficulty establishing himself is that he requires a manager with extraordinary patience. An all-or-nothing style is going to lead to bad stretches, and 2-for-43 just looks worse when it includes 30 strikeouts, as opposed to eight strikeouts and a bunch of groundouts and pop-ups.

The Indians could help Branyan by picking a role for him and sticking with it for a full season. Even a platoon job would allow him to get 400 at-bats without worrying that a bad day will push him to the bench. The moving around—third base, left field, DH—is not helping his development, and he is a player of tremendous potential value.

Ellis Burks DH/OF Bats R Age 37

YEAR	TEAM	LGE	AB	H	DB	TP	HR	BB	SO	R	RBI	SB	CS	OUT	BA	OBP	SLG	EQA	EQR	DEFENSE	
1999	San Fran	NL	394	112	18	0	32	64	80	73	93	6	5	287	.284	.392	.574	.309	76	92-RF	2
2000	San Fran	NL	400	141	22	4	25	51	45	75	95	5	1	260	.352	.427	.615	.336	85	92-RF	3
2001	Clevelnd	AL	440	129	25	1	32	64	73	88	78	5	1	312	.293	.387	.573	.310	83	17-LF	-1
2002	*Clevelnd*	*AL*	*401*	*106*	*22*	*2*	*27*	*64*	*66*	*71*	*82*	*5*	*2*	*297*	*.264*	*.366*	*.531*	*.291*	*68*		

With the need to find at-bats for Branyan and Alex Escobar, and with the acquisitions of Matt Lawton and Brady Anderson, Burks's primary value to the Indians is as trade bait. The argument for keeping him is Milton Bradley, who might find the transition to major-league stardom easier with a veteran African-American player in the same clubhouse. Come to think of it, Burks circa 1987 is a pretty good comp for Bradley right now, at least on the field.

Jolbert Cabrera UT Bats R Age 29

YEAR	TEAM	LGE	AB	H	DB	TP	HR	BB	SO	R	RBI	SB	CS	OUT	BA	OBP	SLG	EQA	EQR	DEFENSE			
1999	Buffalo	Int	279	70	13	3	0	21	40	36	23	15	4	213	.251	.307	.319	.222	25	40-CF	3	21-SS	-2
1999	Clevelnd	AL	37	7	2	0	0	1	7	6	1	3	0	30	.189	.229	.243	.181	2				
2000	Buffalo	Int	74	23	4	1	3	4	8	16	10	2	1	52	.311	.353	.514	.282	11	12-CF	0		
2000	Clevelnd	AL	174	44	3	1	2	6	13	25	14	6	4	134	.253	.286	.316	.205	13	37-OF	4		
2001	Clevelnd	AL	287	80	18	3	1	17	35	53	39	9	4	211	.279	.329	.373	.239	30	40-OF	0	13-3B	0
2002	*Clevelnd*	*AL*	*312*	*87*	*16*	*3*	*3*	*24*	*38*	*52*	*33*	*12*	*4*	*229*	*.279*	*.330*	*.378*	*.241*	*33*				

Cabrera's versatility—he played six positions in 2001—is what allowed Charlie Manuel to carry 12 pitchers for most of the season. He covered for injuries to Kenny Lofton and Travis Fryman, and he gave the middle infielders an occasional inning off. He actually is a good defender, so even though he can't hit or run much, he's worth the roster spot on a team with a short bench. A move to larger rosters would hurt his value, not help it.

Ryan Church RF Bats L Age 23

YEAR	TEAM	LGE	AB	H	DB	TP	HR	BB	SO	R	RBI	SB	CS	OUT	BA	OBP	SLG	EQA	EQR	DEFENSE	
2000	MahngVal	NYP	282	62	8	2	8	23	57	31	38	4	3	223	.220	.286	.348	.214	24	61-RF	-3
2001	Columbus	SAL	382	84	16	1	11	40	84	47	50	2	3	301	.220	.298	.353	.220	34	96-RF	6
2001	Kinston	Car	89	19	5	0	4	15	23	14	12	1	0	70	.213	.330	.404	.250	11	21-RF	-2
2002	*Clevelnd*	*AL*	*443*	*108*	*21*	*2*	*16*	*53*	*103*	*58*	*59*	*6*	*3*	*338*	*.244*	*.325*	*.409*	*.245*	*50*		

Church is a college hitter (UNLV) who has played well enough as a pro, albeit against younger competition, to warrant a prospect label. He's a milder version of Russ Branyan: left-handed, power and walks, will strike out 100 times. Time is not on Church's side: he needs to get to Double-A posthaste if he's going to be Jeromy Burnitz.

Wil Cordero — LF/1B — Bats R — Age 30

YEAR	TEAM	LGE	AB	H	DB	TP	HR	BB	SO	R	RBI	SB	CS	OUT	BA	OBP	SLG	EQA	EQR	DEFENSE
1999	Clevelnd	AL	192	59	11	0	10	13	33	34	32	2	0	133	.307	.367	.521	.292	31	28-LF -2
2000	Pittsbrg	NL	350	98	22	3	16	20	53	44	48	1	2	254	.280	.325	.497	.266	46	73-LF -7
2000	Clevelnd	AL	147	40	11	2	0	5	16	17	16	0	0	107	.272	.310	.374	.230	14	38-LF 3
2001	Clevelnd	AL	268	71	10	1	5	23	43	32	22	0	0	197	.265	.330	.366	.237	27	38-LF -4 20-1B -2
2002	*Clevelnd*	*AL*	*401*	*115*	*24*	*2*	*10*	*35*	*64*	*55*	*47*	*1*	*1*	*287*	*.287*	*.344*	*.431*	*.258*	*48*	

Do you know how long it's been since Wil Cordero was a good player? He had a great 1994 season and a decent year in 1995 before Felipe Alou tired of his defense at shortstop. He's done nothing, really, in the six years since then. His career path looks a bit like that of Gregg Jefferies; the two may be the most disappointing players of the past 15 years.

Marty Cordova — LF — Bats R — Age 32

YEAR	TEAM	LGE	AB	H	DB	TP	HR	BB	SO	R	RBI	SB	CS	OUT	BA	OBP	SLG	EQA	EQR	DEFENSE
1999	Minnesot	AL	420	122	27	3	15	43	84	60	68	12	4	302	.290	.367	.476	.281	63	24-RF -7
2000	Toronto	AL	198	49	5	0	5	16	31	22	18	3	2	151	.247	.314	.348	.226	18	34-LF -7
2001	Clevelnd	AL	409	129	21	2	22	25	70	66	72	0	3	283	.315	.364	.538	.290	64	97-LF 3
2002	*Baltimor*	*AL*	*371*	*98*	*16*	*1*	*16*	*35*	*68*	*48*	*52*	*5*	*4*	*277*	*.264*	*.328*	*.442*	*.262*	*48*	

It was a good story, but Cordova's comeback season really amounted to little more than six weeks of great hitting (he was at .420/.453/.728 on May 10) followed by four months of being Marty Cordova. Credit him for battling back from the plantar fasciitis that nearly ended his career, and for being part of a division winner. Just don't expect another year with an EqA up around .300. The Orioles signed him to a three-year deal. Big shock.

Einar Diaz — C — Bats R — Age 29

YEAR	TEAM	LGE	AB	H	DB	TP	HR	BB	SO	R	RBI	SB	CS	OUT	BA	OBP	SLG	EQA	EQR	DEFENSE
1999	Clevelnd	AL	389	112	23	1	3	20	36	42	31	10	4	281	.288	.330	.375	.240	40	107-C 2
2000	Clevelnd	AL	248	68	15	2	4	8	26	28	24	4	2	182	.274	.319	.399	.240	26	74-C 3
2001	Clevelnd	AL	437	128	34	1	5	19	38	57	58	1	2	311	.293	.340	.410	.250	49	124-C 9
2002	*Clevelnd*	*AL*	*414*	*117*	*24*	*1*	*6*	*20*	*39*	*47*	*39*	*5*	*3*	*300*	*.283*	*.325*	*.389*	*.238*	*41*	

The Indians did well to let Sandy Alomar Jr. walk away and hand the catching job to Diaz, a comparable player who lacked Alomar's health questions. They got a bit excited about having a healthy catcher, though, signing him to a four-year deal. He's Terry Steinbach without the really good years, and you can get that for a lesser commitment.

Mike Edwards — 1B/3B — Bats R — Age 25

YEAR	TEAM	LGE	AB	H	DB	TP	HR	BB	SO	R	RBI	SB	CS	OUT	BA	OBP	SLG	EQA	EQR	DEFENSE
1999	Kinston	Car	478	117	20	2	13	69	117	59	64	4	2	363	.245	.346	.377	.248	56	125-3B -14
2000	Akron	Eas	490	128	18	1	11	53	89	59	50	5	2	364	.261	.337	.369	.242	52	131-3B -8
2001	MahngVal	NYP	74	19	4	0	3	8	8	12	13	0	0	56	.257	.333	.432	.253	9	
2001	Akron	Eas	115	34	6	2	5	12	25	19	20	0	0	81	.296	.362	.513	.286	18	17-1B -1
2002	*Clevelnd*	*AL*	*412*	*119*	*18*	*2*	*16*	*53*	*84*	*61*	*64*	*4*	*1*	*294*	*.289*	*.370*	*.459*	*.277*	*60*	

Edwards, who looked like the Tribe's best hitting prospect a year ago, missed the first half of 2001 after surgery. Even though he hit well in the second half, the lost half-season is the kind of thing that can ruin an older prospect's chances. Edwards is the best of a handful of Indians' third-base prospects, but he could be squeezed out of the organization before getting a real chance.

Travis Fryman — 3B — Bats R — Age 33

YEAR	TEAM	LGE	AB	H	DB	TP	HR	BB	SO	R	RBI	SB	CS	OUT	BA	OBP	SLG	EQA	EQR	DEFENSE
1999	Clevelnd	AL	320	84	15	2	11	22	50	44	47	2	1	237	.262	.312	.425	.244	35	79-3B 3
2000	Clevelnd	AL	563	183	36	4	23	66	98	88	100	1	1	381	.325	.397	.526	.304	97	152-3B 5
2001	Clevelnd	AL	334	93	10	0	5	32	54	36	41	1	2	243	.278	.346	.353	.239	34	86-3B -12
2002	*Clevelnd*	*AL*	*507*	*148*	*20*	*2*	*17*	*63*	*90*	*74*	*76*	*1*	*2*	*361*	*.292*	*.370*	*.440*	*.271*	*69*	

(Travis Fryman *continued*)

He lost the first two months of the season to a torn elbow ligament, and even though he was healthy enough to play 98 games, he was never really 100%. The injury wiped out his power and hampered his throwing, so much so that he had postseason surgery on his shoulder. Injuries aside, he's been all over the place since 1998 or so, and predicting how he'll do in 2002 is a crapshoot.

Karim Garcia RF Bats L Age 26

YEAR	TEAM	LGE	AB	H	DB	TP	HR	BB	SO	R	RBI	SB	CS	OUT	BA	OBP	SLG	EQA	EQR	DEFENSE
1999	Detroit	AL	287	71	9	3	15	17	59	37	31	2	4	220	.247	.289	.456	.239	31	72-RF -1
2000	Detroit	AL	17	3	0	0	0	0	4	1	0	0	0	14	.176	.176	.176	.120	0	
2000	Toledo	Int	156	44	4	1	14	8	31	27	32	2	1	113	.282	.327	.590	.288	25	39-CF -2
2000	Rochestr	Int	273	72	12	1	13	29	69	34	48	2	3	204	.264	.338	.458	.261	35	62-RF -3
2001	Buffalo	Int	467	118	12	3	29	43	98	70	78	3	4	353	.253	.317	.478	.257	59	109-RF -3
2001	Clevelnd	AL	45	15	3	0	5	3	11	8	9	0	0	30	.333	.385	.733	.340	10	10-RF 0
2002	*Clevelnd*	*AL*	*458*	*128*	*18*	*3*	*30*	*45*	*105*	*71*	*70*	*2*	*3*	*333*	*.279*	*.344*	*.528*	*.280*	*69*	

While he's been a prospect forever, Garcia is still just 26 years old, and he hit well enough to get noticed in a September cup of coffee. Let's put it this way: he's still younger than Marty Cordova was when Cordova won the Rookie of the Year Award in 1996. Rather than sign Brady Anderson, the Indians should have given Garcia a clean shot in March. He'll overcome that and restart his career this year.

Juan Gonzalez RF Bats R Age 32

YEAR	TEAM	LGE	AB	H	DB	TP	HR	BB	SO	R	RBI	SB	CS	OUT	BA	OBP	SLG	EQA	EQR	DEFENSE
1999	Texas	AL	554	183	32	1	41	45	92	110	123	3	3	374	.330	.384	.614	.316	105	119-RF -10
2000	Detroit	AL	459	137	29	2	24	26	74	68	66	1	2	324	.298	.339	.527	.279	66	59-RF -5
2001	Clevelnd	AL	533	181	28	1	40	43	81	103	146	1	0	352	.340	.394	.621	.323	104	112-RF -5
2002	*Texas*	*AL*	*503*	*150*	*24*	*1*	*34*	*47*	*83*	*88*	*97*	*1*	*1*	*354*	*.298*	*.358*	*.553*	*.291*	*81*	

Give him credit: taking the one-year deal with the Indians after turning down nine figures from the Tigers could have blown up in his face. He went out and had an MVP-candidate season, something right in line with his Rangers career.

That said, he's an incredibly risky signing. He's going to be expensive and want a ton of years. He's had ongoing back problems, the worst kind of injury for a hitter. Accolades in 2001 aside, he's not much of a defensive outfielder. He's 32, and even if healthy he's unlikely to reach the heights of last year.

Nate Grindell LF/3B Bats R Age 25

YEAR	TEAM	LGE	AB	H	DB	TP	HR	BB	SO	R	RBI	SB	CS	OUT	BA	OBP	SLG	EQA	EQR	DEFENSE
1999	MahngVal	NYP	272	61	13	1	3	15	43	27	27	2	3	214	.224	.269	.313	.196	18	67-3B -7
2000	Columbus	SAL	511	111	22	2	12	37	79	54	61	8	2	402	.217	.275	.339	.210	40	113-3B -16
2001	Kinston	Car	280	67	11	1	6	15	42	37	34	1	2	215	.239	.281	.350	.211	22	47-3B -3 17-1B -1
2001	Akron	Eas	232	59	13	1	8	11	44	30	38	5	3	176	.254	.294	.422	.236	24	40-LF 0 14-1B 1
2002	*Clevelnd*	*AL*	*454*	*117*	*23*	*2*	*14*	*35*	*77*	*59*	*65*	*6*	*4*	*341*	*.258*	*.311*	*.410*	*.237*	*47*	

His errors piled up to the point that the Indians had to move him off of third base, even though he'd gotten raves from Sally League managers in his 39-error 2000. He hit at Double-A, but as a corner outfielder/first baseman, he's a non-prospect. Left at third base, he could be interesting, especially if Branyan continues to frustrate the Tribe.

Maicer Izturis 2B Bats B Age 21

YEAR	TEAM	LGE	AB	H	DB	TP	HR	BB	SO	R	RBI	SB	CS	OUT	BA	OBP	SLG	EQA	EQR	DEFENSE
1999	Columbus	SAL	225	52	5	1	3	14	30	30	16	6	2	175	.231	.277	.302	.202	16	
2000	Columbus	SAL	30	6	1	0	0	2	3	3	1	0	0	24	.200	.250	.233	.170	1	
2001	Kinston	Car	447	97	15	5	1	26	81	39	34	20	6	356	.217	.265	.280	.194	30	98-2B -14
2002	*Clevelnd*	*AL*	*405*	*103*	*16*	*4*	*3*	*32*	*74*	*60*	*26*	*20*	*5*	*307*	*.254*	*.309*	*.336*	*.222*	*36*	

Izturis held his own as he continued to recover from the elbow injury that ruined his 2000 season. He's healthy now, but the lost year of development hurts a player who was going to need a lot of at-bats to become a decent hitter. In his favor is the complete lack of middle-infield prospects in this system.

Kenny Lofton CF Bats L Age 35

YEAR	TEAM	LGE	AB	H	DB	TP	HR	BB	SO	R	RBI	SB	CS	OUT	BA	OBP	SLG	EQA	EQR	DEFENSE
1999	Clevelnd	AL	458	141	29	6	7	74	74	106	37	24	6	323	.308	.410	.443	.296	77	115-CF -2
2000	Clevelnd	AL	534	149	21	5	16	73	63	101	69	30	8	393	.279	.370	.427	.275	78	135-CF 5
2001	Clevelnd	AL	517	142	20	4	16	49	60	95	69	14	9	384	.275	.339	.422	.254	62	130-CF -7
2002	*Clevelnd*	*AL*	*510*	*140*	*22*	*4*	*15*	*65*	*66*	*98*	*52*	*18*	*9*	*378*	*.275*	*.357*	*.422*	*.262*	*67*	

Injuries have reduced him to 60% of the player he was at his peak, but he can still push a team towards a championship. Lofton needs to find a team with enough outfield depth to allow him to play 120 games, with some at DH and lots in left field. His willingness to accept a role other than "starting center fielder and leadoff hitter" will determine the course of his career from this point.

Victor Martinez C Bats B Age 23

YEAR	TEAM	LGE	AB	H	DB	TP	HR	BB	SO	R	RBI	SB	CS	OUT	BA	OBP	SLG	EQA	EQR	DEFENSE
1999	MahngVal	NYP	242	48	4	0	3	16	34	25	22	0	0	194	.198	.249	.252	.175	12	51-C -18
2000	Columbus	SAL	72	20	7	0	1	7	6	8	7	0	0	52	.278	.345	.417	.256	9	20-C -3
2000	Kinston	Car	86	16	6	0	0	8	5	7	6	0	1	71	.186	.259	.256	.178	5	25-C -7
2001	Kinston	Car	440	124	25	2	9	33	60	52	47	2	2	318	.282	.336	.409	.250	49	106-C -14
2002	*Clevelnd*	*AL*	*448*	*129*	*24*	*1*	*12*	*40*	*60*	*66*	*63*	*2*	*2*	*321*	*.288*	*.346*	*.426*	*.257*	*54*	

The Carolina League MVP and organizational player of the year is a converted shortstop with an outsized defensive reputation. Martinez impressed the Indians with his handling of Kinston's pitching staff, which included some of the system's best prospects. He was 22 in the Carolina League, so a dose of skepticism is healthy. Like Josh Bard, he's going to make The Show; the only question is whether he'll be a decent starter or a career backup. How often does a team have two switch-hitting catcher prospects?

John McDonald SS Bats R Age 27

YEAR	TEAM	LGE	AB	H	DB	TP	HR	BB	SO	R	RBI	SB	CS	OUT	BA	OBP	SLG	EQA	EQR	DEFENSE
1999	Akron	Eas	228	60	4	0	3	13	26	25	23	5	2	170	.263	.306	.320	.216	19	55-SS 0
1999	Buffalo	Int	236	70	8	2	0	8	22	25	21	5	3	169	.297	.324	.347	.228	21	59-SS 4
2000	Buffalo	Int	287	73	17	1	1	17	28	34	31	3	2	216	.254	.298	.331	.214	23	67-SS -1
2001	Buffalo	Int	414	98	15	1	2	32	67	50	32	14	9	325	.237	.298	.292	.206	31	109-SS 8
2001	Clevelnd	AL	22	3	1	0	0	1	6	1	0	0	0	19	.136	.200	.182	.138	1	
2002	*Clevelnd*	*AL*	*443*	*121*	*22*	*2*	*3*	*36*	*66*	*58*	*44*	*8*	*5*	*327*	*.273*	*.328*	*.352*	*.229*	*41*	

Glove man who actually could be a good defensive replacement for Omar Vizquel, if not for Vizquel's reputation. All his value is defensive, so even when he finally makes a team, don't get excited. The Indians could have saved themselves a lot of money by plugging McDonald in at second base rather than signing Gutierrez. Over the next two seasons, the difference between the two could be negligible. Well, except for the eight million bucks.

Corey Smith 3B Bats L Age 20

YEAR	TEAM	LGE	AB	H	DB	TP	HR	BB	SO	R	RBI	SB	CS	OUT	BA	OBP	SLG	EQA	EQR	DEFENSE
2000	BlngtnNC	App	214	38	5	1	2	15	60	12	21	3	1	177	.178	.233	.238	.167	10	52-3B -13
2001	Columbus	SAL	514	105	18	2	12	28	158	43	56	5	4	413	.204	.248	.317	.191	33	111-3B -19
2002	*Clevelnd*	*AL*	*461*	*106*	*19*	*2*	*13*	*36*	*147*	*45*	*57*	*7*	*3*	*358*	*.230*	*.286*	*.364*	*.215*	*38*	

A shortstop in high school, Smith has made a ridiculous 77 errors in two seasons as a third baseman, but the Indians nevertheless have no plans to move him. In fact, they're prone to praising his improvement. More worrisome is his pathetic performance at the plate. The scouts insist he has power; it's time to move him to left field and see if it develops.

Zach Sorensen SS Bats B Age 25

YEAR	TEAM	LGE	AB	H	DB	TP	HR	BB	SO	R	RBI	SB	CS	OUT	BA	OBP	SLG	EQA	EQR	DEFENSE
1999	Kinston	Car	525	108	16	4	6	44	126	61	44	13	8	425	.206	.268	.286	.194	35	129-SS 1
2000	Akron	Eas	388	90	16	2	6	32	64	50	30	11	5	303	.232	.292	.330	.215	32	96-SS 1
2000	Buffalo	Int	38	9	1	1	0	3	9	5	2	1	0	29	.237	.293	.316	.214	3	12-SS 3
2001	MahngVal	NYP	54	9	0	1	1	1	9	7	8	1	0	45	.167	.182	.259	.153	2	
2001	Akron	Eas	197	41	5	1	4	11	29	21	14	7	6	162	.208	.250	.305	.188	12	45-SS 2
2002	*Clevelnd*	*AL*	*456*	*116*	*18*	*3*	*9*	*41*	*85*	*65*	*46*	*10*	*5*	*345*	*.254*	*.316*	*.366*	*.229*	*43*	

Sorensen's career looked like it was grinding to a halt when the Indians gave him a shot in the Arizona Fall League. He reestablished himself as a prospect with a .371/.494/.532 line. He's probably a better player than John McDonald, not that either has much chance of a job. The Indians are no longer treating Sorensen and second-base prospect Scott Pratt as a unit; Pratt was moved to the outfield shortly before an injury ended his season.

Eddie Taubensee C Bats L Age 33

YEAR	TEAM	LGE	AB	H	DB	TP	HR	BB	SO	R	RBI	SB	CS	OUT	BA	OBP	SLG	EQA	EQR	DEFENSE
1999	Cincnnti	NL	424	129	22	1	21	24	62	56	81	0	2	297	.304	.343	.509	.276	59	108-C -11
2000	Cincnnti	NL	267	70	9	0	7	17	40	28	23	0	0	197	.262	.311	.375	.230	25	67-C -6
2001	Clevelnd	AL	116	31	3	1	3	10	16	17	11	0	0	85	.267	.329	.388	.242	12	28-C -4
2002	*Clevelnd*	*AL*	*350*	*95*	*15*	*1*	*12*	*28*	*55*	*43*	*47*	*0*	*1*	*256*	*.271*	*.325*	*.423*	*.247*	*39*	

He missed part of the season with a viral infection, and Einar Diaz played so well that Taubensee wasn't going to get many at-bats, anyway. His career is hanging by a thread, because he doesn't have the defensive reputation that gets most backup catchers their jobs, and he has dropped pretty deep into the pool of lefty-hitting backups who can pop a homer.

Jim Thome 1B Bats L Age 31

YEAR	TEAM	LGE	AB	H	DB	TP	HR	BB	SO	R	RBI	SB	CS	OUT	BA	OBP	SLG	EQA	EQR	DEFENSE
1999	Clevelnd	AL	485	138	28	2	34	121	150	99	104	0	0	347	.285	.431	.561	.325	105	105-1B 4
2000	Clevelnd	AL	546	149	29	1	39	110	150	101	101	1	0	397	.273	.399	.544	.308	105	104-1B -1
2001	Clevelnd	AL	528	161	24	1	54	113	160	108	130	0	1	368	.305	.430	.661	.343	127	142-1B -9
2002	*Clevelnd*	*AL*	*541*	*156*	*25*	*1*	*45*	*120*	*166*	*108*	*120*	*0*	*0*	*385*	*.288*	*.418*	*.588*	*.324*	*115*	

Reversing a mid-career decline, Jim Thome's 49-homer season gave him 282 at age 31. He should pass 400 home runs in 2004, and he has to be taken seriously as both a potential 500-homer man and a potential Hall of Fame candidate. His career OBP and career SLG are seventh and 15th among active players, respectively.

Thome, Frank Thomas, and Barry Bonds are probably the most extreme walkers in MLB. All three had terrible starts in 2001. Thomas suffered a season-ending injury, but Thome and Bonds went on to have their best years yet. Checking some other guys . . . Jason Giambi hit well in April . . . so did Edgar Martinez. It's probably not a group trait.

Omar Vizquel SS Bats B Age 35

YEAR	TEAM	LGE	AB	H	DB	TP	HR	BB	SO	R	RBI	SB	CS	OUT	BA	OBP	SLG	EQA	EQR	DEFENSE
1999	Clevelnd	AL	566	192	37	4	5	59	44	108	63	40	9	383	.339	.402	.445	.294	90	138-SS -7
2000	Clevelnd	AL	603	175	27	3	7	79	63	95	62	22	11	439	.290	.377	.380	.262	77	151-SS -4
2001	Clevelnd	AL	611	165	29	8	2	64	62	88	51	11	10	456	.270	.341	.354	.237	63	149-SS 0
2002	*Clevelnd*	*AL*	*539*	*151*	*29*	*4*	*5*	*70*	*56*	*84*	*52*	*15*	*9*	*396*	*.280*	*.363*	*.377*	*.253*	*64*	

His playing time and decent batting average are masking what is a massive decline over the past two seasons. Vizquel's .237 EqA in 2001 was his worst since 1993, and he's no longer the VacuSuck™ at shortstop that he was for so many years. Any rebuilding of the Tribe needs to start with moving this expensive, unproductive player.

PITCHERS (ERA: 4.50, H/9: 9.0, HR/9: 1.0, BB/9: 3.0, K/9: 6.0, KW: 2.0, PERA: 4.50)

Mike Bacsik Throws L Age 24

YEAR	TEAM	LGE	IP	H	ER	HR	BB	K	ERA	W	L	H/9	HR/9	BB/9	K/9	KW	PERA	STUFF
1999	Akron	Eas	147.0	180	116	35	47	59	7.10	5	11	11.0	2.1	2.9	3.6	0.6	5.78	-7
2000	Kinston	Car	66.7	73	34	9	9	32	4.59	3	4	9.9	1.2	1.2	4.3	1.8	6.94	3
2000	Akron	Eas	69.3	72	31	5	10	32	4.02	4	4	9.3	0.6	2.1	4.2	1.0	3.35	8
2000	Buffalo	Int	27.3	37	26	9	7	8	8.56	1	2	12.2	3.0	2.3	2.6	0.6	6.39	-19
2001	Akron	Eas	25.3	27	12	3	4	12	4.26	2	1	9.6	1.1	1.4	4.3	1.5	3.10	7
2001	Buffalo	Int	118.3	128	64	17	28	62	4.87	6	7	9.7	1.3	2.1	4.7	1.1	3.87	5
2001	Clevelnd	AL	10.3	10	4	0	3	4	3.48	1	0	8.7	0.0	2.6	3.5	0.7	8.96	-10

Bacsik is a command left-hander dealt to the Mets as part of the Roberto Alomar deal. He's not ready for the majors yet, which is good, because the Mets need another command lefty in the rotation like they need to hear another plane take off. As pitchers in this class go, Bacsik is a good one. He just needs to end up in front of a good defense to be successful.

Danny Baez Throws R Age 24

YEAR	TEAM	LGE	IP	H	ER	HR	BB	K	ERA	W	L	H/9	HR/9	BB/9	K/9	KW	PERA	STUFF
2000	Kinston	Car	48.0	54	38	12	23	32	7.13	1	4	10.1	2.3	4.3	6.0	0.7	7.31	-4
2000	Akron	Eas	102.7	106	52	10	34	56	4.56	5	6	9.3	0.9	3.0	4.9	0.8	4.65	7
2001	Buffalo	Int	24.3	22	11	3	10	23	4.07	2	1	8.1	1.1	3.7	8.5	1.1	3.55	14
2001	Clevelnd	AL	48.7	41	20	5	19	49	3.70	3	2	7.6	0.9	3.5	9.1	1.3	3.53	19

Not all Cuban imports are immediate successes or abject failures. Baez looked like the latter for a while, but he emerged as the Indians' best reliever in the second half of 2001. There will be pressure to put him into the rotation, although his best chance of success lies with a year of setup relief.

Dave Burba Throws R Age 35

YEAR	TEAM	LGE	IP	H	ER	HR	BB	K	ERA	W	L	H/9	HR/9	BB/9	K/9	KW	PERA	STUFF
1999	Clevelnd	AL	222.7	215	110	26	80	172	4.45	13	12	8.7	1.1	3.2	7.0	1.1	3.86	15
2000	Clevelnd	AL	202.3	179	84	16	74	178	3.74	13	9	8.0	0.7	3.3	7.9	1.2	3.76	24
2001	Clevelnd	AL	164.0	159	74	14	51	112	4.06	10	8	8.7	0.8	2.8	6.1	1.1	6.00	7

Burba's peripherals declined in 2001, but not nearly by as much as his ERA would have you believe. He suffered more than anyone from the decline of the Indians' defense due to injuries and age. Signing with the Rangers—a shaky defensive team in a hitters' park—doesn't bode well for Burba, who would have been a sleeper fantasy pick in a different environment.

Bartolo Colon Throws R Age 27

YEAR	TEAM	LGE	IP	H	ER	HR	BB	K	ERA	W	L	H/9	HR/9	BB/9	K/9	KW	PERA	STUFF
1999	Clevelnd	AL	205.3	195	92	21	63	159	4.03	13	10	8.5	0.9	2.8	7.0	1.3	3.55	20
2000	Clevelnd	AL	193.0	158	79	18	80	210	3.68	13	8	7.4	0.8	3.7	9.8	1.3	3.32	34
2001	Clevelnd	AL	229.0	212	106	24	86	191	4.17	13	12	8.3	0.9	3.4	7.5	1.1	3.85	19

Colon, who has been a very good pitcher for four years, seems destined to suffer the fate of someone like Darryl Strawberry, never appreciated for what he is, perpetually scorned for not living up to expectations. Yes, he could stand to lose a few pounds; then again, so much of his power is generated by his heavy legs that perhaps his doing so would be counterproductive.

Do you think we recognize the biggest moments of our lives as they're happening? It's hard not to think about how much different Colon's life might be had Charlie Manuel relieved him just a little sooner in Game Four of the AL Division Series. Maybe Ricardo Rincon gets out Ichiro, and the Mariners don't take the lead. Maybe the Indians win the game, and with it the series, with Colon as the hero. Maybe Colon sheds the underachiever label for the happier ones that the media likes to distribute in October. You think he knows?

Jose Colon Throws R Age 24

YEAR	TEAM	LGE	IP	H	ER	HR	BB	K	ERA	W	L	H/9	HR/9	BB/9	K/9	KW	PERA	STUFF
1999	BlngtnNC	App	22.3	30	27	10	8	12	10.88	0	2	12.1	4.0	3.2	4.8	0.8	6.57	-29
2000	Columbus	SAL	30.3	31	15	3	11	15	4.45	2	1	9.2	0.9	3.3	4.5	0.7	3.05	-12
2000	Kinston	Car	19.3	26	21	7	9	9	9.78	0	2	12.1	3.3	4.2	4.2	0.5	13.44	-46
2001	Columbus	SAL	46.3	58	37	13	10	21	7.19	1	4	11.3	2.5	1.9	4.1	1.0	5.33	-31

Bartolo's brother served as Kinston's closer last year, racking up 22 saves. He doesn't have his brother's power, relying instead on good control of two breaking pitches. Minor-league closers are generally non-prospects, especially ones who can't strike out a man per inning in the Carolina League. Colon's name will get him an extra chance or two; it's unlikely that it will get him a career.

Dan Denham Throws R Age 19

YEAR	TEAM	LGE	IP	H	ER	HR	BB	K	ERA	W	L	H/9	HR/9	BB/9	K/9	KW	PERA	STUFF
2001	BlngtnNC	App	28.3	41	52	13	39	12	16.52	0	3	13.0	4.1	12.4	3.8	0.2	9.94	-48

After many years of losing their high picks, the Indians had four of the first 43 selections in the 2001 draft. Denham was their highest at #17, a high-school right-hander from Northern California. His command of a fastball/curveball combo didn't overwhelm the Appy League, but he was named the league's #2 prospect anyway. File away the name, and check back in 2004.

Ryan Drese Throws R Age 26

YEAR	TEAM	LGE	IP	H	ER	HR	BB	K	ERA	W	L	H/9	HR/9	BB/9	K/9	KW	PERA	STUFF
1999	MahngVal	NYP	15.0	16	12	3	10	11	7.20	1	1	9.6	1.8	6.0	6.6	0.6	4.93	-16
1999	Columbus	SAL	10.7	14	13	4	6	7	10.97	0	1	11.8	3.4	5.1	5.9	0.6	6.60	-23
1999	Kinston	Car	65.3	63	47	5	64	42	6.47	2	5	8.7	0.7	8.8	5.8	0.3	8.99	-23
2001	Akron	Eas	80.3	83	47	7	43	41	5.27	4	5	9.3	0.8	4.8	4.6	0.5	5.40	-12
2001	Buffalo	Int	60.0	65	38	10	22	35	5.70	3	4	9.8	1.5	3.3	5.3	0.8	5.20	-7
2001	Clevelnd	AL	36.3	35	16	2	14	23	3.96	2	2	8.7	0.5	3.5	5.7	0.8	3.30	5

Drese bounced back nicely after losing the 2000 season when he blew out his ACL covering first base in his first start. While he did pitch well out of the bullpen in September for the Tribe, he's best-suited for starting. If he can just stay healthy—not his strong suit—he can be a good mid-rotation starter.

Tim Drew Throws R Age 23

YEAR	TEAM	LGE	IP	H	ER	HR	BB	K	ERA	W	L	H/9	HR/9	BB/9	K/9	KW	PERA	STUFF
1999	Kinston	Car	163.3	184	107	25	66	73	5.90	7	11	10.1	1.4	3.6	4.0	0.6	5.49	0
2000	Akron	Eas	49.3	52	22	2	16	16	4.01	3	2	9.5	0.4	2.9	2.9	0.5	3.80	0
2000	Buffalo	Int	100.7	113	60	15	30	45	5.36	5	6	10.1	1.3	2.7	4.0	0.8	6.73	0
2000	Clevelnd	AL	11.0	12	7	1	7	5	5.73	0	1	9.8	0.8	5.7	4.1	0.4	9.68	-18
2001	Clevelnd	AL	37.7	46	30	8	15	14	7.17	1	3	11.0	1.9	3.6	3.3	0.5	8.99	-21
2001	Buffalo	Int	108.3	118	63	17	30	58	5.23	5	7	9.8	1.4	2.5	4.8	1.0	4.99	6

Here's hoping the Indians haven't screwed up Tim Drew beyond repair. In 2000, a 21-year-old Drew with about 11 minutes of experience above A ball was brought up to patch the never-ending problems at the back of the Tribe's major-league rotation, and he was hammered in three starts. Last year, the Indians plopped him in the rotation to start the season; he got hammered again and spent the rest of the season shuttling between Cleveland and Buffalo. Drew hasn't pitched all that well at Triple-A yet; until he does, the Tribe needs to stop asking him to be their savior.

This kind of mishandling is one of the hidden costs of waiting on Jaret Wright and Charles Nagy, whose presence prevented the Indians from committing to a real solution at the back of the rotation. The plan was always, "Wait 'til Chuck and Jaret are ready." If they'd just given up on those two and picked up some innings-muncher, Drew might be ready by now, and the Indians might well have met a different fate the past two years.

Chuck Finley   Throws L   Age 39

YEAR	TEAM	LGE	IP	H	ER	HR	BB	K	ERA	W	L	H/9	HR/9	BB/9	K/9	KW	PERA	STUFF
1999	Anaheim	AL	218.3	194	83	20	78	198	3.69	14	10	8.0	.8	3.2	8.2	1.3	3.42	24
2000	Clevelnd	AL	224.7	205	87	19	83	187	3.20	14	11	8.2	.8	3.3	7.5	1.1	3.49	21
2001	Clevelnd	AL	121.3	116	48	13	33	91	4.92	7	6	8.6	1.0	2.4	6.8	1.4	3.56	13

Like Dave Burba's year, Chuck Finley's performance reflected the declining Indians' defense as much as it reflected his own poor pitching. Minor owies are beginning to crop up; he's nearing the end but can still help a team willing to work around the injuries. For 150 innings, he can be a very good pitcher.

Alex Herrera   Throws L   Age 22

YEAR	TEAM	LGE	IP	H	ER	HR	BB	K	ERA	W	L	H/9	HR/9	BB/9	K/9	KW	PERA	STUFF
2000	Columbus	SAL	43.0	43	24	2	27	21	5.02	2	3	9.0	0.4	5.7	4.4	0.4	7.04	-12
2000	Kinston	Car	31.7	29	17	2	21	24	4.83	2	2	8.2	0.6	6.0	6.8	0.6	4.27	5
2001	Kinston	Car	57.0	49	22	2	24	48	3.47	4	2	7.7	0.3	3.8	7.6	1.0	1.34	19
2001	Akron	Eas	27.7	28	13	1	11	14	4.23	2	1	9.1	0.3	3.6	4.6	0.6	3.64	-2

Looking for talent everywhere is the sign of a good organization. Herrera is a product of the Indians' efforts in Venezuela. A short flamethrower with a developing slider, he was awesome at Kinston before dropping off—but still pitching well—at Double-A Akron. With the way the Indians go through pitchers at the back of the staff, it would not be surprising to see Herrera in the majors this year, but he won't be ready for the job for another season at least.

J.D. Martin   Throws R   Age 19

YEAR	TEAM	LGE	IP	H	ER	HR	BB	K	ERA	W	L	H/9	HR/9	BB/9	K/9	KW	PERA	STUFF
2001	BlngtnNC	App	41.3	44	27	8	16	28	5.88	2	3	9.6	1.7	3.5	6.1	0.9	2.86	14

Martin, the Indians' second pick in the 2001 draft, might have had the most impressive debut of any pitcher selected. He threw two no-hitters and had a five-inning, no-hit, 14-strikeout outing. He doesn't project as well as Denham—his fastball isn't as good—but his change-up made him death on young Appy League hitters. Like Denham, he's a long way off, and his lack of a major heater will be a bigger problem at higher levels.

Charles Nagy   Throws R   Age 35

YEAR	TEAM	LGE	IP	H	ER	HR	BB	K	ERA	W	L	H/9	HR/9	BB/9	K/9	KW	PERA	STUFF
1999	Clevelnd	AL	213.3	219	100	22	49	125	4.22	13	11	9.2	0.9	2.1	5.3	1.3	4.46	9
2000	Clevelnd	AL	60.0	66	39	13	17	41	5.85	3	4	9.9	2.0	2.6	6.2	1.2	6.75	0
2001	Buffalo	Int	39.3	40	15	0	11	12	3.43	3	1	9.2	0.0	2.5	2.7	0.5	3.50	-2
2001	Clevelnd	AL	77.3	87	42	9	19	28	4.89	4	5	10.1	1.0	2.2	3.3	0.7	6.08	-10

Just one more year before this saga can be put to rest. Nagy has no cartilage left in his right elbow. While it appears he can occasionally work around this problem and the pain it creates, he's not able to sustain effectiveness over multiple outings. A buyout of the last year of his contract, allowing him to retire, would be the best solution for both him and the team.

Ricardo Rincon   Throws L   Age 32

YEAR	TEAM	LGE	IP	H	ER	HR	BB	K	ERA	W	L	H/9	HR/9	BB/9	K/9	KW	PERA	STUFF
1999	Clevelnd	AL	44.3	45	25	5	20	30	5.08	2	3	9.1	1.0	4.1	6.1	0.8	3.70	-8
2000	Clevelnd	AL	20.3	17	8	1	11	20	3.54	1	1	7.5	0.4	4.9	8.9	0.9	2.54	11
2001	Clevelnd	AL	54.0	46	20	3	20	48	3.33	4	2	7.7	0.5	3.3	8.0	1.2	2.69	11

Like we said a few years ago, this was a great deal for... OK, that's a lost cause. For the first time since being acquired for Brian Giles, though, Rincon made a real contribution to the Indians. By Adjusted Runs Prevented, he was the fourth-best left-handed reliever in baseball last year. He's decades from retirement.

David Riske **Throws R** **Age 25**

YEAR	TEAM	LGE	IP	H	ER	HR	BB	K	ERA	W	L	H/9	HR/9	BB/9	K/9	KW	PERA	STUFF
1999	Akron	Eas	20.3	16	9	1	13	23	3.98	1	1	7.1	0.4	5.8	10.2	0.9	2.60	23
1999	Buffalo	Int	25.3	22	8	0	7	18	2.84	2	1	7.8	0.0	2.5	6.4	1.3	0.93	15
1999	Clevelnd	AL	16.3	14	7	2	5	16	3.86	1	1	7.7	1.1	2.8	8.8	1.6	8.05	15
2001	Buffalo	Int	54.3	45	19	3	20	53	3.15	4	2	7.5	0.5	3.3	8.8	1.3	3.12	16
2001	Clevelnd	AL	26.7	23	14	3	17	28	4.72	1	2	7.8	1.0	5.7	9.4	0.8	2.07	12

Riske missed almost all of 2000 with a shoulder injury. Like Ryan Drese, he came back to perform about as well as he had before. The performances of Riske and Danys Baez meant that the Indians were essentially unharmed by their decision to trade Steve Reed and Steve Karsay for...

John Rocker **Throws L** **Age 27**

YEAR	TEAM	LGE	IP	H	ER	HR	BB	K	ERA	W	L	H/9	HR/9	BB/9	K/9	KW	PERA	STUFF
1999	Atlanta	NL	72.0	51	24	5	31	94	3.00	6	2	6.4	0.6	3.9	11.8	1.5	2.76	35
2000	Atlanta	NL	54.3	41	26	4	40	68	4.31	3	3	6.8	0.7	6.6	11.3	0.9	3.91	17
2001	Atlanta	NL	30.7	26	12	2	14	29	3.52	2	1	7.6	0.6	4.1	8.5	1.0	3.69	11
2001	Clevelnd	AL	37.0	28	16	2	24	41	3.89	2	2	6.8	0.5	5.8	10.0	0.9	5.35	12

With the bad trades the contenders made, it's a wonder anybody won the AL Central. After arriving in Cleveland, Rocker went from closer candidate to mop-up man in about three weeks, and while the line above looks OK, his ARP with the Tribe was −3.4.

To the amusement of the mainstream media, Rocker was traded to the Texas Rangers in December, joined shortly thereafter by Carl Everett. The rush to analyze the potential ramifications of two so-called "bad guys" sharing a postgame spread was sports journalism at its worst, nothing but speculation and innuendo, stuff better fit for the gossip page of a New York tabloid. Both players will help the Rangers, maybe even all the way into October.

Rich Rodriguez **Throws L** **Age 39**

YEAR	TEAM	LGE	IP	H	ER	HR	BB	K	ERA	W	L	H/9	HR/9	BB/9	K/9	KW	PERA	STUFF
1999	San Fran	NL	58.0	59	32	8	23	40	4.97	3	3	9.2	1.2	3.6	6.2	0.9	5.05	-8
2000	NY Mets	NL	41.7	48	26	6	12	16	5.62	2	3	10.4	1.3	2.6	3.5	0.7	9.31	-28
2001	Clevelnd	AL	41.0	37	17	2	16	29	3.73	3	2	8.1	0.4	3.5	6.4	0.9	4.96	-1

The fourth-best bullpen in baseball was a big reason why the Indians were able to win the division despite a rotation that pushed them away from, not towards, a title. Rodriguez, released by the Mets at the end of March, held left-handed batters to a 504 OPS in a spot role while mixing in some mop-up relief. Why pay more?

C.C. Sabathia **Throws L** **Age 21**

YEAR	TEAM	LGE	IP	H	ER	HR	BB	K	ERA	W	L	H/9	HR/9	BB/9	K/9	KW	PERA	STUFF
1999	MahngVal	NYP	18.0	16	10	0	16	13	5.00	1	1	8.0	0.0	8.0	6.5	0.4	3.14	9
1999	Columbus	SAL	15.0	15	9	2	7	10	5.40	1	1	9.0	1.2	4.2	6.0	0.7	1.40	20
1999	Kinston	Car	31.0	35	26	6	21	17	7.55	1	2	10.2	1.7	6.1	4.9	0.4	8.07	-5
2000	Kinston	Car	55.0	56	35	9	26	41	5.73	2	4	9.2	1.5	4.3	6.7	0.8	4.94	18
2000	Akron	Eas	88.7	87	53	10	51	65	5.38	4	6	8.8	1.0	5.2	6.6	0.6	4.72	17
2001	Clevelnd	AL	179.3	160	88	17	90	163	4.42	10	10	8.0	0.9	4.5	8.2	0.9	4.16	28

The single best thing Charlie Manuel did all season was handle C.C. Sabathia wisely. He identified the 20-year-old as the team's best option for the #5 rotation slot, stayed with the rookie when he pitched poorly in May, and didn't overwork him during the surprisingly tight pennant race. Sabathia, for his part, dramatically improved his command as the season progressed, enabling him to work deeper into games.

The most important thing to remember is that Sabathia, while having a full year under his belt, is still just 21. There's no guarantee that he will pitch well in 2002. If he does pitch well, it will again be up to Manuel to use him wisely. The Indians' depth from the right side of the bullpen gives him the luxury of doing so.

Paul Shuey — Throws R — Age 31

YEAR	TEAM	LGE	IP	H	ER	HR	BB	K	ERA	W	L	H/9	HR/9	BB/9	K/9	KW	PERA	STUFF
1999	Clevelnd	AL	84.3	64	30	7	33	102	3.20	6	3	6.8	0.7	3.5	10.9	1.5	3.40	27
2000	Clevelnd	AL	64.7	51	22	3	25	68	3.06	5	2	7.1	0.4	3.5	9.5	1.4	2.85	21
2001	Clevelnd	AL	59.0	43	17	1	25	67	2.59	5	2	6.6	0.2	3.8	10.2	1.3	3.71	26

Shuey, who just keeps getting better, missed much of the summer with a strained elbow. The Tribe re-signed Bob Wickman, a waste of money for a team with a reliever as good as Shuey on the roster and with the depth to back him up during his annual constitutionals. He's made nine trips to the DL in his career, so with his first trip this year he gets the free arthroscopic surgery.

Roy Smith — Throws R — Age 26

YEAR	TEAM	LGE	IP	H	ER	HR	BB	K	ERA	W	L	H/9	HR/9	BB/9	K/9	KW	PERA	STUFF
2000	Kinston	Car	44.0	42	21	0	28	22	4.30	3	2	8.6	0.0	5.7	4.5	0.4	4.91	-23
2000	Akron	Eas	52.3	48	21	0	26	32	3.61	4	2	8.3	0.0	4.5	5.5	0.6	2.99	-6
2001	Buffalo	Int	73.3	65	31	3	37	59	3.80	5	3	8.0	0.4	4.5	7.2	0.8	3.81	-2
2001	Clevelnd	AL	16.7	16	11	3	12	16	5.94	1	1	8.6	1.6	6.5	8.6	0.7	6.93	-5

Baseball's version of Kurt Warner was bagging groceries just two years ago. A stint with the St. Paul Saints led to a job in the Indians' system, and his sidearm delivery took over from there. He gets ground balls and enough strikeouts to be dangerous. What he needs is a team that doesn't have power arms in every nook and cranny of the bullpen.

Brian Tallet — Throws L — Age 24

YEAR	TEAM	LGE	IP	H	ER	HR	BB	K	ERA	W	L	H/9	HR/9	BB/9	K/9	KW	PERA	STUFF
2000	MahngVal	NYP	15.0	14	5	0	4	10	3.00	1	1	8.4	0.0	2.4	6.0	1.3	1.71	11
2001	Kinston	Car	151.3	172	109	31	58	84	6.48	6	11	10.2	1.8	3.4	5.0	0.7	5.82	-8

The Kinston pitching staff that helped win Victor Martinez an MVP award was home to most of the Tribe's best pitching prospects. Tallet is a tall drink of water out of LSU who gets into the 90s and mixes in a slider. The decision to leave him at Kinston all year was conservative, but he could jump forward in a hurry in 2002.

In addition to Tallet and Alex Herrera, Kyle Denney and Shane Wallace both pitched well for Kinston. Unfortunately, both also were shut down due to injuries and subsequently underwent Tommy John surgery. Friends, there really is no such thing as a pitching prospect.

Jake Westbrook — Throws R — Age 24

YEAR	TEAM	LGE	IP	H	ER	HR	BB	K	ERA	W	L	H/9	HR/9	BB/9	K/9	KW	PERA	STUFF
1999	Harrisbg	Eas	173.7	194	102	20	63	63	5.29	8	11	10.1	1.0	3.3	3.3	0.5	4.93	-2
2000	Columbus	Int	92.7	90	40	4	37	52	3.88	6	4	8.7	0.4	3.6	5.1	0.7	5.60	9
2001	Buffalo	Int	64.3	63	29	3	26	35	4.06	4	3	8.8	0.4	3.6	4.9	0.7	4.17	6
2001	Clevelnd	AL	70.0	68	31	5	21	46	3.99	4	4	8.7	0.6	2.7	5.9	1.1	5.36	5

Recalled in late May, Westbrook was doing wonderfully in relief, finally looking like he was ready to stay in the major leagues: 20 innings, a 2.75 ERA, good peripherals, and, best of all, he actually looked comfortable after a couple of years of bouncing around. The Indians tried to use him as a starter again and he collapsed, making six starts, each one a bit worse than the last. The Tribe needs starters more than they need relievers, and Westbrook is still the best solution for the #5 rotation slot.

Bob Wickman — Throws R — Age 33

YEAR	TEAM	LGE	IP	H	ER	HR	BB	K	ERA	W	L	H/9	HR/9	BB/9	K/9	KW	PERA	STUFF
1999	Milwauke	NL	76.7	72	35	6	32	54	4.11	5	4	8.5	0.7	3.8	6.3	0.8	3.42	-1
2000	Milwauke	NL	46.3	39	15	1	16	39	2.91	4	1	7.6	0.2	3.1	7.6	1.2	3.20	12
2000	Clevelnd	AL	27.3	27	11	0	10	11	3.62	2	1	8.9	0.0	3.3	3.6	0.6	3.26	-12
2001	Clevelnd	AL	69.7	59	21	4	13	63	2.71	6	2	7.6	0.5	1.7	8.1	2.4	2.14	19

Like Jeff Shaw, Todd Jones, and Jason Isringhausen, Bob Wickman owes his livelihood to Jerome Holtzman, whose save statistic drives perceptions of value, usage patterns, and salary negotiations. Wickman is a credible relief pitcher who, by dint of being in the right place at the right time for a bad team, picked up a "closer" label that sticks like popcorn in your teeth. The Tribe's aging infield defense is going to hurt Wickman as much as anyone on the staff.

Steve Woodard Throws R Age 27

YEAR	TEAM	LGE	IP	H	ER	HR	BB	K	ERA	W	L	H/9	HR/9	BB/9	K/9	KW	PERA	STUFF
1999	Milwauke	NL	194.3	203	88	21	30	107	4.08	12	10	9.4	1.0	1.4	5.0	1.8	4.47	10
2000	Milwauke	NL	101.7	108	55	14	27	58	4.87	5	6	9.6	1.2	2.4	5.1	1.1	6.11	-4
2000	Clevelnd	AL	54.7	58	28	8	9	35	4.61	3	3	9.5	1.3	1.5	5.8	1.9	4.70	5
2001	Clevelnd	AL	105.7	111	46	9	16	49	3.92	7	5	9.5	0.8	1.4	4.2	1.5	4.91	-2
2001	Buffalo	Int	37.7	38	13	3	1	22	3.11	3	1	9.1	0.7	0.2	5.3	11.0	3.29	15

Frank Thomas didn't do much last season, but he sure ruined Woodard's year. The Big Hurt roped a line drive off Woodard's elbow, sending him to the disabled list right at the point where he was in position to reestablish himself. He's still capable of being a #4 starter, but he needs the support of a good defense and a bullpen that can cover his inability to go deep into games. He's a free agent, and a steal waiting to happen.

Jaret Wright Throws R Age 26

YEAR	TEAM	LGE	IP	H	ER	HR	BB	K	ERA	W	L	H/9	HR/9	BB/9	K/9	KW	PERA	STUFF
1999	Clevelnd	AL	138.3	139	77	16	64	90	5.01	7	8	9.0	1.0	4.2	5.9	0.7	5.56	4
2000	Clevelnd	AL	50.7	49	26	5	23	36	4.62	3	3	8.7	0.9	4.1	6.4	0.8	3.79	11
2001	Buffalo	Int	27.7	29	19	4	17	19	6.18	1	2	9.4	1.3	5.5	6.2	0.6	7.07	-17
2001	Clevelnd	AL	31.3	31	18	2	21	17	5.17	1	2	8.9	0.6	6.0	4.9	0.4	6.40	-12

The shoulder surgery that cut short his 2000 season didn't fix the problem, so the Indians went through most of another season waiting and hoping and watching. Wright was briefly healthy and effective—for about four starts—before disappearing for good in August with more shoulder woes. We've said it before: he needs to take a year off, let everything heal, then try to come back.

Detroit Tigers

It says a lot about the Detroit Tigers that they recently enjoyed their best moment since they swept the Blue Jays to clinch the AL East in 1987. That moment occurred in November, when they gave a five-year contract to a 45-year-old free agent who has never played pro baseball and generally wears a suit to work.

Such is the state of the Tigers that their most pressing need wasn't on the field, but in the front office. The Bermuda Triangle of management—Mike Illitch, Randy Smith, and Phil Garner—had succeeded only in marooning the team. The Detroit Tigers are the second-most storied franchise in the American League, having never suffered through more than four losing seasons in a row. They're now working on a string of eight.

Tigers Prospectus

2001 record: 66-96; Fourth place, AL Central

Pythagenport W/L: 66-96

Runs scored: 724 (11th in AL)

Runs allowed: 876 (12th in AL)

Team EqA: .251 (tenth in AL)

2001 batters age: 27.9 (tied for third-youngest in AL)

2001 pitchers age: 28.2 (fifth-oldest in AL)

Ballpark: Comerica Park; slight pitchers' park; Park Factor of .990

2001: Tried their damndest to disprove the idea that a new park leads to on-field success.

2002: This won't be a good year, but the turnaround is coming now that Dave Dombrowski is on board and their drafting has improved.

Desperate times call for Dave Dombrowski. In luring Dombrowski away from the Marlins, Illitch deserves credit for finally admitting what had been apparent for years: the Tigers are broken, and no one in the organization knows how to fix them. After a decade of being led by football coaches, the sons of other GMs, and last year's cockamamie "advisory committee," (whose main standard for qualification was that you had to have been an All-Star for the Tigers in the 1960s), it is refreshing that they now have an executive in place who actually has experience building a winning franchise.

Don't be fooled by the mediocre overall record of Dombrowski's teams: he is one of the great GMs of the past ten years. His crowning achievement, the 1997 world champion Florida Marlins, is remembered only for its shameful dismantling. Dombrowski has spent his entire career with two of the most difficult franchises of our generation, the Marlins and the Expos. He not only built a championship team from the ground up in five years, but laid the groundwork for the 1994 Expos team that had the best record in baseball when the strike began.

Dombrowski's greatest asset may be his versatility. Some general managers, such as John Hart, have a proven aptitude for the rebuilding process, but they lose patience when the team is ready to compete and start trading Brian Giles for left-handed relievers. Others, such as Brian Sabean, have an uncanny knack for keeping a team in contention by merging unsung veteran talent with Dusty Baker, but they have shown precious little ability to complement those veterans with young talent from within their system.

Dombrowski has done both. In the 1992 expansion draft, a process which has provided little real talent for any new team, Dombrowski picked up Trevor Hoffman, Bryan Harvey, and the real prize, Jeff Conine. In the Rule 5 draft two years later, he acquired Matt Mantei.

He has also shown a knack for converting such hard-won talent into even more valuable commodities. Hoffman was sent to San Diego for Gary Sheffield, giving the first-year Marlins a true superstar hitter. John Burkett was traded for Rick Helling and Ryan Dempster. Journeyman reliever Cris Carpenter, also acquired in the expansion draft, was traded a few months later for Robb Nen. Mantei, after being nurtured into a promising closer, was traded for Brad Penny.

Dombrowski's track record on the free-agent market may be the most impressive line on his resume, given how little practice he has had in that arena. Dombrowski has had only one real opportunity to be an active player in free agency, after the 1995 season, when Wayne Huizenga opened his wallet to finance a winning team. Dombrowski signed Al Leiter and Kevin Brown. Both signings look obvious in retrospect, but at the time Leiter was a 30-year-old left-hander with one of the longest DL rap sheets in the majors, had never recorded more than 11 wins, and had just led the AL in walks allowed. Brown, also 30, had gone 17-18 with a 4.21 ERA the previous two seasons.

The following winter, Dombrowski splurged on six free agents, and all six paid dividends. Moises Alou, Bobby Bonilla, Alex Fernandez, Dennis Cook, Jim Eisenreich, and John Cangelosi each played an integral role in the team's championship, and only Fernandez, who after winning 17 games blew out his rotator cuff, proved to be an unwise investment. In the history of free agency, only Pat Gillick's recent tenure with the Mariners rivals Dombrowski's uncanny run of success in identifying players who would keep their value, while staying clear of the turkeys.

That he was then forced to disband the team in the most disgraceful fire sale in 80 years should not tarnish Dombrowski's reputation. On the contrary, it should enhance it. Forced to start from scratch for the second time in five years, he rebuilt the franchise into a competitive team once again, a team that could very well win the NL East this season.

Dombrowski's ability to build a winner out of nothing is clear. What's not clear is whether he will be given the authority to do so in Detroit. His official title—President and CEO—is imposing, but it's the title he doesn't have that is worrisome. Randy Smith is still the general manager, and as long as he is, Dombrowski's influence is going to be diluted, and the potential for serious front-office discord will loom over the Tigers.

The Tigers have given no indication as to how responsibilities will be divided between the two, but there is a way to make it work. For all of Randy Smith's critical faults as the Tigers' GM—and lord, there are many—he has shown one useful skill: the ability to build a farm system. Let's not forget the depths to which the Tigers' minor-league system had descended at the time Smith arrived from San Diego. Aside from Travis Fryman, the organization had not developed a single everyday player in nearly a decade, and the system was nearly bare. The team had just blown its last four #1 picks on Rick Greene, Matt Brunson, Cade Gaspar, and Mike Drumright.

Smith did inherit some late-round finds, such as Gabe Kapler, Frank Catalanotto, and Daryle Ward, and he added to them in his first year by selecting Rob Fick. Then, in 1998, the Tigers struck gold. They drafted Jeff Weaver in the first round, and if you can come up with a Jeff Weaver every five years, you'll come out ahead no matter how bad your other first-round picks are. But there was more; with their next pick they grabbed Nate Cornejo, who is now their finest pitching prospect. In the second round, the Tigers drafted Brandon Inge and Adam Pettyjohn; late last year, the first three pitchers the team drafted in 1998 made up three-fifths of the Tigers' rotation.

If they struck gold in 1998, though, the Tigers may have found platinum last year. Spurred by one of the most college-player-heavy draft strategies of recent times (their first 11 picks were college players), the Tigers cleaned up. Kenny Baugh, who like Weaver was a college senior that overpowered the low minors in his debut, may arrive as quickly as Weaver did. Baugh is just the foam on the ocean; you have to go down to the Tigers' eighth selection to find a player who wasn't impressive in his first pro season.

Smith's weakness isn't that he's been unable to scout amateur talent; it's that he doesn't know what to do next. But restricted to a carefully defined role, as the de jure GM but the de facto farm director, Smith can be a nice complement for Dombrowski, whose biggest weakness is probably that he hasn't done a particularly good job drafting amateur players. The Marlins have produced some quality players, guys such as Edgar Renteria, Charles Johnson, Livan Hernandez, Luis Castillo, and Mark Kotsay, along with future studs such as Josh Beckett and Adrian Gonzalez. But over a span of nearly a decade, that isn't particularly noteworthy, especially when you consider how high the Marlins were drafting during much of that time. Johnson, Kotsay, Beckett, and Gonzalez were all first-round picks; all but Johnson were top-ten selections. For that matter, so was Josh Booty.

In Detroit, Dombrowski has the luxury of not having to worry about the draft. The Tigers have built the farm system in preparation for his arrival; all he needs to do is convert that talent into the framework of a major-league team. If Dombrowski is willing to let Smith use the strengths that he brings to the table, and if Smith is willing to accept that reduced role, their partnership may not only be harmonious, but symbiotic.

Even before Dombrowski was brought on board, the order had been given to completely clean house. Roger Cedeno, who had been offered a three-year deal during the season, will not be back. Juan Encarnacion was dealt to the Reds for Dmitri Young. Chris Holt and Deivi Cruz were released. Tony Clark, who was not part of the problem but was also deemed not part of the solution, was unceremoniously waived and claimed by the Red Sox.

While the addition of Dombrowski augurs well for the team in the long term, the short-term outlook can be brightened considerably by one simple step: upgrade the defense. The Tigers were brutal in the field last year; Encarnacion, Cruz, and Cedeno were among the worst defenders in baseball at their positions.

There is a way to measure the Tigers' defensive inadequacies. In *Baseball Prospectus 2001*, we discussed Voros McCracken's theory that pitchers have minimal impact on their defense's ability to turn balls in play into outs. Left unsaid was the notion that this stat—batting average on balls in play, or (H-HR)/(AB-HR-K)—can be used to measure a team's defensive ability. Bill James pioneered this concept in the mid-1980s, calling the statistic "Defensive Efficiency," though he used the reciprocal (i.e., if a team allowed a .280 batting average on balls in play, their Defensive Efficiency was .720).

Table 1 lists the Defensive Efficiency of all the teams in the American League. In addition, each team's ballpark effect is calculated by determining the DE for both teams in their home park compared to road games. For example, the Tigers

Table 1.

Team	DE	PF	Adjusted DE
Cleveland Indians	.6772	-.0010	.6777
Detroit Tigers	.6854	+.0055	.6826
Texas Rangers	.6806	-.0077	.6845
New York Yankees	.6934	+.0162	.6853
Toronto Blue Jays	.6876	-.0046	.6899
Baltimore Orioles	.7067	+.0139	.6997
Oakland Athletics	.7125	+.0234	.7008
Boston Red Sox	.6946	-.0135	.7014
Tampa Bay Devil Rays	.6968	-.0133	.7035
Chicago White Sox	.7086	+.0092	.7040
Kansas City Royals	.7013	-.0218	.7122
Anaheim Angels	.7091	-.0077	.7130
Minnesota Twins	.7054	-.0156	.7132
Seattle Mariners	.7052	+.0100	.7262
American League			.6999

and their opponents combined for a DE of .7012 at Comerica Park and .6957 on the road. So the Tigers' park factor is +.0055, and the team's adjusted DE is calculated by subtracting half the park factor.

This study is compelling. The defensive excellence of the Twins is verified, while the declining defense of the Yankees as they age is made clear. The Mariners are so far in front of everyone else that it's almost eerie, and the gap contributes to the sense that their remarkable success last year practically defies explanation.

And there the Tigers are, second only to the Indians as the worst defensive team in the AL.

The problem is probably worse than it looks. For starters, the Tigers employ Steve Sparks, one of only two knuckleballers in the AL. While much research on this subject remains to be done, there is evidence that knuckleball pitchers tend to have lower DE ratings than other pitchers. Sparks' DE rating was just .7083; subtract him from the Tigers' numbers and their adjusted DE inches up to .6781. Furthermore, while the Indians' defensive inadequacies were muted somewhat by a pitching staff that relied on the strikeout, the Tigers struck out just 859 batters, the fewest in the league, meaning there were more balls in play for their defense to screw up.

Depending on whether you count Sparks or not, the Tigers surrendered between 80 and 100 more hits than the league average. Converting 80-100 hits into outs is worth, conservatively, 50 to 70 runs. That's five or seven extra games the Tigers can add to their win total simply by upgrading to a league-average defense.

It's true that teams, on the whole, overrate the importance of a good defense. The flip side is that it is much easier to upgrade a bad defense than to upgrade poor pitching or an anemic lineup. There's truth to the statement that if you shake a tree, a dozen gloves will fall out. While the Tigers have several prospects, notably Omar Infante and Andres Torres, who could help their defense, none of them is ready to play every day in the major leagues. The alternative is to scan the free-agent market for help—in particular, to find a center fielder who can fly. The Tigers are interested in a pair of center fielders on the market, Kenny Lofton and Johnny Damon. While Damon would certainly help and might thrive away from the spotlight in Detroit, Lofton turns 35 this year, and his defense has slipped to where he's nearly unplayable in center field.

The Tigers have a wealth of young pitching. In order to best develop their assets, they need to create the best possible environment for them. They already have the perfect ballpark for that; if they can supplement that park with an above-average defense, a pitching renaissance unseen in Detroit in a generation could carry the team back into contention faster than most anyone realizes.

HITTERS (BA: .270, OBP: .340, SLG: .440, EqA: .260)

Javier Cardona C Bats R Age 26

YEAR	TEAM	LGE	AB	H	DB	TP	HR	BB	SO	R	RBI	SB	CS	OUT	BA	OBP	SLG	EQA	EQR	DEFENSE
1999	Jacksnvl	Sou	421	112	20	0	21	33	70	65	67	3	1	310	.266	.326	.463	.260	53	87-C -7
2000	Toledo	Int	219	58	8	0	10	12	32	26	37	0	1	162	.265	.308	.438	.244	24	50-C -4
2001	Toledo	Int	99	23	1	0	1	8	17	7	10	1	0	76	.232	.290	.273	.198	7	25-C -2
2001	Detroit	AL	96	27	5	0	2	3	10	10	11	0	1	70	.281	.308	.396	.231	9	25-C 1
2002	*Detroit*	*AL*	*345*	*86*	*12*	*0*	*12*	*27*	*55*	*41*	*45*	*1*	*1*	*260*	*.249*	*.304*	*.388*	*.236*	*35*	

The Tigers have more catching options than they know what to do with, so it's surprising that there's talk of keeping Cardona. His main selling point is his mediocrity: no one thinks of him as a potential starter, so no one is worried about stunting his career by making him a backup. Cardona's out-of-character 1999 season should serve as a stern warning to those who want to get overly excited about Mike Rivera on the basis of one power outburst at Double-A.

Roger Cedeno "CF" Bats B Age 27

YEAR	TEAM	LGE	AB	H	DB	TP	HR	BB	SO	R	RBI	SB	CS	OUT	BA	OBP	SLG	EQA	EQR	DEFENSE
1999	NY Mets	NL	456	143	23	4	4	55	93	85	34	57	17	330	.314	.391	.408	.282	70	123-RF 5
2000	Houston	NL	258	69	2	5	5	39	43	49	23	22	11	200	.267	.364	.372	.256	33	61-OF -3
2001	Detroit	AL	526	164	16	11	7	38	72	82	50	52	17	379	.312	.360	.424	.270	72	112-CF -12
2002	*NY Mets*	*NL*	*449*	*129*	*14*	*9*	*7*	*49*	*74*	*83*	*37*	*55*	*18*	*338*	*.287*	*.357*	*.405*	*.274*	*66*	

It is easy to understand why Randy Smith was so eager to acquire Cedeno; the Tigers have been desperate for a true leadoff hitter since Tony Phillips left after 1994, and Cedeno's speed made him doubly attractive for Comerica Park. The move failed for two reasons: 1) Cedeno walked just 36 times in 523 at-bats (after a previous career average of 68 walks per 523 at-bats); 2) in the last 20 years, only Luis Polonia has done as poor a job of converting speed into defensive range. After feuding with Phil Garner, Cedeno didn't so much as walk onto the field the last three weeks of the season, costing him the AL stolen-base title. He has signed with the Mets, with whom he had his best season in 1999.

Tony Clark 1B Bats B Age 30

YEAR	TEAM	LGE	AB	H	DB	TP	HR	BB	SO	R	RBI	SB	CS	OUT	BA	OBP	SLG	EQA	EQR	DEFENSE
1999	Detroit	AL	531	153	25	0	34	58	117	73	98	2	1	379	.288	.364	.527	.290	86	130-1B 1
2000	Detroit	AL	207	59	11	0	15	21	45	31	37	0	0	148	.285	.351	.556	.291	34	53-1B 6
2001	Detroit	AL	431	132	31	3	18	64	93	73	79	0	1	300	.306	.397	.517	.301	75	71-1B -1
2002	*Boston*	*AL*	*481*	*143*	*31*	*2*	*25*	*63*	*108*	*70*	*81*	*1*	*1*	*339*	*.297*	*.379*	*.526*	*.298*	*82*	

Clark is a remarkable streak hitter, which has obscured the fact that his final numbers are as predictable as a Jerry Colangelo cash call. Much maligned in Detroit because of his propensity for slumps and DL stints, he got unfairly lumped with guys like Deivi Cruz and Juan Encarnacion, even though Clark is a good player who may have his best years ahead of him. He could break out big with the Red Sox this season; 40 homers isn't unlikely.

Deivi Cruz SS Bats R Age 26

YEAR	TEAM	LGE	AB	H	DB	TP	HR	BB	SO	R	RBI	SB	CS	OUT	BA	OBP	SLG	EQA	EQR	DEFENSE
1999	Detroit	AL	516	151	26	0	17	7	50	62	59	1	4	369	.293	.307	.442	.243	54	146-SS 20
2000	Detroit	AL	581	182	48	5	11	6	38	67	80	1	4	403	.313	.325	.470	.258	68	150-SS 13
2001	Detroit	AL	415	114	29	1	8	19	40	42	55	4	1	302	.275	.311	.407	.240	42	103-SS -14
2002	*Detroit*	*AL*	*493*	*144*	*36*	*2*	*12*	*21*	*44*	*62*	*60*	*3*	*3*	*352*	*.292*	*.321*	*.446*	*.258*	*59*	

Well, he did walk 17 times, a career high. Cruz's defensive reputation went south like an AARP member in winter, and the numbers back up the change. After being one of the most underrated shortstops in baseball two years ago, Cruz injured his ankle and gained weight. His rehab didn't go well, after which his range deteriorated to the point that he was briefly tried at third base. His career is another data point in the argument that rushing a hitter from A ball to the majors is almost always detrimental to his career.

Damion Easley 2B Bats R Age 32

YEAR	TEAM	LGE	AB	H	DB	TP	HR	BB	SO	R	RBI	SB	CS	OUT	BA	OBP	SLG	EQA	EQR	DEFENSE
1999	Detroit	AL	545	150	29	1	22	46	109	81	64	10	3	398	.275	.350	.453	.269	74	142-2B 7 11-SS -4
2000	Detroit	AL	461	124	28	2	15	50	69	75	57	13	4	341	.269	.355	.436	.268	63	120-2B 12
2001	Detroit	AL	587	160	29	7	13	55	78	83	70	9	6	433	.273	.345	.412	.255	71	151-2B 4
2002	*Detroit*	*AL*	*510*	*135*	*26*	*3*	*16*	*51*	*79*	*73*	*58*	*9*	*4*	*379*	*.265*	*.332*	*.422*	*.259*	*64*	

The cliff approaches. Easley is a slightly above-average second baseman in every department, the kind of player scouts call "solid"—solid hitter, solid power, solid defense. Here's a secret: players who are "solid" in their late twenties collapse in their early thirties. Over the last three years, Easley has gone from hitting .271 to .266 to .259 to .250, from hitting 27 homers to 20 to 14 to 11. You see where this is going: in two years he'll hit about .242 with nine home runs, and a second baseman who hits .242 with 9 homers shouldn't be in the starting lineup, let alone making six million dollars a year.

Juan Encarnacion RF Bats R Age 26

YEAR	TEAM	LGE	AB	H	DB	TP	HR	BB	SO	R	RBI	SB	CS	OUT	BA	OBP	SLG	EQA	EQR	DEFENSE
1999	Detroit	AL	508	133	30	6	20	9	99	60	72	31	12	387	.262	.286	.463	.246	58	127-LF -1
2000	Detroit	AL	545	164	27	6	15	22	79	74	71	16	4	385	.301	.336	.455	.264	69	138-CF 0
2001	Detroit	AL	418	109	21	7	14	27	80	56	56	8	6	315	.261	.313	.445	.248	48	106-RF -4
2002	*Cincnnti*	*NL*	*471*	*134*	*21*	*7*	*17*	*30*	*89*	*62*	*66*	*22*	*8*	*345*	*.285*	*.327*	*.467*	*.263*	*61*	

Talent-wise, he's an embarrassment of riches. On the field, he's just an embarrassment. Encarnacion posted a .296 EqA in a 40-game audition with the Tigers in 1998, a performance many thought heralded a stellar career. Three years later, he's clueless at the plate (with a career strikeout-to-walk ratio of more than four to one) and in the field, where he has one of the worst first steps in the game. Encarnacion didn't make an appearance after September 4, joining Cedeno in Garner's doghouse. He has been traded to the Reds, where he'll battle Ruben Mateo for a fourth-outfielder role.

Robert Fick C/1B Bats L Age 28

YEAR	TEAM	LGE	AB	H	DB	TP	HR	BB	SO	R	RBI	SB	CS	OUT	BA	OBP	SLG	EQA	EQR	DEFENSE
1999	Detroit	AL	41	10	0	0	3	6	5	6	10	1	0	31	.244	.340	.463	.270	6	
2000	Detroit	AL	162	43	8	2	3	20	34	18	21	2	1	120	.265	.350	.395	.254	19	25-1B -1
2001	Detroit	AL	403	116	22	2	21	41	54	67	64	0	3	290	.288	.358	.509	.281	61	74-C -9 19-1B 0
2002	*Detroit*	*AL*	*346*	*91*	*16*	*2*	*17*	*42*	*54*	*55*	*60*	*1*	*2*	*257*	*.263*	*.343*	*.468*	*.273*	*50*	

Credit Phil Garner for swallowing his pride and retracting his statement that Fick's career as a catcher was over. Only an organization stuck in a 1970s mindset would push a hitter like Fick out from behind the plate to make room for a catch-and-throw guy like Brandon Inge. Fick's numbers tumbled after the break (946 OPS before, 680 OPS after). The Tigers still don't think of him as a catcher, so in all likelihood he'll replace Tony Clark at first base until Eric Munson is ready. That could be a few years.

Alejandro Freire DH/OF Bats R Age 27

YEAR	TEAM	LGE	AB	H	DB	TP	HR	BB	SO	R	RBI	SB	CS	OUT	BA	OBP	SLG	EQA	EQR	DEFENSE
1999	Jacksnvl	Sou	245	64	12	0	9	16	45	35	33	1	0	181	.261	.316	.420	.245	27	30-1B 0
2000	Jacksnvl	Sou	490	124	13	0	22	52	110	66	65	1	2	368	.253	.335	.414	.251	58	58-1B 0
2001	Erie	Eas	508	130	18	0	16	42	110	62	70	2	2	380	.256	.320	.386	.238	52	17-RF -1 10-1B 0
2002	*Detroit*	*AL*	*443*	*117*	*12*	*0*	*19*	*42*	*102*	*60*	*61*	*1*	*1*	*327*	*.264*	*.328*	*.420*	*.255*	*54*	

After hitting .323 with 24 home runs for Lakeland in 1997, Freire expected to be on the fast track to Detroit. Instead, the Tigers have left him in Double-A for four straight seasons, even as he has hit close to .300 with slugging averages near .500 every year. When an organization fails to challenge a player and dismisses him as a non-prospect, it can become a self-fulfilling prophecy.

Richard Gomez OF Bats R Age 24

YEAR	TEAM	LGE	AB	H	DB	TP	HR	BB	SO	R	RBI	SB	CS	OUT	BA	OBP	SLG	EQA	EQR	DEFENSE
1999	W Michgn	Mid	489	119	21	6	6	33	133	54	52	32	8	378	.243	.298	.348	.227	46	112-LF -9
2000	Lakeland	Fla	461	104	18	5	7	36	113	53	40	25	6	363	.226	.288	.332	.218	40	117-LF -10
2001	Erie	Eas	349	83	19	1	11	23	73	49	36	17	5	271	.238	.301	.393	.237	37	91-LF -4
2002	*Detroit*	*AL*	*443*	*110*	*19*	*4*	*12*	*43*	*109*	*56*	*51*	*26*	*6*	*339*	*.248*	*.315*	*.391*	*.249*	*53*	

Another one of Erie's many grade-B prospects, Gomez's season was interrupted by a bum knee and later a broken wrist. He continued to develop a little power to go along with a decent batting eye and a knack for stealing bases at an 80% clip. He looks like a classic tweener: too old to develop into a starter, too right-handed to be taken seriously as a supersub outfielder.

Shane Halter 3B/SS Bats R Age 32

YEAR	TEAM	LGE	AB	H	DB	TP	HR	BB	SO	R	RBI	SB	CS	OUT	BA	OBP	SLG	EQA	EQR	DEFENSE
1999	Norfolk	Int	475	119	20	2	5	49	85	63	28	13	15	371	.251	.321	.333	.222	43	67-SS -7 29-CF -2
2000	Detroit	AL	237	64	14	2	3	12	43	26	26	5	2	175	.270	.308	.384	.233	23	35-3B 0 18-1B 2
2001	Detroit	AL	452	137	33	7	14	39	86	57	69	2	3	318	.303	.365	.500	.283	68	66-3B 1 59-SS -7
2002	*Detroit*	*AL*	*419*	*109*	*24*	*4*	*11*	*41*	*83*	*60*	*42*	*6*	*5*	*315*	*.260*	*.326*	*.415*	*.253*	*51*	

(Shane Halter *continued*)
Ladies and gentlemen, your most valuable Tigers position player! His every success can be interpreted as a team failure. He started 60 games apiece at third base and shortstop . . . because Dean Palmer was injured and Deivi Cruz was awful. He led the team in extra-base hits . . . because none of the Tigers' "power hitters" hit even 20 homers, the first time the Tigers have finished without a 20-homer hitter in a full season since 1976. A year ago, Halter was strictly a curiosity, becoming the first Tiger to ever play all nine positions in one game. Now, he's the certified sparkplug of the Tigers' offense, an offense powered by the engine of an Edsel.

John Hannahan 3B Bats L Age 22

YEAR	TEAM	LGE	AB	H	DB	TP	HR	BB	SO	R	RBI	SB	CS	OUT	BA	OBP	SLG	EQA	EQR	DEFENSE
2001	Oneonta	NYP	57	12	5	0	0	3	8	8	5	1	1	46	.211	.250	.298	.186	3	12-3B 0
2001	W Michgn	Mid	178	45	4	0	2	19	43	17	20	2	1	134	.253	.326	.309	.222	16	45-3B 1
2002	*Detroit*	*AL*	*263*	*67*	*7*	*0*	*4*	*31*	*60*	*28*	*25*	*5*	*2*	*198*	*.255*	*.333*	*.327*	*.235*	*26*	

The Big Ten Player of the Year out of the University of Minnesota, Hannahan had a strong debut for a third-round pick. He posted a .409 OBP for West Michigan, and yet he might not be the best third baseman the Tigers drafted; fifth-rounder Ryan Raburn hit .363 and smoked 33 extra-base hits in 44 games. (Raburn also made 23 errors and isn't long for third base.) Hannahan is well-built—he was a prep star as a quarterback—and his power numbers should surge as he gets more experience with wood bats. If the Tigers' 2001 draft class delivers on half the promise it has shown, the rebuilding process in Detroit could be completed in record time.

Bobby Higginson LF Bats L Age 31

YEAR	TEAM	LGE	AB	H	DB	TP	HR	BB	SO	R	RBI	SB	CS	OUT	BA	OBP	SLG	EQA	EQR	DEFENSE
1999	Detroit	AL	373	91	14	0	14	60	58	49	46	4	6	288	.244	.351	.394	.252	46	83-RF -4
2000	Detroit	AL	592	186	45	4	32	66	87	102	100	15	3	409	.314	.385	.566	.309	108	145-LF 10
2001	Detroit	AL	545	162	27	6	20	83	56	89	76	18	14	396	.297	.392	.479	.288	88	142-LF 10
2002	*Detroit*	*AL*	*508*	*148*	*28*	*3*	*25*	*74*	*66*	*84*	*79*	*16*	*8*	*368*	*.291*	*.381*	*.506*	*.299*	*90*	

Higginson, who is consumed with winning, signed a four-year, $34.4-million contract extension with the Tigers last April. Higginson has now completed seven seasons in the major leagues, three in the minors, and three in college at Temple without ever playing for a winning team. It's not surprising, then, that his performance tailed off in the second half, and he started ripping everyone associated with the team in an attempt to get traded out of town. The difference between him and someone like Paul O'Neill is mostly context.

Omar Infante SS Bats R Age 20

YEAR	TEAM	LGE	AB	H	DB	TP	HR	BB	SO	R	RBI	SB	CS	OUT	BA	OBP	SLG	EQA	EQR	DEFENSE
2000	Lakeland	Fla	261	58	5	0	3	14	32	25	18	6	3	206	.222	.263	.276	.188	16	76-SS 0
2001	Erie	Eas	547	142	17	3	2	42	85	73	53	18	8	413	.260	.314	.313	.219	46	130-SS 1
2002	*Detroit*	*AL*	*537*	*142*	*15*	*2*	*5*	*47*	*85*	*65*	*47*	*23*	*8*	*403*	*.264*	*.324*	*.328*	*.232*	*52*	

The single most important piece of advice we can give the Tigers' front office is this: *Omar Infante is not ready.* He's an excellent prospect, a 19-year-old shortstop who hit .302 in Double-A but had a secondary average of just .156. The skills are there, but not the polish, and the majors are not the place to develop that polish. Deivi Cruz, who had to jump from A-ball because he was a Rule 5 draft pick, never did develop it. If the Tigers give Infante a year in Triple-A and a few months in the weight room, he could become the best young player they've developed since Travis Fryman.

Brandon Inge C Bats R Age 25

YEAR	TEAM	LGE	AB	H	DB	TP	HR	BB	SO	R	RBI	SB	CS	OUT	BA	OBP	SLG	EQA	EQR	DEFENSE
1999	W Michgn	Mid	361	72	15	1	7	24	95	35	30	8	2	291	.199	.252	.305	.193	24	95-C 1
2000	Jacksnvl	Sou	307	74	20	1	6	18	72	35	46	7	2	235	.241	.283	.371	.221	27	67-C 2
2000	Toledo	Int	191	40	8	2	5	13	50	22	17	2	1	152	.209	.263	.351	.206	15	49-C 4
2001	Detroit	AL	189	38	12	0	0	10	35	14	16	0	5	156	.201	.241	.265	.168	9	58-C 5
2001	Toledo	Int	91	25	9	1	2	7	22	11	14	1	0	66	.275	.331	.462	.263	12	25-C 1
2002	*Detroit*	*AL*	*417*	*100*	*27*	*2*	*9*	*34*	*102*	*50*	*47*	*6*	*4*	*321*	*.240*	*.297*	*.379*	*.230*	*41*	

The Tigers can look at Inge's lost season to see what might happen if they get giddy and start Infante on Opening Day. Inge is one of the best defensive catchers in baseball, throwing out 46% of base stealers in his rookie season, but the only time he's ever hit was six good weeks in the California Fall League in 1999. His worst-case scenario still involves plenty of big-league service time as the next Mike Matheny or Henry Blanco, but the Tigers stubbornly believe, against all evidence, that he can evolve into something more than that.

Ryan Jackson 1B Bats L Age 30

YEAR	TEAM	LGE	AB	H	DB	TP	HR	BB	SO	R	RBI	SB	CS	OUT	BA	OBP	SLG	EQA	EQR	DEFENSE			
1999	Tacoma	PCL	406	115	22	2	6	30	59	47	50	9	3	294	.283	.334	.392	.246	44	90-1B	-1		
1999	Seattle	AL	68	16	4	0	0	5	17	4	10	3	3	55	.235	.296	.294	.202	5	19-1B	-1		
2000	Durham	Int	507	150	32	2	17	41	110	83	75	5	3	300	.296	.349	.467	.270	68	131-1B	8		
2001	Detroit	AL	118	27	5	2	2	6	22	21	11	3	1	92	.229	.271	.356	.212	10	15-LF	-1	14-1B	2
2002	*Detroit*	*AL*	*413*	*119*	*23*	*2*	*11*	*36*	*85*	*53*	*60*	*9*	*3*	*297*	*.288*	*.345*	*.433*	*.268*	*55*				

Jackson was the worst player on the Tigers' bench, which means he might have been the worst bench player in baseball. A .212-hitting first baseman who stuck around all season because of his defense? Since when did Phil Garner start taking managerial pointers from Tony Muser? It's hard to imagine Jackson will be back, given that he's not even one of the team's four best left-handed-hitting first basemen.

Jose Macias IF/OF Bats B Age 28

YEAR	TEAM	LGE	AB	H	DB	TP	HR	BB	SO	R	RBI	SB	CS	OUT	BA	OBP	SLG	EQA	EQR	DEFENSE			
1999	Toledo	Int	439	101	16	6	2	29	56	37	30	7	4	342	.230	.282	.308	.203	32	107-2B	-4		
2000	Toledo	Int	131	28	5	0	0	15	17	18	7	2	2	105	.214	.298	.252	.196	9	20-CF	-1		
2000	Detroit	AL	172	46	4	5	2	16	21	25	23	2	0	126	.267	.333	.384	.245	19	25-2B	1	17-3B	0
2001	Detroit	AL	490	141	28	6	9	34	47	66	54	19	7	356	.288	.337	.424	.256	59	82-3B	9	28-CF	2
2002	*Detroit*	*AL*	*454*	*125*	*21*	*6*	*8*	*41*	*51*	*60*	*48*	*14*	*5*	*334*	*.275*	*.335*	*.401*	*.256*	*56*				

If there's one area in which the Tigers have managed to corner the market, it's utility infielders. Unable to play both Halter and Macias in the infield at the same time, the Tigers did the predictable: they moved Macias to the outfield and were so pleased with his hustle and defense that he was anointed the team's starting center fielder by season's end. Bill James's principle that bad organizations tend to blame their weaknesses on their best players has a corollary: they also tend to attribute their strengths to their worst ones.

Wendell Magee OF Bats R Age 29

YEAR	TEAM	LGE	AB	H	DB	TP	HR	BB	SO	R	RBI	SB	CS	OUT	BA	OBP	SLG	EQA	EQR	DEFENSE	
1999	Scran-WB	Int	568	151	28	2	18	45	116	80	66	7	7	424	.266	.321	.417	.244	63	138-CF	-4
2000	Detroit	AL	185	53	4	1	8	8	25	30	30	1	0	132	.286	.316	.449	.252	21	40-RF	1
2001	Detroit	AL	208	48	11	4	6	24	38	28	18	3	0	160	.231	.313	.409	.244	23	55-OF	2
2002	*Detroit*	*AL*	*439*	*115*	*19*	*4*	*17*	*48*	*82*	*70*	*56*	*6*	*3*	*327*	*.262*	*.335*	*.440*	*.264*	*59*		

A marginal fourth outfielder in a good year, Magee broke the hamate bone in his left hand in May and had a bad one. He has some pop and can chase the ball down from all three positions, but he has trouble with both contact (140 strikeouts in 738 at-bats) and the twin killing (30 GIDPs), a bad combination. He's likely to return, as much for his salary and prediliction for keeping his mouth shut as for his talent.

Mitch Meluskey C/DH Bats B Age 28

YEAR	TEAM	LGE	AB	H	DB	TP	HR	BB	SO	R	RBI	SB	CS	OUT	BA	OBP	SLG	EQA	EQR	DEFENSE	
1998	New Orln	PCL	402	132	28	0	17	73	55	64	61	2	0	270	.328	.434	.525	.321	79	103-C	-6
1998	Houston	NL	8	2	1	0	0	1	4	1	0	0	0	6	.250	.333	.375	.242	1		
1999	Houston	NL	33	7	1	0	1	5	6	4	3	1	0	26	.212	.316	.333	.231	3		
2000	Houston	NL	335	96	15	0	15	50	68	44	65	1	0	239	.287	.385	.466	.286	52	91-C	-6
2002	*Detroit*	*AL*	*266*	*77*	*9*	*0*	*12*	*39*	*57*	*35*	*40*	*1*	*0*	*189*	*.289*	*.380*	*.459*	*.290*	*43*		

The Meluskey trade nearly got Randy Smith fired, which is ironic in that it was one of the best gambles he's made as the Tigers' GM. Even with Meluskey out all year, the Tigers still got more production from their catchers than the Astros did from Brad Ausmus. Displaying the same arrogance and laziness that got him exiled from Houston, though, Meluskey wore out his welcome in Detroit almost as quickly as he did his shoulder. Even if he comes back healthy this spring, the Tigers don't have a spot for him behind the plate; if they did, it would go to Rob Fick, anyway. Expect a trade; don't expect the Tigers to get fair value.

Ron Merrill SS/2B Bats R Age 23

YEAR	TEAM	LGE	AB	H	DB	TP	HR	BB	SO	R	RBI	SB	CS	OUT	BA	OBP	SLG	EQA	EQR	DEFENSE
2000	Oneonta	NYP	139	33	3	1	1	7	27	13	13	2	2	108	.237	.278	.295	.196	9	31-SS -3
2001	W Michgn	Mid	321	83	8	2	6	26	51	38	38	7	5	243	.259	.320	.352	.229	30	81-SS 3
2001	Erie	Eas	149	38	8	0	4	11	26	19	15	0	1	112	.255	.306	.389	.230	14	31-2B -4
2002	*Detroit*	*AL*	*469*	*124*	*17*	*2*	*12*	*42*	*84*	*57*	*57*	*8*	*6*	*351*	*.264*	*.325*	*.386*	*.244*	*52*	

Merrill was a seventh-rounder out of Tampa in 2000 and was enjoying a fine full-season debut when a brief injury to Infante opened up a spot for him in Double-A. Despite jumping a level and moving to second base, Merrill didn't miss a beat. He is the most-polished and least-heralded of the Tigers' many infield prospects, and he should take down Damion Easley before long.

Lyle Mouton OF Bats R Age 33

YEAR	TEAM	LGE	AB	H	DB	TP	HR	BB	SO	R	RBI	SB	CS	OUT	BA	OBP	SLG	EQA	EQR	DEFENSE
1999	Louisvil	Int	303	100	27	2	16	21	63	52	61	15	0	203	.330	.380	.591	.318	58	75-LF 9
1999	Rochestr	Int	163	34	10	1	3	10	29	21	14	2	1	130	.209	.258	.337	.201	12	33-RF -5
2000	Indianap	Int	198	57	15	0	12	19	40	28	44	3	1	142	.288	.360	.545	.293	33	49-LF -1
2000	Milwauke	NL	98	27	8	1	2	8	27	14	16	1	0	71	.276	.336	.439	.259	12	23-LF 0
2001	Toledo	Int	266	80	14	2	17	28	61	56	45	3	1	187	.301	.374	.560	.302	47	53-RF 0
2002	*Detroit*	*AL*	*424*	*114*	*25*	*2*	*23*	*46*	*102*	*68*	*76*	*1*	*0*	*310*	*.269*	*.340*	*.500*	*.281*	*65*	

Mouton has bounced around after three good seasons as a role player with the White Sox, grabbing just 170 major-league at-bats the last four years. His skill set remains intact: he plays good defense and hit .410 against left-handers in Toledo, with an .836 slugging average. He makes for a better bench player than Wendell Magee.

Eric Munson 1B Bats L Age 24

YEAR	TEAM	LGE	AB	H	DB	TP	HR	BB	SO	R	RBI	SB	CS	OUT	BA	OBP	SLG	EQA	EQR	DEFENSE
1999	W Michgn	Mid	259	56	11	1	9	24	51	28	27	1	1	204	.216	.294	.371	.223	24	32-1B 0
2000	Jacksnvl	Sou	377	90	16	3	14	29	95	46	58	3	1	288	.239	.309	.408	.240	41	74-1B -1
2001	Erie	Eas	532	121	22	1	22	74	137	75	85	0	2	413	.227	.329	.397	.244	61	128-1B -2
2001	Detroit	AL	66	11	5	1	1	3	18	5	7	0	1	56	.167	.203	.318	.170	3	15-1B 1
2002	*Detroit*	*AL*	*525*	*129*	*24*	*1*	*23*	*66*	*141*	*67*	*74*	*2*	*2*	*398*	*.246*	*.330*	*.427*	*.258*	*68*	

How you perceive Munson depends on your expectations. If you expect Munson to live up to his past—the #3 overall pick in 1999, with the potential to become one of the best-hitting catchers in the game—then he's an abject disappointment. If you base your expectations on what he has become—a marginal defensive first baseman with a low batting average and good secondary skills—his upside might just surprise you. He projects as a poor man's Tony Clark, which fits, because the Tigers want him to replace Clark on a poor man's salary.

Dean Palmer DH Bats R Age 33

YEAR	TEAM	LGE	AB	H	DB	TP	HR	BB	SO	R	RBI	SB	CS	OUT	BA	OBP	SLG	EQA	EQR	DEFENSE
1999	Detroit	AL	556	151	25	2	40	51	135	91	98	3	3	408	.272	.342	.540	.283	87	141-3B -5
2000	Detroit	AL	521	138	22	2	31	60	128	72	100	4	2	385	.265	.345	.493	.275	76	107-3B -14 14-1B -4
2001	Detroit	AL	217	52	9	0	13	28	51	37	43	4	1	166	.240	.333	.461	.264	30	
2002	*Detroit*	*AL*	*479*	*118*	*19*	*1*	*29*	*60*	*122*	*73*	*80*	*6*	*2*	*363*	*.246*	*.330*	*.472*	*.271*	*69*	

Palmer illustrates all the dangers of dipping into the mid-tier free-agent market: he was 30 when he signed, so it was likely that all of his skills would erode over the life of his five-year contract. They have. The power that was his calling card has slipped, as his slugging average has dropped from .518 to .471 to .426. His defense, which was bad when he signed, has degenerated to unacceptable levels. His inability to stay healthy cost him most of 2001 and has permanently ended his career at third base. At best, he's a first baseman with a third baseman's stick—a younger version of Todd Zeile—making him a severe albatross on the Tigers' payroll for the next two years.

Jarrod Patterson 3B Bats L Age 28

YEAR	TEAM	LGE	AB	H	DB	TP	HR	BB	SO	R	RBI	SB	CS	OUT	BA	OBP	SLG	EQA	EQR	DEFENSE
1999	El Paso	Tex	243	72	21	1	5	38	47	44	33	2	1	172	.296	.393	.453	.286	38	59-3B -2
1999	Tucson	PCL	266	76	20	2	8	29	34	34	34	3	1	191	.286	.360	.466	.275	38	66-3B -11
2000	Nashvill	PCL	198	51	7	0	5	9	39	21	25	0	1	149	.258	.295	.369	.220	17	43-3B 2
2000	Ottawa	Int	92	24	5	1	0	3	13	8	14	1	0	68	.261	.284	.337	.211	7	25-3B -3
2001	Erie	Eas	72	24	4	1	5	10	11	14	14	0	0	48	.333	.415	.625	.331	15	20-3B -3
2001	Toledo	Int	217	61	14	2	6	29	43	40	23	2	1	157	.281	.368	.447	.274	31	35-3B 1
2001	Detroit	AL	41	12	2	1	2	0	3	7	4	0	1	30	.293	.318	.537	.265	5	
2002	*Detroit*	*AL*	*454*	*126*	*27*	*3*	*13*	*55*	*84*	*65*	*63*	*2*	*1*	*329*	*.278*	*.356*	*.436*	*.273*	*64*	

Patterson has seen more of America than the MaddenCruiser, playing for 15 minor-league teams before making it to the majors. A year in the independent leagues changed his life; since returning to organized baseball in 1998, his stat line includes batting averages of .335, .382, .336, .400, and, most recently, .322 in the Arizona Fall League. In 130 games across four classifications in 2001, he hit .316 with 21 homers and 58 walks. Despite his age (28) and hot-corner defense (not so hot), he could probably start at third base for half the teams in baseball, including the Tigers.

Brian Rios IF Bats R Age 27

YEAR	TEAM	LGE	AB	H	DB	TP	HR	BB	SO	R	RBI	SB	CS	OUT	BA	OBP	SLG	EQA	EQR	DEFENSE
1999	Lakeland	Fla	429	98	23	3	5	17	53	44	30	4	2	333	.228	.262	.331	.200	30	115-3B -2
2000	Jacksnvl	Sou	325	79	22	2	5	20	58	39	32	1	1	247	.243	.295	.369	.223	29	33-SS -4 29-3B -1
2001	Toledo	Int	376	115	24	4	14	22	61	45	58	2	3	264	.306	.349	.503	.276	53	58-3B -6 11-SS -1
2002	*Detroit*	*AL*	*398*	*110*	*22*	*3*	*10*	*29*	*68*	*51*	*42*	*3*	*2*	*290*	*.276*	*.326*	*.422*	*.255*	*47*	

Rios hit .325, popped 48 extra-base hits in limited play, and played all over the infield. He's made at least 30 appearances each at second base, shortstop, and third base the last two years. Somehow, he hasn't so much as sniffed a call-up. Rios was 26 in 2001 and had never hit that well before, but if he can muster a repeat performance he certainly deserves a chance to follow in the exalted footsteps of Halter and Macias as the Tigers' next overrated utility player.

Mike Rivera C Bats R Age 25

YEAR	TEAM	LGE	AB	H	DB	TP	HR	BB	SO	R	RBI	SB	CS	OUT	BA	OBP	SLG	EQA	EQR	DEFENSE
1999	Lakeland	Fla	369	83	13	1	11	14	66	32	49	1	1	287	.225	.256	.355	.203	27	
2000	Lakeland	Fla	244	59	11	2	9	11	50	21	36	1	0	185	.242	.276	.414	.227	23	56-C 0
2000	Jacksnvl	Sou	153	29	6	1	2	4	30	9	8	0	0	124	.190	.210	.281	.165	7	31-C -6
2001	Erie	Eas	422	106	12	1	26	39	93	64	81	1	1	317	.251	.323	.469	.259	54	108-C -8
2002	*Detroit*	*AL*	*427*	*106*	*17*	*2*	*21*	*39*	*94*	*49*	*70*	*1*	*1*	*322*	*.248*	*.311*	*.445*	*.255*	*53*	

Rivera nearly doubled his career-high in walks, and presto!, he was the best hitter in the organization and was named the best power-hitting prospect in the Eastern League. The Tigers suddenly have a peck of catchers. Even ignoring Fick and Meluskey, the Tigers must decide between Inge, a terrific backstop who does less damage at the plate than Lara Flynn Boyle, and Rivera, who can mash but whose glove has more holes than the lone-gunman theory. As always, bet on defense to win out in the spring and for offense to take over in the summer.

Cody Ross OF Bats R Age 21

YEAR	TEAM	LGE	AB	H	DB	TP	HR	BB	SO	R	RBI	SB	CS	OUT	BA	OBP	SLG	EQA	EQR	DEFENSE
2000	W Michgn	Mid	453	102	13	6	6	35	92	52	48	5	2	353	.225	.287	.320	.209	35	120-RF 4
2001	Lakeland	Fla	491	114	23	3	13	30	103	62	57	16	4	381	.232	.280	.371	.221	44	125-LF 5
2002	*Detroit*	*AL*	*501*	*119*	*22*	*4*	*12*	*45*	*110*	*62*	*57*	*12*	*3*	*385*	*.238*	*.300*	*.369*	*.233*	*50*	

Ross stands 5′ 10″ on a good day, but the shadow he casts on the organization continues to grow. He improved every facet of his game in 2001. His combination of speed (28 stolen bases) and power (54 extra-base hits) is unusual for someone so young. Ross is that rare bats-right/throws-left animal, and he has a good chance to become only the fourth B-R/T-L player to get 1,000 at-bats in the majors since Rickey Henderson debuted in 1979.

Ramon Santiago SS Bats B Age 20

YEAR	TEAM	LGE	AB	H	DB	TP	HR	BB	SO	R	RBI	SB	CS	OUT	BA	OBP	SLG	EQA	EQR	DEFENSE
1999	Oneonta	NYP	51	13	0	1	1	1	13	5	5	2	0	38	.255	.274	.353	.217	4	11-SS 1
2000	W Michgn	Mid	393	93	11	1	1	20	66	46	32	19	9	309	.237	.283	.277	.198	27	74-SS 9
2001	Lakeland	Fla	440	101	13	2	2	38	64	46	35	18	6	345	.230	.298	.282	.208	34	
2002	*Detroit*	*AL*	*416*	*106*	*14*	*2*	*4*	*41*	*68*	*48*	*35*	*15*	*5*	*315*	*.255*	*.322*	*.327*	*.231*	*40*	

A year ago, Santiago was a better shortstop prospect than Omar Infante, but after off-season surgery to repair a torn labrum in his throwing shoulder, Santiago spent the entire season as a DH. Long-term, his prospects may still be better: his pre-injury defense was good enough to foster talk of moving Infante to second base, and he made use of his time in 2001 by continuing to refine his batting eye. He's only four months older than his more-touted competition, and his injury means that, unlike Infante, he's in no danger of being rushed to the majors before he's ready.

Randall Simon 1B Bats L Age 27

YEAR	TEAM	LGE	AB	H	DB	TP	HR	BB	SO	R	RBI	SB	CS	OUT	BA	OBP	SLG	EQA	EQR	DEFENSE
1999	Atlanta	NL	219	69	10	0	7	14	23	25	25	2	2	152	.315	.359	.457	.270	29	54-1B -4
2000	Columbus	Int	367	93	17	3	16	29	41	47	65	5	4	278	.253	.308	.447	.247	42	74-1B -9
2001	Toledo	Int	225	71	10	0	10	21	19	26	29	0	3	157	.316	.377	.493	.284	34	51-1B -8
2001	Detroit	AL	257	82	14	2	7	17	24	30	39	0	1	176	.319	.361	.471	.275	35	39-1B -2
2002	*Detroit*	*AL*	*418*	*123*	*18*	*2*	*17*	*44*	*42*	*52*	*60*	*2*	*4*	*299*	*.294*	*.361*	*.469*	*.280*	*62*	

On a good team—such as the 1999 Braves, with whom he spent his rookie season—Simon makes an ideal pinch-hitter: a left-handed line-drive machine with a career .310 batting average. Forced into full-time duty as the Tigers' first baseman, Simon's immobility and lack of power sucked away most of his value. With Meluskey, Fick, and Munson fighting for playing time, that shouldn't be a problem this year.

Andres Torres CF Bats B Age 24

YEAR	TEAM	LGE	AB	H	DB	TP	HR	BB	SO	R	RBI	SB	CS	OUT	BA	OBP	SLG	EQA	EQR	DEFENSE
1999	W Michgn	Mid	425	80	18	2	1	64	127	46	22	19	11	356	.188	.302	.247	.202	32	112-CF -2
2000	Lakeland	Fla	406	99	11	6	3	47	91	55	23	35	12	318	.244	.326	.323	.233	42	104-CF 8
2001	Erie	Eas	258	64	13	2	1	32	49	45	19	13	7	201	.248	.337	.326	.233	26	55-CF 2
2002	*Detroit*	*AL*	*455*	*112*	*17*	*4*	*4*	*56*	*108*	*59*	*30*	*27*	*11*	*354*	*.246*	*.329*	*.327*	*.237*	*48*	

The best of the Tigers' many fleet-footed young outfielders, Torres was voted the best defensive outfielder in the Eastern League and is expected to man center field in Comerica Park no later than 2003. His development was interrupted by an injury to his right (throwing) shoulder that ended his season in July. The Tigers think he's going to be a prototypical leadoff hitter, which is asking too much of Torres: offensively, he's more Gary Pettis than Kenny Lofton.

Chris Wakeland OF Bats L Age 28

YEAR	TEAM	LGE	AB	H	DB	TP	HR	BB	SO	R	RBI	SB	CS	OUT	BA	OBP	SLG	EQA	EQR	DEFENSE
1999	Jacksnvl	Sou	214	58	11	2	10	27	54	32	25	4	3	159	.271	.359	.481	.276	32	54-LF -4
2000	Toledo	Int	496	127	21	1	26	50	145	59	66	3	4	373	.256	.328	.460	.258	63	122-RF -14
2001	Toledo	Int	552	149	29	2	22	39	117	82	78	6	7	410	.270	.324	.449	.253	66	112-RF -4
2001	Detroit	AL	36	10	2	0	2	0	11	5	6	0	0	26	.278	.278	.500	.248	4	10-RF 2
2002	*Detroit*	*AL*	*537*	*144*	*27*	*2*	*24*	*51*	*136*	*73*	*66*	*7*	*6*	*399*	*.268*	*.332*	*.460*	*.266*	*73*	

After having his worst season in a while, Wakeland was rewarded for years of loyal service with a September call-up, which isn't a bad prize as Miss Congeniality awards go. A repeat trip to Detroit seems unlikely; most of his playing time in September came out of spite. Phil Garner would have pencilled John Wockenfuss into the lineup if it allowed him to keep Roger Cedeno and Juan Encarnacion planted firmly on the bench.

Michael Woods 2B Bats R Age 21

YEAR	TEAM	LGE	AB	H	DB	TP	HR	BB	SO	R	RBI	SB	CS	OUT	BA	OBP	SLG	EQA	EQR	DEFENSE
2001	Oneonta	NYP	38	8	1	0	0	3	6	3	2	2	1	31	.211	.275	.237	.187	2	
2001	W Michgn	Mid	172	38	7	2	0	24	48	20	12	6	5	139	.221	.324	.285	.215	15	42-2B -3
2002	*Detroit*	*AL*	*243*	*55*	*12*	*2*	*1*	*32*	*66*	*27*	*18*	*8*	*6*	*194*	*.226*	*.316*	*.305*	*.219*	*22*	

Woods was a collegiate star at Southern University, but the low level of competition at the Division I-AA school made his transition to pro ball far from a sure thing. Those fears proved unfounded when Woods debuted with a .401 OBP in a full-season league. His multidimensional skills and college polish make him the perfect counterpart to Infante's and Santiago's purely athletic approach to the middle infield.

PITCHERS (ERA: 4.50, H/9: 9.0, HR/9: 1.0, BB/9: 3.0, K/9: 6.0, KW: 2.0, PERA: 4.50)

Matt Anderson — Throws R — Age 25

YEAR	TEAM	LGE	IP	H	ER	HR	BB	K	ERA	W	L	H/9	HR/9	BB/9	K/9	KW	PERA	STUFF
1999	Toledo	Int	36.0	40	35	10	30	28	8.75	1	3	10.0	2.5	7.5	7.0	0.5	6.11	-14
1999	Detroit	AL	37.0	37	29	7	29	32	7.05	1	3	9.0	1.7	7.1	7.8	0.6	5.36	-6
2000	Detroit	AL	74.3	65	35	7	37	70	4.24	4	4	7.9	0.8	4.5	8.5	0.9	4.52	11
2001	Detroit	AL	59.0	50	19	2	17	49	2.90	5	2	7.6	0.3	2.6	7.5	1.4	4.93	11

He still throws harder than any other pitcher in the majors, and his walk rate dropped to less than half his previous career rate. That he didn't then blow hitters away is a reflection of the lack of movement on his fastball. Anderson needs to figure out that the title "hardest-thrower" is a poor bridesmaid to "best closer" and sacrifice some velocity for movement. He's getting there; his ERA was 25.07 on April 20 and 2.98 after that. Expect a huge season from him this year.

Kenny Baugh — Throws R — Age 23

YEAR	TEAM	LGE	IP	H	ER	HR	BB	K	ERA	W	L	H/9	HR/9	BB/9	K/9	KW	PERA	STUFF
2001	W Michgn	Mid	35.0	32	13	0	14	21	3.34	3	1	8.2	0.0	3.6	5.4	0.8	5.43	11
2001	Erie	Eas	27.7	31	20	7	8	20	6.51	1	2	10.1	2.3	2.6	6.5	1.3	5.59	10

He's on the serious fast track and could arrive as quickly as Jeff Weaver did. What Baugh does when he gets to Detroit will depend on his health. College baseball researcher Boyd Nation tracked the pitch counts of the top college pitchers in 2001 and found that Baugh was the most abused by far. His PAP^3 score was comparable to that of Randy Johnson, and he finished the season with a whopping 171-pitch effort. The Tigers were very careful with him and shut him down three weeks early as a precaution. Of course, the Mets took good care of Paul Wilson, too.

Adam Bernero — Throws R — Age 25

YEAR	TEAM	LGE	IP	H	ER	HR	BB	K	ERA	W	L	H/9	HR/9	BB/9	K/9	KW	PERA	STUFF
1999	W Michgn	Mid	89.0	103	61	18	27	44	6.17	3	7	10.4	1.8	2.7	4.4	0.8	4.58	-1
2000	Jacksnvl	Sou	58.3	67	42	11	25	29	6.48	2	4	10.3	1.7	3.9	4.5	0.6	5.16	-6
2000	Toledo	Int	44.3	45	22	6	10	31	4.47	3	2	9.1	1.2	2.0	6.3	1.5	3.14	18
2000	Detroit	AL	34.3	34	16	3	11	20	4.19	2	2	8.9	0.8	2.9	5.2	0.9	4.01	1
2001	Toledo	Int	147.7	158	87	17	63	73	5.30	7	9	9.6	1.0	3.8	4.4	0.6	6.71	-7

The fairy tale hit a snag. Bernero, who zoomed from undrafted free agent to the majors in barely a year, was put in his place at Triple-A. The basic utensils—an upper-80s fastball with good movement, command of four pitches—are still there, and he survived the humiliation well enough to get a look-see in September. A career in long relief is his if he wants it.

Nate Cornejo — Throws R — Age 22

YEAR	TEAM	LGE	IP	H	ER	HR	BB	K	ERA	W	L	H/9	HR/9	BB/9	K/9	KW	PERA	STUFF
1999	W Michgn	Mid	177.0	184	88	9	75	72	4.47	10	10	9.4	0.5	3.8	3.7	0.5	5.82	3
2000	Lakeland	Fla	74.0	81	50	11	37	39	6.08	3	5	9.9	1.3	4.5	4.7	0.5	5.28	3
2000	Jacksnvl	Sou	91.0	99	57	11	44	40	5.64	4	6	9.8	1.1	4.4	4.0	0.5	6.62	0
2001	Erie	Eas	119.0	127	74	17	52	69	5.60	5	8	9.6	1.3	3.9	5.2	0.7	4.00	8
2001	Toledo	Int	28.7	28	11	1	8	17	3.45	2	1	8.8	0.3	2.5	5.3	1.1	2.70	20
2001	Detroit	AL	46.7	55	38	9	27	21	7.33	1	4	10.6	1.7	5.2	4.0	0.4	7.44	-16

Cornejo has the highest upside of any pitcher in the organization, including Jeff Weaver. His calling card is the greatest pitch in baseball: a 94-mph fastball with incredible sinking action, a la Kevin Brown. As you might expect a 21-year-old to be, Cornejo was too timid to challenge major-league hitters, with predictable results. Nevertheless, his fastball had more late

(Nate Cornejo *continued*)

movement on it than that of any rookie since at least Juan Guzman. He's built like a horse and has an impeccable health record since he was drafted. The Tigers' ability to mold him into a top starter will have more impact on the team's chances to contend in the next three years than any other factor.

Eric Eckenstahler Throws L Age 25

YEAR	TEAM	LGE	IP	H	ER	HR	BB	K	ERA	W	L	H/9	HR/9	BB/9	K/9	KW	PERA	STUFF
2000	W Michgn	Mid	17.3	27	33	11	14	11	17.13	0	2	14.0	5.7	7.3	5.7	0.4	11.83	-75
2001	Erie	Eas	64.7	69	50	11	44	43	6.96	2	5	9.6	1.5	6.1	6.0	0.5	5.91	-28

The Tigers have high hopes for their 2000 32nd-round draft pick—if a career as a lefty one-out guy, or LOOGY (tm, John Sickels), qualifies as ambitious. Eckenstahler is 6′ 7″ and raw; at this point the only positive on his resume is that he fanned 73 batters in 65 innings in Double-A. He now qualifies as a participant in the LOOGY Lottery, in which bipeds that throw 60 mph with their left arm can win an all-expense-paid trip to various major-league ballparks, with a starting salary of $200,000.

Shane Heams Throws R Age 26

YEAR	TEAM	LGE	IP	H	ER	HR	BB	K	ERA	W	L	H/9	HR/9	BB/9	K/9	KW	PERA	STUFF
1999	W Michgn	Mid	65.7	58	34	2	49	51	4.66	3	4	7.9	0.3	6.7	7.0	0.5	4.97	-12
2000	Jacksnvl	Sou	51.3	52	38	8	39	40	6.66	2	4	9.1	1.4	6.8	7.0	0.5	4.02	-21
2001	Erie	Eas	47.3	44	34	2	55	32	6.46	2	3	8.4	0.4	10.5	6.1	0.3	3.44	-37
2001	Toledo	Int	18.0	21	30	6	34	14	15.00	0	2	10.5	3.0	17.0	7.0	0.2	11.96	-92

There's a lot here to compare with Jeff Nelson, such as Heams's fastball/slider combination, his Double-A performance (110 innings, 67 hits, 71 walks, 124 strikeouts the last two seasons), and his ability to handcuff right-handed hitters (they batted .110 against Heams). In Triple-A, though, Heams has pitched like Harriet Nelson: 28 innings, 33 hits, 39 walks, 28 strikeouts, and a 9.76 ERA. Heams is already older than Nelson was in his rookie season and has neither the gas on his fastball nor the command of his slider to dominate hitters the same way the Mariners setup man does.

Chris Holt Throws R Age 30

YEAR	TEAM	LGE	IP	H	ER	HR	BB	K	ERA	W	L	H/9	HR/9	BB/9	K/9	KW	PERA	STUFF
1999	Houston	NL	175.0	172	73	11	48	104	3.75	11	8	8.8	0.6	2.5	5.3	1.1	4.77	7
2000	Houston	NL	219.7	224	102	19	62	121	4.18	13	11	9.2	0.8	2.5	5.0	1.0	4.88	6
2001	Detroit	AL	163.0	174	87	17	54	76	4.80	8	10	9.6	0.9	3.0	4.2	0.7	5.64	-5

Holt received some attention in Detroit for slamming the dimensions of Comerica Park as too spacious. Coming from a pitcher who had just spent a season at Enron Field, those were strong words. Holt did pitch much worse (6.59 vs. 4.76 ERA) at home, almost entirely because he gave up twice as many walks as he did on other mounds. Why Holt's opinion should matter is a good question; his ERA has jumped three straight years, and his career record is 28-51. He doesn't need a new park, he needs a new league. Like the Texas.

Tim Kalita Throws L Age 23

YEAR	TEAM	LGE	IP	H	ER	HR	BB	K	ERA	W	L	H/9	HR/9	BB/9	K/9	KW	PERA	STUFF
1999	W Michgn	Mid	47.3	51	31	4	30	20	5.89	2	3	9.7	0.8	5.7	3.8	0.3	6.42	-7
2000	Lakeland	Fla	149.0	160	96	16	87	70	5.80	6	11	9.7	1.0	5.3	4.2	0.4	6.83	-6
2001	Erie	Eas	192.3	218	128	35	62	97	5.99	8	13	10.2	1.6	2.9	4.5	0.8	5.19	0

Never heard of him? Neither had most baseball insiders until he led the minor leagues with 200 innings pitched in 2001. This may be cynical, but if you're going to do something as boneheaded as turning a minor-league starter into a galley slave for the greater glory of the Erie Seawolves, it's better to do it with someone who's not a real prospect. Kalita is a left-hander with good control and little else to recommend.

Jose Lima Throws R Age 29

YEAR	TEAM	LGE	IP	H	ER	HR	BB	K	ERA	W	L	H/9	HR/9	BB/9	K/9	KW	PERA	STUFF
1999	Houston	NL	252.0	252	108	28	37	168	3.86	16	12	9.0	1.0	1.3	6.0	2.3	3.73	16
2000	Houston	NL	206.0	235	137	41	56	110	5.99	8	15	10.3	1.8	2.4	4.8	1.0	5.97	-3
2001	Houston	NL	56.3	62	34	10	14	33	5.43	2	4	9.9	1.6	2.2	5.3	1.2	7.62	-7
2001	Detroit	AL	110.7	132	72	21	21	41	5.86	4	8	10.7	1.7	1.7	3.3	1.0	4.90	-7

Instead of criticizing the spacious outfield of Comerica Park as "unnatural" and "punitive," as some have, detractors should look upon those dimensions as a unique home-field advantage. Comerica allowed the Tigers to restore Jose Lima into a marginally useful pitcher almost overnight. Lima's antics and combustible energy reflect a lack of self-confidence, traits aggravated the moment he first saw the left-field fence at Enron. With the comfort level he had in the Astrodome restored, Lima's a good bet to win 15 games with an ERA under 4.00.

Shane Loux **Throws R** **Age 22**

YEAR	TEAM	LGE	IP	H	ER	HR	BB	K	ERA	W	L	H/9	HR/9	BB/9	K/9	KW	PERA	STUFF
1999	W Michgn	Mid	48.3	57	37	11	18	25	6.89	1	4	10.6	2.0	3.4	4.7	0.7	9.64	0
1999	Lakeland	Fla	88.7	105	75	17	57	35	7.61	3	7	10.7	1.7	5.8	3.6	0.3	5.68	-11
2000	Jacksnvl	Sou	155.7	166	91	22	56	87	5.26	7	10	9.6	1.3	3.2	5.0	0.8	5.78	10
2001	Toledo	Int	158.3	188	124	28	82	55	7.05	5	13	10.7	1.6	4.7	3.1	0.3	7.38	-15

A year ago, some considered Loux a better prospect than Nate Cornejo. A year ago, some people didn't know who Harry Potter was. Loux was promoted very aggressively by the Tigers, and the payoff is that he spent the whole season in Triple-A at age 21. The downside is that he pitched like crap. Since he's not on the 40-man roster yet, the Tigers have the luxury of giving him a few more years in Toledo to see whether he sinks or swims.

Matt Miller **Throws L** **Age 27**

YEAR	TEAM	LGE	IP	H	ER	HR	BB	K	ERA	W	L	H/9	HR/9	BB/9	K/9	KW	PERA	STUFF
1999	Lakeland	Fla	105.0	126	94	23	67	45	8.06	3	9	10.8	2.0	5.7	3.9	0.3	7.06	-35
1999	Jacksnvl	Sou	41.0	46	24	5	14	16	5.27	2	3	10.1	1.1	3.1	3.5	0.6	6.37	-12
2000	Jacksnvl	Sou	120.7	138	79	21	38	56	5.89	5	8	10.3	1.6	2.8	4.2	0.7	5.64	-13
2001	Toledo	Int	62.7	63	30	4	23	33	4.31	4	3	9.0	0.6	3.3	4.7	0.7	4.70	-16

The Tigers stopped delaying the inevitable and moved Miller, who had never made a relief appearance before 2001, into the bullpen full time. If Miller wants to carve out a specialist's career, he's going to have to do better against left-handed hitters than he did in 2001, as he had essentially no platoon split in Triple-A. Look at the pitchers two and four spaces ahead if you want an idea of what Miller's career might look like in a few years.

Brian Moehler **Throws R** **Age 30**

YEAR	TEAM	LGE	IP	H	ER	HR	BB	K	ERA	W	L	H/9	HR/9	BB/9	K/9	KW	PERA	STUFF
1999	Detroit	AL	206.0	214	96	19	49	105	4.19	12	11	9.3	0.8	2.1	4.6	1.1	4.46	5
2000	Detroit	AL	191.0	197	83	17	33	102	3.91	12	9	9.3	0.8	1.6	4.8	1.5	4.24	9

Among the many reasons to suspect that the Tigers will improve in 2002, the return of Brian Moehler ranks near the bottom of the list. His reputation in Detroit far exceeds his actual performance, and he was walking on thin ice before the injury: Moehler has never struck out more than 5.2 men per nine innings, a poor mark in today's whiff-happy era. His value comes from bulk innings, which will be of little use to Detroit if the Tigers' young arms have come along as far as Randy Smith thinks they have.

Heath Murray **Throws L** **Age 29**

YEAR	TEAM	LGE	IP	H	ER	HR	BB	K	ERA	W	L	H/9	HR/9	BB/9	K/9	KW	PERA	STUFF
1999	LasVegas	PCL	87.7	90	44	6	37	44	4.52	5	5	9.2	0.6	3.8	4.5	0.6	4.95	-6
1999	San Dieg	NL	52.0	57	32	7	22	23	5.54	2	4	9.9	1.2	3.8	4.0	0.5	5.86	-20
2000	Albuquer	PCL	165.0	169	83	10	71	78	4.53	9	9	9.2	0.5	3.9	4.3	0.5	5.47	-8
2001	Toledo	Int	32.7	33	17	7	3	30	4.68	2	2	9.1	1.9	0.8	8.3	5.0	2.83	12
2001	Detroit	AL	68.0	73	46	10	38	40	6.09	3	5	9.7	1.3	5.0	5.3	0.5	6.34	-19

There comes a point at which you have to say "enough," that being left-handed should only take a player so far. Heath Murray has thrown nearly 150 innings in the majors, with more walks than strikeouts and a 6.32 ERA. Aside from his freakish season in Triple-A (22 hits in 36 innings, a 44-to-2 strikeout-to-walk ratio), he hasn't had an ERA below 4.00 since 1996. Is having a lefty specialist like this really better than keeping a right-handed reliever with far better credentials? Guys like Murray—who has been released—will be the reason why the trend towards left-handed relief at any cost will one day reverse itself.

Danny Patterson Throws R Age 31

YEAR	TEAM	LGE	IP	H	ER	HR	BB	K	ERA	W	L	H/9	HR/9	BB/9	K/9	KW	PERA	STUFF
1999	Texas	AL	66.3	64	26	4	16	43	3.53	4	3	8.7	0.5	2.2	5.8	1.3	4.66	0
2000	Detroit	AL	60.7	62	24	3	11	29	3.56	4	3	9.2	0.4	1.6	4.3	1.3	3.50	-5
2001	Detroit	AL	64.7	68	27	4	11	26	3.76	4	3	9.5	0.6	1.5	3.6	1.2	3.10	-9

Patterson has now had two fine seasons as the Tigers' setup man, making him the most valuable player the Tigers got in the Juan Gonzalez trade. How often does a throw-in end up being the key player in a deal? More often than you think: Frank Catalanotto, who was behind Gabe Kapler and Justin Thompson on the Rangers' wish list, has been the best player in that deal. Cory Lidle, an afterthought in the big Royals/Rays/A's trade last winter, had the best season of anyone involved. Patterson's extreme ground-ball tendencies and terrific control allow him to be effective with one of the lowest strikeout rates in the majors.

Matt Perisho Throws L Age 27

YEAR	TEAM	LGE	IP	H	ER	HR	BB	K	ERA	W	L	H/9	HR/9	BB/9	K/9	KW	PERA	STUFF
1999	Oklahoma	PCL	160.7	158	89	16	84	109	4.99	8	10	8.9	0.9	4.7	6.1	0.6	5.09	3
2000	Texas	AL	113.7	119	72	17	55	73	5.70	5	8	9.4	1.3	4.4	5.8	0.7	6.81	-10
2001	Toledo	Int	41.7	45	22	4	14	19	4.75	2	3	9.7	0.9	3.0	4.1	0.7	2.70	-17
2001	Detroit	AL	42.7	47	23	5	13	18	4.85	2	3	9.9	1.1	2.7	3.8	0.7	6.17	-19

See Heath Murray. The Tigers picked up Perisho, whose 7.37 ERA was unacceptable for even the Rangers, and were apparently surprised when he continued to suck raw eggs for them. Eventually teams will stop the self-immolation that comes with carrying an extra lefty. Tony La Russa's success as a manager has come despite, not because of, his trendsetting penchant for one-batter specialists.

Adam Pettyjohn Throws L Age 25

YEAR	TEAM	LGE	IP	H	ER	HR	BB	K	ERA	W	L	H/9	HR/9	BB/9	K/9	KW	PERA	STUFF
1999	Lakeland	Fla	61.3	62	26	4	14	33	3.82	4	3	9.1	0.6	2.1	4.8	1.2	6.57	8
1999	Jacksnvl	Sou	127.7	140	74	19	35	65	5.22	6	8	9.9	1.3	2.5	4.6	0.9	5.91	3
2000	Jacksnvl	Sou	48.3	52	27	7	13	29	5.03	2	3	9.7	1.3	2.4	5.4	1.1	4.83	7
2000	Toledo	Int	40.0	45	28	6	21	19	6.30	1	3	10.1	1.4	4.7	4.3	0.5	8.09	-11
2001	Toledo	Int	107.0	112	55	12	30	58	4.63	6	6	9.4	1.0	2.5	4.9	1.0	4.97	3
2001	Detroit	AL	69.0	74	38	9	20	38	4.96	4	4	9.7	1.2	2.6	5.0	0.9	6.17	-3

The Tigers have struggled to come up with a left-handed starter since Justin Thompson was traded, which is of particular concern given how tough Comerica Park is on right-handed power. Pettyjohn was called up in July and illustrated that point, posting an ERA of 3.10 at home and an even 8.00 on the road. His broad repertoire is ill-suited for relief work, so he figures to do battle with Mark Redman this spring for the token lefty spot in the rotation.

Luis Pineda Throws R Age 24

YEAR	TEAM	LGE	IP	H	ER	HR	BB	K	ERA	W	L	H/9	HR/9	BB/9	K/9	KW	PERA	STUFF
1999	W Michgn	Mid	39.3	37	25	4	29	32	5.72	2	2	8.5	0.9	6.6	7.3	0.6	5.22	-1
2000	Lakeland	Fla	26.0	27	25	7	23	26	8.65	1	2	9.3	2.4	8.0	9.0	0.6	5.57	-10
2001	Erie	Eas	81.7	83	49	12	37	58	5.40	4	5	9.1	1.3	4.1	6.4	0.8	4.24	6
2001	Detroit	AL	18.0	18	12	2	13	12	6.00	1	1	9.0	1.0	6.5	6.0	0.5	4.57	-12

The frail right-hander breezed through Double- and Triple-A with a great fastball/curveball combination, pitching not at all like a man who had once been released by the Rangers. This is why there is no such thing as a pitching prospect: a guy like Pineda can come out of nowhere just as fast as someone like Jaret Wright can fade into oblivion. Pineda should pitch often—and well—out of the Reds' bullpen this season, after he was thrown in on the Encarnacion trade.

Mark Redman Throws L Age 28

YEAR	TEAM	LGE	IP	H	ER	HR	BB	K	ERA	W	L	H/9	HR/9	BB/9	K/9	KW	PERA	STUFF
1999	SaltLake	PCL	136.7	141	76	14	60	76	5.00	7	8	9.3	0.9	4.0	5.0	0.6	5.66	-7
2000	Minnesot	AL	158.7	156	72	19	37	116	4.08	10	8	8.8	1.1	2.1	6.6	1.6	3.87	13
2001	Minnesot	AL	51.3	53	27	5	18	28	4.73	3	3	9.3	0.9	3.2	4.9	0.8	4.15	2

This is why Branch Rickey once said it's better to trade a player a year too early than a year too late. The Tigers believed their own press clippings about Todd Jones, who led the AL with 42 saves in 2000 but looked ugly in doing so (67 hits, 25 walks in 64 innings). Instead of trading him before the season for a relative bounty of prospects, they waited until he lost his effectiveness and the closer's job before testing the market. They were lucky to find a former #1 pick recovering from a triceps problem and a vote of no-confidence from Tom Kelly. Redman was perhaps the best rookie starter in the AL in 2000, he's in a good ballpark for a lefty fly-ball pitcher, and if he's healthy he's going to surprise people.

Victor Santos — Throws R — Age 25

YEAR	TEAM	LGE	IP	H	ER	HR	BB	K	ERA	W	L	H/9	HR/9	BB/9	K/9	KW	PERA	STUFF
1999	Jacksnvl	Sou	168.0	176	95	23	59	103	5.09	8	11	9.4	1.2	3.2	5.5	0.9	4.97	9
2001	Toledo	Int	37.7	45	29	8	14	16	6.93	1	3	10.8	1.9	3.3	3.8	0.6	7.99	-16
2001	Detroit	AL	73.7	73	46	8	47	49	5.62	3	5	8.9	1.0	5.7	6.0	0.5	3.62	-7

Santos got a lot of press for his excellent debut; he kicked off his career by going 27 1/3 innings without allowing an earned run, the longest such streak since Fernando Valenzuela started with 34 straight. He struggled with his control after that, and his long-term outlook isn't as rosy as Pineda's. In 2002, Santos should work behind Matt Anderson and Danny Patterson to give the Tigers the deepest bullpen they've had in some time.

Steve Sparks — Throws R — Age 36

YEAR	TEAM	LGE	IP	H	ER	HR	BB	K	ERA	W	L	H/9	HR/9	BB/9	K/9	KW	PERA	STUFF
1999	Anaheim	AL	151.3	164	93	18	68	72	5.53	7	10	9.8	1.1	4.0	4.3	0.5	5.18	-8
2000	Toledo	Int	88.3	99	59	11	45	33	6.01	4	6	10.1	1.1	4.6	3.4	0.4	6.12	-21
2000	Detroit	AL	106.3	108	44	6	24	53	3.72	7	5	9.1	0.5	2.0	4.5	1.1	4.04	5
2001	Detroit	AL	235.3	247	112	20	61	110	4.28	14	12	9.4	0.8	2.3	4.2	0.9	3.96	3

Sparks's performance in 2001 illustrates two tenets of the knuckleballer: they are almost always underappreciated—remember, the Tigers signed him as a minor-league free-agent—and because of that, they almost always get their opportunities with second-division clubs, which reinforces the first point. He was voted the Tigers Player of the Year by acclamation, though the press release failed to mention whether he won for his performance or for helping all the beat writers make deadline with his quick pace on the mound.

Andy Van Hekken — Throws L — Age 22

YEAR	TEAM	LGE	IP	H	ER	HR	BB	K	ERA	W	L	H/9	HR/9	BB/9	K/9	KW	PERA	STUFF
1999	Oneonta	NYP	48.7	55	33	8	21	24	6.10	2	3	10.2	1.5	3.9	4.4	0.6	4.40	0
2000	W Michgn	Mid	156.3	158	65	7	41	72	3.74	10	7	9.1	0.4	2.4	4.1	0.9	3.97	11
2001	Lakeland	Fla	108.0	122	71	18	37	51	5.92	4	8	10.2	1.5	3.1	4.3	0.7	4.42	0
2001	Erie	Eas	50.7	58	29	7	10	19	5.15	3	3	10.3	1.2	1.8	3.4	0.9	6.40	0

The Tigers would love to see Van Hekken succeed, both because he's a Michigan boy and to justify wasting two-plus years with Brian Hunter in center field. As a lefty with impeccable control and good movement on a fastball in the upper 80s, he'll get every chance to make it in Detroit. I have a good feeling about him, if only because every prospect that Woody Woodward traded away comes back to haunt the Mariners.

Jeff Weaver — Throws R — Age 25

YEAR	TEAM	LGE	IP	H	ER	HR	BB	K	ERA	W	L	H/9	HR/9	BB/9	K/9	KW	PERA	STUFF
1999	Detroit	AL	168.3	173	88	23	47	113	4.70	9	10	9.2	1.2	2.5	6.0	1.2	4.79	13
2000	Detroit	AL	204.3	205	92	23	43	135	4.05	13	10	9.0	1.0	1.9	5.9	1.6	3.89	17
2001	Detroit	AL	235.3	231	101	18	65	145	3.86	15	11	8.8	0.7	2.5	5.5	1.1	4.23	12

With TV play-by-play man Josh Lewin fleeing Detroit to work for the Rangers, Weaver remains the only compelling reason to tune in to Tiger broadcasts. His stuff remains as untameable as ever; unfortunately, so does his temper. His end-of-season outburst after Garner left him in to absorb a beating in his final start was only the culmination of the heaviest workload Garner had placed on a starting pitcher since Cal Eldred's shoulder broke down in the mid-1990s. The combination of Weaver's consistent mechanics and a pair of relatively light workloads in 1999 and 2000 should keep him healthy. If the Tigers get a real fly-chaser to man center field, Weaver's ERA could drop by a full run.

Kansas City Royals

"Rany on the Royals" (nee "Rob and Rany on the Royals"), which you can read at our Web site, is a wonderful column by Rany Jazayerli on his favorite team. The Royals have a following among analysts, as many of the best-known ones (Jazayerli, Bill James, Rob Neyer, John Sickels) hail from Kansas or spent significant time there.

The problem this creates when it comes to writing about the Royals for *Baseball Prospectus* is that it's hard to find a new angle, something fresh to contribute to the discussion. The Royals have been picked apart and put back together like no team in baseball, and an argument can be made that there's nothing to be said about the Royals that hasn't already been said. We could make up some things, but doing 2,000 words on Joe Randa's amazing cherry cheesecake recipe or Blake Stein's personal quest to bring back the leisure suit would run out of steam around the bottom of this page.

So let's boil the Royals down to two points, really the only two things you—or for that matter, David Glass—need to know for 2002: (1) The Royals have a ton of talent in their system. (2) The Royals aren't going to succeed until they replace their management team.

The Royals have been an irrelevant baseball team since the 1994 strike. They haven't finished over .500 since that season was aborted with the team sitting at 64-51, just four games out of first place. While the Expos get all the sympathy for having a shot at a championship ripped from their hands, the Royals' fate has been forgotten, possibly because they didn't make a spectacle of themselves once things returned to normal.

Going into 2002, the Royals have as much reason to be confident in their future as they have since that summer of '94. From Kansas City through Spokane, the Royals' organization is loaded with talent. Over the past four years, they've brought in a ton of exciting baseball players, primarily though the draft, and are poised to assemble their best team since the mid-1980s.

Royals Prospectus

2001 record: 65–97; Fifth place, AL Central

Pythagenport W/L: 68–94

Runs scored: 729 (tenth in AL)

Runs allowed: 858 (11th in AL)

Team EqA: .243 (tied for 13th in AL)

2001 batters age: 28.1 (tied for sixth-youngest in AL)

2001 pitchers age: 26.8 (tied for second-youngest in AL)

Ballpark: Kauffman Stadium; good hitters' park; Park Factor of 1.058

2001: Questionable decisions hurt, but the bigger problem was that the young pitchers didn't make any progress.

2002: There's enough talent on hand to make them a .500 threat; bad management makes that the upside.

The Royals' greatest concentration of talent is on the mound. In the last few years, they've emphasized pitching in the first-year player draft, and that focus, combined with the compensation picks the Royals acquired as free agents left Kansas City, has filled their system with live arms.

Now, a strategy built around drafting high-school pitchers isn't one about which we're particularly enthusiastic, but the first step is having a plan, and it's clear that the Royals have executed one. Chris George, Jimmy Gobble, and Colt Griffin are the three high-upside arms, and they're backed by a considerable amount of depth in Mike MacDougal, Jeremy Hill, Jeremy Affeldt, and Runelvys Hernandez, just to throw out a few names. The nature of pitching prospects is such that not all of these guys will succeed, which is why quantity is such an important consideration. If the Royals get two mid-rotation starters and some decent trade bait from this group of seven pitchers, that's success.

Past the core group of pitching prospects, the Royals have the same bunch of live arms, injury cases, and long shots that every organization has. OK, theirs is a little bit better, what with a couple of former first-round picks in Kyle Snyder and Jeff Austin, as well as a large collection of hard-throwing right-handers with which any decent manager should be able to assemble a bullpen. The point is that the Royals have quantity and quality, and from this, can expect to build a cheap, effective pitching staff.

The organization has invested less in its hitters, giving the Royals less offensive depth than pitching depth, though some players are making progress at key positions. Catcher Mike Tonis and shortstops Angel Berroa and Alejandro Machado each came into the system through a different door, yet they could be the up-the-middle core of a division winner in 2005. First baseman Ken Harvey is supposed to be a part of that team, but his fragility—especially the possibility that his weight contributes to it—and questions about his plate discipline are troubling. Alexis Gomez, a fast center fielder who could comfortably hide behind Harvey, is young enough to become almost anything, from Steve Finley on down.

With so many young, inexpensive ballplayers coming through the system, the Royals have a few years of cost certainty ahead of them. They need to take advantage of this by locking up their two true stars, Carlos Beltran and Mike Sweeney, to long-term deals. Both players are among the league's best at their positions, and they provide an excellent 3-4 punch around which the Royals can build a winning lineup.

Sounds good, right? Well, what stands in the way of the Royals' success are General Manager Allard Baird and Manager Tony Muser. That sounds harsh, but neither man has proven himself capable of being part of a winning baseball team. The Royals' record under Muser is 309-426, and they haven't sniffed contention in his five seasons. While Baird deserves a share of credit for the talent currently flowing towards Kansas City, his decisions regarding the major-league roster have ranged from puzzling to indefensible.

Baird's errors have been well-covered by Rob Neyer and Rany Jazayerli, among others. His trade record is abysmal, driven by questionable notions of what is important to a winning baseball team. Baird has wasted millions of dollars on veterans whose primary asset was service time, while simultaneously dealing away the team's best players and complaining about how much money they would make. Roberto Hernandez, Doug Henry, Jason Grimsley, and David McCarty combined weren't worth a win to the Royals in 2001, but they cashed checks totalling $10.7 million. Replacing those players with readily available talent for $1 million would be painless, and it would free up nearly ten million bucks for the kind of baseball players a team really needs, such as Jermaine Dye.

The front-office troubles run deeper. Whereas even the much-derided Cam Bonifay did the little things well, like work minor-league free agency and the Rule 5 draft to his advantage, Baird has lost more talent through those processes than he's gained, a sign that he has a poor grip on roster management. Any team that would lose Corey Thurman and Ryan Baerlocher while wasting roster spots on Donnie Sadler and Scott Mullen has a warped idea of what its goals are.

Baird's mistakes at the top of the organization are hampering what has been a good effort by his scouting department, and his poor decisions threaten to scare off players such as Sweeney and Beltran. Already, the trades of Johnny Damon and Jermaine Dye may make it impossible for the Royals to re-sign Sweeney when free agency beckons.

While Baird has weakened the 40-man roster, Tony Muser hasn't done much with what talent he's been given. His childish rant against his players' lifestyles—the infamous "milk and cookies" speech—should have been grounds for dismissal. During Muser's tenure, the Royals have always seemed to be at odds with some player, most notably Carlos Beltran and Mark Quinn over the past two seasons.

Muser might be forgiven for his antagonistic streak if it appeared that he was actually developing the fruit of the Royals' system. However, players such as Jeremy Giambi, Mark Quinn, Dee Brown, Chad Durbin, Dan Reichert, and Blake Stein have stagnated or even regressed upon reaching Kansas City. Mike Sweeney succeeded in spite of Muser, whose disenchantment with Sweeney had the first baseman on the trade block for most of March 1999. It was only an injury to Jeremy Giambi that enabled Sweeney to become the player he is now.

While we can point to a few positive marks in Baird's record, there's virtually nothing Tony Muser has done in five seasons as Royals manager that can be used to build a case for him. He hasn't won, he hasn't developed talent, he hasn't kept the peace in the clubhouse. Unless the standard is "he didn't launch into a profane tirade against the media while brandishing a fifth of vodka," Muser has to be dismissed.

David Glass's to-do list is a short one: fire Baird, fire Muser, hire top-flight management talent. Once those tasks are accomplished, the Royals will be more than halfway to being a relevant baseball team again, rather than just another slide in Bud Selig's never-ending presentation on how to pay players less money.

Like many small-market teams, the Royals can help themselves in other ways. The self-destructive whining about their lot in life is a huge turnoff. No other business would spend the time baseball teams do denigrating their product; the incessant anti-marketing of baseball does as much to dry up revenue streams as any lack of on-field performance. The Royals can build their own "hope and faith" by emphasizing their stars to the citizens of Kansas City.

That's not all they can do. For years, Kauffman Stadium was lionized as a beautiful ballpark, one of the best places in baseball to watch a game. The emergence of mallparks in other cities shouldn't have changed that. In its marketing pitch, the team should play up the ballpark and its unique elements. The average fan doesn't care about luxury boxes; they care about their own experience. For the money, Kauffman provides a great baseball experience. The Royals should also become aggressive about being a regional presence. While Kansas City itself is small, the team has a history of drawing from a wide area, particularly on the weekends.

It's a good time to be a Royals fan. Selling that idea, and not the agenda of victimization handed down by a used-car salesman, will make a bigger difference in the future of the Kansas City Royals than anything that happens in a boardroom or during a contract negotiation.

HITTERS (BA: .270, OBP: .340, SLG: .440, EqA: .260)

Luis Alicea 2B/3B Bats B Age 36

YEAR	TEAM	LGE	AB	H	DB	TP	HR	BB	SO	R	RBI	SB	CS	OUT	BA	OBP	SLG	EQA	EQR	DEFENSE
1999	Texas	AL	162	33	8	0	4	27	28	32	17	2	1	130	.204	.317	.327	.225	16	30-2B -3
2000	Texas	AL	532	158	26	8	6	52	66	81	59	1	3	377	.297	.365	.410	.262	66	119-2B -8
2001	KansasCy	AL	386	109	18	4	4	24	48	46	32	7	6	283	.282	.329	.381	.238	39	61-2B -6 14-3B -1
2002	*KansasCy*	*AL*	*443*	*122*	*22*	*4*	*6*	*44*	*59*	*75*	*48*	*5*	*4*	*325*	*.275*	*.341*	*.384*	*.244*	*48*	

Most utility infielders who can't handle shortstop have the half-life of fresh-baked bread. Alicea stays around because he hits better than the rest of the species, and he has a knack for picking teams with lousy or fragile second basemen. He'll be back in Kansas City, making it all too easy for Tony Muser to screw with Carlos Febles. And just where is Geronimo Pena these days?

Carlos Beltran CF Bats B Age 25

YEAR	TEAM	LGE	AB	H	DB	TP	HR	BB	SO	R	RBI	SB	CS	OUT	BA	OBP	SLG	EQA	EQR	DEFENSE
1999	KansasCy	AL	655	193	27	7	23	39	108	107	103	25	8	470	.295	.338	.463	.266	86	153-CF 0
2000	KansasCy	AL	368	92	16	4	7	30	61	47	41	13	0	276	.250	.307	.372	.235	37	88-CF 1
2001	KansasCy	AL	615	195	32	12	26	54	104	110	103	29	1	421	.317	.376	.535	.303	107	152-CF 14
2002	*KansasCy*	*AL*	*564*	*185*	*28*	*9*	*24*	*54*	*100*	*108*	*99*	*29*	*3*	*382*	*.328*	*.387*	*.537*	*.308*	*100*	

With all due respect to Jason Giambi and Alex Rodriguez, Carlos Beltran might have been the best player in the American League after the All-Star break. He hit .358 with an improved walk rate and an extra-base hit every seven at-bats, went 21-for-22 on the bases, played an awesome center field, and finally perfected his Irish soda bread recipe.

Is this real? Probably. It's a natural progression from his 1999 season, with the across-the-board development you'd expect through aging. His injury- and controversy-riddled 2000 season is a distant memory. Beltran looks like Bernie Williams, v2.0, with more power, speed, and defense.

Brandon Berger OF Bats R Age 27

YEAR	TEAM	LGE	AB	H	DB	TP	HR	BB	SO	R	RBI	SB	CS	OUT	BA	OBP	SLG	EQA	EQR	DEFENSE
1999	Wilmngtn	Car	463	118	21	2	13	31	93	54	53	16	6	351	.255	.308	.393	.237	48	76-LF -5
2000	Wichita	Tex	87	13	3	0	2	4	27	6	6	3	1	75	.149	.197	.253	.160	4	16-LF 0
2000	Wilmngtn	Car	391	97	13	2	13	28	72	49	53	6	3	297	.248	.311	.391	.236	40	100-LF -1
2001	Wichita	Tex	457	122	19	2	30	35	92	74	84	9	5	339	.267	.328	.514	.272	66	83-OF -10
2002	*KansasCy*	*AL*	*461*	*126*	*21*	*2*	*25*	*43*	*97*	*69*	*74*	*10*	*5*	*340*	*.273*	*.335*	*.490*	*.269*	*64*	

Berger's 2001 spike was random. Berger, who had taken the better part of three years to get out of the Carolina League and tanked in his previous trip to Wichita, went nuts last year, blasting 40 bombs. He even had a tasty cup of coffee with the Royals, slugging .875 in 16 at-bats. He's not a prospect, just a guy who found his power stroke once and got himself a line in *The Baseball Encycl*... er, *Total Baseb*... um, a big book of baseball stats.

Angel Berroa SS Bats R Age 22

YEAR	TEAM	LGE	AB	H	DB	TP	HR	BB	SO	R	RBI	SB	CS	OUT	BA	OBP	SLG	EQA	EQR	DEFENSE
2000	Visalia	Cal	432	98	19	3	8	14	71	41	40	5	5	339	.227	.259	.340	.200	30	120-SS -30
2001	Wilmngtn	Car	205	56	13	3	5	9	41	34	20	6	4	153	.273	.321	.439	.250	24	51-SS -2
2001	Wichita	Tex	304	79	17	2	7	14	55	48	32	9	4	229	.260	.315	.398	.240	32	78-SS -2
2001	KansasCy	AL	53	17	2	0	0	3	9	8	4	2	0	36	.321	.357	.358	.253	6	12-SS 0
2002	*KansasCy*	*AL*	*505*	*147*	*30*	*4*	*14*	*31*	*95*	*103*	*62*	*5*	*2*	*360*	*.291*	*.332*	*.450*	*.258*	*61*	

Getting Berroa in what was otherwise a lousy Johnny Damon trade is Allard Baird's best move to date. Berroa has every tool in the shed and is developing skills that apply them to baseball. Most notably, his plate discipline improved in the jump to Wichita, progress that showed in his improved walk rate and was noted by observers. His strong September aside, there's no reason why Berroa shouldn't start the year at Omaha. The Royals still have Neifi Perez, and frankly, keeping Berroa away from what will be a rough couple of months in K.C. will be good for him.

Dee Brown LF Bats L Age 24

YEAR	TEAM	LGE	AB	H	DB	TP	HR	BB	SO	R	RBI	SB	CS	OUT	BA	OBP	SLG	EQA	EQR	DEFENSE
1999	Wilmngtn	Car	232	60	7	1	10	32	56	35	32	11	6	178	.259	.354	.427	.263	31	57-LF -1
1999	Wichita	Tex	235	68	9	2	9	27	42	42	39	6	5	172	.289	.367	.460	.273	34	63-LF -3
1999	KansasCy	AL	25	2	0	0	0	2	6	1	0	0	0	23	.080	.148	.080	.089	0	
2000	Omaha	PCL	477	119	21	4	20	27	108	60	55	15	3	361	.249	.293	.436	.242	52	108-LF -7
2000	KansasCy	AL	25	4	1	0	0	3	8	4	2	0	0	21	.160	.250	.200	.165	1	
2001	KansasCy	AL	379	96	13	0	10	23	70	41	43	5	3	286	.253	.297	.367	.223	34	81-LF -1
2002	*KansasCy*	*AL*	*476*	*129*	*18*	*2*	*19*	*42*	*101*	*71*	*66*	*8*	*2*	*349*	*.271*	*.330*	*.437*	*.256*	*58*	

Something bad has happened here, something that looks like more than a prospect's simple failure to develop. Brown is a completely different hitter than he was two years ago—not just in substance, but in style. He was a power hitter coming through the system, someone who drove the ball and drew a bunch of walks. In 1999 alone, Brown had 54 extra-base hits and took 72 unintentional walks. Now look at last year: 18 unintentional walks in 380 at-bats, a slugging average of .350, and, most damning, he became a ground-ball hitter, with 1.81 ground balls for every fly ball.

Here's the good news: if we're right, then Brown can still become the hitter it seemed he would be. He just needs the right instruction, a hitting coach who can get him back to his strengths. The skill set is there; it looks less like he can't handle the majors and more like he's just screwed up. Whether it's as a Royal, with another MLB team, or in Japan, Brown is going to have some good years.

Endy Chavez OF Bats L Age 24

YEAR	TEAM	LGE	AB	H	DB	TP	HR	BB	SO	R	RBI	SB	CS	OUT	BA	OBP	SLG	EQA	EQR	DEFENSE
1999	Columbia	SAL	262	50	4	1	0	25	38	25	10	9	7	219	.191	.261	.214	.173	14	69-CF 0
1999	St Lucie	Fla	185	46	7	1	2	16	25	23	12	5	2	141	.249	.308	.330	.221	16	39-CF 2
2000	St Lucie	Fla	440	108	16	1	1	34	53	59	31	21	11	342	.245	.300	.293	.209	34	106-CF 2
2001	Wichita	Tex	169	43	3	1	1	13	13	20	10	7	4	130	.254	.308	.302	.213	14	42-CF 1
2001	KansasCy	AL	77	17	2	0	0	3	7	4	5	0	2	62	.221	.250	.247	.166	3	19-LF 1
2001	Omaha	PCL	102	30	5	0	0	1	12	15	4	3	2	74	.294	.301	.343	.216	8	20-CF -2
2002	*Detroit*	*AL*	*422*	*112*	*14*	*2*	*3*	*35*	*49*	*55*	*28*	*13*	*7*	*317*	*.265*	*.322*	*.329*	*.228*	*40*	

Timo Perez Lite was taken from the Mets in the Rule 5 draft, and the Royals eventually traded Michael Curry to the Mets so they could send Chavez to the minors and still keep him. Curry is probably the better player, despite being a lesser physical talent and carrying an "attitude" label. Like the original Timoniel, Chavez's upside is as a fourth outfielder. Waived by the Royals, he'll show up in the Tigers' camp, where he only has to beat out Jose Macias to be the starting center fielder.

Carlos Febles 2B Bats R Age 26

YEAR	TEAM	LGE	AB	H	DB	TP	HR	BB	SO	R	RBI	SB	CS	OUT	BA	OBP	SLG	EQA	EQR	DEFENSE
1999	KansasCy	AL	448	116	21	9	11	42	80	68	51	19	4	336	.259	.333	.420	.257	56	122-2B 3
2000	KansasCy	AL	335	85	12	1	2	32	42	55	27	17	6	257	.254	.337	.313	.232	33	92-2B -3
2000	Omaha	PCL	42	8	2	0	1	6	10	4	4	2	3	37	.190	.302	.310	.205	4	10-2B 4
2001	KansasCy	AL	291	71	9	2	9	23	50	47	26	4	2	222	.244	.301	.381	.229	28	70-2B 1
2001	Omaha	PCL	97	29	5	1	2	8	13	19	8	5	2	70	.299	.368	.433	.272	13	23-2B 2
2002	*KansasCy*	*AL*	*398*	*104*	*18*	*3*	*11*	*45*	*67*	*66*	*43*	*13*	*4*	*298*	*.261*	*.336*	*.405*	*.252*	*47*	

This just isn't going to happen. Febles hasn't been able to stay healthy for more than a month at a time, and the leg injuries he's suffered have wiped out his speed and taken their toll on his range. He's a good enough player to have a random half-season at some point and hit .300/.360/.440 for a few months, but he's unlikely to reach 500 at-bats and could well be out of the majors by 2004.

Alexis Gomez CF Bats L Age 21

YEAR	TEAM	LGE	AB	H	DB	TP	HR	BB	SO	R	RBI	SB	CS	OUT	BA	OBP	SLG	EQA	EQR	DEFENSE
2000	Wilmngtn	Car	475	105	13	2	1	31	122	50	25	11	7	377	.221	.270	.263	.187	29	119-CF -7
2001	Wilmngtn	Car	175	46	6	2	1	10	43	26	8	5	2	131	.263	.304	.337	.220	15	46-CF -1
2001	Wichita	Tex	344	83	13	4	3	22	71	43	25	10	7	268	.241	.291	.328	.211	27	83-CF 0
2002	*KansasCy*	*AL*	*485*	*128*	*19*	*5*	*4*	*41*	*118*	*59*	*41*	*16*	*9*	*365*	*.264*	*.321*	*.348*	*.227*	*45*	

(Alexis Gomez *continued*)

God, the Royals love guys like this. Gomez is a fast, slap-hitting center fielder, young enough to be interesting. Probably the worst thing that could happen would be for him to have a good 2002 and make them think Carlos Beltran is expendable.

A player like Gomez illustrates the importance of an organization-wide approach to player development. If you're able to spot athletic baseball players—not athletes, but athletic *baseball players*—and get them into your system, then instill in them at ages 17, 18, 19 the importance of controlling the strike zone and the value of outs, you can rule the world. Gomez and Berroa have tremendous tools, and you can see them beginning the process of translating them to baseball. Teaching such players plate discipline is like giving them the key to the vault.

Ken Harvey 1B Bats B Age 24

YEAR	TEAM	LGE	AB	H	DB	TP	HR	BB	SO	R	RBI	SB	CS	OUT	BA	OBP	SLG	EQA	EQR	DEFENSE
1999	Spokane	Nwn	198	54	6	0	5	12	35	24	20	3	2	146	.273	.323	.379	.236	20	33-1B -1
2000	Wilmngtn	Car	169	48	6	0	4	9	29	16	19	0	1	122	.284	.332	.391	.242	18	18-1B -2
2001	Wilmngtn	Car	145	47	7	1	5	11	21	19	22	2	1	99	.324	.381	.490	.289	22	20-1B 1
2001	Wichita	Tex	314	91	16	2	7	15	60	43	47	2	0	223	.290	.326	.420	.249	35	53-1B 1
2002	*KansasCy*	*AL*	*432*	*138*	*21*	*2*	*13*	*34*	*81*	*59*	*56*	*1*	*2*	*296*	*.319*	*.369*	*.468*	*.277*	*60*	

Harvey is a big guy—6′4″, 240—who was the subject of considerable internal debate when we were putting together the Top 40 Prospects list. While he hit .338 at Wichita, his walk rate and strikeout-to-walk ratio went to hell, and his power was a disappointment. Some of that is due to bone chips in his right big toe that impacted his mechanics, a problem for which he underwent surgery after the season. Harvey has also had foot problems, so it's worth wondering if his weight is a factor. If so, is that going to mean constant, chronic injuries that hinder, or even halt, his development?

The Royals have a bunch of corner outfield/DH types floating around in Brown, Berger, Harvey, Mark Quinn, Raul Ibanez, Michael Tucker, and Chuck Knoblauch. Sorting through them correctly could be worth 50-70 runs to an offense that sorely needs them.

A.J. Hinch C Bats R Age 28

YEAR	TEAM	LGE	AB	H	DB	TP	HR	BB	SO	R	RBI	SB	CS	OUT	BA	OBP	SLG	EQA	EQR	DEFENSE
1999	Oakland	AL	205	47	4	1	8	9	36	27	25	6	2	160	.229	.268	.376	.216	17	59-C -4
1999	Vancouvr	PCL	60	21	1	0	2	3	11	7	6	1	1	40	.350	.388	.467	.283	9	12-C -1
2000	Sacramen	PCL	416	100	21	1	5	35	65	53	37	4	4	320	.240	.307	.332	.218	36	86-C -2
2001	KansasCy	AL	121	20	2	0	7	8	22	11	16	1	1	102	.165	.230	.355	.194	9	37-C -1
2001	Omaha	PCL	166	48	8	0	9	11	30	23	27	1	0	118	.289	.336	.500	.273	23	24-C -2
2002	*KansasCy*	*AL*	*382*	*95*	*14*	*1*	*18*	*38*	*69*	*57*	*50*	*5*	*3*	*290*	*.249*	*.317*	*.432*	*.247*	*44*	

The good news, if you're a fan of Hinch, is that he found some semblance of his stroke after being demoted to Omaha in July, the first time he'd hit since 1999. With Brent Mayne around to be the #1 catcher and Gregg Zaun gone to Houston, there's an opportunity for Hinch to slide in as a #2 with a bullet. Fair or not, what he does in March may well determine the rest of his professional life. Look for him to succeed.

Raul Ibanez RF Bats L Age 30

YEAR	TEAM	LGE	AB	H	DB	TP	HR	BB	SO	R	RBI	SB	CS	OUT	BA	OBP	SLG	EQA	EQR	DEFENSE	
1999	Seattle	AL	208	55	6	0	10	15	28	23	27	5	1	154	.264	.314	.438	.251	24	37-RF 0	17-1B -2
2000	Seattle	AL	140	35	6	0	3	13	22	21	16	2	0	105	.250	.318	.357	.233	14	36-RF 2	
2001	KansasCy	AL	278	80	11	5	14	33	44	47	55	0	2	200	.288	.363	.514	.284	43	35-RF -4	
2002	*KansasCy*	*AL*	*298*	*84*	*13*	*2*	*13*	*34*	*51*	*42*	*44*	*3*	*1*	*215*	*.282*	*.355*	*.470*	*.274*	*42*		

It's fairly dissatisfying to spend $21.95 on a book about baseball players and find that said book doesn't have all the answers you want. We sympathize, but there's no explanation for Ibanez's performance last year. His power came from pulling the ball more, and he showed an increased willingness to work counts. For $800,000—his 2002 salary—it's a worthwhile gamble to see if the change is permanent.

Alejandro Machado SS Bats R Age 20

YEAR	TEAM	LGE	AB	H	DB	TP	HR	BB	SO	R	RBI	SB	CS	OUT	BA	OBP	SLG	EQA	EQR	DEFENSE
2000	Danville	App	228	49	4	1	0	32	35	22	9	9	6	186	.215	.317	.241	.204	17	59-2B -1
2001	Macon	SAL	320	70	5	1	1	25	59	30	18	9	7	257	.219	.286	.250	.191	20	61-2B -2 12-SS 0
2001	Burlingt	Mid	111	21	3	0	0	7	18	11	8	2	1	91	.189	.242	.216	.165	5	27-SS 6
2002	*KansasCy*	*AL*	*402*	*102*	*11*	*2*	*2*	*40*	*73*	*40*	*27*	*14*	*10*	*310*	*.254*	*.321*	*.306*	*.213*	*33*	

Acquired from the Braves for Rey Sanchez, Machado is a speedy shortstop with an improving glove and all the power of Mr. Roper. What makes him stand out is his strike-zone judgment—117 walks against 845 at-bats as a professional, which is excellent for a teenager. This is a pretty good test case for the Royals. They've been handed a prospect with plate discipline; will they nurture it, or beat it out of him?

Brent Mayne C Bats L Age 34

YEAR	TEAM	LGE	AB	H	DB	TP	HR	BB	SO	R	RBI	SB	CS	OUT	BA	OBP	SLG	EQA	EQR	DEFENSE
1999	San Fran	NL	325	100	21	0	6	39	60	38	41	2	2	227	.308	.390	.428	.278	46	87-C 2
2000	Colorado	NL	325	86	12	0	7	41	44	30	54	1	3	242	.265	.348	.366	.244	35	91-C -3
2001	Colorado	NL	155	48	6	0	0	14	20	14	18	0	0	107	.310	.367	.348	.248	16	44-C 3
2001	KansasCy	AL	165	41	5	1	2	11	15	14	20	1	2	126	.248	.298	.327	.211	13	46-C 0
2002	*KansasCy*	*AL*	*303*	*78*	*8*	*0*	*6*	*32*	*40*	*27*	*37*	*1*	*2*	*237*	*.257*	*.328*	*.343*	*.226*	*20*	

Good idea: having Mayne as your backup catcher. He's good for a .340 OBP, has some defensive skill, and doesn't complain about his playing time. Bad idea: giving him a two-year contract at the age of 34. Teams are slowly learning the lesson that players of a certain caliber are not worthy of guaranteed millions or roster spots, but it's happening in an uneven fashion. That's why Brent Mayne and Vinny Castilla can find jobs that pay well. Baby steps.

Dave McCarty 1B Bats R Age 32

YEAR	TEAM	LGE	AB	H	DB	TP	HR	BB	SO	R	RBI	SB	CS	OUT	BA	OBP	SLG	EQA	EQR	DEFENSE
1999	Toledo	Int	468	117	22	2	26	59	103	71	62	4	5	356	.250	.338	.472	.265	64	111-1B 10 18-OF -1
2000	KansasCy	AL	267	75	14	1	13	18	60	32	51	0	0	192	.281	.326	.487	.265	35	54-1B 7
2001	KansasCy	AL	199	51	9	0	8	25	39	27	27	0	0	148	.256	.341	.422	.256	25	49-1B 1
2002	*KansasCy*	*AL*	*377*	*89*	*17*	*1*	*16*	*44*	*84*	*47*	*48*	*1*	*2*	*290*	*.236*	*.316*	*.414*	*.241*	*41*	

David McCarty isn't bad, it's just that what he does—play defense at first base and hit lefties—is no different from any number of readily available players. If he has a guaranteed two-year contract, you're locked into him, rather than being free to dump him when he tanks and go into the pile of lefty-mashing first-base types to get a replacement. The fear of the unknown is something the Royals are going to have to get past in building a winning team.

Hector Ortiz C Bats R Age 32

YEAR	TEAM	LGE	AB	H	DB	TP	HR	BB	SO	R	RBI	SB	CS	OUT	BA	OBP	SLG	EQA	EQR	DEFENSE
1999	SanAnton	Tex	122	26	3	0	0	8	18	8	10	0	1	97	.213	.262	.238	.174	6	33-C 1
1999	Albuquer	PCL	159	41	5	0	5	6	25	16	15	2	2	120	.258	.288	.384	.222	14	29-C -2 13-1B -1
2000	Omaha	PCL	225	66	7	0	6	16	17	24	19	3	2	161	.293	.342	.404	.251	25	48-C -1
2000	KansasCy	AL	86	33	6	0	0	7	7	14	5	0	0	53	.384	.436	.453	.306	14	23-C 0
2001	KansasCy	AL	153	39	6	1	0	10	21	13	11	1	3	117	.255	.304	.307	.206	11	47-C 4
2001	Omaha	PCL	149	34	5	0	2	14	24	16	13	0	2	117	.228	.294	.302	.203	11	28-C -3
2002	*KansasCy*	*AL*	*300*	*76*	*11*	*1*	*6*	*23*	*40*	*31*	*27*	*2*	*4*	*228*	*.253*	*.307*	*.357*	*.218*	*25*	

Having signed the veteran Mayne to a two-year contract, the Royals have less need for an experienced backup and more room to give Hinch a chance, which hurts Ortiz. He's a catch-and-throw guy who never caught the breaks that people such as Mike Matheny and Alberto Castillo did. He's as good a player as they are.

Neifi Perez SS Bats B Age 27

YEAR	TEAM	LGE	AB	H	DB	TP	HR	BB	SO	R	RBI	SB	CS	OUT	BA	OBP	SLG	EQA	EQR	DEFENSE
1999	Colorado	NL	677	168	23	9	11	20	50	92	58	10	4	513	.248	.271	.357	.211	52	155-SS 8
2000	Colorado	NL	639	162	35	8	9	20	58	78	59	2	5	482	.254	.276	.376	.214	51	158-SS 26
2001	Colorado	NL	373	104	17	7	6	13	42	59	42	5	2	271	.279	.303	.410	.237	37	87-SS 2
2001	KansasCy	AL	198	50	7	1	1	11	16	18	12	2	4	152	.253	.294	.313	.204	14	46-SS -1
2002	*KansasCy*	*AL*	*577*	*156*	*28*	*7*	*9*	*33*	*57*	*85*	*54*	*6*	*4*	*425*	*.270*	*.310*	*.390*	*.231*	*55*	

In the aftermath of the Royals trading Jermaine Dye for Neifi Perez, there was some talk that maybe the trade wasn't so bad, that Perez really could be a good hitter at sea level, that his road stats weren't really indicative of his ability. Such talk was silly, of course; we had five years of evidence, more than 1,200 at-bats, that showed Perez to be a .245/.285/.345 hitter everywhere but at altitude, and even considering his good defense, a generous projection of his offensive peak wouldn't make him worth Dye.

Perez's experience might become a cautionary tale for future Rockies who enter into negotiations with their team. While in Colorado, he was talking about a four-year deal with the Rockies and dickering over numbers ranging from $20 million to $28 million. After two months away from Planet Coors, during which he posted a .241/.277/.302 line, nobody is thinking about giving him a long-term deal. In fact, he's been on the trade market most of the winter. It's something for Juan Pierre to consider come 2004.

Mark Quinn LF Bats R Age 28

YEAR	TEAM	LGE	AB	H	DB	TP	HR	BB	SO	R	RBI	SB	CS	OUT	BA	OBP	SLG	EQA	EQR	DEFENSE
1999	Omaha	PCL	416	130	16	0	21	23	63	51	64	6	7	293	.313	.358	.502	.279	60	101-RF 3
1999	KansasCy	AL	59	20	4	1	6	3	10	11	17	1	0	39	.339	.380	.746	.343	13	13-LF 0
2000	KansasCy	AL	493	146	30	2	21	29	80	72	73	5	2	349	.296	.339	.493	.272	67	81-LF 1
2001	KansasCy	AL	451	125	29	2	19	14	60	59	61	8	5	332	.277	.307	.477	.254	54	97-RF -1
2001	Omaha	PCL	42	7	2	0	1	1	8	3	2	0	0	35	.167	.186	.286	.157	2	
2002	*KansasCy*	*AL*	*524*	*152*	*28*	*2*	*25*	*36*	*81*	*70*	*79*	*8*	*5*	*377*	*.290*	*.336*	*.494*	*.270*	*71*	

Just as Carlos Febles seems unable to get through a season without hurting himself, so Mark Quinn seems unable to get through one without incurring a demotion. He doesn't hit enough to DH, and playing him in the field behind a pitching staff that puts a lot of balls in play is a formula for doubles. Despite the problems he had, Quinn is still projected to be the Royals' starting right fielder in 2002.

Joe Randa 3B Bats R Age 32

YEAR	TEAM	LGE	AB	H	DB	TP	HR	BB	SO	R	RBI	SB	CS	OUT	BA	OBP	SLG	EQA	EQR	DEFENSE
1999	KansasCy	AL	619	196	36	7	17	44	70	89	80	5	4	427	.317	.365	.480	.279	88	152-3B 2
2000	KansasCy	AL	604	185	29	4	15	28	58	83	99	6	3	422	.306	.343	.442	.261	74	155-3B 5
2001	KansasCy	AL	579	152	31	2	15	44	69	62	85	3	2	429	.263	.319	.401	.241	61	136-3B -2
2002	*KansasCy*	*AL*	*538*	*144*	*24*	*3*	*15*	*46*	*62*	*69*	*69*	*5*	*2*	*396*	*.268*	*.325*	*.407*	*.244*	*58*	

Conquering the fear of the unknown would keep the Royals from giving guarantees to people such as David McCarty. The next lesson would be to recognize when a player is peaking, and not simply expect him to repeat his best season. Randa received a contract extension off of his career 1999 season, then another off of his looked-better-than-it-was 2000 season. He's losing 20 points of EqA a year and is signed though 2003. That's a problem.

Donnie Sadler UT Bats R Age 27

YEAR	TEAM	LGE	AB	H	DB	TP	HR	BB	SO	R	RBI	SB	CS	OUT	BA	OBP	SLG	EQA	EQR	DEFENSE
1999	Pawtuckt	Int	172	47	10	3	1	12	34	19	14	3	2	127	.273	.329	.384	.240	18	36-SS -3
1999	Boston	AL	106	31	5	1	0	4	18	18	5	2	1	76	.292	.318	.358	.229	10	
2000	Pawtuckt	Int	317	62	6	4	5	38	59	41	21	8	1	256	.196	.288	.287	.206	25	49-CF 0 34-SS 4
2000	Boston	AL	99	23	2	0	2	4	16	13	10	3	1	77	.232	.269	.313	.201	7	13-SS 3
2001	Cincnnti	NL	84	17	1	0	2	9	17	9	4	3	3	70	.202	.280	.286	.195	6	
2001	KansasCy	AL	101	15	3	0	0	9	15	18	2	4	1	87	.149	.229	.178	.157	4	12-2B 2 11-3B 3
2002	*KansasCy*	*AL*	*345*	*78*	*14*	*3*	*5*	*37*	*65*	*49*	*22*	*10*	*4*	*271*	*.226*	*.301*	*.328*	*.214*	*29*	

Donnie Sadler isn't worth a roster spot, not in this world, not in the next. He might be the worst-hitting position player in baseball. Sadler can run, and he can play the infield fairly well, and you can get that in 50 other guys who at least have a chance of putting up a .250 EqA. He's a free agent as of January.

Mike Sweeney 1B Bats R Age 28

YEAR	TEAM	LGE	AB	H	DB	TP	HR	BB	SO	R	RBI	SB	CS	OUT	BA	OBP	SLG	EQA	EQR	DEFENSE
1999	KansasCy	AL	566	184	41	2	24	48	42	98	98	6	1	383	.325	.387	.532	.302	96	69-1B -10
2000	KansasCy	AL	605	203	23	0	31	63	59	98	135	8	3	405	.336	.412	.527	.311	109	110-1B 1
2001	KansasCy	AL	557	175	37	0	34	66	55	100	103	9	3	385	.314	.388	.564	.308	102	106-1B -3
2002	*KansasCy*	*AL*	*594*	*196*	*30*	*1*	*36*	*73*	*58*	*110*	*123*	*9*	*3*	*401*	*.330*	*.403*	*.566*	*.315*	*112*	

It appears he's settled into autopilot, a mode from which we can expect a .310 EqA for another 4,000 at-bats. Whether Sweeney will accumulate more than 300 of those at-bats as a Royal is unclear. It's beginning to get tiring watching the Royals make minor efforts to sign their best players while the team has some leverage, then make a self-destructive trade and blame the system for their inability to compete. If you were a supremely talented 28-year-old, would you stay in that environment?

Mike Tonis C Bats R Age 23

YEAR	TEAM	LGE	AB	H	DB	TP	HR	BB	SO	R	RBI	SB	CS	OUT	BA	OBP	SLG	EQA	EQR	DEFENSE
2000	Charl-WV	SAL	103	17	6	0	0	6	24	7	11	0	0	86	.165	.214	.223	.153	4	25-C -1
2001	Wilmngtn	Car	129	29	5	0	3	13	34	13	15	0	0	100	.225	.300	.333	.217	11	31-C -1
2001	Wichita	Tex	228	53	9	1	7	18	41	29	32	1	1	176	.232	.294	.373	.224	21	59-C -2
2002	*KansasCy*	*AL*	*345*	*87*	*15*	*1*	*10*	*34*	*77*	*41*	*53*	*1*	*1*	*259*	*.252*	*.319*	*.388*	*.236*	*35*	

Stealth prospect who moved from the draft to Double-A in a little less than a year. He has all the tools defensively, and his offense is getting better as he learns to drive the ball with a wood bat. He's not ready yet, and given all the adjustments that catchers have to make—they're both learning to hit *and* catch better stuff from pitchers at higher levels—it's a good idea to let him get another 500 upper-level at-bats and 1,000 innings behind the plate. Off-season knee surgery was successful. Tonis will be a factor in 2003.

Gregg Zaun C Bats B Age 31

YEAR	TEAM	LGE	AB	H	DB	TP	HR	BB	SO	R	RBI	SB	CS	OUT	BA	OBP	SLG	EQA	EQR	DEFENSE
1999	Texas	AL	92	23	3	1	1	9	6	12	12	1	0	69	.250	.317	.337	.227	8	26-C 2
2000	KansasCy	AL	229	62	8	0	8	40	30	33	31	7	3	170	.271	.386	.410	.275	34	65-C -6
2001	Omaha	PCL	43	11	3	0	1	2	3	4	7	0	0	32	.256	.299	.395	.231	4	
2001	KansasCy	AL	125	41	7	0	7	12	14	15	19	1	2	86	.328	.387	.552	.300	21	32-C -1
2002	*Houston*	*NL*	*234*	*69*	*11*	*0*	*10*	*31*	*28*	*39*	*42*	*6*	*4*	*168*	*.295*	*.377*	*.470*	*.277*	*34*	

It would be nice if a year from now we couldn't call him The Practically Perfect Backup Catcher, because he'd taken the Astros' starting job from Brad Ausmus. They could use another left-handed bat in the lineup anyway, and flipping the two players' roles would be worth 15, maybe 20 runs. That's a lot in a division likely to be decided very late in the season.

PITCHERS (ERA: 4.50, H/9: 9.0, HR/9: 1.0, BB/9: 3.0, K/9: 6.0, KW: 2.0, PERA: 4.50)

Jeremy Affeldt Throws L Age 23

YEAR	TEAM	LGE	IP	H	ER	HR	BB	K	ERA	W	L	H/9	HR/9	BB/9	K/9	KW	PERA	STUFF
1999	Charl-WV	SAL	145.0	152	94	8	109	57	5.83	6	10	9.4	0.5	6.8	3.5	0.3	6.85	-10
2000	Wilmngtn	Car	149.0	165	90	16	65	54	5.44	7	10	10.0	1.0	3.9	3.3	0.4	7.13	-9
2001	Wichita	Tex	149.3	152	76	14	54	88	4.58	8	9	9.2	0.8	3.3	5.3	0.8	5.26	8

Affeldt is a tall, thin left-hander who has been progressing in the shadow of the Royals' better-known prospects. He only gets up around 90 with his fastball, but he mixes it well with a change-up and slurve. He keeps the ball down and in the park, which is how he succeeds without great strikeout numbers. Affeldt was named to the all-Arizona Fall League team despite being used in an unfamiliar role and having a couple of bad outings inflate his ERA to 7.25. His long term outlook is as a swing man/spot starter.

Jeff Austin Throws R Age 25

YEAR	TEAM	LGE	IP	H	ER	HR	BB	K	ERA	W	L	H/9	HR/9	BB/9	K/9	KW	PERA	STUFF
1999	Wilmngtn	Car	109.3	126	79	21	45	54	6.50	4	8	10.4	1.7	3.7	4.4	0.6	5.66	-5
1999	Wichita	Tex	36.3	37	16	1	12	15	3.96	2	2	9.2	0.2	3.0	3.7	0.6	5.32	2
2000	Wichita	Tex	40.3	43	18	5	4	21	4.02	2	2	9.6	1.1	0.9	4.7	2.6	3.70	10
2000	Omaha	PCL	129.3	150	79	19	33	46	5.50	6	8	10.4	1.3	2.3	3.2	0.7	5.80	-8
2001	Omaha	PCL	72.3	84	57	16	32	38	7.09	2	6	10.5	2.0	4.0	4.7	0.6	7.69	-24
2001	KansasCy	AL	27.3	25	14	4	13	26	4.61	1	2	8.2	1.3	4.3	8.6	1.0	5.11	7

The formula for creating a closer isn't "give a guy a lot of save chances in Double-A." It's "take a failed starter with two good pitches and see if he can mow through a lineup once." Austin, a former #1 pick out of Stanford, was at a fork in the road when the Royals moved him to the pen in May. He immediately began pitching better, commanding his mid-90s heater well enough to make his major-league debut in July. He's going to eventually save 30 games and make a ton of money, although not this year.

Ryan Baerlocher Throws R Age 24

YEAR	TEAM	LGE	IP	H	ER	HR	BB	K	ERA	W	L	H/9	HR/9	BB/9	K/9	KW	PERA	STUFF
1999	Spokane	Nwn	74.7	86	56	14	36	36	6.75	2	6	10.4	1.7	4.3	4.3	0.5	5.90	-8
2000	Charl-WV	SAL	109.0	114	64	16	44	69	5.28	5	7	9.4	1.3	3.6	5.7	0.8	5.00	6
2000	Wilmngtn	Car	47.7	50	28	7	20	31	5.29	2	3	9.4	1.3	3.8	5.9	0.8	4.41	7
2001	Wichita	Tex	174.0	211	144	43	67	81	7.45	5	14	10.9	2.2	3.5	4.2	0.6	5.59	-11

Baerlocher is a big guy who doesn't pitch like it, using an average fastball to set up a good curve and change-up. He had some problems with the long ball in each of the past two seasons, something that wasn't helped by the Texas League's good hitters' parks. He'll need another 400 innings or so before he's ready to get out major-league hitters, and he will be fighting the notion that a guy his size should throw harder. The Padres took him in the Rule 5 draft.

Cory Bailey Throws R Age 31

YEAR	TEAM	LGE	IP	H	ER	HR	BB	K	ERA	W	L	H/9	HR/9	BB/9	K/9	KW	PERA	STUFF
1999	Fresno	PCL	47.0	49	30	8	20	35	5.74	2	3	9.4	1.5	3.8	6.7	0.9	4.77	-16
2000	Nashvill	PCL	75.7	72	35	3	37	44	4.16	4	4	8.6	0.4	4.4	5.2	0.6	4.49	-15
2001	KansasCy	AL	68.0	58	27	3	31	58	3.57	5	3	7.7	0.4	4.1	7.7	0.9	3.25	8

Bailey's Comet, which appears in middle relief over Midwestern skies every five years, returned to soak up low-leverage innings for the Royals. It induces ground balls and gives left-handed hitters fits. Next scheduled appearance: 2006, in Chicago.

Ryan Bukvich Throws R Age 24

YEAR	TEAM	LGE	IP	H	ER	HR	BB	K	ERA	W	L	H/9	HR/9	BB/9	K/9	KW	PERA	STUFF
2000	Spokane	Nwn	12.3	11	7	0	11	7	5.11	0	1	8.0	0.0	8.0	5.1	0.3	0.97	-15
2000	Charl-WV	SAL	13.0	11	6	0	9	8	4.15	1	0	7.6	0.0	6.2	5.5	0.4	2.77	-8
2001	Wilmngtn	Car	56.0	51	33	3	47	41	5.30	3	3	8.2	0.5	7.6	6.6	0.4	4.19	-16
2001	Wichita	Tex	11.0	12	8	3	2	9	6.55	0	1	9.8	2.5	1.6	7.4	2.3	5.37	-1

One of a couple of "Closers of the Future" lurking in the Royals' system, Bukvich mostly blows his mid-90s heat past people, a trick that isn't going to work at higher levels. He's working on a splitter and a slider; the Royals should let him start in 2002, because he needs innings to establish that second pitch.

Paul Byrd Throws R Age 31

YEAR	TEAM	LGE	IP	H	ER	HR	BB	K	ERA	W	L	H/9	HR/9	BB/9	K/9	KW	PERA	STUFF
1999	Philadel	NL	197.7	221	121	31	59	95	5.51	9	13	10.1	1.4	2.7	4.3	0.8	4.85	-2
2000	Scran-WB	Int	24.0	27	14	3	7	7	5.25	1	2	10.1	1.1	2.6	2.6	0.5	2.53	-11
2000	Philadel	NL	83.3	92	54	15	29	47	5.83	3	6	9.9	1.6	3.1	5.1	0.8	6.51	-6
2001	Clearwtr	Fla	23.7	26	13	3	7	9	4.94	1	2	9.9	1.1	2.7	3.4	0.6	5.82	-15
2001	Scran-WB	Int	36.0	38	20	6	9	24	5.00	2	2	9.5	1.5	2.3	6.0	1.3	5.75	1
2001	Philadel	NL	9.3	10	5	1	4	2	4.82	0	1	9.6	1.0	3.9	1.9	0.3	8.01	-30
2001	KansasCy	AL	97.7	104	47	10	21	47	4.33	6	5	9.6	0.9	1.9	4.3	1.1	3.77	4

Byrd had a good run after coming over from the Phillies, claiming it was because of a screwball he'd added. He did make 11 good starts in his first 12 with the Royals, but his shoulder couldn't handle the success, and he was shut down in early September. Screwball or no, he's horrid against left-handed batters. All things considered, he can probably be a good reliever.

Tony Cogan Throws L Age 25

YEAR	TEAM	LGE	IP	H	ER	HR	BB	K	ERA	W	L	H/9	HR/9	BB/9	K/9	KW	PERA	STUFF
1999	Spokane	Nwn	37.7	36	15	0	16	19	3.58	2	2	8.6	0.0	3.8	4.5	0.6	2.69	-7
2000	Charl-WV	SAL	74.7	85	42	8	20	24	5.06	4	4	10.2	1.0	2.4	2.9	0.0	3.40	-7
2000	Wilmngtn	Car	39.7	42	23	3	22	16	5.22	2	2	9.5	0.7	5.0	3.6	0.4	7.62	28
2001	KansasCy	AL	26.0	30	21	6	12	16	7.27	1	2	10.4	2.1	4.2	5.5	0.7	5.38	-20
2001	Wichita	Tex	15.7	19	12	4	5	7	6.89	1	1	10.9	2.3	2.9	4.0	0.7	4.04	-28
2001	Omaha	PCL	10.7	11	6	1	4	5	5.06	0	1	9.3	0.8	3.4	4.2	0.6	3.00	-16

We pick on Tony Muser because he does things that just defy explanation. He kept Cogan, a college left-hander with 2⅓ innings of experience above A–ball, on the roster as his only southpaw in the bullpen at the start of the season. How did he introduce the kid to the big leagues? On Opening Day, in Yankee Stadium, against the three-time defending world champions, bringing him in to protect a one-run lead with two runners on, nobody out, and four right-handed hitters scheduled to bat. If that's not the all-time worst introduction to the major leagues, we don't want to know what beats it.

Cogan had been a starter, but the Royals' wealth of left-handed pitching means that he'll be staying in the bullpen. He has little upside and will bounce around for a long, long time as a Mike Magnante type.

Chad Durbin Throws R Age 24

YEAR	TEAM	LGE	IP	H	ER	HR	BB	K	ERA	W	L	H/9	HR/9	BB/9	K/9	KW	PERA	STUFF
1999	Wichita	Tex	155.0	172	102	28	54	88	5.92	6	11	10.0	1.6	3.1	5.1	0.8	5.39	5
2000	Omaha	PCL	72.7	79	43	12	21	43	5.33	3	5	9.8	1.5	2.6	5.3	1.0	4.40	10
2000	KansasCy	AL	76.3	85	51	12	35	37	6.01	3	5	10.0	1.4	4.1	4.4	0.5	7.01	-9
2001	Omaha	PCL	26.0	25	13	4	7	25	4.50	2	1	8.7	1.4	2.4	8.7	1.8	3.80	28
2001	KansasCy	AL	183.7	199	102	23	55	90	5.00	9	11	9.8	1.1	2.7	4.4	0.8	4.76	2

Speaking of Reasons To Fire Tony, his handling of Durbin was nearly as bizarre as his treatment of Cogan. Twice, Muser left a tiring Durbin in games the Royals had in hand in an effort to have him go the distance. On another occasion, he let a tiring Durbin blow a game in which he'd pitched very well for seven innings on his 132nd pitch.

Our objection to Muser's tactics has less to do with the use or abuse of an arm and more to do with the proper way to develop a young pitcher. The notion that a pitcher has to learn how to finish games is antiquated—not because finishing games isn't a good thing, but because even when pitchers are throwing well, they're generally removed for a closer. Seven, even eight good innings is a positive experience for a pitcher, especially one having an up-and-down season. Durbin stayed in the rotation all year, a feat in itself. He'll have to improve his command considerably or find himself lapped by the better pitchers coming up behind him.

Chris George Throws L Age 22

YEAR	TEAM	LGE	IP	H	ER	HR	BB	K	ERA	W	L	H/9	HR/9	BB/9	K/9	KW	PERA	STUFF
1999	Wilmngtn	Car	146.3	152	81	16	58	83	4.98	7	9	9.3	1.0	3.6	5.1	0.7	5.26	10
2000	Wichita	Tex	97.3	97	53	7	51	55	4.90	5	6	9.0	0.6	4.7	5.1	0.5	4.02	10
2000	Omaha	PCL	44.0	52	34	10	19	22	6.95	1	4	10.6	2.0	3.9	4.5	0.6	5.61	-1
2001	Omaha	PCL	110.7	119	73	16	58	60	5.94	4	8	9.7	1.3	4.7	4.9	0.5	4.29	3
2001	KansasCy	AL	74.3	86	46	12	17	30	5.57	3	5	10.4	1.5	2.1	3.6	0.9	5.07	-1

The Big Cheese. George gets raves for his command of good, not great, stuff, especially his ability to change speeds. He's advanced through the system even though his peripherals have not been very impressive, in part because he's posted good primary numbers, in part because scouts love him. He did not pitch well for the Royals, and it's not clear that he's ready for the major leagues. The Royals should give him at least another half-season in Triple-A, at least until they get a new manager.

Jimmy Gobble — Throws L — Age 20

YEAR	TEAM	LGE	IP	H	ER	HR	BB	K	ERA	W	L	H/9	HR/9	BB/9	K/9	KW	PERA	STUFF
2000	Charl-WV	SAL	142.7	165	94	25	43	60	5.93	6	10	10.4	1.6	2.7	3.8	0.7	6.57	1
2001	Wilmngtn	Car	156.7	164	81	19	44	89	4.65	8	9	9.4	1.1	2.5	5.1	1.0	4.79	15

If you have faith in your scouting and player-acquisition program, you should be eager to let all but the best free agents leave and take the draft picks. The Royals took Gobble as a supplemental first rounder in the 1999 draft with a pick they received as compensation for the loss of Dean Palmer. Gobble has some similarities to George but throws harder and has had better numbers so far. He's the best of the Royals' pitching prospects behind George.

Colt Griffin — Throws R — Age 19

YEAR	TEAM	LGE	IP	H	ER	HR	BB	K	ERA	W	L	H/9	HR/9	BB/9	K/9	KW	PERA	STUFF
2001	Spokane	Nwn	2.7	3	6	0	10	0	20.25	0	0	10.1	0.0	33.8	0.0	0.0	39.05	-151

The Royals 2001 #1 pick (#9 overall) is a hard-throwing country boy from Texas. Griffin was rated the hardest thrower in last year's draft, reportedly reaching 100 mph at one point. He's been a full-time pitcher for less than two years, so he has a long learning curve ahead of him.

Jason Grimsley — Throws R — Age 34

YEAR	TEAM	LGE	IP	H	ER	HR	BB	K	ERA	W	L	H/9	HR/9	BB/9	K/9	KW	PERA	STUFF
1999	NY Yanks	AL	74.0	72	37	6	33	49	4.50	4	4	8.8	0.7	4.0	6.0	0.7	4.11	-5
2000	NY Yanks	AL	98.0	101	49	9	34	53	4.50	6	5	9.3	0.8	3.1	4.9	0.8	4.64	-9
2001	KansasCy	AL	80.0	76	36	7	27	58	4.05	5	4	8.6	0.8	3.0	6.5	1.1	3.12	1

Four years ago, Grimsley was one of those bad-joke guys, the poster boy for the kind of replacement-level talent you didn't want to find on your team's NRI list. The Yankees picked him up, stuck him in the pen, and reduced him to a fastball/sinker pitcher. He became a low-leverage innings muncher and graduated to setup man for the Royals last year. He's perhaps the only person who would like to see the Royals keep Neifi Perez.

Junior Guerrero — Throws R — Age 22

YEAR	TEAM	LGE	IP	H	ER	HR	BB	K	ERA	W	L	H/9	HR/9	BB/9	K/9	KW	PERA	STUFF
1999	Charl-WV	SAL	102.3	107	67	12	61	58	5.89	4	7	9.4	1.1	5.4	5.1	0.5	4.70	6
1999	Wilmngtn	Car	48.0	44	25	4	29	40	4.69	2	3	8.3	0.8	5.4	7.5	0.7	2.29	28
2000	Wichita	Tex	129.3	164	127	37	68	55	8.84	3	11	11.4	2.6	4.7	3.8	0.4	6.78	-14
2001	Wichita	Tex	19.3	21	14	2	16	8	6.52	1	1	9.8	0.9	7.4	3.7	0.3	11.83	-34
2001	Wilmngtn	Car	80.0	95	60	16	32	34	6.75	3	6	10.7	1.8	3.6	3.8	0.5	5.60	-6

He's young enough to rebound, but right now, Guerrero is lost. He's lost 8–10 mph off of his fastball over two years and been chased out of the Texas League by a hail of line drives. Returning to Wilmington and the rotation, he got some of his confidence back, if not his velocity. Just 22, he has plenty of time.

Doug Henry — Throws R — Age 38

YEAR	TEAM	LGE	IP	H	ER	HR	BB	K	ERA	W	L	H/9	HR/9	BB/9	K/9	KW	PERA	STUFF
1999	Houston	NL	42.0	43	28	8	20	32	6.00	2	3	9.2	1.7	4.3	6.9	0.8	5.02	-9
2000	Houston	NL	50.0	50	31	9	23	41	5.58	2	4	9.0	1.6	4.1	7.4	0.9	3.78	-3
2000	San Fran	NL	23.7	24	15	2	17	14	5.70	1	2	9.1	0.8	6.5	5.3	0.4	3.52	-18
2001	KansasCy	AL	76.0	78	52	12	43	54	6.16	3	5	9.2	1.4	5.1	6.4	0.6	5.48	-13

Henry has a two-year contract for $2.9 million, which is $2.5 million more than is really necessary to pay for what he does. No team making this kind of signing over and over—the Royals, the Tigers, the Pirates, the Brewers—has any business complaining that the Yankees have an unfair advantage. Unless the Royals can find a bigger fool, Henry will be their #3 right-handed reliever.

Roberto Hernandez — Throws R — Age 37

YEAR	TEAM	LGE	IP	H	ER	HR	BB	K	ERA	W	L	H/9	HR/9	BB/9	K/9	KW	PERA	STUFF
1999	TampaBay	AL	76.7	62	24	1	28	68	2.82	6	3	7.3	0.1	3.3	8.0	1.2	2.83	14
2000	TampaBay	AL	76.3	72	32	8	19	60	3.77	5	3	8.5	0.9	2.2	7.1	1.6	3.39	6
2001	KansasCy	AL	69.0	69	33	6	25	44	4.30	4	4	9.0	0.8	3.3	5.7	0.9	3.93	-5

Wow, imagine how bad the Royals might have been without a Proven Veteran Closer. Not only did they trade Johnny Damon for Hernandez, but Allard Baird's insistence that Hernandez is a major asset led them to not trade him at the deadline and to pick up his $6-million option for 2002. A six-month CD would be a better use of the money. Check that Stuff column: he's deep into a decline, so even expecting saves from him is risky.

Mike MacDougal Throws R Age 25

YEAR	TEAM	LGE	IP	H	ER	HR	BB	K	ERA	W	L	H/9	HR/9	BB/9	K/9	KW	PERA	STUFF
1999	Spokane	Nwn	46.3	48	28	6	20	29	5.44	2	3	9.3	1.2	3.9	5.6	0.7	6.76	1
2000	Wilmngtn	Car	138.3	145	91	13	95	67	5.92	5	10	9.4	0.8	6.2	4.4	0.4	7.44	-18
2001	Omaha	PCL	142.0	149	92	15	90	75	5.83	6	10	9.4	1.0	5.7	4.8	0.4	6.06	-11
2001	KansasCy	AL	16.0	17	8	2	4	7	4.50	1	1	9.6	1.1	2.3	3.9	0.9	5.11	-2

MacDougal is a tall guy who impresses scouts with his velocity but has some issues commanding the heat. He was pushed to Triple-A last year as much for his age and pedigree—he was drafted out of Wake Forest—as anything else. His performance there, and in three MLB starts, was unimpressive, so while he'll be all over prospect lists, there's more sizzle here than steak.

Brian Meadows Throws R Age 26

YEAR	TEAM	LGE	IP	H	ER	HR	BB	K	ERA	W	L	H/9	HR/9	BB/9	K/9	KW	PERA	STUFF
1999	Florida	NL	182.0	213	115	29	48	65	5.69	8	12	10.5	1.4	2.4	3.2	0.7	5.61	-8
2000	San Dieg	NL	127.3	150	87	22	41	47	6.15	5	9	10.6	1.6	2.9	3.3	0.6	5.71	-11
2000	KansasCy	AL	74.3	82	35	7	11	26	4.24	4	4	9.9	0.8	1.3	3.1	1.2	3.88	0
2001	KansasCy	AL	54.3	65	37	11	11	20	6.13	2	4	10.8	1.8	1.8	3.3	0.9	6.38	-14
2001	Omaha	PCL	108.7	133	82	26	26	47	6.79	4	8	11.0	2.2	2.2	3.9	0.9	7.32	-18

He's in the book because he threw 50-odd innings in the majors last year. OK, also because he's part of a great trade chain, all one-for-one deals: Dan Miceli for Brian Meadows for Jay Witasick for D'Angelo Jimenez. That'll look more impressive five years from now. Meadows has very little chance to be anything more than an emergency pitcher.

Orber Moreno Throws R Age 25

YEAR	TEAM	LGE	IP	H	ER	HR	BB	K	ERA	W	L	H/9	HR/9	BB/9	K/9	KW	PERA	STUFF
1999	Omaha	PCL	24.7	22	8	2	4	23	2.92	2	1	8.0	0.7	1.5	8.4	2.9	1.92	27
1999	KansasCy	AL	7.3	6	4	1	5	7	4.91	0	1	7.4	1.2	6.1	8.6	0.7	4.56	7
2001	Wilmngtn	Car	11.0	12	7	3	2	8	5.73	0	1	9.8	2.5	1.6	6.5	2.0	7.66	-22
2001	Wichita	Tex	7.7	6	2	0	3	6	2.35	1	0	7.0	0.0	3.5	7.0	1.0	0.00	10
2001	Omaha	PCL	20.3	21	15	5	9	17	6.64	1	1	9.3	2.2	4.0	7.5	0.9	5.09	-9

People are excited about Moreno, who missed all of 2000 after Tommy John surgery. His velocity has returned, and he impressed observers at three stops along the comeback trail. Rather than waste time on Doug Henry and his ilk, the Royals need to give Moreno and Austin and Shawn Sonnier the opportunity to succeed. The team will improve, and the money saved can be spent on Mike Sweeney and Carlos Beltran. Hiring a manager who can handle young pitchers will go a long way.

Dan Reichert Throws R Age 25

YEAR	TEAM	LGE	IP	H	ER	HR	BB	K	ERA	W	L	H/9	HR/9	BB/9	K/9	KW	PERA	STUFF
1999	Omaha	PCL	111.0	101	52	10	52	93	4.22	6	6	8.2	0.8	4.2	7.5	0.9	3.75	25
1999	KansasCy	AL	40.3	40	23	2	27	20	5.13	2	2	8.9	0.4	6.0	4.5	0.4	7.55	-9
2000	KansasCy	AL	156.7	156	82	13	74	93	4.71	8	9	9.0	0.7	4.3	5.3	0.6	4.29	0
2001	KansasCy	AL	126.3	129	72	12	64	73	5.13	6	8	9.2	0.9	4.6	5.2	0.6	5.28	-3
2001	Omaha	PCL	35.3	37	23	5	19	21	5.86	1	3	9.4	1.3	4.8	5.3	0.6	8.91	-17

Muser's impatience with Reichert's control problems led to the right-hander's demotion in July. He has all the stuff to be a dominant power/ground-ball pitcher, he just hasn't been able to throw enough strikes. Concern about his stamina may lead the Royals to move him to relief, although they have a lot of candidates for bullpen jobs. No matter his role, Reichert belongs in the majors, working on strike one.

Jose Rosado Throws L Age 27

YEAR	TEAM	LGE	IP	H	ER	HR	BB	K	ERA	W	L	H/9	HR/9	BB/9	K/9	KW	PERA	STUFF
1998	KansasCy	AL	179.3	178	88	23	51	131	4.42	10	10	8.9	1.2	2.6	6.6	1.3	4.71	13
1999	KansasCy	AL	209.0	206	96	20	60	140	4.13	12	11	8.9	.9	2.6	6.0	1.2	3.61	15
2000	KansasCy	AL	28.0	30	15	3	7	15	4.82	1	2	9.6	1.0	2.3	4.8	1.1	4.64	3

Rosado has had two shoulder surgeries since his last major-league pitch and is currently expected to try and pitch in spring training. It's a rare pitcher who can make a full return from a torn labrum. His short-term outlook is poor, and his long-term outlook depends on what we see later this year. As a command left-hander, Rosado could take two or three years to come back, then have an entire second career.

Kyle Snyder Throws R Age 24

YEAR	TEAM	LGE	IP	H	ER	HR	BB	K	ERA	W	L	H/9	HR/9	BB/9	K/9	KW	PERA	STUFF
1999	Spokane	Nwn	23.7	24	11	2	8	13	4.18	2	1	9.1	.8	3.0	4.9	.8	5.55	0

Tommy John surgery wiped out Snyder's last two seasons. He's back now, having made an impression on people in instructional league and the Arizona Fall League, and he belongs on prospect lists as a sleeper. Snyder could be in the Royals' bullpen by July.

The difference between Snyder's outlook and Rosado's is entirely due to where we are in the history of medicine. Thirty years ago, they'd have both been looking into other careers. Thirty years forward, maybe we'll have the equivalent of Tommy John surgery for pitchers with torn labrums. Now, though, it's an unfortunate fact that we can fix elbows pretty well, but not shoulders.

Shawn Sonnier Throws R Age 25

YEAR	TEAM	LGE	IP	H	ER	HR	BB	K	ERA	W	L	H/9	HR/9	BB/9	K/9	KW	PERA	STUFF
1999	Wilmngtn	Car	58.7	54	23	2	22	41	3.53	4	3	8.3	0.3	3.4	6.3	0.9	4.12	2
2000	Wichita	Tex	60.3	55	32	9	27	60	4.77	3	4	8.2	1.3	4.0	9.0	1.1	3.42	10
2001	Omaha	PCL	67.7	78	60	17	39	43	7.98	2	6	10.4	2.3	5.2	5.7	0.6	5.61	-25

Another "Closer of the Future." With Moreno, Bukvich, and Sonnier, that's one for each level down to the Carolina League. Makes you wonder why a team would spend six million bucks on Roberto Hernandez, no? Sonnier did not have a good year at Omaha, and with Moreno and Snyder healthy and generating more buzz, his path to a job could be rocky.

Blake Stein Throws R Age 28

YEAR	TEAM	LGE	IP	H	ER	HR	BB	K	ERA	W	L	H/9	HR/9	BB/9	K/9	KW	PERA	STUFF
1999	Vancouvr	PCL	107.7	106	58	12	50	74	4.85	6	6	8.9	1.0	4.2	6.2	0.7	5.23	0
1999	KansasCy	AL	67.7	70	41	9	34	43	5.45	3	5	9.3	1.2	4.5	5.7	0.6	3.42	2
2000	KansasCy	AL	106.3	108	63	16	47	77	5.33	5	7	9.1	1.4	4.0	6.5	0.8	3.78	8
2001	KansasCy	AL	129.0	124	79	18	75	107	5.51	6	8	8.7	1.3	5.2	7.5	0.7	4.36	2

This is all that's left from the Kevin Appier trade, and it's not very good. Stein appeared to have a breakthrough in 2000, but after a terrible start to 2001, he spent the year being jerked in and out of the rotation. After April, he pitched about as well as he had in 2000. Stein is one of Gary Huckabay's one-walk-per-game guys: if he can improve his control by that much, he'll have success.

Jeff Suppan Throws R Age 27

YEAR	TEAM	LGE	IP	H	ER	HR	BB	K	ERA	W	L	H/9	HR/9	BB/9	K/9	KW	PERA	STUFF
1999	KansasCy	AL	211.7	227	108	24	52	102	4.59	12	12	9.7	1.0	2.2	4.3	1.0	3.95	4
2000	KansasCy	AL	223.0	237	123	30	69	127	4.96	11	14	9.6	1.2	2.8	5.1	0.9	3.98	4
2001	KansasCy	AL	220.7	232	115	23	70	114	4.69	12	13	9.5	0.9	2.9	4.6	0.8	4.30	2

Greg Maddux, to whom Suppan was compared coming up in the Red Sox system, had his big control epiphany at ages 26 and 27. Suppan isn't going to become *that* good, but he does have it in him to move from an innings-muncher to a #2 starter. Some day, he'll pitch with a good defense behind him and be a Cy Young candidate.

Corey Thurman Throws R Age 23

YEAR	TEAM	LGE	IP	H	ER	HR	BB	K	ERA	W	L	H/9	HR/9	BB/9	K/9	KW	PERA	STUFF
1999	Wilmngtn	Car	151.7	167	100	23	70	76	5.93	6	11	9.9	1.4	4.2	4.5	0.5	7.00	0
2000	Wilmngtn	Car	111.0	119	67	13	51	57	5.43	5	7	9.6	1.1	4.1	4.6	0.6	3.44	4
2000	Wichita	Tex	47.3	57	45	15	24	33	8.56	1	4	10.8	2.9	4.6	6.3	0.7	6.46	1
2001	Wichita	Tex	145.7	153	100	26	76	101	6.18	6	10	9.5	1.6	4.7	6.2	0.7	4.39	7

As much time, energy, and instruction as the Royals invested in Corey Thurman, you'd think they would have found a way to get him on the 40-man roster now that he's showing improvement. They lost him to the Blue Jays in the Rule 5 draft. Thurman is still a bit raw, but given the opportunity to pitch—and not just watch, like some Rule 5 guys—he can provide the Jays with some good middle-relief innnings.

Brad Voyles Throws R Age 25

YEAR	TEAM	LGE	IP	H	ER	HR	BB	K	ERA	W	L	H/9	HR/9	BB/9	K/9	KW	PERA	STUFF
1999	Macon	SAL	48.0	43	31	0	55	32	5.81	2	3	8.1	0.0	10.3	6.0	0.3	5.07	-21
1999	Myrtle B	Car	10.7	12	10	2	10	7	8.44	0	1	10.1	1.7	8.4	5.9	0.3	3.29	-21
2000	Myrtle B	Car	49.7	45	25	3	31	37	4.53	3	3	8.2	0.5	5.6	6.7	0.6	2.08	-6
2001	Greenvil	Sou	16.0	13	7	0	12	14	3.94	1	1	7.3	0.0	6.8	7.9	0.6	2.14	-2
2001	Wichita	Tex	14.3	12	8	0	13	12	5.02	1	1	7.5	0.0	8.2	7.5	0.5	0.00	-6
2001	KansasCy	AL	8.3	8	6	1	8	6	6.48	0	1	8.6	1.1	8.6	6.5	0.4	3.36	-17

Voyles began the year by breaking his ankle and got healthy just in time to be traded to the Royals for Rey Sanchez. He was a bit lost behind Billy Sylvester and Tim Spooneybarger in the Braves organization; here, he comes to a franchise loaded with live arms better-suited for relief. Voyles was effective when he pitched this year, with good heat and filthy breaking stuff. His lousy AFL stint indicates that he should get some Triple-A experience in 2002.

Kris Wilson Throws R Age 25

YEAR	TEAM	LGE	IP	H	ER	HR	BB	K	ERA	W	L	H/9	HR/9	BB/9	K/9	KW	PERA	STUFF
1999	Wilmngtn	Car	44.0	41	15	0	13	25	3.07	3	2	8.4	0.0	2.7	5.1	1.0	1.78	9
1999	Wichita	Tex	76.7	91	51	16	15	32	5.99	3	6	10.7	1.9	1.8	3.8	1.1	6.60	-13
2000	Wichita	Tex	99.0	114	62	18	22	46	5.64	4	7	10.4	1.6	2.0	4.2	1.0	5.04	-5
2000	KansasCy	AL	35.7	37	16	3	9	17	4.04	2	2	9.3	0.8	2.3	4.3	0.9	3.33	-5
2001	Omaha	PCL	29.0	31	14	2	7	12	4.34	2	1	9.6	0.6	2.2	3.7	0.9	3.01	0
2001	KansasCy	AL	113.0	128	75	23	30	64	5.97	5	8	10.2	1.8	2.4	5.1	1.1	5.58	-6

Wilson was giving the Royals good innings in middle relief when they turned to him to patch the rotation. He pitched well for a while, then tired late in the year. His ERA after August 1 was 8.47, and he pitched just three times in September and October. His role—maybe even his roster spot—depends on the development of the young pitching and the rehab of guys such as Rosado and Snyder. Wilson has value but may need to go elsewhere to get his next opportunity.

Minnesota Twins

Two days after the completion of the World Series, Commissioner Bud Selig announced that baseball would contract from 30 teams to 28 before the beginning of the 2002 season. Up until that time, circulating reports had been somewhat vague, but the presumption was that the two teams that would be eliminated were the Montreal Expos and the Florida Marlins, with some maneuvering of ownership that might put the Devil Rays into the hands of the Montreal ownership group, or, more specifically, Jeffrey Loria.

Instead, Selig's announcement was not specific regarding which teams would be contracted. The presumptive victims became the Expos and the Twins, and the cascade of events (which we don't and can't know at this point) descended from there.

The net effect of the announcement from the commissioner's office was to cripple not two but three franchises, placing them in an environment in which it was all but impossible to do business as usual. Not surprisingly, season-ticket sales for the Twins ground to a halt, and agents for players either suspended negotiations or used the announcement as a fulcrum to create artificial deadlines to increase their clients' leverage. Morale among front-office employees dropped to near zero, and Jim Pohlad wrote to employees of the Twins:

"Baseball has committed itself to economic and competitive reform. Contraction is a response to markets where local revenues are insufficient to contribute to competitiveness. Our willingness to go along with contraction, if the Commissioner so decides, has come from a feeling of hopelessness. Within the context of baseball's commitment, when we are posed the question, 'why should the Minnesota Twins not be contracted?' we are unable to find a plausible answer." (Source: ESPN.com, November 10, 2001)

Contraction aside, no one should find it surprising that morale is low when you get a letter from the de facto chief operating officer saying that you can't be competitive, right after a season in which your team was 85-77, led its division for most of the season, finished six games out, and saw a sharp rise in attendance. Barring some sort of evidence for Pohlad's claims that isn't subject to public scrutiny, you have to wonder whether he's totally clueless—because he didn't realize that the Twins are already competitive—or lying through his teeth. Neither trait is particularly appealing in a COO.

Twins Prospectus

2001 record: 85–77; Second place, AL Central

Pythagenport W/L: 82–80

Runs scored: 771 (eighth in AL)

Runs allowed: 766 (seventh in AL)

Team EqA: .256 (eighth in AL)

2001 batters age: 26.2 (youngest in AL)

2001 pitchers age: 26.8 (second-youngest in AL)

Ballpark: Metrodome; good hitters' park; Park Factor of 1.057

2001: The best story of the year, and if they had just not made the Matt Lawton trade . . .

2002: They will regress, dropping under .500 in a transition year as hitting prospects reach the majors.

The political response in Minnesota to potential contraction was nothing if not spirited. Governor Jesse Ventura basically told MLB to piss off in terms of paying for a new stadium, and the general feeling in the state government is that MLB's move is nothing more than a cynical and transparent attempt to get public financing for a new stadium for the Twins. On November 15, Bud Selig basically confirmed that sentiment when he said:

"I've always said that the road of responsibility runs two ways. I know there are people in the Twin Cities who want to blame Carl [Pohlad], baseball, me, the owners or all of the above. At some point in the past decade, despite 26 or so stadium proposals, there were chances to do something, and nothing got done. So there are a lot of people up there who have to look themselves in the mirror.

"Whether you like it or not, the fact is, to survive in this environment, even if you change other things, you still need a new stadium."

(Source: Minneapolis *Star-Tribune,* November 16, 2001)

You *want* me on that wall! You *need* me on that wall!!

In what seems an odd circumstance, the same attorney is representing both the Twins and Major League Baseball on legal matters relating to contraction. In his brief, the attorney, Roger Magnuson, demonstrated a level of chutzpah not often witnessed by humankind. You really almost have to sit back and bask in the sheer gall of his approach, considering the behavior of Carl Pohlad and MLB:

"All of a sudden, what was a private enterprise is now a public trust.

"The government does not have the right to mandate the continued operation of a business, even if the public likes the services offered by that enterprise."

(Source: AP Report)

On some level, one can certainly understand Magnuson's position. Both sides are guilty of wanting things both ways. It's just awfully hard to accept these kinds of statements after the public trust has been invoked so often around the country by owners trying to get taxpayers to foot the bill for private capital investment. Doubly confusing is the concept that the goals and fiduciary responsibilities of the Twins and MLB overlap so closely that they can share a lawyer on this issue. To quote Milhouse Van Houten, "We're through the looking glass here, people."

By the time you read this chapter, the issue of contraction will probably have been settled for the 2002 season, and people will likely be scrambling for compromises that allow everyone to save face as best they can. A new stadium deal might come out of all this, along with some sort of an agreement to examine other alternatives to baseball's "economic woes." When this happens, hold on to your wallet.

Now on to the team at hand. The reaction among many analysts to the possible dissolution of the Twins was, in tone, almost regretful. No one in the mainstream media really expected the Twins to do much in 2001, and their 85-77 finish, combined with their gaudy grab of first place in the AL Central for much of the first half, was a fantastic David vs. Goliath story that touched off an amazing amount of coverage. The Twins were an attractive team for ESPN in particular, with flashy defenders like Torii Hunter and Doug Mientkiewicz making acrobatic plays, and aggressive base runners taking an extra bag whenever they could. The spin was obvious: "Hey, maybe small-market teams *can* compete!" This period of giddiness lasted for most of the first half of the season.

The Twins were offered up as yet another counter to the constant Chicken Little screed that comes from MLB's central offices. But are the Twins really a data point that supports the argument that baseball's financial playing field is, in fact, even enough for everyone to have a chance to win?

The short answer is probably not. The Twins in 2001 were a very lucky ballclub. They got performances well beyond reasonable expectations from a number of key contributors, particularly on the pitching staff. Joe Mays was a legitimate Cy Young contender, but his peripheral numbers indicate that he has a pretty slim chance of repeating or improving his performance. Doug Mientkiewicz was 79 points of OPS above his career average. Even LaTroy Hawkins had a long run of extremely solid relief outings, until he reverted to form around the All-Star break.

On top of getting a number of performances that are best described as lucky, the Twins also took better advantage of those performances than one would normally expect. They finished at 85-77, despite scoring just five runs more than they allowed. You'd typically expect a team with the Twins' runs scored and runs allowed to win only 81 or 82 games. In other words, a lot of things went right for the Twins in 2001, and they still ended up 17 games out of the wild-card race and six games behind the Indians. If things don't break as well for the Twins in 2002, they could leave a crater in the landscape and win fewer than 70 games.

The Twins roster is strange. They just don't have any huge, gaping holes in the offense, and on the pitching side, they have some question marks, but nothing drastic. Take a look at the lineup likely to take the field for the Twins on Opening Day, 2002:

C	A.J. Pierzynski
1B	Doug Mientkiewicz
2B	Luis Rivas
3B	Corey Koskie
SS	Cristian Guzman
LF	Jacque Jones
CF	Torii Hunter
RF	Bobby Kielty
DH	David Ortiz

There's no one who is a complete disaster. Bobby Kielty may be weak, but he's shown potential and probably has earned a chance to prove that he can grow into a good everyday player. Luis Rivas hasn't hit but is unbelievably young and held his own as a 21-year-old rookie. Are you going to take him out of the lineup? Doug Mientkiewicz and Torii Hunter have their offensive faults, major ones in fact. They're also both wizards with the glove. A.J. Pierzynski hit his way into the lineup last year and at least deserves a shot at hitting his way out of it. In short, dramatic improvement isn't going to be easy; it's not as if the Twins are running Kevin Young out there.

The back end of the rotation is where the Twins can make the biggest improvements in the shortest amount of time. Brad Radke, Eric Milton, and Joe Mays fill out the front of the rotation nicely, but the #4 and #5 spots were notable holes last year, a problem which led to the disastrous Matt Lawton-for-Rick Reed trade. Reed will probably be dealt away by spring training, but the Twins have some internal candidates to fill those spots who could work out nicely, such as Adam Johnson, J.C. Romero, and Kyle Lohse.

The Twins' farm system is in reasonable shape, despite some disappointments. There are, however, some pretty significant problems. The Twins' three best position-playing prospects—Mike Cuddyer, Michael Restovich, and Justin Morneau—are all destined to end up as either corner outfielders or first basemen. That's not a horrible fate, but when most of the offense in your MLB lineup comes from the far left of the defensive spectrum as well, and when that offense is the big club's Achilles' heel, it means that any improvement the team is likely to see will be incremental rather than transformative. The difference between the bat of Doug Mientkiewicz and the bat of Michael Cuddyer is considerably less than the difference between the bat of Cuddyer and, say, Pierzynski or Rivas. The Twins need to convert some of their hitting bounty into something that will really help the club.

General Manager Terry Ryan has done an admirable job building up a farm system that develops quality athletes into ballplayers. He was rumored to be leaving for Toronto but removed his name from consideration for that GM position and elected to stay in Minnesota. The Twins' recent drafts under Ryan have been exceptionally strong, bringing in players such as Adam Johnson, Michael Cuddyer, Joe Mauer, and Justin Morneau, as well as a broad array of guys who may turn out to be able contributors, such as Michael Restovich, B. J. Garbe, and a slew of potential starting pitchers.

Tom Kelly's era in Minnesota came to an end on a high note. Kelly had two reputations in the media, depending on the source: one as a mentor of young players, one as a tormentor of young players. It will be interesting to see what happens in terms of a new manager. The sentimental choice was Paul Molitor, loved by the fans and considered by most baseball insiders to be a nimble, quick learner with the credibility necessary to run a team. Instead, third base coach Ron Gardenhire was chosen. Gardenhire has been with the organization as a player or coach since 1986, and was well-regarded during his stint as a minor league manager.

Together, Gardenhire and Ryan can probably make the most headway by developing the talent already in the Twins system. The organization primarily needs to emphasize the importance of plate discipline to its hitters, but getting people to change is a difficult task. If the Twins can find a manager who can do that, they can not only compete in Minnesota over the long haul, they can grab some more jewelry.

Keep something in mind, though: this team is probably going to crater in 2002, and many people will lament the one-year wonder of 2001 without paying attention to the Twins' kick-ass prospects. The team will have to avoid the perception that it's a disappointment while keeping the focus on developing its hitters and young starters. Then all the Twins need is for MLB's owners to finally decide to solve their revenue-disparity issues without a third party picking up the tab. That might happen as soon as 2003, or it might never happen.

HITTERS (BA: .270, OBP: .340, SLG: .440, EqA: .260)

Chad Allen OF Bats R Age 27

YEAR	TEAM	LGE	AB	H	DB	TP	HR	BB	SO	R	RBI	SB	CS	OUT	BA	OBP	SLG	EQA	EQR	DEFENSE
1999	Minnesot	AL	477	134	20	3	11	32	78	66	45	13	7	350	.281	.328	.405	.246	52	126-LF 2
2000	SaltLake	PCL	380	102	18	3	7	22	70	53	48	7	2	280	.268	.310	.387	.235	37	81-LF -4
2000	Minnesot	AL	49	15	2	0	0	3	12	2	6	0	2	36	.306	.359	.347	.231	5	12-RF 1
2001	Edmonton	PCL	22	7	1	0	1	3	1	3	2	2	0	15	.318	.415	.500	.319	4	
2001	Minnesot	AL	174	47	14	2	4	20	32	21	20	1	2	129	.270	.345	.443	.260	22	27-LF -1
2002	*Minnesot*	*AL*	*391*	*113*	*23*	*3*	*12*	*38*	*72*	*60*	*47*	*6*	*4*	*282*	*.289*	*.352*	*.455*	*.266*	*51*	

Allen came into the season hoping to make the roster as an extra outfielder and ended up with about a quarter season of playing time due to injuries and the Matt Lawton debacle. He's not a bad ballplayer; he's acceptable defensively, can run a little, and is fairly likely to hit about league average, or just a little below. He'll spend most of his career scrambling for that extra-outfielder spot.

Danny Ardoin C Bats B Age 27

YEAR	TEAM	LGE	AB	H	DB	TP	HR	BB	SO	R	RBI	SB	CS	OUT	BA	OBP	SLG	EQA	EQR	DEFENSE
1999	Vancouvr	PCL	338	80	10	2	7	43	71	44	39	2	2	260	.237	.334	.340	.233	34	77-C 6
2000	Sacramen	PCL	233	59	14	1	5	27	70	33	27	4	0	174	.253	.346	.386	.253	28	41-C -2 11-1B 0
2000	Minnesot	AL	32	4	2	0	1	7	9	4	5	0	0	28	.125	.282	.281	.202	3	12-C 1
2001	Edmonton	PCL	299	67	13	1	4	20	73	30	30	2	5	237	.224	.274	.314	.198	21	74-C -1
2002	*Minnesot*	*AL*	*304*	*78*	*15*	*1*	*7*	*36*	*82*	*42*	*38*	*1*	*3*	*229*	*.257*	*.335*	*.382*	*.239*	*32*	

Here's one of several catching options available to Tom Kelly's successor. Ardoin has a reasonable arm, a fair-to-middling batting eye, and some incidental power. He lacks the seal of approval found on players like Joe Oliver, but he's basically the same ballplayer for a considerably lower price.

John Barnes OF Bats R Age 26

YEAR	TEAM	LGE	AB	H	DB	TP	HR	BB	SO	R	RBI	SB	CS	OUT	BA	OBP	SLG	EQA	EQR	DEFENSE	
1999	New Brit	Eas	460	109	17	1	11	36	40	51	47	6	2	353	.237	.296	.350	.220	40	124-OF	-4
2000	SaltLake	PCL	426	133	31	4	10	43	46	81	62	5	4	297	.312	.382	.474	.285	64	111-CF	-2
2000	Minnesot	AL	36	13	3	0	0	2	5	4	2	0	1	24	.361	.425	.444	.288	5	11-RF	2
2001	Edmonton	PCL	307	80	19	1	6	25	25	34	34	2	2	229	.261	.330	.388	.242	33	73-OF	-2
2001	Minnesot	AL	21	2	0	0	0	1	3	1	0	0	0	19	.095	.165	.095	.100	0		
2002	*Minnesot*	*AL*	*411*	*114*	*25*	*2*	*10*	*36*	*40*	*56*	*48*	*5*	*3*	*300*	*.277*	*.336*	*.421*	*.251*	*47*		

He's among the Twins' bumper crop of extra outfielders. Barnes was yet another guy who was run out on the right-field carousel after Lawton was dealt, and he couldn't keep the Twins' offense above water, either. Barnes has some upside and could be a slightly different version of Chad Allen—a little more pop, a little less speed on the base paths.

Casey Blake UT Bats R Age 28

YEAR	TEAM	LGE	AB	H	DB	TP	HR	BB	SO	R	RBI	SB	CS	OUT	BA	OBP	SLG	EQA	EQR	DEFENSE	
1999	Syracuse	Int	387	87	14	2	18	51	77	57	59	7	4	304	.225	.323	.411	.246	46	109-3B	-1
1999	Toronto	AL	39	11	2	0	1	1	6	6	2	0	0	28	.282	.300	.410	.234	4	14-3B	1
2000	Syracuse	Int	106	21	4	1	2	7	23	9	6	0	2	87	.198	.263	.311	.192	7	29-3B	-3
2000	SaltLake	PCL	285	78	15	1	10	31	57	44	37	5	2	209	.274	.354	.439	.266	30	64-3B	-6
2001	Baltimor	AL	15	2	1	0	1	1	3	2	2	1	0	13	.133	.187	.400	.202	1		
2001	Edmonton	PCL	370	102	21	4	8	31	60	52	40	11	3	271	.276	.338	.419	.256	45	81-3B	0
2001	Minnesot	AL	22	7	2	0	0	3	7	2	2	1	0	15	.318	.400	.409	.287	3		
2002	*Minnesot*	*AL*	*429*	*116*	*26*	*3*	*12*	*50*	*84*	*63*	*53*	*0*	*0*	*313*	*.270*	*.347*	*.429*	*.258*	*53*		

A refugee from the Blue Jays' system, Blake is potentially a very useful player on the right club. He can play any infield position for short periods of time, and given 500 at-bats in an emergency situation, could definitely push a team towards a title, a la Randy Velarde.

Brian Buchanan OF Bats R Age 28

YEAR	TEAM	LGE	AB	H	DB	TP	HR	BB	SO	R	RBI	SB	CS	OUT	BA	OBP	SLG	EQA	EQR	DEFENSE	
1999	SaltLake	PCL	380	96	16	1	8	23	78	50	45	8	2	286	.253	.306	.363	.228	36	92-RF	-1
2000	SaltLake	PCL	356	92	14	1	21	31	72	61	74	4	1	265	.258	.322	.480	.263	47	74-RF	-5
2000	Minnesot	AL	81	19	3	0	1	7	19	9	7	0	2	64	.235	.304	.309	.205	6	17-RF	-1
2001	Minnesot	AL	196	55	11	0	11	20	50	29	33	1	1	142	.281	.352	.505	.279	29	37-RF	-7
2002	*Minnesot*	*AL*	*364*	*102*	*16*	*1*	*18*	*36*	*86*	*61*	*63*	*5*	*2*	*264*	*.280*	*.345*	*.478*	*.270*	*50*		

The George Foreman option off the bench. Managers generally like to have one guy on the bench who can win or tie a game with one swing of the bat, no matter what his other skills might or might not be. Buchanan played well enough to earn a longer look as part of a potential platoon or job-share next season, either in the outfield, or, more likely, in the DH role.

Mike Cuddyer 3B/1B/OF Bats R Age 23

YEAR	TEAM	LGE	AB	H	DB	TP	HR	BB	SO	R	RBI	SB	CS	OUT	BA	OBP	SLG	EQA	EQR	DEFENSE			
1999	Ft Myers	Fla	480	120	20	2	13	58	102	65	59	8	3	363	.250	.337	.381	.246	54	128-3B	-13		
2000	New Brit	Eas	499	119	28	5	6	42	96	60	49	3	3	383	.238	.307	.351	.223	45	137-3B	-21		
2001	New Brit	Eas	527	139	28	2	24	66	103	83	72	4	6	394	.264	.349	.461	.267	72	77-3B	-3	54-1B	-7
2001	Minnesot	AL	18	4	3	0	0	2	5	2	1	1	0	14	.222	.300	.389	.241	2				
2002	*Minnesot*	*AL*	*504*	*142*	*30*	*3*	*18*	*67*	*105*	*81*	*73*	*7*	*4*	*366*	*.282*	*.366*	*.460*	*.274*	*72*				

He rebounded nicely from a disappointing 2000 season. Scouts aren't crazy about Cuddyer's potential to ever play the field effectively, but there's almost universal acclaim for his batting stroke. Cuddyer has already begun the slide across the defensive spectrum; he will have a nice career, either as a first baseman or corner outfielder.

The Twins are going to end up with a logjam in the corner outfield/DH spots, particularly since they really like having Mientkiewicz's glove over at first base. That's going to be a problem, especially when everyone on the team who can actually get on base can only play left field.

Edwin Diaz UT Bats R Age 27

YEAR	TEAM	LGE	AB	H	DB	TP	HR	BB	SO	R	RBI	SB	CS	OUT	BA	OBP	SLG	EQA	EQR	DEFENSE	
1999	Tucson	PCL	403	107	18	1	8	14	70	55	37	5	5	301	.266	.298	.375	.224	36	55-2B 1	43-SS -12
2000	Oklahoma	PCL	198	42	6	0	6	8	42	22	23	1	0	156	.212	.245	.333	.194	13	22-2B -4	20-3B -2
2001	Edmonton	PCL	376	90	21	2	9	24	59	49	45	3	5	291	.239	.291	.378	.221	33	69-2B 3	31-3B -4
2002	*Minnesot*	*AL*	*347*	*90*	*18*	*1*	*10*	*27*	*61*	*52*	*40*	*4*	*4*	*261*	*.259*	*.313*	*.403*	*.235*	*35*		

Diaz is a pretty good utility guy, a Luis Sojo-type player with a little more offense in his bat. This is exactly the sort of player that teams can grab to save money and have a winning club. He's not going to push you towards a title if he plays every day, but to spell a regular, fill in for an injured player, or take advantage of a pitcher with big platoon splits, Diaz can be very useful.

Lew Ford CF Bats R Age 25

YEAR	TEAM	LGE	AB	H	DB	TP	HR	BB	SO	R	RBI	SB	CS	OUT	BA	OBP	SLG	EQA	EQR	DEFENSE
1999	Lowell	NYP	256	54	11	1	5	12	39	29	20	6	2	204	.211	.251	.320	.196	17	55-CF 2
2000	Augusta	SAL	530	131	27	6	7	35	89	80	49	23	5	404	.247	.300	.360	.228	50	124-CF 12
2001	Ft Myers	Fla	273	71	14	1	2	14	32	32	19	10	6	208	.260	.310	.341	.222	24	66-CF 0
2001	New Brit	Eas	256	50	8	2	6	19	34	27	21	4	3	209	.195	.260	.313	.196	18	57-CF -5
2002	*Minnesot*	*AL*	*471*	*122*	*24*	*3*	*8*	*36*	*69*	*67*	*43*	*16*	*6*	*355*	*.259*	*.312*	*.374*	*.230*	*45*	

Ford is a quick center fielder on a steady career path. He steals the occasional base, plays above-average defense, and scouts have good things to say about his potential *if* he can shorten his swing just a little. He'll need to hit right from the very beginning in 2002 if he wants to have a shot at being a major-league regular. More likely, he'll be scrambling for roster spots in spring training for a few years as a defensive replacement. The difference between Ford and Doug Glanville is pretty much luck and potential—Glanville has one, Ford the other.

B.J. Garbe RF Bats R Age 21

YEAR	TEAM	LGE	AB	H	DB	TP	HR	BB	SO	R	RBI	SB	CS	OUT	BA	OBP	SLG	EQA	EQR	DEFENSE
1999	Elizbthn	App	172	36	2	0	2	10	38	16	16	1	1	137	.209	.254	.256	.177	9	38-CF -8
2000	Quad Cit	Mid	493	94	10	2	4	41	101	44	36	6	5	404	.191	.259	.243	.179	27	131-CF -18
2001	Ft Myers	Fla	480	103	13	2	6	36	92	44	48	7	5	382	.215	.277	.287	.196	33	127-RF -7
2002	*Minnesot*	*AL*	*457*	*113*	*17*	*2*	*9*	*42*	*94*	*59*	*58*	*7*	*4*	*348*	*.247*	*.311*	*.352*	*.221*	*40*	

Scouts still rave about his tools, and he is just 21 years old, so don't give up on him yet. The Twins' farm system is land-mined with bad places for hitters, and Garbe has shown flashes of brilliance. He's young enough that he can repeat a level somewhere along the way and still be considered a pretty good prospect. He'll probably start the season at high A and could bounce up to New Britain quickly if he hits.

Cristian Guzman SS Bats R Age 24

YEAR	TEAM	LGE	AB	H	DB	TP	HR	BB	SO	R	RBI	SB	CS	OUT	BA	OBP	SLG	EQA	EQR	DEFENSE
1999	Minnesot	AL	418	97	14	3	1	18	79	46	25	8	7	328	.232	.268	.287	.190	26	122-SS -3
2000	Minnesot	AL	626	156	27	20	8	38	89	84	51	27	11	481	.249	.294	.395	.232	62	148-SS -9
2001	Minnesot	AL	491	153	28	14	11	23	67	82	51	23	9	347	.312	.347	.493	.277	70	116-SS -3
2002	*Minnesot*	*AL*	*552*	*162*	*27*	*15*	*12*	*40*	*84*	*99*	*58*	*26*	*12*	*402*	*.293*	*.341*	*.462*	*.264*	*72*	

Losing David Ortiz and Matt Lawton hurt, but losing Guzman for a month was nothing short of brutal for the Twins. Guzman and Miguel Tejada have established themselves as sub-deities in the AL shortstop pantheon, so it's not entirely coincidental that the Twins posted an 8-26 mark during Guzman's absence due to a bum shoulder. His shoulder woes may end up recurring, but if Guzman can stay healthy, he could be a very special player. Scouts love his technique in terms of running the bases, but they drop their jaws at some of the decisions he makes while doing so. He's only 24; it wouldn't be a shock to see him win an MVP Award five or more years down the road.

Denny Hocking UT Bats B Age 32

YEAR	TEAM	LGE	AB	H	DB	TP	HR	BB	SO	R	RBI	SB	CS	OUT	BA	OBP	SLG	EQA	EQR	DEFENSE	
1999	Minnesot	AL	383	104	19	2	7	18	47	45	39	10	7	286	.272	.309	.386	.232	37	37-SS -5	35-2B -4
2000	Minnesot	AL	367	110	24	4	4	43	68	49	44	7	5	262	.300	.373	.420	.268	49	34-OF -1	32-2B -3
2001	Minnesot	AL	326	85	18	2	3	30	58	36	25	5	1	242	.261	.326	.356	.235	32	41-SS 1	13-2B -3
2002	*Minnesot*	*AL*	*337*	*88*	*19*	*2*	*5*	*36*	*60*	*42*	*33*	*8*	*4*	*253*	*.261*	*.332*	*.374*	*.238*	*35*		

Hocking is the very definition of a utility guy. He's useful as long as his cost is low, and as long as you can limit him to time at shortstop and second base. At third base or in the outfield, his bat just isn't enough to keep a club moving along, even in the case of injury. He filled in as well as could be expected when Guzman went down, but the drop-off was still pretty gruesome.

Torii Hunter CF Bats R Age 26

YEAR	TEAM	LGE	AB	H	DB	TP	HR	BB	SO	R	RBI	SB	CS	OUT	BA	OBP	SLG	EQA	EQR	DEFENSE
1999	Minnesot	AL	381	99	15	2	10	23	63	50	34	10	6	288	.260	.311	.308	.234	38	105-CF 9
2000	Minnesot	AL	333	94	15	7	5	14	60	42	41	4	3	242	.282	.315	414	241	35	96-CF 9
2000	SaltLake	PCL	202	63	12	1	14	7	27	42	42	8	2	141	.312	.342	.589	.297	34	48-CF -1
2001	Minnesot	AL	562	151	32	5	29	31	108	86	93	8	6	418	.269	.314	.498	.261	73	147-CF 23
2002	*Minnesot*	*AL*	*503*	*149*	*28*	*5*	*25*	*34*	*95*	*85*	*74*	*10*	*7*	*361*	*.296*	*.341*	*.521*	*.276*	*72*	

The AL's slightly older and even more maddening version of Andruw Jones. Hunter is a superlative defensive center fielder with a long, powerful swing. He yanks Twins fans' chains as if he's Bud Selig's smarter cousin: an amazing catch and throw to save a run, followed by two high-leverage at-bats in which he gets himself out by swinging at balls a foot out of Eric Gregg's strike zone.

Patience at the plate is a virtue for more reasons than drawing walks; just keeping an at-bat alive gives you another shot at a cookie. Hunter did become notably more patient as the season went on (13 walks in the first 2/3 of the season, 16 in the final third) and is working to shake his old platoon role. He is exactly the sort of player who could really break out given more playing time and a new coach. He has absurdly great range going back against his glove side on fly balls.

Jacque Jones LF Bats L Age 27

YEAR	TEAM	LGE	AB	H	DB	TP	HR	BB	SO	R	RBI	SB	CS	OUT	BA	OBP	SLG	EQA	EQR	DEFENSE
1999	SaltLake	PCL	193	49	11	1	3	7	33	24	19	6	2	146	.254	.280	.368	.219	16	52-CF 7
1999	Minnesot	AL	319	93	23	2	10	14	55	53	43	3	4	230	.292	.328	.470	.259	39	87-CF 5
2000	Minnesot	AL	518	148	25	5	20	20	98	63	72	7	5	375	.286	.312	.469	.254	61	137-LF 8
2001	Minnesot	AL	473	134	18	0	17	41	79	57	50	10	10	349	.283	.343	.429	.255	57	122-LF 5
2002	*Minnesot*	*AL*	*455*	*136*	*19*	*2*	*19*	*36*	*83*	*69*	*62*	*11*	*8*	*327*	*.299*	*.350*	*.475*	*.269*	*61*	

Tom Kelly worked hard to protect Jones from left-handed pitching. Like Todd Walker before him, Jones was protected so well that he still doesn't recognize what lefties are doing on the mound. It's time to find out whether he's ever going to be a regular, but on a team filled with right-handed slugs looking for playing time, it's unlikely he'll get the at-bats he needs to develop. Jones would be playing center field on most other clubs; with the Twins, he's just another piece of an amazing overall defense.

Bobby Kielty OF Bats B Age 25

YEAR	TEAM	LGE	AB	H	DB	TP	HR	BB	SO	R	RBI	SB	CS	OUT	BA	OBP	SLG	EQA	EQR	DEFENSE
1999	Quad Cit	Mid	250	56	9	0	8	29	61	32	25	6	2	196	.224	.308	.356	.229	25	56-CF 2
2000	New Brit	Eas	465	109	23	2	13	79	112	65	51	4	3	359	.234	.349	.376	.249	56	121-CF -13
2000	SaltLake	PCL	33	7	3	0	0	5	10	6	1	0	0	26	.212	.316	.303	.218	3	
2001	Edmonton	PCL	339	86	20	1	10	47	69	47	40	4	0	253	.254	.351	.407	.259	43	94-CF 7
2001	Minnesot	AL	104	27	6	0	3	8	22	8	15	3	0	77	.260	.317	.404	.246	12	26-OF -1
2002	*Minnesot*	*AL*	*447*	*119*	*24*	*1*	*17*	*64*	*104*	*69*	*55*	*7*	*2*	*330*	*.266*	*.358*	*.438*	*.267*	*61*	

He's ready to tackle a major-league job. Kielty is a tweener risk, but he can probably hit enough to handle a corner outfield spot. His plate discipline is good, and he has a quick bat, good foot speed, and solid mechanics in the outfield. He's facing an uphill battle for playing time, as the Twins have a veritable avalanche of corner outfielders who will be clawing for at-bats. Kielty probably offers the best mix of offense and defense available. Look for him to peak somewhere in the vicinity of .310/.400/.520 or so, while playing good defense in left field.

Corey Koskie 3B Bats L Age 29

YEAR	TEAM	LGE	AB	H	DB	TP	HR	BB	SO	R	RBI	SB	CS	OUT	BA	OBP	SLG	EQA	EQR	DEFENSE
1999	Minnesot	AL	337	106	16	0	13	36	63	40	57	4	4	235	.315	.388	.478	.287	52	67-3B 7 15-RF -4
2000	Minnesot	AL	465	140	33	4	9	70	91	75	61	5	4	329	.301	.397	.447	.286	72	135-3B 0
2001	Minnesot	AL	560	160	35	2	29	70	102	103	106	24	6	407	.286	.374	.511	.293	95	148-3B 7
2002	*Minnesot*	*AL*	*495*	*151*	*30*	*2*	*21*	*70*	*96*	*76*	*85*	*13*	*5*	*349*	*.305*	*.391*	*.501*	*.295*	*83*	

(Corey Koskie *continued*)

A very fine ballplayer. Koskie's an excellent defender who hits for moderate power, a good average, and draws walks. He's underappreciated in his current market. He takes a great angle on almost every ground ball, and he has the quickest release of any third baseman in baseball except possibly Troy Glaus. Koskie is a good bet to be a top-three third baseman for the next couple of years, along with Eric Chavez and Troy Glaus; after that, he'll likely be overtaken by Hank Blalock.

Matt LeCroy C Bats R Age 26

YEAR	TEAM	LGE	AB	H	DB	TP	HR	BB	SO	R	RBI	SB	CS	OUT	BA	OBP	SLG	EQA	EQR	DEFENSE
1999	Ft Myers	Fla	341	80	14	1	15	31	57	41	48	0	1	262	.235	.301	.413	.236	35	63-C -10
1999	SaltLake	PCL	116	30	4	1	7	4	20	17	21	0	1	87	.259	.287	.491	.247	13	17-C -2
2000	Minnesot	AL	166	29	8	0	6	15	33	17	17	0	0	137	.175	.252	.331	.198	12	47-C -1
2000	New Brit	Eas	199	50	8	1	9	23	35	27	30	0	0	149	.251	.339	.437	.259	25	42-C -5
2000	SaltLake	PCL	63	17	3	0	4	3	11	11	11	0	0	46	.270	.303	.508	.261	8	
2001	Edmonton	PCL	390	113	10	0	17	33	86	43	65	0	2	279	.290	.351	.446	.264	50	20-C -2 10-1B -2
2001	Minnesot	AL	40	17	3	0	4	0	7	6	13	0	1	24	.425	.436	.800	.365	10	
2002	*Minnesot*	*AL*	*403*	*111*	*12*	*1*	*21*	*45*	*85*	*54*	*64*	*0*	*2*	*294*	*.275*	*.348*	*.467*	*.266*	*54*	

LeCroy didn't shed many tears over the departure of Tom Kelly. Kelly didn't like his defense, and that, along with a number of other factors that perhaps shouldn't always matter, led to LeCroy spending the summer pummeling the bejeezus out of PCL pitching as the Edmonton Trappers DH. LeCroy can catch, play first base, or DH. He can also hit. Sensing a theme among the Twins' prospects yet?

Joe Mauer C Bats L Age 19

YEAR	TEAM	LGE	AB	H	DB	TP	HR	BB	SO	R	RBI	SB	CS	OUT	BA	OBP	SLG	EQA	EQR	DEFENSE
2001	Elizbthn	App	117	31	4	1	0	12	11	9	8	2	0	86	.265	.335	.316	.230	11	19-C -6
2002	*Minnesot*	*AL*	*166*	*46*	*5*	*1*	*1*	*20*	*16*	*18*	*13*	*6*	*0*	*120*	*.277*	*.355*	*.337*	*.245*	*18*	

The Twins' front office took some heat for drafting Mauer instead of other heralded prospects such as Mark Prior. Mauer was considered a signability pick, with a bumper for being a hometown boy. The criticism might or might not be justified, but Mauer has certainly played well since signing. He hit .400 in more than 130 plate appearances in rookie ball, walked twice as often as he struck out, showed good footwork behind the plate, and impressed scouts as a polished and surprisingly quick base runner. He might not be Mark Prior, but then again, Mark Prior might not be Joe Mauer.

Jason Maxwell UT Bats R Age 30

YEAR	TEAM	LGE	AB	H	DB	TP	HR	BB	SO	R	RBI	SB	CS	OUT	BA	OBP	SLG	EQA	EQR	DEFENSE
1999	Toledo	Int	421	94	14	2	13	44	82	51	51	5	3	330	.223	.299	.359	.223	39	63-SS 1 36-2B -1
2000	Minnesot	AL	110	27	3	0	2	8	28	13	11	2	1	84	.245	.303	.327	.217	9	19-2B 3 10-3B 2
2001	Minnesot	AL	68	14	1	0	2	9	20	4	11	2	0	54	.206	.299	.309	.217	6	
2002	*Texas*	*AL*	*325*	*81*	*9*	*1*	*12*	*40*	*78*	*42*	*45*	*6*	*2*	*246*	*.249*	*.332*	*.394*	*.243*	*36*	

A solid utility guy, Maxwell has a little pop in his bat, will take a walk, and runs well. The Twins have too many of this type of player, plus young kids at the second base and shortstop who don't need a ton of backup. Maxwell will likely be bouncing around for a few years trying to get the job often held by F.P. Santangelo, Jeff Reboulet, Denny Hocking, or a Crespo brother.

Quinton McCracken OF Bats B Age 32

YEAR	TEAM	LGE	AB	H	DB	TP	HR	BB	SO	R	RBI	SB	CS	OUT	BA	OBP	SLG	EQA	EQR	DEFENSE
1999	TampaBay	AL	147	38	6	1	1	13	20	20	17	6	5	114	.259	.322	.333	.224	13	37-LF 0
2000	Durham	Int	338	85	16	2	2	28	56	49	25	10	6	259	.251	.312	.328	.221	30	81-OF -4
2000	TampaBay	AL	31	4	0	0	0	6	4	4	2	0	1	28	.129	.270	.129	.154	1	
2001	Edmonton	PCL	355	104	23	3	3	20	49	44	36	7	8	259	.293	.332	.400	.242	37	72-CF -1
2001	Minnesot	AL	64	15	2	2	0	5	11	7	3	0	1	50	.234	.290	.328	.206	5	
2002	*Arizona*	*NL*	*387*	*99*	*19*	*3*	*5*	*35*	*62*	*56*	*42*	*11*	*9*	*297*	*.256*	*.318*	*.359*	*.229*	*37*	

Here's a great litmus test for a ballclub. McCracken is a serviceable fifth outfielder but should never be asked to play a larger role than that and should never be paid more than the league minimum. If your local ballclub brings him into camp and signs him to a one-year deal worth $500,000, call the front desk and see if they'll give you a quarter million bucks. Why not? It's obvious they're just throwing it away. McCracken is interchangeable with at least 50 guys in the minors. The decision to let him have even one at-bat at DH during David Ortiz's absence was nothing short of bizarre. He's an appropriate Diamondback.

Doug Mientkiewicz 1B Bats L Age 28

YEAR	TEAM	LGE	AB	H	DB	TP	HR	BB	SO	R	RBI	SB	CS	OUT	BA	OBP	SLG	EQA	EQR	DEFENSE
1999	Minnesot	AL	324	76	23	3	2	40	45	34	31	1	1	249	.235	.325	.343	.230	32	96-1B 1
2000	SaltLake	PCL	471	136	26	2	14	47	66	72	69	0	4	340	.287	.354	.437	.265	61	81-1B 8 36-3B 0
2001	Minnesot	AL	541	171	35	1	18	69	79	80	76	1	7	377	.316	.400	.484	.292	87	142-1B 6
2002	*Minnesot*	*AL*	*520*	*161*	*33*	*2*	*16*	*66*	*77*	*74*	*78*	*4*	*5*	*364*	*.310*	*.387*	*.473*	*.285*	*79*	

We do a fair number of radio spots around the country, and more than one host wanted to compare Mientkiewicz favorably with John Olerud. Sorry. Mientkiewicz is a fine defensive first baseman without enough pop to play the position. A team with lots of outfield power can carry someone like him and be a championship club. The Twins aren't that team. He'll be Mark Grace for a few years, and there are worse fates, but despite how much fun he is to watch on defense, and despite how many singles he slaps, he needs to hit the weight room and find another five to ten home runs and ten walks lying around before he'll be someone you don't think about upgrading.

Dustan Mohr OF Bats R Age 26

YEAR	TEAM	LGE	AB	H	DB	TP	HR	BB	SO	R	RBI	SB	CS	OUT	BA	OBP	SLG	EQA	EQR	DEFENSE
1999	Kinston	Car	438	105	22	2	7	16	104	36	44	3	4	337	.240	.267	.347	.204	32	108-RF 6
1999	Akron	Eas	43	6	2	1	0	4	7	3	2	0	1	38	.140	.213	.233	.153	2	11-RF 2
2000	Ft Myers	Fla	379	87	15	1	9	25	72	45	55	4	3	295	.230	.285	.346	.213	31	89-LF -2
2001	New Brit	Eas	531	156	33	2	19	45	108	79	75	7	6	381	.294	.351	.471	.270	72	133-CF -1
2001	Minnesot	AL	51	12	3	0	0	5	15	7	4	1	1	40	.235	.304	.294	.207	4	15-RF 3
2002	*Minnesot*	*AL*	*543*	*151*	*31*	*2*	*17*	*54*	*119*	*70*	*78*	*7*	*7*	*399*	*.278*	*.343*	*.436*	*.256*	*66*	

Mohr enjoyed a breakout year in New Britain, pounding 68 extra-base hits for the Rock Cats. He's solid defensively on the outfield corners but can't play center field, so he'll need to light up Triple-A early and often to have a chance in what promises to be a crowded corner-outfield situation in Minneapolis.

Mike Moriarty SS Bats R Age 28

YEAR	TEAM	LGE	AB	H	DB	TP	HR	BB	SO	R	RBI	SB	CS	OUT	BA	OBP	SLG	EQA	EQR	DEFENSE
1999	SaltLake	PCL	372	80	16	5	3	47	57	47	37	4	3	295	.215	.310	.309	.216	32	124-SS 4
2000	SaltLake	PCL	384	81	19	2	10	50	56	55	39	1	1	304	.211	.308	.349	.225	36	120-SS 7
2001	Edmonton	PCL	402	86	14	1	11	52	85	54	41	4	3	319	.214	.317	.336	.226	39	122-SS 1
2002	*Minnesot*	*AL*	*393*	*95*	*18*	*2*	*11*	*58*	*76*	*60*	*49*	*4*	*2*	*300*	*.242*	*.339*	*.382*	*.244*	*44*	

Moriarty might be the missing piece to the Ken Phelps All-Star Team. He has moderate plate discipline, a little pop in his bat, and brings a very nice glove to the table. He'd probably hit something like .225/.310/.380 in the majors while playing defense in the top 20% of the league. That's not star production, but it's certainly no worse than you get from the likes of Rey Ordonez. Moriarty should be available as a free agent this off-season and has earned a shot at playing his way onto a big-league club.

Justin Morneau 1B Bats L Age 21

YEAR	TEAM	LGE	AB	H	DB	TP	HR	BB	SO	R	RBI	SB	CS	OUT	BA	OBP	SLG	EQA	EQR	DEFENSE
2000	Elizbthn	App	23	3	2	0	0	1	7	3	1	0	0	20	.130	.167	.217	.133	1	
2001	Quad Cit	Mid	241	66	10	1	8	19	42	35	33	0	0	175	.274	.330	.423	.251	28	56-1B 0
2001	Ft Myers	Fla	205	52	8	2	4	17	44	21	31	0	0	153	.254	.322	.371	.235	21	48-1B -4
2001	New Brit	Eas	39	7	0	0	0	2	8	3	3	0	0	32	.179	.220	.179	.142	1	
2002	*Minnesot*	*AL*	*429*	*120*	*21*	*3*	*11*	*45*	*88*	*60*	*49*	*0*	*0*	*309*	*.280*	*.348*	*.420*	*.256*	*51*	

Ladies and gentlemen, a championship-caliber first baseman. Morneau is one of the best two or three hitting prospects in the minors. He hits hard line drives to all fields, gets some lift on the ball, has reasonable plate discipline, and is only going to fill out over the next couple of years. Scouts compare his swing to Larry Walker's, and one scout says that he's two years away from being as good as Jason Giambi. I don't know if things will happen that quickly, but I think the Twins would be perfectly happy if it took Morneau four years to get that good. He has the most consistent stride you'll ever see in a young hitter.

David Ortiz — DH — Bats L — Age 26

YEAR	TEAM	LGE	AB	H	DB	TP	HR	BB	SO	R	RBI	SB	CS	OUT	BA	OBP	SLG	EQA	EQR	DEFENSE
1999	SaltLake	PCL	462	122	26	2	22	66	96	63	78	2	1	341	.264	.358	.472	.276	68	108-1B -16
2000	Minnesot	AL	408	116	31	1	12	52	71	55	61	1	0	292	.284	.365	.453	.275	58	25-1B 0
2001	Minnesot	AL	302	73	15	1	20	41	59	48	49	1	0	229	.242	.334	.497	.271	44	
2002	*Minnesot*	*AL*	*428*	*116*	*24*	*1*	*23*	*62*	*87*	*62*	*75*	*1*	*0*	*312*	*.271*	*.363*	*.493*	*.281*	*65*	

Ortiz is a reasonable offensive player, which means that as a Twin, he was injured during 2001. He started the season off monstrously before suffering a fractured wrist in early May that kept him out of action for two-and-a-half months. Ortiz looks like he should be some sort of bashing ox, and he began the season that way, but he's never been healthy or played long enough for anyone to find out what he can really do. Some scouts think he can be Mo Vaughn in his prime; others think he'll be the shadow of the Hit Dog on whom the Angels spent a bunch of money. Ortiz is probably in the wrong organization to get the playing time he needs.

A.J. Pierzynski — C — Bats L — Age 25

YEAR	TEAM	LGE	AB	H	DB	TP	HR	BB	SO	R	RBI	SB	CS	OUT	BA	OBP	SLG	EQA	EQR	DEFENSE
1999	SaltLake	PCL	223	48	4	0	2	13	27	21	20	0	0	175	.215	.258	.260	.180	12	61-C -7
1999	Minnesot	AL	22	6	2	0	0	1	4	3	3	0	0	16	.273	.330	.364	.236	2	
2000	New Brit	Eas	229	62	14	1	4	5	23	30	27	0	0	167	.271	.302	.393	.231	21	46-C -6
2000	SaltLake	PCL	151	44	11	1	3	2	21	17	18	1	1	108	.291	.304	.437	.242	16	38-C -2
2000	Minnesot	AL	87	27	5	1	2	4	12	11	10	1	0	60	.310	.355	.460	.273	12	24-C 1
2001	Minnesot	AL	380	113	32	2	8	17	49	52	56	0	8	275	.297	.332	.455	.253	44	100-C 3
2002	*Minnesot*	*AL*	*435*	*134*	*31*	*2*	*11*	*25*	*57*	*68*	*68*	*0*	*4*	*305*	*.308*	*.346*	*.464*	*.263*	*54*	

He was presented with an opportunity, and he seized it. Pierzynski is essentially the same ballplayer as Shea Hillenbrand in Boston. He will hit for a reasonable average, show some line-drive power, but draw only three walks a month, so he will have to hit .300 or close to it to help the team and keep his job. Depending on the skew of the new management regime, even that might not be enough. Pierzynski had a nice 2001 season, though, and it moved him into the column of MLB-approved catchers. Ask the next guy how much money that's worth.

Tom Prince — C — Bats R — Age 37

YEAR	TEAM	LGE	AB	H	DB	TP	HR	BB	SO	R	RBI	SB	CS	OUT	BA	OBP	SLG	EQA	EQR	DEFENSE
1999	Clearwtr	Fla	33	10	1	0	1	2	3	4	6	1	0	23	.303	.351	.424	.266	4	
2000	Philadel	NL	123	29	6	0	3	11	28	13	16	1	0	94	.236	.307	.358	.228	12	35-C 1
2001	Minnesot	AL	195	45	3	1	8	13	34	20	24	3	1	151	.231	.294	.379	.227	19	60-C 8
2002	*Minnesot*	*AL*	*176*	*38*	*7*	*1*	*5*	*16*	*34*	*20*	*21*	*2*	*1*	*139*	*.216*	*.281*	*.352*	*.208*	*14*	

America's Backup Catcher. Prince has a little pop and is well regarded for his ability to work with pitchers. Hard to believe, but Prince has now played in 15 major-league seasons. If he wants a job this year, he'll probably be able to land one somewhere.

Mike Restovich — OF — Bats R — Age 23

YEAR	TEAM	LGE	AB	H	DB	TP	HR	BB	SO	R	RBI	SB	CS	OUT	BA	OBP	SLG	EQA	EQR	DEFENSE
1999	Quad Cit	Mid	501	120	20	3	13	47	109	59	65	3	5	386	.240	.313	.369	.229	49	123-RF -12
2000	Ft Myers	Fla	490	111	21	5	8	45	111	56	48	11	5	384	.227	.294	.339	.217	42	127-RF -10
2001	New Brit	Eas	513	124	26	3	19	49	122	61	71	11	5	394	.242	.312	.415	.243	57	139-RF -3
2002	*Minnesot*	*AL*	*473*	*124*	*26*	*3*	*17*	*55*	*115*	*69*	*70*	*11*	*5*	*354*	*.262*	*.339*	*.438*	*.258*	*60*	

Restovich is veering dangerously towards the precipitous Chad Hermansen career path. He regained some of the power that had vanished during the 2000 season, but without sparkling peripheral numbers. The Twins don't appear thrilled with his defense, which means he'll be competing with eight zillion guys for playing time on the corners. He'll start the year in Triple-A and is unlikely to get a shot at the majors for at least another season or so. The raw bat speed is definitely there for Restovich to be a legitimate power threat.

Luis Rivas — 2B — Bats R — Age 22

YEAR	TEAM	LGE	AB	H	DB	TP	HR	BB	SO	R	RBI	SB	CS	OUT	BA	OBP	SLG	EQA	EQR	DEFENSE
1999	New Brit	Eas	534	122	28	4	6	29	92	62	39	19	10	422	.228	.270	.330	.205	40	120-SS -17
2000	New Brit	Eas	334	76	21	4	3	27	42	45	32	7	3	261	.228	.290	.341	.216	28	73-2B -5
2000	SaltLake	PCL	153	42	11	1	2	9	20	24	18	5	3	114	.275	.321	.399	.241	16	32-2B -1
2000	Minnesot	AL	57	18	3	1	0	2	4	7	5	2	0	39	.316	.339	.404	.256	6	14-2B -2
2001	Minnesot	AL	561	155	20	6	8	42	86	71	48	28	12	418	.276	.332	.376	.243	61	144-2B -16
2002	*Minnesot*	*AL*	*514*	*147*	*31*	*5*	*10*	*51*	*79*	*83*	*53*	*23*	*9*	*376*	*.286*	*.350*	*.424*	*.261*	*65*	

It remains to be seen whether Rivas should be lumped with Alex Gonzalez and Brent Gates, or perhaps in a group above that. There are varying reports and opinions on Rivas's defense, but we're not optimistic. Slow feet at second base means nagging injury problems. Where do you move him? You don't; you focus on fixing those defensive deficiencies to keep him healthy.

Luis Rodriguez — SS/2B — Bats B — Age 22

YEAR	TEAM	LGE	AB	H	DB	TP	HR	BB	SO	R	RBI	SB	CS	OUT	BA	OBP	SLG	EQA	EQR	DEFENSE
1999	Quad Cit	Mid	441	92	8	0	4	33	53	41	34	4	3	352	.209	.267	.254	.183	25	92-2B 4 12-3B -1
2000	Quad Cit	Mid	354	66	7	2	0	24	32	25	20	2	3	291	.186	.243	.218	.164	16	79-2B -8 14-SS 2
2001	Ft Myers	Fla	487	116	17	2	4	60	45	57	50	6	5	376	.238	.325	.306	.221	43	68-SS -2 56-2B -4
2002	*Minnesot*	*AL*	*452*	*110*	*16*	*2*	*5*	*55*	*40*	*58*	*40*	*5*	*4*	*338*	*.281*	*.341*	*.338*	*.231*	*44*	

There's a lot here to like. Rodriguez can play either middle-infield spot reasonably well and is a rare offensive player. He hit an unadjusted .274 at Fort Myers—not exactly a hitters' paradise—led the team in doubles, drew 82 walks, and struck out just 42 times. For a 21-year-old, that's a varied range of skills on which to build. He hasn't received much press, but he is definitely someone to watch at Double-A this year. The Twins could use a hitter who can actually draw walks and play defense.

Mike Ryan — OF/2B — Bats L — Age 24

YEAR	TEAM	LGE	AB	H	DB	TP	HR	BB	SO	R	RBI	SB	CS	OUT	BA	OBP	SLG	EQA	EQR	DEFENSE
1999	Ft Myers	Fla	519	119	21	3	7	47	68	66	52	2	2	402	.229	.296	.322	.212	42	126-2B -21
2000	New Brit	Eas	487	121	19	5	11	24	81	53	55	3	2	368	.248	.285	.376	.220	42	102-LF -3 16-2B -2
2001	Edmonton	PCL	521	133	30	5	14	48	110	73	58	1	5	393	.255	.320	.413	.242	56	85-RF -4 38-2B -10
2002	*Minnesot*	*AL*	*497*	*139*	*24*	*4*	*15*	*44*	*97*	*75*	*68*	*2*	*3*	*361*	*.280*	*.338*	*.435*	*.254*	*59*	

Ryan has performed well at each stop through the organization and had a pretty reasonable year at Edmonton. Defensively, he's a real mystery: quick, not fast, with a throwing motion that requires a long time to generate any heat. He doesn't have the traditional power stroke that you want in an outfielder, but he does hit the ball hard into the gaps. He'll start the season at Triple-A; if he hits, or if the Twins make a bunch of moves, he could end up meeting that projection.

Ruben Salazar — 2B — Bats R — Age 24

YEAR	TEAM	LGE	AB	H	DB	TP	HR	BB	SO	R	RBI	SB	CS	OUT	BA	OBP	SLG	EQA	EQR	DEFENSE
1999	Elizbthn	App	263	67	13	1	6	26	48	31	28	4	2	198	.255	.325	.380	.239	28	27-2B -2 16-3B -2
2000	Ft Myers	Fla	509	134	13	0	11	26	90	63	48	2	3	378	.263	.300	.354	.220	43	100-2B -8
2001	New Brit	Eas	540	145	24	1	9	34	75	63	58	4	1	396	.269	.316	.367	.232	51	108-2B -9
2002	*Minnesot*	*AL*	*487*	*140*	*18*	*1*	*12*	*39*	*78*	*62*	*54*	*5*	*2*	*349*	*.287*	*.340*	*.402*	*.249*	*54*	

Salazar is a solid prospect who hit well at New Britain, increasing his power and plate discipline. Scouts like his tools and think he'll develop more power over the next couple of years. If Luis Rivas craters or gets hurt, Salazar could be in a position to handle second base very capably for the Twins as soon as 2003.

Javier Valentin — C/IF — Bats B — Age 26

YEAR	TEAM	LGE	AB	H	DB	TP	HR	BB	SO	R	RBI	SB	CS	OUT	BA	OBP	SLG	EQA	EQR	DEFENSE
1999	Minnesot	AL	216	55	13	1	5	20	34	22	27	0	0	161	.255	.320	.394	.240	23	64-C 5
2000	SaltLake	PCL	135	41	11	1	6	7	26	18	25	1	0	94	.304	.341	.533	.283	20	24-C 1
2001	Edmonton	PCL	427	106	24	1	14	43	98	44	57	0	1	322	.248	.321	.407	.243	47	49-C 2 25-3B -2
2002	*Minnesot*	*AL*	*394*	*105*	*20*	*1*	*14*	*42*	*90*	*43*	*57*	*0*	*1*	*290*	*.266*	*.337*	*.429*	*.253*	*47*	

(Javier Valentin *continued*)

Valentin could most recently be seen whistling jubilantly while cleaning out Tom Kelly's office. As with Matt LeCroy, Kelly wasn't nuts about Valentin's defense. Valentin spent 2001 learning to keep his hands higher at the plate, as well as playing a little first base and third base. His defense behind the plate is good enough to let him play every day in the majors, and he could well blossom if just left alone to do so. He'll be fighting for a roster spot, presumably behind Pierzynski.

Kevin West RF Bats R Age 22

YEAR	TEAM	LGE	AB	H	DB	TP	HR	BB	SO	R	RBI	SB	CS	OUT	BA	OBP	SLG	EQA	EQR	DEFENSE
1999	Elizbthn	App	230	50	7	2	6	10	76	20	25	1	1	181	.217	.265	.343	.204	17	63-RF -3
2000	Quad Cit	Mid	378	75	10	1	5	20	94	30	38	5	3	306	.198	.249	.270	.181	21	110-RF -4
2001	Quad Cit	Mid	457	98	23	2	6	45	108	52	43	3	1	360	.214	.301	.313	.214	38	117-RF -9
2002	*Minnesot*	*AL*	*438*	*111*	*23*	*2*	*9*	*40*	*113*	*48*	*51*	*5*	*2*	*329*	*.253*	*.316*	*.377*	*.231*	*42*	

Why should you have any interest in a guy who repeated the Midwest League? West has a strange skill set, showing a lot of doubles power at a very young age and, more importantly, getting on base 90 times via walk or hit-by-pitch in only 443 at-bats. Scouts love his instincts and work ethic, and if he develops a little bit of power, he could be the guy to sneak in and grab a corner outfield spot.

PITCHERS (ERA: 4.50, H/9: 9.0, HR/9: 1.0, BB/9: 3.0, K/9: 6.0, KW: 2.0, PERA: 4.50)

Grant Balfour Throws R Age 24

YEAR	TEAM	LGE	IP	H	ER	HR	BB	K	ERA	W	L	H/9	HR/9	BB/9	K/9	KW	PERA	STUFF
1999	Quad Cit	Mid	85.7	92	58	15	42	55	6.09	4	6	9.7	1.6	4.4	5.8	0.7	4.64	3
2000	Ft Myers	Fla	88.7	100	69	20	42	57	7.00	3	7	10.2	2.0	4.3	5.8	0.7	6.56	-14
2001	New Brit	Eas	46.7	38	20	2	29	45	3.86	3	2	7.3	0.4	5.6	8.7	0.8	1.41	12
2001	Edmonton	PCL	16.7	17	11	2	11	12	5.94	1	1	9.2	1.1	5.9	6.5	0.5	6.07	-10

Minor-league closer who had gaudy numbers at New Britain, allowing 26 hits and striking out 72 in only 50 innings. He didn't fare as well at Edmonton, and he'll start the year at Triple-A. Minor-league closers have a spotty history, but Balfour possesses reasonable stuff, and it's not as if LaTroy Hawkins has an ironclad grip on the Twins' closer job.

Doug Bochtler Throws R Age 31

YEAR	TEAM	LGE	IP	H	ER	HR	BB	K	ERA	W	L	H/9	HR/9	BB/9	K/9	KW	PERA	STUFF
1999	Syracuse	Int	26.0	23	11	1	11	20	3.81	2	1	8.0	0.3	3.8	6.9	0.9	3.07	0
1999	Albuquer	PCL	21.3	21	14	3	13	17	5.91	1	1	8.9	1.3	5.5	7.2	0.7	3.48	-15
1999	LosAngls	NL	12.0	14	10	3	5	6	7.50	0	1	10.5	2.3	3.8	4.5	0.6	5.41	-27
2000	Omaha	PCL	39.0	43	30	5	30	20	6.92	1	3	9.9	1.2	6.9	4.6	0.3	4.60	-36
2001	Wichita	Tex	31.0	29	13	2	12	22	3.77	2	1	8.4	0.6	3.5	6.4	0.9	3.91	-6
2001	Edmonton	PCL	45.7	43	26	6	24	41	5.12	2	3	8.5	1.2	4.7	8.1	0.9	3.56	-6

An underrated reliever with a funky delivery, Bochtler has battled injury and control problems. He seemed to get back on the beam last season. Bochtler represents the sort of bargain-basement risk that small-market clubs should take.

Hector Carrasco Throws R Age 32

YEAR	TEAM	LGE	IP	H	ER	HR	BB	K	ERA	W	L	H/9	HR/9	BB/9	K/9	KW	PERA	STUFF
1999	Minnesot	AL	50.3	47	20	3	15	35	3.58	4	2	8.4	0.5	2.7	6.3	1.2	4.38	1
2000	Minnesot	AL	75.3	70	32	5	27	56	3.82	5	3	8.4	0.6	3.2	6.7	1.0	3.81	2
2001	Minnesot	AL	77.3	70	34	7	29	67	3.96	5	4	8.1	0.8	3.4	7.8	1.2	4.25	7

What you see is what you get—a solid guy out of the bullpen who can occasionally have streaks during which he looks like a world-beater, and who occasionally will, well, go the other way. His strikeout rate looks pretty solid; there's no reason to expect a significant change in role for the 2002 season, and he may get a few shots at closing games if the Twins' pen implodes.

Jack Cressend Throws R Age 27

YEAR	TEAM	LGE	IP	H	ER	HR	BB	K	ERA	W	L	H/9	HR/9	BB/9	K/9	KW	PERA	STUFF
1999	New Brit	Eas	147.7	155	82	16	57	78	5.00	7	9	9.4	1.0	3.5	4.8	0.7	6.46	-6
1999	Trenton	Eas	15.0	20	16	5	8	7	9.60	0	2	12.0	3.0	4.8	4.2	0.4	9.52	-38
2000	SaltLake	PCL	90.0	83	39	4	42	62	3.90	6	4	8.3	0.4	4.2	6.2	0.7	4.00	-8
2000	Minnesot	AL	15.7	16	6	0	5	6	3.45	1	1	9.2	0.0	2.9	3.4	0.6	4.22	-12
2001	Edmonton	PCL	17.3	20	12	2	9	6	6.23	1	1	10.4	1.0	4.7	3.1	0.3	6.77	-38
2001	Minnesot	AL	55.7	55	25	5	15	38	4.04	3	3	8.9	0.8	2.4	6.1	1.3	3.34	1

Cressend has been typecast as a junk-balling swing-man, which is certainly a role he's capable of playing. He can probably do more, because his fastball is better than the typical slop-thrower; it has average velocity, and it moves down a little bit in the last moment of flight. Cressend is never going to be a dominant starter, but if a club lets him develop, he could end up being a pleasant surprise at the back end of a rotation. Left in the pen, he could be a DP-inducing righty for the next seven years and make some dough.

Josh Daws Throws R Age 23

YEAR	TEAM	LGE	IP	H	ER	HR	BB	K	ERA	W	L	H/9	HR/9	BB/9	K/9	KW	PERA	STUFF
2001	Elizbthn	App	43.0	46	22	5	8	21	4.60	2	3	9.6	1.0	1.7	4.4	1.3	2.60	-5

We've never really understood the practice of drafting 22-year-old pitchers, particularly ones with command of the strike zone, and then sending them to rookie ball. The Twins assigned Daws to the Appy League, where he dutifully sliced and diced younger competition getting used to wooden bats. Neither we nor the Twins will really know much about Daws as a potential major leaguer until he gets to Double-A.

Eddie Guardado Throws L Age 31

YEAR	TEAM	LGE	IP	H	ER	HR	BB	K	ERA	W	L	H/9	HR/9	BB/9	K/9	KW	PERA	STUFF
1999	Minnesot	AL	47.7	41	21	5	21	50	3.97	3	2	7.7	0.9	4.0	9.4	1.2	3.86	13
2000	Minnesot	AL	60.7	61	36	12	20	52	5.34	3	4	9.0	1.8	3.0	7.7	1.3	3.16	1
2001	Minnesot	AL	65.0	55	24	4	22	64	3.32	5	2	7.6	0.6	3.0	8.9	1.5	3.17	17

Every manager would love to have Everyday Eddie in the pen, a left-hander who can get guys out on a regular basis, pitch 75 games a year, bounce back quickly, and get you a double play or a strikeout when you need one. He's Minnesota's cultural answer to John Franco, and worthy of a big red "S" on his chest.

LaTroy Hawkins Throws R Age 29

YEAR	TEAM	LGE	IP	H	ER	HR	BB	K	ERA	W	L	H/9	HR/9	BB/9	K/9	KW	PERA	STUFF
1999	Minnesot	AL	190.7	204	102	25	50	102	4.81	10	11	9.6	1.2	2.4	4.8	1.0	5.78	0
2000	Minnesot	AL	89.3	86	37	6	26	58	3.73	6	4	8.7	0.6	2.6	5.8	1.1	2.80	1
2001	Minnesot	AL	54.7	52	30	3	37	34	4.94	3	3	8.6	0.5	6.1	5.6	0.5	5.19	-16

Hawkins is solely responsible for 16 of Tom Kelly's diastolic blood-pressure points. He's maddeningly inconsistent with his mechanics, which can result in either a wicked fastball that moves slightly in against right-handers or, just as likely, a dead straight fastball that's about 2 mph slower. His command completely escaped him for large portions of the year, and he's going to have to fight for a meaningful job for the rest of his career. He might well end up in a Todd Van Poppel role somewhere down the line.

Adam Johnson Throws R Age 22

YEAR	TEAM	LGE	IP	H	ER	HR	BB	K	ERA	W	L	H/9	HR/9	BB/9	K/9	KW	PERA	STUFF
2000	Ft Myers	Fla	66.7	58	26	5	24	60	3.51	4	3	7.8	0.7	3.2	8.1	1.3	3.69	34
2001	New Brit	Eas	111.3	114	65	15	50	72	5.25	5	7	9.2	1.2	4.0	5.8	0.7	5.30	11
2001	Edmonton	PCL	23.3	20	9	0	11	18	3.47	2	1	7.7	0.0	4.2	6.9	0.8	5.70	24
2001	Minnesot	AL	26.3	29	19	5	12	16	6.49	1	2	9.9	1.7	4.1	5.5	0.7	7.83	-5

He hasn't disappointed since the Twins drafted him in the first round two years ago. Johnson has very good stuff, and his command is coming around. He should have a shot at the rotation in the spring, depending on the disposition of Rick Reed, and he is probably the best of several pretty good prospects the Twins have to fill rotation spots in the next couple of years. Johnson is definitely the one most likely to be a Front of the Rotation Starter™.

Todd Jones **Throws R** **Age 34**

YEAR	TEAM	LGE	IP	H	ER	HR	BB	K	ERA	W	L	H/9	HR/9	BB/9	K/9	KW	PERA	STUFF
1999	Detroit	AL	68.7	61	30	6	29	63	3.93	5	3	8.0	0.8	3.8	8.3	1.1	3.41	9
2000	Detroit	AL	68.3	58	25	5	20	66	3.29	5	3	7.6	0.7	2.6	8.7	1.6	3.34	16
2001	Detroit	AL	52.7	52	27	6	21	37	4.61	3	3	8.9	1.0	3.6	6.3	0.9	5.32	-5
2001	Minnesot	AL	21.7	22	11	3	7	14	4.57	1	1	9.1	1.2	2.9	5.8	1.0	3.25	-6

Jones was outspoken about how much he loved Detroit and the Tigers organization, which is a little odd considering the Tigers never even sniffed success during his time there. He's been a solid reliever in the past, but his peripheral numbers are getting scary; declining strikeout rates and increasing hit totals are not good trends. Look, someone's going to sign Jason Isringhausen to be their closer; you could do worse than Jones.

Matt Kinney **Throws R** **Age 25**

YEAR	TEAM	LGE	IP	H	ER	HR	BB	K	ERA	W	L	H/9	HR/9	BB/9	K/9	KW	PERA	STUFF
1999	New Brit	Eas	62.0	69	48	12	36	35	6.97	2	5	10.0	1.7	5.2	5.1	0.5	9.34	-14
2000	New Brit	Eas	85.0	85	50	13	38	65	5.29	4	5	9.0	1.4	4.0	6.9	0.9	3.92	11
2000	SaltLake	PCL	53.7	49	26	6	25	47	4.36	3	3	8.2	1.0	4.2	7.9	0.9	3.62	23
2000	Minnesot	AL	42.0	45	27	6	20	24	5.79	2	3	9.6	1.3	4.3	5.1	0.6	4.44	0
2001	Edmonton	PCL	162.3	176	116	28	87	100	6.43	6	12	9.8	1.6	4.8	5.5	0.6	5.85	-6

Kinney was probably the biggest disappointment of the season for the Twins, at least in terms of their prospects. In March, Kinney was a long shot to win a rotation spot with the big club out of spring training. Instead, he spent the year battling control problems and giving up 25 home runs for the Trappers. The Twins have a number of guys who could turn out to be good starters; Kinney can be counted among them, but he'll have to step up and rebuild his rep among scouts and within the organization.

Kyle Lohse **Throws R** **Age 23**

YEAR	TEAM	LGE	IP	H	ER	HR	BB	K	ERA	W	L	H/9	HR/9	BB/9	K/9	KW	PERA	STUFF
1999	Daytona	Fla	51.3	57	33	8	19	28	5.79	2	4	10.0	1.4	3.3	4.9	0.7	4.24	8
1999	Ft Myers	Fla	41.7	50	33	11	11	22	7.13	1	4	10.8	2.4	2.4	4.8	1.0	7.99	0
1999	New Brit	Eas	72.7	85	50	13	23	29	6.19	3	5	10.5	1.6	2.8	3.6	0.6	7.32	-2
2000	New Brit	Eas	170.3	201	130	40	58	90	6.87	6	13	10.6	2.1	3.1	4.8	0.8	7.72	0
2001	New Brit	Eas	35.7	40	21	7	5	21	5.30	2	2	10.1	1.8	1.3	5.3	2.1	2.97	12
2001	Edmonton	PCL	50.0	47	20	3	15	34	3.60	4	2	8.5	0.5	2.7	6.1	1.1	3.86	21
2001	Minnesot	AL	93.7	98	52	14	28	61	5.00	4	6	9.4	1.3	2.7	5.9	1.1	5.20	8

Pressed into service due to a series of injuries, Lohse had a wonderful minor-league season interrupted by a bunch of major-league hitters. He's a control pitcher who needs to keep the ball down; if hitters can make him elevate the ball, they'll hit it hard. Lohse's numbers in the minors are solid, but he doesn't have the strikeout rate you would like to see, making him a long shot to be a successful major-league starter. He will probably start the season at Triple-A.

Joe Mays **Throws R** **Age 26**

YEAR	TEAM	LGE	IP	H	ER	HR	BB	K	ERA	W	L	H/9	HR/9	BB/9	K/9	KW	PERA	STUFF
1999	Minnesot	AL	175.0	177	89	21	56	114	4.58	9	10	9.1	1.1	2.9	5.9	1.0	3.99	5
2000	Minnesot	AL	171.0	174	84	17	55	101	4.42	10	9	9.2	0.9	2.9	5.3	0.9	4.73	5
2001	Minnesot	AL	226.7	237	111	22	61	117	4.41	13	12	9.4	0.9	2.4	4.6	1.0	2.92	6

Mays would have been a deserving Cy Young Award winner. He gets a lot of ground balls, and his strikeout rate improved as the season went on, even as he approached innings-pitched levels that automatically trigger the AndrewsBeacon™. Still, he's a good candidate to slip in 2002; his strikeout rate is still low, his ERA is better than you'd expect given his other numbers, and he's never thrown 233 innings in a season before.

Travis Miller **Throws L** **Age 29**

YEAR	TEAM	LGE	IP	H	ER	HR	BB	K	ERA	W	L	H/9	HR/9	BB/9	K/9	KW	PERA	STUFF
1999	SaltLake	PCL	18.0	17	8	1	7	13	4.00	1	1	8.5	0.5	3.5	6.5	0.9	3.38	-5
1999	Minnesot	AL	53.0	48	19	3	13	40	3.23	4	2	8.2	0.5	2.2	6.8	1.5	2.68	8
2000	Minnesot	AL	74.7	65	28	3	26	61	3.38	5	3	7.8	0.4	3.1	7.4	1.2	3.77	8
2001	Minnesot	AL	50.7	51	25	4	19	29	4.44	3	3	9.1	0.7	3.4	5.2	0.8	4.82	-9

One of the points we often stress is that players we criticize aren't necessarily bad, but they appear that way because they're asked to perform beyond their capabilities. Miller is an excellent example of a guy finding a good niche. He's the second lefty out of the pen, with a more pronounced platoon split than Guardado. His strikeout rate dropped a little, and yes, his ERA was up, but he's a good bet to return to a higher level of success. Like many of the Twins' pitchers, Miller got pasted by the Indians.

Eric Milton Throws L Age 26

YEAR	TEAM	LGE	IP	H	ER	HR	BB	K	ERA	W	L	H/9	HR/9	BB/9	K/9	KW	PERA	STUFF
1999	Minnesot	AL	207.0	199	93	21	53	161	4.04	13	10	8.7	1.0	2.3	7.0	1.5	3.99	22
2000	Minnesot	AL	204.7	203	95	30	36	159	4.18	12	11	8.9	1.3	1.6	7.0	2.2	4.44	20
2001	Minnesot	AL	222.3	229	115	31	58	149	4.66	12	13	9.3	1.3	2.3	6.0	1.3	3.87	11

You have to love that Chuck Knoblauch deal right about now. Milton was one of the top 25 starters in MLB last year, pitching a career-high 220 innings, posting his lowest ERA, and he still appears to be just scraping the surface of his talent. This year, he should take yet another step forward and join the top 10 or 15 MLB starters. A disastrous July and a couple of bad games in October made his second-half numbers look bad, but his strikeout rate increased as the year went along. The idea that a team with Mays, Milton, and Brad Radke at the front of its rotation could be seriously considered as a contraction candidate is laughable.

Brad Radke Throws R Age 29

YEAR	TEAM	LGE	IP	H	ER	HR	BB	K	ERA	W	L	H/9	HR/9	BB/9	K/9	KW	PERA	STUFF
1999	Minnesot	AL	224.7	235	102	24	37	120	4.09	14	11	9.4	1.0	1.5	4.8	1.6	3.29	9
2000	Minnesot	AL	238.7	242	103	23	42	140	3.88	15	12	9.1	0.9	1.6	5.3	1.7	3.79	12
2001	Minnesot	AL	230.3	235	93	21	25	130	3.63	16	10	9.2	0.8	1.0	5.1	2.6	3.64	13

He's a wonderful starting pitcher who keeps hitters off balance and spends the day throwing a two-seam fastball into a teacup. Radke is durable, reliable, and effective, despite not possessing an overpowering fastball. There's no reason to expect a dropoff from him any time soon.

Rick Reed Throws R Age 36

YEAR	TEAM	LGE	IP	H	ER	HR	BB	K	ERA	W	L	H/9	HR/9	BB/9	K/9	KW	PERA	STUFF
1999	NY Mets	NL	152.7	161	82	22	39	94	4.83	8	9	9.5	1.3	2.3	5.5	1.2	4.41	6
2000	NY Mets	NL	186.0	197	91	26	28	108	4.40	11	10	9.5	1.3	1.4	5.2	1.9	4.21	9
2001	NY Mets	NL	125.3	127	53	14	15	80	3.81	8	6	9.1	1.0	1.1	5.7	2.7	3.71	16
2001	Minnesot	AL	73.7	79	38	11	13	41	4.64	4	4	9.7	1.3	1.6	5.0	1.6	5.20	4

The trade for Reed was simply a disastrous deal for Minnesota. For the last three years as a Met, Reed had an ERA 50% higher when pitching anywhere except Shea Stadium. He has no fastball, and, as a control pitcher who gives up a lot of hits, was moving to a league where the ninth hitter he faces is Edgar Martinez, Jeremy Giambi, or someone else who can hit, instead of Omar Daal. For this, you give up a good defensive outfielder who's one of only two guys in your lineup that get on base? Reed will be as good as the umpires let him be. If he has to pitch in the strike zone, he'll get smoked. If he can live in Jimmy Key Land, he'll be effective.

Juan Rincon Throws R Age 23

YEAR	TEAM	LGE	IP	H	ER	HR	BB	K	ERA	W	L	H/9	HR/9	BB/9	K/9	KW	PERA	STUFF
1999	Quad Cit	Mid	161.3	168	92	17	74	88	5.13	8	10	9.4	0.9	4.1	4.9	0.6	4.47	8
2000	Ft Myers	Fla	74.3	78	40	7	27	36	4.84	4	4	9.4	0.8	3.3	4.4	0.7	4.15	5
2000	New Brit	Eas	91.0	98	61	16	41	57	6.03	4	6	9.7	1.6	4.1	5.6	0.7	6.48	6
2001	New Brit	Eas	148.3	150	81	13	72	87	4.91	7	9	9.1	0.8	4.4	5.3	0.6	4.42	4
2001	Minnesot	AL	6.0	6	5	1	5	4	7.50	0	1	9.0	1.5	7.5	6.0	0.4	6.87	-19

Rincon is a three-pitch starter who's been pretty effective and has a chance to be a major-league starter. Scouts think he can add a couple of mph to his fastball by fine-tuning his mechanics. He'll start the year at Triple-A, and if there's another string of injuries to the #4 and #5 guys, he'll get a crack at the rotation late in 2002.

J.C. Romero Throws L Age 26

YEAR	TEAM	LGE	IP	H	ER	HR	BB	K	ERA	W	L	H/9	HR/9	BB/9	K/9	KW	PERA	STUFF
1999	New Brit	Eas	52.7	56	40	9	36	36	6.84	2	4	9.6	1.5	6.2	6.2	0.5	5.16	-18
1999	SaltLake	PCL	20.0	18	11	1	15	15	4.95	1	1	8.1	0.4	6.8	6.8	0.5	4.30	-5
2000	SaltLake	PCL	63.7	68	36	7	25	29	5.09	3	4	9.6	1.0	3.5	4.1	0.6	4.88	-11
2000	Minnesot	AL	63.3	60	31	7	25	50	4.41	4	3	8.5	1.0	3.6	7.1	1.0	6.38	11
2001	Edmonton	PCL	64.3	65	34	5	31	35	4.76	3	4	9.1	0.7	4.3	4.9	0.6	5.26	-7
2001	Minnesot	AL	66.3	71	38	9	23	37	5.16	3	4	9.6	1.2	3.1	5.0	0.8	5.78	-4

This smallish left-hander throws lots of stuff down, and he battled back problems for a large part of the season. Romero was eventually sent down to Edmonton, where he pitched well. He'll be in the mix for the swing-man/fifth-starter role in spring training, and he's capable of pitching well either out of the pen or in the rotation. Most clubs that have seven candidates for the #5 starter job are looking at a bunch of guys who resemble Mike Oquist on a good day, or who've had more stitches in their arms than a box of baseballs. The Twins actually have a few guys with high ceilings vying for those spots.

Johan Santana Throws L Age 23

YEAR	TEAM	LGE	IP	H	ER	HR	BB	K	ERA	W	L	H/9	HR/9	BB/9	K/9	KW	PERA	STUFF
1999	Michigan	Mid	160.0	179	108	29	62	86	6.07	6	12	10.1	1.6	3.5	4.8	0.7	6.22	4
2000	Minnesot	AL	92.0	90	49	9	44	63	4.79	5	5	8.8	0.9	4.3	6.2	0.7	5.38	4
2001	Minnesot	AL	45.7	47	24	5	15	27	4.73	2	3	9.3	1.0	3.0	5.3	0.9	4.48	1

He suffered a torn flexor tendon in June that kept him out of action until near the end of the season. Santana is not really that different from Romero, but he pitched much more effectively in relief (3.00 ERA) than in the rotation (Texas Ranger Country). His likely career is as a lefty specialist; that career might start five years from now, or it could happen this year.

Bob Wells Throws R Age 35

YEAR	TEAM	LGE	IP	H	ER	HR	BB	K	ERA	W	L	H/9	HR/9	BB/9	K/9	KW	PERA	STUFF
1999	Minnesot	AL	85.7	88	40	7	23	44	4.20	5	5	9.2	0.7	2.4	4.6	1.0	3.48	-7
2000	Minnesot	AL	87.0	83	36	12	12	75	3.72	6	4	8.6	1.2	1.2	7.8	3.1	3.26	12
2001	Minnesot	AL	69.7	73	37	11	17	47	4.78	4	4	9.4	1.4	2.2	6.1	1.4	4.45	-4

Wells is a nice guy to have somewhere in the pen. He can throw strikes, get people out without his best stuff, carry a significant workload, and is comfortable with a role in the middle of the bullpen. Bob Wells and pitchers like him may not get a lot of press, but they make their teammates and managers look awfully good.

New York Yankees

It took about one inning of the Division Series for things to truly get back to some semblance of normalcy in the U.S. After that, it was OK for people outside of New York to start hating the Yankees—and by extension, New York—again. For New Yorkers, it was OK to scream with delight and display some of that world-famous disdain. It was very much like being able to get into fights with your big sister again after she came home from the hospital. The sentimentality wore off almost immediately, and then it was time to resume hiding slugs under her pillow.

The story arc for the Yankees in 2001 was fairly serene. Most of the noise in the division came not from the Bronx Zoo, but rather from a Boston Red Sox team that burned hot and finally flamed out after an impressive half-season. Toronto's offense never really came together, and their pitching staff could run on fumes for only so long. The rest of the division's personnel was largely selected by Chuck LaMar, Peter Angelos, and Syd Thrift, so clearly no one else represented a threat to 70 wins, much less to the Yankees. The Yankees were the veteran team, possibly too old to repeat, but clearly geared towards just reaching the playoffs, when they'd be able to crank up the postseason magic and grind through another October.

Yankees Prospectus

2001 record: 95–65; First place, AL East; Lost to Diamondbacks in World Series, 4–3

Pythagenport W/L: 89–73

Runs scored: 804 (fifth in AL)

Runs allowed: 713 (third in AL)

Team EqA: .265 (fifth in AL)

2001 batters age: 30.9 (third-oldest in AL)

2001 pitchers age: 30.5 (second-oldest in AL)

Ballpark: Yankee Stadium; slight pitchers' park; Park Factor of .982

2001: Coasted through the regular season, then had the most thrilling postseason in franchise history, coming two outs shy of a fourpeat.

2002: An upgraded offense makes them the clear favorite in the AL East.

There was just one real change in the Yankees from 2000 to 2001. They signed former Oriole Mike Mussina to a six-year contract for just shy of $90 million, prompting a few cries for mercy around the rest of the league. For Mussina, the Yankees represented what he thought was his best chance for a ring, both immediately and in the foreseeable future. For the Yankees, a team with an aging and questionable rotation, it was a fantastic move that will turn out to be worth every cent, as #1 starters are extremely difficult to come by in any circumstances. New York was going to have a hard time filling out the back end of its rotation; without Mussina, the job would have been much more difficult.

In case you didn't notice, the Yankees managed to avoid the pitfalls that the Red Sox didn't, and they pretty much cruised through the regular season in kind of a low gear. Orlando Hernandez missed a fair amount of the year with a severe toe injury, David Justice missed some time with a strained groin, and Scott Brosius missed about six weeks with a broken finger. By and large, though, the Yankees were pretty healthy and met expectations, winning 95 games and a home series against the upstart Oakland A's in the Division Series.

The Yankees' postseason plan is pretty simple: let the starter go as long as he can while maintaining full effectiveness, then give the ball to Ramiro Mendoza or Mike Stanton (preferably Mendoza), who in turn gives the ball to Mariano Rivera, the human incarnation of quicksand. The plan worked like a charm against the A's, who played like a younger and less prepared team than they did in 2000, and against the Mariners, who had their shortcomings exposed like David Copperfield spending a weekend with Ricky Jay.

Which brings us to the World Series. The media fashioned the libretto for the World Series against the Diamondbacks. The D'Backs would throw the NL's two best starters, Curt Schilling and Randy Johnson, either four or five times in seven games, and it would be up to the Yankees to find a way to beat them at least once or twice. There was no conceit about Arizona being able to win a game with Miguel Batista or soft-tossing Brian Anderson on the mound. The implied subtext was that the Yankees would draw their walks, get the required clutch hits, and simply wear out the lesser pitchers. The Diamondbacks would have to pin their hopes on dominating performances, the specialty of their two big arms. In the end, Arizona won in exactly that fashion, combined with a miracle double by a surprising and impressive Tony Womack, and a bloop single to the edge of the outfield by Luis Gonzalez.

The Yankees were an old team heading into the 2001 season. Are they now just dethroned champions who have to rebuild their base? Absolutely not. When Gonzalez hit his blooper off of Mariano Rivera to win the Series, it didn't really mark an end to a Great Yankee Era; it marked the successful culmination of the Diamondbacks' Desperate Lurch. We're still in the middle of that Great Yankee Era. The team has done an outstanding job of developing talent and identifying where it needs to make stopgap moves. The Yankees are now free of the contracts of a number of aging veterans, including Paul O'Neill, Chuck Knoblauch, Tino Martinez, and Scott Brosius, all on the bad side of 32, and all of whom play positions for which it's easy to find talent.

The Yankees are positively loaded at critical positions. Their up-the-middle position players are the best in baseball; no other team can compete with Jorge Posada, Alfonso Soriano, Derek Jeter, and Bernie Williams. Their rotation has one old guy who has a much greater chance of retiring than of being ineffective in Roger Clemens, another #1 starter behind him in Mussina, a young veteran left-hander who took some steps forward last year in Andy Pettitte, and a number of pretty reasonable options for the #4 and #5 spots. The bullpen's foundation of Rivera and Mendoza is better than anyone else's and provides consistent excellence as well as flexibility on a tactical and strategic level.

The 2002 Yankees will look a bit different, following George Steinbrenner's decision to spend some of his YES Network money. The team signed free agents Jason Giambi and Rondell White to upgrade two lineup holes. They traded for Robin Ventura and John Vander Wal to patch two others and give some of their prospects more time in Triple-A. The DH slot is still open and should belong to Nick Johnson. Johnson can hit for average and power, though it may take some time for him to develop both of those skills, but most importantly, he gets on base and is very much an offensive player in the mold of Williams or Jeter. He's also two years removed from being one of the best hitting prospects the world has ever seen, and all his skills seem to be intact, if a bit rusty.

Ventura, acquired from the Mets for David Justice, is a short-term Yankee because they already have a long-term deal in place with Drew Henson. Henson was overmatched in Triple-A last year, so he will need some time at Columbus to put everything together. While they've brought in White and Vander Wal, the Yankees also have a couple of reasonable corner-outfield prospects in Juan Rivera and Marcus Thames. Rivera is at least a half-season of Triple-A ball away from being ready, and Thames is really more the type of guy who the Yankees use as trade currency to fill an in-season need. No matter who ends up with the playing time in left and right field, the Yankee lineup will be solidly above average with Giambi added to its core.

The rotation is another matter. The front line of starters is entrenched with Clemens, Mussina, and Pettitte. El Duque will hold the #4 spot and can reasonably be expected to be effective now that his toe is healthy. The Yankees have given Sterling Hitchcock $6 million to be the #5 starter, although he hasn't been healthy and effective since 1999. Should he falter, the Yanks have some pitching prospects—guys such as Brandon Claussen, Ted Lilly, and even Brandon Knight (who didn't help his cause in a brief 2001 appearance)—around as spring-training competitors for that spot. No matter what happens with the #5 slot, there are only a couple of AL teams—the A's, and maybe the Twins—with rotations that can stand up against the Yankees' going into next season.

The cries from around the league about revenue disparity are getting pretty old. The media uses the term "high revenue teams" when they mean "the Yankees" whenever discussions—usually underinformed ones—about revenue disparity and competitive balance pop up. Whiny fans from other cities talk about their "inability to keep their players" because of all the money the Yankees spend, but those fans ignore plenty of counterexamples in gigantic markets such as Cleveland, Oakland, Minneapolis, and Seattle. The Yankees do benefit from being the oldest team in the biggest media market in the world. They also benefit from a well-run and well-designed organization. They benefit from management that's creative in terms of developing new markets and revenue streams. They benefit because of hard work.

On the management side, the Yankees are the model of consistency and quiet professionalism, a state of affairs that no one could have fathomed in, say, 1978. Joe Torre is regarded as one of the best and most beloved managers in baseball. Brian Cashman has signed a three-year contract that extends his successful stay in New York, and the Yankees' scouting, business development, and player development programs are the envy of the league. There are no weaknesses on this club at this point. Cashman will be there, and so will all the key front-office players.

The core of this team is Jeter, Williams, Posada, Soriano, Johnson, Rivera, Mendoza, Pettitte, Clemens, and Mussina. Of those ten players, eight are from the Yankees' talent-development system. Clemens was acquired via trade, and Mussina was a free agent who could have been signed by other clubs, ones who instead chose to do things like give comparable salaries to players such as Kevin Appier, Darren Dreifort, Mike Hampton, and Denny Neagle. That's not to mention other clubs who chose to make multiple smaller, dumber signings rather than spend more money on the better players. David Segui? Jeff Shaw? For God's sake, Preston Wilson is scheduled to make $12 million in 2005.

Yes, there are revenue disparities. If owners are serious about fixing them, they have the tools to do so without having to deal with either the players or municipalities. Agree to share a larger portion of local revenues and all revenues from as-yet-undetermined sources. Make whole those clubs whose franchise value is damaged by the deal. Even instituting a salary floor might help. None of it matters. The Yankees are going to keep rolling, and the rest of the clubs in MLB have a number of choices in front of them.

Some clubs have chosen to compete, or at least to make the attempt. The Indians put together a great run based on minor-league development and a willingness to assume the risk that a player would develop sufficiently to make a long-term contract a good value for the team. They've since veered from this strategy and will soon begin to pay for it. The A's did the same thing, only more effectively. The Mariners and Rangers have made investments to broaden and deepen their revenue streams. The Giants and Rockies have made massive marketing investments and tremendous strides in integrating with the wider cultures of their cities.

The Yankees are going to move forward, and they can realistically be called favorites for the World Series again in 2002. Other clubs can choose to whine if they want, or they can begin the hard work of competing.

HITTERS (BA: .270, OBP: .340, SLG: .440, EqA: .260)

Erick Almonte SS Bats R Age 24

YEAR	TEAM	LGE	AB	H	DB	TP	HR	BB	SO	R	RBI	SB	CS	OUT	BA	OBP	SLG	EQA	EQR	DEFENSE
1999	Tampa	Fla	233	50	7	1	4	13	55	27	18	2	1	184	.215	.259	.305	.193	15	61-SS -1
2000	Norwich	Eas	461	114	16	2	14	26	133	46	61	8	2	349	.247	.290	.382	.226	42	125-SS -23
2001	Columbus	Int	353	98	17	2	12	42	83	54	53	3	4	259	.278	.357	.439	.265	47	94-SS -12
2002	*NY Yanks*	*AL*	*421*	*116*	*19*	*2*	*14*	*42*	*115*	*65*	*53*	*4*	*1*	*306*	*.276*	*.341*	*.430*	*.265*	*55*	

Almonte had a breakout year with the bat at Columbus, hitting .287 with reasonable plate discipline and 34 extra-base hits in just under 350 at-bats. Unfortunately, he's not exactly polished on defense. Scouts charitably describe his defense as "erratic," "miserable," and "sloppy." He has neither the range nor the hands to play shortstop in the bigs. He's probably the youngest ballplaying Almonte in the Bronx. . . .

Clay Bellinger UT Bats R Age 33

YEAR	TEAM	LGE	AB	H	DB	TP	HR	BB	SO	R	RBI	SB	CS	OUT	BA	OBP	SLG	EQA	EQR	DEFENSE
1999	Columbus	Int	141	31	7	1	2	11	30	16	12	5	0	110	.220	.283	.326	.215	12	21-3B 0
1999	NY Yanks	AL	45	10	2	0	1	1	9	9	2	1	0	35	.222	.239	.333	.195	3	11-3B 0
2000	NY Yanks	AL	184	40	7	2	7	15	42	32	21	5	0	144	.217	.295	.391	.234	19	23-CF 0 12-3B 1
2001	NY Yanks	AL	81	14	1	1	6	4	20	14	13	1	2	69	.173	.219	.432	.205	7	16-3B 0
2001	Columbus	Int	99	21	7	0	2	5	20	13	10	3	0	78	.212	.255	.343	.206	8	
2002	*NY Yanks*	*AL*	*215*	*43*	*8*	*1*	*7*	*18*	*50*	*30*	*20*	*5*	*1*	*173*	*.200*	*.262*	*.344*	*.207*	*17*	

He's just a defensive fill-in who drank a little Rob Deer elixir in 2001. Bellinger can't hit and won't hit, but he does have some of that World Champion fairy dust on him, so he'll end up with a job as a utility guy for at least another year or so. He does do an excellent job of making the right technical moves when he fills in on defense, and he's not slow, so he can help in the right circumstances.

Scott Brosius 3B Bats R Age 35

YEAR	TEAM	LGE	AB	H	DB	TP	HR	BB	SO	R	RBI	SB	CS	OUT	BA	OBP	SLG	EQA	EQR	DEFENSE
1999	NY Yanks	AL	473	125	24	1	20	34	65	65	74	9	3	351	.264	.321	.446	.254	57	128-3B 13
2000	NY Yanks	AL	469	114	16	0	19	40	64	56	65	0	3	358	.243	.305	.399	.233	47	126-3B 14
2001	NY Yanks	AL	431	133	25	2	15	36	72	62	52	3	1	299	.309	.367	.480	.281	63	115-3B 2
2002	*NY Yanks*	*AL*	*418*	*107*	*17*	*1*	*15*	*43*	*68*	*53*	*56*	*3*	*2*	*313*	*.256*	*.325*	*.409*	*.252*	*50*	

Now retired, Brosius is still a great defensive third baseman who can hit a mediocre fastball out of the park. Given his performance last year and the number of teams looking for third-base help, his decision to walk away probably cost him about $10–15 million over three years.

Michael Coleman OF Bats R Age 26

YEAR	TEAM	LGE	AB	H	DB	TP	HR	BB	SO	R	RBI	SB	CS	OUT	BA	OBP	SLG	EQA	EQR	DEFENSE
1999	Pawtuckt	Int	467	116	25	2	25	41	120	78	59	10	5	356	.248	.312	.471	.256	59	108-CF 4
2000	Pawtuckt	Int	66	16	4	1	5	2	23	10	12	3	0	50	.242	.265	.561	.266	9	14-CF -1
2001	Columbus	Int	103	24	4	2	4	13	32	16	16	2	3	82	.233	.327	.427	.246	12	25-RF -1
2001	NY Yanks	AL	38	9	0	0	1	0	13	5	7	0	1	30	.237	.237	.316	.177	2	
2002	Boston	AL	360	90	17	4	17	39	112	57	49	8	5	275	.250	.323	.461	.259	47	

Coleman pulled a hamstring early in the year and never really got back on track. Just a few years ago, Coleman was considered by many to be one of the best prospects in baseball. He's now wearing the scarlet AAAA, and he'll have to get lucky for a stretch in order to get another opportunity. He's back with the Red Sox, who certainly could use a fourth outfielder with some pop.

Bobby Estalella C Bats R Age 27

YEAR	TEAM	LGE	AB	H	DB	TP	HR	BB	SO	R	RBI	SB	CS	OUT	BA	OBP	SLG	EQA	EQR	DEFENSE
1999	Scran-WB	Int	389	86	20	2	13	47	94	50	52	3	1	304	.221	.311	.383	.235	41	100-C 6
2000	San Fran	NL	304	74	22	3	15	53	84	46	54	3	0	230	.243	.359	.484	.280	48	95-C -1
2001	San Fran	NL	94	21	6	1	3	11	24	12	11	0	0	73	.223	.310	.404	.239	10	27-C 0
2001	Fresno	PCL	22	6	1	0	1	0	8	3	4	0	0	16	.273	.273	.455	.234	2	
2001	Columbus	Int	175	44	9	0	10	20	42	26	36	0	2	133	.251	.333	.474	.261	23	35-C -3
2002	NY Yanks	AL	365	91	21	2	16	52	100	52	60	1	0	274	.249	.343	.449	.271	52	

Sometimes, you get surprised by Paul LoDuca. Unfortunately, sometimes you get surprised by Bobby Estalella. Estalella's bat speed dropped precipitously in 2001, and he looked completely lost at the plate. He could have been one of the more valuable players in baseball last year: he was playing in a pitchers' park, coming into his age-26 season, and coming off a year with an 825 OPS. Instead, he cratered. He could well return to form, or he could be the second coming of Rick Wilkins.

Mike Frank OF Bats L Age 27

YEAR	TEAM	LGE	AB	H	DB	TP	HR	BB	SO	R	RBI	SB	CS	OUT	BA	OBP	SLG	EQA	EQR	DEFENSE
1999	Indianap	Int	432	119	31	5	8	28	52	60	50	7	5	318	.275	.328	.426	.250	50	110-OF 1
2000	Louisvil	Int	198	52	14	1	6	16	26	26	25	6	1	147	.263	.328	.434	.257	25	52-LF 2
2000	Columbus	Int	139	32	5	2	2	14	13	17	10	4	3	110	.230	.311	.338	.223	13	40-OF 3
2001	Columbus	Int	363	90	19	2	10	39	48	44	52	9	3	276	.248	.327	.394	.245	41	87-LF -5
2002	NY Yanks	AL	370	91	20	3	9	43	49	51	42	6	3	282	.246	.324	.389	.247	43	

A replacement-level outfielder with a good glove and a little pop, Frank has been around a long time and has the HTWG (Hustling Telegenic White Guy) tag from his brief time in Cincinnati those many years ago. He's still just 27, can play any outfield position credibly, will pop the occasional home run, and has some speed. Some clubs pay $2 million for this skill set; you can get it for less and spend the extra money where you need it.

Todd Greene C Bats R Age 31

YEAR	TEAM	LGE	AB	H	DB	TP	HR	BB	SO	R	RBI	SB	CS	OUT	BA	OBP	SLG	EQA	EQR	DEFENSE
1999	Edmonton	PCL	73	16	4	0	4	0	11	8	11	0	0	57	.219	.226	.438	.212	6	12-LF 0
1999	Anaheim	AL	320	80	17	0	16	9	55	35	42	1	4	244	.250	.276	.453	.233	32	11-C 0
2000	Syracuse	Int	91	25	3	0	6	5	16	13	12	1	0	66	.275	.313	.505	.266	12	10-LF -1
2000	Toronto	AL	85	20	3	0	5	4	16	11	10	0	0	65	.235	.270	.447	.232	8	
2001	Columbus	Int	132	33	7	0	6	4	18	16	17	3	2	101	.250	.276	.439	.232	13	27-C -2
2001	NY Yanks	AL	96	22	2	0	2	4	18	10	13	0	0	74	.229	.266	.313	.196	6	23-C -5
2002	NY Yanks	AL	316	77	12	0	14	17	55	35	37	2	2	241	.244	.282	.415	.232	31	

Greene finally found his niche, as a backup catcher and lefty smasher. He can fill in at first base or left field, spell your regular catcher, and occasionally pop a Jamie Moyer pitch about 440 feet. He's not going to cut it as a starter, but he can help.

Drew Henson 3B Bats R Age 22

YEAR	TEAM	LGE	AB	H	DB	TP	HR	BB	SO	R	RBI	SB	CS	OUT	BA	OBP	SLG	EQA	EQR	DEFENSE
1999	Tampa	Fla	258	60	8	0	10	19	80	28	26	2	1	199	.233	.286	.380	.223	23	48-3B -15
2000	Chattang	Sou	66	11	5	0	2	2	25	6	9	1	0	55	.167	.191	.333	.176	4	16-3B -1
2000	Tampa	Fla	21	6	0	0	1	1	8	3	1	0	1	16	.286	.318	.429	.232	2	
2000	Norwich	Eas	227	58	6	1	7	15	77	33	31	0	3	172	.256	.303	.383	.226	21	45-3B -6
2001	Tampa	Fla	15	2	0	0	1	1	8	1	3	0	0	13	.133	.234	.333	.192	1	
2001	Norwich	Eas	19	6	1	0	0	1	4	2	2	0	1	14	.316	.367	.368	.236	2	
2001	Columbus	Int	272	60	4	0	11	11	79	29	37	2	1	213	.221	.251	.357	.202	20	66-3B -7
2002	*NY Yanks*	*AL*	*325*	*83*	*8*	*0*	*12*	*26*	*108*	*39*	*38*	*2*	*2*	*244*	*.255*	*.311*	*.391*	*.239*	*34*	

He's considered a top prospect based almost entirely on scouting reports and probably partly because he was a difficult sign, with a football career as an option. Henson is considered the heir apparent to Brosius at third base and is expected to develop significant power. Defensively, he's raw at best, but he has the quickness to improve. He hit .316/.412/.581 in the Arizona Fall League and was a distant second on the league's depth chart at third base behind the obscenely talented Hank Blalock.

Derek Jeter SS Bats R Age 28

YEAR	TEAM	LGE	AB	H	DB	TP	HR	BB	SO	R	RBI	SB	CS	OUT	BA	OBP	SLG	EQA	EQR	DEFENSE
1999	NY Yanks	AL	622	220	39	9	20	85	102	134	102	18	8	401	.368	.452	.585	.340	135	156-SS -13
2000	NY Yanks	AL	587	209	32	4	16	61	87	117	71	23	5	382	.356	.428	.506	.316	108	146-SS -27
2001	NY Yanks	AL	619	206	37	3	24	59	86	119	79	26	3	416	.333	.398	.519	.307	109	145-SS -28
2002	*NY Yanks*	*AL*	*615*	*205*	*33*	*4*	*22*	*75*	*93*	*122*	*82*	*27*	*5*	*415*	*.333*	*.406*	*.507*	*.315*	*115*	

We give Jeter a lot of flack about his dismal defense, and he deserves it. That being said, he may be one of the most UNDERrated ballplayers ever, which is unimaginable for a young, happening Yankee. Jeter's offense is truly outstanding. He hits for a very high average despite playing in a tough ballpark for right-handed hitters; he has the best base-stealing technique this side of Tim Raines; and he will, over the next three to five years, develop significantly more home-run power. Is he Alex Rodriguez? No, but he could be a guy who hits .350/.460/.590 with 35 steals in 40 attempts and plays in 150 games a year for eight years in a row. So he may be 20 runs worse than average with the glove. Big deal.

Nick Johnson 1B Bats L Age 23

YEAR	TEAM	LGE	AB	H	DB	TP	HR	BB	SO	R	RBI	SB	CS	OUT	BA	OBP	SLG	EQA	EQR	DEFENSE
1999	Norwich	Eas	434	131	31	3	11	99	88	94	68	5	4	307	.302	.454	.463	.316	86	129-1B -2
2001	Columbus	Int	372	94	14	0	19	76	97	66	49	7	2	280	.253	.392	.444	.286	61	109-1B -5
2001	NY Yanks	AL	67	14	1	0	3	8	13	7	9	0	0	53	.209	.320	.358	.233	7	12-1B -1
2002	*NY Yanks*	*AL*	*403*	*111*	*21*	*1*	*18*	*82*	*103*	*84*	*68*	*7*	*2*	*294*	*.275*	*.398*	*.467*	*.300*	*72*	

Johnson missed all of 2000 due to a mysterious (and still slightly worrisome) wrist injury. No matter: he's destined for greatness. Johnson possesses a Max Bishop/Rickey Henderson batting eye and a very quick stroke, and he plays a pretty good first base, too. There aren't many players with exactly the same skill set. He'll likely end up as a cross between John Olerud and Barry Bonds. I think most Yankees fans can live with that, even if it takes him a few years to get there.

David Justice LF Bats L Age 36

YEAR	TEAM	LGE	AB	H	DB	TP	HR	BB	SO	R	RBI	SB	CS	OUT	BA	OBP	SLG	EQA	EQR	DEFENSE
1999	Clevelnd	AL	422	124	14	0	23	89	79	73	86	1	3	301	.294	.419	.491	.304	77	91-LF -4
2000	Clevelnd	AL	245	66	14	1	21	35	43	44	54	1	1	180	.269	.361	.592	.301	45	45-OF -3
2000	NY Yanks	AL	272	87	14	0	22	36	37	42	59	1	0	185	.320	.401	.614	.324	55	62-LF -1
2001	NY Yanks	AL	384	100	17	1	20	55	72	64	54	1	2	286	.260	.353	.466	.271	54	25-LF 2
2002	*Oakland*	*AL*	*434*	*115*	*19*	*1*	*27*	*75*	*81*	*72*	*83*	*1*	*2*	*321*	*.265*	*.373*	*.500*	*.295*	*76*	

Justice is still a very productive hitter. He fought through some nagging injuries in 2001, which happens as one ages, but he was fairly effective and can still turn on almost any fastball. Between the writing deadline for this book and the printing, Justice was traded twice and begins the 2002 season as the A's DH. He's capable of playing the same role for them that John Jaha did in 1999.

Chuck Knoblauch LF Bats R Age 33

YEAR	TEAM	LGE	AB	H	DB	TP	HR	BB	SO	R	RBI	SB	CS	OUT	BA	OBP	SLG	EQA	EQR	DEFENSE
1999	NY Yanks	AL	600	186	38	4	20	77	50	120	69	27	9	423	.310	.405	.487	.300	105	147-2B -17
2000	NY Yanks	AL	398	117	25	2	5	41	40	74	25	15	8	289	.294	.372	.405	.265	52	78-2B -10
2001	NY Yanks	AL	524	144	21	3	11	61	63	70	48	36	10	390	.275	.362	.389	.263	69	101-LF -6
2002	*KansasCy*	*AL*	*515*	*140*	*23*	*3*	*11*	*72*	*59*	*91*	*42*	*30*	*11*	*386*	*.272*	*.361*	*.392*	*.261*	*67*	

Wow. Three years from "Legitimate MVP Candidate" to "Not Worth a Roster Spot." He didn't get back on the bike at second base and instead went out to left field, where he just doesn't have the bat to help a club. The rumor is that Knoblauch and the Yankees had a handshake deal on a contract extension, but he's not going to be back in the Bronx. He can be valuable as a pinch hitter, fourth outfielder, and pinch runner at this point, and that's all.

Tino Martinez 1B Bats L Age 34

YEAR	TEAM	LGE	AB	H	DB	TP	HR	BB	SO	R	RBI	SB	CS	OUT	BA	OBP	SLG	EQA	EQR	DEFENSE
1999	NY Yanks	AL	587	164	29	2	30	64	76	97	106	3	4	427	.279	.353	.489	.275	85	150-1B 16
2000	NY Yanks	AL	567	153	39	4	17	46	65	68	89	4	1	415	.270	.334	.443	.258	70	144-1B -2
2001	NY Yanks	AL	592	176	24	2	38	45	77	98	119	1	2	418	.297	.348	.537	.285	91	142-1B 5
2002	*St Louis*	*NL*	*529*	*147*	*28*	*2*	*27*	*58*	*72*	*83*	*96*	*3*	*2*	*384*	*.278*	*.349*	*.491*	*.277*	*78*	

Martinez is holding up to the aging process pretty well, and his clutch hits in the postseason had Yankees fans clamoring for him to be re-signed. The Yankees instead signed Jason Giambi, freeing Martinez to sign a three-year deal with the Cardinals. Martinez probably has two or three more good years in him, both defensively and as someone who can hammer bad breaking pitches from right-handers.

Donzell McDonald OF Bats Age 27

YEAR	TEAM	LGE	AB	H	DB	TP	HR	BB	SO	R	RBI	SB	CS	OUT	BA	OBP	SLG	EQA	EQR	DEFENSE
1999	Norwich	Eas	546	133	20	7	3	70	110	74	26	33	14	427	.244	.333	.322	.233	56	134-CF -8
2000	Norwich	Eas	176	38	6	1	2	28	37	18	8	9	5	143	.216	.324	.295	.221	16	43-CF -3
2000	Columbus	Int	79	19	5	3	1	20	11	15	5	9	0	60	.241	.404	.418	.301	15	22-CF 0
2001	Columbus	Int	381	96	12	8	8	41	73	58	35	16	4	289	.252	.332	.388	.248	44	100-CF -7
2002	*Clevelnd*	*AL*	*454*	*117*	*21*	*7*	*8*	*64*	*93*	*68*	*30*	*23*	*6*	*343*	*.258*	*.349*	*.388*	*.255*	*57*	

Once considered a prize prospect, McDonald has developed into a speedy extra outfielder. He's basically Brian Hunter with more youth, a little bit of upside, some power, and slightly less defense. He can fill a backup role if the Yankees need that, and he probably has more value in that role than Bellinger does.

Deivi Mendez SS Bats R Age 19

YEAR	TEAM	LGE	AB	H	DB	TP	HR	BB	SO	R	RBI	SB	CS	OUT	BA	OBP	SLG	EQA	EQR	DEFENSE
2001	StatenIs	NYP	189	33	6	1	1	6	37	16	14	1	2	158	.175	.205	.233	.150	7	51-SS -5
2001	Greensbr	SAL	177	31	2	0	2	11	37	18	11	2	1	147	.175	.227	.220	.159	7	49-SS -1
2002	*NY Yanks*	*AL*	*394*	*84*	*13*	*1*	*5*	*28*	*85*	*36*	*32*	*6*	*3*	*313*	*.213*	*.265*	*.289*	*.186*	*23*	

Mendez followed up a very promising 2000, in which he hit .300/.382/.433, with an abysmal 2001, when he couldn't crack a 600 OPS in either the New York-Penn or Sally Leagues. Mendez was just 18 last season, so he has time to turn it around, but there's just nothing good to say about his 2001, except that he wasn't disfigured, arrested, or present during the Michael Jackson "Extra-Creepy" 30th Anniversary Special.

Andy Morales 3B Bats R Age 27

YEAR	TEAM	LGE	AB	H	DB	TP	HR	BB	SO	R	RBI	SB	CS	OUT	BA	OBP	SLG	EQA	EQR	DEFENSE
2001	Norwich	Eas	163	35	2	1	1	9	24	14	13	1	1	129	.215	.263	.258	.181	9	22-3B -2
2002	*NY Yanks*	*AL*	*158*	*36*	*2*	*1*	*1*	*13*	*24*	*13*	*12*	*1*	*1*	*123*	*.228*	*.287*	*.272*	*.189*	*9*	

This Cuban bonus baby wasn't a baby, so the Yankees demanded their bonus back after they found out he also couldn't play. Morales is probably out of organized baseball for good, and his situation may have meant a few more bucks for Drew Henson.

Paul O'Neill RF Bats L Age 39

YEAR	TEAM	LGE	AB	H	DB	TP	HR	BB	SO	R	RBI	SB	CS	OUT	BA	OBP	SLG	EQA	EQR	DEFENSE
1999	NY Yanks	AL	595	178	41	4	21	60	78	70	111	10	9	426	.299	.365	.487	.279	88	141-RF -4
2000	NY Yanks	AL	563	165	19	0	22	45	79	76	101	14	10	408	.293	.345	.444	.261	71	124-RF 2
2001	NY Yanks	AL	513	146	31	1	25	50	51	83	75	21	3	370	.285	.350	.495	.282	78	110-RF -10

It was touching to watch the fans at Yankee Stadium see him off during Game Five of the World Series. Of course, in the same game, O'Neill whined about 14 called strikes, two plays on the base paths, concession prices, and global warming. He has enough bat speed left to play but has decided he's had enough. He'll be missed by Yankees fans.

Andy Phillips 2B Bats R Age 25

YEAR	TEAM	LGE	AB	H	DB	TP	HR	BB	SO	R	RBI	SB	CS	OUT	BA	OBP	SLG	EQA	EQR	DEFENSE
1999	StatenIs	NYP	239	53	7	2	5	23	44	22	27	1	2	188	.222	.293	.331	.212	19	62-3B -7
2000	Tampa	Fla	488	117	22	1	12	33	109	51	43	1	0	371	.240	.289	.363	.219	42	124-3B -17
2000	Norwich	Eas	29	7	1	1	0	2	11	4	2	1	0	22	.241	.290	.345	.221	3	
2001	Tampa	Fla	296	76	14	2	9	17	59	34	36	2	2	222	.257	.300	.409	.234	29	71-2B -11
2001	Norwich	Eas	189	46	9	1	5	19	53	21	22	1	0	143	.243	.313	.381	.235	19	46-2B -16
2002	*NY Yanks*	*AL*	*477*	*126*	*23*	*3*	*15*	*46*	*115*	*56*	*61*	*2*	*2*	*353*	*.264*	*.329*	*.419*	*.255*	*58*	

By all accounts, Phillips is a hard worker, and the results are showing up on the field. He started the year in the Florida State League, where he hit the ball well and wasn't overwhelmed by the transition to the Eastern League, posting a .268/.340/.437 in Norwich. Defensively, he's going to have to find a way to be valuable, which probably means learning a few other positions, but he could have a nice career in the bigs as a utility man.

Jorge Posada C Bats B Age 30

YEAR	TEAM	LGE	AB	H	DB	TP	HR	BB	SO	R	RBI	SB	CS	OUT	BA	OBP	SLG	EQA	EQR	DEFENSE
1999	NY Yanks	AL	378	98	21	2	13	49	80	51	58	1	0	280	.259	.348	.429	.262	49	100-C -7
2000	NY Yanks	AL	499	150	31	1	31	101	133	90	85	2	2	351	.301	.426	.553	.321	103	135-C 2
2001	NY Yanks	AL	488	147	27	1	26	64	114	64	104	1	7	348	.301	.387	.520	.294	81	124-C -3
2002	*NY Yanks*	*AL*	*461*	*136*	*23*	*1*	*27*	*73*	*118*	*73*	*88*	*1*	*4*	*329*	*.295*	*.391*	*.525*	*.306*	*85*	

Jorge Posada is a great ballplayer, a switch hitter who actually should be one, hitting for power and average and showing good plate discipline. He's good at working with pitchers and relatively durable, too. Posada is arb-eligible this season and eligible for free agency after the 2002 season. The Yankees would be wise to sign him to a four-year deal.

Juan Rivera RF Bats R Age 23

YEAR	TEAM	LGE	AB	H	DB	TP	HR	BB	SO	R	RBI	SB	CS	OUT	BA	OBP	SLG	EQA	EQR	DEFENSE
1999	Tampa	Fla	429	93	15	1	11	19	75	37	53	3	2	338	.217	.254	.333	.197	29	93-RF -5
2000	Tampa	Fla	416	97	16	1	12	24	62	46	50	6	5	324	.233	.280	.363	.215	35	115-RF -4
2000	Norwich	Eas	63	13	3	0	2	5	15	7	10	0	0	50	.206	.265	.349	.206	5	13-RF -1
2001	Norwich	Eas	322	92	16	2	11	15	49	45	48	4	5	235	.286	.321	.450	.251	37	76-RF 0
2001	Columbus	Int	203	63	8	1	13	15	29	37	37	3	5	145	.310	.360	.552	.287	32	55-RF 1
2002	*NY Yanks*	*AL*	*485*	*130*	*21*	*2*	*18*	*39*	*79*	*61*	*75*	*3*	*2*	*357*	*.268*	*.323*	*.431*	*.256*	*59*	

The Yankees #1 prospect. Rivera swings hard and has a well-developed ability to hit the bad ball. The result is a lot of balls put in play with authority. He's a big guy who gets compared to Vladimir Guerrero in terms of his swing. Rivera doesn't walk a whole lot but has demonstrated that, like Guerrero, he can hit for a high enough average to have a respectable OBP. Comparisons to Juan Gonzalez are probably accurate in terms of the type of player he'll become; then again, by the time Gonzalez was 22, he had been in the majors for a couple of years. Rivera shows good technique in the outfield; in fact, his defense is more technique than raw speed. He should be a good everyday player in the bigs.

Henry Rodriguez OF Bats L Age 34

YEAR	TEAM	LGE	AB	H	DB	TP	HR	BB	SO	R	RBI	SB	CS	OUT	BA	OBP	SLG	EQA	EQR	DEFENSE
1999	ChiCubs	NL	447	133	22	0	28	50	105	69	83	1	4	318	.298	.368	.535	.291	72	104-LF 1
2000	ChiCubs	NL	261	65	14	1	18	19	70	36	49	1	2	198	.249	.306	.517	.262	35	57-LF 1
2000	Florida	NL	109	30	3	0	3	13	21	10	10	0	0	79	.275	.357	.385	.254	13	23-LF -1
2001	Columbus	Int	64	15	1	0	5	7	19	9	13	0	0	49	.234	.316	.484	.260	8	
2002	*NY Yanks*	*AL*	*355*	*90*	*15*	*1*	*19*	*43*	*97*	*47*	*56*	*1*	*2*	*267*	*.254*	*.334*	*.462*	*.268*	*50*	

Everyone seems to have forgotten about Henry. He suffered a back injury in the spring and was designated for assignment by the Yankees in June. If he wants to, he'll have a job somewhere, because he can actually hit right-handed pitchers pretty well. Over the last three seasons, he's posted a 900 OPS against right-handed pitching. He may not be a defensive whiz, and he shouldn't play against lefties, but most clubs can find a spot and a few bucks for someone who can put up a .350 OBP and a .550 SLG against two-thirds of the pitchers in the league.

Luis Sojo UT Bats R Age 36

YEAR	TEAM	LGE	AB	H	DB	TP	HR	BB	SO	R	RBI	SB	CS	OUT	BA	OBP	SLG	EQA	EQR	DEFENSE	
1999	NY Yanks	AL	127	34	4	0	3	3	15	20	17	1	0	93	.268	.285	.370	.219	10	16-3B 0	14-2B 1
2000	Pittsbrg	NL	177	50	7	0	6	9	15	13	20	1	0	127	.282	.320	.424	.248	19	43-3B -2	
2000	NY Yanks	AL	125	38	8	1	2	4	5	19	17	1	0	87	.304	.326	.432	.252	14	19-2B 2	
2001	NY Yanks	AL	79	15	3	0	0	4	10	6	9	1	0	64	.190	.236	.228	.165	4	10-3B 0	
2002	*NY Yanks*	*AL*	*242*	*58*	*6*	*0*	*7*	*16*	*23*	*32*	*33*	*2*	*0*	*184*	*.240*	*.287*	*.351*	*.218*	*20*		

A reflection player: considered good if he's on a good team, bad if he's on a bad one. Sojo is a capable enough 25th guy who can fill in when an infielder is hurt or needs a day off. He brings a little pop, he won't hurt you defensively, and he has a fantastic clubhouse reputation and a bunch of rings. Sojo is indistinguishable from dozens of guys in the minors, so the end of the line could come at any time.

Alfonso Soriano 2B Bats R Age 24

YEAR	TEAM	LGE	AB	H	DB	TP	HR	BB	SO	R	RBI	SB	CS	OUT	BA	OBP	SLG	EQA	EQR	DEFENSE	
1999	Norwich	Eas	366	98	16	2	12	23	67	45	52	15	11	279	.268	.315	.421	.242	40	87-SS -5	
1999	Columbus	Int	82	14	3	1	2	4	17	7	9	1	1	69	.171	.209	.305	.172	4	11-SS 0	
2000	Columbus	Int	461	127	27	5	12	19	83	81	58	11	6	340	.275	.308	.434	.244	50	64-SS -20	40-2B -4
2000	NY Yanks	AL	50	9	1	0	3	1	13	5	3	2	0	41	.180	.196	.380	.195	3		
2001	NY Yanks	AL	577	165	35	3	21	31	108	81	78	40	16	428	.286	.325	.466	.262	75	153-2B -16	
2002	*NY Yanks*	*AL*	*523*	*151*	*26*	*4*	*22*	*37*	*104*	*88*	*80*	*25*	*12*	*383*	*.289*	*.336*	*.480*	*.274*	*76*		

Well, he's exciting to watch, has some amazing physical gifts, and his walk rate is improving. Soriano is overrated by most baseball fans and underrated by most statheads. He's learning to play second base as he goes, and some plate discipline did peek through a couple of times during the season. There's no reason a healthy Soriano can't be the best second baseman in the league. There's also no reason he can't be Carlos Baerga. The projection above looks a little high, at least in terms of batting average, and he should do more work on the base paths than that.

Shane Spencer OF Bats R Age 30

YEAR	TEAM	LGE	AB	H	DB	TP	HR	BB	SO	R	RBI	SB	CS	OUT	BA	OBP	SLG	EQA	EQR	DEFENSE
1999	NY Yanks	AL	205	51	7	0	9	16	45	25	20	0	4	158	.249	.309	.415	.234	21	55-LF 2
1999	Columbus	Int	50	17	1	0	2	7	8	14	9	0	0	33	.340	.421	.480	.305	8	13-LF -1
2000	NY Yanks	AL	247	73	11	3	10	16	40	33	40	1	2	176	.296	.344	.486	.270	33	40-LF 0
2001	Columbus	Int	177	41	9	1	3	22	19	17	14	3	1	137	.232	.321	.345	.231	18	32-LF 0
2001	NY Yanks	AL	284	78	13	2	12	23	50	44	49	4	1	207	.275	.335	.461	.264	37	68-LF 4
2002	*NY Yanks*	*AL*	*394*	*105*	*18*	*2*	*12*	*41*	*66*	*58*	*46*	*5*	*3*	*292*	*.266*	*.336*	*.414*	*.257*	*49*	

What you see is what you get: the right-handed half of a pretty good outfield platoon, probably with John Vander Wal. Spencer will catch the balls hit to him, give you some reasonable pop in the lineup, particularly against lefties, and hit somewhere around league average. If a team is giving him 200-300 at-bats per year in good spots, that's a good sign. If they're giving him 80, or 500, that's a bad sign.

Marcus Thames OF Bats R Age 25

YEAR	TEAM	LGE	AB	H	DB	TP	HR	BB	SO	R	RBI	SB	CS	OUT	BA	OBP	SLG	EQA	EQR	DEFENSE	
1999	Tampa	Fla	271	56	8	2	9	25	65	35	26	2	0	215	.207	.277	.351	.213	23	48-RF	3
1999	Norwich	Eas	186	39	7	1	3	16	40	21	21	0	1	148	.210	.278	.306	.200	13	46-RF	-7
2000	Norwich	Eas	483	105	24	1	14	39	92	61	63	1	4	382	.217	.279	.358	.213	40	109-RF	-9
2001	Norwich	Eas	542	156	36	3	25	65	98	101	82	7	3	389	.288	.368	.504	.287	86	136-CF	8
2002	*NY Yanks*	*AL*	*484*	*128*	*27*	*2*	*20*	*58*	*97*	*82*	*72*	*5*	*3*	*359*	*.264*	*.343*	*.452*	*.271*	*68*		

Thames exploded in his third go'round at Norwich, hitting .321/.410/.598 in 139 games. Even though he's not young, those are hard numbers to ignore. Scouts say that he's learned to turn on inside pitches and lay off breaking balls in the dirt. Thames needs a year of Triple-A to find out how much of what he learned will stay with him; 2001 definitely sticks out in his record.

Randy Velarde 2B Bats R Age 39

YEAR	TEAM	LGE	AB	H	DB	TP	HR	BB	SO	R	RBI	SB	CS	OUT	BA	OBP	SLG	EQA	EQR	DEFENSE	
1999	Anaheim	AL	372	117	14	4	10	39	49	55	47	12	4	259	.315	.385	.454	.284	56	95-2B	7
1999	Oakland	AL	253	88	9	3	8	25	37	48	28	11	4	169	.348	.410	.502	.305	43	59-2B	0
2000	Oakland	AL	483	142	16	0	16	49	84	81	42	10	4	344	.294	.363	.427	.268	64	117-2B	8
2001	Texas	AL	296	93	16	2	10	30	63	49	32	4	2	205	.314	.384	.483	.289	46	52-2B	-3
2001	NY Yanks	AL	46	8	4	0	0	5	11	4	1	2	0	38	.174	.286	.261	.204	4		
2002	*Oakland*	*AL*	*530*	*128*	*18*	*3*	*14*	*56*	*106*	*73*	*47*	*12*	*5*	*407*	*.242*	*.314*	*.366*	*.237*	*56*		

Velarde has been one of the better second basemen in the league for some time now, providing a solid OBP, defense, a little pop, and, by all accounts, a good clubhouse presence. He's 39 years old, but he's in good shape and perhaps has a bit more time left because of all the time he missed when he was younger. (Well, perhaps not.) He's a free agent and could help most teams in the league. He's back in Oakland to reprise his player/coach role.

Bernie Williams CF Bats B Age 33

YEAR	TEAM	LGE	AB	H	DB	TP	HR	BB	SO	R	RBI	SB	CS	OUT	BA	OBP	SLG	EQA	EQR	DEFENSE	
1999	NY Yanks	AL	586	209	30	6	27	94	84	116	114	8	10	387	.357	.446	.567	.330	121	155-CF	2
2000	NY Yanks	AL	532	171	38	6	32	65	74	108	119	13	6	367	.321	.400	.596	.319	105	134-CF	0
2001	NY Yanks	AL	545	183	33	0	32	81	58	111	104	10	6	368	.336	.426	.572	.324	110	145-CF	-2
2002	*NY Yanks*	*AL*	*531*	*166*	*30*	*3*	*30*	*88*	*68*	*104*	*104*	*9*	*7*	*372*	*.313*	*.410*	*.550*	*.320*	*107*		

Bernie Williams makes baseball dull the same way Tiger Woods makes golf dull. Williams might be the most consistently excellent player in the game, and he's a joy to watch. He doesn't get a lot of attention for his performance level, but all he needs to get our Hall of Fame vote is accumulate service time. His career 888 OPS while playing an average or better center field is amazing.

Gerald Williams OF Bats R Age 35

YEAR	TEAM	LGE	AB	H	DB	TP	HR	BB	SO	R	RBI	SB	CS	OUT	BA	OBP	SLG	EQA	EQR	DEFENSE	
1999	Atlanta	NL	424	115	20	1	18	28	62	72	65	16	11	320	.271	.325	.450	.254	52	97-LF	0
2000	TampaBay	AL	629	177	30	2	22	27	91	84	86	12	13	465	.281	.314	.440	.245	69	138-CF	2
2001	TampaBay	AL	232	52	14	0	6	14	36	32	19	10	5	185	.224	.277	.362	.216	20	59-CF	9
2001	NY Yanks	AL	47	9	2	0	0	5	11	11	2	3	1	39	.191	.280	.234	.193	3	13-OF	0
2002	*NY Yanks*	*AL*	*492*	*118*	*21*	*1*	*19*	*41*	*81*	*73*	*63*	*15*	*14*	*388*	*.240*	*.298*	*.402*	*.235*	*52*		

Well, that worked out about as well as could be expected. Someone will give Williams a crack at a fifth-outfielder job during spring training, and there might be worse options, depending on his price. Maybe the Dodgers could sign him and have the dream outfield of Williams, Marquis Grissom, and Tom Goodwin. Mmmm . . . outs.

Enrique Wilson SS/3B Bats B Age 26

YEAR	TEAM	LGE	AB	H	DB	TP	HR	BB	SO	R	RBI	SB	CS	OUT	BA	OBP	SLG	EQA	EQR	DEFENSE
1999	Clevelnd	AL	330	89	23	1	2	22	36	40	23	5	4	245	.270	.317	.364	.230	31	45-3B 1 22-SS -4
2000	Clevelnd	AL	115	37	7	0	3	6	10	15	12	2	1	79	.322	.355	.461	.271	15	
2000	Pittsbrg	NL	123	32	6	1	3	9	12	11	14	0	1	92	.260	.311	.398	.234	12	14-3B -1
2001	Pittsbrg	NL	129	26	3	0	1	3	20	8	8	0	3	106	.202	.220	.248	.155	5	24-SS -3
2001	NY Yanks	AL	99	26	5	1	1	7	12	11	12	0	2	75	.263	.311	.364	.222	9	12-3B 3 11-SS -1
2002	*NY Yanks*	*AL*	*286*	*71*	*15*	*1*	*5*	*23*	*36*	*31*	*24*	*1*	*4*	*219*	*.248*	*.304*	*.360*	*.224*	*26*	

A one-time hot middle-infield prospect for the Indians, Wilson has demonstrated many skills at various levels. It's entirely possible that given 400 carefully selected at bats, he could put up some numbers that would really surprise people. If not, he's a good bench guy and should have a long career as a utility player.

PITCHERS (ERA: 4.50, H/9: 9.0, HR/9: 1.0, BB/9: 3.0, K/9: 6.0, KW: 2.0, PERA: 4.50)

Carlos Almanzar Throws R Age 28

YEAR	TEAM	LGE	IP	H	ER	HR	BB	K	ERA	W	L	H/9	HR/9	BB/9	K/9	KW	PERA	STUFF
1999	LasVegas	PCL	22.3	34	36	13	9	12	14.51	0	2	13.7	5.2	3.6	4.8	0.7	9.96	-65
1999	San Dieg	NL	40.3	42	22	6	13	27	4.91	2	2	9.4	1.3	2.9	6.0	1.0	7.62	-10
2000	San Dieg	NL	71.0	73	39	11	21	50	4.94	4	4	9.3	1.4	2.7	6.3	1.2	4.47	-4
2001	Columbus	Int	34.0	35	15	3	8	18	3.97	2	2	9.3	0.8	2.1	4.8	1.1	3.54	-12
2001	NY Yanks	AL	11.3	13	6	2	2	6	4.76	0	1	10.3	1.6	1.6	4.8	1.5	3.15	-9

Almanzar has a very live arm that, if healthy, could help a team in the back end of the bullpen. He's already had a significant impact on the Yankees: he served up the home run to Mike Piazza that essentially forced the trade of D'Angelo Jimenez to the Padres for Jay Witasick. Almanzar will need to get a hell of a lot of batters out to make up for that.

Randy Choate Throws L Age 26

YEAR	TEAM	LGE	IP	H	ER	HR	BB	K	ERA	W	L	H/9	HR/9	BB/9	K/9	KW	PERA	STUFF
1999	Tampa	Fla	50.7	54	39	10	33	37	6.93	2	4	9.6	1.8	5.9	6.6	0.6	6.49	-25
2000	Columbus	Int	36.7	33	15	3	14	30	3.68	2	2	8.1	0.7	3.4	7.4	1.1	2.22	6
2000	NY Yanks	AL	16.3	17	10	3	7	12	5.51	1	1	9.4	1.7	3.9	6.6	0.9	4.54	-7
2001	NY Yanks	AL	46.7	41	19	0	26	33	3.66	3	2	7.9	0.0	5.0	6.4	0.6	3.66	0

Choate is fun to watch, a Todd Frohwirth or Mark Eichhorn from the left side. He's a promising lefty specialist, and he'll probably spend the next ten to 12 years being asked to retire some nasty lefty bomber or forcing the opposing manager to pinch-hit for one.

Brandon Claussen Throws L Age 23

YEAR	TEAM	LGE	IP	H	ER	HR	BB	K	ERA	W	L	H/9	HR/9	BB/9	K/9	KW	PERA	STUFF
1999	StatenIs	NYP	72.7	77	38	10	16	42	4.71	4	4	9.5	1.2	2.0	5.2	1.3	4.82	15
2000	Greensbr	SAL	94.3	111	83	22	56	51	7.92	2	8	10.6	2.1	5.3	4.9	0.5	6.20	-7
2000	Tampa	Fla	53.0	52	23	2	20	29	3.91	3	3	8.8	0.3	3.4	4.9	0.7	5.44	9
2001	Tampa	Fla	55.7	53	24	5	15	41	3.88	3	3	8.6	0.8	2.4	6.6	1.4	4.86	19
2001	Norwich	Eas	127.7	117	63	9	70	99	4.44	7	7	8.2	0.6	4.9	7.0	0.7	3.76	18

Claussen, a solid rotation prospect, possesses good stuff, isn't afraid to work inside to both left-handers and right-handers, and has greatly improved his ability to change speeds without slowing his arm down. Claussen threw 187 innings during 2001; that might be the upper end of an acceptable workload for him. If he stays healthy, he'll probably get a cup of coffee this year.

Roger Clemens — Throws R — Age 39

YEAR	TEAM	LGE	IP	H	ER	HR	BB	K	ERA	W	L	H/9	HR/9	BB/9	K/9	KW	PERA	STUFF
1999	NY Yanks	AL	194.0	178	88	18	75	161	4.08	12	10	8.3	0.8	3.5	7.5	1.1	4.25	19
2000	NY Yanks	AL	206.7	188	92	23	69	186	4.01	13	10	8.2	1.0	3.0	8.1	1.3	3.62	24
2001	NY Yanks	AL	226.3	199	87	18	69	203	3.46	16	9	7.9	0.7	2.7	8.1	1.5	3.60	27

Is it possible for a guy with six Cy Young Awards to be underrated? In conversations about the best pitchers of a generation, Clemens gets slighted. He's better than Greg Maddux, better than Randy Johnson, and you need to work pretty hard to find any pitcher in history who's unambiguously better than Clemens. He did get some cosmic payback for the 1990 Cy Young Award travesty, when an undeserving Bob Welch won the award thanks to ridiculous run support.

Alex Graman — Throws L — Age 24

YEAR	TEAM	LGE	IP	H	ER	HR	BB	K	ERA	W	L	H/9	HR/9	BB/9	K/9	KW	PERA	STUFF
1999	StatenIs	NYP	78.3	92	57	18	21	40	6.55	3	6	10.6	2.1	2.4	4.6	1.0	4.27	1
2000	Tampa	Fla	138.0	146	84	15	72	70	5.48	6	9	9.5	1.0	4.7	4.6	0.5	5.52	-5
2001	Norwich	Eas	168.7	175	95	16	79	87	5.07	8	11	9.3	0.9	4.2	4.6	0.6	6.10	-2

Once touted as the next big thing, Graman is going to have to improve pretty significantly to have a shot at a big-league career. He has a reasonable fastball, particularly in terms of movement, but if he has to take something off of it to throw strikes, he's going to get hit. Graman could begin the season in either Double-A or Triple-A, depending on what the Yankees need.

Adrian Hernandez — Throws R — Age 22

YEAR	TEAM	LGE	IP	H	ER	HR	BB	K	ERA	W	L	H/9	HR/9	BB/9	K/9	KW	PERA	STUFF
2000	Norwich	Eas	37.3	32	16	2	19	32	3.86	2	2	7.7	0.5	4.6	7.7	0.8	5.08	31
2000	Columbus	Int	30.0	28	16	2	17	25	4.80	1	2	8.4	0.6	5.1	7.5	0.7	5.51	25
2001	Columbus	Int	117.0	122	78	17	68	75	6.00	5	8	9.4	1.3	5.2	5.8	0.6	6.66	4
2001	NY Yanks	AL	19.0	24	20	6	10	10	9.47	0	2	11.4	2.8	4.7	4.7	0.5	3.83	-15

He got a cup of coffee not because he was necessarily better than other options, but because he cost a fair amount of dough. Hernandez's fastball hasn't materialized as promised, but there's a lot of movement on his breaking pitches, and he changes speeds very well for a pitcher his age. He doesn't have great command of his stuff but is young enough to learn. Right now, Hernandez is dealing with culture shock both in the game and outside of it; two years from now, he might be as good as the hype.

Orlando Hernandez — Throws R — Age 32

YEAR	TEAM	LGE	IP	H	ER	HR	BB	K	ERA	W	L	H/9	HR/9	BB/9	K/9	KW	PERA	STUFF
1999	NY Yanks	AL	212.0	204	100	21	73	155	4.25	13	11	8.7	0.9	3.1	6.6	1.1	3.98	14
2000	NY Yanks	AL	195.0	199	99	30	42	140	4.57	11	11	9.2	1.4	1.9	6.5	1.7	4.10	14
2001	NY Yanks	AL	94.0	97	60	18	40	73	5.74	4	6	9.3	1.7	3.8	7.0	0.9	4.54	6

Thirty-two years old? Moving right along.... El Duque had one of those injury seasons that might actually be a good thing in the long term. He suffered a toe injury that required invasive medical attention and spent most of the year rehabbing, a welcome break for his shoulder and elbow. He showed the occasional glimpse of the 17-arm-angle, 22-pitch guy who'd previously baffled hitters, and he is a good bet to return to that form.

Sterling Hitchcock — Throws L — Age 31

YEAR	TEAM	LGE	IP	H	ER	HR	BB	K	ERA	W	L	H/9	HR/9	BB/9	K/9	KW	PERA	STUFF
1999	San Dieg	NL	209.7	201	102	28	64	175	4.38	12	11	8.6	1.2	2.7	7.5	1.4	4.28	19
2000	San Dieg	NL	67.3	68	37	11	21	54	4.95	3	4	9.1	1.5	2.8	7.2	1.3	5.14	13
2001	Lk Elsin	Cal	27.7	33	18	7	1	14	5.86	1	2	10.7	2.3	0.3	4.6	7.0	9.49	-21
2001	Portland	PCL	17.3	19	7	1	3	7	3.63	1	1	9.9	0.5	1.6	3.6	1.2	4.65	0
2001	San Dieg	NL	19.3	18	7	1	3	12	3.26	1	1	8.4	0.5	1.4	5.6	2.0	4.52	16
2001	NY Yanks	AL	55.7	58	27	5	17	27	4.37	3	3	9.4	0.8	2.7	4.4	0.8	6.08	-2

(Sterling Hitchcock *continued*)

Hitchcock is a control freak who battled back from a season lost to injury. He doesn't throw faster than about 25 mph, but he can place the ball wherever he wants, give the hitter 30 different looks, and throw any pitch for a strike at any time. As long as there are human umpires who don't understand where the outside corner is, there will be about ten starters in the league like Hitchcock. He signed a two-year, $12-million deal with the Yankees and should continue to be as effective as he has been for some time to come.

Randy Keisler Throws L Age 26

YEAR	TEAM	LGE	IP	H	ER	HR	BB	K	ERA	W	L	H/9	HR/9	BB/9	K/9	KW	PERA	STUFF
1999	Greensbr	SAL	21.3	19	13	2	15	19	5.48	1	1	8.0	0.8	6.3	8.0	0.6	3.67	9
1999	Tampa	Fla	86.0	86	49	5	55	46	5.13	4	6	9.0	0.5	5.8	4.8	0.4	6.20	-7
1999	Norwich	Eas	44.3	45	22	3	18	22	4.47	3	2	9.1	0.6	3.7	4.5	0.6	6.11	-1
2000	Norwich	Eas	71.7	73	43	8	40	45	5.40	3	5	9.2	1.0	5.0	5.7	0.6	4.80	-3
2000	Columbus	Int	112.7	114	58	11	42	70	4.63	6	7	9.1	0.9	3.4	5.6	0.8	3.80	7
2000	NY Yanks	AL	12.3	13	7	1	7	6	5.11	0	1	9.5	0.7	5.1	4.4	0.4	10.09	-21
2001	NY Yanks	AL	50.3	56	42	11	32	34	7.51	2	4	10.0	2.0	5.7	6.1	0.5	5.98	-11
2001	Columbus	Int	100.7	107	65	15	50	60	5.81	4	7	9.6	1.3	4.5	5.4	0.6	8.12	-15

Ouchie. Keisler started the season as a dark-horse candidate for the #5 spot in the Yankees rotation. He didn't pitch well in either New York or Columbus and was eventually diagnosed with a rotator-cuff tear. He underwent surgery in the off-season and is out of action until at least June or July 2002. His window of opportunity in New York has probably closed.

Brandon Knight Throws R Age 26

YEAR	TEAM	LGE	IP	H	ER	HR	BB	K	ERA	W	L	H/9	HR/9	BB/9	K/9	KW	PERA	STUFF
1999	Oklahoma	PCL	162.7	183	100	25	49	73	5.53	7	11	10.1	1.4	2.7	4.0	0.7	5.23	-2
2000	Columbus	Int	182.0	192	105	27	61	112	5.19	9	11	9.5	1.3	3.0	5.5	0.9	5.56	3
2001	Columbus	Int	167.0	170	91	24	57	118	4.90	9	10	9.2	1.3	3.1	6.4	1.0	5.60	2
2001	NY Yanks	AL	11.7	16	12	5	3	7	9.26	0	1	12.3	3.9	2.3	5.4	1.2	9.45	-28

Knight struck out better than a guy per inning in Columbus, and he has about 18 months to avoid the dreaded "Quadruple-A" label. He can help a major-league club, either as a back-of-the-rotation starter or perhaps as a setup guy out of the pen. Knight needs to have a great outing in front of a decision maker, something he didn't do in 2001, when he faced the Orioles in three of his four MLB appearances and somehow found a way to allow ten runs in ten innings. That's not the way to make a good impression.

Ted Lilly Throws L Age 26

YEAR	TEAM	LGE	IP	H	ER	HR	BB	K	ERA	W	L	H/9	HR/9	BB/9	K/9	KW	PERA	STUFF
1999	Ottawa	Int	88.0	89	45	13	22	63	4.60	5	5	9.1	1.3	2.3	6.4	1.4	3.79	16
1999	Montreal	NL	25.7	26	17	6	8	25	5.96	1	2	9.1	2.1	2.8	8.8	1.6	6.91	11
2000	Columbus	Int	145.3	145	74	18	48	103	4.58	8	8	9.0	1.1	3.0	6.4	1.1	5.49	10
2001	Columbus	Int	23.7	22	12	3	10	20	4.56	1	2	8.4	1.1	3.8	7.6	1.0	4.66	6
2001	NY Yanks	AL	125.0	121	67	19	49	107	4.82	7	7	8.7	1.4	3.5	7.7	1.1	5.66	10

People seem to have completely forgotten about Lilly as a prospect. He's still young, with good strikeout rates and solid control, and his career could develop in a couple of ways. With most clubs, he'd be an effective back-of-the-rotation starter with the potential to improve. With this one, he'll have to wait for an injury.

Ramiro Mendoza Throws R Age 30

YEAR	TEAM	LGE	IP	H	ER	HR	BB	K	ERA	W	L	H/9	HR/9	BB/9	K/9	KW	PERA	STUFF
1999	NY Yanks	AL	130.3	130	54	12	23	79	3.73	8	6	9.0	0.8	1.6	5.5	1.7	4.34	2
2000	NY Yanks	AL	65.3	71	35	8	16	30	4.82	3	4	9.8	1.1	2.2	4.1	0.9	3.76	-2
2001	NY Yanks	AL	99.7	97	41	8	22	67	3.70	7	4	8.8	0.7	2.0	6.1	1.5	3.68	4

Mendoza is an outstanding pitcher who keeps the ball down, can take the mound for four innings if you need him to, or pitch on short rest for a few days. He's a lot like Ivan Rodriguez or Pedro Martinez in that he's structurally very important to the club, providing flexibility and durability to the pitching staff, which allows Joe Torre to make moves and adapt as needs arise.

Mike Mussina — Throws R — Age 33

YEAR	TEAM	LGE	IP	H	ER	HR	BB	K	ERA	W	L	H/9	HR/9	BB/9	K/9	KW	PERA	STUFF
1999	Baltimor	AL	212.7	192	75	14	43	170	3.17	16	8	8.1	0.6	1.8	7.2	2.0	3.45	25
2000	Baltimor	AL	245.7	226	91	25	38	208	3.33	17	10	8.3	0.9	1.4	7.6	2.7	3.47	27
2001	NY Yanks	AL	231.3	205	79	19	40	204	3.07	18	8	8.0	0.7	1.6	7.9	2.5	3.21	30

The voting didn't show it, but Mussina was the most deserving Cy Young Award candidate on the Yankees last year. After signing the big contract, Mussina didn't disappoint, pitching exceptionally well and consistently throughout the season. A lack of run support made his win/loss record a little anemic, but he was nevertheless the best pitcher on the staff. Moose didn't do anything in 2001 that would indicate that his run of excellence is nearing its end.

Christian Parker — Throws R — Age 26

YEAR	TEAM	LGE	IP	H	ER	HR	BB	K	ERA	W	L	H/9	HR/9	BB/9	K/9	KW	PERA	STUFF
1999	Harrisbg	Eas	85.0	102	66	16	39	30	6.99	3	6	10.8	1.7	4.1	3.2	0.4	4.48	-27
1999	Ottawa	Int	10.7	11	5	0	7	4	4.22	1	0	9.3	0.0	5.9	3.4	0.3	7.10	-23
2000	Norwich	Eas	204.0	213	101	16	69	95	4.46	12	11	9.4	0.7	3.0	4.2	0.7	5.07	-2

Parker's arm didn't respond well to pitching 204 innings in 2000, and he missed the majority of last season after undergoing shoulder surgery in July. He's expected to be back for the 2002 season; if he's healthy, he'll be filling out the roster in Triple-A, waiting for the inevitable injuries.

Andy Pettitte — Throws L — Age 30

YEAR	TEAM	LGE	IP	H	ER	HR	BB	K	ERA	W	L	H/9	HR/9	BB/9	K/9	KW	PERA	STUFF
1999	NY Yanks	AL	201.0	202	99	18	74	120	4.43	11	11	9.0	0.8	3.3	5.4	0.8	4.33	6
2000	NY Yanks	AL	212.3	210	94	15	65	124	3.98	13	11	8.9	0.6	2.8	5.3	1.0	4.18	9
2001	NY Yanks	AL	214.0	198	75	13	39	156	3.15	16	8	8.3	0.5	1.6	6.6	2.0	4.33	21

His fastball actually had a bit more pop than in the previous year, something Pettitte used to good advantage, working inside more to right-handed hitters. His numbers moved with the league's as the strike zone expanded: he lost about a walk per nine innings and added a strikeout per nine. Pettitte still has one of the best moves to first base in the game, and he will be an excellent #3 starter again this year.

Mariano Rivera — Throws R — Age 32

YEAR	TEAM	LGE	IP	H	ER	HR	BB	K	ERA	W	L	H/9	HR/9	BB/9	K/9	KW	PERA	STUFF
1999	NY Yanks	AL	65.3	57	20	2	15	51	2.76	5	2	7.9	0.3	2.1	7.0	1.7	1.72	13
2000	NY Yanks	AL	74.0	66	26	3	20	57	3.16	5	3	8.0	0.4	2.4	6.9	1.4	2.65	10
2001	NY Yanks	AL	80.3	66	23	5	11	79	2.58	7	2	7.4	0.6	1.2	8.9	3.6	2.51	25

Rivera is the best closer of his generation. Cool Papa Bell once said, "The best pitchers are the ones who can tell you what pitch they're going to throw, and you still can't hit it." People aren't in shock about the bloop single Luis Gonzalez hit to win the World Series; they're in shock about the Tony Womack double down the right-field line two batters prior. Rivera is absolute death on lefties, throwing a cut fastball that moves about three inches towards their hands in the last ten feet of flight. It's a thing of beauty to watch, and it's responsible for more sawed-off lumber than Paul Bunyan on a meth bender.

Matt J. Smith — Throws L — Age 23

YEAR	TEAM	LGE	IP	H	ER	HR	BB	K	ERA	W	L	H/9	HR/9	BB/9	K/9	KW	PERA	STUFF
2000	StatenIs	NYP	76.3	80	36	4	25	29	4.24	4	4	9.4	0.5	2.9	3.4	0.6	5.10	0
2001	Greensbr	SAL	94.0	88	42	2	47	57	4.02	6	4	8.4	0.2	4.5	5.5	0.6	5.26	9
2001	Tampa	Fla	66.7	65	31	5	26	42	4.18	4	3	8.8	0.7	3.5	5.7	0.8	3.99	12

Smith, a lefty with good polish and good stuff, was taken in the fourth round of the 2000 draft, and he has done nothing since signing except keep hitters out on their front foot. He's a big guy, athletic, compared by scouts to Eric Milton. The big hurdle for Smith will be Double-A; if he can make the adjustment there quickly, look out.

Mike Stanton Throws L Age 35

YEAR	TEAM	LGE	IP	H	ER	HR	BB	K	ERA	W	L	H/9	HR/9	BB/9	K/9	KW	PERA	STUFF
1999	NY Yanks	AL	67.7	60	23	4	15	58	3.06	5	3	8.0	0.5	2.0	7.7	1.9	3.81	13
2000	NY Yanks	AL	72.7	59	23	4	20	74	2.85	6	2	7.3	0.5	2.5	9.2	1.9	3.63	21
2001	NY Yanks	AL	84.7	72	29	4	28	74	3.08	6	3	7.7	0.4	3.0	7.9	1.3	2.62	13

The lefty set-up man for Rivera, Stanton is signed to a fairly low-cost deal through the 2002 season. He took on a heavier load in 2000, as the Yankees lacked a right-handed counterpart for him for much of the season; as expected, he handled the workload. Like Arthur Rhodes, Stanton is effective against hitters on both sides of the plate. There's no reason to expect much change in his role or effectiveness.

Jay Witasick Throws R Age 29

YEAR	TEAM	LGE	IP	H	ER	HR	BB	K	ERA	W	L	H/9	HR/9	BB/9	K/9	KW	PERA	STUFF
1999	KansasCy	AL	168.0	173	94	20	69	101	5.04	8	11	9.3	1.1	3.7	5.4	0.7	4.97	0
2000	KansasCy	AL	95.7	97	50	13	31	66	4.70	5	6	9.1	1.2	2.9	6.2	1.1	5.20	3
2000	San Dieg	NL	64.0	63	36	8	29	48	5.06	3	4	8.9	1.1	4.1	6.8	0.8	6.15	6
2001	San Dieg	NL	38.0	30	13	3	13	43	3.08	3	1	7.1	0.7	3.1	10.2	1.7	3.46	25
2001	NY Yanks	AL	44.7	37	18	5	17	50	3.63	3	2	7.5	1.0	3.4	10.1	1.5	5.65	18

In June of 1999, you could buy stock in drkoop.com for just under $40 per share. Right before Christmas 1999, you could pick up a piece of the amazon.com goldmine for just under $120 a share. On June 23, 2001, the Yankees picked up Jay Witasick for D'Angelo Jimenez. Witasick had been a serviceable back-of-the-bullpen guy for a couple of years, and he has good stuff. He'll probably make a fine set-up man over the next few years. But he's also not noticeably better than many other, cheaper options. This is the sort of advantage the Yankees do get from having a lot of cash: they can afford to make a mistake or two like this more easily than, say, the Royals can.

Witasick was flipped for John Vander Wal in December. He's behind Robb Nen and Felix Rodriguez in the Giants' pecking order, but he's still valuable to a team that doesn't get a ton of innings from its good starters.

Mark Wohlers Throws R Age 32

YEAR	TEAM	LGE	IP	H	ER	HR	BB	K	ERA	W	L	H/9	HR/9	BB/9	K/9	KW	PERA	STUFF
2000	Louisvil	Int	22.7	27	18	5	10	12	7.15	1	2	10.7	2.0	4.0	4.8	0.6	10.38	-40
2000	Cincnnti	NL	26.0	26	15	3	14	18	5.19	1	2	9.0	1.0	4.8	6.2	0.6	4.00	-8
2001	Cincnnti	NL	31.3	34	16	4	6	17	4.60	1	2	9.8	1.1	1.7	4.9	1.4	5.61	-10
2001	NY Yanks	AL	36.7	33	17	3	17	31	4.17	2	2	8.1	0.7	4.2	7.6	0.9	4.72	3

Wohlers fought his way back from well-chronicled control problems. He still has pretty good stuff, but iffy control. He should be battling for a job somewhere for the foreseeable future, but the Indians signed him to two years, guaranteed, plus an option for 2004.

Oakland Athletics

If someone had told us at the start of the 2001 season that the A's would win 102 games in the regular season, we probably would have said something along the lines of, "That may be a little high, but that's probably about right." If you had told us that the A's would win 102 games and finish 14 games behind the Seattle Mariners in the AL West, we would have said, "Please don't hurt us. Here's some more drug money. Please leave us alone now."

> **Athletics Prospectus**
>
> **2001 record:** 102–60; Second place, AL West; AL wild card, Lost to Yankees in Division Series, 3–2
>
> **Pythagenport W/L:** 105–57
>
> **Runs scored:** 884 (fourth in AL)
>
> **Runs allowed:** 645 (second in AL)
>
> **Team EqA:** .271 (fourth in AL)
>
> **2001 batters age:** 27.1 (second-youngest in AL)
>
> **2001 pitchers age:** 27.4 (tied for sixth-youngest in AL)
>
> **Ballpark:** Network Associates Coliseum; slight pitchers' park; Park Factor of .976
>
> **2001:** The quietest 102 wins you'll ever see led to the unanswered question: why didn't Jeremy slide?
>
> **2002:** They'll miss Jason Giambi, but not as much as you might think. The favorite in a tough division.

The A's were out of contention for the division title almost immediately. They started the season horribly, particularly at the plate, where their much-vaunted patience appeared totally destroyed by a new and dancing interpretation of the strike zone. They got crushed in the season's first two weeks, winning just two games. The A's foundered to an 8-17 April and were written off as a factor in the AL West, hopelessly behind the streaking Mariners. The pitchers weren't pitching, the hitters weren't hitting, and pretty much nothing was going right. The local press began calling for Art Howe's head on a platter, and attendance dropped to around 10,000-14,000 a game for the early May series against the Blue Jays.

Things started to come together in May, particularly on the pitching side. The A's ripped off a seven-game winning streak, characterized by the rotation smothering the opposing offense. The A's fought back to .500 and pretty much stayed there through the All-Star break, finishing the first half at 44-43.

After that, the A's became an Unholy Juggernaut of Unstoppable Death and Destruction™. Incidentally, this is easier to do if you face the Tigers, Royals, Devil Rays, Orioles, Rockies, and Rangers a bunch of times. The A's were a collective 30-5 against those six teams in the second half.

Check out the post-break performances of the A's rotation in Table 1.

That's nothing short of obscene. Behind starting pitching that was the envy of the league, the A's rolled to a 58-17 second half, leaving a disintegrating Boston Red Sox team far back in the wild-card chase, which was effectively over at the end of August.

The postseason was a different matter. The A's went into an emotionally charged Yankee Stadium and beat the Yankees in the first two games of the Division Series behind outstanding pitching by Mark Mulder and Tim Hudson. The A's were a horrendous 0-for-19 with runners in scoring position, and their hitters looked positively overmatched at the plate against Yankees pitchers. The A's were leading 2-0, though, so their anemic hitting was just sort of a pleasant amusement, not reason to worry. They came home, ostensibly to knock off the Yankees and take their rightful place as youthful heirs to the AL throne. The Mariners were a sideshow; sure, they won the division, but they were a "soft" 116-win team, if such a thing was possible, and they just didn't stack up to the A's.

Then the unthinkable happened.

Game 3. Bottom of the seventh, two out. Terrence Long at the plate. Jeremy Giambi on first. Long rips a double down the line in right field, and Giambi is off and running. Shane Spencer's throw is over both cutoff men, but it's snagged by Jeter crossing the first-base line moving towards the dugout. He shovel passes to Posada, who tags Giambi—who is inexplicably ignoring Ramon Hernandez's signal to slide to the outside of the plate—for the third out of the inning. The A's

Table 1. After the All-Star Break

Pitcher	IP	ERA	Record
Tim Hudson	104	3.81	9-4
Mark Mulder	110	3.11	12-2
Barry Zito	102	2.29	11-2
Cory Lidle	97	2.96	11-2
Erik Hiljus	58	3.57	4-0

go on to lose 1-0. Hey, no biggie, they'll win tomorrow. Or the next day. Right? Yeah. (Uncomfortable chortle.)

Well, they didn't. The Yankees systematically beat the A's down, and Jermaine Dye broke his leg. The A's looked like an entirely different team, and, most ominously, they looked like they had simply been out-prepared. The cries for Art Howe's head became much louder. Why was Eric Byrnes on the bench when tying-run Giambi was on first base with two outs in the seventh? Why were the A's hitters swinging at pitches so obviously out of the strike zone? Why didn't the A's play more little ball? This team wasn't prepared. This team was overconfident and cocky.

All of this is a great lesson in expectations management. Two weeks into the season, A's fans would have been very happy with 102 wins and the wild card. After two wins at Yankee Stadium in October, suddenly the entire season is a disappointment. Either way, it's over, and it's time to move forward.

There's a lot of change in the air around the A's. In addition to being a darkhorse candidate for contraction (don't lose any sleep over it), the A's were reported in the middle of the season as having been sold to a group from Las Vegas. Most importantly to the fans, they lost their best player and their closer to free agency in the off-season. Yes, Jason Isringhausen is gone, but most A's fans are more concerned over the loss of the team's heart and soul, Jason Giambi. Giambi and the A's could not come to an agreement on an extension before the 2001 season, reportedly because the A's were unwilling to give him the no-trade clause he wanted. They eventually came around, but too late; Giambi signed a seven-year, $120-million deal with the Yankees in December.

A's fans shouldn't worry. The loss of Big G is not the biggest danger facing the team. Giambi is 31 years old, coming off his peak season, and required at least a six-year commitment. He plays a position at which it's relatively easy to find an acceptable substitute. The A's should be concentrating on putting the best team they can on the field for 2002 and beyond.

The foundation for a successful club over the medium and long term is in place, with key players such as Hudson, Mulder, Long, Miguel Tejada, Eric Chavez, Ramon Hernandez, and Jim Mecir locked into contracts through 2004 or longer, at costs that will allow the A's some financial flexibility, without having to sell new products like Jeremy Giambi Sliding Pants. Billy Beane said after the 2000 season that the 2000 club would be the worst he'd put on the field for the next several years, and he wasn't just whistling Dixie. Giambi, Isringhausen, and Damon are gone; if the A's do nothing more to replace them, their team for 2002 looks like this:

C	Ramon Hernandez/Greg Myers
1B	Mario Valdez/Adam Piatt/Olmedo Saenz
2B	Frank Menechino
3B	Eric Chavez
SS	Miguel Tejada
LF	Jeremy Giambi/Adam Piatt
CF	Terrence Long
RF	Jermaine Dye
DH	David Justice
SP	Tim Hudson
SP	Mark Mulder
SP	Barry Zito
SP	Cory Lidle
SP	Erik Hiljus
RP	Billy Koch
RP	Jim Mecir
RP	Chad Bradford
RP	Jeff Tam
RP	Luis Vizcaino
RP	Chad Harville

They also have six compensation draft picks and increased financial flexibility.

For those positions that appear soft, consider the strength of the prospects in the A's system. If Frank Menechino is healthy, he's a good option who can hit .270/.380/.420 and play solid defense. If not, the A's have Esteban German, Mark Ellis, and Bobby Crosby coming up fast. In the outfield, Ryan Ludwick is probably a year away at most. Mario Valdez is a capable major-league first baseman. If Adam Piatt has recovered from his unfortunate illness and its aftereffects, he's a quality right-handed bat to complement Valdez. If Erik Hiljus implodes, the A's have a number of prospects who have a chance to be very good, particularly Mario Ramos. This team would have been better in the short term with Jason Giambi, but not in the long term. Right now, worst-case scenario, this is one of the three best teams in the AL, and it has depth.

Off the field, the team is facing some less obvious concerns. The A's have lost former Director of Player Personnel J.P. Ricciardi to the Blue Jays. Another key to the A's success, Scouting Director Grady Fuson, has been hired away by Tom Hicks (a move for which the A's tried to grab Hank Blalock as compensation, a maneuver that deserves nothing if not bemused admiration. Who knows? Maybe they get Travis Hafner in the deal instead. Nothing wrong with that). Network Associates Coliseum is not a competitive venue, and the A's need a better place to play. The club may move to the South Bay, but the Giants don't want to give up their spurious claim on the San Jose/Santa Clara market without receiving heaps o'cash as part of the deal, so that will eventually head to court.

Billy Beane and the A's front office have positioned the A's to be successful through a time of great upheaval, so fans probably shouldn't be overly worried about any of these extraneous factors.

If you're an A's fan and you really want something about which to worry, be concerned about the A's plate discipline. Yes, you read that correctly. The A's led the AL in walks with

Table 2.

Player	AB	BB
Jason Giambi	520	129
Frank Menechino	471	79
Jeremy Giambi	371	63
Eric Chavez	552	41 (9 intentional)
Miguel Tejada	622	43
Ramon Hernandez	453	37
Terrence Long	629	52
Johnny Damon	644	61
Jermaine Dye	232	27 (with Oakland)

640, but the distribution of those walks, as shown in Table 2, is a cause for concern.

Menechino's elbow injury prevented him from swinging the bat effectively for most of the second half of the season, and his walk rate increased during that span. The rest of the regulars were not that impressive.

Strategically, the A's have been able to build good offenses despite financial constraints by focusing on secondary average (walks and power), which is basically less expensive and more effective than batting average (singles). If they want to keep building a good offense, they're going to need to draw those walks. Right now, the team as a whole isn't doing that: the aggregate team numbers are inflated by Jason Giambi's league-leading total.

The A's are probably the favorite to win the AL West this year. The Mariners got career years from a number of players, most of whom will return to earth in 2002. The A's rotation is arguably the best in baseball, having both quality and depth. The core of the offense should be entering its prime soon. The front office of the A's, despite the losses, is one of the most respected and professional in the game. They got here through sound understanding of baseball and business principles, and that's unlikely to change. There are jobs on the line, though. Art Howe is definitely going to face a great deal of pressure and scrutiny from day one. Another April like last year's, and there's a reasonable chance for a Bob Geren May.

Longer term, the A's need to stick to the plan that's gotten them this far. That means diligent research and homework before drafting and negotiating. Mitigating development risk through the selection of different types of players, including low-risk college pitchers like Mulder and Zito, as well as development projects like Miguel Tejada. It means continuing to instill plate discipline into hitters' heads throughout the system and rewarding them with promotion and playing time for executing on a good plan in the batter's box.

The A's do their homework in the weight room, the film room, on the road watching young kids, and at computers in the front office. No matter where they end up or what kind of financial straitjacket they may or may not wear, they'll be in good shape if they stick to their philosophical guns and work hard. The fact that they put a little pinprick in the commissioner's view of the baseball world (the one he tries so desperately to sell) is a nice little bonus.

HITTERS (BA: .270, OBP: .340, SLG: .440, EqA: .260)

Mark Bellhorn UT Bats B Age 27

YEAR	TEAM	LGE	AB	H	DB	TP	HR	BB	SO	R	RBI	SB	CS	OUT	BA	OBP	SLG	EQA	EQR	DEFENSE	
1999	Midland	Tex	57	14	0	0	2	8	13	9	6	1	0	43	.246	.338	.351	.242	6	15-2B -3	
2000	Sacramen	PCL	436	105	15	7	21	77	117	87	56	14	4	335	.241	.359	.452	.274	66	90-3B -3	10-2B 2
2001	Sacramen	PCL	156	38	5	0	10	20	54	25	30	2	0	118	.244	.339	.468	.269	22	16-2B 4	15-OF 0
2001	Oakland	AL	74	12	2	2	1	7	32	13	4	0	0	62	.162	.235	.284	.179	4		
2002	*ChiCubs*	*NL*	*368*	*90*	*12*	*4*	*18*	*62*	*127*	*73*	*50*	*8*	*2*	*280*	*.245*	*.353*	*.446*	*.272*	*54*		

The Mickey Tettleton of middle infielders, Bellhorn can play pretty much any position, draw a bunch of walks, hit a surprising number of bombs, and strike out every third at-bat. He's been on the periphery of the A's plans for several years but never seemed to be fully in favor. He'll probably end up somewhere fighting for a 25th-man spot, and if he gets one, he could definitely win a full-time job given the right circumstances.

Freddie Bynum SS Bats L Age 22

YEAR	TEAM	LGE	AB	H	DB	TP	HR	BB	SO	R	RBI	SB	CS	OUT	BA	OBP	SLG	EQA	EQR	DEFENSE	
2000	Vancouvr	Nwn	294	61	6	1	1	17	63	32	17	10	8	241	.207	.255	.245	.176	16	67-SS -15	
2001	Modesto	Cal	446	95	17	4	1	30	91	41	32	15	8	359	.213	.263	.276	.189	28	57-SS -14	51-2B -15
2002	*Oakland*	*AL*	*417*	*99*	*14*	*3*	*3*	*38*	*91*	*48*	*33*	*17*	*10*	*328*	*.237*	*.301*	*.307*	*.213*	*34*		

A speed-burning shortstop drafted out of a North Carolina junior college, Bynum struggled at Modesto, hitting just .261/.325/.350 and making 41 errors at shortstop and second base. He's still young and raw, and scouts think he could be a Johnny Damon-type hitter once he develops his skills. Hopefully, they don't mean the 2001 vintage.

Eric Byrnes OF Bats R Age 26

YEAR	TEAM	LGE	AB	H	DB	TP	HR	BB	SO	R	RBI	SB	CS	OUT	BA	OBP	SLG	EQA	EQR	DEFENSE
1999	Modesto	Cal	363	95	15	1	5	39	37	52	42	14	5	273	.262	.340	.350	.241	39	89-LF -6
1999	Midland	Tex	163	31	6	0	2	13	33	17	17	4	2	134	.190	.258	.264	.185	10	39-LF -6
2000	Midland	Tex	257	62	18	1	4	30	38	33	25	12	7	202	.241	.322	.366	.235	27	66-RF -2
2000	Sacramen	PCL	241	73	17	1	8	24	29	43	37	9	4	172	.303	.370	.481	.282	36	50-LF 0
2001	Sacramen	PCL	412	108	19	1	17	31	60	68	42	21	3	307	.262	.319	.437	.257	51	93-LF -2
2001	Oakland	AL	38	10	2	0	3	4	5	10	5	1	0	28	.263	.345	.553	.291	6	
2002	*Oakland*	*AL*	*501*	*132*	*25*	*1*	*16*	*51*	*74*	*82*	*68*	*20*	*4*	*373*	*.263*	*.332*	*.413*	*.261*	*65*	

He's known throughout the East Bay as "The Guy Who Should Have Been Running For Jeremy." Byrnes gets surprisingly little press for someone who has a shot at being a solid major-league regular. He has speed and power, he hits for a reasonable average, and he can play good defense. He's more likely to have a solid career as a very good extra outfielder, a la Dave Martinez.

Eric Chavez 3B Bats L Age 24

YEAR	TEAM	LGE	AB	H	DB	TP	HR	BB	SO	R	RBI	SB	CS	OUT	BA	OBP	SLG	EQA	EQR	DEFENSE
1999	Oakland	AL	355	92	23	2	14	42	49	48	50	1	1	264	.259	.338	.454	.262	46	94-3B -5
2000	Oakland	AL	499	145	24	4	28	56	83	88	85	2	2	356	.291	.363	.523	.288	79	134-3B -3
2001	Oakland	AL	556	171	37	0	38	44	86	98	123	8	2	387	.308	.362	.579	.301	96	145-3B 11
2002	*Oakland*	*AL*	*497*	*155*	*33*	*2*	*32*	*60*	*82*	*89*	*95*	*6*	*2*	*344*	*.312*	*.386*	*.579*	*.319*	*99*	

Probably the most improved defensive player in baseball, Chavez had a reasonable consolidation year—all in the second half. Despite appearing overmatched and impatient in the postseason, Chavez had a great second half, hitting .340/.382/.664 after the All-Star break. What is worrisome is the lack of progress Chavez made in terms of selectivity. He drew just 32 unintentional walks and gave away a lot of at-bats. He is self-critical and will work to correct the problem. He's another key to the A's that Beane has locked in through 2004.

Bobby Crosby SS Bats R Age 22

YEAR	TEAM	LGE	AB	H	DB	TP	HR	BB	SO	R	RBI	SB	CS	OUT	BA	OBP	SLG	EQA	EQR	DEFENSE
2001	Modesto	Cal	38	12	2	0	1	2	8	5	2	0	0	26	.316	.350	.447	.265	5	
2002	*Oakland*	*AL*	*91*	*27*	*2*	*0*	*4*	*7*	*20*	*10*	*11*	*0*	*0*	*64*	*.297*	*.347*	*.451*	*.272*	*12*	

The A's moved Crosby, the former Big West Player of the Year, directly to high-A ball in Modesto, where he proceeded to hit the snot out of the ball until a hip flexor injury knocked him out for a month. Crosby is polished, athletic, and could end up playing any position where there's a need. For now, he'll be in the middle infield, and he'll probably battle Esteban German over the next few years for the spot in Oakland next to Miguel Tejada.

Johnny Damon CF Bats L Age 28

YEAR	TEAM	LGE	AB	H	DB	TP	HR	BB	SO	R	RBI	SB	CS	OUT	BA	OBP	SLG	EQA	EQR	DEFENSE
1999	KansasCy	AL	573	177	38	9	15	61	44	97	73	34	6	402	.309	.378	.485	.292	93	140-LF 3
2000	KansasCy	AL	642	210	39	10	17	57	53	128	82	46	10	442	.327	.383	.498	.297	106	133-CF 8
2001	Oakland	AL	648	181	36	4	11	64	60	116	53	25	14	481	.279	.348	.398	.253	77	154-CF 8
2002	*Boston*	*AL*	*588*	*177*	*36*	*6*	*16*	*62*	*54*	*101*	*69*	*30*	*11*	*421*	*.301*	*.368*	*.464*	*.281*	*88*	

It was strange to see balls in the gaps actually get caught. Damon was fantastic to watch defensively, but he didn't come close to hitting as expected. His swing was devoid of weight transfer via a pivot; he instead slid his hips through the hitting zone, preventing him from generating any power. His defense will be missed; his bat won't be. Damon signed a four-year deal to play center field for the Red Sox.

Jermaine Dye RF Bats R Age 28

YEAR	TEAM	LGE	AB	H	DB	TP	HR	BB	SO	R	RBI	SB	CS	OUT	BA	OBP	SLG	EQA	EQR	DEFENSE
1999	KansasCy	AL	600	178	44	8	28	51	105	93	114	2	3	425	.297	.353	.537	.286	93	153-RF 9
2000	KansasCy	AL	589	190	39	2	34	61	87	101	111	0	1	400	.323	.389	.569	.309	106	135-RF -6
2001	KansasCy	AL	366	104	10	0	15	31	59	52	49	7	1	263	.284	.347	.434	.264	47	84-RF -2
2001	Oakland	AL	234	74	17	1	15	28	38	45	63	2	0	160	.316	.391	.590	.316	45	55-RF -4
2002	*Oakland*	*AL*	*582*	*176*	*34*	*3*	*30*	*66*	*99*	*94*	*108*	*5*	*1*	*407*	*.302*	*.373*	*.526*	*.302*	*102*	

Dye is an excellent, versatile ballplayer who can hit, field, run, and generally stay healthy. He suffered a very scary injury during Game 4 of the Division Series, fouling a ball off of his knee. The twisting nature of the fracture caused some initial concern, but Dye is expected to be ready for spring training and should be in right field from day one, giving the A's some much-needed power from the right side.

Mark Ellis SS Bats R Age 25

YEAR	TEAM	LGE	AB	H	DB	TP	HR	BB	SO	R	RBI	SB	CS	OUT	BA	OBP	SLG	EQA	EQR	DEFENSE
1999	Spokane	Nwn	280	62	4	0	5	26	46	32	24	8	4	222	.221	.290	.289	.204	21	71-SS 1
2000	Wilmngtn	Car	505	131	21	2	6	57	73	65	48	13	6	379	.259	.338	.345	.238	52	127-SS -3
2001	Sacramen	PCL	471	116	22	0	11	49	71	58	46	18	6	361	.246	.322	.363	.237	49	129-SS 0
2002	*Oakland*	*AL*	*459*	*117*	*19*	*1*	*12*	*56*	*73*	*68*	*51*	*17*	*6*	*348*	*.255*	*.336*	*.379*	*.253*	*56*	

Ellis came to the A's as change for Angel Berroa in last winter's three-way deal. He's a legitimate prospect in his own right, playing nice defense at shortstop, stealing bases at a good clip, and hitting .273/.351/.417 in Sacramento at age 24. He's not going to move Tejada aside, but if this is a legitimate increase in his performance level, he'll be a very nice utility guy.

Ron Gant LF/DH Bats Age 37

YEAR	TEAM	LGE	AB	H	DB	TP	HR	BB	SO	R	RBI	SB	CS	OUT	BA	OBP	SLG	EQA	EQR	DEFENSE
1999	Philadel	NL	516	132	25	5	17	79	104	103	72	11	3	387	.256	.356	.422	.265	70	128-LF 5
2000	Philadel	NL	345	86	16	1	20	31	67	51	36	4	4	263	.249	.313	.475	.255	43	83-LF 0
2000	Anaheim	AL	81	19	3	1	6	19	16	14	15	1	2	64	.235	.380	.519	.288	14	20-LF 0
2001	Colorado	NL	166	39	7	1	7	23	47	28	19	3	1	128	.235	.328	.416	.251	20	43-LF -1
2001	Oakland	AL	82	23	7	1	2	11	21	17	14	2	0	59	.280	.366	.463	.281	12	
2002	*San Dieg*	*NL*	*432*	*96*	*19*	*3*	*18*	*72*	*107*	*78*	*54*	*8*	*4*	*340*	*.222*	*.333*	*.405*	*.261*	*59*	

Gant played well in a limited role, splitting time with Jeremy Giambi in the outfield and at DH. Gant still has significant pop and will latch on somewhere where he's got a shot at the postseason. Well-spotted, he can definitely give a club 250 good at-bats. He could make for a great platoon partner with Ray Lankford for the Padres.

Esteban German 2B Bats R Age 23

YEAR	TEAM	LGE	AB	H	DB	TP	HR	BB	SO	R	RBI	SB	CS	OUT	BA	OBP	SLG	EQA	EQR	DEFENSE
1999	Modesto	Cal	502	122	15	6	3	71	130	68	33	20	9	389	.243	.340	.315	.232	51	110-2B -23
2000	Visalia	Cal	435	97	13	6	2	38	87	48	24	35	7	345	.223	.289	.294	.214	37	106-2B -18
2000	Midland	Tex	75	12	0	0	1	14	21	9	4	3	2	65	.160	.301	.200	.191	5	18-2B -2
2001	Midland	Tex	337	78	15	2	5	51	67	58	22	19	8	267	.231	.342	.332	.240	38	78-2B -5
2001	Sacramen	PCL	149	51	5	0	4	16	18	33	12	14	2	100	.342	.420	.456	.308	26	35-2B 0
2002	*Oakland*	*AL*	*476*	*124*	*15*	*4*	*9*	*63*	*100*	*75*	*37*	*34*	*9*	*361*	*.261*	*.347*	*.366*	*.259*	*62*	

German, one of the fastest players in baseball, had a great season at the plate and in the field, improving his power, base-stealing prowess, and footwork around the bag at second base. He'll begin the season in Sacramento but is one of two candidates, along with Bobby Crosby, to be the A's long-term solution at second base. German has a slightly less extreme version of the Lance Blankenship skill set: speed and a great eye. His home-run totals won't ever be huge, but he could be a Luis Castillo-type player.

Jason Giambi 1B Bats L Age 31

YEAR	TEAM	LGE	AB	H	DB	TP	HR	BB	SO	R	RBI	SB	CS	OUT	BA	OBP	SLG	EQA	EQR	DEFENSE
1999	Oakland	AL	569	188	32	1	37	100	93	115	124	1	1	382	.330	.436	.585	.333	122	136-1B -9
2000	Oakland	AL	502	176	25	1	47	130	84	106	135	2	0	326	.351	.492	.685	.376	142	123-1B -3
2001	Oakland	AL	529	195	45	1	45	133	72	119	130	2	0	334	.369	.503	.713	.387	156	129-1B 0
2002	*NY Yanks*	*AL*	*501*	*166*	*27*	*1*	*39*	*116*	*78*	*106*	*118*	*2*	*0*	*335*	*.331*	*.457*	*.623*	*.358*	*128*	

Giambi is a fantastic hitter, combining the ability to hit the ball hard to all fields, a great batting eye, and the willingness to execute a plan at the plate. As has been well chronicled, Giambi wanted a no-trade clause to sign a six-year, $90-million deal during the spring, but the A's wouldn't give him the clause. Beane's best course of action was to let him walk; now the A's can find a reasonable solution at first base for a lot less money and spend the savings either on pitching help, or on locking Barry Zito into a long-term deal.

Jeremy Giambi DH Bats L Age 27

YEAR	TEAM	LGE	AB	H	DB	TP	HR	BB	SO	R	RBI	SB	CS	OUT	BA	OBP	SLG	EQA	EQR	DEFENSE
1999	KansasCy	AL	283	82	13	1	3	37	59	33	32	0	0	201	.290	.377	.375	.261	35	24-1B -4
1999	Omaha	PCL	124	38	3	1	9	26	27	24	21	1	1	87	.306	.429	.565	.323	26	20-LF 2 15-1B 0
2000	Oakland	AL	259	69	10	2	11	29	54	42	50	0	0	190	.266	.347	.448	.265	34	44-RF -6
2001	Oakland	AL	375	115	21	0	16	65	72	69	63	0	1	261	.307	.413	.491	.303	66	38-RF -9
2002	*Oakland*	*AL*	*398*	*115*	*16*	*1*	*17*	*64*	*84*	*63*	*63*	*1*	*1*	*284*	*.289*	*.387*	*.462*	*.293*	*66*	

He showed flashes of the offensive brilliance that was expected of him after punishing the ball in the minors. He's going to break out in a big way sooner rather than later. Giambi can't play defense in the outfield any better than his brother could, and he may be the solution to replace Jason at first base. If he can be signed to a four-year deal at a reasonable price, the A's should go for it.

Jason Hart 1B Bats R Age 24

YEAR	TEAM	LGE	AB	H	DB	TP	HR	BB	SO	R	RBI	SB	CS	OUT	BA	OBP	SLG	EQA	EQR	DEFENSE
1999	Modesto	Cal	546	131	29	1	14	36	106	63	77	1	3	418	.240	.289	.374	.221	48	127-1B 1
2000	Midland	Tex	538	143	32	2	21	46	112	70	79	2	0	395	.266	.327	.450	.257	66	126-1B 0
2001	Sacramen	PCL	493	110	20	1	16	52	93	60	62	3	2	385	.223	.301	.365	.225	46	132-1B 0
2002	*Texas*	*AL*	*506*	*136*	*25*	*1*	*20*	*53*	*105*	*70*	*82*	*2*	*2*	*372*	*.269*	*.338*	*.441*	*.256*	*62*	

Hart is a big kid, once called "Little Mac" in Southern Oregon because of his ability to hit prodigious drives. He had lots of trouble with off-speed pitches in Sacramento, and as soon as scouts noticed this trend, he saw the same pattern at the plate as Pedro Cerrano did. He'll have to improve his plate discipline a tad, swing at better pitches, and hit about .290 to get a shot at a first-base job anywhere, let alone with the Rangers and their crowd at first base and DH.

Ramon Hernandez C Bats R Age 26

YEAR	TEAM	LGE	AB	H	DB	TP	HR	BB	SO	R	RBI	SB	CS	OUT	BA	OBP	SLG	EQA	EQR	DEFENSE
1999	Vancouvr	PCL	291	71	9	3	11	19	34	32	46	1	2	222	.244	.301	.409	.234	29	44-C 1 11-3B -4
1999	Oakland	AL	135	40	5	0	4	17	10	13	22	1	0	95	.296	.379	.422	.274	19	40-C -3
2000	Oakland	AL	419	107	15	0	17	33	56	51	64	1	0	312	.255	.321	.413	.245	46	122-C -2
2001	Oakland	AL	456	125	20	0	19	39	59	60	66	1	1	332	.274	.337	.443	.259	57	130-C 3
2002	*Oakland*	*AL*	*403*	*104*	*14*	*1*	*15*	*41*	*54*	*46*	*60*	*1*	*1*	*300*	*.258*	*.327*	*.409*	*.253*	*48*	

This is a very underrated ballplayer. Hernandez is a good defensive catcher who handles the pitching staff well and is undervalued as a hitter, thanks in large part to the cavernous outfield in Oakland. Hernandez is a very similar player to former A's backstop Terry Steinbach, a league-average hitter with some durability and strong defense. He got beat up throughout the season, as catchers are prone to do, and still finished strong: .291/.339/.522 after the All-Star break.

Eric Hinske 3B Bats L Age 24

YEAR	TEAM	LGE	AB	H	DB	TP	HR	BB	SO	R	RBI	SB	CS	OUT	BA	OBP	SLG	EQA	EQR	DEFENSE
1999	Daytona	Fla	450	106	20	3	14	45	101	53	52	9	6	350	.236	.308	.387	.233	46	54-1B 5 53-3B -7
2000	WestTenn	Sou	456	109	18	6	18	61	132	67	61	9	4	351	.239	.331	.423	.253	57	113-3B -9
2001	Sacramen	PCL	435	111	19	1	21	49	103	59	65	17	6	330	.255	.339	.448	.264	59	114-3B -11
2002	*Toronto*	*AL*	*476*	*128*	*23*	*3*	*20*	*64*	*125*	*69*	*66*	*12*	*5*	*353*	*.269*	*.356*	*.456*	*.273*	*69*	

Breaks come and go. A year ago Hinske, a 22-year-old left-handed-hitting third baseman waiting for his shot at the bigs, was traded to a club with a 22-year-old left-handed-hitting third baseman with 1,000 plate appearances in the big leagues coming off a season in which he hit 26 home runs. That was a bad break. This winter, Hinske was traded again, this time to a team with a hole at third base and a GM who understands that he's a very good ballplayer who might eventually be one of the better third basemen in the league. That was a good break. Picking up Hinske was a great way for J.P. Ricciardi to begin his career as the Blue Jays' GM.

Terrence Long OF Bats L Age 26

YEAR	TEAM	LGE	AB	H	DB	TP	HR	BB	SO	R	RBI	SB	CS	OUT	BA	OBP	SLG	EQA	EQR	DEFENSE
1999	Norfolk	Int	303	92	17	3	6	18	39	34	38	11	5	216	.304	.344	.439	.262	38	75-RF 7
1999	Vancouvr	PCL	154	35	3	2	2	8	27	13	18	6	4	123	.227	.269	.312	.198	11	38-CF 0
2000	Sacramen	PCL	59	21	2	0	3	3	4	8	11	0	2	40	.356	.387	.542	.291	9	13-CF -3
2000	Oakland	AL	583	176	34	4	20	36	68	103	80	5	0	407	.302	.344	.477	.271	78	137-CF -10
2001	Oakland	AL	633	191	38	4	14	56	89	98	90	9	3	445	.302	.358	.441	.269	83	160-OF -3
2002	*Oakland*	*AL*	*606*	*182*	*36*	*4*	*18*	*50*	*85*	*89*	*87*	*8*	*2*	*426*	*.300*	*.354*	*.462*	*.279*	*88*	

Long is a tweener outfielder; he plays either corner very well and is a bit stretched in center. The A's signed him to a four-year deal towards the end of the season, a move that met with mixed reviews among the pundits but was well received among A's fans. The A's do expect him to hit for more power than he's demonstrated thus far, but for now, they're happy with his progress hitting left-handers and his ability to take the field every day.

Ryan Ludwick CF Bats R Age 23

YEAR	TEAM	LGE	AB	H	DB	TP	HR	BB	SO	R	RBI	SB	CS	OUT	BA	OBP	SLG	EQA	EQR	DEFENSE
1999	Modesto	Cal	171	38	9	1	3	12	46	19	22	1	1	134	.222	.279	.339	.209	13	39-CF -4
2000	Modesto	Cal	501	109	17	1	21	43	130	59	63	5	3	395	.218	.285	.381	.223	46	118-CF 8
2001	Midland	Tex	443	90	10	2	18	45	114	81	88	6	7	352	.221	.298	.388	.228	44	116-CF -8
2001	Sacramen	PCL	56	11	2	0	1	3	15	9	6	2	0	45	.196	.237	.286	.186	3	17-CF 4
2002	*Texas*	*AL*	*502*	*125*	*21*	*2*	*24*	*58*	*137*	*74*	*86*	*7*	*5*	*382*	*.249*	*.327*	*.442*	*.251*	*60*	

Here's the guy the A's would like to see in center field pretty soon. Ludwick is a masher with a legitimate set of skills for center field. Still, some scouts are not sold on his ability to play center, particularly if he fills out much more physically, but his fundamentals are sound, he has a reasonable arm, and he goes back well on balls. Scouts compare his bat to Paul Konerko's. He's put up pretty good numbers in some hitters' paradises. Now that he's a Ranger, he has a good shot at being their center fielder by 2003 after a good year in the PCL.

Billy McMillon OF Bats L Age 30

YEAR	TEAM	LGE	AB	H	DB	TP	HR	BB	SO	R	RBI	SB	CS	OUT	BA	OBP	SLG	EQA	EQR	DEFENSE
1999	Scran-WB	Int	466	134	33	3	14	55	74	83	70	9	2	334	.288	.368	.461	.279	69	122-LF -5
2000	Toledo	Int	383	124	23	1	13	61	64	55	44	2	1	260	.324	.419	.491	.306	67	100-LF 2
2000	Detroit	AL	122	38	9	1	4	17	17	20	23	1	0	84	.311	.400	.500	.301	21	14-RF -1
2001	Detroit	AL	34	4	2	0	1	2	10	2	5	0	0	30	.118	.184	.265	.154	1	
2001	Oakland	AL	58	18	8	1	0	6	11	7	10	1	0	40	.310	.382	.483	.291	9	12-LF -1
2002	*Oakland*	*AL*	*423*	*120*	*28*	*2*	*14*	*63*	*77*	*67*	*63*	*6*	*1*	*304*	*.284*	*.377*	*.459*	*.290*	*69*	

Some guys just have bad luck. McMillon went from the Hades of Detroit to the Land of OBP Enlightenment. He got a chance to play, hit the ball well, then promptly had his shoulder wear out. He's undergone arthroscopic surgery and should be ready for the start of next season. Things are crowded in Oakland, but if some club needs an inexpensive outfielder to give them 450 good plate appearances, they should call McMillon. At this point, I expect he'd suit up for free to get the playing time.

Frank Menechino 2B Bats R Age 31

YEAR	TEAM	LGE	AB	H	DB	TP	HR	BB	SO	R	RBI	SB	CS	OUT	BA	OBP	SLG	EQA	EQR	DEFENSE
1999	Vancouvr	PCL	502	144	27	8	12	62	89	86	72	3	4	362	.287	.372	.444	.273	71	53-3B 3 40-SS 10
2000	Sacramen	PCL	38	11	0	0	2	4	4	6	3	1	0	27	.289	.357	.447	.274	5	
2000	Oakland	AL	144	38	10	1	6	19	40	31	25	1	4	111	.264	.354	.472	.265	20	37-2B 3
2001	Oakland	AL	475	127	24	2	14	81	84	89	66	1	3	351	.267	.390	.415	.276	70	130-2B 5
2002	*Oakland*	*AL*	*424*	*112*	*20*	*3*	*13*	*63*	*84*	*73*	*57*	*2*	*4*	*316*	*.264*	*.359*	*.417*	*.268*	*59*	

Menechino played well enough to let the A's part with Jose Ortiz in the deal that brought Jermaine Dye to Oakland (and heartburn to Royals fans). Menechino played great in the first half, showing the plate discipline and power that we saw from him in the minors. He suffered an injury to his left elbow that prevented him from really extending his arms, and he hit a miserable .192/.340/.254 in the second half. If healthy, he's a very good ballplayer. With German and Crosby nipping at his heels, he better get healthy quickly.

Greg Myers C Bats L Age 36

YEAR	TEAM	LGE	AB	H	DB	TP	HR	BB	SO	R	RBI	SB	CS	OUT	BA	OBP	SLG	EQA	EQR	DEFENSE
1999	San Dieg	NL	130	39	2	0	4	11	13	9	16	0	0	91	.300	.355	.408	.258	15	31-C -2
1999	Atlanta	NL	72	16	2	0	2	12	15	10	9	0	0	56	.222	.333	.333	.233	7	22-C 3
2000	Baltimor	AL	125	30	4	0	4	7	26	9	13	0	0	95	.240	.280	.368	.216	10	27-C -1
2001	Baltimor	AL	75	22	1	0	5	8	15	12	20	0	0	53	.293	.361	.507	.285	11	
2001	Oakland	AL	87	17	1	0	8	14	18	15	14	0	0	70	.195	.307	.483	.256	12	23-C 2
2002	*Oakland*	*AL*	*192*	*46*	*5*	*0*	*10*	*30*	*40*	*21*	*27*	*0*	*0*	*146*	*.240*	*.342*	*.422*	*.264*	*26*	

The A's and Myers agreed to a deal for 2002 with a club option for 2003, so he'll be back in Oakland as Ramon Hernandez's backup and a left-handed bat off the bench. Myers plays solid defense, waits for a pitch in his zone, and swings hard. He makes a great complement for Hernandez.

Adam Piatt OF Bats R Age 26

YEAR	TEAM	LGE	AB	H	DB	TP	HR	BB	SO	R	RBI	SB	CS	OUT	BA	OBP	SLG	EQA	EQR	DEFENSE
1999	Midland	Tex	471	130	31	2	26	71	104	89	87	4	2	343	.276	.376	.516	.292	79	114-3B -13 10-SS 1
2000	Sacramen	PCL	253	66	9	0	8	20	55	28	34	2	2	189	.261	.322	.391	.239	26	21-3B -2 19-RF -1
2000	Oakland	AL	156	49	5	5	6	21	39	24	23	0	1	108	.314	.399	.526	.302	27	22-RF -3
2001	Oakland	AL	96	23	6	1	0	13	22	10	7	0	0	73	.240	.330	.323	.228	9	26-RF 0
2001	Sacramen	PCL	109	25	4	0	2	10	24	11	14	2	0	84	.229	.305	.321	.220	10	25-RF -4
2002	*Oakland*	*AL*	*412*	*113*	*21*	*3*	*15*	*53*	*100*	*61*	*60*	*2*	*2*	*301*	*.274*	*.357*	*.449*	*.276*	*60*	

Anything can happen. You can be an underappreciated prospect who has demonstrated success everywhere you've played, change positions, go through a brutal conditioning and strengthening regimen, and then get hit with a freak illness. Piatt missed virtually all season after getting knocked out by viral meningitis, which completely sapped his strength. He played briefly in Mexico over the winter, not hitting all that well. He has a lot to prove in spring training.

Rob Ryan OF Bats L Age 29

YEAR	TEAM	LGE	AB	H	DB	TP	HR	BB	SO	R	RBI	SB	CS	OUT	BA	OBP	SLG	EQA	EQR	DEFENSE
1999	Tucson	PCL	404	100	23	4	14	47	64	54	64	3	2	306	.248	.338	.428	.256	51	104-RF -7
1999	Arizona	NL	29	7	0	0	2	1	7	4	5	0	0	22	.241	.267	.448	.231	3	
2000	Tucson	PCL	325	87	12	1	7	35	34	43	41	1	1	239	.268	.353	.375	.250	37	84-LF -1
2000	Arizona	NL	27	8	0	1	0	4	6	4	2	0	0	19	.296	.404	.370	.273	4	
2001	Tucson	PCL	212	60	15	3	9	26	31	36	38	1	2	154	.283	.370	.509	.286	34	47-LF -4
2001	Sacramen	PCL	219	44	7	2	6	35	46	30	26	1	2	177	.201	.316	.333	.224	21	52-OF -3
2002	*Oakland*	*AL*	*423*	*106*	*18*	*4*	*15*	*66*	*74*	*60*	*63*	*1*	*1*	*318*	*.251*	*.352*	*.418*	*.267*	*59*	

Acquired from the Diamondbacks, Ryan is a potential Ken Phelps All-Stars platoon mate for a right-handed glove man. He can hit right-handed pitching well enough to be a fourth outfielder. The A's have a lot of depth when it comes to guys like this, each with a slightly different skill set. The Yankees hold their depth on the major-league roster and pay more for it.

Olmedo Saenz 3B/1B Bats R Age 31

YEAR	TEAM	LGE	AB	H	DB	TP	HR	BB	SO	R	RBI	SB	CS	OUT	BA	OBP	SLG	EQA	EQR	DEFENSE
1999	Oakland	AL	254	74	15	0	13	20	41	41	42	1	1	181	.291	.373	.504	.288	40	43-3B -1 18-1B 2
2000	Oakland	AL	213	70	12	2	10	22	35	40	33	1	0	143	.329	.410	.545	.314	40	16-3B -2 14-1B -1
2001	Oakland	AL	306	74	20	1	11	21	55	36	35	0	1	233	.242	.311	.422	.242	34	22-1B 0
2002	*Oakland*	*AL*	*284*	*78*	*15*	*1*	*13*	*26*	*52*	*44*	*41*	*1*	*1*	*207*	*.275*	*.335*	*.472*	*.272*	*40*	

Hopefully, it was just an off year. Saenz was the latest in an A's string of DHs/corner guys, following Geronimo Berroa and Matt Stairs, pulled from organizations that focused on limitations rather than capabilities. Saenz, who always looks like he's in pain, can fill in at either corner without killing you defensively and hits lots of hard line drives. If he doesn't recover quickly with the bat, the A's will start looking at other options.

Oscar Salazar IF Bats R Age 24

YEAR	TEAM	LGE	AB	H	DB	TP	HR	BB	SO	R	RBI	SB	CS	OUT	BA	OBP	SLG	EQA	EQR	DEFENSE	
1999	Modesto	Cal	520	123	22	8	13	24	107	65	64	7	4	401	.237	.271	.385	.217	44	29-2B -2	28-3B -9
2000	Midland	Tex	422	103	19	1	10	25	71	51	39	2	2	321	.244	.288	.365	.218	36	93-SS -18	
2001	Midland	Tex	519	114	22	2	14	40	101	57	67	6	2	407	.220	.277	.351	.213	42	77-SS -10	34-3B -3
2002	*Oakland*	*AL*	*484*	*116*	*20*	*3*	*13*	*44*	*99*	*62*	*56*	*5*	*2*	*370*	*.240*	*.303*	*.374*	*.233*	*49*		

Salazar is a middle infielder with (bonk) a very solid bat, improving plate discipline (fling), and enough youth to be a very intriguing prospect. The organization is pretty well stocked with (boot) middle infielders, and Salazar is probably well behind Crosby and German, although he could hit his way into the picture. The problem is 37 errors in Double-A and footwork that scouts describe as being "as good as it's going to get."

F.P. Santangelo UT Bats B Age 34

YEAR	TEAM	LGE	AB	H	DB	TP	HR	BB	SO	R	RBI	SB	CS	OUT	BA	OBP	SLG	EQA	EQR	DEFENSE	
1999	San Fran	NL	256	67	18	3	3	51	50	48	25	10	4	193	.262	.405	.391	.281	40	58-CF 0	
2000	LosAngls	NL	144	30	2	0	2	19	30	19	10	3	2	116	.208	.322	.264	.212	12	30-OF -2	
2001	Sacramen	PCL	189	35	5	1	4	27	44	26	14	4	3	157	.185	.306	.286	.211	16	33-CF 2	21-2B 2
2001	Oakland	AL	71	16	5	0	0	12	15	18	9	1	1	56	.225	.366	.296	.238	8	15-2B -1	
2002	*NY Yanks*	*AL*	*250*	*52*	*11*	*1*	*3*	*37*	*57*	*38*	*19*	*6*	*3*	*201*	*.208*	*.310*	*.296*	*.216*	*22*		

He's gritty. He's tough. He'll draw walks. He can play lots of positions. If necessary, he'll gnaw through a wall of epoxy and ground glass for the team. Is it enough? Probably not. There appears to be a trend among 25th guys on the A's roster, one that requires more time, attention, and gravitas than we have time to give it.

Miguel Tejada SS Bats R Age 26

YEAR	TEAM	LGE	AB	H	DB	TP	HR	BB	SO	R	RBI	SB	CS	OUT	BA	OBP	SLG	EQA	EQR	DEFENSE
1999	Oakland	AL	592	157	35	4	23	51	83	93	85	7	7	442	.265	.333	.454	.258	75	155-SS 4
2000	Oakland	AL	605	175	28	1	34	59	90	104	116	6	0	430	.289	.356	.507	.284	93	157-SS -4
2001	Oakland	AL	626	180	31	3	35	46	77	116	120	10	6	452	.288	.346	.514	.279	93	159-SS -6
2002	*Oakland*	*AL*	*555*	*150*	*29*	*2*	*28*	*56*	*78*	*96*	*94*	*8*	*4*	*401*	*.285*	*.350*	*.495*	*.285*	*87*	

Causality is a difficult and slippery concept. An oversimplified version of the central stathead tenet is that hitters should be more disciplined at the plate—as if that were a matter of a simple choice. It's the snake oil we push. But sometimes, the effects are so compelling that you wonder whether it really is that simple.

Here are Miguel Tejada's month-by-month breakdowns for 2001.

Month	BA	OBP	SLG	OB-BA
April	.237	.308	.443	.071
May	.295	.373	.571	.078
June	.274	.294	.425	.020
July	.267	.333	.476	.066
August	.216	.238	.371	.022
September	.329	.429	.571	.100

What drives what? Do Miguel Tejada's hitting numbers jump because of his increased patience, or does the arrow go the other way? Or both ways? "How can players improve?" is really the key issue for any baseball analysis. I'm inclined to believe that there's a method that drives successful offensive performance, and we see the effects across the board. It's not just a question of deciding to walk more.

Mario Valdez 1B Bats L Age 27

YEAR	TEAM	LGE	AB	H	DB	TP	HR	BB	SO	R	RBI	SB	CS	OUT	BA	OBP	SLG	EQA	EQR	DEFENSE	
1999	Charlott	Int	401	100	13	1	22	64	85	64	60	1	0	301	.249	.365	.451	.274	59	90-1B -3	18-LF -1
2000	SaltLake	PCL	305	95	16	1	14	45	44	56	60	1	1	211	.311	.404	.508	.302	53	38-1B 2	
2000	Sacramen	PCL	61	13	2	0	2	7	13	9	9	0	0	48	.213	.309	.344	.225	6	14-1B 0	
2001	Oakland	AL	55	17	1	0	1	12	16	8	8	0	0	38	.309	.439	.382	.294	9		
2001	Modesto	Cal	19	6	2	0	1	2	1	2	3	0	1	14	.316	.394	.579	.295	3		
2002	*Oakland*	*AL*	*328*	*90*	*13*	*1*	*15*	*51*	*66*	*51*	*51*	*0*	*1*	*239*	*.274*	*.372*	*.457*	*.285*	*52*		

(Mario Valdez *continued*)

Valdez was kind of a forgotten man after his broken hand, but don't be surprised to see him as a major part of the A's first-base situation in 2002. Valdez can hit for average, draw walks, play solid defense, and pop the occasional home run. He's good enough to start for at least five or ten major-league clubs, more than that if you consider platoons.

Tom Wilson C Bats R Age 31

YEAR	TEAM	LGE	AB	H	DB	TP	HR	BB	SO	R	RBI	SB	CS	OUT	BA	OBP	SLG	EQA	EQR	DEFENSE
1999	Orlando	Sou	106	27	3	0	5	13	35	10	17	0	0	79	.255	.346	.425	.259	13	18-C -4
1999	Durham	Int	216	56	14	0	14	42	55	34	35	0	2	162	.259	.380	.519	.292	37	57-C 1
2000	Columbus	Int	335	87	15	0	19	64	112	57	62	2	2	250	.260	.382	.475	.286	55	76-C -10
2001	Sacramen	PCL	260	66	11	1	7	43	56	36	40	0	1	195	.254	.365	.385	.258	33	46-C -8
2001	Oakland	AL	21	4	1	0	2	1	4	5	4	0	0	17	.190	.253	.524	.244	3	
2002	*Toronto*	*AL*	*328*	*91*	*16*	*0*	*18*	*59*	*90*	*49*	*55*	*1*	*2*	*239*	*.277*	*.388*	*.491*	*.293*	*56*	

A long-time *BP* favorite, Wilson is a minor-league veteran with talent to help a big-league club in at least a backup role and perhaps more than that. He probably won't get an opportunity in Oakland; the A's have re-signed Greg Myers to back up Ramon Hernandez, so unless Wilson is interested in being injury insurance, he's likely to move somewhere else. Another nice pickup by the Blue Jays, where he'll stick.

PITCHERS (ERA: 4.50, H/9: 9.0, HR/9: 1.0, BB/9: 3.0, K/9: 6.0, KW: 2.0, PERA: 4.50)

Shane Bazzell Throws R Age 23

YEAR	TEAM	LGE	IP	H	ER	HR	BB	K	ERA	W	L	H/9	HR/9	BB/9	K/9	KW	PERA	STUFF
1999	So Oregn	Nwn	28.7	31	15	2	10	9	4.71	1	2	9.7	0.6	3.1	2.8	0.4	5.17	-3
1999	Visalia	Cal	42.0	48	31	7	21	17	6.64	2	3	10.3	1.5	4.5	3.6	0.4	6.45	-9
2000	Modesto	Cal	76.7	84	48	12	30	42	5.63	4	5	9.9	1.4	3.5	4.9	0.7	8.17	-12
2001	Modesto	Cal	131.3	141	76	17	48	68	5.21	6	9	9.7	1.2	3.3	4.7	0.7	4.26	-1
2001	Midland	Tex	10.0	13	9	3	2	3	8.10	0	1	11.7	2.7	1.8	2.7	0.8	21.91	-43

Bazzell had a great year at Modesto after spending a year and a half in the California League. His raw numbers were encouraging, with 129 walks and 38 strikeouts in 135 innings, but that's a long time to spend in A ball. He'll head to the Texas League meat grinder for the 2002 season. Bazzell needs to spend a year consolidating last season's gains; if he can do that, he's young enough to have a career, although probably out of the bullpen.

Chad Bradford Throws R Age 27

YEAR	TEAM	LGE	IP	H	ER	HR	BB	K	ERA	W	L	H/9	HR/9	BB/9	K/9	KW	PERA	STUFF
1999	Charlott	Int	73.7	70	25	2	15	43	3.05	5	3	8.6	0.2	1.8	5.3	1.4	2.17	3
2000	Charlott	Int	51.0	49	20	3	13	31	3.53	4	2	8.6	0.5	2.3	5.5	1.2	3.40	-6
2000	ChiSox	AL	14.0	13	3	0	1	9	1.93	2	0	8.4	0.0	0.6	5.8	4.5	2.17	12
2001	Sacramen	PCL	22.0	19	6	0	3	15	2.45	2	0	7.8	0.0	1.2	6.1	2.5	0.89	12
2001	Oakland	AL	38.7	37	17	6	6	32	3.96	2	2	8.6	1.4	1.4	7.4	2.7	2.77	9

Sometimes, you wonder how Billy Beane sleeps at night. When he talks to Kenny Williams about a potential trade, it's a little like watching Garry Kasparov show up for a quick game of chess with Matthew Perry. Bradford is a truly great reliever, inducing ground balls and strikeouts at a high rate and seldom walking a batter. He'll be in the A's pen in a middle-inning role.

Mark Guthrie Throws L Age 36

YEAR	TEAM	LGE	IP	H	ER	HR	BB	K	ERA	W	L	H/9	HR/9	BB/9	K/9	KW	PERA	STUFF
1999	Boston	AL	47.7	49	27	8	17	36	5.10	2	3	9.3	1.5	3.2	6.8	1.1	5.24	-5
1999	ChiCubs	NL	11.3	11	5	1	3	8	3.97	1	0	8.7	0.8	2.4	6.4	1.3	3.98	1
2000	ChiCubs	NL	19.0	17	8	1	8	15	3.79	1	1	8.1	0.5	3.8	7.1	0.9	4.86	2
2000	TampaBay	AL	33.3	32	17	3	15	26	4.59	2	2	8.6	0.8	4.1	7.0	0.9	4.24	-1
2000	Toronto	AL	21.3	19	10	3	7	20	4.22	1	1	8.0	1.3	3.0	8.4	1.4	4.25	8
2001	Oakland	AL	53.3	49	25	6	19	49	4.22	3	3	8.3	1.0	3.2	8.3	1.3	4.70	7

When Guthrie was first signed, there were some mumblings about moving him into the rotation. He stayed in the pen and was bitten by the home-run bug. His other numbers were pretty reasonable, but he allowed seven bombs in 53 innings; that's not an acceptable performance in his role at Network Associates Coliseum. Guthrie's sustained strikeout rate bodes well for some improvement in 2002, and the move to Shea Stadium—he was dealt for David Justice—will help him.

Aaron Harang Throws R Age 24

YEAR	TEAM	LGE	IP	H	ER	HR	BB	K	ERA	W	L	H/9	HR/9	BB/9	K/9	KW	PERA	STUFF
1999	Pulaski	App	75.3	84	45	12	22	37	5.38	3	5	10.0	1.4	2.0	4.4	0.0	3.05	1
2000	Charlott	Fla	149.3	162	97	25	62	86	5.85	6	11	9.8	1.5	3.7	5.2	0.7	5.23	0
2001	Midland	Tex	156.7	165	78	14	45	74	4.48	9	8	9.5	0.8	2.6	4.3	0.8	5.29	0

The A's going to the Rangers for pitching talent is a little bit like Paul Allen mugging a homeless guy. Who can't see. Or move. Harang pitched remarkably well in Midland and should spend this season in Sacramento. His repertoire isn't filled with amazing stuff, but he has good command of his pitches, changes speeds well, and scouts like his compact delivery. If he had been in Texas last season, he might well have ended up in Arlington for eight or ten gruesome starts.

Chad Harville Throws R Age 25

YEAR	TEAM	LGE	IP	H	ER	HR	BB	K	ERA	W	L	H/9	HR/9	BB/9	K/9	KW	PERA	STUFF
1999	Midland	Tex	21.7	17	8	1	10	25	3.32	1	1	7.1	0.4	4.2	10.4	1.3	2.39	30
1999	Vancouvr	PCL	27.3	21	8	0	11	27	2.63	2	1	6.9	0.0	3.6	8.9	1.2	1.83	27
1999	Oakland	AL	16.0	14	8	2	8	15	4.50	1	1	7.9	1.1	4.5	8.4	0.9	6.04	9
2000	Sacramen	PCL	63.3	58	36	10	33	62	5.12	3	4	8.2	1.4	4.7	8.8	0.9	4.74	7
2001	Sacramen	PCL	40.0	37	20	6	14	38	4.50	2	2	8.3	1.4	3.2	8.6	1.4	4.81	6

Biceps tendinitis landed Harville on the DL at the start of the season, but testing revealed no significant damage to arm, elbow, or shoulder. He's a small right-hander who can flat out bring heat, and he'll be in the mix for a bullpen slot on the big club. He's often called a right-handed Billy Wagner, but that's overstating the case. Harville has the stuff to be a closer in the bigs, and for as long as people have been paying attention to him, he's just 25 this year.

Gil Heredia Throws R Age 36

YEAR	TEAM	LGE	IP	H	ER	HR	BB	K	ERA	W	L	H/9	HR/9	BB/9	K/9	KW	PERA	STUFF
1999	Oakland	AL	209.3	215	88	19	28	116	3.78	13	10	9.2	0.8	1.2	5.0	2.1	4.66	10
2000	Oakland	AL	203.0	215	102	21	54	100	4.52	11	12	9.5	0.9	2.4	4.4	0.9	4.16	3
2001	Oakland	AL	114.0	138	82	25	28	46	6.47	4	9	10.9	2.0	2.2	3.6	0.8	5.80	-15

Heredia was the definition of a classy professional, accepting his demotion to the pen and performing admirably once asked to be the long reliever. He pitched horribly as a starter, with an ERA just under 6.00. In limited work as a reliever, he posted a 3.27 ERA. He also got better as the season progressed. Heredia is a free agent and will likely land elsewhere, but he was an important part of the A's success while he was in Oakland, and the fans will miss him.

Erik Hiljus Throws R Age 29

YEAR	TEAM	LGE	IP	H	ER	HR	BB	K	ERA	W	L	H/9	HR/9	BB/9	K/9	KW	PERA	STUFF
1999	Jacksnvl	Sou	15.0	13	6	2	6	17	3.60	1	1	7.8	1.2	3.6	10.2	1.4	2.71	11
1999	Toledo	Int	59.3	54	25	6	17	52	3.79	4	3	8.2	0.9	2.6	7.9	1.5	5.07	3
2000	Toledo	Int	73.3	65	27	4	22	61	3.31	5	3	8.0	0.5	2.7	7.5	1.4	4.89	3
2001	Sacramen	PCL	93.0	103	68	23	33	68	6.58	3	7	10.0	2.2	3.2	6.6	1.0	4.80	-3
2001	Oakland	AL	70.0	62	28	6	20	64	3.60	5	3	8.0	0.8	2.6	8.2	1.6	3.73	22

Hiljus works off of a plus fastball, mixing in breaking balls to keep hitters off balance and changing speeds fairly well. Hiljus's peripheral numbers are very good, and if he's past his injury problems, there's no reason to think he can't be an effective member of what could be the best overall rotation in baseball in 2002.

Tim Hudson Throws R Age 26

YEAR	TEAM	LGE	IP	H	ER	HR	BB	K	ERA	W	L	H/9	HR/9	BB/9	K/9	KW	PERA	STUFF
1999	Midland	Tex	16.7	14	5	0	3	12	2.70	1	1	7.6	0.0	1.6	6.5	2.0	0.51	30
1999	Vancouvr	PCL	49.0	41	19	2	22	46	3.49	3	2	7.5	0.4	4.0	8.4	1.0	3.07	31
1999	Oakland	AL	140.0	117	51	7	52	131	3.28	10	6	7.5	0.4	3.3	8.4	1.3	3.22	33
2000	Oakland	AL	200.0	186	90	21	67	167	4.05	12	10	8.4	0.9	3.0	7.5	1.2	3.86	22
2001	Oakland	AL	236.7	223	98	19	68	172	3.73	15	11	8.5	0.7	2.6	6.5	1.3	3.61	18

Hudson's workload got a bit heavy in terms of innings, but Howe did a good job throughout the year of protecting his arm. Hudson is the ace of the staff, throwing nasty forkballs and keeping hitters off stride with some wicked changes of speed. His strikeout rate dropped just a bit last year; it'd be nice to see that trendline go a different direction in 2002. He's very reminiscent of Dave Stewart on the mound.

Eric Ireland Throws R Age 25

YEAR	TEAM	LGE	IP	H	ER	HR	BB	K	ERA	W	L	H/9	HR/9	BB/9	K/9	KW	PERA	STUFF
1999	Kissimme	Fla	162.3	180	95	27	38	86	5.27	8	10	10.0	1.5	2.1	4.8	1.1	4.16	5
1999	Jackson	Tex	16.3	16	6	1	2	11	3.31	1	1	8.8	0.6	1.1	6.1	2.8	6.25	17
2000	Round Ro	Tex	175.7	192	104	22	66	82	5.33	8	12	9.8	1.1	3.4	4.2	0.6	4.99	-2
2001	Sacramen	PCL	173.0	199	116	28	66	70	6.03	7	12	10.4	1.5	3.4	3.6	0.5	6.97	-13

Ireland has logged a boatload of innings each of the last three years, and he's probably ready for a chance to make a big-league rotation, a chance he may have to go elsewhere to get. The A's rotation is completely set, and Ireland is probably behind Mario Ramos on the organizational depth chart. He has very good command of what scouts call "ordinary" stuff; there are a lot of guys making a lot of money who fit that description.

Jason "White Knuckle" Isringhausen Throws R Age 29

YEAR	TEAM	LGE	IP	H	ER	HR	BB	K	ERA	W	L	H/9	HR/9	BB/9	K/9	KW	PERA	STUFF
1999	Norfolk	Int	47.7	46	24	5	21	36	4.53	2	3	8.7	0.9	4.0	6.8	0.9	3.40	1
1999	NY Mets	NL	40.3	42	26	7	18	28	5.80	2	2	9.4	1.6	4.0	6.2	0.8	6.32	-7
1999	Oakland	AL	25.0	23	11	2	10	20	3.96	2	1	8.3	0.7	3.6	7.2	1.0	1.86	6
2000	Oakland	AL	71.0	65	30	5	26	56	3.80	5	3	8.2	0.6	3.3	7.1	1.1	3.85	4
2001	Oakland	AL	70.7	59	25	5	22	70	3.18	5	3	7.5	0.6	2.8	8.9	1.6	2.85	19

Isringhausen mixes true 95-mph heat with the occasional knee-buckling curveball to torture opposing hitters and A's fans alike. He blew a league-leading nine saves in 43 opportunities, but that didn't stop the Cardinals from giving him a big contract to close for them.

Cory Lidle Throws R Age 30

YEAR	TEAM	LGE	IP	H	ER	HR	BB	K	ERA	W	L	H/9	HR/9	BB/9	K/9	KW	PERA	STUFF
1999	TampaBay	AL	6.0	5	2	0	2	4	3.00	1	0	7.5	0.0	3.0	6.0	1.0	6.15	0
2000	Durham	Int	51.7	51	20	4	9	33	3.48	4	2	8.9	0.7	1.6	5.7	1.8	3.23	12
2000	TampaBay	AL	102.3	105	48	11	24	61	4.22	6	5	9.2	1.0	2.1	5.4	1.3	4.75	0
2001	Oakland	AL	184.3	189	89	21	45	112	4.35	10	10	9.2	1.0	2.2	5.5	1.2	3.79	10

Check out that "KW" column. Lidle has always been an effective pitcher when given the opportunity, and kudos once again to A's management for acquiring him and building an inexpensive winner. Lidle has great control and keeps the ball down, and he adapted well to the heaviest workload of his career. Art Howe handled him masterfully, limiting his time in each game pretty harshly as the season went along. There is absolutely no reason to expect Lidle to suddenly fall off a cliff.

Mike Magnante Throws L Age 37

YEAR	TEAM	LGE	IP	H	ER	HR	BB	K	ERA	W	L	H/9	HR/9	BB/9	K/9	KW	PERA	STUFF
1999	Anaheim	AL	71.3	67	27	2	24	44	3.41	5	3	8.5	0.3	3.0	5.6	0.9	3.28	0
2000	Oakland	AL	42.7	45	21	3	16	17	4.43	3	2	9.5	0.6	3.4	3.6	0.5	4.33	-19
2001	Oakland	AL	53.0	59	29	6	12	22	4.92	3	3	10.0	1.0	2.0	3.7	0.9	3.53	-15

Magnante is a lefty specialist who lives off the ground ball and the outside corner. He wanted some stability, so he settled for less money to stay in Oakland on a club option in 2002. Once a winner of the Binaca Blast Deep Drive Derby, he's been effective at keeping the ball down for the last two seasons. He'll be back in the same role this year.

Jim Mecir — Throws R — Age 32

YEAR	TEAM	LGE	IP	H	ER	HR	BB	K	ERA	W	L	H/9	HR/9	BB/9	K/9	KW	PERA	STUFF
1999	TampaBay	AL	20.3	17	8	0	12	15	3.54	1	1	7.5	0.0	5.3	6.6	0.6	2.60	1
2000	TampaBay	AL	47.7	44	19	2	18	33	3.59	3	2	8.3	0.4	3.4	6.2	0.9	2.58	3
2000	Oakland	AL	37.7	31	12	2	11	37	2.87	3	1	7.4	0.5	2.6	8.8	1.7	3.10	21
2001	Oakland	AL	64.0	55	25	4	25	58	3.52	4	3	7.7	0.6	3.5	8.2	1.2	3.37	11

The screwball-throwing right-hander has always been effective when healthy. Mecir could end up in the closer role, and that would work out just fine. He's under contract at a very low price through 2003, with a club option for 2004. He'll be effective for the life of the contract.

Justin Miller — Throws R — Age 24

YEAR	TEAM	LGE	IP	H	ER	HR	BB	K	ERA	W	L	H/9	HR/9	BB/9	K/9	KW	PERA	STUFF
1999	Salem VA	Car	36.3	40	23	6	12	20	5.70	2	2	9.9	1.5	3.0	5.0	0.8	5.46	0
2000	Midland	Tex	84.3	86	51	11	41	57	5.44	4	5	9.2	1.2	4.4	6.1	0.7	5.04	5
2000	Sacramen	PCL	52.0	53	22	4	12	27	3.81	3	3	9.2	0.7	2.1	4.7	1.1	2.85	14
2001	Sacramen	PCL	162.7	179	111	29	72	95	6.14	6	12	9.9	1.6	4.0	5.3	0.7	5.35	0

Miller hasn't translated his stuff into results yet. If he can stay healthy, he definitely has the repertoire—plus fastball, slider, curve, and change-up—to succeed. The A's have a number of these C+/B– pitching prospects. One or two are likely to pan out, with others used as trade bait. Miller was sent to the Jays in the Billy Koch deal, a boon for his career opportunities.

Mark Mulder — Throws L — Age 24

YEAR	TEAM	LGE	IP	H	ER	HR	BB	K	ERA	W	L	H/9	HR/9	BB/9	K/9	KW	PERA	STUFF
1999	Vancouvr	PCL	134.0	145	68	15	32	61	4.57	7	8	9.7	1.0	2.1	4.1	1.0	5.04	6
2000	Oakland	AL	164.0	173	90	19	56	87	4.94	8	10	9.5	1.0	3.1	4.8	0.8	5.37	4
2001	Oakland	AL	230.3	223	89	15	49	146	3.48	16	10	8.7	0.6	1.9	5.7	1.5	3.40	18

Mulder mixes three very good pitches, executes the game plan, and just flat out pitches exceptionally well. He and the A's agreed on a contract extension through 2005, with a club option for 2006. With that kind of arrangement and a deep bullpen, look for a slightly quicker hook on Mulder, Hudson, and Barry Zito in 2002.

Wayne Nix — Throws R — Age 25

YEAR	TEAM	LGE	IP	H	ER	HR	BB	K	ERA	W	L	H/9	HR/9	BB/9	K/9	KW	PERA	STUFF
1999	Modesto	Cal	116.0	128	89	18	79	60	6.91	4	9	9.9	1.4	6.1	4.7	0.4	6.57	-19
2000	Visalia	Cal	136.7	143	90	16	85	76	5.93	5	10	9.4	1.1	5.6	5.0	0.4	8.17	-18
2001	Visalia	Cal	144.7	176	124	40	54	75	7.71	4	12	10.9	2.5	3.4	4.7	0.7	7.33	-25
2001	Midland	Tex	14.0	15	6	2	1	7	3.86	1	1	9.6	1.3	0.6	4.5	3.5	15.47	-13

There's an entire silo of pitchers who are one walk per nine innings away from being prospects. Sometimes they find their way, usually they don't. Wayne Nix took a big step forward in 2001, posting his best strikeout-to-walk ratio yet at Visalia: 167 whiffs and 36 walks in 148 innings. He has a great fastball that he never harnessed until last year; sometimes, it takes a long time to find the control of a really good pitch. Nix will start the year in Double-A; if he really has found his control, he could have a good career as a starter.

Juan Pena — Throws L — Age 23

YEAR	TEAM	LGE	IP	H	ER	HR	BB	K	ERA	W	L	H/9	HR/9	BB/9	K/9	KW	PERA	STUFF
1999	Visalia	Cal	140.7	154	89	17	67	64	5.69	6	10	9.9	1.1	4.3	4.1	0.5	7.77	-8
2000	Modesto	Cal	152.3	148	81	14	75	104	4.79	8	9	8.7	0.8	4.4	6.1	0.7	5.69	10
2001	Midland	Tex	151.7	165	89	20	54	72	5.28	7	10	9.8	1.2	3.2	4.3	0.7	5.58	-1

Pena made the adjustment to Double-A pretty well for a guy who doesn't throw that hard. His ERA might be a little misleading, as nearly 25% of the runs he allowed were unearned. He needs to improve his command and changes of speed to succeed at higher levels, and he is fairly far down on the depth chart in the organization. His future is probably as a lefty out of the pen.

Mario Ramos Throws L Age 24

YEAR	TEAM	LGE	IP	H	ER	HR	BB	K	ERA	W	L	H/9	HR/9	BB/9	K/9	KW	PERA	STUFF
2000	Modesto	Cal	148.0	153	74	13	52	76	4.50	8	8	9.3	0.8	3.2	4.6	0.7	4.45	4
2000	Midland	Tex	27.0	26	9	0	6	13	3.00	2	1	8.7	0.0	2.0	4.3	1.1	1.97	15
2001	Midland	Tex	87.7	94	52	11	34	45	5.34	4	6	9.7	1.1	3.5	4.6	0.7	3.87	0
2001	Sacramen	PCL	80.0	75	35	6	31	58	3.94	5	4	8.4	0.7	3.5	6.5	0.9	3.74	18

Ramos throws an 87-mph fastball and 70-mph change-up with exactly the same motion and arm speed. He's very polished for his age and underrated by scouts because of his small stature. The A's picked him up in the sixth round out of Rice, and now he'll be the circling vulture in Sacramento, waiting for either an injury or for Erik Hiljus to falter.

Jeff Tam Throws R Age 31

YEAR	TEAM	LGE	IP	H	ER	HR	BB	K	ERA	W	L	H/9	HR/9	BB/9	K/9	KW	PERA	STUFF
1999	Buffalo	Int	25.0	27	14	2	9	9	5.04	1	2	9.7	0.7	3.2	3.2	0.5	3.36	-23
1999	Norfolk	Int	21.3	23	9	1	3	7	3.80	1	1	9.7	0.4	1.3	3.0	1.2	3.32	-16
1999	NY Mets	NL	9.7	11	8	3	3	7	7.45	0	1	10.2	2.8	2.8	6.5	1.2	3.03	-11
2000	Oakland	AL	87.7	86	32	3	19	46	3.29	7	3	8.8	0.3	2.0	4.7	1.2	2.73	-1
2001	Oakland	AL	74.7	72	31	3	28	42	3.74	5	3	8.7	0.4	3.4	5.1	0.8	3.07	-5

Tam is the A's righty sinker specialist, often called on to get tough right-handed hitters or to induce the occasional double play. He bounces back from appearances quickly, can go two innings comfortably, doesn't cost a lot, and gets plenty of ground balls. In other words, he's a guy who can help any club, and the type of guy that low-payroll clubs have to go out and find. See also Bradford, Chad.

Luis Vizcaino Throws R Age 25

YEAR	TEAM	LGE	IP	H	ER	HR	BB	K	ERA	W	L	H/9	HR/9	BB/9	K/9	KW	PERA	STUFF
1999	Midland	Tex	107.0	123	86	25	53	63	7.23	3	9	10.3	2.1	4.5	5.3	0.6	6.28	-9
1999	Vancouvr	PCL	13.3	13	6	0	6	5	4.05	1	0	8.8	0.0	4.1	3.4	0.4	2.89	-10
2000	Sacramen	PCL	49.0	48	25	5	20	33	4.59	2	3	8.8	0.9	3.7	6.1	0.8	4.85	-2
2000	Oakland	AL	21.7	20	10	2	9	18	4.15	1	1	8.3	0.8	3.7	7.5	1.0	6.88	5
2001	Sacramen	PCL	41.0	38	19	6	12	38	4.17	3	2	8.3	1.3	2.6	8.3	1.6	2.33	12
2001	Oakland	AL	37.0	39	23	7	11	29	5.59	2	2	9.5	1.7	2.7	7.1	1.3	4.39	0

He throws really hard. There's not a lot of subtlety when Vizcaino is on the mound. He telegraphs his change-up from time to time, so he compensates for that by not throwing it. His slider is inconsistent, so he doesn't throw it. The result is at-bats in which Vizcaino fires fastball after fastball with increasing effort, and the batter swings harder and harder until he either strikes out, pops up, or lashes a ball. It's entertaining to watch, but it's not really high baseball art.

Mike Wood Throws R Age 22

YEAR	TEAM	LGE	IP	H	ER	HR	BB	K	ERA	W	L	H/9	HR/9	BB/9	K/9	KW	PERA	STUFF
2001	Vancouvr	Nwn	21.7	20	7	0	6	11	2.91	1	1	8.3	0.0	2.5	4.6	0.9	2.63	10
2001	Modesto	Cal	54.7	62	35	11	12	29	5.76	2	4	10.2	1.8	2.0	4.8	1.2	4.09	6

Wood was obviously too polished for the Northwest League, so the A's moved him to Modesto, where he only got better. Wood has great command, particularly for his age. He'll be facing the Double-A barrier this season. He keeps the ball down, so he may be able to get through the Texas League without actually suffering post-traumatic stress disorder.

Barry Zito Throws L Age 24

YEAR	TEAM	LGE	IP	H	ER	HR	BB	K	ERA	W	L	H/9	HR/9	BB/9	K/9	KW	PERA	STUFF
1999	Visalia	Cal	37.0	33	22	5	24	37	5.35	2	2	8.0	1.2	5.8	9.0	0.8	3.11	25
1999	Midland	Tex	23.3	20	10	1	12	21	3.86	2	1	7.7	0.4	4.6	8.1	0.9	6.06	27
2000	Sacramen	PCL	101.7	93	43	5	43	73	3.81	6	5	8.2	0.4	3.8	6.5	0.8	3.75	20
2000	Oakland	AL	89.3	78	36	5	37	77	3.63	6	4	7.9	0.5	3.7	7.8	1.0	2.53	29
2001	Oakland	AL	216.0	189	87	17	76	195	3.63	15	9	7.9	0.7	3.2	8.1	1.3	3.64	29

Somewhere, Jim Thome's knees just buckled. One of the A's three young guns, Zito relies on working his reasonable fastball in and out, then dropping a positively unhittable curveball as an out pitch. He changes speeds well but does so primarily to improve his fastball. Nothing in his record points anywhere near fluke; he will likely be one of the top five left-handers in baseball for the next several years and will get the concomitant media attention for allegedly being a flake.

Seattle Mariners

> A lot of people thought it was wacko, but usually when someone tries something new people think it's a little crazy. No doubt going to the Dominican when other teams weren't that interested gave us a big boost.
>
> — Pat Gillick, on building the Blue Jays' formidable Dominican "baseball factory" with Epy Guerrero in the 1980s

Gillick's statement could likewise apply to the way the Mariners have turned their Pacific Rim recruiting into a well-oiled machine. In courting regular free agents, the Mariners are hampered by their location: the Pacific Northwest doesn't produce nearly as many players as other regions, the commute sucks for people who want to live in a gated, Isleworth-style community, and the area isn't known for the kind of activities Mo Vaughn appreciates. Seattle is the closest MLB city to Japan (it's a ten-hour flight to Tokyo, which isn't that bad) and has deep Japanese ties including a growing and merchandise-scarfing fan base.

Mariners Prospectus

2001 record: 116–46; First place, AL West; Lost to Yankees in Championship Series, 4–1

Pythagenport W/L: 110–52

Runs scored: 927 (first in AL)

Runs allowed: 627 (first in AL)

Team EqA: .286 (first in AL)

2001 batters age: 31.3 (oldest in AL)

2001 pitchers age: 30.3 (third-oldest in AL)

Ballpark: Safeco Field; excellent pitchers' park; Park Factor of .933

2001: Simply a dominant performance, regardless of the postseason outcome.

2002: Pitching, defense, and OBP will keep them in contention; the team's age is a source of concern.

Along with the other West Coast teams, the Mariners operate at an advantage recruiting out of Korea and China as well. But their Pacific focus doesn't stop there: the Mariners have also recruited heavily in Australia, producing a trio of solid prospects in Chris Snelling, Craig Anderson, and Travis Blackley.

The Mariners have poured an enormous amount of time and money into their Pacific Rim operations. Just as Gillick did in the Dominican a decade ago, he's created a player development pipeline outside the draft. The Mariners spent $1.3 million to sign Chinese outfielder Shin-Soo Choo out of high school, and he's displayed seven skills, albeit in rookie ball. That $1.3 million is less than the signing bonuses alone shelled out to 22 of 2001's first-round picks. The Devil Rays spent $4.2 million to sign pitcher Dewon Brazelton, and the Cubs spent $4 million on Mark Prior. Spending $13 million for Ichiro Suzuki, who was about the 30th-most valuable player in all of baseball in his rookie season, was a bargain move.

Teams that can find an untapped or underutilized source of players have an easier path to winning. The teams that broke the color barrier in the late 1940s got fine players at low cost. Today, the Astros aren't afraid to draft and develop right-handed pitchers under six feet tall, for instance, a plan that has yielded some great talent. There are few large talent pools that remain untapped, the most obvious one being women. As baseball works to increase its international scope, we can expect to see the teams at the forefront of smart player-development strategies continue to find success.

A side benefit of recruiting in Pacific Rim countries as opposed to Latin America is greater age certainty. Even within the Mariners system we can see examples of why it's risky to recruit out of Latin America and, in particular, the Dominican Republic (proclaimed in February of 1865, though it can produce documents placing its inception in 1983 if necessary). Rumors about Antonio Perez's age continue to dog him. Alquino Lopez put up good numbers pitching in the Texas League, but no one cares, because he's not his listed age of 20. Gustavo Martinez is likely older than 20, too.

Even if you could carbon-date guys before they sign, there's also the problem of stiff competition in Latin America; many teams having strong scouting programs there, and even the bad organizations pay attention. Finding kids in the Dominican who don't have an agent is nearly impossible without going door-to-door in small towns. By contrast, the Mariners' Pacific Rim scouting not only provides a talent and cost advantage, it also allows them to better project a prospect's future development.

International scouting takes on increased importance because baseball's free-agent compensation system, designed to help teams that lose players to other teams, requires the Mariners to give up a draft pick when they sign a player like Arthur Rhodes. The Mariners have signed a lot of free agents in the past couple of years and have been penalized by losing draft picks to needy teams such as the Yankees and Mets (for signing Jeff Nelson and John Olerud, respectively). The Mariners have used their remaining picks to select players who fall in the draft due to signability concerns. In 2000, their first pick came in the fourth round; they took and inked Sam Hays, who was regarded by some teams as unsignable. After Alex Rodriguez left, giving the M's a supplemental first-rounder in the 2001 draft, the M's took Michael Garciaparra, whose knee injury in the spring scared other teams away.

The result of this well-planned strategy has been that the Mariners fielded a competitive team built almost entirely from free agents and trades, while at the same time cultivating a farm system as chock-full of interesting prospects as any in baseball, with a huge crop of young talent in Double-A and A ball. The organization is also deep: the Mariners' Triple-A rotation could have supplied four back-of-the-rotation starters (Kevin Hodges, Rob Ramsay, Dennis Stark, and Jason Turman) in addition to Brett Tomko, who could have been a #3 starter for most teams.

The Mariners could make a smooth transition from their current roster to a homegrown one in 2003-2005. If they succeed, they will have fielded a competitive club every year for more than a decade, even if it didn't always turn out so well (as in 1998 and 1999). Pat Gillick, though, hasn't presided over any kind of youth movement in ages. Even in Toronto, he became Trader Pat, hyping his prospects before turning them into useful players for the major-league roster. Lou Piniella isn't known for his patience with young players, though he's certainly mellowed. Gillick's contract expires after next year; Piniella's runs through 2003. No one in the organization seems an obvious candidate for succession to either position, a situation that bears monitoring.

How the Mariners manage their roster this year will determine the team's fortunes for a long time to come. Extended contracts with free agents will block prospects who could contribute at far less cost, and that in turn could lead to the Mariners trading those prospects for older, more expensive talent. Additionally, trading off prospects recruited from the Pacific Rim could negate some of the Mariners' advantage: if prospects think they might end up in some hellhole like Tampa Bay, why should they favor the Mariners?

The Rangers are rich and are going to get much smarter, the A's are going to continue to be the A's, and the unbalanced schedule means the Mariners are going to face a brutal schedule for the foreseeable future. As the team makes a run for the pennant in 2002, they absolutely must keep an eye towards continuing competitiveness in order to ensure that the Mariners of 2005 don't resemble the Mariners of 1985.

Things didn't look this good for the Mariners a year ago. The Rangers had paid Alex Rodriguez a lot of money to leave Seattle—a move worth a projected swing of about 15 games between the division rivals—and the A's off-season maneuvers had made them the divisional favorite. The Red Sox and Yankees were expected to contend for the AL East with the runner-up taking the wild card. Both had payrolls approaching $110 million, more than $30 million above what the Mariners spent, and were viewed as having bought contenders. The Mariners, having traded or lost three Hall-of-Famers in 18 months, were labeled a team adrift.

The departure of Rodriguez was particularly traumatic because his leaving did not yield a bounty of new players. So the Mariners took stock of the team and filled a couple of holes. They signed the top two players on the "Least Likely to Play for Lou Piniella Again" list: Jeff Nelson, who frequently feuded with the "throw strikes, dammit!" version of Piniella, and Bret Boone, who Piniella had run out of town for refusing to shorten his swing or play hard. They picked up Ichiro, and they hoped a healthy Jamie Moyer would return to form.

It was reasonable to figure the Mariners would win 85 games. They hit that mark on August 12 and kept on winning. Boone was a different player than he'd been before, and Ichiro was a different player than anyone in this country under the age of 85 had seen before. Freddy Garcia improved, Moyer was better than ever, and the M's were lucky throughout the regular season.

For 162 games, the Mariners were the best team in baseball. They had the game's best offense, powered by Ichiro, plus an age-defying Edgar Martinez, an unheralded Mike Cameron, and unlikely performances from players such as Boone and Mark McLemore. The Mariners' lineup rarely included a player much below average for his position. Their starting rotation was sixth-best in the majors, and their bullpen was the AL's best by a wide margin.

Pundits like to say the Mariners won with speed, pitching, and defense, but in truth they were equally adept at pounding their opponents as they were at keeping opponents off the scoreboard. Their run differential was an eye-popping +300. The A's, with the second-best record in baseball, had a differential of +239. That's dominance.

None of this helped them in the playoffs, though. The lineup went dead, hitting a paltry .228/.359/.307 in the postseason. Every regular but Ichiro performed significantly worse than he had in the regular season. On the mound, only Jamie Moyer was effective as the pitching staff put too many runners on base, and the league's best defense botched plays that might have rescued the pitchers.

Did the Mariners fail to make moves that might have helped them extend their season? Only Gillick himself knows for certain if he could have made a deal to find another big hitter, be it Robin Ventura, Phil Nevin, or even Jermaine Dye. No one knows if those players would have hit well in the playoffs. The team made some strange decisions in October, such as starting Paul Abbott over Joel Piniero, and playing Mark McLemore at shortstop instead of Ramon Vazquez in the absence of the tuberculosis-stricken Carlos Guillen.

Still, it's doubtful that any of these decisions changed the final outcome of the Mariners' postseason run. The Indians gave them too much trouble, and the M's went up against the Yankees having to make rotation adjustments, having used Freddy Garcia twice against the Tribe. The result was the Yankees, suffering an offensive outage themselves, beat the Mariners in just five games, the last a 12-3 drubbing that ended the season. That ignoble end has quieted much of the talk about the Mariners having one of the greatest seasons ever, but their playoff defeat shouldn't overshadow what they accomplished.

Keith Woolner wrote a fine article that placed the 2001 Mariners as one of the five best teams of all time, as measured by value over replacement player (VORP). In fact, they're second behind only the 1927 Yankees, as Table 1 shows.

That trophy with all the little flags isn't given to the team with the best performance in the regular season, though, so the Mariners get to raise a third division pennant in April and make another run at the big prize. Baseball's all about winning the World Series, so there's no reason to criticize a team, such as the Diamondbacks or even the Marlins before them, that takes a shot at greatness, even at the expense of its future. The Mariners should be applauded, however, for potentially setting themselves up to turn over their roster while heading to the playoffs again and again.

Table 1.

Year	Team	League	VORP
1927	New York Yankees	AL	760.3
2001	Seattle Mariners	AL	703.4
1936	New York Yankees	AL	682.8
1939	New York Yankees	AL	680.7
1896	Baltimore Orioles	NL	680.1
1897	Baltimore Orioles	NL	674.4
1998	New York Yankees	AL	647.9
1898	Baltimore Orioles	NL	635.9
1948	Cleveland Indians	AL	634.3
1891	Boston Red Sox	AA	629.9

HITTERS (BA: .270, OBP: .340, SLG: .440, EqA: .260)

Manny Alexander 2B Bats R Age 31

YEAR	TEAM	LGE	AB	H	DB	TP	HR	BB	SO	R	RBI	SB	CS	OUT	BA	OBA	SLG	EQA	EQR	DEFENSE			
1999	ChiCubs	NL	178	48	12	2	0	7	35	16	14	3	0	130	.270	.297	.360	.224	15	18-SS	1	12-3B	-4
2000	Boston	AL	194	43	5	3	4	10	36	29	18	2	0	151	.222	.260	.340	.203	14	44-3B	-2	11-SS	2
2001	Tacoma	PCL	343	89	22	1	7	14	50	40	43	5	7	261	.259	.291	.391	.223	31	51-2B	-1	17-SS	-8
2002	*NY Yanks*	*AL*	*299*	*75*	*15*	*2*	*7*	*19*	*50*	*35*	*30*	*3*	*4*	*228*	*.251*	*.296*	*.385*	*.228*	*28*				

You could close this book right now, throw it out the nearest window, and hit another all-glove, no-hit Triple-A infielder. Criminal charges related to steroids found in Alexander's car in Boston never materialized. He didn't suddenly start hitting for power and have a career year, so we can assume if the chemicals were his, he gave up on them.

David Bell 3B Bats R Age 29

YEAR	TEAM	LGE	AB	H	DB	TP	HR	BB	SO	R	RBI	SB	CS	OUT	BA	OBA	SLG	EQA	EQR	DEFENSE			
1999	Seattle	AL	592	163	32	2	22	53	79	91	76	7	4	433	.275	.337	.448	.260	75	148-2B	-10		
2000	Seattle	AL	455	121	26	2	12	37	58	58	48	2	3	337	.266	.330	.411	.247	51	78-3B	3	39-2B	-1
2001	Seattle	AL	475	135	23	0	20	30	51	69	72	2	1	341	.284	.330	.459	.260	59	123-3B	19		
2002	*Seattle*	*AL*	*542*	*153*	*26*	*1*	*23*	*51*	*68*	*81*	*72*	*3*	*3*	*392*	*.282*	*.344*	*.461*	*.276*	*78*				

Bell looks like the generic actors who take the field in commercials that feature baseball. His performance is equally forgettable, good with the glove and slightly below-average for his position with the bat. Players like David Bell are good to have in the organization, because when your team can't trade for Phil Nevin or Robin Ventura, you're still getting a positive contribution, and you're not forced to give 500 at-bats to Shea Hillenbrand. With the Mariners' off-season trade for Jeff Cirillo, Bell no longer has a place in Seattle. He accepted the team's arbitration offer, though, putting the Mariners in an awkward situation.

Willie Bloomquist 2B Bats R Age 24

YEAR	TEAM	LGE	AB	H	DB	TP	HR	BB	SO	R	RBI	SB	CS	OUT	BA	OBA	SLG	EQA	EQR	DEFENSE
1999	Everett	Nwn	177	34	7	1	1	11	29	16	13	6	3	146	.192	.241	.260	.177	10	34-2B -5
2000	Lancastr	Cal	250	71	17	2	1	22	27	38	28	9	6	185	.284	.342	.380	.244	27	49-2B -2 11-SS -1
2000	Tacoma	PCL	192	42	4	1	1	4	27	14	20	4	0	150	.219	.235	.266	.175	10	50-2B 1
2001	SanAnton	Tex	497	115	15	2	1	23	55	47	23	24	8	389	.231	.266	.276	.193	32	69-SS 0 49-2B 2
2002	*Seattle*	*AL*	*492*	*122*	*19*	*3*	*3*	*35*	*61*	*55*	*42*	*19*	*7*	*377*	*.248*	*.298*	*.317*	*.219*	*43*	

You can't spell Bloomquist without "bust." Scouts like to talk about his makeup and how he does the things that don't show up in box scores... and they don't mean his failure to hit. His ability to do all the little things the team likes, from hustling to bunting, means he may well get a chance to hit a hollow .270 and stick with the M's for two or three painful years. But hey, he looks great in uniform, and his midriff? Stunning. You can't teach that.

Bret Boone 2B Bats R Age 33

YEAR	TEAM	LGE	AB	H	DB	TP	HR	BB	SO	R	RBI	SB	CS	OUT	BA	OBA	SLG	EQA	EQR	DEFENSE
1999	Atlanta	NL	612	154	32	1	22	39	104	98	61	12	9	467	.252	.302	.415	.236	63	146-2B -1
2000	San Dieg	NL	471	123	20	2	20	44	89	62	75	7	4	352	.261	.330	.439	.255	58	123-2B -5
2001	Seattle	AL	633	227	38	3	43	43	95	131	154	4	6	412	.359	.405	.632	.327	126	152-2B 13
2002	*Seattle*	*AL*	*586*	*165*	*26*	*2*	*35*	*54*	*101*	*106*	*93*	*8*	*6*	*427*	*.282*	*.342*	*.512*	*.287*	*94*	

At age 32, Boone suddenly started hitting for huge power and had a career year, one of the best seasons in recent memory by a second baseman. He showed up at camp heavier and more powerful after what must have been a hellacious winter weight-training program.

His season was a fluke, though. Boone hit .444/.497/.715 against left-handed pitchers last year, wildly out of line with his career performance. From 1998 through 2000 he hit .251/.317/.406 against southpaws, making his 2001 totals 489 points of OPS goodness better, nearly four times the improvement he made against right-handers. Against all pitchers, Boone still hacks at high pitches out of the strike zone and isn't patient at the plate. He won't be worth the $8–9 million per season over four years he tried to get in free agency. The strength and the power will persist, though, so that 2002 projection is accurate. Boone accepted arbitration after contentious negotiations with the Mariners produced no agreement on a multi-year contract.

Jay Buhner DH/RF Bats R Age 37

YEAR	TEAM	LGE	AB	H	DB	TP	HR	BB	SO	R	RBI	SB	CS	OUT	BA	OBA	SLG	EQA	EQR	DEFENSE
1999	Seattle	AL	262	60	10	0	15	66	88	36	37	0	0	202	.229	.392	.439	.284	44	66-RF -4
2000	Seattle	AL	364	99	19	0	29	55	86	50	84	0	2	267	.272	.374	.563	.299	65	85-RF -3
2001	Seattle	AL	46	11	1	0	3	8	8	4	6	0	0	35	.239	.352	.457	.270	7	

Bone spent the year rehabbing a bum left foot. His timing was off when he returned, but he could still take a walk with his patented "swing at two, look at four" technique. One of the most generous and good-natured players in the sport, Buhner is the kind of guy who'll conduct charity auctions when he hears of tragedy befalling people he barely knows, or go shopping wearing a Mariners cap and sign autographs for kids as he tries to buy linens or a coffee. After two years of pain, he retired in December.

Mike Cameron CF Bats R Age 29

YEAR	TEAM	LGE	AB	H	DB	TP	HR	BB	SO	R	RBI	SB	CS	OUT	BA	OBA	SLG	EQA	EQR	DEFENSE
1999	Cincnnti	NL	541	135	32	8	21	73	134	87	61	32	12	418	.250	.345	.455	.268	78	144-CF 2
2000	Seattle	AL	543	157	29	4	22	72	117	97	81	25	8	394	.289	.382	.479	.289	89	148-CF 5
2001	Seattle	AL	548	162	33	4	30	72	134	109	122	33	6	392	.296	.385	.535	.305	101	147-CF 11
2002	*Seattle*	*AL*	*498*	*135*	*28*	*4*	*24*	*73*	*125*	*87*	*71*	*23*	*7*	*370*	*.271*	*.364*	*.488*	*.295*	*87*	

We told you last year's projection was way low, and that Cameron would continue to improve as he learns from Edgar Martinez. Identifiable by his slightly askew hat, Cameron is an elite two-way center fielder, the best outfielder on the team, and the Mariner most likely to pie Boone's face during postgame interviews. He was fed a diet of wicked breaking stuff in the ALCS and didn't do much with it. He's likely taking batting practice right now, working to ensure that it never happens again. Or he's playing Sega.

Ryan Christianson C Bats R Age 21

YEAR	TEAM	LGE	AB	H	DB	TP	HR	BB	SO	R	RBI	SB	CS	OUT	BA	OBA	SLG	EQA	EQR	DEFENSE
1999	Everett	Nwn	106	21	3	0	4	8	36	9	8	1	1	86	.198	.261	.340	.202	8	12-C -5
2000	Wisconsn	Mid	433	88	11	1	10	31	108	44	40	0	4	349	.203	.259	.303	.190	28	94-C -5
2001	San Bern	Cal	538	111	30	3	9	40	107	49	60	2	1	428	.206	.264	.323	.200	38	109-C 0
2002	*Seattle*	*AL*	*519*	*116*	*25*	*2*	*15*	*53*	*120*	*56*	*48*	*2*	*3*	*406*	*.224*	*.295*	*.366*	*.229*	*51*	

The translation doesn't look all that great, but Christianson did show plate discipline and hit 42 doubles, which is a good indicator of future power. He'll start to put the package together next year. He's played a lot for a young catcher, which means he's either durable or an injury risk, depending on your bent.

Jermaine Clark 2B Bats L Age 25

YEAR	TEAM	LGE	AB	H	DB	TP	HR	BB	SO	R	RBI	SB	CS	OUT	BA	OBA	SLG	EQA	EQR	DEFENSE
1999	Lancastr	Cal	489	113	20	3	4	38	81	66	35	16	8	384	.231	.288	.309	.207	38	119-2B 3
2000	New Havn	Eas	460	122	24	6	2	70	71	64	35	25	7	345	.265	.372	.357	.260	59	127-2B 1
2001	Tacoma	PCL	218	52	7	2	1	24	35	31	23	11	2	168	.239	.320	.303	.225	20	65-2B 0
2002	*Seattle*	*AL*	*394*	*101*	*18*	*4*	*3*	*52*	*67*	*61*	*33*	*19*	*5*	*298*	*.256*	*.343*	*.345*	*.253*	*48*	

As punishment for making organizational teacher's pet Bloomquist look bad last year, Clark was left unprotected by the Mariners in the Rule 5 draft and didn't shed a tear when he was picked. Later, the Tigers offered Clark back during a roster crunch, and the M's were reluctant to pony up the token cash. He was injured this year, so add "fragile" to the inexplicably bad scouting reports filed on Clark. While his upside isn't tremendous, at worst he'd be a league-average second baseman with a decent glove, much better than what ten teams field.

Charles Gipson UT Bats R Age 29

YEAR	TEAM	LGE	AB	H	DB	TP	HR	BB	SO	R	RBI	SB	CS	OUT	BA	OBA	SLG	EQA	EQR	DEFENSE
1999	Tacoma	PCL	173	47	7	2	0	12	22	21	17	13	3	129	.272	.326	.335	.236	18	21-SS -9 14-CF 1
1999	Seattle	AL	80	19	5	2	0	5	11	16	9	3	4	65	.237	.290	.350	.210	7	17-3B 5 11-OF 1
2000	Tacoma	PCL	216	50	6	5	1	25	37	22	18	12	6	172	.231	.318	.319	.224	20	38-CF 4 13-3B 7
2000	Seattle	AL	29	9	1	1	0	4	8	7	3	2	3	23	.310	.394	.414	.255	4	
2001	Seattle	AL	65	16	3	2	0	4	17	15	6	1	1	50	.246	.305	.354	.222	6	14-LF 3
2002	*Seattle*	*AL*	*227*	*53*	*7*	*5*	*1*	*22*	*46*	*35*	*20*	*8*	*6*	*180*	*.233*	*.301*	*.322*	*.219*	*20*	

Early in life, Gipson was offered a Faustian deal: excel in three tools at the cost of two. He took the deal, but instead of power, average, and fielding, he got running, throwing, fielding, and a laughing djin. He's good enough at enough positions to justify the roster spot.

Carlos Guillen SS Bats B Age 26

YEAR	TEAM	LGE	AB	H	DB	TP	HR	BB	SO	R	RBI	SB	CS	OUT	BA	OBA	SLG	EQA	EQR	DEFENSE
2000	Tacoma	PCL	87	24	3	1	2	10	16	16	9	3	1	64	.276	.355	.402	.260	11	13-3B -1
2000	Seattle	AL	289	80	17	2	8	25	47	46	43	1	3	212	.277	.339	.433	.254	35	68-3B -7 17-SS -2
2001	Seattle	AL	462	132	24	4	6	56	77	81	58	4	1	331	.286	.364	.394	.260	57	124-SS 6
2002	*Seattle*	*AL*	*421*	*120*	*22*	*3*	*9*	*58*	*75*	*66*	*58*	*4*	*2*	*303*	*.285*	*.372*	*.416*	*.279*	*62*	

Piniella never liked Guillen, though he managed to keep from trashing him openly while trying to push the team to find a different replacement for Alex Rodriguez. That's all changed now that he knows Guillen played much of last season with tuberculosis, which cost Guillen strength, weight, and playoff time. Piniella has a thing for guys who play through flu, illnesses, and broken bones; in camp this spring, don't be surprised if borderline prospects are bolting on fake neck braces, casts, and splints. Guillen can now expect every chance to succeed, which is what it looks like he'll do.

Stan Javier OF Bats B Age 38

YEAR	TEAM	LGE	AB	H	DB	TP	HR	BB	SO	R	RBI	SB	CS	OUT	BA	OBA	SLG	EQA	EQR	DEFENSE
1999	San Fran	NL	336	94	16	1	3	26	51	48	29	11	6	248	.280	.333	.360	.237	34	76-LF -1
1999	Houston	NL	64	21	3	1	0	9	7	12	4	3	1	44	.328	.411	.406	.286	10	16-OF 0
2000	Seattle	AL	342	100	18	5	6	39	56	61	40	4	3	245	.292	.365	.427	.267	45	72-OF -3
2001	Seattle	AL	286	92	15	1	5	37	41	49	37	11	1	195	.322	.402	.434	.291	45	59-LF 2

(Stan Javier *continued*)

Used as a fourth outfielder, Javier made Ichiro and Cameron look good and Al Martin look worse, to the point of costing Martin his job. Over 17 seasons, eight teams, and two World Series, Javier had a career that, while not spectacular, certainly demands respect. He's going to return to his native Dominican Republic and attempt to replant destroyed forests, which also merits respect.

Kenny Kelly OF Bats R Age 23

YEAR	TEAM	LGE	AB	H	DB	TP	HR	BB	SO	R	RBI	SB	CS	OUT	BA	OBA	SLG	EQA	EQR	DEFENSE
1999	St Pete	Fla	208	48	8	2	3	13	52	28	15	8	3	163	.231	.282	.332	.212	17	51-CF 1
2000	Orlando	Sou	507	118	17	6	3	43	118	64	25	20	14	403	.233	.297	.308	.209	40	124-CF -2
2001	SanAnton	Tex	487	113	16	3	10	37	112	59	37	12	9	383	.232	.288	.339	.213	40	120-CF -8
2002	*Seattle*	*AL*	*466*	*113*	*17*	*4*	*8*	*47*	*114*	*63*	*32*	*13*	*9*	*362*	*.242*	*.312*	*.348*	*.232*	*47*	

Kelly is a natural athlete slowly rounding into a baseball player. Remember that he was the University of Miami's quarterback prior to Ken Dorsey and has only been a full-time baseball player for two years. After buying him away from the gridiron, the Devil Rays gave up on him last spring. Kelly signed with the Mariners, finished the season smoking hot, and was arguably the second-best player in the Arizona Fall League behind Hank Blalock. He still needs work on what is a long swing, so his ETA is mid-2003.

Eugene Kingsale CF Bats B Age 25

YEAR	TEAM	LGE	AB	H	DB	TP	HR	BB	SO	R	RBI	SB	CS	OUT	BA	OBA	SLG	EQA	EQR	DEFENSE
1999	Bowie	Eas	273	56	11	3	2	24	46	34	18	8	6	224	.205	.271	.289	.194	19	67-CF 1
1999	Rochestr	Int	190	54	3	0	3	10	22	25	17	8	8	144	.284	.327	.347	.226	17	47-CF 0
1999	Baltimor	AL	85	23	2	0	0	4	11	9	7	1	3	65	.271	.317	.294	.205	6	21-CF -1
2000	Baltimor	AL	88	23	2	1	0	1	12	13	9	1	2	67	.261	.270	.307	.190	5	24-CF -1
2001	Rochestr	Int	247	50	12	2	0	25	41	30	15	13	2	199	.202	.279	.267	.201	18	57-OF -2
2001	Tacoma	PCL	214	58	11	3	3	9	23	26	21	11	4	159	.271	.306	.393	.237	22	51-CF 2
2002	*Seattle*	*AL*	*472*	*125*	*18*	*4*	*7*	*44*	*71*	*75*	*46*	*2*	*2*	*349*	*.265*	*.328*	*.364*	*.243*	*51*	

Syd Thrift's rejuvenation of the Orioles farm system produced too many middling outfield prospects, so they had to try and sneak Kingsale out on waivers, and the M's snagged him. After being injured for much of 2000, Kingsale didn't look as bad as he has in the past. He does play a respectable center field, so his upside is as a defensive replacement, although not for the Mariners.

Craig Kuzmic 2B Bats B Age 25

YEAR	TEAM	LGE	AB	H	DB	TP	HR	BB	SO	R	RBI	SB	CS	OUT	BA	OBA	SLG	EQA	EQR	DEFENSE
1999	Wisconsn	Mid	333	61	10	1	7	41	92	31	34	3	2	274	.183	.275	.282	.196	23	44-3B 0 23-LF -5
1999	Lancastr	Cal	108	16	2	0	3	14	44	12	8	2	1	93	.148	.249	.250	.179	6	13-C -2
2000	Lancastr	Cal	518	116	18	4	14	43	125	68	60	2	4	406	.224	.290	.355	.217	44	78-1B -3 25-2B 2
2001	SanAnton	Tex	492	124	27	3	13	55	134	67	73	5	3	371	.252	.331	.398	.246	56	83-2B -10 38-3B -3
2002	*Seattle*	*AL*	*451*	*107*	*21*	*3*	*14*	*55*	*128*	*60*	*60*	*4*	*3*	*347*	*.237*	*.320*	*.390*	*.248*	*53*	

Kuzmic switch-hits and can play every position passably except shortstop and center field, including catcher. This means he offers enormous value and flexibility to a manager who likes to use his utility players and play a lot of matchup games. Unlike Kingsale, Kuzmic is in the right organization for an opportunity.

Tom Lampkin C Bats L Age 38

YEAR	TEAM	LGE	AB	H	DB	TP	HR	BB	SO	R	RBI	SB	CS	OUT	BA	OBA	SLG	EQA	EQR	DEFENSE
1999	Seattle	AL	205	61	10	2	10	11	28	29	34	1	3	147	.298	.347	.512	.275	29	48-C 5
2000	Seattle	AL	103	28	5	1	8	8	15	15	23	0	0	75	.272	.343	.573	.291	17	24-C 0
2001	Seattle	AL	206	52	9	0	7	19	35	31	26	1	0	154	.252	.331	.398	.247	23	57-C 1
2002	*San Dieg*	*NL*	*208*	*46*	*9*	*1*	*8*	*20*	*36*	*25*	*26*	*1*	*1*	*163*	*.221*	*.289*	*.389*	*.235*	*22*	

Lampkin hits left-handed and is fair defensively, so he has some value. He's over 70 in catcher years, though, and he's not going to get healthier. Using him as part of the package for Ben Davis was a good move. Lampkin will platoon with Wiki Gonzalez in San Diego, making for a fairly inexpensive and effective catching platoon.

Al Martin LF Bats L Age 34

YEAR	TEAM	LGE	AB	H	DB	TP	HR	BB	SO	R	RBI	SB	CS	OUT	BA	OBA	SLG	EQA	EQR	DEFENSE
1999	Pittsbrg	NL	542	148	34	7	25	43	110	93	60	17	3	397	.273	.328	.500	.272	77	123-LF -12
2000	San Dieg	NL	352	110	15	6	11	24	50	62	27	5	8	250	.313	.359	.483	.272	48	74-LF -7
2000	Seattle	AL	135	34	1	4	5	6	27	19	10	4	1	102	.252	.294	.430	.241	14	33-LF 1
2001	Seattle	AL	287	77	17	2	8	38	51	45	46	8	3	213	.268	.357	.425	.265	39	61-LF 0
2002	*Seattle*	*AL*	*443*	*109*	*19*	*5*	*15*	*50*	*83*	*68*	*41*	*10*	*4*	*338*	*.246*	*.323*	*.413*	*.257*	*57*	

When Al Martin was arrested in Scottsdale in 1999 for getting into a tussle with his backup wife, the 32-year-old outfielder told police that he and 21-year-old Shawn Haggerty-Martin had been "going out" for six years, which means their star-crossed romance began when Martin was 26 and his eventual backup wife was 15. Hopefully, he made that up. Last year, Martin was lying about attending USC on a football scholarship, playing safety there, never playing baseball before signing with the Braves, and being acquitted of beating his backup wife, all stories as devoid of value as Martin himself. A free agent, it's possible that his career is over.

Edgar Martinez DH Bats R Age 39

YEAR	TEAM	LGE	AB	H	DB	TP	HR	BB	SO	R	RBI	SB	CS	OUT	BA	OBA	SLG	EQA	EQR	DEFENSE
1999	Seattle	AL	493	171	29	1	27	91	87	83	84	7	2	324	.347	.454	.574	.339	109	
2000	Seattle	AL	554	192	27	0	42	90	84	100	148	3	0	362	.347	.442	.623	.344	126	
2001	Seattle	AL	480	163	36	2	29	97	78	89	131	4	1	318	.340	.457	.604	.346	112	
2002	*Seattle*	*AL*	*494*	*138*	*25*	*1*	*28*	*92*	*85*	*77*	*91*	*5*	*1*	*357*	*.279*	*.392*	*.504*	*.309*	*95*	

Martinez should be the first designated hitter elected to the Hall of Fame. His career is a study in consistent hitting excellence: he's a seven-time All-Star; his batting average of .319 is 51st all-time; his on-base percentage of .425 is 12th all-time; his slugging percentage of .530 is 41st all-time. This year he'll pass 2,000 hits to go with his more than 1,000 RBI, 1,000 walks, and 3,000 total bases. Though he's spent the vast majority of his career as a designated hitter, he is one of the best hitters ever, and his contributions would guarantee his selection were it not for the deep uncertainty about whether a player who doesn't take the field should be recognized with the game's highest honor.

Mark McLemore UT Bats B Age 37

YEAR	TEAM	LGE	AB	H	DB	TP	HR	BB	SO	R	RBI	SB	CS	OUT	BA	OBA	SLG	EQA	EQR	DEFENSE
1999	Texas	AL	558	155	21	7	6	77	69	101	43	15	8	411	.278	.365	.373	.255	68	133-2B 4
2000	Seattle	AL	481	128	24	1	4	76	69	72	48	31	16	369	.266	.367	.345	.251	58	123-2B 2 12-LF 0
2001	Seattle	AL	416	135	20	10	6	72	73	86	64	38	8	289	.325	.424	.464	.309	77	40-LF -1 29-3B -2
2002	*Seattle*	*AL*	*473*	*112*	*19*	*5*	*6*	*76*	*78*	*83*	*39*	*29*	*10*	*371*	*.237*	*.342*	*.336*	*.251*	*58*	

Piniella used McLemore to rest everyone else in the lineup, playing him at every fielding position but catcher and first base. His defense was average on the corners and bad up the middle, but he had a career year with the bat, a performance that was critical to the Mariners' league-best offense. He won't come close to that output again.

John Olerud 1B Bats L Age 33

YEAR	TEAM	LGE	AB	H	DB	TP	HR	BB	SO	R	RBI	SB	CS	OUT	BA	OBA	SLG	EQA	EQR	DEFENSE
1999	NY Mets	NL	585	175	29	0	23	118	61	106	96	3	0	410	.299	.426	.467	.306	106	153-1B 12
2000	Seattle	AL	564	172	35	0	20	96	84	83	109	0	2	394	.305	.410	.473	.298	95	152-1B 19
2001	Seattle	AL	583	194	28	2	26	98	60	101	106	3	1	390	.333	.432	.521	.319	112	149-1B 4
2002	*Seattle*	*AL*	*578*	*164*	*26*	*1*	*25*	*100*	*71*	*94*	*100*	*2*	*1*	*415*	*.284*	*.389*	*.462*	*.298*	*101*	

Olerud is part of a class of unheralded players who have control of the strike zone, some power, and who play good defense but are not regarded as team leaders despite being quite valuable to a championship drive. He's never been the best at his position, but he pushes his teams towards pennants year after year.

Antonio Perez SS Bats R Age 20

YEAR	TEAM	LGE	AB	H	DB	TP	HR	BB	SO	R	RBI	SB	CS	OUT	BA	OBA	SLG	EQA	EQR	DEFENSE
1999	Rockford	Mid	390	85	15	1	5	26	87	41	25	16	13	318	.218	.278	.300	.199	28	54-SS -12 53-2B -12
2000	Lancastr	Cal	394	83	25	2	11	36	100	54	35	12	9	319	.211	.283	.368	.219	36	92-SS -2
2001	SanAnton	Tex	21	3	0	0	0	0	7	1	0	0	0	18	.143	.143	.143	.097	0	
2002	*Seattle*	*AL*	*348*	*80*	*20*	*2*	*9*	*34*	*92*	*53*	*29*	*16*	*11*	*279*	*.230*	*.298*	*.376*	*.234*	*37*	

(Antonio Perez *continued*)

Perez came to spring training out of shape, then promptly broke his hand and was shut down for the season. Don't believe the hype: Perez is older than listed, and there's no evidence he'll become more than a good, but unremarkable, player.

Chris Snelling LF Bats L Age 20

YEAR	TEAM	LGE	AB	H	DB	TP	HR	BB	SO	R	RBI	SB	CS	OUT	BA	OBA	SLG	EQA	EQR	DEFENSE
1999	Everett	Nwn	262	54	9	1	5	17	28	23	23	3	4	212	.206	.260	.305	.192	17	69-CF 0
2000	Wisconsn	Mid	268	66	6	3	7	22	38	31	37	3	3	205	.246	.310	.369	.228	26	66-CF -7
2001	San Bern	Cal	458	127	24	5	6	33	60	66	52	6	4	335	.277	.339	.391	.247	51	106-LF -1
2002	*Seattle*	*AL*	*426*	*119*	*19*	*4*	*10*	*38*	*59*	*54*	*54*	*8*	*4*	*311*	*.279*	*.338*	*.413*	*.263*	*55*	

The Force is strong with this one. A legitimate five-talent prospect, Snelling hits for average and power, has decent plate discipline, surfs, and is a hawk in the thrift stores. One of the youngest players in the California League, Snelling was also the circuit's second-best hitter. Slow to start, he came on strong to win the league batting title. Snelling played on a broken foot for the last couple weeks of the season, another of the minor injuries he's suffered. He's constantly compared to Lenny Dykstra for his hard-nosed play, though Dykstra never hit for the kind of power Snelling already displays.

The only reason Snelling isn't widely regarded as one of the best prospects in baseball is that he stands 5′9″, and there's a ridiculous "you must be this high to ride the hype machine" requirement.

Ed Sprague 1B Bats R Age 34

YEAR	TEAM	LGE	AB	H	DB	TP	HR	BB	SO	R	RBI	SB	CS	OUT	BA	OBA	SLG	EQA	EQR	DEFENSE
1999	Pittsbrg	NL	491	129	25	2	22	44	86	68	76	2	6	368	.263	.344	.456	.262	65	131-3B -20
2000	San Dieg	NL	160	43	11	0	11	11	37	19	27	0	0	117	.269	.326	.544	.278	24	22-1B -7
2000	Boston	AL	110	25	4	0	2	11	16	11	9	0	0	85	.227	.298	.318	.212	9	26-3B 1
2001	Seattle	AL	96	32	5	0	3	11	16	10	18	0	0	64	.333	.406	.479	.298	16	
2002	*Seattle*	*AL*	*380*	*94*	*17*	*1*	*17*	*43*	*74*	*47*	*54*	*1*	*2*	*288*	*.247*	*.324*	*.432*	*.260*	*49*	

After the Padres dumped him (again) in March, Sprague spent two months playing Perfect Dark before the M's called. His eye-hand coordination thus honed, Sprague swung a hot bat initially. Because the team already had a pretty good DH, Piniella had to try to hide Sprague on the field. At third base, he was terrible; at first base, wretched; in left field, a failure; and he was too big to hide under the resin bag, so his playing time suffered.

Jamal Strong CF Bats R Age 23

YEAR	TEAM	LGE	AB	H	DB	TP	HR	BB	SO	R	RBI	SB	CS	OUT	BA	OBA	SLG	EQA	EQR	DEFENSE
2000	Everett	Nwn	306	73	4	2	1	31	31	34	17	25	10	242	.239	.312	.275	.215	26	74-CF 2
2001	Wisconsn	Mid	194	53	8	1	0	29	30	25	13	16	4	145	.273	.374	.325	.256	24	46-CF -5
2001	San Bern	Cal	340	86	8	2	0	39	57	49	24	25	7	261	.253	.334	.288	.228	33	81-CF -2
2002	*Seattle*	*AL*	*488*	*128*	*16*	*2*	*2*	*60*	*77*	*60*	*37*	*33*	*10*	*370*	*.262*	*.343*	*.316*	*.246*	*56*	

Jamal Strong is a smarter, more personable version of Brian L. Hunter. One of the fastest players in baseball, Strong doesn't have any power but is a great base stealer, like Hunter. Strong, however, maximizes that one skill by drawing walks. Double-A is going to be particularly hard on Strong as he faces pitchers with better stuff who give up fewer freebies. The worst-case scenario is that by 2003 Strong will be an interesting spare-outfielder option for steal-obsessed Piniella. The best-case scenario is that he'll be an outstanding leadoff hitter.

Ichiro Suzuki RF Bats L Age 28

YEAR	TEAM	LGE	AB	H	DB	TP	HR	BB	SO	R	RBI	SB	CS	OUT	BA	OBA	SLG	EQA	EQR	DEFENSE
1999	Orix	JpP	417	144	28	2	22	40	43	84	68	11	1	274	.345	.411	.580	.324	82	
2000	Orix	JpP	395	155	21	1	13	44	34	62	61	20	1	241	.392	.458	.549	.343	83	
2001	Seattle	AL	703	270	37	8	10	34	46	139	75	55	16	449	.384	.417	.502	.311	121	144-RF 3
2002	*Seattle*	*AL*	*627*	*227*	*34*	*5*	*18*	*59*	*49*	*113*	*84*	*38*	*11*	*411*	*.362*	*.417*	*.518*	*.325*	*124*	

Along with Vladimir Guerrero, Cliff Floyd, and Chipper Jones, Ichiro is hugely productive despite not seeing many pitches: these guys swing at and hit the first good pitch they see. Jones somehow managed to walk nearly 100 times, but the others weren't even close.

Ichiro is one of the best reasons in baseball to buy a ticket. While he's not as productive as some other players—and was a lousy MVP selection—Ichiro's crazy bat artwork, base-stealing, and his sometimes brilliant defense all combine to make him an entertainment bargain.

Juan Thomas DH Bats R Age 30

YEAR	TEAM	LGE	AB	H	DB	TP	HR	BB	SO	R	RBI	SB	CS	OUT	BA	OBA	SLG	EQA	EQR	DEFENSE
1999	New Havn	Eas	270	60	11	0	13	9	92	39	40	0	0	210	.222	.256	.407	.217	23	14-1B -1
2000	New Havn	Eas	503	126	22	2	23	33	132	54	77	3	0	377	.250	.303	.439	.245	56	27-1B -3
2001	Tacoma	PCL	504	141	32	2	20	38	128	66	82	2	2	365	.280	.332	.470	.263	65	25-1B 1
2002	*Seattle*	*AL*	*473*	*122*	*25*	*2*	*17*	*40*	*132*	*68*	*67*	*2*	*1*	*352*	*.258*	*.316*	*.427*	*.256*	*58*	

Juan Thomas in left field wouldn't have done much for the Mariners, but boy, would it have been entertaining. "Large Human" hits towering, jaw-dropping blasts. Baseball is entertainment, after all; if we're going to watch an outfielder who can't play defense, why not have it be a hustling, underpaid, crowd-pleasing man of the people instead of Al Martin?

Ramon Vazquez SS Bats L Age 25

YEAR	TEAM	LGE	AB	H	DB	TP	HR	BB	SO	R	RBI	SB	CS	OUT	BA	OBA	SLG	EQA	EQR	DEFENSE	
1999	New Havn	Eas	448	105	24	2	4	46	77	48	36	5	1	344	.234	.310	.324	.220	39	67-SS -1	41-3B -2
2000	New Havn	Eas	414	105	22	2	8	40	78	49	47	1	4	313	.254	.321	.374	.233	41	123-SS 4	
2001	Tacoma	PCL	472	131	23	1	9	68	76	75	69	8	6	347	.278	.369	.388	.259	60	126-SS 14	
2001	Seattle	AL	35	9	0	0	0	0	3	4	4	0	0	26	.257	.257	.257	.174	2		
2002	*San Dieg*	*NL*	*485*	*133*	*27*	*2*	*9*	*61*	*88*	*65*	*54*	*7*	*4*	*356*	*.274*	*.355*	*.394*	*.266*	*65*		

Vazquez put up good numbers in Triple-A, improving both his power and plate discipline. He continued to play good defense, although he rushes throws from shortstop, sometimes before he's entirely planted, at the cost of accuracy. He'd be a natural at second base, and if he can get on Boone's weight-training program, look out. Traded to the Padres in the Davis deal, he should combine with D'Angelo Jimenez to form a great young double-play combination.

Dan Wilson C Bats R Age 33

YEAR	TEAM	LGE	AB	H	DB	TP	HR	BB	SO	R	RBI	SB	CS	OUT	BA	OBA	SLG	EQA	EQR	DEFENSE
1999	Seattle	AL	412	113	23	2	8	25	73	46	38	5	0	299	.274	.319	.398	.242	43	113-C -5
2000	Seattle	AL	269	69	8	0	7	19	45	31	29	1	2	202	.257	.306	.364	.224	24	75-C 3
2001	Seattle	AL	381	111	20	1	12	22	60	49	46	3	2	272	.291	.333	.444	.257	45	104-C 3
2002	*Seattle*	*AL*	*381*	*98*	*15*	*1*	*12*	*33*	*66*	*45*	*39*	*3*	*2*	*285*	*.257*	*.316*	*.396*	*.248*	*43*	

Early in the season, especially against pitchers with good heat or movement, Wilson appeared lost and scared at the plate, as if he wasn't sure what he wasn't supposed to be doing. He came around as the season wore on, eventually putting up his best numbers in years, which made him an average catcher. His defensive reputation far exceeds his performance and has for years. Watch how frequently good pitchers, such as Jamie Moyer, shake him off.

PITCHERS (ERA: 4.50, H/9: 9.0, HR/9: 1.0, BB/9: 3.0, K/9: 6.0, KW: 2.0, PERA: 4.50)

Paul Abbott Throws R Age 34

YEAR	TEAM	LGE	IP	H	ER	HR	BB	K	ERA	W	L	H/9	HR/9	BB/9	K/9	KW	PERA	STUFF
1999	Seattle	AL	69.7	62	32	8	27	67	4.13	4	4	8.0	1.0	3.5	8.7	1.2	3.22	17
2000	Seattle	AL	175.7	184	97	21	65	99	4.97	9	11	9.4	1.1	3.3	5.1	0.8	4.03	0
2001	Seattle	AL	160.3	160	95	20	83	112	5.33	7	11	9.0	1.1	4.7	6.3	0.7	4.30	4

He's injured. His release points and mechanics were all over the place last season, and as a result, the wheels would fly off, and he never seemed to have easy outings. Maybe it's a torn rotator cuff, a strained tendon . . . it doesn't matter. The Mariners, if they're smart and ruthless, will hurry and sign him and his 17-4 record to a contract to avoid arbitration and then immediately trade him to someone who doesn't do his medical homework, like Gord Ash . . . shoot, too late.

Ryan Anderson Throws L Age 22

YEAR	TEAM	LGE	IP	H	ER	HR	BB	K	ERA	W	L	H/9	HR/9	BB/9	K/9	KW	PERA	STUFF
1999	New Havn	Eas	138.7	128	77	13	87	114	5.00	7	8	8.3	0.8	5.6	7.4	0.7	6.04	22
2000	Tacoma	PCL	105.3	85	46	10	52	117	3.93	7	5	7.3	0.9	4.4	10.0	1.1	4.56	42

Last year, we made an exception to our "no pitcher can be the best prospect in baseball because they're too risky" rule. Like people who ignored financial fundamentals so they could turn little Billy's college fund into Yahoo! stock, it turns out we weren't so wise.

While pitching injuries aren't the death sentence they used to be, a torn labrum is bad news. Anderson will be treated gingerly on his long road to recovery. We're not going to know if he'll be the same pitcher until 2003, when hopefully he'll have avoided injury for a year.

Norm Charlton Throws L Age 39

YEAR	TEAM	LGE	IP	H	ER	HR	BB	K	ERA	W	L	H/9	HR/9	BB/9	K/9	KW	PERA	STUFF
1999	Durham	Int	29.7	35	25	8	11	21	7.58	1	2	10.6	2.4	3.3	6.4	1.0	3.98	-20
1999	TampaBay	AL	52.7	47	25	3	30	45	4.27	3	3	8.0	0.5	5.1	7.7	0.8	4.39	2
2001	Seattle	AL	47.0	40	16	4	10	46	3.06	3	2	7.7	0.8	1.9	8.8	2.3	3.54	19

There's a point in every horror series where after the monster has been burned, buried, run off cliffs, and tossed into vats of molten steel, he comes back as the hero. The reform of Norm Norm by Bryan Price was greeted with great gnashing and wailing in Seattle, but it turned out pretty well. If I remember my *Leprechaun* movies, though, he turns evil again in the next installment.

Charlton's mid-90s heat comes from grabbing little Norm, which he does a major-league-leading 3.1 times per pitch thrown. This makes him hard on families with kids as well as on opposing batters. He also suffered two groin injuries that put him on the DL and limited his innings. Coincidence?

Ryan Franklin Throws L Age 29

YEAR	TEAM	LGE	IP	H	ER	HR	BB	K	ERA	W	L	H/9	HR/9	BB/9	K/9	KW	PERA	STUFF
1999	Tacoma	PCL	135.0	152	82	21	39	63	5.47	6	9	10.1	1.4	2.6	4.2	0.8	6.14	-14
2000	Tacoma	PCL	156.0	179	112	39	37	101	6.46	6	11	10.3	2.3	2.1	5.8	1.4	5.44	-7
2001	Seattle	AL	78.3	80	43	12	23	57	4.94	4	5	9.2	1.4	2.6	6.5	1.2	3.63	1

At the start of the season it looked like Franklin was going to be sold to a Japanese team. Then an injury to Paul Abbott gave Franklin an opening, and he served as a long reliever until an overstocked bullpen caused his playing time and performance to suffer. It's good to see Franklin get his chance, and I hope his example opens the doors for many other players to get the opportunity to shake off undeserved "career minor leaguer" labels.

Brian Fuentes Throws L Age 26

YEAR	TEAM	LGE	IP	H	ER	HR	BB	K	ERA	W	L	H/9	HR/9	BB/9	K/9	KW	PERA	STUFF
1999	New Havn	Eas	59.7	59	42	8	48	45	6.34	2	5	8.9	1.2	7.2	6.8	0.5	6.57	-8
2000	New Havn	Eas	140.7	137	81	14	83	98	5.18	7	9	8.8	0.9	5.3	6.3	0.6	6.86	-5
2001	Tacoma	PCL	49.0	44	28	5	32	44	5.14	2	3	8.1	0.9	5.9	8.1	0.7	4.18	-8

His delivery—a quick, short-motion, side-arm sling—produces heat in the 90s and makes him murder on left-handed hitters. Jeff Bower calls Fuentes "Mike Venafro with better stuff." If rosters do expand to 27 players, you'll never be able to get Fuentes out of a uniform. He was traded to the Rockies as part of the Cirillo package.

Freddy Garcia Throws R Age 25

YEAR	TEAM	LGE	IP	H	ER	HR	BB	K	ERA	W	L	H/9	HR/9	BB/9	K/9	KW	PERA	STUFF
1999	Seattle	AL	210.0	192	88	16	75	168	3.77	14	9	8.2	0.7	3.2	7.2	1.1	3.60	25
2000	Seattle	AL	122.3	124	68	14	52	78	5.00	6	8	9.1	1.0	3.8	5.7	0.8	4.04	8
2001	Seattle	AL	234.0	224	95	15	66	155	3.65	16	10	8.6	0.6	2.5	6.0	1.2	3.27	17

Garcia's control and movement both improved, and he stepped up to claim the "ace" label, suffering only three disaster outings all year. Aces get ridden hard, though: he went fewer than six innings just four times. His only obvious weakness is his tendency to get rattled by inconsistent umpires, something he'll get over.

Kevin Gryboski Throws R Age 28

YEAR	TEAM	LGE	IP	H	ER	HR	BB	K	ERA	W	L	H/9	HR/9	BB/9	K/9	KW	PERA	STUFF
1999	New Havn	Eas	62.7	71	39	9	24	25	5.60	3	4	10.2	1.3	3.4	3.6	0.5	5.35	-33
2000	New Havn	Eas	18.3	16	7	0	10	12	3.44	1	1	7.9	0.0	4.9	5.9	0.6	3.47	-12
2000	Tacoma	PCL	42.7	43	26	4	25	25	5.48	2	3	9.1	0.8	5.3	5.3	0.5	5.89	-25
2001	Tacoma	PCL	59.3	66	40	10	24	32	6.07	2	5	10.0	1.5	3.6	4.9	0.7	5.53	-27

Groomed as a closer in the minors, Gryboski's shot at a job hinges on the entire Mariners bullpen being decimated by injuries. He throws in the mid-90s, touching 96, and has good sinking movement on his fastball. As the lines above show, it hasn't brought him success yet.

John Halama Throws L Age 30

YEAR	TEAM	LGE	IP	H	ER	HR	BB	K	ERA	W	L	H/9	HR/9	BB/9	K/9	KW	PERA	STUFF
1999	Seattle	AL	184.3	188	86	17	47	104	4.20	11	9	9.2	0.8	2.3	5.1	1.1	3.71	5
2000	Seattle	AL	177.3	187	86	17	46	86	4.36	10	10	9.5	0.9	2.3	4.4	0.9	5.25	0
2001	Seattle	AL	113.7	129	66	17	25	48	5.23	6	7	10.2	1.3	2.0	3.8	1.0	5.56	-11

The Mariners were unwise to not take advantage of Halama's gaudy 14-9 record in 2000 by trading him for some minor-league position players with upside. Halama looked bad in his 17 starts in 2001. This got him demoted to Tacoma, where he tossed a perfect game. After his recall, he pitched well out of the bullpen; he should be a swing man for the Mariners in 2002.

Jeff Heaverlo Throws R Age 24

YEAR	TEAM	LGE	IP	H	ER	HR	BB	K	ERA	W	L	H/9	HR/9	BB/9	K/9	KW	PERA	STUFF
1999	Wisconsn	Mid	17.7	17	9	2	8	14	4.58	1	1	8.7	1.0	4.1	7.1	0.9	3.71	21
2000	Lancastr	Cal	156.3	180	114	35	54	90	6.56	5	12	10.4	2.0	3.1	5.2	0.8	5.00	0
2000	Tacoma	PCL	12.7	16	10	2	6	3	7.11	0	1	11.4	1.4	4.3	2.1	0.3	5.00	-17
2001	SanAnton	Tex	177.3	180	88	21	49	114	4.47	10	10	9.1	1.1	2.5	5.8	1.2	4.92	11

Last year, Heaverlo had success as he relied less on his fastball—which isn't great—trusted his curve, and worked to develop his change-up on the side. It works now. The Texas League failed to challenge him: he finished first in strikeouts, second in ERA, and walked two batters a game. He's not going to find the next levels more challenging, and will certainly be in the majors by midseason barring injury.

Justin Kaye Throws R Age 26

YEAR	TEAM	LGE	IP	H	ER	HR	BB	K	ERA	W	L	H/9	HR/9	BB/9	K/9	KW	PERA	STUFF
1999	Lancastr	Cal	63.7	67	46	7	50	35	6.50	2	5	9.5	1.0	7.1	4.9	0.3	6.69	-34
2000	New Havn	Eas	87.3	79	40	6	43	70	4.12	5	5	8.1	0.6	4.4	7.2	0.8	4.55	-3
2001	Tacoma	PCL	73.0	64	44	7	59	68	5.42	3	5	7.9	0.9	7.3	8.4	0.6	4.01	-12

A Vegas skate punk, Kaye sported maroon-tinted hair for a while. It looked good. His control isn't there yet, but the side-to-side movement on his pitches is incredible and makes him worth the wait. He'll have a fruitful career in relief, but it may not start until 2004.

Gil Meche Throws R Age 23

YEAR	TEAM	LGE	IP	H	ER	HR	BB	K	ERA	W	L	H/9	HR/9	BB/9	K/9	KW	PERA	STUFF
1999	New Havn	Eas	58.7	56	28	4	26	39	4.30	4	3	8.6	0.6	4.0	6.0	0.8	4.28	20
1999	Tacoma	PCL	31.3	32	17	3	13	18	4.88	1	2	9.2	0.9	3.7	5.2	0.7	3.53	10
2000	Seattle	AL	85.3	81	39	6	33	59	4.11	5	4	8.5	0.6	3.5	6.2	0.9	3.50	18

When he was cracked open for the second time by Dr. James Andrews, Meche said, "The first time . . . he didn't really know what to look for, and he didn't see a big problem. So when I was trying to come back, it was the same thing all over again. Hopefully, this time they got it."

Meche's shoulder saga has been going on since mid-2000, when "strained right shoulder" was the best diagnosis a team of baffled specialists could offer. The M's said his most recent surgery was "exploratory," just as the last one was initially described. Meche's comments indicate the presence of an impingement that the first operation was supposed to fix and didn't, necessitating the second one. He managed that 2000 line despite something deeply wrong with his shoulder, with his velocity coming and going.

(Gil Meche *continued*)

Meche may return eventually, but history is littered with amazing pitching prospects made mortal by injury; Roger Salkeld immediately comes to mind. If Meche ever comes back, the team will likely have to put him on a Bill Swift-like protection program, either with extremely low pitch counts or a conversion to relief. Depending on his health, Meche could become another Troy Percival or a young version of the older Terry Mullholland.

Jamie Moyer Throws L Age 39

YEAR	TEAM	LGE	IP	H	ER	HR	BB	K	ERA	W	L	H/9	HR/9	BB/9	K/9	KW	PERA	STUFF
1999	Seattle	AL	233.0	234	97	20	40	136	3.75	15	11	9.0	0.8	1.5	5.3	1.7	3.58	13
2000	Seattle	AL	160.0	166	81	20	43	97	4.56	9	9	9.3	1.1	2.4	5.5	1.1	5.42	6
2001	Seattle	AL	204.3	213	97	23	42	113	4.27	12	11	9.4	1.0	1.8	5.0	1.3	3.56	8

One of the most laughable elements of the postseason was the Fox radar gun telling us that Jamie Moyer was throwing 85-mph heat. Moyer couldn't throw 85 downhill with gale-force winds behind him. He's lucky to get over 80, and his best fastball is about 82. He became the oldest pitcher to win 20 games for the first time. Moyer's all about preparation and control. Watching him is a joyous, baffling experience as he sets up and sits down batters with stuff that would be average in the PCL.

Jeff Nelson Throws R Age 35

YEAR	TEAM	LGE	IP	H	ER	HR	BB	K	ERA	W	L	H/9	HR/9	BB/9	K/9	KW	PERA	STUFF
1999	NY Yanks	AL	31.7	25	13	2	18	35	3.69	2	2	7.1	0.6	5.1	9.9	1.0	3.65	16
2000	NY Yanks	AL	67.7	52	25	2	37	70	3.33	5	3	6.9	0.3	4.9	9.3	0.9	2.65	16
2001	Seattle	AL	62.0	42	24	3	42	84	3.48	4	3	6.1	0.4	6.1	12.2	1.0	2.86	29

Nelson is a lights-out sidearmer with unreasonable movement on his pitches. Every so often, though, he'll come to the mound with no control; that's when he gets rocked. You can predict the outcome of his appearance based on the first three or four pitches: if he's pitching right to where the catcher is setting up, it's over. If his pitches are riding in or out of the zone as the count swings ever further in favor of the batter, hang on to your hat.

Jose Paniagua Throws R Age 28

YEAR	TEAM	LGE	IP	H	ER	HR	BB	K	ERA	W	L	H/9	HR/9	BB/9	K/9	KW	PERA	STUFF
1999	Seattle	AL	81.3	69	35	4	43	73	3.87	5	4	7.6	0.4	4.8	8.1	0.8	3.60	7
2000	Seattle	AL	80.7	71	33	5	31	70	3.68	5	4	7.9	0.6	3.5	7.8	1.1	3.13	10
2001	Seattle	AL	65.3	65	38	7	36	44	5.23	3	4	9.0	1.0	5.0	6.1	0.6	4.71	-11

When Paniagua didn't come in to set Carl Everett on his ass for Everett's crotch-grabbing, foul-mouthed performance August 14, it was obvious the last coals in Mt. Piniella had cooled, and there was no reason to carry Paniagua any longer. He was part of the Cirillo deal, banished to pitchers' hell one mile above sea level.

Joel Piniero Throws R Age 23

YEAR	TEAM	LGE	IP	H	ER	HR	BB	K	ERA	W	L	H/9	HR/9	BB/9	K/9	KW	PERA	STUFF
1999	New Havn	Eas	170.0	190	104	26	52	82	5.51	8	11	10.1	1.4	2.8	4.3	0.8	6.65	5
2000	New Havn	Eas	49.0	55	32	11	13	31	5.88	2	3	10.1	2.0	2.4	5.7	1.2	5.07	10
2000	Tacoma	PCL	59.7	60	27	4	21	33	4.07	4	3	9.1	0.6	3.2	5.0	0.8	3.05	14
2000	Seattle	AL	20.7	23	14	3	11	10	6.10	1	1	10.0	1.3	4.8	4.4	0.5	5.46	-13
2001	Tacoma	PCL	73.7	76	45	9	37	46	5.50	3	5	9.3	1.1	4.5	5.6	0.6	4.08	3
2001	Seattle	AL	71.7	64	24	2	20	53	3.01	6	2	8.0	0.3	2.5	6.7	1.3	2.83	22

Pronounced JO-el, Piniero throws a fastball with eye-popping movement and three other pitches for strikes, and he goes to any of them in any count, making predictions by color men even more inaccurate. He looks like a gunslinger on the mound, working quickly, the shadow from the brim of his cap covering his eyes as he takes the signs without emotion. You can see how tired he is by how much time he takes between pitches: early in the game, he can't wait to throw the next pitch; later, he'll walk the long way around the mound. The organizational thought is that his control and durability would make him better out of the pen.

Robert Ramsay Throws L Age 28

YEAR	TEAM	LGE	IP	H	ER	HR	BB	K	ERA	W	L	H/9	HR/9	BB/9	K/9	KW	PERA	STUFF
1999	Pawtuckt	Int	111.0	131	84	25	39	56	6.81	4	8	10.6	2.0	3.2	4.5	0.7	6.73	-17
1999	Tacoma	PCL	31.0	28	15	3	16	25	4.35	2	1	8.1	0.9	4.6	7.3	0.8	1.85	11
2000	Seattle	AL	49.7	47	27	3	33	32	4.89	3	3	8.5	0.5	6.0	5.8	0.5	3.55	-11
2001	Tacoma	PCL	144.3	172	124	34	77	71	7.73	4	12	10.7	2.1	4.8	4.4	0.5	7.51	-26

Ramsay is a big left-hander who doesn't throw hard. Unless he wakes up one morning to discover he's gained 7–8 mph on his fastball, he's Brian Meadows with some hits traded for walks. Unlike Meadows, Ramsay didn't luck into a rotation spot with a bad team and a big contract early in his career. He's in the Padres' camp now.

Arthur Rhodes Throws L Age 32

YEAR	TEAM	LGE	IP	H	ER	HR	BB	K	ERA	W	L	H/9	HR/9	BB/9	K/9	KW	PERA	STUFF
1999	Baltimor	AL	52.7	46	33	8	38	58	5.64	2	4	7.9	1.4	6.5	9.9	0.8	5.56	3
2000	Seattle	AL	69.0	55	25	5	24	76	3.26	5	3	7.2	0.7	3.1	9.9	1.6	3.98	22
2001	Seattle	AL	67.0	51	18	5	11	79	2.42	5	2	6.9	0.7	1.5	10.6	3.6	1.83	35

Rhodes cooks with 95-octane gas and throws an 85-mph breaking ball that dives on the plate like a Stuka on an infantry column. Rhodes is one of the few relievers who is paid millions and worth every penny. Because right-handed hitters don't fare well against him, the Mariners might be better served using him in longer, higher-leverage situations. Rhodes pitched more than an inning about as often (11 times) as he was brought in for one out (15 times).

Kazuhiro Sasaki Throws R Age 34

YEAR	TEAM	LGE	IP	H	ER	HR	BB	K	ERA	W	L	H/9	HR/9	BB/9	K/9	KW	PERA	STUFF
1999	Yokohama	JpC	23.7	15	5	1	6	33	1.90	3	0	5.7	0.4	2.3	12.5	2.8	2.04	45
2000	Seattle	AL	61.0	49	28	9	25	77	4.13	4	3	7.2	1.3	3.7	11.4	1.5	3.23	25
2001	Seattle	AL	64.7	57	22	6	10	59	3.06	5	2	7.9	0.8	1.4	8.2	3.0	3.20	17

When he's spotting his fastball and dropping his forkball on batters, Sasaki is as unhittable as anyone in baseball. Other times... not so much. Cutting down on the dingers and walks made him less impressive but much more effective. When Ichiro signed with the team, he told everyone that while he was happy to play with Sasaki, he wouldn't be drinking with the notorious master of alcohol. If someone wants to bet you on a Sasaki/David Wells drink-off, take Kazu and try to act surprised when you're collecting the rube's money.

Aaron Sele Throws R Age 32

YEAR	TEAM	LGE	IP	H	ER	HR	BB	K	ERA	W	L	H/9	HR/9	BB/9	K/9	KW	PERA	STUFF
1999	Texas	AL	223.7	204	87	18	58	184	3.50	16	9	8.2	0.7	2.3	7.4	1.6	4.15	23
2000	Seattle	AL	219.0	214	92	15	60	136	3.78	14	10	8.8	0.6	2.5	5.6	1.1	4.21	12
2001	Seattle	AL	215.0	228	106	24	49	108	4.44	12	12	9.5	1.0	2.1	4.5	1.1	3.84	4

Sele's luck gauge may have reached "E". He is by far the luckiest starter of the last five years (his Support-Neutral record is 61-57, his actual record 82-47) and third-luckiest of the last ten years, behind Kirk Rueter and Tom Glavine. His improvement in the second half was masked by poor run support, so Sele was criticized for "slumping." Then he kept losing in the playoffs and looked bad while doing it. That end to his season likely cost Sele more than $10 million on his next contract. Someone needing an above-average innings muncher should contact his agent.

Rafael Soriano Throws R Age 22

YEAR	TEAM	LGE	IP	H	ER	HR	BB	K	ERA	W	L	H/9	HR/9	BB/9	K/9	KW	PERA	STUFF
1999	Everett	Nwn	70.0	79	65	16	55	44	8.36	2	6	10.2	2.1	7.1	5.7	0.4	4.36	0
2000	Wisconsn	Mid	117.3	122	62	7	56	52	4.76	6	7	9.4	0.5	4.3	4.0	0.5	4.11	4
2001	San Bern	Cal	81.3	80	46	7	48	54	5.09	4	5	8.9	0.8	5.3	6.0	0.6	3.54	11
2001	SanAnton	Tex	45.0	46	27	8	16	36	5.40	2	3	9.2	1.6	3.2	7.2	1.1	4.19	22

Holy smokes. Soriano's great start got him bumped a level in mid-season, when he seemingly got nastier, his strikeout rate jumping and his walk rate dropping. The consensus seems to be that he needs to work on his slider and change-up, so he'll start 2002 in Double-A. Then again, his potentially dominant stuff, highlighted by a high-90s moving heater, might catch Piniella's eye and cause Soriano to break camp with the team.

Dennis Stark Throws R Age 27

YEAR	TEAM	LGE	IP	H	ER	HR	BB	K	ERA	W	L	H/9	HR/9	BB/9	K/9	KW	PERA	STUFF
1999	New Havn	Eas	146.0	165	103	23	71	64	6.35	5	11	10.2	1.4	4.4	3.9	0.5	6.60	-18
2000	New Havn	Eas	46.0	45	21	2	21	26	4.11	3	2	8.8	0.4	4.1	5.1	0.6	3.29	0
2001	Tacoma	PCL	143.0	148	76	16	52	82	4.78	8	8	9.3	1.0	3.3	5.2	0.8	3.92	0
2001	Seattle	AL	16.0	19	13	5	4	11	7.31	1	1	10.7	2.8	2.3	6.2	1.4	9.06	-12

His raw stats in Tacoma look great and come with a 14-2 record and PCL Pitcher of the Year honors. Stark has battled injuries that cost him a lot of development time. He could still bloom into a #4 starter; someone with patience will need to give him that chance, but Stark's not the kind of pitcher with obviously amazing stuff that will necessarily convince a team to do so. He has a clearer path to a job with the Rockies, but overall, the trade doesn't give him a better chance of success.

Brett Tomko Throws R Age 29

YEAR	TEAM	LGE	IP	H	ER	HR	BB	K	ERA	W	L	H/9	HR/9	BB/9	K/9	KW	PERA	STUFF
1999	Cincnnti	NL	173.0	181	98	28	50	119	5.10	8	11	9.4	1.5	2.6	6.2	1.2	4.79	6
2000	Seattle	AL	93.3	95	49	11	33	58	4.72	5	5	9.2	1.1	3.2	5.6	0.9	4.66	-3
2001	Seattle	AL	35.7	41	28	9	14	21	7.07	1	3	10.3	2.3	3.5	5.3	0.8	6.14	-16
2001	Tacoma	PCL	124.7	130	64	16	32	74	4.62	7	7	9.4	1.2	2.3	5.3	1.2	5.76	0

After Tomko struggled in May, the M's demoted him and told him to go increase his value so they could trade him. Tomko stumbled initially at Tacoma but pitched better as he gained strength. Like Roosevelt Brown, Tomko is a good player screwed out of a chance he deserves and too obviously valuable for his organization to let him off the hook. Tomko's stuff is better than it was in 1997, and he could be a quality starter for nearly any team in baseball.

Greg Wooten Throws R Age 28

YEAR	TEAM	LGE	IP	H	ER	HR	BB	K	ERA	W	L	H/9	HR/9	BB/9	K/9	KW	PERA	STUFF
1999	Lancastr	Cal	111.3	140	92	26	40	35	7.44	3	9	11.3	2.1	3.2	2.8	0.4	5.72	-30
2000	New Havn	Eas	175.3	192	81	19	19	71	4.16	10	9	9.9	1.0	1.0	3.6	1.9	3.48	0
2001	Tacoma	PCL	172.0	192	97	24	41	73	5.08	8	11	10.0	1.3	2.1	3.8	0.9	6.15	-9

By using his control to throw strikes almost exclusively, Wooten ends up with eye-popping strikeout-to-walk ratios. He still doesn't have heat, and he puts a lot of balls in play, most of them ground balls. Put the package together and you have a guy who can succeed given a great infield defense behind him.

Tampa Bay Devil Rays

The Devil Rays experienced the best thing that could have happened to them last year: failure. Complete and utter failure, the likes of which sometimes is the only thing that can force an organization to face up to the fact that it's been going full speed in the wrong direction.

In previous seasons the Devil Rays had spent a considerable amount of money to bring in veteran talent. Their hope was to become a contender and establish a fan base while building the farm system for the long haul. Whatever the merits of the plan, the execution was fundamentally flawed. Players such as Wilson Alvarez, Juan Guzman, Gerald Williams, Jose Canseco, Greg Vaughn, and Vinny Castilla not only leeched the club's resources, they failed to either improve the team or set the turnstiles a-spinning.

As the 2001 season opened, the Devil Rays' commitment to that core of high-priced veterans was wavering. Sometimes, after a club comes to grips with the fact that it must abandon its plan—but before it is able to pull itself together and chart a new course—it simply staggers around aimlessly for a bit. The D-Rays displayed all the symptoms of such delirium in the opening days of the season: (1) Second-base prospect Brent Abernathy out-hit perennial project Bobby Smith during spring training, but the team chose to send down Abernathy and give the second-base job to Smith. After Smith went 2-for-19 over his first six games, they designated him for assignment. A sudden reversal, perhaps, but then Abernathy had deserved the job all along. Yet the job did not go to Abernathy; it went to veteran backup Russ Johnson. (2) Third baseman Vinny Castilla was elbowed out almost as abruptly as Smith was. Castilla showed signs of life with a .315 average in March, but when he hit .206 and committed three errors in his first nine games, the club benched him and gave his job to Aubrey Huff. Castilla, feeling scapegoated, demanded to be traded or released. They shopped him for a few weeks and, finding no takers, ate his contract and released him. (3) Center fielder Gerald Williams, whose early-season performance should have left him grateful merely to remain in the major leagues, berated manager Larry Rothschild in the dugout after the manager pinch-hit for him in the final inning of a blowout. Rothschild benched Williams. (4) Over the winter, general manager Chuck LaMar had defended Rothschild, blaming injuries for the club's 93-loss season in 2000, and had said Rothschild deserved the chance to turn the team around. But days after the Williams benching, LaMar fired Rothschild and replaced him with Hal McRae.

Devil Rays Prospectus

2001 record: 62–100; Fifth place, AL East

Pythagenport W/L: 60–102

Runs scored: 672 (14th in AL)

Runs allowed: 887 (13th in AL)

Team EqA: .243 (tied for 13th in AL)

2001 batters age: 28.1 (tied for sixth-youngest in AL)

2001 pitchers age: 26.9 (fourth-youngest in AL)

Ballpark: Tropicana Field; neutral park; Park Factor of 1.003

2001: Finished better than they started, thanks to an infusion of younger players.

2002: There are reasons to be optimistic long term; short-term, look for another 90 losses.

Admittedly, the club had performed abominably to begin the season, but it was awfully early to start making drastic moves. Though their record stood at 4-10, another way to look at it was that they were only three games below .500. Like the Smith demotion and the Castilla benching, firing Rothschild may have been the right move, but it smacked of panic, a knee-jerk reaction to a deteriorating situation.

Then *The New York Times* alleged that the team was in danger of failing to make payroll. Major League Baseball was about to intervene, the story went, and the club might be moved or contracted at season's end if things didn't get straightened out.

Commissioner Bud Selig saw fit to get involved. This wasn't necessarily a positive development from the point of view of Devil Rays fans. Many recalled that a meeting between Selig and owner Vince Naimoli during the winter of 1999–2000 had preceded the club's ill-fated free-agent spending spree.

This time, whether out of guilt or the best interests of the Tampa Bay franchise, Selig provided much more effective leadership—by arranging for someone else to lead. He orchestrated the hiring of Tigers president John McHale Jr. as Tampa Bay's new chief operating officer. McHale's arrival marked the turning point. From that point onward, the club backed away even more completely from the quick-fix approach and instead focused upon promoting and developing the young players who could become the core of a contender down the road.

In June, Williams was released just before his $4-million option for 2002 would have vested. Jason Tyner replaced him. Soon after, Abernathy was promoted and installed as the starting second baseman. In July, catcher Toby Hall was promoted. He had put up MVP numbers at Triple-A Durham, and he kept hitting as the D-Rays' regular catcher for the remainder of the season. Albie Lopez was dealt to Arizona for a package including young left-hander Nick Bierbrodt, and Fred McGriff's contract was unloaded on the Cubs. The latter move enabled Steve Cox to get more at-bats.

Aubrey Huff continued to see regular time at third base; when his glove work proved unacceptable, McRae gave the job to Jared Sandberg, while continuing to find at-bats for Huff. Though Huff suffered though a disappointing season at the plate and in the field, he eventually found his stroke late in the year, thanks in part to McRae's willingness to stick with him.

After setting an American League record for losses in the first half, the D-Rays actually played close to .500 ball over the second half. Rookie relievers Travis Phelps, Victor Zambrano, and Jesus Colome each contributed in a big way, and rookie southpaw Joe Kennedy became the most effective member of the starting rotation. Paul Wilson, after his early-season control problems, went to the bullpen, found himself, and returned to the rotation to pitch brilliantly down the stretch.

We don't mean to imply that all of McRae's moves were inspired. He's still prone to pull stunts like removing furniture from the clubhouse as a motivational technique, and his obsession with glove men is particularly ironic for a guy who was a career designated hitter. Neither do we mean to nitpick. All in all, he accomplished the goal of working young players into the lineup, and he showed laudable restraint for someone who hadn't been noted for excessive patience.

Going into 2002, the Devil Rays have some of the elements of a workable batting order. The most critical issue is whether Jason Tyner will be able to reach base consistently from the leadoff spot. (If Tyner can't fit the bill, they just might have to wait until Carl Crawford is ready. Come to think of it, he might already be more ready to contribute than Tyner is.) With a little improvement, Randy Winn can be a decent #2 hitter; if they choose to go with a more traditional right-field bat, Brent Abernathy might fit in the two hole.

The biggest question mark in the heart of the order is Ben Grieve, who slugged a ridiculously bad .387 last season. It must be assumed he'll return to his power-hitting ways; players like him don't just stop hitting at age 25. If he rebounds, there's decent power and good balance in the middle of the order with Grieve, Greg Vaughn, Toby Hall, and Steve Cox. If Vaughn is unloaded, Aubrey Huff can DH, although he'll need to take his game up a notch as well. Hall is every bit as good as he looked last year and is capable of having an All-Star season immediately. The Rays' preoccupation with "little ball," as illustrated by their willingness to play a guy like Randy Winn in right field, can be a bit disturbing. But they do have enough power on hand to work around it, if Grieve gets back to swinging the way he can.

The bottom third of the order can consist of either Winn or Abernathy, then Hal McRae's obligatory glove man Sandberg, and the shortstop, perhaps Chris Gomez. If Gomez turns back into Clark Kent, or even if he doesn't, they might do better to promote young shortstop Jorge Cantu. At this point, Cantu is a virtual carbon copy of Gomez, capable of being a .260 hitter and steady defender in the majors.

Cantu is just one of the Rays' talented minor leaguers who are just a year or two away. Outfielders Josh Hamilton and Carl Crawford are very young and have serious upside. The lower rungs of the system are loaded with power arms such as Seth McClung, Evan Rust, and Jamie Shields. The Rays have several other varieties of intriguing pitching prospects, such as left-handed 6′9″ control artist Hans Smith, clever lefty Derek Anderson, and the master of winning without impressing the scouts, Jim Magrane. At the upper levels of the system, they have several guys who could help this year, including Bobby Seay, Matt White, Delvin James, Jason Standridge, and Travis Harper. As Branch Rickey said, out of quantity comes quality.

After the Devil Rays spent most of the season correcting for the mistakes of 1999 and 2000, they announced in November that ex-Pirates GM Cam Bonifay had been hired as director of player personnel. "The Devil Rays are extremely fortunate to have someone with Cam's baseball background and expertise joining our organization. He is an extremely respected baseball man," GM Chuck LaMar said, apparently with a straight face.

It would be easy to spend a few paragraphs making up more punch lines, but the truth is just about all the good ones have already been used. At the risk of appearing to defend Bonifay (analytic heresy!) let's take a more balanced, less sarcastic look at what he did in Pittsburgh and what he might bring to the Devil Rays.

First, the bad stuff. Bonifay's taste in free agents ran to the masochistic. Lavishing millions on mediocrities such as Derek Bell, Pat Meares, and Mike Benjamin not only pissed away the capital of a cash-poor team, but it legitimately raised the question of whether Bonifay could tell a ballplayer from an accountant in double knits.

In some cases, Bonifay was able to trade the free agents to extract younger players from contenders. Wil Cordero was dealt for Enrique Wilson, who was dealt for Damaso Marte. Terry Mulholland brought Adrian Burnside from the Dodgers.

As far as playing the small-market GM's game, Bonifay's track record in other areas was defensible. He made some of the better minor-league free-agent signings of recent years, including Todd Ritchie and Josias Manzanillo. He got a few decent years out of minor-league free agent Kevin Young (although he later signed Young to a Meares-type deal). He picked up Luis Sojo and later dealt him to the Yanks for Chris Spurling, a decent pitching prospect. Danny Darwin was signed in 1996 and later used to acquire Rich Loiselle, who pitched pretty well before blowing out his arm. In the Rule 5 draft, he acquired Emil Brown and Scott Sauerbeck, two useful bit players, at minimal cost.

On several occasions, Bonifay unloaded expensive veterans before their trade value plummeted. Carlos Garcia and Orlando Merced were sent to Toronto (with Dan Plesac) for a package that included Craig Wilson, Jose Silva, and Abraham Nunez; the deal was panned at the time, but Merced and Garcia subsequently grew old in hurry. Al Martin was dispatched to San Diego for John Vander Wal.

His record on straight talent-for-talent trades is mixed. Getting Jon Lieber and Dan Miceli for Stan Belinda, and Brian Giles for Ricardo Rincon, were winning moves; dealing Lieber for Brant Brown was a loser.

All in all, Bonifay's record suggests that he's more than a mere buffoon who thinks the key to success is to sign enough Derek Bells. He's shown he can make the kind of low-risk moves that help replenish a club's talent pool while keeping its payroll manageable. That's exactly the kind of expertise the Devil Rays need. Since it's likely they won't give him the authority to sign free agents, they'll be taking advantage of his strengths rather than his weaknesses. In the right role, Bonifay might be able to help the Devil Rays.

No one is pretending that the D-Rays are ready to vault into contention, but at least, for the first time in years, they're moving in the right direction.

HITTERS (BA: .270, OBP: .340, SLG: .440, EqA: .260)

Brent Abernathy 2B Bats R Age 24

YEAR	TEAM	LGE	AB	H	DB	TP	HR	BB	SO	R	RBI	SB	CS	OUT	BA	OBP	SLG	EQA	EQR	DEFENSE
1999	Knoxvill	Sou	576	141	28	1	11	38	48	79	45	21	10	445	.245	.295	.354	.222	51	131-2B -8
2000	Durham	Int	92	24	2	0	2	9	11	12	15	8	2	70	.261	.347	.348	.250	11	24-2B -5
2000	Syracuse	Int	358	98	18	1	4	20	31	41	30	11	11	271	.274	.314	.363	.225	33	89-2B 1
2001	Durham	Int	256	75	13	0	6	16	21	44	23	10	4	185	.293	.338	.414	.254	30	58-2B 6
2001	TampaBay	AL	305	88	17	1	6	28	30	46	36	7	3	220	.289	.348	.410	.257	37	79-2B 0
2002	*TampaBay*	*AL*	*515*	*151*	*24*	*1*	*12*	*49*	*49*	*79*	*52*	*20*	*9*	*372*	*.293*	*.355*	*.414*	*.263*	*66*	

It says a lot about the organization that they'd sour on Miguel Cairo, then get all excited about Abernathy, a player with pretty much the same skills. Maybe that's a tad harsh; Abernathy might have a little more power and a little more patience. If he can't play second base, it won't make a bit of difference, because he doesn't have the power or the on-base skills to be much of an asset anywhere else. If you can hit .280 but you don't have speed, power potential, or a good batting eye, where do you go? If you're Brent Gates or Warren Morris, the answer, ultimately, is "nowhere," even if your batting average charms a team into keeping you around for a few years.

Rocco Baldelli CF Bats R Age 20

YEAR	TEAM	LGE	AB	H	DB	TP	HR	BB	SO	R	RBI	SB	CS	OUT	BA	OBP	SLG	EQA	EQR	DEFENSE
2000	Princetn	App	234	35	7	1	1	6	67	17	13	4	2	201	.150	.176	.201	.135	7	60 CF 3
2001	Charl-SC	SAL	417	85	18	3	6	18	95	42	39	12	6	338	.204	.244	.305	.189	26	112-CF -4
2002	*TampaBay*	*AL*	*394*	*87*	*20*	*2*	*6*	*23*	*101*	*45*	*37*	*16*	*6*	*313*	*.221*	*.264*	*.327*	*.198*	*27*	

Baldelli, the club's first-round pick in the 2000 draft, could go either way. He's a marvelous athlete, a great pure center fielder who hasn't yet proven he can't hit. A Rhode Islander who'd never played below the Mason-Dixon Line, he wilted in the South Carolina heat in the second half. The Rays are hoping he'll show better stamina at Bakersfield—not exactly a milder clime—because he'll need to learn to avoid sunstroke if he's going to make it through Double-A Orlando. At least the Devil Rays play indoors.

Jace Brewer SS Bats R Age 23

YEAR	TEAM	LGE	AB	H	DB	TP	HR	BB	SO	R	RBI	SB	CS	OUT	BA	OBP	SLG	EQA	EQR	DEFENSE
2000	Charl-SC	SAL	139	25	6	1	0	3	30	7	10	1	0	114	.180	.199	.237	.151	5	27-SS -2
2001	Charl-SC	SAL	422	73	11	2	2	15	79	40	25	3	3	352	.173	.204	.223	.149	15	101-SS -20
2002	*TampaBay*	*AL*	*387*	*88*	*15*	*3*	*3*	*20*	*78*	*32*	*32*	*3*	*3*	*302*	*.227*	*.265*	*.305*	*.184*	*22*	

(Jace Brewer *continued*)

Brewer had surgery on his throwing shoulder over the winter and played in pain during the first half. His bat started to come around late in the year. He's such a terrific glove man that he won't need to hit much to be valuable. He's older than Jorge Cantu and will need to pick it up in a hurry to keep Cantu from beating him to the majors.

Jorge Cantu SS Bats R Age 20

YEAR	TEAM	LGE	AB	H	DB	TP	HR	BB	SO	R	RBI	SB	CS	OUT	BA	OBP	SLG	EQA	EQR	DEFENSE
1999	HudsnVal	NYP	287	54	10	1	1	12	65	22	20	1	2	235	.188	.223	.240	.160	12	72-SS -7
2000	Charl-SC	SAL	188	44	10	1	1	7	42	18	15	1	2	146	.234	.266	.314	.194	12	45-SS -2
2000	St Pete	Fla	130	32	4	1	1	2	14	13	10	2	1	99	.246	.260	.315	.194	8	32-SS -9
2001	Orlando	Sou	517	119	24	2	3	12	91	52	38	3	6	404	.230	.254	.302	.186	30	120-SS -34
2002	*TampaBay*	*AL*	*506*	*131*	*25*	*2*	*6*	*24*	*96*	*57*	*51*	*4*	*6*	*381*	*.259*	*.292*	*.352*	*.212*	*39*	

Cantu was one of the youngest players in Double-A last year and didn't embarrass himself. He won't wow people with his tools, but he is known for his steadiness at the plate and in the field. He has a good chance to make the jump to the majors sometime this year, since he'll probably hit for a better average than he did last season, and the only guy in front of him may be Chris Gomez. Cantu won't be anything special at the major-league level for a few years, but he's young enough to develop into a fine hitter.

Jason Conti OF Bats L Age 27

YEAR	TEAM	LGE	AB	H	DB	TP	HR	BB	SO	R	RBI	SB	CS	OUT	BA	OBP	SLG	EQA	EQR	DEFENSE
1999	Tucson	PCL	508	125	18	6	7	45	81	75	43	16	6	389	.246	.312	.346	.227	48	126-CF 2
2000	Tucson	PCL	375	101	18	3	9	16	55	57	42	7	2	276	.269	.306	.405	.238	38	90-CF -15
2000	Arizona	NL	92	21	5	3	1	5	28	11	15	3	0	71	.228	.275	.380	.224	8	24-RF 2
2001	Tucson	PCL	355	103	20	4	7	29	49	55	41	2	4	256	.290	.357	.428	.261	45	89-CF 0
2001	Durham	Int	159	47	7	0	6	9	29	23	18	3	1	113	.296	.336	.453	.262	20	36-CF -1
2002	*TampaBay*	*AL*	*502*	*141*	*24*	*5*	*13*	*43*	*85*	*81*	*56*	*7*	*2*	*363*	*.281*	*.338*	*.426*	*.258*	*61*	

The D-Rays say they'll be looking for players who can do the little things, and Conti can. Plus, unlike Jason Tyner, he can do some of the big things—just not enough of them to justify full-time play. Like Randy Winn, Conti could be a role player for a good team or a below-average regular for a bad one.

Steve Cox 1B Bats L Age 27

YEAR	TEAM	LGE	AB	H	DB	TP	HR	BB	SO	R	RBI	SB	CS	OUT	BA	OBP	SLG	EQA	EQR	DEFENSE
1999	Durham	Int	533	169	44	3	21	55	69	90	103	2	3	367	.317	.385	.529	.298	89	123-1B 4
2000	TampaBay	AL	314	92	17	1	12	43	41	42	34	1	2	224	.293	.385	.468	.285	48	55-RF -6 19-1B -3
2001	TampaBay	AL	343	94	18	0	15	25	65	39	55	2	2	251	.274	.337	.458	.262	44	74-1B -1
2002	*TampaBay*	*AL*	*461*	*141*	*28*	*1*	*21*	*54*	*77*	*70*	*77*	*2*	*3*	*323*	*.306*	*.379*	*.508*	*.293*	*75*	

Would you like a hand basket for that strikeout-to-walk ratio, Mr. Cox? For whatever reason, the high strike seemed to hurt him more than it does most hitters, and he was fortunate to hang on to as much of his 2000 production as he did. It's hard to envision a scenario this year in which he wouldn't be able to get 500 at-bats.

Carl Crawford CF Bats L Age 20

YEAR	TEAM	LGE	AB	H	DB	TP	HR	BB	SO	R	RBI	SB	CS	OUT	BA	OBP	SLG	EQA	EQR	DEFENSE
1999	Princetn	App	257	54	7	2	0	4	53	28	12	6	3	206	.210	.223	.253	.165	11	58-RF -5
2000	Charl-SC	SAL	572	138	17	6	5	20	109	65	39	25	8	442	.241	.268	.318	.204	41	131-RF -11
2001	Orlando	Sou	546	133	23	2	3	27	88	54	43	24	15	428	.244	.282	.310	.204	40	130-CF 0
2002	*TampaBay*	*AL*	*516*	*140*	*23*	*3*	*5*	*33*	*94*	*80*	*39*	*23*	*9*	*385*	*.271*	*.315*	*.357*	*.231*	*49*	

Don't make the mistake of dismissing this guy as all hype and no performance. For a teenager in Double-A, he did just fine, without any help from his park or league. Yes, it would be nice if he learned to draw more walks, but he has plenty of time to work on that. It will be a surprise if he isn't playing regularly sometime in 2003. Expect him to eventually be Kenny Lofton.

John Flaherty C Bats R Age 34

YEAR	TEAM	LGE	AB	H	DB	TP	HR	BB	SO	R	RBI	SB	CS	OUT	BA	OBP	SLG	EQA	EQR	DEFENSE
1999	TampaBay	AL	445	130	14	0	17	14	56	52	73	0	2	317	.292	.322	.438	.249	49	112-C 8
2000	TampaBay	AL	393	107	11	0	12	15	50	35	39	0	0	286	.272	.299	.392	.229	36	101-C -2
2001	TampaBay	AL	248	63	16	1	5	11	29	22	31	1	0	185	.254	.288	.387	.225	22	68-C -5
2002	*TampaBay*	*AL*	*368*	*95*	*17*	*1*	*10*	*20*	*48*	*38*	*46*	*0*	*1*	*274*	*.258*	*.298*	*.391*	*.227*	*34*	

Flaherty missed most of September with a herniated disc in his neck, the result, no doubt, of having watched Toby Hall zoom past him. He has played for seven last-place teams in his ten major-league seasons, and it's no coincidence. Note how well the club played once Hall finally replaced him as the starting catcher.

Jonny Gomes OF Bats L Age 21

YEAR	TEAM	LGE	AB	H	DB	TP	HR	BB	SO	R	RBI	SB	CS	OUT	BA	OBP	SLG	EQA	EQR	DEFENSE
2001	Princetn	App	217	45	7	1	8	21	80	30	23	5	3	175	.207	.300	.359	.225	21	60-CF -7
2002	*TampaBay*	*AL*	*253*	*59*	*9*	*0*	*10*	*26*	*99*	*31*	*30*	*6*	*3*	*197*	*.233*	*.305*	*.387*	*.233*	*26*	

A year older than most Appy League players, Gomes surprised folks by winning the league's MVP award. Great bat speed is his one tool. He'll need to hope for a chance at quick advancement, and he'd better do something with the opportunity if they give it to him. The cards are already stacked against him in this organization; the club's experiences with Vinny Castilla, Jose Canseco, et al, have apparently taught them that power is bad and speed is good.

Chris Gomez SS Bats R Age 31

YEAR	TEAM	LGE	AB	H	DB	TP	HR	BB	SO	R	RBI	SB	CS	OUT	BA	OBP	SLG	EQA	EQR	DEFENSE
1999	San Dieg	NL	237	63	8	1	1	24	45	20	15	1	2	176	.266	.336	.321	.227	22	67-SS 1
2000	San Dieg	NL	55	13	0	0	0	6	5	4	3	0	0	42	.236	.311	.236	.197	4	13-SS -1
2001	Portland	PCL	40	11	2	0	1	2	4	4	4	1	0	29	.275	.310	.400	.241	4	
2001	San Dieg	NL	113	24	4	0	0	8	12	7	8	1	0	89	.212	.264	.248	.181	6	23-SS -5
2001	Durham	Int	95	27	4	1	4	11	5	16	16	1	1	69	.284	.358	.474	.274	14	20-SS 5
2001	TampaBay	AL	190	61	13	0	10	8	21	33	38	3	0	129	.321	.353	.547	.293	30	51-SS -1
2002	*TampaBay*	*AL*	*373*	*105*	*17*	*1*	*12*	*37*	*42*	*43*	*41*	*2*	*1*	*269*	*.282*	*.346*	*.429*	*.262*	*47*	

From the "Why didn't I think of that?" Department: Before Gomez left San Diego, manager Bruce Bochy casually suggested to him that he might think about trying to hit the ball a little harder. Gomez signed with the Devil Rays, went down to Triple-A and hit four home runs in 93 at-bats, got recalled, and hit eight in 189 at-bats for the big club. We're left with two theories: (1) We've been wrong about Gomez all this time—he was perfectly capable of being a productive hitter, it just never occurred to him to do so; and (2) it was a fluke.

Ben Grieve LF Bats L Age 26

YEAR	TEAM	LGE	AB	H	DB	TP	HR	BB	SO	R	RBI	SB	CS	OUT	BA	OBP	SLG	EQA	EQR	DEFENSE
1999	Oakland	AL	484	135	17	0	32	58	95	80	88	4	0	349	.279	.364	.512	.288	78	110-LF 5
2000	Oakland	AL	591	174	36	2	30	66	114	91	104	3	0	417	.294	.368	.514	.290	94	129-LF -4
2001	TampaBay	AL	545	154	31	2	13	89	137	78	77	7	1	392	.283	.389	.418	.279	80	113-RF -5
2002	*TampaBay*	*AL*	*507*	*147*	*23*	*1*	*23*	*73*	*121*	*80*	*82*	*6*	*0*	*360*	*.290*	*.379*	*.475*	*.289*	*81*	

It's very rare—not to mention distressing—to see a hitter to take such a major step backward at age 25. For some reason, Grieve went back to hitting way too many ground balls and ended up slugging 14 points below his father's lifetime mark. Perhaps the A's knew something everyone else didn't? After all, it's a little suspicious that the power-and-walk-lovin' A's would deal away a young hitter who provides both those qualities. Maybe Greg Vaughn can teach Grieve to uppercut a little more.

Jose Guillen RF Bats R Age 26

YEAR	TEAM	LGE	AB	H	DB	TP	HR	BB	SO	R	RBI	SB	CS	OUT	BA	OBP	SLG	EQA	EQR	DEFENSE
1999	Pittsbrg	NL	120	32	2	0	2	9	19	17	18	1	0	88	.267	.318	.333	.225	11	29-RF -2
1999	Nashvill	PCL	130	39	6	0	5	6	19	22	18	0	1	92	.300	.337	.462	.261	16	30-RF 0
1999	TampaBay	AL	168	43	9	0	3	8	32	24	14	0	0	125	.256	.314	.363	.229	16	43-RF -3
2000	Durham	Int	78	31	7	1	8	7	11	18	26	0	1	48	.397	.452	.821	.378	21	17-RF -4
2000	TampaBay	AL	315	83	16	5	11	14	57	39	40	3	1	233	.263	.322	.451	.255	38	79-RF 1
2001	TampaBay	AL	135	39	4	0	4	7	22	15	12	2	3	100	.289	.334	.407	.243	15	36-RF 3
2001	Durham	Int	120	34	7	0	7	3	26	18	28	0	0	86	.283	.301	.517	.262	15	26-RF 0
2002	*Arizona*	*NL*	*403*	*114*	*17*	*2*	*16*	*30*	*78*	*65*	*62*	*3*	*2*	*291*	*.283*	*.333*	*.454*	*.262*	*51*	

Guillen opened the year as the club's starting right fielder. He hit .252 in 28 games in April and May before tripping over first base and spraining his left knee. They sent him down to rehab it, he was sidelined on and off for the next three months, got suspended for ten games for using a corked bat, and smoked the ball whenever he was able to hobble to the plate. He'll open 2002 as a Diamondback, most likely as a fourth outfielder.

Toby Hall C Bats R Age 26

YEAR	TEAM	LGE	AB	H	DB	TP	HR	BB	SO	R	RBI	SB	CS	OUT	BA	OBP	SLG	EQA	EQR	DEFENSE
1999	St Pete	Fla	214	52	10	1	3	12	10	18	25	0	1	163	.243	.286	.341	.210	17	29-C -3
1999	Orlando	Sou	173	39	5	0	7	2	10	16	25	1	1	135	.225	.237	.376	.200	12	36-C -3
2000	Orlando	Sou	279	86	9	0	9	11	24	33	43	2	1	194	.308	.336	.437	.256	32	55-C -14
2000	Durham	Int	185	54	10	0	8	1	19	19	32	0	0	131	.292	.302	.476	.252	21	41-C -2
2001	Durham	Int	380	122	21	1	19	29	20	57	68	1	3	261	.321	.372	.532	.292	60	64-C 4
2001	TampaBay	AL	188	59	13	0	6	5	14	30	33	2	2	131	.314	.339	.479	.267	24	46-C 1
2002	*TampaBay*	*AL*	*539*	*169*	*23*	*1*	*22*	*35*	*38*	*67*	*94*	*2*	*3*	*373*	*.314*	*.355*	*.482*	*.277*	*75*	

Hall started hitting in 2000 and won't stop until, oh, 2014 or thereabouts. Outstanding hitters rarely reach the majors this late in life, but Hall is a legitimate exception to the rule. What makes him so exciting is that he's an exception to another rule, the one that says that it's pretty much impossible to hit for power without striking out more than 50 times a year. If there are any disbelievers in your fantasy league, outbid them.

Josh Hamilton OF Bats L Age 21

YEAR	TEAM	LGE	AB	H	DB	TP	HR	BB	SO	R	RBI	SB	CS	OUT	BA	OBP	SLG	EQA	EQR	DEFENSE
1999	Princetn	App	232	53	14	1	4	5	48	23	21	6	2	181	.228	.245	.349	.200	16	53-CF -5
1999	HudsnVal	NYP	72	10	2	0	0	1	16	4	4	0	1	63	.139	.155	.167	.110	1	16-CF 5
2000	Charl-SC	SAL	398	94	16	1	9	17	76	42	39	6	4	308	.236	.269	.349	.207	30	81-CF -6
2001	Orlando	Sou	90	15	5	0	0	4	22	4	4	1	0	75	.167	.202	.222	.150	3	22-CF -2
2002	*TampaBay*	*AL*	*390*	*101*	*20*	*1*	*9*	*24*	*86*	*45*	*40*	*8*	*3*	*292*	*.259*	*.302*	*.385*	*.231*	*37*	

Hamilton hurt his back in a spring auto accident, and it affected him all year, although he did hit well enough in spring training to make the team consider taking him north. Realistically, he needs at least another full season in the minors before we should start thinking about him as a major-league regular. The Devil Rays are more willing than most organizations to let a player advance as quickly as he can, so it's possible Hamilton could hit his way up to Tampa sometime this year. Health will be the key; his back is not expected to be a problem again.

Aubrey Huff 3B Bats L Age 25

YEAR	TEAM	LGE	AB	H	DB	TP	HR	BB	SO	R	RBI	SB	CS	OUT	BA	OBP	SLG	EQA	EQR	DEFENSE
1999	Orlando	Sou	497	131	29	2	18	46	78	67	58	1	2	368	.264	.329	.439	.254	60	132-3B 8
2000	Durham	Int	412	124	30	2	19	43	71	66	66	2	3	291	.301	.369	.522	.289	66	89-3B -11
2000	TampaBay	AL	121	36	4	0	5	4	16	11	14	0	0	85	.298	.326	.455	.256	14	31-3B -5
2001	Durham	Int	67	19	4	0	3	5	6	13	9	0	0	48	.284	.333	.478	.266	9	16-3B 2
2001	TampaBay	AL	412	108	26	1	9	25	62	46	47	1	3	307	.262	.304	.396	.231	39	64-3B 1 17-1B -1
2002	*TampaBay*	*AL*	*519*	*155*	*32*	*2*	*21*	*47*	*83*	*75*	*71*	*1*	*3*	*367*	*.299*	*.357*	*.489*	*.279*	*75*	

Huff's defense at third base was so poor that he essentially lost his job late in the year to no-hit, good-field Jared Sandberg. We shouldn't be all that surprised: Hal McRae displayed a strong preference for gloves over bats when he managed the Royals.

The Fred McGriff deal allowed Steve Cox to move back to first base and might free up the DH role for Huff if the D-Rays can get out from under Greg Vaughn's contract. Huff will need to get back to hitting the way he did in 2000.

Chairon Isenia C Bats R Age 23

YEAR	TEAM	LGE	AB	H	DB	TP	HR	BB	SO	R	RBI	SB	CS	OUT	BA	OBP	SLG	EQA	EQR	DEFENSE	
1999	Princetn	App	102	18	4	1	1	4	18	9	6	2	1	85	.176	.212	.265	.165	5	24-C -6	
1999	HudsnVal	NYP	119	23	5	0	2	2	24	11	9	0	0	96	.193	.209	.286	.166	5	29-C -4	
2000	Charl-SC	SAL	387	81	9	0	6	11	58	26	40	2	2	308	.200	.230	.279	.175	20	88-C -16	
2001	Bakrsfld	Cal	291	68	7	0	7	12	39	30	35	1	2	225	.234	.268	.330	.200	20	37-C -5	
2001	Orlando	Sou	44	7	1	0	0	2	7	2	4	0	0	37	.159	.196	.182	.134	1	14-C -3	
2002	*TampaBay*	*AL*	*361*	*91*	*8*	*1*	*8*	*23*	*56*	*38*	*37*	*2*	*2*	*272*	*.252*	*.297*	*.346*	*.214*	*29*		

An easily overlooked catching prospect, Isenia is a free swinger who is developing into a respectable hitter. Pitchers like to work with him, and his ability to speak several languages helps him get the most out of moundmen of every extraction. He'll get his first real test above A ball this year; if he passes it, he could have a future as Toby Hall's backup.

Russ Johnson IF Bats R Age 29

YEAR	TEAM	LGE	AB	H	DB	TP	HR	BB	SO	R	RBI	SB	CS	OUT	BA	OBP	SLG	EQA	EQR	DEFENSE	
1999	New Orln	PCL	77	24	4	0	1	14	12	14	10	1	2	55	.312	.422	.403	.282	12	12-2B 0	
1999	Houston	NL	157	44	8	0	6	18	29	23	23	1	3	116	.280	.354	.446	.262	20	24-3B 0	
2000	Houston	NL	45	7	0	0	0	2	9	4	2	1	1	39	.156	.191	.156	.126	1		
2000	TampaBay	AL	183	49	5	0	3	23	26	27	17	4	1	135	.268	.353	.344	.245	20	29-3B 5	14-2B 3
2001	TampaBay	AL	249	77	18	2	5	36	49	34	34	2	2	174	.309	.398	.458	.288	39	31-2B 2	29-3B -1
2002	*TampaBay*	*AL*	*266*	*80*	*15*	*1*	*7*	*42*	*51*	*45*	*36*	*4*	*3*	*189*	*.301*	*.396*	*.444*	*.286*	*41*		

Johnson represents no part of Tampa Bay's future and only takes away at-bats from the guys who do. It was kind of odd that the Devil Rays didn't make more of an effort last year to deal him to a team that could have used him, such as the Astros. During the playoffs, the Astros' bench contained Orlando Merced and a couple of pine-tar rags. Johnson could have done for them what he does so well for the Devil Rays: pinch-hit and play all over the infield. And for once, it would have mattered.

Felix Martinez SS Bats B Age 28

YEAR	TEAM	LGE	AB	H	DB	TP	HR	BB	SO	R	RBI	SB	CS	OUT	BA	OBP	SLG	EQA	EQR	DEFENSE
1999	Wichita	Tex	328	73	18	1	3	28	44	42	27	12	7	262	.223	.288	.311	.208	26	76-SS 0
2000	Durham	Int	150	35	6	2	3	5	27	15	15	2	3	118	.233	.269	.360	.207	11	42-SS 4
2000	TampaBay	AL	298	67	13	4	2	28	60	41	17	9	3	234	.225	.309	.315	.220	27	106-SS 9
2001	TampaBay	AL	219	58	15	1	1	11	40	26	15	5	5	167	.265	.311	.356	.223	20	61-SS -9
2002	*TampaBay*	*AL*	*368*	*92*	*19*	*3*	*5*	*34*	*70*	*49*	*31*	*8*	*6*	*282*	*.250*	*.313*	*.359*	*.227*	*35*	

See, you have to keep Felix Martinez around, or you won't have any leverage when you try to re-sign Chris Gomez. It all makes sense. Martinez is a good defensive shortstop, but it's been a few decades since hitters of his ilk were able to hold full-time jobs in the majors, snappy glove work or not. If you ever go to a game and see someone cheering for this guy, don't freak; it's probably just Nelson Norman.

Toe Nash OF Bats B Age 20

YEAR	TEAM	LGE	AB	H	DB	TP	HR	BB	SO	R	RBI	SB	CS	OUT	BA	OBP	SLG	EQA	EQR	DEFENSE
2001	Princetn	App	177	30	6	0	4	12	75	14	15	0	0	147	.169	.223	.271	.170	9	35-LF -1
2002	*TampaBay*	*AL*	*208*	*42*	*7*	*0*	*6*	*16*	*93*	*18*	*19*	*0*	*0*	*166*	*.202*	*.259*	*.322*	*.188*	*13*	

When a guy becomes front-page news before he plays his first professional game, it's always going to be hard to separate the reality from the hype. No, Nash didn't walk off the sandlots and immediately zoom up the ladder, but the Devil Rays were quite satisfied with what he accomplished, especially since he had virtually zero experience in competitive baseball. As to the later reports of his past off-field issues, he proved to be a model citizen and a highly motivated student of the game. He has power, he has speed, he has a great arm, and he has a future. In a year or two we'll have a much better idea of how bright it will be.

Josh Pressley 1B Bats L Age 22

YEAR	TEAM	LGE	AB	H	DB	TP	HR	BB	SO	R	RBI	SB	CS	OUT	BA	OBP	SLG	EQA	EQR	DEFENSE
1999	Charl-SC	SAL	452	85	12	0	7	35	85	36	44	0	2	369	.188	.250	.261	.178	25	100-1B -9
2000	Charl-SC	SAL	500	116	19	0	8	33	65	43	42	1	1	385	.232	.282	.318	.205	36	80-1B 2
2001	Orlando	Sou	113	29	1	1	1	4	22	9	11	0	0	84	.257	.282	.310	.201	8	17-1B 0
2002	*TampaBay*	*AL*	*427*	*107*	*16*	*1*	*8*	*34*	*72*	*43*	*49*	*1*	*1*	*321*	*.251*	*.306*	*.349*	*.220*	*36*	

Pressley, the club's first-round pick in 1998, was working on learning to pull the ball when a broken wrist ended his season. He already makes excellent contact and only needs to turn some of his doubles into homers. Orlando is a tough place for hitters, so he'll be doing just fine if he can get into double digits in home runs. Wrist injuries can linger, so he'll need to prove he's fully recovered.

Damian Rolls IF Bats R Age 24

YEAR	TEAM	LGE	AB	H	DB	TP	HR	BB	SO	R	RBI	SB	CS	OUT	BA	OBP	SLG	EQA	EQR	DEFENSE
1999	Vero Bch	Fla	474	113	17	1	8	26	74	47	37	13	8	369	.238	.287	.329	.210	37	113-3B -3
2000	Orlando	Sou	53	13	4	0	0	5	6	5	3	1	1	41	.245	.317	.321	.219	5	
2001	TampaBay	AL	237	66	13	1	2	11	41	35	12	11	4	176	.278	.310	.367	.231	23	38-2B 1 18-CF -1
2002	*TampaBay*	*AL*	*436*	*124*	*25*	*1*	*6*	*31*	*75*	*55*	*34*	*21*	*8*	*320*	*.284*	*.332*	*.388*	*.247*	*48*	

Rolls made a nice comeback after missing almost all of the 2000 season following shoulder surgery. He won the second-base job for a stretch in the first half, and he hit for a good average for a month or so before falling back to his true level. A former Rule 5 pick, Rolls had never played a full season above A ball, so his ability to hold his own against major-league pitching was a pleasant surprise. He isn't expected to play regularly in 2002, so it wouldn't be a surprise if the Rays sent him to Triple-A to get more playing time.

Jared Sandberg 3B Bats R Age 24

YEAR	TEAM	LGE	AB	H	DB	TP	HR	BB	SO	R	RBI	SB	CS	OUT	BA	OBP	SLG	EQA	EQR	DEFENSE
1999	St Pete	Fla	511	117	16	1	17	37	150	53	67	4	1	395	.229	.286	.364	.220	45	134-3B 3
2000	Orlando	Sou	253	60	13	1	5	25	54	27	31	3	2	195	.237	.308	.356	.226	24	59-3B 6
2001	Durham	Int	328	78	12	0	16	37	75	38	49	0	1	251	.238	.323	.421	.247	38	85-3B 9
2001	TampaBay	AL	136	30	5	0	2	11	39	14	17	1	0	106	.221	.283	.301	.203	10	38-3B 1
2002	*TampaBay*	*AL*	*490*	*127*	*19*	*1*	*18*	*57*	*131*	*59*	*72*	*3*	*1*	*364*	*.259*	*.336*	*.412*	*.254*	*59*	

Hal McRae's irrepressible giddiness over Sandberg, even as he struggled to hit .200, smacked of the Terry Shumpert fiasco back in Kansas City. Perhaps, like Shumpert, Sandberg will be allowed to throw away at-bats by the gross for several years before he'll be held accountable for his batting average. Sandberg might pop a dozen homers or so, but his average will likely be downright Shumpertian.

Bobby Smith 2B Bats R Age 28

YEAR	TEAM	LGE	AB	H	DB	TP	HR	BB	SO	R	RBI	SB	CS	OUT	BA	OBP	SLG	EQA	EQR	DEFENSE
1999	TampaBay	AL	199	39	5	1	3	14	56	18	19	4	4	164	.196	.252	.276	.182	12	44-3B 5
1999	Durham	Int	225	70	14	2	12	22	57	43	38	10	4	159	.311	.380	.551	.302	40	54-3B 3
2000	Durham	Int	263	73	18	1	16	19	60	43	51	12	2	192	.278	.332	.536	.283	41	54-2B 0
2000	TampaBay	AL	174	42	7	0	7	12	52	20	26	2	2	134	.241	.294	.402	.230	17	42-2B 1
2001	TampaBay	AL	19	3	0	0	0	3	9	1	1	0	0	16	.158	.273	.158	.165	1	
2001	Durham	Int	405	118	22	2	21	43	84	65	67	8	2	289	.291	.367	.511	.289	65	71-LF 0 24-2B 0
2002	*TampaBay*	*AL*	*393*	*112*	*19*	*2*	*23*	*43*	*97*	*67*	*70*	*11*	*4*	*285*	*.285*	*.356*	*.519*	*.288*	*63*	

The organization's designated yo-yo, Smith won the second-base job in spring training, held it for all of six games, and spent most of the year at Triple-A before being restored to the 40-man roster after the season. Apparently the D-Rays haven't yet figured out whether he's good enough, and they want to jerk him around among second base, third base, shortstop, the bench, and Triple-A for a few more years before deciding where he best fits.

Jason Smith — SS — Bats L — Age 24

YEAR	TEAM	LGE	AB	H	DB	TP	HR	BB	SO	R	RBI	SB	CS	OUT	BA	OBP	SLG	EQA	EQR	DEFENSE
1999	Daytona	Fla	143	31	3	1	4	8	33	15	18	5	2	114	.217	.265	.336	.206	11	38-SS -18
2000	WestTenn	Sou	492	109	18	5	12	13	129	49	53	11	7	390	.222	.243	.352	.198	34	114-SS -18
2001	Iowa	PCL	239	51	8	5	3	11	64	27	13	5	2	190	.213	.250	.326	.196	16	67-SS 2
2001	Durham	Int	31	6	2	0	0	0	10	3	3	0	0	25	.194	.194	.258	.151	1	
2002	*TampaBay*	*AL*	*435*	*106*	*20*	*5*	*10*	*24*	*123*	*50*	*50*	*7*	*4*	*333*	*.244*	*.283*	*.382*	*.220*	*38*	

Smith was the less useless of the two players obtained from the Cubs for Fred McGriff. He has a mixed bag of talents: a strong arm, a little pop, and he bats from the left side. He possesses little range and gets to a three-ball count about as often as he gets to a Cabinet meeting. If Chris Gomez hits the way he's supposed to and gets what he deserves, Smith might help bridge the gap until Jorge Cantu is ready.

Ramon Soler — 2B/SS — Bats B — Age 20

YEAR	TEAM	LGE	AB	H	DB	TP	HR	BB	SO	R	RBI	SB	CS	OUT	BA	OBP	SLG	EQA	EQR	DEFENSE
1999	Charl-SC	SAL	405	76	12	1	1	41	98	47	20	22	9	338	.188	.265	.230	.184	25	89-SS -10
2001	Bakrsfld	Cal	425	91	13	2	1	34	72	50	19	13	4	338	.214	.275	.261	.192	27	69-2B -6
2002	*TampaBay*	*AL*	*389*	*94*	*14*	*2*	*3*	*40*	*75*	*53*	*26*	*16*	*5*	*300*	*.242*	*.312*	*.311*	*.218*	*33*	

A shoulder injury wiped out Soler's 2000 season and limited him to second base in 2001, but he might be able to return to shortstop this year. He's a switch-hitter with terrific speed, and he has enough offensive potential to develop into a top-of-the-order hitter; he even takes a few walks. Soler will probably make the jump to Double-A this year and will be one of the youngest players in the Southern League.

Jason Tyner — LF/CF — Bats L — Age 25

YEAR	TEAM	LGE	AB	H	DB	TP	HR	BB	SO	R	RBI	SB	CS	OUT	BA	OBP	SLG	EQA	EQR	DEFENSE
1999	Binghmtn	Eas	518	139	13	3	1	45	46	67	26	30	11	390	.268	.327	.311	.227	48	121-CF -5
2000	Norfolk	Int	329	100	6	1	0	25	31	47	25	26	12	241	.304	.356	.328	.241	35	80-CF 1
2000	NY Mets	NL	42	9	2	0	0	0	4	3	5	1	1	34	.214	.230	.262	.167	2	11-LF 0
2000	TampaBay	AL	83	21	2	0	0	3	11	6	8	6	1	63	.253	.288	.277	.207	6	23-LF 4
2001	Durham	Int	160	48	2	1	0	15	9	24	12	9	4	117	.300	.365	.325	.244	17	37-CF 0
2001	TampaBay	AL	397	119	7	5	1	17	36	54	22	30	7	285	.300	.332	.350	.241	41	93-LF 1
2002	*TampaBay*	*AL*	*489*	*151*	*14*	*3*	*2*	*42*	*46*	*75*	*34*	*31*	*9*	*347*	*.309*	*.363*	*.362*	*.257*	*58*	

If Jason Tyner batted against a team with no fielders, could he record an extra-base hit? Almost all of his hits were singles, 34 of them of the infield variety. It certainly is possible to be a productive hitter while hitting mostly singles—Luis Castillo could get rich giving clinics on the topic—but to do it, you have to draw walks. Tyner simply hasn't shown he can do that. One thing he did vow to do at the end of last season was add weight over the winter in order to drive the ball more. We'll see; Juan Pierre added some muscle before last season, then proved that learning to use it is a different challenge entirely.

Greg Vaughn — DH/LF — Bats R — Age 36

YEAR	TEAM	LGE	AB	H	DB	TP	HR	BB	SO	R	RBI	SB	CS	OUT	BA	OBP	SLG	EQA	EQR	DEFENSE
1999	Cincnnti	NL	550	132	18	2	44	77	127	99	109	13	2	420	.240	.336	.520	.279	86	128-LF 4
2000	TampaBay	AL	456	120	25	1	30	74	113	80	72	8	1	337	.263	.368	.520	.292	78	72-LF 4
2001	TampaBay	AL	487	122	23	0	28	73	112	79	88	10	6	371	.251	.351	.470	.271	71	57-LF 2
2002	*TampaBay*	*AL*	*472*	*115*	*21*	*1*	*29*	*82*	*117*	*79*	*78*	*8*	*3*	*360*	*.244*	*.356*	*.477*	*.278*	*73*	

Homers and walks are all Greg Vaughn contributes, but they are two great tastes that taste great together. He continues to supply enough of each to keep his production palatable, even as his average slips and his age creeps toward 40. The club already has gotten rid of the rest of the veteran mercenaries it brought in with Vaughn, so you have to think he'll be gone as soon as they find a taker. If the Rays got Manny Aybar and Jason Smith for Fred McGriff, what will Vaughn bring? Carlos Castillo and Lou Merloni?

Randy Winn — OF — Bats B — Age 28

YEAR	TEAM	LGE	AB	H	DB	TP	HR	BB	SO	R	RBI	SB	CS	OUT	BA	OBP	SLG	EQA	EQR	DEFENSE
1999	Durham	Int	206	67	17	2	3	12	25	31	25	7	5	144	.325	.365	.471	.274	28	46-CF 1
1999	TampaBay	AL	302	83	18	4	2	14	55	43	23	8	9	228	.275	.309	.381	.227	28	76-CF 1
2000	Durham	Int	307	95	22	4	7	41	52	60	35	14	4	217	.309	.395	.476	.294	51	76-LF -1
2000	TampaBay	AL	157	40	2	0	2	25	22	26	16	6	8	125	.255	.364	.306	.232	16	43-LF 2
2001	TampaBay	AL	430	125	26	6	7	40	70	57	52	10	11	316	.291	.357	.428	.260	54	107-RF -1
2002	*TampaBay*	*AL*	*435*	*127*	*27*	*5*	*8*	*46*	*73*	*72*	*46*	*15*	*9*	*317*	*.292*	*.360*	*.432*	*.267*	*58*	

If this is as good as it gets, why are the Devil Rays still interested? Ah, it's probably a moot point. By the time they play any meaningful games they'll have Carl Crawford in center field and Josh Hamilton in right. Winn is well-suited to be a fourth outfielder, a Danny Bautista, but to play him regularly is a sign of both a disturbing lack of quality players on the roster and a manager who is preoccupied with speed and defense.

Ron Wright — 1B — Bats R — Age 26

YEAR	TEAM	LGE	AB	H	DB	TP	HR	BB	SO	R	RBI	SB	CS	OUT	BA	OBP	SLG	EQA	EQR	DEFENSE
1999	Altoona	Eas	82	17	5	0	0	6	27	4	3	0	0	65	.207	.266	.268	.186	5	10-1B 3
2000	Chattang	Sou	247	60	13	0	11	28	69	32	42	1	1	188	.243	.323	.429	.249	29	53-1B -3
2000	Louisvil	Int	61	12	4	0	2	6	18	9	12	0	0	49	.197	.269	.361	.211	5	13-1B -1
2001	Durham	Int	448	115	19	0	21	49	95	62	73	2	2	335	.257	.333	.440	.256	56	113-1B 0
2002	*Seattle*	*AL*	*382*	*94*	*15*	*0*	*18*	*48*	*94*	*38*	*49*	*1*	*1*	*289*	*.246*	*.330*	*.427*	*.262*	*51*	

"Remember me? I used to be a prospect, before my back went haywire. No, no, you're thinking of Bob Hamelin. Japan, last I heard, but that was a while ago. Anyway, I'm back. No, I don't hit left-handed. Got lotsa power, though. Don't mind playing part-time, either. Could pinch-hit, teach the kids how to have a good attitude, do that Kevin Millar thing for ya. What do you mean your manager doesn't like power? I thought I'd heard 'em all. OK, well, if you change your mind, you know where I'll be."

PITCHERS (ERA: 4.50, H/9: 9.0, HR/9: 1.0, BB/9: 3.0, K/9: 6.0, KW: 2.0, PERA: 4.50)

Wilson Alvarez — Throws L — Age 32

YEAR	TEAM	LGE	IP	H	ER	HR	BB	K	ERA	W	L	H/9	HR/9	BB/9	K/9	KW	PERA	STUFF
1999	TampaBay	AL	163.7	158	84	19	66	127	4.62	9	9	8.7	1.0	3.6	7.0	1.0	4.42	12
2001	Orlando	Sou	20.3	23	14	4	8	10	6.20	1	1	10.2	1.8	3.5	4.4	0.6	6.86	-25
2001	Durham	Int	18.3	20	12	3	8	11	5.89	1	1	9.8	1.5	3.9	5.4	0.7	5.23	-12

The Devil Rays must decide if it's better to pay Wilson Alvarez $7 million and have him pitch for you, or if it's better to pay him $7 million and send him home. Of course, there's no guarantee that they'll get to make that choice. Even after recovering from shoulder surgery last year, Alvarez—who was never a paragon of physical fitness—encountered numerous setbacks and shut it down for good in August.

Derek Andersen — Throws L — Age 24

YEAR	TEAM	LGE	IP	H	ER	HR	BB	K	ERA	W	L	H/9	HR/9	BB/9	K/9	KW	PERA	STUFF
1999	HudsnVal	NYP	55.0	53	20	0	19	26	3.27	4	2	8.7	0.0	3.1	4.3	0.7	4.39	-1
2000	Charl-SC	SAL	20.0	26	19	8	3	11	8.55	0	2	11.7	3.6	1.4	4.9	1.8	7.24	-26
2001	Charl-SC	SAL	36.3	41	22	8	5	22	5.45	2	2	10.2	2.0	1.2	5.4	2.2	3.84	-12
2001	Bakrsfld	Cal	23.3	24	12	2	8	13	4.63	1	2	9.3	0.8	3.1	5.0	0.8	4.60	-14

Andersen turns the ball over, sinks it, cuts it, compresses it into a diamond, teleports it through other dimensions, makes it disappear up his sleeve, and throws it past the hitter after pointing to the stands and shouting at him, "Hey, who's that guy hitting on your girlfriend?" He can't crack 90 mph, so it is perhaps inevitable that he gets compared to Tom Glavine. We'll see how his act plays at the higher levels.

Manny Aybar — Throws R — Age 27

YEAR	TEAM	LGE	IP	H	ER	HR	BB	K	ERA	W	L	H/9	HR/9	BB/9	K/9	KW	PERA	STUFF
1999	St Louis	NL	100.0	101	50	12	30	67	4.50	6	5	9.1	1.1	2.7	6.0	1.1	5.66	-2
2000	Florida	NL	24.7	26	14	3	11	12	5.11	1	2	9.5	1.1	4.0	4.4	0.5	2.50	-15
2000	Cincnnti	NL	50.3	53	28	6	18	28	5.01	3	3	9.5	1.1	3.2	5.0	0.8	4.93	-11
2001	Iowa	PCL	40.3	49	36	10	20	20	8.03	1	3	10.9	2.2	4.5	4.5	0.5	6.57	-26
2001	ChiCubs	NL	22.7	25	18	4	15	13	7.15	1	2	9.9	1.6	6.0	5.2	0.4	7.59	-28
2001	Durham	Int	33.0	38	24	7	11	20	6.55	1	3	10.4	1.9	3.0	5.5	0.9	9.28	-24

What can you say about Manny Aybar that hasn't already been said about any other eminently forgettable right-hander? He's the kind of pitcher who gets sent out to eat meaningless innings, so the amount of work he gets has little do with how well he performs. If the pitching staff has injuries and there's no one interesting at Triple-A, they call for Aybar.

Brandon Backe — Throws R — Age 24

YEAR	TEAM	LGE	IP	H	ER	HR	BB	K	ERA	W	L	H/9	HR/9	BB/9	K/9	KW	PERA	STUFF
2001	Charl-SC	SAL	22.0	27	19	5	11	9	7.77	1	1	11.0	2.0	4.5	3.7	0.4	4.94	-37
2001	Bakrsfld	Cal	22.7	22	12	2	11	16	4.76	1	2	8.7	0.8	4.4	6.4	0.7	3.48	-8
2001	Orlando	Sou	21.3	21	12	2	12	12	5.06	1	1	8.9	0.8	5.1	5.1	0.5	7.85	-19

Backe, a converted outfielder, did very well in his first season on the mound. He hit the low 90s consistently and didn't have any problems until he got to Double-A. Understandably, he's still learning to set up hitters and use his secondary pitches. Staying healthy this year will be the key for him; converted position players sometimes break down after their first season of professional pitching, because their arms haven't been built up yet.

Nick Bierbrodt — Throws L — Age 24

YEAR	TEAM	LGE	IP	H	ER	HR	BB	K	ERA	W	L	H/9	HR/9	BB/9	K/9	KW	PERA	STUFF
1999	El Paso	Tex	78.3	78	40	4	41	39	4.60	4	5	9.0	0.5	4.7	4.5	0.5	5.03	3
1999	Tucson	PCL	46.7	50	37	9	31	33	7.14	1	4	9.6	1.7	6.0	6.4	0.5	7.58	-2
2000	El Paso	Tex	37.0	34	19	1	24	25	4.62	2	2	8.3	0.2	5.8	6.1	0.5	7.26	4
2000	Tucson	PCL	16.7	19	15	3	13	9	8.10	0	2	10.3	1.6	7.0	4.9	0.3	4.22	-11
2001	El Paso	Tex	18.3	18	9	2	7	12	4.42	1	1	8.8	1.0	3.4	5.9	0.9	1.43	10
2001	Tucson	PCL	48.3	40	13	0	10	40	2.42	4	1	7.4	0.0	1.9	7.4	2.0	2.86	34
2001	Arizona	NL	23.0	26	18	5	11	14	7.04	1	2	10.2	2.0	4.3	5.5	0.6	8.03	-9
2001	TampaBay	AL	65.0	64	37	10	26	53	5.12	3	4	8.9	1.4	3.6	7.3	1.0	5.12	15

When the Devil Rays cashed in Albie Lopez, the take was Bierbrodt, a young left-hander with a history of injuries and inconsistency. With Tampa Bay, he showed none of the former but plenty of the latter, alternating gems and torchings with a randomness that would make Jason Bere envious. There's a school of thought, though, that says you're better off taking a guy who runs hot and cold than a guy who's unfailingly mediocre, because a hot-and-cold guy has at least shown that he's capable of pitching very well. Bierbrodt has shown that; how often he'll actually do it is anyone's guess.

Jesus Colome — Throws R — Age 22

YEAR	TEAM	LGE	IP	H	ER	HR	BB	K	ERA	W	L	H/9	HR/9	BB/9	K/9	KW	PERA	STUFF
1999	Modesto	Cal	130.7	131	71	11	66	76	4.89	7	8	9.0	0.8	4.5	5.2	0.6	4.85	6
2000	Midland	Tex	107.7	112	65	14	50	66	5.43	5	7	9.4	1.2	4.2	5.5	0.7	5.03	11
2000	Orlando	Sou	15.0	18	13	4	7	6	7.80	0	2	10.8	2.4	4.2	3.6	0.4	9.58	-15
2001	Durham	Int	19.0	18	8	1	7	14	3.79	1	1	8.5	0.5	3.3	6.6	1.0	7.83	5
2001	TampaBay	AL	45.7	48	31	7	24	29	6.11	2	3	9.5	1.4	4.7	5.7	0.6	3.73	-5

Lordy, this kid throws hard—and he's only 22. A true Armando Benitez-in-progress, with high-90s heat, a never-ending quest for a reliable second pitch, and inconsistent command. A hamstring injury sidelined him early in the year and kept his workload down to a safe level. If he addresses his weaknesses, he could come very quickly; that might happen this year or three years from now. It's nice to think that the only thing standing between him and the closer's job is Esteban Yan.

Chad Coward Throws R Age 23

YEAR	TEAM	LGE	IP	H	ER	HR	BB	K	ERA	W	L	H/9	HR/9	BB/9	K/9	KW	PERA	STUFF
2000	Princetn	App	30.3	30	19	3	21	18	5.64	1	2	8.9	0.9	6.2	5.3	0.4	5.39	-1
2000	HudsnVal	NYP	34.0	37	22	4	17	15	5.82	1	3	9.8	1.1	4.5	4.0	0.4	8.60	-8
2001	Charl-SC	SAL	10.7	10	5	0	6	6	4.22	1	0	8.4	0.0	5.1	5.1	0.5	4.22	-7
2001	Bakrsfld	Cal	67.3	66	29	2	28	34	3.88	4	3	8.8	0.3	3.7	4.5	0.6	3.36	-6

He pronounces it COE-ward, and he's probably damned tired of correcting people. Coward was one of the most effective pitchers at Bakersfield last year, and while he was a little old for the league and isn't regarded as much of a prospect, you have to respect a guy who puts up a 2.00 ERA in the California League. He'll have to keep surprising people in order to stay ahead of the organization's wave of youthful hard throwers.

Doug Creek Throws L Age 33

YEAR	TEAM	LGE	IP	H	ER	HR	BB	K	ERA	W	L	H/9	HR/9	BB/9	K/9	KW	PERA	STUFF
1999	Iowa	PCL	127.3	134	93	25	72	94	6.57	4	10	9.5	1.8	5.1	6.6	0.7	4.98	-9
2000	Durham	Int	17.0	15	10	1	15	16	5.29	1	1	7.9	0.5	7.9	8.5	0.5	2.94	-8
2000	TampaBay	AL	61.0	51	31	9	32	72	4.57	3	4	7.5	1.3	4.7	10.6	1.1	4.10	17
2001	TampaBay	AL	62.7	54	36	6	47	63	5.17	3	4	7.8	0.9	6.8	9.0	0.7	4.47	1

Like the 14-year-old who smokes to prove he's cool enough to hang out with the big kids, the Devil Rays carried Creek all year to show that they were major league enough to have a situational lefty. Perhaps this year they'll figure out that Creek is worth ten times more to a contender (not to mention 100 times more to Tony La Russa). He's 33 years old, and he gets left-handed hitters out; cash him in for a prospect already.

Neal Frendling Throws R Age 22

YEAR	TEAM	LGE	IP	H	ER	HR	BB	K	ERA	W	L	H/9	HR/9	BB/9	K/9	KW	PERA	STUFF
1999	Princetn	App	17.7	20	11	2	6	8	5.60	1	1	10.2	1.0	3.1	4.1	0.7	4.89	0
1999	HudsnVal	NYP	47.3	50	25	5	13	24	4.75	2	3	9.5	1.0	2.5	4.6	0.9	5.44	9
2000	Charl-SC	SAL	151.0	170	109	32	59	91	6.50	6	11	10.1	1.9	3.5	5.4	0.8	5.79	7
2001	Bakrsfld	Cal	111.3	119	67	14	46	59	5.42	5	7	9.6	1.1	3.7	4.8	0.6	6.02	1

Frendling is a low-round draft pick and overachiever who led the organization in strikeouts in 2000, using a broad arsenal rather than sheer velocity. He continued to whiff guys last year, but a case of tendinitis knocked him out of action at the end of the season. He didn't need surgery and is expected to be fine for 2002. The strikeouts haven't been sufficient to win him much respect as a prospect, and he'll need to keep putting up good numbers to stay ahead of the guys in the system with better raw stuff.

Travis Harper Throws R Age 26

YEAR	TEAM	LGE	IP	H	ER	HR	BB	K	ERA	W	L	H/9	HR/9	BB/9	K/9	KW	PERA	STUFF
1999	St Pete	Fla	82.3	86	46	10	31	47	5.03	4	5	9.4	1.1	3.4	5.1	0.8	5.69	-1
1999	Orlando	Sou	71.7	80	51	15	27	46	6.40	3	5	10.0	1.9	3.4	5.8	0.9	6.56	-3
2000	Orlando	Sou	51.0	53	21	2	13	19	3.71	4	2	9.4	0.4	2.3	3.4	0.7	4.91	-3
2000	Durham	Int	99.3	118	68	19	26	39	6.16	4	7	10.7	1.7	2.4	3.5	0.8	5.06	-9
2000	TampaBay	AL	31.0	35	19	4	12	14	5.52	1	2	10.2	1.2	3.5	4.1	0.6	4.00	-5
2001	Durham	Int	146.0	174	115	37	48	78	7.09	5	11	10.7	2.3	3.0	4.8	0.8	5.29	-14

Harper must have gotten on somebody's bad side last year. The big-league club dropped out of contention before the season was a month old, with a pitching staff impersonating arsonists on meth, but the D-Rays turned up their noses at the thought of promoting Harper. Mickey Callaway got called up, and Tony Fiore got a look, as did Brian Rose, Dan Wheeler, Ken friggin' Hill, and Martin Gramatica. By July, Durham's entire pitching staff had been called up except Harper, who got to stay in Triple-A and go 12-6.

Delvin James Throws R Age 24

YEAR	TEAM	LGE	IP	H	ER	HR	BB	K	ERA	W	L	H/9	HR/9	BB/9	K/9	KW	PERA	STUFF
1999	Charl-SC	SAL	151.3	179	102	26	45	54	6.07	6	11	10.6	1.5	2.7	3.2	0.6	5.92	-6
1999	St Pete	Fla	17.3	18	7	0	5	4	3.63	1	1	9.3	0.0	2.6	2.1	0.4	4.02	-3
2000	St Pete	Fla	134.7	161	90	25	33	47	6.01	5	10	10.8	1.7	2.2	3.1	0.7	6.51	-9
2000	Orlando	Sou	35.0	39	20	5	7	17	5.14	2	2	10.0	1.3	1.8	4.4	1.2	4.76	5
2001	Orlando	Sou	38.3	38	16	2	10	19	3.76	2	2	8.9	0.5	2.3	4.5	0.9	2.26	10
2001	Durham	Int	07.0	95	50	10	30	39	5.17	4	6	9.8	1.0	3.1	4.0	0.6	6.30	-13

Look for this guy to get a shot in middle relief sometime this year. He won't be great, but he could pitch well enough to earn a setup role. James throws hard with good control and has pitched fairly well while being moved along rather slowly. His conversion from starting to relief midway through last season seemed to agree with him, as he was more effective out of the pen in the second half.

Joe Kennedy Throws L Age 23

YEAR	TEAM	LGE	IP	H	ER	HR	BB	K	ERA	W	L	H/9	HR/9	BB/9	K/9	KW	PERA	STUFF
1999	HudsnVal	NYP	93.3	94	43	5	35	48	4.15	5	5	9.1	0.5	3.4	4.6	0.7	4.44	11
2000	Charl-SC	SAL	135.0	141	68	15	37	74	4.53	7	8	9.4	1.0	2.5	4.9	1.0	5.39	9
2001	Orlando	Sou	43.7	38	10	0	3	33	2.06	4	1	7.8	0.0	0.6	6.8	5.5	0.78	38
2001	Durham	Int	25.3	25	13	3	10	18	4.62	1	2	8.9	1.1	3.6	6.4	0.9	3.21	18
2001	TampaBay	AL	119.7	123	60	15	32	74	4.51	6	7	9.3	1.1	2.4	5.6	1.2	4.42	12

It is not our intent to damn with faint praise when we point out that Joe Kennedy was Tampa Bay's most effective starter last season. He zoomed through the minors by making Double-A and Triple-A hitters look foolish for a couple of months, and he proved to be more than good enough to hold a rotation spot for the rest of the season. A left-hander who throws in the low 90s with a sharp curve, he seemed to learn as he went along, and he strung together a number of good starts near the end of the season. He could take a big step forward as he builds stamina; one weakness last season was that he tended to lose his edge after the 60-pitch mark.

Jim Magrane Throws R Age 23

YEAR	TEAM	LGE	IP	H	ER	HR	BB	K	ERA	W	L	H/9	HR/9	BB/9	K/9	KW	PERA	STUFF
2000	Charl-SC	SAL	170.0	184	97	22	55	84	5.14	8	11	9.7	1.2	2.9	4.4	0.8	4.61	4
2001	Orlando	Sou	171.7	189	103	23	61	80	5.40	8	11	9.9	1.2	3.2	4.2	0.7	5.66	0

Though Magrane sounds like a lefty and pitches like one, he isn't. He's a dedicated finesse pitcher, working with a repertoire that would put any scout to sleep. Another way of looking at it is that he has everything but stuff: command, intelligence, and an ability to set up hitters. Unlike some finesse guys who dominate the lower levels by getting overaggressive A-ball hitters to fish for balls out of the zone, Magrane didn't hit the wall at Double-A, a good sign for his continued success.

Mark Malaska Throws L Age 24

YEAR	TEAM	LGE	IP	H	ER	HR	BB	K	ERA	W	L	H/9	HR/9	BB/9	K/9	KW	PERA	STUFF
2000	HudsnVal	NYP	41.7	45	25	4	18	17	5.40	2	3	9.7	0.9	3.9	3.7	0.5	9.20	-17
2001	Charl-SC	SAL	153.7	178	108	29	56	69	6.33	6	11	10.4	1.7	3.3	4.0	0.6	6.89	-13
2001	Bakrsfld	Cal	16.7	19	10	2	7	6	5.40	1	1	10.3	1.1	3.8	3.2	0.4	5.55	-13

Here's a guy who has a chance to surprise. Malaska, a converted outfielder, doesn't throw that hard, but he has excellent movement on his fastball and slider. Unlike a lot of pitchers who rely on movement, he doesn't struggle with walks, posting a strikeout-to-walk ratio better than four-to-one in his first full professional season. He's a lefty, so if he stays healthy he'll land a spot somewhere eventually.

Seth McClung Throws R Age 21

YEAR	TEAM	LGE	IP	H	ER	HR	BB	K	ERA	W	L	H/9	HR/9	BB/9	K/9	KW	PERA	STUFF
1999	Princetn	App	47.7	54	51	7	61	19	9.63	1	4	10.2	1.3	11.5	3.6	0.2	11.32	-34
2000	HudsnVal	NYP	43.3	42	19	0	21	19	3.95	3	2	8.7	0.0	4.4	3.9	0.5	5.43	4
2000	Charl-SC	SAL	31.7	31	17	0	24	14	4.83	2	2	8.8	0.0	6.8	4.0	0.3	5.62	-2
2001	Charl-SC	SAL	161.3	166	88	14	75	84	4.91	8	10	9.3	0.8	4.2	4.7	0.6	5.92	6

(Seth McClung *continued*)

McClung is the most impressive of all the Devil Rays' young pitchers. A big guy—6′6″ and 235 pounds—his fastball was voted the best in the South Atlantic League in *Baseball America*'s survey. He tries to rear back and blow people away when he ought to be trying to set them up, but come on: if you were 21 and threw in the mid- to upper 90s, wouldn't you try to blow people away, too? His will eventually reach a level at which he won't always be able to get away with that, and he might struggle for a bit as he learns to get his breaking ball over more consistently. But once he learns, look out. The only major concern is that he threw a fair number of innings last year at age 20.

Travis Phelps **Throws R** **Age 24**

YEAR	TEAM	LGE	IP	H	ER	HR	BB	K	ERA	W	L	H/9	HR/9	BB/9	K/9	KW	PERA	STUFF
1999	St Pete	Fla	138.3	145	71	13	47	68	4.62	7	8	9.4	0.8	3.1	4.4	0.7	5.96	3
2000	Orlando	Sou	104.7	102	53	9	47	71	4.56	6	6	8.8	0.8	4.0	6.1	0.8	4.78	10
2000	Durham	Int	28.7	33	25	7	15	18	7.85	1	2	10.4	2.2	4.7	5.7	0.6	5.46	-3
2001	Durham	Int	15.0	14	4	0	1	9	2.40	2	0	8.4	0.0	0.6	5.4	4.5	0.00	15
2001	TampaBay	AL	61.7	57	27	5	23	51	3.94	4	3	8.3	0.7	3.4	7.4	1.1	3.99	9

Phelps was an 89th-round pick, making him the lowest-drafted player ever to reach the majors, so it's a bit redundant to say he lacks overpowering stuff. He mixes a decent fastball with an above-average slider and change-up, hits his spots, and stays away from the middle of the plate. Hitters seemed to catch on to him a bit in the second half, so he might not be quite as effective this season. He probably won't ever be entrusted with a high-profile role.

Bryan Rekar **Throws R** **Age 30**

YEAR	TEAM	LGE	IP	H	ER	HR	BB	K	ERA	W	L	H/9	HR/9	BB/9	K/9	KW	PERA	STUFF
1999	Durham	Int	33.7	35	17	4	9	19	4.54	2	2	9.4	1.1	2.4	5.1	1.1	4.16	1
1999	TampaBay	AL	101.7	108	56	12	34	54	4.96	5	6	9.6	1.1	3.0	4.8	0.8	5.52	-7
2000	Durham	Int	21.0	20	8	1	4	13	3.43	1	1	8.6	0.4	1.7	5.6	1.6	2.45	13
2000	TampaBay	AL	181.0	190	83	19	32	94	4.13	11	9	9.4	0.9	1.6	4.7	1.5	4.00	7
2001	TampaBay	AL	147.3	156	80	19	43	83	4.89	7	9	9.5	1.2	2.6	5.1	1.0	6.10	0

Rekar was awarded a $1.4-million salary in arbitration last winter, after which everything that could go wrong, did. He pitched halfway decently over the first three months of the season, but nevertheless dropped ten of his first 11 decisions. Every time he took the mound, it seemed that the D-Rays' hitters turned into Ray Oylers, and their fielders turned into Dave Kingmans. Then Rekar hurt his shoulder, missed a month, and pitched poorly upon his return. Speculation that the club will non-tender him turned into a spring training invitation with the Royals.

Ryan Rupe **Throws R** **Age 27**

YEAR	TEAM	LGE	IP	H	ER	HR	BB	K	ERA	W	L	H/9	HR/9	BB/9	K/9	KW	PERA	STUFF
1999	Orlando	Sou	24.7	25	11	2	7	14	4.01	2	1	9.1	0.7	2.6	5.1	1.0	5.63	0
1999	TampaBay	AL	143.0	142	70	15	48	96	4.41	8	8	8.9	0.9	3.0	6.0	1.0	4.37	12
2000	TampaBay	AL	98.3	106	57	16	25	60	5.22	5	6	9.7	1.5	2.3	5.5	1.2	6.21	0
2000	Durham	Int	20.3	22	14	4	8	13	6.20	1	1	9.7	1.8	3.5	5.8	0.8	8.92	-19
2001	TampaBay	AL	149.0	153	87	27	46	117	5.26	7	10	9.2	1.6	2.8	7.1	1.3	6.39	7

Conspiracy theorists who speculate that there were multiple Lee Harvey Oswalds must have a field day with Rupe. He gave up two earned runs or less in 11 of his 26 starts, but he gave up five earned runs or more nine times—including outings of seven, eight, nine, and ten earned runs allowed, a true "straight from hell." That doesn't even include his two relief appearances: he gave up six runs each time, working a total of one and two-thirds innings. It seems like only yesterday he was a promising young pitcher; now he's 27 years old. Those six-run outings will age you quickly.

Bobby Seay **Throws L** **Age 24**

YEAR	TEAM	LGE	IP	H	ER	HR	BB	K	ERA	W	L	H/9	HR/9	BB/9	K/9	KW	PERA	STUFF
1999	St Pete	Fla	58.7	56	24	0	28	30	3.68	4	3	8.6	0.0	4.3	4.6	0.5	5.00	4
1999	Orlando	Sou	18.3	20	15	3	15	11	7.36	1	1	9.8	1.5	7.4	5.4	0.4	8.90	-16
2000	Orlando	Sou	130.7	146	89	23	54	71	6.13	5	10	10.1	1.6	3.7	4.9	0.7	5.68	-1
2001	Orlando	Sou	65.3	78	53	15	30	30	7.30	2	5	10.7	2.1	4.1	4.1	0.5	9.15	-23
2001	TampaBay	AL	13.0	13	8	3	5	11	5.54	0	1	9.0	2.1	3.5	7.6	1.1	6.98	-1

It wasn't entirely a lost season. Seay had raised expectations by enjoying his first winning season in 2000, at Double-A Orlando. He returned to Orlando in 2001, strained his index finger in May, and wound up missing almost two months. He pitched poorly upon his return, but he got called up anyway in August and fared pretty well before tiring in September. Regardless of how good the D-Rays thought he'd be four years ago, the fact is that he hasn't been consistently successful at any level. Until he shows he's mastered Triple-A, we can't expect much from him.

Hans Smith Throws L Age 23

YEAR	TEAM	LGE	IP	H	ER	HR	BB	K	ERA	W	L	H/9	HR/9	BB/9	K/9	KW	PERA	STUFF
2000	Charl-SC	SAL	32.3	32	12	0	8	12	3.34	3	1	8.9	0.0	2.2	3.3	0.8	3.21	-7
2001	Bakrsfld	Cal	38.0	39	22	4	19	22	5.21	2	2	9.2	0.9	4.5	5.2	0.6	3.04	-11

Smith is 6′9″ and left-handed. A Randy Johnson clone, right? Not even close. His stuff is nothing special, and his height is the only scary thing about him. He simply delivers strike after strike and makes batters put the ball in play, mostly on the ground. He had a ridiculous 1.45 ERA at Bakersfield last year, but that probably won't hold up, as he allowed almost a hit an inning. God, I wish the D-Rays had a reliever named "Franz" with whom to pair him.

Jason Standridge Throws R Age 23

YEAR	TEAM	LGE	IP	H	ER	HR	BB	K	ERA	W	L	H/9	HR/9	BB/9	K/9	KW	PERA	STUFF
1999	Charl-SC	SAL	107.3	116	60	10	42	43	5.03	5	7	9.7	0.8	3.5	3.6	0.5	3.72	-2
1999	St Pete	Fla	49.3	50	23	0	24	17	4.20	3	2	9.1	0.0	4.4	3.1	0.4	4.95	0
2000	St Pete	Fla	52.3	59	43	9	37	27	7.39	2	4	10.1	1.5	6.4	4.6	0.4	5.80	-9
2000	Orlando	Sou	93.7	100	53	7	44	37	5.09	4	6	9.6	0.7	4.2	3.6	0.4	5.57	-2
2001	Durham	Int	106.0	124	80	17	56	37	6.79	4	8	10.5	1.4	4.8	3.1	0.3	7.44	-17
2001	TampaBay	AL	18.3	22	18	5	13	9	8.84	0	2	10.8	2.5	6.4	4.4	0.3	4.28	-26

Standridge made good progress during 2000 but seemed to give it all back last year. He pitched poorly at Triple-A, got called up anyway, and stunk even worse with the big club. His numbers always have been something of a mystery, because he's said to have good stuff—a low-90s fastball and hard curve—but he posts distinctly unimpressive strikeout-to-walk ratios. He might get a chance to open the season on the major-league roster, but don't expect much.

Tanyon Sturtze Throws R Age 31

YEAR	TEAM	LGE	IP	H	ER	HR	BB	K	ERA	W	L	H/9	HR/9	BB/9	K/9	KW	PERA	STUFF
1999	Charlott	Int	102.3	96	48	8	44	76	4.22	6	5	8.4	0.7	3.9	6.7	0.9	4.67	-2
2000	ChiSox	AL	17.3	21	16	3	12	6	8.31	0	2	10.9	1.6	6.2	3.1	0.3	10.86	-46
2000	TampaBay	AL	53.0	50	20	3	11	38	3.40	4	2	8.5	0.5	1.9	6.5	1.7	2.29	13
2001	TampaBay	AL	197.0	206	107	21	75	105	4.89	10	12	9.4	1.0	3.4	4.8	0.7	4.14	-1

No offense to Sturtze, who's battled hard and long to establish himself as a major leaguer, but the Devil Rays' best use for Sturtze would be as trade bait. Admittedly, to go 11-12 with a 100-loss club is a hell of an accomplishment, probably equivalent to 14-9 with an average team or 16-7 with a division winner. It's important to remember, though, that Sturtze is 31 years old and until last year hadn't thrown 150 innings in a season since 1994, due to chronic injuries and chronic ineffectiveness.

Jeff Wallace Throws L Age 26

YEAR	TEAM	LGE	IP	H	ER	HR	BB	K	ERA	W	L	H/9	HR/9	BB/9	K/9	KW	PERA	STUFF
1999	Nashvill	PCL	15.0	17	12	3	8	11	7.20	1	1	10.2	1.8	4.8	6.6	0.7	9.16	-16
1999	Pittsbrg	NL	37.7	31	20	2	32	37	4.78	2	2	7.4	0.5	7.6	8.8	0.6	3.55	6
2000	Nashvill	PCL	13.3	13	7	1	6	9	4.72	0	1	8.8	0.7	4.1	6.1	0.8	0.67	-2
2000	Pittsbrg	NL	37.7	38	26	4	28	24	6.21	1	3	9.1	1.0	6.7	5.7	0.4	7.31	-21
2001	TampaBay	AL	49.7	47	29	4	35	36	5.26	3	3	8.5	0.7	6.3	6.5	0.5	4.27	-9

Wallace had Tommy John surgery in 1998 and hasn't been quite the same since. He wore out in the second half in both 1999 and 2000, after which the Pirates gave up and released him. The Rays picked him up, stuck him in middle relief, and he ended up carrying one of the staff's lowest ERAs well into the season. After a couple of long relief outings, he got a spot start in August, but the strain was too much for his elbow, and he hardly pitched for the rest of the season. He did hold left-handed hitters to a .161 average and two extra-base hits in 62 at-bats, but he hadn't done well against lefties the previous two years, so it's far from clear whether he'd make a good specialist. Claimed on waivers by the Red Sox.

Matt White Throws R Age 23

YEAR	TEAM	LGE	IP	H	ER	HR	BB	K	ERA	W	L	H/9	HR/9	BB/9	K/9	KW	PERA	STUFF
1999	St Pete	Fla	117.0	123	63	13	40	62	4.85	6	7	9.5	1.0	3.1	4.8	0.8	7.56	5
2000	Orlando	Sou	112.7	122	77	18	59	65	6.15	5	8	9.7	1.4	4.7	5.2	0.6	5.48	3
2000	Durham	Int	36.7	34	15	1	15	24	3.68	2	2	8.3	0.2	3.7	5.9	0.8	3.81	19
2001	Durham	Int	29.7	35	29	5	28	12	8.80	1	2	10.6	1.5	8.5	3.6	0.2	9.73	-31

White had something of a breakthrough season in 2000, then came down with Steve Blass-like symptoms last year. It was perhaps a relief to learn that there was a physical cause, a shoulder problem that required season-ending surgery in May. It's impossible to know what kind of shape his arm will be in this season; we'd advise extreme caution, at least until he shows he still can get it into the mid-90s and get his hard curve over.

Paul Wilson Throws R Age 29

YEAR	TEAM	LGE	IP	H	ER	HR	BB	K	ERA	W	L	H/9	HR/9	BB/9	K/9	KW	PERA	STUFF
2000	St Lucie	Fla	25.3	25	9	0	6	10	3.20	2	1	8.9	0.0	2.1	3.6	0.8	4.87	-3
2000	Norfolk	Int	83.7	89	45	10	27	42	4.84	4	5	9.6	1.1	2.9	4.5	0.8	5.11	-6
2000	TampaBay	AL	50.0	43	15	1	13	40	2.70	4	2	7.7	0.2	2.3	7.2	1.5	2.95	23
2001	TampaBay	AL	157.3	156	78	19	49	113	4.46	9	8	8.9	1.1	2.8	6.5	1.2	5.13	6

Wilson pitched horribly over the first two months, suffering from bouts of wildness: falling behind, walking guys, hitting guys. It was so disturbing it was hard to believe he wasn't pitching hurt. The D-Rays sent him to the bullpen in June, used him once in two weeks, and nursed him back by pitching him in the late innings of lost causes. It worked: he turned it around, and they returned him to the rotation in late July. Wilson made 12 more starts and pitched extremely well in all but three of them, going 6-2 with a 2.55 ERA and a 64-to-19 strikeout-to-walk ratio. That's obviously something to get excited about; the caveat is that he had done pretty much the same thing over the last two months of 2000. Wilson is high-risk/high-upside.

Esteban Yan Throws R Age 28

YEAR	TEAM	LGE	IP	H	ER	HR	BB	K	ERA	W	L	H/9	HR/9	BB/9	K/9	KW	PERA	STUFF
1999	TampaBay	AL	66.3	66	34	7	27	46	4.61	3	4	9.0	0.9	3.7	6.2	0.9	5.16	-5
2000	TampaBay	AL	145.0	146	74	22	34	110	4.59	8	8	9.1	1.4	2.1	6.8	1.6	5.36	6
2001	TampaBay	AL	65.7	58	23	6	10	61	3.15	5	2	7.9	0.8	1.4	8.4	3.0	4.50	17

When the Devil Rays made Esteban Yan their closer, should we have foreseen that he'd hold the job more or less all season? Sure, he'd pitched decently in relief over the last two months of 2000, but he'd also posted a 6.60 ERA as a starter for the four months before that. No, we think it only confirms what we learned in the World Series: sometimes you can make all the wrong moves and things still will turn out all right. That's more true in a seven-game series than in a 162-game season, though, and we expect Yan to get his butt kicked backed to middle relief before 2002 is over.

Victor Zambrano Throws R Age 27

YEAR	TEAM	LGE	IP	H	ER	HR	BB	K	ERA	W	L	H/9	HR/9	BB/9	K/9	KW	PERA	STUFF
1999	Orlando	Sou	70.3	131	198	70	43	51	25.34	0	8	16.8	9.0	5.5	6.5	0.6	7.61	-91
2000	Durham	Int	64.7	71	47	13	32	41	6.54	2	5	9.9	1.8	4.5	5.7	0.6	6.52	-28
2001	Durham	Int	29.7	29	16	3	15	20	4.85	1	2	8.8	0.9	4.6	6.1	0.7	3.88	-16
2001	TampaBay	AL	50.7	42	20	5	17	55	3.55	4	2	7.5	0.9	3.0	9.8	1.6	3.38	22

How does a guy go from having a 5.03 ERA at Triple-A one year to a 3.16 ERA in the majors the next? Well, for one thing, his ERA at Durham in 2000 was deceptively high. He pitched well for most of the year but came down with a sore shoulder and got hit hard in the second half before going on the DL. Plus, he probably pitched a bit over his head last year. That's not to say he wasn't terrific: he undoubtedly was the D-Rays' top reliever in the second half. It's just that his performance was so far above and beyond what he'd done in any of his previous seasons that it's hard to trust it.

Texas Rangers

Like nearly all baseball barons, Texas Rangers' boss Tom Hicks considers owning a major-league ballclub a personal indulgence. Team ownership isn't a constant act of pouring money into a bottomless pit, which is what Bud Selig would have us believe, but there are plenty of business ventures more profitable than owning a ball club. This modest profitability is balanced by the fact that owning a baseball team carries virtually no risk.

What buying a sports team does like no other investment is to put the owner in a position of high visibility, enabling him to capture the public's attention in a way that less glamorous business enterprises can't. Whereas before he was an anonymous, cold-hearted suit forging hostile takeovers and displacing employees, now he's the man who cares enough about his community to pay the salaries of the local sports heroes.

Unlike many of baseball's owners, Hicks does care about his community. He is as Texan as a ten-gallon hat. Born and raised in the Lone Star State, he earned his undergraduate degree at the University of Texas and rooted his merger-and-acquisitions firm in Dallas. He feels fortunate to be able to give back to his home state, and he wants Texas to feel fortunate to call him one of its own. While he has the connections and financial wherewithal to run for governor or the Senate, owning sports teams brings him a much greater outpouring of affection. After all, when was the last time a city held a parade celebrating the passage of a new clean-water bill?

Hicks wasn't seeking ownership aggressively when he bought his first team, the NHL Dallas Stars, in 1995. He stepped forward only after three other potential buyers passed once they got a look at the team's books. In less than four years, the Stars rose from last place to the Stanley Cup. The string of sellouts and the fevered celebration in a town with less hockey tradition than Rio de Janeiro had to have whetted Hicks's imagination for what could happen if his newly acquired baseball club brought home the World Series trophy.

Rangers Prospectus

2001 record: 73–89, Fourth place, AL West

Pythagenport W/L: 74–88

Runs scored: 890 (third in AL)

Runs allowed: 968 (14th in AL)

Team EqA: .272 (tied for second in AL)

2001 batters age: 29.9 (fifth-oldest in AL)

2001 pitchers age: 28.6 (fourth-youngest in AL)

Ballpark: The Ballpark in Arlington; moderate hitters' park; Park Factor of 1.033

2001: Oops. Everything collapsed around Alex Rodriguez, who was the only free agent to make a contribution.

2002: The start of something big, as system begins coughing up talent to support Tom Hicks's checkbook. The AL West is loaded.

Like Major League Baseball, the NHL has no salary cap. Signing free agents at least 31 years old (at the time of Hicks's moves, this age was 32) with a minimum of four years of experience doesn't require any compensation to the former team. Hicks took full advantage of the free market and assembled a championship squad the old-fashioned way—he bought it. He filled gaping holes by throwing gobs of greenbacks at key free agents, and he turned around the floundering Stars overnight.

What does all this puck talk have to do with the Texas Rangers? Plenty. The Rangers had dabbled in the free-agent market since Hicks's Southwest Sports Group (SSG) bought the club in 1998. The biggest splash of the first two SSG-sponsored shopping sessions was bringing back Rafael Palmeiro to play first base after the 1998 season. Aside from that, they've shied away from big-ticket items, mainly scouring the bins for pitching help that didn't.

Last year's blockbuster signing of Alex Rodriguez signaled a change. Hicks wants results, and he is going to take the approach he used with the Stars to transform the team.

The Rangers weren't expected to join the A-Rod Auction; their more pressing need was pitching, having finished last in the American League in ERA in 2000. By the time Rodriguez's signature had dried on his contract, the team didn't have the resources—time, not money—to sign any front-line pitching. As the Rangers wooed Rodriguez around the clock, other teams scooped up the free-agent pitching jewels. General Manager Doug Melvin saw this happening and deployed Plan B.

Plan B basically amounted to trying to bludgeon other teams into submission. It seemed reasonable to assume the Rangers' pitching couldn't be any worse in 2001 and that normal performance fluctuation would lead to some improvement in that department, so the plan was to add more big bats to the lineup. Having already traded for Randy Velarde,

Melvin inked free agents Andres Galarraga and Ken Caminiti during baseball's winter meetings. All three players carried considerable risk, since none was younger than 38, and all had had trouble staying healthy of late.

Leaving spring training, it seemed that Patton couldn't have drawn up a better plan. The Rangers ripped through their Florida foes, with the mound staff fashioning the best ERA in the Grapefruit League. Then, demonstrating that March records are as useful a forecasting tool as the Psychic Friends Network, the Rangers came apart at the seams. By May 4, they were six games under .500 and ten and one-half games behind the streaking Mariners despite ranking second in the AL in runs scored. The team ERA was pushing 7.00 and the staff was on pace to set all-time records for hits allowed, earned runs allowed, and home runs allowed. Manager Johnny Oates resigned, presumably just before the axe was to fall on him.

Though Oates had guided the ball club to three division titles in his six years at the helm, it was time for a change. With the Rangers clearly on track to finish out of the postseason, they needed to turn lemons into lemonade. Youngsters needed to play so they could be evaluated, and Oates's preference was for a set veteran lineup that allowed reserves to atrophy on the bench. Jerry Narron was moved from the third-base coaching box to fill the vacancy. The kids began to see considerable action, and though the team still occupied the AL West basement at season's end, there were some encouraging developments.

When Velarde made his annual trip to the DL in mid-May, Michael Young was handed the second-base job and showed that he could be Rodriguez's double-play partner for the remainder of the decade. Even before Melvin disposed of Caminiti's remnants in early July, Narron had given most of his at-bats to Mike Lamb, greatly increasing Lamb's value whether he stays in Texas or becomes trade bait. Narron was committed to finding more playing time for Frank Catalanotto, who responded with the best on-base percentage of any leadoff hitter in the Junior Circuit. The pitching staff was more than a run per game better under the new skipper, even as newly-acquired Rob Bell and Aaron Myette learned their lessons the hard way.

The Rangers were pleased enough with Narron's job performance under difficult conditions that they extended his contract through the 2003 season. In case anyone thought that the extension meant Hicks was at ease with a second straight last-place finish, he put that notion to rest when he fired Melvin hours before the season finale.

At first blush, the firing might seem unjustified. Melvin inherited a bone-dry farm system when he arrived in 1995. It's now stocked with as many blue-chippers as any system in the game. He more than held his own on the trade front, occasionally pulling off shrewd and inspired deals. Most notably, after 24 years of futility in Arlington, the Rangers reached the playoffs in 1996, 1998, and 1999.

The nucleus of those division winners—Juan Gonzalez, Ivan Rodriguez, Rusty Greer, Will Clark, and Dean Palmer—was in place before Melvin arrived. His biggest shortcoming as general manager was the failure of his draft picks to provide any real help at the big-league level in his seven years with the club. While there is now a gusher ready to blow at the upper levels of the system, it's too late to save Melvin's job.

Melvin's first two June drafts, in 1995 and 1996, were ultimately his undoing. He dove in headlong for pitching, expending four first-round picks on Jonathan Johnson, R.A. Dickey, Sam Marsonek, and Corey Lee. None of them has ever gotten more than a bitter taste of coffee in the majors.

The team's previous owner, current leader of the free world George W. Bush, experienced the jolt of doling out signing bonuses to the underachieving quartet, but Hicks has definitely felt the aftershocks. When the youngsters should have been arriving in Texas, instead there was a massive void, which forced the Rangers to buy arms on the free-agent market. Melvin proved an equally poor judge of pitching talent in that arena, signing Mark Clark, Mike Munoz, Kenny Rogers, Darren Oliver, and Mark Petkovsek. Assembling a quality pitching staff is no easy feat, and while the organization does have some promising hurlers in the minors, Melvin's recent inability to put together a group that even approached adequacy couldn't be swept under the rug.

So, who gets to harvest the bumper crop of prospects that Melvin sowed? John Hart. Hicks targeted Hart from the outset, and following a cursory interview process, signed him to the largest contract ever given to a general manager.

Hart walks into a situation that is both similar to and different from the one he encountered as the Indians' new GM in 1991. The Rangers already have a cash-cow ballpark, so money isn't an issue in obtaining or retaining players. The youthful foundation for a high-powered offense is already in place, just as it was when he took over in Cleveland. There, he inherited Albert Belle, Carlos Baerga, Jim Thome, and Sandy Alomar Jr. Now, he's been gifted with Alex Rodriguez, Carlos Pena, Hank Blalock, and Mark Teixeira. The lumber is in place for a dominant run if Hart can find some pitching to support it.

Curiously, that task was precisely Hart's Achilles' heel with the Tribe. While he was able to squeeze a couple good years out of the aging limbs of Dennis Martinez and Orel Hershiser in the mid-1990s, he spent the next five years trying to duplicate the feat. In the process, he gave up many of the Indians' best young position players, such as Sean Casey, Brian Giles, and Richie Sexson, for less than equal value. When Hart bolted the south shore of Lake Erie last fall, the

Indians still lacked pitching and were an old team in need of a serious overhaul, with few parts in their minor-league garage with which to perform the work.

To cover Hart's blind spot in the search for pitching, Hicks couldn't resist hiring the A's director of scouting, Grady Fuson, to be the Rangers' assistant general manager. The hiring was controversial: Hicks had been granted permission to interview Fuson only for the GM vacancy. Hicks tripled Fuson's previous salary and is enamored with Fuson's ability to identify pitchers who can work effectively at the major-league level within a year or two of being drafted out of college.

The hiring frenzy didn't stop there. The Rangers also secured Orel Hershiser's services in the nebulous capacity of "associate to the general manager." He supposedly will have a hand in all things arm-related, acting as a scout, special instructor, and a consultant to Hart. To complete the behind-the-scenes makeover, Oscar Acosta was brought in as the new pitching coach. Though Don Baylor won't admit it, Acosta may have been the most valuable coach in baseball last year. He put some bite in a Cubs' staff that vaulted from 14th to fourth in the National League in ERA and set an all-time record for strikeouts in a season.

When Hicks announced Narron's contract extension in June, he said that the Rangers had entered into a rebuilding program. After four months of auditioning prospects and another two assembling a veritable who's who in the front office and coaching ranks, is the rebuilding over?

Surely, Hicks won't have the patience to wait and see if the young pitching in the system develops. Though Hart talks bravely of building for the future, it's been nearly a decade since he operated in that mode, and he only has a three-year contract. Unlike his situation in Cleveland, if Hart doesn't put a winner on the field by 2004, he probably won't be on the job beyond then. Does anyone really think he'll adopt a long-term approach for the greater glory of the next Rangers' GM?

The best-case scenario for which Rangers' fans can reasonably hope is that Hicks continues his free-spending ways, enabling Hart to find immediate mound reinforcements on the free-agent market. It will cost the organization its premium draft picks, but Fuson has shown he can unearth jewels later in the draft, snaring both Tim Hudson and Mario Ramos in round six. The Rangers could also draft premium high schoolers who have declared their intention to attend college in the later rounds, tempting them with first-round-caliber bonuses. Alternatively, the money saved on draft day could be plowed into worldwide scouting and development. As long as the financial commitment is there, Fuson will make it work.

At the other end of the spectrum is the chilling thought of Hart repeating the mistakes he made in Cleveland by giving away Rangers gems such as Carlos Pena, Hank Blalock, Mark Teixeira, or Kevin Mench for replaceable commodities like Dustin Hermanson or Felix Heredia.

Under Tom Hicks's ownership, the Rangers operate differently than most teams in that salaries don't drive the decision-making process. With Alex Rodriguez and a group of young sluggers knocking at the door, Texas will have the best offense in baseball in the latter half of the decade as long as they don't fritter it away now to obtain pitching. Early indications are positive, as the Rangers signed Todd Van Poppel, Jay Powell, and Chan Ho Park rather than make trades.

It's an odd sentiment to be expressed in *Baseball Prospectus*, but here's to more free-agent pitchers landing in Arlington.

HITTERS (BA: .270, OBP: .340, SLG: .440, EqA: .260)

Hank Blalock 3B Bats L Age 21

YEAR	TEAM	LGE	AB	H	DB	TP	HR	BB	SO	R	RBI	SB	CS	OUT	BA	OBP	SLG	EQA	EQR	DEFENSE
2000	Savannah	SAL	532	127	22	1	8	43	57	46	53	14	6	411	.239	.298	.329	.217	45	133-3B 0
2001	Charlott	Fla	243	75	13	1	6	18	33	35	34	4	3	171	.309	.357	.444	.267	31	62-3B 8
2001	Tulsa	Tex	275	76	14	2	9	32	38	40	45	2	2	201	.276	.354	.440	.265	36	65-3B -1
2002	*Texas*	*AL*	*482*	*147*	*24*	*2*	*18*	*52*	*64*	*63*	*59*	*10*	*6*	*340*	*.305*	*.373*	*.475*	*.279*	*70*	

Blalock is the best hitting prospect in the game, and there's not anybody particularly close. Despite being one of the youngest players in his leagues, he has mashed at every level and made seamless transitions upon promotion. His minor-league numbers are very similar to Vladimir Guerrero's, though they're very different players. Mark Teixeira's presence has set off talk of moving Blalock to another position due to his athleticism. That will ultimately happen, but this March he'll be a non-roster invitee to spring training, and it wouldn't be a shock to see him leave Florida with the Rangers' hot-corner job.

Need further verification of how good he is? When Billy Beane raised the issue of compensation for the Rangers' illegal hiring of Grady Fuson, he immediately floated Blalock's name. Smart guy, that Beane.

Jason Botts OF/1B Bats B Age 21

YEAR	TEAM	LGE	AB	H	DB	TP	HR	BB	SO	R	RBI	SB	CS	OUT	BA	OBP	SLG	EQA	EQR	DEFENSE
2001	Savannah	SAL	419	105	18	1	7	40	93	49	38	6	4	318	.251	.328	.348	.232	41	59-1B -5 42-RF -4
2002	*Texas*	*AL*	*420*	*115*	*20*	*1*	*9*	*56*	*99*	*53*	*45*	*7*	*4*	*309*	*.274*	*.359*	*.390*	*.254*	*50*	

Botts, a draft-and-follow taken in the 46th round of the 1999 draft, is full of surprises. The Rangers didn't know he could switch-hit, and he further shocked the team with his agility and speed. He is the fastest player in the system despite carrying 245 pounds on a 6′6″ frame. With first basemen coming out of their ears, the Rangers are taking advantage of Botts's athleticism and making him an outfielder. Botts led the Sally League in on-base percentage and showed good power, which was masked by Savannah's Grayson Stadium. Keep an eye on this guy.

Jason Bourgeois 2B Bats B Age 20

YEAR	TEAM	LGE	AB	H	DB	TP	HR	BB	SO	R	RBI	SB	CS	OUT	BA	OBP	SLG	EQA	EQR	DEFENSE
2001	Pulaski	App	259	54	8	1	3	16	51	32	18	8	4	209	.208	.259	.282	.189	16	61-2B -8
2002	*Texas*	*AL*	*284*	*69*	*12*	*1*	*4*	*22*	*58*	*32*	*25*	*11*	*4*	*219*	*.243*	*.297*	*.335*	*.212*	*23*	

Bourgeois was named the most exciting player in the Appalachian League. Alfredo Griffin was exciting, too, but we're not talking about that kind of excitement. Only 5′9″, the Rangers' second-round pick in 2000 shed his slap-and-dash style and began driving the ball last year. Bourgeois is a little rough around second base, but he has the tools and puts in the effort to improve. He could mature into a dynamite leadoff hitter.

Frank Catalanotto UT Bats L Age 28

YEAR	TEAM	LGE	AB	H	DB	TP	HR	BB	SO	R	RBI	SB	CS	OUT	BA	OBP	SLG	EQA	EQR	DEFENSE
1999	Detroit	AL	284	80	15	0	13	13	43	40	35	3	4	208	.282	.331	.472	.260	36	25-1B -1 18-2B -1
2000	Texas	AL	278	82	13	2	10	29	32	52	39	6	2	198	.295	.374	.464	.281	42	39-2B -7 14-1B -4
2001	Texas	AL	463	160	31	5	13	41	48	81	56	14	5	308	.346	.406	.518	.307	80	87-LF 1
2002	*Texas*	*AL*	*412*	*132*	*26*	*3*	*14*	*42*	*49*	*73*	*52*	*11*	*4*	*284*	*.320*	*.383*	*.500*	*.291*	*65*	

Last year, we said of Frank Catalanotto, "If some organization finds a way to give him 500 plate appearances, they'll be very pleased with the results." Catalanotto added playing the outfield to his skill set last year, seeing most of his action there as Rangers fly chasers fell like dominoes. Jerry Narron batted him leadoff in the second half of the season to take advantage of his knack for getting on base. There's some thought that Catalanotto should be made a regular at one position, but he has more value as an "everyday utility man," spelling a variety of players while gaining the platoon advantage for the team.

Chad Curtis OF Bats R Age 33

YEAR	TEAM	LGE	AB	H	DB	TP	HR	BB	SO	R	RBI	SB	CS	OUT	BA	OBP	SLG	EQA	EQR	DEFENSE
1999	NY Yanks	AL	194	54	4	0	6	41	31	36	24	8	4	144	.278	.411	.392	.282	30	55-LF -3
2000	Texas	AL	331	91	22	1	9	32	62	45	46	3	3	243	.275	.341	.429	.256	40	71-LF -9
2001	Texas	AL	115	31	4	0	3	14	18	25	10	6	1	85	.270	.353	.383	.258	14	32-OF 1
2002	*Texas*	*AL*	*289*	*79*	*9*	*0*	*9*	*40*	*53*	*47*	*36*	*7*	*3*	*213*	*.273*	*.362*	*.398*	*.258*	*36*	

Chad Curtis has been an idiot for years, going back to his famous snub of NBC's Jim Gray during the 1999 World Series. With the Rangers, his combination of religious zeal and boorish intensity has led to run-ins with Royce Clayton and Pudge Rodriguez. At this point in his career, Curtis simply isn't worth the hassle. The Rangers recognized that fact and gladly let him file for free agency.

Rusty Greer LF Bats L Age 33

YEAR	TEAM	LGE	AB	H	DB	TP	HR	BB	SO	R	RBI	SB	CS	OUT	BA	OBP	SLG	EQA	EQR	DEFENSE
1999	Texas	AL	546	167	40	3	21	90	59	104	97	2	2	381	.306	.408	.505	.304	97	145-LF -2
2000	Texas	AL	387	116	35	3	8	46	54	62	61	4	1	272	.300	.379	.468	.284	58	92-LF -3
2001	Texas	AL	245	70	17	0	10	28	28	40	31	1	2	177	.286	.361	.478	.276	35	60-LF -3
2002	*Texas*	*AL*	*458*	*131*	*37*	*2*	*15*	*63*	*59*	*78*	*71*	*4*	*2*	*329*	*.286*	*.372*	*.474*	*.279*	*68*	

For the second straight season, Rusty Greer missed extensive time due to injury. Last year, surgery for a pinched nerve in his hip took away the final four months of his season. His crash-and-burn style of play is reminiscent of Lenny Dykstra's, and his career is taking a similar, ominous direction. Dykstra played his last full campaign at age 30 and was tying flies instead of catching them when he was 34. The Rangers are praying that Greer's path diverges from Dykstra's: last March they inked Greer to a hefty extension through the 2004 season.

Travis Hafner 1B Bats L Age 25

YEAR	TEAM	LGE	AB	H	DB	TP	HR	BB	SO	R	RBI	SB	CS	OUT	BA	OBP	SLG	EQA	EQR	DEFENSE
1999	Savannah	SAL	504	117	23	2	17	49	160	66	71	2	2	389	.232	.306	.387	.232	51	106-1B -4
2000	Charlott	Fla	447	125	18	1	18	50	95	66	75	0	2	324	.280	.364	.445	.270	62	59-1B -4 18-3B -2
2001	Tulsa	Tex	329	79	16	0	16	48	83	46	54	2	1	251	.240	.340	.435	.259	43	78-1B -1
2002	*Texas*	*AL*	*433*	*123*	*22*	*1*	*21*	*57*	*113*	*70*	*79*	*1*	*2*	*312*	*.284*	*.367*	*.485*	*.279*	*64*	

Travis Hafner can flat out mangle a pitched baseball. He played through pain last year following surgery for a broken hamate bone and still posted the fourth-best on-base percentage and third-highest slugging percentage in the Texas League. Hafner had the wrist cleaned out last November and should be back at full strength this season. First base in Arlington is as backed up as the airspace over DFW, so a team in need of a power bat should offer Hart a Ricky Rincon-type arm to see if he still takes that kind of bait.

Bill Haselman C Bats R Age 36

YEAR	TEAM	LGE	AB	H	DB	TP	HR	BB	SO	R	RBI	SB	CS	OUT	BA	OBP	SLG	EQA	EQR	DEFENSE
1999	Detroit	AL	142	40	6	0	5	9	23	13	14	2	0	102	.282	.325	.430	.253	16	36-C 0
2000	Texas	AL	191	53	12	0	8	13	32	21	26	0	1	139	.277	.327	.466	.258	24	55-C 0
2001	Texas	AL	130	39	4	0	4	8	23	13	27	0	1	92	.300	.344	.423	.254	15	36-C 1
2002	*Texas*	*AL*	*198*	*54*	*6*	*0*	*8*	*18*	*38*	*17*	*24*	*0*	*1*	*145*	*.273*	*.333*	*.424*	*.248*	*22*	

The final tally looks like an ordinary Bill Haselman season; however, getting there was anything but ordinary. In a six-month period, Haselman was cut more than Chuck Wepner, undergoing surgery on his rotator cuff, labrum, and elbow. If the Rangers have designs on dealing Ivan Rodriguez, they shouldn't count on Haselman picking up the slack.

Scott Heard C Bats L Age 20

YEAR	TEAM	LGE	AB	H	DB	TP	HR	BB	SO	R	RBI	SB	CS	OUT	BA	OBP	SLG	EQA	EQR	DEFENSE
2001	Savannah	SAL	282	53	8	1	4	23	75	20	27	0	1	230	.188	.251	.266	.179	16	66-C -18
2001	Pulaski	App	118	24	6	0	2	7	34	14	10	1	1	95	.203	.248	.305	.187	7	28-C -7
2002	*Texas*	*AL*	*367*	*88*	*14*	*1*	*7*	*36*	*105*	*37*	*37*	*1*	*2*	*281*	*.240*	*.308*	*.341*	*.214*	*30*	

Heard is one of the youngest examples of the Nichols Law of Catcher Defense, which states that a catcher's perceived defensive skill is inversely proportional to his hitting skill. The Rangers rave about the way Heard handles a pitching staff, but his defensive numbers were dwarfed by those of fellow Sand Gnat Branden Pack, and his bat speed looks like it was mixed by the late DJ Screw. Can anyone name another high-school first-rounder who didn't even hit .300 his senior year?

Gabe Kapler CF Bats R Age 26

YEAR	TEAM	LGE	AB	H	DB	TP	HR	BB	SO	R	RBI	SB	CS	OUT	BA	OBP	SLG	EQA	EQR	DEFENSE
1999	Toledo	Int	54	16	4	1	3	8	9	9	11	0	1	39	.296	.387	.574	.303	10	14-CF 0
1999	Detroit	AL	413	104	22	4	19	38	65	59	48	10	5	314	.252	.318	.462	.256	52	121-CF 0
2000	Texas	AL	437	133	29	1	15	37	50	56	62	8	4	308	.304	.359	.478	.277	62	116-CF -4
2001	Texas	AL	483	136	25	1	20	63	60	80	76	22	7	354	.282	.367	.462	.279	73	131-CF 2
2002	*Texas*	*AL*	*498*	*146*	*29*	*2*	*20*	*69*	*66*	*78*	*66*	*18*	*8*	*360*	*.293*	*.379*	*.480*	*.284*	*77*	

We're beginning to have doubts that Kapler will reach the heights we've been predicting. Although he boosted his walk rate by 30% last year, his stiff, mechanical swing looks like it could be prone to the kind of extended slump he suffered in June and July, which marred his season totals. Kapler's extra work with coach Reid Nichols paid dividends in center field; nevertheless, he is better suited for right and will move there if the Rangers can find a ball hawk to patrol the generous expanses at The Ballpark.

Mike Lamb 3B Bats L Age 26

YEAR	TEAM	LGE	AB	H	DB	TP	HR	BB	SO	R	RBI	SB	CS	OUT	BA	OBP	SLG	EQA	EQR	DEFENSE
1999	Tulsa	Tex	544	149	38	3	16	40	67	75	72	3	2	397	.274	.329	.443	.255	65	136-3B -2
2000	Texas	AL	488	138	25	2	6	28	53	62	44	0	2	352	.283	.327	.379	.237	48	128-3B -13
2000	Oklahoma	PCL	55	13	2	1	2	4	6	6	4	2	1	43	.236	.288	.418	.234	6	12-3B -6
2001	Oklahoma	PCL	271	74	15	2	7	13	28	30	34	0	2	199	.273	.311	.421	.240	28	69-3B -9
2001	Texas	AL	284	91	10	0	7	15	23	43	38	2	1	194	.320	.363	.430	.266	36	67-3B -4
2002	*Texas*	*AL*	*530*	*156*	*29*	*2*	*17*	*41*	*56*	*75*	*68*	*2*	*3*	*377*	*.294*	*.345*	*.453*	*.261*	*65*	

(Mike Lamb *continued*)

Is there any player in the majors who is as young, good, and inexpensive as Mike Lamb with less chance of being in the same organization a year from now? With Blalock and Mark Teixeira in the fold, Lamb's days in Texas are numbered. Unless the Rangers want to stunt someone's career, the law of supply and demand dictates that some smart GM will get a line-drive hitter with improving hot-corner defense at a wholesale price.

Ricky Ledee LF Bats L Age 28

YEAR	TEAM	LGE	AB	H	DB	TP	HR	BB	SO	R	RBI	SB	CS	OUT	BA	OBP	SLG	EQA	EQR	DEFENSE
1999	Columbus	Int	116	27	8	1	3	14	27	15	12	3	2	91	.233	.315	.397	.239	13	30-CF -3
1999	NY Yanks	AL	249	72	14	5	10	26	64	46	40	4	3	180	.289	.356	.506	.281	38	73-LF -5
2000	NY Yanks	AL	190	48	9	1	8	24	34	22	31	7	3	145	.253	.340	.437	.260	25	45-LF -2
2000	Clevelnd	AL	62	14	1	1	2	8	8	12	7	0	0	48	.226	.314	.371	.233	6	18-LF 2
2000	Texas	AL	211	50	7	3	4	22	44	22	36	6	3	164	.237	.312	.355	.229	21	53-RF -1
2001	Texas	AL	242	59	24	1	2	24	50	35	37	2	3	186	.244	.318	.376	.233	24	60-RF -4
2002	*Texas*	*AL*	*418*	*109*	*26*	*4*	*12*	*52*	*88*	*63*	*61*	*5*	*4*	*313*	*.261*	*.343*	*.428*	*.255*	*51*	

Ledee's return from a torn hamstring tendon coincided with Greer's season-ending injury, but Ledee failed to take advantage of a golden opportunity to establish himself as something more than an extra outfielder. The fact that he hasn't shown the ability to hit right-handers consistently precludes using him in even a platoon role. Not that long ago, Ledee seemed poised to be a very good big leaguer; he might soon be clinging to a spot on a 40-man roster.

Chris Magruder OF Bats B Age 25

YEAR	TEAM	LGE	AB	H	DB	TP	HR	BB	SO	R	RBI	SB	CS	OUT	BA	OBP	SLG	EQA	EQR	DEFENSE
1999	Shrevprt	Tex	483	106	18	2	5	54	88	61	46	11	8	385	.219	.305	.296	.211	39	124-RF -3
2000	Shrevprt	Tex	501	123	27	2	3	47	75	64	29	11	7	385	.246	.316	.325	.222	45	129-CF -5
2001	Shrevprt	Tex	151	34	5	2	2	12	27	18	9	3	2	119	.225	.289	.325	.210	12	39-RF 0
2001	Fresno	PCL	210	51	5	1	8	17	41	29	24	2	1	160	.243	.313	.390	.237	22	53-CF 1
2001	Oklahoma	PCL	127	42	12	3	4	19	17	23	17	1	2	87	.331	.428	.567	.321	25	31-CF 1
2002	*Texas*	*AL*	*499*	*138*	*25*	*3*	*13*	*55*	*87*	*78*	*59*	*6*	*4*	*365*	*.277*	*.348*	*.417*	*.255*	*60*	

Magruder was one of three middling prospects given to Melvin when he foisted $2 million worth of Big Cat on the Giants. His showing at Oklahoma was way out of line with anything he had done previously and demonstrates that virtually anything can happen in a month's worth of at-bats. Show Magruder a wall and he'll run through it; however, his upside is as a fifth outfielder: a poor man's Chad Curtis, without the spiritual baggage.

Kevin Mench OF Bats R Age 24

YEAR	TEAM	LGE	AB	H	DB	TP	HR	BB	SO	R	RBI	SB	CS	OUT	BA	OBP	SLG	EQA	EQR	DEFENSE
1999	Pulaski	App	257	60	13	0	7	14	54	29	26	4	1	199	.233	.275	.366	.215	21	51-LF 3
2000	Charlott	Fla	505	138	26	4	22	57	80	85	83	11	5	372	.273	.351	.471	.272	72	122-LF -1
2001	Tulsa	Tex	476	109	23	1	21	28	77	61	61	3	4	371	.229	.276	.414	.225	45	117-RF 0
2002	*Texas*	*AL*	*478*	*130*	*23*	*2*	*25*	*44*	*83*	*72*	*74*	*6*	*4*	*352*	*.272*	*.333*	*.485*	*.264*	*63*	

Coming off a tremendous 2000, Kevin Mench seemed in need of just a smidge of polish to be ready for The Show. However, off-season wrist surgery led to a slow start with Tulsa, causing him to press at the plate and cut his walk rate in half. This year is a crucial one; a strong start in Oklahoma returns him front and center as a prospect and an answer to the Rangers' outfield questions. Because of his Incaviglian frame, Mench is always going to have to hit a ton to overcome the associated prejudices about his defense.

Craig Monroe OF Bats R Age 25

YEAR	TEAM	LGE	AB	H	DB	TP	HR	BB	SO	R	RBI	SB	CS	OUT	BA	OBP	SLG	EQA	EQR	DEFENSE
1999	Charlott	Fla	486	105	14	0	14	31	115	54	57	23	11	392	.216	.266	.331	.205	37	130-CF 0
2000	Tulsa	Tex	466	110	27	3	15	46	91	67	62	8	8	364	.236	.306	.403	.235	49	111-RF -11
2001	Oklahoma	PCL	410	104	21	3	17	42	77	51	62	9	7	313	.254	.328	.444	.254	51	97-LF 1
2001	Texas	AL	52	12	1	0	2	6	16	8	5	2	0	40	.231	.310	.365	.237	5	16-RF 3
2002	*Texas*	*AL*	*440*	*119*	*22*	*2*	*18*	*53*	*94*	*65*	*68*	*12*	*7*	*327*	*.270*	*.349*	*.452*	*.264*	*58*	

Monroe appears to be the rare bird whose game elevates as the competition gets better. Except for hitting for average, Monroe meets or exceeds all design specifications for a spare outfielder, and his defense makes him very popular with the pitching staff. The Rangers liked what they saw last September, so a strong camp should land him in Arlington in April.

Jose Morban SS Bats R Age 22

YEAR	TEAM	LGE	AB	H	DB	TP	HR	BB	SO	R	RBI	SB	CS	OUT	BA	OBP	SLG	EQA	EQR	DEFENSE
2000	Savannah	SAL	286	52	8	2	3	28	84	20	20	11	0	243	.182	.259	.255	.182	17	78-SS -4
2000	Pulaski	App	123	19	2	0	2	6	42	11	9	2	2	106	.154	.194	.220	.145	4	30-SS -1
2001	Savannah	SAL	496	103	18	6	6	32	126	51	34	22	12	405	.208	.257	.304	.195	34	116-SS -6
2002	*Texas*	*AL*	*459*	*109*	*18*	*5*	*8*	*43*	*130*	*56*	*43*	*23*	*14*	*364*	*.237*	*.303*	*.351*	*.217*	*40*	

With Kelly Dransfeldt's career moldering in the Sooner State, the sword passes to Jose Morban to challenge for the shortstop job in Texas. Please stifle your guffaws. Morban is a pure shortstop, very raw for his age, with a decent grasp of the strike zone, gap-plus power, and blazing speed. Last year was a return engagement in Savannah; he can't afford any more mulligans if he is to become primo trade bait for John Hart.

Laynce Nix OF Bats L Age 21

YEAR	TEAM	LGE	AB	H	DB	TP	HR	BB	SO	R	RBI	SB	CS	OUT	BA	OBP	SLG	EQA	EQR	DEFENSE
2001	Savannah	SAL	427	97	21	4	6	28	100	39	43	4	4	334	.227	.276	.337	.207	32	103-RF -1
2002	*Texas*	*AL*	*447*	*113*	*25*	*5*	*7*	*36*	*115*	*49*	*45*	*4*	*4*	*338*	*.253*	*.308*	*.378*	*.225*	*41*	

On the one hand, the Rangers' system is oozing with corner infield prospects; on the other, there's a lack of outfield depth. Rangers whiz Jamey Newberg *(http://www.newbergreport.com)* says Nix is charging hard, behind only Mench in terms of potential impact. Nix brings above-average tools across the board and a strong work ethic. He draws frequent comparisons to Rusty Greer, but while their minor-league numbers are similar, Greer had superior plate discipline at a similar age.

Rafael Palmeiro 1B/DH Bats L Age 37

YEAR	TEAM	LGE	AB	H	DB	TP	HR	BB	SO	R	RBI	SB	CS	OUT	BA	OBP	SLG	EQA	EQR	DEFENSE
1999	Texas	AL	554	182	26	1	49	90	61	93	142	2	4	376	.329	.425	.644	.337	124	28-1B 1
2000	Texas	AL	554	162	27	3	40	95	68	97	113	2	1	393	.292	.399	.569	.313	108	105-1B -10
2001	Texas	AL	601	172	30	0	52	103	78	104	128	1	1	430	.286	.395	.596	.316	121	112-1B -2
2002	*Texas*	*AL*	*575*	*153*	*26*	*1*	*46*	*104*	*75*	*91*	*123*	*1*	*2*	*424*	*.266*	*.378*	*.555*	*.298*	*103*	

His name doesn't often come up in discussions of the subject, but Rafael Palmeiro is a Hall of Famer. Bill James's Favorite Toy pegs his likelihood of hitting 500 home runs at 97% and his chance of 3,000 hits at 28%. Either milestone will make him a lock, as we're not talking about Jose Canseco or Harold Baines. The only phase of his game that has slipped appreciably from a decade ago is his range at first base. Palmeiro is a perfect fit to move into the full-time designated-hitter role, but he's not buying into it, creating a potential clash due to the presence of...

Carlos Pena 1B Bats L Age 24

YEAR	TEAM	LGE	AB	H	DB	TP	HR	BB	SO	R	RBI	SB	CS	OUT	BA	OBP	SLG	EQA	EQR	DEFENSE
1999	Charlott	Fla	513	110	24	4	14	55	152	63	71	1	3	406	.214	.300	.359	.223	47	135-1B -8
2000	Tulsa	Tex	532	135	24	1	22	75	108	86	74	7	0	397	.254	.351	.427	.264	71	136-1B -15
2001	Oklahoma	PCL	434	115	32	2	19	72	115	60	61	9	3	322	.265	.376	.479	.286	70	115-1B 2
2001	Texas	AL	62	17	5	1	3	10	15	7	12	0	0	45	.274	.375	.532	.296	11	16-1B 2
2002	*Oakland*	*AL*	*488*	*127*	*30*	*2*	*21*	*73*	*128*	*80*	*79*	*8*	*2*	*363*	*.260*	*.357*	*.459*	*.281*	*76*	

He's ready. If nothing else positive can be said about signing Andres Galarraga, at least it enabled Carlos Pena to get a full season of Triple-A under his belt. Pena battled a sore rib cage and started slowly at Oklahoma, then scorched the PCL at a .324/.437/.629 clip over the final three months. Last year was the first season in which his fielding numbers matched his lofty defensive reputation. The Rangers had Pena play the outfield in winter ball in hopes of averting a job-sharing arrangement similar to that used by the local gridsters in 1971, when Roger Staubach and Craig Morton alternated starts at quarterback. Now that he's in Oakland, he's in the right place to blossom into a star.

Alex Rodriguez SS Bats R Age 26

YEAR	TEAM	LGE	AB	H	DB	TP	HR	BB	SO	R	RBI	SB	CS	OUT	BA	OBP	SLG	EQA	EQR	DEFENSE
1999	Seattle	AL	497	145	23	0	44	51	96	107	108	20	7	359	.292	.363	.604	.306	93	126-SS 3
2000	Seattle	AL	552	190	35	2	46	94	106	137	136	16	5	367	.344	.446	.665	.352	135	146-SS 17
2001	Texas	AL	633	210	29	1	58	77	113	140	141	17	3	426	.332	.414	.656	.339	142	156-SS 4
2002	*Texas*	*AL*	*571*	*188*	*26*	*1*	*50*	*82*	*109*	*132*	*131*	*18*	*4*	*387*	*.329*	*.413*	*.641*	*.333*	*124*	

For the third time in his career, Alex Rodriguez had an MVP-type season and failed to win the award, finishing a laughable sixth in the Baseball Writers Association voting. Rodriguez's season was all the more impressive for the way he handled the media scrutiny and the abusive fans who came out of the woodwork after he signed the richest contract in sports history. Remember when we used to speak of the Trinity? It no longer exists. There's only one shortstop god, and he plays in Texas.

Ivan Rodriguez C Bats R Age 30

YEAR	TEAM	LGE	AB	H	DB	TP	HR	BB	SO	R	RBI	SB	CS	OUT	BA	OBP	SLG	EQA	EQR	DEFENSE
1999	Texas	AL	593	198	25	1	37	18	56	111	108	24	12	407	.334	.354	.567	.294	95	137-C 15
2000	Texas	AL	357	124	25	4	28	15	42	63	78	5	5	238	.347	.375	.675	.323	70	85-C 8
2001	Texas	AL	442	142	24	1	28	25	63	74	67	9	3	303	.321	.362	.570	.299	74	103-C 17
2002	*Texas*	*AL*	*538*	*180*	*28*	*2*	*33*	*36*	*72*	*97*	*96*	*11*	*7*	*365*	*.335*	*.376*	*.578*	*.302*	*92*	

In baseball history, only Johnny Bench caught more games through age 29 than Ivan Rodriguez has. Of the catchers in the top ten for games caught though age 29, only Gary Carter subsequently managed even four seasons of more than 100 contests behind the plate, and almost without exception, none of those catchers were much more than average offensively by the time they reached 33. Using similarity scores, the three players judged "essentially similar" to Pudge at age 29—Ted Simmons, Yogi Berra, and Joe Torre—were all at various stages of a position switch by 33.

The effects of Rodriguez's heavy workload are beginning to show, namely the patella tendinitis that required surgery and shortened his 2001 season. He is a free agent after this season; if the Rangers decide to try to re-sign him, they need to be aware that history shows he'll soon be a liability, not an asset, especially at the salary he'll command.

Jason Romano CF/2B Bats R Age 23

YEAR	TEAM	LGE	AB	H	DB	TP	HR	BB	SO	R	RBI	SB	CS	OUT	BA	OBP	SLG	EQA	EQR	DEFENSE
1999	Charlott	Fla	463	118	22	7	11	29	81	58	48	19	10	355	.255	.307	.404	.238	49	107-2B -9
2000	Tulsa	Tex	537	125	27	1	7	38	84	64	52	15	7	419	.233	.288	.326	.211	43	123-2B -9
2001	Tulsa	Tex	187	39	6	1	1	13	31	15	15	5	2	150	.209	.262	.267	.187	11	44-2B -9
2001	Oklahoma	PCL	149	42	5	1	3	18	25	28	11	3	3	110	.282	.359	.389	.253	18	17-2B 1 12-CF 0
2002	*Texas*	*AL*	*478*	*131*	*29*	*3*	*9*	*48*	*82*	*66*	*50*	*14*	*7*	*353*	*.274*	*.340*	*.404*	*.249*	*55*	

A lack of outfield depth in the system, coupled with Romano's clumsy footwork around second base, prompted the move to center field. The Rangers are impressed with his outfield instincts and believe that his strong work ethic will lead to a smooth transition. We actually have more doubts about his bat. Romano's reputation as a frontline top-of-the-order hitter is based on one outstanding season in 1999. He needs a good campaign in Triple-A to reemerge as a genuine prospect.

Scott Sheldon UT Bats R Age 33

YEAR	TEAM	LGE	AB	H	DB	TP	HR	BB	SO	R	RBI	SB	CS	OUT	BA	OBP	SLG	EQA	EQR	DEFENSE
1999	Oklahoma	PCL	449	126	28	2	23	47	103	74	76	9	2	325	.281	.351	.506	.282	68	57-2B 5 31-SS -1
2000	Texas	AL	123	35	9	0	5	8	33	20	19	0	0	88	.285	.333	.480	.266	16	13-SS 0 12-3B 3
2001	Texas	AL	120	26	3	0	4	3	30	12	12	1	1	95	.217	.236	.342	.191	8	33-3B -2
2002	*Texas*	*AL*	*365*	*90*	*21*	*1*	*16*	*33*	*94*	*53*	*51*	*5*	*2*	*277*	*.247*	*.309*	*.441*	*.245*	*41*	

Jerry Narron is a carbon copy of Johnny Oates when it comes to playing his regulars every day. Sheldon can handle every position on the diamond, hit a little bit, and, given the chance, help keep a team fresh. Fortunately, last year's unsightly line hasn't soured the Rangers, so Sheldon will continue to receive a biweekly major-league paycheck to go with his biweekly plate appearance.

Ruben Sierra — DH/OF — Bats B — Age 36

YEAR	TEAM	LGE	AB	H	DB	TP	HR	BB	SO	R	RBI	SB	CS	OUT	BA	OBP	SLG	EQA	EQR	DEFENSE
2000	Oklahoma	PCL	437	131	21	2	16	44	61	57	65	4	2	308	.300	.364	.467	.276	62	80-LF -3
2000	Texas	AL	60	14	1	0	1	3	8	5	7	1	0	46	.233	.270	.300	.198	4	
2001	Oklahoma	PCL	94	23	3	1	2	9	13	13	10	2	0	71	.245	.311	.362	.232	9	
2001	Texas	AL	344	104	21	1	25	20	45	58	69	2	0	240	.302	.341	.587	.295	57	31-RF -7
2002	*Seattle*	*AL*	*438*	*116*	*20*	*3*	*19*	*46*	*62*	*57*	*62*	*4*	*1*	*323*	*.265*	*.335*	*.454*	*.272*	*62*	

Like Lazarus, John Travolta, and Tony Bennett before him, Ruben Sierra has returned from the dead. He still won't take a free pass, and scouts swear that his bat speed is gone, but his slugging percentage last year was the highest of his career. Although Sierra is a free agent and wants to return to the Rangers, there simply is no place for him. Under no circumstances should he ever be allowed to play the outfield again. Man, that was ugly. He signed a one-year deal with the Mariners, who already have Edgar Martinez at DH, so Sierra's at-bats will have to come as a left fielder.

Mark Teixeira — 3B — Bats B — Age 22

One advantage of having a good working relationship with Scott Boras is that the best player in the June draft can fall into your lap with the fifth pick. Teixeira was the 2000 College Player of the Year and a shoo-in to repeat before breaking his ankle early last season. He hits for average, draws walks, and has light-tower power from both sides of the plate. Some scouts have minor questions about his glove, but his bat will more than answer them. By next spring, Teixeira may not only inherit Blalock's spot as the game's top prospect, he may also force Blalock to the outfield.

Corey Wright — CF — Bats L — Age 22

YEAR	TEAM	LGE	AB	H	DB	TP	HR	BB	SO	R	RBI	SB	CS	OUT	BA	OBP	SLG	EQA	EQR	DEFENSE
1999	Savannah	SAL	337	68	13	2	1	47	77	44	16	6	7	276	.202	.304	.261	.201	25	90-CF -6
2000	Charlott	Fla	385	82	13	3	1	60	90	54	18	17	8	310	.213	.327	.270	.218	35	98-CF 2
2000	Tulsa	Tex	70	12	0	0	0	3	20	5	2	1	1	59	.171	.212	.171	.138	2	17-CF 1
2001	Tulsa	Tex	424	92	12	2	1	47	104	47	20	15	10	342	.217	.304	.262	.203	32	107-CF -3
2002	*Texas*	*AL*	*473*	*118*	*17*	*3*	*3*	*62*	*120*	*69*	*28*	*19*	*12*	*367*	*.249*	*.336*	*.317*	*.224*	*44*	

Corey Wright has five of John Sickels's seven skills. Unfortunately, the two he lacks—hitting for average and hitting for power—are among the three most important. Scouts often fuss too much over strikeouts; in Wright's case, if he could cut his whiffs by half, the increased contact would produce enough base hits to make him a handy commodity.

Mike Young — 2B — Bats R — Age 25

YEAR	TEAM	LGE	AB	H	DB	TP	HR	BB	SO	R	RBI	SB	CS	OUT	BA	OBP	SLG	EQA	EQR	DEFENSE
1999	Dunedin	Fla	498	123	26	2	4	45	88	59	56	16	4	379	.247	.312	.331	.225	45	67-2B -1 45-SS -6
2000	Tennesse	Sou	353	87	20	3	6	26	71	43	39	10	4	270	.246	.299	.371	.227	33	88-2B -2
2000	Tulsa	Tex	187	51	11	3	1	12	28	23	23	6	2	138	.273	.317	.380	.237	19	41-SS -1
2001	Oklahoma	PCL	189	50	5	0	7	18	31	24	23	3	2	141	.265	.331	.402	.246	21	40-2B -3
2001	Texas	AL	386	101	19	4	12	27	79	61	51	3	1	286	.262	.314	.425	.245	43	101-2B 0
2002	*Texas*	*AL*	*557*	*157*	*30*	*4*	*15*	*53*	*109*	*80*	*85*	*9*	*3*	*403*	*.282*	*.344*	*.431*	*.258*	*68*	

When stopgap Randy Velarde pulled a hamstring in late-May, Young was retrieved from Oklahoma sooner than expected. There was some initial anxiety about his ability to handle the right side of second base, but his steady play at the keystone quickly dispelled those concerns. Young is cut from Robby Thompson cloth, and he's beginning what should be a sturdy ten-year career. Most importantly, he'll do his job for just $500 a plate appearance over the next two seasons, freeing up money to be spent elsewhere.

PITCHERS (ERA: 4.50, H/9: 9.0, HR/9: 1.0, BB/9: 3.0, K/9: 6.0, KW: 2.0, PERA: 4.50)

Rob Bell Throws R Age 25

YEAR	TEAM	LGE	IP	H	ER	HR	BB	K	ERA	W	L	H/9	HR/9	BB/9	K/9	KW	PERA	STUFF
1999	Chattang	Sou	73.7	76	37	10	17	48	4.52	4	4	9.3	1.2	2.1	5.9	1.4	3.98	16
2000	Louisvil	Int	40.7	39	21	7	13	40	4.65	2	3	8.6	1.5	2.9	8.9	1.5	3.98	29
2000	Cincnnti	NL	137.0	147	95	28	60	100	6.24	5	10	9.7	1.8	3.9	6.6	0.8	4.79	6
2001	Louisvil	Int	28.0	30	16	5	5	19	5.14	1	2	9.6	1.6	1.6	6.1	1.9	3.81	9
2001	Cincnnti	NL	42.3	46	27	8	15	27	5.74	2	3	9.8	1.7	3.2	5.7	0.9	5.67	0
2001	Texas	AL	110.0	123	77	21	45	61	6.30	4	8	10.1	1.7	3.7	5.0	0.7	6.62	-5

Doesn't it seem strange that a small-payroll team light on pitching and heavy on outfielders would trade a young power arm who isn't even arbitration-eligible for a struggling outfield prospect? That's what the Reds did when they dealt Bell to the Rangers for Ruben Mateo. Bell's subsequent performance indicates that maybe Jim Bowden hadn't gone on a YooHoo-and-Cuervo bender. In four months with Texas, Bell had command of his power curve for one inning. With that curveball in tow, Bell could become something special; without it, he's Mike Loynd.

Joaquin Benoit Throws R Age 22

YEAR	TEAM	LGE	IP	H	ER	HR	BB	K	ERA	W	L	H/9	HR/9	BB/9	K/9	KW	PERA	STUFF
1999	Charlott	Fla	109.0	114	67	11	60	56	5.53	5	7	9.4	0.9	5.0	4.6	0.5	7.31	0
2000	Tulsa	Tex	80.7	82	42	9	30	50	4.69	4	5	9.1	1.0	3.3	5.6	0.8	4.77	14
2001	Tulsa	Tex	22.7	22	10	2	7	16	3.97	2	1	8.7	0.8	2.8	6.4	1.1	3.76	21
2001	Oklahoma	PCL	127.3	123	79	16	83	101	5.58	6	8	8.7	1.1	5.9	7.1	0.6	4.66	15

Entering last season, the main goal for Benoit was to work through the minor elbow twinges caused by his throwing slightly across his body. He did that, logging 152 $^{2}/_{3}$ innings—47 more than his previous season high. However, command of his nasty fastball, slider, and change-up became an issue as he faced tougher competition. Benoit is out of options after this season, making it likely that he'll move to the bullpen by next spring.

Jovanny Cedeno Throws R Age 22

YEAR	TEAM	LGE	IP	H	ER	HR	BB	K	ERA	W	L	H/9	HR/9	BB/9	K/9	KW	PERA	STUFF
2000	Savannah	SAL	127.3	118	56	3	68	80	3.96	8	6	8.3	0.2	4.8	5.7	0.6	4.05	14
2001	Charlott	Fla	8.7	7	4	0	6	7	4.15	1	0	7.3	0.0	6.2	7.3	0.6	2.46	13

The stat lines, or lack of, tell the story. Cedeno is a dazzling young twirler whose body hasn't stood up to the rigors of the job despite careful handling. Given time to mature, he could develop into a front-of-the-rotation starter. However, time is the problem. Cedeno may miss part of this season because of last June's surgery on a partially torn labrum, and he is out of options after 2003. The Rangers need to push him aggressively, while at the same time being cautious. It's Russian roulette with three chambers loaded.

Francisco Cordero Throws R Age 24

YEAR	TEAM	LGE	IP	H	ER	HR	BB	K	ERA	W	L	H/9	HR/9	BB/9	K/9	KW	PERA	STUFF
1999	Jacksnvl	Sou	49.7	46	24	4	22	41	4.35	3	3	8.3	0.7	4.0	7.4	0.9	1.72	13
1999	Detroit	AL	20.0	17	11	2	15	19	4.95	1	1	7.7	0.9	6.8	8.6	0.6	2.78	10
2000	Texas	AL	80.7	83	47	9	39	49	5.24	4	5	9.3	1.0	4.4	5.5	0.6	4.77	-7
2001	Oklahoma	PCL	14.3	11	3	0	3	14	1.88	2	0	6.9	0.0	1.9	8.8	2.3	1.27	30

It was a lost season for Francisco Cordero, twice sidelined with stress fractures in his lower back. Despite the injuries, the Rangers believe that he will eventually assume a setup role and pump some of the gas that's been missing in the bullpen. Cordero still has an option remaining, so he'll likely open the season as a RedHawk so he can rebuild arm strength and hunt for his command, which has always been his bugaboo.

Tim Crabtree Throws R Age 32

YEAR	TEAM	LGE	IP	H	ER	HR	BB	K	ERA	W	L	H/9	HR/9	BB/9	K/9	KW	PERA	STUFF
1999	Texas	AL	69.3	62	23	3	15	53	2.99	6	2	8.0	0.4	1.9	6.9	1.8	2.96	10
2000	Texas	AL	83.7	81	36	6	25	53	3.87	5	4	8.7	0.6	2.7	5.7	1.1	4.68	-2
2001	Texas	AL	27.0	28	16	3	13	15	5.33	1	2	9.3	1.0	4.3	5.0	0.6	6.19	-18

Crabtree entered last season as the closer for the first time in his career, inheriting the job when John Wetteland retired. Naturally, the media emphasized that Crabtree had four times as many blown saves as saves in his career, failing to mention that those figures are not unusual for setup men, as they seldom work the ninth inning. He nevertheless proceeded to live down to the media's expectations, chiefly because he was pitching with a painful back and shoulder. Crabtree ultimately underwent season-ending rotator-cuff surgery and will be forever labeled as someone who can't close games. A free agent, he can help a team if given time to mend.

Doug Davis **Throws L** **Age 26**

YEAR	TEAM	LGE	IP	H	ER	HR	BB	K	ERA	W	L	H/9	HR/9	BB/9	K/9	KW	PERA	STUFF
1999	Tulsa	Tex	72.7	76	46	13	29	54	5.70	3	5	9.4	1.6	3.6	6.7	0.9	3.59	10
1999	Oklahoma	PCL	80.3	75	35	4	32	56	3.92	5	4	8.4	0.4	3.6	6.3	0.9	3.08	18
2000	Oklahoma	PCL	67.7	72	44	10	34	41	5.85	3	5	9.6	1.3	4.5	5.5	0.6	4.29	-1
2000	Texas	AL	102.7	104	58	12	47	65	5.08	5	6	9.1	1.1	4.1	5.7	0.7	4.46	-2
2001	Texas	AL	198.0	197	89	13	66	109	4.05	12	10	9.0	0.6	3.0	5.0	0.8	4.44	6

Last year's numbers look tidy, but they don't tell the story of Davis's season. His ERA stood at 7.00 in mid-May, when he was demoted to Triple-A briefly. Upon returning, he began throwing a cut fastball underneath hitters' hands to gain control of the inside half of the plate, and he posted an ERA of 3.84 the rest of the way. Davis's soft-tossing ways won't allow him to be ace material, but he's the only member of the 2001 rotation who will be part of the next good Rangers team.

R.A. Dickey **Throws R** **Age 27**

YEAR	TEAM	LGE	IP	H	ER	HR	BB	K	ERA	W	L	H/9	HR/9	BB/9	K/9	KW	PERA	STUFF
1999	Tulsa	Tex	94.3	115	81	21	50	38	7.73	3	7	11.0	2.0	4.8	3.6	0.4	7.02	-38
1999	Oklahoma	PCL	23.3	23	10	1	8	12	3.86	2	1	8.9	0.4	3.1	4.6	0.8	4.89	-2
2000	Oklahoma	PCL	158.3	176	98	18	69	61	5.57	7	11	10.0	1.0	3.9	3.5	0.4	5.31	-17
2001	Oklahoma	PCL	159.7	172	89	18	57	76	5.02	8	10	9.7	1.0	3.2	4.3	0.7	5.16	-7

Dickey is the best of four hurlers that the Rangers chose in the first rounds of the 1995 and 1996 drafts, a fact that goes a long way towards explaining the pitching shortage at the big-league level. Best known for not having an ulnar collateral ligament in his right arm, Dickey has great makeup and gets the most out of what he has, but he has lost five mph off the average fastball he brought from the University of Tennessee. If things break just right, he could latch on as the last man in the bullpen.

Ryan Dittfurth **Throws R** **Age 22**

YEAR	TEAM	LGE	IP	H	ER	HR	BB	K	ERA	W	L	H/9	HR/9	BB/9	K/9	KW	PERA	STUFF
1999	Pulaski	App	80.0	87	57	9	54	36	6.41	3	6	9.8	1.0	6.1	4.1	0.3	4.57	-1
2000	Savannah	SAL	152.0	163	120	20	126	82	7.11	5	12	9.7	1.2	7.5	4.9	0.3	6.90	-6
2001	Charlott	Fla	141.7	151	95	21	74	83	6.04	6	10	9.6	1.3	4.7	5.3	0.6	5.34	1

Ryan Dittfurth won the Nolan Ryan Award as the Rangers' best minor-league pitcher last year, and he has a bit of the young Express in him, ranking in the top ten of the Florida State League in strikeouts, walks, hit batters, and wild pitches. A boring two-seamer launched from a 6′6″ frame is Dittfurth's calling card, and he has the workings of a good curveball and change-up. His ceiling is as high as that of any pitcher in the organization.

Justin Duchscherer **Throws R** **Age 24**

YEAR	TEAM	LGE	IP	H	ER	HR	BB	K	ERA	W	L	H/9	HR/9	BB/9	K/9	KW	PERA	STUFF
1999	Augusta	SAL	37.7	35	13	0	11	20	3.11	3	1	8.4	0.0	2.6	4.8	0.9	0.31	20
1999	Sarasota	Fla	106.7	125	87	30	36	71	7.34	3	9	10.5	2.5	3.0	6.0	1.0	6.10	3
2000	Trenton	Eas	144.3	142	63	12	37	92	3.93	9	7	8.9	0.7	2.3	5.7	1.2	4.37	16
2001	Trenton	Eas	67.3	70	35	9	19	44	4.68	3	4	9.4	1.2	2.5	5.9	1.2	4.12	11
2001	Tulsa	Tex	43.7	41	19	5	12	36	3.92	3	2	8.5	1.0	2.5	7.4	1.5	3.44	23
2001	Oklahoma	PCL	50.0	50	24	7	11	37	4.32	3	3	9.0	1.3	2.0	6.7	1.7	3.82	20

The Red Sox panicked when Jason Varitek broke his elbow, allowing Melvin to swoop in and pilfer Duchscherer for Doug Mirabelli. Some scouts say that none of his pitches is major-league average, but his fastball has good darting movement, and he mixes it with a curveball and change-up that always seem to paint the black. His recent near-dominance at every rung of the ladder buoys his chances of being the rare finesse pitcher who bucks the odds and succeeds in The Show.

Ryan Glynn Throws R Age 27

YEAR	TEAM	LGE	IP	H	ER	HR	BB	K	ERA	W	L	H/9	HR/9	BB/9	K/9	KW	PERA	STUFF
1999	Oklahoma	PCL	87.7	93	49	8	39	40	5.03	4	6	9.5	0.8	4.0	4.1	0.5	4.71	-5
1999	Texas	AL	59.3	62	37	9	29	39	5.61	3	4	9.4	1.4	4.4	5.9	0.7	6.22	-3
2000	Oklahoma	PCL	81.7	82	42	7	35	47	4.63	4	5	9.0	0.8	3.9	5.2	0.7	4.35	-2
2000	Texas	AL	91.7	105	58	13	34	33	5.69	4	6	10.3	1.3	3.3	3.2	0.5	5.29	-12
2001	Texas	AL	48.0	56	34	6	25	14	6.38	2	3	10.5	1.1	4.7	2.6	0.3	6.62	-27
2001	Oklahoma	PCL	77.7	89	63	13	52	33	7.30	2	7	10.3	1.5	6.0	3.8	0.3	8.58	-30

That Ryan Glynn had never been a strikeout pitcher already made his chance for success in the majors slim. Slim met none when his control took a hiatus last year. Glynn was out of options when demoted to Oklahoma, so he became a minor-league free agent after the season. Though he's only 27, any shot he had at a big-league career has already come and gone.

Rick Helling Throws R Age 31

YEAR	TEAM	LGE	IP	H	ER	HR	BB	K	ERA	W	L	H/9	HR/9	BB/9	K/9	KW	PERA	STUFF
1999	Texas	AL	220.3	238	131	35	71	130	5.35	10	14	9.7	1.4	2.9	5.3	0.9	4.28	3
2000	Texas	AL	218.7	219	113	24	81	145	4.65	12	12	9.0	1.0	3.3	6.0	0.9	4.06	9
2001	Texas	AL	226.7	238	123	34	60	146	4.88	11	14	9.5	1.4	2.4	5.8	1.2	4.98	7

Nobody in the AL has thrown more pitches over the past three seasons than Rick Helling. The effects of the heavy workload showed last year, when he would intermittently lose 4–5 mph off his high-80s fastball. He compensated by throwing more strikes, slicing his walks, and yielding more base hits. The drop in velocity, combined with the perils of being a fly-ball pitcher in the hot climes of Texas, leaves him walking an increasingly thin tightrope. The Rangers non-tendered Helling in advance of signing Chan Ho Park, making him a free agent.

Travis Hughes Throws R Age 24

YEAR	TEAM	LGE	IP	H	ER	HR	BB	K	ERA	W	L	H/9	HR/9	BB/9	K/9	KW	PERA	STUFF
1999	Savannah	SAL	151.0	162	94	19	73	77	5.60	7	10	9.7	1.1	4.4	4.6	0.5	4.99	-1
2000	Charlott	Fla	123.3	140	93	22	67	60	6.79	4	10	10.2	1.6	4.9	4.4	0.4	7.26	-20
2001	Tulsa	Tex	89.0	93	62	13	55	56	6.27	3	7	9.4	1.3	5.6	5.7	0.5	6.33	-18

The Rangers like whatever is in the water at Cowley County Community College, having found both a booming bat, Travis Hafner, and possibly the hardest thrower in the organization, Travis Hughes, there. Though Hughes is very raw, Texas added him to the 40-man roster last winter rather than expose his arm to the Rule 5 draft. He brings gas out of the bullpen, but at this stage, his control is an oxidizer, creating a highly combustible mixture.

Danny Kolb Throws R Age 27

YEAR	TEAM	LGE	IP	H	ER	HR	BB	K	ERA	W	L	H/9	HR/9	BB/9	K/9	KW	PERA	STUFF
1999	Tulsa	Tex	40.0	38	18	0	22	20	4.05	2	2	8.6	0.0	5.0	4.5	0.5	4.60	-3
1999	Oklahoma	PCL	62.7	70	37	5	29	15	5.31	3	4	10.1	0.7	4.2	2.2	0.3	5.40	-19
1999	Texas	AL	32.0	32	15	2	13	15	4.22	2	2	9.0	0.6	3.7	4.2	0.6	4.29	-10
2000	Oklahoma	PCL	17.3	15	6	0	9	13	3.12	1	1	7.8	0.0	4.7	6.7	0.7	3.32	-2
2001	Charlott	Fla	19.0	22	10	3	3	8	4.74	1	1	10.4	1.4	1.4	3.8	1.3	6.24	-23
2001	Oklahoma	PCL	17.7	17	7	1	5	13	3.57	1	1	8.7	0.5	2.5	6.6	1.3	1.73	3
2001	Texas	AL	15.7	14	9	2	10	14	5.17	1	1	8.0	1.1	5.7	8.0	0.7	4.19	-2

Yes, he's still hanging around. Danny Kolb returned from elbow surgery with his good heat intact, and he is working from ahead in the count more often since becoming a reliever and dumping his off-speed junk. Kolb is free to sign with another organization, but he'd be wise to stay put, as there should be opportunities galore in the Junior Circuit's worst bullpen.

Colby Lewis Throws R Age 22

YEAR	TEAM	LGE	IP	H	ER	HR	BB	K	ERA	W	L	H/9	HR/9	BB/9	K/9	KW	PERA	STUFF
1999	Pulaski	App	61.7	64	38	7	34	35	5.55	3	4	9.3	1.0	5.0	5.1	0.5	4.02	4
2000	Charlott	Fla	165.7	177	97	26	53	100	5.27	8	10	9.6	1.4	2.9	5.4	0.9	5.88	11
2001	Tulsa	Tex	156.3	160	96	24	73	111	5.53	7	10	9.2	1.4	4.2	6.4	0.8	5.56	14

Colby Lewis has emerged as the organization's best homegrown pitching prospect, which isn't quite like being the most eligible bachelor in a leper colony now that the Rangers have assembled a fair group of green arms. Lewis is a Tommy John surgery survivor, and the team is currently monitoring his tender right shoulder and prudently chose not to have him work in the Arizona Fall League. If Lewis stays healthy, his 2003 ETA dovetails nicely with the free-agent exodus of up to 60% of last year's rotation.

Pat Mahomes — Throws R — Age 31

YEAR	TEAM	LGE	IP	H	ER	HR	BB	K	ERA	W	L	H/9	HR/9	BB/9	K/9	KW	PERA	STUFF
1999	Norfolk	Int	37.7	44	26	7	13	17	6.21	1	3	10.5	1.7	3.1	4.1	0.7	4.23	-12
1999	NY Mets	NL	59.7	58	33	7	31	46	4.98	3	4	8.7	1.1	4.7	6.9	0.7	3.49	-2
2000	NY Mets	NL	95.3	97	62	14	54	68	5.85	4	7	9.2	1.3	5.1	6.4	0.6	5.77	-11
2001	Texas	AL	108.7	117	70	15	52	58	5.80	5	7	9.7	1.2	4.3	4.8	0.6	5.30	-17

Mahomes opened last season with a random stretch of effectiveness that caused the Rangers to raise the ante, pitching him more frequently and stretching out his innings. The bluff was called when he was dropped into the rotation in late May, and he was disrobed in four starts. Mahomes has managed an ERA under 5.00 but twice in a nine-year career, so it's hard to fathom why he keeps getting chances. It isn't as if his stuff is so sexy that teams can't resist giving it a romp.

Chris Michalak — Throws B? — Age 31

YEAR	TEAM	LGE	IP	H	ER	HR	BB	K	ERA	W	L	H/9	HR/9	BB/9	K/9	KW	PERA	STUFF
1999	Edmonton	PCL	28.3	30	18	4	16	17	5.72	1	2	9.5	1.3	5.1	5.4	0.5	6.57	-28
1999	Tucson	PCL	63.7	69	39	7	30	28	5.51	3	4	9.8	1.0	4.2	4.0	0.5	4.13	-21
2000	Albuquer	PCL	138.3	159	97	23	59	59	6.31	5	10	10.3	1.5	3.8	3.8	0.5	4.81	-16
2001	Toronto	AL	119.0	128	67	13	47	54	5.07	6	7	9.7	1.0	3.6	4.1	0.6	4.58	-7
2001	Texas	AL	21.7	26	15	5	6	10	6.23	1	1	10.8	2.1	2.5	4.2	0.8	2.95	-17

Journeyman Michalak won the Blue Jays' fifth-starter job with a surprising spring. The mirage evaporated as the weather grew warmer, and by August he was off to Texas. Michalak isn't tough enough on left-handed hitters to be a specialist, so he'll be in the March mix for a long-relief job. If nothing else, he has novelty value; he owns the best pickoff move in the game and is ambidextrous enough to become only the second pitcher in modern baseball history to throw with both hands.

Juan Moreno — Throws L — Age 27

YEAR	TEAM	LGE	IP	H	ER	HR	BB	K	ERA	W	L	H/9	HR/9	BB/9	K/9	KW	PERA	STUFF
1999	Tulsa	Tex	57.3	53	37	8	40	53	5.81	2	4	8.3	1.3	6.3	8.3	0.7	3.55	-8
2001	Tulsa	Tex	8.3	7	3	0	4	6	3.24	1	0	7.6	0.0	4.3	6.5	0.8	1.38	-2
2001	Oklahoma	PCL	8.3	8	4	1	3	8	4.32	1	0	8.6	1.1	3.2	8.6	1.3	2.25	6
2001	Texas	AL	37.3	35	25	5	27	34	6.03	1	3	8.4	1.2	6.5	8.2	0.6	4.07	-5

Here is another example of why teams don't need to overpay for relief pitching. Cut loose from the A's organization after the 1996 season, Moreno was stumbled upon by the Rangers in the Venezuelan winter league two years later. Rotator-cuff surgery in 2000 delayed his Rangers debut until last May, but it was worth the wait. Moreno throws hard, has a filthy slider, and could see his role expanded since he is also effective against right-handed hitters.

Aaron Myette — Throws R — Age 24

YEAR	TEAM	LGE	IP	H	ER	HR	BB	K	ERA	W	L	H/9	HR/9	BB/9	K/9	KW	PERA	STUFF
1999	Birmnghm	Sou	157.0	171	111	28	78	95	6.36	6	11	9.8	1.6	4.5	5.4	0.6	4.76	5
1999	ChiSox	AL	16.3	16	11	2	12	11	6.06	1	1	8.8	1.1	6.6	6.1	0.5	5.33	-1
2000	Charlott	Int	108.7	118	79	22	54	72	6.54	4	8	9.8	1.8	4.5	6.0	0.7	4.66	6
2001	Oklahoma	PCL	69.7	65	34	6	34	54	4.39	4	4	8.4	0.8	4.4	7.0	0.8	4.43	16
2001	Texas	AL	85.7	84	46	11	35	64	4.83	5	5	8.8	1.2	3.7	6.7	0.9	6.45	7

Previously lost in the sea of pitching prospects on the south side of Chicago, Myette gives the Rangers' staff a legitimate power arm. He is very aggressive on the mound; the Rangers like his willingness to pitch inside and protect their hitters. He isn't guaranteed a starting job heading into spring training, but given the competition, you have to like his chances.

Darren Oliver Throws L Age 31

YEAR	TEAM	LGE	IP	H	ER	HR	BB	K	ERA	W	L	H/9	HR/9	BB/9	K/9	KW	PERA	STUFF
1999	St Louis	NL	198.3	201	92	15	62	107	4.17	12	10	9.1	0.7	2.8	4.9	0.9	4.01	6
2000	Oklahoma	PCL	30.0	29	16	3	15	20	4.80	1	2	8.7	0.9	4.5	6.0	0.7	3.48	-3
2000	Texas	AL	118.3	130	65	13	34	49	4.94	6	7	9.9	1.0	2.6	3.7	0.7	6.35	-7
2001	Texas	AL	164.0	170	92	21	62	99	5.05	8	10	9.3	1.2	3.4	5.4	0.8	5.67	0

In his short tenure as pitching coach, Larry Hardy made significant adjustments to the mechanics of nearly every Rangers starting pitcher. When he quit in early June, all had ERAs that over a full season would have been the worst of their careers. After his resignation, the starters' ERAs improved by nearly a run and a half during the rest of the campaign. Hardy's tinkering may not have been the cause, but it is an interesting coincidence.

This has little to do with Darren Oliver, who would be mediocre if God or, better yet, Leo Mazzone were his coach. Joe Kerrigan—a minor deity—will get his shot at Oliver in 2002; the left-hander was sent to the Red Sox for Carl Everett.

Mark Petkovsek Throws R Age 36

YEAR	TEAM	LGE	IP	H	ER	HR	BB	K	ERA	W	L	H/9	HR/9	BB/9	K/9	KW	PERA	STUFF
1999	Anaheim	AL	84.7	86	35	5	18	43	3.72	5	4	9.1	0.5	1.9	4.6	1.2	3.38	-4
2000	Anaheim	AL	82.0	89	39	7	19	31	4.28	5	4	9.8	0.8	2.1	3.4	0.8	3.59	-14
2001	Texas	AL	82.3	92	50	13	27	40	5.47	4	5	10.1	1.4	3.0	4.4	0.7	6.37	-19

Bypassing the Mikes, Mussina and Hampton, Doug Melvin lassoed Mark Petkovsek from the 2000 class of Type A free agents. It seems only fitting that the Elias Bureau would have its name attached to a rating system so comical. For a cool $2 million, Petkovsek did a bang-up imitation of Dave Eiland. The bottom line is that the Rangers forfeited a couple of early-round draft choices in exchange for two years of sporadically adequate middle relief. Blech.

Andy Pratt Throws L Age 22

YEAR	TEAM	LGE	IP	H	ER	HR	BB	K	ERA	W	L	H/9	HR/9	BB/9	K/9	KW	PERA	STUFF
1999	Savannah	SAL	72.7	72	35	8	22	51	4.33	4	4	8.9	1.0	2.7	6.3	1.2	5.47	21
2000	Charlott	Fla	86.0	94	59	19	31	62	6.17	3	7	9.8	2.0	3.2	6.5	1.0	4.63	16
2000	Tulsa	Tex	55.0	62	43	10	33	29	7.04	2	4	10.1	1.6	5.4	4.7	0.4	9.01	-6
2001	Tulsa	Tex	168.0	186	111	29	67	90	5.95	7	12	10.0	1.6	3.6	4.8	0.7	6.02	3

With the help of his dad, a pitching coach in the Cubs' chain, Pratt was fairly polished coming out of high school. That sheen enabled him to succeed at the lower levels of the system, but he found the sledding tougher at Tulsa last year. Pratt has average stuff, is adept at changing speeds, and needs to sharpen his curveball. The last couple steps will be a tougher climb; by 2004, he'll have made the adjustments and be in the big leagues to stay.

Nick Regilio Throws R Age 23

YEAR	TEAM	LGE	IP	H	ER	HR	BB	K	ERA	W	L	H/9	HR/9	BB/9	K/9	KW	PERA	STUFF
1999	Pulaski	App	46.0	48	26	5	20	24	5.09	2	3	9.4	1.0	3.9	4.7	0.6	2.62	4
2000	Charlott	Fla	85.7	101	66	19	34	41	6.93	3	7	10.6	2.0	3.6	4.3	0.6	7.31	-12
2001	Charlott	Fla	59.0	66	40	12	19	36	6.10	2	5	10.1	1.8	2.9	5.5	0.9	3.10	5
2001	Tulsa	Tex	55.3	56	27	3	23	27	4.39	3	3	9.1	0.5	3.7	4.4	0.6	6.68	0

A nearly finished product when drafted in the second round in 1999, Regilio's progress was slowed by shoulder and elbow woes in 2000. He avoided the knife and bounced back nicely last year, dominating the Florida State League before a mid-season promotion to Double-A. Regilio's stuff and command are both a tick above average, but neither is good enough to Express Mail him to the majors or to guarantee him once he gets there.

Kenny Rogers Throws L Age 37

YEAR	TEAM	LGE	IP	H	ER	HR	BB	K	ERA	W	L	H/9	HR/9	BB/9	K/9	KW	PERA	STUFF
1999	Oakland	AL	125.7	125	53	7	34	67	3.80	8	6	9.0	0.5	2.4	4.8	1.0	4.34	8
1999	NY Mets	NL	76.0	75	35	8	23	52	4.14	4	4	8.9	0.9	2.7	6.2	1.1	3.94	13
2000	Texas	AL	238.0	241	105	17	64	126	3.97	15	11	9.1	0.6	2.4	4.8	1.0	4.00	7
2001	Texas	AL	128.3	136	73	16	47	70	5.12	6	8	9.5	1.1	3.3	4.9	0.7	5.84	0

For a guy who does a fair impression of "Old Aches and Pains," Luke Appling, it's shocking that last year was the first time in Rogers's 13-year career that he was placed on the disabled list. His injury was a rib that was impinging on a muscle in his shoulder area, which likely explains his loss of command. Expect him to return to form this season.

Justin Thompson Throws L Age 29

YEAR	TEAM	LGE	IP	H	ER	HR	BB	K	ERA	W	L	H/9	HR/9	BB/9	K/9	KW	PERA	STUFF
1999	Detroit	AL	144.7	155	84	21	49	82	5.23	7	9	9.6	1.3	3.0	5.1	0.8	4.50	1

This will likely be the last time Justin Thompson gets an entry in the book. Thompson has had four shoulder operations since he last pitched in the majors, his left arm now a testament to how unnatural an act it is to throw a baseball. The Rangers declined their 2002 option on his contract, though they may still offer him an incentive-laden one-year deal. Moms and dads, if you're looking for a safe career for your kids, have them try knife juggling instead of pitching.

Domingo Valdez Throws R Age 22

YEAR	TEAM	LGE	IP	H	ER	HR	BB	K	ERA	W	L	H/9	HR/9	BB/9	K/9	KW	PERA	STUFF
1999	Pulaski	App	16.3	21	17	5	9	6	9.37	0	2	11.6	2.8	5.0	3.3	0.3	9.49	-20
2000	Pulaski	App	58.7	57	30	3	33	32	4.60	3	4	8.7	0.5	5.1	4.9	0.5	4.69	7
2001	Savannah	SAL	77.0	84	65	17	54	55	7.60	2	7	9.8	2.0	6.3	6.4	0.5	5.52	1
2001	Charlott	Fla	40.7	44	29	7	21	25	6.42	2	3	9.7	1.5	4.6	5.5	0.6	7.32	-2

Valdez was an overweight underachiever until dedicating himself to his profession two years ago. Since then, he's been blowing away overmatched hitters. He views himself as a starter, but the Rangers are probably going to chop his high-strikeout, low-hit servings into one-inning bites. Now that he's overcome the initial inertia, Valdez should move quickly and reach the Rangers' bullpen in 2003.

Mike Venafro Throws L Age 28

YEAR	TEAM	LGE	IP	H	ER	HR	BB	K	ERA	W	L	H/9	HR/9	BB/9	K/9	KW	PERA	STUFF
1999	Texas	AL	68.0	67	28	3	18	37	3.71	5	3	8.9	0.4	2.4	4.9	1.0	3.14	-3
2000	Texas	AL	59.7	58	23	2	17	32	3.47	4	3	8.7	0.3	2.6	4.8	0.9	3.46	-5
2001	Texas	AL	59.3	59	27	2	27	28	4.10	4	3	8.9	0.3	4.1	4.2	0.5	4.67	-15

Some ominous signs began to appear in lefty-getter Venafro's line last season. Over the final two months, his ERA skyrocketed to 9.15, and he walked twice as many batters as he struck out. Venafro, not a large man, has worked in 212 games over the past three seasons. While he's never been on the disabled list, he did complain of shoulder stiffness and may not bounce back this year.

Jeff Zimmerman Throws R Age 29

YEAR	TEAM	LGE	IP	H	ER	HR	BB	K	ERA	W	L	H/9	HR/9	BB/9	K/9	KW	PERA	STUFF
1999	Texas	AL	80.3	74	32	8	19	66	3.59	6	3	8.3	0.9	2.1	7.4	1.7	2.02	12
2000	Texas	AL	75.7	67	34	8	28	73	4.04	4	4	8.0	1.0	3.3	8.7	1.3	4.66	10
2001	Texas	AL	68.0	61	28	9	15	68	3.71	5	3	8.1	1.2	2.0	9.0	2.3	2.14	19

The nasty bite returned to Jeff Zimmerman's slider last year, along with the dominance he flashed during the first half of his rookie season. He was especially lights out after the All-Star break, when batters hit an Oyler-esque .118/.217/.226 off of him. New GM John Hart is making noise about acquiring a "proven closer." How much proof does he need?

Toronto Blue Jays

In 1998, the average age of the Blue Jays' starting position players was 28. While that's not exceptionally noteworthy, the team's core—Carlos Delgado, Shawn Green, Shannon Stewart, Jose Cruz Jr., and Alex Gonzalez—ranged in age from 24 to 26. By the end of that season, the Jays had also assembled a trio of starting pitchers—Chris Carpenter, Kelvim Escobar, and Roy Halladay—of whom the oldest was 23, with ceilings as high as a Victorian schoolhouse. That team won 88 games under the guidance of first-year manager Tim Johnson, a 12-game improvement from the previous year.

In many ways the 1998 Blue Jays resembled their 1983 team. Led by then-young manager Bobby Cox, the 1983 club improved by 11 games in posting an 89-win season—the first winning campaign in franchise history. It too had a lineup powered by a nucleus of up-and-coming young players. That team hit postseason pay dirt two years later, and the organization produced winning seasons for more than a decade, eventually morphing into the unit that won consecutive World Series in 1992 and 1993.

While it may have been optimistic to expect a repeat of the successes of the 1983 cast, one could look at the two rosters and make a compelling argument that General Manager Gord Ash's club had a better talent base than that assembled from scratch by the team's original GM, Pat Gillick. Unquestionably, Toronto was poised for a nice run.

Since then, however, the Blue Jays have "built on" their success with yearly totals of 84, 83, and 80 victories. Whispers that began in 2000 about making changes to shake up the clubhouse swelled into a relentless din by the end of last season. A team that had efficiently retooled since admitting after 1994 that every drop of glory had been squeezed out of its aging roster now seems on the verge of self-disembowelment. What in the name of the late BJ Birdy happened?

There is no question as to the popular explanation: just as Manuel Noriega's name is never heard without the phrase "Panamanian strongman," so the current Blue Jays are inextricably linked with the adjective "underachieving." Because underachievement is generally associated with young people who don't reach their predicted level of success, we can assume that the individuals being targeted are the young turks who were supposed to propel the Blue Jays into the postseason. By and large, that is the picture being painted by the Toronto sports media. Is it a fair assessment?

Blue Jays Prospectus

2001 record: 80–82; Third place, AL East

Pythagenport W/L: 82–80

Runs scored: 767 (ninth in AL)

Runs allowed: 753 (sixth in AL)

Team EqA: .254 (ninth in AL)

2001 batters age: 28 (fifth-youngest in AL)

2001 pitchers age: 28.1 (tied for sixth-youngest in AL)

Ballpark: Skydome; moderate hitters' park; Park Factor of 1.038

2001: Transition year began with a change in ownership and ended with changes in the front office, all to the good.

2002: Not quite ready to challenge the Yankees, but on the right track for 2003.

Table 1 lists projected 2001 Equivalent Averages for various Blue Jays, using only statistics up to and including the 1998 season. Raul Mondesi is also included because he was essentially traded straight up for Shawn Green after the 1999 campaign and replaced Green in right field. The final column is a list of the actual 2001 EqAs for those players.

Overall, the Fab Five position players have improved offensively since 1998 and actually did slightly better last year than would have been projected three years ago. While the organization may have anticipated their rising to loftier heights, to heap blame for the team's recent failures on a group that has basically performed up to expectations is neither fair nor accurate.

Of the five, only Delgado projected to be a star. Although Stewart, Cruz, and Green/Mondesi looked to become well-above-average players, they weren't going to be productive enough to push an offense to the upper strata of the league if not buttressed by solid contributions throughout the lineup. That support simply hasn't been there. Over the past three

Table 1.

Player	1998 EqA	Projected 2001 EqA	Actual 2001 EqA
Carlos Delgado	.322	.316	.323
Shannon Stewart	.278	.293	.289
Jose Cruz Jr.	.265	.282	.291
Alex Gonzalez	.222	.239	.242
Shawn Green	.280	.295	.325
Raul Mondesi	.268	.282	.275

seasons, Toronto has typically had three lightweight bats in its lineup: Alex Gonzalez and, depending on the year, holes at catcher, designated hitter, second base, and third base. As a result, the team has finished in the middle of the pack in run scoring despite getting exactly what it should have expected from its offensive core.

Of course, the position players aren't the only flock of Blue Jays accused of underachieving; Carpenter, Escobar, and Halladay have also been fingered in the indictment. Admittedly, it's impossible to claim that they've reached the level of success they should have achieved by now. Then again, predicting the development of hurlers in their early 20s is as exact a science as locating underground water with a divining rod. Arm injuries aren't as much a question of "if"as "when." Then there are the mental rigors of pitching, which in extreme cases can cause a pitcher to go Ankiel. The Jays' young guns have experienced both of these problems.

The struggles of Carpenter and Escobar likely trace back to 1998, when Johnson went to the whip the final two months in a futile effort to win the AL wild card. Both pitchers were worked extremely hard, and both showed the effects of overuse the following year. Carpenter spent most of 1999 battling arm problems before having surgery to clean out his elbow. Escobar made every start, but his nasty stuff lost its bite, and he was hit hard. Halladay's problems have been more mental than physical. Some time between 1999 and 2000, he lost all confidence in his ability to get hitters out, and it showed in the results.

It's easy—and not wholly inaccurate—to attribute the deterioration of the third-best starting staff in the league in 1998 to the struggles of the young trio. However, other causes have had an equal, if not greater, effect. Roger Clemens, fresh off back-to-back Cy Young Awards in 1997 and 1998, was exchanged for the bigger, but not better, David Wells. The fact that Dave Stewart recommended trading Woody Williams for Joey Hamilton should alone be enough to disqualify him from becoming a major-league GM. Even last year, when Carpenter, Escobar, and Halladay all returned to their 1998 level, the impact was negated by preseason moves: Wells was dealt for damaged goods, and Frank Castillo left town as a free agent and wasn't adequately replaced.

Developments and organizational decisions regarding managers and coaches have also helped stall the club's progress. Ash couldn't have foreseen Johnson's penchant for telling tall tales about nonexistent Vietnam experiences, but taking four months—until the middle of spring training in 1999—to recognize that the lies would undermine the team's respect for Johnson was clearly a mistake. Ash had to scramble to find a new skipper and ended up hiring Jim Fregosi, an old-school, hands-off manager whose main selling point was that he could start work immediately. Whereas Johnson's best quality was his lack of allegiances to fading veterans and his faith in the kids, Fregosi prefers his meat aged and inserted it into the lineup whenever the opportunity arose.

In fairness to Fregosi, he walked into a messy situation. While he may have been a decent choice to lead a veteran team, or even to lead these same Blue Jays a few years later, his lack of communication and teaching skills were a poor match for a young ball club.

Ash showed worse judgment after the 1999 campaign when he brought Cito Gaston back to Toronto as the hitting coach. Gaston had managed the 1992-93 World Champions, remaining at the helm through 1997. It is well known that at the time of his leaving, a lot of the players didn't get along with him. One of them was Green, who was traded to the Dodgers for Mondesi, an inferior player, within a month of Gaston's return.

Coach Gaston preaches aggressive hitting, with predictable results. The walk rates of Cruz and Stewart are half what they were prior to Gaston's arrival. Gonzalez, who seemed to be on the right track in 1999, has gone back to his free-swinging ways. Only Delgado had the self-assurance to retain a patient approach, one that has enabled him to become one of the most dangerous hitters in baseball. Gaston received a fair amount of credit when the 2000 Blue Jays led the AL in home runs; largely ignored was the fact that their on-base percentage plummeted to 12th in the AL, causing a 5% drop in runs scored.

Hiring broadcasters as managers is one of the more inexplicable recent trends in the game. The Jays jumped on this bandwagon after the 2000 season, plucking managerial neophyte Buck Martinez from their announcing booth for his media savvy and hoping that his popularity in Toronto would put fannies in the Skydome seats. It's not clear whether in-game philosophy was ever discussed at his job interview. "Bucky Ball" focuses on contact hitting and speed rather than swinging for the fences; Martinez inherited a lineup that in 2000 led the league in homers, finished fourth in strikeouts, and tenth in stolen bases. Oil and water didn't mix, as the offense remained mired in the bottom half of the AL in run scoring. On the other hand, Martinez displayed a willingness to play prospects when he needed a replacement rather than hauling in a decaying exoskeleton, and he did a nice job handling the starting pitchers.

The Blue Jays are at a crossroads. The franchise's inability to build on its firm foundation has patrons speaking with their wallets and staying away from the ballpark. Attendance last year was up 5% over the 2000 season but still totaled less than half of what the club drew in the early 1990s. As long as the correct targets are identified, the impulse to drastically shake up the team is not misplaced. On that front, score the Jays' first major off-season move a direct hit. After a hiring process that lasted longer than the gestation period of the average placental mammal, the Blue Jays appointed J.P.

Ricciardi to replace Gord Ash as general manager. Ricciardi was previously the Athletics' dircctor of player development, and he brings several attractive qualities to the organization:

- **An ability to work with a limited budget.** The Blue Jays' ownership group, Rogers Communications, intends to keep the team's payroll at $75 million in 2002. Coming from Oakland, where finding change on the sidewalk is considered a cash infusion, Ricciardi will feel like he's hit the winning Powerball numbers. Proven young players will be signed to long-term, below-market contracts.
- **A deep conviction in the importance of on-base percentage.** Ricciardi didn't waste any time before introducing the topic, talking at length about the subject at his first news conference. The mantra, "OBP is life," will echo in the halls throughout his tenure. Gaston's firing occurred prior to Ricciardi's arrival, so that's one less axe that has to drop. Immediately, if not sooner, the Blue Jays will have in place a consistent approach to teaching plate discipline throughout their system.
- **A strong belief and background in scouting, drafting, and development.** As a co-creator of "The Oakland Model" that produced most of the front-line talent on back-to-back playoff teams, Ricciardi knows that player development is the lifeblood of an organization. Money, coaching, innovation, and a cohesive instruction plan will produce a steady stream of effective, low-cost talent. Baseball players will be preferred to athletes.

As for less philosophical, more tangible moves to satisfy those fans lusting for head-rolling action, Ricciardi needs to, and likely will, identify and remove the real barriers to the Blue Jays' success. The middle infield is a great place to start. Gonzalez has been traded to the Cubs, to be replaced by Felipe Lopez, and Homer Bush isn't guaranteed a job, as the Jays have Orlando Hudson, who is both better and cheaper. While Mondesi's performance is tolerable, his $11 million salary isn't; dumping it is a priority.

Cruz and Stewart are both eligible to drink from the free-agency chalice after 2003. The organization ought to use the upcoming season to evaluate them—how they fit into the lineup, how they fit into the budget, and whether they're interested in staying in Toronto. Should either opt for free agency, it wouldn't be the worst thing to let them play out their final year, secure in the knowledge that high draft choices are the compensation. Thanks in large part to the penurious final days of Interbrew ownership, the lower levels of the Blue Jays' farm system are among the worst in baseball and desperately need replenishing.

The Jays' rotation has a solid front four, and the trade for Luke Prokopec should settle the fifth-starter question. There isn't enough available depth to survive a 162-game schedule, but consistent with Ricciardi's background, a Cory Lidle/Erik Hiljus-type alternative can provide a low-cost reinforcement with some upside.

Shedding the "underachieving" label isn't going to happen overnight; there is too much dead weight and too many burdensome contracts on the Blue Jays' payroll. However, even after three years of empty promises, it's hard to not be buoyed by the decision to have J.P. Ricciardi chart the team's course. As a first step, expect a return to the Jays' 1998 level of play this year. After that, it gets better. It's a brave new world north of the border; the rest of the American League East had better start paying attention.

HITTERS (BA: .270, OBP: .340, SLG: .440, EqA: .260)

Homer Bush 2B Bats R Age 29

YEAR	TEAM	LGE	AB	H	DB	TP	HR	BB	SO	R	RBI	SB	CS	OUT	BA	OBP	SLG	EQA	EQR	DEFENSE
1999	Toronto	AL	481	158	27	4	5	16	72	67	53	31	8	331	.328	.357	.432	.270	63	109-2B 8 17-SS -3
2000	Toronto	AL	296	66	3	0	3	14	53	35	19	9	5	235	.223	.270	.264	.188	18	75-2B 12
2001	Toronto	AL	271	87	12	1	3	9	43	33	27	12	4	188	.321	.353	.406	.259	32	76-2B 6
2002	*Toronto*	*AL*	*406*	*122*	*15*	*2*	*5*	*25*	*70*	*54*	*38*	*13*	*5*	*289*	*.300*	*.341*	*.384*	*.249*	*45*	

Batting average fluctuates significantly from year-to-year—it's the nature of the beast. Bush's average has dipped below .298 only four times in 11 professional seasons, so most years he isn't a total cipher, despite his hack-tastic ways. A more persistent problem is his inability to stay healthy, and not even Martinez's infatuation with Bush's little-ball skills can begin to justify paying big money to somebody who is essentially a part-time player.

Kevin Cash C Bats R Age 24

YEAR	TEAM	LGE	AB	H	DB	TP	HR	BB	SO	R	RBI	SB	CS	OUT	BA	OBP	SLG	EQA	EQR	DEFENSE
2000	Hagerstn	SAL	201	38	6	0	7	15	58	19	17	2	2	165	.189	.247	.323	.192	13	49-C 6
2001	Dunedin	Fla	380	90	15	0	11	30	86	42	48	2	2	292	.237	.299	.363	.223	34	78-C 6
2002	*Toronto*	*AL*	*366*	*93*	*18*	*1*	*12*	*36*	*92*	*43*	*42*	*2*	*2*	*275*	*.254*	*.321*	*.407*	*.244*	*40*	

A non-drafted free agent out of Florida State, Cash is the dark horse in the Blue Jays' wild catching scramble. Cash has adapted quickly to the move from third base to catcher, leading both his minor leagues in throwing out base thieves. He's no slouch with the bat either, posting an EqA 21% better than the average Florida State League backstop. Similar success at Double-A will vault Cash to within a few lengths of the other masked men in the organization.

Alberto Castillo C Bats R Age 32

YEAR	TEAM	LGE	AB	H	DB	TP	HR	BB	SO	R	RBI	SB	CS	OUT	BA	OBP	SLG	EQA	EQR	DEFENSE
1999	St Louis	NL	256	67	5	0	5	21	44	20	30	0	0	189	.262	.322	.340	.227	23	
2000	Toronto	AL	184	40	5	0	2	19	32	13	16	0	0	144	.217	.291	.277	.199	13	45-C 3
2001	Toronto	AL	131	28	2	0	2	7	26	9	5	1	1	104	.214	.266	.275	.187	8	47-C 0
2002	*NY Yanks*	*AL*	*213*	*49*	*2*	*0*	*4*	*21*	*41*	*15*	*20*	*1*	*1*	*165*	*.230*	*.299*	*.296*	*.205*	*16*	

Castillo is a throwback to the glory days of Bill Plummer and Ken Rudolph, players with no ability to hit who carved out major-league careers as backup catchers because of good defensive reputations. Today's high-octane offenses and shortened benches due to pitcher specialization make such catchers a vanishing breed. Castillo's contract expired after last season, and he, too, will likely disappear, moving the species one step closer to the fate of the passenger pigeon. Unless he beats out Todd Greene for the backup-catcher job with the Yankees, that is.

Jose Cruz CF Bats B Age 28

YEAR	TEAM	LGE	AB	H	DB	TP	HR	BB	SO	R	RBI	SB	CS	OUT	BA	OBP	SLG	EQA	EQR	DEFENSE
1999	Toronto	AL	345	85	18	3	15	61	80	61	44	13	4	264	.246	.360	.446	.273	51	103-CF 7
1999	Syracuse	Int	104	18	3	1	2	24	19	14	11	4	0	86	.173	.328	.279	.227	11	29-LF 5
2000	Toronto	AL	597	147	31	5	32	64	113	87	72	15	5	455	.246	.321	.476	.262	80	159-CF 0
2001	Toronto	AL	576	164	38	4	37	48	119	96	90	30	6	418	.285	.341	.557	.291	95	135-CF -7
2002	*Toronto*	*AL*	*565*	*155*	*36*	*4*	*32*	*74*	*121*	*104*	*85*	*29*	*5*	*415*	*.274*	*.358*	*.522*	*.293*	*97*	

Cruz's time in Toronto has been one of extremes. It reached a peak by the end of last season, when the local media voted him the team's best player. Of course, the assessment wasn't accurate, but why clutter a good story with facts? However, Cruz did show the best power of his career and was among the top five center fielders in the American League. With hitting coach Cito Gaston and his aggressive approach out the door, Cruz could regain some of his old plate discipline and take another leap forward.

Carlos Delgado 1B Bats L Age 30

YEAR	TEAM	LGE	AB	H	DB	TP	HR	BB	SO	R	RBI	SB	CS	OUT	BA	OBP	SLG	EQA	EQR	DEFENSE
1999	Toronto	AL	567	159	34	0	48	80	124	111	133	1	1	409	.280	.382	.594	.311	110	147-1B 2
2000	Toronto	AL	554	195	46	1	45	114	91	108	131	0	1	360	.352	.474	.682	.367	147	161-1B -8
2001	Toronto	AL	574	168	26	1	44	114	117	108	107	3	0	406	.293	.420	.571	.323	121	159-1B 0
2002	*Toronto*	*AL*	*540*	*162*	*28*	*1*	*42*	*98*	*110*	*102*	*117*	*1*	*1*	*379*	*.300*	*.408*	*.589*	*.323*	*112*	

When heads start rolling, the finger pointing follows. With Delgado suffering an off-year and carrying the team's heftiest contract, many digits were aimed his way in the off-season. Being the best player on the Blue Jays' roster wasn't enough; management expected him to take responsibility for everybody else's performance as well. Most of Delgado's problems last year were due to his struggles against left-handers—his OPS against southpaws fell nearly 180 points from his 1998–2000 performance. There is nothing in Delgado's peripheral numbers to suggest he won't return a monster in 2002.

Shawn Fagan 3B Bats R Age 24

YEAR	TEAM	LGE	AB	H	DB	TP	HR	BB	SO	R	RBI	SB	CS	OUT	BA	OBP	SLG	EQA	EQR	DEFENSE
2000	Queens	NYP	93	19	4	0	2	8	26	12	8	0	0	74	.204	.276	.312	.202	7	22-3B -6
2000	Hagerstn	SAL	176	37	8	0	1	12	30	14	14	2	1	140	.210	.262	.273	.186	10	43-3B -2
2001	Dunedin	Fla	491	120	12	3	9	63	122	53	51	4	1	372	.244	.331	.336	.232	48	113-3B -2
2002	*Toronto*	*AL*	*456*	*119*	*15*	*2*	*13*	*54*	*115*	*55*	*54*	*5*	*1*	*338*	*.261*	*.339*	*.388*	*.250*	*53*	

Fagan makes the book as the recipient of BP's Max Bishop Award for the best batting eye among Toronto's minor leaguers. His strong arm and limited range prompted the Blue Jays to station him behind the plate after drafting him in 2000, but their catching backlog forced a return to third base, the position he manned at Penn State. Fagan has fair straight-ahead speed, but he needs to improve his agility to become a viable option at the hot corner.

Tony Fernandez PH/3B Bats B Age 40

YEAR	TEAM	LGE	AB	H	DB	TP	HR	BB	SO	R	RBI	SB	CS	OUT	BA	OBP	SLG	EQA	EQR	DEFENSE
1999	Toronto	AL	477	160	27	0	11	72	55	69	76	6	7	324	.335	.432	.461	.303	82	119-3B -5
2000	Seibu	JpP	372	124	22	1	13	48	44	55	63	2	4	252	.333	.417	.503	.305	65	
2001	Milwauke	NL	64	18	0	0	1	7	8	6	3	1	2	48	.281	.352	.328	.231	6	10-3B 3
2001	Toronto	AL	59	19	1	0	2	2	7	5	13	0	1	41	.322	.352	.441	.258	7	
2002	*Toronto*	*AL*	*388*	*101*	*18*	*1*	*10*	*53*	*51*	*48*	*53*	*4*	*5*	*292*	*.260*	*.349*	*.389*	*.251*	*46*	

After being released by the Brewers, Fernandez called ex-teammate Buck Martinez and wormed his way onto the Jays' roster for a farewell tour. Fernandez rewarded the sentimentality by setting a franchise-record with 16 pinch hits. Though he exited the game as a no-range third sacker and will always be remembered for kicking a potential game-ending grounder in Game 7 of the 1997 World Series, in the pre-Trinity era, Fernandez was ice with the glove and a good-hitting shortstop. Anybody trying to assemble a case for Dave Concepcion for the Hall of Fame should instead be pumping Fernandez, who was a similar, but better, player.

Darrin Fletcher C Bats L Age 35

YEAR	TEAM	LGE	AB	H	DB	TP	HR	BB	SO	R	RBI	SB	CS	OUT	BA	OBP	SLG	EQA	EQR	DEFENSE
1999	Toronto	AL	409	123	20	0	21	22	41	47	80	0	0	286	.301	.344	.504	.277	58	102-C -4
2000	Toronto	AL	412	134	19	1	21	14	40	41	56	1	0	278	.325	.355	.529	.288	62	104-C -4
2001	Toronto	AL	415	99	14	0	14	26	37	38	60	0	1	317	.239	.291	.373	.222	37	111-C 2
2002	*Toronto*	*AL*	*380*	*100*	*12*	*0*	*16*	*28*	*37*	*36*	*56*	*0*	*0*	*280*	*.263*	*.314*	*.421*	*.245*	*41*	

Fletcher played all of last season with severe back pain. While a rigorous stretching and strengthening regimen helped him pick up his numbers after the All-Star break, he never came close to approaching his career-best 2000 form. With high mileage on his odometer and oodles of catching depth in the organization, Fletcher's days in Toronto are numbered. Last year was not an aberration; the sooner the Jays trade him, the better.

Jeff Frye 2B/3B Bats R Age 35

YEAR	TEAM	LGE	AB	H	DB	TP	HR	BB	SO	R	RBI	SB	CS	OUT	BA	OBP	SLG	EQA	EQR	DEFENSE
1999	Boston	AL	113	33	1	0	2	13	10	14	13	2	2	82	.292	.369	.354	.249	13	22-2B -2
2000	Boston	AL	236	70	7	0	3	25	33	32	13	1	3	169	.297	.366	.364	.249	26	45-2B -3 11-RF -1
2000	Colorado	NL	84	27	5	0	0	7	15	12	4	3	0	57	.321	.379	.381	.269	11	20-2B 0
2001	Toronto	AL	175	46	8	1	2	12	16	26	16	2	1	130	.263	.318	.354	.229	16	37-2B 2 12-3B 0
2002	*Toronto*	*AL*	*266*	*70*	*11*	*1*	*4*	*33*	*33*	*36*	*22*	*7*	*2*	*198*	*.263*	*.344*	*.357*	*.245*	*29*	

Frye is an MS-DOS system slogging along in a Windows world. Bloated pitching staffs make multi-tasking a prerequisite for today's middle-infield bench men, yet Frye was signed for the lone duty of carrying on the legacy of Mickey Morandini. Aside from the missing mullet, he was virtually indistinguishable from The Mick. Frye's advancing age and diminished skills, along with his inability to adequately handle any position besides second base, should put an end to his surprisingly long major-league career.

Brad Fullmer DH Bats L Age 27

YEAR	TEAM	LGE	AB	H	DB	TP	HR	BB	SO	R	RBI	SB	CS	OUT	BA	OBP	SLG	EQA	EQR	DEFENSE
1999	Ottawa	Int	141	41	5	0	10	10	15	25	26	2	2	102	.291	.347	.539	.283	22	23-1B -1
1999	Montreal	NL	348	95	34	2	9	18	32	37	44	1	3	256	.273	.312	.460	.250	40	84-1B -9
2000	Toronto	AL	477	143	25	1	34	25	60	73	100	3	1	335	.300	.343	.570	.291	77	
2001	Toronto	AL	521	148	30	2	20	41	76	75	85	5	2	375	.284	.342	.464	.267	69	
2002	*Anaheim*	*AL*	*478*	*139*	*30*	*2*	*23*	*39*	*67*	*68*	*78*	*5*	*2*	*341*	*.291*	*.344*	*.506*	*.282*	*72*	

The Blue Jays' 3-4-5 hitters all endured down years compared to 2000, accounting for most of the offense's 96-run decrease. Martinez handed Fullmer the full-time DH job out of spring training, and, like Delgado, Fullmer couldn't solve lefties, hitting a wretched .202/.233/.286 against them. However, unlike Delgado, Fullmer never has hit them. The Blue Jays could add two wins for $200,000 if they tap the keg of free lefty mashers in the minors to platoon with Fullmer. He gives the Angels the same blend of strengths and weaknesses.

Alex Gonzalez SS Bats R Age 29

YEAR	TEAM	LGE	AB	H	DB	TP	HR	BB	SO	R	RBI	SB	CS	OUT	BA	OBP	SLG	EQA	EQR	DEFENSE			
1999	Toronto	AL	153	46	11	0	3	14	20	21	12	4	2	109	.301	.369	.431	.270	21	37-SS	12		
2000	Toronto	AL	523	134	31	2	16	37	99	66	66	4	4	393	.256	.310	.415	.240	55	138-SS	-8		
2001	Toronto	AL	635	168	24	5	19	46	129	82	78	16	12	479	.265	.319	.408	.242	69	151-SS	16		
2002	*ChiCubs*	*NL*	*568*	*149*	*28*	*3*	*19*	*56*	*120*	*77*	*58*	*14*	*9*	*428*	*.262*	*.329*	*.423*	*.252*	*68*				

Despite our using career curves to project offensive performance, nobody conforms precisely to the norm, and some players aren't even close. Gonzalez was in the big leagues to stay in 1995 at age 22 and survived, but he has flat-lined ever since then. Ricciardi's first move was to trade Gonzalez and the last three years on his contract to the Cubs. Rotoheads: playing in the NL Central should help Gonzalez post his best counting stats ever.

Gabe Gross OF Bats L Age 22

YEAR	TEAM	LGE	AB	H	DB	TP	HR	BB	SO	R	RBI	SB	CS	OUT	BA	OBP	SLG	EQA	EQR	DEFENSE			
2001	Dunedin	Fla	131	32	5	1	4	19	31	17	11	2	1	100	.244	.344	.389	.251	16	34-RF	-7		
2001	Tennesse	Sou	42	9	2	0	2	4	12	7	8	0	1	34	.214	.307	.405	.231	4				
2002	*Toronto*	*AL*	*220*	*56*	*8*	*1*	*8*	*31*	*57*	*28*	*27*	*2*	*3*	*167*	*.255*	*.347*	*.409*	*.255*	*27*				

This never would've happened in the latter days of the Belgian beer-makers' reign. Gross was signed for a sum equal to the combined contracts given to the last two first-rounders taken on Interbrew's watch. Fresh out of Auburn, he ravaged the Florida State League before getting a quick look-see at Double-A Tennessee. Gross combines great plate discipline with light-tower power, and he should be banging on the players' entrance at Skydome by next year.

Orlando Hudson 2B Bats B Age 24

YEAR	TEAM	LGE	AB	H	DB	TP	HR	BB	SO	R	RBI	SB	CS	OUT	BA	OBP	SLG	EQA	EQR	DEFENSE			
1999	Hagerstn	SAL	523	105	26	3	4	30	90	46	47	4	3	421	.201	.245	.285	.182	30	101-3B	11	20-LF	0
2000	Dunedin	Fla	362	83	12	1	6	27	47	40	34	5	3	282	.229	.285	.318	.207	27	77-3B	4	16-2B	-8
2000	Tennesse	Sou	137	29	4	2	2	11	18	15	12	2	1	109	.212	.275	.314	.203	10	39-3B	3		
2001	Tennesse	Sou	309	81	18	6	3	29	41	42	41	5	2	230	.262	.329	.388	.243	34	65-2B	8	11-3B	2
2001	Syracuse	Int	196	56	13	2	4	22	31	29	25	9	3	143	.286	.362	.434	.270	27	49-2B	7		
2002	*Toronto*	*AL*	*476*	*128*	*25*	*5*	*8*	*46*	*72*	*64*	*59*	*12*	*4*	*352*	*.269*	*.333*	*.393*	*.248*	*54*				

The Jays seemed to have exhausted much of their stockpile of middle infielders with the July 2000 trades of Mike Young and Brent Abernathy. Hudson's emergence brought quick reinforcements. Hudson made a seamless transition from third base to the keystone and exploded at the plate with improved patience and gap power. He has a decent chance to be the Jays' Opening Day starter, and should have the job by midseason at the latest.

Cesar Izturis 2B/SS Bats B Age 22

YEAR	TEAM	LGE	AB	H	DB	TP	HR	BB	SO	R	RBI	SB	CS	OUT	BA	OBP	SLG	EQA	EQR	DEFENSE			
1999	Dunedin	Fla	532	131	25	6	3	15	65	53	52	17	10	411	.246	.271	.333	.204	39	84-SS	-5	45-2B	3
2000	Syracuse	Int	436	90	12	4	1	15	43	47	24	17	10	355	.206	.234	.259	.173	22	128-SS	22		
2001	Syracuse	Int	342	94	16	2	2	11	20	30	32	19	8	256	.275	.299	.351	.223	30	57-SS	-1	24-2B	3
2001	Toronto	AL	134	38	7	2	2	2	13	20	9	7	1	97	.284	.294	.410	.239	14	31-2B	3		
2002	*LosAngls*	*NL*	*477*	*123*	*20*	*4*	*5*	*24*	*44*	*62*	*44*	*29*	*10*	*364*	*.258*	*.293*	*.348*	*.228*	*45*				

Historically, the Blue Jays haven't been shy about pushing their better middle-infield prospects up the ladder, so it wasn't a shock to see Izturis debut in The Show last June at age 21. Although his numbers with Toronto look OK, Izturis's bat is not major-league ready; he's a free swinger with a long stroke that puts the ball in the air and doesn't enable him to utilize his speed. Izturis is good to go defensively, but it's doubtful that he'll ever experience the Vizquelian transformation required to make him an adequate hitter. The Dodgers traded Luke Prokopec for Izturis, who will battle Alex Cora for the shortstop job in Chavez Ravine.

Reed Johnson OF Bats R Age 25

YEAR	TEAM	LGE	AB	H	DB	TP	HR	BB	SO	R	RBI	SB	CS	OUT	BA	OBP	SLG	EQA	EQR	DEFENSE
1999	St Cath	NYP	199	36	6	1	1	15	34	16	14	2	3	166	.181	.241	.236	.167	9	57-OF 2
2000	Hagerstn	SAL	337	75	17	2	6	43	52	45	45	6	2	264	.223	.321	.338	.230	33	95-RF 1
2000	Dunedin	Fla	134	35	7	1	3	10	30	19	19	2	1	100	.261	.338	.396	.249	15	36-CF 0
2001	Tennesse	Sou	556	151	24	3	10	34	77	82	59	26	9	414	.272	.324	.379	.241	59	131-LF -1
2002	*Toronto*	*AL*	*475*	*126*	*23*	*3*	*12*	*47*	*75*	*69*	*65*	*17*	*6*	*355*	*.265*	*.331*	*.402*	*.251*	*56*	

In a franchise castigated for its recent underachieving, Johnson is as out of place as Chris Kahrl at the World Hot Latin Rhythm Championship. A 17th-round pick drafted out of Cal State-Fullerton in 1999, Johnson was named the best hustler in the Southern League. Better yet, he can actually play, finishing as the league bridesmaid in batting average and stolen bases. Add fair power, a knack for getting on base, and outfield versatility, then shake and let ferment until 2003. You've just fashioned the perfect fourth outfielder.

Chris Latham OF Bats B Age 29

YEAR	TEAM	LGE	AB	H	DB	TP	HR	BB	SO	R	RBI	SB	CS	OUT	BA	OBP	SLG	EQA	EQR	DEFENSE
1999	SaltLake	PCL	370	99	18	5	11	45	87	68	36	13	9	280	.268	.348	.432	.260	48	94-CF 13
2000	ColSprin	PCL	333	68	11	4	6	57	101	55	35	20	6	270	.204	.323	.315	.231	35	102-CF -4
2001	Syracuse	Int	293	74	17	7	12	48	83	52	48	11	9	228	.253	.359	.481	.274	45	77-OF -1
2001	Toronto	AL	73	21	4	1	2	10	24	12	10	4	1	53	.288	.379	.452	.284	11	22-OF 2
2002	*Toronto*	*AL*	*379*	*95*	*18*	*7*	*14*	*63*	*114*	*74*	*47*	*16*	*10*	*294*	*.251*	*.357*	*.446*	*.270*	*56*	

The Jays promoted Latham at the All-Star break after Brian Simmons's performance made it clear that it was best not to remind fans he was all the team had to show for David Wells. Because all of the Jays' starting outfielders are durable and play every day, the club doesn't have to carry two extra fly chasers as long as the primary backup can handle all three outfield positions. Latham can, and he also supplies a nice mix of on-base skills and gap power off the bench. He enters camp as the favorite to win the fourth-outfielder job.

Joe Lawrence C Bats R Age 25

YEAR	TEAM	LGE	AB	H	DB	TP	HR	BB	SO	R	RBI	SB	CS	OUT	BA	OBP	SLG	EQA	EQR	DEFENSE
1999	Knoxvill	Sou	252	55	13	1	5	43	49	39	17	4	4	201	.218	.336	.337	.234	27	64-3B -4
2000	Dunedin	Fla	384	93	18	1	11	51	82	49	46	12	5	296	.242	.335	.380	.245	44	68-C -16
2000	Tennesse	Sou	138	33	8	0	0	24	27	19	8	4	1	106	.239	.358	.297	.239	15	29-C -3
2001	Syracuse	Int	321	67	11	3	1	34	57	26	24	5	7	261	.209	.292	.271	.197	22	75-C -8
2002	*Toronto*	*AL*	*442*	*108*	*23*	*2*	*8*	*60*	*89*	*62*	*37*	*11*	*7*	*341*	*.244*	*.335*	*.360*	*.239*	*48*	

Even on the heels of Lawrence's pathetic-looking 2001, "No Vacancy" signs behind home plate at Syracuse's P&C Stadium may force a job share with Fletcher at the major-league level. It's an arrangement with which Martinez should be comfortable, as he was the non-productive platoon mate of Ernie Whitt for six years. The deterioration of Lawrence's batting eye is distressing, but he's a better hitter than he showed last year, when he played with a left wrist condition that caused his hand to go numb. The injury could require surgery, in which case Lawrence might not be ready for spring training.

Felipe Lopez 3B/SS Bats B Age 22

YEAR	TEAM	LGE	AB	H	DB	TP	HR	BB	SO	R	RBI	SB	CS	OUT	BA	OBP	SLG	EQA	EQR	DEFENSE
1999	Hagerstn	SAL	552	116	21	2	8	43	166	59	51	10	8	444	.210	.269	.299	.196	38	127-SS -22
2000	Tennesse	Sou	471	108	15	3	8	20	109	45	34	8	7	370	.229	.261	.325	.197	32	122-SS -40
2001	Tennesse	Sou	73	13	2	0	2	7	23	10	3	3	3	63	.178	.250	.288	.184	5	
2001	Syracuse	Int	360	94	17	4	16	29	87	61	40	10	4	270	.261	.320	.464	.258	46	58-SS -5 18-2B 4
2001	Toronto	AL	177	48	4	4	6	12	34	22	24	3	3	132	.271	.317	.441	.248	20	42-3B 0
2002	*Toronto*	*AL*	*547*	*146*	*20*	*5*	*21*	*46*	*141*	*79*	*71*	*8*	*5*	*406*	*.267*	*.324*	*.437*	*.253*	*65*	

Talk about on-the-job training. Felipe Lopez was inserted at third base in the wake of the Tony Batista affair despite just two games' preparation at Syracuse. Not surprisingly, his defense was shaky. Lopez has a quick, short stroke and is rapidly developing power. The trades of Gonzalez and Izturis clear his path to the shortstop job.

Luis Lopez 1B/3B Bats R Age 28

YEAR	TEAM	LGE	AB	H	DB	TP	HR	BB	SO	R	RBI	SB	CS	OUT	BA	OBP	SLG	EQA	EQR	DEFENSE	
1999	Syracuse	Int	526	155	30	2	3	31	54	64	56	1	0	371	.295	.335	.376	.241	53	81-1B 4	26-3B 1
2000	Syracuse	Int	490	149	22	1	7	40	32	57	69	2	1	342	.304	.358	.396	.257	57	50-3B -2	31-1B -1
2001	Syracuse	Int	343	103	21	2	10	37	29	54	68	1	1	241	.300	.371	.461	.278	49	80-1B 3	
2001	Toronto	AL	119	31	2	0	4	8	14	11	11	0	0	88	.261	.307	.378	.230	11	26-3B -1	
2002	*Toronto*	*AL*	*481*	*143*	*24*	*2*	*12*	*50*	*43*	*67*	*70*	*1*	*1*	*339*	*.297*	*.363*	*.430*	*.269*	*64*		

Luis Lopez hits enough to help a team anywhere on the diamond other than first base and DH. Unfortunately, those are the only positions that he can handle defensively. Lopez is in line to join the late Hank Sauer as the only players in Syracuse history to have their numbers retired, but he lacks the long-ball stroke to mimic Sauer's late-career coming out party in the majors.

Raul Mondesi RF Bats R Age 31

YEAR	TEAM	LGE	AB	H	DB	TP	HR	BB	SO	R	RBI	SB	CS	OUT	BA	OBP	SLG	EQA	EQR	DEFENSE
1999	LosAngls	NL	608	157	30	5	34	64	124	97	97	31	9	460	.258	.332	.492	.272	89	154-RF -3
2000	Toronto	AL	384	105	22	1	25	28	64	75	63	22	7	286	.273	.328	.531	.279	59	94-RF -6
2001	Toronto	AL	572	150	25	4	30	75	111	91	87	27	12	434	.262	.352	.477	.275	86	143-RF -7
2002	*Toronto*	*AL*	*529*	*144*	*23*	*3*	*20*	*64*	*106*	*87*	*82*	*23*	*10*	*395*	*.272*	*.351*	*.491*	*.279*	*81*	

Mondesi established himself as a Martinez favorite with his hustle and aggressiveness. "The Buffalo" is actually no more than a league-average right fielder, despite the excitement he generates with his physical tools. Mondesi would be the best outfielder to make disappear to open a spot for Vernon Wells, although the contract the Jays inherited from the Dodgers will make doing so difficult. Mondesi is like the velvet nude hanging on the living room wall; ridding yourself of it requires admitting that nobody else thinks it's remotely worth what you paid for it.

Josh Phelps C/DH Bats R Age 24

YEAR	TEAM	LGE	AB	H	DB	TP	HR	BB	SO	R	RBI	SB	CS	OUT	BA	OBP	SLG	EQA	EQR	DEFENSE
1999	Dunedin	Fla	404	105	18	2	15	20	117	50	57	3	2	301	.260	.301	.426	.239	42	23-C -2
2000	Tennesse	Sou	188	40	8	1	7	10	65	20	22	1	0	148	.213	.266	.378	.215	16	38-C -10
2000	Dunedin	Fla	114	29	5	0	8	9	38	18	21	0	0	85	.254	.312	.509	.264	15	16-C 0
2001	Tennesse	Sou	494	123	22	1	25	63	124	77	75	2	2	373	.249	.345	.449	.264	67	68-C -10
2002	*Toronto*	*AL*	*474*	*121*	*19*	*1*	*25*	*54*	*138*	*69*	*74*	*2*	*2*	*355*	*.255*	*.331*	*.458*	*.262*	*62*	

By laying off pitches out of the strike zone, Phelps turned his power into a weapon last year, doubling his career walk rate and almost taking home the Southern League triple crown. Unfortunately, Phelps threw out just 18% of the runners who tried to steal on him, reinforcing anxieties about his defense behind the plate and drawing comparisons to the Pirates' Craig Wilson. Fortunately, the Blue Jays are in the right league if those concerns are valid. Phelps usually struggles when first exposed to a new level, so he'll be spending most of this season solving Triple-A pitching.

Alexis Rios OF Bats R Age 21

YEAR	TEAM	LGE	AB	H	DB	TP	HR	BB	SO	R	RBI	SB	CS	OUT	BA	OBP	SLG	EQA	EQR	DEFENSE
1999	Med Hat	Pio	231	40	5	1	0	8	37	16	6	2	2	193	.173	.202	.203	.143	7	67-CF -4
2000	Hagerstn	SAL	74	13	2	1	0	1	15	4	3	1	2	63	.176	.191	.230	.141	2	
2000	Queens	NYP	210	42	6	1	1	5	26	14	15	2	3	171	.200	.224	.252	.162	9	39-RF -5
2001	Charl-WV	SAL	494	105	18	5	1	19	63	30	41	10	8	397	.213	.244	.275	.179	27	123-RF -12
2002	*Toronto*	*AL*	*440*	*105*	*16*	*4*	*3*	*24*	*62*	*42*	*26*	*11*	*9*	*343*	*.239*	*.278*	*.314*	*.195*	*29*	

Interbrew wanted to pay below market value for its top draft picks the final two years it owned the team, ostensibly so that more money would be available to pay other upper-round selections. In reality, the goal was to improve the bottom line to make the club more attractive to prospective buyers. As a result, Alexis Rios and Miguel Negron were drafted in 1999 and 2000 and were the only first-rounders in either draft to sign for less than seven figures. Rios is the better of the two, which is akin to saying that the gas chamber is preferable to the gallows.

Deion Sanders OF Bats L Age 34

YEAR	TEAM	LGE	AB	H	DB	TP	HR	BB	SO	R	RBI	SB	CS	OUT	BA	OBP	SLG	EQA	EQR	DEFENSE	
2000	Louisvil	Int	106	20	1	0	3	12	9	11	6	8	4	90	.189	.271	.283	.199	8	25-LF	0
2001	Louisvil	Int	75	32	5	4	1	2	4	11	8	4	2	46	.427	.456	.640	.346	16	18-LF	-1
2001	Cincnnti	NL	75	14	2	0	1	4	8	6	4	3	4	65	.187	.242	.253	.170	4	16-LF	2
2001	Syracuse	Int	107	25	6	1	1	7	11	14	6	4	3	85	.234	.285	.336	.210	9	11-LF	-1
2002	*Toronto*	*AL*	*231*	*56*	*10*	*3*	*4*	*20*	*21*	*26*	*19*	*6*	*4*	*179*	*.242*	*.303*	*.364*	*.224*	*21*		

In what would have been a nifty little job of cross-marketing, Syracuse could have lured fans from all four major sports had they added hockey goon Tie Domi to the roster to go with non-contact footballer Sanders and failed hoopster Mark Hendrickson. Deion groupie Dave Stewart signed Pine Time to a contract that enabled him to continue using his "baseball career" as negotiating leverage to extract millions from the Washington Redskins. Baseball has served Sanders well, but don't look for any more comebacks until the time comes to rework his deal with CBS.

Shannon Stewart LF Bats R Age 28

YEAR	TEAM	LGE	AB	H	DB	TP	HR	BB	SO	R	RBI	SB	CS	OUT	BA	OBP	SLG	EQA	EQR	DEFENSE	
1999	Toronto	AL	602	187	29	2	11	53	73	98	64	35	14	429	.311	.373	.420	.271	82	136-LF	-9
2000	Toronto	AL	589	191	43	5	23	31	69	105	68	20	6	404	.324	.364	.531	.293	94	136-LF	7
2001	Toronto	AL	637	209	46	7	13	49	62	106	61	24	11	439	.328	.383	.484	.289	98	142-LF	-2
2002	*Toronto*	*AL*	*575*	*184*	*40*	*5*	*16*	*52*	*64*	*103*	*67*	*24*	*10*	*401*	*.320*	*.376*	*.490*	*.290*	*91*		

Despite a solid season, Stewart's reluctance to hit third in the batting order didn't sit well with Martinez, so he is now the odds-on favorite to leave town to make room for Vernon Wells. Stewart's career line is very similar to Bernie Williams's, who didn't blossom into an offensive force until he turned 28. Instead of missing out on a potential explosion, the Jays should consider shifting Stewart to designated hitter, a move that would both free up space in the outfield and eliminate the constant criticism of Stewart's weak throwing arm.

Richard Thompson OF Bats L Age 23

YEAR	TEAM	LGE	AB	H	DB	TP	HR	BB	SO	R	RBI	SB	CS	OUT	BA	OBP	SLG	EQA	EQR	DEFENSE	
2000	Queens	NYP	265	54	9	2	1	28	66	25	17	11	5	216	.204	.286	.264	.198	19	67-CF	-8
2001	Dunedin	Fla	462	121	12	4	1	30	77	64	44	21	8	349	.262	.313	.312	.220	39	108-OF	3
2001	Syracuse	Int	53	12	0	1	0	4	11	5	3	4	1	42	.226	.281	.264	.201	4	17-LF	4
2002	*Toronto*	*AL*	*465*	*123*	*17*	*3*	*3*	*45*	*91*	*53*	*39*	*19*	*7*	*349*	*.265*	*.329*	*.333*	*.232*	*45*		

Ball clubs remain very much infatuated with batting average and speed, virtues that enabled Thompson to be named team MVP at Dunedin. A contact hitter with little power, Thompson managed just 21 extra-base hits, most of them leg doubles, in more than 450 at-bats. He has the potential to be a terrific fly chaser in center field, but he needs to work on getting a better jump on the ball. Put Jason Tyner on the rack, and the result is Rich Thompson.

Vernon Wells CF Bats R Age 23

YEAR	TEAM	LGE	AB	H	DB	TP	HR	BB	SO	R	RBI	SB	CS	OUT	BA	OBP	SLG	EQA	EQR	DEFENSE	
1999	Dunedin	Fla	265	72	11	1	8	19	38	29	28	7	2	195	.272	.322	.411	.247	30	69-CF	-4
1999	Knoxvill	Sou	105	29	5	1	2	9	15	13	11	4	1	77	.276	.333	.400	.251	12	26-CF	1
1999	Syracuse	Int	128	36	8	1	3	8	21	17	17	4	1	93	.281	.327	.430	.254	15	33-CF	-1
1999	Toronto	AL	88	24	2	0	2	3	16	7	8	1	1	65	.273	.297	.364	.220	7	21-CF	1
2000	Syracuse	Int	495	114	28	5	15	39	86	67	57	18	4	385	.230	.291	.398	.233	51	119-CF	3
2001	Syracuse	Int	415	108	22	3	12	29	63	53	48	12	10	317	.260	.313	.414	.239	44	97-CF	-5
2001	Toronto	AL	96	31	6	0	2	5	13	14	6	5	0	65	.323	.361	.448	.279	13	26-CF	0
2002	*Toronto*	*AL*	*523*	*145*	*29*	*4*	*16*	*41*	*86*	*71*	*62*	*16*	*7*	*385*	*.277*	*.330*	*.440*	*.258*	*65*		

The Blue Jays intend to shake things up this season, which means that Wells will open the season as the starting center fielder. Wells has made very little progress since his breakout 1999 campaign, still hacking at pitches early in the count and trying to pull everything. He says he'll be an improved hitter in the majors, a feat that will entail making major adjustments at the plate. If it's going to be such a snap, why didn't he do it in his two-year stint at Syracuse?

Jayson Werth C/1B Bats R Age 23

YEAR	TEAM	LGE	AB	H	DB	TP	HR	BB	SO	R	RBI	SB	CS	OUT	BA	OBP	SLG	EQA	EQR	DEFENSE
1999	Frederck	Car	244	62	9	1	2	27	37	31	22	9	2	184	.254	.332	.324	.233	24	61-C -8
1999	Bowie	Eas	123	30	4	1	1	13	26	14	9	4	1	94	.244	.322	.317	.226	11	29-C -2
2000	Bowie	Eas	283	58	13	1	5	43	52	38	21	6	2	227	.205	.315	.311	.222	26	76-C -12
2000	Frederck	Car	86	20	2	0	2	7	15	13	14	3	1	67	.233	.290	.326	.214	7	16-C -2
2001	Dunedin	Fla	73	12	0	0	2	13	20	7	10	1	1	62	.164	.291	.247	.195	5	
2001	Tennesse	Sou	375	91	16	1	14	50	91	42	53	8	2	286	.243	.334	.403	.251	45	46-C 0 25-1B -1
2002	*Toronto*	*AL*	*424*	*111*	*18*	*1*	*14*	*63*	*99*	*64*	*54*	*10*	*3*	*316*	*.262*	*.357*	*.408*	*.264*	*57*	

Orioles' super-genius Syd Thrift gave away former first-rounder Werth after he seemed to stall in Double-A. Throughout his struggles, Werth retained excellent control of the strike zone, and everything jelled the second half of last season. Despite the catching logjam at the upper levels, the immediate plan is to keep Lawrence, Phelps, and Werth sporting the tools of ignorance and see what shakes out, though Werth's athleticism and rough defense may ultimately lead to a position switch.

Chris Woodward UT Bats R Age 26

YEAR	TEAM	LGE	AB	H	DB	TP	HR	BB	SO	R	RBI	SB	CS	OUT	BA	OBP	SLG	EQA	EQR	DEFENSE
1999	Syracuse	Int	280	75	17	2	1	31	46	38	16	3	1	206	.268	.342	.354	.241	29	56-SS 4 16-2B -1
2000	Syracuse	Int	143	43	11	1	5	8	29	20	21	2	0	100	.301	.338	.497	.275	20	20-2B 1 10-3B 1
2000	Toronto	AL	104	20	5	0	4	8	25	15	15	1	0	84	.192	.250	.356	.204	8	18-SS -1
2001	Toronto	AL	63	13	3	2	2	0	12	9	5	0	1	51	.206	.206	.413	.194	4	12-2B 2
2001	Syracuse	Int	194	55	12	1	11	16	37	27	28	0	0	139	.284	.340	.526	.280	29	21-3B 2 11-SS 0
2002	*Toronto*	*AL*	*292*	*79*	*17*	*2*	*11*	*25*	*59*	*43*	*31*	*2*	*1*	*214*	*.271*	*.328*	*.455*	*.260*	*37*	

Martinez used his bench sparingly last year, mainly because it offered very little in terms of flexibility. That situation will improve with the exit of Frye and Fernandez, as Woodward and Ryan Freel are legitimate utility players. With both out of options and room for only one on the roster, Freel was outrighted to Syracuse last fall (and is now in the Devil Rays' system). It was the right choice; Woodward is a natural infielder and has some juice in his bat.

PITCHERS (ERA: 4.50, H/9: 9.0, HR/9: 1.0, BB/9: 3.0, K/9: 6.0, KW: 2.0, PERA: 4.50)

Chris Baker Throws R Age 24

YEAR	TEAM	LGE	IP	H	ER	HR	BB	K	ERA	W	L	H/9	HR/9	BB/9	K/9	KW	PERA	STUFF
1999	Med Hat	Pio	9.0	8	3	0	2	5	3.00	1	0	8.0	0.0	2.0	5.0	1.3	4.53	6
1999	St Cath	NYP	50.3	64	49	16	19	26	8.76	1	5	11.4	2.9	3.4	4.6	0.7	10.03	-19
2000	Dunedin	Fla	97.3	117	82	26	36	53	7.58	3	8	10.8	2.4	3.3	4.9	0.7	5.48	-18
2001	Tennesse	Sou	165.0	195	116	34	48	74	6.33	6	12	10.6	1.9	2.6	4.0	0.8	4.54	-5

Baker is one of a number of draft afterthoughts who have pitched their way to the top of the Blue Jays' chain. Toronto's 29th-round pick in 1999 had no problem adjusting to Double-A competition, his strikeout-to-walk ratio holding steady at three to one. Baker pounds the strike zone and sometimes catches too much of the plate—he gave up the most round-trippers in his league. He could pull on a big-league jersey later this summer if International League sluggers don't further expose his weakness.

Pete Bauer Throws R Age 23

YEAR	TEAM	LGE	IP	H	ER	HR	BB	K	ERA	W	L	H/9	HR/9	BB/9	K/9	KW	PERA	STUFF
2000	Hagerstn	SAL	33.0	38	21	5	10	11	5.73	2	2	10.4	1.4	2.7	3.0	0.6	10.02	-20
2001	Charl-WV	SAL	36.7	33	13	0	15	23	3.19	3	1	8.1	0.0	3.7	5.6	0.8	5.71	13
2001	Tennesse	Sou	127.3	146	79	18	40	45	5.58	6	8	10.3	1.3	2.8	3.2	0.6	6.97	-8

On the other hand, Toronto's player-development staff hasn't fared well with its recent taste in early-round moundsmen. Bauer was taken in the second round of the 2000 draft as compensation for Graeme Lloyd's leaving. Bauer's stuff isn't as overpowering as his massive 6′7″, 250-pound frame would suggest, and he was hit hard after the organization challenged him with an in-season, two-level jump to Tennessee. The Blue Jays desperately need some of their higher-ceiling arms to step up, because their pitching reserves are low.

Pedro Borbon **Throws L** **Age 34**

YEAR	TEAM	LGE	IP	H	ER	HR	BB	K	ERA	W	L	H/9	HR/9	BB/9	K/9	KW	PERA	STUFF
1999	LosAngls	NL	48.0	48	27	5	24	30	5.06	2	3	9.0	0.9	4.5	5.6	0.6	3.99	-12
2000	Toronto	AL	43.3	43	28	4	31	29	5.82	2	3	8.9	0.8	6.4	6.0	0.5	6.50	-19
2001	Toronto	AL	53.0	51	24	7	11	43	4.08	3	3	8.7	1.2	1.9	7.3	2.0	3.59	6

Coming off an ugly 2000 season, Borbon took a unique route in his return to respectability: he slashed his walk rate by more than six per game, the greatest single-year decrease in baseball history. Borbon's wonky elbow is never going to be completely healthy, and it's impossible for him to duplicate last year's improvement, so this is about as good as it gets.

Brian Bowles **Throws R** **Age 25**

YEAR	TEAM	LGE	IP	H	ER	HR	BB	K	ERA	W	L	H/9	HR/9	BB/9	K/9	KW	PERA	STUFF
1999	Hagerstn	SAL	79.0	83	54	8	55	39	6.15	3	6	9.5	0.9	6.3	4.4	0.4	6.33	-25
2000	Tennesse	Sou	79.7	75	35	2	38	46	3.95	5	4	8.5	0.2	4.3	5.2	0.6	4.25	-7
2001	Syracuse	Int	74.7	67	39	4	52	60	4.70	4	4	8.1	0.5	6.3	7.2	0.6	3.90	-5

Fiftieth-round draft choices who work as minor-league middle men for seven years don't often earn an entry in *Total Baseball* (or in *Baseball Prospectus,* for that matter). Bowles has become an effective hurler by pruning his pitch selection way back, basically throwing only a plus fastball and a splitter. For success at the big-league level, the combination must be thrown with Sasaki-like precision. Bowles's walk rate has never been below four a game, so the command is still lacking.

Chris Carpenter **Throws R** **Age 27**

YEAR	TEAM	LGE	IP	H	ER	HR	BB	K	ERA	W	L	H/9	HR/9	BB/9	K/9	KW	PERA	STUFF
1999	Toronto	AL	160.3	157	69	14	40	105	3.87	10	8	8.8	0.8	2.2	5.9	1.3	4.08	15
2000	Toronto	AL	183.3	192	106	25	68	112	5.20	9	11	9.4	1.2	3.3	5.5	0.8	5.43	0
2001	Toronto	AL	222.0	223	112	26	71	149	4.54	12	13	9.0	1.1	2.9	6.0	1.0	4.14	10

There were many positives about Carpenter's season last year, but the biggest was that he threw pain-free and didn't miss a turn. Carpenter went Ankiel for half a dozen starts in late July and early August, allowing 36 runs in 30 innings while losing control of all his pitches. He then pulled it together and finished strong. Carpenter has #1 starter stuff and is a good candidate to chop another half a run off his ERA as long as his head doesn't interfere.

Scott Cassidy **Throws R** **Age 26**

YEAR	TEAM	LGE	IP	H	ER	HR	BB	K	ERA	W	L	H/9	HR/9	BB/9	K/9	KW	PERA	STUFF
1999	Hagerstn	SAL	165.3	187	105	29	46	81	5.72	7	11	10.2	1.6	2.5	4.4	0.9	6.06	-6
2000	Dunedin	Fla	79.7	84	55	11	49	48	6.21	3	6	9.5	1.2	5.5	5.4	0.5	2.29	-9
2000	Tennesse	Sou	42.0	53	41	14	17	23	8.79	1	4	11.4	3.0	3.6	4.9	0.7	8.54	-27
2001	Tennesse	Sou	87.7	101	64	17	35	44	6.57	3	7	10.4	1.7	3.6	4.5	0.6	5.84	-17
2001	Syracuse	Int	61.7	67	41	9	33	33	5.98	3	4	9.8	1.3	4.8	4.8	0.5	4.15	-12

A non-drafted free agent, Cassidy has steadily progressed through the system by spotting a marginal fastball and mixing it with workable off-speed stuff. Though the final results continue to look promising, Cassidy's strikeout and walk ratios have deteriorated as he's advanced. An optimistic projection places him as a useful long reliever/spot starter; given the initial cash outlay, even that return on investment would make a pyramid schemer envious.

Gustavo Chacin **Throws L** **Age 21**

YEAR	TEAM	LGE	IP	H	ER	HR	BB	K	ERA	W	L	H/9	HR/9	BB/9	K/9	KW	PERA	STUFF
1999	Med Hat	Pio	63.7	76	51	13	29	25	7.21	2	5	10.7	1.8	4.1	3.5	0.4	5.08	-9
2000	Dunedin	Fla	125.0	156	121	32	76	50	8.71	3	11	11.2	2.3	5.5	3.6	0.3	5.92	-14
2001	Tennesse	Sou	132.0	156	93	25	43	54	6.34	5	10	10.6	1.7	2.9	3.7	0.6	5.02	-1

Venezuelan Gustavo Chacin is a short left-hander whom the Jays have pushed aggressively due to his solid winter-ball performances against good competition. Chacin has an average fastball, a big yellow hammer, and a deceptive delivery that makes both offerings appear better than they actually are. Left-handed batters hit him for a .184/.236/.350 line, as compared to .274/.324/.431 for righties, so there's little doubt where Chacin's future lies.

Pasqual Coco — Throws R — Age 24

YEAR	TEAM	LGE	IP	H	ER	HR	BB	K	ERA	W	L	H/9	HR/9	BB/9	K/9	KW	PERA	STUFF
1999	Hagerstn	SAL	91.3	96	48	8	34	43	4.73	5	5	9.5	0.8	3.4	4.2	0.6	3.49	5
1999	Dunedin	Fla	75.3	86	60	15	43	40	7.17	2	6	10.3	1.8	5.1	4.8	0.5	7.13	-6
2000	Tennesse	Sou	163.0	178	108	28	69	95	5.96	7	11	9.8	1.5	3.8	5.2	0.7	5.33	2
2001	Syracuse	Int	122.7	130	73	14	56	63	5.36	6	8	9.5	1.0	4.1	4.6	0.6	5.31	-2
2001	Toronto	AL	14.3	13	5	0	6	9	3.14	1	1	8.2	0.0	3.8	5.7	0.8	4.46	3

Coco is a fastball/change-up pitcher who last year learned that he needs a quality third pitch to succeed as a starter at the game's higher levels. He will likely begin the season a SkyChief, but as the mound prospect closest to graduation, he'll see considerable time at Skydome this year because a team's rotation almost never stays intact for an entire season. If the Blue Jays are anticipating immediate success, they'll be disappointed.

Matt DeWitt — Throws R — Age 24

YEAR	TEAM	LGE	IP	H	ER	HR	BB	K	ERA	W	L	H/9	HR/9	BB/9	K/9	KW	PERA	STUFF
1999	Arkansas	Tex	146.7	169	111	30	65	77	6.81	5	11	10.4	1.8	4.0	4.7	0.6	5.92	-1
2000	Syracuse	Int	68.3	72	37	7	24	35	4.87	4	4	9.5	0.9	3.2	4.6	0.7	5.80	-7
2000	Toronto	AL	14.7	18	13	3	7	6	7.98	0	2	11.0	1.8	4.3	3.7	0.4	6.95	-26
2001	Syracuse	Int	55.3	55	27	5	10	34	4.39	3	3	9.0	0.8	[illegible]	5.5	0.9	3.31	-3
2001	Toronto	AL	20.0	20	11	2	10	12	4.95	1	1	9.0	0.9	4.5	5.4	0.6	3.36	-7

White Sox GM Kenny Williams said returning DeWitt to Toronto was the "honorable thing to do" when the lesser Mike (Williams) in the Wells trade was also diagnosed with a bum shoulder. DeWitt proceeded to lead the International League in saves, which sounds fancy until you check the list and find that recent leaders include Dave Pavlas, Eddie Gaillard, and Bob Scanlan. Apparently the Blue Jays saw the list, too, outrighting DeWitt to Syracuse after the season.

John Dillinger — Throws R — Age 28

YEAR	TEAM	LGE	IP	H	ER	HR	BB	K	ERA	W	L	H/9	HR/9	BB/9	K/9	KW	PERA	STUFF
2001	Syracuse	Int	154.0	162	88	14	74	74	5.14	7	10	9.5	0.8	4.3	4.3	0.5	5.52	-10

John Dillinger was a prospect in the Pirates' chain the last time a divisional pennant was hoisted in the Steel City. Ten years later, armed with a new elbow ligament and tales from the independent leagues, he is throwing harder with better bite and command of his off-speed pitches than ever before. Assuming Chris Michalak's return to pumpkindom hasn't soured the Blue Jays on high-mileage rookies, Dillinger could be the next Mike Fyhrie.

Kelvim Escobar — Throws R — Age 26

YEAR	TEAM	LGE	IP	H	ER	HR	BB	K	ERA	W	L	H/9	HR/9	BB/9	K/9	KW	PERA	STUFF
1999	Toronto	AL	186.0	180	88	16	68	128	4.26	11	10	8.7	0.8	3.3	6.2	0.9	5.12	12
2000	Toronto	AL	185.7	181	94	22	69	141	4.56	10	11	8.8	1.1	3.3	6.8	1.0	4.80	9
2001	Toronto	AL	123.7	105	48	7	49	115	3.49	9	5	7.6	0.5	3.6	8.4	1.2	3.23	16

Frustrated as a setup man, Escobar was dropped into the rotation when Steve Parris's shoulder gave out. He proceeded to go on a roll reminiscent of his 1998 stretch run. Escobar is still too wild for sustained effectiveness, but an even bigger concern is the repeated forearm numbness he suffered late in the year. No substantive diagnosis has been made, but since the ailment doesn't flare up when he works in short stints, a return to the bullpen may be in the cards.

Scott Eyre — Throws L — Age 30

YEAR	TEAM	LGE	IP	H	ER	HR	BB	K	ERA	W	L	H/9	HR/9	BB/9	K/9	KW	PERA	STUFF
1999	Charlott	Int	72.3	69	30	4	25	45	3.73	5	3	8.6	0.5	3.1	5.6	0.9	4.31	5
1999	ChiSox	AL	28.0	31	20	5	13	17	6.43	1	2	10.0	1.6	4.2	5.5	0.7	6.70	-19
2000	Charlott	Int	46.3	41	19	1	22	34	3.69	3	2	8.0	0.2	4.3	6.6	0.8	3.80	-6
2000	ChiSox	AL	22.0	22	12	3	10	16	4.91	1	1	9.0	1.2	4.1	6.5	0.8	5.85	-7
2001	Syracuse	Int	78.0	75	43	11	33	65	4.96	4	5	8.7	1.3	3.8	7.5	1.0	4.12	-7
2001	Toronto	AL	16.3	14	6	1	7	15	3.31	1	1	7.7	0.6	3.9	8.3	1.1	3.05	11

(Scott Eyre *continued*)

Not even Buck Martinez needs four left-handers in the bullpen, so Eyre spent last summer sampling Finger Lakes wines and blowing away Triple-A hitters. This year, following Lance Painter's release, Eyre will relocate to the north shore of Lake Ontario. However, his outlook remains the same—a slinger with good stuff and a wild streak that makes rent-to-own furniture a good idea.

Bob File **Throws R** **Age 25**

YEAR	TEAM	LGE	IP	H	ER	HR	BB	K	ERA	W	L	H/9	HR/9	BB/9	K/9	KW	PERA	STUFF
1999	Dunedin	Fla	48.0	47	23	4	18	31	4.31	3	2	8.8	0.8	3.4	5.8	0.9	2.73	-2
2000	Tennesse	Sou	34.7	32	14	2	14	26	3.63	2	2	8.3	0.5	3.6	6.7	0.9	6.46	-1
2000	Syracuse	Int	18.0	19	7	1	2	8	3.50	1	1	9.5	0.5	1.0	4.0	2.0	0.93	-1
2001	Toronto	AL	70.3	72	35	5	28	36	4.48	4	4	9.2	0.6	3.6	4.6	0.6	3.00	-9

We're going to go out on a limb and flatly state that File is the best big leaguer ever to emerge from the Philadelphia College of Textiles. He was a power-hitting third baseman in college. The Jays were smitten with his arm and drafted him in the 19th round in 1998. Last year, File was worked longer and harder than he'd ever been before, and it showed, his ERA soaring from 1.74 before the break to 5.18 afterwards. He has yet to master a second pitch to complement his power sinker. File may grab some save opportunities now that Billy Koch has been sent to Oakland.

Roy Halladay **Throws R** **Age 25**

YEAR	TEAM	LGE	IP	H	ER	HR	BB	K	ERA	W	L	H/9	HR/9	BB/9	K/9	KW	PERA	STUFF
1999	Toronto	AL	151.3	159	86	16	66	81	5.11	7	10	9.5	1.0	3.9	4.8	0.6	3.85	0
2000	Syracuse	Int	75.3	86	46	12	20	32	5.50	3	5	10.3	1.4	2.4	3.8	0.8	5.58	-3
2000	Toronto	AL	77.7	84	50	12	34	44	5.79	3	6	9.7	1.4	3.9	5.1	0.6	9.42	-11
2001	Dunedin	Fla	23.7	27	13	3	4	8	4.94	1	2	10.3	1.1	1.5	3.0	1.0	7.38	-29
2001	Tennesse	Sou	31.0	33	15	3	7	16	4.35	2	1	9.6	0.9	2.0	4.6	1.1	3.19	4
2001	Syracuse	Int	13.3	14	7	3	0	10	4.72	0	1	9.5	2.0	0.0	6.8	-1.0	3.58	19
2001	Toronto	AL	109.0	92	32	3	24	91	2.64	9	3	7.6	0.2	2.0	7.5	1.9	3.10	31

It was a bold move and a rousing success. After Halladay came off one of the worst seasons ever by a starting pitcher, the Blue Jays sent him all the way back to A ball, overhauled his mechanics, and assigned two sports psychologists to rebuild his confidence. Three months later he was back in the majors and pitching like a top prospect, exactly what he was three years ago. Best of all, he is striking out more batters and walking fewer than ever before. Still just 25 years old, Halladay is suddenly back on track to becoming one of the better pitchers in the game.

Jarrod Kingrey **Throws R** **Age 25**

YEAR	TEAM	LGE	IP	H	ER	HR	BB	K	ERA	W	L	H/9	HR/9	BB/9	K/9	KW	PERA	STUFF
1999	Hagerstn	SAL	58.3	64	45	10	37	34	6.94	2	4	9.9	1.5	5.7	5.2	0.5	4.81	-22
2000	Dunedin	Fla	37.7	41	30	5	31	20	7.17	1	3	9.8	1.2	7.4	4.8	0.3	6.29	-38
2000	Tennesse	Sou	16.0	15	10	0	16	10	5.63	1	1	8.4	0.0	9.0	5.6	0.3	3.96	-20
2001	Tennesse	Sou	49.3	55	44	10	39	29	8.03	1	4	10.0	1.8	7.1	5.3	0.4	3.75	-37

Kingrey has been making late-game entrances since signing out of the University of Alabama, amassing 84 saves over the past three seasons at various outposts south of the Mason-Dixon Line. He doesn't flash heat like a prototypical closer, instead getting it done with a wicked change-up and a large set of cojones. It's a stretch to imagine Kingrey closing in the big leagues; if he tightens his control, he should eventually find a niche in middle relief.

Billy Koch **Throws R** **Age 27**

YEAR	TEAM	LGE	IP	H	ER	HR	BB	K	ERA	W	L	H/9	HR/9	BB/9	K/9	KW	PERA	STUFF
1999	Syracuse	Int	26.3	27	14	3	10	17	4.78	1	2	9.2	1.0	3.4	5.8	0.9	3.67	5
1999	Toronto	AL	64.3	56	26	4	25	56	3.64	4	3	7.8	0.6	3.5	7.8	1.1	3.08	11
2000	Toronto	AL	81.3	75	29	5	15	59	3.21	6	3	8.3	0.6	1.7	6.5	2.0	2.61	9
2001	Toronto	AL	71.0	68	35	6	31	52	4.44	4	4	8.6	0.8	3.9	6.6	0.8	4.49	-2

Nobody in the history of the game reached 100 saves faster than Koch did. That fact and two bucks will get him a latte in T.O., now that the Jays have sent him to the A's. Despite three-digit heat, Koch goofs around with five different pitches. Unless he's as stubborn as his billy-goat beard implies, he'll pare back the menu options and rise to the ranks of the elite.

Esteban Loaiza — Throws R — Age 30

YEAR	TEAM	LGE	IP	H	ER	HR	BB	K	ERA	W	L	H/9	HR/9	BB/9	K/9	KW	PERA	STUFF
1999	Texas	AL	125.0	122	52	9	33	76	3.74	8	6	8.8	0.6	2.4	5.5	1.2	4.00	6
2000	Texas	AL	114.3	120	61	18	25	74	4.80	6	7	9.4	1.4	2.0	5.8	1.5	4.51	7
2000	Toronto	AL	95.0	92	38	7	21	61	3.60	7	4	8.7	0.7	2.0	5.8	1.5	3.58	15
2001	Toronto	AL	202.3	216	99	24	38	105	4.40	11	11	9.6	1.1	1.7	4.7	1.4	4.74	3

For seven seasons, Loaiza has teased clubs with his talent and frustrated them with his complacency. If great stuff were the only requirement for success, Mike Moore would be in the Hall of Fame. Loaiza may yet replicate Moore's fleeting late-1980s success, but the Blue Jays don't care to wait him out. Loaiza's $6-million salary this season almost guarantees they'll have to try.

Brandon Lyon — Throws R — Age 22

YEAR	TEAM	LGE	IP	H	ER	HR	BB	K	ERA	W	L	H/9	HR/9	BB/9	K/9	KW	PERA	STUFF
2000	Queens	NYP	57.0	59	23	4	7	27	3.63	4	2	9.3	0.6	1.1	4.3	1.9	4.36	6
2001	Tennesse	Sou	56.0	63	34	10	10	28	5.46	2	4	10.1	1.6	1.6	4.5	1.4	4.55	7
2001	Syracuse	Int	68.0	71	33	9	11	41	4.37	4	4	9.4	1.2	1.5	5.4	1.9	4.66	17
2001	Toronto	AL	63.3	65	28	5	14	33	3.98	4	3	9.2	0.7	2.0	4.7	1.2	3.92	11

No pitcher in team history ever reached the majors faster than Brandon Lyon. A 14th-round pick in 2000, Lyon was in Toronto 13 months after his professional debut, bettering Dave Stieb's mark by a month. Although Lyon's stuff will never be confused with Stieb's overpowering collection, he throws four pitches for strikes and has tremendous poise. After walking just 25 batters in 187 minor-league innings, Lyon sustained his control in Toronto, issuing but 15 free passes in 63 innings. He is penciled in as the fourth starter; note that more than half of his MLB innings last year came against league bantamweights Baltimore and Detroit.

Steve Parris — Throws R — Age 34

YEAR	TEAM	LGE	IP	H	ER	HR	BB	K	ERA	W	L	H/9	HR/9	BB/9	K/9	KW	PERA	STUFF
1999	Indianap	Int	36.7	39	21	6	10	22	5.15	2	2	9.6	1.5	2.5	5.4	1.1	4.26	0
1999	Cincnnti	NL	128.3	132	67	15	44	77	4.70	7	7	9.3	1.1	3.1	5.4	0.9	3.66	6
2000	Cincnnti	NL	200.7	216	111	26	58	104	4.90	10	12	9.7	1.2	2.6	4.7	0.9	4.52	1
2001	Toronto	AL	109.0	123	69	16	39	47	5.70	5	7	10.2	1.3	3.2	3.9	0.6	4.53	-7

The Jays were faced with the exodus of 60% of the starting rotation after the 2000 season, as Frank Castillo and Steve Trachsel were free agents, while an angry mob of thin-skinned fans chased Jumbo Wells over the Peace Bridge. In response, Ash traded for and overpaid Parris to be the Blue Jays' version of the Dutch Boy for two years. No more than a journeyman starter, Parris killed the club all season before labrum and rotator-cuff damage finished him in July. It's unlikely that he'll pitch at all in 2002.

Dan Plesac — Throws L — Age 40

YEAR	TEAM	LGE	IP	H	ER	HR	BB	K	ERA	W	L	H/9	HR/9	BB/9	K/9	KW	PERA	STUFF
1999	Toronto	AL	25.0	22	11	3	8	26	3.96	2	1	7.9	1.1	2.9	9.4	1.6	6.99	11
1999	Arizona	NL	23.0	20	9	3	7	24	3.52	2	1	7.8	1.2	2.7	9.4	1.7	3.35	16
2000	Arizona	NL	40.7	35	19	4	21	40	4.20	3	2	7.7	0.9	4.6	8.9	1.0	4.23	7
2001	Toronto	AL	46.7	32	16	4	23	65	3.09	3	2	6.2	0.8	4.4	12.5	1.4	3.17	33

Though Plesac pitched well in a limited role and met the clauses guaranteeing his contract for 2002, all indications are that the best active threat to Jesse Orosco's appearance record is hanging 'em up. In his career, Plesac made the adjustments from starting rotation to the bullpen, from closer to situational left-hander, and from flamethrower to finesse pitcher, so there's no doubt he could've effectively wangled his way through another season or seven. He's young enough that he could always come back in a couple of years should he need pocket money.

Paul Quantrill — Throws R — Age 33

YEAR	TEAM	LGE	IP	H	ER	HR	BB	K	ERA	W	L	H/9	HR/9	BB/9	K/9	KW	PERA	STUFF
1999	Toronto	AL	50.3	51	23	4	14	28	4.11	3	3	9.1	0.7	2.5	5.0	1.0	2.95	-4
2000	Toronto	AL	89.3	90	38	6	20	47	3.83	6	4	9.1	0.6	2.0	4.7	1.2	3.94	-5
2001	Toronto	AL	86.0	83	30	5	11	55	3.14	7	3	8.7	0.5	1.2	5.8	2.5	2.79	5

(Paul Quantrill *continued*)

Quantrill was the Jays' lone All-Star, and he led the AL in appearances thanks to Martinez's revolving-door bullpen. Quantrill's stuff is eminently hittable; he compensates by not walking batters and keeping the ball down and in the yard. He signed a three-year contract extension in August, and while his "put it in play" style of pitching is subject to considerable year-to-year fluctuation, there's no reason to expect a collapse any time soon. Traded to the Dodgers, his numbers will improve even if he doesn't actually pitch better.

Mike Sirotka **Throws L** **Age 31**

YEAR	TEAM	LGE	IP	H	ER	HR	BB	K	ERA	W	L	H/9	HR/9	BB/9	K/9	KW	PERA	STUFF
1999	ChiSox	AL	218.0	223	99	21	48	124	4.09	13	11	9.2	0.9	2.0	5.1	1.3	3.93	9
2000	ChiSox	AL	201.7	202	94	20	56	127	4.20	12	10	9.0	0.9	2.5	5.7	1.1	3.80	11

A third consecutive disappointing season may have hammered the nails in Uncle Fester's coffin, but only after the Sirotka debacle had slammed the cover. Ash's insistence on Sirotka as the key component in the David Wells trade, despite Sirotka's sporadic arm troubles in 2000, was certainly a mistake. However, the bigger gaffe was the misdiagnosis by the team physician that allowed the trade to go through. Make no mistake—Sirotka's south paw is a major mess. While he'll toe the slab at some point this summer, it's hard to imagine him regaining any sort of effectiveness before 2003.

Mike Smith **Throws R** **Age 24**

YEAR	TEAM	LGE	IP	H	ER	HR	BB	K	ERA	W	L	H/9	HR/9	BB/9	K/9	KW	PERA	STUFF
2000	Queens	NYP	49.7	51	27	4	22	26	4.89	3	3	9.2	0.7	4.0	4.7	0.6	4.83	-6
2001	Charl-WV	SAL	91.7	95	44	5	34	38	4.32	5	5	9.3	0.5	3.3	3.7	0.6	5.28	-4
2001	Tennesse	Sou	87.7	93	49	11	30	47	5.03	4	6	9.5	1.1	3.1	4.8	0.8	3.83	3

Mike Smith is quite likely the best pitching prospect about whom you've never heard. Though probably shorter than his listed 5′11″, performance-wise he towers over his peers in the Blue Jays' system. Smith's hard-boring stuff and mental makeup draw comparisons to Roy Oswalt, and he would've led the Southern League in ERA but for the fact that he didn't log enough innings to qualify after jumping two levels to Tennessee. Smith will be in camp as a non-roster invitee; if the Jays don't fill their hole at fifth starter over the winter, it's not inconceivable that he could head north with the job.

Arizona Diamondbacks

The belief in many quarters that a veteran team is the way to win has now been burned into the minds of baseball executives, written in stone, sent to Cooperstown, and etched in Mount Rushmore. The 2001 Arizona Diamondbacks won the World Series with one of the oldest teams in the history of the postseason, and watching the geezers shuffle onto the field after their dramatic Game Seven victory probably goaded a few GMs to age their rosters over the off-season.

The problem is that assembling a team this old is an enormous gamble. It rarely works no matter how it's executed, and it usually requires mortgaging the future. That's not to mention the extraordinary expense and low return on investment involved in crafting a roster nearly devoid of players in the bargain three-years-and-under category. That the Diamondbacks pulled it off is a credit to their player selection, their health record in 2001, and their overall luck. That they did it does not make it a good recipe for other teams to follow.

> **Diamondbacks Prospectus**
>
> **2001 record:** 92–70; First place, NL West; Beat the Yankees in the World Series, 4–3
>
> **Pythagenport W/L:** 95–67
>
> **Runs scored:** 818 (third in NL)
>
> **Runs allowed:** 677 (second in NL)
>
> **Team EqA:** .267 (fourth in NL)
>
> **2001 batters age:** 32.2 (oldest in NL)
>
> **2001 pitchers age:** 31.4 (oldest in NL)
>
> **Ballpark:** Bank One Ballpark; slight hitters' park; Park Factor of 1.014
>
> **2001:** Big gamble, big payoff: any season that ends with your two best pitchers hugging on the field is a good one.
>
> **2002:** Look at those ages and draw your own conclusions. The tough competition won't help.

On Opening Day 2001, the Diamondbacks had 28 players with major-league contracts earning a total of $81.2 million, the eighth-highest Opening Day payroll in baseball. While it's easy to assume that the Snakes bought their championship, that assumption is belied by the terrible return the Diamondbacks received on most of their investments.

They paid more than $9.3 million to four players who missed all or most of the season due to injuries: Todd Stottlemyre, Matt Mantei, Russ Springer ($1.8 million for a middle reliever?), and Armando Reynoso. Nearly every team has major injuries—they're the nature of the baseball beast. The Snakes were fortunate in that only one of the injuries they suffered affected a player expected to make a significant contribution. That injury, Mantei's torn ulnar collateral ligament, cost them a player in an overvalued role for whom they had a superior backup already on the roster.

Setting aside those four, that left $71.9 million to spend on useful players. Unfortunately, more than two-thirds of the money Arizona spent on hitters went to players who produced less than the average player at their positions. That's largely the fault of Jay ($8 million) Bell, Tony ($4 million) Womack, Steve ($5.4 million) Finley, and Matt ($9 million) Williams, who were a collective 23.5 runs below average in 2001. Most damning, none of those performances was a surprise, as Bell, Williams, and Finley were all old and declining when they first came to Arizona, and Womack has never been a valuable hitter. It was all money poorly spent for the sake of spending money. In fact, only one regular hitter on the 2001 Diamondbacks earned less than $1 million (Craig Counsell, $425,000), and he wasn't originally expected to be an everyday player.

The Diamondbacks' purse strings weren't nearly as loose with pitchers, but they still ponied up for a few who turned out to be duds. Brian Anderson was pricey at just over $4 million, while Greg Swindell's $2 million salary as part of a multiyear deal indicated an organization ignorant of the ready availability of comparable left-handed relievers on waivers and via minor-league free agency.

No Diamondbacks pitcher was as overpaid as Matt Mantei was. Mantei's injury was hardly a surprise for a player who has been on the disabled list in every season since 1993, including shoulder and biceps injuries that held him to 45 innings in 2000. The Snakes ignored Mantei's long injury history and gave him a four-year, $22-million deal in January 2001; it's a ridiculous overpayment for any kind of reliever, but particularly for one who had reached 60 innings in a major-league season just once.

So how did the Diamondbacks win, given the rampant misallocation of their allegedly limited funds? Be it prescience or luck, the Diamondbacks hit three tape-measure home runs amid all their multi-million-dollar contracts, and those homers made all the difference in their season.

Luis Gonzalez came to Arizona from Detroit after the 1998 season in exchange for prospect-turned-suspect Karim Garcia and a half-million dollars. Gonzalez was a serviceable, perhaps even good, corner outfielder at the time, but he had posted a career-best .475 slugging percentage in his last season with the Tigers, and his OBP had seen the .360 mark just once. He was already 31 years old when he played his first game at the BOB. The trade was a good one for Arizona, but there was no reason to get excited, and the three-year, $12.5-million extension Gonzalez signed in August 1999 looked like more D'backs' extravagance.

It turned out to be the biggest bargain in the franchise's short history. In 1999, Gonzalez topped .300 for the first time; in 2000, he hit 30 homers for the first time; and in 2001, he had what would have been an MVP season in just about any other year, creating 65 runs more than the average left fielder while earning less than $5 million. If the Snakes saw this coming when they acquired Gonzalez, our hats are off to them.

The other two contracts that paid off for the Diamondbacks belonged to World Series co-MVPs Randy Johnson and Curt Schilling. For just short of $20 million between them, they were the top two starting pitchers in baseball in 2001, providing 15.7 wins above replacement-level pitchers, a performance that more than justified their high salaries. Johnson, in particular, was a marvel, posting the best season by an MLB starting pitcher last year and one of the best seasons of his career, all in the year in which he turned 38. Schilling provided an even better return on investment, as he earned just $6.5 million last year, and the team didn't miss the four players they had dealt to acquire him.

Three outstanding successes, however, don't mean that a team understands the concept of maximizing its return on investment, which is critical to any team that likes to call itself "small market" or otherwise complain publicly about its financial situation. The best evidence a team can provide that it does grasp the concept is heavy use of quality players who have less than three years of experience. On that test, the Diamondbacks failed.

The salary structure in place under the collective bargaining agreement that expired in October of 2001 holds player compensation down for at least a player's first three seasons in the majors, and potentially his fourth depending on how much major-league service time he accumulates during those three seasons. This salary structure provides any team concerned about holding down its expenditures on player salaries—and really, is there a team in baseball that shouldn't be?—with a strong incentive to fill as many roster spots as possible with players in that sub-three-years category. A rookie earning $200,000 can easily produce as much as a veteran reserve earning $1 million; a third-year player earning $600,000 can produce as much as a free-agent signee earning several million dollars. In both cases, the veteran's production is usually a known quantity, but the younger player generally offers the chance of a whole lot more.

The Diamondbacks failed to make much use of this GM's best friend, building a team that blew a lot of money on overpaid veteran hitters. Bell, Womack, Williams, Finley, and newly-minted millionaire Danny Bautista were all below average for their positions and less than 15 runs above replacement level in 2001.

Even when the Diamondbacks did consider cheaper options, they misused them. Erubiel Durazo was scarcely used in a reserve role, sitting behind newly acquired Mark Grace, who cost $3 million and posted a lower EqA and OPS than did Durazo. Junior Spivey, already 26 and clearly ready for a major-league role, posted a .271 EqA in 188 plate appearances; that was better than the EqAs of Jay Bell and Tony Womack, who both received at least 20 times Spivey's salary. The Snakes cried poverty several times during the 2001 season, but is there any reason to bail out a team that spends money so unwisely?

The World Championship should provide the Diamondbacks with a financial boost in 2002, as ticket prices, ticket sales, and merchandise sales all increase. For the first time, the Snakes will receive their share of the national television contract, which was denied to them and to the Devil Rays as part of their hazing, er, expansion agreement. If Arizona really couldn't produce the cash needed to pay its aging players in 2001, it might have enough to do so in 2002—just in time for the team to fall apart.

To fill out their roster, the Diamondbacks didn't just spend money; they sacrificed much of what was becoming a productive farm system. Matt Mantei cost the team Brad Penny, who would have given the Diamondbacks the third starter they frequently needed in the postseason and would have spared Arizona the need to acquire another starter in July. That deal, to acquire starting pitcher Albie Lopez, cost the Diamondbacks pitching prospect Nick Bierbrodt just as the left-hander had recovered from elbow surgery. Outfield prospects Abraham Nunez and Paul Weichard were also traded, although Nunez has been hurt and Weichard has been lost in the vortex of the Pirates' system. By signing many top free agents, including dubious selections such as Finley, Stottlemyre, and Swindell, the Diamondbacks have surrendered high picks in the last four drafts. Only one player selected by the Diamondbacks in the first 15 rounds of any draft appeared on their expanded major-league roster in September, and just six other drafted players were on the roster at all.

The Diamondbacks' farm system now includes two types of prospects: first basemen who can beat the heck out of the ball and catchers with pop. The first basemen include Jack Cust (making a valiant attempt to play left field), Lyle Overbay, Billy Martin, and, of course, Erubiel Durazo, all of whom are blocked by Mark Grace through 2003. The catchers include Brad Cresse, J.D. Closser, and Craig Ansman. The Diamondbacks can obviously play only one each day, so unless they acknowledge Cresse's defensive flaws and try to move him to third base, they won't have much use for two of the three. Arizona has two or three pitching prospects worth your attention, but no one who we might expect to contribute until at least 2003, meaning that we're likely to see a lot more overpaid talent on the Diamondbacks' roster as they attempt to paper over the lack of talent coming from the farm system.

The Snakes won the World Series with luck, money, and luck. They faced flawed competition in all three rounds of the playoffs. Their most important players stayed healthy. They went out and acquired two of the best starting pitchers in baseball, resulting in a team that was much tougher to beat in the playoffs than it was during the regular season. They overcame some of the worst postseason managing you'll ever see, refusing to roll over and die when the Yankees' Terminator, Mariano Rivera, came in to close out the Bombers' fourth straight championship. Tip your cap to the Diamondbacks, and bow your heads as well, because it will be a long time before this Phoenix rises again.

HITTERS (BA: .270, OBP: .340, SLG: .440, EqA: .260)

Craig Ansman — C — Bats R — Age 24

YEAR	TEAM	LGE	AB	H	DB	TP	HR	BB	SO	R	RBI	SB	CS	OUT	BA	OBP	SLG	EQA	EQR	DEFENSE
2000	Missoula	Pio	67	12	3	0	0	7	25	4	3	0	0	55	.179	.263	.224	.176	4	15-C -1
2001	Sth Bend	Mid	351	91	19	2	14	21	93	49	51	2	1	261	.259	.313	.444	.249	40	66-C 1
2002	*Arizona*	*NL*	*340*	*93*	*20*	*2*	*14*	*28*	*100*	*43*	*47*	*3*	*1*	*248*	*.274*	*.329*	*.468*	*.264*	*45*	

An organization player who started the year on South Bend's disabled list with a phantom injury, Ansman went from being the third catcher on a low-A team to a possible prospect with an explosive year. He slugged .623 and posted the best EqA of any catcher in the Diamondbacks' system. Ansman was drafted out of SUNY-Stony Brook, so he was old for the Midwest League at 23 and wasn't promoted because J.D. Closser and Brad Cresse are ahead of him. Ansman is worth someone's attention.

Rod Barajas — C — Bats R — Age 26

YEAR	TEAM	LGE	AB	H	DB	TP	HR	BB	SO	R	RBI	SB	CS	OUT	BA	OBP	SLG	EQA	EQR	DEFENSE
1999	El Paso	Tex	498	127	26	1	11	17	75	55	66	1	0	371	.255	.287	.378	.221	43	110-C -3
2000	Tucson	PCL	412	81	15	0	12	8	63	32	57	3	2	333	.197	.219	.320	.180	23	84-C 2 12-1B -1
2001	Tucson	PCL	158	45	6	0	8	9	21	18	26	3	1	114	.285	.331	.475	.265	21	20-1B 0 17-C -1
2001	Arizona	NL	106	18	4	0	3	4	22	10	9	0	0	88	.170	.200	.292	.165	5	24-C -2
2002	*Arizona*	*NL*	*421*	*104*	*15*	*0*	*16*	*22*	*72*	*47*	*64*	*4*	*1*	*318*	*.247*	*.284*	*.397*	*.227*	*39*	

Barajas would be the ideal backup catcher for a team whose starter was a defensive whiz but a little lacking at the plate, especially against left-handers. The Diamondbacks aren't that team. He hasn't walked much in the minors but has pop, smacking the PCL around as a repeater this year; he's worth a second look to see if he can hit enough to overcome his defensive shortcomings.

Danny Bautista — OF — Bats R — Age 30

YEAR	TEAM	LGE	AB	H	DB	TP	HR	BB	SO	R	RBI	SB	CS	OUT	BA	OBP	SLG	EQA	EQR	DEFENSE
1999	Calgary	PCL	130	35	6	0	6	9	16	18	20	2	2	97	.269	.320	.454	.252	15	36-CF 3
1999	Florida	NL	207	61	10	1	5	1	28	32	23	3	0	146	.295	.301	.425	.241	21	53-OF 5
2000	Florida	NL	90	18	4	0	4	4	18	9	12	1	0	72	.200	.234	.378	.203	7	21-LF 1
2000	Arizona	NL	263	82	16	6	7	16	28	43	44	5	2	183	.312	.357	.498	.281	38	66-RF 1
2001	Arizona	NL	219	67	12	2	5	13	25	27	26	3	2	154	.306	.347	.447	.263	27	50-RF 0
2002	*Arizona*	*NL*	*307*	*92*	*16*	*3*	*9*	*21*	*41*	*49*	*42*	*6*	*2*	*217*	*.300*	*.345*	*.459*	*.270*	*41*	

When Bautista started for the Diamondbacks, he was the only member of the lineup under 30. While that does show that you can win with a lineup that has Noah in left, Israel in right, and Methuselah at first base (due to reduced mobility at his age), it isn't a recipe for long-term success. Bautista is stretched in a full-time role but is a great fourth outfielder given his bat and ability to play center field almost as well as Steve Finley does. He signed a three-year deal to stay in Arizona and goes into camp as the starting right fielder.

Jay Bell 2B/3B Bats R Age 36

YEAR	TEAM	LGE	AB	H	DB	TP	HR	BB	SO	R	RBI	SB	CS	OUT	BA	OBP	SLG	EQA	EQR	DEFENSE
1999	Arizona	NL	589	166	31	5	38	74	122	128	104	6	4	427	.282	.366	.545	.294	100	146-2B -14
2000	Arizona	NL	567	150	29	5	18	62	81	83	64	6	3	420	.265	.340	.429	.257	70	141-2B -1
2001	Arizona	NL	428	109	22	1	14	63	67	61	47	0	1	320	.255	.354	.409	.259	54	72-2B 0 33-3B -2
2002	*Arizona*	*NL*	*486*	*122*	*27*	*3*	*18*	*71*	*84*	*82*	*59*	*4*	*2*	*366*	*.251*	*.346*	*.430*	*.263*	*65*	

In the climactic scene of *Return of the Jedi,* in which Darth Vader saves Luke Skywalker from torture and death at the hands of the Emperor, Vader throws the Emperor into an apparently bottomless column, avoiding on-screen bloodshed but giving us a frightening picture nonetheless. About halfway down, the Emperor passed Jay Bell, who will hit bottom after his contract runs out at the end of the 2002 season. Our guess is that the bottom of that column is in Tampa Bay.

Kevan Burns LF Bats L Age 25

YEAR	TEAM	LGE	AB	H	DB	TP	HR	BB	SO	R	RBI	SB	CS	OUT	BA	OBP	SLG	EQA	EQR	DEFENSE
1999	Missoula	Pio	54	13	1	2	0	3	12	7	6	1	0	41	.241	.281	.333	.211	4	
1999	Sth Bend	Mid	158	39	7	0	1	8	29	14	15	1	2	121	.247	.283	.310	.200	11	40-CF 0
2000	Sth Bend	Mid	414	91	14	4	3	28	72	43	37	13	5	328	.220	.270	.295	.197	28	89-LF -8
2001	Lancastr	Cal	250	67	14	3	7	17	40	31	27	6	3	186	.268	.316	.432	.248	28	48-LF -3
2002	*Arizona*	*NL*	*385*	*99*	*17*	*4*	*8*	*31*	*70*	*51*	*49*	*12*	*6*	*292*	*.257*	*.313*	*.384*	*.236*	*40*	

Burns is among the Snakes' best hitting prospects, which is more of an indictment of their farm system than praise for Burns. He's a patient hitter with a good line-drive stroke but without the power to be a major-league left fielder or the arm to play right field. Having two farm teams in good hitting environments has masked Arizona's lack of hitting prospects, so Tucson will tell the tale for Burns as it has for the others.

Alex Cintron SS Bats B Age 23

YEAR	TEAM	LGE	AB	H	DB	TP	HR	BB	SO	R	RBI	SB	CS	OUT	BA	OBP	SLG	EQA	EQR	DEFENSE
1999	High Des	Cal	483	107	18	1	2	9	66	46	37	7	4	380	.222	.238	.275	.176	25	120-SS -12
2000	El Paso	Tex	512	123	24	3	3	16	56	59	39	5	5	394	.240	.265	.316	.196	33	124-SS -25
2001	Tucson	PCL	416	105	20	2	2	15	44	43	27	7	5	316	.252	.281	.325	.205	30	91-SS -20 14-2B -2
2002	*Arizona*	*NL*	*466*	*124*	*21*	*3*	*4*	*25*	*56*	*61*	*42*	*10*	*6*	*348*	*.266*	*.303*	*.350*	*.220*	*40*	

Baseball tools come without instructions. Cintron has natural abilities that don't really translate well on the baseball field. He hits for nice averages, never walks, and has no power and minimal speed, making him a liability at the plate. He has the capacity for good range in the field, but he doesn't field shortstop well at all and will probably end up as part of the organizational logjam at second base. Cintron is in the wrong organization and will probably end up traveling the waiver highway.

J.D. Closser C Bats B Age 22

YEAR	TEAM	LGE	AB	H	DB	TP	HR	BB	SO	R	RBI	SB	CS	OUT	BA	OBP	SLG	EQA	EQR	DEFENSE
1999	Missoula	Pio	277	57	8	0	6	42	68	34	25	3	2	222	.206	.312	.300	.216	24	63-C -8
1999	Sth Bend	Mid	179	33	3	0	3	23	40	19	18	0	1	147	.184	.279	.251	.188	11	30-C -8
2000	Sth Bend	Mid	347	64	13	1	6	40	67	39	25	3	1	284	.184	.271	.280	.194	24	71-C -11
2001	Lancastr	Cal	467	101	16	3	14	48	101	57	53	3	5	371	.216	.291	.353	.217	41	94-C -12
2002	*Colorado*	*NL*	*447*	*120*	*21*	*3*	*15*	*61*	*100*	*72*	*60*	*5*	*5*	*332*	*.268*	*.356*	*.430*	*.237*	*46*	

Although Closser has largely been passed on prospect lists by Brad Cresse, Closser has a much better defensive profile than Cresse does, and he showed some ability to hit last year in the friendly confines of the California League. He has the emotional, clubhouse-leader personality that counts for too much in the Arizona organization, so he'll get an extra chance or two to get his bat up to major-league caliber. Traded to the Rockies for lefty Mike Myers, with Jack Cust.

Greg Colbrunn 1B/PH Bats R Age 32

YEAR	TEAM	LGE	AB	H	DB	TP	HR	BB	SO	R	RBI	SB	CS	OUT	BA	OBP	SLG	EQA	EQR	DEFENSE
1999	Arizona	NL	135	43	4	3	5	10	21	19	22	1	1	93	.319	.382	.504	.291	21	26-1B 0
2000	Arizona	NL	330	102	20	1	15	38	41	46	54	0	1	229	.309	.395	.512	.299	56	82-1B 1
2001	Arizona	NL	97	29	5	0	5	9	12	12	19	0	0	68	.299	.376	.505	.291	15	
2002	*Arizona*	*NL*	*286*	*83*	*15*	*1*	*11*	*34*	*38*	*38*	*43*	*0*	*1*	*204*	*.290*	*.366*	*.465*	*.278*	*42*	

Colbrunn is a great bench guy to have if he's inexpensive, and one way to keep him inexpensive is to use him properly: as your first pinch hitter against lefties and as your first or second against righties, but never as a starter. He's also an emergency catcher, and given the fear of being caught without a catcher that paralyzes most managers, that has value. Colbrunn could probably keep filling this role at about $250,000 a year until he's 40, and it would be a good deal for all parties concerned.

Craig Counsell 2B Bats L Age 31

YEAR	TEAM	LGE	AB	H	DB	TP	HR	BB	SO	R	RBI	SB	CS	OUT	BA	OBP	SLG	EQA	EQR	DEFENSE			
1999	Florida	NL	67	11	1	0	0	4	9	4	2	0	0	56	.164	.211	.179	.140	2	10-2B	1		
1999	LosAngls	NL	109	29	7	0	0	8	13	21	9	1	0	80	.266	.316	.330	.223	9	27-2B	0		
2000	Tucson	PCL	193	58	14	2	2	16	19	35	20	3	1	136	.301	.356	.425	.264	24	18-3B	1	18-2B	-1
2000	Arizona	NL	152	47	7	1	2	18	17	22	10	3	3	108	.309	.389	.408	.270	21	17-2B	0	13-3B	5
2001	Arizona	NL	458	129	21	3	4	59	64	78	38	6	8	337	.282	.366	.367	.250	53	47-SS	0	47-2B	9
2002	*Arizona*	*NL*	*389*	*106*	*17*	*2*	*4*	*52*	*55*	*71*	*33*	*7*	*6*	*289*	*.272*	*.358*	*.357*	*.248*	*44*				

What the Snakes do with Counsell this off-season will tell us a lot about just how clueless their front office is. Yes, Counsell is a postseason hero, a seasoned veteran, aged to perfection like a Black Angus or a tawny Porto. All three of those things go bad if you leave them out too long. Counsell is 31, has a career OPS of 716, and is about to become expensive. The Free Junior Spivey campaign will begin shortly; check our Web site for details.

Brad Cresse C Bats R Age 23

YEAR	TEAM	LGE	AB	H	DB	TP	HR	BB	SO	R	RBI	SB	CS	OUT	BA	OBP	SLG	EQA	EQR	DEFENSE	
2000	High Des	Cal	170	42	3	0	11	9	51	22	31	0	0	128	.247	.298	.459	.246	19	36-C	-9
2000	El Paso	Tex	42	9	0	0	1	4	12	6	7	0	0	33	.214	.308	.286	.210	3		
2001	El Paso	Tex	425	101	22	1	12	35	117	40	58	0	1	325	.238	.309	.379	.231	42	92-C	-12
2002	*Arizona*	*NL*	*395*	*99*	*17*	*1*	*16*	*41*	*119*	*49*	*57*	*0*	*1*	*297*	*.251*	*.321*	*.420*	*.248*	*46*		

He started to live up to the hype this year, but hardly enough to justify it all. Cresse showed some promise at the plate, and he clearly has the potential to be a top power hitter. But El Paso pitchers preferred throwing to Mike Rose, John Hernandez, or Mr. Bonkers the syphilitic monkey, a situation that hasn't improved much. With Closser and Ansman coming up behind him and a hole in the organization at third base, a move to the hot corner may be best for all concerned.

Midre Cummings PH/OF Bats L Age 30

YEAR	TEAM	LGE	AB	H	DB	TP	HR	BB	SO	R	RBI	SB	CS	OUT	BA	OBP	SLG	EQA	EQR	DEFENSE	
1999	New Brit	Eas	95	32	4	0	2	13	14	22	12	2	1	64	.337	.423	.442	.297	15	24-CF	0
1999	SaltLake	PCL	253	69	13	3	10	19	39	37	49	3	3	187	.273	.328	.466	.259	32	58-LF	-7
1999	Minnesot	AL	38	11	0	0	1	2	6	2	8	2	0	27	.289	.325	.368	.245	4		
2000	Minnesot	AL	179	50	8	0	5	9	22	27	22	0	0	129	.279	.325	.408	.245	19	33-RF	-2
2000	Boston	AL	25	8	0	0	0	5	3	1	2	0	0	17	.320	.433	.320	.276	3		
2001	Tucson	PCL	258	74	20	6	4	21	44	31	30	2	2	186	.287	.341	.457	.263	33	46-LF	-1
2002	*Arizona*	*NL*	*337*	*96*	*19*	*4*	*9*	*39*	*57*	*54*	*51*	*3*	*1*	*242*	*.285*	*.359*	*.445*	*.272*	*47*		

If pinch-hitting is an actual skill, then Cummings probably has it. But is that marginal benefit worth burning a roster spot, rather than using it on someone who brings a second skill, such as familiarity with a baseball glove? With Colbrunn and Durazo on the bench already, what did Cummings bring to the postseason roster that Arizona didn't already have in spades?

Jack Cust LF/1B Bats L Age 23

YEAR	TEAM	LGE	AB	H	DB	TP	HR	BB	SO	R	RBI	SB	CS	OUT	BA	OBP	SLG	EQA	EQR	DEFENSE	
1999	High Des	Cal	441	104	23	1	19	66	147	63	59	1	2	339	.236	.337	.422	.254	55	100-LF	-19
2000	El Paso	Tex	441	100	22	3	14	87	151	69	47	7	6	346	.227	.356	.385	.254	56	123-LF	-13
2001	Tucson	PCL	438	104	19	0	21	90	145	64	60	5	2	336	.237	.371	.425	.272	65	110-RF	-15
2002	*Colorado*	*NL*	*486*	*140*	*26*	*2*	*24*	*84*	*168*	*83*	*73*	*8*	*4*	*350*	*.288*	*.393*	*.498*	*.270*	*66*		

Cust is probably ready for the majors with the bat. He swatted 27 homers in a reasonably tough home-run park in Tucson, and he drew 102 walks to lead the minors. Two things are holding him back: his propensity to whiff (160 strikeouts in 2001), which has the Snakes justifiably, if excessively, concerned; and his dexterity with the glove in left field, or lack thereof, which needs to improve unless he ends up on an AL squad. Already traded to the Rockies, he'll hit wherever he ends up, but there's only a 50/50 chance he stays in Colorado.

David Dellucci OF Bats L Age 28

YEAR	TEAM	LGE	AB	H	DB	TP	HR	BB	SO	R	RBI	SB	CS	OUT	BA	OBP	SLG	EQA	EQR	DEFENSE
1999	Arizona	NL	108	42	6	1	1	10	22	26	14	2	0	66	.389	.454	.491	.325	20	22-RF -3
2000	Tucson	PCL	121	24	4	2	3	10	14	12	13	3	0	97	.198	.260	.339	.207	9	27-RF -2
2000	Arizona	NL	50	14	3	0	0	4	8	2	2	0	2	38	.280	.333	.340	.220	4	
2001	Arizona	NL	217	62	10	2	10	21	44	29	41	2	1	156	.286	.353	.488	.277	31	47-RF -6
2002	*Arizona*	*NL*	*206*	*58*	*10*	*2*	*7*	*24*	*41*	*37*	*28*	*1*	*1*	*149*	*.282*	*.357*	*.451*	*.271*	*29*	

Dellucci stays healthy about as long as Carl Everett keeps his mouth shut. Dellucci's career has been interrupted by surgery to correct a congenital wrist problem, a blown-out ankle, and numerous knee injuries. What all that means is that Dellucci is 28 years old with just 903 plate appearances in his career and a lot of lost development time. Right now, he's a very good fourth outfielder/pinch hitter who can handle both corners, and he may still have a small spike ahead of him.

Doug Devore RF Bats L Age 24

YEAR	TEAM	LGE	AB	H	DB	TP	HR	BB	SO	R	RBI	SB	CS	OUT	BA	OBP	SLG	EQA	EQR	DEFENSE
1999	Missoula	Pio	116	19	3	1	2	7	43	11	10	1	0	97	.164	.220	.259	.168	6	27-RF -5
2000	Sth Bend	Mid	465	109	18	2	12	29	112	46	40	4	4	360	.234	.281	.359	.214	38	117-RF -12
2001	El Paso	Tex	471	112	22	6	12	37	119	49	51	7	2	361	.238	.296	.386	.230	46	120-RF -7
2002	*Arizona*	*NL*	*429*	*109*	*20*	*4*	*11*	*40*	*117*	*56*	*52*	*7*	*3*	*323*	*.254*	*.318*	*.396*	*.242*	*46*	

Talk to any baseball person about Devore and they start babbling as if they're discussing Heidi Klum, talking first about Devore's body and then about everything else. While Devore really looks like a baseball player, he still has a fair amount of work to do to become one. After jumping a level from South Bend—a move the Diamondbacks too often have their prospects try—he was nearly sent down to Lancaster before he started hitting, just barely earning consideration for a 2002 promotion. Devore needs to develop skills that this organization doesn't teach well.

Erubiel Durazo 1B Bats L Age 28

YEAR	TEAM	LGE	AB	H	DB	TP	HR	BB	SO	R	RBI	SB	CS	OUT	BA	OBP	SLG	EQA	EQR	DEFENSE
1999	El Paso	Tex	219	69	14	1	9	33	38	37	35	1	1	151	.315	.408	.511	.305	39	63-1B -10
1999	Tucson	PCL	113	39	4	0	8	11	16	20	21	1	0	74	.345	.406	.593	.323	22	29-1B 2
1999	Arizona	NL	154	50	5	2	10	24	40	30	27	1	1	105	.325	.419	.578	.322	31	39-1B 1
2000	Arizona	NL	197	52	7	0	9	31	39	33	32	1	0	145	.264	.366	.437	.272	28	52-1B -3
2001	Arizona	NL	175	48	9	0	13	27	42	35	39	0	0	127	.274	.376	.549	.299	31	32-1B -1
2002	*Arizona*	*NL*	*388*	*121*	*18*	*1*	*26*	*64*	*89*	*74*	*73*	*1*	*0*	*267*	*.312*	*.409*	*.564*	*.320*	*77*	

Free Erubiel Durazo! He's a prisoner of conscience, held by sadistic autocrats in a desert kingdom. Removed from the position that was his birthright, he was exiled to an emirate many miles to the south, only to find himself summoned when the king found it expedient to have him nearby. Although he has not taken well to his martyr status, he has continued to spread the forbidden gospel of walks and power. His bat will do the talking.

Steve Finley CF Bats L Age 37

YEAR	TEAM	LGE	AB	H	DB	TP	HR	BB	SO	R	RBI	SB	CS	OUT	BA	OBP	SLG	EQA	EQR	DEFENSE
1999	Arizona	NL	591	153	32	9	34	55	87	97	96	6	4	442	.259	.325	.516	.271	84	155-CF 4
2000	Arizona	NL	541	149	27	4	34	57	80	95	90	11	6	398	.275	.352	.529	.285	86	144-CF -1
2001	Arizona	NL	495	139	26	4	14	45	57	67	73	11	7	363	.281	.342	.434	.258	61	126-CF 3
2002	*Arizona*	*NL*	*513*	*119*	*27*	*4*	*23*	*56*	*72*	*75*	*70*	*9*	*7*	*401*	*.232*	*.308*	*.435*	*.246*	*60*	

Finley had a dismal start in 2001, eventually finding his singles stroke but none of his power. He turns 37 during spring training, so there's no reason to expect that the surprise power he found in his thirties will suddenly reappear. The fielding ability is still there, so it's not as if Finley is useless, but he's not going to be worth the $6 million he's owed in this, the last year of his bloated contract.

Luis Gonzalez LF Bats L Age 34

YEAR	TEAM	LGE	AB	H	DB	TP	HR	BB	SO	R	RBI	SB	CS	OUT	BA	OBP	SLG	EQA	EQR	DEFENSE
1999	Arizona	NL	613	201	43	4	26	58	58	108	104	7	5	417	.328	.392	.538	.303	106	143-LF -2
2000	Arizona	NL	619	189	42	2	31	70	78	101	107	2	4	434	.305	.385	.530	.298	105	152-LF -2
2001	Arizona	NL	609	203	35	7	57	96	70	130	143	1	1	407	.333	.433	.695	.351	149	150-LF 3
2002	*Arizona*	*NL*	*551*	*171*	*34*	*4*	*35*	*85*	*69*	*105*	*106*	*3*	*3*	*383*	*.310*	*.403*	*.577*	*.318*	*109*	

The National League MVP... in any year other than 2001, when he was arguably just the third-best player in the league. Gonzalez had a sizable lead over everyone other than Barry Bonds and Sammy Sosa in EqA and EqR. He's also 34 and coming off a career year for a team that desperately needs to rebuild. Trading him would be a daring and unpopular move. It would also refill a farm system left barren by trades and bad drafting. It's the right move.

Mark Grace 1B Bats L Age 38

YEAR	TEAM	LGE	AB	H	DB	TP	HR	BB	SO	R	RBI	SB	CS	OUT	BA	OBP	SLG	EQA	EQR	DEFENSE
1999	ChiCubs	NL	593	180	43	5	16	75	41	104	85	2	4	417	.304	.384	.474	.285	90	156-1B 0
2000	ChiCubs	NL	513	143	37	1	12	88	26	73	79	1	2	372	.279	.390	.425	.278	76	137-1B 3
2001	Arizona	NL	476	146	31	2	15	64	31	68	79	1	0	330	.307	.392	.475	.291	76	121-1B 2
2002	*Arizona*	*NL*	*528*	*134*	*33*	*2*	*15*	*83*	*35*	*80*	*71*	*2*	*2*	*396*	*.254*	*.355*	*.409*	*.261*	*69*	

Credit where it's due: Grace had a fine season, better than we expected him to have. Signing him was a dumb idea, nevertheless. Durazo was ready and is just as ready now even though Grace will be blocking him again. It was also an unwise use of funds by a team that loves to cry poverty; if they were so bleeping poor, why did they waste $4 million filling a hole that didn't exist? Grace will make an interesting Hall of Fame case if he can get regular playing time for another three years.

Billy Martin 1B Bats R Age 26

YEAR	TEAM	LGE	AB	H	DB	TP	HR	BB	SO	R	RBI	SB	CS	OUT	BA	OBP	SLG	EQA	EQR	DEFENSE
1999	Columbia	SAL	227	43	12	1	5	17	87	26	20	0	1	185	.189	.254	.317	.193	15	56-3B -15
2000	Sth Bend	Mid	435	98	19	2	17	57	144	55	56	3	1	338	.225	.322	.395	.243	49	57-1B 0
2001	Lancastr	Cal	474	104	21	2	16	70	124	66	63	0	2	372	.219	.324	.373	.237	51	56-1B 1 47-3B -8
2002	*Arizona*	*NL*	*408*	*112*	*28*	*2*	*20*	*66*	*146*	*71*	*60*	*2*	*2*	*358*	*.239*	*.333*	*.432*	*.257*	*60*	

Martin is in the wrong organization for a guy with his profile. He has hit everywhere he's played but has always been old for his leagues, and he won't be promoted because the Snakes have better first-base prospects ahead of him. Martin played some third base this year and didn't impress anyone with his defense. He'll have to work at it, because moving to the hot corner is the only way he'll see any light in this organization. He needs to reach Triple-A this year to have a career.

Damian Miller C Bats R Age 32

YEAR	TEAM	LGE	AB	H	DB	TP	HR	BB	SO	R	RBI	SB	CS	OUT	BA	OBP	SLG	EQA	EQR	DEFENSE
1999	Arizona	NL	297	79	13	0	13	15	72	34	46	0	0	218	.266	.306	.441	.245	32	83-C 2
2000	Arizona	NL	325	88	16	0	12	32	68	40	43	2	2	239	.271	.338	.431	.256	39	89-C 5
2001	Arizona	NL	380	107	14	1	14	33	68	46	49	0	1	274	.282	.344	.434	.259	47	117-C 2
2002	*Arizona*	*NL*	*369*	*97*	*16*	*1*	*16*	*36*	*77*	*46*	*54*	*1*	*1*	*273*	*.263*	*.328*	*.442*	*.257*	*46*	

Miller's stats dipped slightly as he played much of the year in pain from two injuries, a nagging rotator-cuff strain and a slight tear in an Achilles' tendon. Despite that, he remained above replacement level at the plate. His glove work is adequate, but not as special as the Snakes believe it is. Miller has been a good value up to now; given his age and quality, the Snakes should probably non-tender him before he gets too expensive.

Chad Moeller C Bats R Age 27

YEAR	TEAM	LGE	AB	H	DB	TP	HR	BB	SO	R	RBI	SB	CS	OUT	BA	OBP	SLG	EQA	EQR	DEFENSE
1999	New Brit	Eas	254	58	11	2	3	14	44	25	19	0	0	196	.228	.278	.323	.204	18	76-C -10
2000	SaltLake	PCL	164	41	9	1	4	6	43	22	15	0	1	124	.250	.276	.390	.218	14	40-C -8
2000	Minnesot	AL	127	27	4	1	1	8	29	13	9	1	0	100	.213	.259	.283	.188	8	39-C 0
2001	Tucson	PCL	270	63	13	0	7	23	49	33	29	1	3	210	.233	.297	.359	.219	24	65-C -9
2001	Arizona	NL	56	13	1	1	1	6	10	9	3	0	0	43	.232	.306	.339	.221	5	14-C 0
2002	*Arizona*	*NL*	*299*	*75*	*14*	*2*	*8*	*25*	*63*	*39*	*29*	*2*	*2*	*226*	*.251*	*.309*	*.391*	*.234*	*30*	

(Chad Moeller *continued*)

If Barajas is wrong for this team, then Moeller shouldn't even be on its 40-man roster. Pitchers like throwing to him, and he's a decent plate-blocker. On the other hand, he doesn't hit at all and doesn't do much against the running game. If things break right for him, he'll be the new Joe Girardi, trying to make a team that already has a turbocharged Girardi in Damian Miller.

Lyle Overbay 1B Bats L Age 25

YEAR	TEAM	LGE	AB	H	DB	TP	HR	BB	SO	R	RBI	SB	CS	OUT	BA	OBP	SLG	EQA	EQR	DEFENSE
1999	Missoula	Pio	301	69	14	2	6	22	63	31	44	4	2	234	.229	.283	.349	.214	25	68-1B -6
2000	Sth Bend	Mid	266	71	12	2	5	17	40	33	32	5	2	197	.267	.313	.383	.235	26	64-1B -5
2000	El Paso	Tex	237	66	10	1	6	19	39	30	32	2	1	172	.278	.335	.405	.249	27	60-1B -8
2001	El Paso	Tex	525	147	34	2	10	53	93	61	70	3	3	381	.280	.349	.410	.255	63	106-1B -3 21-LF -6
2002	*Arizona*	*NL*	*504*	*144*	*27*	*2*	*12*	*52*	*94*	*64*	*80*	*6*	*3*	*363*	*.286*	*.353*	*.419*	*.262*	*64*	

The next Mark Grace? Overbay bears a strong resemblance to Grace at the plate, with a good combination of walks and doubles, and a similarly strong work ethic. Overbay kept a notebook on opposing pitchers throughout the season, helping him improve his performance as the year progressed. While he's probably ready for the majors now, he's blocked by Grace, Durazo, and perhaps Cust as well, making the Grace signing look even worse than it already did.

Reggie Sanders RF Bats R Age 34

YEAR	TEAM	LGE	AB	H	DB	TP	HR	BB	SO	R	RBI	SB	CS	OUT	BA	OBP	SLG	EQA	EQR	DEFENSE
1999	San Dieg	NL	484	139	24	7	27	60	100	90	70	31	13	358	.287	.373	.533	.295	84	118-LF -4
2000	Atlanta	NL	343	80	22	1	11	27	72	42	35	20	4	267	.233	.293	.399	.237	37	83-LF -3
2001	Arizona	NL	441	118	22	3	32	44	107	85	89	14	10	333	.268	.339	.549	.281	70	108-RF 3
2002	*San Fran*	*NL*	*423*	*98*	*21*	*3*	*20*	*54*	*104*	*65*	*53*	*21*	*11*	*336*	*.232*	*.319*	*.437*	*.261*	*59*	

Sanders set career highs in homers and RBI last year, but he didn't draw the walks he had in 1999, so it wasn't his best season. Grabbing him for $1.5 million was one of Garagiola's best moves, and one that probably deserves a lot of credit for pushing the Snakes to the top of their division, since it gave them a third hitter who wasn't an automatic out. That said, Sanders is 34 and has never played 140 games in a season, so whoever bites this winter will get bitten back tenfold.

Junior Spivey 2B Bats R Age 27

YEAR	TEAM	LGE	AB	H	DB	TP	HR	BB	SO	R	RBI	SB	CS	OUT	BA	OBP	SLG	EQA	EQR	DEFENSE
1999	El Paso	Tex	162	35	8	2	2	28	28	27	12	8	6	133	.216	.336	.327	.231	17	35-2B -4
2000	Tucson	PCL	115	29	6	2	3	8	16	16	12	2	1	87	.252	.301	.417	.238	12	21-2B 0
2001	Tucson	PCL	192	38	3	0	5	24	29	20	21	8	5	159	.198	.287	.292	.204	15	50-2B 0
2001	Arizona	NL	163	43	7	3	5	22	40	34	21	3	0	120	.264	.357	.436	.270	23	44-2B 0
2002	*Arizona*	*NL*	*329*	*83*	*13*	*3*	*10*	*46*	*66*	*56*	*34*	*14*	*7*	*253*	*.252*	*.344*	*.401*	*.256*	*42*	

Spivey's debut wasn't outstanding, but it got him out of the mess he'd made for himself by failing to hit in his first extended Triple-A time. If we consider economics, Spivey should be the clear choice for the second-base job in 2001. If we consider the Arizona organization as a whole and its need to shift to younger hitters, Spivey should be the clear choice for the second-base job in 2001. We expect Jay Bell to play second base for Arizona this year.

Luis Terrero CF Bats B Age 22

YEAR	TEAM	LGE	AB	H	DB	TP	HR	BB	SO	R	RBI	SB	CS	OUT	BA	OBP	SLG	EQA	EQR	DEFENSE
1999	Missoula	Pio	271	53	11	2	4	17	108	33	18	9	6	224	.196	.248	.295	.187	17	71-CF -3
2000	Missoula	Pio	273	50	3	0	5	1	90	20	22	8	7	230	.183	.194	.249	.152	10	67-RF -2
2000	High Des	Cal	79	11	3	0	0	1	16	6	2	2	2	70	.139	.155	.177	.118	2	19-CF 1
2001	Sth Bend	Mid	89	12	1	0	1	0	32	3	6	2	0	77	.135	.142	.180	.116	2	21-RF 0
2001	Yakima	Nwn	42	9	3	0	0	1	9	5	1	0	1	34	.214	.233	.286	.169	2	
2001	Lancastr	Cal	68	23	7	0	2	1	13	10	6	3	0	45	.338	.352	.529	.293	10	17-CF -2
2001	El Paso	Tex	144	35	11	2	2	4	45	21	8	5	2	111	.243	.271	.389	.220	13	34-CF -1
2002	*Arizona*	*NL*	*354*	*88*	*15*	*2*	*8*	*15*	*117*	*48*	*30*	*13*	*7*	*273*	*.249*	*.279*	*.370*	*.217*	*30*	

Terrero gets raves for his tools everywhere he plays, but he has yet to show any discernible development as a baseball player. He never walks and has trouble with even mediocre breaking pitches. He doesn't always concentrate when he's on the field, and he hasn't done well with the organization's attempts to teach him about this "base ball" game. While the D'backs don't have a great track record of developing young hitters, it's not clear that anyone could succeed with Terrero.

Matt Williams 3B Bats R Age 36

YEAR	TEAM	LGE	AB	H	DB	TP	HR	BB	SO	R	RBI	SB	CS	OUT	BA	OBP	SLG	EQA	EQR	DEFENSE
1999	Arizona	NL	628	187	34	1	36	33	86	95	134	2	0	441	.298	.335	.527	.279	90	152-3B 10
2000	Arizona	NL	373	101	18	2	12	15	47	42	45	1	2	274	.271	.304	.426	.239	38	94-3B 2
2001	Arizona	NL	408	115	24	0	18	20	59	59	67	1	0	293	.282	.319	.473	.260	60	00 3B 7
2002	*Arizona*	*NL*	*538*	*147*	*29*	*1*	*21*	*38*	*79*	*71*	*83*	*3*	*1*	*392*	*.273*	*.321*	*.448*	*.256*	*65*	

His Baldness didn't bounce back much from his disappointing, injury-riddled 2000 campaign in a 2001 season riddled with still more injuries. Entering the last season of his contract, Williams is probably looking at retirement if he doesn't play well, which is the most likely occurrence at this point. He's not helping the team much when he does play, since he doesn't walk at all and his range at third base is diminishing. Arizona has too many guys like this to win the NL West again. Say, anybody know if Williams is married?

Tony Womack SS Bats L Age 32

YEAR	TEAM	LGE	AB	H	DB	TP	HR	BB	SO	R	RBI	SB	CS	OUT	BA	OBP	SLG	EQA	EQR	DEFENSE
1999	Arizona	NL	615	169	26	10	4	44	63	103	39	61	13	459	.275	.325	.369	.247	70	110-RF 5 15-2B -3
2000	Arizona	NL	621	166	22	13	7	21	68	90	54	41	11	466	.267	.296	.378	.232	61	143-SS -9
2001	Arizona	NL	481	132	19	5	3	21	46	68	31	28	7	356	.274	.311	.353	.232	46	113-SS -4
2002	*Arizona*	*NL*	*542*	*141*	*21*	*7*	*6*	*40*	*59*	*84*	*38*	*43*	*12*	*413*	*.260*	*.311*	*.358*	*.236*	*56*	

Wo-hack finally had the year statheads expected of him. With a slight drop in his foot speed and a little random chance, his average dropped to a point at which even the Diamondbacks realized he was a problem. He set career lows in walks, steals, OBP, and slugging percentage. That didn't stop Bob Brenly from putting Womack atop the Snakes' World Series lineup, making him among the worst leadoff hitters in Series history. As Womack heads into his walk year, the Snakes should give him a push.

PITCHERS (ERA: 4.50, H/9: 9.0, HR/9: 1.0, BB/9: 3.0, K/9: 6.0, KW: 2.0, PERA: 4.50)

Brian Anderson Throws L Age 30

YEAR	TEAM	LGE	IP	H	ER	HR	BB	K	ERA	W	L	H/9	HR/9	BB/9	K/9	KW	PERA	STUFF
1999	Arizona	NL	133.0	143	66	17	23	68	4.47	8	7	9.7	1.2	1.6	4.6	1.5	4.29	0
2000	Arizona	NL	212.3	241	119	34	32	92	5.04	11	13	10.2	1.4	1.4	3.9	1.4	3.82	0
2001	Arizona	NL	127.7	150	79	21	27	44	5.57	6	8	10.6	1.5	1.9	3.1	0.8	6.14	-14

Anderson wasn't healthy all season, and it showed in his disappointing performance. Back spasms and a groin strain cost him most of April and June. He couldn't keep the ball down at all, and he had a hard time putting hitters away on the rare occasions he reached two strikes. Anderson looked like a breakout candidate after a strong finish in 2000; if he's healthy this year, he could easily be the Snakes' #4 starter.

Miguel Batista Throws R Age 31

YEAR	TEAM	LGE	IP	H	ER	HR	BB	K	ERA	W	L	H/9	HR/9	BB/9	K/9	KW	PERA	STUFF
1999	Montreal	NL	140.3	137	63	9	49	86	4.04	9	7	8.8	0.6	3.1	5.5	0.9	5.35	0
2000	Omaha	PCL	29.3	34	23	8	7	19	7.06	1	2	10.4	2.5	2.1	5.8	1.4	6.90	-24
2000	KansasCy	AL	57.3	68	49	14	28	30	7.69	2	4	10.7	2.2	4.4	4.7	0.5	6.77	-20
2000	Montreal	NL	11.0	12	6	2	2	6	4.91	0	1	9.8	1.6	1.6	4.9	1.5	13.84	-20
2001	Arizona	NL	126.7	128	66	11	54	72	4.69	7	7	9.1	0.8	3.8	5.1	0.7	3.60	-5

The Desert Mendoza had his best year yet, something he has credited to increased concentration on the mound. It also likely has to do with the opportunities he received. Batista was equally effective as a starter and a reliever and will probably remain in that swing-man role for the time being. That said, a little bit of bad luck will find him putting too many men on base, and he could really stand to drop his walk rate.

Troy Brohawn Throws L Age 29

YEAR	TEAM	LGE	IP	H	ER	HR	BB	K	ERA	W	L	H/9	HR/9	BB/9	K/9	KW	PERA	STUFF
1999	Tucson	PCL	16.0	16	7	1	4	8	3.94	1	1	9.0	0.6	2.3	4.5	1.0	5.15	-3
2000	Tucson	PCL	16.0	21	17	6	5	11	9.56	0	2	11.8	3.4	2.8	6.2	1.1	3.73	-29
2001	Arizona	NL	48.3	50	26	4	21	24	4.84	2	3	9.3	0.7	3.9	4.5	0.6	4.82	-17

The soft-tosser came back from two years almost completely lost to injuries to spend almost the entire year in the majors, despite not being very effective. Most damning was his resounding awfulness against left-handed hitters, who tagged him to the tune of .386/.476/.600 last year. He was actually effective against righties, but the Snakes had a few other relievers in that category as well. He had no business being on the World Series roster and was designated for assignment in December.

Chris Capuano Throws L Age 23

YEAR	TEAM	LGE	IP	H	ER	HR	BB	K	ERA	W	L	H/9	HR/9	BB/9	K/9	KW	PERA	STUFF
2000	Sth Bend	Mid	96.3	92	47	5	50	60	4.39	6	5	8.6	0.5	4.7	5.6	0.6	4.21	11
2001	El Paso	Tex	169.0	169	98	19	88	114	5.22	8	11	9.0	1.0	4.7	6.1	0.6	6.18	6

Capuano has a good arm with a mixed track record. His strikeout rate was excellent this year, but he was nevertheless very hittable. He was inconsistent from start to start, and while working with Cresse may have been part of the problem, Capuano's stuff wasn't always there when he took the mound. In a system largely devoid of pitching prospects, there's a temptation to rush the ones you have up the ladder. Capuano really needs another year at Double-A.

Robert Ellis Throws R Age 31

YEAR	TEAM	LGE	IP	H	ER	HR	BB	K	ERA	W	L	H/9	HR/9	BB/9	K/9	KW	PERA	STUFF
1999	New Orln	PCL	158.0	179	105	26	60	70	5.98	7	11	10.2	1.5	3.4	4.0	0.6	7.28	-17
2000	Syracuse	Int	18.0	18	14	3	16	13	7.00	1	1	9.0	1.5	8.0	6.5	0.4	5.61	-34
2001	Tucson	PCL	25.0	28	13	2	6	8	4.68	1	2	10.1	0.7	2.2	2.9	0.7	4.45	-10
2001	Arizona	NL	89.0	100	52	10	30	33	5.26	4	6	10.1	1.0	3.0	3.3	0.6	5.83	-12

The Snakes messed around with this guy for four months and still managed to win the division. Ellis had been a mediocre—or simply bad—Triple-A pitcher for years before he lucked into a spot with Arizona last spring. For some reason, Brenly left him in the rotation for 17 starts despite mounting evidence that he couldn't do the job. With all of the pitchers who've done well in Triple-A without getting chances in the bigs, why on earth did Arizona waste so much time on Ellis?

Geraldo Guzman Throws R Age 29

YEAR	TEAM	LGE	IP	H	ER	HR	BB	K	ERA	W	L	H/9	HR/9	BB/9	K/9	KW	PERA	STUFF
2000	El Paso	Tex	50.7	49	26	3	26	31	4.62	3	3	8.7	0.5	4.6	5.5	0.6	4.59	-13
2000	Tucson	PCL	35.3	32	15	4	11	31	3.82	2	2	8.2	1.0	2.8	7.9	1.4	1.64	21
2000	Arizona	NL	63.0	62	29	7	18	46	4.14	4	3	8.9	1.0	2.6	6.6	1.3	4.81	10
2001	Tucson	PCL	93.0	97	52	11	38	54	5.03	4	6	9.4	1.1	3.7	5.2	0.7	5.76	-9

The Dominican carpenter didn't have his best stuff all year, although he posted decent numbers for Tucson. In August, Guzman was diagnosed with a torn ligament in his right elbow, leading to the dreaded ligament-replacement surgery. When healthy, Guzman throws hard with good control, getting ground balls and strikeouts; in other words, he's a pretty good fifth-starter candidate. Check back in 2003.

Randy Johnson Throws L Age 38

YEAR	TEAM	LGE	IP	H	ER	HR	BB	K	ERA	W	L	H/9	HR/9	BB/9	K/9	KW	PERA	STUFF
1999	Arizona	NL	273.0	215	88	28	59	328	2.90	21	9	7.1	0.9	1.9	10.8	2.8	2.56	47
2000	Arizona	NL	255.7	195	77	20	63	308	2.71	21	7	6.9	0.7	2.2	10.8	2.4	2.88	47
2001	Arizona	NL	243.7	181	70	16	63	299	2.59	20	7	6.7	0.6	2.3	11.0	2.4	2.61	49

The best pitcher in baseball. What Johnson has done at his age is remarkable, given that most pitchers in their late 30s answer to "Coach." He was more than two wins better than every pitcher in baseball except teammate Curt Schilling and the Twins' Joe Mays. He has an excellent chance to become the fourth pitcher in history with 4,000 strikeouts, assuming Roger Clemens gets there first. Johnson has made the four-year deal the Snakes gave him three years ago look like a brilliant move. He will be the most coveted 39-year-old in history after this season.

Byung-Hyun Kim Throws R Age 23

YEAR	TEAM	LGE	IP	H	ER	HR	BB	K	ERA	W	L	H/9	HR/9	BB/9	K/9	KW	PERA	STUFF
1999	El Paso	Tex	19.3	13	6	0	10	23	2.79	1	1	6.1	0.0	4.7	10.7	1.1	1.99	45
1999	Tucson	PCL	29.3	24	13	2	16	30	3.99	2	1	7.4	0.6	4.9	9.2	0.9	2.34	31
1999	Arizona	NL	27.0	22	12	2	17	28	4.00	2	1	7.3	0.7	5.7	9.3	0.8	4.44	21
2000	Arizona	NL	71.7	52	30	8	38	99	3.77	5	3	6.5	1.0	4.8	12.4	1.3	4.45	40
2001	Arizona	NL	88.3	75	39	8	39	91	3.97	6	4	7.6	0.8	4.0	9.3	1.2	2.87	22

Kim ranked second in Michael Wolverton's Adjusted Runs Prevented among major-league closers last year, behind the Rangers' Jeff Zimmerman and ahead of many higher-paid pitchers. He did tire badly in September and was horribly misused in the postseason; it remains to be seen what effect the overwork and lack of success will have on him mentally and physically. Kim's combination of unhittable stuff and improving control reminds observers of Dan Quisenberry; Kim throws harder than Quiz did and has an upside beyond even Quisenberry's career. He'll be considered with the Riveras and Hoffmans of the world by the end of the season, assuming his World Series experience hasn't ruined him.

Eric Knott Throws L Age 27

YEAR	TEAM	LGE	IP	H	ER	HR	BB	K	ERA	W	L	H/9	HR/9	BB/9	K/9	KW	PERA	STUFF
1999	El Paso	Tex	169.3	190	93	17	52	53	4.94	9	10	10.1	0.9	2.8	2.8	0.5	5.65	-12
2000	Tucson	PCL	43.3	52	20	0	9	15	5.82	2	3	10.8	1.7	1.9	3.1	0.8	6.72	-24
2001	El Paso	Tex	26.7	29	17	4	11	12	5.74	1	2	9.8	1.4	3.7	4.1	0.5	5.31	-31
2001	Tucson	PCL	73.3	81	34	7	10	27	4.17	4	4	9.9	0.9	1.2	3.3	1.4	4.52	-13

Knott bounced to Taiwan in 1999, returning to the Diamondbacks system a little more developed. His control and left-handedness are his best attributes and a rare combination among relievers in this organization. He has worked as a starter for most of his minor-league career, but he doesn't project as much more than a short reliever in the majors.

Mike Koplove Throws R Age 25

YEAR	TEAM	LGE	IP	H	ER	HR	BB	K	ERA	W	L	H/9	HR/9	BB/9	K/9	KW	PERA	STUFF
1999	Sth Bend	Mid	82.0	84	47	11	34	54	5.16	4	5	9.2	1.2	3.7	5.9	0.8	3.14	-4
2000	High Des	Cal	23.7	21	9	0	11	16	3.42	2	1	8.0	0.0	4.2	6.1	0.7	1.56	-1
2000	El Paso	Tex	45.7	43	21	3	20	31	4.14	3	2	8.5	0.6	3.9	6.1	0.8	5.38	-5
2001	El Paso	Tex	44.7	46	28	5	25	26	5.64	2	3	9.3	1.0	5.0	5.2	0.5	4.17	-22
2001	Tucson	PCL	21.3	20	10	1	12	15	4.22	1	1	8.4	0.4	5.1	6.3	0.6	2.82	-4
2001	Arizona	NL	9.7	8	5	1	8	11	4.66	0	1	7.4	0.9	7.4	10.2	0.7	6.16	8

A sidearmer with a hard-breaking slider, Koplove slipped onto the playoff roster for the first two rounds without making an appearance. His motion doesn't put much strain on his arm, so he's able to pitch in back-to-back games when it's needed. If the Snakes retool their major-league roster, Koplove will probably find a place in the bullpen this year. He could use a year of Triple-A to refine his control.

Sean Lawrence Throws L Age 31

YEAR	TEAM	LGE	IP	H	ER	HR	BB	K	ERA	W	L	H/9	HR/9	BB/9	K/9	KW	PERA	STUFF
1999	Vancouvr	PCL	42.7	44	27	5	25	25	5.70	2	3	9.3	1.1	5.3	5.3	0.5	6.75	-27
2001	Portland	PCL	36.0	32	15	1	17	28	3.75	2	2	8.0	0.3	4.3	7.0	0.8	5.06	-4
2001	Tucson	PCL	22.7	21	12	2	11	20	4.76	1	2	8.3	0.8	4.4	7.9	0.9	6.44	-7

Released from Portland early in the year after arm injuries ended his tenure in the Pirates' system, Lawrence found himself as a lefty specialist and short reliever with Tucson. His sweeping curve has largely returned, and his control seems to be better when he pitches in relief. He fanned half the left-handed batters he faced as a Sidewinder. In other words, Lawrence belonged on the World Series roster in Brohawn's stead.

Albie Lopez Throws R Age 30

YEAR	TEAM	LGE	IP	H	ER	HR	BB	K	ERA	W	L	H/9	HR/9	BB/9	K/9	KW	PERA	STUFF
1999	TampaBay	AL	65.0	67	33	7	20	37	4.57	3	4	9.3	1.0	2.8	5.1	0.9	4.80	-9
2000	TampaBay	AL	189.0	200	99	21	57	95	4.71	10	11	9.5	1.0	2.7	4.5	0.8	3.86	-3
2001	TampaBay	AL	131.3	141	73	15	49	64	5.00	7	8	9.7	1.0	3.4	4.4	0.7	5.76	-3
2001	Arizona	NL	77.0	75	36	8	21	55	4.21	5	4	8.8	0.9	2.5	6.4	1.3	3.91	15

(Albie Lopez *continued*)
Talent for talent, the Devil Rays took the Diamondbacks to school in the Lopez deal, getting top prospect Nick Bierbrodt in exchange for the free-agent-to-be. Given the Diamondbacks' situation, it's hard to blame them for making the deal: their core talent was old and declining, and the team's top two pitchers were both in the throes of incredible seasons. Bierbrodt might be ready to contribute this year, which would probably be too late. Lopez pitched well for the D'backs, so it's a win all around. One of the beneficiaries of the Braves' bizarre largesse this winter, he's pencilled in as their #4 starter this year.

Matt Mantei **Throws R** **Age 28**

YEAR	TEAM	LGE	IP	H	ER	HR	BB	K	ERA	W	L	H/9	HR/9	BB/9	K/9	KW	PERA	STUFF
1999	Florida	NL	35.7	27	16	4	21	45	4.04	2	2	6.8	1.0	5.3	11.4	1.1	2.59	23
1999	Arizona	NL	30.0	18	9	1	16	44	2.70	2	1	5.4	0.3	4.8	13.2	1.4	2.79	40
2000	Arizona	NL	44.3	36	21	4	29	47	4.26	3	2	7.3	0.8	5.9	9.5	0.8	4.27	8
2001	Arizona	NL	7.0	6	4	2	4	10	5.14	0	1	7.7	2.6	5.1	12.9	1.3	2.51	23

Mantei got hurt. In other news, air is made of nitrogen and oxygen, the sun rose in the east this morning, and the Berkeley city council opposed the bombing of Afghanistan. The Mantei deal is probably Joe Garagiola Jr.'s defining accomplishment, the move that made it clear to fans that he didn't understand the first thing about building a baseball team. Even if Mantei had been healthy all year, couldn't Arizona have used a third starter like Brad Penny in the playoffs?

Mike Mohler **Throws L** **Age 33**

YEAR	TEAM	LGE	IP	H	ER	HR	BB	K	ERA	W	L	H/9	HR/9	BB/9	K/9	KW	PERA	STUFF
1999	Memphis	PCL	16.0	14	5	0	6	11	2.81	1	1	7.9	0.0	3.4	6.2	0.9	3.29	0
1999	St Louis	NL	49.7	49	23	3	19	28	4.17	3	3	8.9	0.5	3.4	5.1	0.7	4.32	-8
2000	St Louis	NL	21.0	22	12	1	12	7	5.14	1	1	9.4	0.4	5.1	3.0	0.3	8.55	-33
2000	Sacramen	PCL	17.7	24	28	8	17	10	14.26	0	2	12.2	4.1	8.7	5.1	0.3	7.07	-73
2001	Tucson	PCL	47.3	47	24	5	18	30	4.56	2	3	8.9	1.0	3.4	5.7	0.8	6.02	-16
2001	Arizona	NL	12.7	15	11	3	8	6	7.82	0	1	10.7	2.1	5.7	4.3	0.4	7.06	-36

The Snakes had problems with left-handed relief all season, and this is how desperate they got. Mohler wasn't even pitching well in Triple-A, surrendering 28 runs in 45 1/3 innings there. More appalling is that when rosters expanded on September 1, the Diamondbacks recalled Mohler because he was on the 40-man roster, rather than designate him for assignment and bring up the superior Sean Lawrence. Brilliant.

Mike Morgan **Throws R** **Age 42**

YEAR	TEAM	LGE	IP	H	ER	HR	BB	K	ERA	W	L	H/9	HR/9	BB/9	K/9	KW	PERA	STUFF
1999	Texas	AL	149.0	169	88	21	40	60	5.32	7	10	10.2	1.3	2.4	3.6	0.8	5.70	-12
2000	Arizona	NL	107.7	113	53	9	33	50	4.43	6	6	9.4	0.8	2.8	4.2	0.8	4.36	-11
2001	Arizona	NL	38.7	38	18	2	15	19	4.19	2	2	8.8	0.5	3.5	4.4	0.6	4.63	-12

Morgan wants to pitch until he's 50, saying that his arm is still healthy and he has a new palm ball he has yet to introduce. One wonders what he's waiting for. Morgan hasn't been particularly effective in his swing-man role the last two years, and there's very little reason to continue to employ a pitcher his age when equal or better arms are available for free elsewhere. Then again, there's always Tampa Bay.

John Patterson **Throws R** **Age 24**

YEAR	TEAM	LGE	IP	H	ER	HR	BB	K	ERA	W	L	H/9	HR/9	BB/9	K/9	KW	PERA	STUFF
1999	El Paso	Tex	100.7	104	69	21	46	84	6.17	4	7	9.3	1.9	4.1	7.5	0.9	5.18	18
1999	Tucson	PCL	34.7	34	19	3	19	22	4.93	2	2	8.8	0.8	4.9	5.7	0.6	6.61	4
2000	Tucson	PCL	16.7	17	9	1	9	8	4.86	1	1	9.2	0.5	4.9	4.3	0.4	7.36	-4
2001	El Paso	Tex	26.3	29	16	3	11	12	5.47	1	2	9.9	1.0	3.8	4.1	0.5	5.58	-8
2001	Tucson	PCL	69.0	77	47	10	35	28	6.13	3	5	10.0	1.3	4.6	3.7	0.4	6.38	-14

Patterson came back quickly from the Tommy John surgery he had in April of 2000, so his struggles as he climbed the ladder shouldn't be a surprise. He was inconsistent, he tired easily, and he didn't always bring his money pitch—a big, looping curveball—to the park. His velocity was down 5–6 mph as well. None of this is unexpected for a pitcher in his first year back from ligament-replacement surgery; 2002 will be the test. It's way too early to give up on him.

Beltran Perez **Throws R** **Age 20**

YEAR	TEAM	LGE	IP	H	ER	HR	BB	K	ERA	W	L	H/9	HR/9	BB/9	K/9	KW	PERA	STUFF
2001	Sth Bend	Mid	157.3	167	86	21	46	90	4.92	8	9	9.6	1.2	2.6	5.1	1.0	4.32	14

The Diamondbacks' Minor League Pitcher of the Year, Beltran went from "good arm" to "top prospect" in 2001, a change the coaches attribute to the work he did on speeding up his game. Perez's stuff is electric, and his control improved dramatically in 2001, leading him to make short work of the Midwest League. He probably should have been promoted to the California League in July, but the Snakes are likely to just bump him to Double-A this year instead. Watch him

Bret Prinz **Throws R** **Age 25**

YEAR	TEAM	LGE	IP	H	ER	HR	BB	K	ERA	W	L	H/9	HR/9	BB/9	K/9	KW	PERA	STUFF
1999	Sth Bend	Mid	131.0	164	120	35	61	54	8.24	3	12	11.3	2.4	4.2	3.7	0.4	6.78	-23
2000	El Paso	Tex	64.3	65	32	9	17	46	4.48	4	3	9.1	1.3	2.4	6.4	1.4	3.52	0
2001	Arizona	NL	37.3	38	20	3	17	22	4.82	2	2	9.2	0.7	4.1	5.3	0.6	2.79	-8

Briefly considered the closer before Kim smacked some sense into everyone, Prinz nonetheless had a strong rookie season. However, he got hurt at the wrong time, suffering from rotator-cuff tendinitis just as Kim started his September swoon. An MRI showed no structural damage, so if that diagnosis holds, Prinz should give Arizona a second reliable reliever in 2002.

Armando Reynoso **Throws R** **Age 36**

YEAR	TEAM	LGE	IP	H	ER	HR	BB	K	ERA	W	L	H/9	HR/9	BB/9	K/9	KW	PERA	STUFF
1999	Arizona	NL	168.0	183	93	18	56	71	4.98	9	10	9.8	1.0	3.0	3.8	0.6	4.35	-5
2000	Arizona	NL	171.7	186	89	19	43	79	4.67	9	10	9.8	1.0	2.3	4.1	0.9	4.82	-1
2001	Arizona	NL	44.3	57	37	11	12	12	7.51	1	4	11.6	2.2	2.4	2.4	0.5	6.03	-24

After establishing a career high with two consecutive years in which he threw more than 100 innings, Reynoso hurt his shoulder early in 2001 and missed the rest of the season. Gambling on a pitcher such as Reynoso, who has had periods of effectiveness when healthy, isn't necessarily a bad idea; signing him to a two-year deal with an option for a third year is. When the D'backs complain about their financial woes, the press needs to trot out every one of these stupid signings as its rebuttal.

Erik Sabel **Throws R** **Age 27**

YEAR	TEAM	LGE	IP	H	ER	HR	BB	K	ERA	W	L	H/9	HR/9	BB/9	K/9	KW	PERA	STUFF
1999	Tucson	PCL	74.3	79	36	4	26	28	4.36	4	4	9.6	0.5	3.1	3.4	0.5	4.03	-11
2000	Tucson	PCL	108.3	128	75	21	33	43	6.23	4	8	10.6	1.7	2.7	3.6	0.7	8.15	-29
2001	Tucson	PCL	38.0	39	18	4	9	20	4.26	2	2	9.2	0.9	2.1	4.7	1.1	3.44	-9
2001	Arizona	NL	49.0	55	27	7	11	20	4.96	2	3	10.1	1.3	2.0	3.7	0.9	4.46	-17

He finally had his first effective stretch in Triple-A in his third year at that level, so the Diamondbacks continued their revolving-door bullpen policy and gave Sabel a chance to have his head handed to him. Sabel is a step above the Robert Ellises of the world; he's younger, he has better control, and he can generate ground balls when he has his command. He's a worthwhile project at the back of the bullpen, not the solution to the Snakes' real relief problem.

Curt Schilling **Throws R** **Age 35**

YEAR	TEAM	LGE	IP	H	ER	HR	BB	K	ERA	W	L	H/9	HR/9	BB/9	K/9	KW	PERA	STUFF
1999	Philadel	NL	178.0	174	81	23	37	137	4.10	11	9	8.8	1.2	1.9	6.9	1.9	3.34	20
2000	Philadel	NL	114.0	113	54	15	26	85	4.26	7	6	8.9	1.2	2.1	6.7	1.6	3.50	17
2000	Arizona	NL	98.7	97	38	9	11	64	3.47	7	4	8.8	0.8	1.0	5.8	2.9	3.38	18
2001	Arizona	NL	250.7	228	96	31	35	236	3.45	18	10	8.2	1.1	1.3	8.5	3.4	2.95	32

It's hard to believe that all the abuse Schilling suffered at the hands of Terry Francona in Philadelphia hasn't had any ill effects on him, but it's clear that that's the case. After a decade of effectiveness between injuries, Schilling has been healthy for most of the last five years and is coming off of a year in which he was the second-best starting pitcher in baseball. That success is not likely to last, given his history, so it's hard to blame the Diamondbacks for looking at 2001 as a one-shot deal.

Greg Swindell Throws R Age 37

YEAR	TEAM	LGE	IP	H	ER	HR	BB	K	ERA	W	L	H/9	HR/9	BB/9	K/9	KW	PERA	STUFF
1999	Arizona	NL	63.0	62	30	7	18	46	4.29	4	3	8.9	1.0	2.6	6.6	1.3	2.37	2
2000	Arizona	NL	77.0	72	30	6	16	57	3.51	6	3	8.4	0.7	1.9	6.7	1.8	3.08	7
2001	Arizona	NL	50.0	54	29	10	7	34	5.22	3	3	9.7	1.8	1.3	6.1	2.4	4.42	-4

Although Swindell turned in another decent relief season, there was enough slippage in his peripherals to give us some concern. He gave up 12 home runs in just 53 1/3 innings, his worst ratio since becoming a full-time reliever in 1997. He was more hittable and saw his strikeout rate dip slightly. Unfortunately for Arizona, before last season they signed Swindell through 2003, a really spacey move to make with a 36-year-old middle reliever. He could reach the cliff at any moment.

Brandon Webb Throws R Age 23

YEAR	TEAM	LGE	IP	H	ER	HR	BB	K	ERA	W	L	H/9	HR/9	BB/9	K/9	KW	PERA	STUFF
2000	Sth Bend	Mid	15.7	14	7	0	10	10	4.02	1	1	8.0	0.0	5.7	5.7	0.5	5.12	-4
2001	Lancastr	Cal	168.3	176	86	16	56	83	4.60	9	10	9.4	0.9	3.0	4.4	0.7	5.35	1

Lancaster's staff this year didn't feature much consistency in either its composition or in the performances of its pitchers. Webb was the staff's main season-long member. He showed good movement on his pitches along with some remaining problems controlling them. Andrew Good had a good first half with Lancaster, then struggled at Double-A. June draftees Brandon Medders and James Bellflower joined Webb in the second half, with Bellflower competing with Webb for the "best stuff" label. One or two of these guys will survive the move to Double-A and become prospects.

Bobby Witt Throws R Age 38

YEAR	TEAM	LGE	IP	H	ER	HR	BB	K	ERA	W	L	H/9	HR/9	BB/9	K/9	KW	PERA	STUFF
1999	TampaBay	AL	191.7	193	102	20	80	122	4.79	10	11	9.1	0.9	3.8	5.7	0.8	5.54	3
2000	Clevelnd	AL	18.0	22	12	3	5	6	6.00	1	1	11.0	1.5	2.5	3.0	0.6	6.17	-24
2001	Tucson	PCL	21.0	21	11	1	10	11	4.71	1	1	9.0	0.4	4.3	4.7	0.6	4.81	-9
2001	Arizona	NL	39.3	41	25	5	22	25	5.72	2	2	9.4	1.1	5.0	5.7			

In the little time Witt spent on the mound, he was right around replacement level. Aside from Guzman, who was hurt, the Snakes had one of the worst Triple-A rotations you'll see, so Witt's performance was the best they were going to get from the system. The resurrection of Bobby Witt is used to support the contention that there are too many teams and not enough pitching, but it really just demonstrates that some teams are incredibly lazy when it comes to scouting talent beyond the All-Stars.

Atlanta Braves

Did anything really change for the Braves in 2001? After all, it was just another year, another seemingly effortless glide into the postseason, another total defeat of Shermanesque proportions for Atlanta, followed by yet another grumpy assertion that the South will, indeed, rise again.

This rehash belies the fact that these aren't the Terry Pendleton miracle Braves of '91, or the Dynasty Braves of the late '90s. For ten years, you could argue that John Schuerholz had simply glommed onto the successful organization built by Bobby Cox and Paul Snyder. He didn't draft Chipper Jones or Tom Glavine, he didn't trade for John Smoltz, and if it hadn't been for the Tribune Corporation's ham-handed dopiness, he might not have landed Greg Maddux.

Baseball Prospectus 2001 pointed out that it's an open question whether Schuerholz's acquisitions at the major-league level have done the Braves any good. Charged with the mission of cementing the Braves' annual drive toward postseason glory by adding talent to the team's core (which was assembled through the Braves player-development program under Cox and Snyder and now under Roy Clark), Schuerholz has generally come up short. He's given big-money multi-year contracts to Brian Jordan and John Smoltz. Trading Denny Neagle, Michael Tucker, and Rob Bell for Bret Boone flopped. Dealing Boone and Ryan Klesko for Quilvio Veras, Wally Joyner, and Reggie Sanders created the team's subsequent hole in left field that B.J. Surhoff was never going to be able to plug. Stretch-drive deals such as coughing up Bruce Chen to get two months from a fourth starter like Andy Ashby, or taking on a couple extra years of Surhoff's contract, were disasters that cost the Braves playing time, talent, and cash beyond all reason. Reacquiring Terry Pendleton in 1996 was perhaps the nadir of all Braves moves, reflecting a poverty of ideas that few management teams deserve to outlive.

Amid this litany of bad decision-making, there are two deals that need to be remembered above the others, because of what they say about analysis and potentially about the Braves.

> **Braves Prospectus**
>
> **2001 record:** 88–74; First place, NL East; Lost to Diamondbacks in Championship Series, 4–1
>
> **Pythagenport W/L:** 90–72
>
> **Runs scored:** 729 (13th in NL)
>
> **Runs allowed:** 643 (first in NL)
>
> **Team EqA:** .256 (11th in NL)
>
> **2001 batters age:** 29.9 (seventh-oldest in NL)
>
> **2001 pitchers age:** 31.2 (second-oldest in NL)
>
> **Ballpark:** Turner Field; slight pitchers' park; Park Factor of .982
>
> **2001:** They squeaked into the playoffs with their worst team since 1990.
>
> **2002:** Five through eight: Brian Jordan, Vinny Castilla, Javy Lopez, Wes Helms. It might be a good time to be a Mets fan.

First, there's the Jermaine Dye deal. Having made the mistake of sticking with Mark Lemke about two years past his expiration date, Schuerholz attempted to patch the hole at second base by trading Dye to the Royals to bring in Keith Lockhart and Michael Tucker. At the time, the deal was interpreted as a good move for the Braves. Tucker looked like a better prospect than Dye, and Lockhart was pretty useful in his own right. Imagine everyone's surprise when Dye exploded into a significantly better player than was expected by most projection tools or sabermetric analysis, while Tucker remained merely a decent fourth outfielder, and Lockhart remained the kind of player who can be hustled up on waivers. The scouts who had Dye pegged definitely look good in hindsight. Similarly, when Ryan Klesko went to the Padres, he did not look like the player he subsequently became. Surprising everybody, Klesko got into shape and became much better than expected; initially it just looked like the Braves were giving up a chunky, slow left fielder under contract for two years, but he became a better five-year investment for the Padres than Brian Jordan can ever be for the Braves. If there's a question to be asked, it's why no Braves' hitters find themselves having the sort of mid-career renaissances enjoyed by Dye and Klesko.

While losing Dye and Klesko cost the Braves the corner outfielders they so desperately needed in 2000 and 2001, what about the pitching deals? Consider the trades of Rob Bell and Bruce Chen. In both cases, the Braves were rightly criticized for surrendering high-upside talent for adequate veterans, but both pitchers turned into disappointments who first angered and then alienated their new pitching coaches. Coincidence? Among the other pitchers Schuerholz has traded, Ruben Quevedo's bulk is a source of concern, and the small print on Jason Schmidt's warning label turned out to be prophetic.

Perhaps it has been too easy to criticize Schuerholz. It's important to remember that several of his moves have turned out significantly better than expected. He got rid of

Marquis Grissom right when Grissom's value was at its highest and when he was about to become expensive. While the acquisitions of Ashby and Surhoff look bad, Schuerholz's other stretch-drive pickups include Alejandro Pena in 1991, Fred McGriff in 1993, Denny Neagle in 1996, and Jose Hernandez and Terry Mulholland in 1999. He has reason to feel good about the free-agent signings of Terry Pendleton in 1991 and Andres Galarraga in 1998. Reggie Sanders was a reasonable risk going into 2000, no less sensible a pickup than when the Diamondbacks' Joe Garagiola Jr. signed him for 2001.

Are these good moves a function of genius, or of opportunity? Evaluating Schuerholz fairly requires not only judging him in terms of his failures, but also in the much more difficult terms of his twin responsibilities to the Braves' present and future. Remember, being the Braves GM entails a far greater responsibility than being the GM for a team that gets to strip itself down and rebuild from scratch. The Braves have to blend constant success with relatively constant change, and Schuerholz's defenders can reasonably point out that he achieves that balance every year.

Schuerholz has had to confront this challenge before, in his previous incarnation as a Royals general manager. Schuerholz's tenure in Kansas City is usually remembered for its lone success, the World Series victory of 1985. More critically, it was characterized by Schuerholz's spectacular failure to balance the requirements of the present with the Royals' future. Indeed, 1985 might have taught Schuerholz the dangerous lesson that as long as you have enough pitching, you can get by with guys like Willie Wilson and Darryl Motley playing regularly in the outfield. In trying to wring another championship out of the George Brett Royals, Schuerholz would waste time and money bringing in people like Bill Buckner, Pat Tabler, and Gerald Perry, playing Frank White years beyond the useful portion of his career, and trying to get by with the likes of Angel Salazar.

What's troubling is that those decisions have analogues in Schuerholz's history with the Braves, whether it was being stubborn about Mark Lemke's usefulness, trying to get by with Rico Brogna and Wally Joyner and B.J. Surhoff in key offensive roles, or trading for Rey Sanchez in 2001. The dead hand of history stretches into this winter. Thinking back on Schuerholz's failures with the Royals, it isn't hard to understand the decision to give John Smoltz an awful lot of money, apparently to be a closer. Remember how Mark Davis was supposed to propel the Royals past the Sandy Alderson/Tony LaRussa A's? The Royals treated the acquisition of Davis as their perfect foil for the invention of The Eck. Not only did it fail, it missed the point of what separated the A's and the Royals, which was that Alderson fielded a team that was superior in just about every phase of the game. The decision to overpay Smoltz also represents a failure to appreciate the success the Braves have had in assembling useful, cost-effective bullpens built from homegrown pitchers.

Missing from Schuerholz's present is a signature error of the kind that ruined his Royals past. In 1987, Schuerholz made what is arguably the worst trade in the last 20 years—David Cone for Ed Hearn—a mistake borne of desperation. It is to Schuerholz's credit that so far he has not made such a mistake in Atlanta, and that is the fundamental difference between the Schuerholz Royals and the Schuerholz Braves.

Success breeds confidence, and the Braves have been nothing if not successful during their decade-long run of divisional dominance. Is that confidence justified? The Braves, like the Yankees, have the advantage of competing in their league's weakest division. They can't guarantee that Ed Wade will continue to spend money badly or that Steve Phillips will be stuck with Todd Zeile and Rey Ordonez and the Fantabulous No-Hit Outfield forever, but there's no reason to believe either of them, or the Expos, are a threat to the Braves dynasty. The main competition within the division should be the Marlins. Having just reached the point of being dangerous, though, they're being threatened with extinction and have already been abandoned by their architect, Dave Dombrowski.

Having lousy competition, a young offensive core, and good starting pitching is not enough, however. The Braves were lucky to get out of the first round of the 2001 playoffs, beating an Astros team whose pitching staff was a collection of walking wounded, handicapped all the more by Larry Dierker's decision to get a little too cute.

Unfortunately, the Braves' freedom of action is severely limited in the wake of the decision to give John Smoltz an eight-figure salary. If they stick to their budget of $90 million, there is practically no money left to spend filling the hole at first base. The decision to waste money on Vinny Castilla, exactly the kind of player this team didn't need, further hampers an offense that has been the Braves' biggest problem in recent years. In the long term, young talent such as Wilson Betemit or Kelly Johnson will eventually plug one hole by taking over at third base, but there's nobody in the system likely to make a significant impact on the Braves' lineup in 2002.

So the Braves will have to once again rely on their rotation. Greg Maddux is Greg Maddux and doesn't seem likely to slip any time soon. Behind him, there are reasons for concern. Tom Glavine and Kevin Millwood have been less than reliable over the last three years. John Burkett, 2001's big surprise, has moved on to Boston. John Smoltz might be able to start, but if he does, it isn't hard to envision a Bret Saberhagen-like "20 starts and out" kind of year. Jason Marquis has proven himself, and Odalis Perez should be able to step in, but there are ongoing rumors that Marquis might be dealt for offensive help. With the talent deeper down in the farm system and the number of starters who might be useful in 2002, it sounds like a workable proposition. Is it?

Any decision to trade Jason Marquis should set off alarm bells. There are too many warning signs among the established starters, and the wave of young talent in the organization does not look ready to break through in 2002. There's a very real danger that the 2002 and 2003 Braves will resemble the late-'80s Royals in another respect: as pitchers such as Bret Saberhagen and Mark Gubicza started breaking down, youngsters such as Kevin Appier and Tom Gordon were good, but not good enough to make up the difference. That was pretty much the cue for John Schuerholz to skip town. The question is whether he'll choose a similarly suitable moment to launch his retirement and make room for Frank Wren at the top, or whether he'll take an active part in helping shape what should be another good decade for the organization.

The Braves understand better than most organizations that there is no such thing as a pitching prospect. There is pitching talent, and the only way to measure that is in depth. They've had the usual litany of breakdowns, but if guys such as Matt Belisle, Matt McClendon, Derrick Lewis, Horacio Ramirez, and Christian Parra break down, is that a sign that the Braves are doing something wrong? No. The organization monitors its young pitchers closely, starting them at 80-85 pitches at the beginning of the season, never having them top 120, and rarely letting them top 110. In keeping with what has worked at the major-league level, all Braves farmhands throw live batting practice one day between starts. Relievers never throw more than two days in a row.

The next year or two represent a fragile time, but there's the right kind of young pitching depth and premium offensive talent under 30 to fire up a new period of Braves dominance. The challenge for John Schuerholz, as always, will be to balance the needs of the present against those of the future. The question is whether personal ambition to win now will take precedence over that need for balance.

HITTERS (BA: .270, OBP: .340, SLG: .440, EqA: .260)

Paul Bako C Bats L Age 30

YEAR	TEAM	LGE	AB	H	DB	TP	HR	BB	SO	R	RBI	SB	CS	OUT	BA	OBP	SLG	EQA	EQR	DEFENSE
1999	Houston	NL	217	56	15	1	2	23	53	16	17	1	1	162	.258	.329	.364	.236	22	61-C 3
2000	Florida	NL	163	41	6	1	0	20	44	10	14	0	0	122	.252	.336	.301	.225	15	48-C 1
2000	Atlanta	NL	59	11	5	0	2	4	14	8	6	0	0	48	.186	.238	.373	.201	4	17-C 0
2001	Atlanta	NL	138	31	11	1	2	19	29	20	16	1	0	107	.225	.318	.362	.234	14	44-C 0
2002	*Atlanta*	*NL*	*234*	*54*	*13*	*1*	*3*	*32*	*59*	*20*	*20*	*1*	*0*	*180*	*.231*	*.323*	*.333*	*.230*	*23*	

"Bits" is your basic good backup to a slugging right-handed-hitting catcher with a few defensive limitations. In other words, he's a great guy to have when Javy Lopez is your regular starter. Lopez's return to Atlanta should guarantee another year of employment for Bako, catching Greg Maddux every fifth game.

Wilson Betemit SS Bats B Age 20

YEAR	TEAM	LGE	AB	H	DB	TP	HR	BB	SO	R	RBI	SB	CS	OUT	BA	OBP	SLG	EQA	EQR	DEFENSE
1999	Danville	App	260	55	10	1	2	13	71	19	25	2	2	207	.212	.250	.281	.182	15	67-SS -11
2000	Jamestwn	NYP	277	66	9	1	4	17	43	36	22	1	2	213	.238	.283	.321	.204	20	68-SS -18
2001	Myrtle B	Car	333	83	14	1	7	21	71	35	37	6	4	253	.249	.295	.360	.221	29	83-SS -5
2001	Greenvil	Sou	183	55	8	0	5	8	35	18	15	4	2	130	.301	.332	.426	.252	21	45-SS -3
2002	*Atlanta*	*NL*	*464*	*126*	*19*	*1*	*13*	*35*	*103*	*58*	*62*	*3*	*1*	*339*	*.272*	*.323*	*.401*	*.247*	*51*	

Betemit is the organization's lone hitting prospect above A ball. While there's some concern that he doesn't have a great left-handed stroke, keep in mind that he only started switch-hitting in 1998. He was named the best defensive shortstop in the Carolina League, with his chief asset being a great arm. Some scouts have speculated he'll outgrow shortstop, but the Braves are better off leaving him there until he proves he can't handle it. If there's an area of concern, it's that Betemit doesn't walk enough. He's likely to improve, but it's not guaranteed.

Ken Caminiti 3B/1B Bats B Age 39

YEAR	TEAM	LGE	AB	H	DB	TP	HR	BB	SO	R	RBI	SB	CS	OUT	BA	OBP	SLG	EQA	EQR	DEFENSE	
1999	Houston	NL	275	79	12	1	13	42	54	45	54	5	2	198	.287	.387	.480	.290	45	70-3B -5	
2000	Houston	NL	206	60	11	0	14	39	34	39	40	3	0	146	.291	.406	.549	.314	40	49-3B -7	
2001	Texas	AL	185	45	8	1	10	23	35	26	26	0	0	140	.243	.332	.459	.261	24	49-3B -1	
2001	Atlanta	NL	172	40	8	0	7	20	37	13	17	0	1	133	.233	.313	.401	.237	18	30-1B -7	13-3B -1
2002	*Atlanta*	*NL*	*333*	*75*	*15*	*1*	*16*	*47*	*70*	*47*	*53*	*3*	*1*	*259*	*.225*	*.321*	*.420*	*.252*	*41*		

One of the baseball industry's unhappiest blind spots is how it treats people with problems. A quick review of what's known publicly makes it pretty clear that Ken Caminiti is a mess and needs help. Will he get it, or will this be another situation where people expect that he's rich enough to get his own help? Let's just hope he gets his life straightened out.

Ramon Castro SS Bats R Age 22

YEAR	TEAM	LGE	AB	H	DB	TP	HR	BB	SO	R	RBI	SB	CS	OUT	BA	OBP	SLG	EQA	EQR	DEFENSE	
1999	Macon	SAL	356	71	8	2	2	17	58	21	22	6	3	288	.199	.238	.250	.171	17	37-2B -3	24-SS -1
2000	Myrtle B	Car	402	93	16	2	5	31	77	43	36	7	4	313	.231	.296	.318	.212	32	91-SS 3	11-2B -1
2001	Greenvil	Sou	262	67	16	3	5	19	55	29	24	3	5	200	.256	.318	.397	.236	27	59-SS -5	
2001	Richmond	Int	136	29	8	2	1	7	28	14	14	1	2	109	.213	.255	.324	.193	9	27-SS 3	
2002	*Atlanta*	*NL*	*389*	*97*	*18*	*3*	*9*	*36*	*84*	*41*	*41*	*8*	*6*	*298*	*.249*	*.313*	*.380*	*.236*	*40*		

Signed out of Venezuela in 1997, Castro was a starter on both the Double-A and Southern League All-Star teams, but he still hasn't shown up on any prospect lists. He gets good marks for his work ethic, and given his age, he's a good bet to have a career in the same way Alvaro Espinoza and Ricky Gutierrez had careers. He just needs to land on the right team at the right time, because he'll end up being good enough to hold the job for three or four years.

Mark DeRosa SS Bats R Age 27

YEAR	TEAM	LGE	AB	H	DB	TP	HR	BB	SO	R	RBI	SB	CS	OUT	BA	OBP	SLG	EQA	EQR	DEFENSE	
1999	Richmond	Int	363	91	14	1	1	15	46	34	33	5	5	277	.251	.287	.303	.201	25	94-SS -6	
2000	Richmond	Int	371	102	20	2	3	32	35	55	30	10	4	272	.275	.336	.364	.241	39	88-SS 1	
2001	Richmond	Int	189	54	10	0	4	16	20	29	17	6	3	138	.286	.344	.402	.252	22	24-SS 1	18-3B -1
2001	Atlanta	NL	165	50	6	0	4	11	16	28	22	2	1	116	.303	.361	.412	.262	20	38-SS 3	
2002	*Atlanta*	*NL*	*348*	*95*	*17*	*1*	*5*	*32*	*39*	*50*	*37*	*11*	*4*	*257*	*.273*	*.334*	*.371*	*.246*	*39*		

DeRosa's window of opportunity for a full-time career with the Braves borders on nonexistent. He has a pair of younger players (Marcus Giles and Rafael Furcal) already ahead of him, and guys such as Betemit and Kelly Johnson coming up behind him. If Furcal isn't 100% in camp, DeRosa could get real playing time in April and May, but it's more likely that he'll settle into a role as one of the better utility infielders in the game.

Julio Franco AARP Bats R Age 40

YEAR	TEAM	LGE	AB	H	DB	TP	HR	BB	SO	R	RBI	SB	CS	OUT	BA	OBP	SLG	EQA	EQR	DEFENSE
2001	MexCty	Mex	396	126	25	4	10	34	75	59	55	10	5	275	.318	.376	.477	.284	59	
2001	Atlanta	NL	90	28	4	0	3	10	17	14	11	0	0	62	.311	.385	.456	.283	13	22-1B -1
2002	*Atlanta*	*NL*	*90*	*23*	*3*	*0*	*2*	*13*	*18*	*10*	*9*	*0*	*0*	*67*	*.256*	*.350*	*.356*	*.248*	*10*	

So you're a perennial contender with a problem. Rico Brogna was a victim of catastrophic career-ending ossification, and Sid Bream's dried remains have long since disappeared into the voracious Asian black market for aphrodisiacs. If you're John Schuerholz, who you gonna call? Mexico City, apparently. Franco isn't 40. He also isn't 50, and if he can do this well in a pinch, he could put past geezer gimmicks such as Satchel Paige, Minnie Minoso, and Pete Rose to shame.

Rafael Furcal SS Bats B Age 21

YEAR	TEAM	LGE	AB	H	DB	TP	HR	BB	SO	R	RBI	SB	CS	OUT	BA	OBP	SLG	EQA	EQR	DEFENSE	
1999	Macon	SAL	345	90	8	1	1	30	38	43	20	34	15	269	.261	.324	.299	.224	32	74-SS -12	
1999	Myrtle B	Car	190	50	8	2	0	10	42	24	9	14	6	146	.263	.300	.326	.219	16	38-SS 6	
2000	Atlanta	NL	458	133	21	3	4	66	73	83	35	37	14	339	.290	.383	.376	.268	63	97-SS -9	25-2B 1
2001	Atlanta	NL	326	94	13	0	6	22	47	40	32	23	6	238	.288	.335	.383	.250	37	79-SS 2	
2002	*Atlanta*	*NL*	*467*	*132*	*18*	*2*	*9*	*54*	*75*	*74*	*38*	*40*	*12*	*347*	*.283*	*.357*	*.388*	*.266*	*63*		

Furcal's shoulder injury probably goes back to December of 2000, when he hurt it in winter ball. Whether he'll still have his great arm when he gets back remains to be seen. Even if he doesn't, that's not necessarily the end of his career as a shortstop. If Ozzie Smith and Alan Trammell could compensate for their shoulder problems, Furcal is young enough to get the benefit of the doubt. He'll keep his small power spike while recovering his walks and retaining his steals, becoming the best shortstop in the league behind Rich Aurilia.

Marcus Giles 2B Bats R Age 24

YEAR	TEAM	LGE	AB	H	DB	TP	HR	BB	SO	R	RBI	SB	CS	OUT	BA	OBP	SLG	EQA	EQR	DEFENSE
1999	Myrtle B	Car	519	147	34	4	11	37	89	65	55	5	4	376	.283	.333	.428	.253	60	120-2B -9
2000	Greenvil	Sou	471	121	22	1	15	55	70	61	50	15	4	354	.257	.336	.403	.252	57	123-2B -4
2001	Richmond	Int	256	80	17	1	6	21	44	45	42	10	4	180	.313	.368	.457	.277	36	61-2B -2
2001	Atlanta	NL	245	67	10	2	9	27	31	37	32	2	5	183	.273	.346	.441	.257	31	57-2B 1
2002	*Atlanta*	*NL*	*506*	*148*	*26*	*3*	*16*	*66*	*84*	*75*	*60*	*14*	*7*	*365*	*.292*	*.374*	*.451*	*.282*	*77*	

As good as Furcal might grow up to be, Giles is a better bet to be an offensive star at his position for the next few years. To combat concerns that Giles wasn't going to be an adequate second baseman, the Braves had Glenn Hubbard, one of the great unheralded glove men at second base, work with him in 1998. As a result, Giles has gone from genuinely awful to adequate, with the chance to get better. His power and ability to drive the ball to all fields should make him an excellent addition to the heart of the order. For the people who have been waiting since we started touting him four years ago, it's all good from here on out.

Bernard Gilkey OF Bats R Age 35

YEAR	TEAM	LGE	AB	H	DB	TP	HR	BB	SO	R	RBI	SB	CS	OUT	BA	OBP	SLG	EQA	EQR	DEFENSE
1999	Arizona	NL	204	58	15	1	8	26	39	27	36	2	2	148	.284	.371	.485	.282	31	46-RF -3
2000	Arizona	NL	74	8	1	0	2	6	15	6	6	0	0	66	.108	.175	.203	.135	2	16-RF -1
2000	Boston	AL	90	21	6	1	1	9	11	11	9	0	0	69	.233	.324	.356	.233	9	20-RF -1
2001	Atlanta	NL	107	31	4	0	3	10	26	8	16	0	1	77	.290	.355	.411	.256	13	22-LF -3
2002	*Atlanta*	*NL*	*194*	*42*	*9*	*1*	*5*	*19*	*41*	*19*	*22*	*2*	*2*	*154*	*.216*	*.286*	*.351*	*.215*	*17*	

Gilkey has had flashes of usefulness in a platoon and spot-starter role. At his age, though, seasons like 2001 aren't good enough to make a team put up with his defensive limitations or his off-field distractions. The move of Chipper Jones to left field eliminates Gilkey's role with the Braves. He'll be elsewhere this year.

Nick Green 2B Bats R Age 23

YEAR	TEAM	LGE	AB	H	DB	TP	HR	BB	SO	R	RBI	SB	CS	OUT	BA	OBP	SLG	EQA	EQR	DEFENSE
1999	Jamestwn	NYP	280	60	8	0	7	16	73	31	24	5	3	223	.214	.260	.318	.197	19	72-2B -4
2000	Macon	SAL	344	67	14	2	7	14	80	32	27	4	3	280	.195	.231	.308	.182	20	83-SS -17
2000	Myrtle B	Car	95	21	4	0	1	7	23	11	5	2	1	75	.221	.284	.295	.202	7	13-SS -9
2001	Myrtle B	Car	315	77	15	1	9	27	70	44	37	6	2	240	.244	.310	.384	.235	32	69-2B -5
2002	*Atlanta*	*NL*	*399*	*97*	*15*	*1*	*12*	*35*	*101*	*55*	*40*	*12*	*3*	*305*	*.243*	*.304*	*.376*	*.235*	*41*	

A 1998 draft-and-follow, Green is one of a gaggle of good middle infielders in the organization. He is considered athletic enough to move back to shortstop if the situation warranted it, but with Furcal and Betemit around, that seems unlikely. His season ended early when he tore up his knee. Like everybody in the system not named Betemit or Kelly Johnson, he's hoping to grow up to be Mark DeRosa.

Wes Helms 3B/1B Bats R Age 26

YEAR	TEAM	LGE	AB	H	DB	TP	HR	BB	SO	R	RBI	SB	CS	OUT	BA	OBP	SLG	EQA	EQR	DEFENSE
1999	Greenvil	Sou	112	28	4	0	6	4	35	11	18	1	0	84	.250	.279	.446	.237	12	28-1B -1
2000	Richmond	Int	539	146	22	5	19	21	90	66	76	0	5	398	.271	.304	.436	.240	56	125-3B -10
2001	Atlanta	NL	217	51	10	4	10	20	47	30	38	1	1	167	.235	.302	.456	.247	25	51-1B -2
2002	*Atlanta*	*NL*	*427*	*115*	*20*	*5*	*19*	*31*	*91*	*51*	*68*	*2*	*3*	*315*	*.269*	*.319*	*.473*	*.261*	*55*	

By himself, Wes Helms is not a problem. If the Braves had a real first baseman and real corner outfielders, carrying a hitter such as Helms at third base and batting him seventh or eighth is not a real liability. For the next year or two, he'll hit for reasonable power, and by the time he's primed for some serious arbitration cash, either Wilson Betemit or Kelly Johnson should be ready to make him a Devil Ray.

Kelly Johnson SS Bats L Age 20

YEAR	TEAM	LGE	AB	H	DB	TP	HR	BB	SO	R	RBI	SB	CS	OUT	BA	OBP	SLG	EQA	EQR	DEFENSE
2001	Macon	SAL	442	100	14	1	15	53	118	53	44	12	4	346	.226	.315	.364	.234	46	110-SS -26
2002	*Atlanta*	*NL*	*420*	*101*	*11*	*1*	*18*	*59*	*121*	*56*	*52*	*15*	*4*	*323*	*.240*	*.334*	*.400*	*.256*	*53*	

Johnson's explosive development as a hitter fully justified Roy Clark's decision to draft him in the first round in 2000. He has a strong arm and good hands, so a move to third base seems like it would be a good fit. Johnson possesses a smooth swing, and he already has an idea of how to work the count. He's the Braves' second-best prospect behind Betemit.

Andruw Jones CF Bats R Age 25

YEAR	TEAM	LGE	AB	H	DB	TP	HR	BB	SO	R	RBI	SB	CS	OUT	BA	OBP	SLG	EQA	EQR	DEFENSE
1999	Atlanta	NL	594	161	35	5	26	69	95	94	79	20	12	445	.271	.355	.478	.274	88	162-CF 27
2000	Atlanta	NL	661	199	37	5	36	50	92	118	99	19	6	468	.301	.357	.536	.290	106	161-CF 19
2001	Atlanta	NL	628	166	26	2	35	53	120	109	108	11	4	466	.264	.324	.479	.263	83	161-CF 18
2002	*Atlanta*	*NL*	*576*	*171*	*33*	*3*	*29*	*62*	*106*	*101*	*85*	*20*	*7*	*412*	*.297*	*.365*	*.516*	*.294*	*96*	

The easy thing is to just blame Merv Rettenmund, because Andruw Jones was not supposed to give up his walks for a couple of years. Jones signed a six-year extension after the season, a contract that will run through his 30th birthday. It's not exactly a gamble for either party, although the deflating effect on other people's salaries probably got Jones scratched off of a few Christmas-card lists. He'll be fine, and he is still headed for superstardom.

Chipper Jones 3B/Wherever He Wants Bats B Age 30

YEAR	TEAM	LGE	AB	H	DB	TP	HR	BB	SO	R	RBI	SB	CS	OUT	BA	OBP	SLG	EQA	EQR	DEFENSE
1999	Atlanta	NL	567	179	33	1	47	119	87	112	105	22	3	391	.316	.436	.626	.343	134	150-3B -14
2000	Atlanta	NL	582	178	32	1	37	87	59	113	106	13	7	411	.306	.398	.555	.309	109	147-3B -3
2001	Atlanta	NL	575	196	33	6	38	95	70	117	104	9	10	389	.341	.436	.617	.334	126	140-3B -8
2002	*Atlanta*	*NL*	*534*	*173*	*31*	*4*	*32*	*91*	*69*	*98*	*90*	*14*	*8*	*369*	*.324*	*.422*	*.577*	*.328*	*114*	

Chipper Jones generally gets what Chipper Jones wants, and apparently being something less than a great third baseman makes him want to move to an easier defensive position. The decision may hurt how he's perceived historically, because right now he's having a Hall of Fame career at the hot corner. The question is whether he'll age well. Assuming Andruw Jones and Rafael Furcal bounce back, and Marcus Giles becomes as good as expected, Jones is likely to have better run and RBI totals in the next three years than he's had in the previous three. This will be cited as evidence that players peak in their early thirties, and/or that Jones is clutch. He's great enough to deserve whatever compliments come his way, even the wrong-headed ones.

Brian Jordan RF Bats R Age 35

YEAR	TEAM	LGE	AB	H	DB	TP	HR	BB	SO	R	RBI	SB	CS	OUT	BA	OBP	SLG	EQA	EQR	DEFENSE
1999	Atlanta	NL	579	162	26	4	24	44	75	97	110	11	8	425	.280	.340	.463	.264	76	138-RF -1
2000	Atlanta	NL	493	130	21	0	19	31	73	68	76	9	2	365	.264	.313	.422	.246	55	130-RF 5
2001	Atlanta	NL	562	172	33	3	25	29	75	85	99	3	2	392	.306	.345	.509	.278	80	140-RF 7
2002	*LosAngls*	*NL*	*505*	*135*	*23*	*2*	*21*	*44*	*75*	*81*	*88*	*8*	*3*	*373*	*.267*	*.326*	*.446*	*.265*	*67*	

Jordan just gave the Braves his first good perfomance in the third year of a five-year deal. That it came in the season they played without a first baseman or a left fielder meant that it was timed perfectly, but the Braves can't count on a repeat performance. Jordan can disappear against right-handed pitching for seasons at a time, and his age and past breakdowns are reasons to worry. He's still one of the great first-pitch hitters in the game.

Ryan Langerhans RF Bats L Age 22

YEAR	TEAM	LGE	AB	H	DB	TP	HR	BB	SO	R	RBI	SB	CS	OUT	BA	OBP	SLG	EQA	EQR	DEFENSE
1999	Macon	SAL	461	93	19	1	6	38	105	44	32	9	6	375	.202	.267	.286	.193	30	109-RF -6
2000	Myrtle B	Car	406	80	14	4	6	21	105	43	30	13	8	334	.197	.244	.296	.186	25	85-RF -8
2001	Myrtle B	Car	481	123	25	3	7	46	104	59	43	14	9	367	.256	.325	.364	.235	49	121-RF 2
2002	*Atlanta*	*NL*	*441*	*106*	*20*	*3*	*9*	*46*	*109*	*56*	*39*	*15*	*9*	*344*	*.240*	*.312*	*.361*	*.232*	*44*	

An outstanding fielder with a good arm, Langerhans scuffled in 2000. In some respects it was a lost season as he recovered from a really ugly beaning at the end of 1999. He made progress across the board in 2001 and might be the best outfield prospect in the organization. Naturally, you'd like to do better than developing the next Mike Kingery, and Langerhans is young enough to become something more.

Keith Lockhart PH/2B Bats L Age 37

YEAR	TEAM	LGE	AB	H	DB	TP	HR	BB	SO	R	RBI	SB	CS	OUT	BA	OBP	SLG	EQA	EQR	DEFENSE			
1999	Atlanta	NL	162	42	4	1	1	17	19	19	20	2	1	121	.259	.333	.315	.227	15	19-2B	2		
2000	Atlanta	NL	277	74	12	3	2	25	28	31	31	4	1	204	.267	.328	.354	.235	27	50-2B	1	13-3B	0
2001	Atlanta	NL	179	42	4	0	4	15	19	18	13	1	2	139	.235	.299	.324	.212	14	34-2B	-1		
2002	*Atlanta*	*NL*	*236*	*49*	*6*	*1*	*4*	*26*	*27*	*26*	*25*	*3*	*2*	*189*	*.208*	*.286*	*.292*	*.198*	*17*				

Lockhart has had a nice five-year run with the Braves as a spare part. There's no way to adequately quantify the value of a guy who is able to handle the difficulties of being a bench player and pinch hitter. It's impossible to consistently succeed in the role, and harder still to post numbers that impress people. Lockhart didn't stick in the majors until after his 30th birthday. Every minor-league free agent can think of him as they wonder if they can make it after six or eight years in the bushes.

George Lombard OF Bats L Age 26

YEAR	TEAM	LGE	AB	H	DB	TP	HR	BB	SO	R	RBI	SB	CS	OUT	BA	OBP	SLG	EQA	EQR	DEFENSE	
1999	Richmond	Int	234	45	10	2	6	29	92	20	23	16	5	194	.192	.287	.329	.219	22	59-LF	-4
2000	Richmond	Int	426	110	22	5	10	47	128	63	42	25	8	324	.258	.339	.404	.255	53	106-LF	-8
2000	Atlanta	NL	39	4	0	0	0	1	13	8	2	4	0	35	.103	.143	.103	.118	1		
2001	Richmond	Int	45	13	2	0	4	6	13	6	7	2	2	34	.289	.389	.600	.305	9	11-LF	0
2002	*Atlanta*	*NL*	*370*	*90*	*15*	*3*	*10*	*49*	*127*	*43*	*39*	*31*	*9*	*289*	*.243*	*.332*	*.381*	*.254*	*47*		

Even if you overlook the fragility that keeps him off the field, Lombard isn't really a prospect. He might be worth starting ahead of B.J. Surhoff, but that's setting the bar low enough to entertain a Ralph Garr comeback. Lombard could be a solid fourth outfielder, but defense isn't one of his strengths, so he's not about to seamlessly replace somebody like Dave Martinez.

Javy Lopez C Bats R Age 31

YEAR	TEAM	LGE	AB	H	DB	TP	HR	BB	SO	R	RBI	SB	CS	OUT	BA	OBP	SLG	EQA	EQR	DEFENSE	
1999	Atlanta	NL	247	77	18	1	11	17	38	34	42	0	3	173	.312	.363	.526	.285	38	56-C	-3
2000	Atlanta	NL	485	139	18	1	25	28	73	58	86	0	0	346	.287	.330	.482	.266	63	122-C	-5
2001	Atlanta	NL	440	123	16	1	18	26	70	47	69	1	0	317	.280	.331	.443	.257	53	116-C	-1
2002	*Atlanta*	*NL*	*449*	*130*	*17*	*1*	*20*	*36*	*76*	*54*	*71*	*0*	*1*	*320*	*.290*	*.342*	*.465*	*.270*	*61*		

Lopez's decision to sign a one-year, $6-million contract with the Braves was one of the first signs that last winter was going to be different for mid-level free agents. Granted, he's been declining steadily, but he was the best catcher on the market by far, and he came with all sorts of "winner" cachet. The Braves saved a bunch of money on the Javy Lopez and Andruw Jones deals; it's a shame they wasted the savings on junk like Vinny Castilla and Albie Lopez.

Pat Manning 2B/3B Bats R Age 22

YEAR	TEAM	LGE	AB	H	DB	TP	HR	BB	SO	R	RBI	SB	CS	OUT	BA	OBP	SLG	EQA	EQR	DEFENSE			
1999	Macon	SAL	174	35	10	1	2	10	44	17	12	1	1	140	.201	.250	.305	.188	11	38-SS	0		
2000	Macon	SAL	451	71	12	0	7	43	88	33	34	4	2	382	.157	.235	.231	.167	22	119-2B	0		
2001	Macon	SAL	225	50	9	1	8	28	49	29	19	3	1	176	.222	.315	.378	.236	24	35-2B	-2	19-3B	-2
2001	Myrtle B	Car	233	49	8	0	9	24	41	21	26	2	2	186	.210	.290	.361	.219	21	44-2B	-5	16-3B	0
2002	*Atlanta*	*NL*	*423*	*92*	*15*	*1*	*14*	*53*	*91*	*50*	*42*	*5*	*2*	*333*	*.217*	*.305*	*.357*	*.228*	*41*				

Manning didn't have the arm or range for shortstop, so he joins the organizational logjam at second base and third base. Although he was accused of getting overly pull-conscious last year, he did hit a total of 23 home runs, and he's drawn more than 60 walks in each of the last two years. He's young, so he's worth remembering.

Dave Martinez OF Bats L Age 37

YEAR	TEAM	LGE	AB	H	DB	TP	HR	BB	SO	R	RBI	SB	CS	OUT	BA	OBP	SLG	EQA	EQR	DEFENSE
1999	TampaBay	AL	510	151	24	5	7	55	67	78	65	13	6	365	.296	.370	.404	.265	66	128-RF -8
2000	TampaBay	AL	103	27	4	2	1	9	15	11	11	1	4	80	.262	.321	.369	.224	10	24-RF 1
2000	ChiCubs	NL	55	10	2	1	0	1	7	5	2	1	0	45	.182	.196	.255	.157	2	
2000	Texas	AL	117	32	3	1	2	13	18	13	11	2	1	86	.274	.351	.368	.248	13	30-RF 4
2000	Toronto	AL	177	56	10	1	2	22	25	28	21	4	2	123	.316	.395	.418	.279	25	47-RF 1
2001	Atlanta	NL	238	71	12	3	2	20	37	35	21	3	3	170	.298	.355	.399	.254	28	41-RF -6
2002	*Atlanta*	*NL*	*411*	*103*	*17*	*4*	*6*	*47*	*64*	*56*	*42*	*10*	*5*	*312*	*.251*	*.328*	*.355*	*.238*	*43*	

While Martinez is eminently well-suited for a backup role, he's no longer good enough to provide the Braves with an easy way to replace Surhoff. Given his past experience as a regular, Martinez is useful as a spot starter for Jordan and Andruw Jones against tough right-handers.

Eddie Perez C Bats R Age 34

YEAR	TEAM	LGE	AB	H	DB	TP	HR	BB	SO	R	RBI	SB	CS	OUT	BA	OBP	SLG	EQA	EQR	DEFENSE
1999	Atlanta	NL	311	78	11	0	9	13	37	29	30	0	1	234	.251	.294	.373	.222	27	81-C 1
2001	Greenvil	Sou	37	11	0	0	3	0	9	5	4	0	0	26	.297	.307	.541	.270	5	
2001	Atlanta	NL	10	3	0	0	0	0	2	0	0	0	0	7	.300	.300	.300	.203	1	
2002	*Atlanta*	*NL*	*235*	*56*	*7*	*0*	*9*	*11*	*40*	*21*	*27*	*0*	*1*	*180*	*.238*	*.272*	*.383*	*.216*	*20*	

Perez and Bako should be considered mutually exclusive, even given Bobby Cox's occasional taste for a third catcher. It might not matter: Perez has missed most of the past two seasons with right shoulder problems, undergoing two surgeries on his rotator cuff that have failed to repair the damage. If he can't throw, he can't play; he just doesn't bring anything else to the table.

Rey Sanchez SS Bats R Age 34

YEAR	TEAM	LGE	AB	H	DB	TP	HR	BB	SO	R	RBI	SB	CS	OUT	BA	OBP	SLG	EQA	EQR	DEFENSE
1999	KansasCy	AL	474	142	18	6	2	17	42	63	53	10	5	337	.300	.329	.376	.238	47	130-SS 24
2000	KansasCy	AL	504	139	18	2	1	22	48	64	36	7	3	368	.276	.311	.325	.219	41	133-SS 28
2001	KansasCy	AL	388	121	12	5	1	13	29	48	28	9	1	268	.312	.337	.376	.244	40	92-SS 34
2001	Atlanta	NL	155	38	4	1	0	3	13	11	10	2	0	117	.245	.259	.284	.187	9	44-SS 13
2002	*Atlanta*	*NL*	*501*	*131*	*17*	*4*	*3*	*27*	*45*	*62*	*43*	*10*	*2*	*372*	*.261*	*.299*	*.329*	*.217*	*41*	

How good was Rey Sanchez's defense last season? Insanely great, to the tune of 43 runs above average. That figure ties him for the second-best season of all-time with Everett Scott's 1921 and Honus Wagner's 1912. (Top honors go to Hughie Jennings's 1895 season, which was 46 runs above average.) Sanchez's year blows away any post-1950 performance:

1. Rey Sanchez, 2001 43
2t. Dave Concepcion, 1975 31
2t. Mark Belanger, 1975 31
4. Orlando Cabrera, 2001 29
5t. Roy McMillan, 1956 28
5t. Ron Hansen, 1963 28
5t. Dal Maxvill, 1969 28
5t. Mark Belanger, 1976 28
5t. Dave Concepcion, 1977 28
5t. Ozzie Smith, 1982 28
5t. Jose Uribe, 1989 28
5t. Rey Sanchez, 2000 28

Is Sanchez's figure legit? Clay Davenport played around with the team pitch/field splits (a factor not included in these ratings), and even a reasonable adjustment would still leave Sanchez in the upper 20s, which is where he's been the last two years. If there's one player who justifies being on the field for his defense, it's Sanchez.

B.J. Surhoff LF Bats L Age 37

YEAR	TEAM	LGE	AB	H	DB	TP	HR	BB	SO	R	RBI	SB	CS	OUT	BA	OBP	SLG	EQA	EQR	DEFENSE
1999	Baltimor	AL	672	217	33	2	32	37	69	105	109	5	1	456	.323	.360	.521	.288	101	148-LF 11
2000	Baltimor	AL	410	125	19	0	17	25	40	55	58	8	2	287	.305	.348	.476	.273	56	102-LF 4
2000	Atlanta	NL	129	37	10	2	1	10	11	13	11	3	0	92	.287	.342	.419	.259	16	28-LF -1
2001	Atlanta	NL	486	138	32	1	11	36	41	71	61	9	3	351	.284	.334	.422	.254	57	108-LF -2
2002	*Atlanta*	*NL*	*557*	*143*	*28*	*2*	*17*	*45*	*55*	*74*	*66*	*11*	*2*	*416*	*.257*	*.312*	*.406*	*.246*	*62*	

The sucking vortex of doom in left field worked its way down from Ryan Klesko to Ice Williams to Reggie Sanders to Surhoff. Details can be found in the dictionary under "entropy." Surhoff has saved his career once before, busting out for a great 1995 when it seemed like he was never going to escape a cycle of injuries and disappointing seasons. He's now seven years older and hasn't posted an OBP above .350 in six years. If not for his good 1999, he'd be wrestling with Orlando Merced for the tastiest non-roster invitations each winter.

Steve Torrealba C Bats R Age 24

YEAR	TEAM	LGE	AB	H	DB	TP	HR	BB	SO	R	RBI	SB	CS	OUT	BA	OBP	SLG	EQA	EQR	DEFENSE	
1999	Myrtle B	Car	181	36	4	0	6	8	47	19	18	1	0	145	.199	.237	.320	.188	11	47-C	-1
2000	Myrtle B	Car	348	84	8	0	8	21	80	36	29	3	1	265	.241	.285	.333	.211	27	90-C	-5
2001	Greenvil	Sou	298	69	12	0	8	25	53	31	28	0	0	220	.232	.282	.352	.210	25	81-C	-8
2002	*Atlanta*	*NL*	*367*	*91*	*10*	*0*	*11*	*32*	*80*	*45*	*38*	*3*	*0*	*276*	*.248*	*.308*	*.365*	*.232*	*36*		

You might have missed it, but Torrealba was on last year's postseason roster because of Javy Lopez's injuries. That's not too shabby for a guy who missed a month after fouling a pitch off of his knee. With Lopez and Bako both coming back, he'll hang out in Richmond and wait for injuries.

Travis Wilson 2B Bats R Age 24

YEAR	TEAM	LGE	AB	H	DB	TP	HR	BB	SO	R	RBI	SB	CS	OUT	BA	OBP	SLG	EQA	EQR	DEFENSE			
1999	Macon	SAL	364	87	14	2	7	7	70	42	40	6	5	282	.239	.266	.346	.204	27	70-2B	-7		
2000	Myrtle B	Car	496	122	26	3	11	8	112	51	49	3	6	380	.246	.264	.377	.209	38	119-2B	-2		
2001	Greenvil	Sou	122	33	4	1	2	2	24	10	16	1	3	92	.270	.285	.369	.212	9	23-2B	-2		
2001	Richmond	Int	383	90	23	2	3	9	75	34	36	3	2	295	.235	.258	.329	.197	25	42-LF	-7	33-2B	-4
2002	*Atlanta*	*NL*	*507*	*132*	*26*	*3*	*12*	*22*	*112*	*63*	*60*	*6*	*7*	*382*	*.260*	*.291*	*.394*	*.228*	*47*				

The official flavor of last spring's sensation was kiwi, as Bobby Cox took a shine to New Zealand's greatest fast-pitch softball player-turned-pro baseball project. The Braves think Wilson is a good enough athlete to play anywhere; he may not be a good enough hitter to play anywhere but Richmond. He is obviously raw, a work in progress, and until he learns to take a pitch, he will be nothing more than a curiosity.

A.J. Zapp 1B Bats L Age 24

YEAR	TEAM	LGE	AB	H	DB	TP	HR	BB	SO	R	RBI	SB	CS	OUT	BA	OBP	SLG	EQA	EQR	DEFENSE	
1999	Macon	SAL	438	79	16	1	13	29	172	41	40	2	1	360	.180	.236	.311	.186	27	114-1B	-8
2000	Myrtle B	Car	406	97	21	1	8	41	107	51	40	2	1	310	.239	.316	.355	.229	39	96-1B	-4
2001	Greenvil	Sou	294	60	11	0	7	16	85	29	27	3	1	235	.204	.252	.313	.193	19	72-1B	4
2002	*Atlanta*	*NL*	*399*	*93*	*16*	*1*	*11*	*36*	*129*	*46*	*41*	*4*	*1*	*307*	*.233*	*.297*	*.361*	*.225*	*37*		

Considered one of the organization's better hitting prospects ever since being picked in the first round in 1996, Zapp hasn't turned out well, in no small part because he keeps getting hurt. A broken hand slowed him in '98, while a back injury hampered him in 2001 before shutting him down. He needs a break in 2002 about as badly as Mr. Mister does.

PITCHERS (ERA: 4.50, H/9: 9.0, HR/9: 1.0, BB/9: 3.0, K/9: 6.0, KW: 2.0, PERA: 4.50)

Matt Belisle Throws R Age 22

YEAR	TEAM	LGE	IP	H	ER	HR	BB	K	ERA	W	L	H/9	HR/9	BB/9	K/9	KW	PERA	STUFF
1999	Danville	App	76.0	84	44	7	29	25	5.21	3	5	9.9	.8	3.4	3.0	.4	8.01	-8
2000	Macon	SAL	96.0	107	58	17	23	50	5.44	4	7	10.0	1.6	2.2	4.7	1.1	4.39	9
2000	Myrtle B	Car	77.0	83	40	12	12	42	4.68	4	5	9.7	1.4	1.4	4.9	1.8	5.31	13

Belisle went from everyone's top-prospect lists to MIA, as he missed all of 2001 with surgery to repair a ruptured disc in his back. He showed up in instructional league with his big, moving sinker intact and made an appearance in the Arizona Fall League. With several free agents potentially leaving the pen, Belisle might join the bullpen in the same way Kevin McGlinchy did.

Jung Bong Throws L Age 21

YEAR	TEAM	LGE	IP	H	ER	HR	BB	K	ERA	W	L	H/9	HR/9	BB/9	K/9	KW	PERA	STUFF
1999	Macon	SAL	109.3	122	80	16	68	51	6.59	4	8	10.0	1.3	5.6	4.2	0.4	6.68	-7
2000	Macon	SAL	115.3	124	68	10	57	47	5.31	5	8	9.7	0.8	4.4	3.7	0.4	6.99	-2
2000	Myrtle B	Car	40.0	40	16	2	8	22	3.60	2	2	9.0	0.4	1.8	4.9	1.4	4.43	18
2001	Myrtle B	Car	165.0	174	90	17	63	84	4.91	8	10	9.5	0.9	3.4	4.6	0.7	5.84	7

Originally scouted as an outfielder at the World Championships in 1997, Bong is turning into as good a left-handed pitching prospect as you'll find. He throws in the low 90s, which is usually newsworthy enough, but he also has command of a couple of different curves and a change-up, and he is aggressive about working on his command. There have been more position player-turned-pitcher disappointments than breakthroughs (Tris Jerue, anyone?), but Bong looks like one who will make it.

John Burkett Throws R Age 37

YEAR	TEAM	LGE	IP	H	ER	HR	BB	K	ERA	W	L	H/9	HR/9	BB/9	K/9	KW	PERA	STUFF
1999	Texas	AL	159.0	161	72	15	38	95	4.08	10	8	9.1	0.8	2.2	5.4	1.3	4.77	6
2000	Atlanta	NL	145.0	140	63	12	42	98	3.91	9	7	8.7	0.7	2.6	6.1	1.2	4.87	8
2001	Atlanta	NL	207.0	194	85	15	63	150	3.70	14	9	8.4	0.7	2.7	6.5	1.2	3.44	18

The multimillion-dollar question is whether Burkett was really something special in 2001. There are a lot of similarities between his 2000 and 2001 translations in terms of rate stats, so he was arguably just healthier. Mostly, you can explain his 2001 as the result of his being the beneficiary of the best bullpen support of any starter in baseball, seeing only two of the 23 runners he left for his relievers score. After some confusion, he really did sign a two-year deal with the Red Sox.

Jose Cabrera Throws R Age 30

YEAR	TEAM	LGE	IP	H	ER	HR	BB	K	ERA	W	L	H/9	HR/9	BB/9	K/9	KW	PERA	STUFF
1999	New Orln	PCL	47.3	47	22	4	14	28	4.18	3	2	8.9	0.8	2.7	5.3	1.0	3.77	-9
1999	Houston	NL	28.3	25	11	3	8	25	3.49	2	1	7.9	1.0	2.5	7.9	1.6	2.03	13
2000	Houston	NL	63.0	67	33	9	14	36	4.71	3	4	9.6	1.3	2.0	5.1	1.3	5.20	-9
2001	Atlanta	NL	55.3	55	27	4	22	35	4.39	3	3	8.9	0.7	3.6	5.7	0.8	3.68	-5

Cabrera is an example of the easy availability of good relief help at less than the Ed Wade rate. He was snagged from the Astros on waivers in April. For a couple of months, Cabrera was the best right-handed reliever in the pen. He'll make a mistake against lefties more often than you'd like; other than that, he's a useful middle reliever.

John Ennis Throws R Age 22

YEAR	TEAM	LGE	IP	H	ER	HR	BB	K	ERA	W	L	H/9	HR/9	BB/9	K/9	KW	PERA	STUFF
1999	Danville	App	65.3	82	57	17	27	25	7.85	2	5	11.3	2.3	3.7	3.4	0.5	8.00	-13
2000	Macon	SAL	94.3	99	52	12	32	55	4.96	5	5	9.4	1.1	3.1	5.2	0.9	4.55	11
2001	Myrtle B	Car	130.0	146	99	29	60	83	6.85	4	10	10.1	2.0	4.2	5.7	0.7	6.67	1

A '98 draft pick, Ennis reflects the organization's commitment to drafting pitching with the understanding that anybody can develop. Ennis is big 6′5″; possesses good mechanics; has command of his fastball, breaking stuff, and change-up; and knows how to pitch. Ennis, Bong, and Trey Hodges will make a very interesting trio to watch in Double-A this year. Ennis has the most upside of the three.

Brett Evert Throws R Age 21

YEAR	TEAM	LGE	IP	H	ER	HR	BB	K	ERA	W	L	H/9	HR/9	BB/9	K/9	KW	PERA	STUFF
2000	Jamestwn	NYP	77.3	101	73	25	24	32	8.50	2	7	11.8	2.9	2.8	3.7	0.7	8.78	-12
2000	Macon	SAL	42.0	59	48	17	11	15	10.29	1	4	12.6	3.6	2.4	3.2	0.7	7.67	-15
2001	Macon	SAL	34.7	33	10	0	4	17	2.60	3	1	8.6	0.0	1.0	4.4	2.1	1.84	21
2001	Myrtle B	Car	70.7	74	38	10	20	43	4.84	4	4	9.4	1.3	2.5	5.5	1.1	5.06	13

Evert is another one of the big, young flamethrowers that the Braves like to pick out of high school. There are concerns about his mechanics and command of his breaking stuff, but he's expected to improve as he fills out. He had to be shut down in July with shoulder problems, then he was fine in instructional league in the fall. Evert was named the best pitching prospect in the Carolina League in *Baseball America*'s poll; the Braves are hoping he has a better year than last year's poll winner, Christian Parra.

Tom Glavine — Throws L — Age 36

YEAR	TEAM	LGE	IP	H	ER	HR	BB	K	ERA	W	L	H/9	HR/9	BB/9	K/9	KW	PERA	STUFF
1999	Atlanta	NL	242.7	247	109	17	69	124	4.04	15	12	9.2	0.6	2.6	4.6	0.9	4.09	5
2000	Atlanta	NL	238.3	242	106	21	54	135	4.00	15	11	9.1	0.8	2.0	5.1	1.3	3.47	10
2001	Atlanta	NL	205.0	219	117	21	87	93	5.14	10	13	9.6	0.9	3.8	4.1	0.5	3.81	-3

If Glavine's 1999 season was enough to inspire a sense of doom, the first half of his 2001 season was enough to summon up visions from Gibbon's *Decline and Fall of the Roman Empire*, or maybe just Carson Daly. Anyway, Glavine's walk rate rose, his strikeout rate plummeted, and he wasn't as durable. Then he logged quality starts in 13 of 16 second-half outings while cutting his walk rate from 4.8 walks per nine innings to 3.1. Was it just an adjustment period, as Glavine learned to take advantage of the high strike? Maybe, although two out of three years he has given people reason to worry. Glavine has 224 wins and should hang on long enough to get into the 270s.

Buddy Hernandez — Throws R — Age 23

YEAR	TEAM	LGE	IP	H	ER	HR	BB	K	ERA	W	L	H/9	HR/9	BB/9	K/9	KW	PERA	STUFF
2000	Jamestwn	NYP	23.0	20	8	0	9	17	3.13	2	1	7.8	0.0	3.5	6.7	0.9	2.84	11
2001	Macon	SAL	14.3	14	6	2	1	14	3.77	1	1	8.8	1.3	0.6	8.8	7.0	7.93	18
2001	Myrtle B	Car	50.0	43	21	3	25	43	3.78	4	2	7.7	0.5	4.5	7.7	0.9	1.99	10

An undrafted free agent signed out of Division III North Carolina Wesleyan, Hernandez might turn into a useful big-league reliever pretty quickly. He works in the low 90s and has command of four pitches, but he was easily overlooked by scouts because he stands 5′9″. The Braves are taking a wait-and-see approach with Hernandez, who has done more with what he has than Billy Sylvester has done with his great arm.

Trey Hodges — Throws R — Age 24

YEAR	TEAM	LGE	IP	H	ER	HR	BB	K	ERA	W	L	H/9	HR/9	BB/9	K/9	KW	PERA	STUFF
2000	Jamestwn	NYP	17.3	30	41	13	16	6	21.29	0	2	15.6	6.7	8.3	3.1	0.2	9.66	-89
2001	Myrtle B	Car	164.0	196	110	36	27	71	6.04	6	12	10.8	2.0	1.5	3.9	1.3	6.12	-8

You might remember Hodges as one of LSU's stars in the 2000 College World Series. Because he was worked so hard down the stretch of that college season, the Braves avoided working him much after signing him and were uncertain about what might happen in 2001. A 139-to-18 strikeout-to-walk ratio ought to impress anybody. He doesn't throw particularly hard, so the danger here is that he could wind up like "command" prospects Christian Parra and Horacio Ramirez, scuffling at higher levels.

Steve Karsay — Throws R — Age 30

YEAR	TEAM	LGE	IP	H	ER	HR	BB	K	ERA	W	L	H/9	HR/9	BB/9	K/9	KW	PERA	STUFF
1999	Clevelnd	AL	80.0	71	31	5	25	67	3.49	6	3	8.0	0.6	2.8	7.5	1.3	2.77	12
2000	Clevelnd	AL	81.0	72	28	4	20	65	3.11	6	3	8.0	0.4	2.2	7.2	1.6	3.12	11
2001	Clevelnd	AL	42.3	33	10	1	8	42	2.13	4	1	7.0	0.2	1.7	8.9	2.6	1.12	29
2001	Atlanta	NL	43.7	41	19	3	15	31	3.92	3	2	8.5	0.6	3.1	6.4	1.0	4.27	0

Karsay has reason to be unhappy with his lot in life. While less talented people get to be closers (at what point does somebody like John Rocker or Jason Isringhausen finally receive a little less benefit of the doubt?), Karsay gets an occasional multi-week trial. Invariably, all it takes is a blown save and a reminder that Karsay's elbow is less reliable than an Elvis sighting, and his team immediately rousts somebody else for the role. The perception that Karsay has somehow fallen short and the concerns about his health have both been overstated. He's been one of the best relievers in the game for three years; the Yankees will get 80 quality high-leverage innings for their investment in him.

Nathan Kent — Throws R — Age 23

YEAR	TEAM	LGE	IP	H	ER	HR	BB	K	ERA	W	L	H/9	HR/9	BB/9	K/9	KW	PERA	STUFF
1999	Jamestwn	NYP	54.0	58	28	5	15	23	4.67	3	3	9.7	0.8	2.5	3.8	0.8	7.47	-5
2000	Myrtle B	Car	128.3	133	56	7	33	52	3.93	8	6	9.3	0.5	2.3	3.6	0.8	4.75	4
2001	Greenvil	Sou	158.3	172	83	18	41	70	4.72	9	9	9.8	1.0	2.3	4.0	0.9	6.07	1

A gentle giant in the Mike Smithson mold, Kent doesn't throw hard, but he does have good command of a range of breaking stuff and his change-up. Breaking with organizational form, Kent is a college pitcher, taken out of the University of Kentucky in the 49th round in 1999. He's been nothing but successful so far, and if he simply survives as well as succeeds, he will show up in the majors by 2003.

Ben Kozlowski **Throws L** **Age 21**

YEAR	TEAM	LGE	IP	H	ER	HR	BB	K	ERA	W	L	H/9	HR/9	BB/9	K/9	KW	PERA	STUFF
2000	Macon	SAL	75.7	88	64	15	50	35	7.61	2	6	10.5	1.8	5.9	4.2	0.3	8.35	-11
2001	Macon	SAL	143.3	154	77	18	38	75	4.83	7	9	9.7	1.1	2.4	4.7	1.0	5.50	8
2001	Myrtle B	Car	14.3	16	9	2	4	8	5.65	1	1	10.0	1.3	2.5	5.0	1.0	7.17	8

Picked out of a Florida community college in 1999, Kozlowski is another one of the organization's big (6′6″), projectable pitchers. After struggling as a 19-year-old in 2000, he came into 2001 taking his career a little more seriously and showed outstanding command and low-90s heat. He still has a reputation for being hyper, but no longer in an unfocused way.

Kerry Ligtenberg **Throws R** **Age 31**

YEAR	TEAM	LGE	IP	H	ER	HR	BB	K	ERA	W	L	H/9	HR/9	BB/9	K/9	KW	PERA	STUFF
2000	Atlanta	NL	51.3	48	25	6	20	45	4.38	3	3	8.4	1.1	3.5	7.9	1.1	3.33	5
2001	Atlanta	NL	56.7	51	25	3	27	45	3.97	3	3	8.1	0.5	4.3	7.1	0.8	3.35	3

After starting off badly, Ligtenberg posted a 1.79 ERA over the final four months of the season in a comeback that was a lot more significant than Mark Wohlers's. By season's end, Cox was even comfortable using him on consecutive nights. With Karsay gone and Smoltz's durability and job description up in the air, Ligtenberg has an opportunity to slip back into the closer's role he held in 1998. He'll be better at it than John Rocker. Again.

Greg Maddux **Throws R** **Age 36**

YEAR	TEAM	LGE	IP	H	ER	HR	BB	K	ERA	W	L	H/9	HR/9	BB/9	K/9	KW	PERA	STUFF
1999	Atlanta	NL	232.3	234	88	15	31	122	3.41	17	9	9.1	0.6	1.2	4.7	2.0	3.91	12
2000	Atlanta	NL	249.3	238	89	17	35	169	3.21	19	9	8.6	0.6	1.3	6.1	2.4	3.02	21
2001	Atlanta	NL	222.3	218	82	17	24	139	3.32	16	9	8.8	0.7	1.0	5.6	2.9	3.35	18

We could just as easily address this issue in the Roger Clemens comment, but how could anybody, from advertisers to fans, mistake Nolan Ryan for the best right-handed starter in baseball history? Clemens and Maddux are arguably *the* greatest tandem anyone has ever seen, yet you're more likely to find some whiskey-soaked New York journalist blathering about almost anybody but Clemens or Maddux. In part, that's a matter of choice by the athletes themselves. Maddux's historical legacy lies in his performance, not his chattiness with some writer trying to bring an athlete's story to life for the right compensation.

The crime lies in the way that journalists pretend that workaday mythmaking has nothing to do with popular perception. Trying to make a buck is all well and good, but when there's nothing to support an argument for Ryan or Tom Seaver or anybody else who happened to be good when you were under 40, why pretend? Parochial or generational hosannas are not victimless crimes. Worse than being mere back scratching, they obfuscate genuine greatness. Maddux has 20 more wins than Tom Seaver had at the same age, and a lower career ERA to boot, despite never getting the benefit of pitching in the low-offense 1970s. Ryan, for what it's worth, wasn't even as good as Seaver.

In terms of career value, if Clemens isn't the best right-handed pitcher we've ever seen, Maddux is. Pedro Martinez would have to be Pedro Martinez for another six full seasons or so before he really enters the discussion. Do we have to be polite about this?

Jason Marquis **Throws R** **Age 23**

YEAR	TEAM	LGE	IP	H	ER	HR	BB	K	ERA	W	L	H/9	HR/9	BB/9	K/9	KW	PERA	STUFF
1999	Myrtle B	Car	31.3	27	13	0	19	24	3.73	2	1	7.8	0.0	5.5	6.9	0.6	0.79	26
1999	Greenvil	Sou	53.0	61	41	10	29	25	6.96	2	4	10.4	1.7	4.9	4.2	0.4	5.43	-5
2000	Greenvil	Sou	65.3	80	54	17	23	33	7.44	2	5	11.0	2.3	3.2	4.5	0.7	5.53	-1
2000	Richmond	Int	22.0	22	13	2	13	15	5.32	1	1	9.0	0.8	5.3	6.1	0.6	9.55	0
2000	Atlanta	NL	23.3	24	14	4	10	15	5.40	1	2	9.3	1.5	3.9	5.8	0.8	5.69	-5
2001	Atlanta	NL	120.7	120	64	12	53	79	4.77	6	7	9.0	0.9	4.0	5.9	0.7	4.36	4

While epicures can appreciate the graybeards dissecting opposing hitters, there's something about Marquis that makes him the staff's most entertaining pitcher. He's got good velocity and a nice hard curve, and he mixes in a couple of different change-ups. Mostly, he's just fun because he stomps around looking combative. Right now, he's "just" a very good fourth starter.

Matt McClendon Throws R Age 24

YEAR	TEAM	LGE	IP	H	ER	HR	BB	K	ERA	W	L	H/9	HR/9	BB/9	K/9	KW	PERA	STUFF
1999	Jamestwn	NYP	21.3	25	20	5	15	11	8.44	0	2	10.5	2.1	6.3	4.6	0.4	6.03	-21
2000	Myrtle B	Car	37.0	35	15	2	9	24	3.65	2	2	8.5	0.5	2.2	5.8	1.3	2.40	20
2000	Greenvil	Sou	130.0	136	69	10	55	60	4.78	7	7	9.4	0.7	3.8	4.2	0.5	4.84	1
2001	Myrtle B	Car	9.0	8	8	0	14	5	8.00	0	1	8.0	0.0	14.0	5.0	0.2	17.78	-67
2001	Greenvil	Sou	10.3	11	8	2	8	5	6.97	0	1	9.6	1.7	7.0	4.4	0.3	7.19	-22
2001	Richmond	Int	40.7	51	36	6	35	24	6.94	1	4	9.8	1.2	6.8	4.6	0.3	9.80	-20

Another product off of the Braves' assembly line of big kids who throw hard and have sharp breaking stuff—and another one who broke down. Initially, the acquisition of McClendon was touted as an example of organizational vision: he was a top high-school talent who went to college, flopped, hired Scott Boras, dropped to the fifth round, and still got fair value from the Braves. However, the non-Boras reason he dropped in the draft became an issue this year. McClendon's mechanics have been a headache from the start, so when his elbow went bad, it should not have been a surprise. It's not really an indicator of anything, good or bad, just another reason to hold back your enthusiasm for pitching prospects.

Kevin Millwood Throws R Age 27

YEAR	TEAM	LGE	IP	H	ER	HR	BB	K	ERA	W	L	H/9	HR/9	BB/9	K/9	KW	PERA	STUFF
1999	Atlanta	NL	219.3	203	88	22	40	105	3.01	15	9	8.3	0.9	2.0	7.6	1.9	2.92	27
2000	Atlanta	NL	216.7	214	97	23	51	149	4.03	13	11	8.9	1.0	2.1	6.2	1.5	4.48	14
2001	Atlanta	NL	114.3	122	66	17	36	68	5.20	6	7	9.6	1.3	2.8	5.4	0.9	4.96	2

Millwood declined for yet another year as he lost time to shoulder stiffness, so things look bleak, right? Keep in mind that he's also coming off of a year in which he posted quality starts in 12 of his 21 opportunities, and at the end of the year, he was throwing his curve and reaching the low 90s. While tendinitis can be anything from serious to annoying, we like the odds that Millwood will return to his 2000 form.

Trey Moore Throws L Age 29

YEAR	TEAM	LGE	IP	H	ER	HR	BB	K	ERA	W	L	H/9	HR/9	BB/9	K/9	KW	PERA	STUFF
2000	Ottawa	Int	58.3	60	29	5	20	32	4.47	3	3	9.3	0.8	3.1	4.9	0.8	6.44	-6
2000	Montreal	NL	40.0	44	26	6	17	21	5.85	1	3	9.9	1.4	3.8	4.7	0.6	7.21	-12
2001	Richmond	Int	157.7	162	77	13	52	83	4.40	9	9	9.2	0.7	3.0	4.7	0.8	4.47	0

Claimed off of waivers from the Expos, Moore had a nifty comeback season from shoulder surgery that cost him all of 1999. His year might translate into a viable candidacy for somebody's fifth-starter slot. You just know that every minor-league lefty pushing 30 noticed Chris Michalak get his day in the sun, and every one of them would like to get off of the Rick Krivda Triple-A Treadmill.

Damian Moss Throws L Age 25

YEAR	TEAM	LGE	IP	H	ER	HR	BB	K	ERA	W	L	H/9	HR/9	BB/9	K/9	KW	PERA	STUFF
1999	Macon	SAL	37.3	50	48	17	21	24	11.57	1	3	12.1	4.1	5.1	5.8	0.6	5.94	-27
1999	Greenvil	Sou	36.0	44	32	8	21	16	8.00	1	3	11.0	2.0	5.3	4.0	0.4	9.13	-22
2000	Richmond	Int	155.3	155	98	17	102	104	5.68	7	10	9.0	1.0	5.9	6.0	0.5	3.79	3
2001	Richmond	Int	86.3	86	53	13	45	69	5.53	4	6	9.0	1.4	4.7	7.2	0.8	4.02	7

Moss suffered a knee injury early last season and later had shoulder trouble caused by sleeping on his arm wrong. He was in his third year after Tommy John surgery, and his control was just beginning to improve enough to make him interesting. Moss doesn't throw hard, but he's difficult to time because of his effectiveness at mixing his pitches. He might get lost in the shuffle, given the Braves' collection of young pitchers.

Kenny "Bubba" Nelson Throws R Age 20

YEAR	TEAM	LGE	IP	H	ER	HR	BB	K	ERA	W	L	H/9	HR/9	BB/9	K/9	KW	PERA	STUFF
2001	Macon	SAL	145.7	173	130	37	81	79	8.03	4	12	10.7	2.3	5.0	4.9	0.5	6.71	-1

Another one of the Braves' "types," Nelson is a big hard-throwing high-school pitcher with as much chance of flameout as development. That's not an indictment of Nelson, who throws in the low 90s and spins a great curve. It's important to remember that the organization is just as rich in touted young pitchers coming off of their first major surgeries as in guys who have

(Kenny "Bubba" Nelson *continued*)
been able to withstand normal workloads. Nelson impressed almost as much as teammates Ben Kozlowski and Adam Wainwright did, but the Sally League is a long way off from the majors, and the odds that one of the three will make it are long, just as a matter of course.

Christian Parra Throws R Age 24

YEAR	TEAM	LGE	IP	H	ER	HR	BB	K	ERA	W	L	H/9	HR/9	BB/9	K/9	KW	PERA	STUFF
1999	Jamestwn	NYP	49.7	51	29	5	25	29	5.26	3	3	9.2	0.9	4.5	5.3	0.6	5.37	4
1999	Macon	SAL	33.0	36	24	6	16	19	6.55	1	3	9.8	1.6	4.4	5.2	0.6	5.46	0
2000	Myrtle B	Car	145.3	145	78	15	64	92	4.83	7	9	9.0	0.9	4.0	5.7	0.7	3.97	9
2001	Greenvil	Sou	86.3	94	68	14	64	50	7.09	3	7	9.8	1.5	6.7	5.2	0.4	7.14	-16

After going undrafted in 1998, Parra pitched in a Mexican semipro league before signing with the Braves in '99. When healthy, he can throw four pitches for strikes, changing speeds and location effectively and getting into the low 90s with a strong drop-and-drive delivery. His introduction to Double-A never got on track because of a thumb injury he had from the start. He's not a premium prospect, just someone who knows how to pitch and bears watching.

Odalis Perez Throws L Age 24

YEAR	TEAM	LGE	IP	H	ER	HR	BB	K	ERA	W	L	H/9	HR/9	BB/9	K/9	KW	PERA	STUFF
1999	Atlanta	NL	97.0	94	52	11	44	74	4.82	5	6	8.7	1.0	4.1	6.9	0.8	5.81	15
2001	Richmond	Int	23.7	22	7	1	2	17	2.66	2	1	8.4	0.4	0.8	6.5	4.3	3.07	24
2001	Atlanta	NL	96.0	94	43	6	35	57	4.03	6	5	8.8	0.6	3.3	5.3	0.8	5.24	3

After elbow surgery, Perez is still throwing hard and still has the nice curveball that made him a great prospect from the get-go. Having lost his job to Marquis (in part because of a poorly-timed fielding injury), he'll go into camp fighting Albie Lopez for a spot in the rotation. Even then, Perez will be the first guy to get bumped for any of the organization's young pitchers, so despite his talent, his job description is up in the air.

Steve Reed Throws R Age 36

YEAR	TEAM	LGE	IP	H	ER	HR	BB	K	ERA	W	L	H/9	HR/9	BB/9	K/9	KW	PERA	STUFF
1999	Clevelnd	AL	64.3	65	32	9	17	44	4.48	4	3	9.1	1.3	2.4	6.2	1.3	4.02	-2
2000	Clevelnd	AL	57.7	57	27	6	17	39	4.21	3	3	8.9	0.9	2.7	6.1	1.1	3.89	-1
2001	Clevelnd	AL	26.7	25	13	3	10	20	4.39	2	1	8.4	1.0	3.4	6.8	1.0	3.25	0
2001	Atlanta	NL	30.0	29	14	3	12	20	4.20	2	1	8.7	0.9	3.6	6.0	0.8	4.10	-6

Reed limited right-handed batters to a .149/.192/.220 line while rolling over for lefties to the tune of .519/.629/.904. In other words, the average right-handed hitter hit about as well when facing Reed as an almost-dangerous pitcher, while the average left-handed batter hitting against Reed fared better than Barry Bonds did in the best offensive season ever. There is a reason to believe that having right-handed situational pitchers makes more sense than having left-handed ones, in that they're more likely to get the matchup (Reed faced more than twice as many right-handed hitters as lefties). However, it would be hard for anyone to have splits like Reed and not give his manager the willies, worrying about whether or not the other guy's bench has any lefty-hitting pitchers or batboys.

Mike Remlinger Throws L Age 36

YEAR	TEAM	LGE	IP	H	ER	HR	BB	K	ERA	W	L	H/9	HR/9	BB/9	K/9	KW	PERA	STUFF
1999	Atlanta	NL	82.0	74	36	8	29	73	3.95	5	4	8.1	0.9	3.2	8.0	1.3	2.38	10
2000	Atlanta	NL	71.3	62	31	5	30	64	3.91	5	3	7.8	0.6	3.8	8.1	1.1	3.30	9
2001	Atlanta	NL	73.7	64	29	8	21	75	3.54	5	3	7.8	1.0	2.6	9.2	1.8	3.03	18

Some of the pitchers who came up with Remlinger in San Francisco during the tail end of the Al Rosen/Roger Craig days include teammates John Burkett and Steve Reed, plus Rod Beck, Gil Heredia, and Pat Rapp. They were the kids on a staff that had Rick Reuschel and Don Robinson and Dan Quisenberry, as well as future pitching coaches such as Bud Black and Dave Righetti. Given all of the complaints about Craig and his methods back in the day, it would be interesting to see what they'd say now about coming up with the Giants back then.

Rudy Seanez Throws R Age 33

YEAR	TEAM	LGE	IP	H	ER	HR	BB	K	ERA	W	L	H/9	HR/9	BB/9	K/9	KW	PERA	STUFF
1999	Atlanta	NL	53.7	50	21	3	18	37	3.52	4	2	8.4	0.5	3.0	6.2	1.0	3.25	1
2000	Atlanta	NL	20.0	19	10	3	7	18	4.50	1	1	8.6	1.4	3.2	8.1	1.3	4.34	5
2001	San Dieg	NL	21.3	20	13	3	13	19	5.48	1	1	8.4	1.3	5.5	8.0	0.7	3.18	-1
2001	Atlanta	NL	11.3	9	4	1	4	14	3.18	1	0	7.1	0.8	3.2	11.1	1.0	3.03	29

Seanez is in danger of becoming the Braves' version of what Darryl Strawberry was to the Yankees for a few years. Is the team in need of some help down the stretch? Heck, dig up old what's his face—he's never very expensive, everybody knows him, and the staff knows what he can do. Seanez's primary value to anyone other than the Braves is that he might bring you a live arm out of Macon or Myrtle Beach on the last day of July.

John Smoltz Throws R Age 35

YEAR	TEAM	LGE	IP	H	ER	HR	BB	K	ERA	W	L	H/9	HR/9	BB/9	K/9	KW	PERA	STUFF
1999	Atlanta	NL	187.3	174	67	13	33	140	3.22	14	7	8.4	0.6	1.6	6.7	2.1	3.12	24
2001	Atlanta	NL	56.7	53	22	6	9	46	3.49	4	2	8.4	1.0	1.4	7.3	2.6	3.70	11

Smoltz is three years older than Dennis Eckersley was when he became The Eck in 1988. At that point, Eckersley had 157 wins; Smoltz has 160. Given that we don't yet know how Hall of Fame voters will treat Eck, it's hard to guess which course might help Smoltz the most. From a team perspective, getting 80 or 90 high-leverage innings is great, but do you pay a premium for that because this good reliever used to be John Smoltz? If he tries to start, he'll fall into the same pattern as Bret Saberhagen, having a good season in one of the three years during his deal.

Tim Spooneybarger Throws R Age 22

YEAR	TEAM	LGE	IP	H	ER	HR	BB	K	ERA	W	L	H/9	HR/9	BB/9	K/9	KW	PERA	STUFF
1999	Danville	App	23.3	21	12	0	18	15	4.63	1	2	8.1	0.0	6.9	5.8	0.4	5.17	-1
2000	Myrtle B	Car	44.0	38	16	0	21	34	3.27	3	2	7.8	0.0	4.3	7.0	0.8	1.84	19
2001	Greenvil	Sou	21.0	20	8	1	4	15	3.43	1	1	8.6	0.4	1.7	6.4	1.9	6.03	10
2001	Richmond	Int	49.0	40	18	1	24	45	3.31	3	2	7.3	0.2	4.4	8.3	0.9	0.99	23

Billy Sylvester might get the saves and the touts, but his setup man is the better prospect. Spooneybarger is young, throws hard with a deceptive delivery, and mixes two- and four-seam fastballs effectively with a slurve. He's been much more dominant than Sylvester at the same levels despite being three years younger, but because Sylvester flirts with triple digits once in a blue moon, and because some people think saves reflect an ability, Spooneybarger seems to be slipping under the radar.

Billy Sylvester Throws R Age 25

YEAR	TEAM	LGE	IP	H	ER	HR	BB	K	ERA	W	L	H/9	HR/9	BB/9	K/9	KW	PERA	STUFF
1999	Macon	SAL	83.7	88	51	6	52	37	5.49	4	5	9.5	0.6	5.6	4.0	0.4	5.48	-22
2000	Myrtle B	Car	38.3	40	23	5	19	25	5.40	2	2	9.4	1.2	4.5	5.9	0.7	2.58	-13
2001	Greenvil	Sou	27.0	27	25	5	30	23	8.33	1	2	9.0	1.7	10.0	7.7	0.4	3.15	-31
2001	Richmond	Int	36.0	32	22	3	32	30	5.50	2	2	8.0	0.8	8.0	7.5	0.5	5.96	-14

Sylvester gets touted as a closer prospect because he throws in the high 90s and has been successful since being moved into the role in 2000. There's no questioning that he has good stuff, but his great heat and his splitter aren't translating into a lot of dominance. His jerky, three-quarters delivery makes him easy to run on.

Adam Wainwright Throws R Age 20

YEAR	TEAM	LGE	IP	H	ER	HR	BB	K	ERA	W	L	H/9	HR/9	BB/9	K/9	KW	PERA	STUFF
2000	Danville	App	28.3	34	21	8	3	18	6.67	1	2	10.8	2.5	1.0	5.7	3.0	5.79	12
2001	Macon	SAL	161.7	170	95	21	68	94	5.29	8	10	9.5	1.2	3.8	5.2	0.7	7.20	9

Courtesy of the fantabulous official cockamamie free-agent compensation scheme, the Braves got two 2000 first-round picks for Russ Springer and with the first one chose Wainwright. At 6′6″, Wainwright is a big guy who already throws in the low 90s. He may pick up more velocity as he gets older and fills out. He also has a good curve and change-up. Anyone who translates this well from a low A-ball league bears watching.

Chicago Cubs

We've been guilty of rushing to praise the Cubs for the things that they've done well in the last couple of years. As the Cubs' player-development pipeline gets closer to pumping talented young players onto the big-league roster, our unstated message has been that you should pay less attention to events at the major-league level. We've focused on giving credit to what is already the best player-development program the organization has had since the mid-'80s.

We don't mean to say that the work Jim Hendry, Oneri Fleita, Leon Lee, Jim Stockstill, and the rest of the Cubs' player development and scouting crew do not deserve the praise we've lavished on them. But just as 1998 raised questions of whether or not Andy MacPhail understood what it would take to build a real contender, the Cubs' failed bid for the NL Central title in 2001 underscored the fact that those questions are still relevant. The Cubs must learn from what they did not do well at the major-league level.

Cubs Prospectus

2001 record: 88–74; Third place, NL Central

Pythagenport W/L: 89–73

Runs scored: 777 (seventh in NL)

Runs allowed: 701 (fourth in NL)

Team EqA: .265 (sixth in NL)

2001 batters age: 31 (third-oldest in NL)

2001 pitchers age: 29.3 (fifth-oldest in NL)

Ballpark: Wrigley Field; slight pitchers' park; Park Factor of .984

2001: Sammy Sosa and a great pitching staff made for a great summer in Chicago.

2002: They'll score more runs, and have young pitching coming up; it wouldn't be an upset if they played into October.

The only thing consistent about the Cubs is their inconsistency. The MacPhail regime has reshuffled Sammy Sosa's sidekicks on an almost annual basis and sacrificed MacPhail's lieutenants whenever necessary. The Cubs have been little more than an amusing sideshow, careening back and forth between misery and near-relevance. Years like this past one, in which the Cubs obviously had an opportunity and blew it, force us to review the organization's goals and how effective they have been at achieving them.

One obvious goal going into 2001 was getting Sammy Sosa re-signed. In no small part because of their direct relationship with the media—as the linchpin of their corporate parent's television and radio programming—the Cubs understand better than most organizations that they're in the entertainment industry. There was no way that the Cubs were going to let their star attraction and the centerpiece of their advertising campaigns walk away over something as trivial as a lot of money, not when even more money was at stake. Sosa signed a four-year extension in the spring but added an incentive for the organization to try and matter sometime soon by insisting on a player option after the 2003 season. Compared to the money flushed by Tribune Media's participation in the WB network's ongoing effort to find out how much Nikki Cox America can take (and some of us can take a lot), money spent on Sosa was money well spent.

Another important goal was to provide a semblance of a contending team, so as to keep the restless natives from getting cranky. In 2000, Don Baylor treated the pitching staff as little more than a necessary evil; in 2001, the Cubs tried a little harder in the pitching department. They went out and spent money, briefly chasing after Mike Hampton before settling for a broader swag of mid-tier talent, hauling in Jason Bere, Julian Tavarez, Jeff Fassero, and Flash Gordon. Such gateway free agents usually don't pay off as well as these guys did. However, the Cubs were both lucky and smart. They identified good risks, and in the cases of Fassero and Tavarez, had some freedom going into spring training about how they used them.

The Cubs also seemed to appreciate that they had offensive problems that they needed to address. As they have in years past, they mostly acquired expensive mediocrities such as Bill Mueller and Ron Coomer, but they also shelled out good money to Todd Hundley after having blown bad money on Joe Girardi. They spent time and money convincing Rondell White that Chicago was a place to feel good about for another year, and when all was said and done, the Cubs had made a pretty thorough overhaul. The only skimping was at first base, where Hee Choi was expected to eventually inherit the job that was stocked for the time being with a platoon of temps, Matt Stairs and Julio Zuleta.

On paper, it all made sense. The Cubs would field an improved team that would keep people happy and focused on the big-league club, while allowing Hendry's staff to continue to minister to a burgeoning farm system. The problem is that it worked too well. The Cubs did not merely threaten to contend, they were winning, putting everyone in the organization on the spot. Anybody can build a sand castle in the sky; the Cubs managed to keep it up there for four months.

It's worth noting that the Cubs led the Central throughout the first half despite a number of unforeseen problems. Bill Mueller broke his kneecap a month into the season, and Eric Young regressed from adequate leadoff man to Knoblauchian uselessness, exacerbating the Cubs' OBP issues. Center field became too obvious a hole, as the previous year's commitment to Damon Buford looked about as bad as it should have. Worst of all, Hundley didn't merely struggle—he hit so badly that Joe Girardi was a plausible option to start ahead of him. Hundley's implosion inspired the latest version of Don Baylor's unique brand of compassionate conservatism: the manager sought solace and sympathy from Chicago's "big four" beat writers while engaging in his usual blaming of the victim. Hundley needed help, and Baylor did nothing to help get him back on track beyond whatever tough love Hundley got to read about in the paper.

The lineup's sudden dependence on people such as Coomer and Girardi and Robert Machado was made worse by Baylor's formulaic response to not scoring runs, which was to rely on tactics that produced even fewer runs. Baylor overmanaged a weakened lineup to even worse results, asking position players to bunt a major-league-leading 67 times, two more times than the equally inexplicable White Sox, and 15 ahead of the Cardinals' second-place tally within the National League. If Ricky Gutierrez's primary strength is that he's a better offensive player than your average National League shortstop, what's the point of having him make almost six innings' worth of outs on purpose?

The Cubs committed other gaffes that helped undermine what was a real opportunity to pull off a surprise and win the division. Most of these gaffes revolved around Baylor's failure to appreciate his team's strengths and weaknesses. On a team where Eric Young's offensive shortcomings were an issue, and his defensive contributions were negligible, why pass up the chance to use Delino DeShields at second base? On a team missing Rondell White's power, why avoid Roosevelt Brown and bench Matt Stairs? Once you consider these choices, the disasters behind the plate, and the loss of Mueller for most of the year, is it any wonder that the Cubs' offense struggled? It's easy to defend Baylor by saying that he had lost half of his lineup by July, but contingency planning is part of a manager's job, and it's not like the Cubs didn't have the pieces with which to cobble together a worthwhile lineup. They needed a leadoff hitter; in DeShields, they found one. They needed power even after the acquisition of Fred McGriff; they had Matt Stairs lying around. Don Baylor just couldn't let it be that easy.

Another significant barrier to success was Andy MacPhail's case of the slows, which have been a problem for years. A combination of miserliness and general pokiness kept Gary Gaetti off of the roster when he was desperately needed for nearly two weeks in 1998. In 2000, the Cubs flubbed their chance to nab a bundle of talent from the Yankees in exchange for Sammy Sosa, entirely because of their lack of preparation. In 2001, their failure to get the Fred McGriff deal done for more than a month after the players had been agreed upon was inexcusable.

Furthermore, MacPhail's other stretch-drive maneuvers garnered frustratingly little in the way of impact talent. Nabbing Michael Tucker to paper over the gaping hole in center field was sensible in some ways. Three of the Cubs' starters (Tavarez, Kevin Tapani, and Jon Lieber) were ground-ball pitchers, and the other two (Bere and Kerry Wood) weren't guys who let a lot of balls get into play. Sacrificing some outfield defense to help the lineup was a worthwhile risk, except that Tucker has never been an especially valuable hitter and contributed little towards fixing either the club's power shortage or its OBP problem. The acquisition of David Weathers resembled the kind of move that contenders are supposed to make, except that the bullpen was already a source of strength, probably the team's best feature. More critically, in getting Weathers, the Cubs gave up one of their best deadline bargaining chips in Ruben Quevedo, just to bring in a supernumerary middle reliever whose value was at its highest.

In effect, the Cubs' management team failed to take themselves or their opportunity seriously enough. They acquired talent that would not make a difference (Tucker and Weathers) while dragging their feet in acquiring the talent that would (McGriff). They failed to best utilize the talent they had on hand. The Astros' hot August run was out of the Cubs' control, but the Cubs' failure to do what was within their power made the month's 8 1/2-game swing which saw a 4 1/2-game lead over the Astros on August 1 turn into a four-game deficit by August 31—pretty predictable. By the end of the season, all that was left to be accomplished was Baylor's decision to throw his pitching coach, Oscar Acosta, overboard for the unforgivable sin of annoying competence.

Weeping over the past comes easily in Wrigleyville, but the Cubs need to learn from these failures at the management level now, because they're one of the four contenders in the most competitive division in baseball. The Cubs have the talent to win, but they need to demonstrate the ability to commit to something more than a year-to-year cycle of contingencies and overlapping crises. Just as the Mets' dependence on Mike Piazza and the Giants' reliance on Barry Bonds have defined the win-now focus of those teams, the Cubs must take advantage of having Sammy Sosa. Unlike the Giants or the Mets, though, the Cubs have the farm system to build on what they achieve now, or to use in trade to put them over the top.

The decision to trade for Alex Gonzalez at the winter meetings commits the Cubs to a legitimately poor offensive player. With center field, catcher, and second base all up in the air, there's the danger that if Baylor gets his way, the team will field mostly harmless veterans to support McGriff, Sosa, and Moises Alou. Just as they did in 2001, the Cubs have useful alternatives. In particular, Bill Mueller provides the Cubs with an elegant solution to the problem Mark Grace had always represented. Grace's best offensive role would have been as a leadoff hitter, but among today's tin-eared, risk-averse managers, how many would bat their first baseman at the top of the order? In 2002, the Cubs can carry a slow leadoff man such as Mueller to maximize Sosa's at-bats with runners on base, and with McGriff in the cleanup slot, followed by Alou, they're closer to the kind of old-fashioned, tub-thumping softball team that has been most successful in Wrigley Field. A lineup stocked with good on-base threats such as DeShields and Mark Bellhorn has the makings of a really good offense. A comeback season from Todd Hundley would just be gravy. With Bobby Hill and Corey Patterson not far off, there's an opportunity to start breaking in legitimately good young talent while the team contends. It's worked for the Braves.

A large part of the Cubs' future success rests on the outstanding collection of young pitching within the organization. Beyond the headliners, Lieber and Wood, there's a bullpen stocked with Gordon, Fassero, and Kyle Farnsworth. The balance of the staff consists of useful veterans (guys such as Bere and Jesus Sanchez), talented sophomores (Will Ohman and Courtney Duncan), and the best group of rookie pitchers who might plausibly push their way onto a big-league staff this year, notably Mark Prior, Juan Cruz, Carlos Zambrano, and Scott Chiasson. That list barely touches on the pitching talent that Hendry and company have assembled at every level. The key is that the organization has depth. Individual prospects will flame out, but weight of numbers and the continued identification of prospects will produce an unprecedented wave of homegrown pitching talent.

Baylor remains a major problem. His ham-handed catering to the press managed to alienate those few remaining players who had anything positive to say about him. The confrontation with Acosta inspired a near-mutiny among the pitching staff. Baylor's credibility goes no further than the press box. This situation isn't as hopeless as it sounds, but it says a lot about the state of the game today that a manager's acumen is judged by his facility with the fourth estate and not on the basis of anything he actually does involving a ball club. If Baylor cannot identify the veterans he should be using, and if he keeps trashing everyone under the age of 30, he will continue to be an obstacle to North Side success.

Can the Cubs win this year? Surprisingly, the answer is yes, but they'll need to catch a few breaks. The Astros might be retrenching, but they're still the class of the division, and the Cardinals and Reds have reasons to feel good. Until the Cubs demonstrate the ability to connect their player-development skills with an effective plan for big-league success, though, their productive farm system could be as irrelevant as those of the late-'80s Brewers or the mid-'90s Royals.

HITTERS (BA: .270, OBP: .340, SLG: .440, EqA: .260)

Roosevelt Brown OF Bats L Age 26

YEAR	TEAM	LGE	AB	H	DB	TP	HR	BB	SO	R	RBI	SB	CS	OUT	BA	OBP	SLG	EQA	EQR	DEFENSE
1999	WestTenn	Sou	126	33	7	0	3	10	29	9	9	4	1	94	.262	.322	.389	.243	14	31-RF -1
1999	Iowa	PCL	263	85	19	1	18	16	49	40	61	3	2	180	.323	.367	.608	.308	47	66-LF -3
2000	Iowa	PCL	361	102	19	0	13	29	58	53	45	8	3	262	.283	.345	.443	.264	47	89-RF -10
2000	ChiCubs	NL	92	32	6	0	4	2	20	11	14	0	1	61	.348	.368	.543	.292	14	19-LF 0
2001	Iowa	PCL	360	114	23	1	19	14	61	56	64	3	4	250	.317	.351	.544	.286	55	79-LF -4
2001	ChiCubs	NL	83	23	6	1	4	7	10	14	22	0	0	60	.277	.339	.518	.278	12	15-LF -3
2002	*ChiCubs*	*NL*	*450*	*137*	*25*	*1*	*21*	*34*	*83*	*62*	*74*	*6*	*3*	*316*	*.304*	*.353*	*.504*	*.283*	*67*	

In a world in which corner outfielders who slug .500 don't exactly grow on trees, it defies logic that Rosie Brown isn't getting a shot. The Cubs burned 35 left-field starts on Delino DeShields, Michael Tucker, and Corey Patterson. In the two games that Sammy Sosa didn't start in right field, Todd Dunwoody did. If Brown ate Don Baylor's dog and mailed him the bones, I doubt he'd get treated much worse.

Hee Choi 1B Bats L Age 23

YEAR	TEAM	LGE	AB	H	DB	TP	HR	BB	SO	R	RBI	SB	CS	OUT	BA	OBP	SLG	EQA	EQR	DEFENSE	
1999	Lansing	Mid	292	70	12	2	11	32	74	44	38	1	1	223	.240	.317	.408	.242	32	79-1B -5	
2000	Daytona	Fla	350	85	16	3	12	26	86	43	47	2	1	266	.243	.301	.409	.236	36	84-1B -1	
2000	WestTenn	Sou	128	35	7	0	8	20	38	22	20	2	1	94	.273	.372	.516	.290	21	35-1B 0	
2001	Iowa	PCL	267	56	9	0	11	31	61	32	38	4	1	212	.210	.292	.367	.224	25	68-1B 1	
2002	*ChiCubs*	*NL*	*429*	*111*	*20*	*2*	*20*	*49*	*113*	*68*	*65*	*5*	*2*	*320*	*.259*	*.335*	*.455*	*.264*	*57*		

Choi came into 2001 with a chance to be the Cubs' first baseman by midsummer. Instead, he suffered a hand injury, tried to play through it without telling anybody, and ended up visiting the DL twice. His Arizona Fall League stint was cut short by another hand injury, although it's supposed to be reassuring that it was not the same hand that killed his season at Iowa. While Choi's power stroke is still the organization's long-term answer at first base, Fred McGriff's decision to stick around will give Choi plenty of time to bounce back. There's apparently an agreement in place that will release him from his military-service requirement in Korea if he does eventually make the majors to stay.

Ron Coomer 1B/3B Bats R Age 35

YEAR	TEAM	LGE	AB	H	DB	TP	HR	BB	SO	R	RBI	SB	CS	OUT	BA	OBP	SLG	EQA	EQR	DEFENSE	
1999	Minnesot	AL	464	125	22	1	18	25	61	52	64	2	1	340	.269	.308	.438	.245	51	60-1B 4	48-3B 6
2000	Minnesot	AL	539	148	28	1	17	29	44	81	78	2	0	391	.275	.317	.425	.246	59	121-1B 4	
2001	ChiCubs	NL	351	96	20	1	8	27	59	26	55	0	0	255	.274	.328	.405	.246	38	64-3B -1	19-1B -1
2002	*ChiCubs*	*NL*	*469*	*121*	*23*	*1*	*14*	*44*	*68*	*50*	*61*	*1*	*0*	*348*	*.258*	*.322*	*.401*	*.244*	*51*		

As easy as it is to bash the Cubs, remember that they did put Coomer into a role for which he's well suited, which is backup corner infielder. When Bill Mueller broke down, Coomer provided the Cubs with everything they could have expected, offensively and defensively. Could they have gotten similar quality from somebody like Kevin Orie or Cole Liniak or Chris Snopek? Probably, but a lack of confidence in a player can be just as debilitating as a lack of talent. The Cubs wanted safety, security, and mediocrity. They got it.

Jim Deschaine SS/3B Bats R Age 24

YEAR	TEAM	LGE	AB	H	DB	TP	HR	BB	SO	R	RBI	SB	CS	OUT	BA	OBP	SLG	EQA	EQR	DEFENSE	
1999	Eugene	Nwn	271	55	6	0	6	15	69	26	24	3	3	220	.203	.245	.292	.182	16	26-LF -2	14-SS -12
2000	Lansing	Mid	491	112	22	2	12	44	101	55	47	9	6	385	.228	.295	.354	.220	44	106-SS -12	
2001	Daytona	Fla	499	119	17	1	17	43	110	52	58	3	6	386	.238	.301	.379	.226	47	57-SS -11	48-3B -1
2002	*Toronto*	*AL*	*469*	*123*	*20*	*1*	*17*	*46*	*108*	*64*	*58*	*6*	*6*	*352*	*.262*	*.328*	*.418*	*.249*	*54*		

Deschaine is a sleeper, drafted in 1999 out of Division III Brandeis. During the first half, he was the All-Star shortstop in the Florida State League, but he was never expected to stick at the position as long as he has. In the second half, the Cubs tipped their hand by moving him to third base. He generates good power from a line-drive stroke, and he has the arm strength for third. Traded to the Blue Jays in the Alex Gonzalez deal, his future will depend on how well Eric Hinske succeeds.

Delino DeShields UT Bats L Age 33

YEAR	TEAM	LGE	AB	H	DB	TP	HR	BB	SO	R	RBI	SB	CS	OUT	BA	OBP	SLG	EQA	EQR	DEFENSE	
1999	Baltimor	AL	329	92	10	2	7	34	46	46	34	11	8	245	.280	.349	.386	.249	38	85-2B -8	
2000	Baltimor	AL	558	174	45	5	11	63	72	83	85	38	11	395	.312	.383	.470	.289	89	90-2B -6	39-LF -2
2001	Baltimor	AL	189	41	8	2	4	32	36	32	23	11	1	149	.217	.333	.344	.244	22	45-LF -3	
2001	ChiCubs	NL	164	47	10	3	2	27	30	27	17	12	1	118	.287	.387	.421	.286	26	22-LF -1	12-2B -4
2002	*ChiCubs*	*NL*	*494*	*131*	*29*	*5*	*13*	*73*	*85*	*85*	*61*	*33*	*8*	*371*	*.265*	*.360*	*.423*	*.273*	*72*		

DeShields is useful in a regular role as a platoon leadoff man, playing second base, third base, or left field, not every day at any one position, but starting at the top of the order against right-handed pitching. Tony Phillips and Mark McLemore have already blazed the trail for the utility leadoff hitter, and DeShields could be similarly useful for a couple of years.

Nate Frese SS Bats R Age 24

YEAR	TEAM	LGE	AB	H	DB	TP	HR	BB	SO	R	RBI	SB	CS	OUT	BA	OBP	SLG	EQA	EQR	DEFENSE
1999	Lansing	Mid	378	74	18	2	3	37	73	43	29	5	2	306	.196	.272	.278	.194	25	102-SS 27
2000	Daytona	Fla	434	104	19	3	6	47	93	52	37	5	4	334	.240	.318	.339	.226	40	108-SS 16
2001	WestTenn	Sou	241	41	4	1	4	30	61	23	18	0	1	201	.170	.269	.245	.184	15	70-SS 6
2002	*ChiCubs*	*NL*	*423*	*96*	*17*	*2*	*7*	*53*	*104*	*55*	*39*	*6*	*3*	*330*	*.227*	*.313*	*.326*	*.221*	*38*	

Frese is kind of a latter-day Eddie Joost, in that his basic strengths are his glove and his willingness to take a walk. His power would have been notable in a time before today's power-hitting shortstops came along. Having his season shortened by a broken finger cost him a second half to catch up to Double-A. Despite the injury, Frese was named the best defensive shortstop in the Southern League, showing off the strong arm and range to the hole that will be his ticket to the majors.

Joe Girardi C Bats R Age 37

YEAR	TEAM	LGE	AB	H	DB	TP	HR	BB	SO	R	RBI	SB	CS	OUT	BA	OBP	SLG	EQA	EQR	DEFENSE
1999	NY Yanks	AL	209	53	18	1	2	8	23	24	27	3	1	157	.254	.281	.378	.220	18	61-C -4
2000	ChiCubs	NL	366	102	15	1	6	27	56	46	39	1	0	264	.279	.333	.374	.240	37	96-C 5
2001	ChiCubs	NL	230	61	10	1	3	20	42	23	26	0	1	170	.265	.324	.357	.231	22	60-C 3
2002	*ChiCubs*	*NL*	*304*	*70*	*14*	*1*	*5*	*28*	*54*	*32*	*33*	*1*	*1*	*235*	*.230*	*.295*	*.332*	*.212*	*24*	

Joltless Joe Girardi is a little more than halfway to Bob Boone's all-time games caught record, which is a lot further than anyone probably would have expected. Never, ever underestimate the power of nice. Girardi might lose to Ditka if dey both ran for mayor, but dat's assuming dat Da Coach could move Mayor Daley outta da way.

Ross Gload OF/1B Bats L Age 26

YEAR	TEAM	LGE	AB	H	DB	TP	HR	BB	SO	R	RBI	SB	CS	OUT	BA	OBP	SLG	EQA	EQR	DEFENSE
1999	Brevard	Fla	499	123	21	2	8	39	86	61	53	2	1	377	.246	.304	.345	.221	43	130-1B 0
2000	Portland	Eas	404	102	22	2	14	21	55	48	49	3	1	303	.252	.291	.421	.235	40	49-LF -4 47-1B 0
2000	Iowa	PCL	102	37	7	1	12	7	13	19	29	1	1	66	.363	.408	.804	.359	26	25-LF -5
2000	ChiCubs	NL	31	6	0	1	1	3	9	4	3	0	0	25	.194	.265	.355	.208	2	
2001	Iowa	PCL	473	128	28	8	12	32	80	60	77	8	6	351	.271	.319	.440	.250	55	66-RF -3 46-1B 6
2002	*NY Mets*	*NL*	*466*	*126*	*28*	*4*	*16*	*40*	*81*	*69*	*68*	*5*	*3*	*343*	*.270*	*.328*	*.451*	*.264*	*62*	

After his breakthrough in 2000, Gload stuck with what worked, trying to uppercut everything. At least it's a plan, and he performed very well against right-handed pitching, pasting almost 50 extra-base hits and slugging .536. He has no defensive value in the outfield, but he might be a nifty pinch hitter and spare part. Nabbed by the Rockies off of waivers after the season, he was then traded to the Mets. He has a shot to step in after Mo Vaughn's next breakdown.

Jeff Goldbach C Bats R Age 22

YEAR	TEAM	LGE	AB	H	DB	TP	HR	BB	SO	R	RBI	SB	CS	OUT	BA	OBP	SLG	EQA	EQR	DEFENSE
1999	Lansing	Mid	404	82	16	1	12	42	72	52	41	0	2	324	.203	.283	.337	.210	33	82-C -13
2000	Daytona	Fla	425	71	10	1	8	22	84	36	43	3	3	357	.167	.215	.252	.163	19	99-C -23
2001	Daytona	Fla	149	25	4	1	3	10	30	11	12	0	0	124	.168	.225	.268	.170	7	28-C -4
2001	WestTenn	Sou	100	19	2	1	3	7	17	10	5	1	0	81	.190	.247	.320	.194	7	26-C -5
2002	*ChiCubs*	*NL*	*388*	*84*	*13*	*2*	*13*	*35*	*79*	*49*	*44*	*3*	*2*	*306*	*.216*	*.281*	*.361*	*.215*	*33*	

While the Cubs have made huge strides in player development, catcher is still not one of their strong positions. They have Goldbach, who has inexplicably scuffled since his promising 1999; they have Ryan Jorgensen, the glove man who caddied for Brad Cresse at LSU; and they have Yoon-Min Kweon, a good catch-and-throw Korean who has a lot of work to do as a hitter. Collectively, they're why Todd Hundley was locked up in a long-term deal. Part of the problem is that Goldbach has been temperamental at best, struggling in all phases of the game. He might break out of it; right now, he's struggling to be as successful as Pat Cline.

Ryan Gripp 3B Bats R Age 24

YEAR	TEAM	LGE	AB	H	DB	TP	HR	BB	SO	R	RBI	SB	CS	OUT	BA	OBP	SLG	EQA	EQR	DEFENSE
1999	Eugene	Nwn	264	58	10	1	6	14	76	21	23	1	1	207	.220	.268	.333	.203	19	68-3B 1
2000	Lansing	Mid	509	131	17	0	16	43	95	60	59	2	0	378	.257	.318	.385	.237	52	122-3B -1
2001	Daytona	Fla	247	60	10	0	6	19	61	26	38	3	3	190	.243	.305	.356	.223	22	61-3B -4
2001	WestTenn	Sou	261	55	13	0	8	19	59	27	40	1	0	206	.211	.274	.352	.212	21	62-3B -8
2002	*ChiCubs*	*NL*	*507*	*134*	*19*	*0*	*18*	*46*	*123*	*56*	*62*	*4*	*2*	*375*	*.264*	*.325*	*.408*	*.248*	*57*	

Gripp started slowly at Daytona, then got promoted after a hot month, only to struggle at West Tenn. He also had a defensive slump at the end of the year, finishing with 31 errors. Nevertheless, promoting him is pretty defensible from an organizational perspective. Jim Deschaine needed to be moved to third base, and the Cubs are considering moving Dave Kelton to left field. Gripp's age and defensive limitations make it important for the Cubs to make a decision about him by 2003.

Ricky Gutierrez SS Bats R Age 32

YEAR	TEAM	LGE	AB	H	DB	TP	HR	BB	SO	R	RBI	SB	CS	OUT	BA	OBP	SLG	EQA	EQR	DEFENSE
1999	Houston	NL	270	71	7	5	1	34	42	32	24	1	5	204	.263	.350	.337	.235	27	69-SS -6
2000	ChiCubs	NL	452	125	18	2	11	60	53	71	54	8	2	329	.277	.369	.398	.265	59	116-SS -7
2001	ChiCubs	NL	530	161	25	3	10	38	47	80	69	4	3	372	.304	.359	.419	.262	65	138-SS -8
2002	*Clevelnd*	*AL*	*457*	*128*	*19*	*3*	*10*	*47*	*50*	*67*	*53*	*6*	*3*	*332*	*.280*	*.347*	*.400*	*.252*	*53*	

Gutierrez is a useful player, especially in the league that has Rich Aurilia and a bunch of other guys at shortstop. His basic value is as a stopgap. He's not a good defensive shortstop, but he can play the position, and he can be a valuable hitter in the #2 slot, and obviously not just because of his ability to drop a bunt. The Indians picked him up to replace Roberto Alomar at second base. It could work for one year, but by the time Gutierrez's three-year deal is up, he should be done as a regular.

Bobby Hill 2B Bats B Age 24

YEAR	TEAM	LGE	AB	H	DB	TP	HR	BB	SO	R	RBI	SB	CS	OUT	BA	OBP	SLG	EQA	EQR	DEFENSE
2000	NWK	ATL	397	97	14	4	7	65	56	55	38	33	9	309	.244	.353	.353	.253	50	
2001	WestTenn	Sou	216	57	8	1	2	25	38	25	17	13	6	165	.264	.343	.338	.239	23	50-2B -2
2002	*ChiCubs*	*NL*	*377*	*105*	*12*	*3*	*9*	*58*	*64*	*59*	*41*	*41*	*11*	*283*	*.279*	*.375*	*.398*	*.276*	*57*	

Despite losing more than half of the year to a groin pull, Hill is almost ready to be the Cubs' second baseman and everyday leadoff hitter. However, there's the feeling that he needs to be a little more appreciative, so he has already been condemned to Iowa before camp even opens. He played very well in the Arizona Fall League while hurt, but he was accused of jaking. If Scott Boras hadn't held him out on the White Sox after they drafted him in 1999, would this stuff even get mentioned?

Todd Hundley C Bats B Age 33

YEAR	TEAM	LGE	AB	H	DB	TP	HR	BB	SO	R	RBI	SB	CS	OUT	BA	OBP	SLG	EQA	EQR	DEFENSE
1999	LosAngls	NL	380	81	12	0	26	40	105	50	55	3	0	299	.213	.295	.450	.245	44	101-C -10
2000	LosAngls	NL	303	88	14	0	25	42	63	49	69	0	1	216	.290	.380	.584	.307	56	79-C -8
2001	ChiCubs	NL	247	49	9	0	13	24	75	24	33	0	0	198	.198	.276	.393	.222	23	65-C -8
2002	*ChiCubs*	*NL*	*326*	*69*	*12*	*0*	*18*	*47*	*99*	*40*	*44*	*1*	*0*	*257*	*.212*	*.311*	*.414*	*.245*	*38*	

The sad thing about Hundley's season is that not even his late recovery was useful. He punched seven home runs after September 1, but that was almost all he did; he added a pair of singles and drew three walks in 51 at-bats. Hundley struggled with "dehydration" problems, even on cool days and during night games, and neither his early slump nor his running spat with Baylor helped. Baylor isn't going away, but some players have managed to get from his bad side to his good side (ask Kyle Farnsworth). As organizational disasters go, Hundley isn't likely to out-hit that projection, and he's under contract for more than $18 million over the next three years.

Nic Jackson OF Bats L Age 22

YEAR	TEAM	LGE	AB	H	DB	TP	HR	BB	SO	R	RBI	SB	CS	OUT	BA	OBP	SLG	EQA	EQR	DEFENSE
2000	Eugene	Nwn	302	60	7	4	5	10	69	23	29	11	3	245	.199	.225	.298	.182	17	73-RF -4
2001	Daytona	Fla	512	127	21	3	16	26	103	64	60	13	7	392	.248	.290	.395	.228	49	129-CF -5
2002	*ChiCubs*	*NL*	*502*	*124*	*18*	*3*	*16*	*33*	*113*	*59*	*60*	*20*	*7*	*385*	*.247*	*.293*	*.390*	*.232*	*50*	

"Action" Jackson was named the most exciting player in the Florida State League, and he gets high marks for his quick bat and good speed, so you know he's toolsy. However, as excited as the Cubs are about him, his arm isn't really sufficient for right field, his range may not cut it in center field, and he's going to have to improve offensively to end up in left field. If he does anything at West Tenn, watch him, because he's popular in the organization.

Dave Kelton 3B/LF Bats R Age 22

YEAR	TEAM	LGE	AB	H	DB	TP	HR	BB	SO	R	RBI	SB	CS	OUT	BA	OBP	SLG	EQA	EQR	DEFENSE
1999	Lansing	Mid	510	104	11	2	9	21	132	46	41	10	6	411	.204	.237	.286	.180	28	113-3B -25
2000	Daytona	Fla	527	115	21	3	15	27	133	55	58	4	5	417	.218	.258	.355	.203	39	97-3B -17
2001	WestTenn	Sou	229	63	8	2	10	19	54	29	36	1	2	168	.275	.332	.459	.259	29	47-3B -5
2002	*ChiCubs*	*NL*	*460*	*121*	*16*	*3*	*19*	*37*	*122*	*62*	*63*	*7*	*6*	*345*	*.263*	*.318*	*.435*	*.250*	*54*	

Kelton had been the organizational golden child at third base until this year. A bad streak in the field got the Cubs to thinking about moving him to another position, even after the trades of Eric Hinske and Cole Liniak. A strained wrist cut his season short and temporarily squelched the Cubs' attempt to test him in left field. They aren't giving up on him as a third baseman, but how he looks in camp will make a big impact on whether he stays at the hot corner or moves to left field. The good news is that his command of the strike zone showed some signs of improvement. Given his power and his age, he might turn into the young right-handed-hitting slugger the Cubs will need.

Robert Machado C Bats R Age 29

YEAR	TEAM	LGE	AB	H	DB	TP	HR	BB	SO	R	RBI	SB	CS	OUT	BA	OBP	SLG	EQA	EQR	DEFENSE
1999	Charlott	Int	54	10	2	0	2	3	12	3	6	0	0	44	.185	.248	.333	.196	4	16-C 3
1999	Ottawa	Int	74	15	5	0	0	0	12	5	2	0	1	60	.203	.218	.270	.162	3	20-C -1
2000	Tacoma	PCL	331	92	12	0	10	21	42	34	49	1	4	243	.278	.325	.405	.241	35	71-C 8
2001	Iowa	PCL	179	47	8	0	7	10	33	17	25	0	0	132	.263	.306	.425	.241	19	45-C 0
2001	ChiCubs	NL	136	32	8	0	3	6	22	13	14	0	0	104	.235	.272	.360	.211	11	37-C 1
2002	*ChiCubs*	*NL*	*300*	*77*	*12*	*0*	*12*	*20*	*53*	*31*	*36*	*0*	*1*	*224*	*.257*	*.303*	*.417*	*.239*	*31*	

Part of the "bad Latin element" that had the White Sox upset for a while in the mid-1990s (along with Olmedo Saenz and Mario Valdez), Machado can have value as a caddy for Hundley. With the amount of money committed to Hundley, there isn't a lot of danger that Machado will get a chance to be the new Henry Blanco, which is sort of a good thing.

Fred McGriff 1B Bats L Age 38

YEAR	TEAM	LGE	AB	H	DB	TP	HR	BB	SO	R	RBI	SB	CS	OUT	BA	OBP	SLG	EQA	EQR	DEFENSE
1999	TampaBay	AL	523	168	28	1	35	80	94	75	103	1	0	355	.321	.412	.579	.322	104	122-1B -1
2000	TampaBay	AL	559	160	16	0	29	84	106	79	103	2	0	399	.286	.379	.470	.285	87	143-1B -11
2001	TampaBay	AL	345	116	14	0	22	42	60	43	64	1	1	230	.336	.408	.568	.317	65	73-1B 2
2001	ChiCubs	NL	171	50	8	2	12	25	31	28	42	0	1	122	.292	.390	.573	.308	32	46-1B -3
2002	*ChiCubs*	*NL*	*526*	*138*	*19*	*1*	*30*	*80*	*102*	*66*	*90*	*1*	*1*	*389*	*.262*	*.360*	*.473*	*.279*	*80*	

After taking his time allowing himself to be made a Cub, McGriff then decided to stick around, exercising his option for 2002. He's a good risk, in that he's been available for at least 90% of his team's games since the Reagan administration. McGriff defies the characterization of guys with old players' skills fading in their early thirties, and he's not getting fragile with age. Being a Devil Ray didn't help his legacy any, but he has been a significantly more valuable player than Don Mattingly or Tony Perez or Orlando Cepeda. McGriff's curse is that he's the guy who has no excuses, no what-ifs. Fred McGriff simply is, and has always been, the player you see on the field.

Ty Meadows OF Bats R Age 24

YEAR	TEAM	LGE	AB	H	DB	TP	HR	BB	SO	R	RBI	SB	CS	OUT	BA	OBP	SLG	EQA	EQR	DEFENSE	
1999	Lansing	Mid	452	102	20	3	11	42	93	48	43	8	6	356	.226	.299	.356	.222	41	107-LF -9	
2000	Daytona	Fla	169	43	7	1	5	12	40	21	17	6	3	129	.254	.312	.396	.238	18	43-LF -4	
2000	WestTenn	Sou	256	62	12	3	5	14	71	30	28	3	1	195	.242	.287	.371	.221	22	64-LF -3	
2001	WestTenn	Sou	205	49	9	1	9	32	56	37	24	0	1	157	.239	.354	.424	.261	27	54-LF -3	
2002	*KansasCy*	*AL*	*414*	*112*	*20*	*3*	*13*	*49*	*109*	*57*	*47*	*6*	*4*	*306*	*.271*	*.348*	*.428*	*.259*	*52*		

Drafted out of Vanderbilt, Meadows is known for his unorthodox swing and his work ethic: even noted machismo crank Oscar Acosta grudgingly admitted that he liked him. He's developing the patience to contribute on almost any level, and the good job he's done beating up lefties means that a future as a platoon outfielder might be in the cards. The Royals did well to grab him in the Rule 5 draft; he's a better left-field candidate than Chuck Knoblauch is.

Chad Meyers 2B Bats R Age 26

YEAR	TEAM	LGE	AB	H	DB	TP	HR	BB	SO	R	RBI	SB	CS	OUT	BA	OBP	SLG	EQA	EQR	DEFENSE	
1999	WestTenn	Sou	240	61	18	1	2	19	41	34	22	13	5	185	.254	.324	.363	.237	25	58-2B -4	
1999	Iowa	PCL	173	54	10	2	0	24	18	31	13	13	5	124	.312	.402	.393	.279	26	39-2B -1	
1999	ChiCubs	NL	143	33	9	0	0	7	25	16	5	3	2	112	.231	.281	.294	.198	10	24-2B 1	11-CF 0
2000	Iowa	PCL	301	73	6	0	3	34	40	41	22	25	12	240	.243	.327	.289	.222	28	62-2B -13	15-OF -4
2001	Iowa	PCL	446	122	28	3	8	53	65	77	46	22	7	331	.274	.372	.404	.269	62	101-2B -17	
2002	*Oakland*	*AL*	*470*	*123*	*23*	*2*	*7*	*55*	*73*	*79*	*41*	*25*	*12*	*359*	*.262*	*.339*	*.364*	*.249*	*56*		

Have you ever noticed how rarely somebody like this works out? Second basemen with leadoff skills who can't really field the position always seem to get considered for moves to the outfield. For every arguable success like Eric Owens, there's a passel of guys like Meyers and Keith Miller and Bobby Morris littering the boneyard. He's been signed by the A's, so at least Sacramento will have a good leadoff man.

Luis Montanez SS Bats R Age 20

YEAR	TEAM	LGE	AB	H	DB	TP	HR	BB	SO	R	RBI	SB	CS	OUT	BA	OBP	SLG	EQA	EQR	DEFENSE
2000	Lansing	Mid	30	4	0	0	0	2	7	1	0	0	1	27	.133	.188	.133	.113	1	
2001	Lansing	Mid	503	98	25	3	3	24	132	46	34	9	5	410	.195	.238	.274	.178	27	112-SS -30
2002	*ChiCubs*	*NL*	*429*	*96*	*24*	*2*	*6*	*34*	*121*	*48*	*33*	*14*	*6*	*339*	*.224*	*.281*	*.331*	*.208*	*34*	

The good news is that Montanez is still very young, so he will get better. The club's top pick in 2000 has excellent quickness afield, with good mobility and a strong arm. He opened the year trying to pull everything, but he improved once he got over that and started taking advantage of his quick wrists to flick pitches all over the diamond. The bad news is that he's being compared to Alex S. Gonzalez; there's reason to hope for more. Now that the Cubs have acquired Gonzalez from the Jays, Montanez has three years to work on his game and be ready to replace him in 2005.

Adam Morrissey UT Bats R Age 21

YEAR	TEAM	LGE	AB	H	DB	TP	HR	BB	SO	R	RBI	SB	CS	OUT	BA	OBP	SLG	EQA	EQR	DEFENSE	
2000	Eugene	Nwn	281	57	9	1	5	25	54	20	21	5	6	230	.203	.271	.295	.194	19	45-3B -3	12-2B 0
2001	Lansing	Mid	431	99	18	5	10	58	90	59	39	4	6	338	.230	.326	.364	.234	45	46-2B -9	31-OF -1
2002	*Oakland*	*AL*	*451*	*111*	*17*	*4*	*13*	*61*	*97*	*53*	*49*	*7*	*8*	*348*	*.246*	*.336*	*.388*	*.250*	*54*		

Morrissey might be the best-hitting Aussie import since Dave Nilsson, even though he doesn't have a position yet. He's played second base, third base, and shortstop, but he is best in the outfield. Obviously, his value changes dramatically if he's not an infielder. He's young enough to learn a position, and even if he moves to the outfield, he has enough breakout potential to be valuable. Morrissey was traded to the A's for Mark Bellhorn after the season.

Bill Mueller 3B Bats B Age 31

YEAR	TEAM	LGE	AB	H	DB	TP	HR	BB	SO	R	RBI	SB	CS	OUT	BA	OBP	SLG	EQA	EQR	DEFENSE
1999	San Fran	NL	418	124	13	0	6	60	48	60	38	4	2	296	.297	.389	.371	.266	54	109-3B -3
2000	San Fran	NL	570	159	29	4	11	44	57	98	56	4	2	413	.279	.336	.402	.249	64	136-3B -1
2001	ChiCubs	NL	211	65	12	1	6	36	16	39	24	1	1	147	.308	.414	.460	.297	35	56-3B -1
2002	*ChiCubs*	*NL*	*443*	*125*	*22*	*2*	*9*	*55*	*44*	*72*	*45*	*4*	*2*	*320*	*.282*	*.361*	*.402*	*.263*	*57*	

(Bill Mueller *continued*)

While the Cubs' legacy at third base is much bemoaned, you could interpret their patchwork over the years as occasionally ingenious. Ron Cey, Vance Law, Steve Buechele, and Gary Gaetti all had their moments. The problem isn't with turnover, it's with commitments, as the Cubs never cut bait in time. Bill Mueller is a wonderful player, with generally solid defense, on-base skills, and the ability to spray hits all over the park. But it won't be in the Cubs' interest to keep him beyond 2002, especially if he gets more expensive.

Augie Ojeda IF Bats B Age 27

YEAR	TEAM	LGE	AB	H	DB	TP	HR	BB	SO	R	RBI	SB	CS	OUT	BA	OBP	SLG	EQA	EQR	DEFENSE
1999	Bowie	Eas	468	112	17	3	8	42	47	61	48	4	1	357	.239	.310	.340	.224	42	132-SS 5
2000	Iowa	PCL	395	102	22	1	7	24	26	45	34	11	5	298	.258	.309	.372	.231	38	101-SS -3
2000	ChiCubs	NL	78	17	3	1	2	9	8	10	8	0	1	62	.218	.299	.359	.220	7	19-SS 5
2001	ChiCubs	NL	145	32	5	1	1	11	17	17	13	1	0	113	.221	.283	.290	.200	10	22-SS -1 17-3B 1
2002	*ChiCubs*	*NL*	*397*	*101*	*18*	*2*	*7*	*39*	*40*	*55*	*40*	*9*	*3*	*299*	*.254*	*.321*	*.363*	*.236*	*40*	

He's one of the easy favorites in any "coolest name" contest. Spot duty as a utility infielder is no way to build a respectable-looking season as a hitter, but Ojeda switch hits, he can handle any position, he's a good bunter, and he can drop a fly ball in the Wrigley Field basket once in a while.

Corey Patterson CF Bats L Age 22

YEAR	TEAM	LGE	AB	H	DB	TP	HR	BB	SO	R	RBI	SB	CS	OUT	BA	OBP	SLG	EQA	EQR	DEFENSE
1999	Lansing	Mid	471	116	23	7	14	12	93	56	45	17	7	361	.246	.269	.414	.226	44	102-CF -2
2000	WestTenn	Sou	459	111	21	4	19	32	114	62	68	17	10	357	.242	.299	.429	.240	50	118-CF 4
2000	ChiCubs	NL	42	7	0	0	2	3	13	8	2	1	1	36	.167	.237	.310	.185	3	11-CF -1
2001	Iowa	PCL	366	84	18	2	6	27	59	53	27	16	7	289	.230	.284	.339	.214	31	86-CF -5
2001	ChiCubs	NL	132	31	4	0	4	5	28	28	15	4	0	101	.235	.275	.356	.217	11	37-CF -2
2002	*ChiCubs*	*NL*	*468*	*121*	*23*	*4*	*18*	*40*	*101*	*72*	*54*	*22*	*7*	*354*	*.259*	*.317*	*.440*	*.256*	*59*	

Another year, another time to say Corey Patterson is still one of the best prospects in the game, *but*...

Baylor sent Patterson down after spring training to have him work on his plate coverage. The problem is that he's still trying to cover too much of it. Patterson can occasionally paste a bad pitch, but on what level is that skill just negative reinforcement? If he doesn't learn to lay off bad pitches, he's going to continue to struggle to identify the pitches he should wait for and hurt. He's dropping into Steve Finley/Devon White territory in terms of what can be expected of him, which is still very good. The Cubs need to stick him at a level and leave him alone.

Sammy Sosa RF Bats R Age 33

YEAR	TEAM	LGE	AB	H	DB	TP	HR	BB	SO	R	RBI	SB	CS	OUT	BA	OBP	SLG	EQA	EQR	DEFENSE
1999	ChiCubs	NL	626	176	25	2	61	70	158	110	130	5	8	458	.281	.356	.620	.302	115	162-RF 2
2000	ChiCubs	NL	607	191	31	1	51	83	154	102	132	7	4	420	.315	.399	.621	.323	124	150-RF -10
2001	ChiCubs	NL	580	197	35	5	65	112	130	152	164	0	2	385	.340	.450	.753	.368	158	156-RF -1
2002	*ChiCubs*	*NL*	*545*	*162*	*27*	*3*	*51*	*94*	*139*	*105*	*119*	*4*	*5*	*388*	*.297*	*.401*	*.639*	*.327*	*119*	

There's a lot that's fun about Sosa's career. He blew past 400 home runs in 2001, and with 50 to go before he reaches 500, does anyone really want to say he can't get there in 2002? If he does, he'd also break his tie with Mark McGwire and Babe Ruth for most 50-homer seasons. While his defenders in the MVP debate are right to celebrate the nifty confluence between Sosa's numbers and the unavoidable impression that, at the end of the day, he would beat you, you don't turn a blind eye to the best season ever by a hitter. Left-handers intentionally walked Sosa more than 10% of the time they faced him. Can you blame them?

Matt Stairs 1B/OF Bats L Age 34

YEAR	TEAM	LGE	AB	H	DB	TP	HR	BB	SO	R	RBI	SB	CS	OUT	BA	OBP	SLG	EQA	EQR	DEFENSE
1999	Oakland	AL	528	143	26	3	41	84	109	95	102	2	7	392	.271	.373	.564	.297	94	126-RF -6
2000	Oakland	AL	474	114	22	0	24	73	107	73	82	5	2	362	.241	.343	.439	.262	64	96-RF -8
2001	ChiCubs	NL	342	91	17	0	19	50	64	50	65	2	3	254	.266	.368	.482	.280	53	68-1B 4 16-LF 1
2002	*ChiCubs*	*NL*	*447*	*111*	*21*	*1*	*26*	*77*	*98*	*71*	*75*	*4*	*5*	*341*	*.248*	*.359*	*.474*	*.277*	*69*	

Stairs was everything the Cubs should have expected him to be and then some, but apparently they didn't know what they were getting. Don Baylor's whining about Stairs's pull-hitting ways was probably the single silliest thing any manager said all year (Non-Brenly Division). Did Baylor think he was getting Gerald Perry? A team like the Braves would have killed to have Stairs at first base in 2001. The Wonder Hamster is still a valuable platoon player and will be a great pickup for some team.

Michael Tucker — OF — Bats L — Age 31

YEAR	TEAM	LGE	AB	H	DB	TP	HR	BB	SO	R	RBI	SB	CS	OUT	BA	OBP	SLG	EQA	EQR	DEFENSE
1999	Cincnnti	NL	206	73	9	1	11	33	75	52	41	9	1	227	.247	.328	.416	.250	36	78-RF 5
2000	Cincnnti	NL	270	70	14	3	14	41	59	52	33	12	6	206	.259	.369	.489	.283	44	70-OF 0
2001	Cincnnti	NL	232	58	11	1	7	22	47	32	31	12	5	179	.250	.317	.397	.242	26	57-OF 1
2001	ChiCubs	NL	206	57	9	7	5	22	40	32	32	4	3	152	.277	.349	.461	.267	28	53-OF -1
2002	*KansasCy*	*AL*	*391*	*105*	*18*	*5*	*13*	*48*	*86*	*69*	*51*	*14*	*8*	*293*	*.269*	*.349*	*.440*	*.263*	*52*	

A completely serviceable fourth outfielder often miscast as a regular, Tucker exercised his contract option for 2002 after the season. Considering his talent level and the unfriendliness of the free-agent market, that was as sensible as it gets. The Cubs dumped him on the Royals, who will no doubt ask him to play more often than he should, at the expense of younger players with more upside.

Rondell White — OF — Bats R — Age 30

YEAR	TEAM	LGE	AB	H	DB	TP	HR	BB	SO	R	RBI	SB	CS	OUT	BA	OBP	SLG	EQA	EQR	DEFENSE
1999	Montreal	NL	540	165	28	5	22	26	79	81	60	8	6	381	.306	.350	.498	.276	76	131-LF -6
2000	Montreal	NL	292	89	17	0	13	24	61	50	53	5	1	204	.305	.361	.497	.284	44	74-LF 5
2000	ChiCubs	NL	67	21	2	0	2	5	11	7	7	0	2	48	.313	.376	.433	.263	9	18-LF 2
2001	ChiCubs	NL	324	103	20	1	17	25	47	45	51	1	0	221	.318	.376	.543	.299	54	71-LF -1
2002	*NY Yanks*	*AL*	*447*	*135*	*23*	*2*	*21*	*39*	*77*	*70*	*60*	*5*	*3*	*315*	*.302*	*.358*	*.503*	*.289*	*70*	

It was a worthwhile gamble to give White a spin, and the Cubs got both the best and the worst of it. In the first half, he was the great all-around hitter he can be; in the second half, he was essentially unavailable thanks to a pulled groin. At the time he broke down, White was the Cubs' second banana, but with his fragility, he needs to be fourth or fifth in the bunch for a team to be able to enjoy him when he's around and not miss him when he's inevitably gone. The Yankees, who gave him a two-year, $10-million deal, fit that description to a T.

Eric Young — 2B — Bats R — Age 35

YEAR	TEAM	LGE	AB	H	DB	TP	HR	BB	SO	R	RBI	SB	CS	OUT	BA	OBP	SLG	EQA	EQR	DEFENSE
1999	LosAngls	NL	461	131	25	2	2	58	24	69	40	43	22	352	.284	.370	.360	.255	58	110-2B -11
2000	ChiCubs	NL	611	180	40	2	6	55	36	95	45	51	7	438	.295	.360	.396	.268	82	147-2B -3
2001	ChiCubs	NL	606	176	44	4	6	39	38	102	43	31	14	444	.290	.340	.406	.253	71	139-2B -6
2002	*Milwauke*	*NL*	*565*	*152*	*34*	*3*	*6*	*65*	*36*	*88*	*45*	*47*	*16*	*428*	*.269*	*.344*	*.372*	*.253*	*69*	

We're at a point in the game's history when there aren't a lot of great leadoff hitters. Young is one of the reasons why, although we can haggle about the chicken/egg element of the problem. Are we short on great leadoff men because guys like Eric Young and Tony Womack are being used in the role, or are they being used because we're short on great leadoff men? At his best, Young is adequate leading off, good enough for a team with star talent in the heart of the order. By failing to draw walks all season, Young became a player whose faults were a little more noticeable.

Julio Zuleta — 1B — Bats R — Age 27

YEAR	TEAM	LGE	AB	H	DB	TP	HR	BB	SO	R	RBI	SB	CS	OUT	BA	OBP	SLG	EQA	EQR	DEFENSE	
1999	WestTenn	Sou	484	126	30	3	16	23	124	58	71	2	2	360	.260	.310	.434	.244	53	118-1B -6	
2000	Iowa	PCL	390	112	19	1	22	22	74	61	73	4	3	281	.287	.336	.510	.274	55	82-1B -10	18-LF -1
2000	ChiCubs	NL	69	20	5	0	4	1	17	12	12	0	1	50	.290	.325	.536	.271	10	10-1B -2	
2001	ChiCubs	NL	106	24	4	0	6	8	27	12	25	0	1	83	.226	.295	.434	.237	11	27-1B -4	
2001	Iowa	PCL	145	41	7	0	7	7	30	15	25	3	1	105	.283	.324	.476	.263	19	20-1B -1	11-3B -5
2002	*ChiCubs*	*NL*	*399*	*107*	*22*	*1*	*18*	*28*	*95*	*53*	*66*	*4*	*3*	*295*	*.268*	*.316*	*.464*	*.257*	*49*		

Zuleta opened the year sharing the first base job with Matt Stairs, then wasn't given much of an opportunity to build on his 2000 performance. He doesn't really have a position, since he's immobile almost anywhere he's placed. He'd be an adequate DH for a team that was simply looking for right-handed power for a year, but if he can't adapt to a part-time or bench role, he won't have value to an NL team.

PITCHERS (ERA: 4.50, H/9: 9.0, HR/9: 1.0, BB/9: 3.0, K/9: 6.0, KW: 2.0, PERA: 4.50)

Francis Beltran Throws R Age 21

YEAR	TEAM	LGE	IP	H	ER	HR	BB	K	ERA	W	L	H/9	HR/9	BB/9	K/9	KW	PERA	STUFF
1999	Eugene	Nwn	31.7	35	21	4	16	15	5.97	1	3	9.9	1.1	4.5	4.3	0.5	11.89	-18
2000	Eugene	Nwn	41.0	41	23	3	23	24	5.05	2	3	9.0	0.7	5.0	5.3	0.5	4.80	-4
2000	Lansing	Mid	20.0	19	13	0	21	9	5.85	1	1	8.6	0.0	9.5	4.1	0.2	14.16	-32
2001	Daytona	Fla	91.7	111	81	23	45	45	7.95	2	8	10.9	2.3	4.4	4.4	0.5	7.58	-11

The Cubs' Dominican scouting doesn't get a lot of attention, but Oneri Fleita's Latin American player-development program has done a good job producing results that top the team's earlier commitment to Venezuela. Beltran joins Juan Cruz and Wilton Chavez as one of the more prominent signings by scout Jose Serra. Beltran's tool is that he can pump gas up around 97 mph; he's been added to the 40-man roster for that reason alone.

Jason Bere Throws R Age 31

YEAR	TEAM	LGE	IP	H	ER	HR	BB	K	ERA	W	L	H/9	HR/9	BB/9	K/9	KW	PERA	STUFF
1999	Louisvil	Int	26.0	23	8	0	9	19	2.77	2	1	8.0	0.0	3.1	6.6	1.1	2.93	15
1999	Cincnnti	NL	46.7	49	33	5	33	25	6.36	2	3	9.5	1.0	6.4	4.8	0.4	6.83	-19
1999	Milwauke	NL	23.7	23	12	3	8	17	4.56	1	2	8.7	1.1	3.0	6.5	1.1	5.27	6
2000	Milwauke	NL	116.7	117	68	17	52	87	5.25	6	7	9.0	1.3	4.0	6.7	0.8	4.70	7
2000	Clevelnd	AL	58.7	56	27	5	21	44	4.14	4	3	8.6	0.8	3.2	6.8	1.0	5.48	10
2001	ChiCubs	NL	179.7	172	90	21	69	141	4.51	10	10	8.6	1.1	3.5	7.1	1.0	4.77	13

Shame on us for being completely unfair to Bere last year. More than for any other pitcher, tip your cap to Oscar Acosta for getting a worthwhile season out of Jason Bere. Not only did Bere stay pretty healthy, he produced 18 quality starts in 32 tries. Yes, he still has his limitations—any moderately patient lineup or one with some left-handed sock can hurt him quickly and thoroughly—but Bere has finally become a good fourth starter.

Matthew Bruback Throws R Age 23

YEAR	TEAM	LGE	IP	H	ER	HR	BB	K	ERA	W	L	H/9	HR/9	BB/9	K/9	KW	PERA	STUFF
1999	Lansing	Mid	136.3	161	126	30	98	68	8.32	3	12	10.6	2.0	6.5	4.5	0.3	6.98	-11
2000	Lansing	Mid	53.7	58	30	5	21	21	5.03	3	3	9.7	0.8	3.5	3.5	0.5	4.74	-1
2000	Daytona	Fla	91.7	101	69	14	59	45	6.77	3	7	9.9	1.4	5.8	4.4	0.4	7.11	-11
2001	Daytona	Fla	82.7	82	38	7	25	52	4.14	5	4	8.9	0.8	2.7	5.7	1.0	4.77	13
2001	WestTenn	Sou	43.3	44	25	5	22	27	5.19	2	3	9.1	1.0	4.6	5.6	0.6	13.73	-9

A successful draft-and-follow picked in '97 and signed in '98, Bruback was one of the least-heralded members of the famed '99 Lansing Lugnuts. He's essentially a huge (6′ 7″) kid who throws hard with good movement. The Cubs feel his collapse upon promotion to Double-A was a crisis of confidence as much as anything else. He'll need to develop some sort of breaking pitch or face a conversion to relief.

Wilton Chavez Throws R Age 21

YEAR	TEAM	LGE	IP	H	ER	HR	BB	K	ERA	W	L	H/9	HR/9	BB/9	K/9	KW	PERA	STUFF
2000	Eugene	Nwn	89.0	83	32	0	29	48	3.24	7	3	8.4	0.0	2.9	4.9	0.8	4.07	18
2001	Lansing	Mid	45.7	47	37	8	36	34	7.29	1	4	9.3	1.6	7.1	6.7	0.5	5.61	8
2001	Daytona	Fla	88.7	106	68	19	34	37	6.90	3	7	10.8	1.9	3.5	3.8	0.5	5.98	-6

Hard-throwing and lanky, Chavez sometimes gets compared to Juan Cruz, except that Chavez is a little less savvy. He relies heavily on an especially nasty slider and his low-90s heat, but he hasn't shown a lot of touch on his change-up yet. Because of the Cruz comparison, some people are expecting a huge breakthrough for Chavez, like Cruz's 2000; it's worth remembering that Cruz's development is the exception, not the rule.

Scott Chiasson — Throws R — Age 24

YEAR	TEAM	LGE	IP	H	ER	HR	BB	K	ERA	W	L	H/9	HR/9	BB/9	K/9	KW	PERA	STUFF
1999	So Oregn	Nwn	70.7	83	57	12	44	27	7.26	2	6	10.6	1.5	5.6	3.4	0.3	7.53	-20
2000	Visalia	Cal	149.7	174	116	35	59	85	6.98	5	12	10.5	2.1	3.5	5.1	0.7	4.49	-5
2001	WestTenn	Sou	57.0	54	25	3	23	38	3.95	3	3	8.5	0.5	3.6	6.0	0.8	3.02	-1
2001	Iowa	PCL	12.0	11	4	1	0	10	3.00	1	0	8.3	0.8	0.0	7.5	-1.0	2.41	20
2001	ChiCubs	NL	6.0	7	5	2	2	5	7.50	0	1	10.5	3.0	3.0	7.5	1.3	2.71	-2

Chiasson was drafted from the A's in the Rule 5 draft. The Cubs liked him well enough to secure his rights in a subsequent deal involving Eric Hinske. They claim he can touch 97 mph at times, but he's usually throwing his hard sinker in the low 90s, supplemented with a good slider. With Todd Van Poppel and David Weathers out of the picture, Chiasson is good enough to break into the big-league pen this year and contribute in the way that Courtney Duncan did in 2001.

Ben Christensen — Throws R — Age 24

YEAR	TEAM	LGE	IP	H	ER	HR	BB	K	ERA	W	L	H/9	HR/9	BB/9	K/9	KW	PERA	STUFF
1999	Eugene	Nwn	21.0	24	18	4	16	11	7.71	1	1	10.3	1.7	6.9	4.7	0.3	6.84	-17
1999	Daytona	Fla	22.0	29	26	8	13	12	10.64	0	2	11.9	3.3	5.3	4.9	0.5	7.55	-17
2000	Daytona	Fla	58.0	66	43	14	19	40	6.67	2	4	10.2	2.2	2.9	6.2	1.1	3.24	8
2000	WestTenn	Sou	41.7	41	20	4	15	28	4.32	3	2	8.9	0.9	3.2	6.0	0.9	5.01	14
2001	WestTenn	Sou	16.3	20	14	3	10	5	7.71	1	1	11.0	1.7	5.5	2.8	0.3	8.87	-29

Christensen's stuff can be excellent: his slider hangs out in the mid-80s, while his sinker gets into the mid-90s. He never got on track in 2001, as shoulder tendinitis turned into surgery (stridently labeled "not reconstructive"). He seems brazenly unrepentant for the beaning incident that got him suspended for the last few months of his college career, so it's hard to extend him much sympathy. If he's healthy, Christensen could break out in a big way, potentially pushing someone such as Julian Tavarez out of the rotation by August.

Juan Cruz — Throws R — Age 21

YEAR	TEAM	LGE	IP	H	ER	HR	BB	K	ERA	W	L	H/9	HR/9	BB/9	K/9	KW	PERA	STUFF
1999	Eugene	Nwn	81.3	103	76	22	37	34	8.41	2	7	11.4	2.4	4.1	3.8	0.5	7.64	-9
2000	Lansing	Mid	92.0	96	68	14	67	61	6.65	3	7	9.4	1.4	6.6	6.0	0.5	5.94	7
2000	Daytona	Fla	40.3	44	34	12	21	35	7.59	1	3	9.8	2.7	4.7	7.8	0.8	5.51	18
2001	WestTenn	Sou	119.3	113	62	9	65	87	4.68	6	7	8.5	0.7	4.9	6.6	0.7	5.48	18
2001	ChiCubs	NL	42.7	40	19	3	15	31	4.01	3	2	8.4	0.6	3.2	6.5	1.0	3.25	23

Cruz didn't merely blossom in 2000, he suddenly transmogrified from somebody with talent to one of the best pitching prospects on the planet. He can throw his mid-90s heat, change-up, and slider for strikes at any point in the count, all from a deceptive three-quarters delivery that makes it difficult to pick up anything, and he's shown no real problems in his platoon splits. The organization absolutely loves his intensity and his willingness to work inside. He's going to be very, very good.

Jose Cueto — Throws R — Age 23

YEAR	TEAM	LGE	IP	H	ER	HR	BB	K	ERA	W	L	H/9	HR/9	BB/9	K/9	KW	PERA	STUFF
1999	Eugene	Nwn	24.3	28	15	4	6	11	5.55	1	2	10.4	1.5	2.2	4.1	0.9	5.64	4
2000	Eugene	Nwn	45.3	46	27	3	28	24	5.36	2	3	9.1	0.6	5.6	4.8	0.4	7.93	-10
2000	Lansing	Mid	27.7	26	20	2	28	20	6.51	1	2	8.5	0.7	9.1	6.5	0.4	8.11	-15
2001	Lansing	Mid	91.7	91	57	9	61	58	5.60	4	6	8.9	0.9	6.0	5.7	0.5	6.02	-5
2001	Daytona	Fla	35.0	45	40	15	15	25	10.29	1	3	11.6	3.9	3.9	6.4	0.8	5.96	-8

Added to the 40-man roster, Cueto is a conversion project who was once an outfielder in the Rangers' organization. He is a straight power pitcher who reminds some of Juan Cruz, though like Wilton Chavez, he's not as polished as Cruz. He can snap off a good slider once in a while, but he lacks consistent command of his fastball and does not change speeds well. After logging enough experience to gain some sort of consistency, he's probably going to be converted to relief.

Courtney Duncan — Throws R — Age 27

YEAR	TEAM	LGE	IP	H	ER	HR	BB	K	ERA	W	L	H/9	HR/9	BB/9	K/9	KW	PERA	STUFF
1999	Daytona	Fla	64.0	78	65	15	50	26	9.14	1	6	11.0	2.1	7.0	3.7	0.3	12.10	-56
1999	WestTenn	Sou	43.0	44	37	5	48	26	7.74	1	4	9.2	1.0	10.0	5.4	0.3	11.37	-42
2000	WestTenn	Sou	71.0	70	37	4	39	41	4.69	4	4	8.9	0.5	4.9	5.2	0.5	6.04	-25
2001	ChiCubs	NL	42.7	38	21	4	22	39	4.43	3	2	8.0	0.8	4.6	8.2	0.9	5.10	3

A definite feel-good story. Duncan's struggles when he initially reached Double-A should not have been a surprise. He essentially went uncoached in college at Grambling, and there was a conflict between what some in the Cubs organization expected of him—he was labeled a flamethrower—versus what he was capable of doing. Moving him to the bullpen gave him back his career. He works in the low 90s, changes speeds well, and should be a fine setup man for Flash Gordon and Kyle Farnsworth.

Kyle Farnsworth — Throws R — Age 26

YEAR	TEAM	LGE	IP	H	ER	HR	BB	K	ERA	W	L	H/9	HR/9	BB/9	K/9	KW	PERA	STUFF
1999	Iowa	PCL	38.7	41	21	5	9	22	4.89	2	2	9.5	1.2	2.1	5.1	1.2	3.56	10
1999	ChiCubs	NL	129.0	149	91	26	44	63	6.35	5	9	10.4	1.8	3.1	4.4	0.7	5.02	-7
2000	Iowa	PCL	25.7	24	14	1	18	17	4.91	1	2	8.4	0.4	6.3	6.0	0.5	3.64	-12
2000	ChiCubs	NL	81.7	81	50	13	41	66	5.51	4	5	8.9	1.4	4.5	7.3	0.8	6.22	-3
2001	ChiCubs	NL	79.3	65	29	7	26	86	3.29	6	3	7.4	0.8	2.9	9.8	1.7	2.87	22

Farnsworth is already being compared to Robb Nen; like Nen, he was a mechanical mess as a starter who, forced to focus in a relief role, developed better command of his high-90s heat and splitter. It won't be too long before the Cubs can dispense with the veterans and simply turn over the closer job to Farnsworth. Unlike in previous years, the battle won't be over Farnsworth's confidence level, but over the organization's confidence in itself.

Jeff Fassero — Throws L — Age 39

YEAR	TEAM	LGE	IP	H	ER	HR	BB	K	ERA	W	L	H/9	HR/9	BB/9	K/9	KW	PERA	STUFF
1999	Seattle	AL	150.7	164	102	29	61	100	6.09	6	11	9.8	1.7	3.6	6.0	0.8	6.68	-4
1999	Texas	AL	18.7	17	8	1	8	13	3.86	1	1	8.2	0.5	3.9	6.3	0.8	5.13	1
2000	Boston	AL	139.0	136	64	14	41	96	4.14	8	7	8.8	0.9	2.7	6.2	1.2	4.11	6
2001	ChiCubs	NL	72.0	63	27	5	21	64	3.38	5	3	7.9	0.6	2.6	8.0	1.5	3.81	11

Fassero had a nice run in April and May as the closer, even showing off low-90s velocity that nobody thought he had left in him. Fassero had made 58 appearances by August 1, his highest total since 1992, and a trio of game-blowing outings in August didn't get as much attention as the implosions of one-man wrecking crews such as Turk Wendell. Fassero isn't a situational reliever; he just knows how to pitch, has a good assortment, and usually keeps the ball in the infield.

Chris Gissell — Throws R — Age 24

YEAR	TEAM	LGE	IP	H	ER	HR	BB	K	ERA	W	L	H/9	HR/9	BB/9	K/9	KW	PERA	STUFF
1999	WestTenn	Sou	102.0	116	76	15	63	40	6.71	3	8	10.2	1.3	5.6	3.5	0.3	7.78	-15
2000	WestTenn	Sou	89.3	96	55	11	42	43	5.54	4	6	9.7	1.1	4.2	4.3	0.5	4.94	-1
2001	WestTenn	Sou	155.7	168	98	21	72	83	5.67	7	10	9.7	1.2	4.2	4.8	0.6	7.04	-5

Gissell's failure to develop since being a highly-touted high-school pitcher is the result of a litany of minor injuries and struggles with his command. Since having his shoulder 'scoped in 1999, his heat isn't consistently getting into the low 90s anymore, although he still has a good curve. Being a survivor up to this point is good enough for most; he's at the right age to take a step forward now that he's logged a full season.

Tom Gordon — Throws R — Age 34

YEAR	TEAM	LGE	IP	H	ER	HR	BB	K	ERA	W	L	H/9	HR/9	BB/9	K/9	KW	PERA	STUFF
1999	Boston	AL	19.0	14	8	2	10	24	3.79	1	1	6.6	0.9	4.7	11.4	1.2	4.71	22
2001	ChiCubs	NL	43.7	33	14	3	14	54	2.89	4	1	6.8	0.6	2.9	11.1	1.9	3.60	31

Gordon's elbow is still a major problem. He started off hurting, and he ended up with tendinitis and soreness, missing a third of the season in all. He still throws hard, and he still has the great curve that is the source of the problem. Gordon is pretty much reduced to the Eckersley role, in which he should just be handed ninth-inning leads. Working him on consecutive days isn't always a good idea.

Felix Heredia — Throws L — Age 26

YEAR	TEAM	LGE	IP	H	ER	HR	BB	K	ERA	W	L	H/9	HR/9	BB/9	K/9	KW	PERA	STUFF
1999	ChiCubs	NL	54.7	52	27	6	21	45	4.45	3	3	8.6	1.0	3.5	7.4	1.1	5.49	3
2000	ChiCubs	NL	57.3	53	28	5	27	46	4.40	3	3	8.3	0.8	4.2	7.2	0.9	4.36	1
2001	ChiCubs	NL	36.0	38	21	5	14	23	5.25	2	2	9.5	1.3	3.5	5.8	0.8	6.99	-14

Rather than give Heredia an opportunity to stretch out his arm and really work on harnessing his plus fastball, Baylor and Acosta rooted him even more firmly in the situational role, using him in 14 of the season's first 24 games. It was pretty much downhill from there. Now that he's in Toronto, he has the opportunity to finally transcend the specialist role. Don't be surprised when he embarrasses the Cubs.

Aaron Krawiec — Throws L — Age 23

YEAR	TEAM	LGE	IP	H	ER	HR	BB	K	ERA	W	L	H/9	HR/9	BB/9	K/9	KW	PERA	STUFF
2000	Eugene	Nwn	73.7	80	48	13	30	46	5.86	3	5	9.8	1.6	3.7	5.6	0.8	4.71	6
2001	Lansing	Mid	160.7	181	117	32	70	94	6.55	6	12	10.1	1.8	3.9	5.3	0.7	8.06	-5

It's been a long time since Kenny Holtzman was a Cub, and that long since the Cubs have had a really good left-handed starter. Unfair as it is to bring up that legacy in conjunction with a low-A ball pitcher, Krawiec cooks with gas using a low-90s sinker, and he flashes a great overhand curve and change-up. He has the most upside of any left-handed starter in the organization.

Jon Lieber — Throws R — Age 32

YEAR	TEAM	LGE	IP	H	ER	HR	BB	K	ERA	W	L	H/9	HR/9	BB/9	K/9	KW	PERA	STUFF
1999	ChiCubs	NL	214.0	207	92	26	39	167	3.87	14	10	8.7	1.1	1.6	7.0	2.1	4.29	20
2000	ChiCubs	NL	253.0	256	116	32	44	171	4.13	15	13	9.1	1.1	1.6	6.1	1.9	4.28	14
2001	ChiCubs	NL	220.0	227	97	22	37	119	3.97	14	10	9.3	0.9	1.5	4.9	1.6	4.06	9

While it seems as if he's just been noticed, Lieber hasn't really taken a step forward so much as he's stayed healthy. His declining strikeout rates are a reason to be concerned, especially as he has yet to come up with something that works consistently against left-handed hitters. He reached 20 wins in no small part because of the unbalanced schedule, beating the Reds five times in six starts. He's a *BP* favorite, but those are all warning signs for a worse year in 2002.

Mike Meyers — Throws R — Age 24

YEAR	TEAM	LGE	IP	H	ER	HR	BB	K	ERA	W	L	H/9	HR/9	BB/9	K/9	KW	PERA	STUFF
1999	Daytona	Fla	98.3	100	66	19	48	82	6.04	4	7	9.2	1.7	4.4	7.5	0.9	2.99	18
1999	WestTenn	Sou	32.7	25	10	1	10	36	2.76	3	1	6.9	0.3	2.8	9.9	1.8	1.52	53
2000	WestTenn	Sou	54.7	57	33	7	26	34	5.43	2	4	9.4	1.2	4.3	5.6	0.7	3.59	8
2000	Iowa	PCL	62.3	69	43	11	28	35	6.21	2	5	10.0	1.6	4.0	5.1	0.6	7.60	-4
2001	Iowa	PCL	143.0	140	74	10	72	88	4.66	8	8	8.8	0.6	4.5	5.5	0.6	3.78	8

The meteoric rises of Juan Cruz and Carlos Zambrano have dropped Meyers out of the organization's immediate plans. Don't worry: he's going to be a big-league starter somewhere. He mixes his snapping curve with adequate heat and an effective change-up, which just isn't very sexy compared to the mid-90s heat with great movement that seems to be standard issue among so many Cubs farmhands.

Roberto Miniel — Throws R — Age 22

YEAR	TEAM	LGE	IP	H	ER	HR	BB	K	ERA	W	L	H/9	HR/9	BB/9	K/9	KW	PERA	STUFF
1999	Ogden	Pio	89.3	98	57	11	42	39	5.74	4	6	9.9	1.1	4.2	3.9	0.5	6.48	0
2000	Ogden	Pio	83.0	95	56	16	24	41	6.07	3	6	10.3	1.7	2.6	4.4	0.9	4.83	2
2001	Beloit	Mid	106.3	109	56	13	36	67	4.74	6	6	9.2	1.1	3.0	5.7	0.9	6.33	4
2001	Lansing	Mid	29.3	37	28	8	15	13	8.59	1	2	11.4	2.5	4.6	4.0	0.4	6.18	-20

Miniel was the hidden bonus of the Quevedo/Weathers trade with the Brewers. He's a stringbean out of the Dominican Republic who can throw in the low 90s, and he has five pitches: the heater, a curve, a slider, a forkball, and a change-up. In terms of value, he's what the Cubs really got for Quevedo, in that the Cubs landed a prospect who might be ready in two or three years for one who's ready now.

Phil Norton — Throws L — Age 26

YEAR	TEAM	LGE	IP	H	ER	HR	BB	K	ERA	W	L	H/9	HR/9	BB/9	K/9	KW	PERA	STUFF
1999	WestTenn	Sou	85.0	84	46	8	44	55	4.87	4	5	8.9	0.8	4.7	5.8	0.6	3.84	6
1999	Iowa	PCL	81.7	97	70	22	34	46	7.71	2	7	10.7	2.4	3.7	5.1	0.7	6.91	-8
2000	Iowa	PCL	162.0	168	108	20	103	97	6.00	6	12	9.3	1.1	5.7	5.4	0.5	5.76	-7
2001	Iowa	PCL	72.7	69	41	4	52	47	5.08	4	4	8.5	0.5	6.4	5.8	0.5	3.98	-20

Norton throws hard and has a nice curve. With Fassero and Ohman ahead of him, Norton is, at best, on the 40-man roster to create depth to help MacPhail make a trade. He'll be more than just a good situational reliever; his sinker is really tough to get out of the infield, particularly for left-handers.

Will Ohman — Throws L — Age 24

YEAR	TEAM	LGE	IP	H	ER	HR	BB	K	ERA	W	L	H/9	HR/9	BB/9	K/9	KW	PERA	STUFF
1999	Daytona	Fla	104.0	117	80	23	50	65	6.92	4	8	10.1	2.0	4.3	5.6	0.6	5.92	-6
2000	WestTenn	Sou	69.3	63	34	5	37	57	4.41	4	4	8.2	0.6	4.8	7.4	0.8	3.30	6
2001	Iowa	PCL	51.3	51	32	10	20	47	5.61	2	4	8.9	1.8	3.5	8.2	1.2	4.53	5
2001	ChiCubs	NL	12.0	12	7	2	5	10	5.25	0	1	9.0	1.5	3.8	7.5	1.0	7.75	-1

One of the many targets of the hard-hitting comedy *Acosta Unplugged,* Ohman has a good sinking fastball that gets into the 90s and a good curve. Assuming there's nobody left in the organization who gets angry when a young pitcher asks to see a trainer in spring training, Ohman might have a shot at replacing Felix Heredia as the second lefty in the pen.

Mark Prior — Throws R — Age 21

He's here as a courtesy to remind you that he's around, that he's arguably the greatest college pitcher of all time, and that he might be in the majors before the end of the season. Prior has great heat, a power curve, and enough command that people thought he was ready to step into the major leagues straight from USC. With $10.5 million guaranteed up front, the pressure will be on for him to produce right away.

Steve Smyth — Throws L — Age 24

YEAR	TEAM	LGE	IP	H	ER	HR	BB	K	ERA	W	L	H/9	HR/9	BB/9	K/9	KW	PERA	STUFF
1999	Eugene	Nwn	25.3	30	17	4	8	7	6.04	1	2	10.7	1.4	2.8	2.5	0.4	7.16	-16
1999	Lansing	Mid	54.7	62	44	10	34	26	7.24	2	4	10.2	1.6	5.6	4.3	0.4	8.08	-14
2000	Daytona	Fla	135.7	153	97	22	70	63	6.43	5	10	10.1	1.5	4.6	4.2	0.4	5.18	-8
2001	WestTenn	Sou	114.3	124	68	15	45	57	5.35	5	8	9.8	1.2	3.5	4.5	0.6	3.90	0

The Cubs had initially considered Smyth a future reliever, and they are only now taking him more seriously as a starter as he continues to succeed in the role. He's already wearing the usual labels applied to lefties, such as "scrappy" and "crafty." In English, that means he can throw four pitches for strikes, he keeps the ball low, and he doesn't throw hard. Smyth had to be shut down early to have his shoulder 'scoped, but he's in good shape for 2002.

Kevin Tapani — Throws R — Age 38

YEAR	TEAM	LGE	IP	H	ER	HR	BB	K	ERA	W	L	H/9	HR/9	BB/9	K/9	KW	PERA	STUFF
1999	ChiCubs	NL	140.3	146	62	11	28	66	3.98	9	7	9.4	0.7	1.8	4.2	1.2	4.85	4
2000	ChiCubs	NL	199.3	208	103	31	39	133	4.65	11	11	9.4	1.4	1.8	6.0	1.7	4.77	11
2001	ChiCubs	NL	168.0	167	77	21	36	120	4.13	10	9	8.9	1.1	1.9	6.4	1.7	5.01	14

While Tapani isn't the workhorse he used to be, he's become a very valuable third or fourth starter. Reliance on his splitter makes him bass-ackwards, so not surprisingly, he struggled against right-handed-hitting lineups such as the Astros, which is exactly what the Cubs didn't need down the stretch. He's definitely valuable for a team that can spot him against the right kind of opponents.

Julian Tavarez Throws R Age 29

YEAR	TEAM	LGE	IP	H	ER	HR	BB	K	ERA	W	L	H/9	HR/9	BB/9	K/9	KW	PERA	STUFF
1999	San Fran	NL	57.3	61	32	7	21	30	5.02	3	3	9.6	1.1	3.3	4.7	0.7	6.03	-16
2000	Colorado	NL	121.7	127	60	9	44	55	4.44	7	7	9.4	0.7	3.3	4.1	0.6	3.66	-10
2001	ChiCubs	NL	158.0	159	77	11	62	86	4.39	9	9	9.1	0.6	3.5	4.9	0.7	5.51	-1

Tavarez has never been consistent enough as a reliever to be as useful in the pen as he is at the bottom of a rotation. To the Cubs' credit, they signed him to be the #4 starter. He did not wear down during the season and was throwing in the mid-90s in September. He's simply a five-inning starter. If you accept him as a good fifth starter with some anger-management issues, you won't be disappointed. Even with Tapani's departure, Tavarez might get squeezed out of the rotation by July.

Todd Van Poppel Throws R Age 30

YEAR	TEAM	LGE	IP	H	ER	HR	BB	K	ERA	W	L	H/9	HR/9	BB/9	K/9	KW	PERA	STUFF
1999	Nashvill	PCL	166.0	178	109	28	72	105	5.91	7	11	9.7	1.5	3.9	5.7	0.7	5.72	-6
2000	Iowa	PCL	42.0	37	15	3	11	37	3.21	3	2	7.9	0.6	2.4	7.9	1.7	4.41	15
2000	ChiCubs	NL	87.0	82	44	9	40	68	4.55	5	5	8.5	0.9	4.1	7.0	0.9	3.64	1
2001	ChiCubs	NL	72.3	63	34	8	34	72	4.23	4	4	7.8	1.0	4.2	9.0	1.1	2.66	12

Van Poppel is only six years removed from the point at which Art Howe decided he'd either have to start or die, and it took until 2000 for a team to put him back into the relief role in which he'd enjoyed his only big-league success. As much as Van Poppel might still be thought of as one of the great first-round disasters of all time, he's a good reliever. Signed by the Rangers, he's being reunited with Oscar Acosta in Texas. He's a good bet to win a dozen games in middle relief.

Dave Weathers Throws R Age 32

YEAR	TEAM	LGE	IP	H	ER	HR	BB	K	ERA	W	L	H/9	HR/9	BB/9	K/9	KW	PERA	STUFF
1999	Milwauke	NL	96.3	98	51	13	32	67	4.76	5	6	9.2	1.2	3.0	6.3	1.0	4.32	-3
2000	Milwauke	NL	76.3	77	36	6	26	44	4.24	4	4	9.1	0.7	3.1	5.2	0.8	3.11	-6
2001	Milwauke	NL	51.3	47	22	3	22	37	3.86	3	3	8.2	0.5	3.9	6.5	0.8	2.16	1
2001	ChiCubs	NL	27.0	27	13	3	8	16	4.33	2	1	9.0	1.0	2.7	5.3	1.0	3.20	-6

Acquiring Weathers was a bad move. Weathers's value isn't as your best setup man, because he's not consistent enough against left-handed hitters. There's a danger that he'll be the next Russ Springer, commanding top dollar because someone's going to look at that good four-month run he had with the Brewers in 2001 and think he's about to become Jeff Nelson. The focus should be on his successful career as a long/middle reliever. The Mets will be paying him more than $9 million over the next three years, expecting more than long/middle relief.

John Webb Throws R Age 23

YEAR	TEAM	LGE	IP	H	ER	HR	BB	K	ERA	W	L	H/9	HR/9	BB/9	K/9	KW	PERA	STUFF
2000	Lansing	Mid	134.3	139	64	9	44	62	4.29	8	7	9.3	0.6	2.9	4.2	0.7	4.48	6
2000	Daytona	Fla	17.3	18	8	2	4	12	4.15	1	1	9.3	1.0	2.1	6.2	1.5	7.18	11
2001	Daytona	Fla	21.7	20	8	0	8	12	3.32	1	1	8.3	0.0	3.3	5.0	0.8	7.89	0

Webb is a sinker/slider guy who already has low-90s heat and a plus change-up. The Cubs think he could add even more velocity as he fills out. He had to have Tommy John surgery early on in 2001, so he won't resurface until late in 2002. He's a name to remember.

Kerry Wood Throws R Age 25

YEAR	TEAM	LGE	IP	H	ER	HR	BB	K	ERA	W	L	H/9	HR/9	BB/9	K/9	KW	PERA	STUFF
2000	ChiCubs	NL	135.0	125	72	15	72	117	4.80	7	8	8.3	1.0	4.8	7.8	0.8	4.64	19
2001	ChiCubs	NL	165.3	136	72	14	82	175	3.92	10	8	7.4	0.8	4.5	9.5	1.1	3.64	32

Wood missed a month with shoulder tendinitis, producing plenty of shrieking that his problem was "normal," not "structural." This shrieking was followed by almost daily twittering about whether he'd save the club's playoff chances this week or next. The trouble with Wood is that his curve, one of the game's best, generates a dangerous amount of torque. His overall numbers don't give him enough credit; he had a higher percentage of quality starts than Jon Lieber did. While we probably all still think of Wood as a young kid, he's older than Roger Clemens was when the Rocket finally got straightened out in 1986.

Michael Wuertz **Throws R** **Age 23**

YEAR	TEAM	LGE	IP	H	ER	HR	BB	K	ERA	W	L	H/9	HR/9	BB/9	K/9	KW	PERA	STUFF
1999	Lansing	Mid	168.7	187	97	22	49	73	5.18	8	11	10.0	1.2	2.6	3.9	0.7	6.60	1
2000	Daytona	Fla	167.3	191	126	35	76	93	6.78	6	13	10.3	1.9	4.1	5.0	0.6	5.12	0
2001	WestTenn	Sou	153.7	174	112	31	63	85	6.56	5	12	10.2	1.8	3.7	5.0	0.7	5.93	-1

Wuertz would get much higher billing in other organizations. Although he was picked out of high school, he's a command-and-control sinker/slider guy with low-90s velocity. The icing will be when he perfects a change-up, which will help him freeze lefties and avoid an easy souvenir or two. Within the organization, he's compared to the Twins' Kyle Lohse, in that he's a good bet to be at least a fourth or fifth starter. He's young, and he has yet to really struggle, so the Cubs may be selling him short.

Carlos Zambrano **Throws R** **Age 21**

YEAR	TEAM	LGE	IP	H	ER	HR	BB	K	ERA	W	L	H/9	HR/9	BB/9	K/9	KW	PERA	STUFF
1999	Lansing	Mid	151.3	170	97	18	70	56	5.77	6	11	10.1	1.1	4.2	3.3	0.4	5.81	-2
2000	WestTenn	Sou	55.3	56	27	4	21	29	4.39	3	3	9.1	0.7	3.4	4.7	0.7	2.73	14
2000	Iowa	PCL	57.3	55	32	4	38	37	5.02	3	3	8.6	0.6	6.0	5.8	0.5	4.68	-1
2001	Iowa	PCL	146.3	135	72	10	77	110	4.43	8	8	8.3	0.6	4.7	6.8	0.7	4.66	21

The Cubs are done flirting with making Zambrano a closer, at least for now. He throws two-seam and four-seam heat from a couple of arm slots with great movement, and his breaking stuff, when it shows up, can be excellent. That's the rub, and the reason why he may yet return to the pen. Since his age is in doubt, he could end up doing almost anything; a long-relief role in the big-league pen would be a good way to get him acclimated.

Cincinnati Reds

Is there a more enigmatic franchise in baseball than the Cincinnati Reds? Usually we would be falling all over ourselves to praise an organization that has the vision to acquire top-tier talent such as Ken Griffey Jr., coupled with the recognition that it can rehabilitate and retread pitchers or tarnished hitting prospects at low cost. When said franchise is doing all that in the face of cost controls implemented in response to Cincinnati's medium-market status, it's not only an important concession to fiscal reality, it's smart baseball business.

How do you shoehorn the Reds into the big-market/small-market paradigm? Is there any structure here that would lend itself to a tidy description?

Perhaps more than any other franchise, the Reds make it clear that an organization is nothing more than a collection of individuals. The Reds also reflect the danger of trying to lump organizations, front-office personnel, or players into easily understood boxes labeled "good" and "bad." Instead, the Reds are defined by fuzzier notions of contingency, possibility, and chance. In this, they are an expression of the strange combination of strengths and weaknesses of their general manager, Jim Bowden.

Reds Prospectus

2001 record: 66–96; Fifth place, NL Central

Pythagenport W/L: 70–92

Runs scored: 735 (12th in NL)

Runs allowed: 850 (14th in NL)

Team EqA: .253 (13th in NL)

2001 batters age: 28.1 (sixth-youngest in NL)

2001 pitchers age: 27.6 (fifth-youngest in NL)

Ballpark: Cinergy Field; neutral park; Park Factor of 0.994

2001: Lousy numbers hid a lot of good developments in 2001, led by Adam Dunn's debut.

2002: They're not as good as the best teams in the Central this year, but will be in the mix starting in 2003.

Bowden is probably the most interesting GM in the game today, a status that has as much to do with his unpredictability as anything else. Unlike Roland Hedley's search for Ronald Reagan's brain in *Doonesbury* in the 1980s, however, the search for a method to Bowden's madness might not be completely hopeless.

Bowden has not been shy about taking risks. By trying to breathe life into the careers of Ruben Sierra and Deion Sanders and Dante Bichette, or by helping to keep Terry Pendleton out of street clothes, Bowden has made more than his share of roster boo-boos. Balanced against those boo-boos is his outstanding record of nabbing talented young hitters coming off of bad seasons. Whether it was Bret Boone, Paul Konerko, Mike Cameron, Jeffrey Hammonds, Todd Walker, Michael Tucker, or Dmitri Young, Bowden and his staff correctly identified young hitters capable of doing better things if freed from their old circumstances.

You might characterize some of these guys as toolsy, but Dmitri Young and Paul Konerko aren't known for their cat-like swiftness, and Bret Boone was not known for his athleticism coming up in the Mariners organization. All of these guys were south of 30 years old, and most of them were picked up when they were around 26 to 28, exactly the right time for them to bust out and make the Reds look good. Most of them came out of organizations known for poor instruction, and the Reds are confident in their ability to help guys like this. While Juan Encarnacion isn't anyone's idea of a great risk, as a 26-year-old refugee from the drifting Tigers, he fits the pattern.

Bowden's sweet tooth for tools isn't necessarily a bad thing in itself. If there's any lesson to be learned from last summer's pathetic final spin with Deion Sanders, it is that flyers on tools players have to be just that, flyers, and not investments. Tools goofs have to be harvested the same way that an organization develops pitching prospects—by the fistful—in the hope that somewhere amidst those jangling tool belts a single worthwhile Jermaine Dye lingers.

While we can sort these players into neat piles—the ones we thought were good ideas at the time (and who usually meet our expectations) and those other guys (such as Freon Deion)—you have to see both groups as products of the same organizational thought process. Clearly, Bowden likes to take a chance on guys who are down on their luck, but his willingness to take anybody at the right price indicates that Bowden may be more of a bargain shopper than a GM with a rigorous philosophy of getting and retaining young players who will break out. Jon Nunnally got a break in 1997 and rewarded the Reds for it. He was also dumped a couple of months into 1998, before his 27th birthday.

Bowden's capacity for finding bargain-bin talent extends to the pitching staff. Here, the role of Don Gullett as one of the game's great reconditioners of pre-owned hurlers is instrumental to what success the Reds have enjoyed. Obviously talented pitchers such as Pete Harnisch, Steve Parris,

Ron Villone, Elmer Dessens, Stan Belinda, Mike Remlinger, and Jeff Shaw have all become wealthy and successful thanks to the Reds' willingness to take chances. However, pitching is by its nature combustible, and no matter how good Gullett is, the Reds couldn't save David Weathers or Jason Bere, couldn't breathe new life into the careers of Gabe White or Mark Wohlers, and couldn't turn around low-risk projects such as Andy Larkin or Manny Aybar.

The Reds have also suffered a few high-profile disappointments. Rob Bell had to be traded when it became obvious that he wasn't going to able to work with Gullett and manager Bob Boone. Ed Yarnall disappointed a lot of people with his indifference to his future. Were the Reds smart to take a chance on Gabe White, or were they dumb to trade him too soon for so little? It's not necessary to get bogged down in the specifics. The organization deserves credit for treating all of these guys as being virtually interchangeable (though this is less true for Reds pitchers than hitters). As long as the Reds do not have to commit big money, they've demonstrated a willingness to sift through as many cereal boxes as it takes to cobble together an adequate big-league staff, with the 2001 season being an important exception for reasons we'll explain in a bit.

One of the perils of haphazardly labeling teams by market size is that the labels contribute to a circular reasoning in regard to the teams' success or failure. In 2001, when the Reds slipped even further from their 1999 breakout, the inevitable hand-wringing and poor-mouthing began. Their failure was explained away as the inevitable product of a small-market team's need of heaping helpings of luck and health to win. Injuries were used as an early, easy excuse. The breakdowns of Harnisch, Griffey, and Barry Larkin were only the pointed edge of the scythe of injuries that cut through the Reds in 2001. A contributing problem was the team's failure to acquire adequate talent in the trades of Denny Neagle, Steve Parris, and Ron Villone. Scott Williamson's breakdown had to have been anticipated for years, but when both Yarnall and Bell washed out, and only Elmer Dessens and Jim Brower were even moderately useful from Bowden's latest group of interesting project pitchers, it became pretty clear that the Reds were in for a long and disappointing year. Keep in mind that the Reds weren't merely unhealthy: they also endured a lot of bad luck, as upper-level prospects such as Yarnall, Bell, Clayton Andrews, Osvaldo Fernandez, and Leo Estrella fell flat on their collective face.

The simultaneous failure of so many of the potential temps serves as a valid reminder that Bowden's relentless experimentation comes with risks. A larger problem than the injuries themselves—after all, Harnisch had been a risk since 2000—was that most of the contingencies failed. This brings up the question of whether Bowden needs a foil within the organization. A general manager can turn over his roster as often as it strikes his fancy, but it is the manager who has to guide a team through that turnover, and it is the manager who has to adapt to circumstances. If Bowden is willing to take a chance on almost any player's strengths, what kind of manager would provide the best complementary perspective? Ideally, you'd like somebody who can accept Bowden's commitment to flexibility while injecting some element of patience. That is exactly who Bob Boone is not.

In his resurrection as a manager, Boone narrowly beat out Ron Oester, mostly due to the Reds' unwillingness to meet Oester's modest salary request. The mystery is why Boone was considered at all. In his spectacular failures as a manager at Tacoma and at Kansas City, Boone demonstrated a wide-ranging appreciation of almost everything under the sun, but very little grasp of how to handle a pitching staff, run a lineup, try to win now, or successfully develop young players to win later.

More shocking, Boone walked into the Reds job claiming he'd learned nothing from failure, because to his way of thinking, he hadn't failed. The Reds didn't give appropriate consideration to firing him at that point. Ask Boone who best handled young pitchers, and he'll modestly say he did. Ask Boone if he's a great manager, and he'll tell you that of course he is. Some people earn the right to be arrogant, and I don't think any of us can understand what life is like if you're the smartest person you've ever met. But when there's so little in the way of supporting evidence, bravado withers into phony chutzpah.

A Bowden/Boone management tandem is problematic in that it turns a roster into something less than the sum of its parts. For the sake of argument, Boone and Bowden can both find value in almost anybody, from Deion Sanders to Brady Clark to Wilton Guerrero to D.T. Cromer to Donnie Sadler to Bill Selby. But Bowden and Boone get paid to identify who they need most from that group. Instead, the Reds opened the season without carrying anybody on the bench who could hit, in no small part because Boone and Bowden couldn't choose from among Guerrero, Sadler, and Juan Castro for one roster spot.

Bob Boone is like television; every few hours, you see something worthwhile, but those gems are lost in a tidal wave of mind-numbing dreck. Wooing beat writers, Boone spent his spring yammering about his personal anguish over having to demote people such as Clark and Cromer or minor-league veterans such as Chris Nichting. Soon he began bubbling about how he really liked Wilton Guerrero, if only he'd get to see more of Guerrero's speed, entirely missing the point that Guerrero's second major problem—behind not having a position—is that he doesn't get on base.

With Boone, though, you need only flip the channel to find a good idea. Also during spring training, he claimed that he'd use Dennis Reyes in more than just a situational role.

Reyes was once one of the best left-handed starting-pitcher prospects in baseball, so stretching out his arm seemed like a sensible plan. Unfortunately, like most of Bob Boone's good ideas, this one was abandoned; instead of giving Reyes a bigger role in the bullpen, Boone moved him into the rotation. The problem isn't that Boone doesn't have good ideas; the problem is he can't stick with any *one* good idea.

The injuries the Reds suffered in 2001 caused a secondary problem: the team was held hostage by some of the injured players. Ken Griffey Jr. had no business spending the first month of the season on the active roster, but he didn't want to be placed on the DL, and the Reds lacked the courage to tell him to live with it. Similar attempts to cater to Larkin and Harnisch achieved nothing. In May, Boone was babbling about how, after personally catching Harnisch, he could state for a fact that Harnisch was fine. Arguing from a position of authority isn't worth much when you're flat-out wrong. The Reds were worse than they had to be because Bowden and Boone and the players dithered, and nobody who was supposed to be in charge made anything resembling a decision.

Flogging Boone, while a worthy use of time, ignores a more important point. 2001 was the year in which the Reds served notice that they don't intend to endlessly cycle through journeymen and non-roster invitees. With the team already spinning out of contention by May, the Reds were in position to dish out more of the same, entrusting the rest of the season to retreads such as Frankie Rodriguez and minor-league veterans such as Larry Luebbers. Doing so would have created a marginally more competitive team, and the season might have looked superficially better.

To the Reds' credit, they didn't do that. Instead of calling up their low-ceiling, low-risk guys from Louisville, the Reds showed that their player-development program was able to produce something more than guys named Pokey, Gookie, and Gumby. By mid-June, the Reds had four rookies in the rotation, and while Chris Reitsma and Brian Reith were the best parts of the Bichette and Neagle deals, Lance Davis and Jose Acevedo were homegrown and looked reasonably ready. Although Bob Boone whined that "we need to find our own Roy Oswalts," the Reds got quality starts half of the time they sent Juan Acevedo and Lance Davis to the mound.

Davis and Acevedo are just the front end of a wave of homegrown pitching talent. A 16th-round pick, Davis is sort of a poster boy for a commitment to developing pitching by drafting depth. Guys like Acevedo, Scott Dunn, and even Ryan Mottl aren't as sexy as Ty Howington, Dustin Moseley, or David Gil, but the point is that the Reds are getting more meat out of their drafts, and the cumulative strength means they won't have to settle for the next Elmer Dessens.

At the plate, either by design or luck, the Reds are in the same boat as the Cardinals. They may not have many hitting prospects, but with Adam Dunn, Austin Kearns, and Ben Broussard, how many do they need? Kearns and Dunn can be major stars, Broussard will be a good major-league regular, and Ruben Mateo might be one of the most interesting retread experiments in the game today. The retread cycle will always be able to generate the Brady Clarks of the world, but scoring prospects the caliber of Dunn and Kearns gives the Reds the foundation of a great offensive team.

It would be hard to describe the Reds as an organization that has come to grips with its suspected financial limitations. Many of their actions might be directed by fiscal restraints. Did they draft Brent Sowers in the first round in 2001 because they'd already borrowed against their 2001 budget to sign 2000 pick Dustin Moseley, and Sowers wasn't going to sign for what the Reds could theoretically offer? And if they are that handicapped, how do you explain big chunks of change committed to past-peak veterans such as Larkin or to dubious prospects such as Alejandro Diaz and Dane Sardinha?

This is not solely Jim Bowden's responsibility; last winter's 11th-hour agreement with Barry Larkin was a decision made for the organization by owner Carl Lindner. The organization faces a problem with Sean Casey right now, and if Lindner again hijacks the final decision, especially with Ben Broussard nearly ready to step into Casey's role, then it's hard to extend much sympathy to the Reds for their financial limitations.

The Reds are poised on the brink of a most fundamental organizational change: accepting that they can both build and exist in a constant cycle of renewal and contention. They must not merely embrace change, as they have; they must have the courage to embody it. There are reasons to be confident they'll do so. The Reds have their own R&D department and are trying to do things such as track how defense impacts pitching. With the 2003 opening of the Great American Ballpark looming, the Reds are in the difficult position of fielding a potential contender in the next two years while breaking in the raft of talent that can make the Reds a legitimate homegrown contender during the middle of this decade. Whether the Reds have the patience to let it happen is another matter. Jim Bowden might not be with Cincinnati on Opening Day 2003, and Bob Boone shouldn't be, but as an organization, the ingredients are here for a team that will give the Astros, Cardinals, and Cubs a run for NL Central supremacy from 2003 through 2006.

HITTERS (BA: .270, OBP: .340, SLG: .440, EqA: .260)

Aaron Boone 3B Bats R Age 29

YEAR	TEAM	LGE	AB	H	DB	TP	HR	BB	SO	R	RBI	SB	CS	OUT	BA	OBP	SLG	EQA	EQR	DEFENSE
1999	Cincnnti	NL	472	129	26	4	14	25	73	53	67	14	6	349	.273	.320	.434	.251	55	126-3B 12
2000	Cincnnti	NL	292	82	14	0	13	20	48	42	41	6	1	211	.281	.345	.462	.270	40	81-3B 7
2001	Cincnnti	NL	382	117	28	2	14	27	60	56	64	6	3	268	.306	.362	.500	.283	57	101-3B -2
2002	*Cincnnti*	*NL*	*428*	*128*	*27*	*2*	*17*	*40*	*72*	*60*	*69*	*8*	*5*	*305*	*.299*	*.359*	*.491*	*.279*	*62*	

Can Boone stay healthy? After blowing out a knee in 2000, he had both his hamate and his ulna broken by pitches last season, and not even a piece of Bagwell Armor™ prescribed after the first injury could protect him from the second. Boone is one of those lonely few players still called "Boy" by his manager, but at least the Reds aren't being run by Cap Anson. Boone is underrated; a healthy season would end that.

Ben Broussard 1B Bats L Age 25

YEAR	TEAM	LGE	AB	H	DB	TP	HR	BB	SO	R	RBI	SB	CS	OUT	BA	OBP	SLG	EQA	EQR	DEFENSE	
1999	Billings	Pio	142	38	5	1	6	19	36	17	19	0	0	104	.268	.360	.444	.270	20	31-LF -2	
1999	Chattang	Sou	128	24	4	0	6	8	42	20	15	1	0	104	.188	.245	.359	.203	10	18-LF -1	12-1B 1
2000	Chattang	Sou	302	71	6	3	13	58	77	56	44	9	2	233	.235	.364	.404	.266	43	65-LF -9	14-1B -2
2001	Mudville	Cal	106	22	3	0	4	12	30	11	15	0	0	84	.208	.299	.349	.221	10	30-1B 1	
2001	Chattang	Sou	363	101	18	0	19	49	68	68	55	7	2	264	.278	.371	.485	.285	57	92-1B -2	
2002	*Cincnnti*	*NL*	*440*	*124*	*18*	*1*	*23*	*67*	*107*	*82*	*68*	*8*	*2*	*318*	*.282*	*.377*	*.484*	*.287*	*70*		

After Broussard struggled through 2000 with a wrist injury, the Reds didn't like what they saw in spring training and shipped him to A ball at the start of the year to make a point. After he had a good month, they moved him back to Chattanooga. He has pole-to-pole power, hits to all fields, and could step into a big-league lineup right now without missing a beat. The question is whether the Reds will take a chance on him over Casey, who is popular but has less power than Broussard and will carry a hefty price tag.

Damon Buford CF Bats R Age 32

YEAR	TEAM	LGE	AB	H	DB	TP	HR	BB	SO	R	RBI	SB	CS	OUT	BA	OBP	SLG	EQA	EQR	DEFENSE
1999	Boston	AL	296	75	14	2	7	18	65	39	38	9	2	223	.253	.300	.385	.233	29	81-CF 0
2000	ChiCubs	NL	499	125	17	3	15	40	108	61	46	3	6	380	.251	.315	.387	.234	50	136-CF -1
2001	ChiCubs	NL	85	16	3	0	3	4	20	12	8	0	0	69	.188	.225	.329	.185	5	24-CF -1
2001	Rochestr	Int	152	38	6	0	5	21	24	20	12	3	1	115	.250	.349	.388	.253	19	32-OF 3
2001	Louisvil	Int	55	18	4	1	3	10	16	13	13	0	1	38	.327	.431	.600	.326	12	13-LF -1
2002	*Boston*	*AL*	*433*	*103*	*17*	*2*	*14*	*46*	*96*	*57*	*50*	*5*	*3*	*333*	*.238*	*.311*	*.383*	*.234*	*44*	

Buford isn't quite the joke that Marc Sullivan was, although being Don Buford's son did get him a few breaks. One year, he even got a full-time job. When that didn't work out, he was picked up by his dad's organization (the Orioles), but even his old man had to let him go. Buford's best skills are that he can occasionally hurt a lefty, and he can play the outfield. That's Henry Cotto Lite in a world that finally noticed.

Sean Casey 1B Bats L Age 27

YEAR	TEAM	LGE	AB	H	DB	TP	HR	BB	SO	R	RBI	SB	CS	OUT	BA	OBP	SLG	EQA	EQR	DEFENSE
1999	Cincnnti	NL	592	191	40	3	25	53	81	100	92	0	2	403	.323	.387	.527	.299	98	144-1B -9
2000	Cincnnti	NL	481	149	30	2	20	45	73	66	80	1	0	332	.310	.376	.505	.291	76	122-1B -4
2001	Cincnnti	NL	535	171	30	0	17	40	53	70	95	3	1	365	.320	.374	.471	.282	77	126-1B -4
2002	*Cincnnti*	*NL*	*562*	*186*	*32*	*2*	*23*	*61*	*72*	*89*	*92*	*3*	*1*	*377*	*.331*	*.396*	*.518*	*.302*	*95*	

At a point in Casey's career when you would have expected a breakout season, it just didn't happen. Despite arriving at camp in great shape, he suffered a collection of nagging minor injuries—an ankle turned, an elbow hit by a pitch, a back strained. He just didn't have as good a year as anyone would have projected. The Reds aren't in a position to give him a big multiyear contract if he's working his way down to being Hal Morris.

Juan Castro — 2B/SS — Bats R — Age 30

YEAR	TEAM	LGE	AB	H	DB	TP	HR	BB	SO	R	RBI	SB	CS	OUT	BA	OBP	SLG	EQA	EQR	DEFENSE	
1999	Albuquer	PCL	413	95	20	3	5	28	64	40	37	2	2	320	.230	.279	.329	.206	31	51-SS 2	40-3B 0
2000	Louisvil	Int	60	17	3	1	2	11	12	8	8	0	1	44	.283	.394	.467	.285	10	13-SS 0	
2000	Cincnnti	NL	225	53	12	2	4	11	30	19	22	0	2	174	.236	.271	.360	.208	17	38-SS 8	17-2B 1
2001	Cincnnti	NL	243	57	8	0	4	12	42	28	14	0	0	186	.235	.271	.317	.199	16	27-SS -2	21-2B -1
2002	*Cincnnti*	*NL*	*337*	*83*	*16*	*2*	*7*	*30*	*59*	*38*	*33*	*2*	*2*	*256*	*.246*	*.308*	*.368*	*.225*	*31*		

Castro's value as a player is directly tied to Barry Larkin's status as a shortstop. If the Reds stick with Larkin at short, then there's room on the roster for a defensive replacement. If the Reds replace Larkin, Castro will need to start nagging teammate Jose Rijo about coaching opportunities in the Dominican Republic.

Brady Clark — OF — Bats R — Age 29

YEAR	TEAM	LGE	AB	H	DB	TP	HR	BB	SO	R	RBI	SB	CS	OUT	BA	OBP	SLG	EQA	EQR	DEFENSE
1999	Chattang	Sou	508	137	29	2	13	67	59	77	53	15	11	382	.270	.356	.411	.258	65	132-RF -3
2000	Louisvil	Int	489	138	36	4	15	61	50	79	67	9	7	358	.282	.370	.464	.277	72	131-RF 2
2001	Louisvil	Int	169	43	5	1	2	17	16	23	17	5	2	128	.254	.337	.331	.234	17	46-RF 2
2001	Cincnnti	NL	129	35	3	0	6	22	14	23	18	4	1	95	.271	.381	.434	.279	20	29-LF -2
2002	*Cincnnti*	*NL*	*429*	*118*	*23*	*2*	*13*	*64*	*48*	*68*	*50*	*11*	*7*	*318*	*.275*	*.369*	*.429*	*.269*	*60*	

Clark is an outstanding fourth outfielder and would prove it if Bob Boone would just leave him alone and accept that there's space on the roster for Clark instead another one of the freak shows. There isn't a lot of playing time for the Reds' fourth and fifth outfielders, Austin Kearns should be up before long, and Ruben Mateo and Robin Jennings aren't chopped liver. Clark might arrive just in time to rot on the bench.

D.T. Cromer — 1B — Bats L — Age 31

YEAR	TEAM	LGE	AB	H	DB	TP	HR	BB	SO	R	RBI	SB	CS	OUT	BA	OBP	SLG	EQA	EQR	DEFENSE	
1999	Indianap	Int	533	154	33	3	25	34	92	69	86	3	2	381	.289	.334	.503	.272	73	57-RF -11	46-1B -2
2000	Louisvil	Int	416	105	23	2	13	27	82	52	58	5	3	314	.252	.299	.411	.235	42	51-1B -2	15-LF -3
2000	Cincnnti	NL	47	16	3	0	2	1	13	7	7	0	0	31	.340	.366	.532	.292	7		
2001	Louisvil	Int	244	66	11	2	10	15	44	34	45	3	2	180	.270	.316	.455	.253	29	42-1B 2	
2001	Cincnnti	NL	57	16	4	0	5	3	16	7	12	0	0	41	.281	.317	.614	.290	9		
2002	*Cincnnti*	*NL*	*448*	*128*	*24*	*2*	*19*	*35*	*94*	*59*	*71*	*4*	*3*	*323*	*.286*	*.337*	*.475*	*.266*	*59*		

Rather than accept assignment to the minors, Cromer elected to become a free agent. Can you blame him? He's been an effective spot starter and pinch hitter for a team that needed him, and then he watched as the Reds committed money and roster space to Wilton Guerrero, a man on a quest to be a crummier version of Lenny Harris. Cromer is too old to be catching a Brian Daubach-sized break, but he is a better option than digging up Wally Joyner or Rico Brogna.

Gookie Dawkins — SS — Bats R — Age 23

YEAR	TEAM	LGE	AB	H	DB	TP	HR	BB	SO	R	RBI	SB	CS	OUT	BA	OBP	SLG	EQA	EQR	DEFENSE	
1999	Rockford	Mid	309	66	7	3	6	22	41	34	20	19	9	251	.214	.266	.314	.203	23	75-SS -14	
1999	Chattang	Sou	128	40	3	0	2	10	17	17	10	10	4	91	.313	.362	.383	.260	16	31-SS -3	
2000	Chattang	Sou	380	82	17	5	6	29	70	47	27	14	7	305	.216	.274	.334	.209	30	54-SS -6	39-2B -3
2000	Cincnnti	NL	41	9	1	0	0	2	6	4	3	0	0	32	.220	.256	.244	.174	2	13-SS 1	
2001	Chattang	Sou	401	82	14	2	7	24	86	51	34	9	3	322	.204	.251	.302	.191	26	96-SS -5	
2002	*Cincnnti*	*NL*	*452*	*108*	*18*	*3*	*10*	*40*	*94*	*63*	*36*	*11*	*3*	*347*	*.239*	*.301*	*.358*	*.223*	*41*		

Dawkins was hobbled by a knee injury for most of the year. It's expected that he's going to hit for more power; even so, he desperately needs to improve his walk rate. At worst, he might develop into the next Pokey Reese, in which case he'll be useful until he reaches arbitration. If the Reds want to do their young pitchers any favors, they'll call up Dawkins after Larkin's next breakdown.

Alejandro Diaz — CF — Bats R — Age 23

YEAR	TEAM	LGE	AB	H	DB	TP	HR	BB	SO	R	RBI	SB	CS	OUT	BA	OBP	SLG	EQA	EQR	DEFENSE
1999	Clinton	Mid	221	49	11	1	4	6	38	23	25	13	7	179	.222	.245	.335	.197	15	55-CF -1
1999	Chattang	Sou	220	51	6	5	6	4	31	20	25	4	2	171	.232	.251	.386	.210	17	55-CF 6
2000	Chattang	Sou	500	121	16	6	12	6	76	61	55	12	13	392	.242	.254	.370	.203	37	122-CF 8
2001	Chattang	Sou	88	23	3	0	2	1	12	12	8	0	1	66	.261	.274	.364	.208	7	23-CF -1
2002	*Cincnnti*	*NL*	*457*	*120*	*17*	*6*	*12*	*17*	*74*	*58*	*54*	*17*	*9*	*346*	*.263*	*.289*	*.405*	*.229*	*43*	

(Alejandro Diaz *continued*)

Diaz blew out his shoulder, costing him another year of learning something about the strike zone. He has major problems staying back. He commits his hands early, which prevents him from hurting any pitcher who knows what he's doing. Even so, he's the organization's best defensive outfielder, and the Reds spent almost $1.2 million on him, so they're not about to give up.

Adam Dunn OF Bats L Age 22

YEAR	TEAM	LGE	AB	H	DB	TP	HR	BB	SO	R	RBI	SB	CS	OUT	BA	OBP	SLG	EQA	EQR	DEFENSE
1999	Rockford	Mid	318	75	13	1	7	29	70	39	27	10	6	249	.236	.309	.349	.225	30	64-LF -8
2000	Dayton	Mid	442	97	17	1	12	69	112	68	51	12	4	349	.219	.332	.344	.237	48	115-LF -6
2001	Chattang	Sou	144	42	5	0	10	19	30	24	24	4	2	104	.292	.380	.535	.297	25	39-LF -1
2001	Louisvil	Int	215	66	9	0	19	36	47	41	49	4	1	150	.307	.414	.614	.329	46	54-LF 0
2001	Cincnnti	NL	245	67	18	1	20	36	63	56	45	4	2	180	.273	.373	.600	.308	47	63-RF 2
2002	*Cincnnti*	*NL*	*533*	*154*	*25*	*1*	*36*	*84*	*135*	*105*	*90*	*12*	*5*	*384*	*.289*	*.386*	*.542*	*.302*	*96*	

Dunn is the best young hitting prospect in the game right now, because he has the sense to wait on a pitch and the wrists to catch up to anything and drive it. Called up in July after Alex Ochoa was traded, Dunn totaled 51 home runs among Double-A, Triple-A, and the majors. His time on the gridiron as a quarterback shows up on the diamond, in that he's not yet a natural outfielder. He flashes a good arm at times, but he also takes poor routes to the ball. Experience and patience will help him improve.

It's fun to start kicking around comparisons between the Austin Kearns/Ken Griffey/Adam Dunn outfield that should be in place by the end of the year and that tantalizing Kal Daniels/Paul O'Neill/Eric Davis group of the late '80s. O'Neill was 25 when he joined Davis and Daniels in the outfield in 1988; Davis was 26 with just two full seasons under his belt (thanks again, Mr. Rose), while Daniels was six months younger than O'Neill and already had a full season of experience. By contrast, Griffey is older than any of that trio, but he's also everything Davis might have been and then some. Dunn and Kearns are both significantly younger than their 1988 counterparts, which makes them more likely to turn into superstars instead of merely stars of the caliber of O'Neill and Daniels.

David Espinosa SS Bats B Age 20

YEAR	TEAM	LGE	AB	H	DB	TP	HR	BB	SO	R	RBI	SB	CS	OUT	BA	OBP	SLG	EQA	EQR	DEFENSE
2001	Dayton	Mid	504	102	23	4	5	40	131	62	24	7	6	409	.202	.263	.294	.192	33	120-SS -30
2002	*Cincnnti*	*NL*	*475*	*114*	*24*	*5*	*6*	*43*	*133*	*55*	*42*	*13*	*8*	*369*	*.240*	*.303*	*.349*	*.219*	*42*	

Along with Dane Sardinha, Espinosa was given one of the creative multiyear major-league contracts that the Reds came up with after the 2000 draft. There was some early talk of moving him to second base because of the organization's depth at shortstop, but how deep are the Reds, really? Antonio Perez is in the Mariners system, Pokey Reese is the Red Sox' problem, and Gookie Dawkins's slow development is the Reds' problem. Espinosa started the year pressing and making some bad decisions in the field, but he made significant progress during the season. There have been some silly comparisons to Chipper Jones; hey, at least he isn't being compared to Freddie Benavides.

Ken Griffey Jr. CF Bats L Age 32

YEAR	TEAM	LGE	AB	H	DB	TP	HR	BB	SO	R	RBI	SB	CS	OUT	BA	OBP	SLG	EQA	EQR	DEFENSE
1999	Seattle	AL	599	175	25	3	50	85	95	120	130	23	7	431	.292	.386	.594	.313	119	149-CF 2
2000	Cincnnti	NL	521	138	20	3	39	86	107	95	110	5	4	387	.265	.377	.539	.297	93	141-CF 9
2001	Cincnnti	NL	365	108	21	2	22	42	61	59	66	2	0	257	.296	.373	.545	.299	63	83-CF -6
2002	*Cincnnti*	*NL*	*531*	*143*	*26*	*3*	*34*	*88*	*102*	*95*	*98*	*11*	*3*	*391*	*.269*	*.373*	*.522*	*.294*	*91*	

The Reds have learned what the Mariners knew, which is that Griffey requires catering. This doesn't make him a bad guy or a clubhouse cancer or any of that nonsense, just somebody who brings to the table his own collection of issues and needs. Because he's Ken Griffey Jr., his sneezes become news. Griffey needs to take heart in the fact that the Reds have improved as far as developing pitching talent, and that he's about to become the dean of what might be the best outfield in the majors for the next several years.

Wilton Guerrero PH Bats B Age 27

YEAR	TEAM	LGE	AB	H	DB	TP	HR	BB	SO	R	RBI	SB	CS	OUT	BA	OBP	SLG	EQA	EQR	DEFENSE
1999	Montreal	NL	316	91	17	6	2	9	35	40	29	5	6	231	.288	.312	.399	.233	30	39-2B -14 14-LF -3
2000	Montreal	NL	290	78	6	2	2	15	38	29	22	8	1	213	.269	.305	.324	.219	24	61-LF -6
2001	Louisvil	Int	228	65	13	2	0	13	28	22	26	10	4	168	.285	.326	.360	.235	22	34-2B -7 11-SS -4
2001	Cincnnti	NL	142	49	5	1	1	3	14	17	8	5	2	95	.345	.359	.415	.262	17	13-SS -5
2002	*Cincnnti*	*NL*	*361*	*106*	*18*	*4*	*3*	*21*	*45*	*46*	*31*	*13*	*6*	*261*	*.294*	*.332*	*.391*	*.244*	*38*	

Guerrero is another one of Bob Boone's silly experiments, but one with a semblance of a point. Guerrero may well be one of the best positionless, punchless pinch hitters around. He can run, he can hit for a decent average, and he can put the ball in play. He can play badly anywhere on the field, and he's already under contract for $850,000. These are all good things, aren't they? He might have value if rosters go to 27 men.

Robin Jennings — OF — Bats L — Age 30

YEAR	TEAM	LGE	AB	H	DB	TP	HR	BB	SO	R	RBI	SB	CS	OUT	BA	OBP	SLG	EQA	EQR	DEFENSE
1999	Iowa	PCL	256	71	16	4	7	21	31	37	33	5	3	188	.277	.334	.453	.260	32	61-RF 2
2000	Louisvil	Int	122	42	11	1	5	7	15	16	23	0	2	82	.344	.387	.574	.304	21	29-LF -2
2000	SaltLake	PCL	337	89	26	4	9	26	43	53	44	3	1	249	.264	.321	.445	.253	40	60-OF -10
2001	Oakland	AL	52	14	4	0	0	2	5	5	4	0	0	38	.269	.296	.346	.216	4	
2001	Sacramen	PCL	143	40	10	2	4	8	24	22	21	4	2	105	.280	.324	.462	.258	18	25-CF -4
2001	Louisvil	Int	114	32	6	0	7	9	20	17	13	2	2	84	.281	.333	.518	.272	16	25-LF -3
2001	Cincnnti	NL	77	23	4	2	3	5	9	10	14	0	0	54	.299	.341	.519	.279	11	12-RF -1
2002	*Cincnnti*	*NL*	*408*	*115*	*28*	*4*	*13*	*34*	*63*	*59*	*56*	*1*	*1*	*294*	*.282*	*.337*	*.466*	*.264*	*53*	

Jennings might have a shot at the job in left field now that Dmitri Young has been traded for Juan Encarnacion, who is about as close to useless as a player can get. The key factor isn't Encarnacion, it's how soon until Austin Kearns is ready. America's canal system was in full working order almost before they started building railroads, which didn't make canals bad, just not as good. Very few players can survive being not as good.

Austin Kearns — RF — Bats R — Age 22

YEAR	TEAM	LGE	AB	H	DB	TP	HR	BB	SO	R	RBI	SB	CS	OUT	BA	OBP	SLG	EQA	EQR	DEFENSE
1999	Rockford	Mid	433	88	25	2	9	31	131	45	29	10	5	350	.203	.263	.333	.203	33	112-RF -10
2000	Dayton	Mid	504	121	22	1	19	60	103	74	65	9	4	387	.240	.325	.401	.245	57	129-RF -8
2001	Chattang	Sou	210	50	11	1	5	20	42	26	30	5	3	164	.238	.314	.371	.232	21	52-RF -5
2002	*Cincnnti*	*NL*	*449*	*116*	*24*	*1*	*17*	*55*	*107*	*66*	*51*	*15*	*6*	*339*	*.258*	*.339*	*.430*	*.259*	*58*	

Before 2001, if you were going to pick the Reds farmhand most likely to be on this book's cover, it would have been Kearns. He's a big, athletic outfielder who was perceived to be a more natural baseball player than Adam Dunn. That was before a thumb injury cost him three months, but he bounced back to have a great AFL campaign. He pitched in high school, so you know he has the arm for right field. He'll complete the Reds' outfield of stars before the end of the year, although it would be unrealistic to expect Kearns to provide anything like Dunn's explosive breakthrough.

Barry Larkin — SS — Bats R — Age 38

YEAR	TEAM	LGE	AB	H	DB	TP	HR	BB	SO	R	RBI	SB	CS	OUT	BA	OBP	SLG	EQA	EQR	DEFENSE
1999	Cincnnti	NL	581	166	29	4	12	85	53	102	70	25	8	423	.286	.379	.411	.273	82	150-SS 8
2000	Cincnnti	NL	396	120	26	4	11	43	28	68	38	13	6	282	.303	.373	.472	.281	59	97-SS -9
2001	Cincnnti	NL	157	42	10	0	3	26	21	30	19	3	2	117	.268	.377	.389	.264	21	41-SS -10
2002	*Cincnnti*	*NL*	*450*	*112*	*26*	*3*	*10*	*72*	*46*	*78*	*46*	*18*	*7*	*345*	*.249*	*.352*	*.387*	*.255*	*57*	

There's some anger in Cincinnati about Joe Nuxhall's criticisms of Larkin's decline in the field, but the criticism is overdue. Let's face it: Larkin will never be what he was, in no small part because he was one of the all-time great shortstops. Just because he can't make a play going to his right isn't the end of the world; some guys never really can make that play. Unfortunately, most of them aren't asked to play shortstop. You can forgive Larkin for trying; raging against the dying of the light is part of the human condition.

Brandon Larson — 3B — Bats R — Age 26

YEAR	TEAM	LGE	AB	H	DB	TP	HR	BB	SO	R	RBI	SB	CS	OUT	BA	OBP	SLG	EQA	EQR	DEFENSE
1999	Rockford	Mid	252	59	9	1	9	15	73	23	31	6	2	195	.234	.281	.385	.223	23	64-3B -1
1999	Chattang	Sou	172	42	6	0	9	6	52	21	29	3	3	133	.244	.277	.436	.230	17	42-3B -4
2000	Chattang	Sou	439	110	18	0	19	21	121	53	55	10	4	333	.251	.291	.421	.236	45	104-3B -23
2000	Louisvil	Int	63	17	5	1	2	3	16	10	5	0	0	46	.270	.303	.476	.253	7	16-3B 3
2001	Louisvil	Int	426	104	19	2	13	25	114	58	51	4	5	327	.244	.298	.390	.228	41	108-3B 11
2001	Cincnnti	NL	33	4	3	0	0	2	8	2	1	0	0	29	.121	.171	.212	.134	1	
2002	*Cincnnti*	*NL*	*437*	*110*	*22*	*1*	*17*	*33*	*128*	*54*	*57*	*10*	*5*	*332*	*.252*	*.304*	*.423*	*.240*	*47*	

Larson was healthy for a second straight season; he just isn't making progress. He's credited with a good work ethic, shows decent range and a plus arm at the hot corner, and has absolutely no idea what he's supposed to be doing at the plate. He's been accused of pressing, but the accusation just lowers him into the Ryan Minor class of disappointments.

Jason LaRue C Bats R Age 28

YEAR	TEAM	LGE	AB	H	DB	TP	HR	BB	SO	R	RBI	SB	CS	OUT	BA	OBP	SLG	EQA	EQR	DEFENSE
1999	Indianap	Int	263	61	11	2	10	11	49	36	30	0	2	204	.232	.271	.403	.219	23	65-C 2
1999	Cincnnti	NL	90	19	3	0	4	10	30	11	10	4	1	72	.211	.304	.378	.235	10	26-C 3
2000	Louisvil	Int	308	74	18	1	13	18	51	48	42	2	2	236	.240	.296	.432	.238	33	73-C -6
2000	Cincnnti	NL	99	23	4	0	5	3	17	12	12	0	0	76	.232	.280	.424	.230	10	29-C 0
2001	Cincnnti	NL	365	91	24	2	12	25	90	41	45	3	3	277	.249	.310	.425	.242	40	94-C 12
2002	*Cincnnti*	*NL*	*383*	*98*	*21*	*2*	*15*	*35*	*90*	*58*	*47*	*4*	*3*	*288*	*.256*	*.318*	*.439*	*.249*	*45*	

One element of the catcher's job that gets overlooked is the difficulty of adapting to catching major-league-quality breaking stuff. How much of that does a catcher really see in the minors? How many of those breaking balls are thrown for strikes so that you can work on framing them effectively? LaRue has yet to fully make the adjustment, but he has improved. He's rumored to be on the block, and his trade value will never get much higher than it is now.

Ruben Mateo OF Bats R Age 24

YEAR	TEAM	LGE	AB	H	DB	TP	HR	BB	SO	R	RBI	SB	CS	OUT	BA	OBP	SLG	EQA	EQR	DEFENSE
1999	Oklahoma	PCL	249	76	10	0	14	12	33	42	48	5	2	175	.305	.351	.514	.282	37	59-CF 2
1999	Texas	AL	122	30	10	1	5	2	25	16	17	3	0	92	.246	.263	.467	.239	13	28-CF 0
2000	Texas	AL	204	60	9	0	8	7	30	30	18	6	0	144	.294	.334	.456	.266	26	52-CF 0
2001	Texas	AL	129	34	7	2	1	9	24	20	14	1	0	95	.264	.333	.372	.242	14	31-RF -2
2001	Louisvil	Int	252	61	17	3	2	13	42	35	24	2	0	191	.242	.293	.357	.221	22	57-RF -8
2002	*Cincnnti*	*NL*	*446*	*129*	*25*	*3*	*14*	*32*	*78*	*68*	*57*	*8*	*1*	*318*	*.289*	*.337*	*.453*	*.264*	*57*	

Acquired from the Rangers for Rob Bell in an exchange of problems, Mateo spent September working his way into shape in a tailored conditioning program; after fully evaluating him medically, the Reds feel he merely needed another year of conditioning to recuperate. They expect him to be at full strength in 2002, though there is some concern about whether he's still treating the broken leg cautiously. Before the Reds blew it and traded for Encarnacion, Mateo had a shot at the job in right field.

Jackson Melian OF Bats R Age 22

YEAR	TEAM	LGE	AB	H	DB	TP	HR	BB	SO	R	RBI	SB	CS	OUT	BA	OBP	SLG	EQA	EQR	DEFENSE
1999	Tampa	Fla	474	110	17	7	6	36	110	49	44	6	5	369	.232	.293	.335	.214	39	124-CF -12
2000	Norwich	Eas	294	68	6	2	9	13	71	27	31	12	1	227	.231	.268	.357	.216	25	78-CF -4
2001	Chattang	Sou	433	92	15	0	14	28	93	54	43	7	5	346	.212	.269	.344	.207	34	108-OF -10
2002	*Cincnnti*	*NL*	*476*	*122*	*17*	*3*	*14*	*39*	*114*	*58*	*53*	*14*	*6*	*360*	*.256*	*.313*	*.393*	*.237*	*49*	

Melian has been touted as the next big thing from the Yankees fine stable of outfield prospects, following in the footsteps of Pine Time, Ruben Rivera, and Ricky Ledee. Melian is supposed to be an all-tools player, but he doesn't run well, he can be brutally indifferent in the outfield, and he's not hitting. He even earned a benching in winter ball. He's too young to give up on, but he needs to start snuffing coffee and get a clue.

Corky Miller C Bats R Age 26

YEAR	TEAM	LGE	AB	H	DB	TP	HR	BB	SO	R	RBI	SB	CS	OUT	BA	OBP	SLG	EQA	EQR	DEFENSE
1999	Rockford	Mid	199	44	5	0	7	22	46	26	24	1	3	158	.221	.328	.352	.231	20	66-C -1
1999	Chattang	Sou	105	21	5	0	4	8	30	15	12	0	0	84	.200	.296	.362	.223	10	33-C 1
2000	Chattang	Sou	328	73	11	0	10	31	50	35	40	3	5	260	.223	.319	.348	.227	32	101-C 3
2001	Chattang	Sou	174	43	7	0	8	20	31	21	35	1	1	132	.247	.359	.425	.264	24	54-C 6
2001	Louisvil	Int	145	48	8	0	7	10	18	28	26	2	0	97	.331	.405	.531	.310	26	41-C 5
2001	Cincnnti	NL	49	10	2	0	3	4	14	5	7	1	0	39	.204	.285	.429	.238	5	16-C 2
2002	*Cincnnti*	*NL*	*328*	*81*	*12*	*0*	*15*	*38*	*62*	*49*	*48*	*3*	*2*	*249*	*.247*	*.325*	*.421*	*.248*	*38*	

Miller is an outstanding defender who gets good marks for his receiving, plate-blocking, and game-calling, from Bob Boone himself no less. He's not the athlete that Jason LaRue is, but that might not be the criterion the Reds use in choosing between them. The Reds are intrigued enough to consider going with a Stinnett/Miller combination if the right deal for LaRue comes along, and it would be cheap and effective to do so.

Rainer Olmedo — SS — Bats R — Age 21

YEAR	TEAM	LGE	AB	H	DB	TP	HR	BB	SO	R	RBI	SB	CS	OUT	BA	OBP	SLG	EQA	EQR	DEFENSE
2000	Dayton	Mid	378	77	14	1	3	17	77	34	28	8	7	308	.204	.239	.270	.175	20	92-SS -10 15-2B 4
2001	Mudville	Cal	542	113	15	3	1	18	116	40	22	21	13	442	.208	.239	.253	.173	28	126-SS -10
2002	*Cincnnti*	*NL*	*529*	*129*	*18*	*2*	*4*	*36*	*120*	*56*	*40*	*28*	*14*	*413*	*.244*	*.292*	*.308*	*.204*	*39*	

Breathlessly described as a guy who might be the next Rey Ordonez or Omar Vizquel, Olmedo is one of the Reds' Venezuelan imports. Because Vizquel came up incapable of doing anything but field, and because he's one of the few players who learned how to hit in the majors, he ends up being the poster boy for a hundred guys like Olmedo. Vizquel was essentially unique, so don't get excited about Olmedo, who is fast, young, and raw, just yet.

Wily Mo Pena — CF — Bats R — Age 20

YEAR	TEAM	LGE	AB	H	DB	TP	HR	BB	SO	R	RBI	SB	CS	OUT	BA	OBP	SLG	EQA	EQR	DEFENSE
2000	StatenIs	NYP	73	17	1	1	0	0	27	4	6	1	0	56	.233	.248	.274	.180	4	20-CF -1
2000	Greensbr	SAL	254	42	5	1	6	12	97	28	17	2	3	215	.165	.209	.264	.162	11	57-CF -5
2001	Dayton	Mid	517	110	18	3	17	24	194	58	72	12	7	414	.213	.257	.358	.206	40	127-CF 3
2002	*Cincnnti*	*NL*	*464*	*108*	*16*	*2*	*14*	*31*	*188*	*57*	*52*	*13*	*7*	*363*	*.233*	*.281*	*.366*	*.214*	*39*	

After Pena had reportedly signed with the Mets, Marlins, Taco Bell, and the Denver Gold, baseball turned to Maury Povich for a tear-jerking episode in which blood tests confirmed that Pena was indeed the father of all of the deals. Instead of boot camp, Pena was punished with a big-league contract with the Yankees that will force him to be in the majors by 2003. That timetable will push the Reds to put him in Double-A in 2002, where he will struggle. The person who deserves to be criticized for this is Pena's agent. How does forcing his client to be promoted before he's ready help him have a real career? He has a good shot at growing up to be Jose Guillen. Does that represent success?

Pokey Reese — 2B/SS — Bats R — Age 29

YEAR	TEAM	LGE	AB	H	DB	TP	HR	BB	SO	R	RBI	SB	CS	OUT	BA	OBP	SLG	EQA	EQR	DEFENSE
1999	Cincnnti	NL	585	164	36	5	10	28	75	80	49	32	7	428	.280	.320	.410	.249	66	140-2B 27
2000	Cincnnti	NL	520	130	21	5	12	38	79	73	43	27	3	393	.250	.308	.379	.239	55	129-2B 13
2001	Cincnnti	NL	430	102	23	2	9	31	70	52	42	24	4	332	.237	.292	.363	.228	41	74-SS -4 47-2B 1
2002	*Boston*	*AL*	*532*	*140*	*24*	*4*	*12*	*43*	*86*	*71*	*46*	*25*	*4*	*396*	*.263*	*.318*	*.391*	*.245*	*59*	

Reese should not be missed. He threw tantrums when the Reds didn't reward his mediocrity with zillions, and he pouted after being pinch-hit for. Now that he's gone, the question is whether holding onto Reese instead of Antonio Perez in the Griffey trade was ever really defensible. Reese might have some value as a shortstop; as a second baseman, he's not an asset, and he's certainly not worth as much as he thinks he is. He was non-tendered by the Red Sox after being traded twice in 48 hours, and he is expected to sign with the team as Nomar Garciaparra insurance.

Ruben Rivera — CF — Bats R — Age 28

YEAR	TEAM	LGE	AB	H	DB	TP	HR	BB	SO	R	RBI	SB	CS	OUT	BA	OBP	SLG	EQA	EQR	DEFENSE
1999	San Dieg	NL	416	84	16	1	24	51	132	65	47	16	7	339	.202	.296	.418	.239	47	123-CF 4
2000	San Dieg	NL	430	95	20	6	18	38	126	63	58	7	4	339	.221	.297	.421	.238	47	121-CF 5
2001	Cincnnti	NL	264	70	15	1	10	20	70	39	35	6	3	197	.265	.326	.443	.255	32	69-CF 2
2002	*San Fran*	*NL*	*373*	*86*	*15*	*3*	*17*	*43*	*116*	*58*	*45*	*11*	*4*	*291*	*.231*	*.310*	*.424*	*.255*	*48*	

Plugged into a part-time role, Ruben Rivera turned in a season that looked useful. His strikeout and walk rates did not really change, so there isn't reason to believe he's improved. He will not be an All-Star or a good regular, but he can be a nice caddy for a left-handed-hitting center fielder who needs a defensive replacement. He may get a chance to do exactly that for Marvin Benard, as Rivera was claimed on waivers by the Giants in November. Non-tendered, and a free agent at this writing.

Dane Sardinha — C — Bats R — Age 23

YEAR	TEAM	LGE	AB	H	DB	TP	HR	BB	SO	R	RBI	SB	CS	OUT	BA	OBP	SLG	EQA	EQR	DEFENSE
2001	Mudville	Cal	425	85	18	1	7	9	93	35	40	0	1	341	.200	.219	.296	.173	21	109-C 1
2002	*Cincnnti*	*NL*	*400*	*95*	*19*	*1*	*7*	*18*	*94*	*36*	*38*	*0*	*1*	*306*	*.237*	*.270*	*.343*	*.198*	*27*	

The good news is that the scouting reports on Sardinha from his Pepperdine days were accurate. He's a great catch-and-throw guy. The bad news is that he was even worse at the plate than expected. He tried to hack his way out of slumps and spent the whole year doing so. The Reds did not sign him to be just a good backup catcher, so the pressure is still on. To his credit, Sardinha is aware of the problem and knows he needs to work on it.

Steve Smitherman LF Bats R Age 23

YEAR	TEAM	LGE	AB	H	DB	TP	HR	BB	SO	R	RBI	SB	CS	OUT	BA	OBP	SLG	EQA	EQR	DEFENSE
2000	Billings	Pio	296	65	11	2	7	8	81	28	29	5	1	232	.220	.245	.341	.198	20	59-LF -4
2001	Dayton	Mid	505	112	27	1	14	32	124	60	47	8	5	398	.222	.274	.362	.213	42	126-LF -9
2002	*Cincnnti*	*NL*	*467*	*115*	*24*	*2*	*12*	*32*	*127*	*54*	*50*	*11*	*5*	*357*	*.246*	*.295*	*.383*	*.226*	*43*	

Not really a tools guy so much as a ballplayer, Smitherman out-hit prospect/strikeout celebrity Samone Peters. His best tool on defense is a strong arm. Guys like Smitherman or first baseman Randy Ruiz need Chris Kattan-sized breaks before they'll be more than good organizational soldiers. It can happen.

Kelly Stinnett C Bats R Age 32

YEAR	TEAM	LGE	AB	H	DB	TP	HR	BB	SO	R	RBI	SB	CS	OUT	BA	OBP	SLG	EQA	EQR	DEFENSE
1999	Arizona	NL	285	65	10	0	15	20	77	35	37	2	1	221	.228	.290	.421	.234	29	75-C 0
2000	Arizona	NL	242	53	6	0	8	15	51	21	32	0	1	190	.219	.279	.343	.209	19	70-C 0
2001	Cincnnti	NL	188	50	10	0	10	16	52	28	27	2	2	140	.266	.336	.479	.266	25	52-C -6
2002	*Cincnnti*	*NL*	*269*	*64*	*9*	*0*	*16*	*26*	*74*	*36*	*41*	*3*	*2*	*207*	*.238*	*.305*	*.450*	*.247*	*31*	

Stinnett was traded by the Snakes to keep him away from the Giants, which was great for Benito Santiago and for the Reds, but it didn't do much for the Giants or Stinnett. His season ended early due to elbow and knee problems, but the Reds came away sufficiently impressed. If they decide to hold on to LaRue, they can just as easily convert Stinnett into a prospect by trading him to whatever team loses its starting catcher to a spring-training injury.

Todd Walker 2B Bats L Age 29

YEAR	TEAM	LGE	AB	H	DB	TP	HR	BB	SO	R	RBI	SB	CS	OUT	BA	OBP	SLG	EQA	EQR	DEFENSE
1999	Minnesot	AL	525	148	38	4	6	47	73	60	44	17	10	387	.282	.342	.404	.251	61	94-2B -3
2000	SaltLake	PCL	242	67	10	1	2	25	31	38	28	5	2	177	.277	.345	.351	.241	25	59-2B -3
2000	Colorado	NL	166	46	9	3	6	17	17	24	29	3	1	121	.277	.347	.476	.272	23	42-2B -5
2001	Colorado	NL	282	77	17	2	10	23	34	48	38	1	3	208	.273	.328	.454	.255	34	73-2B -4
2001	Cincnnti	NL	262	80	11	0	7	24	36	41	34	0	5	187	.305	.365	.427	.261	33	62-2B -5
2002	*Cincnnti*	*NL*	*481*	*143*	*26*	*3*	*16*	*51*	*65*	*70*	*60*	*6*	*7*	*345*	*.297*	*.365*	*.464*	*.273*	*67*	

Walker isn't fading away so much as he's continuing to be what he is. Because of his miserable defense, he may not even settle into a Keith Lockhart career path as he gets older. At some point, he's going to have a bad year that wipes out his career faster than you can say "Carlos Baerga." He's useful right now on a team that doesn't have a defensive problem at shortstop and can use the help on offense. The Reds fill only half that bill.

Dmitri Young OF/1B/3B Bats B Age 28

YEAR	TEAM	LGE	AB	H	DB	TP	HR	BB	SO	R	RBI	SB	CS	OUT	BA	OBP	SLG	EQA	EQR	DEFENSE
1999	Cincnnti	NL	373	110	29	2	14	25	66	61	52	2	1	264	.295	.342	.496	.274	52	77-RF -3
2000	Cincnnti	NL	550	164	36	5	18	28	73	65	83	0	3	389	.298	.335	.480	.265	70	90-LF -3 28-1B -2
2001	Cincnnti	NL	542	170	29	3	21	34	65	71	71	8	5	377	.314	.358	.494	.280	78	72-LF 1 27-3B -2
2002	*Detroit*	*AL*	*522*	*158*	*31*	*3*	*18*	*45*	*72*	*76*	*71*	*6*	*4*	*368*	*.303*	*.358*	*.477*	*.282*	*78*	

Young's value is pretty much grounded in the right now. Right now, he makes a perfectly adequate first baseman, DH, or corner outfielder for a contender. Right now, he's a good guy to stick in the fifth or sixth slot in the lineup, because he drives the ball consistently. Playing at third base last year gave him a sort of Pedro Guerrero cachet, but that only works on a team with a shortstop who can go about a dozen feet into the hole. Right now, Dmitri Young has been inexplicably traded to the Tigers, where he'll play first base regularly.

PITCHERS (ERA: 4.50, H/9: 9.0, HR/9: 1.0, BB/9: 3.0, K/9: 6.0, KW: 2.0, PERA: 4.50)

Jose Acevedo Throws R Age 24

YEAR	TEAM	LGE	IP	H	ER	HR	BB	K	ERA	W	L	H/9	HR/9	BB/9	K/9	KW	PERA	STUFF
1999	Clinton	Mid	128.7	146	95	29	48	78	6.65	4	10	10.2	2.0	3.4	5.5	0.8	5.21	3
2000	Dayton	Mid	134.3	167	127	39	61	68	8.51	3	12	11.2	2.6	4.1	4.6	0.6	6.52	-14
2001	Chattang	Sou	75.0	76	41	10	28	50	4.92	4	4	9.1	1.2	3.4	6.0	0.9	5.24	4
2001	Cincnnti	NL	92.0	99	55	15	30	55	5.38	4	6	9.7	1.5	2.9	5.4	0.9	5.70	2

Even after a good showing in his debut season, Acevedo is fighting for the fifth slot in the rotation, his opportunity depending on how many retreads take the Reds' offers to jump-start their careers by working with Don Gullett. It's just as well, because Acevedo didn't do much against good lineups or playoff teams, mostly beating weaker teams such as the Expos and Pirates. A four-pitch starter with no single dominant offering, Acevedo was credited with doing a better job of trusting his fastball. His long-term future looks good.

Ricardo Aramboles Throws R Age 20

YEAR	TEAM	LGE	IP	H	ER	HR	BB	K	ERA	W	L	H/9	HR/9	BB/9	K/9	KW	PERA	STUFF
1999	Greensbr	SAL	33.0	33	17	2	16	17	4.64	2	2	9.0	0.5	4.4	4.6	0.5	3.19	11
2000	Greensbr	SAL	139.7	159	105	29	60	78	6.77	5	11	10.2	1.9	3.9	5.0	0.6	7.27	4
2001	Dayton	Mid	19.7	25	15	4	5	5	6.86	1	1	11.4	1.8	2.3	2.3	0.5	4.67	-12
2001	Chattang	Sou	9.3	11	5	2	0	3	4.82	0	1	10.6	1.9	0.0	2.9	-1.0	10.27	-9
2001	Columbus	Int	24.0	26	12	3	5	11	4.50	2	1	9.8	1.1	1.9	4.1	1.1	4.85	8

The Reds are excited about Aramboles despite the sprained elbow that shut him down early. He throws hard and has a pretty good change-up, so with his popularity, he's going to arrive a lot faster than you'd expect for a kid with next to no experience above A ball. While the Yankees spent $1.5 million to sign him, the Reds are the team who will get the benefit of the Yankees outspending everyone, essentially using the Yankees' bankroll as working capital in exchange for time spent on Mark Wohlers's none-too-successful comeback.

Chris Booker Throws R Age 25

YEAR	TEAM	LGE	IP	H	ER	HR	BB	K	ERA	W	L	H/9	HR/9	BB/9	K/9	KW	PERA	STUFF
1999	Daytona	Fla	72.3	79	56	13	47	44	6.97	2	6	9.8	1.6	5.8	5.5	0.5	6.87	-21
2000	Daytona	Fla	28.7	25	13	0	19	20	4.08	2	1	7.8	0.0	6.0	6.3	0.5	5.43	-13
2000	WestTenn	Sou	14.0	13	10	2	13	13	6.43	1	1	8.4	1.3	8.4	8.4	0.5	6.67	-12
2001	WestTenn	Sou	48.0	51	47	12	44	43	8.81	1	4	9.6	2.3	8.3	8.1	0.5	7.47	-33
2001	Chattang	Sou	15.7	14	10	2	14	14	5.74	1	1	8.0	1.1	8.0	8.0	0.5	5.70	-20

Part of the bounty received for Michael Tucker (along with Ben Shaffar, a decent young starter), Booker throws wild, heavy, high-90s heat, which got him onto the 40-man roster this winter. The timing worked out poorly, because he was then diagnosed with a frayed rotator cuff. The Reds hope he can avoid surgery, but the 60-day DL looks more likely than a real shot at a bullpen job.

Jim Brower Throws R Age 29

YEAR	TEAM	LGE	IP	H	ER	HR	BB	K	ERA	W	L	H/9	HR/9	BB/9	K/9	KW	PERA	STUFF
1999	Buffalo	Int	156.3	186	114	28	63	54	6.56	5	12	10.7	1.6	3.6	3.1	0.4	6.13	-22
1999	Clevelnd	AL	25.3	29	20	7	8	18	7.11	1	2	10.3	2.5	2.8	6.4	1.1	3.80	-6
2000	Buffalo	Int	101.3	106	49	10	26	51	4.35	6	5	9.4	0.9	2.3	4.5	1.0	4.23	0
2000	Clevelnd	AL	66.0	73	41	9	25	32	5.59	3	4	10.0	1.2	3.4	4.4	0.6	5.27	-11
2001	Cincnnti	NL	121.0	124	69	15	54	76	5.13	6	7	9.2	1.1	4.0	5.7	0.7	4.51	-6

In terms of straight value, Eddie Taubensee for Jim Brower worked out a lot better than expected for the Reds, so if Rob Pugmire, the other pitcher in the deal, develops, so much the better. Brower gave the Reds 22 games in which he worked two or more innings in relief, and with the Reds' rotation in a shambles, that was exactly what they needed to either finish off lost causes or get games to Danny Graves and Scott Sullivan. Like Gene Nelson before him, Brower was forced out of his best role by the team's need for a starter, but he'll be a valuable long reliever if the Reds let him.

Lance Davis Throws L Age 25

YEAR	TEAM	LGE	IP	H	ER	HR	BB	K	ERA	W	L	H/9	HR/9	BB/9	K/9	KW	PERA	STUFF
1999	Rockford	Mid	128.0	146	88	20	57	52	6.19	5	9	10.3	1.4	4.0	3.7	0.5	5.54	-10
2000	Chattang	Sou	112.7	112	58	7	55	63	4.63	6	7	8.9	0.6	4.4	5.0	0.6	4.30	0
2000	Louisvil	Int	31.3	36	19	5	8	12	5.46	1	2	10.3	1.4	2.3	3.4	0.8	5.38	-5
2001	Louisvil	Int	79.0	86	41	9	18	35	4.67	4	5	9.8	1.0	2.1	4.0	1.0	4.00	1
2001	Cincnnti	NL	104.3	113	55	10	30	43	4.74	6	6	9.7	0.9	2.6	3.7	0.7	5.07	-3

Everyone is hung up on Davis going 8-4, even though he's not fooling hitters very often. He's reliant on his outfield defense, so you might say he's an interested party in seeing someone like Austin Kearns replace Dmitri Young. Davis doesn't have a dominant pitch, but he'll go inside on anybody and use his curve at any point in the count. He wouldn't have a lot of job security on most teams, but Bob Boone loves control, and Davis has that.

Elmer Dessens **Throws R** **Age 30**

YEAR	TEAM	LGE	IP	H	ER	HR	BB	K	ERA	W	L	H/9	HR/9	BB/9	K/9	KW	PERA	STUFF
2000	Louisvil	Int	23.3	24	11	1	8	10	4.24	2	1	9.3	0.4	3.1	3.9	0.6	4.51	-4
2000	Cincnnti	NL	155.0	157	64	9	35	76	3.72	10	7	9.1	0.5	2.0	4.4	1.1	3.96	0
2001	Cincnnti	NL	197.0	214	108	27	50	103	4.93	10	12	9.8	1.2	2.3	4.7	1.0	4.51	2

Dessens is a perfect example of the payoff you can get by having Don Gullett as your pitching coach. Gullett turned a reclamation project into a really good fourth starter. Unfortunately, Dessens is the best the Reds have until the kids develop or Pete Harnisch reappears. To his credit, he had as many quality starts as Ryan Dempster did. Dessens has a huge platoon split—which could make him handy against some teams if Boone spots him—and he controls the running game.

Scott Dunn **Throws R** **Age 24**

YEAR	TEAM	LGE	IP	H	ER	HR	BB	K	ERA	W	L	H/9	HR/9	BB/9	K/9	KW	PERA	STUFF
1999	Billings	Pio	38.7	44	33	7	30	18	7.68	1	3	10.2	1.6	7.0	4.2	0.3	5.98	-19
2000	Clinton	Mid	142.7	152	108	22	103	88	6.81	5	11	9.6	1.4	6.5	5.6	0.4	6.54	-7
2001	Mudville	Cal	58.0	57	36	4	43	35	5.59	2	4	8.8	0.6	6.7	5.4	0.4	3.79	-5
2001	Chattang	Sou	94.7	104	82	16	81	53	7.80	3	8	9.9	1.5	7.7	5.0	0.3	6.24	-17

Dunn is wild, mixing low-90s heat with a good curve, a change-up, and even a knuckler. It isn't often that you find someone this wild with good mechanics, but what Dunn lacks is command, not form. It's an interesting distinction that presents a difficult dilemma. I don't envy the Reds; Dunn is a science project that could turn into almost anything from fridge fuzz to cold fusion.

Seth Etherton **Throws R** **Age 25**

YEAR	TEAM	LGE	IP	H	ER	HR	BB	K	ERA	W	L	H/9	HR/9	BB/9	K/9	KW	PERA	STUFF
1998	Midland	Tex	49.3	58	35	11	13	26	6.39	2	3	10.6	2.0	2.4	4.7	1.0	6.23	1
1999	Erie	Eas	166.3	168	81	19	43	108	4.38	9	9	9.1	1.0	2.3	5.8	1.3	4.10	16
1999	Edmonton	PCL	21.3	26	20	7	6	14	8.44	0	2	11.0	3.0	2.5	5.9	1.2	5.02	1
2000	Edmonton	PCL	59.7	60	30	7	18	40	4.53	3	4	9.1	1.1	2.7	6.0	1.1	4.29	14
2000	Anaheim	AL	60.7	71	44	14	18	32	6.53	2	5	10.5	2.1	2.7	4.7	.9	4.70	-2

Etherton was shut down with shoulder tendinitis in August 2000, so when he came up with a case of shoulder weakness last spring, all sorts of alarm bells rang. It turned out to be a damaged labrum and a bone spur in his shoulder. A polished USC product, Etherton was never a power prospect so much as a command pitcher, relying on a nice curve and a fastball that only occasionally touched 90. He's expected to be at full strength in spring training and is already penciled into the Opening Day rotation.

Jared Fernandez **Throws R** **Age 30**

YEAR	TEAM	LGE	IP	H	ER	HR	BB	K	ERA	W	L	H/9	HR/9	BB/9	K/9	KW	PERA	STUFF
1999	Pawtuckt	Int	161.7	188	99	24	42	54	5.51	7	11	10.5	1.3	2.3	3.0	0.6	5.12	-13
2000	Pawtuckt	Int	109.7	121	64	14	39	49	5.25	5	7	9.9	1.1	3.2	4.0	0.6	4.69	-17
2001	Louisvil	Int	195.7	228	134	34	69	80	6.16	8	14	10.5	1.6	3.2	3.7	0.6	5.97	-16
2001	Cincnnti	NL	11.7	13	7	1	5	4	5.40	0	1	10.0	0.8	3.9	3.1	0.4	6.57	-23

Fernandez was released and re-signed to a minor-league deal after the season, so the Reds will have the opportunity to see whether he's going to become a useful commodity in his thirties. Reds Director of Player Development Tim Naehring claimed that just having a knuckleballer makes other pitchers' stuff better, but the research that's been done by BP doesn't support that claim. A study by Chris Kahrl revealed that there are no day-after effects on hitters in the next couple of games after facing a knuckleballer. So while the idea sounds cool, it just isn't true, at least not in a way we can detect.

Osvaldo Fernandez **Throws R** **Age 33**

YEAR	TEAM	LGE	IP	H	ER	HR	BB	K	ERA	W	L	H/9	HR/9	BB/9	K/9	KW	PERA	STUFF
2000	Louisvil	Int	58.0	58	27	4	21	33	4.19	3	3	9.0	0.6	3.3	5.1	0.8	4.87	0
2000	Cincnnti	NL	77.0	81	38	5	26	32	4.44	5	4	9.5	0.6	3.0	3.7	0.6	3.31	-2
2001	Cincnnti	NL	80.3	88	44	7	30	28	4.93	4	5	9.9	0.8	3.4	3.1	0.5	7.02	-17
2001	Louisvil	Int	52.3	60	33	9	15	21	5.68	2	4	10.3	1.5	2.6	3.6	0.7	5.40	-13

He doesn't dominate, and last winter's excitement over his comeback was overstated, but when Fernandez is on, he can throw strikes, change speeds, and use his breaking stuff effectively. When he can't do that, he's dangerous to fans, even on Complimentary Hard Hat Night.

David Gil — Throws R — Age 23

YEAR	TEAM	LGE	IP	H	ER	HR	BB	K	ERA	W	L	H/9	HR/9	BB/9	K/9	KW	PERA	STUFF
2000	Dayton	Mid	24.7	27	15	2	12	9	5.47	1	2	9.9	0.7	4.4	3.3	0.4	5.81	-6
2000	Chattang	Sou	23.0	22	12	2	13	17	4.70	1	2	8.6	0.8	5.1	6.7	0.7	3.26	13
2001	Dayton	Mid	12.3	11	4	0	4	8	2.92	1	0	8.0	0.0	2.9	5.8	1.0	1.02	22
2001	Chattang	Sou	61.3	63	36	6	33	35	5.28	3	4	9.2	0.9	4.8	5.1	0.5	4.36	2

The Reds were concerned that Gil was overworked at the University of Miami, so they tried to bring him along slowly. Nevertheless, he strained his forearm on the cusp of being called up in June, and he never really healed in his scramble to rehabilitate and get back to the mound. Gil has a good sinker/splitter combo, getting into the low 90s, but he needs to be more consistent with his change-up.

Danny Graves — Throws R — Age 28

YEAR	TEAM	LGE	IP	H	ER	HR	BB	K	ERA	W	L	H/9	HR/9	BB/9	K/9	KW	PERA	STUFF
1999	Cincnnti	NL	106.7	107	53	9	41	62	4.47	6	6	9.0	0.8	3.5	5.2	0.8	3.02	-6
2000	Cincnnti	NL	89.3	91	45	7	35	47	4.53	5	5	9.2	0.7	3.5	4.7	0.7	2.72	-9
2001	Cincnnti	NL	77.3	79	33	6	16	39	3.84	5	4	9.2	0.7	1.9	4.5	1.2	4.58	-7

There's some talk about moving Graves into the rotation in 2002, which makes sense when you consider that it's easier to find relievers than starters, and the Reds will be paying him a pretty penny if they keep him through this winter's arbitration confrontation. He junked around with perfecting a new slider before finally falling back on the one he'd been using all along. Tighter infield defense would help him in any role, while a Walker/Larkin combo up the middle will fire up a lot of opponent's rallies.

Josh Hall — Throws R — Age 21

YEAR	TEAM	LGE	IP	H	ER	HR	BB	K	ERA	W	L	H/9	HR/9	BB/9	K/9	KW	PERA	STUFF
2001	Dayton	Mid	132.0	133	63	9	52	70	4.30	8	7	9.1	0.6	3.5	4.8	0.7	4.52	11

Hall was a seventh-round draft pick out of a Virginia high school in 1998. He developed slowly, in part because of a high-school knee injury followed by minor shoulder surgery. Even as he finally broke out last year, his season was ended prematurely by a freak accident that caused a stress fracture in his foot. He doesn't throw especially hard, relying on a good curveball. Hall is a major sleeper.

Joey Hamilton — Throws R — Age 31

YEAR	TEAM	LGE	IP	H	ER	HR	BB	K	ERA	W	L	H/9	HR/9	BB/9	K/9	KW	PERA	STUFF
1999	Toronto	AL	103.7	109	54	11	33	55	4.69	6	6	9.5	1.0	2.9	4.8	0.8	5.63	-3
2000	Syracuse	Int	40.0	42	18	1	13	13	4.05	2	2	9.5	0.2	2.9	2.9	0.5	4.62	-6
2000	Toronto	AL	31.7	33	15	3	10	15	4.26	2	2	9.4	0.9	2.8	4.3	0.8	2.89	1
2001	Toronto	AL	135.7	141	67	15	36	78	4.44	8	7	9.4	1.0	2.4	5.2	1.1	5.74	4
2001	Cincnnti	NL	17.7	20	11	3	5	8	5.60	1	1	10.2	1.5	2.5	4.1	0.8	6.23	-11

The Reds took a calculated risk, in that having Hamilton work with Don Gullett might make it clear to Hamilton that he could get something out of pitching for the Reds besides money. For the team, it's a worthwhile exercise to give a struggling veteran the chance to be the next Pete Harnisch or Elmer Dessens. If the player treats the opportunity as an investment in his career, everyone comes out ahead. Hamilton is supposed to be all the way back from his '99 rotator-cuff repair, so wherever he winds up, he might turn in a serviceable season. With longtime believer Dave Stewart now the pitching coach in Milwaukee, don't bet against his becoming a Brewer.

Pete Harnisch — Throws R — Age 35

YEAR	TEAM	LGE	IP	H	ER	HR	BB	K	ERA	W	L	H/9	HR/9	BB/9	K/9	KW	PERA	STUFF
1999	Cincnnti	NL	196.0	206	98	23	48	108	4.50	11	11	9.5	1.1	2.2	5.0	1.1	3.47	7
2000	Cincnnti	NL	129.7	144	78	20	38	63	5.41	6	8	10.0	1.4	2.6	4.4	0.8	4.64	-2
2001	Cincnnti	NL	35.3	43	29	8	15	14	7.39	1	3	11.0	2.0	3.8	3.6	0.5	7.37	-22

Harnisch has given the Reds two good seasons and two injury seasons. Considering his track record, that's about as good as it can get. The last two years have seen him endure a frayed rotator cuff (which still hasn't been repaired), plus elbow damage that required surgery. At this point, all he should expect is an incentive-laden deal, but he's threatening to retire if the Reds lowball him. Since it was the Reds who resurrected his career, how gracious is that?

Ty Howington Throws L Age 21

YEAR	TEAM	LGE	IP	H	ER	HR	BB	K	ERA	W	L	H/9	HR/9	BB/9	K/9	KW	PERA	STUFF
2000	Dayton	Mid	144.7	156	100	17	96	68	6.22	5	11	9.7	1.1	6.0	4.2	0.4	7.66	-5
2001	Dayton	Mid	35.0	30	11	0	12	27	2.83	3	1	7.7	0.0	3.1	6.9	1.1	2.07	34
2001	Mudville	Cal	37.0	37	23	4	24	24	5.59	2	2	9.0	1.0	5.8	5.8	0.5	5.73	7
2001	Chattang	Sou	39.3	41	26	5	26	24	5.95	1	3	9.4	1.1	5.9	5.5	0.5	5.03	8

Howington bounced back quickly from having bone chips removed from his elbow in March, shooting through three levels while showing off the tight-breaking curve and low-90s moving fastball that have the Reds excited. He's had his delivery changed to eliminate the cross-body motion that caused concerns, and now his heat runs in on right-handed hitters a little more effectively. Young pitchers are a crapshoot, but Howington's the guy in the organization with the best balance of upside and proximity to the majors. If he's healthy, he'll be up before September.

Larry Luebbers Throws R Age 32

YEAR	TEAM	LGE	IP	H	ER	HR	BB	K	ERA	W	L	H/9	HR/9	BB/9	K/9	KW	PERA	STUFF
1999	Memphis	PCL	129.0	144	77	18	39	56	5.37	6	8	10.0	1.3	2.7	3.9	0.7	4.55	-8
1999	St Louis	NL	44.3	52	30	7	13	14	6.09	2	3	10.6	1.4	2.6	2.8	0.5	4.84	-13
2000	Louisvil	Int	110.0	118	63	12	43	52	5.15	5	7	9.7	1.0	3.5	4.3	0.6	4.46	-7
2000	Cincnnti	NL	22.0	23	11	1	10	8	4.50	1	1	9.4	0.4	4.1	3.3	0.4	5.91	-22
2001	Chattang	Sou	52.0	53	24	4	15	26	4.15	3	3	9.2	0.7	2.6	4.5	0.9	5.75	-2
2001	Louisvil	Int	121.0	134	63	11	31	41	4.69	6	7	10.0	0.8	2.3	3.0	0.7	4.98	-9

He's baseball's answer to the aptly-named Aspire: "Proud owners will tell you, they Aspire to own some other car." Luebbers's skill set is pretty straightforward: he has good control, and he can handle a regular workload. He's been qualified, ready, and waiting for a fifth-starter's job for years. He's also never going to break out and perform better than a fifth starter.

Scott MacRae Throws R Age 27

YEAR	TEAM	LGE	IP	H	ER	HR	BB	K	ERA	W	L	H/9	HR/9	BB/9	K/9	KW	PERA	STUFF
1999	Chattang	Sou	126.3	154	106	29	56	51	7.55	4	10	11.0	2.1	4.0	3.6	0.5	6.39	-32
2000	Chattang	Sou	77.0	83	52	8	48	35	6.08	3	6	9.7	0.9	5.6	4.1	0.4	5.64	-37
2001	Chattang	Sou	57.0	64	33	7	18	23	5.21	3	3	10.1	1.1	2.8	3.6	0.6	6.71	-24
2001	Louisvil	Int	20.0	20	10	1	8	10	4.50	1	1	9.0	0.4	3.6	4.5	0.6	2.54	-13
2001	Cincnnti	NL	31.0	30	10	0	7	14	2.90	2	1	8.7	0.0	2.0	4.1	1.0	4.30	-5

Up to this year, MacRae was just an organizational soldier, selected in the 32nd round of the 1995 draft. He would have gone unnoticed if Bob Boone hadn't spotted him while scouting Jose Rijo. His best weapon is a sinker that gets into the low 90s. While it's good to see MacRae finally make it, he's a tenth or 11th man at best.

Hector Mercado Throws L Age 28

YEAR	TEAM	LGE	IP	H	ER	HR	BB	K	ERA	W	L	H/9	HR/9	BB/9	K/9	KW	PERA	STUFF
2000	Louisvil	Int	77.7	72	40	3	52	50	4.64	4	5	8.3	0.3	6.0	5.8	0.5	3.46	-16
2000	Cincnnti	NL	14.0	13	8	2	7	12	5.14	1	1	8.4	1.3	4.5	7.7	0.9	4.00	0
2001	Louisvil	Int	13.7	12	6	0	8	9	3.95	1	1	7.9	0.0	5.3	5.9	0.6	1.68	-9
2001	Cincnnti	NL	53.7	48	26	5	27	47	4.36	3	3	8.0	0.8	4.5	7.9	0.9	4.57	2

Mercado throws hard enough to be something more than just a situational left-hander. Not all left-handed hitters struggle with lefty heat, and there are plenty of right-handed hitters who really do their business killing off-speed lefty junk. There are a lot of reasons to believe that scouting-driven situational usage patterns are more useful than conventional platoons. The failure to utilize such information is a blind spot for as many analysts as managers today. The best performance analysis requires a synthesis of scouting and statistical information.

Dustin Moseley Throws R Age 20

YEAR	TEAM	LGE	IP	H	ER	HR	BB	K	ERA	W	L	H/9	HR/9	BB/9	K/9	KW	PERA	STUFF
2001	Dayton	Mid	150.0	169	95	21	55	62	5.70	7	10	10.1	1.3	3.3	3.7	0.6	6.46	0

The Reds love Moseley's command and poise. He reaches 90 mph once in a while, spots his fastball well, and has a great curve. He'll probably struggle to adapt as his body fills out, so it's a little early to predict anything for him. A supplemental first-round pick in 2000, he's projectable, which is baseball-speak for "he could be absolutely anything you wishcast for him." Comparisons to Greg Maddux have been ridiculously premature.

Michael Neu   Throws R   Age 24

YEAR	TEAM	LGE	IP	H	ER	HR	BB	K	ERA	W	L	H/9	HR/9	BB/9	K/9	KW	PERA	STUFF
1999	Rockford	Mid	18.3	18	12	2	13	13	5.89	1	1	8.8	1.0	6.4	6.4	0.5	6.07	-7
2000	Clinton	Mid	64.7	66	56	12	60	52	7.79	2	5	9.2	1.7	8.4	7.2	0.4	4.85	-18
2001	Mudville	Cal	64.0	60	37	6	41	50	5.20	3	4	8.4	0.8	5.8	7.0	0.6	4.31	-11

A short right-hander (5′10″), Neu impressed some people with his performance as a minor-league closer. He does throw 90 with a good slider, and relievers aren't generally a predictable lot, so he could work out. It's considerably more likely than a team of sled bulldogs winning the Iditarod.

Brian Reith   Throws R   Age 24

YEAR	TEAM	LGE	IP	H	ER	HR	BB	K	ERA	W	L	H/9	HR/9	BB/9	K/9	KW	PERA	STUFF
1999	Tampa	Fla	146.0	167	95	26	42	68	5.86	6	10	10.3	1.6	2.6	4.2	0.8	7.16	-3
2000	Tampa	Fla	116.7	119	58	10	41	63	4.47	7	6	9.2	0.8	3.2	4.9	0.8	4.02	7
2000	Dayton	Mid	34.0	37	20	5	9	17	5.29	2	2	9.8	1.3	2.4	4.5	0.9	4.35	3
2000	Chattang	Sou	30.3	33	19	5	11	19	5.64	1	2	9.8	1.5	3.3	5.6	0.9	5.43	7
2001	Chattang	Sou	101.0	111	68	16	48	54	6.06	4	7	9.9	1.4	4.3	4.8	0.6	7.26	-7
2001	Cincnnti	NL	40.3	50	35	11	14	18	7.81	1	3	11.2	2.5	3.1	4.0	0.6	8.24	-19

Reith was pressed into action after other potential call-ups broke down, and the extent to which he'd been rushed showed. He made a good initial impression on Boone for his gutsy performances under fire, but the self-immolation got to be a bit too much of a habit. Reith has good mechanics for a big pitcher, but he doesn't dial up his heat much higher than 90 to complement a slider and change-up. It's likely that he'll spend 2002 regrouping in Louisville.

Chris Reitsma   Throws R   Age 24

YEAR	TEAM	LGE	IP	H	ER	HR	BB	K	ERA	W	L	H/9	HR/9	BB/9	K/9	KW	PERA	STUFF
1999	Sarasota	Fla	99.0	116	77	24	37	53	7.00	3	8	10.5	2.2	3.4	4.8	0.7	8.15	-7
2000	Sarasota	Fla	62.3	67	35	7	21	30	5.05	3	4	9.7	1.0	3.0	4.3	0.7	5.37	0
2000	Trenton	Eas	87.0	96	49	12	22	42	5.07	4	6	9.9	1.2	2.3	4.3	1.0	3.27	5
2001	Cincnnti	NL	177.7	193	92	20	44	77	4.66	10	10	9.8	1.0	2.2	3.9	0.9	5.97	-2

We were right in pegging Reitsma as a sleeper for last year's rotation, but that's one of the last times "right" and Reitsma will appear in the same sentence in reference to 2001. He made a good first impression with the velocity and movement on his fastball, his good change-up, and a couple of starts against the Pirates. It was downhill from there. Since coming back from losing two years to a broken elbow, he's not throwing in the high 90s any more, but he is regularly in the low 90s. He's not really in any danger of losing his rotation spot, it's just that he has to improve to do the Reds much good.

Dennys Reyes   Throws L   Age 25

YEAR	TEAM	LGE	IP	H	ER	HR	BB	K	ERA	W	L	H/9	HR/9	BB/9	K/9	KW	PERA	STUFF
1999	Cincnnti	NL	63.0	52	27	5	33	65	3.86	4	3	7.4	0.7	4.7	9.3	1.0	3.89	18
2000	Cincnnti	NL	44.7	43	25	4	24	32	5.04	2	3	8.7	0.8	4.8	6.4	0.7	5.67	-6
2001	Louisvil	Int	34.7	34	20	4	19	25	5.19	2	2	8.8	1.0	4.9	6.5	0.7	4.50	2
2001	Cincnnti	NL	52.0	48	28	4	31	42	4.85	3	3	8.3	0.7	5.4	7.3	0.7	5.93	-1

Stuck in a situational role for which he was overqualified, Reyes got a brief trial in the rotation, but Boone couldn't commit to that for longer than a few weeks. His control problems, especially when facing right-handed hitters, won't go away until he gets work on a more regular basis. Reyes did not pitch in winter ball, which might mean he'll show up to camp ready to work a lot of innings, or it might mean he'll show up ready for sumo season.

John Riedling   Throws R   Age 26

YEAR	TEAM	LGE	IP	H	ER	HR	BB	K	ERA	W	L	H/9	HR/9	BB/9	K/9	KW	PERA	STUFF
1999	Chattang	Sou	42.7	42	22	3	21	26	4.64	2	3	8.9	0.6	4.4	5.5	0.6	5.45	-12
1999	Indianap	Int	32.0	30	15	1	17	21	4.22	2	2	8.4	0.3	4.8	5.9	0.6	2.17	0
2000	Louisvil	Int	74.0	70	37	9	30	61	4.50	4	4	8.5	1.1	3.6	7.4	1.0	3.02	3
2000	Cincnnti	NL	15.0	12	6	1	7	16	3.60	1	1	7.2	0.6	4.2	9.6	1.1	3.66	19
2001	Cincnnti	NL	29.7	28	12	1	13	18	3.64	2	1	8.5	0.3	3.9	5.5	0.7	2.40	-3

(John Riedling *continued*)
After minor shoulder surgery, Riedling is expected to be ready to return to the majors by May at the latest, and possibly as early as March. However, when the doctors opened him up, they discovered that the damage was more severe than initially expected. When healthy, Riedling can flash dominant breaking stuff and good heat, although he falls in love with his curve. His condition in the spring could affect whether the Reds trade Danny Graves.

Jose Rijo **Throws R** **Age 37**

YEAR	TEAM	LGE	IP	H	ER	HR	BB	K	ERA	W	L	H/9	HR/9	BB/9	K/9	KW	PERA	STUFF
2001	Louisvil	Int	14.0	17	11	3	6	5	7.07	1	1	10.9	1.9	3.9	3.2	0.4	7.17	-39
2001	Cincnnti	NL	16.7	17	10	2	8	10	5.40	1	1	9.2	1.1	4.3	5.4	0.6	3.17	-11

Cut through the nostalgia surrounding Jose Rijo's comeback, and it's not hard to accept that he can provide value as more than just a celebrity to finish up a blowout now and again. The Marlins get some benefit from having Ricky Bones in the bullpen as a combination of a Spanish-speaking coach and a mentor, and Rijo was credited with playing a similar role with Acevedo and Reyes. On 11- or 12-man pitching staffs, you can find room for somebody like that.

Ryan Snare **Throws L** **Age 23**

YEAR	TEAM	LGE	IP	H	ER	HR	BB	K	ERA	W	L	H/9	HR/9	BB/9	K/9	KW	PERA	STUFF
2001	Dayton	Mid	113.0	120	70	16	51	65	5.58	5	8	9.6	1.3	4.1	5.2	0.6	4.69	0

Snare was the Reds' second-round pick in 2000, nabbed fresh from being an ace at North Carolina. There was concern that his fascination with bodybuilding was going to hinder his development, but he seems to have curbed that. He can get up to 91 mph at times, and he supplements the fastball with a curve and change-up. The Reds didn't push him hard in 2001, but they have high expectations for him this year.

Scott Sullivan **Throws R** **Age 31**

YEAR	TEAM	LGE	IP	H	ER	HR	BB	K	ERA	W	L	H/9	HR/9	BB/9	K/9	KW	PERA	STUFF
1999	Cincnnti	NL	108.7	107	51	9	39	70	4.22	6	6	8.9	0.7	3.2	5.8	0.9	2.88	-1
2000	Cincnnti	NL	104.0	99	48	12	31	85	4.15	6	6	8.6	1.0	2.7	7.4	1.4	3.31	6
2001	Cincnnti	NL	98.0	95	45	9	32	66	4.13	6	5	8.7	0.8	2.9	6.1	1.0	3.82	-1

Unobjectivity Alert: Sullivan is a favorite, in the same way that you had to love other sidearmers such as Kent Tekulve, Dan Quisenberry, and even Todd Frohwirth. With a tradition like that, it's almost a sin that Sullivan isn't funny-looking and doesn't bear an even funnier moniker. What matters is that it looks like his work on developing an off-speed pitch to freeze left-handed hitters was relatively successful, making him a better option for the primary setup role than he had been.

Travis Thompson **Throws R** **Age 24**

YEAR	TEAM	LGE	IP	H	ER	HR	BB	K	ERA	W	L	H/9	HR/9	BB/9	K/9	KW	PERA	STUFF
1999	Billings	Pio	20.3	18	6	0	4	14	2.66	1	1	8.0	0.0	1.8	6.2	1.8	0.48	18
2000	Clinton	Mid	35.3	39	25	7	15	23	6.37	1	3	9.9	1.8	3.8	5.9	0.8	2.44	6
2000	Dayton	Mid	136.3	146	74	15	45	63	4.89	7	8	9.6	1.0	3.0	4.2	0.7	4.74	1
2001	Chattang	Sou	163.3	176	86	16	52	72	4.74	9	9	9.7	0.9	2.9	4.0	0.7	5.91	-2

An undrafted free agent who played shortstop at East Carolina University, Thompson throws strikes and changes speeds. He doesn't throw hard for a big guy, reaching only 90 mph, but he has a good slider. Thompson will never impress scouts, but the organization likes him for his durability and command. He's somewhere between Cory Lidle and Jon Ratliff at this point, on his way to being a good guy to have at the bottom of your rotation or being a valuable member of a few Triple-A playoff teams.

Scott Williamson **Throws R** **Age 26**

YEAR	TEAM	LGE	IP	H	ER	HR	BB	K	ERA	W	L	H/9	HR/9	BB/9	K/9	KW	PERA	STUFF
1999	Cincnnti	NL	88.3	72	34	7	36	96	3.46	6	4	7.3	0.7	3.7	9.8	1.3	2.48	26
2000	Cincnnti	NL	114.3	91	46	6	62	121	3.62	8	5	7.2	0.5	4.9	9.5	1.0	3.21	22
2001	Cincnnti	NL	0.7	1	1	0	2	0	13.50	0	0	13.5	0.0	27.0	0.0	0.0	0.00	-116

Do we chalk up another win for skeptics of short pitchers, or do we just blame Williamson for not coming clean about how his arm felt? We'll have to see if he still has his mid-90s heat, his power slider, and his forkball when he returns. While elbow reconstructions turn out well more often than not these days, there are never any guarantees. He might be ready by Opening Day, and he might be in the rotation; don't bet much on either outcome.

Colorado Rockies

Is this an impossible task?

The Rockies play in an environment unique in MLB history. It's not just that they have a good hitters' park in Coors Field. Any non-domed park in Denver would be a good place to hit. It's the altitude, and not the ballpark's characteristics, that make the difference. Batted balls fly farther and land faster, affecting all aspects of offense. The thinner air creates less friction over the seams of a baseball, causing breaking balls to move less. All told, pitches are easier to hit and, once put in play, more likely to result in good things for the team at the plate.

Ever since Denver was granted an expansion team, we've kicked around ideas about how to build a winning team there. The altitude and its effects on all parts of the game have to be factored into every decision. Ideas that we liked in the abstract seem to have less value as time goes by, and ones we didn't consider have gained credence.

What we do know is that the Rockies have struggled to win on the road since their inception. It's possible that the demands of baseball at altitude are so different from the demands of "regular" baseball that it's impossible for the franchise to build a consistent winner. Are the Rockies doomed no matter how many trades Dan O'Dowd executes? We doubt it; it's just that building a winner in Colorado will require accepting a different type of baseball, and an adherence to putting together a team that can play it. Here's how we would attack the problem:

Rockies Prospectus

2001 record: 73–89; Fifth place, NL West

Pythagenport W/L: 83–79

Runs scored: 923 (first in NL)

Runs allowed: 906 (16th in NL)

Team EqA: .268 (tied for second in NL)

2001 batters age: 28 (fifth-youngest in NL)

2001 pitchers age: 28.3 (eighth-youngest in NL)

Ballpark: Coors Field; obscene hitters' park; Park Factor of 1.265

2001: Year One of The Great Change-up Experiment flopped. Dan O'Dowd made some trades.

2002: They weren't nearly as bad as they looked and should be in the hunt this year. O'Dowd will make more trades.

Hitting

Despite a persistent notion that altitude affects fly-ball hitters and not other types, the conditions at Coors Field benefit all batters. Walt Weiss was helped, just as Dante Bichette was. This is because the conditions don't just affect fly balls meeting less resistance as they climb into the night; they make bloopers drop faster, leading to more singles. And remember: every batter gets a shot at those hanging curveballs and flat sliders.

"Hitting" is the key element at Coors Field. The worst thing you can do is strike out, because the outcome of putting a bat on the ball is better there than it is anywhere else. Players hitting in Coors Field batted .312 last season, with a .535 slugging percentage. When they didn't strike out, though, those numbers jumped to .378 and .649. Think about that: simply not striking out makes you a .380 hitter with great power at Coors Field.

The extra boost given to batted balls also made walks relatively less valuable. The positive expectation of a ball in play—.378 OBP, .649 slugging—takes away much of the incentive to work deep counts, because deep counts increase the odds of a costly strikeout.

Given the decreased value of walks in Coors, the aggressive approach of Vinny Castilla and Dante Bichette—the greatest beneficiaries of Coorsflation—almost makes sense. In their home park, there was a big advantage to getting a ball in play early in the count, rather than risk a whiff. This approach killed their walk totals and was terrible on the road, where walks had more value, but it made Castilla and Bichette very, very good at Coors Field.

The Rockies should therefore choose players who put the ball in play, all else being equal, and they should encourage approaches at the plate that reduce strikeouts without having a detrimental affect on OBP. Todd Helton and Larry Walker are going to help a team no matter what, but on the margins, it's better for the Rockies to have a player who strikes out 50 times rather than 80, even if there's a slight loss in expected walks. The extra balls in play will help them win games at home. Someone like Juan Pierre, with 41 walks and 29 strikeouts in 600-odd at-bats, really is a worthwhile player in Coors Field.

Pitching

If putting balls in play is the best approach for hitters in Denver, then it makes sense for the Rockies to favor pitchers who strike out a bunch of guys. This is difficult: the effect of

Coors Field on breaking pitches makes it hard for pitchers to get the batter to swing and miss, much less do so three times. Coors is not a good strikeout park, reducing them by 15% a year (source: Stats, Inc.).

To combat this, the Rockies would be best off assembling a staff of hard throwers who blow people away with great heat, even if they're lacking in other areas. They should discourage the use of curves and sliders except as show pitches to be dropped in on occasion. Rockies' pitchers need fastballs in the 90s and straight change-ups in the 80s, although the former is much more important, and more plentiful.

What types of pitchers are we talking about? Think early Chuck Finley and David Cone or, even better, any version of Nolan Ryan. The Rockies will have to take some chances and be patient with the pitchers they acquire. Most importantly, they'll have to adjust their mind-set on walks, which will be the hardest part of this plan. The Rockies want a staff that will strike out 1,300 batters, even if it walks 700, because it's that important to keep the opposition from putting the ball in play.

At some point, the Rockies are going to have to entertain new notions on how to run a pitching staff. The conventional methods don't work, in large part because Rockies pitchers have to do things so much differently at home than on the road. The Rockies would be well served to start thinking about how to partition their innings not by situation, carrying setup men and closers and situational left-handers, but by location: at home they should use hard throwers who walk guys but don't give up hits, and on the road they should use pitchers with a normal arsenal.

Defense

One of the early ideas about winning at altitude was that the Rockies would need a fast outfield, able to cover the gaps and reach balls that would be plummeting towards earth much faster than they would be elsewhere. While this isn't a bad idea, it's also possible that the physics issues may preclude *anyone* from being a good defender at altitude.

With that in mind, the Rockies should worry less about defense. They have to score 1,000-1,100 runs to win, and playing guys who don't contribute to that goal is counterproductive, given that the marginal benefit of a good defender will be less in Denver than at sea level. Additionally, they should worry less about range and more about handedness, especially in the infield. The value of an out is such that blowing an easy play is more detrimental in Coors Field than anywhere else. Finally, a properly constructed Rockies pitching staff will put fewer balls in play than any other staff in baseball, minimizing the impact of diminished defensive ability.

Yes, Virginia, Jack Cust should play left field.

Roster

This is thc hard part. Because the Rockies need different types of players at home than on the road, it becomes very difficult to construct a roster capable of winning in both places. Those hard throwers are going to be walking a hell of a lot of hitters at sea level, in places where it's better to just let guys swing the bat. The Juan Pierres of the world are going to go from batting .370 on balls in play to .270 and suddenly have a .300 OBP.

Ideally, you would have a team—or develop a team—capable of shifting gears. While this might work with hitters, who can conceivably modify their approach from night to night, it's unlikely to be a successful strategy with pitchers. There aren't many pitchers capable of striking out eight or nine men per nine innings with just their fastball, *and* who are capable of using good breaking stuff to get outs when they go on the road.

With that in mind, the Rockies are going to want, say, three pitchers and one reliever who can and do pitch anywhere. This is where they'll make the bulk of their financial investment, and these pitchers would be used in much the way a team uses its regular rotation and best reliever.

The other seven or eight pitchers on the staff would be "home" or "road" guys, selected for how well they fit the criterion listed and, in general, for their low cost. Four would do the bulk of their work at Coors Field, starting or working in high-leverage relief situations for multiple innings. The others would pitch mostly on the road. Each group would, of course, be available to throw low-leverage innings as needed both at home and on the road.

There are other things the Rockies can do. They need to carry 12 pitchers, so their short bench has to be long on guys with multiple talents. They can't carry a no-hit backup catcher or a Lenny Harris-style pinch hitter. Terry Shumpert, who has played all over the place in his time with the Rockies while hitting reasonably well, is an excellent example of a good Rockies' bench player.

The Rockies can't platoon at more than one position, and they would be best served to have eight everyday players, if possible. Again, this is a function of a short bench, which makes it harder to do much within a National League game but hit for your pitchers. Speaking of which, the Rockies should try and have pitchers who can hit, because they'll want to be able to leave an effective pitcher in longer than most, as well as occasionally use a pitcher as a pinch hitter to bolster the short bench. Of course, a pitcher who can hit a little gets more out of Coors Field than he would elsewhere.

Most of the solutions for making mile-high baseball more like baseball in the rest of the country involve physics.

Building a pressurized dome is the really expensive solution with no chance of happening. Other notions involve changing the baseball itself, either altering its properties to make it carry less or raising its seams to help pitchers throw better breaking balls.

The problem with changing the baseball is the same as the problems with changing the strike zone: it sounds like a small thing, but it would alter the heart of the game, and the effects of such changes are always greater than anticipated. The intent in modifying the baseball used in Rockies' home games would be to lower offense, to make the 13-11 games into 6-5 games. It's a cosmetic solution.

Of course, we don't know what altering the ball itself would really do. Calibrating such a change properly would be difficult at best and could lead to some strange results. Additionally, the Rockies would be at a perpetual disadvantage: it's one thing to be a visiting team that plays three to nine games a year in Denver's environment with a different baseball; it's another to play half your games with a different ball. Pitching is a difficult, high-risk endeavor under the best of circumstances; using a different baseball in every other start would introduce a set of problems almost certain to end in injury.

Let's just accept that baseball games in Denver are going to be high-scoring. That's not a bad thing, notwithstanding the reactionary element that gets fired up whenever baseball gets too far from looking like it did in 1968. You can't fight physics, at least not without inviting The Law of Unintended Consequences to wreak havoc.

What you can do is address the Rockies' disadvantage. It's been established that pitching in Denver is harder, physically, than it is anywhere else, because of the additional effort required on every pitch, and the additional pitches required to get through a game.

So give the Rockies an extra player.

Currently, the Rockies use 11 pitchers, often going to 12. Allowing the Rockies to carry 26 players would permit them to always have 12 pitchers—really the minimum necessary in Denver's environment—and on occasion, 13. This would allow the Rockies to implement innovative pitching patterns without sacrificing the in-game value of a six-man bench.

It's an unusual solution, to be sure. However, it would be the one least intrusive on the entire league, while best protecting the health of the Rockies' pitchers. To get around the inevitable squawking, a modified version of the rule would allow teams playing the Rockies in Denver to use a 26-man roster in those games. Just about every team in baseball adds a pitcher when heading for the mountains anyway, so this would put both the Rockies and their opponents on even ground in every game.

Don't change the baseball, don't build a dome, don't complain about how the game is going to hell in a hand basket. Just allow a 26-man roster, then step back and see if the Rockies can innovate well enough to take advantage of it.

HITTERS (BA: .270, OBP: .340, SLG: .440, EqA: .260)

Garrett Atkins 1B Bats R Age 22

YEAR	TEAM	LGE	AB	H	DB	TP	HR	BB	SO	R	RBI	SB	CS	OUT	BA	OBP	SLG	EQA	EQR	DEFENSE
2000	Portland	Nwn	265	61	5	0	6	27	52	23	30	1	0	204	.230	.303	.317	.215	22	35-1B -3 10-3B 0
2001	Salem VA	Car	494	135	34	4	5	62	98	61	55	4	3	361	.273	.358	.389	.255	60	125-1B -1
2002	*Colorado*	*NL*	*465*	*150*	*32*	*4*	*9*	*63*	*95*	*64*	*62*	*4*	*1*	*316*	*.323*	*.403*	*.467*	*.269*	*59*	

Being a first-base prospect behind Todd Helton can be hazardous to your health. The Rockies want to find a spot for Atkins, so they're moving him to third base. Unfortunately, he has elbow problems that flare up when he's asked to make a lot of throws, which is how he ended up at first originally. He'll need to turn his doubles into homers *and* find a way to stay healthy playing third base. Look for the elbow to make Atkins trade bait before he reaches the majors.

Gary Bennett C Bats R Age 30

YEAR	TEAM	LGE	AB	H	DB	TP	HR	BB	SO	R	RBI	SB	CS	OUT	BA	OBP	SLG	EQA	EQR	DEFENSE
1999	Philadel	NL	88	24	3	0	1	3	10	7	16	0	0	64	.273	.297	.341	.215	7	20-C -2
2000	Scran-WB	Int	321	94	17	0	13	34	43	43	48	1	0	227	.293	.370	.467	.280	47	75-C -3
2000	Philadel	NL	74	18	4	0	2	12	14	7	5	0	0	56	.243	.362	.378	.256	9	24-C 1
2001	Philadel	NL	75	17	3	1	1	9	16	8	6	0	0	58	.227	.310	.333	.221	7	22-C 0
2001	Norfolk	Int	68	20	4	0	2	4	11	7	13	0	0	48	.294	.339	.441	.259	8	14-C 0
2001	Colorado	NL	54	14	2	0	1	2	4	6	4	0	0	40	.259	.295	.352	.218	4	14-C -1
2002	*Colorado*	*NL*	*337*	*104*	*18*	*1*	*10*	*39*	*53*	*41*	*69*	*0*	*0*	*233*	*.309*	*.380*	*.457*	*.256*	*38*	

(Gary Bennett *continued*)

If Kirt Manwaring and Brent Mayne can keep Ben Petrick from getting 500 at-bats, Gary Bennett sure can, too. He's the kind of backup catcher we're always touting: decent defensively, with some pop and plate discipline. The Rockies have to make sure all their bench players can hit a little; Bennett qualifies.

Brent Butler 2B Bats R Age 24

YEAR	TEAM	LGE	AB	H	DB	TP	HR	BB	SO	R	RBI	SB	CS	OUT	BA	OBP	SLG	EQA	EQR	DEFENSE
1999	Arkansas	Tex	528	123	15	1	10	19	49	54	41	0	2	407	.233	.265	.322	.197	35	55-SS 0 46-3B 3
2000	ColSprin	PCL	427	105	23	1	7	33	44	54	39	1	2	324	.246	.304	.354	.222	38	94-2B -12 25-SS -2
2001	ColSprin	PCL	264	75	16	2	5	14	24	39	29	3	2	191	.284	.326	.417	.247	29	51-2B -9
2001	Colorado	NL	117	26	6	1	1	6	6	16	13	1	1	92	.222	.265	.316	.196	8	19-2B -3
2002	*Colorado*	*NL*	*513*	*156*	*33*	*3*	*13*	*40*	*47*	*84*	*59*	*5*	*4*	*361*	*.304*	*.354*	*.456*	*.243*	*52*	

The trade of Jeff Cirillo means that there's a job open for Butler at third base. At worst, he should be able to move into a platoon with Greg Norton, while also serving as the backup for the middle infielders. Though Butler has been a disappointment to date, he is still just 24, and he is playing in the right environment for a low-strikeout hitter with power. He's going to make some money.

Jeff Cirillo 3B Bats R Age 32

YEAR	TEAM	LGE	AB	H	DB	TP	HR	BB	SO	R	RBI	SB	CS	OUT	BA	OBP	SLG	EQA	EQR	DEFENSE
1999	Milwauke	NL	607	195	30	2	16	67	77	95	84	6	4	416	.321	.393	.456	.286	91	148-3B 10
2000	Colorado	NL	579	168	43	2	10	57	66	94	95	2	4	415	.290	.359	.423	.262	73	151-3B -1
2001	Colorado	NL	512	149	24	3	15	39	53	66	74	11	2	365	.291	.346	.438	.264	65	135-3B 20
2002	*Seattle*	*AL*	*527*	*142*	*25*	*2*	*14*	*56*	*61*	*77*	*72*	*7*	*3*	*388*	*.269*	*.340*	*.404*	*.261*	*68*	

Wilton projects Cirillo to lose three points of EqA, a slight decline consistent with his age and recent performance. However, he's moving from one extreme to the other in terms of hitting environments; he could be the same hitter and drop 100 points of OPS, anyway. Cirillo's problems hitting on the road the past two years have been documented; he'll get some of that performance back and hit closer to his pre-Rockies numbers.

Jacob Cruz LF Bats L Age 29

YEAR	TEAM	LGE	AB	H	DB	TP	HR	BB	SO	R	RBI	SB	CS	OUT	BA	OBP	SLG	EQA	EQR	DEFENSE
1999	Buffalo	Int	202	52	5	2	6	17	37	24	25	3	2	152	.257	.322	.391	.240	21	40-LF -2
1999	Clevelnd	AL	87	29	5	1	3	4	11	13	16	0	2	60	.333	.369	.517	.282	13	21-CF 1
2000	Clevelnd	AL	29	7	4	0	0	4	4	3	5	1	0	22	.241	.354	.379	.258	4	
2001	Clevelnd	AL	68	16	2	0	4	5	20	12	12	0	2	54	.235	.309	.441	.238	7	17-CF -1
2001	Colorado	NL	74	13	1	0	1	10	23	6	6	0	2	63	.176	.280	.230	.179	4	17-LF -3
2001	ColSprin	PCL	83	23	3	1	5	2	21	14	19	1	0	60	.277	.299	.518	.264	11	19-OF 4
2002	*Detroit*	*AL*	*260*	*65*	*9*	*1*	*11*	*25*	*69*	*31*	*44*	*1*	*3*	*198*	*.250*	*.316*	*.419*	*.247*	*30*	

Cruz has had more joint problems than Lamar Odom. He was crushing the ball in 1999 when he tore a ligament in his thumb, ending his season. Then he blew out his ACL in 2000. The rust of having just 319 at-bats in two years showed, as he didn't even hit after being traded to paradise in June. If Cruz can stay healthy for 18 months, he can get on the John Vander Wal career track. He's in a bad spot in Detroit, fighting with a number of similar players for DH/RF at-bats.

Mario Encarnacion OF Bats R Age 24

YEAR	TEAM	LGE	AB	H	DB	TP	HR	BB	SO	R	RBI	SB	CS	OUT	BA	OBP	SLG	EQA	EQR	DEFENSE
1999	Midland	Tex	349	86	15	2	13	36	89	50	48	6	5	269	.246	.318	.413	.242	39	72-CF -12
1999	Vancouvr	PCL	145	32	3	0	3	5	40	15	14	4	3	116	.221	.254	.303	.189	9	37-RF 4
2000	Sacramen	PCL	300	73	14	2	11	28	92	40	47	11	5	232	.243	.313	.413	.243	34	74-RF 4
2001	Sacramen	PCL	185	48	6	1	10	16	55	24	27	4	3	139	.259	.327	.465	.259	24	40-RF -4
2001	ColSprin	PCL	43	14	2	0	2	4	7	6	8	0	1	30	.326	.391	.512	.290	7	13-OF 0
2001	Colorado	NL	61	12	1	0	0	4	12	3	3	2	1	50	.197	.246	.213	.167	3	16-LF 2
2002	*Colorado*	*NL*	*450*	*137*	*20*	*2*	*21*	*45*	*127*	*71*	*76*	*12*	*6*	*319*	*.304*	*.368*	*.498*	*.259*	*54*	

Encarnacion's star had fallen a bit in the A's system, so they used him to acquire the player he could become—Jermaine Dye—in July's three-way deal. He strikes out a lot, which makes him less likely to take advantage of playing at altitude. A good spring could earn him a share of the Rockies' left-field job, probably with Todd Hollandsworth.

Josue Espada IF Bats R Age 26

YEAR	TEAM	LGE	AB	H	DB	TP	HR	BB	SO	R	RBI	SB	CS	OUT	BA	OBP	SLG	EQA	EQR	DEFENSE
1999	Midland	Tex	429	110	12	1	4	47	53	61	35	13	10	322	.270	.344	.331	.234	43	80-SS -25 24-2B -6
2000	Sacramen	PCL	145	31	6	0	0	22	22	16	8	5	2	116	.214	.320	.255	.211	12	34-2B 6
2000	Midland	Tex	97	20	6	0	0	9	12	13	5	1	1	78	.206	.281	.268	.193	6	11-2B -2
2001	Calgary	PCL	283	70	17	1	2	34	44	48	22	10	5	218	.247	.333	.336	.234	29	66-SS -5
2001	ColSprin	PCL	27	6	0	0	1	4	5	6	2	3	2	22	.222	.323	.333	.231	3	
2002	*Colorado*	*NL*	*387*	*115*	*24*	*1*	*5*	*50*	*59*	*72*	*36*	*20*	*10*	*282*	*.297*	*.378*	*.403*	*.242*	*41*	

The Rockies picked up Espada from the Marlins for Juan Acevedo. As you might expect for a refugee from the A's system, he's shown good plate discipline at almost every stop. He's not a real good shortstop, which hurts his chance to be a utility infielder, as does Brent Butler's presence. The next year is critical; guys like this become Jeff Gardner more often than they become Frank Menechino.

Sal Fasano C Bats R Age 30

YEAR	TEAM	LGE	AB	H	DB	TP	HR	BB	SO	R	RBI	SB	CS	OUT	BA	OBP	SLG	EQA	EQR	DEFENSE
1999	Omaha	PCL	276	67	10	0	17	35	63	48	37	3	2	211	.243	.364	.464	.276	42	82-C -6
1999	KansasCy	AL	59	14	1	0	5	7	15	10	15	0	1	46	.237	.376	.508	.285	10	23-C 0
2000	Oakland	AL	126	28	5	0	8	13	41	21	19	0	0	98	.222	.310	.452	.251	15	38-C 0
2001	Oakland	AL	21	2	0	0	0	1	10	2	0	0	0	19	.095	.165	.095	.100	0	
2001	ColSprin	PCL	80	21	3	0	5	8	24	12	17	0	0	59	.262	.348	.488	.275	12	22-C -2
2001	Colorado	NL	62	15	3	0	3	3	16	9	8	0	0	47	.242	.301	.435	.242	7	21-C 1
2002	*Colorado*	*NL*	*294*	*82*	*11*	*0*	*19*	*31*	*86*	*52*	*48*	*2*	*1*	*213*	*.279*	*.348*	*.510*	*.253*	*34*	

No, it just seems like everyone in this chapter was with a different team a year ago. Fasano, a backup catcher in the Mark Parent tradition, has never been able to establish himself as a legitimate major leaguer. Even the A's, who favor walks-and-power guys, had to say "uncle" after his 1-for-21 start. Jazayerli's Rule of Backup Catchers says he'll hit .300 at some point. Fasano's career depends on it happening real soon.

Choo Freeman CF Bats R Age 22

YEAR	TEAM	LGE	AB	H	DB	TP	HR	BB	SO	R	RBI	SB	CS	OUT	BA	OBP	SLG	EQA	EQR	DEFENSE
1999	Ashevlle	SAL	489	98	16	2	8	28	140	53	40	7	3	394	.200	.248	.290	.186	29	130-CF -8
2000	Salem VA	Car	439	99	14	4	5	25	105	56	40	8	6	346	.226	.270	.310	.198	30	125-CF -12
2001	Salem VA	Car	530	113	13	4	7	27	108	54	35	12	5	422	.213	.256	.292	.190	33	123-CF -4
2002	*Colorado*	*NL*	*495*	*135*	*18*	*4*	*12*	*36*	*117*	*75*	*56*	*14*	*6*	*366*	*.273*	*.322*	*.398*	*.217*	*40*	

The Rockies appear to be moving away from drafting high-school football players. This is one reason why. Freeman, a wide receiver who chose the Rockies over Texas A&M—forfeiting a chance to be immortalized in *Sidelines*—hasn't shown any improvement in three professional seasons. He's a non-prospect, the kind who should be used in an instructional video for scouting departments.

Darryl Hamilton OF Bats L Age 37

YEAR	TEAM	LGE	AB	H	DB	TP	HR	BB	SO	R	RBI	SB	CS	OUT	BA	OBP	SLG	EQA	EQR	DEFENSE
1999	Colorado	NL	327	87	9	2	4	33	19	54	20	3	4	244	.266	.335	.343	.232	32	82-CF 1
1999	NY Mets	NL	169	57	9	1	5	17	17	19	20	1	3	115	.337	.401	.491	.293	27	44-CF 1
2000	NY Mets	NL	106	30	4	1	1	13	18	20	6	2	0	76	.283	.361	.368	.255	13	23-OF -1
2001	NY Mets	NL	127	30	8	1	1	19	17	16	6	3	1	98	.236	.343	.339	.240	14	32-LF 1
2002	*Colorado*	*NL*	*374*	*96*	*15*	*3*	*6*	*47*	*46*	*55*	*26*	*5*	*4*	*282*	*.257*	*.340*	*.361*	*.213*	*30*	

(Darryl Hamilton *continued*)

Inside *Baseball Prospectus:* There are certain rules we follow in choosing the players for this book, one of which is that anybody with a reasonable amount of major-league playing time is included. Another is that players are listed with the organization they were playing for at the end of the season. That's how Darryl Hamilton, who had 126 at-bats for the Mets, makes the book as part of this chapter, even though he was released by the Rockies just a week after signing with them.

That's a long way of saying Hamilton's career is over.

Todd Helton 1B Bats L Age 28

YEAR	TEAM	LGE	AB	H	DB	TP	HR	BB	SO	R	RBI	SB	CS	OUT	BA	OBP	SLG	EQA	EQR	DEFENSE
1999	Colorado	NL	560	159	32	4	31	59	71	98	93	5	5	406	.284	.358	.521	.285	88	148-1B -3
2000	Colorado	NL	553	181	45	2	36	90	56	115	118	4	3	375	.327	.424	.611	.332	119	152-1B 18
2001	Colorado	NL	564	175	43	2	44	90	88	119	129	6	5	394	.310	.409	.628	.327	120	153-1B 8
2002	*Colorado*	*NL*	*539*	*197*	*44*	*3*	*45*	*94*	*75*	*130*	*128*	*6*	*5*	*347*	*.365*	*.460*	*.709*	*.335*	*113*	

Todd Helton: 2000s ↔ Sandy Koufax: 1960s. Discuss. Helton is an excellent hitter playing in the best hitters' environment and best hitters' era in history. Koufax was an excellent pitcher whose prime years were spent in Dodger Stadium during Dead Ball Era II, the complete opposite end of the spectrum. Both players are very good, among the best in the game, but it's easy to overestimate *how* good, because their stats are wildly distorted.

There are people who have an emotional attachment to the idea that Sandy Koufax was one of the greatest pitchers in baseball history, rather than a good one with a high peak and some fortuitous timing. It would be interesting to ask those people how they rank Todd Helton, because Helton 2000–03 is going to have a lot in common with Koufax 1963–66.

Todd Hollandsworth LF Bats L Age 29

YEAR	TEAM	LGE	AB	H	DB	TP	HR	BB	SO	R	RBI	SB	CS	OUT	BA	OBP	SLG	EQA	EQR	DEFENSE
1999	LosAngls	NL	264	77	13	2	9	21	56	39	31	4	2	189	.292	.346	.458	.267	35	56-OF 0 10-1B 0
2000	LosAngls	NL	265	64	10	0	9	26	56	42	24	11	4	205	.242	.311	.381	.236	28	67-CF 0
2000	Colorado	NL	163	47	6	0	10	8	35	33	19	6	3	119	.288	.322	.509	.268	22	39-LF 2
2001	Colorado	NL	113	39	14	1	5	7	17	19	17	4	0	74	.345	.383	.619	.323	22	26-LF -1
2002	*Colorado*	*NL*	*357*	*116*	*24*	*1*	*18*	*34*	*73*	*69*	*49*	*14*	*4*	*245*	*.325*	*.384*	*.549*	*.278*	*50*	

An underrated factor in the Rockies' first-half collapse last season was the loss of Hollandsworth, who was off to a career-best start when he fouled a pitch off his right leg May 11. He never returned; the diagnosis changed a few times, and the injury was eventually called a stress fracture of his right shin. Hollandsworth should be healthy this spring and will be the platoon left fielder.

Matt Holliday LF Bats R Age 22

YEAR	TEAM	LGE	AB	H	DB	TP	HR	BB	SO	R	RBI	SB	CS	OUT	BA	OBP	SLG	EQA	EQR	DEFENSE
1999	Ashevlle	SAL	452	87	13	0	11	38	123	49	40	5	2	367	.192	.261	.294	.193	30	107-3B -32
2000	Salem VA	Car	471	110	22	1	6	29	75	51	53	6	4	365	.234	.279	.323	.205	35	104-3B -16
2001	Salem VA	Car	268	64	11	1	9	27	42	30	41	7	2	206	.239	.311	.388	.238	28	27-LF -2
2002	*Colorado*	*NL*	*469*	*133*	*24*	*1*	*16*	*46*	*88*	*71*	*70*	*12*	*4*	*340*	*.284*	*.348*	*.441*	*.239*	*48*	

The Rockies have already spent $1.5 million to keep Holliday playing baseball rather than football. That includes a six-year, $700,000 contract signed last summer, about 15 minutes before he underwent season-ending elbow surgery. He's a better baseball prospect than Freeman is, which is damning with faint praise. It's hard to call him a prospect until we see what the surgery did to his power.

Mark Little OF Bats R Age 29

YEAR	TEAM	LGE	AB	H	DB	TP	HR	BB	SO	R	RBI	SB	CS	OUT	BA	OBP	SLG	EQA	EQR	DEFENSE
1999	Memphis	PCL	193	51	10	4	2	8	44	31	17	9	4	146	.264	.308	.389	.235	20	51-CF 1
2000	Memphis	PCL	426	112	24	5	14	40	95	56	52	16	9	323	.263	.338	.441	.259	55	104-CF 4
2001	ColSprin	PCL	39	12	2	0	0	2	8	5	3	0	1	28	.308	.351	.359	.235	4	
2001	Colorado	NL	83	26	2	0	4	0	17	16	13	5	2	59	.313	.337	.482	.270	11	19-OF 1
2002	*Colorado*	*NL*	*363*	*115*	*19*	*4*	*14*	*29*	*83*	*72*	*47*	*19*	*8*	*256*	*.317*	*.367*	*.507*	*.261*	*45*	

More marginal players seem to be trying to get an entry in the Coors Lottery. The Rockies had Little, Brooks Kieschnick, Butch Huskey, Darryl Hamilton, Lance Johnson, Roberto Kelly, and Melvin Nieves signed to minor-league contracts and playing at Triple-A last season. The idea is sound: get to Coors Field, put up some numbers, and have a career. Even the downside—put up numbers at the elevation of Colorado Springs and enhance the resume—is a pretty good plan. Little can play all three outfield spots and provide some right-handed pop behind the three lefty starters; Mario Encarnacion does those things and has upside, so Little has a problem.

Adam Melhuse C/PH Bats R Age 30

YEAR	TEAM	LGE	AB	H	DB	TP	HR	BB	SO	R	RBI	SB	CS	OUT	BA	OBP	SLG	EQA	EQR	DEFENSE
1999	Knoxvill	Sou	377	90	14	0	15	84	77	58	48	3	4	291	.239	.381	.395	.267	54	42-LF -2 25-1B -2
1999	Syracuse	Int	71	18	4	0	2	8	19	13	13	1	1	54	.254	.329	.394	.242	8	17-C -1
2000	Albuquer	PCL	105	30	4	0	2	18	20	15	15	3	2	77	.286	.390	.381	.268	14	15-C -1 10-1B 0
2000	ColSprin	PCL	137	32	4	1	2	16	34	17	13	1	2	107	.234	.314	.321	.217	12	22-LF 1
2001	ColSprin	PCL	181	40	8	1	5	27	38	20	24	0	1	142	.221	.326	.359	.234	19	36-C -4
2001	Colorado	NL	70	11	2	0	1	5	15	5	7	1	0	59	.157	.213	.229	.158	3	16-C -4
2002	*ChiCubs*	*NL*	*379*	*91*	*13*	*1*	*12*	*63*	*87*	*54*	*48*	*3*	*2*	*290*	*.240*	*.348*	*.375*	*.251*	*46*	

Melhuse has value because he can almost play third base and left field. His problem is that he's a fairly lousy catcher, so he needs to be the "hitting" backup for a guy like Henry Blanco. He's migrated to the Cubs and Don Baylor, who prefers guys like Robert Machado and Sandy Martinez as his backup catcher.

Jayson Nix SS Bats R Age 19

YEAR	TEAM	LGE	AB	H	DB	TP	HR	BB	SO	R	RBI	SB	CS	OUT	BA	OBP	SLG	EQA	EQR	DEFENSE
2001	Casper	Pio	152	28	7	0	2	13	50	13	10	0	2	126	.184	.253	.270	.179	9	38-SS -6
2002	*Colorado*	*NL*	*195*	*51*	*10*	*0*	*5*	*19*	*68*	*21*	*21*	*1*	*5*	*149*	*.262*	*.327*	*.390*	*.208*	*15*	

The Rockies' first pick in 2001—a compensation selecton for the Matt Harrington fiasco—is the brother of Rangers' prospect Laynce Nix. A shortstop in high school, Nix projects as a second baseman in the pros and will play the keystone full-time in 2002. More importantly, he represents a shift away from the Rockies' history of drafting athletes and projectable high-school pitchers, and a shift towards taking high-upside baseball players. Good move.

Greg Norton UT Bats B Age 29

YEAR	TEAM	LGE	AB	H	DB	TP	HR	BB	SO	R	RBI	SB	CS	OUT	BA	OBP	SLG	EQA	EQR	DEFENSE
1999	ChiSox	AL	432	114	20	0	19	65	82	61	50	4	4	322	.264	.362	.442	.269	60	108-3B -1 10-1B -5
2000	ChiSox	AL	199	50	7	1	6	24	41	24	27	1	0	149	.251	.338	.387	.247	23	36-3B -7 11-1B 1
2000	Charlott	Int	98	26	2	0	5	21	23	16	15	1	0	72	.265	.403	.439	.290	16	24-3B 3
2001	Colorado	NL	220	54	13	2	11	17	55	28	35	1	0	166	.245	.300	.473	.251	26	16-3B -3 15-LF -4
2002	*Colorado*	*NL*	*366*	*106*	*20*	*1*	*19*	*53*	*86*	*58*	*56*	*3*	*1*	*261*	*.290*	*.379*	*.505*	*.266*	*48*	

Norton is a left-handed hitter masquerading as a switch-hitter, with a .324 slugging percentage from the right side over the past four seasons. Somewhat pigeonholed as a bench player, he brings enough to the table that he could be part of a valuable third-base platoon now that Cirillo is gone.

Alex Ochoa RF/LF Bats R Age 30

YEAR	TEAM	LGE	AB	H	DB	TP	HR	BB	SO	R	RBI	SB	CS	OUT	BA	OBP	SLG	EQA	EQR	DEFENSE
1999	Milwauke	NL	277	81	16	3	8	41	40	45	37	5	4	200	.292	.393	.458	.286	44	67-LF -3
2000	Cincnnti	NL	244	75	18	3	13	21	25	47	54	7	4	173	.307	.368	.566	.298	42	59-LF 1
2001	Cincnnti	NL	350	104	20	4	7	22	45	49	36	12	9	255	.297	.341	.437	.257	43	82-RF 0
2001	Colorado	NL	183	41	10	2	1	19	20	23	15	4	3	145	.224	.302	.317	.214	15	47-LF 2
2002	*Milwauke*	*NL*	*481*	*130*	*27*	*5*	*12*	*50*	*62*	*72*	*61*	*14*	*9*	*360*	*.270*	*.339*	*.422*	*.256*	*60*	

When Ochoa was traded to the Rockies, it was hard to not think of Dante Bichette. Both were 29 upon arriving in Denver, both were toolsy corner outfielders with good arms, and neither had been much of a player to that point. Unlike Bichette, Ochoa didn't hit in his first exposure to the thin air. That, the return of Hollandsworth, and the acquisition of Encarnacion are going to make it difficult for Ochoa to replicate Fonzie's career. Moving to Milwaukee pretty much ends his bid for park-inflated stardom.

Jose Ortiz **2B** **Bats R** **Age 25**

YEAR	TEAM	LGE	AB	H	DB	TP	HR	BB	SO	R	RBI	SB	CS	OUT	BA	OBP	SLG	EQA	EQR	DEFENSE
1999	Vancouvr	PCL	376	99	24	2	8	25	46	55	38	10	3	280	.263	.320	.402	.244	41	96-SS -5
2000	Sacramen	PCL	511	162	28	3	21	36	62	84	83	16	7	356	.317	.365	.507	.286	78	75-2B 2 48-SS -8
2001	Oakland	AL	42	8	0	0	0	3	4	4	3	1	0	34	.190	.244	.190	.162	2	
2001	Sacramen	PCL	255	63	12	3	6	23	45	34	32	6	3	195	.247	.314	.388	.237	27	54-2B -6
2001	Colorado	NL	200	47	6	1	12	12	31	35	32	3	1	154	.235	.288	.455	.243	22	45-2B -1
2002	*Colorado*	*NL*	*479*	*158*	*27*	*4*	*21*	*43*	*73*	*88*	*74*	*12*	*4*	*325*	*.330*	*.385*	*.534*	*.275*	*64*	

As roller coasters go, this was a seven-screamer. Ortiz went from Rookie of the Year favorite to Triple-A, then to a tremendous opportunity with the Rockies. He's didn't hit that well after the deal, which shouldn't affect his standing going into 2002. He's a very valuable property and a big part of any success the Rockies are going to have. Wilton's off on both the average (it'll be lower) and the power (it'll be much higher).

Ben Petrick **C** **Bats R** **Age 25**

YEAR	TEAM	LGE	AB	H	DB	TP	HR	BB	SO	R	RBI	SB	CS	OUT	BA	OBP	SLG	EQA	EQR	DEFENSE
1999	Carolina	Sou	68	18	2	1	3	7	15	13	15	2	1	51	.265	.338	.456	.263	9	15-C -5
1999	ColSprin	PCL	273	70	12	3	14	36	53	41	45	7	4	207	.256	.347	.476	.271	40	62-C -10
1999	Colorado	NL	60	17	1	0	4	9	12	11	10	1	0	43	.283	.377	.500	.292	10	16-C -4
2000	ColSprin	PCL	241	65	16	2	7	24	39	28	33	5	2	178	.270	.336	.440	.259	30	57-C -7
2000	Colorado	NL	141	40	7	1	3	17	30	27	17	1	2	103	.284	.367	.411	.262	18	40-C -4
2001	Colorado	NL	238	52	12	2	10	29	57	37	34	3	3	189	.218	.309	.412	.239	26	66-C -8
2001	ColSprin	PCL	63	13	1	0	1	11	19	9	7	1	0	50	.206	.324	.270	.217	6	10-LF -1
2002	*Colorado*	*NL*	*364*	*106*	*20*	*4*	*14*	*52*	*84*	*63*	*59*	*6*	*4*	*262*	*.291*	*.380*	*.484*	*.260*	*45*	

It was a disappointing year for Petrick, who didn't hit, was pretty bad behind the plate, and suffered biceps tendinitis that gave the Rockies an excuse to bury him again, this after they'd finally committed to him by trading Brent Mayne. Asked to play some outfield during his rehab assignment, he did poorly, and his hitting suffered. As much grief as we've given the Rockies for their handling of him, they gave Petrick the job last year, and he didn't perform. They will try again in 2002.

Juan Pierre **CF** **Bats L** **Age 24**

YEAR	TEAM	LGE	AB	H	DB	TP	HR	BB	SO	R	RBI	SB	CS	OUT	BA	OBP	SLG	EQA	EQR	DEFENSE
1999	Ashevlle	SAL	586	140	17	3	1	27	39	56	36	30	12	458	.239	.276	.283	.198	40	139-LF -7
2000	Carolina	Sou	450	135	12	3	1	22	26	52	28	29	9	324	.300	.336	.347	.240	46	103-CF 3
2000	Colorado	NL	195	52	2	0	0	10	14	21	16	5	5	148	.267	.305	.277	.201	13	49-CF -1
2001	Colorado	NL	598	179	24	9	2	37	25	98	49	40	15	434	.299	.348	.380	.252	69	151-CF -2
2002	*Colorado*	*NL*	*598*	*202*	*23*	*8*	*3*	*45*	*31*	*94*	*54*	*41*	*15*	*411*	*.338*	*.384*	*.418*	*.250*	*64*	

Slap-and-dash hitter who can be valuable in this environment, because he puts so many balls in play. The downside is that the break-even rate for stealing is up around 80% because of the value of an out in Coors, so he's hurting the team on the bases. If Pierre can squeeze out another 30 walks without screwing himself up, he'll be a great leadoff hitter.

Rene Reyes **OF/1B** **Bats B** **Age 24**

YEAR	TEAM	LGE	AB	H	DB	TP	HR	BB	SO	R	RBI	SB	CS	OUT	BA	OBP	SLG	EQA	EQR	DEFENSE
1999	Ashevlle	SAL	159	41	5	0	2	4	23	18	12	0	0	118	.258	.278	.327	.203	11	
2001	Ashevlle	SAL	489	117	18	1	7	21	85	45	40	23	8	380	.239	.277	.323	.209	38	58-RF -6 57-1B 0
2002	*Colorado*	*NL*	*442*	*134*	*21*	*1*	*13*	*27*	*79*	*82*	*47*	*32*	*9*	*317*	*.303*	*.343*	*.443*	*.241*	*45*	

The Sally League MVP won the title by hitting a soft .322 and stealing 53 bases. It might have been more impressive if he weren't a 23-year-old in middle-A ball. Reyes came into baseball as a catcher, but he has been moved to the outfield after having his right knee reconstructed, a surgery that cost him the 2000 season. He's not a prospect and will get a rude awakening in Double-A this year.

Terry Shumpert UT Bats R Age 35

YEAR	TEAM	LGE	AB	H	DB	TP	HR	BB	SO	R	RBI	SB	CS	OUT	BA	OBP	SLG	EQA	EQR	DEFENSE	
1999	ColSprin	PCL	75	24	6	1	4	4	8	11	12	2	1	52	.320	.354	.587	.298	13		
1999	Colorado	NL	253	78	22	2	9	26	38	49	30	11	0	175	.308	.377	.518	.300	43	44-2B 5	12-OF -3
2000	Colorado	NL	258	58	11	5	8	23	37	44	33	6	4	204	.225	.301	.399	.233	27	29-LF 0	16-2B -2
2001	Colorado	NL	236	64	11	4	4	13	37	34	22	13	3	175	.271	.315	.403	.246	26	26-2B -2	19-LF 2
2002	*Colorado*	*NL*	*294*	*85*	*20*	*6*	*9*	*29*	*46*	*53*	*36*	*12*	*2*	*211*	*.289*	*.353*	*.490*	*.255*	*35*		

He's the kind of bench player the Rockies need: capable of playing both the infield and outfield, can hit a little, run a little. He's not getting back to 1999, and the Rockies can use his roster spot on players with a bit more upside who will make the minimum, so it's time to cut him loose.

Juan Uribe SS Bats R Age 22

YEAR	TEAM	LGE	AB	H	DB	TP	HR	BB	SO	R	RBI	SB	CS	OUT	BA	OBP	SLG	EQA	EQR	DEFENSE
1999	Ashevlle	SAL	430	84	21	1	5	15	84	37	28	5	4	350	.195	.227	.284	.174	22	124-SS -16
2000	Salem VA	Car	496	108	17	4	11	25	101	49	47	12	4	392	.218	.258	.335	.202	36	131-SS -14
2001	ColSprin	PCL	273	71	22	5	5	12	39	31	36	9	6	208	.260	.294	.432	.237	29	73-SS -6
2001	Colorado	NL	266	74	12	10	7	7	47	29	47	3	0	192	.278	.301	.477	.254	31	67-SS -4
2002	*Colorado*	*NL*	*515*	*157*	*33*	*10*	*18*	*33*	*95*	*77*	*69*	*12*	*3*	*361*	*.305*	*.347*	*.501*	*.253*	*58*	

Uribe accelerated the departure of Neifi Perez with a good showing during the incumbent's thumb injury in April. He is a similar player to Perez, with a lot more power, less speed, and less glove. With Uribe, Petrick, Ortiz, and Pierre, the Rockies have the inexpensive up-the-middle core of a contender. What they need is 100 more walks a year from those guys, collectively.

Larry Walker RF Bats L Age 35

YEAR	TEAM	LGE	AB	H	DB	TP	HR	BB	SO	R	RBI	SB	CS	OUT	BA	OBP	SLG	EQA	EQR	DEFENSE
1999	Colorado	NL	419	144	24	3	32	50	48	94	95	8	4	279	.344	.427	.644	.339	93	104-RF -2
2000	Colorado	NL	304	82	18	5	8	40	37	54	41	4	5	227	.270	.368	.441	.270	43	82-RF 4
2001	Colorado	NL	476	155	32	2	33	76	87	97	108	12	4	325	.326	.429	.609	.334	105	123-RF -4
2002	*Colorado*	*NL*	*441*	*153*	*31*	*4*	*25*	*74*	*73*	*103*	*89*	*15*	*5*	*293*	*.347*	*.441*	*.605*	*.311*	*79*	

Walker stayed as healthy as he's ever going to—his 142 games played were his third-highest total—and he returned to his established level of offense. He has four years to go at about $13 million per year; between natural decline and his constant physical ailments, he's going to be a problem for this team down the road. For 2002, that Wilton looks pretty accurate.

PITCHERS (ERA: 4.50, H/9: 9.0, HR/9: 1.0, BB/9: 3.0, K/9: 6.0, KW: 2.0, PERA: 4.50)

Todd Belitz Throws L Age 26

YEAR	TEAM	LGE	IP	H	ER	HR	BB	K	ERA	W	L	H/9	HR/9	BB/9	K/9	KW	PERA	STUFF
1999	Orlando	Sou	158.7	186	125	35	68	80	7.09	5	13	10.6	2.0	3.9	4.5	0.6	7.45	-12
2000	Durham	Int	45.7	39	20	1	28	37	3.94	3	2	7.7	0.2	5.5	7.3	0.7	5.07	-1
2000	Sacramen	PCL	12.0	13	9	3	5	8	6.75	0	1	9.8	2.3	3.8	6.0	0.8	4.41	-17
2001	Sacramen	PCL	52.0	54	30	8	20	34	5.19	3	3	9.3	1.4	3.5	5.9	0.9	7.65	-21
2001	ColSprin	PCL	12.7	15	9	2	4	5	6.39	0	1	10.7	1.4	2.8	3.6	0.6	12.54	-43
2001	Colorado	NL	8.7	10	6	2	3	4	6.23	0	1	10.4	2.1	3.1	4.2	0.7	6.07	-25

The forgotten man in the Encarnacion/Ortiz acquisition, Belitz is a good candidate to replace Mike Myers as the Rockies' lefty specialist. If he's successful, it would be like getting Jack Cust for nothing. Well, the Rockies got J.D. Closser, too, and the money they're not paying Myers. Hell, Belitz could have an ERA of 23.51, start a mild influenza epidemic, and make fun of John Elway's teeth, and the Cust trade would still be a good one.

Brian Bohanon Throws L Age 33

YEAR	TEAM	LGE	IP	H	ER	HR	BB	K	ERA	W	L	H/9	HR/9	BB/9	K/9	KW	PERA	STUFF
1999	Colorado	NL	206.7	220	117	25	77	108	5.10	10	13	9.6	1.1	3.4	4.7	0.7	4.88	0
2000	Colorado	NL	177.7	189	97	19	65	87	4.91	9	11	9.6	1.0	3.3	4.4	0.7	3.68	-2
2001	Colorado	NL	97.3	112	67	15	42	38	6.20	4	7	10.4	1.4	3.9	3.5	0.5	5.74	-16

Bohanon is a lousy pitcher, but he makes a decent lefty bat off the bench. His OPSs for the last four years, working backwards, are 796, 609, 518, 683. He'd be worth a roster spot because of that if he could do anything on the mound, or if rosters expand to 26. He's in camp with the Reds, hoping for a Don Gullett laying on of hands.

Shawn Chacon Throws R Age 24

YEAR	TEAM	LGE	IP	H	ER	HR	BB	K	ERA	W	L	H/9	HR/9	BB/9	K/9	KW	PERA	STUFF
1999	Salem VA	Car	72.3	74	41	6	37	39	5.10	4	4	9.2	0.7	4.6	4.9	0.5	6.86	2
2000	Carolina	Sou	171.3	170	95	18	86	115	4.99	9	10	8.9	0.9	4.5	6.0	0.7	4.65	10
2001	ColSprin	PCL	22.7	22	11	3	8	20	4.37	2	1	8.7	1.2	3.2	7.9	1.3	2.04	27
2001	Colorado	NL	153.7	154	91	20	78	108	5.33	7	10	9.0	1.2	4.6	6.3	0.7	4.23	9

Because the Rockies always believe they need pitching, they tend to rush their better prospects through Triple-A to the majors. Chacon arrived in April and was battered in his first two outings before settling in, making 13 quality starts and a handful of other near-quality ones. While he has an above-average fastball and breaking ball, he still will need a change-up and improved command to stick around. It's doubtful he'll survive 2002 in the rotation without at least one of those.

Tim Christman Throws L Age 27

YEAR	TEAM	LGE	IP	H	ER	HR	BB	K	ERA	W	L	H/9	HR/9	BB/9	K/9	KW	PERA	STUFF
1999	Salem VA	Car	48.3	44	16	0	16	31	2.98	3	2	8.2	0.0	3.0	5.8	1.0	5.12	-8
2000	Carolina	Sou	10.0	9	5	0	8	7	4.50	1	0	8.1	0.0	7.2	6.3	0.4	3.75	-20
2001	ColSprin	PCL	43.0	44	27	5	27	27	5.65	2	3	9.2	1.0	5.7	5.7	0.5	7.12	-29

Christman will be battling Belitz for a job in the back of the Rockies' bullpen. He throws harder than Belitz, which is something of a miracle given that he's undergone six surgeries, four on his arm. Regardless of who wins in March, both pitchers will spend time in the majors this year.

Aaron Cook Throws R Age 23

YEAR	TEAM	LGE	IP	H	ER	HR	BB	K	ERA	W	L	H/9	HR/9	BB/9	K/9	KW	PERA	STUFF
1999	Ashevlle	SAL	125.3	161	116	32	57	37	8.33	3	11	11.6	2.3	4.1	2.7	0.3	8.80	-23
2000	Ashevlle	SAL	138.0	157	83	23	29	61	5.41	6	9	10.2	1.5	1.9	4.0	1.1	4.10	3
2000	Salem VA	Car	44.7	51	30	9	13	22	6.04	2	3	10.3	1.8	2.6	4.4	0.8	8.87	-2
2001	Salem VA	Car	157.3	164	75	10	53	68	4.29	9	8	9.4	0.6	3.0	3.9	0.6	6.39	-1

Cook, the Rockies' second-round pick in 1997, has moved very slowly through the system. He has the best fastball in the Rockies' chain, topping out at 98 mph. His good year was helped by his development from thrower to pitcher, as he used his slider more. Cook looks good but will need to strike out more batters to become a serious prospect.

Kane Davis Throws R Age 27

YEAR	TEAM	LGE	IP	H	ER	HR	BB	K	ERA	W	L	H/9	HR/9	BB/9	K/9	KW	PERA	STUFF
1999	Altoona	Eas	95.0	104	57	8	47	33	5.40	5	6	9.9	0.8	4.5	3.1	0.4	6.52	-17
1999	Nashvill	PCL	52.0	60	35	9	18	23	6.06	2	4	10.4	1.6	3.1	4.0	0.6	7.01	-16
2000	Akron	Eas	18.7	22	14	4	6	8	6.75	1	1	10.6	1.9	2.9	3.9	0.7	4.28	-24
2000	Buffalo	Int	30.0	32	17	3	13	14	5.10	1	2	9.6	0.9	3.9	4.2	0.5	5.58	-13
2000	Clevelnd	AL	12.7	16	11	3	7	2	7.82	0	1	11.4	2.1	5.0	1.4	0.1	13.86	-57
2000	Indianap	Int	19.7	22	12	3	8	9	5.49	1	1	10.1	1.4	3.7	4.1	0.6	4.07	-14
2001	Colorado	NL	64.3	68	38	8	29	38	5.32	3	4	9.5	1.1	4.1	5.3	0.7	3.72	-12

Traded twice in eight months, Davis took Juan Acevedo's place in the Rockies' bullpen and pitched surprisingly well. He had one of the biggest platoon splits you'll see from an overhand thrower: 1067 OPS vs. left-handed batters, 618 vs. righties. It's hard to have guys like this on a team that needs its relievers to go two and three innings at a time.

Randey Dorame Throws L Age 23

YEAR	TEAM	LGE	IP	H	ER	HR	BB	K	ERA	W	L	H/9	HR/9	BB/9	K/9	KW	PERA	STUFF
1999	San Bern	Cal	151.0	152	71	16	41	95	4.23	9	8	9.1	1.0	2.4	5.7	1.2	3.34	20
2000	Vero Bch	Fla	55.7	58	29	7	15	32	4.69	3	3	9.4	1.1	2.4	5.2	1.1	2.87	13
2000	SanAnton	Tex	55.3	64	35	8	18	19	5.69	2	4	10.4	1.3	2.9	3.1	0.5	5.32	-4
2001	Carolina	Sou	28.0	32	17	5	7	11	5.46	1	2	10.3	1.6	2.3	3.5	0.8	6.93	-7
2001	Salem VA	Car	78.7	102	80	24	39	32	9.15	2	7	11.7	2.7	4.5	3.7	0.4	8.62	-28

Dorame had his first taste of failure, scuffling in Double-A before pitching a bit better on his return to A ball. It's not that big a surprise: for a command lefty who relies on location and breaking stuff, Double-A was going to be a challenge. He didn't pitch much better at Salem and was unimpressive in the Mexican winter league (27 walks, 21 strikeouts in 54 innings), so his prospect status is mostly just our wishcasting.

Scott Elarton Throws R Age 26

YEAR	TEAM	LGE	IP	H	ER	HR	BB	K	ERA	W	L	H/9	HR/9	BB/9	K/9	KW	PERA	STUFF
1999	Houston	NL	126.3	110	45	8	36	109	3.21	9	5	7.8	0.6	2.6	7.8	1.5	3.77	20
2000	Houston	NL	194.7	203	108	25	69	116	4.99	10	12	9.4	1.2	3.2	5.4	0.8	4.68	5
2001	Houston	NL	106.3	120	77	22	44	61	6.52	4	8	10.2	1.9	3.7	5.2	0.7	6.75	-8
2001	Colorado	NL	19.7	25	20	6	9	9	9.15	0	2	11.4	2.7	4.1	4.1	0.5	5.21	-21

He was worked very, very hard in the last two months of 2000, less than a year removed from surgery. He sucked volleyballs through a Crazy Straw in 2001. You decide if there's causation. What we do know is that Elarton's performance led to the disabled list in June—biceps tendinitis—and a trade to hell in July. All of his statistical trends are negative, so the best bet is to see him pitch in April before drawing a conclusion. It might be time to move him back to the bullpen for good; Elarton would be nasty for 60 appearances and 95 innings.

Horacio Estrada Throws L Age 26

YEAR	TEAM	LGE	IP	H	ER	HR	BB	K	ERA	W	L	H/9	HR/9	BB/9	K/9	KW	PERA	STUFF
1999	Louisvil	Int	131.3	138	86	22	62	90	5.89	6	9	9.5	1.5	4.2	6.2	0.7	5.57	3
2000	Indianap	Int	157.3	165	81	18	45	84	4.63	8	9	9.4	1.0	2.6	4.8	0.9	3.76	4
2000	Milwauke	NL	25.3	29	20	4	16	12	7.11	1	2	10.3	1.4	5.7	4.3	0.4	6.06	-21
2001	ColSprin	PCL	92.0	100	51	13	26	49	4.99	4	6	9.8	1.3	2.5	4.8	0.9	5.14	-4

Check back in three years. Estrada bounced through waivers twice at the end of spring training, ending up in the Rockies' chain. A sore shoulder kept him from making an impression in Denver, but he pitched fairly well for the SkySox late in the season. He's not well suited to altitude, so he'll eventually migrate elsewhere and settle into a rotation slot.

Mike Hampton Throws L Age 29

YEAR	TEAM	LGE	IP	H	ER	HR	BB	K	ERA	W	L	H/9	HR/9	BB/9	K/9	KW	PERA	STUFF
1999	Houston	NL	237.3	222	97	11	85	159	3.68	16	10	8.4	0.4	3.2	6.0	0.9	3.06	15
2000	NY Mets	NL	217.3	206	91	9	81	134	3.77	14	10	8.5	0.4	3.4	5.5	0.8	3.52	11
2001	Colorado	NL	200.0	215	115	24	76	98	5.18	9	13	9.7	1.1	3.4	4.4	0.6	4.79	-2

You can't just excuse Hampton's performance by chalking it up to altitude. He had a 5.10 ERA on the road, and his peripherals away from Colorado weren't good. Like Elarton, all his trend lines point down, although in this case no health reasons have emerged. With seven years and $105 million left on his deal, the Rockies have to be nervous: you can hear Hampton ticking.

Craig House Throws R Age 24

YEAR	TEAM	LGE	IP	H	ER	HR	BB	K	ERA	W	L	H/9	HR/9	BB/9	K/9	KW	PERA	STUFF
1999	Portland	Nwn	35.7	29	12	0	16	30	3.03	3	1	7.3	0.0	4.0	7.6	0.9	4.38	12
2000	Salem VA	Car	14.7	12	7	0	11	14	4.30	1	1	7.4	0.0	6.8	8.6	0.6	3.01	8
2000	Carolina	Sou	21.0	17	9	0	15	19	3.86	1	1	7.3	0.0	6.4	8.1	0.6	5.88	6
2000	ColSprin	PCL	8.0	7	2	0	2	6	2.25	1	0	7.9	0.0	2.3	6.8	1.5	3.59	14
2000	Colorado	NL	13.3	15	13	2	14	7	8.78	0	1	10.1	1.4	9.5	4.7	0.3	5.18	-33
2001	ColSprin	PCL	57.7	53	30	4	35	44	4.68	3	3	8.3	0.6	5.5	6.9	0.6	4.44	-2

(Craig House *continued*)

House is exactly the kind of pitcher the Rockies need to get to the big leagues. He throws in the mid-90s and strikes out a lot of guys, minimizing balls in play. His motion is still unusual, although he's tamed it some. He might have been rushed in 2000, so the fact that he didn't pitch in Denver in 2001 isn't a negative. He'll get there this spring and be as good as you can expect a Rockies' reliever to be.

Jason Jennings **Throws R** **Age 23**

YEAR	TEAM	LGE	IP	H	ER	HR	BB	K	ERA	W	L	H/9	HR/9	BB/9	K/9	KW	PERA	STUFF
1999	Ashevlle	SAL	59.0	60	26	6	11	35	3.97	4	3	9.2	0.9	1.7	5.3	1.6	5.01	14
2000	Salem VA	Car	148.7	153	72	13	46	78	4.36	9	8	9.3	0.8	2.8	4.7	0.8	5.07	8
2000	Carolina	Sou	35.0	39	23	7	11	22	5.91	1	3	10.0	1.8	2.8	5.7	1.0	5.89	10
2001	Carolina	Sou	25.0	24	11	2	9	15	3.96	2	1	8.6	0.7	3.2	5.4	0.8	4.11	12
2001	ColSprin	PCL	135.3	134	62	9	46	78	4.12	8	7	8.9	0.6	3.1	5.2	0.8	4.95	12
2001	Colorado	NL	38.7	38	18	2	17	21	4.19	2	2	8.8	0.5	4.0	4.9	0.6	3.77	7

The Rockies 1999 #1 pick out of Baylor reached the big leagues before he forgot how to hit, batting .267/.313/.533 in his brief stint. As we've said many times, pitchers who can hit really help when a team has to carry 12 arms. Jennings's numbers above are skewed a bit: he made just two of his seven starts at Coors, getting hammered both times. He's big, he throws hard, he gets ground balls, and he's that rarest of things: a Rockies pitcher worth getting a little bit excited about.

Jose Jimenez **Throws R** **Age 28**

YEAR	TEAM	LGE	IP	H	ER	HR	BB	K	ERA	W	L	H/9	HR/9	BB/9	K/9	KW	PERA	STUFF
1999	Memphis	PCL	28.3	28	11	0	11	12	3.49	2	1	8.9	0.0	3.5	3.8	0.5	3.63	0
1999	St Louis	NL	168.0	168	81	15	59	102	4.34	10	9	9.0	0.8	3.2	5.5	0.9	5.73	4
2000	Colorado	NL	70.0	68	29	3	23	39	3.73	5	3	8.7	0.4	3.0	5.0	0.8	2.47	-4
2001	Colorado	NL	53.0	54	26	5	20	30	4.42	3	3	9.2	0.8	3.4	5.1	0.8	3.46	-9

A one-inning closer is a luxury that the Rockies can't afford. Putting Jimenez, an ex-starter who would be a reasonable candidate to throw 90–100 innings in relief, in that role is a waste of resources. Shoulder problems limited him to 18 innings after the All-Star break; when he's healthy, he gets a ton of ground-ball outs. Look for him to bounce back in 2002.

Josh Kalinowski **Throws L** **Age 25**

YEAR	TEAM	LGE	IP	H	ER	HR	BB	K	ERA	W	L	H/9	HR/9	BB/9	K/9	KW	PERA	STUFF
1999	Salem VA	Car	157.0	148	73	6	81	99	4.18	9	8	8.5	0.3	4.6	5.7	0.6	3.38	11
2000	Carolina	Sou	28.3	26	11	0	13	17	3.49	2	1	8.3	0.0	4.1	5.4	0.7	10.03	-2
2001	Carolina	Sou	135.0	156	109	26	80	65	7.27	4	11	10.4	1.7	5.3	4.3	0.4	7.13	-24

Kalinowski's first year after elbow surgery was a mixed bag, as he missed time with minor injuries, dealt with reduced velocity, and didn't get positive results. The good news is that his best pitch, a nasty deuce, survived the surgery. He's no longer a top prospect, just a guy with one plus pitch who will show up in middle relief by the end of the year.

Ryan Kibler **Throws R** **Age 21**

YEAR	TEAM	LGE	IP	H	ER	HR	BB	K	ERA	W	L	H/9	HR/9	BB/9	K/9	KW	PERA	STUFF
2000	Ashevlle	SAL	158.3	180	111	21	86	57	6.31	6	12	10.2	1.2	4.9	3.2	0.3	7.48	-8
2001	Ashevlle	SAL	59.0	62	39	6	38	30	5.95	3	4	9.5	0.9	5.8	4.6	0.4	4.91	1
2001	Salem VA	Car	72.0	69	26	0	21	35	3.25	5	3	8.6	0.0	2.6	4.4	0.8	3.27	15
2001	Carolina	Sou	45.3	42	18	0	21	26	3.57	3	2	8.3	0.0	4.2	5.2	0.6	4.13	17

That "click" you heard was Ryan Kibler becoming a good pitcher. A second-round pick in 1999, he became more aggressive early in the season, throwing more strikes, and carrying that approach through three levels. Command of the strike zone isn't just for hitters; pitchers who can get ahead in the count garner all kinds of benefits beyond an improved strikeout-to-walk ratio. Kibler's at least a year away, and some time lost to injury is probably inevitable.

Dan Miceli — Throws R — Age 31

YEAR	TEAM	LGE	IP	H	ER	HR	BB	K	ERA	W	L	H/9	HR/9	BB/9	K/9	KW	PERA	STUFF
1999	San Dieg	NL	70.0	67	35	7	30	53	4.50	4	4	8.6	0.9	3.9	6.8	0.9	5.04	-2
2000	Florida	NL	49.3	46	20	4	15	36	3.65	3	2	8.4	0.7	2.7	6.6	1.2	4.03	2
2001	Florida	NL	25.7	24	14	4	10	25	4.91	1	2	8.4	1.4	3.5	8.8	1.3	7.95	2
2001	Colorado	NL	19.3	18	8	2	4	14	3.72	1	1	8.4	0.9	1.9	6.5	1.8	2.70	4

One of the season's more bizarre story lines was Miceli's rant against John Boles, in which he claimed the Marlins' manager couldn't garner respect because he hadn't played in the major leagues. The evidence that managers don't need MLB experience to succeed is overwhelming, so Miceli looked pretty silly. The fallout wasn't as amusing: Boles was fired, Miceli was exiled to Colorado, and both teams fell apart. Miceli is a free agent as we go to press; he can help a team, but so can a lot of guys who come without his baggage.

Mike Myers — Throws L — Age 33

YEAR	TEAM	LGE	IP	H	ER	HR	BB	K	ERA	W	L	H/9	HR/9	BB/9	K/9	KW	PERA	STUFF
1999	Milwauke	NL	43.0	44	22	6	11	32	4.60	2	3	9.2	1.3	2.3	6.7	1.5	4.76	-1
2000	Colorado	NL	42.0	36	17	2	20	36	3.64	3	2	7.7	0.4	4.3	7.7	0.9	1.43	8
2001	Colorado	NL	37.7	34	17	2	21	29	4.06	2	2	8.1	0.5	5.0	6.9	0.7	3.00	-1

He's good at what he does, with a ridiculous sidearm motion that makes him very hard on left-handed batters. That doesn't make him worth Jack Cust and J.D. Closser, which is what the Diamondbacks traded to get him. Joe Garagiola Jr. has done a good job in picking free agents, but he's dealt Cust, Closser, Tony Batista, Brad Penny, and Vlad Nunez for three short relievers. That's a brutal record. Given what we know about the two players, that Ray Lankford hit a home run off of Myers is one of last year's more random occurrences.

Denny Neagle — Throws L — Age 33

YEAR	TEAM	LGE	IP	H	ER	HR	BB	K	ERA	W	L	H/9	HR/9	BB/9	K/9	KW	PERA	STUFF
1999	Cincnnti	NL	106.0	116	69	21	33	68	5.86	4	8	9.8	1.8	2.8	5.8	1.0	3.86	3
2000	Cincnnti	NL	117.7	118	60	13	41	78	4.59	6	7	9.0	1.0	3.1	6.0	1.0	3.26	10
2000	NY Yanks	AL	93.3	99	51	14	25	57	4.92	5	5	9.5	1.3	2.4	5.5	1.1	5.15	4
2001	Colorado	NL	169.7	173	89	22	54	112	4.72	9	10	9.2	1.2	2.9	5.9	1.0	4.42	8

Like Hampton, Neagle didn't pitch particularly well on the road (5.11 ERA), so you can't blame his season on the Coors Effect. He did, as expected, give up a ton of home runs at home: 15 in 79 innings. When you account for everything, though, his performance is right in line with previous seasons. Expecting four more years of the same is folly.

Jay Powell — Throws R — Age 30

YEAR	TEAM	LGE	IP	H	ER	HR	BB	K	ERA	W	L	H/9	HR/9	BB/9	K/9	KW	PERA	STUFF
1999	Houston	NL	81.0	69	30	3	33	69	3.33	6	3	7.7	0.3	3.7	7.7	1.0	4.31	8
2000	Houston	NL	28.0	28	14	1	16	14	4.50	2	1	9.0	0.3	5.1	4.5	0.4	5.14	-18
2001	Houston	NL	36.3	36	19	3	17	23	4.71	2	2	8.9	0.7	4.2	5.7	0.7	4.17	-9
2001	Colorado	NL	35.7	37	18	4	11	21	4.54	2	2	9.3	1.0	2.8	5.3	1.0	3.28	-7

Frying pan to fire: Powell, just getting his stuff back after missing most of 2000 with a rotator-cuff tear, was dealt from Houston to Colorado in June. He actually pitched better after the deal and emerged as the Rockies' closer in August. Having conquered the two best hitting environments in baseball, Powell moved to what may be the third-best, The Ballpark in Arlington, signing a three-year deal to help set up Jeff Zimmerman. He's the best alternate closer candidate, rotoheads.

Justin Speier — Throws R — Age 28

YEAR	TEAM	LGE	IP	H	ER	HR	BB	K	ERA	W	L	H/9	HR/9	BB/9	K/9	KW	PERA	STUFF
1999	Richmond	Int	45.0	45	26	5	24	28	5.20	2	3	9.0	1.0	4.8	5.6	0.6	6.31	-22
1999	Atlanta	NL	27.7	32	22	7	11	20	7.16	1	2	10.4	2.3	3.6	6.5	0.9	5.22	-13
2000	Clevelnd	AL	68.3	60	29	8	23	68	3.82	5	3	7.9	1.1	3.0	9.0	1.5	2.87	16
2001	Clevelnd	AL	21.3	23	15	5	8	14	6.33	1	1	9.7	2.1	3.4	5.9	0.9	6.24	-14
2001	ColSprin	PCL	12.3	10	5	0	9	10	3.65	1	0	7.3	0.0	6.6	7.3	0.6	1.49	-5
2001	Colorado	NL	52.0	51	23	6	11	38	3.98	3	3	8.8	1.0	1.9	6.6	1.7	3.02	5

(Justin Speier *continued*)
Speier, along with Kane Davis, Jay Powell, and Dan Miceli, was acquired during the season as Dan O'Dowd rebuilt his bullpen. All four pitched well for the Rockies, who let the more expensive of the four leave over the winter and kept Speier and Davis, who should again provide 120–130 useful innings. Relievers are fungible, and given what altitude does to pitchers, the Rockies need to invest as little in them as possible.

John Thomson Throws R Age 28

YEAR	TEAM	LGE	IP	H	ER	HR	BB	K	ERA	W	L	H/9	HR/9	BB/9	K/9	KW	PERA	STUFF
1999	ColSprin	PCL	24.0	26	15	3	9	13	5.63	1	2	9.8	1.1	3.4	4.9	0.7	10.52	-20
1999	Colorado	NL	67.7	75	43	9	30	31	5.72	3	5	10.0	1.2	4.0	4.1	0.5	6.52	-14
2001	ColSprin	PCL	68.3	73	34	7	17	33	4.48	4	4	9.6	0.9	2.2	4.3	1.0	3.92	-1
2001	Colorado	NL	87.0	90	44	11	22	55	4.55	5	5	9.3	1.1	2.3	5.7	1.3	3.46	10

The best pitcher the Rockies have ever developed made it back to the rotation last year, following a year lost to surgery on a torn labrum. Three starts in May proved only that he wasn't ready yet. Coming back in August, he had a 3.62 ERA in 11 starts down the stretch, with a three-to-one strikeout-to-walk ratio. They'll have to monitor him, and they should be prepared to accept 150 good innings rather than risk further injury. Handled gently, he'll be a real asset.

Chin-Hui Tsao Throws R Age 21

YEAR	TEAM	LGE	IP	H	ER	HR	BB	K	ERA	W	L	H/9	HR/9	BB/9	K/9	KW	PERA	STUFF
2000	Ashevlle	SAL	142.0	144	76	18	51	97	4.82	7	9	9.1	1.1	3.2	6.1	1.0	4.03	21
2001	Salem VA	Car	19.0	20	10	2	7	10	4.74	1	1	9.5	0.9	3.3	4.7	0.7	8.28	0

Ouchie. Tsao missed almost all of 2001 after blowing out his elbow and undergoing Tommy John surgery. He threw in the mid-90s with a great slider before the surgery, and while he's young enough to make a full return, it will be 2003 before we have an idea of his chances. The Rockies aren't done in Taiwan: they've signed 16-year-old Ching-Ling Lo for $1.4 million over the winter.

Gabe White Throws L Age 30

YEAR	TEAM	LGE	IP	H	ER	HR	BB	K	ERA	W	L	H/9	HR/9	BB/9	K/9	KW	PERA	STUFF
1999	Cincnnti	NL	63.7	64	33	12	12	55	4.66	3	4	9.0	1.7	1.7	7.8	2.3	4.06	6
2000	Colorado	NL	81.7	70	23	4	12	73	2.53	7	2	7.7	0.4	1.3	8.0	3.0	1.63	22
2001	Colorado	NL	63.7	72	46	14	23	38	6.50	2	5	10.2	2.0	3.3	5.4	0.8	4.90	-17

That's more like it. When White, one of the more extreme fly-ball pitchers in baseball, was dealt to the Rockies in April 2000, we expected truly taterrific results. Instead, he was the best reliever in the league. Last year, he, uh, wasn't, allowing 18 long balls in 67 2/3 innings. He's been traded back to the Reds; if Danny Graves is dumped for salary reasons, White will be a good bet to back into 15 saves.

Colin Young Throws L Age 24

YEAR	TEAM	LGE	IP	H	ER	HR	BB	K	ERA	W	L	H/9	HR/9	BB/9	K/9	KW	PERA	STUFF
1999	Portland	Nwn	58.0	68	54	17	32	39	8.38	1	5	10.6	2.6	5.0	6.1	0.6	7.18	-9
2000	Ashevlle	SAL	59.7	56	29	5	29	45	4.37	4	3	8.4	0.8	4.4	6.8	0.8	1.76	3
2001	Salem VA	Car	51.0	57	38	13	18	37	6.71	2	4	10.1	2.3	3.2	6.5	1.0	2.84	-14

The Rockies added Colin Young to their 40-man roster over the winter, after he spent the year closing for Salem. He's been beating up on younger hitters for a couple of seasons, despite not having an impressive repertoire. Pitchers who get by in A ball on guile and an unusual delivery don't generally have long shelf lives.

Jason Young Throws R Age 22

YEAR	TEAM	LGE	IP	H	ER	HR	BB	K	ERA	W	L	H/9	HR/9	BB/9	K/9	KW	PERA	STUFF
2001	Salem VA	Car	103.3	116	69	18	38	53	6.01	4	7	10.1	1.6	3.3	4.6	0.7	5.85	1

Jason Young is a hard thrower drafted out of Stanford in 2000. He impresses scouts with a mid-90s fastball, a good curve, and above-average control. His strikeout rate, for a college pitcher with his stuff, was low, which is the primary concern. Young is behind Kibler and Cook, but a decent prospect in his own right.

Florida Marlins

The primary concern of baseball team owners has shifted dramatically in the past 15 to 20 years. There was a time, believe it or not, when the men who owned baseball teams spent their time trying to get those teams to win games, in order to bring fans to the park and make money. For much of baseball history, owners did so under rules that heavily favored them, but the dawning of free agency showed just how much these men wanted to win, and how much they would be willing to invest in their product to do so.

Now, many owners care only about one thing: getting governments to build publicly financed stadiums and turn the stadiums over to the owners, so they can make lots and lots of money. And in the pursuit of that unholy grail, owners of baseball teams across the country have done the exact opposite of what their predecessors did: they've stopped trying to win, stopped investing in their product, and done everything to discourage fan interest but post armed guards outside of Gate C.

The Marlins stand as the shining example of this phenomenon. Not even ten years old, they've been built, risen to the top of the game, been torn apart, and built up again. And for almost the entirety of the team's existence, Marlins ownership has complained about how awful their situation is, and how they must have taxpayer money for the construction of a baseball-only playground. The argument is that they need a new stadium to "compete"; the reality is something more like, "but everybody ELSE is getting one." (For full effect, tell your seven-year old he can't have a Playstation, and listen to the response.)

It's downright pathetic the way the Marlins have been run since the end of 1997. You remember 1997, right? The season that ended with Edgar Renteria as a World Series hero, as the Marlins became the greatest expansion success story since Wal-Mart? The hangovers from the postgame celebration weren't yet cured when Marlins' owner Wayne Huizenga began to tear the team apart, frustrated that his demands for a ballpark had been once again denied. He proceeded to gut the Marlins in a tantrum the likes of which we hadn't seen in sports since John McEnroe retired.

Now, understand that the economic benefit of winning a World Series turns up in two places: in postseason revenue, with 8–10 sold-out home games bringing in $10–$20 million, and in the next season. After a championship, ticket sales increase, and the anticipation of heightened demand causes ticket prices to be raised. The team is in better position to negotiate media rights, or if the team and its broadcast outlets are owned by the same entity, ad rates can be increased to reflect the team's increased popularity. Winning the World Series is worth anywhere from $25–$50 million over two years, and if that money is put back into the team, it can perpetuate the success, increasing revenues for the better part of a decade.

> ### Marlins Prospectus
>
> **2001 record:** 76–86; Fourth place, NL East
> **Pythagenport W/L:** 81–81
> **Runs scored:** 742 (tenth in NL)
> **Runs allowed:** 744 (tied for seventh in NL)
> **Team EqA:** .262 (ninth in NL)
> **2001 batters age:** 27.3 (second-youngest in NL)
> **2001 pitchers age:** 26 (youngest in NL)
> **Ballpark:** Pro Player Stadium; moderate pitchers' park; Park Factor of .954
> **2001:** Despite management's insistence that no one should watch, an interesting baseball team came together.
> **2002:** On talent, a budding dynasty. On Selig's PDA, a problem to be eliminated.

Huizenga forfeited much of that benefit. By not even pretending to bring back a contending team, and by loudly announcing he was doing so, in essence, to spite the people of South Florida, he cost the Marlins tens of millions of dollars in 1998. A team that had drawn 2.36 million people in winning the World Series in 1997 drew just 1.75 million to the park the next year.

At the time, Huizenga claimed to have lost nearly $30 million on building that championship team. It only came to light later, but the Marlins were quite profitable in 1997. That profitability was hidden in related-party transactions: Huizenga owned both the Marlins and their park, Pro Player Stadium, and he allowed the ballpark to be credited with almost all baseball-related revenue. It was all his money, and it was all baseball money, but the lines were drawn to make the team look like it was hemorrhaging cash. In reality, the team made about a $14-million profit in 1997.

Huizenga would eventually sell the Marlins to John Henry, who took up the task of getting South Florida to build him a stadium. Henry was left in an impossible situation; his team was a couple of years from being competitive, and his fan base had been chased away by the purge and by marketing that all but told people to stay away. Henry's chances of getting a stadium were no better, and probably worse, than Huizenga's had been, because of resentment over the purge.

Finally, Henry had inherited the Marlins' lease agreements, which still funneled money the team was generating to the Huizenga-owned ballpark. So now the team really wasn't going to be profitable, as the money it made essentially went into someone else's pockets. He was also stuck with a sweetheart broadcast deal with a Huizenga-owned cable network as part of the sale agreement.

(Aside: The Twins have a similar situation in Minnesota, where their lease agreement looks like something drawn up between Billy Beane and Allard Baird. The Twins are essentially tenants of the Vikings, and as such get a shamefully low percentage of the revenue generated during baseball games.

(In both Florida and Minnesota, the problem is not that the park or the market is not viable; the problem is horrific leases that screw the baseball team. Renegotiating the agreements in each case would be a much less expensive solution than building a new ballpark with taxpayer funds.)

The Marlins are not John Henry's problem anymore, as he's left the team behind to be part of the new Red Sox ownership group. That he was allowed to bid on one team while owning another is a sign of just how far out of control the owners' side of the baseball business, led by Bud Selig, has gotten. Rules in place for the better part of a century that prevented the ownership of multiple teams were violated as Selig tossed decorum, decency, and honesty out the window, desperately courting ownership support for his revenue-sharing plan. Selig's endorsement of these shenanigans left the Marlins twisting in the wind all winter, a potential contraction candidate with no real owner, virtually no front office, and no ability to make itself better.

Even with all that, Henry may regret leaving, because the Marlins have a team that might be better than the Red Sox right now, and is certain to be better than them in the future. Last year, we discussed the Marlins' young lineup and its chances of developing into a championship-caliber offense. The Fish got a mixed bag last season, posting a .262 Equivalent Average that left them ninth in the National League. They can do better, and will be helped by returns to form by Charles Johnson and Luis Castillo, and continued improvement from Preston Wilson and Derrek Lee. They can win with the lineup they already have in place.

You can be that confident because the Marlins have an amazing collection of young pitching on hand. Two years ago, Ryan Dempster had a breakthrough season. Last year, it was Brad Penny who established himself as a front-of-the-rotation starter. This year, all eyes are on Josh Beckett, who had a year for the ages in charging from the Florida State League to Pro Player Stadium in five months. Along with Matt Clement and A.J. Burnett, the Marlins could feature an Opening Day rotation that includes five pitchers under the age of 28, all the caliber of a #3 starter or better. There's a "Braves, circa 1990" feel to this pitching staff, and with the competition in the NL East growing older by the day, it doesn't take much wishcasting to see an extended run of success, fueled by a strong young rotation.

Young pitchers carry risk, so it's entirely possible—probable, in the case of Dempster—that 2002 is not going to be a banner year for these guys. At least one will get hurt, and there's always the risk that none of the healthy pitchers will take the step forward that Penny did in 2001. Even so, the Marlins have depth behind the five aces. Kevin Olsen is a control freak who pitched well in a late-season cameo. Hansel Izquierdo—a refugee from Cuba and, even worse, the Western League—could steal a rotation spot with a big spring training. Chuck Smith and Jason Grilli, each expected to help last year, are working their way back from injuries. The Fish also have developed a tremendous bullpen, filled with live arms such as Vlad Nunez, Blaine Neal, and Armando Almanza.

With most franchises, we worry about the front office putting a good team on the field. The Marlins have a good team on the field in search of a front office that will not screw it up, one that will get the word out to South Florida. While the rumored sale of the franchise to Expos' owner Jeffrey Loria is another black mark in a winter of black marks, getting any ownership group in place and hiring management and marketing teams has to be better than the limbo the franchise occupied all winter.

Once the Marlins have an owner, they can begin making Miami work again as a baseball market. That's going to involve actually trying to win. It's going to involve rebuilding the fan base with a positive message that gets people excited again, and not conditioning everything on extorting hundreds of millions of dollars from the taxpayers of Florida.

Equally important, marketing the Marlins is also going to involve coming clean about the real reasons that the team has financial difficulties, which have more to do with Wayne Huizenga's shenanigans than with any inherent market or stadium problems. Perhaps nothing can be done about the Marlins' lease with Pro Player Stadium, but it can't hurt to shine a bright light on the rat in the corner, and to explain to the team's fans that the man who screwed them four years ago has never really stopped doing so.

HITTERS (BA: .270, OBP: .340, SLG: .440, EqA: .260)

Jeff Abbott OF Bats R Age 29

YEAR	TEAM	LGE	AB	H	DB	TP	HR	BB	SO	R	RBI	SB	CS	OUT	BA	OBP	SLG	EQA	EQR	DEFENSE	
1999	Charlott	Int	274	79	18	1	8	12	25	34	30	1	3	198	.288	.318	.449	.249	31	65-CF	-4
1999	ChiSox	AL	57	10	0	0	2	4	11	5	6	1	1	48	.175	.230	.281	.175	3	12-LF	-1
2000	ChiSox	AL	213	60	16	1	3	18	33	30	28	2	1	154	.282	.343	.408	.254	25	51-OF	-4
2001	Calgary	PCL	160	45	6	0	7	6	30	19	10	1	1	125	.200	.291	.420	.294	17	30-CF	-4
2001	Florida	NL	42	12	3	0	0	3	6	5	5	0	0	30	.286	.344	.357	.241	4	11-OF	0
2002	*Florida*	*NL*	*277*	*77*	*14*	*1*	*9*	*23*	*43*	*36*	*34*	*1*	*1*	*201*	*.278*	*.333*	*.433*	*.261*	*35*		

What looked like a good trade for both teams turned into an irrelevancy the size of "Larouche for President." Abbott spent most of the year fighting patellar tendinitis and watching Kevin Millar take the right-field at-bats that might have been his. Julio Ramirez, sent to Chicago for Abbott, lasted less than a month in Chicago. Abbott can help a team with a lefty-heavy outfield.

Chip Ambres CF Bats R Age 22

YEAR	TEAM	LGE	AB	H	DB	TP	HR	BB	SO	R	RBI	SB	CS	OUT	BA	OBP	SLG	EQA	EQR	DEFENSE	
1999	Utica	NYP	111	22	2	1	4	13	28	13	8	4	3	92	.198	.284	.342	.213	10	25-CF	-3
2000	KaneCnty	Mid	334	64	13	2	5	34	80	31	19	13	6	276	.192	.269	.287	.197	24	81-CF	1
2001	KaneCnty	Mid	389	80	20	4	4	39	89	53	27	8	9	318	.206	.286	.308	.204	30	91-CF	-1
2002	*Florida*	*NL*	*376*	*84*	*19*	*3*	*7*	*42*	*95*	*45*	*26*	*13*	*9*	*301*	*.223*	*.301*	*.346*	*.225*	*36*		

Ambres has developed rather strangely for a tools prospect. His walk rates have become pretty respectable, but he hasn't been able to generate the power projected for him. He broke his leg late in the year, an injury that could spell the end of his days as a prospect if it means he can no longer cover center field.

Rich Becker OF Bats L Age 30

YEAR	TEAM	LGE	AB	H	DB	TP	HR	BB	SO	R	RBI	SB	CS	OUT	BA	OBP	SLG	EQA	EQR	DEFENSE	
1999	Milwauke	NL	139	35	5	2	5	31	35	14	15	4	0	104	.252	.388	.424	.283	22	33-OF	-4
1999	Oakland	AL	124	35	0	0	2	24	38	20	11	3	2	91	.282	.406	.331	.264	16	33-CF	-1
2000	Oakland	AL	47	12	2	0	1	10	15	11	5	1	0	35	.255	.397	.362	.273	7	15-CF	0
2000	Detroit	AL	235	60	8	0	9	53	62	46	35	1	2	177	.255	.392	.404	.274	35	60-RF	-6
2001	Calgary	PCL	160	35	7	0	6	24	36	27	21	2	1	126	.219	.321	.375	.237	17	41-LF	-6
2001	Toledo	Int	240	57	8	2	5	45	58	36	16	6	3	186	.237	.361	.350	.250	29	42-LF	-3
2002	*Detroit*	*AL*	*340*	*82*	*11*	*0*	*11*	*69*	*89*	*52*	*36*	*8*	*3*	*261*	*.241*	*.369*	*.371*	*.266*	*47*		

We're cheating here: Becker finished the year in the Tigers' system, having been released by the Fish during the season. Whatever his limitations—he can't hit lefties, he can't carry center field, he's not a good end-of-inning pinch hitter—he will give a team a .360 OBP off the bench and can pinch-run. The right manager can make Becker an important contributor to a good team.

Dave Berg IF Bats R Age 31

YEAR	TEAM	LGE	AB	H	DB	TP	HR	BB	SO	R	RBI	SB	CS	OUT	BA	OBP	SLG	EQA	EQR	DEFENSE			
1999	Florida	NL	306	88	19	1	3	24	55	42	24	2	2	220	.288	.343	.386	.246	33	28-SS	2	25-2B	3
2000	Florida	NL	212	55	14	1	1	23	42	23	21	3	0	157	.259	.344	.349	.243	23	37-SS	-2		
2001	Florida	NL	217	56	14	1	4	13	33	28	17	0	1	162	.258	.305	.387	.230	20	28-2B	0	11-SS	-1
2002	*Toronto*	*AL*	*267*	*70*	*15*	*1*	*4*	*27*	*48*	*34*	*23*	*2*	*1*	*198*	*.262*	*.330*	*.371*	*.239*	*28*				

The Marlins seem to print utility players. Berg has been around for a while. Chris Clapinski has never gotten a clean shot because of Berg. Craig Counsell spent some time here, although he wasn't developed in this system. Amaury Garcia and Cesar Crespo were dealt away because there was no place for them to play. Matt Erickson and Pablo Ozuna are now on that track. Weird . . . anyway, Berg is gone, non-tendered by the Fish and trying to latch on with the Blue Jays.

Miguel Cabrera SS Bats R Age 19

YEAR	TEAM	LGE	AB	H	DB	TP	HR	BB	SO	R	RBI	SB	CS	OUT	BA	OBP	SLG	EQA	EQR	DEFENSE
2000	Utica	NYP	33	6	2	0	0	1	7	2	4	0	0	27	.182	.206	.242	.153	1	
2001	KaneCnty	Mid	430	90	14	2	5	27	83	44	44	1	0	340	.209	.257	.286	.187	26	87-SS -8
2002	*Florida*	*NL*	*387*	*91*	*16*	*2*	*7*	*30*	*81*	*41*	*44*	*3*	*0*	*296*	*.235*	*.290*	*.341*	*.218*	*33*	

The youngest player in last year's Futures Game, Cabrera started the year booting just about everything at shortstop. He settled down as the season went on and improved at the plate as well, so take his overall line above with a grain of salt. The consensus is that Cabrera will eventually move to third base, an opinion based partially on his physique—he's not a small man—and partially on the power he's projected to have. He's a good prospect at either position.

Luis Castillo 2B Bats B Age 26

YEAR	TEAM	LGE	AB	H	DB	TP	HR	BB	SO	R	RBI	SB	CS	OUT	BA	OBP	SLG	EQA	EQR	DEFENSE
1999	Florida	NL	491	148	21	4	1	61	79	72	27	43	17	360	.301	.379	.367	.263	64	121-2B -8
2000	Florida	NL	545	181	16	3	2	71	79	97	27	59	23	387	.332	.409	.383	.280	81	134-2B -12
2001	Florida	NL	539	150	18	10	2	63	76	80	48	33	16	405	.278	.355	.360	.248	62	133-2B -1
2002	*Florida*	*NL*	*499*	*138*	*16*	*7*	*4*	*68*	*78*	*81*	*29*	*51*	*19*	*380*	*.277*	*.363*	*.361*	*.264*	*68*	

Here's the problem with Luis Castillo: so much of his value is tied up in his OBP that if he doesn't reach base at a .370 clip or so, he's not an asset. He didn't last year, scuffling at the plate while battling an assortment of nagging injuries. Castillo's career will parallel Quilvio Veras's from here: some very good years interspersed with injury-riddled ones, and an early decline.

Ramon Castro C Bats R Age 26

YEAR	TEAM	LGE	AB	H	DB	TP	HR	BB	SO	R	RBI	SB	CS	OUT	BA	OBP	SLG	EQA	EQR	DEFENSE
1999	Calgary	PCL	340	73	13	0	12	20	59	31	44	0	0	267	.215	.261	.359	.207	26	86-C 0
1999	Florida	NL	68	13	1	0	3	9	13	4	4	0	0	55	.191	.286	.338	.213	6	19-C 2
2000	Calgary	PCL	211	60	13	0	12	11	37	32	32	0	0	151	.284	.320	.517	.270	28	55-C -1
2000	Florida	NL	140	34	2	0	3	14	33	10	15	0	0	106	.243	.316	.321	.220	12	42-C 1
2001	Calgary	PCL	378	107	20	0	21	33	67	61	67	1	1	272	.283	.342	.503	.275	54	85-C 0
2002	*Florida*	*NL*	*351*	*91*	*13*	*0*	*19*	*40*	*69*	*43*	*54*	*0*	*0*	*260*	*.259*	*.335*	*.459*	*.269*	*49*	

The Fish were able to sneak Castro through waivers in April, raising questions as to whether anybody in MLB actually watches the waiver wire. Whatever chance Castro had at a career with the Marlins died when Charles Johnson passed on exercising his out clause. Hopefully, Castro will be traded this spring and allowed to win the starting job for which he's been qualified for two years. He'd be worth two or three wins to a team like the Cardinals.

Cliff Floyd LF Bats L Age 29

YEAR	TEAM	LGE	AB	H	DB	TP	HR	BB	SO	R	RBI	SB	CS	OUT	BA	OBP	SLG	EQA	EQR	DEFENSE
1999	Florida	NL	253	76	16	1	12	27	43	36	47	4	6	183	.300	.372	.514	.285	40	57-LF -3
2000	Florida	NL	425	129	24	1	24	44	75	74	91	23	3	299	.304	.378	.534	.303	75	92-LF -5
2001	Florida	NL	560	186	47	4	32	57	86	130	108	18	3	377	.332	.401	.602	.324	112	142-LF 1
2002	*Florida*	*NL*	*482*	*150*	*33*	*2*	*26*	*55*	*84*	*86*	*97*	*21*	*4*	*336*	*.311*	*.382*	*.550*	*.313*	*92*	

He can hit a little. Like a lot of National Leaguers, Floyd had a season that could have won the MVP Award in some years. As it was, he was the third-best left fielder in the league. Any chance the Marlins have to be interesting in 2002 requires that they retain Floyd. Oddity: over the past five seasons, Floyd is actually a slightly reverse-platoon hitter.

Andy Fox UT Bats L Age 31

YEAR	TEAM	LGE	AB	H	DB	TP	HR	BB	SO	R	RBI	SB	CS	OUT	BA	OBP	SLG	EQA	EQR	DEFENSE
1999	Arizona	NL	274	69	11	2	6	30	56	32	31	3	1	206	.252	.345	.372	.247	31	68-SS -6
2000	Arizona	NL	87	18	1	0	2	3	15	9	11	2	1	70	.207	.233	.287	.178	5	16-3B 0
2000	Florida	NL	166	41	4	2	3	16	34	19	10	8	3	128	.247	.323	.349	.234	17	27-SS -2
2001	Calgary	PCL	40	14	1	2	1	3	2	8	6	1	1	27	.350	.404	.550	.306	7	
2001	Florida	NL	82	17	1	1	3	14	14	9	8	1	0	65	.207	.334	.354	.241	9	11-SS -1
2002	*Florida*	*NL*	*238*	*59*	*8*	*2*	*7*	*29*	*44*	*30*	*26*	*4*	*2*	*181*	*.248*	*.330*	*.387*	*.250*	*28*	

Fox, one of the game's better bench players, broke his right pinky in April and missed most of the season. Dave Berg is gone, so Fox will take over as the primary utility man. While he hasn't played well since 1999, his skills all seem to be intact, so you can expect him to contribute in a variety of ways this year.

Adrian Gonzalez 1B Bats L Age 20

YEAR	TEAM	LGE	AB	H	DB	TP	HR	BB	SO	R	RBI	SB	CS	OUT	BA	OBP	SLG	EQA	EQR	DEFENSE
2000	Utica	NYP	31	7	2	0	0	4	7	5	2	0	0	24	.226	.314	.290	.213	3	
2001	KaneCnty	Mid	528	127	20	1	13	42	91	60	68	2	3	404	.241	.299	.356	.221	46	116 1B 11
2002	*Florida*	*NL*	*463*	*121*	*20*	*1*	*14*	*45*	*87*	*60*	*52*	*3*	*3*	*345*	*.261*	*.327*	*.400*	*.250*	*54*	

He's the best first-base prospect in the game, with developing power and a glove that is already major-league ready. Comparisons have thus far centered on doubles hitters like Keith Hernandez and Mark Grace. Just 20, his power could develop better than that, making him another Todd Helton. He'll start the 2002 season in Double-A and should force Derrek Lee to another team over next winter.

Alex Gonzalez SS Bats R Age 25

YEAR	TEAM	LGE	AB	H	DB	TP	HR	BB	SO	R	RBI	SB	CS	OUT	BA	OBP	SLG	EQA	EQR	DEFENSE
1999	Florida	NL	565	158	27	8	15	8	105	80	58	2	5	412	.280	.304	.435	.240	58	132-SS -15
2000	Florida	NL	390	81	19	4	7	8	71	36	42	7	1	310	.208	.227	.331	.189	24	97-SS -6
2001	Florida	NL	522	140	36	1	10	29	91	60	51	2	2	384	.268	.316	.398	.238	53	141-SS -9
2002	*Florida*	*NL*	*507*	*131*	*30*	*4*	*14*	*32*	*98*	*70*	*56*	*5*	*3*	*379*	*.258*	*.302*	*.416*	*.244*	*56*	

At least the other Alex Gonzalez is a legitimate glove man. This one doesn't field nearly well enough to carry his anemic bat, even in a comeback season. He's the type of player who has enough natural ability to accidentally have things go his way and hit .290/.340/.460 for a year. For that reason, there's a large error bar to that Wilton projection; tread carefully.

Kevin Hooper 2B Bats R Age 25

YEAR	TEAM	LGE	AB	H	DB	TP	HR	BB	SO	R	RBI	SB	CS	OUT	BA	OBP	SLG	EQA	EQR	DEFENSE
1999	Utica	NYP	299	60	13	3	0	25	39	32	13	5	5	243	.201	.266	.264	.185	18	72-2B 6
2000	KaneCnty	Mid	476	97	21	4	2	48	92	52	26	8	2	381	.204	.280	.277	.198	33	120-2B -1
2001	KaneCnty	Mid	67	15	1	0	0	9	14	7	3	1	1	53	.224	.316	.239	.200	5	17-2B -1
2001	Portland	Eas	481	130	16	4	2	52	76	60	34	16	8	359	.270	.346	.333	.238	49	114-2B 1
2002	*Florida*	*NL*	*483*	*121*	*19*	*4*	*3*	*54*	*89*	*65*	*29*	*17*	*7*	*369*	*.251*	*.326*	*.325*	*.233*	*48*	

Luis Castillo is fragile enough that it's worth listing Hooper here. Drafted in the eighth round in 1999, he's a similar player in style to Castillo: minimal power, decent glove, steals some bases, not afraid to walk. Hooper lacks Castillo's speed, although he would slug a bit better than the incumbent. With Berg gone, Hooper is a Castillo owie from major-league playing time, and he could surprise some people.

Charles Johnson C Bats R Age 30

YEAR	TEAM	LGE	AB	H	DB	TP	HR	BB	SO	R	RBI	SB	CS	OUT	BA	OBP	SLG	EQA	EQR	DEFENSE
1999	Baltimor	AL	425	113	19	1	18	51	94	59	55	0	0	312	.266	.349	.442	.265	56	124-C 6
2000	Baltimor	AL	285	88	15	0	23	29	61	52	55	2	0	197	.309	.373	.604	.311	53	78-C 0
2000	ChiSox	AL	133	45	8	0	10	18	33	23	34	0	0	88	.338	.421	.624	.334	28	36-C 2
2001	Florida	NL	455	125	27	0	21	36	113	54	81	0	0	330	.275	.332	.473	.264	59	120-C 6
2002	*Florida*	*NL*	*400*	*111*	*18*	*0*	*22*	*48*	*103*	*59*	*63*	*1*	*0*	*289*	*.278*	*.355*	*.488*	*.285*	*63*	

His 14-month contract with the President of Hades appeared to expire around Memorial Day. Johnson hit .228/.288/.356 after May 31, perhaps the biggest reason the Marlins dropped out of the NL East race. His strikeout-to-walk ratio fell completely apart—he walked only 11 times after the All-Star break. The collapse, and the soft free-agent market this winter, convinced him to not void the last four years of his contract, so he'll be the catcher. Look for a bounce back to his 1999 level.

Derrek Lee 1B Bats R Age 26

YEAR	TEAM	LGE	AB	H	DB	TP	HR	BB	SO	R	RBI	SB	CS	OUT	BA	OBP	SLG	EQA	EQR	DEFENSE
1999	Calgary	PCL	329	78	14	1	14	25	82	44	52	2	3	254	.237	.296	.413	.233	33	88-1B 0
1999	Florida	NL	220	47	10	1	5	14	65	21	20	2	1	174	.214	.261	.336	.201	16	55-1B 4
2000	Florida	NL	482	137	17	3	29	57	113	70	69	0	3	348	.284	.364	.512	.285	75	126-1B 7
2001	Florida	NL	566	168	39	4	22	47	107	88	79	4	2	400	.297	.357	.496	.280	83	146-1B 12
2002	*Florida*	*NL*	*536*	*153*	*29*	*3*	*25*	*57*	*123*	*81*	*82*	*4*	*3*	*386*	*.285*	*.354*	*.491*	*.284*	*83*	

Lee represents an organizational problem. He's been improving, and with his good defense, he's not someone a team has to think actively about replacing. At the same time, he's not likely to take a big step forward and really be worth five or six wins. Lee is durable, so his counting stats are going to make him expensive. The Marlins should get what they can from him this season, then deal him to make room for Adrian Gonzalez.

Mike Lowell 3B Bats R Age 28

YEAR	TEAM	LGE	AB	H	DB	TP	HR	BB	SO	R	RBI	SB	CS	OUT	BA	OBP	SLG	EQA	EQR	DEFENSE
1999	Calgary	PCL	80	21	0	0	2	7	17	8	7	0	0	59	.262	.322	.338	.226	7	21-3B 3
1999	Florida	NL	311	80	13	0	13	22	64	32	46	0	0	231	.257	.316	.424	.246	35	76-3B 5
2000	Florida	NL	514	141	31	0	25	47	69	72	92	4	0	373	.274	.344	.481	.273	72	134-3B 2
2001	Florida	NL	556	167	28	0	22	40	67	67	108	1	2	391	.300	.356	.469	.272	76	142-3B 9
2002	*Florida*	*NL*	*470*	*134*	*18*	*0*	*22*	*46*	*68*	*58*	*78*	*3*	*1*	*337*	*.285*	*.349*	*.464*	*.277*	*68*	

See Derrek Lee. It's not quite as bad, in that Lowell has less service time than Lee, so he's less expensive and his offense—comparable to Lee's—is more valuable at third base. Lowell is comparable to Tim Wallach in his prime, an above-average hitter and good defender. The Marlins need a couple of their young veterans—Lowell, Lee, Alex Gonzalez, Preston Wilson—to take it up a notch.

John Mabry RF Bats L Age 31

YEAR	TEAM	LGE	AB	H	DB	TP	HR	BB	SO	R	RBI	SB	CS	OUT	BA	OBP	SLG	EQA	EQR	DEFENSE	
1999	Seattle	AL	261	66	10	0	11	17	53	33	34	2	1	196	.253	.299	.418	.237	27	34-RF 4	24-3B -8
2000	Seattle	AL	103	27	3	0	2	9	27	18	8	0	1	77	.262	.334	.350	.232	10	11-3B -1	10-RF 0
2000	San Dieg	NL	125	30	6	0	8	3	35	17	26	0	0	95	.240	.258	.480	.235	13	25-RF -2	
2001	Florida	NL	148	35	6	0	7	12	37	15	22	1	0	113	.236	.310	.419	.243	17	28-RF -4	
2002	*Florida*	*NL*	*233*	*57*	*7*	*0*	*10*	*20*	*61*	*29*	*31*	*0*	*1*	*177*	*.245*	*.304*	*.403*	*.240*	*25*		

Mabry started each of the last two seasons with teams that eventually reached the playoffs, only to be traded during the year. That's gotta sting a little. He started 2001 with the Cardinals and lasted a week, spending the remainder of the year pinch-hitting for pitchers and Alex Gonzalez. He's not the worst benchie out there, just limited in how he can contribute. Free agent as of mid-January.

Kevin Millar RF/1B Bats R Age 30

YEAR	TEAM	LGE	AB	H	DB	TP	HR	BB	SO	R	RBI	SB	CS	OUT	BA	OBP	SLG	EQA	EQR	DEFENSE	
1999	Calgary	PCL	138	35	8	1	5	9	17	17	19	1	0	103	.254	.299	.435	.242	15	21-LF 0	
1999	Florida	NL	354	102	18	4	9	36	59	48	65	1	0	252	.288	.365	.438	.271	48	86-1B -5	
2000	Florida	NL	262	69	15	3	14	33	43	36	41	0	0	193	.263	.361	.504	.284	41	29-1B 2	14-LF -1
2001	Florida	NL	453	149	40	5	21	37	59	66	89	0	0	304	.329	.384	.578	.310	81	78-RF -4	14-1B 0
2002	*Florida*	*NL*	*423*	*125*	*30*	*4*	*18*	*49*	*64*	*62*	*78*	*1*	*0*	*298*	*.296*	*.369*	*.513*	*.297*	*71*		

Making lemons out of lemonade: the difficult year Preston Wilson endured created an opportunity for Millar, who outhit even our highest expectations. He needs someone to caddy for him in right field; other than that, there's no reason not to make him the starter and give him 500 at-bats.

Abraham Nunez CF Bats B Age 22

YEAR	TEAM	LGE	AB	H	DB	TP	HR	BB	SO	R	RBI	SB	CS	OUT	BA	OBP	SLG	EQA	EQR	DEFENSE
1999	High Des	Cal	480	95	18	2	14	58	123	61	51	20	8	393	.198	.286	.331	.215	42	130-RF 0
2000	Brevard	Fla	109	19	3	0	1	21	38	12	7	6	2	92	.174	.313	.229	.207	9	
2000	Portland	Eas	226	53	13	1	6	35	66	30	32	5	4	177	.235	.337	.381	.244	26	
2001	Portland	Eas	483	100	12	6	14	73	161	64	44	18	13	396	.207	.313	.344	.226	40	134-CF 0
2002	*Florida*	*NL*	*482*	*107*	*18*	*4*	*14*	*77*	*159*	*69*	*56*	*23*	*11*	*386*	*.222*	*.329*	*.363*	*.246*	*58*	

He's finally healthy again after the shoulder problem that kept him from playing the field in 2000. Even though he's had two lost seasons, he's still just 22 years old, and he walked 83 times in Double-A last year. He'll put up some very good numbers in Calgary, and he provides insurance against Cliff Floyd walking away after the season. Matt Mantei keeps on giving.

Eric Owens RF Bats R Age 31

YEAR	TEAM	LGE	AB	H	DB	TP	HR	BB	SO	R	RBI	SB	CS	OUT	BA	OBP	SLG	EQA	EQR	DEFENSE
1999	San Dieg	NL	446	122	22	3	10	33	46	54	61	29	7	331	.274	.328	.404	.252	53	95-OF 0
2000	San Dieg	NL	593	180	22	6	6	37	58	86	51	27	15	428	.304	.348	.391	.250	67	144-OF 6
2001	Florida	NL	403	109	18	1	5	27	50	55	30	8	6	300	.270	.316	.357	.228	37	90-RF -4
2002	*Florida*	*NL*	*523*	*140*	*19*	*3*	*8*	*45*	*63*	*63*	*53*	*19*	*10*	*393*	*.268*	*.326*	*.361*	*.241*	*56*	

The Padres' Kevin Towers did a good job of trading Owens when his value had peaked, receiving a real outfielder—Mark Kotsay—in exchange for a blown-up utility player (and Matt Clement). It appears that Owens's days of playing the infield are over, leaving him an extra outfielder with about one-and-a-half skills; in other words, he's not worth the roster spot.

Pablo Ozuna IF Bats R Age 23

YEAR	TEAM	LGE	AB	H	DB	TP	HR	BB	SO	R	RBI	SB	CS	OUT	BA	OBP	SLG	EQA	EQR	DEFENSE
1998	Peoria	Mid	546	155	22	5	7	19	60	79	41	29	17	407	.284	.314	.381	.234	54	123-SS -16
1999	Portland	Eas	501	123	22	5	5	6	50	47	35	18	11	388	.246	.265	.339	.204	36	114-SS -21
2000	Portland	Eas	467	123	22	4	6	30	57	57	44	23	17	361	.263	.313	.366	.228	45	113-2B -2
2000	Florida	NL	24	8	1	0	0	0	2	2	1	1	0	16	.333	.333	.375	.246	2	
2002	*Florida*	*NL*	*448*	*121*	*20*	*4*	*6*	*28*	*55*	*55*	*37*	*25*	*14*	*341*	*.270*	*.313*	*.373*	*.238*	*47*	

Ozuna broke his wrist playing winter ball after the 2000 season, then eventually underwent surgery to repair torn cartilage in the wrist. He missed the entire 2001 season due to the injury and may have been passed by Kevin Hooper in the line of guys waiting for Luis Castillo to get hurt. He's off the prospect track.

Mike Redmond C Bats R Age 31

YEAR	TEAM	LGE	AB	H	DB	TP	HR	BB	SO	R	RBI	SB	CS	OUT	BA	OBP	SLG	EQA	EQR	DEFENSE
1999	Florida	NL	244	75	3	0	3	23	31	21	28	0	0	169	.307	.378	.357	.256	28	74-C 5
2000	Florida	NL	213	56	6	2	0	10	17	17	15	0	0	157	.263	.317	.310	.217	17	66-C 1
2001	Florida	NL	142	46	2	0	5	13	11	20	15	0	0	96	.324	.387	.444	.281	20	41-C 2
2002	*Florida*	*NL*	*223*	*59*	*4*	*1*	*4*	*22*	*21*	*21*	*22*	*0*	*0*	*164*	*.265*	*.331*	*.345*	*.237*	*22*	

Redmond is one of the game's better backup catchers, in a group with Tom Lampkin and Bill Haselman, all behind Gregg Zaun. Most teams obsess over having a good glove behind the plate; they should realize that you can get 90% of the defensive skill of the Mike DiFelices of the world in a package capable of posting an EqA 40 points higher. It's a sustained advantage for the teams that get it right.

Nate Rolison 1B Bats L Age 25

YEAR	TEAM	LGE	AB	H	DB	TP	HR	BB	SO	R	RBI	SB	CS	OUT	BA	OBP	SLG	EQA	EQR	DEFENSE
1999	Portland	Eas	442	113	14	1	14	52	112	57	52	0	1	330	.256	.339	.387	.246	50	112-1B -8
2000	Calgary	PCL	429	119	26	2	18	54	113	64	62	2	1	311	.277	.361	.473	.277	63	112-1B -2
2001	Brevard	Fla	48	15	2	0	1	7	8	6	5	0	0	33	.313	.405	.417	.284	7	12-1B 4
2001	Portland	Eas	19	4	0	0	0	1	7	1	2	0	0	15	.211	.250	.211	.162	1	
2001	Calgary	PCL	12	2	0	0	0	1	3	1	1	0	0	10	.167	.231	.167	.146	0	
2002	*Florida*	*NL*	*368*	*100*	*17*	*1*	*15*	*52*	*101*	*54*	*51*	*1*	*1*	*269*	*.272*	*.362*	*.446*	*.278*	*55*	

(Nate Rolison *continued*)
After a huge 2000 season at Calgary, Rolison looked ready to challenge Derrek Lee for the Marlins' first-base job. Like Osuna, though, he suffered an off-season injury—a broken hamate bone—that ruined the next 12 months. Hand injuries like this can kill a player's power; at best, it will take Rolison most of 2002 just to get back to where he was a year ago. By that time, Adrian Gonzalez, not Derrek Lee, will be his problem.

Will Smith LF Bats L Age 20

YEAR	TEAM	LGE	AB	H	DB	TP	HR	BB	SO	R	RBI	SB	CS	OUT	BA	OBP	SLG	EQA	EQR	DEFENSE
2001	KaneCnty	Mid	541	119	18	1	11	24	81	66	60	2	3	425	.220	.256	.318	.193	35	111-LF -3
2002	*Florida*	*NL*	*495*	*120*	*17*	*1*	*14*	*30*	*80*	*52*	*55*	*3*	*3*	*378*	*.242*	*.286*	*.366*	*.221*	*43*	

The Marlins' sixth-round pick in 2000 comes from the Wild Wild West. He spent his first Summertime as a pro Gettin' Jiggy Wit' It at the plate, but that all changed after Independence Day last year, when his numbers dropped badly. His walk rate declined, possibly a sign that he didn't agree often with the Men in Black. Regardless, his whole second half was A Nightmare on His Street. Smith sought comfort in the off-season, even though we know that Parents Just Don't Understand what goes on during a slump. He's young enough to learn and recover his stroke, and he should eventually find a job in Miami.

(Mr. Smith, here's hoping we've ruined it for everyone, and you'll never have to deal with this again.)

Derek Wathan SS Bats B Age 25

YEAR	TEAM	LGE	AB	H	DB	TP	HR	BB	SO	R	RBI	SB	CS	OUT	BA	OBP	SLG	EQA	EQR	DEFENSE
1999	KaneCnty	Mid	476	95	12	2	1	33	59	43	32	16	8	389	.200	.255	.239	.178	26	122-SS 5
2000	Brevard	Fla	374	81	15	3	6	33	60	40	36	11	7	300	.217	.282	.321	.207	29	90-SS 3
2000	Portland	Eas	143	29	4	1	0	9	21	11	13	2	1	115	.203	.253	.245	.176	7	41-SS -3
2001	Portland	Eas	478	106	11	6	3	40	81	56	30	17	11	382	.222	.283	.289	.200	34	116-SS 1
2002	*Florida*	*NL*	*487*	*117*	*14*	*4*	*5*	*44*	*84*	*58*	*45*	*21*	*10*	*380*	*.240*	*.303*	*.316*	*.219*	*43*	

One of two sons of former Royals catcher John Wathan in the Marlins' system, Derek is the better prospect of the two. He's a speedy shortstop, good defensively, and he's coming along about 30 years too late to be a great prospect. His speed and name should get him a roster spot later this year.

Preston Wilson CF Bats R Age 27

YEAR	TEAM	LGE	AB	H	DB	TP	HR	BB	SO	R	RBI	SB	CS	OUT	BA	OBP	SLG	EQA	EQR	DEFENSE
1999	Florida	NL	486	137	21	3	27	40	144	66	68	9	4	353	.282	.347	.504	.278	72	127-CF 1
2000	Florida	NL	612	163	35	3	31	47	172	91	117	33	14	463	.266	.326	.485	.266	84	156-CF 4
2001	Florida	NL	472	137	31	2	24	34	91	74	75	20	8	343	.290	.344	.517	.280	71	121-CF 5
2002	*Florida*	*NL*	*520*	*142*	*30*	*3*	*26*	*55*	*133*	*83*	*80*	*33*	*10*	*388*	*.273*	*.343*	*.492*	*.284*	*83*	

Wilson had a horrible year, as he and his wife Trista lost a newborn child in July, for which we offer them our deepest condolences.

On the field, Wilson had perhaps his best season, making much more contact and increasing all his numbers accordingly. His five-year, $45-million contract still looks excessive, but perhaps less so than it did a year ago.

PITCHERS (ERA: 4.50, H/9: 9.0, HR/9: 1.0, BB/9: 3.0, K/9: 6.0, KW: 2.0, PERA: 4.50)

Juan Acevedo Throws R Age 32

YEAR	TEAM	LGE	IP	H	ER	HR	BB	K	ERA	W	L	H/9	HR/9	BB/9	K/9	KW	PERA	STUFF
1999	St Louis	NL	103.7	116	67	16	40	47	5.82	4	8	10.1	1.4	3.5	4.1	0.6	5.69	-20
2000	Milwauke	NL	81.3	85	43	10	26	45	4.76	4	5	9.4	1.1	2.9	5.0	0.9	3.76	-9
2001	Colorado	NL	32.3	32	18	3	17	21	5.01	2	2	8.9	0.8	4.7	5.8	0.6	5.29	-12
2001	Florida	NL	28.3	28	14	2	14	17	4.45	2	1	8.9	0.6	4.4	5.4	0.6	3.64	-8

With Braden Looper and Antonio Alfonseca, the Marlins really didn't need another right-handed reliever with issues against left-handed batters. They dealt for Acevedo at midseason anyway. He's an interchangeable part, and he's trying to make the Tigers' bullpen this spring. Comerica Park could make him look valuable.

Antonio Alfonseca Throws R Age 30

YEAR	TEAM	LGE	IP	H	ER	HR	BB	K	ERA	W	L	H/9	HR/9	BB/9	K/9	KW	PERA	STUFF
1999	Florida	NL	79.3	79	33	4	24	41	3.74	5	4	9.0	0.5	2.7	4.7	0.9	3.08	-6
2000	Florida	NL	74.0	75	34	6	20	42	4.14	4	4	9.1	0.7	2.4	5.1	1.0	4.27	-6
2001	Florida	NL	60.7	62	27	5	13	32	4.01	4	3	9.2	0.7	1.9	4.7	1.2	3.64	-6

There are 50 or 60 relief pitchers better than Alfonseca, whose perceived value is entirely a function of his usage pattern, which maximizes one particular statistic. He had back surgery in October, so he'll be watched carefully this spring. Once he proves he's healthy, the Fish need to trade him for something of actual value.

Armando Almanza Throws R Age 29

YEAR	TEAM	LGE	IP	H	ER	HR	BB	K	ERA	W	L	H/9	HR/9	BB/9	K/9	KW	PERA	STUFF
1999	Portland	Eas	10.3	9	5	2	5	12	4.35	1	0	7.8	1.7	4.4	10.5	1.2	5.08	0
1999	Calgary	PCL	20.3	22	19	3	21	13	8.41	0	2	9.7	1.3	9.3	5.8	0.3	13.12	-55
1999	Florida	NL	14.7	11	6	1	8	18	3.68	1	1	6.8	0.6	4.9	11.0	1.1	2.18	25
2000	Florida	NL	46.3	40	25	3	35	41	4.86	2	3	7.8	0.6	6.8	8.0	0.6	4.98	-4
2001	Florida	NL	38.3	37	26	7	23	36	6.10	1	3	8.7	1.6	5.4	8.5	0.8	5.47	-4

One-batter lefties have to be able to get, well, one batter. Almanza coughed up a .333/.423/.711 line to first batters in 2001, hurting the Marlins more than he helped. He's good enough against lefties to have value; he just needs to be better about throwing strikes.

Wes Anderson Throws R Age 22

YEAR	TEAM	LGE	IP	H	ER	HR	BB	K	ERA	W	L	H/9	HR/9	BB/9	K/9	KW	PERA	STUFF
1999	KaneCnty	Mid	132.3	139	78	17	57	77	5.30	6	9	9.5	1.2	3.9	5.2	0.7	4.35	12
2000	Brevard	Fla	114.7	120	77	12	78	60	6.04	5	8	9.4	0.9	6.1	4.7	0.4	5.70	-1
2001	Brevard	Fla	35.0	43	32	7	24	11	8.23	1	3	11.1	1.8	6.2	2.8	0.2	10.20	-33

Anderson was within shouting distance of Josh Beckett when the year began. He couldn't get anyone out in the Florida State League, though, and his velocity was way down. He was eventually diagnosed with a torn labrum and underwent surgery in September. He won't pitch until midseason at best, and he won't be a factor until 2003 at the earliest.

Benito Baez Throws L Age 25

YEAR	TEAM	LGE	IP	H	ER	HR	BB	K	ERA	W	L	H/9	HR/9	BB/9	K/9	KW	PERA	STUFF
1999	Midland	Tex	59.0	60	29	7	16	37	4.42	4	3	9.2	1.1	2.4	5.6	1.2	5.73	-2
1999	Vancouvr	PCL	18.3	18	10	2	7	14	4.91	1	1	8.8	1.0	3.4	6.9	1.0	3.66	7
2000	Midland	Tex	56.0	57	32	6	28	33	5.14	3	3	9.2	1.0	4.5	5.3	0.6	6.12	-15
2001	Calgary	PCL	57.7	57	23	5	8	38	3.59	4	2	8.9	0.8	1.2	5.9	2.4	3.09	3
2001	Florida	NL	12.7	13	8	3	5	11	5.68	0	1	9.2	2.1	3.6	7.8	1.1	14.08	-12

After six and a half seasons in the minors, Baez used six-year free agency—and the best two months of his life—to reach the majors with the Marlins. He's a fastball/change-up lefty, and his command has improved ever since he went to the bullpen. He can help the Fish, although the memory of his lousy cameo last summer won't help.

Denny Bautista Throws R Age 19

YEAR	TEAM	LGE	IP	H	ER	HR	BB	K	ERA	W	L	H/9	HR/9	BB/9	K/9	KW	PERA	STUFF
2001	Utica	NYP	36.7	36	13	0	8	16	3.19	3	1	8.8	0.0	2.0	3.9	1.0	5.64	11
2001	KaneCnty	Mid	40.0	46	26	4	18	11	5.85	1	3	10.4	0.9	4.1	2.5	0.3	6.25	-11

He's picked up a halo on the basis of his association with Pedro Martinez, with whom he's trained in the off-season. Bautista throws in the mid-90s with a good curve and is rapidly growing into his 6′5″ frame. There are a lot of pitches between here and ESPN; just remember the name, because you're going to be hearing about him.

Josh Beckett **Throws R** **Age 22**

YEAR	TEAM	LGE	IP	H	ER	HR	BB	K	ERA	W	L	H/9	HR/9	BB/9	K/9	KW	PERA	STUFF
2000	KaneCnty	Mid	56.0	60	33	10	17	35	5.30	3	3	9.6	1.6	2.7	5.6	1.0	3.68	10
2001	Brevard	Fla	62.3	47	15	0	17	63	2.17	6	1	6.8	0.0	2.5	9.1	1.9	2.49	43
2001	Portland	Eas	70.0	66	37	12	24	67	4.76	4	4	8.5	1.5	3.1	8.6	1.4	2.37	34
2001	Florida	NL	21.0	19	11	3	10	19	4.71	1	1	8.1	1.3	4.3	8.1	0.9	3.51	27

Stud. He shook off concerns about the shoulder tendinitis that cut short his 2000 season to have one of the great pitching-prospect years of recent times. He'll open 2002 in the Marlins' rotation; hopes are high, but Beckett is still basically a two-pitch pitcher, and he has fewer than 100 innings above A ball. Be realistic in your expectations for 2002.

Ricky Bones **Throws R** **Age 33**

YEAR	TEAM	LGE	IP	H	ER	HR	BB	K	ERA	W	L	H/9	HR/9	BB/9	K/9	KW	PERA	STUFF
1999	Baltimor	AL	47.7	51	27	6	16	26	5.10	2	3	9.6	1.1	3.0	4.9	0.8	5.28	-12
2000	Florida	NL	83.7	81	34	5	22	52	3.66	5	4	8.7	0.5	2.4	5.6	1.2	4.75	-1
2001	Florida	NL	62.7	65	36	6	30	33	5.17	3	4	9.3	0.9	4.3	4.7	0.6	5.70	-18

He's a garbage-time pitcher, doing little more than soaking up the lowest-leverage innings on the staff. The Marlins were 20-41 in games when Bones took the mound, because he generally came in when the team was behind and pitched until they had to hit for him. He gets credit for bringing along some of the Marlins' Latin pitchers, which has value, just not enough to warrant the roster spot.

A.J. Burnett **Throws R** **Age 25**

YEAR	TEAM	LGE	IP	H	ER	HR	BB	K	ERA	W	L	H/9	HR/9	BB/9	K/9	KW	PERA	STUFF
1999	Portland	Eas	124.3	131	87	21	72	85	6.30	5	9	9.5	1.5	5.2	6.2	0.6	7.37	-2
1999	Florida	NL	41.3	39	20	3	21	30	4.35	3	2	8.5	0.7	4.6	6.5	0.7	4.76	15
2000	Florida	NL	83.3	83	43	7	36	51	4.64	4	5	9.0	0.8	3.9	5.5	0.7	4.75	8
2001	Florida	NL	159.3	160	89	18	74	103	5.03	8	10	9.0	1.0	4.2	5.8	0.7	4.43	6

One of the better mysteries in baseball right now is A.J. Burnett's strikeout rate. He throws hard, with a good knuckle-curve as a pitch he can use for strike three, and he's shown himself to be hard to hit at times. He's a hairsbreadth from exploding on the National League, and he's a better candidate for the All-Star team this year than Beckett is.

Matt Clement **Throws R** **Age 27**

YEAR	TEAM	LGE	IP	H	ER	HR	BB	K	ERA	W	L	H/9	HR/9	BB/9	K/9	KW	PERA	STUFF
1999	San Dieg	NL	186.3	184	92	17	72	122	4.44	11	10	8.9	0.8	3.5	5.9	0.8	5.21	9
2000	San Dieg	NL	207.0	199	110	20	103	151	4.78	11	12	8.7	0.9	4.5	6.6	0.7	5.68	7
2001	Florida	NL	165.3	161	83	13	76	108	4.52	9	9	8.8	0.7	4.1	5.9	0.7	5.63	4

Speaking of mysteries... Clement has excellent stuff that hasn't yet translated into success. He's plateaued following a strong rookie season in 1999, unable to get his control together or learn a pitch he can use to get out lefties. While Clement still has upside as a starter, he really fits the profile of a pitcher who would adapt well to the bullpen, and the Marlins have the rotation depth to move him.

Vic Darensbourg **Throws L** **Age 31**

YEAR	TEAM	LGE	IP	H	ER	HR	BB	K	ERA	W	L	H/9	HR/9	BB/9	K/9	KW	PERA	STUFF
1999	Florida	NL	38.7	41	21	3	18	14	4.89	2	2	9.5	0.7	4.2	3.3	0.4	8.86	-31
2000	Florida	NL	63.7	59	29	6	23	52	4.10	4	3	8.3	0.8	3.3	7.4	1.1	4.41	3
2001	Florida	NL	47.7	48	19	4	9	27	3.59	3	2	9.1	0.8	1.7	5.1	1.5	4.61	-4

Intentional walks haven't been pulled out of the DTs this year, so that line is a bit deceptive. Darensbourg actually walked just four men in nearly 50 innings last season, the culmination of a steady improvement in his control. It might be *too* good: he gave up a .541 slugging average to left-handed batters last year. He's one of the keepers in the Marlins pen.

Ryan Dempster — Throws R — Age 25

YEAR	TEAM	LGE	IP	H	ER	HR	BB	K	ERA	W	L	H/9	HR/9	BB/9	K/9	KW	PERA	STUFF
1999	Florida	NL	149.3	147	88	20	78	113	5.30	7	10	8.9	1.2	4.7	6.8	0.7	4.47	13
2000	Florida	NL	228.0	217	111	27	80	186	4.38	13	12	8.6	1.1	3.2	7.3	1.2	3.85	21
2001	Florida	NL	207.3	203	109	18	100	138	4.73	11	12	8.8	0.8	4.3	6.0	0.7	5.44	7

Dempster wasn't right all year, fighting his control even during his periods of relative effectiveness. He was particularly bad in September and October, an indication that the number of pitches his wildness had forced him to throw—he ranked 14th in the majors in Pitcher Abuse Points—had taken its toll. If he makes 25 starts in 2002, it'll be an upset.

One of the arguments for signing Charles Johnson was his impact on the Marlins' young rotation. Given the performances of Dempster, Burnett, Clement, and Chuck Smith, it's hard to see where he had any positive impact. None of the pitchers showed improvement in 2001. This doesn't mean Johnson was a negative; it just means there's no evidence that his "veteran leadership" helped these pitchers.

Jason Grilli — Throws R — Age 25

YEAR	TEAM	LGE	IP	H	ER	HR	BB	K	ERA	W	L	H/9	HR/9	BB/9	K/9	KW	PERA	STUFF
1999	Calgary	PCL	44.0	50	32	7	24	20	6.55	2	3	10.2	1.4	4.9	4.1	0.4	8.72	-12
1999	Fresno	PCL	104.0	120	78	23	40	58	6.75	4	8	10.4	2.0	3.5	5.0	0.7	5.58	-1
2000	Calgary	PCL	45.3	50	20	4	22	17	5.56	2	3	9.9	0.8	4.4	3.4	0.4	6.69	-12
2001	Florida	NL	25.7	29	18	5	10	14	6.31	1	2	10.2	1.8	3.5	4.9	0.7	6.30	-9
2001	Calgary	PCL	46.0	48	27	4	24	24	5.28	2	3	9.4	0.8	4.7	4.7	0.5	4.60	-3
2001	Brevard	Fla	13.7	13	6	0	7	7	3.95	1	1	8.6	0.0	4.6	4.6	0.5	4.49	-8

Grilli's career is in serious jeopardy following two seasons' worth of injury problems. Elbow surgery cut 2000 short; he was healthy enough to win the Marlins' #5 starter job last spring, but he pitched poorly and was subsequently hampered by a strained muscle in his arm and back problems. He'll be forced out of the Marlins' system shortly.

Hansel Izquierdo — Throws R — Age 25

YEAR	TEAM	LGE	IP	H	ER	HR	BB	K	ERA	W	L	H/9	HR/9	BB/9	K/9	KW	PERA	STUFF
1999	WnstnSlm	Car	81.0	88	57	10	53	40	6.33	3	6	9.8	1.1	5.9	4.4	0.4	6.45	-14
2000	Kinston	Car	39.3	48	34	10	16	18	7.78	1	3	11.0	2.3	3.7	4.1	0.6	9.53	-30
2001	KaneCnty	Mid	43.3	45	23	3	21	20	4.78	2	3	9.3	0.6	4.4	4.2	0.5	2.40	-22
2001	Brevard	Fla	22.0	30	25	9	8	11	10.23	0	2	12.3	3.7	3.3	4.5	0.7	4.61	-31
2001	Portland	Eas	51.0	65	47	16	14	26	8.29	1	5	11.5	2.8	2.5	4.6	0.9	5.26	-17

Izquierdo would make the book on back story alone, having been cut twice in 2000 and ending up in the Western League. The Fish brought him in over the winter, and he shot through the system, ending the year with 24 good innings in the Arizona Fall League. He throws a hard sinker/slider combination. While he needs some experience at the upper levels, the Marlins are going to take a serious look at him this spring for a major-league job.

Braden Looper — Throws R — Age 27

YEAR	TEAM	LGE	IP	H	ER	HR	BB	K	ERA	W	L	H/9	HR/9	BB/9	K/9	KW	PERA	STUFF
1999	Florida	NL	87.0	89	40	7	26	45	4.14	5	5	9.2	0.7	2.7	4.7	0.9	4.43	-8
2000	Florida	NL	68.7	71	34	3	30	26	4.46	4	4	9.3	0.4	3.9	3.4	0.4	5.20	-21
2001	Florida	NL	66.3	67	35	7	27	42	4.75	3	4	9.1	0.9	3.7	5.7	0.8	3.69	-7

Looper addressed two major problems, striking out a few more people and doing better against left-handed batters, thanks to a new slider. He's signed through 2003 at less than a $1 million per year, so there's no danger of him becoming too expensive for his role. He's first in line for the closer job should anything happen to Alfonseca, at least until the next guy in this chapter is ready.

Blaine Neal **Throws R** **Age 24**

YEAR	TEAM	LGE	IP	H	ER	HR	BB	K	ERA	W	L	H/9	HR/9	BB/9	K/9	KW	PERA	STUFF
1999	KaneCnty	Mid	28.7	30	17	4	11	18	5.34	1	2	9.4	1.3	3.5	5.7	0.8	2.81	-4
2000	Brevard	Fla	53.3	48	25	2	30	41	4.22	3	3	8.1	0.3	5.1	6.9	0.7	6.20	-2
2001	Portland	Eas	51.7	50	25	2	28	28	4.35	3	3	8.7	0.3	4.9	4.9	0.5	3.66	-13

We've seen position player-to-pitcher, and we've occasionally seen pitcher-to-position player. Neal is vying to become the first pitcher-to-first-base-to-pitcher conversion. He's had a long road, with two position changes and elbow surgery, but he's now the Marlins' designated closer prospect. Nothing fancy, just a good fastball/slider combination. He should make the Opening Day bullpen.

Vladimir Nunez **Throws R** **Age 27**

YEAR	TEAM	LGE	IP	H	ER	HR	BB	K	ERA	W	L	H/9	HR/9	BB/9	K/9	KW	PERA	STUFF
1999	Arizona	NL	34.0	31	15	2	17	25	3.97	2	2	8.2	0.5	4.5	6.6	0.7	3.56	0
1999	Florida	NL	73.7	73	38	9	28	52	4.64	4	4	8.9	1.1	3.4	6.4	0.9	5.49	5
2000	Florida	NL	73.0	79	45	11	28	40	5.55	3	5	9.7	1.4	3.5	4.9	0.7	7.88	-11
2000	Calgary	PCL	92.3	91	51	11	41	68	4.97	5	5	8.9	1.1	4.0	6.6	0.8	4.04	4
2001	Florida	NL	85.0	85	41	8	27	51	4.34	5	4	9.0	0.8	2.9	5.4	0.9	3.35	-3

Like Looper, Nunez got his act together against lefties last season, holding them to a .213/.290/.356 line. It appears that he's settled in as a reliever, having pitched very well in that role from May onward. He's just another reason for the Fish to ditch Alfonseca and use the other arms in their pen to pitch the ninth inning.

Some day in 2003, Brad Penny is going to throw seven shutout innings, Vlad Nunez is going to come in and set the middle of a lineup down 1-2-3, and Abraham Nunez is going to hit a two-run home run, all for a 3-0 win. On that same day, Matt Mantei is going be on the disabled list.

Kevin Olsen **Throws R** **Age 25**

YEAR	TEAM	LGE	IP	H	ER	HR	BB	K	ERA	W	L	H/9	HR/9	BB/9	K/9	KW	PERA	STUFF
1999	KaneCnty	Mid	62.7	67	33	7	19	29	4.74	3	4	9.6	1.0	2.7	4.2	0.8	4.62	2
1999	Brevard	Fla	57.7	73	52	18	16	29	8.12	1	5	11.4	2.8	2.5	4.5	0.9	7.91	-14
2000	Brevard	Fla	107.0	111	48	5	33	45	4.04	7	5	9.3	0.4	2.8	3.8	0.7	4.92	0
2000	Portland	Eas	52.7	62	45	14	23	33	7.69	2	4	10.6	2.4	3.9	5.6	0.7	5.81	-5
2001	Portland	Eas	146.3	153	72	18	30	84	4.43	8	8	9.4	1.1	1.8	5.2	1.4	4.50	4
2001	Florida	NL	14.0	12	3	0	2	10	1.93	2	0	7.7	0.0	1.3	6.4	2.5	1.25	24

This is not the organization in which to be a command right-hander, but Olsen managed to garner some attention in the wake of Beckett's Comet, thanks to a 144-to-21 strikeout-to-walk ratio. He's needed adjustment periods at high-A and Double-A, so don't overproject the 1.20 major-league ERA he posted last year in a cup of coffee. Olsen is the guy who'll take Dempster's rotation slot when Dempster goes on the DL. He has a very good long-term outlook.

Brad Penny **Throws R** **Age 24**

YEAR	TEAM	LGE	IP	H	ER	HR	BB	K	ERA	W	L	H/9	HR/9	BB/9	K/9	KW	PERA	STUFF
1999	El Paso	Tex	97.7	96	47	12	27	72	4.33	6	5	8.8	1.1	2.5	6.6	1.3	5.29	20
1999	Portland	Eas	32.0	31	18	4	14	25	5.06	2	2	8.7	1.1	3.9	7.0	0.9	4.54	19
2000	Calgary	PCL	13.7	12	7	1	9	13	4.61	1	1	7.9	0.7	5.9	8.6	0.7	3.98	24
2000	Florida	NL	121.0	123	64	12	49	71	4.76	6	7	9.1	0.9	3.6	5.3	0.7	5.00	5
2001	Florida	NL	193.7	187	78	13	48	124	3.62	13	9	8.7	0.6	2.2	5.8	1.3	4.20	17

If you've gone through this chapter page by page and are tired of reading about great young Marlins pitchers, you're in luck: Penny is the last one. He was very good from start to finish, with only a strained rib cage marring an otherwise fine season. The massive improvement in his control kept his workload ridiculously low: Penny's Stress score of 4 was among the four lowest among pitchers with at least 200 innings. He inherits the staff ace mantle from Dempster.

Johnny Ruffin Throws R Age 30

YEAR	TEAM	LGE	IP	H	ER	HR	BB	K	ERA	W	L	H/9	HR/9	BB/9	K/9	KW	PERA	STUFF
1999	Albuquer	PCL	52.0	51	33	8	30	44	5.71	2	4	8.8	1.4	5.2	7.6	0.7	3.41	-12
2000	Tucson	PCL	57.0	52	28	5	27	47	4.42	3	3	8.2	0.8	4.3	7.4	0.9	3.26	-4
2000	Arizona	NL	9.7	13	10	4	2	4	9.31	0	1	12.1	3.7	1.9	3.7	1.0	8.06	-37
2001	Calgary	PCL	35.7	31	13	1	13	30	3.28	3	1	7.8	0.3	3.3	7.6	1.2	4.64	1
2001	Florida	NL	4.0	3	2	0	4	3	4.50	0	0	6.8	0.0	9.0	6.8	0.4	10.11	-20

Like a dog with a bone, *Baseball Prospectus* will promote its pet projects until they retire. For the second straight season, Ruffin was unimpressive in a brief major-league trial, after which the Marlins cut him loose, and he ended up in the Reds' system. Some team has to have use for a pitcher who can post a 3.00 ERA in 80 innings, right? Until one does, Ruffin is worth $35 in your International League roto auction.

Jesus Sanchez Throws L Age 27

YEAR	TEAM	LGE	IP	H	ER	HR	BB	K	ERA	W	L	H/9	HR/9	BB/9	K/9	KW	PERA	STUFF
1999	Florida	NL	78.0	83	60	15	50	56	6.92	3	6	9.6	1.7	5.8	6.5	0.6	5.93	-16
2000	Florida	NL	185.0	199	111	29	63	109	5.40	9	12	9.7	1.4	3.1	5.3	0.9	5.54	0
2001	Calgary	PCL	71.3	72	40	5	42	37	5.05	4	4	9.1	0.6	5.3	4.7	0.4	3.81	-12
2001	Florida	NL	60.0	60	33	6	28	37	4.95	3	4	9.0	0.9	4.2	5.6	0.7	4.92	-3

A few years back, when the Cubs acquired Jon Lieber, there was some concern because of his fly-ball tendencies. That seems to have worked out, so it pays to be optimistic about Sanchez's chances in Wrigley Field. He'll provide inexpensive insurance for both Juan Cruz in the rotation and Jeff Fassero in the bullpen. Sanchez is very good against the running game, so it will be interesting to see if he can cancel out Todd Hundley.

Chuck Smith Throws R Age 32

YEAR	TEAM	LGE	IP	H	ER	HR	BB	K	ERA	W	L	H/9	HR/9	BB/9	K/9	KW	PERA	STUFF
1999	Oklahoma	PCL	83.0	84	44	9	33	51	4.77	4	5	9.1	1.0	3.6	5.5	0.8	3.66	-10
2000	Oklahoma	PCL	71.0	66	35	4	41	52	4.44	4	4	8.4	0.5	5.2	6.6	0.6	4.71	3
2000	Florida	NL	125.7	109	46	5	44	105	3.29	6	6	7.8	0.4	3.2	7.5	1.2	3.69	24
2001	Calgary	PCL	12.7	12	4	0	3	6	2.84	1	0	8.5	0.0	2.1	4.3	1.0	2.84	8
2001	Florida	NL	85.7	85	43	9	31	57	4.52	5	5	8.9	0.9	3.3	6.0	0.9	4.99	8

The great story of 2000 fell apart in 2001, starting the season late with a sprained shoulder and ending it early with ligament damage in his elbow. He eschewed surgery, opting for rest and rehab. That doesn't usually go well, but it doesn't really matter: Smith's window of opportunity here is closed, and he's just another thirtysomething with an injury problem.

Mike Tejera Throws L Age 25

YEAR	TEAM	LGE	IP	H	ER	HR	BB	K	ERA	W	L	H/9	HR/9	BB/9	K/9	KW	PERA	STUFF
1999	Portland	Eas	153.0	152	75	18	45	107	4.41	9	8	8.9	1.1	2.6	6.3	1.2	3.48	18
1999	Calgary	PCL	11.3	13	8	2	4	4	6.35	0	1	10.3	1.6	3.2	3.2	0.5	11.59	-20
2001	Portland	Eas	138.3	157	101	28	59	76	6.57	5	10	10.2	1.8	3.8	4.9	0.6	5.38	-12

He made a reasonably successful return from Tommy John surgery, staying healthy and at one level all year. Yes, that's success. He didn't have a ton of velocity to lose, so it's just a matter of sorting through what works and getting his command—which used to be very good—back. By 2004, he'll have a job and some pretty good press.

Claudio Vargas Throws R Age 23

YEAR	TEAM	LGE	IP	H	ER	HR	BB	K	ERA	W	L	H/9	HR/9	BB/9	K/9	KW	PERA	STUFF
1999	KaneCnty	Mid	98.7	110	69	17	46	51	6.29	4	7	10.0	1.6	4.2	4.7	0.6	5.12	0
2000	Brevard	Fla	141.0	150	87	24	52	94	5.55	6	10	9.6	1.5	3.3	6.0	0.9	5.28	11
2000	Portland	Eas	15.7	16	8	2	6	9	4.60	1	1	9.2	1.1	3.4	5.2	0.8	6.02	5
2001	Portland	Eas	145.7	165	125	36	85	99	7.72	4	12	10.2	2.2	5.3	6.1	0.6	5.33	0

Scouts love Vargas, who gets his heat into the low 90s and has the beginnings of two other pitches. Neither is there yet, which is why he wound up surrendering 25 homers in 159 innings. His command is good, but it's not as good as Olsen's, so you can add him to the long list of current Marlins prospects just waiting for six-year free agency and a chance to control their destiny.

Houston Astros

The Astros have been a Baseball Prospectus favorite for some time. They've managed to win their division four out of the last five years while doing all of the things we like to see. They employ a smart management team, they spend top dollar for premier talent, they usually avoid blowing money in the areas where cash evaporates quickly (mid-tier free agents and the early rounds of the draft), and they commit significant resources to scouting. Better than most organizations, they've managed to sustain the difficult long-term balancing act of winning now while developing talent for the future.

However, in 2000, the Astros fell flat on their collective face, and 2001 saw only the latest in a long stretch of postseason disappointments. Are the Astros on their way out? The mainstream media are generally treating 2001 as a last hurrah for Houston; the Cubs and Cardinals are spending money hand over fist to buy the credibility that the Astros have earned with those four division titles in five years.

Astros Prospectus

2001 record: 93–69; Second place, NL Central, NL wild card, lost to Braves 3–0 in Division Series

Pythagenport W/L: 89–73

Runs scored: 847 (second in NL)

Runs allowed: 769 (tenth in NL)

Team EqA: .266 (fifth in NL)

2001 batters age: 30.4 (fourth-oldest in NL)

2001 pitchers age: 27.9 (sixth-youngest in NL)

Ballpark: Enron Field; excellent hitters' park; Park Factor of 1.060

2001: Some explosive performances by young players pushed the Astros back to the top of the division.

2002: The best team in the game's deepest division, fully capable of making it five out of six.

The 2000 Astros were one of the unluckiest teams of all time, with a 15-31 record in one-run games that helped make a down year look like a disastrous one. Some of the bad fortune was rightfully blamed on their bullpen, and losing Craig Biggio and Billy Wagner to injuries didn't help. Organizational missteps added to the problem, especially trading Mike Hampton and Carl Everett for little immediate gain. In 2001, the Astros returned with a vengeance, assuming their proper place atop the National League Central. Big spenders such as the Mets and Giants went back to their familiar position of being squeezed out by a pair of better organizations from the league's strongest division.

That the Astros made it to the playoffs at all in 2001 was a bit of a surprise. After a pair of extra-inning losses to the Reds on June 21 and 22, their record was a mediocre 36-35, and they trailed the first-place Cubs by seven games. The previous winter's acquisitions had gone universally bad. The hoped-for middle relief savior, Doug Brocail, broke down in spring training. Veteran pitchers such as Kent Bottenfield and Mike Jackson struggled from the outset. Jeff Bagwell's catcher of choice, Brad Ausmus, plumbed Girardian depths of uselessness. The ghost of Charlie Hayes lingered before melting away under direct sunlight.

A combination of factors helped the summertime push. First, the Cubs were leading the division, and practically speaking, that means it was anybody's race. Second, by June the rotation was finally taking shape. Shane Reynolds was rounding into form after rushing back from a winter knee injury, Wade Miller was turning into one of the league's finest starters, and, best of all, Roy Oswalt had moved from a middle-relief audition in May to instant success in the big-league rotation. Jose Lima and Kent Bottenfield were gone, leaving only Scott Elarton's ugly immolation every five days (until Elarton finally broke down in July). The offense deserves a lot of credit for helping push the Astros to within 4 1/2 games of the Cubs on August 1, but it was pitching that put the Astros in first place to stay, fueling a 21-7 month with a staff ERA of 2.86.

Perhaps what was most compelling about the Astros' charge was how it dispelled any notion that the organization needed the Astrodome to win. Moving from an extreme pitchers' park to an extreme hitters' park does not make winning impossible; it simply pushes management to reconsider how it constructs the roster. During the course of 2001, the Astros acted on some of the lessons their new environment was teaching them. Jose Lima went from being a commodity to being useless. Before the end of June, he was gone. Glen Barker went from being a handy spare part in a runs-scarce environment to a New Orleans Zephyr, leaving Lance Berkman to take center field on Richard Hidalgo's off days.

After their great second half, though, the Astros made another all-too-familiar quick exit from the postseason. While the injuries in the rotation were an obvious problem, it wasn't starting pitching that killed the Astros in October, and it wasn't the famed struggles of the Killer Bs. It was managing.

We've hemmed and hawed over Larry Dierker's value as a manager over the years, especially in the wake of the firing of pitching coach Vern Ruhle in 2000. Dierker had already failed to command what Bill James labeled the one indispensable quality for any manager: the respect of his players. His handling of his pitching staffs went from effective (with Ruhle) to questionable. While Dierker's openness to the sabermetric work of the last 20 years makes him a sympathetic figure for outfits like BP, he really needed to win if he was going to command any respect from above in the Astros chain of command, let alone regain any in the clubhouse.

Dierker can't say he didn't have his fate in his hands. The Astros were leading 3-2 going into the eighth inning in the first game of the Division Series. Octavio Dotel had been a significant part of the Astros' drive to the postseason, and he was available to face the bottom of the Braves order. Rather than go with his best, though, Dierker called on Mike Jackson with Paul Bako, the pitcher's slot, and Marcus Giles due to bat.

Because the bottom of the order was due up, and because the middle of the Braves lineup was likely to bat in the ninth, the eighth was the inning in which Bobby Cox was going to have to use his bench. On that bench, he had Keith Lockhart and Ken Caminiti from the left side, and Bernard Gilkey from the right. So why did Dierker bring in Jackson, who had let left-handed hitters tattoo him to the tune of .294/.387/.513 with an Enron ERA of 6.06? By comparison, Dotel had limited lefties to .238/.347/.291 and had an Enron ERA of 1.70. Dierker had to know that if Cox was going to use his left-handed pinch hitters, it was now or never. Dotel has a moving fastball and two effective breaking pitches to tie up lefties; Jackson does not. Whether you went by the numbers, the physical skills, or Dierker's established usage patterns, Dotel was the obvious choice and the best bet to keep the Astros out of trouble.

Jackson came in, Lockhart doubled, and Giles drove him home, tying the game. Given Bobby Cox's slender range of tactical options, it was Dierker who created the potential for the subsequent big inning that put the Astros behind one game into the series, a hole from which they would never recover.

The sad thing is that the Astros were probably the best team in baseball in mid-August. If the playoffs had started before Labor Day, the Astros might have won everything, but baseball isn't a five-month game. In the act of propelling the Astros into first place, the pitching staff started coming apart at the seams, mostly due to unforeseeable accidents. Pedro Astacio tore up his shoulder four starts into his Astros' career. Carlos Hernandez, the organization's best possible replacement for Astacio, jammed his shoulder running the bases. Shane Reynolds had to put in time on the DL with a strained back, and Wade Miller missed starts after getting spiked in the hand covering first base. By the time Roy Oswalt's hamstring gave out, the Astros' source of strength had reverted to being a weakness.

The Astros really did give it their best shot. They made the big stretch trade for Astacio, correctly identifying their desperate need for a starter whom they could turn to in a short series. Outside of Miller, Reynolds, Oswalt, and Astacio, the Astros got 19 quality starts out of 78 tries (24.4%) from their other ten starters. That's unacceptably bad. Like the 1998 acquisition of Randy Johnson, trading for Astacio was a worthwhile gamble that didn't pay. That doesn't make the gamble bad, but it might affect how Gerry Hunsicker feels about making a stretch-drive trade for an ace starter in years to come.

In the wake of the Division Series sweep, the Astros had another off-season in which they didn't do much to help themselves. Adding players such as the Brian Hunter who can run and T.J. Mathews and C.J. Nitkowski looks pretty insignificant compared to losing Moises Alou. Finally handing Larry Dierker his walking papers is a pretty important move, and replacing him with Jimy Williams will have an impact. Sabermetric orthodoxy has put forth the claim that managers are relatively minor figures in how well or poorly a team performs. Like most tidy theories, this one ignores a fundamental fact—the manager determines who plays and how much, and he dictates the structure of each player's workload.

Will Jimy Williams work his starting pitchers hard like Dierker did? With the Red Sox, he was for the most part handed graybeards who needed (and got) gentle handling. The exception was Pedro Martinez, who was babied with extra rest between starts, but who was not particularly sheltered from high-pitch outings. Williams is coming over having had considerable experience with starters who need special treatment, albeit ones on the other end of their careers from guys such as Wade Miller and Roy Oswalt. With those two, plus Tim Redding and Carlos Hernandez in the mix, Williams has to contend and develop at once. As the Athletics and White Sox have shown in recent years, those are not mutually exclusive goals.

To get a sense of what could happen, remember Williams's earlier incarnation as a manager, during his three-plus years at the helm of the Blue Jays. Dave Stieb lost his command during the first two of those years, but Williams shouldn't be held responsible for that, as he inherited an overworked Stieb from Bobby Cox. Jimmy Key continued to develop, enjoying a pair of outstanding seasons before running into elbow trouble in 1988. Key was 25 in 1986, or only slightly older than Oswalt and Miller will be in 2002. Under Williams, Jim Clancy had a couple of great years, including the best season of his career in 1986, but it was Clancy's new forkball—not

Williams—that deserves the credit. In general, it would be hard to attribute much of the performance of the Jays' big three to Williams.

More interesting was what happened at the margins of the Blue Jays' pitching staff. Williams carved out a few neat roles, using lefty John Cerutti as a swing man in all three seasons. While Cerutti was basically the fourth starter, he never opened more than 21 games. In part, this was because Williams also squeezed in work for young flamethrowers such as Jose Nunez and Todd Stottlemyre, and promising sinkerballer Joe Johnson. Nunez and Johnson didn't work out, and we're all still pretty familiar with Stottlemyre.

Nobody should pretend that young pitching isn't a crapshoot, but Tim Redding is no Jose Nunez. Because the Astros have so much young pitching talent on the way up, and because the team has three established starters in Miller, Oswalt, and Reynolds, it's going to require creativity to balance contending with development. Based on Williams's time with the Blue Jays, there's some small reason to believe that he'll carve out overlapping jobs for Redding and Hernandez, and eventually for guys such as Chad Qualls, Mike Nannini, or Rodrigo Rosario.

The more basic issue is whether Williams will succeed where Dierker failed. One component of Dierker's failure to win friends and influence people was his admirable—but ultimately self-destructive—frankness with the press. Because Jimy Williams treats language as an extended ruse to hide whatever he really thinks, there's little chance of his bruising the easily-bruised feelings of the Astros clubhouse. Where Williams should get credit is for his willingness to tackle pressing questions. When he ran the Blue Jays, he braved the whining that accompanied the necessary decision to move Damaso Garcia out of the leadoff slot. When running the Red Sox, he refused to cater to Carl Everett. Whether Williams gets through to Bagwell and Biggio remains to be seen, but it won't be for lack of trying.

Of greater concern is the question of whether Williams favors old players, especially in bench roles. Such a predisposition might go far in explaining the Astros' strange offseason fascination with hoarding journeymen such as Orlando Merced, Jose Vizcaino, Brian Hunter, and even Scott Servais. Merced has value as a tactical weapon, but the other three aren't worth more than the minimum salary. However, in recent years Williams did give breaks to young players such as Brian Daubach and Shea Hillenbrand, and Trot Nixon seems to have turned out all right. Morgan Ensberg and Jason Lane shouldn't have to worry about too much bias on behalf of veterans. Best yet, Williams built some nice combinations behind the plate in his years in Boston, which hopefully means he'll be flexible enough to play Gregg Zaun at Brad Ausmus's expense.

Williams's arrival in the wake of Larry Dierker also means that somebody is going to have to re-explain the facts of life to Jeff Bagwell. Houston's Hamlet spends his time griping about the talent on hand and the need for more players his own age. When he received his enormous contract, Bagwell claimed he understood what his salary meant for the future shape of the team, but he still spends time wishing the front office was keeping the Pastros together, instead of being a standard bearer for teams that have a lot to look forward to.

Bagwell is apparently turning a blind eye to what this organization has accomplished in the recent past. The organization's homegrown talent—the Roy Oswalts and the Lance Berkmans—is why the Astros won in 2001. Vinny Castilla was available for a reason, and Moises Alou had to sign elsewhere for a Bagwell-sized reason. The Astros are going to continue to contend not because of players like Castilla and Alou, but because of the talent on the roster and the intelligence to put that talent to work.

We've lauded the Astros for past successes with Andres Reiner's voracious Venezuelan program, a program that is now being expanded to the Dominican Republic. But the Astros have also done better than most organizations in the amateur draft. There are few gambits that the Astros don't employ better than almost every other team: they draft-and-follow well, they dig up small college pitchers with breakout potential, and they draft college seniors who not only wind up being cheaper, but often better, than juniors drafted around them. The Astros' success is also a product of their willingness to make their own assumptions about what makes a player valuable. Along with the Athletics, the Astros draft for the ability to pitch, not merely picking hurlers for height and hoping that they throw hard when they fill out. It is all to the credit of the best scouting effort in baseball.

As a result of this winter's inaction, the Astros might be considered underdogs by some. That would be a mistake. With a lineup built around Bagwell, Berkman, and Hidalgo, with Daryle Ward finally getting his shot, with an outstanding pair of young aces and the best reliever in the division (that's Octavio Dotel, folks), the Astros have fashioned a formula for continued success. Unlike the Cubs and the Cardinals, the Astros aren't depending on the recently famous or the over-30 crowd. The Astros have shown the ability to swing the big deals, develop the best talent, and field the best lineup in the division, year after year. Feel sorry for the other five teams in the NL Central, because the Astros aren't going away.

HITTERS (BA: .270, OBP: .340, SLG: .440, EqA: .260)

Moises Alou   RF   Bats R   Age 35

YEAR	TEAM	LGE	AB	H	DB	TP	HR	BB	SO	R	RBI	SB	CS	OUT	BA	OBP	SLG	EQA	EQR	DEFENSE
2000	Houston	NL	451	154	25	2	29	45	41	77	105	3	3	300	.341	.403	.599	.320	87	97-RF -6
2001	Houston	NL	509	169	27	1	27	54	48	79	106	5	1	341	.332	.399	.548	.310	91	108-RF -2
2002	*ChiCubs*	*NL*	*458*	*138*	*21*	*1*	*24*	*56*	*46*	*70*	*81*	*5*	*2*	*322*	*.301*	*.377*	*.509*	*.295*	*76*	

Alou has more lives than a cat. Year after year, you think he'll start losing it. While injuries have affected him in just about every year of his career, costing him two complete seasons, it's important to remember that his big-league career didn't really get started until he was almost 26, after only 90 games apiece at Double-A and Triple-A. His defense gets panned, but it's not like he's in the same boat as Juan Gonzalez, despite being three years older than Gonzalez. Consistently betting against him might work one of these years, but that's weak. Wrigley Field won't hurt him as much as park factors might have you believe.

Brad Ausmus   C   Bats R   Age 33

YEAR	TEAM	LGE	AB	H	DB	TP	HR	BB	SO	R	RBI	SB	CS	OUT	BA	OBP	SLG	EQA	EQR	DEFENSE
1999	Detroit	AL	454	128	25	6	10	46	62	60	53	11	9	335	.282	.364	.430	.265	61	121-C 5
2000	Detroit	AL	519	144	25	3	8	63	69	73	50	11	6	381	.277	.362	.383	.256	63	142-C 13
2001	Houston	NL	421	99	22	4	5	28	64	45	34	4	1	323	.235	.284	.342	.219	34	118-C 11
2002	*Houston*	*NL*	*481*	*125*	*23*	*5*	*7*	*56*	*68*	*60*	*46*	*10*	*6*	*362*	*.260*	*.337*	*.372*	*.236*	*49*	

Ausmus kills the running game, but there hasn't been a lot of evidence to support the claim that he's saving his team runs by how he calls a game. While there's speculation that his lousy season was the product of a first-half eye problem, he was an offensive zero all year except for August, denying the Astros even the little bit of OBP he'd been good for in the recent past. Like Joe Girardi, Ausmus will be around forever, but he's done as a useful offensive player. Consider him a hidden cost of having Jeff Bagwell.

Jeff Bagwell   1B   Bats R   Age 34

YEAR	TEAM	LGE	AB	H	DB	TP	HR	BB	SO	R	RBI	SB	CS	OUT	BA	OBP	SLG	EQA	EQR	DEFENSE
1999	Houston	NL	565	170	28	0	44	142	118	138	121	26	11	406	.301	.450	.584	.338	133	155-1B 3
2000	Houston	NL	586	174	30	1	46	97	106	141	121	8	6	418	.297	.408	.587	.319	120	153-1B 6
2001	Houston	NL	596	172	41	4	38	101	115	126	127	11	3	427	.289	.396	.562	.311	115	157-1B 9
2002	*Houston*	*NL*	*537*	*161*	*32*	*2*	*40*	*110*	*109*	*129*	*114*	*17*	*6*	*382*	*.300*	*.419*	*.590*	*.320*	*111*	

With Alou headed out of town and Biggio not what he was, you would think that Bagwell would be the Astros top dog, but Berkman seems to have already eclipsed him, Bagwell's pronouncements to the contrary notwithstanding. As a ten-and-five guy, he's not going anywhere, and the real problem is that his salary escalates from $8 million in 2002 to more than twice that in 2006. It's possible that Bagwell could retain a significant portion of his value when he's pushing 40, but he's untradeable, and he's going to handicap the front office's ability to pay market rates for other significant talent.

Glen Barker   CF   Bats B   Age 31

YEAR	TEAM	LGE	AB	H	DB	TP	HR	BB	SO	R	RBI	SB	CS	OUT	BA	OBP	SLG	EQA	EQR	DEFENSE
1999	Houston	NL	73	21	1	0	1	11	18	21	10	15	6	58	.288	.388	.342	.266	11	22-CF 1
2000	Houston	NL	67	14	1	1	2	6	21	16	5	8	6	59	.209	.282	.343	.211	6	23-CF 2
2000	New Orln	PCL	108	28	4	0	2	8	12	12	9	8	3	83	.259	.310	.352	.231	11	25-CF 1
2001	Houston	NL	24	2	0	0	0	3	5	5	1	4	6	28	.083	.229	.083	.128	1	12-CF 3
2001	New Orln	PCL	169	45	1	3	2	11	41	24	18	6	3	127	.266	.316	.343	.226	15	42-CF 2
2002	*Houston*	*NL*	*193*	*50*	*5*	*2*	*4*	*19*	*46*	*38*	*23*	*18*	*10*	*153*	*.259*	*.325*	*.368*	*.231*	*20*	

With Daryle Ward likely to move into a starting role in the outfield, Barker might have had a good shot at getting a little more job security in his fifth-outfielder/pinch-runner/defensive-replacement slot. After all, Jimy Williams never did get tired of Darren Lewis. The signing of Brian L. Hunter pushed Barker off of the 40-man roster, but he's just as deserving as Hunter or Lewis of a big-league job.

Lance Berkman OF Bats B Age 26

YEAR	TEAM	LGE	AB	H	DB	TP	HR	BB	SO	R	RBI	SB	CS	OUT	BA	OBP	SLG	EQA	EQR	DEFENSE
1999	New Orln	PCL	227	68	13	0	8	33	43	34	42	6	1	160	.300	.388	.463	.289	36	56-LF -1
1999	Houston	NL	94	23	2	0	4	11	19	10	15	4	1	72	.245	.324	.394	.246	11	23-LF -1
2000	New Orln	PCL	114	35	5	1	5	26	19	15	21	3	3	82	.307	.439	.500	.311	22	25-LF 1
2000	Houston	NL	351	100	23	1	21	51	67	71	62	6	2	253	.285	.377	.536	.298	61	83-RF -2
2001	Houston	NL	572	188	51	5	33	88	103	108	122	7	9	393	.329	.427	.608	.329	122	155-LF -2
2002	*Houston*	*NL*	*510*	*175*	*40*	*4*	*32*	*88*	*99*	*101*	*122*	*14*	*7*	*342*	*.343*	*.440*	*.625*	*.335*	*111*	

By the end of the year, what hadn't Berkman done? Anybody who ropes almost 50 extra-base hits on the road is no creation of his environment. There have been some attempts to label him a platoon hitter, even though he hit .308/.400/.467 against left-handers. He was supposed to be a bad outfielder after spending his college career at first base, but last year the Astros were starting him in center field now and again. He's probably headed to Enron's roomier right field in 2002, because he covers more ground than Ward does. Strap in for an incredible four-year run, and if you hear Berkman can't do something, don't believe it.

Craig Biggio 2B Bats R Age 36

YEAR	TEAM	LGE	AB	H	DB	TP	HR	BB	SO	R	RBI	SB	CS	OUT	BA	OBP	SLG	EQA	EQR	DEFENSE
1999	Houston	NL	643	188	40	0	22	81	99	117	73	24	15	470	.292	.381	.457	.280	97	147-2B 2
2000	Houston	NL	376	98	12	4	8	55	67	63	32	11	2	280	.261	.375	.378	.265	51	96-2B 3
2001	Houston	NL	614	181	34	3	20	62	85	118	70	7	4	437	.295	.379	.458	.281	91	149-2B -13
2002	*Houston*	*NL*	*579*	*161*	*36*	*3*	*17*	*72*	*92*	*104*	*60*	*16*	*7*	*425*	*.278*	*.358*	*.439*	*.263*	*75*	

Last year, we said that Biggio would get back to his '99 levels, while noting that's still below where he used to be. He did, and it is, and the projection above bodes ill for what we should expect in 2002. Biggio was moved back to the leadoff slot in June, but it did not significantly impact the team's runs-scored rates. Questions about whether his wounded knee will let him get back to being an effective second baseman have no easy answers. He's not a good bet to go to third base, and offensively, he wouldn't hold up his end as a left fielder, especially if it meant blocking Daryle Ward and Jason Lane. Unless the Astros make a big mistake, Biggio will be a problem only through 2003.

Eric Bruntlett SS Bats R Age 24

YEAR	TEAM	LGE	AB	H	DB	TP	HR	BB	SO	R	RBI	SB	CS	OUT	BA	OBP	SLG	EQA	EQR	DEFENSE
2000	Martnsvl	App	180	35	7	1	1	18	26	21	12	5	1	146	.194	.281	.261	.197	13	45-SS 0
2001	Round Ro	Tex	510	121	18	2	3	42	77	67	32	15	5	394	.237	.300	.298	.211	40	111-SS 3
2002	*Houston*	*NL*	*459*	*112*	*18*	*2*	*4*	*50*	*72*	*56*	*37*	*16*	*4*	*351*	*.244*	*.318*	*.318*	*.217*	*39*	

Bruntlett was the shortstop on the Stanford team that lost to Skip Bertman's LSU squad in the 2000 College World Series. He's gotten very little attention despite similar skills (speed and defense) to Adam Everett. He's in the same boat that John McDonald is in with the Indians; he can play big-league defense, but he might spend the bulk of his career playing it in the minors.

John Buck C Bats R Age 21

YEAR	TEAM	LGE	AB	H	DB	TP	HR	BB	SO	R	RBI	SB	CS	OUT	BA	OBP	SLG	EQA	EQR	DEFENSE
1999	Auburn	NYP	240	43	7	0	3	15	53	22	18	3	1	198	.179	.233	.246	.169	12	63-C -7
2000	Michigan	Mid	402	89	17	0	9	35	90	40	47	1	2	315	.221	.287	.331	.210	32	100-C -2
2001	Lexingtn	SAL	459	101	15	0	15	28	89	54	49	2	5	363	.220	.272	.351	.207	36	112-C -8
2002	*Houston*	*NL*	*469*	*116*	*17*	*1*	*17*	*44*	*103*	*63*	*64*	*3*	*5*	*358*	*.247*	*.312*	*.397*	*.229*	*45*	

Buck gets good marks for working on his catching, but it's his power potential that makes him a prospect. Having him in the organization made the inclusion of Garett Gentry in the Pedro Astacio deal a little easier to swallow. The jump to Double-A is going to be rough after two years in low-A leagues, especially considering that Buck, who can get overly pull-conscious, did not make big strides in 2001. Given his age, power, and position, he's still a good prospect.

Chris Burke SS/2B Bats R Age 22

YEAR	TEAM	LGE	AB	H	DB	TP	HR	BB	SO	R	RBI	SB	CS	OUT	BA	OBP	SLG	EQA	EQR	DEFENSE
2001	Michigan	Mid	237	54	10	3	2	19	34	30	11	9	5	188	.228	.288	.321	.210	19	55-SS -10
2002	*Houston*	*NL*	*299*	*78*	*13*	*3*	*5*	*27*	*46*	*38*	*28*	*17*	*7*	*228*	*.261*	*.322*	*.375*	*.233*	*30*	

Long before the Astros made Burke their top pick in the 2001 draft out of the University of Tennessee, he was being compared to Craig Biggio. He'll probably end up being moved to second, making it that much cleaner a comparison. Burke made an easy transition to the pro game and hitting with wood, showing patience and the ability to drive the ball well. With experience, he'll add power. Biggio is under contract through 2003, and Burke is the leading candidate to be the starter in 2004.

Vinny Castilla 3B Bats R Age 34

YEAR	TEAM	LGE	AB	H	DB	TP	HR	BB	SO	R	RBI	SB	CS	OUT	BA	OBP	SLG	EQA	EQR	DEFENSE
1999	Colorado	NL	602	146	17	1	30	44	69	71	85	1	3	459	.243	.295	.424	.235	62	153-3B -9
2000	TampaBay	AL	331	77	8	1	7	10	36	22	42	1	2	256	.233	.262	.326	.197	22	83-3B 6
2001	TampaBay	AL	93	22	4	0	3	3	19	7	10	0	0	71	.237	.266	.376	.212	7	24-3B 1
2001	Houston	NL	443	120	25	1	23	30	73	62	81	1	4	327	.271	.320	.488	.260	56	120-3B 2
2002	*Atlanta*	*NL*	*496*	*119*	*18*	*1*	*19*	*39*	*80*	*53*	*70*	*2*	*3*	*380*	*.240*	*.295*	*.395*	*.231*	*49*	

We can understand how time spent with the Devil Rays might suck the will to live right out of you, and the subsequent euphoria of being liberated from that perdition might explain a decent year at the plate. So tip your cap to Vinny Castilla, because in returning to relevant baseball, he gave the Astros a better four-month stretch than anybody really believed he had left in him. Also note that his performance only translated into adequacy. Castilla should be an easy winner of the Gary Gaetti Weasel Pop Award, regressing back to the above projection now that the Braves have thrown oodles of cash his way.

Morgan Ensberg 3B Bats R Age 26

YEAR	TEAM	LGE	AB	H	DB	TP	HR	BB	SO	R	RBI	SB	CS	OUT	BA	OBP	SLG	EQA	EQR	DEFENSE
1999	Kissimme	Fla	439	88	19	1	12	51	101	52	49	9	4	355	.200	.290	.330	.215	38	115-3B -12
2000	Round Ro	Tex	489	125	22	0	22	69	107	71	64	6	8	372	.256	.353	.436	.262	65	136-3B 7
2001	New Orln	PCL	320	93	16	0	20	41	54	56	52	5	3	230	.291	.375	.528	.294	54	76-3B 5
2002	*Houston*	*NL*	*436*	*125*	*20*	*0*	*26*	*58*	*91*	*74*	*76*	*10*	*6*	*317*	*.287*	*.370*	*.511*	*.283*	*67*	

Ensberg broke his left wrist at the end of June, which cost him six weeks and might have saved him from being dangled as trade bait. He bounced back to have a great August and a huge winter season. Although he's not toolsy, his defense has gotten generally good marks. While the Astros are almost falling over themselves denying that they're considering Ensberg their third baseman, don't be surprised if he's starting by May 1. You could make a glib comparison to Sean Berry, because like Berry, Ensberg was relatively old before breaking in. The difference is that Ensberg does everything just a wee bit better than Berry did.

Tony Eusebio C Bats R Age 35

YEAR	TEAM	LGE	AB	H	DB	TP	HR	BB	SO	R	RBI	SB	CS	OUT	BA	OBP	SLG	EQA	EQR	DEFENSE
1999	Houston	NL	325	89	10	0	6	37	62	31	33	0	0	236	.274	.348	.360	.244	35	86-C 4
2000	Houston	NL	218	59	14	0	8	21	41	22	32	0	0	159	.271	.344	.445	.263	28	59-C -4
2001	Houston	NL	153	39	5	0	6	16	29	16	15	0	0	114	.255	.334	.405	.249	18	40-C -1
2002	*Colorado*	*NL*	*267*	*76*	*9*	*0*	*11*	*35*	*53*	*30*	*37*	*0*	*0*	*191*	*.285*	*.368*	*.442*	*.247*	*29*	

No longer an Astro because of the team's decision to sign Gregg Zaun, Eusebio was the senior player in the organization (he signed in 1985). He's a fun player to have around as a right-handed version of Spanky LaValliere. He'll be a valuable backup wherever he lands, and there are several worse catchers playing regularly.

Adam Everett SS Bats R Age 25

YEAR	TEAM	LGE	AB	H	DB	TP	HR	BB	SO	R	RBI	SB	CS	OUT	BA	OBP	SLG	EQA	EQR	DEFENSE
1999	Trenton	Eas	345	83	8	0	9	30	64	44	36	13	4	266	.241	.312	.342	.228	33	98-SS -6
2000	New Orln	PCL	459	108	24	1	5	62	97	70	32	10	3	354	.235	.337	.325	.234	47	123-SS 1
2001	New Orln	PCL	444	106	20	7	4	36	67	61	36	20	5	343	.239	.311	.342	.229	43	113-SS -5
2002	*Houston*	*NL*	*455*	*120*	*23*	*3*	*9*	*55*	*85*	*76*	*46*	*24*	*6*	*341*	*.264*	*.343*	*.387*	*.248*	*52*	

(Adam Everett *continued*)

The defensive wunderkind spent another year at New Orleans, in part because the circumstances for a promotion never developed. After a hot start, Everett sprained his thumb in May. He's shown flashes of on-base skills, so he has more offensive upside than you see here, and he can be a better fit in the #2 slot than Julio Lugo is. Some of his problems at the plate ought to be correctable, especially learning to lay off of pitches low and outside. If he sorts that out, Everett will have an even better shot at winning the shortstop job in camp.

Garett Gentry C Bats L Age 21

YEAR	TEAM	LGE	AB	H	DB	TP	HR	BB	SO	R	RBI	SB	CS	OUT	BA	OBP	SLG	EQA	EQR	DEFENSE
1999	Martnsvl	App	119	20	3	1	1	4	29	8	7	1	0	99	.168	.199	.235	.152	4	18-C -5
2000	Auburn	NYP	238	50	10	0	4	16	31	25	20	2	0	188	.210	.261	.303	.194	16	32-C -7
2001	Michigan	Mid	364	84	13	1	15	28	49	42	62	2	0	280	.231	.292	.396	.230	35	66-C -11
2002	*Colorado*	*NL*	*361*	*103*	*17*	*1*	*14*	*33*	*53*	*49*	*49*	*3*	*0*	*258*	*.285*	*.345*	*.454*	*.241*	*37*	

Gentry generates good power from a quick bat, and if you can put the words "power" and "catcher" together, you've got a prospect. There are concerns about his defense; he has a slow release, but he has put in a lot of work on his throwing and plate blocking. A slight shoulder tear ended his season in August, although he checked out and was made the PTBNL in the Astacio deal. He's an outstanding pickup for the Rockies.

Ramon German 3B Bats B Age 22

YEAR	TEAM	LGE	AB	H	DB	TP	HR	BB	SO	R	RBI	SB	CS	OUT	BA	OBP	SLG	EQA	EQR	DEFENSE
2000	Martnsvl	App	231	51	12	1	4	12	77	22	23	6	5	185	.221	.260	.333	.199	16	40-1B 1 14-3B -1
2001	Lexingtn	SAL	483	102	26	2	9	41	114	53	65	10	6	387	.211	.278	.329	.208	38	122-3B -4
2002	*Houston*	*NL*	*447*	*113*	*28*	*2*	*9*	*43*	*122*	*56*	*53*	*14*	*8*	*342*	*.253*	*.318*	*.385*	*.231*	*44*	

German is part of the organization's "second wave" of Latin American talent, Dominicans coming up behind the front wave of Venezuelans developed by Andres Reiner over the last ten years. German's chief asset is good bat speed, which should lead to more power as he matures. He also made a decent conversion from first base to third base, significantly improving his chances within the organzation. He's not particularly impatient, drawing walks in around 10% of his plate appearances since the start of his career in the Dominican Summer Leagues. He has a lot more upside than the DTs indicate.

Keith Ginter 2B/LF Bats R Age 26

YEAR	TEAM	LGE	AB	H	DB	TP	HR	BB	SO	R	RBI	SB	CS	OUT	BA	OBP	SLG	EQA	EQR	DEFENSE
1999	Kissimme	Fla	386	84	12	2	10	46	101	48	32	5	6	308	.218	.310	.337	.221	35	102-2B -5
2000	Round Ro	Tex	466	133	24	2	20	60	128	80	66	14	7	340	.285	.383	.474	.286	75	122-2B -7
2001	New Orln	PCL	462	118	27	4	14	56	133	66	61	7	5	349	.255	.355	.422	.262	61	84-2B -2 32-LF 0
2002	*Houston*	*NL*	*429*	*121*	*21*	*4*	*16*	*64*	*128*	*76*	*55*	*10*	*6*	*314*	*.282*	*.375*	*.462*	*.274*	*62*	

After warming up at third base in the 2000 Arizona Fall League, Ginter came into camp hacking to try and win the job with the Astros. Even though he had a good camp, the team sent him back to shuttle between second base and left field in Triple-A, as the Astros explored ways to get him to the majors. Ginter generates good opposite-field power from an uppercut stroke, which is probably what you don't want from a right-handed hitter in Enron. To claim a job in spring training, he'd have to outshine Ensberg or hope that Daryle Ward's defense in left field was a complete disaster. With Burke in the system and Biggio locked in for two more years, Ginter's primary value to the Astros is as trade bait, because his future is right now.

Richard Hidalgo CF Bats R Age 26

YEAR	TEAM	LGE	AB	H	DB	TP	HR	BB	SO	R	RBI	SB	CS	OUT	BA	OBP	SLG	EQA	EQR	DEFENSE
1999	Houston	NL	386	88	23	2	16	51	68	48	54	7	5	303	.228	.324	.422	.249	47	107-LF 9
2000	Houston	NL	556	168	40	2	42	48	101	110	111	11	6	394	.302	.376	.608	.311	106	150-CF 20
2001	Houston	NL	509	141	30	3	18	51	91	70	79	3	5	373	.277	.357	.454	.268	70	144-CF 8
2002	*Houston*	*NL*	*484*	*147*	*35*	*2*	*26*	*60*	*92*	*78*	*86*	*9*	*7*	*344*	*.304*	*.381*	*.545*	*.293*	*80*	

Hidalgo is a fixture now, but it took an injury to Roger Cedeno in 2000 to really create the opportunity for him. In prior seasons, Hidalgo had a great reputation as a gamer and a hard worker. Last year, there were some grumbles that he came into camp out of shape after getting his multiyear contract. The grousing looks like it was overstated. Hip, knee, and groin problems hampered him early, and acute tonsilitis left him weak for a stretch in June, and he basically never got comfortable. He's primed for a great bounce-back season.

Royce Huffman 3B Bats R Age 25

YEAR	TEAM	LGE	AB	H	DB	TP	HR	BB	SO	R	RBI	SB	CS	OUT	BA	OBP	SLG	EQA	EQR	DEFENSE	
1999	Martnsvl	App	201	41	9	3	1	17	33	18	17	7	2	162	.204	.270	.294	.199	14	25-3B -1	15-LF -2
2000	Kissimme	Fla	466	117	26	2	5	63	54	61	41	17	4	353	.251	.344	.348	.244	52	64-3B -2	47-2B -6
2001	Round Ro	Tex	518	141	27	1	4	42	91	61	39	9	6	383	.272	.334	.351	.235	51	128-3B -10	
2002	*Houston*	*NL*	*484*	*135*	*27*	*2*	*6*	*57*	*81*	*60*	*50*	*16*	*6*	*355*	*.279*	*.355*	*.380*	*.248*	*55*		

Huffman is a good athlete, having been a punter and punt returner at Texas Christian. He can handle second base or left field (even shortstop in a pinch), and he's made a good impression by working seriously at mastering all of them. He's obviously being groomed as a utility man, but with Jose Vizcaino inked to be the utility infielder, and with both Keith Ginter and Julio Lugo being considered for utility roles as well, Huffman might end up getting no further than did Tim Forkner, a similarly useful positionless OBP guy.

Jason Lane OF Bats R Age 25

YEAR	TEAM	LGE	AB	H	DB	TP	HR	BB	SO	R	RBI	SB	CS	OUT	BA	OBP	SLG	EQA	EQR	DEFENSE	
1999	Auburn	NYP	293	59	10	2	8	24	51	28	33	2	2	236	.201	.264	.331	.201	21	71-1B -12	
2000	Michigan	Mid	524	125	19	0	18	39	101	66	68	10	5	404	.239	.296	.378	.227	49	89-LF -4	23-1B -1
2001	Round Ro	Tex	535	148	25	1	31	50	99	81	94	9	2	389	.277	.350	.501	.280	81	132-LF -2	
2002	*Houston*	*NL*	*512*	*145*	*24*	*1*	*29*	*54*	*102*	*80*	*92*	*11*	*3*	*370*	*.283*	*.352*	*.504*	*.276*	*74*		

Lane was a teammate of Eric Munson and Morgan Ensberg at USC, and you know which one was considered the best prospect in college. Meanwhile, the Astros got a pair of guys who can play in the big leagues. Lane was USC's hero in the 1998 College World Series, pasting a grand slam and winning the championship game as a reliever. Initially, they tried to move Lane to first base, then thought better of it. One corner outfield job is up for grabs, and while the Astros would clearly love to have Daryle Ward add his lefty bat to their predominantly right-handed lineup, a good camp could push Lane into a job-sharing arrangement.

Julio Lugo SS Bats R Age 26

YEAR	TEAM	LGE	AB	H	DB	TP	HR	BB	SO	R	RBI	SB	CS	OUT	BA	OBP	SLG	EQA	EQR	DEFENSE	
1999	Jackson	Tex	447	123	19	3	8	34	55	59	32	16	8	332	.275	.329	.385	.242	48	113-SS -12	
2000	New Orln	PCL	102	30	2	1	3	8	19	17	10	9	5	77	.294	.345	.422	.257	13	17-2B 5	
2000	Houston	NL	420	115	21	4	10	30	85	72	37	20	9	314	.274	.327	.414	.249	49	57-SS -8	43-2B -4
2001	Houston	NL	511	134	18	3	10	43	98	92	36	12	11	388	.262	.324	.368	.233	51	124-SS 2	
2002	*Houston*	*NL*	*460*	*131*	*24*	*3*	*12*	*43*	*91*	*78*	*38*	*23*	*13*	*342*	*.285*	*.346*	*.428*	*.253*	*55*		

Despite dramatic improvements in Lugo's defense this year, his long-term future isn't at shortstop. He has a good arm, but he's never had exceptional footwork, and the Astros have had him play the outfield in spring training in previous seasons. Like Jose Hernandez, there's a chance that he's never going to be appreciated for what he is, either in the field or at the plate.

David Matranga 2B/SS Bats R Age 25

YEAR	TEAM	LGE	AB	H	DB	TP	HR	BB	SO	R	RBI	SB	CS	OUT	BA	OBP	SLG	EQA	EQR	DEFENSE
1999	Kissimme	Fla	484	93	18	2	5	51	133	51	35	9	6	397	.192	.277	.269	.193	33	122-SS 4
2000	Round Ro	Tex	378	78	13	2	5	34	99	39	34	3	3	303	.206	.289	.291	.202	28	109-SS -7
2001	Round Ro	Tex	394	105	26	1	9	37	92	62	47	11	5	294	.266	.340	.406	.253	47	97-2B 10
2002	*Houston*	*NL*	*419*	*111*	*23*	*2*	*12*	*51*	*112*	*65*	*51*	*13*	*6*	*314*	*.265*	*.345*	*.415*	*.252*	*50*	

Matranga is similar to Russ Johnson in that he'd make an excellent utility infielder, the kind you could actually start two or three times per week and get some runs. He slugged over .600 against lefties, not that the Astros need help from the right side of the plate. Matranga deserves more consideration than Royce Huffman because of his defensive skills, getting extremely good marks for his glove work at second base.

Jason Maule IF Bats L Age 24

YEAR	TEAM	LGE	AB	H	DB	TP	HR	BB	SO	R	RBI	SB	CS	OUT	BA	OBP	SLG	EQA	EQR	DEFENSE	
1999	Auburn	NYP	91	15	2	0	0	14	22	7	7	4	1	77	.165	.279	.187	.182	5	25-2B -5	
2000	Michigan	Mid	251	58	8	0	0	32	52	30	18	13	5	198	.231	.320	.263	.214	21	62-2B -8	
2001	Michigan	Mid	424	112	15	3	1	53	68	63	42	26	6	318	.264	.350	.321	.243	46	49-3B 3	47-2B -3
2002	*Houston*	*NL*	*432*	*122*	*18*	*2*	*2*	*59*	*80*	*56*	*55*	*34*	*7*	*317*	*.282*	*.369*	*.347*	*.254*	*51*		

(Jason Maule *continued*)

BP blind spot alert: we love guys who walk, which is why we get excited about hitters like Jackie Rexrode. Even though Maule was repeating the level, and even though he was old for the league, a guy who hits .347, draws a ton of walks, and steals 56 bases in 62 attempts gets our motor running. If Eric Yelding had ever hit this well, people would have gone ga-ga.

Orlando Merced PH Bats L Age 35

YEAR	TEAM	LGE	AB	H	DB	TP	HR	BB	SO	R	RBI	SB	CS	OUT	BA	OBP	SLG	EQA	EQR	DEFENSE
1999	Montreal	NL	194	51	12	1	8	24	25	25	24	2	1	144	.263	.344	.459	.266	26	37-LF -1
2000	Orix	JpP	81	19	3	1	2	2	13	8	13	0	0	62	.235	.253	.370	.205	6	
2000	New Orln	PCL	67	17	1	0	2	1	4	7	13	0	1	51	.254	.265	.358	.202	5	12-RF 1
2001	Houston	NL	136	36	5	1	6	14	27	19	29	5	1	101	.265	.337	.449	.264	18	24-RF -4
2002	*Houston*	*NL*	*179*	*46*	*8*	*1*	*5*	*19*	*31*	*22*	*24*	*6*	*1*	*134*	*.257*	*.328*	*.397*	*.243*	*20*	

Merced gave the Astros exactly what they needed from a pinch hitter, given their right-leaning lineup. Daryle Ward was clearly less comfortable in the role, while Merced led the majors in pinch-hit RBI. There's some credibility to the belief that a veteran spare part can do more for you in the role than a younger player, and when it comes to stocking the last five roster spots on a contender, that sort of thing matters.

Mike Rosamond OF Bats R Age 24

YEAR	TEAM	LGE	AB	H	DB	TP	HR	BB	SO	R	RBI	SB	CS	OUT	BA	OBP	SLG	EQA	EQR	DEFENSE
1999	Auburn	NYP	236	46	6	1	4	14	70	20	14	9	4	194	.195	.243	.280	.184	14	61-CF 6
2000	Kissimme	Fla	459	80	10	4	13	44	167	45	42	10	8	387	.174	.248	.298	.189	30	127-CF 0
2001	Lexingtn	SAL	410	88	14	1	11	27	119	43	38	15	9	330	.215	.266	.334	.204	31	101-CF -7
2001	Round Ro	Tex	109	27	4	1	1	10	27	11	9	2	3	85	.248	.311	.330	.216	9	31-CF 5
2002	*Houston*	*NL*	*474*	*112*	*21*	*3*	*14*	*40*	*155*	*55*	*44*	*21*	*11*	*373*	*.236*	*.296*	*.382*	*.222*	*43*	

Picked in the first round in 1999, Rosamond is an athletic center fielder with a good arm. He gets polite mentions on prospect lists, even though he hasn't earned them. He struggles mightily against breaking stuff, and while he's shown improved patience, he still strikes out a ton and doesn't hit for the kind of power that makes a team put up with his faults. The Astros pushed him up to Double-A to get a sense of whether he'd be worth adding to the 40-man roster, then didn't do so.

Scott Servais C Bats R Age 35

YEAR	TEAM	LGE	AB	H	DB	TP	HR	BB	SO	R	RBI	SB	CS	OUT	BA	OBP	SLG	EQA	EQR	DEFENSE
1999	San Fran	NL	200	56	7	0	6	11	29	21	21	0	0	144	.280	.327	.405	.245	21	52-C -4
2000	ColSprin	PCL	63	16	1	1	2	3	8	5	8	0	1	48	.254	.296	.397	.225	6	12-C 0
2000	Colorado	NL	100	18	3	0	1	5	15	5	11	0	1	83	.180	.225	.240	.160	4	31-C -1
2001	New Orln	PCL	149	47	9	1	5	11	19	19	27	0	0	102	.315	.370	.490	.285	22	41-C 2
2002	*San Fran*	*NL*	*187*	*46*	*6*	*1*	*5*	*16*	*28*	*17*	*21*	*0*	*0*	*141*	*.246*	*.305*	*.369*	*.235*	*19*	

Servais is harder to get rid of than Strom Thurmond, although at least he isn't quite old enough to share stories about his days fighting in the War of Northern Aggression. Servais no longer has the defensive skills of his youth, but there are worse backup catchers with jobs. In terms of accomplishments, Servais topped ten years of service time; he needs to choose his next employer carefully if he wants to add to that.

Bill Spiers IF Bats L Age 36

YEAR	TEAM	LGE	AB	H	DB	TP	HR	BB	SO	R	RBI	SB	CS	OUT	BA	OBP	SLG	EQA	EQR	DEFENSE
1999	Houston	NL	396	115	18	5	4	42	42	54	37	8	5	286	.290	.358	.391	.255	47	59-3B 6 26-LF -5
2000	Houston	NL	353	102	16	3	3	44	35	38	40	6	4	255	.289	.369	.377	.257	43	43-3B 3 23-SS 0

The back injury that shelved Spiers all season forced his decision to retire. Like so many of the prospects coming out of the Brewers' organization in the late '80s, Spiers didn't enjoy a full career, but he didn't wash out either. Gary Sheffield and Greg Vaughn both became stars, and guys such as Spiers, B.J. Surhoff, Dave Nilsson, and John Jaha all had their moments. That they didn't have very many of those moments as Brewers is another issue altogether, one with little relationship to small marketdom.

Jon Topolski Bats L Age 25

YEAR	TEAM	LGE	AB	H	DB	TP	HR	BB	SO	R	RBI	SB	CS	OUT	BA	OBP	SLG	EQA	EQR	DEFENSE
1999	Auburn	NYP	268	47	10	2	1	33	80	27	22	10	8	228	.175	.269	.239	.184	16	59-LF -10
2000	Michigan	Mid	497	98	17	7	2	72	137	57	26	11	13	412	.197	.301	.272	.202	38	129-CF -8
2001	Lexingtn	SAL	580	131	19	3	17	56	136	71	66	13	7	456	.226	.296	.357	.222	53	106-LF 0
2002	*Houston*	*NL*	*491*	*123*	*20*	*5*	*12*	*66*	*132*	*70*	*60*	*20*	*12*	*380*	*.251*	*.339*	*.385*	*.241*	*54*	

One of the only bad things about the Astros' organization is that they don't have a high A affiliate, so they're stuck keeping college hitters like Topolski and Mike Hill in leagues for which they're clearly overqualified. Topolski is a good example of the Astros picking a college senior high (in the fourth round out of Baylor in '99). Some of the selections, such as Morgan Ensberg, push their way into the picture, while the others generally get to be good regulars on competitive minor-league affiliates, costing the Astros little as an organization. Topolski's power is a nice return to his days as a college slugger; Round Rock will make or break him as an organizational soldier and fringe prospect.

Chris Truby 3B Bats R Age 28

YEAR	TEAM	LGE	AB	H	DB	TP	HR	BB	SO	R	RBI	SB	CS	OUT	BA	OBP	SLG	EQA	EQR	DEFENSE
1999	Jackson	Tex	467	115	17	2	21	27	91	59	64	13	6	358	.246	.290	.426	.236	49	118-3B 12
2000	New Orln	PCL	270	74	10	2	2	12	31	26	25	5	2	198	.274	.305	.348	.222	23	62-3B 4
2000	Houston	NL	259	66	14	3	11	6	51	26	55	2	1	194	.255	.283	.459	.241	28	66-3B -1
2001	Houston	NL	136	28	6	1	8	12	32	11	23	1	2	110	.206	.274	.441	.230	14	30-3B -2
2001	New Orln	PCL	322	93	24	4	10	23	60	46	60	9	4	233	.289	.341	.481	.270	44	56-3B -1 27-1B -3
2002	*Houston*	*NL*	*454*	*125*	*23*	*5*	*20*	*35*	*90*	*61*	*76*	*9*	*6*	*335*	*.275*	*.327*	*.480*	*.258*	*56*	

Shame on the Astros for not waiting. Vinny Castilla didn't give them much more than what you could have reasonably expected from Truby. Truby's defense gets favorable reviews, and since he raised his hands at the plate, he's been consistently successful at driving the ball. He's a similar player to Castilla, except that he'll be good for the next few years, while Castilla won't.

Jose Vizcaino IF Bats B Age 34

YEAR	TEAM	LGE	AB	H	DB	TP	HR	BB	SO	R	RBI	SB	CS	OUT	BA	OBP	SLG	EQA	EQR	DEFENSE
1999	LosAngls	NL	269	71	3	0	3	17	21	26	31	2	1	199	.264	.310	.309	.214	21	38-SS -1 21-2B 1
2000	LosAngls	NL	94	20	3	1	0	9	14	9	4	1	0	74	.213	.288	.266	.197	6	13-SS 3
2000	NY Yanks	AL	174	50	7	2	0	9	25	22	10	5	8	132	.287	.322	.351	.221	15	43-2B 3
2001	Houston	NL	255	71	7	3	1	14	28	38	14	3	2	186	.278	.320	.341	.225	22	36-SS -1 12-2B -3
2002	*Houston*	*NL*	*250*	*67*	*7*	*2*	*2*	*20*	*31*	*31*	*22*	*6*	*3*	*186*	*.268*	*.322*	*.336*	*.219*	*21*	

Having Vizcaino around as a veteran caddy for an inexperienced shortstop might make sense, but Julio Lugo has a couple of seasons under his belt, and Adam Everett is as ready as he's going to get. So either Vizcaino's one-year deal for $1.7 million does not bode well for Everett, or it means that the plan to convert Lugo to a utility role will be accelerated. Or perhaps it's just the next best thing to publicly burning currency, because after all, that's still illegal.

Daryle Ward LF Bats L Age 27

YEAR	TEAM	LGE	AB	H	DB	TP	HR	BB	SO	R	RBI	SB	CS	OUT	BA	OBP	SLG	EQA	EQR	DEFENSE
1999	New Orln	PCL	240	79	14	1	22	19	39	46	51	1	1	162	.329	.383	.671	.327	49	59-1B -1
1999	Houston	NL	151	42	6	0	8	7	29	11	29	0	0	109	.278	.310	.477	.256	18	22-LF -4
2000	Houston	NL	264	66	9	2	19	12	56	34	43	0	0	198	.250	.283	.515	.254	32	36-LF -1
2001	Houston	NL	212	56	11	0	10	18	41	21	40	0	0	156	.264	.324	.458	.257	26	37-LF -3
2002	*Houston*	*NL*	*337*	*99*	*18*	*1*	*22*	*30*	*70*	*46*	*62*	*0*	*0*	*238*	*.294*	*.351*	*.549*	*.284*	*51*	

Ward has been ready to be a big-league regular for at least three years, arguably four. It hasn't been until now that he's gotten an opportunity while simultaneously demonstrating a commitment to making himself nimble enough to thunder around the outfield. As a hitter, he may not be as patient as you'd want, but he's really good at keeping his hands back and shifting his weight quickly to drive the ball. Expect him to hold up those rate projections over 500 plate appearances. The question is whether Jimy Williams is the kind of manager who will just let him play and turn a blind eye to his defense. Given Williams's preferences for veterans and glove work, it's doubtful.

Tom Whiteman SS Bats R Age 22

YEAR	TEAM	LGE	AB	H	DB	TP	HR	BB	SO	R	RBI	SB	CS	OUT	BA	OBP	SLG	EQA	EQR	DEFENSE
2000	Auburn	NYP	239	45	9	1	1	12	60	21	14	2	3	197	.188	.228	.247	.164	11	64-SS -14
2001	Lexingtn	SAL	405	100	18	4	12	26	113	41	38	8	8	313	.247	.297	.400	.229	39	105-SS -5
2002	*Houston*	*NL*	*397*	*104*	*22*	*3*	*12*	*33*	*116*	*52*	*45*	*8*	*7*	*300*	*.262*	*.319*	*.423*	*.239*	*42*	

The Astros were already being touted for their shortstops, but they nevertheless nabbed Whiteman in the sixth round of the 2000 draft. He is perceived as more of an offensive player, but he has the physical tools to be a good shortstop, with a good arm and smooth mechanics. Although the Astros are saying they'd like to keep Chris Burke at shortstop, Whiteman might force him to second base.

PITCHERS (ERA: 4.50, H/9: 9.0, HR/9: 1.0, BB/9: 3.0, K/9: 6.0, KW: 2.0, PERA: 4.50)

J.D. Arteaga Throws L Age 27

YEAR	TEAM	LGE	IP	H	ER	HR	BB	K	ERA	W	L	H/9	HR/9	BB/9	K/9	KW	PERA	STUFF
1999	Binghmtn	Eas	29.0	32	21	5	16	15	6.52	1	2	9.9	1.6	5.0	4.7	0.5	7.89	-30
2000	Binghmtn	Eas	115.7	126	60	12	31	47	4.67	6	7	9.8	0.9	2.4	3.7	0.8	5.94	-19
2001	New Orln	PCL	135.7	148	70	14	34	57	4.64	7	8	9.8	0.9	2.3	3.8	0.8	5.06	-11

Stolen from the Mets in the minor-league portion of the 2000 Rule 5 draft, Arteaga does a couple of things well: he throws strikes and keeps the ball on the ground. He couldn't break a grapefruit by throwing it against a wall, but he mixes his curve and change-up effectively. While he's probably doomed to be nothing more than a Triple-A stalwart, he'd be a decent fifth starter on a team that doesn't play in a park with a short porch in left field.

Pedro Astacio Throws R Age 32

YEAR	TEAM	LGE	IP	H	ER	HR	BB	K	ERA	W	L	H/9	HR/9	BB/9	K/9	KW	PERA	STUFF
1999	Colorado	NL	243.7	238	115	32	63	189	4.25	14	13	8.8	1.2	2.3	7.0	1.5	3.98	18
2000	Colorado	NL	207.3	197	97	25	63	172	4.21	12	11	8.6	1.1	2.7	7.5	1.4	3.91	20
2001	Colorado	NL	140.0	137	68	16	45	101	4.37	8	8	8.8	1.0	2.9	6.5	1.1	4.55	13
2001	Houston	NL	28.3	27	9	1	4	15	2.86	2	1	8.6	0.3	1.3	4.8	1.9	2.93	15

Skip Jumbo Wells and Chan Ho Park. If healthy, Pedro Astacio is the top big-ticket free-agent pitcher on the market. That he isn't considered as such says a lot about the disregard for Denver's effect on statistics, although the condition of Astacio's labrum is definitely a source of concern. He was one of the best stretch-drive pickups, right up to the point where he broke down instead of being the veteran ace the Astros so desperately needed. Nevertheless, Astacio was a significant component of the great August run that won the division. If he's healthy, he will be the best free-agent buy.

Kent Bottenfield Throws R Age 33

YEAR	TEAM	LGE	IP	H	ER	HR	BB	K	ERA	W	L	H/9	HR/9	BB/9	K/9	KW	PERA	STUFF
1999	St Louis	NL	193.3	198	102	19	74	112	4.75	10	11	9.2	0.9	3.4	5.2	0.8	3.92	4
2000	Anaheim	AL	131.0	143	81	21	46	74	5.56	6	9	9.8	1.4	3.2	5.1	0.8	4.78	0
2000	Philadel	NL	43.7	44	23	4	17	28	4.74	2	3	9.1	0.8	3.5	5.8	0.8	4.40	6
2001	Houston	NL	50.3	59	39	13	14	31	6.97	2	4	10.5	2.3	2.5	5.5	1.1	7.12	-10

A palate can be defined by what one chooses to taste, so you have to wonder if settling for Bottenfield predetermined the Astros' subsequent interest in Dave Mlicki. I mean, after one aorta-busting Dairy Queen chili cheese dog, what's one more? Bottenfield can be a perfectly acceptable swing man, flitting between fourth starter and closer with aplomb. The shame is that some people thought he'd turned a corner in 1999, when he had simply stayed healthy and gotten good run support. Coming off of shoulder surgery, he's far from being a certain contributor for anybody in 2002.

Doug Brocail — Throws R — Age 35

YEAR	TEAM	LGE	IP	H	ER	HR	BB	K	ERA	W	L	H/9	HR/9	BB/9	K/9	KW	PERA	STUFF
1999	Detroit	AL	80.3	68	28	6	21	77	3.14	6	3	7.6	0.7	2.4	8.6	1.8	2.12	19
2000	Detroit	AL	54.0	51	21	4	11	41	3.50	4	2	8.5	0.7	1.8	6.8	1.9	3.76	7

Brocail was hailed as the middle reliever who would solve all of the Astros' bullpen problems, but instead he became one of those unanswerable "what might have beens," like whether or not Napoleon would have beaten Godzilla in Greco-Roman wrestling. Brocail needed Tommy John surgery before the end of April. The Astros declined his option, and while he might be useful to a team in the second half of 2002, betting on it would be like counting on the big lizard to cover the spread.

Nelson Cruz — Throws R — Age 29

YEAR	TEAM	LGE	IP	H	ER	HR	BB	K	ERA	W	L	H/9	HR/9	BB/9	K/9	KW	PERA	STUFF
1999	Toledo	Int	58.7	62	32	6	23	29	4.91	3	4	9.5	0.9	3.5	4.4	0.6	3.10	-3
1999	Detroit	AL	69.0	71	36	10	19	46	4.70	4	4	9.3	1.3	2.5	6.0	1.2	4.98	-1
2000	Toledo	Int	51.3	60	40	12	18	29	7.01	2	4	10.5	2.1	3.2	5.1	0.8	7.41	-19
2000	Detroit	AL	42.0	39	16	3	11	34	3.43	3	2	8.4	0.6	2.4	7.3	1.5	2.61	11
2001	Houston	NL	77.7	75	36	9	21	60	4.17	5	4	8.7	1.0	2.4	7.0	1.4	4.19	3

Cruz started off the season as the finisher, or what you might consider the anti-closer, the guy brought in when the Astros were losing by a lot. That changed during the course of the season, as it became more apparent how unreliable Mike Jackson was. What do you say about a guy who was great in Enron and awful on the road? Cruz posted a 2.74 ERA in the unfriendly railyard, while getting smacked around for a 5.94 ERA on the road; his home-run rates were one every 15.3 innings at home and one every 4.5 innings on the road.

Octavio Dotel — Throws R — Age 26

YEAR	TEAM	LGE	IP	H	ER	HR	BB	K	ERA	W	L	H/9	HR/9	BB/9	K/9	KW	PERA	STUFF
1999	Norfolk	Int	68.7	61	35	10	32	73	4.59	4	4	8.0	1.3	4.2	9.6	1.1	4.00	29
1999	NY Mets	NL	83.7	78	46	11	41	77	4.95	4	5	8.4	1.2	4.4	8.3	0.9	5.22	16
2000	Houston	NL	129.0	122	72	22	50	126	5.02	6	8	8.5	1.5	3.5	8.8	1.3	4.94	13
2001	Houston	NL	102.7	77	33	4	42	117	2.89	8	3	6.8	0.4	3.7	10.3	1.4	2.81	28

Dotel opened the year in the rotation, then was demoted to the bullpen in May. The argument was that Dotel might not be able to start until he develops a change-up, but the movement on his fastball borders on untouchable, and he has a useful slider and curve. There's nothing wrong with being one of baseball's best relievers, unless it potentially keeps you from being a great starter. Between the Astros' wealth in talented young starters and the chance that Wagner might go away in a huff, we may never get to see how good Dotel would be starting every fifth day. He'll end up really wealthy, regardless; it's just a poor application of resources.

Wayne Franklin — Throws L — Age 28

YEAR	TEAM	LGE	IP	H	ER	HR	BB	K	ERA	W	L	H/9	HR/9	BB/9	K/9	KW	PERA	STUFF
1999	Kissimme	Fla	17.0	15	7	0	9	12	3.71	1	1	7.9	0.0	4.8	6.4	0.7	3.19	-11
1999	Jackson	Tex	45.7	48	27	5	21	24	5.32	2	3	9.5	1.0	4.1	4.7	0.6	2.62	-24
2000	New Orln	PCL	46.7	49	27	6	20	26	5.21	2	3	9.5	1.2	3.9	5.0	0.6	7.04	-26
2000	Houston	NL	23.0	21	10	2	10	19	3.91	2	1	8.2	0.8	3.9	7.4	0.9	5.07	1
2001	Houston	NL	12.3	15	12	3	8	7	8.76	0	1	10.9	2.2	5.8	5.1	0.4	6.31	-32
2001	New Orln	PCL	48.3	51	31	8	23	32	5.77	2	3	9.5	1.5	4.3	6.0	0.7	6.55	-24

There are three kinds of players for whom time has almost no meaning: catchers, knuckleballers, and left-handed relievers. Like Taoists, all they have to do in order to be rewarded is exist. It's been scientifically proven that if you lock an empty room, a year later you'll find a left-handed reliever infestation. Feed them, and they'll live in the room over the garage until they're 38, at which point Tony LaRussa might take them off of your hands.

Carlos Hernandez Throws L Age 22

YEAR	TEAM	LGE	IP	H	ER	HR	BB	K	ERA	W	L	H/9	HR/9	BB/9	K/9	KW	PERA	STUFF
1999	Martnsvl	App	52.7	52	30	5	29	35	5.13	3	3	8.9	0.9	5.0	6.0	0.6	4.53	9
2000	Michigan	Mid	106.3	115	82	19	70	66	6.94	4	8	9.7	1.6	5.9	5.6	0.5	5.99	0
2001	Round Ro	Tex	137.0	131	82	18	81	114	5.39	6	9	8.6	1.2	5.3	7.5	0.7	4.68	20
2001	Houston	NL	16.0	14	6	1	6	14	3.38	1	1	7.9	0.6	3.4	7.9	1.2	0.95	34

Generally ranked behind Wilfredo Rodriguez before this year, Hernandez is a short Venezuelan left-hander. Although his outstanding curve gets the most press, he throws in the low 90s and has a good change-up, so we're not talking about Doug Johns. Brought up in mid-August, he might have been the Astros' savior down the stretch, but he had to sit out the rest of the year after injuring his shoulder diving into second base. In part because it wasn't a pitching injury, he hasn't had surgery, instead spending the winter rehabbing. Considering his age and his history of nagging arm problems, there's a lot to worry about here. He might be good for a few weeks or months, but he will break down.

Mike Jackson Throws R Age 37

YEAR	TEAM	LGE	IP	H	ER	HR	BB	K	ERA	W	L	H/9	HR/9	BB/9	K/9	KW	PERA	STUFF
1999	Clevelnd	AL	67.7	66	35	9	22	54	4.66	4	4	8.8	1.2	2.9	7.2	1.2	3.50	2
2001	Houston	NL	64.3	71	41	12	20	37	5.74	3	4	9.9	1.7	2.8	5.2	0.9	4.39	-14

Jackson's steady transformation from a wild thing with the Phillies (anyone else besides bitter Phillies fans remember his being traded with Glenn Wilson to the Mariners for Phil Bradley?) to one of the game's best setup men in the '90s was one of those good little untold stories of a pitcher's development over time. Jackson has enjoyed a great career. At his age, and after his struggles coming off of shoulder surgery, this might be it.

Brad Lidge Throws R Age 25

YEAR	TEAM	LGE	IP	H	ER	HR	BB	K	ERA	W	L	H/9	HR/9	BB/9	K/9	KW	PERA	STUFF
1999	Kissimme	Fla	20.0	18	10	0	14	12	4.50	1	1	8.1	0.0	6.3	5.4	0.4	4.51	-3
2000	Kissimme	Fla	38.0	41	29	8	20	27	6.87	1	3	9.7	1.9	4.7	6.4	0.7	4.45	-5
2001	Round Ro	Tex	26.3	22	10	2	9	25	3.42	2	1	7.5	0.7	3.1	8.5	1.4	2.36	24

Health problems have been a consistent issue for Lidge, as he's missed most of the past three seasons. Last year, it was shoulder problems that required surgery. Although he can deal in the mid-90s, he's had to change his throwing motion, and he dropped his curve for a slider. Nothing has helped keep him healthy. Lidge is a prospect in the same way that Jeff D'Amico (the big one on the Brewers) is a Cy Young candidate, but he's talented enough to become an outstanding reliever someday.

Scott Linebrink Throws R Age 25

YEAR	TEAM	LGE	IP	H	ER	HR	BB	K	ERA	W	L	H/9	HR/9	BB/9	K/9	KW	PERA	STUFF
1999	Shrevprt	Tex	43.7	51	33	10	15	24	6.80	2	3	10.5	2.1	3.1	4.9	0.8	7.33	-8
2000	Fresno	PCL	59.3	64	35	12	11	39	5.31	3	4	9.7	1.8	1.7	5.9	1.8	5.45	-1
2000	New Orln	PCL	16.3	12	5	0	7	18	2.76	1	1	6.6	0.0	3.9	9.9	1.3	2.56	29
2001	New Orln	PCL	67.7	64	31	5	28	49	4.12	4	4	8.5	0.7	3.7	6.5	0.9	4.17	-1
2001	Houston	NL	9.3	8	4	0	5	7	3.86	1	0	7.7	0.0	4.8	6.8	0.7	3.27	3

Linebrink would be a fine candidate to step into the bullpen and give the Astros a solid reliever at the minimum salary, if Drayton McLane would just let someone as low-profile as Linebrink take the job. He has a moving sinker/splitter combo that would be effective in the majors, but shoulder problems have hampered him in both 1998 and 1999, in part because of a cross-body throwing motion. The longer Gerry Hunsicker pretends that some magic pixie dust makes the likes of T.J. Mathews better than Linebrink, the more McLane's money disappears unnecessarily.

Jim Mann Throws R Age 27

YEAR	TEAM	LGE	IP	H	ER	HR	BB	K	ERA	W	L	H/9	HR/9	BB/9	K/9	KW	PERA	STUFF
1999	Syracuse	Int	63.7	64	45	12	39	56	6.36	2	5	9.0	1.7	5.5	7.9	0.7	4.55	-7
2000	Norfolk	Int	77.3	78	46	11	36	55	5.35	4	5	9.1	1.3	4.2	6.4	0.8	3.51	-13
2001	New Orln	PCL	64.3	63	34	9	22	51	4.76	3	4	8.8	1.3	3.1	7.1	1.2	3.59	-5

If the awful Willie Nelson vehicle *Barbarossa* had a point, perhaps it was as an allegory about the life of a Triple-A closer. After all, is life worth living without a flair for the dramatic, even in the grimiest hovel? Mann is known as something of an intense character. He was born with the knowledge that the play's the thing, and that there is no stage too small on which to star.

Greg Miller Throws L Age 22

YEAR	TEAM	LGE	IP	H	ER	HR	BB	K	ERA	W	L	H/9	HR/9	BB/9	K/9	KW	PERA	STUFF
1999	Augusta	SAL	131.7	139	86	17	76	75	5.88	6	9	9.5	1.2	5.2	5.1	0.5	5.05	5
2000	Kissimme	Fla	138.7	162	106	31	55	71	6.88	4	11	10.5	2.0	3.6	4.6	0.6	5.07	2
2001	Round Ro	Tex	51.0	53	37	5	41	25	6.53	2	4	9.4	0.9	7.2	4.4	0.3	4.32	-11

The other player in the double-Everett deal, Miller throws hard for a left-hander, topping out a little above 90 mph at times. His back caused problems in 2001, but he's supposed to be good to go for 2002. With Carlos Hernandez a serious candidate for a breakdown, Miller is the Astros' best internal option to get a lefty into the fifth starter's slot. It would be a big surprise if he broke camp with the team; if Hernandez has already broken down and Mlicki is inescapably Mlicki-like, Miller might get a look by July.

Wade Miller Throws R Age 25

YEAR	TEAM	LGE	IP	H	ER	HR	BB	K	ERA	W	L	H/9	HR/9	BB/9	K/9	KW	PERA	STUFF
1999	New Orln	PCL	162.3	165	88	18	66	102	4.88	8	10	9.1	1.0	3.7	5.7	0.8	4.96	11
2000	New Orln	PCL	104.7	102	47	8	36	65	4.04	7	5	8.8	0.7	3.1	5.6	0.9	4.20	12
2000	Houston	NL	107.0	104	52	12	35	79	4.37	6	6	8.7	1.0	2.9	6.6	1.1	4.85	17
2001	Houston	NL	198.0	196	102	26	68	147	4.64	11	11	8.9	1.2	3.1	6.7	1.1	3.61	15

Miller should not be relegated to wallflower status just because Roy Oswalt gets all the attention. Miller pumps his four-seamer and his sinker into the 90s, and he has good command of his slider, change-up, and curve. Dierker has worked him hard, but the time Miller has lost has been to non-throwing injuries—finger surgery in '98, getting his hand stepped on last August—rather than arm problems. His raw stats come out looking a little better because he made more starts on the road, so if the 2002 schedule sets him up for a few more home games, his numbers might suffer. Focus on the basics: he's the same pitcher regardless of the changes in his stat line, and he's getting close to being one of the league's best. He pitched five good games, including four quality starts, against the Cardinals last year, which should make for some more divisional fun this year.

Dave Mlicki Throws R Age 34

YEAR	TEAM	LGE	IP	H	ER	HR	BB	K	ERA	W	L	H/9	HR/9	BB/9	K/9	KW	PERA	STUFF
1999	Detroit	AL	198.0	202	97	21	58	118	4.41	11	11	9.2	1.0	2.6	5.4	1.0	4.25	7
2000	Detroit	AL	124.7	136	68	15	36	56	4.91	6	8	9.8	1.1	2.6	4.0	0.8	5.05	-5
2001	Detroit	AL	88.7	102	65	18	39	46	6.60	3	7	10.4	1.8	4.0	4.7	0.6	7.12	-13
2001	Houston	NL	79.7	91	55	15	30	39	6.21	3	6	10.3	1.7	3.4	4.4	0.6	5.15	-11

As you would expect for a guy who was bumped for all sorts of rookies in both Detroit and Houston, Mlicki is at best insurance, if only of the anvil-in-the-parachute variety. Since he's going to earn close to $6 million in 2002 for being little more than an emergency fifth starter, the punishment for acquiring him for last year's stretch run speaks for itself. The Astros would be better off exploring whether they can turn Mlicki's contract into a personal services agreement. Who doesn't need a clean car?

Mike Nannini Throws R Age 21

YEAR	TEAM	LGE	IP	H	ER	HR	BB	K	ERA	W	L	H/9	HR/9	BB/9	K/9	KW	PERA	STUFF
1999	Auburn	NYP	72.7	73	33	5	23	41	4.09	4	4	9.0	0.6	2.8	5.1	0.9	3.13	19
1999	Michigan	Mid	91.0	106	64	16	35	39	6.33	3	7	10.5	1.6	3.5	3.9	0.6	6.80	0
2000	Michigan	Mid	98.3	103	52	9	37	49	4.76	5	6	9.4	0.8	3.4	4.5	0.7	5.17	9
2000	Kissimme	Fla	80.0	85	37	7	17	37	4.16	5	4	9.6	0.8	1.9	4.2	1.1	5.10	10
2001	Lexingtn	SAL	181.7	217	132	39	51	77	6.54	6	14	10.8	1.9	2.5	3.8	0.8	4.91	0

An example of the Astros' willingness to look at a player's skills instead of his packaging, Nannini is another one of Houston's right-handed command pitchers short of six feet tall. Nannini has been throwing in the low to mid-90s since he was a teenager. The Astros have been very careful with him, working to improve his off-speed and breaking stuff. Given his age and his workload, I'd be concerned about a breakdown, although he has demonstrated the kind of command that should have kept his pitch counts down.

Roy Oswalt Throws R Age 24

YEAR	TEAM	LGE	IP	H	ER	HR	BB	K	ERA	W	L	H/9	HR/9	BB/9	K/9	KW	PERA	STUFF
1999	Michigan	Mid	151.7	158	84	16	61	82	4.98	8	9	9.4	0.9	3.6	4.9	0.7	5.47	5
2000	Kissimme	Fla	48.7	47	19	2	14	30	3.51	3	2	8.7	0.4	2.6	5.5	1.1	4.05	14
2000	Round Ro	Tex	128.3	117	43	8	22	98	3.02	10	4	8.2	0.6	1.5	6.9	2.2	2.93	29
2001	New Orln	PCL	31.3	31	15	5	7	24	4.31	2	1	8.9	1.4	2.0	6.9	1.7	5.32	18
2001	Houston	NL	137.0	123	47	11	21	116	3.09	10	5	8.1	0.7	1.4	7.6	2.8	2.85	30

What's better, his mid-90s heat or his jaw-dropping curve? Oswalt is smart, uses both pitches and a change-up effectively, and gives every right-handed pitcher straining to reach six feet reason to believe they can beat scouting biases. If there's a limitation, it's that Oswalt isn't known for sweating the details of fielding or holding runners, but that's small beer. Oswalt was better prepared for the new strike zone than most, because he wasn't shy about working high before last year. Elbow problems cropped up in August before he suffered the strained groin that effectively killed the Astros' season as well as his own. Like Tim Hudson two years ago, Oswalt is about to become one of the best pitchers in the game.

Tony Pluta Throws R Age 19

YEAR	TEAM	LGE	IP	H	ER	HR	BB	K	ERA	W	L	H/9	HR/9	BB/9	K/9	KW	PERA	STUFF
2001	Lexingtn	SAL	127.0	135	105	16	122	70	7.44	4	10	9.6	1.1	8.6	5.0	0.3	5.24	-3

Pluta is that rare bird in the Astros' organization. They didn't nab him from Venezuela or in the late rounds or sign him as a draft-and-follow. He's just a plain old third-rounder worth following. He throws in the mid-90s and can reach higher when he wants. Having pitched regularly only since his sophomore year of high school four years ago, he needs work on his breaking and off-speed stuff. That he is this dominant this soon is a sign that he's going to be something special.

Brandon Puffer Throws R Age 26

YEAR	TEAM	LGE	IP	H	ER	HR	BB	K	ERA	W	L	H/9	HR/9	BB/9	K/9	KW	PERA	STUFF
1999	Clinton	Mid	62.0	64	34	5	30	31	4.94	3	4	9.3	0.7	4.4	4.5	0.5	3.82	-21
2000	Ashevlle	SAL	14.0	22	30	8	17	6	19.29	0	2	14.1	5.1	10.9	3.9	0.2	14.83	-122
2000	Kissimme	Fla	21.7	19	11	0	16	14	4.57	1	1	7.9	0.0	6.6	5.8	0.4	4.05	-22
2001	Round Ro	Tex	76.7	75	46	8	48	53	5.40	4	5	8.8	0.9	5.6	6.2	0.6	2.93	-20

The Astros are always on the prowl for low-cost pickups on the domestic front as well as in Venezuela. Puffer was rescued from the independent leagues after washing out of four different organizations. He throws sidearm, using a good sinker/slider combo, but unlike most sidearmers, he doesn't have serious trouble with left-handed hitters. At Round Rock, he was the setup man for Travis Wade, another indy-league vet. Puffer has been added to the 40-man roster, and while the organization is being cautious, the shortage of experienced and useful right-handed relief might create an opportunity for Puffer in the second half.

Chad Qualls Throws R Age 23

YEAR	TEAM	LGE	IP	H	ER	HR	BB	K	ERA	W	L	H/9	HR/9	BB/9	K/9	KW	PERA	STUFF
2001	Michigan	Mid	159.7	174	84	17	43	69	4.73	9	9	9.8	1.0	2.4	3.9	0.8	5.48	0

Qualls was a second-round pick in 2000 out of the University of Nevada who signed too late to pitch professionally that year. Qualls throws a low-90s sinker, supplemented by a good slider and change-up; he's developing a splitter as well. Working from a three-quarters motion, he's virtually untouchable against right-handed hitters. He doesn't have mechanical problems, and considering his college experience, he should move up to Double-A in 2002, with a good shot at moving up faster than a level per year.

Tim Redding Throws R Age 24

YEAR	TEAM	LGE	IP	H	ER	HR	BB	K	ERA	W	L	H/9	HR/9	BB/9	K/9	KW	PERA	STUFF
1999	Michigan	Mid	104.3	97	65	8	85	81	5.61	5	7	8.4	0.7	7.3	7.0	0.5	6.97	-3
2000	Kissimme	Fla	152.0	145	75	12	70	107	4.44	9	8	8.6	0.7	4.1	6.3	0.8	4.90	13
2000	Round Ro	Tex	22.3	26	25	6	22	15	10.07	0	2	10.5	2.4	8.9	6.0	0.3	4.73	-15
2001	Round Ro	Tex	87.3	80	39	9	30	74	4.02	6	4	8.2	0.9	3.1	7.6	1.2	3.24	23
2001	New Orln	PCL	34.0	32	21	5	21	30	5.56	2	2	8.5	1.3	5.6	7.9	0.7	5.74	14
2001	Houston	NL	55.7	56	32	9	21	44	5.17	3	3	9.1	1.5	3.4	7.1	1.0	5.74	9

Redding can't quite send his seven fielders to the dugout, but he induces so few ground-ball outs that he could probably get by with a catcher and three outfielders. He throws in the mid-90s, mixing in a good slider and a curve that frightens many hitters. Unfortunately, he lacks anything like an effective change-up, a flaw that ought to make him a great candidate for relief work until he masters something off-speed. He'll get a look as the fifth starter, depending on how healthy Carlos Hernandez is and how much Dave Mlicki the Astros can stand.

Shane Reynolds Throws R Age 34

YEAR	TEAM	LGE	IP	H	ER	HR	BB	K	ERA	W	L	H/9	HR/9	BB/9	K/9	KW	PERA	STUFF
1999	Houston	NL	242.7	231	90	22	31	177	3.34	17	10	8.6	0.8	1.1	6.6	2.9	3.97	22
2000	Houston	NL	136.7	142	70	17	37	83	4.61	7	8	9.4	1.1	2.4	5.5	1.1	5.06	6
2001	Houston	NL	178.7	193	87	20	32	82	4.38	10	10	9.7	1.0	1.6	4.1	1.3	4.38	3

Reynolds would be better off in almost any other park. He relies heavily on command of his fastball, and when he's on, he can wipe out left-handed hitters with a great splitter. Since Reynolds doesn't have an off-speed or breaking pitch to consistently freeze righties, Enron's short left-field porch is problematic for him. He's one of the game's great conditioning demons, managing to get back from a December knee injury to pitch by the end of April. Reynolds isn't an ace, and he isn't a workhorse anymore, but he has value as the graybeard/role model for the avalanche of kids.

Wilfredo Rodriguez Throws L Age 23

YEAR	TEAM	LGE	IP	H	ER	HR	BB	K	ERA	W	L	H/9	HR/9	BB/9	K/9	KW	PERA	STUFF
1999	Kissimme	Fla	144.3	144	85	17	75	99	5.30	7	9	9.0	1.1	4.7	6.2	0.7	4.14	16
2000	Kissimme	Fla	50.0	56	45	12	36	34	8.10	1	5	10.1	2.2	6.5	6.1	0.5	6.43	-2
2000	Round Ro	Tex	55.3	64	60	15	52	38	9.76	1	5	10.4	2.4	8.5	6.2	0.4	7.46	-10
2001	Round Ro	Tex	93.0	98	72	16	66	64	6.97	3	7	9.5	1.5	6.4	6.2	0.5	7.17	-13

Talk about cruelty: in his second big-league game, Rodriguez was brought in to face Barry Bonds with Bonds sitting on 69 home runs. Considering he throws hard and doesn't have great command of his breaking stuff, was it any surprise he had a date with destiny? Rodriguez has been one of the most touted prospects in the organization but has fallen well short of the hype. Between nagging injuries and trouble maintaining a consistent release point, he's no further along than he was three years ago. He's in the early phases of a conversion to relief; like most young left-handed flamethrowers, he needs to stay out of the situational role to be successful.

Rodrigo Rosario Throws R Age 22

YEAR	TEAM	LGE	IP	H	ER	HR	BB	K	ERA	W	L	H/9	HR/9	BB/9	K/9	KW	PERA	STUFF
1999	Martnsvl	App	76.7	96	75	22	41	36	8.80	2	7	11.3	2.6	4.8	4.2	0.4	6.97	-9
2000	Auburn	NYP	73.0	83	55	12	40	33	6.78	2	6	10.2	1.5	4.9	4.1	0.4	6.20	-6
2001	Lexingtn	SAL	136.3	149	82	18	51	67	5.41	6	9	9.8	1.2	3.4	4.4	0.7	4.17	0

A non-Venezuelan Latin—yes, the Astros have Dominicans too—Rosario started the year in Lexington's bullpen, then moved into the rotation early in the season. He throws a moving fastball in the low 90s, and he can throw a slurve and change-up for strikes. He has a jangly Oil Can Boyd quality on the mound, all limbs and motion, that should make him hard to hit at every level.

Kirk Saarloos Throws R Age 23

YEAR	TEAM	LGE	IP	H	ER	HR	BB	K	ERA	W	L	H/9	HR/9	BB/9	K/9	KW	PERA	STUFF
2001	Lexingtn	SAL	28.3	27	13	2	10	20	4.13	2	1	8.6	0.6	3.2	6.4	1.0	2.26	2

The Astros' third-round pick in 2001 out of Cal State Fullerton, Saarloos has a good shot at cracking the majors before the end of 2002. After signing somebody like T.J. Mathews, the Astros are still short of relief help, so a good first couple of months in the minors could get Saarloos up by July, which is about when the Astros will need to decide whether to trade for a veteran at the deadline. Saarloos has an outstanding change-up without being a Doug Jones type, so he'll move up fast.

Tom Shearn — Throws R — Age 24

YEAR	TEAM	LGE	IP	H	ER	HR	BB	K	ERA	W	L	H/9	HR/9	BB/9	K/9	KW	PERA	STUFF
1999	Kissimme	Fla	143.3	160	99	24	64	72	6.22	6	10	10.0	1.5	4.0	4.5	0.6	5.95	-1
2000	Round Ro	Tex	134.0	148	92	21	66	71	6.18	5	10	9.9	1.4	4.4	4.8	0.5	5.94	-4
2001	Round Ro	Tex	109.7	103	61	12	62	89	5.01	5	7	8.5	1.0	5.1	7.3	0.7	5.55	0

Another of the Astros' late-round picks, Shearn was nabbed in the 29th round out of an Ohio high school in 1996. Because of the organization's wealth in pitching talent, he's been pushed into a long-relief/swing role. He got a lot nastier as a reliever, although he was also repeating the Texas League. Shearn isn't a top prospect so much as a guy who might turn into a bullpen asset.

Ron Villone — Throws L — Age 32

YEAR	TEAM	LGE	IP	H	ER	HR	BB	K	ERA	W	L	H/9	HR/9	BB/9	K/9	KW	PERA	STUFF
1999	Cincnnti	NL	138.3	132	63	7	61	87	4.10	8	7	8.6	0.5	4.0	5.7	0.7	3.92	5
2000	Cincnnti	NL	143.0	157	91	19	64	68	5.73	6	10	9.9	1.2	4.0	4.3	0.5	5.39	-13
2001	Colorado	NL	48.7	46	25	5	26	39	4.62	2	3	8.5	0.9	4.8	7.2	0.8	5.29	0
2001	Houston	NL	68.3	68	36	10	21	52	4.74	4	4	9.0	1.3	2.8	6.8	1.2	5.69	0

Will Villone ever get put into a role for which he's suited? The question isn't whether he has value, because as a spot starter and left-handed long reliever, he does. A bizarre side effect of the drive towards the 12- and 13-man pitching staff is that it crowds out guys who can handle multiple innings, as the overpropagation of specialists creates demand for even more specialists to compensate for the limitations of the other specialists. Villone is best in a role in which he tosses a hundred innings, and he'd be especially handy on a staff with four or five right-handed starters.

Billy Wagner — Throws L — Age 30

YEAR	TEAM	LGE	IP	H	ER	HR	BB	K	ERA	W	L	H/9	HR/9	BB/9	K/9	KW	PERA	STUFF
1999	Houston	NL	72.3	45	17	5	19	112	2.12	7	1	5.6	0.6	2.4	13.9	2.9	1.59	53
2000	Houston	NL	28.3	28	18	5	15	25	5.72	1	2	8.9	1.6	4.8	7.9	0.8	5.29	-4
2001	Houston	NL	59.3	48	20	4	18	64	3.03	5	2	7.3	0.6	2.7	9.7	1.8	2.55	24

Is Wagner as valuable as he's supposed to be? He reinjured his elbow in June, and while it wasn't related to his 2000 injury, that's two elbow injuries in two years. Worse yet, Wagner has a track record of not coming clean when the elbow gives him trouble. Is a potential employer supposed to just smile and cough up tens of millions of dollars to suit Wagner's fancy while pretending those concerns don't exist? Wagner is expecting Robb Nen money, even though Nen has been significantly more durable.

Mike Williams — Throws R — Age 33

YEAR	TEAM	LGE	IP	H	ER	HR	BB	K	ERA	W	L	H/9	HR/9	BB/9	K/9	KW	PERA	STUFF
1999	Pittsbrg	NL	62.7	54	31	8	31	68	4.45	4	3	7.8	1.1	4.5	9.8	1.1	5.03	11
2000	Pittsbrg	NL	70.7	64	34	7	33	63	4.33	4	4	8.2	0.9	4.2	8.0	1.0	3.85	5
2001	Pittsbrg	NL	40.3	38	22	5	19	35	4.91	2	2	8.5	1.1	4.2	7.8	0.9	3.86	1
2001	Houston	NL	21.0	22	13	2	13	13	5.57	1	1	9.4	0.9	5.6	5.6	0.5	3.77	-15

If there's a pitcher who has contributed more to debunking the perceived value of the closer—besides a desperately old Jeff Reardon—it might be Mike Williams. He went from being a popular organizational soldier with the Phillies to nice fifth starter to steely closer through little more than changes of scenery. Williams is extremely tough on right-handed hitters, but his problems with lefties make him better suited for co-chairman in a bullpen by committee than for relief ace.

Los Angeles Dodgers

At its core, baseball is a pretty simple game. Some of the rules are a little arcane, but by and large, there are two core conflicts, one inside the other.

There's the batter/pitcher matchup, in which one guy tries to get a ball past another guy within a small, haphazardly-defined space. The larger conflict is the game as a whole, where you try to capitalize on the opportunities created by the batter/pitcher conflict to outscore your opponent. The offense uses shrewd baserunning and tactics to play this "outer game"; the defense uses acrobatic moves and deception where it can to prevent runners from scoring. It's simple and somewhat nuanced, and the result is nothing short of a borderline religious experience.

Unfortunately, as happens with most religions, other systems have been built up around baseball's core. The profit motive emerged, and the perceived stakes got higher and higher. The same politics that go on in every business crept into what is basically a kid's game, and the resulting pollution and disturbances inevitably found their way onto the field. For better or worse, baseball has organized itself into franchises, each with its own set of peculiarities, foibles, and strengths that inevitably are reflected by the team on the field.

> **Dodgers Prospectus**
>
> **2001 record:** 86–76; Third place, NL West
>
> **Pythagenport W/L:** 82–80
>
> **Runs scored:** 758 (eighth in NL)
>
> **Runs allowed:** 744 (tied for seventh in NL)
>
> **Team EqA:** .264 (eighth in NL)
>
> **2001 batters age:** 30.1 (sixth-oldest in NL)
>
> **2001 pitchers age:** 29.6 (fourth-oldest in NL)
>
> **Ballpark:** Dodger Stadium; good pitchers' park; Park Factor of .938
>
> **2001:** Jim Tracy did a phenomenal job to keep a flawed team in contention deep into September.
>
> **2002:** They'll be healthier, but it's hard to see how they're going to be much better, unless Tracy really is Joe McCarthy in blue.

The Dodgers have a more complicated situation than most. They're part of the same corporate family as the Fox News Channel and everything else News Corporation owns. There are plusses and minuses to this type of relationship. MLB wanted to be affiliated with a deep-pocketed owner in the media business, particularly in a large and prestigious market such as Los Angeles. Well, MLB got it, along with the turf wars, committees, and petty struggles that come with such an affiliation.

News Corp is in the media business, where operations are largely project-based. There's not really a stable of producers and show developers who are nurtured before getting a chance to put together shows for Fox. Products are pitched to executives, cranked out, and put on the air. If they draw eyeballs, they're hits, and they stay on the air and make money. If not, they're gone, sometimes after as little as one week.

Baseball doesn't work that way. It requires patience and persistence. One of the most important skills a baseball organization can have is the ability to develop talent. It allows for flexibility, both on the field and on the balance sheet. Developed talent can either be deployed on the field, or it can be traded to meet immediate needs.

The Dodgers farm system is completely dead. There's nothing there. Kevin Malone failed to establish a program for identifying and developing talent. The result is a club with many immediate needs working within a corporate culture that demands immediate results and offers little flexibility. You don't need to be an organizational behavior expert to figure out what kind of decisions get made under those circumstances. Bad ones. Bad, expensive ones.

So what happened in 2001? The Dodgers entered the season with the roster and payroll shown in Table 1.

What happens in your company when a manager spends a lot of money on something that ends up being useless or counterproductive? Does the manager say, "Gosh, I blew that, but let's learn from that, and make sure we're smart here. Write off the mistake as a sunk cost, and find the smartest way to do what we need to do from here on out"? Generally, that only happens in a sole proprietorship run by a highly enlightened individual. In the real world, one covers one's booty after such a gaffe. So when a team has really expensive players who are not only easily replaceable, but also downright counterproductive, you nevertheless see them on the field, rending the hope of the hometown faithful like so much flesh from a sacrificial lamb.

Speaking of which, let's examine the Dodgers' center-field situation. Wanting to get younger, Kevin Malone traded 38-year-old Devon White to the Brewers for 34-year-old Marquis Grissom. Grissom cost $1,000,000 more than White in 2001, had piled up an eye-popping number of outs over the previous two seasons, and his offensive skills were nothing

Table 1. Your Opening Day 2001 Dodgers

Kevin Brown	$15,714,286	Mark Grudzielanek	$4,000,000	Chris Donnels	$300,000
Shawn Green	$12,166,667	Tom Goodwin	$3,416,667	Matt Herges	$250,000
Gary Sheffield	$9,916,667	Terry Adams	$2,600,000	Alex Cora	$240,000
Chan Ho Park	$9,900,000	Gregg Olson	$1,750,000	Paul LoDuca	$230,000
Darren Dreifort	$9,400,000	Mike Fetters	$1,725,000	Eric Gagne	$220,000
Carlos Perez	$7,833,333	Adrian Beltre	$1,250,000	Angel Pena	$210,000
Eric Karros	$7,375,000	Chad Kreuter	$900,000	Hiram Bocachica	$200,000
Jeff Shaw	$6,383,333	Dave Hansen	$625,000	Jose Nunez	$200,000
Andy Ashby	$6,000,000	Tim Bogar	$525,000	Luke Prokopec	$200,000
Marquis Grissom	$5,000,000	Jeff Reboulet	$450,000		

but a fading memory. No one in the United States except Kevin Malone and Mama Grissom would possibly have given him a job, much less allowed him to amass 425 outs. Of course, the other center-field option is noted run producer Tom Goodwin, who wasn't even that good during his one good season, several years ago. He's also signed to a contract that probably made his agent do a spit take in joyful disbelief when the Rockies tendered the offer.

The other outfield spots are manned by two of the best hitters in baseball, Shawn Green and Gary Sheffield. Both are excellent players, but both also cost a great deal of money. The result is an outfield with a total salary that exceeds the payroll of a number of small-market teams, an outfield that would have been better, and much less expensive, by the simple exclusion of Grissom and Goodwin.

The infield isn't exactly the Garden of Eden, either. Adrian Beltre's freak appendix problems are now a thing of the past, and there's every reason to believe that he'll soon be part of an amazing cohort of third basemen. At catcher, there's an overnight sensation who surprised everyone and helped keep the club above water last year. Paul LoDuca is not young, and he may not repeat his performance. Those are the high points. There's also Alex Cora, a prototypical good-field/no-hit shortstop who might be a little light on the fielding, but at least he doesn't cost much. He's also not going to push a team towards a title. At second base, Mark Grudzielanek is a serviceable, if unspectacular, second baseman who can help a championship club in a supporting role, but that's pretty much the limit of his ability. Receiving throws from all these guys is first baseman Eric Karros, an aging mediocrity whose offense has fallen below that of a number of Triple-A first basemen.

All told, the Dodgers paid a fortune for a middle-of-the-pack offense, and even that performance required career years from Green and LoDuca.

How about the pitching staff? Kevin Brown is three years into his historic contract, but he's a top-tier pitcher, so his contract is at least excusable. Given Darren Dreifort's track record when the Dodgers handed him a five-year, $55-million deal, you have wonder not only what Kevin Malone was thinking, but also how you can get Scott Boras to negotiate your next pay raise. Dreifort had never thrown more than 199 innings in a season, had a long and terrifying injury history, and, quite honestly, had never really come close to performing like a #1 starter. What on god's green Earth convinced the Dodgers to sign him to that kind of deal, especially when the insurance on the contract would be limited and difficult to get? Chan Ho Park was under contract for 2001 at $9.9 million, or about .9 Dreifort. To fill the other rotation spots, the Dodgers signed Andy Ashby, he of the declining strikeout rate, to a three-year deal starting at $5.5 million in 2001. Beyond that, Tracy filled out the rotation with a bargain-basement youngster, either Eric Gagne or Luke Prokopec, depending on which one was hot at any given time.

The rotation sounded good in March; by June, the sounds were elbows a'poppin'. Dreifort and Ashby missed the bulk of the season, with Dreifort undergoing his second Tommy John surgery. Brown's elbow got torn up in September, and he pitched through the pain for a couple of starts before undergoing surgery after the Dodgers finally gave up on the pennant race. The bullpen survived, thanks to some journeyman work and a couple of role players from surprising places.

After a couple of particularly embarrassing incidents, the sheriff was finally run out of town on a rail. Malone's mouth was more prominent than his actual performance, and the Dodgers eventually replaced him with Dan Evans from the Chicago White Sox organization. The News Corp brass is hoping that the Dodgers can emulate some of the player-development success of the White Sox. The minor-league performances of several Dodgers prospects were nothing short of depressing, with only Chin-Feng Chen as any sort of bright spot. Everywhere else in the farm system, there's pretty much no good news to be had.

The amazing part of the Dodgers' 2001 season is that despite the team's lack of concern about costs or return on investment, despite a player-development system that makes Branch Rickey spin and cry out in his grave, despite a full season of the G&G boys in center field, and despite more bad performances in the front office than in a Mario Van Peebles film, the Dodgers were in the race until the season's very last weekend.

For this, we offer some fair amount of credit to new manager Jim Tracy. Tracy dealt with everything from Gary Sheffield's spring-training litany of whining about his financial future to Kevin Malone's overdue firing in May. In between, he juggled the bullpen well, allowed LoDuca to emerge from his cocoon, insulated his players from the malaise and intrigue of the front office, and went about his business in a relatively quiet and professional manner. This was a nice change from the usual modus operandi of the Dodgers front office.

From here, his job gets harder. Going into the 2002 season, the Dodgers face some challenges:

- 3 pitchers coming off of surgery whose combined salary is comparable to the GNP of Chad
- A virtual prison of contract commitments to bad offensive players
- A player-development apparatus best described as "Bonifesque"
- News Corp execs floating trial balloons about wanting to get out of the baseball business

Balanced against those challenges are a few important strengths:

- Two of the best hitters in baseball in Green and Sheffield
- A catcher who may provide a sustained advantage over the competition
- Deep enough pockets to simply spend their way through rough patches
- A promising manager in Jim Tracy
- One prospect who can probably hit, but who can't play defense

All that should keep Tracy and Evans busy for at least the next few months. Add in all the exciting meetings the Commissioner's likely to call regarding labor negotiations and intra-MLB squabbling, and it should be an interesting year or three. The intrigue and constant change endemic to News Corp should give the whole situation a certain zest.

Fortunately, the Dodgers find themselves in a competitive environment that's on the soft side. The Diamondbacks have little hope in the minors, the Giants even less. The Dodgers are actually somewhat spry compared to those two, and they may get lucky in terms of health. It's possible that Kevin Brown and Andy Ashby could be healthy; it's less likely that Pedro Feliz and Benito Santiago will be good.

It's a race to the bottom in the NL West, and everyone appears to be tunnelling diligently. None of the top three teams in the division really has much help coming up in the farm system, and both the Giants and D'Backs have significant financial constraints. The Dodgers' best short-term hope is to start spending money repairing Kevin Malone's mess on the player-development side, and to bite the bullet and pay for some short-term talent at the big-league level. Here's a hint for new GM Dan Evans—avoid out-munching center fielders.

HITTERS (BA: .270, OBP: .340, SLG: .440, EqA: .260)

Luke Allen RF Bats L Age 23

YEAR	TEAM	LGE	AB	H	DB	TP	HR	BB	SO	R	RBI	SB	CS	OUT	BA	OBP	SLG	EQA	EQR	DEFENSE
1999	SanAnton	Tex	539	134	13	8	12	33	105	71	63	9	5	410	.249	.293	.369	.222	48	133-3B -34
2000	SanAnton	Tex	344	81	14	3	6	28	71	43	46	9	4	267	.235	.294	.346	.219	30	86-3B -9
2001	Jacksnvl	Sou	493	126	27	4	13	32	109	63	59	9	3	370	.256	.302	.406	.236	50	119-RF -5
2002	*LosAngls*	*NL*	*479*	*130*	*22*	*5*	*15*	*45*	*109*	*74*	*69*	*9*	*3*	*352*	*.271*	*.334*	*.432*	*.265*	*64*	

Allen is probably the Dodgers' second-best prospect above rookie ball. His defense at third base was somewhat reminiscent of a three-legged yak on Demerol, so the Dodgers moved him to the OF, and he responded with a very respectable year. He showed good power and speed, and coaches liked the way he was able to grind through slumps with careful and diligent work on his swing. Allen will begin the year in Triple-A and will have a shot to break camp with the Dodgers in 2003.

Bruce Aven OF Bats R Age 30

YEAR	TEAM	LGE	AB	H	DB	TP	HR	BB	SO	R	RBI	SB	CS	OUT	BA	OBP	SLG	EQA	EQR	DEFENSE
1999	Florida	NL	384	112	17	2	13	39	76	57	68	3	0	272	.292	.370	.448	.276	55	87-LF -3
2000	Pittsbrg	NL	149	37	7	0	6	3	28	17	25	2	3	115	.248	.263	.416	.218	13	29-OF -2
2000	Albuquer	PCL	31	7	1	0	0	5	6	5	2	0	0	24	.226	.333	.258	.215	3	
2000	LosAngls	NL	20	5	0	0	2	3	7	2	4	0	0	15	.250	.348	.550	.288	3	
2001	LasVegas	PCL	288	65	9	0	8	22	54	34	27	4	1	224	.226	.288	.340	.215	24	67-LF -3
2001	LosAngls	NL	24	9	2	0	1	0	4	3	2	0	0	15	.375	.412	.583	.323	4	
2002	*LosAngls*	*NL*	*332*	*87*	*13*	*1*	*11*	*33*	*70*	*44*	*48*	*4*	*2*	*247*	*.262*	*.329*	*.407*	*.255*	*41*	

Aven is the type of player who can fill a platoon/pinch-hitter role fairly inexpensively. He has some sock, and in what amounts to one full season in the bigs, has hit .277/.344/.441 despite playing in some pretty bad hitters' parks. While most clubs like to get more defense than this from their 24th or 25th guy, Aven would be better on the bench than at least two dozen guys who have regular big-league jobs.

Adrian Beltre 3B Bats R Age 23

YEAR	TEAM	LGE	AB	H	DB	TP	HR	BB	SO	R	RBI	SB	CS	OUT	BA	OBP	SLG	EQA	EQR	DEFENSE
1999	LosAngls	NL	544	153	27	5	16	55	97	83	66	15	7	398	.281	.354	.438	.266	72	148-3B -6
2000	LosAngls	NL	518	155	29	2	21	49	73	71	85	12	5	368	.299	.362	.485	.280	76	135-3B 4
2001	LosAngls	NL	480	136	23	4	14	25	70	63	64	13	4	348	.283	.324	.435	.253	56	124-3B -2
2002	*LosAngls*	*NL*	*545*	*162*	*30*	*4*	*16*	*48*	*88*	*81*	*72*	*19*	*5*	*388*	*.297*	*.354*	*.455*	*.281*	*81*	

A couple of things that should scare Dodgers opponents: first, Beltre may be a year younger than indicated. Second, despite undergoing two surgeries related to his appendix, Beltre came back relatively quickly and demonstrated a full skill set, hitting for average and power, drawing walks, stealing bases, and playing very good defense. He never showed all his skills at the same time, but that consolidation will definitely come. The Dodgers have not yet signed Beltre to a long-term contract. He is arbitration-eligible, so this is their very last shot at signing him at a reasonable cost. He will be one of the big four or five third basemen in baseball for the next several years, along with Eric Chavez, Troy Glaus, and Hank Blalock. Beltre will end up underrated if he stays in Chavez Ravine.

Hiram Bocachica 2B Bats R Age 26

YEAR	TEAM	LGE	AB	H	DB	TP	HR	BB	SO	R	RBI	SB	CS	OUT	BA	OBP	SLG	EQA	EQR	DEFENSE
1999	SanAnton	Tex	485	124	20	6	9	47	73	65	46	19	10	371	.256	.332	.377	.242	54	121-2B -14
2000	Albuquer	PCL	471	130	28	2	19	29	97	74	61	7	10	351	.276	.332	.465	.258	59	115-2B -12
2001	LosAngls	NL	134	34	12	1	2	9	28	16	10	4	1	101	.254	.304	.403	.239	14	14-2B -2
2002	*LosAngls*	*NL*	*396*	*106*	*22*	*3*	*11*	*37*	*83*	*58*	*41*	*14*	*9*	*299*	*.268*	*.330*	*.422*	*.259*	*51*	

Bocachica has been around so long as a borderline prospect that it's hard to believe he's just 26. A similar player to Mark Grudzielanek, his defense has been the primary impediment to him having a greater role in the bigs. If he gets 300 at-bats, he could post something in the .270/.330/.440 range, even in Dodger Stadium. A utility guy who can do that would fill a big gap for the Dodgers.

Chin-Feng Chen LF Bats R Age 24

YEAR	TEAM	LGE	AB	H	DB	TP	HR	BB	SO	R	RBI	SB	CS	OUT	BA	OBP	SLG	EQA	EQR	DEFENSE
1999	San Bern	Cal	508	125	17	4	21	51	131	61	73	16	5	388	.246	.318	.419	.248	59	111-LF -5
2000	SanAnton	Tex	524	128	24	2	5	42	132	51	51	14	10	406	.244	.302	.326	.216	44	127-LF 2
2001	Vero Bch	Fla	240	54	11	2	4	20	60	29	29	1	0	186	.225	.292	.338	.215	20	11-LF 1
2001	Jacksnvl	Sou	230	62	12	1	13	33	64	38	38	3	3	171	.270	.364	.500	.282	36	49-LF -3
2002	*LosAngls*	*NL*	*462*	*119*	*20*	*2*	*16*	*62*	*130*	*60*	*64*	*13*	*5*	*348*	*.258*	*.345*	*.413*	*.266*	*64*	

No one who's seen Chen play likes his defense, but everyone likes his stroke. When it's working, his stroke is unbelievably quick, somewhat reminiscent of Mark McGwire's. The bat doesn't travel very far, and it comes down through the bottom-center of the ball, creating vicious line drives with a ton of backspin that makes the ball just take off. His defensive statistics aren't really that bad, yet we can't find one person to say anything good about his glove work, and the Dodgers already have him DHing a little in the minors. They should give him a shot to take Eric Karros's job, but they won't, given the contract Karros signed.

McKay Christensen CF Bats L Age 26

YEAR	TEAM	LGE	AB	H	DB	TP	HR	BB	SO	R	RBI	SB	CS	OUT	BA	OBP	SLG	EQA	EQR	DEFENSE
1999	Birmnghm	Sou	297	77	8	5	2	22	47	41	22	11	4	224	.259	.320	.340	.230	28	74-CF 4
1999	ChiSox	AL	53	13	1	0	1	3	6	10	6	2	1	41	.245	.286	.321	.209	4	17-CF -1
2000	Charlott	Int	338	85	11	1	6	26	50	42	25	22	6	258	.251	.306	.343	.229	32	83-CF -6
2001	Charlott	Int	276	71	14	5	7	29	48	49	23	13	3	208	.257	.331	.420	.256	34	68-CF -3
2001	LasVegas	PCL	56	12	0	1	1	5	10	7	3	3	1	45	.214	.286	.304	.210	5	15-CF -1
2001	LosAngls	NL	50	18	2	0	1	2	8	7	8	3	2	34	.360	.411	.460	.290	8	12-CF -3
2002	*LosAngls*	*NL*	*382*	*98*	*16*	*4*	*8*	*35*	*69*	*65*	*34*	*14*	*4*	*288*	*.257*	*.319*	*.382*	*.248*	*44*	

Acquired from the ChiSox for long-shot pitching prospect Wade Parrish, Christensen was basically brought up to cover for Marquis Grissom while Grissom served a suspension, and he saw little action outside of that. Christensen's upside is a fourth outfielder on a team that needs a lefty pinch hitter and a good glove. He fits here.

Alex Cora SS Bats L Age 26

YEAR	TEAM	LGE	AB	H	DB	TP	HR	BB	SO	R	RBI	SB	CS	OUT	BA	OBP	SLG	EQA	EQR	DEFENSE
1999	Albuquer	PCL	293	77	9	5	3	10	34	39	27	7	4	220	.263	.299	.358	.222	26	76-SS -2
1999	LosAngls	NL	30	5	2	0	0	0	4	2	3	0	0	25	.167	.193	.233	.146	1	
2000	Albuquer	PCL	107	35	7	2	0	4	10	13	15	3	2	74	.327	.360	.430	.263	13	30-SS -3
2000	LosAngls	NL	358	88	20	6	4	22	49	40	32	4	1	271	.246	.301	.369	.227	33	97-SS -9
2001	LosAngls	NL	409	98	21	3	4	29	49	42	32	0	2	313	.240	.300	.335	.215	34	116-SS -1
2002	*LosAngls*	*NL*	*427*	*107*	*22*	*5*	*5*	*34*	*57*	*55*	*41*	*5*	*3*	*323*	*.251*	*.306*	*.361*	*.232*	*42*	

Cora is best suited for a bench role. He's quick enough to play shortstop and second base, has enough of an arm to play third base, and the one thing he can do at the plate is make contact. He makes a terrible regular and could lose his job to Cesar Izturis this spring. Explain again how this team stayed in contention until the final couple weeks of the season?

Bubba Crosby CF Bats L Age 25

YEAR	TEAM	LGE	AB	H	DB	TP	HR	BB	SO	R	RBI	SB	CS	OUT	BA	OBP	SLG	EQA	EQR	DEFENSE
1999	San Bern	Cal	369	86	16	1	1	28	72	34	24	10	5	288	.233	.292	.290	.204	27	86-CF -3
2000	Vero Bch	Fla	278	60	10	4	7	22	45	34	35	14	7	225	.216	.282	.356	.218	25	68-LF -7
2001	Jacksnvl	Sou	390	104	18	4	5	29	59	56	39	14	5	291	.267	.324	.372	.239	41	100-LF -1
2001	LasVegas	PCL	41	7	2	1	0	1	7	4	4	1	1	35	.171	.190	.268	.155	2	12-CF 3
2002	*LosAngls*	*NL*	*403*	*99*	*16*	*4*	*6*	*37*	*71*	*51*	*39*	*22*	*8*	*312*	*.246*	*.309*	*.350*	*.236*	*42*	

Highly touted coming out of Rice, Crosby hasn't adjusted to pro ball as well as the Dodgers hoped he would. His bat speed has really disappointed scouts. Crosby was pretty much an average hitter in the Southern League this year, and he'll begin his age-25 season in Triple-A. In reality, he's probably a better option for center field in Dodger Stadium than Grissom and Goodwin are. If he hits at all early in the season, look for him to get a shot with the big club.

Tom Goodwin CF Bats L Age 33

YEAR	TEAM	LGE	AB	H	DB	TP	HR	BB	SO	R	RBI	SB	CS	OUT	BA	OBP	SLG	EQA	EQR	DEFENSE
1999	Texas	AL	401	106	12	6	3	36	54	60	31	37	11	306	.264	.325	.347	.239	43	105-CF 0
2000	Colorado	NL	308	73	8	6	4	44	70	55	37	33	7	241	.237	.334	.341	.247	36	85-CF 1
2000	LosAngls	NL	214	56	3	1	1	15	38	29	11	16	3	161	.262	.310	.299	.222	19	55-CF 6
2001	LosAngls	NL	289	72	11	5	4	21	49	55	24	22	8	225	.249	.300	.363	.230	28	71-CF -2
2002	*LosAngls*	*NL*	*443*	*101*	*14*	*6*	*5*	*47*	*86*	*70*	*34*	*42*	*12*	*353*	*.228*	*.302*	*.321*	*.232*	*46*	

All that production for only $3.4 million? That hardly seems fair. Note the cool, consistent OBPs, the soporific slugging, the prodigious out-making capability. No sane team would have both Goodwin and Marquis Grissom on the same field. It's hard to blame Jim Tracy when he's been handed such ballplayers. The Dodgers center fielders would be good fourth outfielders in an independent league.

Shawn Green RF Bats L Age 29

YEAR	TEAM	LGE	AB	H	DB	TP	HR	BB	SO	R	RBI	SB	CS	OUT	BA	OBP	SLG	EQA	EQR	DEFENSE
1999	Toronto	AL	607	192	37	1	46	60	103	130	121	19	7	422	.316	.387	.608	.316	119	149-RF 0
2000	LosAngls	NL	619	172	45	4	25	82	111	98	99	23	5	452	.278	.369	.485	.286	99	151-RF -7
2001	LosAngls	NL	626	197	34	4	51	69	91	129	132	20	4	433	.315	.386	.626	.322	127	159-RF -1
2002	*LosAngls*	*NL*	*557*	*164*	*31*	*3*	*38*	*72*	*95*	*111*	*105*	*19*	*4*	*397*	*.294*	*.375*	*.566*	*.314*	*110*	

We wonder if Cito Gaston thinks Green is ready to play every day yet. He's a solid defensive outfielder, one of the best offensive performers in baseball, durable, good with the fans, and possesses a swing that's beautiful to watch. Despite Bud Selig, Carl Pohlad, $15 parking, Carl Everett, and Bermanisms, this is a great era in which to be a baseball fan. Green will hit for more power than the projection above indicates.

Marquis Grissom CF Bats R Age 35

YEAR	TEAM	LGE	AB	H	DB	TP	HR	BB	SO	R	RBI	SB	CS	OUT	BA	OBP	SLG	EQA	EQR	DEFENSE
1999	Milwauke	NL	605	160	24	1	21	42	101	88	79	20	6	451	.264	.312	.412	.244	66	145-CF -3
2000	Milwauke	NL	600	145	18	2	14	31	91	64	59	18	10	465	.242	.279	.348	.212	48	139-CF 2
2001	LosAngls	NL	452	109	19	1	22	14	91	61	64	7	5	348	.241	.266	.434	.227	43	108-CF 1
2002	*LosAngls*	*NL*	*539*	*122*	*15*	*1*	*22*	*43*	*105*	*71*	*67*	*15*	*8*	*425*	*.226*	*.284*	*.380*	*.229*	*53*	

There is absolutely no reason for Marquis Grissom to be in the major leagues. There are dozens of guys in the minors with similar or superior skills, and when you consider that he cost the Dodgers $5 million during the 2001 season, it makes you wonder why Kevin Malone was given the GM job in the first place. When you start making decisions like that, you should spend less time around offices and more time around padded walls and noisy baubles from Fisher-Price. Whoo-ee! Look at that out column! Them's good eatin'.

Mark Grudzielanek 2B Bats R Age 32

YEAR	TEAM	LGE	AB	H	DB	TP	HR	BB	SO	R	RBI	SB	CS	OUT	BA	OBP	SLG	EQA	EQR	DEFENSE
1999	LosAngls	NL	494	164	23	5	8	25	60	73	46	5	6	336	.332	.376	.447	.274	66	113-SS -4
2000	LosAngls	NL	626	181	38	6	7	37	74	102	49	11	3	448	.289	.337	.403	.250	70	146-2B -8
2001	LosAngls	NL	544	158	21	3	14	26	70	88	59	4	4	390	.290	.333	.417	.249	61	132-2B -3
2002	*LosAngls*	*NL*	*535*	*143*	*26*	*4*	*10*	*39*	*72*	*80*	*44*	*8*	*4*	*396*	*.267*	*.317*	*.387*	*.244*	*58*	

Grudzielanek is a consistent, average ballplayer. If he is the sixth- or seventh-best player on the field at any given time, the team has a shot to make the playoffs and advance. He tore a ligament in his left ankle in June and never fully recovered, fading badly after the All-Star break. He can still help a club in the right circumstances, but you wouldn't want him under contract for more than a year.

Dave Hansen PH/3B Bats L Age 33

YEAR	TEAM	LGE	AB	H	DB	TP	HR	BB	SO	R	RBI	SB	CS	OUT	BA	OBP	SLG	EQA	EQR	DEFENSE
1999	LosAngls	NL	108	28	9	1	2	25	19	14	17	0	0	80	.259	.407	.417	.286	18	
2000	LosAngls	NL	123	37	6	2	8	24	29	18	25	0	1	87	.301	.415	.577	.318	25	
2001	LosAngls	NL	142	36	9	0	3	31	25	14	23	0	1	107	.254	.387	.380	.266	20	20-1B -1 14-3B 3
2002	*LosAngls*	*NL*	*165*	*40*	*8*	*1*	*6*	*36*	*34*	*19*	*27*	*0*	*1*	*126*	*.242*	*.378*	*.412*	*.279*	*26*	

Not a career wasted, per se, but an opportunity missed. Hansen has always been good enough to play more, but he got typecast as "too valuable on the bench" very early in his career. He's a disciplined hitter with power, and he'd help the Dodgers considerably if they would find him another 150 plate appearances at the expense of one of the lead weights, such as Eric Karros, who trudged to the batter's box in 2001.

Phil Hiatt 3B/1B Bats R Age 33

YEAR	TEAM	LGE	AB	H	DB	TP	HR	BB	SO	R	RBI	SB	CS	OUT	BA	OBP	SLG	EQA	EQR	DEFENSE
1999	Indianap	Int	311	69	7	0	16	25	97	38	44	0	0	242	.222	.283	.399	.226	29	35-1B 3 16-LF 1
2000	ColSprin	PCL	493	129	23	1	28	48	144	77	76	10	2	366	.262	.332	.483	.268	68	117-1B -4
2001	LasVegas	PCL	428	124	22	3	34	47	99	84	76	5	3	307	.290	.364	.593	.303	78	84-3B -3 16-1B -3
2001	LosAngls	NL	50	13	3	0	2	3	16	6	6	0	0	37	.260	.302	.440	.243	5	
2002	*LosAngls*	*NL*	*427*	*109*	*20*	*2*	*27*	*49*	*122*	*71*	*70*	*7*	*2*	*320*	*.255*	*.332*	*.501*	*.281*	*67*	

Yes, that's Phil Hiatt, here to demonstrate that the difference between someone like him and Eric Karros is, well, several million bucks, but nothing in terms of performance. Hiatt is a perfect example of a "replacement level" player—one available for little or no cost, capable of saving the Dodgers $7 million to be spent on better players.

Eric Karros 1B Bats R Age 34

YEAR	TEAM	LGE	AB	H	DB	TP	HR	BB	SO	R	RBI	SB	CS	OUT	BA	OBP	SLG	EQA	EQR	DEFENSE
1999	LosAngls	NL	585	182	32	0	38	46	110	74	112	7	5	408	.311	.383	.561	.296	97	145-1B 7
2000	LosAngls	NL	593	153	26	0	33	55	112	84	106	4	3	443	.258	.325	.469	.260	76	149-1B 10
2001	LosAngls	NL	442	112	17	0	18	39	86	44	69	3	1	331	.253	.317	.414	.244	49	111-1B 7
2002	*LosAngls*	*NL*	*547*	*137*	*21*	*1*	*26*	*57*	*114*	*62*	*83*	*6*	*3*	*413*	*.250*	*.321*	*.435*	*.259*	*71*	

Karros is an underrated defensive first baseman, but he is nevertheless a sinkhole on a team with playoff aspirations. He hasn't hit well since 1999, he's never drawn many bases on balls, never really hit for average, and had problems with his back in 2001. Considering his age and likely cost, he's someone the Dodgers should be looking to upgrade at the first opportunity. The Dodgers would be better off with Dave Hansen playing first base full-time. Inexplicably, Karros is signed through 2003 for $24 million, with a $9 million option for 2004 that kicks in if he gets to the plate 500 times in 2003. Dodger fans, you may commence abdominal cramping.

Chad Kreuter C Bats B Age 37

YEAR	TEAM	LGE	AB	H	DB	TP	HR	BB	SO	R	RBI	SB	CS	OUT	BA	OBP	SLG	EQA	EQR	DEFENSE
1999	KansasCy	AL	321	74	10	0	7	31	57	30	35	0	0	247	.231	.309	.327	.219	28	87-C 2
2000	LosAngls	NL	215	58	11	0	7	52	44	32	28	1	0	157	.270	.416	.419	.291	36	67-C 4
2001	LosAngls	NL	193	45	13	1	6	40	44	23	18	0	0	148	.233	.367	.404	.265	27	61-C 2
2002	*LosAngls*	*NL*	*243*	*47*	*11*	*1*	*6*	*52*	*56*	*27*	*24*	*0*	*0*	*196*	*.193*	*.336*	*.321*	*.239*	*27*	

His walk rate jumped as his batting average dropped. Kreuter is now a card-carrying member of the Mark Parent MLB-Approved Backup Catcher Society, along with Greg Myers, Tom Lampkin, Tom Prince, and many others. He might have a hard time finding a job with that batting average, particularly if you look at his seasonal splits—a 787 OPS before the All-Star break, 608 afterwards.

Paul LoDuca C Bats R Age 30

YEAR	TEAM	LGE	AB	H	DB	TP	HR	BB	SO	R	RBI	SB	CS	OUT	BA	OBP	SLG	EQA	EQR	DEFENSE
1999	Albuquer	PCL	73	23	5	0	1	8	1	12	6	1	1	51	.315	.412	.425	.286	11	17-C -3
1999	LosAngls	NL	96	23	1	0	3	9	8	11	11	1	2	75	.240	.318	.344	.223	9	27-C 1
2000	Albuquer	PCL	271	83	22	2	3	25	14	36	39	6	4	192	.306	.368	.435	.269	36	46-C -1
2000	LosAngls	NL	66	17	2	0	2	5	7	6	8	0	2	51	.258	.310	.379	.222	6	15-C 3
2001	LosAngls	NL	465	156	24	0	28	37	25	75	96	2	4	313	.335	.390	.568	.307	82	85-C 3 23-1B 0
2002	*LosAngls*	*NL*	*425*	*129*	*20*	*1*	*20*	*45*	*26*	*70*	*68*	*6*	*6*	*302*	*.304*	*.370*	*.496*	*.292*	*70*	

Uh . . . okay. We don't know where his 2001 performance came from, but we're impressed. LoDuca came out of nowhere to have a great, insanely strange season, and he was a big part of keeping the Dodgers in contention when they really didn't belong there. LoDuca is solid defensively, and most of the pitchers like working with him behind the plate. His fundamental skills are very good, so there's no reason to believe that he won't perform as well as the projection above indicates.

Lamont Matthews RF Bats L Age 24

YEAR	TEAM	LGE	AB	H	DB	TP	HR	BB	SO	R	RBI	SB	CS	OUT	BA	OBP	SLG	EQA	EQR	DEFENSE
1999	Yakima	Nwn	254	42	7	1	9	18	101	24	25	2	2	214	.165	.223	.307	.179	15	66-CF 3
1999	San Bern	Cal	15	3	0	0	1	1	7	1	2	0	1	13	.200	.250	.400	.196	1	
2000	San Bern	Cal	485	98	20	4	18	59	172	54	55	6	7	394	.202	.292	.371	.222	46	128-OF 7
2001	Vero Bch	Fla	365	89	19	2	8	71	114	48	40	1	2	278	.244	.370	.373	.257	47	102-RF -9
2001	Jacksnvl	Sou	57	8	3	0	0	10	24	4	5	0	1	50	.140	.269	.193	.170	3	15-RF 1
2002	*LosAngls*	*NL*	*471*	*105*	*24*	*3*	*13*	*74*	*175*	*58*	*50*	*4*	*5*	*371*	*.223*	*.328*	*.369*	*.245*	*55*	

Like Rob Deer, he plays right field—a lot like Rob Deer, come to think of it. Matthews once struck out while playing Parcheesi, and he can draw walks off John Tudor, Bob Tewksbury, and Greg Maddux with Eric Gregg umpiring. He's old for his league, but he can play a creditable corner outfield, has some pop, and if everything breaks right for him, he could have a career as

(Lamont Matthews *continued*)

a first baseman/fourth outfielder off of someone's bench, or possibly even become a platoon mate for some right-handed hitter who doesn't walk, runs well, and plays indifferent defense. He's one of the Dodgers' many outfield options no worse than Marquis Grissom, along with Tucker Carlson, Marilyn Manson, a Benjamin Bufano Panda Sculpture, and June Chadwick.

Angel Pena C Bats R Age 27

YEAR	TEAM	LGE	AB	H	DB	TP	HR	BB	SO	R	RBI	SB	CS	OUT	BA	OBP	SLG	EQA	EQR	DEFENSE			
1999	LosAngls	NL	121	26	4	0	5	11	22	14	22	0	1	96	.215	.280	.372	.216	10	34-C	0		
1999	Albuquer	PCL	124	30	7	1	1	8	22	11	18	2	1	95	.242	.288	.339	.213	10	28-C	0		
2000	Albuquer	PCL	309	83	9	2	14	20	72	40	45	2	1	227	.269	.313	.447	.250	35	60-C	0	14-1B	-1
2001	LasVegas	PCL	194	53	7	1	12	17	47	31	31	1	0	141	.273	.334	.505	.273	28	29-C	1	14-1B	-4
2001	LosAngls	NL	54	12	2	0	1	1	14	4	2	0	0	42	.222	.236	.315	.184	3	15-C	1		
2002	*LosAngls*	*NL*	*273*	*70*	*8*	*1*	*14*	*27*	*69*	*35*	*52*	*3*	*1*	*204*	*.256*	*.323*	*.447*	*.264*	*36*				

LoDuca had a great year, but Pena isn't a bad second option. He hasn't done anything in the majors yet, but he demonstrated some power in the minors, catches a reasonable game, and hits lefties pretty hard, making him a nice end-game option to run to the plate against spot relievers. A serviceable backup.

Jeff Reboulet IF Bats R Age 38

YEAR	TEAM	LGE	AB	H	DB	TP	HR	BB	SO	R	RBI	SB	CS	OUT	BA	OBP	SLG	EQA	EQR	DEFENSE			
1999	Baltimor	AL	154	29	4	0	0	31	25	25	4	1	0	125	.188	.331	.214	.207	12	28-3B	1	24-2B	5
2000	KansasCy	AL	180	44	8	0	0	20	28	28	13	3	1	137	.244	.320	.289	.216	15	41-2B	5		
2001	LosAngls	NL	217	62	16	2	3	32	41	37	23	0	1	156	.286	.379	.419	.271	30	43-SS	-8	14-2B	-1
2002	*LosAngls*	*NL*	*194*	*40*	*9*	*1*	*2*	*31*	*38*	*33*	*10*	*1*	*1*	*155*	*.206*	*.316*	*.294*	*.219*	*17*				

Reboulet can't really play shortstop anymore; his arm strength and mobility have dropped to a point where he simply can't go to his right and make a play. Still, he's a pinch hitter who can draw a walk and a guy who can turn the double play pretty well at second base; there are worse options, many already in the organization. The Dodgers have picked up his $450,000 option for the 2002 season.

David Ross C Bats R Age 25

YEAR	TEAM	LGE	AB	H	DB	TP	HR	BB	SO	R	RBI	SB	CS	OUT	BA	OBP	SLG	EQA	EQR	DEFENSE	
1999	Vero Bch	Fla	380	67	12	1	6	34	125	34	27	3	5	319	.176	.250	.261	.178	21	96-C	0
2000	San Bern	Cal	194	42	8	1	5	9	44	19	14	1	1	153	.216	.253	.345	.199	14	42-C	6
2000	SanAnton	Tex	68	13	2	1	2	7	17	9	9	1	0	55	.191	.272	.338	.210	6	21-C	-3
2001	Jacksnvl	Sou	252	60	10	1	9	26	71	30	37	1	1	193	.238	.322	.393	.241	27	69-C	-2
2002	*LosAngls*	*NL*	*318*	*77*	*14*	*1*	*11*	*38*	*97*	*41*	*36*	*3*	*2*	*243*	*.242*	*.323*	*.396*	*.250*	*38*		

Ross has some skills. His defense is considered solid, he can hit for some power, and he will draw some walks. Catcher isn't exactly where this organization needs help. Ross has a shot at a pretty good major-league career, be it in L.A. or somewhere else. If he can bump up his production 10% or so, he has a shot to be Robert Fick off the bench for some team for a long time.

Gary Sheffield LF Bats R Age 33

YEAR	TEAM	LGE	AB	H	DB	TP	HR	BB	SO	R	RBI	SB	CS	OUT	BA	OBP	SLG	EQA	EQR	DEFENSE	
1999	LosAngls	NL	555	170	18	0	36	95	59	103	100	9	5	390	.306	.411	.533	.311	105	134-LF	-6
2000	LosAngls	NL	509	169	26	3	43	95	65	105	106	3	6	346	.332	.440	.648	.343	119	119-LF	-8
2001	LosAngls	NL	522	171	29	2	38	92	57	104	106	10	4	355	.328	.431	.609	.335	115	124-LF	-5
2002	*Atlanta*	*NL*	*540*	*160*	*24*	*2*	*38*	*101*	*66*	*105*	*100*	*10*	*6*	*386*	*.296*	*.407*	*.559*	*.318*	*110*		

Baseball's Dale Carnegie might also be its most consistent player. Once again, Sheffield played the vast majority of the season, hit the snot out of the ball, played indifferent defense, and had a relationship with the media that can best be described as "bipolar." His numbers will once again look like those of Edgar Martinez. His departure to Atlanta pretty much guts the Dodgers' offense.

Shane Victorino CF Bats R Age 21

YEAR	TEAM	LGE	AB	H	DB	TP	HR	BB	SO	R	RBI	SB	CS	OUT	BA	OBP	SLG	EQA	EQR	DEFENSE
1999	GreatFls	Pio	223	41	6	2	1	10	37	23	11	7	3	185	.184	.219	.242	.164	10	55-CF 11
2000	Yakima	Nwn	244	48	4	1	2	10	48	19	13	9	6	202	.197	.232	.246	.168	12	60-2B -3
2001	WilmngNC	SAL	457	109	19	5	3	27	65	52	24	23	9	357	.239	.284	.322	.211	36	109-CF 4
2002	*LosAngls*	*NL*	*420*	*103*	*17*	*5*	*5*	*35*	*71*	*58*	*29*	*22*	*8*	*325*	*.245*	*.303*	*.345*	*.231*	*42*	

Young speed burner Victorino is a legitimate center fielder who stole 47 bases in 60 chances at Wilmington. He has some pop in his bat but hasn't yet developed the timing or the patience to drive the ball. He did hit 30 doubles and triples, but with his kind of speed, almost any hit that isn't fielded cleanly and quickly can become a double. It will be interesting to see how Victorino's speed-based game is affected by his move to the pitcher-friendly Florida State League.

PITCHERS (ERA: 4.50, H/9: 9.0, HR/9: 1.0, BB/9: 3.0, K/9: 6.0, KW: 2.0, PERA: 4.50)

Terry Adams Throws R Age 29

YEAR	TEAM	LGE	IP	H	ER	HR	BB	K	ERA	W	L	H/9	HR/9	BB/9	K/9	KW	PERA	STUFF
1999	ChiCubs	NL	65.0	63	33	8	23	51	4.57	3	4	8.7	1.1	3.2	7.1	1.1	4.14	1
2000	LosAngls	NL	84.7	83	39	6	32	50	4.15	5	4	8.8	0.6	3.4	5.3	0.8	4.36	-7
2001	LosAngls	NL	165.7	154	63	8	48	113	3.42	11	7	8.4	0.4	2.6	6.1	1.2	4.80	9

Adams moved into the rotation in response to a bevy of injuries and responded well. He's likely to be in a similar role in 2002, except that he'll start the season in the rotation and move to the bullpen if he can't handle the workload. Adams has a drastic home/away split that would worry me in terms of making him a starter—a 3.46 ERA in Chavez Ravine, 5.09 on the road. Very dangerous, and another obvious pickup for Ed Wade and the Phillies.

Victor Alvarez Throws L Age 25

YEAR	TEAM	LGE	IP	H	ER	HR	BB	K	ERA	W	L	H/9	HR/9	BB/9	K/9	KW	PERA	STUFF
1999	Vero Bch	Fla	68.7	73	37	9	20	37	4.85	4	4	9.6	1.2	2.6	4.8	0.9	3.20	7
1999	SanAnton	Tex	57.0	61	29	7	11	31	4.58	3	3	9.6	1.1	1.7	4.9	1.4	5.09	9
2000	Vero Bch	Fla	18.0	32	46	15	15	12	23.00	0	2	16.0	7.5	7.5	6.0	0.4	7.59	-71
2000	SanAnton	Tex	47.7	48	30	5	31	29	5.66	2	3	9.1	0.9	5.9	5.5	0.5	6.22	-8
2001	Jacksnvl	Sou	40.3	39	15	2	9	22	3.35	3	1	8.7	0.4	2.0	4.9	1.2	1.71	10
2001	LasVegas	PCL	115.3	121	66	13	48	64	5.15	6	7	9.4	1.0	3.7	5.0	0.7	4.83	0

There's a wide range of opinion among scouts on Alvarez's potential. He buzzed through Jacksonville early in the year, then had a pretty solid 20 starts in Las Vegas, combining for 134 strikeouts and 48 walks in 163 innings between the two levels. He hasn't been highly touted, but he's got a live arm, good movement on a mid-range fastball, and hitters seem to have trouble picking the ball up out of his hand. He's probably the only short pitcher not drafted by the Houston Astros. Alvarez is definitely worth keeping an eye on, despite some injury problems.

Andy Ashby Throws R Age 34

YEAR	TEAM	LGE	IP	H	ER	HR	BB	K	ERA	W	L	H/9	HR/9	BB/9	K/9	KW	PERA	STUFF
1999	San Dieg	NL	205.7	215	101	25	45	119	4.42	12	11	9.4	1.1	2.0	5.2	1.3	4.10	8
2000	Philadel	NL	102.7	115	62	15	31	45	5.44	4	7	10.1	1.3	2.7	3.9	0.7	5.97	-6
2000	Atlanta	NL	99.0	105	47	11	19	49	4.27	6	5	9.5	1.0	1.7	4.5	1.3	4.14	5
2001	LosAngls	NL	11.7	13	6	2	1	6	4.63	0	1	10.0	1.5	0.8	4.6	3.0	4.06	5

(Andy Ashby *continued*)

Getting information about Ashby's elbow injury was like interviewing G. Gordon Liddy about the break-in. In mid-April, the rotation was altered to give Ashby an extra day of rest. Well, the next day: "We'll skip a start to relieve the soreness." And then: "Maybe a trip to the 15-day DL because of the muscle strain." The trickle and stop-action mudslide of Ashby's elbow continued for two months, until the team finally found a torn flexor tendon on an MRI performed in June. He's expected to be ready for spring training.

At some point, people in baseball are going to realize that pitching is an unnatural act and start paying more attention to little aches and pains. The tough-guy mentality is part of sports, but it can be very counterproductive for everyone involved. Ask Billy Wagner.

James Baldwin **Throws R** **Age 30**

YEAR	TEAM	LGE	IP	H	ER	HR	BB	K	ERA	W	L	H/9	HR/9	BB/9	K/9	KW	PERA	STUFF
1999	ChiSox	AL	204.3	217	117	30	68	122	5.15	10	13	9.6	1.3	3.0	5.4	0.9	4.55	2
2000	ChiSox	AL	179.7	191	101	29	48	115	5.06	9	11	9.6	1.5	2.4	5.8	1.2	4.00	8
2001	ChiSox	AL	97.3	110	61	14	36	40	5.64	4	7	10.2	1.3	3.3	3.7	0.6	4.72	-9
2001	LosAngls	NL	76.3	80	39	9	22	43	4.60	4	4	9.4	1.1	2.6	5.1	1.0	4.68	4

Baldwin and his salary were shipped to the Dodgers as a rental just before the deadline, and he pitched about as well as could be expected. His trip to the free-agent market this winter will make him an ambulatory example of a phenomenon the oil industry calls "The Winner's Curse," although no one had signed him as of the new year.

Kevin Brown **Throws R** **Age 37**

YEAR	TEAM	LGE	IP	H	ER	HR	BB	K	ERA	W	L	H/9	HR/9	BB/9	K/9	KW	PERA	STUFF
1999	LosAngls	NL	250.0	228	90	18	49	199	3.24	18	10	8.2	0.6	1.8	7.2	2.0	3.45	25
2000	LosAngls	NL	225.7	204	81	19	39	192	3.23	16	9	8.1	0.8	1.6	7.7	2.5	2.89	29
2001	LosAngls	NL	108.7	99	43	7	34	84	3.56	7	5	8.2	0.6	2.8	7.0	1.2	3.37	20

Brown is a really underrated pitcher, not often mentioned in epochal discussions about great pitchers, although he should be. He underwent surgery in September to repair a flexor muscle in his pitching elbow. In late September, he already knew about the tear, but he pitched through it anyway (ouch), and he was prepared to go on three days' rest if the Dodgers were still realistically in the race. He should be ready to go by Opening Day.

Giovanni Carrara **Throws R** **Age 34**

YEAR	TEAM	LGE	IP	H	ER	HR	BB	K	ERA	W	L	H/9	HR/9	BB/9	K/9	KW	PERA	STUFF
1999	Indianap	Int	153.3	168	99	24	62	81	5.81	6	11	9.9	1.4	3.6	4.8	0.7	4.09	-14
2000	ColSprin	PCL	96.3	96	47	10	32	63	4.39	6	5	9.0	0.9	3.0	5.9	1.0	3.39	4
2000	Colorado	NL	15.3	16	13	4	9	13	7.63	1	1	9.4	2.3	5.3	7.6	0.7	9.22	-17
2001	LasVegas	PCL	28.0	30	19	6	11	22	6.11	1	2	9.6	1.9	3.5	7.1	1.0	3.38	-1
2001	LosAngls	NL	79.0	79	40	11	21	56	4.56	4	5	9.0	1.3	2.4	6.4	1.3	3.35	1

Carrara has more frequent-flier miles than Pamela Des Barres. He also has great control, reasonable stuff, and a very good ability to change speeds. Despite his less-than-four-star itinerary, Carrara can pitch, and he could definitely help a championship club in a Ramiro Mendoza role.

Darren Dreifort **Throws R** **Age 30**

YEAR	TEAM	LGE	IP	H	ER	HR	BB	K	ERA	W	L	H/9	HR/9	BB/9	K/9	KW	PERA	STUFF
1999	LosAngls	NL	181.3	178	89	19	64	126	4.42	10	10	8.8	0.9	3.2	6.3	1.0	5.16	10
2000	LosAngls	NL	190.7	191	106	29	72	146	5.00	9	12	9.0	1.4	3.4	6.9	1.0	4.77	11
2001	LosAngls	NL	91.7	87	47	10	42	73	4.61	5	5	8.5	1.0	4.1	7.2	0.9	6.23	11

At this point, the question is whether Dreifort will be able to live a normal life and play catch with his kids. He could well make it back from another Tommy John surgery; Dr. Frank Jobe thinks he'll be pitching by the second half of this season. Dr. Jobe knows more about orthopedia than we do. It would be great to see Dreifort get back on the mound; we just don't know how likely it is, particularly given his power-based repertoire.

Eric Gagne Throws R Age 26

YEAR	TEAM	LGE	IP	H	ER	HR	BB	K	ERA	W	L	H/9	HR/9	BB/9	K/9	KW	PERA	STUFF
1999	SanAnton	Tex	159.0	160	98	26	73	128	5.55	7	11	9.1	1.5	4.1	7.2	0.9	3.62	13
1999	LosAngls	NL	28.0	25	13	3	13	27	4.18	2	1	8.0	1.0	4.2	8.7	1.0	2.34	30
2000	LosAngls	NL	102.3	109	69	18	49	70	6.07	4	7	9.6	1.6	4.3	6.2	0.7	5.36	0
2000	Albuquer	PCL	56.7	57	30	10	15	46	4.76	3	3	9.1	1.6	2.4	7.3	1.5	4.42	10
2001	LosAngls	NL	144.3	146	76	21	41	105	4.74	8	8	9.1	1.3	2.6	6.5	1.3	5.64	6
2001	LasVegas	PCL	22.0	20	11	2	10	20	4.50	1	1	8.2	0.8	4.1	8.2	1.0	1.65	18

Gagne was pitted against Luke Prokopec in a sort of Mark Burnett-on-peyote cage match for the final spot in the rotation. He was jerked around considerably by Kevin Malone, Dave Wallace, and Jim Tracy, and, given the circumstances, he didn't pitch too badly. All the requisite skills are there for Gagne to be a very good starting pitcher. It's just a matter of opportunity and patience. With Prokopec a Blue Jay and Chan Ho Park a Ranger, Gagne should settle in this year.

Matt Herges Throws R Age 32

YEAR	TEAM	LGE	IP	H	ER	HR	BB	K	ERA	W	L	H/9	HR/9	BB/9	K/9	KW	PERA	STUFF
1999	Albuquer	PCL	130.0	146	86	20	55	59	5.95	5	9	10.1	1.4	3.8	4.1	0.5	5.48	-14
1999	LosAngls	NL	24.0	26	15	5	7	16	5.63	1	2	9.8	1.9	2.6	6.0	1.1	4.70	-8
2000	LosAngls	NL	110.3	107	40	6	33	67	3.75	7	5	8.7	0.5	2.7	5.5	1.0	3.40	0
2001	LosAngls	NL	96.0	93	46	7	41	61	4.31	6	5	8.7	0.7	3.8	5.7	0.7	3.74	-5

Herges was the foundation of the bullpen, logging nearly 100 innings, including several stretches in which he was asked to pitch in high-leverage situations. History hasn't been particularly kind to pitchers who've had this kind of workload, but Herges held up fairly well, partially because of a lighter workload late in the season. He takes great advantage of Dodger Stadium; if Herges ever signs anywhere else, his career could definitely explode into a froth of wild run scoring.

Steve Langone Throws R Age 24

YEAR	TEAM	LGE	IP	H	ER	HR	BB	K	ERA	W	L	H/9	HR/9	BB/9	K/9	KW	PERA	STUFF
2000	Yakima	Nwn	80.0	99	56	21	6	35	6.30	3	6	11.1	2.4	0.7	3.9	2.9	5.05	-3
2001	Vero Bch	Fla	95.7	111	65	21	23	49	6.11	4	7	10.4	2.0	2.2	4.6	1.1	4.14	-10
2001	Jacksnvl	Sou	5.3	4	1	0	0	5	1.69	1	0	6.8	0.0	0.0	8.4	-1.0	1.97	46

He throws three pitches: an average fastball and a wicked curve and change-up. Langone delivers all three pitches with identical arm speed, and he can vary the change-up by as much as five or six mph as needed. Already very polished, he'll start the season at Double-A, which could be his biggest challenge. If he doesn't make the bigs as a starter, his change-up could make him a devastating weapon out of the bullpen.

Terry Mulholland Throws L Age 39

YEAR	TEAM	LGE	IP	H	ER	HR	BB	K	ERA	W	L	H/9	HR/9	BB/9	K/9	KW	PERA	STUFF
1999	ChiCubs	NL	114.3	131	65	15	27	40	5.12	6	7	10.3	1.2	2.1	3.1	0.7	5.26	-12
1999	Atlanta	NL	62.0	62	25	5	11	35	3.63	4	3	9.0	0.7	1.6	5.1	1.6	3.31	6
2000	Atlanta	NL	165.3	184	89	21	34	69	4.84	8	10	10.0	1.1	1.9	3.8	1.0	5.07	-11
2001	Pittsbrg	NL	34.3	38	19	4	9	14	4.98	2	2	10.0	1.0	2.4	3.7	0.8	3.70	-15
2001	LosAngls	NL	30.3	33	18	6	6	20	5.34	1	2	9.8	1.8	1.8	5.9	1.7	6.49	-7

Mulholland's contract probably has clauses about flexibility of use. He gets thrown into almost every situation, from being the #2 starter to being the one-out lefty brought in to hold Speedy Guy on first and get Lefty Slugger to ground one to the second baseman. He hasn't thrown hard for years, so he'll probably end up in the same assortment of roles in 2002. Last year's broken finger should not impact his effectiveness.

Gregg Olson Throws R Age 35

YEAR	TEAM	LGE	IP	H	ER	HR	BB	K	ERA	W	L	H/9	HR/9	BB/9	K/9	KW	PERA	STUFF
1999	Arizona	NL	59.3	61	33	8	21	41	5.01	3	4	9.3	1.2	3.2	6.2	1.0	3.73	-5
2000	LosAngls	NL	18.7	20	12	4	6	13	5.79	1	1	9.6	1.9	2.9	6.3	1.1	5.44	-9
2001	LosAngls	NL	24.3	24	17	4	18	19	6.29	1	2	8.9	1.5	6.7	7.0	0.5	9.24	-21

(Gregg Olson *continued*)
Remember what Olson's curveball looked like about ten years ago? It's always impressive when someone who's at the top of the heap gets knocked down, then hangs around and works his butt off to stay in the game. Olson has done exactly that for the last several years. It was ugly in 2002, and Olson was released just before the All-Star break. Even if he can't hook on anywhere, it was a pretty good run.

Jesse Orosco **Throws L** **Age 45**

YEAR	TEAM	LGE	IP	H	ER	HR	BB	K	ERA	W	L	H/9	HR/9	BB/9	K/9	KW	PERA	STUFF
1999	Baltimor	AL	32.3	28	17	4	17	35	4.73	2	2	7.8	1.1	4.7	9.7	1.0	5.22	8
2001	LasVegas	PCL	7.0	5	2	0	3	7	2.57	1	0	6.4	0.0	3.9	9.0	1.2	0.00	15
2001	LosAngls	NL	16.3	15	8	3	6	17	4.41	1	1	8.3	1.7	3.3	9.4	1.4	4.16	9

During spring training, Orosco's agent cast one of the first stones at Kevin Malone, claiming his client had been misled about his role, and basically calling Malone a liar. Orosco had a tailbone injury for much of the year, but when he was healthy, he did what he's been doing since the Eisenhower administration—get out left-handed hitters. He will spend February and March trolling for a job. Just think: if Bud Selig's contraction bluff actually gets called, and teams end up with 27 guys on the roster, Orosco could be pitching for Tony LaRussa until he's 52 or 53 years old.

Chan Ho Park **Throws R** **Age 29**

YEAR	TEAM	LGE	IP	H	ER	HR	BB	K	ERA	W	L	H/9	HR/9	BB/9	K/9	KW	PERA	STUFF
1999	LosAngls	NL	200.7	200	114	30	84	157	5.11	10	12	9.0	1.3	3.8	7.0	0.9	5.43	9
2000	LosAngls	NL	221.0	198	103	19	102	193	4.19	13	12	8.1	0.8	4.2	7.9	0.9	3.56	20
2001	LosAngls	NL	217.3	202	99	20	81	175	4.10	13	11	8.4	0.8	3.4	7.2	1.1	3.98	18

The pitching prize of the free-agent market. There are whispers of Park being "mentally soft" and "not ready to be a front-of-the-rotation starter." Well, that may or may not be the case, but Park has been a successful pitcher, learned a fair amount of English, and seems to be a solid, confident guy. The real problem is his significant home/road split: since 1997, he's posted a 4.66 ERA away from Chavez Ravine. The Rangers, spending $65 million on Park over the next five years, might be quite disappointed.

Luke Prokopec **Throws R** **Age 24**

YEAR	TEAM	LGE	IP	H	ER	HR	BB	K	ERA	W	L	H/9	HR/9	BB/9	K/9	KW	PERA	STUFF
1999	SanAnton	Tex	161.0	176	98	27	50	92	5.48	7	11	9.8	1.5	2.8	5.1	0.9	7.61	5
2000	SanAnton	Tex	128.3	126	53	12	23	86	3.72	8	6	8.8	0.8	1.6	6.0	1.9	3.32	21
2000	LosAngls	NL	20.7	21	10	2	7	11	4.35	1	1	9.1	0.9	3.0	4.8	0.8	4.17	2
2001	LosAngls	NL	131.3	146	82	24	36	73	5.62	6	9	10.0	1.6	2.5	5.0	1.0	5.50	0

Prokopec made the unholy circuit of rotation to bullpen to disabled list to Las Vegas. He has good stuff in a small frame, and good command up and down in the strike zone. There were some concerns that he was tipping his pitches early in the season. He had a few blister problem days through the season, but he definitely has the pitches to be a front-line starter. The A's Jeremy Giambi said, "He had some of the best stuff I've ever seen." He'll be the #4 starter in Toronto, another steal by J.P. Ricciardi.

Al Reyes **Throws R** **Age 31**

YEAR	TEAM	LGE	IP	H	ER	HR	BB	K	ERA	W	L	H/9	HR/9	BB/9	K/9	KW	PERA	STUFF
1999	Louisvil	Int	10.7	10	5	0	8	6	4.22	1	0	8.4	0.0	6.8	5.1	0.4	8.83	-28
1999	Milwauke	NL	35.0	31	20	5	21	35	5.14	2	2	8.0	1.3	5.4	9.0	0.8	3.87	5
1999	Baltimor	AL	29.0	26	15	4	13	28	4.66	1	2	8.1	1.2	4.0	8.7	1.1	4.29	7
2000	Rochestr	Int	12.3	12	10	3	10	13	7.30	0	1	8.8	2.2	7.3	9.5	0.6	10.05	-26
2000	Baltimor	AL	13.3	13	9	2	9	10	6.08	0	1	8.8	1.4	6.1	6.8	0.6	6.05	-15
2000	Albuquer	PCL	37.3	39	26	6	22	28	6.27	1	3	9.4	1.4	5.3	6.8	0.6	4.59	-20
2000	LosAngls	NL	6.0	4	1	0	1	7	1.50	1	0	6.0	0.0	1.5	10.5	3.5	0.00	41
2001	LasVegas	PCL	28.3	27	15	4	13	23	4.76	1	2	8.6	1.3	4.1	7.3	0.9	3.68	-7
2001	LosAngls	NL	25.7	25	13	3	12	18	4.56	1	2	8.8	1.1	4.2	6.3	0.8	4.81	-6

After Gregg Olson pitched his way off the roster, Reyes was summoned to Chavez Ravine and did journeyman's work for half a season. He has never really mastered his mechanics, and he has a tendency to open up a little bit on his delivery, which can result in what is technically called "Excessive Pitch Elevation." This causes things like "Whiplash" and "Losses." Still, he does have reasonable stuff and will be at least an option worth considering for a lot of clubs. His next stop may be in your town.

Chad Ricketts — Throws R — Age 27

YEAR	TEAM	LGE	IP	H	ER	HR	BB	K	ERA	W	L	H/9	HR/9	BB/9	K/9	KW	PERA	STUFF
1999	WestTenn	Sou	64.3	68	42	13	24	50	5.88	3	4	9.5	1.8	3.4	7.0	1.0	4.21	-12
2000	Albuquer	PCL	67.0	65	41	9	38	53	5.51	3	4	8.7	1.2	5.1	7.1	0.7	4.60	-15
2001	LasVegas	PCL	57.0	54	32	6	32	44	5.05	3	3	8.5	0.9	5.1	6.9	0.7	4.01	-13

A cash-strapped club could improve its bullpen by taking a chance on Ricketts. Acquired from the Cubs in the Terry Adams deal, Ricketts has a reasonable repertoire and is what can best be described as "effectively wild." He moves the ball a lot both in and out of the strike zone, using a plus fastball and north-south movement to fool hitters. Ricketts has a big body with mechanics that can get a little loose, but he definitely possesses the fastball and know-how to be a solid major-league contributor right now. He was thrown into the same deal with Prokopec and will be part of a wide-open fight for jobs in the Blue Jays bullpen.

Ricardo Rodriguez — Throws R — Age 23

YEAR	TEAM	LGE	IP	H	ER	HR	BB	K	ERA	W	L	H/9	HR/9	BB/9	K/9	KW	PERA	STUFF
2000	GreatFls	Pio	93.0	86	35	5	26	66	3.39	6	4	8.3	0.5	2.5	6.4	1.3	3.47	24
2001	Vero Bch	Fla	147.7	165	111	31	70	92	6.77	5	11	10.1	1.9	4.3	5.6	0.7	5.11	0

The Dodgers love his stuff. Rodriguez struck out a man per inning in Vero Beach and spent the season trying to work the ball inside on the hands of right-handed hitters. His stuff is good enough for him to make the majors as a potential #3 starter. He will have to tune his mechanics, work on his move to first base, and, most importantly, stay healthy.

Jeff Shaw — Throws R — Age 35

YEAR	TEAM	LGE	IP	H	ER	HR	BB	K	ERA	W	L	H/9	HR/9	BB/9	K/9	KW	PERA	STUFF
1999	LosAngls	NL	67.7	68	28	6	13	39	3.72	5	3	9.0	0.8	1.7	5.2	1.5	3.23	-2
2000	LosAngls	NL	58.7	60	28	6	13	35	4.30	4	3	9.2	0.9	2.0	5.4	1.3	4.43	-5
2001	LosAngls	NL	68.7	70	33	9	16	47	4.33	4	4	9.2	1.2	2.1	6.2	1.5	4.07	-1

The Dodgers opted not to pick up Shaw's option for 2002, adding him to the mix of closers looking for inflated contracts. There's nothing in his record to suggest a significant change in his level of performance. While he's a reliable, consistent reliever, there's no reason to pay him anywhere near $3 million. The fact that he made $6.4 million last year is hysterical. At a reduced rate, he could be a very good setup man. Shaw is exactly the sort of player whose market value would be crushed by a universal free-agent structure. He spent much of the winter trying to join the Reds, to no avail.

Dennis Springer — Throws R — Age 37

YEAR	TEAM	LGE	IP	H	ER	HR	BB	K	ERA	W	L	H/9	HR/9	BB/9	K/9	KW	PERA	STUFF
1999	Florida	NL	202.3	225	109	22	54	75	4.85	10	12	10.0	1.0	2.4	3.3	0.7	5.27	-8
2000	Norfolk	Int	112.7	140	84	21	38	26	6.71	4	9	11.2	1.7	3.0	2.1	0.3	5.89	-30
2001	LasVegas	PCL	114.7	138	79	19	36	32	6.20	4	9	10.8	1.5	2.8	2.5	0.4	6.35	-22
2001	LosAngls	NL	17.3	20	10	3	2	6	5.19	1	1	10.4	1.6	1.0	3.1	1.5	3.50	-7

One of the great difficulties about doing this book is that we need to have at least a similar number of players for each team, in order to make the chapters look relatively balanced. Some organizations simply don't have 50 players who warrant a comment, while others have 60 or more. Springer, as you probably know, is a durable knuckleballer, and he might just be entering his prime. A contender could do worse than take a chance on him. OK, that's 42.

Mike Trombley — Throws R — Age 35

YEAR	TEAM	LGE	IP	H	ER	HR	BB	K	ERA	W	L	H/9	HR/9	BB/9	K/9	KW	PERA	STUFF
1999	Minnesot	AL	91.3	86	43	13	23	81	4.24	5	5	8.5	1.3	2.3	8.0	1.8	3.56	9
2000	Baltimor	AL	72.7	69	42	13	31	71	5.20	3	5	8.5	1.6	3.8	8.8	1.1	3.71	6
2001	Baltimor	AL	52.3	47	24	4	26	43	4.13	3	3	8.1	0.7	4.5	7.4	0.8	3.61	2
2001	LosAngls	NL	23.7	23	14	4	9	22	5.32	1	2	8.7	1.5	3.4	8.4	1.2	6.94	1

Trombley is a durable right-handed relief pitcher. He still has very good stuff, and his main weakness is the same one he's always had: occasionally, the hard sinker he throws stays about thigh high and gets hit harder than Bill O'Reilly at an NAACP meeting. Even with that flaw, Trombley is a nice building block for a bullpen and should be an asset in 2002.

Milwaukee Brewers

If we are to believe the wheedling, whining, and hand-wringing of Clan Selig, it was the best of times in Milwaukee in 2001. Baseball's second-smallest market is, according to the game's own cooked books, the home of its most lucrative franchise. While this transparent attempt to lend a patina of legitimacy to the claim that baseball franchises are made or broken by publicly financed stadia was treated with less contempt than it deserved (both on Capitol Hill and by a news media compromised by its dependence on access), it provides a lens through which to view baseball's family affair. Can the Seligs, a family that doesn't even competently run the parking lot outside its new monster park, be trusted with a baseball franchise?

Brewers Prospectus

2001 record: 68–94; Fourth place, NL Central

Pythagenport W/L: 74–88

Runs scored: 740 (11th in NL)

Runs allowed: 806 (11th in NL)

Team EqA: .254 (12th in NL)

2001 batters age: 29.6 (eighth-youngest in NL)

2001 pitchers age: 26.6 (second-youngest in NL)

Ballpark: Miller Park, neutral park, Park Factor of 1.001

2001: New park helped them make a bunch of money even while the team had a lousy year.

2002: There's no reason to think they'll be a factor any time soon, especially given the competition in the division.

Having shaken down most of southeastern Wisconsin to get it built, the Brewers opened Miller Park a year behind schedule. Sadly, it may not have been worth the wait. It is, for all intents and purposes, a domed stadium with a moon roof, New Comiskey with a concrete comb-over. The steep pagoda-like interior is innovative, but the resulting seating tends to be remote. While the revenues the team is willing to report jumped from $50 million in 2000 to anywhere between $80 and $100 million in 2001, the Brewers are claiming that they have to raise ticket prices for 2002. With a straight face. After all, the family's head is happy to try and mislead Congress under oath, so what's some small-time burgling?

Just as the Brewers claim it's necessary to raise ticket prices, they're also claiming that the roof (which added $100 million to the cost of the stadium) is an asset that guarantees that the good people of Sheboygan or Eau Claire or Prairie du Chien will be more inclined to make the long road trip to Miller Park now that they don't have to worry about a rainout. The Brewers have consistently tried to market themselves as a regional franchise, spending time stumping in the backwoods of Wisconsin in a way that every team needs to take to heart. Those efforts and the new ballpark combined to put 2.8 million fannies in the seats in 2001.

The Brewers aren't alone in working the various Smallvilles scattered throughout the Midwest, though. The Cubs don't exactly have a problem getting people to pour into Wrigley from hundreds of miles away. The Brewers should have focused on making the ballpark a core element of the baseball experience, instead of focusing on keeping up with the Colangelos. If the dome is supposed to protect fans from exposure in October, well, that won't be a problem any time soon. Besides, these are people who don't mind watching the Packers outdoors in December.

Family factotum Wendy Selig-Prieb describes the state of the franchise breezily: "When you look at the bigger picture and what we set out to do two years ago, I think we are absolutely on the right path. I believe there is a lot of reason for optimism." On one level, she's right. The Brewers have been making money hand over fist. The problem is that there's more to pro baseball than that. As the White Sox and New Comiskey—along with three of the last four expansion franchises—demonstrate, fan interest in a new park should not be mistaken for a real commitment to the team. When the novelty of Miller Park wears off, Brewers fans will be left with expensive seats, a bad team, less sunshine, and an obvious attempt by the franchise to encroach on the Wisconsin ritual of tailgating in the parking lot. What does it mean for Czar Bud's arguments about the game's economics if Milwaukee is the most profitable franchise in baseball, but that profitability has nothing to do with whether they field a competitive team? Then again, if the Brewers don't put together a winning team, they won't have to worry for long about having to reconcile their financial success with the product on the field.

The organization has made all of the appropriate noises about fielding a better team. General Manager Dean Taylor came in at the end of 1999 talking about establishing a "winning mindset," while Davey Lopes was brought in last year to manage, a clean break from Phil Garner's whiny claims of victimization. Taylor and Lopes's first year together produced a third-place finish that sounds more impressive than it was; the team's record was just 73-89, and they finished closer to last place than to second. However, there were reasons for hope. The revenues generated by the new ballpark changed the Brewers' modus operandi: Geoff Jenkins, Richie Sexson, and Jeromy Burnitz all got multiyear deals in the spring before the 2001 season. Jeff D'Amico was coming off of a superb, almost healthy, season. The farm system had Ben Sheets and Nick Neugebauer to brag about. In an especially neat trick, Taylor even managed to undo the worst of Sal Bando's errors, making Marquis Grissom and the final two years of his contract go away. You could start to see the outlines of a plan in which the franchise would make money, plow it back into the product, and set off the kind of self-sustaining success that teams like the Indians made famous.

That vision extended into the season's early months. Not surprisingly, D'Amico broke down, but Sheets was ready from the opening bell, and Paul Rigdon had a good pair of months. The offense wasn't dominating, but Richie Sexson and Jeromy Burnitz were going strong, Ronnie Belliard seemed to have overcome his back problem, Jose Hernandez and Tyler Houston were doing well while playing regularly, and, most importantly, the lineup was entirely Grissom-free. Lopes's squad put together a good first half, posting a record of 38-34 going into a road trip.

The team-wide meltdown started June 25 in Pittsburgh with a four-game sweep at the hands of the division's patsies. By the time the smoke cleared, the Brewers had lost 31 of 40 games, and the idea that the Brewers were going to build something in 2001 was dead. The problems that contributed to the collapse weren't surprises. Rigdon, Jenkins, and Houston broke down, while both Sheets and Jamey Wright struggled terribly before going onto the DL.

In the end, all that was left for the Brewers to do was play recordball. While they could not avoid the MLB team record for strikeouts in a season (with 1,399), they benched Hernandez so he could avoid the single-season strikeout mark, and Jimmy Haynes conveniently disappeared onto the DL for a month so as to fall short of 20 losses. The strangest decision of the season was reactivating everybody for a going-away special: the Brewers tried to send Sheets, D'Amico, Houston and as many of the other walking wounded as they could back onto the field.

At this point, you have to ask if there is a program in place that justifies Wendy Selig-Prieb's confidence. The results are not so consistently rosy as she's determined to portray. On the major-league level, we need to assess how well Taylor has done in assembling a team. To his credit, deleting Grissom bordered on miraculous, and acquiring Richie Sexson for a few journeymen pitchers gave the Brewers the first baseman they've been missing ever since Cecil Cooper got a career-ending case of the olds. Acquiring Ruben Quevedo for David Weathers was a great return on the waiver claim that brought in Weathers. Overall, though, Taylor's pickups have been a mixed bag. His other trades have brought in Jimmy Haynes, Jamey Wright, and Henry Blanco for Jeff Cirillo, and Jaime Navarro and John Snyder for Jose Valentin and Cal Eldred. The Cirillo deal has boiled down to Cirillo for Wright; Blanco is easily replaceable, and Haynes was non-tendered after two adequate seasons.

Replacing Jose Valentin brings us to Taylor's sore spot, his big-ticket free-agent acquisitions, Jose Hernandez and Jeffrey Hammonds. Hernandez has just been a replacement to help cover for the losses of Cirillo and Valentin, and while he has value, he's never going to be as valuable as either of those two.

The decision to sign Jeffrey Hammonds last winter is far more troubling. Taylor talks a lot about how he's rebuilding, and how the Brewers are newly committed to player development. If the Brewers had saved the money and concentrated on drafting well, they could have hope and faith, but Taylor had money to spend, so the Brewers got caught up in making some off-season noise. Instead of following what was supposed to be their mission, they blew big money on Hammonds to play a position he can't handle. Over the course of his career, Hammonds has been called all sorts of things he isn't—versatile, dangerous, useful—but at the end of the day, he's fragile, doesn't hit for much power, doesn't walk, doesn't run as much as you'd expect from hearing people talk about his running, and he can't really play center field on an everyday basis. The Brewers have focused on the decent week he had leading off before his inevitable breakdown. Pretending that one week, and not the rest of his career, tells them something is just the Brewers' way of avoiding an admission that signing Hammonds was bad. Franklin Stubbs bad.

What about the farm system? One of the most common complaints about it is its dearth of position-playing prospects. Taylor's crew usually plays up the evils of the franchise's past to protect themselves from criticism of what they've accomplished in their two years. While we shouldn't pretend that the past was a happy time for Brewers player development, the team did manage to develop Mark Loretta, Geoff Jenkins, and Ronnie Belliard before the Taylor regime. Is there any hitter drafted in the last two years who will be as good as any member of that trio? Since Epy Guerrero was signing people such as Cristian Guerrero before Taylor brought in his gang, Taylor can't even take credit for the progress the Brewers have made south of the border.

While the Brewers proudly point to the pitching in their system, it wasn't current Director of Scouting Jack Zduriencik who picked Ben Sheets and Nick Neugebauer. His predecessor,

Ken Califano, drafted both of them, as well as J.M. Gold. While Califano was creating hope and faith for the Brewers, Zduriencik 1) helped run a Dodgers international scouting effort that got caught cheating, 2) participated in a Mets player-development effort that can best be described as dead, and 3) ran the Pirates' drafts for the three years that got them Jason Kendall and nothing else. This is undoubtedly an unfair assessment of Zduriencik. Perhaps he adds intangibles. Nevertheless, there should be some level of concern that he's been part of three of the worst-run player-development efforts of the past decade. The early returns on his first two drafts with the Brewers are, to be polite, mixed.

Beyond Zduriencik, Taylor has people such as Chuck Tanner and Larry Doughty on the payroll. Taylor's crew will look good in the short term, when Califano's picks are manning the rotation, but long term, the new crew had better come to the dance with more than just Dave Krynzel in their pockets.

In addition to beefing up the Brewers' player-development program, Taylor also needs to get a little more aggressive in using his 40-man and big-league roster spots with an eye towards the future. When Ronnie Belliard broke down, the Brewers needed somebody for the top of the order who could play second base. Why wasn't Marcos Scutaro called up? A bullpen on a non-contender should not be stocked with guys such as Gus Gandarillas and Mike Buddie. While either might be useful as an 11th man, the Brewers should be stocking their bullpen with guys like David Weathers, on the off chance that they can be turned into prospects as good as Ruben Quevedo. That means getting aggressive in the minor-league free-agent market, and watching the waiver wire with a sense of hunger.

The Brewers aren't anywhere close to being able to contend with the Astros over the next few years, and the Cubs and Cardinals are both built to win now. The Reds are further along than the Brewers in their efforts to re-tool. The Brewers' offense has only one keeper in the near term, Richie Sexson. Every other hitter should be bait for teams in contention. The happier news is the pitching staff. By the All-Star break, Brewers fans will be treated to a rotation built around Ben Sheets, Nick Neugebauer, Ruben Quevedo, and Jamey Wright. Sheets and Wright are both power/ground-ball guys, while Neugebauer is just pure power. There has been a long-standing complaint that the team needs a veteran starter to show guys such as Jamey Wright and Jimmy Haynes how to carry themselves. The hope is that new pitching coach Dave Stewart has picked another great job in which to build his resume, and that he'll lend the right element of frowning gravitas.

If the Brewers can come out of 2002 having assembled a good rotation—the most difficult task for any organization—then the opportunity to contend will be there. A smart GM can scare up a bullpen and offensive help on the cheap and through player development. If the Brewers are taking notes from organizations such as the Athletics, Yankees, and Padres, they could give the Astros a fight by 2004. However, the NL Central isn't sitting still, and the Brewers are not operating in a vacuum. Realistically, their goals should be to convert current major-league talent into guys who can be part of the next good Brewers team, and to let the rotation grow and develop.

HITTERS (BA: .270, OBP: .340, SLG: .440, EqA: .260)

Ron Belliard 2B Bats R Age 27

YEAR	TEAM	LGE	AB	H	DB	TP	HR	BB	SO	R	RBI	SB	CS	OUT	BA	OBP	SLG	EQA	EQR	DEFENSE	
1999	Louisvil	Int	108	24	3	0	1	12	12	11	7	9	3	87	.222	.304	.278	.214	9	26-2B	-4
1999	Milwauke	NL	457	133	28	4	8	59	55	58	54	3	5	329	.291	.372	.422	.267	61	111-2B	-1
2000	Milwauke	NL	574	150	30	8	8	74	77	80	51	6	5	429	.261	.348	.383	.249	67	149-2B	2
2001	Milwauke	NL	365	100	32	3	11	33	55	72	37	5	2	267	.274	.341	.468	.267	49	95-2B	3
2002	*Milwauke*	*NL*	*518*	*147*	*33*	*5*	*12*	*68*	*77*	*77*	*59*	*9*	*6*	*377*	*.284*	*.367*	*.436*	*.272*	*73*		

Belliard will never become a superstar, but like Ray Durham, he can still be one of the best mere mortals in the non-Alomar/Kent stratosphere. His future as a Brewer is a little less assured these days, between losing two months to a sprained ankle and the huge financial commitment to Mark Loretta. Questions about his conditioning echo earlier sentiments from scouts that Belliard's chunky build would affect his development. He has power and patience, and he's not the slouch defensively that he usually is perceived to be. He'll outslug that projection, keeping last year's power spike.

Henry Blanco C Bats R Age 30

YEAR	TEAM	LGE	AB	H	DB	TP	HR	BB	SO	R	RBI	SB	CS	OUT	BA	OBP	SLG	EQA	EQR	DEFENSE
1999	Colorado	NL	258	51	12	2	5	30	35	26	22	1	1	208	.198	.284	.318	.207	20	83-C 7
2000	Milwauke	NL	286	67	17	0	9	32	55	27	31	0	3	222	.234	.311	.388	.232	29	81-C 13
2001	Milwauke	NL	315	70	19	3	6	32	61	35	32	3	1	246	.222	.297	.359	.223	29	96-C 5
2002	*Milwauke*	*NL*	*306*	*72*	*16*	*2*	*8*	*38*	*61*	*34*	*32*	*3*	*2*	*236*	*.235*	*.320*	*.379*	*.230*	*33*	

A respectable backup catcher employed beyond his ability. Now, there's nothing wrong with respectability, after all, Shannon Tweed has had an acting career that employed the full range of her talents. The difference between Tweed and Blanco is that nobody put Tweed in a role she wasn't capable of filling, while the Brewers keep trying to talk themselves into believing that Blanco is the new Jim Sundberg.

Jeromy Burnitz RF Bats L Age 33

YEAR	TEAM	LGE	AB	H	DB	TP	HR	BB	SO	R	RBI	SB	CS	OUT	BA	OBP	SLG	EQA	EQR	DEFENSE
1999	Milwauke	NL	467	124	31	1	33	85	115	84	96	6	3	346	.266	.396	.548	.307	90	122-RF -4
2000	Milwauke	NL	567	131	28	1	31	91	111	87	93	5	4	440	.231	.349	.448	.266	80	149-RF -1
2001	Milwauke	NL	564	147	33	4	35	76	127	108	103	0	4	421	.261	.352	.520	.281	88	149-RF -3
2002	*NY Mets*	*NL*	*548*	*129*	*30*	*2*	*30*	*89*	*130*	*86*	*92*	*4*	*4*	*423*	*.235*	*.342*	*.462*	*.273*	*82*	

The question has never been whether Burnitz contributes, even in a year as poor as his 2000. It's more a matter of cost. He's sort of baseball's Macy Gray: without a really good collection of backup singers, you might notice that he's not as good as he's cracked up to be. He's a classic "old player's skills" guy, which makes him a candidate for an early career fade. Burnitz is under contract for a huge chunk of change in 2003, and the clock is ticking, so chances are the Brewers won't get a good package for him before his decline becomes apparent.

Raul Casanova C Bats B Age 29

YEAR	TEAM	LGE	AB	H	DB	TP	HR	BB	SO	R	RBI	SB	CS	OUT	BA	OBP	SLG	EQA	EQR	DEFENSE
1999	Toledo	Int	160	31	6	0	6	5	26	18	20	0	0	129	.194	.222	.344	.187	10	29-C -1
2000	Milwauke	NL	233	58	12	3	6	22	44	19	35	1	2	177	.249	.323	.403	.242	25	58-C -4
2001	Milwauke	NL	192	51	8	0	12	12	25	22	34	0	0	141	.266	.311	.495	.261	24	47-C -4
2002	*Milwauke*	*NL*	*268*	*68*	*11*	*1*	*11*	*24*	*44*	*33*	*41*	*0*	*1*	*201*	*.254*	*.315*	*.425*	*.246*	*30*	

Just when it began to look like Davey Lopes was getting a clue, in that Lopes recognized that his lineup was better off with Casanova than with Henry Blanco, a knee injury ended Casanova's season in mid-August. Casanova had some good times in Miller Park that might heighten people's expectations, but he is better off as a solid caddy.

Daryl Clark 3B Bats L Age 22

YEAR	TEAM	LGE	AB	H	DB	TP	HR	BB	SO	R	RBI	SB	CS	OUT	BA	OBP	SLG	EQA	EQR	DEFENSE	
2000	Ogden	Pio	216	45	6	1	7	39	64	24	25	2	2	173	.208	.331	.343	.234	23	34-3B -11	20-1B -5
2001	Beloit	Mid	514	113	16	1	14	44	148	54	59	2	3	404	.220	.285	.337	.211	41	119-3B -27	
2002	*Milwauke*	*NL*	*491*	*119*	*16*	*1*	*16*	*64*	*153*	*56*	*58*	*4*	*3*	*375*	*.242*	*.330*	*.377*	*.242*	*54*		

Have things in Milwaukee really changed since the days of Sal Bando? Clark, like Mike Kinkade before him, can really hit, and like Kinkade, he's a disaster at the hot corner. He will get a ton of publicity for the big year he's about to post in High Desert; if you have to pick somebody most likely to win the Triple Crown for the entire minor leagues, pick Clark. He may end up in an outfield corner, and he should have a better career than Kinkade has had.

Lou Collier UT Bats R Age 28

YEAR	TEAM	LGE	AB	H	DB	TP	HR	BB	SO	R	RBI	SB	CS	OUT	BA	OBP	SLG	EQA	EQR	DEFENSE	
1999	Milwauke	NL	135	34	6	0	3	13	30	17	21	3	2	103	.252	.318	.363	.231	13	17-SS -2	
2000	Huntsvil	Sou	180	45	4	1	2	23	44	26	25	5	2	137	.250	.337	.317	.231	18	31-3B 0	
2001	Indianap	Int	315	87	14	2	13	23	59	45	33	7	3	231	.276	.335	.457	.262	41	62-CF 1	14-2B 0
2001	Milwauke	NL	127	33	8	1	2	17	25	20	14	5	1	95	.260	.351	.386	.256	16	19-LF 0	14-3B -1
2002	*NY Mets*	*NL*	*371*	*99*	*17*	*2*	*11*	*48*	*78*	*62*	*53*	*8*	*3*	*275*	*.267*	*.351*	*.412*	*.267*	*51*		

The last player cut in spring training, Collier is a little like Terry Shumpert. He has more power than your average utility man, and he can actually contribute a little in the field. That's a big improvement for Collier, who had one of the slowest first steps you were ever going to see at shortstop when he first broke in with the Pirates.

Mike Coolbaugh 3B/SS Bats R Age 30

YEAR	TEAM	LGE	AB	H	DB	TP	HR	BB	SO	R	RBI	SB	CS	OUT	BA	OBP	SLG	EQA	EQR	DEFENSE
1999	Columbus	Int	391	100	25	2	13	31	105	54	54	4	6	297	.256	.313	.430	.243	43	61-3B -8 36-RF -4
2000	Columbus	Int	392	101	21	0	22	58	94	57	54	5	3	294	.258	.357	.480	.276	59	54-SS -6 26-2B -1
2001	Indianap	Int	351	90	21	2	10	38	85	47	47	2	2	263	.256	.335	.413	.250	41	79-3B 9 15-SS 4
2001	Milwauke	NL	70	15	3	0	3	5	14	10	8	0	0	55	.214	.281	.386	.222	6	16-3B -1
2002	*St Louis*	*NL*	*412*	*109*	*23*	*1*	*18*	*49*	*107*	*60*	*58*	*4*	*3*	*306*	*.265*	*.343*	*.456*	*.266*	*56*	

Like a lot of minor-league journeymen hauled in by the Brewers lately, Coolbaugh was touted by Davey Lopes as somebody he liked. Of course, Lopes really only liked him in principle. He didn't like Coolbaugh enough to give him a shot once Ron Belliard and Tyler Houston were out of action. After the year, Coolbaugh signed a minor-league deal with the Cardinals, who might give him a look at third base in their crazed drive to put Albert Pujols anywhere other than at his natural position. He's a fine replacement for Craig Paquette.

Jeff Deardorff RF/1B Bats R Age 23

YEAR	TEAM	LGE	AB	H	DB	TP	HR	BB	SO	R	RBI	SB	CS	OUT	BA	OBP	SLG	EQA	EQR	DEFENSE
1999	Stockton	Cal	438	94	17	1	7	26	152	41	31	1	4	348	.215	.263	.306	.193	28	117-3B -17
2000	Mudville	Cal	429	89	19	3	8	16	121	35	36	3	5	345	.207	.237	.322	.186	26	68-3B 0 28-1B -2
2001	High Des	Cal	257	59	9	1	10	16	67	26	35	3	3	201	.230	.278	.389	.220	23	35-RF -2 29-1B -1
2001	Huntsvil	Sou	203	50	8	1	11	10	65	25	34	1	1	154	.246	.285	.458	.240	22	39-RF -3
2002	*Milwauke*	*NL*	*438*	*110*	*17*	*2*	*16*	*33*	*138*	*52*	*48*	*5*	*6*	*334*	*.251*	*.304*	*.409*	*.235*	*45*	

One of the most interesting discoveries Clay Davenport has made over the years is that if there's a type of player that improves dramatically, it's the guy who strikes out a ton. This isn't as counterintuitive as it sounds. Striking out a lot is an obvious problem, but it's one that some guys can correct. Deardorff is a great example of a high-school hitter who stumbled along for years, and who is finally starting to figure out what pitches he can hammer. The problem for Deardorff is that while he has improved dramatically, he needs to improve even more if he's going to be more than just a successful minor-league slugger.

Angel Echevarria OF Bats R Age 31

YEAR	TEAM	LGE	AB	H	DB	TP	HR	BB	SO	R	RBI	SB	CS	OUT	BA	OBP	SLG	EQA	EQR	DEFENSE
1999	Colorado	NL	186	48	4	0	10	15	31	24	29	1	3	141	.258	.323	.441	.248	22	35-RF -2
2000	ColSprin	PCL	275	78	17	1	6	19	43	34	36	1	1	198	.284	.338	.418	.253	32	51-RF -2 13-1B -1
2000	Milwauke	NL	42	9	1	0	1	7	8	3	4	0	0	33	.214	.327	.310	.224	4	
2001	Milwauke	NL	133	35	9	0	6	8	25	12	14	0	1	99	.263	.316	.466	.253	16	19-LF -4
2002	*ChiCubs*	*NL*	*290*	*80*	*11*	*0*	*11*	*28*	*54*	*34*	*38*	*0*	*2*	*212*	*.276*	*.340*	*.428*	*.257*	*35*	

Echevarria was a failure as one of the Brewers' primary pinch hitters, hitting .139/.220/.306. In the rest of his playing time, Echevarria hit .299 and slugged over .500. There are worse people being employed as regulars at first base. He signed as a minor-league free agent with the Cubs, with whom he'll be fighting for the pinch-hitting role in which he has yet to thrive.

Cristian Guerrero RF Bats R Age 21

YEAR	TEAM	LGE	AB	H	DB	TP	HR	BB	SO	R	RBI	SB	CS	OUT	BA	OBP	SLG	EQA	EQR	DEFENSE
1999	Ogden	Pio	222	45	4	1	3	12	70	22	13	9	2	179	.203	.246	.270	.184	13	55-RF -2
2000	Ogden	Pio	250	55	8	1	6	18	51	24	23	9	4	199	.220	.276	.332	.209	20	58-RF 0
2001	High Des	Cal	321	75	14	1	4	13	76	32	25	11	7	253	.234	.264	.321	.199	22	75-RF -9
2002	*Milwauke*	*NL*	*329*	*82*	*12*	*1*	*8*	*24*	*87*	*41*	*30*	*16*	*7*	*254*	*.249*	*.300*	*.365*	*.227*	*31*	

Vladimir's cousin hasn't really hit the way a prospect should, but his youth and his bloodline will keep him around. Guerrero has enormous holes in his swing, so unlike some high-strikeout guys who might improve if they learn a little bit about selectivity, Guerrero has to rework his stroke *and* master the strike zone. High Desert is a lousy place to learn, because the ball carries even when it's not struck very well. In another organization, he might have a better chance of turning his obvious tools into skills.

Will Hall SS Bats Age 22

YEAR	TEAM	LGE	AB	H	DB	TP	HR	BB	SO	R	RBI	SB	CS	OUT	BA	OBP	SLG	EQA	EQR	DEFENSE	
1999	Ogden	Pio	274	51	8	1	3	6	72	17	14	6	5	228	.186	.206	.255	.158	11		
2000	Beloit	Mid	477	101	25	3	2	6	140	40	27	4	7	382	.212	.222	.289	.171	23	129-SS -9	
2001	High Des	Cal	341	79	12	3	10	15	75	38	31	9	6	268	.232	.267	.372	.212	28	89-SS -14	
2001	Huntsvil	Sou	161	37	7	1	2	3	45	12	11	3	2	126	.230	.244	.323	.190	10	41-SS -3	
2002	*Milwauke*	*NL*	*456*	*106*	*18*	*3*	*11*	*23*	*127*	*46*	*36*	*11*	*9*	*359*	*.232*	*.269*	*.357*	*.206*	*35*		

Hall was named the California League's Most Exciting Player, although it's unlikely that the votes of the people sitting behind first base were counted. While he's athletic, his arm is wildly inaccurate for short, leading to 40 errors in 2000 and 45 more in 2001. Unfortunately, his defense might be his strong suit; the power that appears to be his only hitting skill was a High Desert illusion. Hall was named the Arizona Fall League's top prospect; before you get excited, recall that one year James Mouton was the AFL's star.

Jeffrey Hammonds OF Bats R Age 31

YEAR	TEAM	LGE	AB	H	DB	TP	HR	BB	SO	R	RBI	SB	CS	OUT	BA	OBP	SLG	EQA	EQR	DEFENSE	
1999	Cincnnti	NL	262	71	10	0	17	24	59	40	38	2	6	197	.271	.334	.504	.266	36	66-OF 7	
2000	Colorado	NL	440	131	20	2	17	36	76	79	87	11	6	315	.298	.356	.468	.273	61	106-RF -2	
2001	Milwauke	NL	174	44	12	1	6	14	36	21	21	5	3	133	.253	.320	.437	.250	21	45-CF 0	
2002	*Milwauke*	*NL*	*359*	*100*	*16*	*1*	*16*	*37*	*75*	*57*	*53*	*11*	*7*	*266*	*.279*	*.346*	*.462*	*.268*	*50*		

If ever you worried about the ghost of Sal Bando reaching from beyond deserved oblivion and spiting the organization with another turkey of a deal, we give you the Brewers' decision to sign Hammonds. Ever the porcelain mouse, he strained his shoulder in June. The Brewers tried to bring him back in July, and he only hurt himself worse. If the Brewers trade Burnitz, Hammonds might at least get moved to an outfield corner so that somebody such as Rule 5 pick Ryan Christenson could play center field. Then the problem would be that Hammonds doesn't hit enough to hold a corner job on a good team.

Jose Hernandez SS/3B Bats R Age 32

YEAR	TEAM	LGE	AB	H	DB	TP	HR	BB	SO	R	RBI	SB	CS	OUT	BA	OBP	SLG	EQA	EQR	DEFENSE	
1999	ChiCubs	NL	343	92	12	2	15	35	93	55	41	6	2	253	.268	.344	.446	.264	45	79-SS 10	13-CF -3
1999	Atlanta	NL	167	42	5	0	5	10	41	21	19	4	1	126	.251	.294	.371	.225	15	39-SS 3	
2000	Milwauke	NL	449	109	21	1	11	35	115	49	56	2	7	347	.243	.305	.367	.223	41	91-3B -2	33-SS 0
2001	Milwauke	NL	543	140	26	3	25	37	157	70	80	5	4	407	.258	.307	.455	.248	63	142-SS 3	
2002	*Milwauke*	*NL*	*469*	*124*	*21*	*2*	*22*	*47*	*140*	*71*	*68*	*6*	*5*	*350*	*.264*	*.331*	*.458*	*.261*	*61*		

Is Robin Yount the only shortstop good enough for the snobs of Milwaukee? Jose Valentin was constantly belittled for his much-exaggerated faults. Hernandez had to spend another year listening to whining about his strikeouts and reminders of his admittedly bad 2000, as if his performance in 2001 was unprecedented. He's a good glove and a power source. Why ask why? It isn't like we're talking Dale Sveum here. At least Hernandez is projected to be the starting shortstop in 2002, as he should be.

Tyler Houston 3B/1B Bats L Age 31

YEAR	TEAM	LGE	AB	H	DB	TP	HR	BB	SO	R	RBI	SB	CS	OUT	BA	OBP	SLG	EQA	EQR	DEFENSE	
1999	ChiCubs	NL	250	58	8	1	9	25	62	25	25	1	1	193	.232	.302	.380	.229	24	51-3B -12	13-C -2
2000	Milwauke	NL	286	71	12	0	19	13	66	29	42	2	1	216	.248	.281	.490	.247	33	29-1B -2	21-3B 3
2001	Milwauke	NL	236	71	7	0	12	16	53	37	39	0	0	165	.301	.347	.483	.273	32	55-3B -2	
2002	*Milwauke*	*NL*	*258*	*69*	*9*	*0*	*13*	*23*	*64*	*29*	*34*	*1*	*1*	*190*	*.267*	*.327*	*.453*	*.259*	*32*		

Houston is projected to be the starting third baseman, which is not as laughable as it might have been two years ago. He's worked hard on his defense, and while he still doesn't have much range, he can start a double play now and again. Houston was hampered by hamstring problems before breaking down with a foot injury. The Brewers tried to rush him back in time for the September 1 roster expansion, but he only hurt the foot worse.

Bucky Jacobsen 1B Bats R Age 26

YEAR	TEAM	LGE	AB	H	DB	TP	HR	BB	SO	R	RBI	SB	CS	OUT	BA	OBP	SLG	EQA	EQR	DEFENSE
1999	Stockton	Cal	158	32	5	0	4	14	40	15	15	2	2	128	.203	.275	.310	.201	12	11-LF -1
1999	Huntsvil	Sou	153	27	3	1	3	14	33	15	15	2	1	127	.176	.253	.268	.184	9	24-LF -6 13-1B -1
2000	Huntsvil	Sou	280	70	8	0	16	41	68	39	41	3	1	211	.250	.350	.450	.268	39	75-1B -8
2001	Huntsvil	Sou	95	34	5	0	8	12	14	17	21	1	1	62	.358	.433	.663	.343	21	22-1B -1
2001	Indianap	Int	303	72	14	1	12	25	72	41	50	0	0	231	.238	.301	.409	.236	31	76-1B -1
2002	*Milwauke*	*NL*	*348*	*94*	*15*	*1*	*19*	*45*	*84*	*53*	*59*	*4*	*2*	*256*	*.270*	*.354*	*.483*	*.278*	*52*	

Jacobsen bounced back and forth between Indianapolis and Huntsville, creating longer commutes and confusion among the loyal little legion of Buckybackers. That projection looks a bit optimistic for a guy who's struggled with his introductions to new leagues. Nevertheless, he can be a nice homegrown replacement for Angel Echevarria. The problem is that he's a right-handed-hitting first baseman in the organization that has Richie Sexson, a much better right-handed-hitting first baseman. Sadly, the International League's pension plan isn't any better than Enron's.

Geoff Jenkins LF Bats L Age 27

YEAR	TEAM	LGE	AB	H	DB	TP	HR	BB	SO	R	RBI	SB	CS	OUT	BA	OBP	SLG	EQA	EQR	DEFENSE
1999	Milwauke	NL	448	138	43	3	21	29	81	68	77	4	1	311	.308	.359	.558	.296	74	115-LF 8
2000	Milwauke	NL	515	155	36	3	34	26	124	97	89	10	1	361	.301	.350	.581	.298	88	130-LF 5
2001	Milwauke	NL	398	110	20	1	21	34	102	62	65	4	2	290	.276	.343	.490	.273	56	104-LF 7
2002	*Milwauke*	*NL*	*448*	*133*	*29*	*2*	*25*	*40*	*116*	*73*	*75*	*8*	*1*	*316*	*.297*	*.355*	*.538*	*.293*	*73*	

Jenkins never really got started, spending most of the year fighting hand and shoulder injuries before going onto the DL with a torn thumb. When he came back in September he struggled, like a lot of the "hey, we'll be around next year" reactivations. At the plate, he's got a great coiled stance that conjures visions of the original Cobra, Dave Parker. The decision to bat him third is conventional, but why not plug somebody like Burnitz into that slot, someone who can both drive in runs and set them up by drawing a walk or two, and have the high-average hitter as a finisher for a big inning? Yes, lineup order isn't supposed to matter, but given the primitive computer programming that advanced that conclusion, it's hard not to believe that some runs can't be gained by optimizing a lineup.

Kade Johnson C Bats R Age 23

YEAR	TEAM	LGE	AB	H	DB	TP	HR	BB	SO	R	RBI	SB	CS	OUT	BA	OBP	SLG	EQA	EQR	DEFENSE
2000	Ogden	Pio	97	21	5	0	4	7	24	7	14	1	1	77	.216	.278	.392	.221	9	
2001	High Des	Cal	368	72	12	1	13	26	113	37	40	5	2	298	.196	.261	.340	.204	28	49-C -10 15-LF -2
2002	*Milwauke*	*NL*	*351*	*76*	*10*	*1*	*16*	*35*	*114*	*37*	*46*	*7*	*2*	*277*	*.217*	*.288*	*.387*	*.228*	*34*	

After rotator-cuff surgery in 2000, Johnson bounced back to play regularly in the high-A California League in his first full season as a pro. If he isn't a catcher, he isn't a prospect, but fortunately Johnson has the physical talent to catch, and the Brewers are confident his footwork and receiving skills will improve.

David Krynzel CF Bats L Age 20

YEAR	TEAM	LGE	AB	H	DB	TP	HR	BB	SO	R	RBI	SB	CS	OUT	BA	OBP	SLG	EQA	EQR	DEFENSE
2000	Ogden	Pio	127	30	6	1	0	8	28	11	13	3	2	99	.236	.290	.299	.204	9	32-CF -3
2001	Beloit	Mid	142	33	1	0	1	7	31	14	13	5	3	112	.232	.276	.261	.189	9	34-CF -4
2001	High Des	Cal	379	78	16	2	3	19	117	40	20	16	11	312	.206	.247	.282	.184	23	89-CF 3
2002	*Milwauke*	*NL*	*462*	*116*	*14*	*3*	*5*	*34*	*138*	*50*	*43*	*26*	*16*	*362*	*.251*	*.302*	*.327*	*.215*	*39*	

Assistant GM Dave Wilder says Krynzel has the feel for hitting leadoff, and that he's a natural for the job. This is like when your mother tells you you're a natural to be an astronaut. After all, even though you may not have any of the actual skills required, somebody believes in you, and that's enough, isn't it? Krynzel is young enough to become more than just the next Chad Green, but not if the Brewers promote him too aggressively, as they did in his first full season. He covers the gaps well afield, and he can fly on the bases. He's going to have to hit, though, and High Desert is no place to get ready for Double-A.

Luis Lopez IF Bats B Age 31

YEAR	TEAM	LGE	AB	H	DB	TP	HR	BB	SO	R	RBI	SB	CS	OUT	BA	OBP	SLG	EQA	EQR	DEFENSE	
1999	NY Mets	NL	105	23	4	0	2	11	31	11	13	1	1	83	.219	.311	.314	.217	9	16-SS -1	
2000	Milwauke	NL	203	54	10	0	7	6	32	23	27	1	2	151	.266	.302	.419	.235	20	36-SS -4	14-2B 1
2001	Milwauke	NL	223	63	9	3	4	12	37	23	19	0	1	161	.283	.330	.404	.244	24	37-3B -7	11-SS -2
2002	*Milwauke*	*NL*	*221*	*60*	*9*	*1*	*6*	*16*	*42*	*26*	*31*	*2*	*2*	*163*	*.271*	*.321*	*.403*	*.242*	*24*		

One of the Brewers' basic problems is identifying what's good about a player, within his limits. Lopez is a good hitter for a utility infielder, and that's as far as it goes. If Lopez can't hold off Elvis Pena in camp, he'll have to be traded or go through waivers. Keeping both would waste space on both the 25- and 40-man rosters, and with this team, you have to expect that a non-roster invitee or two will come north from spring training.

Mark Loretta IF Bats R Age 30

YEAR	TEAM	LGE	AB	H	DB	TP	HR	BB	SO	R	RBI	SB	CS	OUT	BA	OBP	SLG	EQA	EQR	DEFENSE	
1999	Milwauke	NL	589	169	35	5	5	44	55	91	64	3	1	421	.287	.347	.389	.250	66	69-SS -6	55-1B -2
2000	Milwauke	NL	354	99	20	1	7	32	35	47	38	0	3	258	.280	.341	.401	.248	39	81-SS 13	
2001	Milwauke	NL	385	116	15	2	2	26	39	42	30	1	2	271	.301	.354	.366	.246	41	50-2B -2	31-3B -2
2002	*Milwauke*	*NL*	*479*	*140*	*23*	*3*	*7*	*41*	*53*	*69*	*51*	*2*	*2*	*341*	*.292*	*.348*	*.397*	*.253*	*55*		

Loretta got hurt again, starting off with an injured thumb that cost him the first couple of months, and finishing with a broken leg that has people concerned going into 2002. With Houston and Hernandez coming off of good seasons, Loretta will be shoehorned into a roving infielder role, starting at second base, third base, and shortstop as needed. That's not an ideal role for him; at third base, he's too ready to let the ball play him, while giving you less offense than you'd want from the position. After he shows he's healthy, he'll be very valuable to a contender looking for a starter at second or short.

James Mouton OF Bats R Age 33

YEAR	TEAM	LGE	AB	H	DB	TP	HR	BB	SO	R	RBI	SB	CS	OUT	BA	OBP	SLG	EQA	EQR	DEFENSE
1999	Montreal	NL	122	31	5	1	2	17	29	17	12	5	2	93	.254	.354	.361	.250	15	27-LF -3
2000	Milwauke	NL	160	37	6	1	2	28	39	26	16	12	4	127	.231	.355	.319	.245	19	40-OF -1
2001	Milwauke	NL	130	35	8	0	3	11	34	20	11	7	3	106	.254	.329	.362	.239	15	37-OF 0
2002	*Milwauke*	*NL*	*170*	*40*	*6*	*1*	*4*	*26*	*45*	*25*	*16*	*11*	*3*	*133*	*.235*	*.337*	*.353*	*.246*	*20*	

Mouton is one of Davey Lopes's favorites, which isn't a bad thing. He has value as a pinch hitter, pinch runner, defensive sub, and spot starter against left-handers. That's a handy guy to have as your fifth outfielder on a team where the starters in both outfield corners bat left-handed. The problem is that Mouton and Alex Sanchez are mutually exclusive, not complementary, bench players.

Elvis Pena 2B/SS Bats B Age 25

YEAR	TEAM	LGE	AB	H	DB	TP	HR	BB	SO	R	RBI	SB	CS	OUT	BA	OBP	SLG	EQA	EQR	DEFENSE	
1999	Carolina	Sou	358	93	19	4	2	35	65	43	23	13	4	269	.260	.332	.352	.238	37	77-2B -15	24-SS 0
2000	Carolina	Sou	494	136	16	5	3	52	75	77	32	30	10	367	.275	.351	.346	.247	55	115-SS -18	10-2B -1
2001	Indianap	Int	440	103	15	2	1	29	70	54	27	10	4	341	.234	.289	.284	.202	31	103-SS -16	12-2B -3
2001	Milwauke	NL	40	9	3	0	0	6	5	5	6	2	0	31	.225	.337	.300	.236	4		
2002	*Milwauke*	*NL*	*476*	*126*	*22*	*3*	*3*	*53*	*80*	*64*	*31*	*20*	*6*	*356*	*.265*	*.338*	*.342*	*.240*	*50*		

A useful throw-in in the Acevedo trade with the Rockies, Pena is a Cuban who fled to this country as a teenager. Pena doesn't really have the arm for shortstop, so he's essentially a second baseman. There's a chance that he can turn into a useful utility man, sort of a poor man's Mark McLemore, although McLemore was a couple of years younger when he broke into the majors.

Jeff Pickler — 2B — Bats L — Age 26

YEAR	TEAM	LGE	AB	H	DB	TP	HR	BB	SO	R	RBI	SB	CS	OUT	BA	OBP	SLG	EQA	EQR	DEFENSE
1999	Stockton	Cal	309	84	11	1	1	14	29	27	28	4	3	228	.272	.303	.324	.213	24	72-2B -8
1999	Huntsvil	Sou	184	45	5	1	1	10	25	15	18	6	3	142	.245	.284	.299	.202	13	46-2B 0
2000	Huntsvil	Sou	263	72	6	0	1	22	28	29	23	10	8	199	.274	.331	.308	.221	23	66-2B -3
2000	Indianap	Int	190	55	5	1	1	20	27	30	18	11	3	138	.289	.360	.342	.250	22	48-2B -2
2001	Huntsvil	Sou	533	134	11	2	1	46	50	61	28	23	11	410	.251	.312	.285	.212	42	130-2B -12
2002	*Texas*	*AL*	*473*	*133*	*14*	*2*	*3*	*44*	*51*	*54*	*42*	*22*	*14*	*354*	*.281*	*.342*	*.338*	*.231*	*45*	

Sometimes, an employer isn't subtle about letting you know you're not part of the company's long-term plan. It can start off with something as simple as the employer forgetting to give you a T-shirt at the company picnic, or not listing your extension in the company directory. For Pickler, it was the chance to be a Southern League All-Star in both 2000 and 2001 that showed him his future. Not even the rash of injuries in the big-league infield could get him back to Indianapolis. Being taken by the Rangers in the minor-league portion of the Rule 5 draft is an escape of sorts, except that second base is pretty well covered in Texas. Pickler has limited defensive value and no power. He'll take a walk, so he might be a useful temp for somebody.

Jim Rushford — OF — Bats L — Age 28

YEAR	TEAM	LGE	AB	H	DB	TP	HR	BB	SO	R	RBI	SB	CS	OUT	BA	OBP	SLG	EQA	EQR	DEFENSE
2000	Duluth	Nth	287	75	12	2	8	16	37	34	34	6	4	216	.261	.305	.401	.234	29	
2001	High Des	Cal	256	68	13	1	9	27	34	44	37	1	2	190	.266	.341	.430	.256	31	38-LF 0 26-1B 6
2001	Huntsvil	Sou	190	56	11	1	6	18	22	29	24	2	1	135	.295	.364	.458	.274	27	46-RF -2
2002	*Milwauke*	*NL*	*392*	*109*	*18*	*2*	*15*	*43*	*54*	*54*	*53*	*6*	*5*	*288*	*.278*	*.349*	*.449*	*.267*	*53*	

Rushford was undrafted coming out of San Diego State, so he put in four years in the independent leagues before being signed by the Brewers to provide some grizzled, bus-weary bust-ass leadership. He did more than just that, leading all of the minor leagues in batting average in 2001. What would the world be like if organizations spent more time fielding minor-league teams that featured "non-prospects" like this who can play ball? Next thing you know, minor-league pennant races might matter again.

Alex Sanchez — CF — Bats L — Age 25

YEAR	TEAM	LGE	AB	H	DB	TP	HR	BB	SO	R	RBI	SB	CS	OUT	BA	OBP	SLG	EQA	EQR	DEFENSE
1999	Orlando	Sou	503	111	9	3	2	16	89	50	22	30	18	410	.221	.245	.262	.179	28	121-CF 0
2000	Orlando	Sou	87	23	1	1	0	0	13	11	3	2	4	67	.264	.269	.299	.185	5	19-LF -1
2000	Durham	Int	449	125	18	2	2	24	65	66	29	40	17	341	.278	.321	.341	.231	44	107-CF -1
2001	Indianap	Int	337	100	13	4	1	23	41	49	24	22	7	244	.297	.344	.368	.248	37	76-CF -7
2001	Milwauke	NL	68	14	4	2	0	5	11	7	4	6	2	56	.206	.260	.324	.207	5	14-CF -1
2002	*Milwauke*	*NL*	*483*	*139*	*15*	*4*	*3*	*38*	*73*	*77*	*30*	*48*	*19*	*362*	*.288*	*.340*	*.354*	*.246*	*54*	

A worse player than his numbers show, Sanchez is one of those speed guys with very little idea about what he's doing in any phase of the game. He gets caught flat-footed in the outfield, especially coming in on line drives, and then he forgets which base to throw to. He can slap a single and he can run, so he's only useful as the last man on the bench on a team with a good center fielder and a couple of better pinch hitters.

Marcos Scutaro — 2B — Bats R — Age 26

YEAR	TEAM	LGE	AB	H	DB	TP	HR	BB	SO	R	RBI	SB	CS	OUT	BA	OBP	SLG	EQA	EQR	DEFENSE
1999	Buffalo	Int	463	118	20	2	7	51	65	63	42	16	5	350	.255	.335	.352	.239	49	122-2B 3
2000	Buffalo	Int	429	112	18	4	5	52	52	61	48	7	5	322	.261	.351	.357	.244	47	109-2B -1 17-SS -7
2001	Indianap	Int	502	139	25	2	11	59	77	83	47	9	9	372	.277	.361	.400	.257	62	117-2B -11
2002	*Milwauke*	*NL*	*483*	*133*	*24*	*3*	*10*	*61*	*74*	*76*	*53*	*14*	*7*	*357*	*.275*	*.357*	*.400*	*.260*	*62*	

If there's a guy primed to be the next Frankie Menechino, it's Scutaro. He already has more than three years of experience in the International League, he has solid on-base skills, and he's picking up power as he matures. He should have been starting at second base and hitting at the top of the order after Belliard broke down. He was finally added to the 40-man roster after the season, about three months too late to do the 2001 Brewers any good.

Richie Sexson 1B Bats R Age 27

YEAR	TEAM	LGE	AB	H	DB	TP	HR	BB	SO	R	RBI	SB	CS	OUT	BA	OBP	SLG	EQA	EQR	DEFENSE	
1999	Clevelnd	AL	476	124	16	7	33	30	103	71	114	3	3	355	.261	.309	.532	.267	66	58-1B 3	43-LF -3
2000	Clevelnd	AL	321	83	15	1	17	21	84	43	42	1	0	238	.259	.312	.470	.256	39	47-LF -2	25-1B 3
2000	Milwauke	NL	214	63	12	0	14	31	58	42	44	1	0	151	.294	.390	.547	.306	39	56-1B 10	
2001	Milwauke	NL	599	168	24	3	46	57	151	98	128	2	4	435	.280	.348	.561	.289	97	154-1B 7	
2002	*Milwauke*	*NL*	*571*	*161*	*23*	*3*	*39*	*66*	*154*	*93*	*122*	*3*	*3*	*413*	*.282*	*.356*	*.538*	*.290*	*94*		

Baseball's Lerch busted out about as well as expected when handed an everyday job. Even so, it's impressive that in his first full season as a Brewer, Sexson tied the franchise's single-season mark for home runs (45), originally set by Gorman Thomas, and fell one short of the team's RBI record, set by Cecil Cooper. Sexson also homered better than once every 12 plate appearances in Miller Park, and he hit .293/.370/.625 in the second half. He's in the middle of what should be a really good five-year run.

Mark Sweeney OF Bats L Age 32

YEAR	TEAM	LGE	AB	H	DB	TP	HR	BB	SO	R	RBI	SB	CS	OUT	BA	OBP	SLG	EQA	EQR	DEFENSE	
1999	Indianap	Int	310	92	14	1	10	50	38	55	41	2	2	220	.297	.399	.445	.287	48	53-RF -1	16-1B -4
2000	Indianap	Int	55	25	3	0	3	8	8	11	13	0	0	30	.455	.524	.673	.392	14		
2000	Milwauke	NL	73	16	3	0	2	11	17	8	6	0	0	57	.219	.328	.342	.233	7		
2001	Indianap	Int	411	113	30	1	6	52	66	63	66	2	1	299	.275	.358	.397	.258	50	49-LF 1	
2001	Milwauke	NL	89	24	2	1	3	12	20	9	11	2	1	66	.270	.356	.416	.262	12	18-LF -1	
2002	*NY Mets*	*NL*	*415*	*109*	*20*	*1*	*11*	*57*	*76*	*60*	*49*	*4*	*2*	*308*	*.263*	*.352*	*.395*	*.262*	*54*		

What's worse, that the Brewers traded Alex Ochoa to get Sweeney (and thus avoid arbitration with Ochoa), or that they didn't use Sweeney after getting him? In 2000, he was hurt, but what about in 2001, when the bench desperately needed a lefty bat? A useful fourth outfielder and pinch hitter, Sweeney is not primed to be the next Warren Newson or anything, he's just a good spare part on a team that wasted time on Alex Sanchez. Now that he's a Met, he'll fight for a pinch-hitting job.

Devon White CF Bats B Age 39

YEAR	TEAM	LGE	AB	H	DB	TP	HR	BB	SO	R	RBI	SB	CS	OUT	BA	OBP	SLG	EQA	EQR	DEFENSE
1999	LosAngls	NL	480	132	20	2	15	33	81	60	68	17	5	353	.275	.336	.419	.256	58	120-CF -4
2000	LosAngls	NL	160	43	6	1	4	7	28	25	13	2	6	123	.269	.303	.394	.223	14	35-CF -6
2001	Milwauke	NL	391	113	27	2	14	26	81	54	48	17	3	281	.289	.348	.476	.276	56	91-CF -5
2002	*Milwauke*	*NL*	*390*	*93*	*20*	*2*	*12*	*31*	*81*	*55*	*45*	*14*	*6*	*303*	*.238*	*.295*	*.392*	*.232*	*39*	

GM Dean Taylor's master stroke of 2001 was unloading Marquis Grissom, whom he traded for Devo; White's good season was just gravy. White even did well in the leadoff slot, posting a .365 OBP during the third of a season that he was at the top of the order. Unfortunately, his days as a primo defender are gone, and his chances of doing this well again are remote. The Brewers declined to pick up their option on Devo for 2002.

PITCHERS (ERA: 4.50, H/9: 9.0, HR/9: 1.0, BB/9: 3.0, K/9: 6.0, KW: 2.0, PERA: 4.50)

Mike Buddie Throws R Age 31

YEAR	TEAM	LGE	IP	H	ER	HR	BB	K	ERA	W	L	H/9	HR/9	BB/9	K/9	KW	PERA	STUFF
1999	Columbus	Int	81.7	77	30	2	24	49	3.31	6	3	8.5	0.2	2.6	5.4	1.0	3.69	-4
2000	Columbus	Int	28.7	39	38	11	22	12	11.93	0	3	12.2	3.5	6.9	3.8	0.3	10.61	-59
2000	Indianap	Int	54.0	56	33	5	32	29	5.50	2	4	9.3	0.8	5.3	4.8	0.5	3.54	-22
2001	Indianap	Int	43.3	47	33	6	32	21	6.85	2	3	9.8	1.2	6.6	4.4	0.3	3.10	-34
2001	Milwauke	NL	38.0	38	18	2	15	18	4.26	2	2	9.0	0.5	3.6	4.3	0.6	4.27	-12

A nondescript reliever straight from the Age of Clutterbuck, Buddie is not to be confused for the next David Weathers. He's more of a command pitcher, and he has next to no upside. At best, he provides some value as an eleventh pitcher who can be designated for assignment at any time without real concern about losing him.

Carlos Chantres Throws R Age 26

YEAR	TEAM	LGE	IP	H	ER	HR	BB	K	ERA	W	L	H/9	HR/9	BB/9	K/9	KW	PERA	STUFF
1999	Birmnghm	Sou	135.7	148	89	20	64	71	5.90	6	9	9.8	1.3	4.2	4.7	0.6	4.87	-6
2000	Charlott	Int	141.0	150	78	15	54	69	4.98	7	9	9.6	1.0	3.4	4.4	0.6	3.87	-4
2001	Indianap	Int	165.3	188	128	22	118	59	6.97	5	13	10.2	1.2	6.4	3.2	0.3	6.18	-29

Imagine that you're a young free-agent pitcher who won't cost his new employer draft picks or really big money. You'd have the freedom to pitch in just about any organization you want, right? So who in his right mind chooses the Brewers? Chantres is a command pitcher who reentered minor-league free agency this winter with an uglier resume. He signed with the Devil Rays, showing that his taste in organizations hasn't gotten any better. He will have a shot at the #5 slot in the rotation.

Matt Childers Throws R Age 23

YEAR	TEAM	LGE	IP	H	ER	HR	BB	K	ERA	W	L	H/9	HR/9	BB/9	K/9	KW	PERA	STUFF
1999	Beloit	Mid	104.3	127	74	19	34	30	6.38	4	8	11.0	1.6	2.9	2.6	0.4	7.76	-15
2000	Beloit	Mid	70.0	79	41	9	19	27	5.27	3	5	10.2	1.2	2.4	3.5	0.7	5.42	-1
2000	Mudville	Cal	85.0	108	73	21	32	25	7.73	2	7	11.4	2.2	3.4	2.6	0.4	7.67	-19
2001	High Des	Cal	121.3	156	105	33	37	40	7.79	3	10	11.6	2.4	2.7	3.0	0.5	7.74	-20
2001	Huntsvil	Sou	38.0	43	23	5	13	13	5.45	2	2	10.2	1.2	3.1	3.1	0.5	5.47	-8

Childers's main claim to fame is his mid-90s heat, and like a lot of high-school draftees, he's taken a long time to gain any kind of command. His future is as a reliever unless he picks up command of any pitch that wiggles or moves slower than his fastball. Childers is a better prospect than Gene Altman, another favored flamethrower in the organization.

Will Cunnane Throws R Age 28

YEAR	TEAM	LGE	IP	H	ER	HR	BB	K	ERA	W	L	H/9	HR/9	BB/9	K/9	KW	PERA	STUFF
1999	LasVegas	PCL	38.0	29	13	0	19	36	3.08	3	1	6.9	0.0	4.5	8.5	0.9	1.23	10
1999	San Dieg	NL	31.0	36	23	8	10	20	6.68	1	2	10.5	2.3	2.9	5.8	1.0	5.45	-15
2000	LasVegas	PCL	99.3	96	44	9	28	69	3.99	6	5	8.7	0.8	2.5	6.3	1.2	4.29	9
2000	San Dieg	NL	39.0	35	16	2	17	30	3.69	2	2	8.1	0.5	3.9	6.9	0.9	4.88	2
2001	Milwauke	NL	53.3	55	27	5	20	30	4.56	3	3	9.3	0.8	3.4	5.1	0.8	5.86	-10
2001	Indianap	Int	24.0	24	12	3	8	17	4.50	2	1	9.0	1.1	3.0	6.4	1.1	4.77	-3

How often does a guy get sent down as he's finally shaking off a bad start, just because his cumulative numbers still look terrible? Cunnane was beginning to pitch well in late June and July, but because he had been so awful before then, it was hard for the Brewers to see the trees for the forest. Cunnane's fastball is good but has no movement. In the '80s, he'd have been the kind of guy to whom Roger Craig would teach a forkball, set him loose, and watch him blow out his elbow after a great year and a half. Cunnane signed with the Cubs as a minor-league free agent.

Jeff D'Amico Throws R Age 26

YEAR	TEAM	LGE	IP	H	ER	HR	BB	K	ERA	W	L	H/9	HR/9	BB/9	K/9	KW	PERA	STUFF
2000	Indianap	Int	28.7	34	24	8	11	16	7.53	1	2	10.7	2.5	3.5	5.0	0.7	3.34	-9
2000	Milwauke	NL	159.3	160	69	12	38	90	3.90	10	8	9.0	0.7	2.1	5.1	1.2	2.77	13
2001	Milwauke	NL	47.3	54	32	9	14	26	6.08	2	3	10.3	1.7	2.7	4.9	0.9	7.91	-9

How much sunshine are you expecting to find in this space? D'Amico had arm problems in high school and has had them in every year since, he's a really oversized human being, and he's coming off of a shoulder surgery that only Orel Hershiser has ever been able to survive professionally. D'Amico is an awful lot of fun to watch when he's on a roll, but the likelihood that he'll enjoy another roll like 2001 is remote.

Mike DeJean Throws R Age 31

YEAR	TEAM	LGE	IP	H	ER	HR	BB	K	ERA	W	L	H/9	HR/9	BB/9	K/9	KW	PERA	STUFF
1999	Colorado	NL	65.3	75	45	11	27	28	6.20	2	5	10.3	1.5	3.7	3.9	0.5	6.60	-27
2000	ColSprin	PCL	15.0	14	5	0	4	9	3.00	1	1	8.4	0.0	2.4	5.4	1.1	2.35	-1
2000	Colorado	NL	53.3	57	33	7	25	30	5.57	2	4	9.6	1.2	4.2	5.1	0.6	3.76	-15
2001	Milwauke	NL	80.7	75	34	3	35	55	3.79	5	4	8.4	0.3	3.9	6.1	0.8	3.28	0

DeJean was picked up in the Juan Acevedo trade along with Mark Leiter, a deal in which two teams desperate for right-handed relief depth exchanged some. It sort of worked out. Liberated from pitching at altitude, DeJean was healthy and successful in long relief. Kane Davis had a good year for the Rockies, while Acevedo, who was supposed to be the best player in the deal, flopped. In terms of middle-relief subcultures, there's little you'll find here that wasn't already written in *Rich Bordi: A Life.*

Chad Fox **Throws R** **Age 31**

YEAR	TEAM	LGE	IP	H	ER	HR	BB	K	ERA	W	L	H/9	HR/9	BB/9	K/9	KW	PERA	STUFF
1999	Milwauke	NL	8.3	6	3	1	3	11	3.24	1	0	6.5	1.1	3.2	11.9	1.8	9.78	24
2001	Milwauke	NL	61.7	51	27	5	32	64	3.94	4	3	7.4	0.7	4.7	9.3	1.0	2.14	15

After watching him miss two years with elbow problems, the Brewers are crowing about Fox's potential as a closer. Do not get carried away. Like Matt Mantei, he's an injury risk waiting for his next breakdown. The difference between the Brewers and the Marlins is that the Fish understood when to sell high, while the Brewers are talking multiyear deal. Question for Davey Lopes: why did you have one of the most unhittable relievers in the league issue seven intentional walks?

Gus Gandarillas **Throws R** **Age 30**

YEAR	TEAM	LGE	IP	H	ER	HR	BB	K	ERA	W	L	H/9	HR/9	BB/9	K/9	KW	PERA	STUFF
1999	New Brit	Eas	33.3	37	27	5	25	16	7.29	1	3	10.0	1.4	6.8	4.3	0.3	12.23	-53
1999	SaltLake	PCL	63.7	70	39	9	23	32	5.51	3	4	9.9	1.3	3.3	4.5	0.7	5.25	-24
2000	SaltLake	PCL	94.0	99	53	11	35	53	5.07	4	6	9.5	1.1	3.4	5.1	0.8	4.81	-18
2001	Pawtuckt	Int	16.0	16	9	0	13	5	5.06	1	1	9.0	0.0	7.3	2.8	0.2	6.96	-42
2001	Indianap	Int	65.7	67	30	6	17	35	4.11	4	3	9.2	0.8	2.3	4.8	1.0	5.00	-10
2001	Milwauke	NL	19.7	22	12	2	9	6	5.49	1	1	10.1	0.9	4.1	2.7	0.3	5.88	-30

The 2001 Brewers might not have accomplished much in terms of their record or player development, but they did get minor-league lifers such as Gus Gandarillas and Mike Coolbaugh into the majors. That may not mean much to Brewers fans, but if getting such guys major-league playing time helps the team to land future minor-league free agents, then something was accomplished. Gandarillas quickly re-signed with the Brewers, that's for certain.

Jose Garcia **Throws R** **Age 24**

YEAR	TEAM	LGE	IP	H	ER	HR	BB	K	ERA	W	L	H/9	HR/9	BB/9	K/9	KW	PERA	STUFF
2000	Huntsvil	Sou	103.3	113	69	14	55	52	6.01	4	7	9.8	1.2	4.8	4.5	0.5	5.88	-5
2001	Huntsvil	Sou	105.7	111	62	10	56	51	5.28	5	7	9.5	0.9	4.8	4.3	0.5	5.52	-7

Garcia has been really slow in shaking off the rust caused by missing '99 with an elbow injury that resulted in Tommy John surgery. Although he throws in the low 90s and owns a good curve, he works behind in the count far too often to inspire confidence as a starter. He doesn't get hit hard, so he might work out as a reliever, but you can say that about a lot of guys. Garcia was removed from the 40-man roster after the Rule 5 draft.

J.M. Gold **Throws R** **Age 22**

YEAR	TEAM	LGE	IP	H	ER	HR	BB	K	ERA	W	L	H/9	HR/9	BB/9	K/9	KW	PERA	STUFF
1999	Beloit	Mid	109.3	138	111	33	61	53	9.14	2	10	11.4	2.7	5.0	4.4	0.4	7.92	-11
2000	Beloit	Mid	33.7	31	14	0	18	19	3.74	2	2	8.3	0.0	4.8	5.1	0.5	4.59	9
2001	Ogden	Pio	28.0	26	13	2	12	21	4.18	2	1	8.4	0.6	3.9	6.8	0.9	4.22	14

The Brewers' top pick (and eighth selection overall) in 1998, Gold missed most of the previous two seasons after blowing out his elbow. He returned in 2001, showing flashes of his mid-90s velocity and sharp-breaking curve, but we won't really know how well he's bounced back until this summer. He used to throw cross-body, something the Brewers are trying to correct. It's worth remembering that they also tried with Kyle Peterson, and it didn't work.

Jimmy Haynes **Throws R** **Age 29**

YEAR	TEAM	LGE	IP	H	ER	HR	BB	K	ERA	W	L	H/9	HR/9	BB/9	K/9	KW	PERA	STUFF
1999	Oakland	AL	147.3	152	86	19	67	92	5.25	7	9	9.3	1.2	4.1	5.6	0.7	6.19	-3
2000	Milwauke	NL	205.0	223	115	19	82	78	5.05	10	13	9.8	0.8	3.6	3.4	0.5	5.26	-8
2001	Milwauke	NL	167.0	174	92	17	70	90	4.96	9	10	9.4	0.9	3.8	4.9	0.6	5.06	-1

(Jimmy Haynes *continued*)

Haynes's struggles are less frustrating than Jamey Wright's, in that the expectations are lower. A strained oblique at the end of August saved Haynes from a 20-loss season and cost him his shot at the 2001 DeLeon Award for the largest difference between losses and wins. Haynes exasperates all sorts of people with his soft-spoken nature, and his future will depend heavily on whether his next pitching coach can find a way to turn Haynes's great stuff into results. Stranger things have happened, but it's about as likely as Michael Bolton opening for an Oingo Boingo reunion tour. Non-tendered in December, Haynes could be your team's fifth starter by the time you read this.

Ben Hendrickson — Throws R — Age 21

YEAR	TEAM	LGE	IP	H	ER	HR	BB	K	ERA	W	L	H/9	HR/9	BB/9	K/9	KW	PERA	STUFF
2000	Ogden	Pio	48.7	62	55	16	32	25	10.17	1	4	11.5	3.0	5.9	4.6	0.4	7.16	-17
2001	Beloit	Mid	135.0	132	77	6	95	76	5.13	7	8	8.8	0.4	6.3	5.1	0.4	5.01	4

Hendrickson flits between 88 and 92 mph with his fastball, but it's his curveball that makes people stare. In the *Baseball America* tools poll, it was named the best breaking pitch in the Midwest League. The question, as with all Brewers pitching prospects, is whether to send him to High Desert's charnel house for some pastings, or push him up to Double-A to avoid a bad ballpark and instead face a tougher league.

Michael Jones — Throws R — Age 19

YEAR	TEAM	LGE	IP	H	ER	HR	BB	K	ERA	W	L	H/9	HR/9	BB/9	K/9	KW	PERA	STUFF
2001	Ogden	Pio	33.3	34	17	2	14	16	4.59	2	2	9.2	0.5	3.8	4.3	0.6	5.14	1

Generally speaking, it's premature to get excited about a high-school pitcher in the year he is drafted. The Brewers, though, have terribly few prospects, and Jones's debut was outstanding. The organization's first-rounder in 2001, Jones throws in the low 90s already. Like Jeff D'Amico, he had shoulder problems in high school. Given the Brewers' track record with young pitchers with arm problems, you can only hope Jones beats history instead of repeating it.

Ray King — Throws L — Age 28

YEAR	TEAM	LGE	IP	H	ER	HR	BB	K	ERA	W	L	H/9	HR/9	BB/9	K/9	KW	PERA	STUFF
1999	Iowa	PCL	41.3	38	20	1	26	28	4.35	3	2	8.3	0.2	5.7	6.1	0.5	2.52	-12
1999	ChiCubs	NL	10.3	12	9	2	8	5	7.84	0	1	10.5	1.7	7.0	4.4	0.3	6.09	-37
2000	Indianap	Int	26.3	26	13	1	13	15	4.44	2	1	8.9	0.3	4.4	5.1	0.6	6.02	-20
2000	Milwauke	NL	26.7	25	10	1	8	17	3.38	2	1	8.4	0.3	2.7	5.7	1.1	2.00	1
2001	Milwauke	NL	52.7	49	25	4	22	39	4.27	3	3	8.4	0.7	3.8	6.7	0.9	3.57	-1

King is probably a perfectly fine situational lefty in a world where scheduling might keep him from seeing the same team or the same hitters too often. He's a one-trick pony, pedalling up his fastball while trying to get people to chase a slider he keeps outside. As routines go, it should wear out pretty quickly; King would get killed in a seven-game series, not that the Brewers have to worry about that any time soon. As long as baseball sticks with a schedule in which NL teams can face as many as 20 different opponents, King won't have to worry about becoming overly familiar to anybody, and he will continue to be a useful situational guy.

Brandon Kolb — Throws R — Age 28

YEAR	TEAM	LGE	IP	H	ER	HR	BB	K	ERA	W	L	H/9	HR/9	BB/9	K/9	KW	PERA	STUFF
1999	LasVegas	PCL	66.3	63	32	4	34	42	4.34	4	3	8.5	0.5	4.6	5.7	0.6	5.28	-16
2000	LasVegas	PCL	57.7	53	23	3	22	42	3.59	4	2	8.3	0.5	3.4	6.6	1.0	5.65	-7
2000	San Dieg	NL	15.3	13	6	0	9	11	3.52	1	1	7.6	0.0	5.3	6.5	0.6	5.08	-2
2001	Indianap	Int	53.0	56	37	10	28	39	6.28	2	4	9.5	1.7	4.8	6.6	0.7	5.69	-22
2001	Milwauke	NL	10.0	14	15	5	7	6	13.50	0	1	12.6	4.5	6.3	5.4	0.4	14.70	-61

Kolb has been just about ready to break through for several years now, and because he throws in the mid-90s, there's always the hope that he will finally turn into something. He has a chance at breaking camp in a setup role, and between Fox's fragility and Leskanic's off-season surgery, there's a long shot that he might impress Lopes and Stewart enough to sneak into a few save opportunities.

Curt Leskanic Throws R Age 34

YEAR	TEAM	LGE	IP	H	ER	HR	BB	K	ERA	W	L	H/9	HR/9	BB/9	K/9	KW	PERA	STUFF
1999	Colorado	NL	88.7	81	40	6	41	69	4.06	6	4	8.2	0.6	4.2	7.0	0.8	4.19	1
2000	Milwauke	NL	75.3	67	37	6	42	67	4.42	4	4	8.0	0.7	5.0	8.0	0.8	2.43	5
2001	Milwauke	NL	65.7	65	37	9	28	51	5.07	3	4	8.9	1.2	3.8	7.0	0.9	3.86	-2

Leskanic's heavily incentive laden contract might put the Brewers in a bit of a pickle, in that he hasn't been able to hold onto the closer's job, and replacing him with Chad Fox might lead to some squawking. It will be less of an issue at the start of the year, as Leskanic recuperates from off-season surgery to repair several small tears in his shoulder. By June, either he'll be asking for a trade, or he'll be closing. Fox's unreliable elbow should get Leskanic back into the closer's role soon enough.

Allen Levrault Throws R Age 24

YEAR	TEAM	LGE	IP	H	ER	HR	BB	K	ERA	W	L	H/9	HR/9	BB/9	K/9	KW	PERA	STUFF
1999	Huntsvil	Sou	93.7	101	59	16	33	58	5.67	4	6	9.7	1.5	3.2	5.6	0.9	4.37	11
1999	Louisvil	Int	37.3	42	29	10	15	27	6.99	1	3	10.1	2.4	3.6	6.5	0.9	9.10	0
2000	Indianap	Int	107.0	108	57	11	44	66	4.79	6	6	9.1	0.9	3.7	5.6	0.8	4.64	8
2000	Milwauke	NL	12.0	11	5	0	6	8	3.75	1	0	8.3	0.0	4.5	6.0	0.7	4.77	4
2001	Indianap	Int	29.7	26	11	1	9	23	3.34	2	1	7.9	0.3	2.7	7.0	1.3	2.89	26
2001	Milwauke	NL	125.3	142	88	23	53	64	6.32	5	9	10.2	1.7	3.8	4.6	0.6	6.34	-11

Levrault had a great winter-ball campaign before 2001, showed up to camp slimmed down, and was rewarded with an April call-up when Jeff D'Amico broke down. He's not about to develop into a good starting pitcher; he relies on low-90s heat and a nice change-up, and none of his breaking stuff is reliable. He gets good marks for his attitude, since he's cut from the stubborn bulldoggy mold. That and his limited assortment suggests that he'll make a great replacement for David Weathers in the long-relief role.

Brian Mallette Throws R Age 27

YEAR	TEAM	LGE	IP	H	ER	HR	BB	K	ERA	W	L	H/9	HR/9	BB/9	K/9	KW	PERA	STUFF
1999	Stockton	Cal	37.0	38	21	2	22	17	5.11	2	2	9.2	0.5	5.4	4.1	0.4	5.76	-33
2000	Mudville	Cal	65.7	73	66	15	63	45	9.05	1	6	10.0	2.1	8.6	6.2	0.4	6.69	-54
2001	Huntsvil	Sou	52.0	52	33	7	29	38	5.71	2	4	9.0	1.2	5.0	6.6	0.7	3.14	-19
2001	Indianap	Int	15.7	15	11	3	10	16	6.32	1	1	8.6	1.7	5.7	9.2	0.8	2.62	-6

At six feet tall, Mallette is short by professional standards. In this organization, though, a decent year is enough to vault a minor-league reliever onto the 40-man roster. He has a reasonably good shot at making the team out of spring training. One of the many sad things about the Brewers' farm system is that relievers are among their best homegrown prospects.

Luis Martinez Throws L Age 22

YEAR	TEAM	LGE	IP	H	ER	HR	BB	K	ERA	W	L	H/9	HR/9	BB/9	K/9	KW	PERA	STUFF
1999	Ogden	Pio	54.7	61	42	7	42	22	6.91	2	4	10.0	1.2	6.9	3.6	0.3	12.38	-25
2000	Beloit	Mid	85.3	100	81	19	68	44	8.54	2	7	10.5	2.0	7.2	4.6	0.3	6.34	-18
2001	High Des	Cal	114.3	120	80	15	78	66	6.30	4	9	9.4	1.2	6.1	5.2	0.4	5.46	-3
2001	Huntsvil	Sou	10.7	9	6	0	10	8	5.06	0	1	7.6	0.0	8.4	6.8	0.4	8.51	-6

Martinez is a beanpole who throws in the low 90s, and when you're a lefty who throws that hard, you get more attention than Pamela Anderson's home-cooking video. There's already some talk about trying to turn Martinez into a situational reliever. The Brewers pen needs more than just another Ray King, and with Valerio De Los Santos coming back in 2002, they'd be better off seeing whether Martinez can continue to make progress as a starter in the minors.

Jose Mieses Throws R Age 22

YEAR	TEAM	LGE	IP	H	ER	HR	BB	K	ERA	W	L	H/9	HR/9	BB/9	K/9	KW	PERA	STUFF
1999	Helena	Pio	101.3	110	57	11	35	44	5.06	5	6	9.8	1.0	3.1	3.9	0.6	3.43	6
2000	Beloit	Mid	128.7	137	74	19	41	76	5.18	6	8	9.6	1.3	2.9	5.3	0.9	3.82	14
2000	Mudville	Cal	33.0	31	16	2	18	24	4.36	2	2	8.5	0.5	4.9	6.5	0.7	3.59	20
2001	Huntsvil	Sou	24.0	22	9	3	3	22	3.38	2	1	8.3	1.1	1.1	8.3	3.7	3.26	36
2001	Indianap	Int	15.0	19	15	5	8	10	9.00	0	2	11.4	3.0	4.8	6.0	0.6	8.89	-8

(Jose Mieses *continued*)

One of the products of Epy Guerrero's attempts to get the organization a better toehold in the Dominican, Mieses isn't what you'd expect from somebody with those strikeout rates. Like the Orioles' John Stephens, he relies on command, in this case using a curve and an outstanding palmball. The discovery of a cracked vertebra in his back sidelined him and was followed by surgery to correct a minor shoulder problem. Mieses shouldn't win a rotation slot out of camp, but he'll enter the picture by July, and he should be the fifth starter by spring training 2003.

Nick Neugebauer **Throws R** **Age 21**

YEAR	TEAM	LGE	IP	H	ER	HR	BB	K	ERA	W	L	H/9	HR/9	BB/9	K/9	KW	PERA	STUFF
1999	Beloit	Mid	77.0	69	60	8	90	72	7.01	3	6	8.1	0.9	10.5	8.4	0.4	5.48	15
2000	Mudville	Cal	74.0	58	44	0	87	69	5.35	3	5	7.1	0.0	10.6	8.4	0.4	5.74	16
2000	Huntsvil	Sou	48.7	45	33	4	48	38	6.10	2	3	8.3	0.7	8.9	7.0	0.4	6.44	9
2001	Huntsvil	Sou	106.7	95	52	9	57	94	4.39	6	6	8.0	0.8	4.8	7.9	0.8	4.88	28
2001	Indianap	Int	21.3	18	9	1	10	20	3.80	1	1	7.6	0.4	4.2	8.4	1.0	2.05	39
2001	Milwauke	NL	6.3	5	4	1	5	9	5.68	0	1	7.1	1.4	7.1	12.8	0.9	7.43	39

The flamethrower with a name Milwaukee was meant to love, Neugebauer could be what Bobby Witt was supposed to be before Bobby Valentine overworked him. He showed tremendous improvement last year as he stopped trying to hit triple digits on the radar gun, instead concentrating on throwing mid-90s strikes and improving his mechanics. When his slider is working, he's a no-hitter kind of guy.

A shoulder strain suffered after his promotion turned into arthroscopic surgery to repair his rotator cuff. How soon he'll be ready to join the rotation is up in the air, but once he does, he'll be overpowering. Like the Cubs with Kerry Wood, the Brewers are going to have to be careful about pushing Neugebauer too hard, because he can be one of the best pitchers of his generation.

Ruben Quevedo **Throws R** **Age 23**

YEAR	TEAM	LGE	IP	H	ER	HR	BB	K	ERA	W	L	H/9	HR/9	BB/9	K/9	KW	PERA	STUFF
1999	Richmond	Int	106.0	118	78	27	32	79	6.62	4	8	10.0	2.3	2.7	6.7	1.2	5.12	14
1999	Iowa	PCL	44.0	37	17	1	22	38	3.48	3	2	7.6	0.2	4.5	7.8	0.9	3.55	33
2000	Iowa	PCL	75.0	71	37	9	29	62	4.44	4	4	8.5	1.1	3.5	7.4	1.1	4.38	25
2000	ChiCubs	NL	89.0	98	67	19	44	58	6.78	3	7	9.9	1.9	4.4	5.9	0.7	7.60	-3
2001	Iowa	PCL	138.7	132	68	15	54	107	4.41	8	7	8.6	1.0	3.5	6.9	1.0	3.67	22
2001	Milwauke	NL	55.7	53	31	8	27	48	5.01	3	3	8.6	1.3	4.4	7.8	0.9	4.72	19

The best acquisition the Brewers made all year. Quevedo may fall short of being an ace, but he's going to be very good. He throws five pitches for strikes, the usual four (fastball, curve, slider, change-up), plus a forkball. He doesn't pump gas the way Neugebauer and Sheets do, but he's in the low 90s. What's not to like? A couple of things, actually: his workloads at such a young age, and his bulk. Until the weight starts affecting his knees (and subsequently his delivery), he'll be a good third starter in what is shaping up to be a good young rotation.

Paul Rigdon **Throws R** **Age 26**

YEAR	TEAM	LGE	IP	H	ER	HR	BB	K	ERA	W	L	H/9	HR/9	BB/9	K/9	KW	PERA	STUFF
1999	Akron	Eas	42.0	45	19	3	10	17	4.07	3	2	9.6	0.6	2.1	3.6	0.9	1.07	6
1999	Buffalo	Int	105.7	114	55	12	27	48	4.68	6	6	9.7	1.0	2.3	4.1	0.9	4.99	0
2000	Buffalo	Int	72.0	74	32	5	18	33	4.00	4	4	9.3	0.6	2.3	4.1	0.9	3.67	4
2000	Clevelnd	AL	18.7	19	11	3	7	15	5.30	1	1	9.2	1.4	3.4	7.2	1.1	6.15	5
2000	Milwauke	NL	68.7	75	43	12	21	43	5.64	3	5	9.8	1.6	2.8	5.6	1.0	4.34	5
2001	Milwauke	NL	76.3	83	52	11	41	39	6.13	3	5	9.8	1.3	4.8	4.6	0.5	5.84	-11

Rigdon opened up with two good months, posting a 4.06 ERA and making six quality starts in 11 tries. Then his elbow gave out, and he tried to pitch through it, with ugly results. He's already had Tommy John surgery; this latest procedure removed scar tissue and bone spurs and shifted his ulnar nerve. He shouldn't be a factor in spring training, and he may not be able to pitch until after the All-Star break.

Ben Sheets — Throws R — Age 23

YEAR	TEAM	LGE	IP	H	ER	HR	BB	K	ERA	W	L	H/9	HR/9	BB/9	K/9	KW	PERA	STUFF
1999	Stockton	Cal	27.3	27	15	2	15	17	4.94	1	2	8.9	0.7	4.9	5.6	0.6	4.21	11
2000	Huntsvil	Sou	68.3	70	36	7	25	40	4.74	4	4	9.2	0.9	3.3	5.3	0.8	2.75	12
2000	Indianap	Int	82.7	80	36	5	30	50	3.92	5	4	8.7	0.5	3.3	5.4	0.8	3.47	16
2001	Indianap	Int	11.7	12	4	0	3	5	3.09	1	0	9.3	0.0	2.3	3.9	0.8	4.60	7
2001	Milwauke	NL	146.3	158	82	20	43	76	5.04	7	9	9.7	1.2	2.6	4.7	0.9	5.24	4

The Olympic hero broke camp with the team as the fifth starter, mostly out of respect for his being Ben Sheets, Olympic Hero. He promptly made the decision look great, opening the year with a 10-5 run that got him into the All-Star game. Sheets throws his sinker in the low 90s and his four-seamer in the mid-90s, and he has an outstanding 12-to-6 curve that whistles in like a Blyleven special. The absence of an effective change-up was a major problem against left-handed hitters; once he masters one, he'll be a power/ground-ball pitcher around whom you can build a rotation. Rotator-cuff tendinitis shut him down for six weeks, and as they did with just about all of their injured players, the Brewers reactivated him for the last couple of weeks of the season to no good end. Assuming the shoulder is sound, Sheets is good and about to get much better.

Mac Suzuki — Throws R — Age 27

YEAR	TEAM	LGE	IP	H	ER	HR	BB	K	ERA	W	L	H/9	HR/9	BB/9	K/9	KW	PERA	STUFF
1999	Seattle	AL	44.0	44	29	6	20	32	5.93	2	3	9.0	1.2	5.7	6.5	0.6	8.45	-10
1999	KansasCy	AL	70.3	75	38	8	25	36	4.86	4	4	9.6	1.0	3.2	4.6	0.7	4.82	-7
2000	KansasCy	AL	193.7	192	101	22	77	134	4.69	11	11	8.9	1.0	3.6	6.2	0.9	3.78	9
2001	KansasCy	AL	56.7	62	39	11	24	35	6.19	2	4	9.8	1.7	3.8	5.6	0.7	5.31	-8
2001	Milwauke	NL	53.7	51	30	4	33	38	5.03	3	3	8.6	0.7	5.5	6.4	0.6	5.89	-3

It's hard to believe Suzuki was traded, waived, claimed, and released only a year after it looked like he was the Royals' best starter. The Brewers released him after the season, and he's been re-signed by the Royals. He still hasn't mastered an off-speed pitch, which keeps him from succeeding as a starter, and his lack of command keeps him from being worth much in relief. Until he adds one or the other, he'll be a fringe fifth starter/mop-up man.

Jamey Wright — Throws R — Age 27

YEAR	TEAM	LGE	IP	H	ER	HR	BB	K	ERA	W	L	H/9	HR/9	BB/9	K/9	KW	PERA	STUFF
1999	ColSprin	PCL	108.3	117	63	14	41	55	5.23	5	7	9.7	1.2	3.4	4.6	0.7	6.73	-4
1999	Colorado	NL	98.3	104	55	8	45	44	5.03	5	6	9.5	0.7	4.1	4.0	0.5	3.64	-2
2000	Milwauke	NL	164.7	166	83	11	72	85	4.54	9	9	9.1	0.6	3.9	4.6	0.6	4.02	1
2001	Milwauke	NL	186.7	196	111	22	88	104	5.35	9	12	9.5	1.1	4.2	5.0	0.6	5.26	-2

As unpredictable as pitchers can be, Wright's failure to improve has been especially maddening. When he starts struggling, you can see him get frustrated and make it worse, alternating between guiding his pitches—which include a great sinker and curve—and beaning people. Wright completely collapsed in the second half last year, with a 6.70 ERA after the All-Star break. Postseason surgery to remove a bone spur from his elbow is not supposed to affect him in 2002.

Montreal Expos

By the time you read this, Bud Selig's cockamamie scheme for the first contraction of big-league teams since 1899 will be on hold, if not snuffed out altogether. However, while the Expos will almost certainly play in Montreal in 2002, it's no longer a question of if the city will lose its team, but when.

Major League Baseball held its 100th birthday party in 1969 and celebrated by adding four franchises. It was an era of risk-taking in the United States, and MLB was in lockstep with the spirit, expanding outside the country's borders for the first time. Of the four new venues, Montreal was by far the most intriguing and eagerly anticipated. The decision to expand into Montreal may seem puzzling now, but it wasn't then. The city has a rich baseball history dating back to the 19th century and is most famous for warmly welcoming Jackie Robinson to professional baseball in 1946. In the 1960s, long-time mayor Jean Drapeau wanted to transform Montreal into a metropolis of international reknown. The city had just pulled off a hugely successful World's Fair, Expo '67, and a year later would win the bid to host the 1976 Summer Olympics. At the time, Canada had a "fixed exchange rate," which kept the value of the Canadian dollar within prescribed limits relative to the U.S. dollar.

Expos Prospectus

2001 record: 68–94; Fifth place, NL East

Pythagenport W/L: 66–96

Runs scored: 670 (14th in NL)

Runs allowed: 812 (12th in NL)

Team EqA: .246 (15th in NL)

2001 batters age: 27.4 (third-youngest in NL)

2001 pitchers age: 27.2 (third-youngest in NL)

Ballpark: Olympic Stadium; slight hitters' park; Park Factor of 1.027

2001: The Alou Era ended, Vladimir Guerrero rocked, and a city shrugged.

2002: Probably baseball's first lame-duck franchise in a century, the culmination of seven years of self-mutilation. Baseball should be ashamed of itself.

The fledgling Expos were an easy bunch to like. From their nifty tri-color hats, to "Le Grande Orange," to players with goofy names like "Coco," "Boots," and "Mack," to Ron Hunt's knack for getting plunked by pitches, the club was always entertaining, if seldom successful.

In 1977, Toronto was awarded a major-league franchise. Even though Dick Williams had been hired as Expos manager and Montreal would soon field a competitive ball club, the Blue Jays became Canada's team. Their fresh, new smell and eight years of Expos' losses contributed to the rapid passing of the torch, but it was mainly due to political turmoil in Quebec. The 1976 elections gave the Parti Quebecois control of the provincial parliament, a move seen by many Canadians as a huge step towards Quebec seceding from the dominion. Although the political situation didn't immediately hurt the Expos at the turnstiles—attendance more than tripled by the early 1980s as the franchise went through its most successful period—it did affect them on a national scale, as they played second fiddle to the Blue Jays on non-Quebec-based media outlets.

It was painful to watch a once-proud organization under the ownership of Charles Bronfman be systematically ripped apart by consortium frontman Claude Brochu. Brochu's selling off of players coincided with the post-1994 implementation of a revenue-sharing system that benefited the teams with the lowest payrolls, irrespective of market size or revenues. Brochu's fire sales only became more blatant with each passing year as the stream of free cash, combined with national television and merchandising monies, guaranteed the Expos a healthy profit if the payroll was kept low. Brochu himself received multi-million-dollar bonuses tied directly to the club's profits, rather than to its on-field performance.

In December of 1999, Jeffrey Loria and his partners paid $35 million to buy 24% of the team, with Loria replacing Brochu as principal owner and managing general partner. As despicable as Brochu's actions were, Loria's haven't been any better. At the time, Loria was portrayed as riding into Montreal on a white horse to save the franchise. That horse might well prove to be of the trojan variety.

A conspiracy theorist could make a persuasive argument that Loria was sent by Major League Baseball to finish off the Expos once and for all. Taken at face value and in isolation, most of his actions have been credible. Taken as a whole, they have methodically gored the beast. The trouble with conspiracy theories is that there are always missing links, and in the case of the Expos, there are absolutely no facts that indicate such a connection between MLB and Loria. But just for fun, let's look at the other evidence:

Within two weeks of Loria assuming control, the Expos dove into the player market, signing free agent Graeme Lloyd and trading prospects for Hideki Irabu. In spring training, they participated in a menage à trois, giving up Brad Fullmer and gaining Lee Stevens, a lesser player who was ten times as expensive as Fullmer. The acquisitions were designed to show Montreal that the new ownership was serious about winning. However, even at the time the deals were consummated, it was obvious that it would've been tough to commit $25 million to three players with less impact than these guys: an adequate situational left-hander, an underachieving fourth starter, and a replacement-level first baseman.

In February 2000, Loria unveiled a model of Labatt Park and kicked off a drive to raise $100 million toward construction of the ballpark. Both the city of Montreal and the province of Quebec made some financial concessions as part of a plan to get the stadium built. Just six months later, with fund-raising falling short of the goal and with no public subsidies, Loria let a $1-million lease option expire, claiming that nobody else was interested in the property. Last July, a real-estate developer purchased it. Without any chance of erecting a new ballpark, it becomes much easier to move or fold a team.

Not surprisingly, the Expos' local broadcast revenues were the lowest in the game. Loria decided to change that and refused to accept the fees that were being offered. As a result, Montreal played the 2000 season without television or English-radio broadcasts. That caused many advertisers, including the team's main sponsor, Labatt, to cancel their agreements. The Expos ultimately signed broadcast packages last year, but at one-third the sum Loria had hoped to receive. For a ball club teetering on the brink of extinction, deep-sixing its primary marketing tool was beyond reckless.

The Expos haven't had a director of marketing since the change in ownership. Executive vice-president and Loria's son-in-law, David Samson, maintains that nobody in Quebec will take the job, which is patently absurd. Without any marketing presence, attendance increased 20% from 1999 to 2000. Imagine how much better things could've been with someone on board who had real ideas about how to get fans out to the ballpark.

After taking control of the team in 1999, Loria's group decided to not bring back hitting coach Tommy Harper, manager Felipe Alou's most trusted assistant, for the 2000 season. Six months later, they fired bench coach Luis Pujols and pitching coach Bobby Cuellar. When undermining Alou failed to achieve the desired result of getting him to resign, Loria took a more direct approach, firing him after a 21-32 start last year. While Alou had clearly lost his passion for the job, the team fared little better under new skipper and close friend of Loria, Jeff Torborg. By eliminating Alou—who had been with the organization for 27 years, lived year-round in Montreal, and was more popular than the Expos' players—Loria severed the team's most visible link to the community.

The agreement between Loria and the local shareholders gave him the power, as managing general partner, to put out a cash call anytime he reasonably determines that more money is needed to run the ball club. If any of the partners refuses to meet the call, any of the other shareholders can pay that partner's share and increase their equity. At this point, it gets complicated, but through a "valuation notice" (a statement of how much the team is worth) process and clauses in the contract, if nobody pays that partner's share, the valuation is reduced by $25 million and the cash-call process starts again. Via this dilution mechanism, it's possible for a single shareholder to acquire majority holdings at a bargain price if repeated cash calls aren't met.

That's exactly what has happened. Loria issued numerous cash calls in one year, totaling somewhere between $40 and $70 million. Naturally, the local owners thought the requests were excessive and balked at fronting the money. Loria was the only partner to meet the calls and, as a result, effectively owned 92% of the Expos by May 2001. Baseball rules prohibit a franchise from moving unless owners holding at least a two-thirds majority of the team's shares approve it. Loria now has his majority of one.

All in all, there is enough fishy behavior in Montreal to keep Kenn Thomas swarming for years. As for motive, the rumored $250-million buyout offered by Selig and the baseball lords as part of the contraction scheme should more than suffice. With a total investment of no more than $100 million, Loria stands to reap a windfall profit whether the team is contracted or sold and relocated.

As if to grind salt into the wounds of Expos' fans—and despite the spin that's been spun, there are many—the team is primed to end its run of four straight 90-loss seasons. With the return of a healthy and motivated Fernando Tatis and the imminent arrival of Brandon Phillips, the Expos' infield is equaled only by the Braves in the NL East. Whichever club fills its yawning void at first base wins the tiebreaker. Brad Wilkerson's on-base skills and Vladimir Guerrero's booming bat make for a terrific pair of bookends in the outfield corners, flanking Peter Bergeron. If Bergeron flubs what is likely his final shot at regular playing time, Gold Glove shortstop Orlando Cabrera could be used as trade bait for a center fielder.

On the mound, only the Marlins have a better young one-two punch than Javier Vazquez and Tony Armas, Jr. Behind them, there's a dropoff. If baling wire and duct tape can hold Carl Pavano's elbow together, that will help, and Justin Wayne should be ready to step into the rotation at the All-Star break. Six-inning starts will be the norm every fifth day from Tomokazu Ohka, and there is enough filler for fifth starter that Torborg won't have to dumpster-dive again for Bobby Munoz and Chris Peters. The bullpen will be exciting, if not necessarily effective.

The Expos don't have much depth, making them vulnerable to injuries stunting what should be a year of sizeable growth. A few smart minor-league free-agent signings could greatly hedge the risk; they can't afford to enter the season with a collection of washouts similar to those stationed in Ottawa last year. Of course, Selig's contraction gewgaw put the Expos at a spectacular disadvantage in filling out their minor-league rosters.

There are signs of promise on the player-development front, too. The minor-league cupboards are not nearly as chock full as they were a decade ago, nor are they as barren as many people believe them to be. Phillips and Wayne are clearly the plums and are close to being ripe. The system's best talent is in the low minors, but in the upper two levels there are some big right-handed throwers and a few hitters who could carve out roles if they can improve certain facets of their performance, most commonly centered around winning the battle for control of the strike zone.

It's at that very fulcrum of the game where the most encouraging news emerges. While teams have long recognized the value of pitchers not walking batters, only in recent years have some teams begun to emphasize the obvious corollary. The Expos have been particularly slow learners, taking the tenets of aggressive hitting to laughable extremes. However, last year, under the guidance of new Director of Player Development Tony LaCava, the organization started reversing its course and focusing on plate discipline. The results aren't yet obvious on a large-scale basis, but players such as Val Pascucci, Matt Watson, and Grady Sizemore are gaining attention within the organization for their ability to work the count in their favor, then hit the ball hard.

If the men in blue yell "Play ball!" in Olympic Stadium this year, there won't be many folks on hand to hear it, even if the Expos do put a much-improved product on the field. It's too late for miracles. Numerous factors, from the language barrier to the floating Canadian dollar, conspire to make baseball in Quebec a difficult proposition. However, Major League Baseball itself administered the poison of an ill-conceived revenue-sharing scheme that removed the financial incentive to try and caused the patient to take a fatal turn for the worse.

Contraction? Relocation? Those terms are too kind. More accurately, the commissioner's office and the lords of baseball are performing euthanasia to finish something they started years ago.

HITTERS (BA: .270, OBP: .340, SLG: .440, EqA: .260)

Michael Barrett C Bats R Age 25

YEAR	TEAM	LGE	AB	H	DB	TP	HR	BB	SO	R	RBI	SB	CS	OUT	BA	OBP	SLG	EQA	EQR	DEFENSE	
1999	Montreal	NL	434	126	31	3	8	27	36	52	49	0	2	310	.290	.336	.431	.254	50	62-3B -7	50-C -5
2000	Montreal	NL	273	58	15	1	1	20	32	27	21	0	1	216	.212	.268	.286	.191	17	47-3B -7	25-C -3
2000	Ottawa	Int	120	40	3	0	3	11	10	19	18	1	0	80	.333	.397	.433	.285	17	24-3B 0	
2001	Montreal	NL	472	121	33	2	6	23	46	43	39	2	1	352	.256	.293	.373	.223	41	126-C -13	
2002	*Montreal*	*NL*	*411*	*112*	*23*	*2*	*8*	*32*	*43*	*49*	*44*	*1*	*1*	*300*	*.273*	*.325*	*.397*	*.246*	*45*		

The Expos came to their senses, stationing Barrett behind home plate and leaving him there all season. In last year's book, we theorized that such a move would cause Barrett's offense to resurface, but we were mistaken—at least so far. There is a school of thought that says catchers develop more slowly with the bat because they have to focus so much on their defense. The Expos hope that Barrett is enrolled there; if not, he won't graduate to the level he appeared headed towards in 1999.

Jason Bay OF Bats R Age 23

YEAR	TEAM	LGE	AB	H	DB	TP	HR	BB	SO	R	RBI	SB	CS	OUT	BA	OBP	SLG	EQA	EQR	DEFENSE
2000	Vermont	NYP	138	31	2	0	2	6	29	10	8	7	3	110	.225	.259	.283	.191	9	13-LF 0
2001	Jupiter	Fla	128	23	3	1	1	13	28	9	8	6	2	107	.180	.260	.242	.185	8	35-RF -2
2001	Clinton	Mid	327	89	13	2	9	35	68	45	39	7	2	240	.272	.345	.407	.256	40	78-RF 10
2002	*Montreal*	*NL*	*413*	*104*	*12*	*2*	*12*	*49*	*94*	*49*	*42*	*15*	*4*	*313*	*.252*	*.331*	*.378*	*.249*	*48*	

Bay was allowed to skip a level after a tremendous spring at the team's minor-league complex. He proved to be in over his head and was sent down to Clinton six weeks later, where he led the Midwest League in batting. The former 22nd-round pick has a well-rounded offensive game, good speed, and plays an excellent corner outfield. Bay will attempt another Jupiter landing this year; at his age, he can't afford to scrub the mission again.

Peter Bergeron OF Bats L Age 24

YEAR	TEAM	LGE	AB	H	DB	TP	HR	BB	SO	R	RBI	SB	CS	OUT	BA	OBP	SLG	EQA	EQR	DEFENSE
1999	Harrisbg	Eas	163	44	12	1	3	18	29	22	13	5	4	124	.270	.343	.411	.251	20	39-LF -3
1999	Ottawa	Int	193	55	12	2	2	19	38	29	16	10	7	144	.285	.351	.399	.253	23	38-LF 0
2000	Montreal	NL	522	126	26	6	5	51	92	76	29	9	13	409	.241	.309	.343	.219	46	129-CF 4
2001	Montreal	NL	375	82	12	4	3	26	74	55	17	10	7	300	.219	.276	.296	.190	20	96-CF 2
2001	Ottawa	Int	209	49	6	2	0	19	39	28	8	12	6	166	.234	.300	.282	.208	16	50-CF -1
2002	*Montreal*	*NL*	*502*	*124*	*21*	*5*	*5*	*51*	*102*	*75*	*31*	*18*	*11*	*389*	*.247*	*.316*	*.339*	*.228*	*48*	

The pain caused by the failings of much of the Expos' homegrown talent is intensified by the fact that for the team to succeed, they need a steady flow of young players who can contribute promptly upon arriving in the big leagues. Bergeron doesn't at all resemble the player he was a few years ago; his plate discipline has vanished, taking his OBP with it, and his confidence is shattered. Just 24, Bergeron still has time to resurrect his career, but he desperately needs a change of scenery.

Geoff Blum UT Bats B Age 29

YEAR	TEAM	LGE	AB	H	DB	TP	HR	BB	SO	R	RBI	SB	CS	OUT	BA	OBP	SLG	EQA	EQR	DEFENSE	
1999	Ottawa	Int	268	66	14	1	8	31	37	36	30	4	1	203	.246	.328	.396	.246	30	54-SS -7	
1999	Montreal	NL	133	31	7	2	8	16	23	21	17	1	0	102	.233	.315	.496	.264	18	31-SS -8	
2000	Montreal	NL	345	96	20	2	11	22	55	[illegible]	43	1	4	253	.278	.326	.443	.251	40	48-3B -1	29-SS 2
2001	Montreal	NL	453	111	17	0	12	40	80	57	54	9	5	347	.245	.317	.362	.231	45	71-3B -4	26-LF 0
2002	*Montreal*	*NL*	*396*	*101*	*15*	*1*	*14*	*46*	*72*	*51*	*45*	*7*	*5*	*299*	*.255*	*.333*	*.404*	*.252*	*48*		

Blum is a quality utility man who spent much of 2001 masquerading as a regular due to Jose Vidro's various ailments and Fernando Tatis's season-ending surgery. Like Old Overholt rye whiskey, Blum is agreeable in small doses. If you're drinking it every day, you need to seek help.

Orlando Cabrera SS Bats R Age 27

YEAR	TEAM	LGE	AB	H	DB	TP	HR	BB	SO	R	RBI	SB	CS	OUT	BA	OBP	SLG	EQA	EQR	DEFENSE
1999	Montreal	NL	384	97	23	5	8	13	35	47	37	2	2	289	.253	.282	.401	.225	35	102-SS 6
2000	Montreal	NL	426	101	24	1	13	19	20	40	53	4	4	329	.237	.271	.390	.217	36	107-SS 14
2001	Montreal	NL	626	177	40	6	14	39	46	65	97	19	7	456	.283	.328	.433	.254	74	158-SS 28
2002	*Montreal*	*NL*	*529*	*141*	*30*	*4*	*13*	*40*	*42*	*68*	*60*	*11*	*7*	*395*	*.267*	*.318*	*.412*	*.247*	*60*	

Which is the sadder statement about the Expos' offense: Cabrera batting cleanup for most of August and September, or, given the options, that he was arguably the best choice? Cabrera is worthy of his Gold Glove at shortstop and is a nice asset if he is average offensively at the position, which he was last year. His increased output doesn't appear to be more than a few extra bloopers falling each month, so look for him to regress toward his mean.

Ron Calloway CF Bats L Age 25

YEAR	TEAM	LGE	AB	H	DB	TP	HR	BB	SO	R	RBI	SB	CS	OUT	BA	OBP	SLG	EQA	EQR	DEFENSE
1999	High Des	Cal	191	42	9	0	2	20	34	22	13	10	4	153	.220	.297	.298	.212	16	43-CF -10
1999	Jupiter	Fla	213	47	6	2	3	11	51	22	18	3	4	170	.221	.262	.310	.192	14	51-CF 12
2000	Jupiter	Fla	542	127	19	3	6	40	99	57	48	19	10	425	.234	.289	.314	.209	42	117-CF 6
2001	Harrisbg	Eas	282	79	18	3	7	22	45	39	38	16	5	208	.280	.336	.440	.262	36	62-CF -6
2001	Ottawa	Int	241	62	10	0	10	16	59	26	34	9	1	180	.257	.314	.423	.250	28	56-CF -5
2002	*Montreal*	*NL*	*477*	*123*	*21*	*3*	*14*	*43*	*101*	*71*	*54*	*23*	*7*	*361*	*.258*	*.319*	*.403*	*.250*	*57*	

Entering last season, Calloway wasn't even expected to start in Harrisburg, let alone emerge as a prospect. He ended up posting career highs in virtually every offensive category, belting more home runs than in his previous four professional seasons combined. Calloway is now on the team's radar screen, but his static strikeout-to-walk ratio indicates that his 2001 performance will prove to be an anomaly. If it isn't, his ability to play anywhere in the outfield would make him a dandy reserve outfielder, bringing speed and extra-base pop off the bench.

Matt Cepicky LF Bats L Age 24

YEAR	TEAM	LGE	AB	H	DB	TP	HR	BB	SO	R	RBI	SB	CS	OUT	BA	OBP	SLG	EQA	EQR	DEFENSE
1999	Vermont	NYP	328	73	11	2	7	12	54	32	30	4	5	260	.223	.251	.332	.194	21	50-LF -1
2000	Jupiter	Fla	541	136	25	4	5	17	71	45	64	18	9	414	.251	.276	.340	.209	41	106-LF -1
2001	Harrisbg	Eas	460	104	18	5	15	22	94	50	61	4	8	364	.226	.263	.385	.211	37	104-LF 0
2002	*Montreal*	*NL*	*480*	*126*	*20*	*4*	*14*	*32*	*91*	*57*	*62*	*12*	*8*	*362*	*.262*	*.309*	*.408*	*.242*	*52*	

To witness Cepicky's prodigious power, you'll need to get to the ballpark early—at least 90 minutes before the first pitch. He maintains his batting practice mentality when the game starts, swinging at everything that's thrown. The Expos think highly enough of him to have sent him to the Arizona Fall League, but he continued to show that he just doesn't get it. Wilton is being way too charitable; Cepicky won't begin to approach that projection until he realizes that the strike zone exists for a reason.

Tomas de la Rosa SS Bats R Age 24

YEAR	TEAM	LGE	AB	H	DB	TP	HR	BB	SO	R	RBI	SB	CS	OUT	BA	OBP	SLG	EQA	EQR	DEFENSE
1999	Harrisbg	Eas	470	106	17	2	5	30	64	54	33	17	10	374	.226	.273	.302	.199	33	127-SS 4
2000	Ottawa	Int	343	68	10	1	1	25	42	25	33	8	3	278	.198	.256	.242	.179	19	95-SS -12
2000	Montreal	NL	66	19	2	1	2	6	10	7	8	2	1	48	.288	.355	.439	.266	9	21-SS -2
2001	Ottawa	Int	426	98	15	1	9	38	58	54	30	10	8	336	.230	.298	.333	.216	36	118-SS 1
2002	*Montreal*	*NL*	*428*	*102*	*16*	*2*	*8*	*44*	*62*	*56*	*41*	*19*	*8*	*334*	*.238*	*.309*	*.341*	*.228*	*42*	

Clever marketing can sell just about anything branded "lite." Actual people have spent legal tender on products such as Spam Lite, Milky Way Lite, and Aunt Jemima Butter Lite syrup. As difficult as those promotions were, imagine being de la Rosa's agent and trying to peddle Felix Martinez Lite.

Rob Ducey OF Bats L Age 37

YEAR	TEAM	LGE	AB	H	DB	TP	HR	BB	SO	R	RBI	SB	CS	OUT	BA	OBP	SLG	EQA	EQR	DEFENSE
1999	Philadel	NL	188	48	9	2	8	35	53	28	31	2	1	141	.255	.372	.452	.277	29	45-LF -1
2000	Philadel	NL	153	30	3	1	6	27	43	23	24	1	0	123	.196	.317	.346	.230	16	28-LF -6
2001	Philadel	NL	27	6	2	0	1	6	9	5	4	0	0	21	.222	.364	.407	.264	4	
2001	Montreal	NL	46	11	2	0	2	10	12	6	8	0	1	36	.239	.383	.413	.268	7	12-LF 0
2002	*Montreal*	*NL*	*181*	*35*	*6*	*1*	*7*	*35*	*55*	*24*	*26*	*1*	*0*	*146*	*.193*	*.324*	*.354*	*.239*	*20*	

Exactly how did Don Ho come to be a Vegas headliner? Surely, it took more than "Tiny Bubbles." The best we can reckon is that he hails from Hawaii. A similar conclusion can be reached about Ducey; given his performance, there's no way the Blue Jays would have carried him on their roster from 1987 to 1991 if he hadn't been from Toronto. It established him as a "major leaguer," enabling him to have a 13-year career. After tearing an Achilles tendon in July, Ducey's playing days may be over, but his story reinforces the idea that where you come from matters.

Vladimir Guerrero RF Bats R Age 26

YEAR	TEAM	LGE	AB	H	DB	TP	HR	BB	SO	R	RBI	SB	CS	OUT	BA	OBP	SLG	EQA	EQR	DEFENSE
1999	Montreal	NL	611	190	36	4	42	47	57	98	123	11	7	428	.311	.367	.589	.303	108	151-RF -7
2000	Montreal	NL	574	194	29	10	43	50	68	97	115	8	10	390	.338	.398	.648	.324	117	138-RF -3
2001	Montreal	NL	598	184	44	4	33	56	75	107	106	36	15	429	.308	.374	.560	.301	106	152-RF -3
2002	*Montreal*	*NL*	*542*	*175*	*34*	*6*	*35*	*59*	*70*	*99*	*106*	*29*	*13*	*380*	*.323*	*.389*	*.601*	*.319*	*110*	

Should Bud Selig and his cronies make good on their threat of contraction, one of the few real benefits would be increased exposure for Guerrero. He is the most exciting player in baseball; his actions in the course of a single game can range from daringly brilliant to aggressively foolish. Guerrero's numbers dropped last year as opponents took advantage of the fact that he's never seen a pitch he didn't think he could hit. Mock contraction drafts land Guerrero in Pittsburgh, where his play would immediately evoke images of Roberto Clemente, another visually spectacular right fielder whose production never quite matched his jaw-dropping play.

Scott Hodges 3B Bats L Age 23

YEAR	TEAM	LGE	AB	H	DB	TP	HR	BB	SO	R	RBI	SB	CS	OUT	BA	OBP	SLG	EQA	EQR	DEFENSE
1999	CapeFear	SAL	463	91	22	1	5	32	111	44	39	4	8	380	.197	.250	.281	.181	27	121-3B -2
2000	Jupiter	Fla	433	111	20	1	12	35	73	57	60	5	2	324	.256	.314	.390	.237	44	105-3B 4
2001	Harrisbg	Eas	308	73	10	1	4	23	54	27	26	2	1	236	.237	.290	.315	.208	23	72-3B -2
2002	*Montreal*	*NL*	*419*	*105*	*18*	*1*	*12*	*40*	*84*	*53*	*52*	*5*	*3*	*317*	*.251*	*.316*	*.384*	*.239*	*44*	

Don't judge Hodges's poor season at Harrisburg too harshly—he played much of the year with colitis, which wasn't diagnosed until early August. Prior to the diagnosis, he lost almost 40 pounds, absolutely draining him of his power. In addition to the physical problems, Hodges didn't win any advocates in the organization with an attitude that was perceived as immature and selfish. He remains the best third-base prospect in the system, although Vince Rooi is closing quickly.

Terry Jones OF Bats B Age 31

YEAR	TEAM	LGE	AB	H	DB	TP	HR	BB	SO	R	RBI	SB	CS	OUT	BA	OBP	SLG	EQA	EQR	DEFENSE
1999	Ottawa	Int	332	81	14	2	0	18	62	39	19	22	9	260	.244	.284	.298	.206	25	77-CF -2
1999	Montreal	NL	63	16	1	1	0	3	13	4	3	1	2	49	.254	.288	.302	.196	4	17-CF 3
2000	Montreal	NL	169	42	7	2	0	8	29	29	12	7	2	129	.249	.282	.314	.208	13	42-LF 1
2001	Ottawa	Int	69	19	2	0	0	3	12	6	5	2	3	53	.275	.306	.304	.203	5	13-RF 1
2001	Montreal	NL	77	20	6	0	0	2	9	9	3	3	0	57	.260	.278	.338	.214	6	19-CF 0
2002	*Montreal*	*NL*	*315*	*76*	*14*	*2*	*1*	*20*	*55*	*39*	*19*	*11*	*4*	*243*	*.241*	*.287*	*.308*	*.206*	*23*	

Remember Justice League of America member and quintessential one-tool superhero, Flash? Think how utterly worthless he would have been if he had hamstring problems. That's what Terry Jones was up against last year. However, unlike the underrated Flash, Jones was never deserving of league membership. Jones's jig is up with the Expos, and he should suffer the same fate as DC Comics' Black Lightning and Metamorpho, finally disappearing from our pages.

Henry Mateo 2B Bats B Age 25

YEAR	TEAM	LGE	AB	H	DB	TP	HR	BB	SO	R	RBI	SB	CS	OUT	BA	OBP	SLG	EQA	EQR	DEFENSE
1999	Jupiter	Fla	454	97	23	4	4	33	126	49	42	17	10	367	.214	.274	.308	.202	33	100-2B -15
2000	Harrisbg	Eas	535	134	23	7	5	44	100	69	48	31	12	413	.250	.312	.348	.229	52	130-2B -2
2001	Ottawa	Int	505	131	14	11	5	33	82	67	41	38	13	387	.259	.311	.360	.234	51	116-2B -7
2002	*Montreal*	*NL*	*467*	*119*	*19*	*7*	*6*	*42*	*92*	*65*	*46*	*34*	*13*	*361*	*.255*	*.316*	*.364*	*.240*	*51*	

Although they get the adrenaline pumping, triples and stolen bases have only a weak correlation to run scoring. Mateo led the International League in triples and stolen bases, making some prospect lists thanks to his legs. Like the leaves changing colors, he'll be no more than a September event in Quebec until he learns how to walk to first base and adds another infield position to his resume.

Josh McKinley 2B Bats B Age 22

YEAR	TEAM	LGE	AB	H	DB	TP	HR	BB	SO	R	RBI	SB	CS	OUT	BA	OBP	SLG	EQA	EQR	DEFENSE
1999	Vermont	NYP	293	54	8	1	3	20	58	30	20	3	3	242	.184	.237	.249	.170	14	44-SS -19 16-2B -3
1999	CapeFear	SAL	173	35	7	0	0	12	40	12	11	4	4	142	.202	.254	.243	.174	9	20-SS -10
2000	CapeFear	SAL	495	101	23	2	4	37	107	48	44	21	11	404	.204	.262	.283	.192	33	94-3B -21 18-2B -6
2001	Jupiter	Fla	484	107	18	1	2	51	89	49	43	16	7	384	.221	.297	.275	.205	36	127-2B -8
2002	*Montreal*	*NL*	*455*	*108*	*23*	*1*	*4*	*47*	*97*	*55*	*42*	*19*	*9*	*356*	*.237*	*.309*	*.319*	*.221*	*41*	

McKinley was the first of the Expos' signability picks in the final years of the Brochu regime. The 11th pick in the 1998 draft, he was selected immediately after Carlos Pena and before talents such as Jeff Weaver and C.C. Sabathia. After failed trials on the left side of the infield, the organization has settled on playing him at second base. Though McKinley will take a walk, he has shown little progress in making consistent, hard contact. It certainly seems the Expos got what they paid for.

Mike Mordecai IF Bats R Age 34

YEAR	TEAM	LGE	AB	H	DB	TP	HR	BB	SO	R	RBI	SB	CS	OUT	BA	OBP	SLG	EQA	EQR	DEFENSE			
1999	Montreal	NL	227	53	9	2	5	17	29	27	23	1	5	179	.233	.290	.357	.213	19	24-SS	4	22-3B	3
2000	Montreal	NL	170	48	12	0	5	10	31	19	16	2	2	124	.282	.325	.441	.252	20	37-3B	-3		
2001	Montreal	NL	254	73	17	2	3	17	45	29	33	2	2	183	.287	.334	.406	.247	28	32-3B	-3	24-2B	-4
2002	*Montreal*	*NL*	*228*	*56*	*15*	*1*	*4*	*21*	*42*	*29*	*22*	*3*	*3*	*175*	*.246*	*.309*	*.373*	*.232*	*23*				

One of the more bizarre moments of last season was Torborg scheming in September about how to get Mordecai and Geoff Blum to both play nine positions in the same game this March. It's disturbing enough that a major-league manager would spend time plotting a spring-training stunt during the regular season, but perhaps even more distressing is that Torborg plans to have Mordecai on the roster again this year.

Valentino Pascucci OF/1B Bats R Age 23

YEAR	TEAM	LGE	AB	H	DB	TP	HR	BB	SO	R	RBI	SB	CS	OUT	BA	OBP	SLG	EQA	EQR	DEFENSE			
1999	Vermont	NYP	273	69	12	1	5	34	51	37	29	7	2	206	.253	.347	.359	.246	31	65-RF	-5		
2000	CapeFear	SAL	73	18	3	0	2	11	16	12	6	2	0	55	.247	.345	.370	.251	9	19-RF	-1		
2000	Jupiter	Fla	419	100	21	1	12	49	109	52	48	8	4	323	.239	.327	.379	.241	46	89-RF	-7		
2001	Harrisbg	Eas	486	103	12	1	17	57	111	68	55	6	5	388	.212	.302	.346	.222	45	109-RF	-5	15-1B	0
2002	*Montreal*	*NL*	*457*	*114*	*18*	*1*	*16*	*57*	*115*	*67*	*56*	*11*	*4*	*347*	*.249*	*.333*	*.398*	*.253*	*56*				

While position-player-to-pitcher conversions are fairly common, switches going the other way aren't. Pascucci is one example, having mainly toed the slab in college. The step up to Double-A is a steep one, and Pascucci's numbers were down across the board last year. Three straight years of declining Equivalent Averages can't be considered progress, but his control of the strike zone keeps hope alive. The Expos plan to move Pascucci to first base and stationed him there exclusively in the Arizona Fall League.

Brandon Phillips SS Bats R Age 21

YEAR	TEAM	LGE	AB	H	DB	TP	HR	BB	SO	R	RBI	SB	CS	OUT	BA	OBP	SLG	EQA	EQR	DEFENSE	
2000	CapeFear	SAL	495	96	14	4	8	25	104	50	47	10	6	405	.194	.238	.287	.181	28	121-SS	-16
2001	Jupiter	Fla	204	50	10	1	4	29	48	27	18	9	3	157	.245	.347	.363	.249	24	55-SS	-4
2001	Harrisbg	Eas	266	68	11	0	7	12	41	29	31	9	4	202	.256	.293	.376	.226	24	62-SS	-1
2002	*Montreal*	*NL*	*496*	*124*	*19*	*3*	*14*	*49*	*105*	*66*	*59*	*20*	*8*	*380*	*.250*	*.317*	*.385*	*.243*	*55*		

This is the reason teams continue to draft raw athletes. If, like Phillips, they can translate their tools into skills, it makes for a potentially dominating player. When the organization challenged Phillips to walk more than he struck out, he made the intelligent choice—he decided to be more patient at the plate rather than cut down on his swing. Though he found Eastern League competition tougher, he followed up with a dynamite stint in the Arizona Fall League, playing mostly third base. The defensive switch was made only so that he could participate; he projects to be an above-average shortstop, with plus range, soft hands, and a strong arm. Phillips is coming like a freight train and could be in the Expos' 2003 Opening Day lineup.

Wilken Ruan CF Bats R Age 22

YEAR	TEAM	LGE	AB	H	DB	TP	HR	BB	SO	R	RBI	SB	CS	OUT	BA	OBP	SLG	EQA	EQR	DEFENSE	
1999	CapeFear	SAL	403	72	11	2	1	13	84	28	33	14	10	341	.179	.209	.223	.154	16	112-CF	9
2000	CapeFear	SAL	581	136	21	6	1	15	80	61	36	30	9	454	.234	.257	.296	.195	38	131-CF	2
2001	Jupiter	Fla	298	73	7	1	2	6	38	30	20	14	10	235	.245	.263	.295	.191	19	71-CF	-3
2001	Harrisbg	Eas	117	26	6	0	0	3	18	12	5	4	0	91	.222	.248	.274	.186	7	28-CF	4
2002	*Montreal*	*NL*	*546*	*132*	*23*	*3*	*3*	*26*	*86*	*62*	*52*	*33*	*11*	*425*	*.242*	*.276*	*.311*	*.206*	*41*		

How tough is a scout's job? Imagine trying to assess a player's potential on the basis of a single game. Then again, you could get a full whiff of Eau de Ruan on just one play at last year's Futures Game. He lunged at a pitch well off the plate, dinked it into right field, foolishly tried stretching it into a double, was thrown out, and fractured his ring finger with a head-first slide. Ruan does play a mean center field, though.

Brian Schneider C Bats L Age 25

YEAR	TEAM	LGE	AB	H	DB	TP	HR	BB	SO	R	RBI	SB	CS	OUT	BA	OBP	SLG	EQA	EQR	DEFENSE
1999	Harrisbg	Eas	423	97	14	0	14	22	56	38	50	1	1	327	.229	.269	.362	.210	33	106-C 4
2000	Ottawa	Int	239	57	20	2	4	13	41	20	27	1	0	182	.238	.278	.389	.221	21	59-C 1
2000	Montreal	NL	116	27	7	0	0	5	22	6	11	0	1	90	.233	.264	.293	.188	7	32-C -3
2001	Ottawa	Int	342	91	26	1	6	27	61	33	41	2	0	251	.266	.325	.398	.244	37	89-C 7
2001	Montreal	NL	41	13	0	0	2	6	3	4	7	0	0	28	.317	.404	.463	.294	7	11-C 1
2002	*Montreal*	*NL*	*369*	*99*	*22*	*1*	*9*	*36*	*59*	*37*	*46*	*1*	*1*	*271*	*.268*	*.333*	*.407*	*.253*	*43*	

Schneider impressed former second-string backstop Torborg with his work behind the plate in September, putting a hammerlock on the backup-catcher job. The power he showed a couple of years ago in Harrisburg raises concerns about temporary genetic mutation occurring on tours of Three Mile Island, but even without that sock, Schneider's left-handed bat still makes him handy off the bench. He is embarking on what should be a nice little career, logging a few seasons as a starter before it's over.

Fernando Seguignol 1B/LF Bats B Age 27

YEAR	TEAM	LGE	AB	H	DB	TP	HR	BB	SO	R	RBI	SB	CS	OUT	BA	OBP	SLG	EQA	EQR	DEFENSE
1999	Ottawa	Int	312	81	16	2	19	33	90	45	58	2	6	238	.260	.346	.506	.272	46	49-1B -2
1999	Montreal	NL	105	27	5	0	6	4	31	13	10	0	0	78	.257	.326	.476	.263	14	20-1B -3
2000	Ottawa	Int	142	37	12	0	8	10	26	18	27	1	1	106	.261	.327	.514	.270	20	24-1B 0 12-RF -3
2000	Montreal	NL	163	45	7	0	10	7	42	21	21	0	1	119	.276	.316	.503	.263	21	17-1B -1 14-LF -6
2001	Montreal	NL	50	8	2	0	0	2	14	2	5	0	0	42	.160	.204	.200	.143	2	
2001	Ottawa	Int	245	73	8	0	14	15	45	35	43	0	1	173	.298	.347	.502	.276	35	51-1B 0
2002	*Montreal*	*NL*	*383*	*105*	*17*	*1*	*22*	*35*	*92*	*51*	*60*	*2*	*3*	*281*	*.274*	*.335*	*.496*	*.274*	*55*	

There is no performance-based explanation for Panamanian Seguignol to have spent large chunks of the last four years in the capital of Canada. Sometimes you have to dig a little deeper for the answer. Think about the strategic importance of the Panama Canal. Think Moe Berg. The complete story may never come to light, but sources tell us it involves maple syrup, woven straw hats, and the inexplicable popularity of the MacKenzie Brothers.

Grady Sizemore CF Bats L Age 19

YEAR	TEAM	LGE	AB	H	DB	TP	HR	BB	SO	R	RBI	SB	CS	OUT	BA	OBP	SLG	EQA	EQR	DEFENSE
2001	Clinton	Mid	468	98	14	2	1	59	101	43	42	14	8	378	.209	.300	.254	.201	34	113-CF -7
2002	*Montreal*	*NL*	*438*	*101*	*14*	*2*	*2*	*56*	*102*	*47*	*34*	*22*	*8*	*345*	*.231*	*.318*	*.285*	*.219*	*39*	

The Expos picked Sizemore in the third round of the 2000 draft and wooed him away from the University of Washington with a $2-million signing bonus. So far, they are ecstatic with the returns. Sizemore held his own in low-A ball as an 18-year-old, exhibiting tremendous plate discipline, a trait the organization is starting to emphasize. He hit only two balls out of the park, but the Expos liken him to Jim Edmonds, who didn't show much power until his early twenties.

Mark Smith OF Bats R Age 32

YEAR	TEAM	LGE	AB	H	DB	TP	HR	BB	SO	R	RBI	SB	CS	OUT	BA	OBP	SLG	EQA	EQR	DEFENSE
1999	Yakult	JpC	290	73	11	1	19	20	80	37	53	3	1	218	.252	.314	.493	.262	38	
2000	Florida	NL	194	48	9	1	5	15	50	22	26	2	0	146	.247	.307	.381	.233	19	38-LF -2
2001	Ottawa	Int	147	30	7	0	6	14	35	19	17	3	2	119	.204	.279	.374	.219	13	38-RF -1
2001	Montreal	NL	194	48	14	1	6	22	32	29	18	0	2	148	.247	.329	.423	.248	23	49-LF 1
2002	*Montreal*	*NL*	*302*	*70*	*12*	*1*	*13*	*32*	*59*	*27*	*28*	*4*	*2*	*234*	*.232*	*.305*	*.407*	*.242*	*34*	

Smith got much of his playing time as a result of the Expos jerking Bergeron, Brad Wilkerson, and Milton Bradley back and forth between Montreal and Ottawa. Smith has limited talents; he can hit lefties a bit, keeps fans interested when balls aren't hit right at him, and makes a killer three-egg omelet. He'll be using that resume to try to find work after opting for free agency.

Lee Stevens 1B Bats L Age 34

YEAR	TEAM	LGE	AB	H	DB	TP	HR	BB	SO	R	RBI	SB	CS	OUT	BA	OBP	SLG	EQA	EQR	DEFENSE
1999	Texas	AL	511	146	28	1	26	47	116	74	79	2	3	368	.286	.346	.497	.274	73	130-1B -1
2000	Montreal	NL	452	119	27	2	22	42	96	59	72	0	0	333	.263	.328	.478	.264	60	118-1B 10
2001	Montreal	NL	542	137	33	1	26	70	133	79	97	2	1	406	.253	.342	.461	.266	74	149-1B -6
2002	*Montreal*	*NL*	*480*	*122*	*25*	*1*	*22*	*63*	*121*	*67*	*70*	*1*	*1*	*359*	*.254*	*.341*	*.448*	*.267*	*66*	

The Expos don't recognize that Stevens isn't providing anything they couldn't get from Fernando Seguignol for one-twentieth the cost. Stevens's steady defense went in the tank after he took a couple of Big-O bad hops to the noggin. The organization values his leadership, but it's an unnecessary commodity on this ball club, even if his $4-million salary is supposed to show ownership's commitment to winning.

Fernando Tatis 3B Bats R Age 27

YEAR	TEAM	LGE	AB	H	DB	TP	HR	BB	SO	R	RBI	SB	CS	OUT	BA	OBP	SLG	EQA	EQR	DEFENSE
1999	St Louis	NL	537	156	29	2	34	75	118	99	100	17	9	390	.291	.393	.542	.304	99	142-3B -3
2000	St Louis	NL	325	81	19	1	18	53	86	57	61	2	3	247	.249	.369	.480	.280	51	75-3B 1
2001	Montreal	NL	145	38	7	0	3	15	36	20	12	0	0	107	.262	.344	.372	.245	16	34-3B -9
2002	*Montreal*	*NL*	*442*	*120*	*22*	*1*	*22*	*61*	*118*	*74*	*70*	*10*	*5*	*326*	*.271*	*.360*	*.475*	*.282*	*69*	

Tatis rubbed Tony LaRussa the wrong way, causing him to be briefly reunited with Felipe Alou, who played with Tatis's father in the Dominican Republic and is a close family friend. One injury after another (strained groin, partially torn labrum, back problems) marred his season before knee surgery scuttled it altogether. A healthy body and a focused attitude are all that Tatis needs to regain his 1999 form, but the unforgiving turf at Olympic Stadium and the turmoil surrounding the team don't make either a sure thing.

Jose Vidro 2B Bats B Age 27

YEAR	TEAM	LGE	AB	H	DB	TP	HR	BB	SO	R	RBI	SB	CS	OUT	BA	OBP	SLG	EQA	EQR	DEFENSE
1999	Montreal	NL	495	148	41	2	13	23	47	65	56	0	4	351	.299	.335	.469	.261	61	106-2B -3
2000	Montreal	NL	609	199	45	2	25	41	63	97	93	5	4	414	.327	.371	.530	.293	96	148-2B -1
2001	Montreal	NL	485	158	31	1	16	29	42	83	60	4	1	328	.326	.373	.493	.287	72	117-2B -11
2002	*Montreal*	*NL*	*523*	*164*	*33*	*2*	*20*	*42*	*53*	*81*	*68*	*6*	*3*	*362*	*.314*	*.365*	*.499*	*.289*	*81*	

The Expos can point to Vidro as a successful product of the organization's aggressive, contact-hitting philosophy. He is one of very few, however, as not many players possess the hand-eye coordination needed to put good wood on bad chucks. For the second year in the last three, Vidro couldn't stay out of harm's way; a gaggle of injuries caused him to miss large blocks of time and hampered his performance. If, by some miracle, the team stays in Montreal, some enterprising bean counter should run the numbers to see how quickly a new $2-million playing surface would pay for itself in terms of players' health and associated synergies.

Matt Watson LF Bats L Age 23

YEAR	TEAM	LGE	AB	H	DB	TP	HR	BB	SO	R	RBI	SB	CS	OUT	BA	OBP	SLG	EQA	EQR	DEFENSE
1999	Vermont	NYP	291	77	9	1	4	19	30	33	27	6	4	218	.265	.312	.344	.223	26	63-CF -4
2000	Jupiter	Fla	141	22	6	1	0	13	25	8	6	2	2	121	.156	.230	.213	.159	6	18-LF -2
2001	Jupiter	Fla	465	129	28	2	5	46	48	55	56	9	6	342	.277	.346	.378	.247	52	104-LF -1
2002	*Montreal*	*NL*	*424*	*120*	*20*	*2*	*7*	*45*	*51*	*52*	*43*	*10*	*6*	*310*	*.283*	*.352*	*.389*	*.257*	*52*	

Over the years, Montreal has earned a reputation as an organization that focuses too much on tools. However, they do have a few players who don't grab much attention while being honest-to-goodness ballplayers. Watson is one of them. Last year, he won his second batting title in three tries, and you can basically throw out his 2000 season, which was ravaged by a shoulder injury. Watson makes lots of hard contact and could surface as a 20-homer guy once he gets away from the pitcher-friendly humidity of Florida.

Brad Wilkerson LF Bats L Age 25

YEAR	TEAM	LGE	AB	H	DB	TP	HR	BB	SO	R	RBI	SB	CS	OUT	BA	OBP	SLG	EQA	EQR	DEFENSE	
1999	Harrisbg	Eas	430	86	19	2	6	69	100	54	37	2	3	347	.200	.316	.295	.216	38	116-RF	-2
2000	Harrisbg	Eas	232	66	26	1	6	33	39	41	33	5	3	169	.284	.379	.483	.286	37	57-LF	-2
2000	Ottawa	Int	215	50	10	0	11	39	59	36	30	4	3	168	.233	.356	.433	.265	30	62-LF	-1
2001	Ottawa	Int	241	61	7	0	12	57	63	41	46	10	4	184	.253	.400	.432	.287	41	55-LF	1
2001	Montreal	NL	117	25	7	2	1	16	35	11	5	2	1	93	.214	.308	.333	.222	11	32-LF	0
2002	*Montreal*	*NL*	*392*	*99*	*20*	*2*	*12*	*72*	*108*	*63*	*49*	*5*	*3*	*296*	*.253*	*.369*	*.406*	*.270*	*56*		

Having sent Rondell White and Milton Bradley packing, the Expos have placed all of their outfield eggs in Brad Wilkerson's basket. Shoulder surgery kept Wilkerson out of action until mid-May, delaying his Montreal debut until the All-Star break. Although he struggled after arriving, he continued to control the strike zone—making him something of an anomaly in this organization. Wilkerson has shown that he needs time to gather himself at each new level, so Torborg must stick with him if he gets off to a slow start. Come the summer solstice, both will be reaping the benefits of patience.

PITCHERS (ERA: 4.50, H/9: 9.0, HR/9: 1.0, BB/9: 3.0, K/9: 6.0, KW: 2.0, PERA: 4.50)

Tony Armas Jr. Throws R Age 24

YEAR	TEAM	LGE	IP	H	ER	HR	BB	K	ERA	W	L	H/9	HR/9	BB/9	K/9	KW	PERA	STUFF
1999	Harrisbg	Eas	143.3	150	77	14	55	75	4.83	7	9	9.4	0.9	3.5	4.7	0.7	4.05	8
2000	Ottawa	Int	19.3	22	12	4	4	10	5.59	1	1	10.2	1.9	1.9	4.7	1.3	5.35	0
2000	Montreal	NL	90.3	92	50	9	41	52	4.98	4	6	9.2	0.9	4.1	5.2	0.6	4.23	5
2001	Montreal	NL	189.0	177	89	15	81	142	4.24	11	10	8.4	0.7	3.9	6.8	0.9	4.46	16

It's hard to be anything but optimistic about Armas following last season's performance. He improved upon everything within his control: his strikeouts skyrocketed, while his walks and home runs allowed decreased. Additionally, after elbow and shoulder woes in 2000, he stayed healthy and made 34 starts. Armas has great mechanics and improving command of four above-average pitches. The franchise has plenty of problems; the top of the rotation isn't one of them.

Donnie Bridges Throws R Age 23

YEAR	TEAM	LGE	IP	H	ER	HR	BB	K	ERA	W	L	H/9	HR/9	BB/9	K/9	KW	PERA	STUFF
1999	CapeFear	SAL	45.3	47	26	4	23	23	5.16	2	3	9.3	0.8	4.6	4.6	0.5	3.16	7
1999	Jupiter	Fla	103.0	113	61	11	43	42	5.33	5	6	9.9	1.0	3.8	3.7	0.5	6.23	-2
2000	Jupiter	Fla	72.3	66	25	0	24	43	3.11	5	3	8.2	0.0	3.0	5.4	0.9	4.72	17
2000	Harrisbg	Eas	123.3	126	62	9	52	61	4.52	7	7	9.2	0.7	3.8	4.5	0.6	3.01	8
2001	Harrisbg	Eas	15.7	17	15	3	17	9	8.62	0	2	9.8	1.7	9.8	5.2	0.3	6.32	-19
2001	Ottawa	Int	55.0	63	56	14	48	38	9.16	1	5	10.3	2.3	7.9	6.2	0.4	9.21	-15

Montreal has oodles of farm arms that project as mid-range starters, while only Bridges has top-of-the-rotation stuff. Unfortunately, the organization is paying the price for having him work more than 200 innings as a 21-year-old. Bridges tried pitching through a strained right shoulder last year and lost the timing in his delivery, trashing what was already inconsistent command. The good news? The arsenal is still there, evidenced by the best strikeout rate of his career.

Ronald Chiavacci Throws R Age 24

YEAR	TEAM	LGE	IP	H	ER	HR	BB	K	ERA	W	L	H/9	HR/9	BB/9	K/9	KW	PERA	STUFF
1999	CapeFear	SAL	62.3	68	50	10	46	34	7.22	2	5	9.8	1.4	6.6	4.9	0.4	7.74	-18
1999	Jupiter	Fla	43.7	52	38	11	21	22	7.83	1	4	10.7	2.3	4.3	4.5	0.5	3.61	-4
2000	Jupiter	Fla	152.7	173	114	30	73	82	6.72	5	12	10.2	1.8	4.3	4.8	0.6	6.28	-7
2001	Harrisbg	Eas	146.7	146	97	18	100	102	5.95	6	10	9.0	1.1	6.1	6.3	0.5	5.74	0

A 44th-round draft pick with a Body by Beck (the reliever, not the mutating musician), Chiavacci needed an extreme season to get noticed. Mission accomplished. He finished three walks shy of leading the Eastern League in both strikeouts and bases on balls. While that double is generally the province of hurlers with blistering heat, Chiavacci's best pitch is a huge curveball. He's a bulldog who insists on taking the ball every fifth day and desperately needs the work to develop some control.

Zach Day Throws R Age 24

YEAR	TEAM	LGE	IP	H	ER	HR	BB	K	ERA	W	L	H/9	HR/9	BB/9	K/9	KW	PERA	STUFF
2000	Greensbr	SAL	82.3	90	59	15	41	50	6.45	3	6	9.8	1.6	4.5	5.5	0.6	4.37	0
2000	Tampa	Fla	34.3	36	22	5	19	23	5.77	2	2	9.4	1.3	5.0	6.0	0.6	7.91	-3
2000	Akron	Eas	45.7	42	20	2	22	31	3.94	3	2	8.3	0.4	4.3	6.1	0.7	4.52	14
2001	Akron	Eas	132.0	141	75	12	60	59	5.11	7	8	9.6	0.8	4.1	4.0	0.5	5.05	-4
2001	Ottawa	Int	29.3	32	15	3	9	12	4.60	1	2	9.8	0.9	2.8	3.7	0.7	8.78	-10

Although the Indians aren't exactly flush with mound hopefuls, they were willing to give up Day for Milton Bradley after Day regressed from an outstanding 2000 season. Most disturbing is his plummeting strikeout rate. Day's best pitch is a sinker, so strikeouts aren't vital to his success, but their relative paucity indicates something was wrong. Having learned from the L'Affaire Bridges, the Expos turned off the innings spigot at 160. They hope a quiet off-season will cure whatever ails Day.

Scott Downs Throws L Age 26

YEAR	TEAM	LGE	IP	H	ER	HR	BB	K	ERA	W	L	H/9	HR/9	BB/9	K/9	KW	PERA	STUFF
1999	Daytona	Fla	46.7	49	24	5	15	24	4.63	2	3	9.5	1.0	2.9	4.6	0.8	3.02	2
1999	WestTenn	Sou	78.3	67	28	3	29	68	3.22	6	3	7.7	0.3	3.3	7.8	1.2	1.69	30
2000	ChiCubs	NL	100.3	105	52	12	30	56	4.66	5	6	9.4	1.1	2.7	5.0	0.9	5.18	2

There were mild outcries in the hamlets of Quebec when Rondell White, the best bargaining chip the Expos had, brought only Downs in return at the 2000 trading deadline. Eighteen months later, the topic seldom even comes up, thanks to Downs's continued absence. Out of sight, out of mind, you know. Tommy John surgery was the culprit last year. TJ survivors usually regain their velocity ahead of their command; since Downs is a control freak, don't expect a shower of happy returns this season.

Joey Eischen Throws L Age 32

YEAR	TEAM	LGE	IP	H	ER	HR	BB	K	ERA	W	L	H/9	HR/9	BB/9	K/9	KW	PERA	STUFF
1999	Tucson	PCL	46.7	52	37	8	30	24	7.14	1	4	10.0	1.5	5.8	4.6	0.4	9.94	-42
2000	Ottawa	Int	56.7	66	42	11	24	25	6.67	2	4	10.5	1.7	3.8	4.0	0.5	5.45	-18
2001	Ottawa	Int	49.7	52	28	9	14	37	5.07	3	3	9.4	1.6	2.5	6.7	1.3	3.52	-7
2001	Montreal	NL	28.0	30	17	3	14	15	5.46	1	2	9.6	1.0	4.5	4.8	0.5	4.97	-17

Since being traded as a teenager for Oil Can Boyd, Eischen has logged more miles than hobo-wannabe Boxcar Willie ever did. Eischen lives the seesaw existence of the typical disposable lefty—toiling in the Adirondack Lumberjacks' rotation one year, facing Ken Griffey Jr. with the ball game on the line the next. The road is calling, as Eischen refused assignment to the minors after the season, becoming a free agent.

Anthony Ferrari Throws L Age 24

YEAR	TEAM	LGE	IP	H	ER	HR	BB	K	ERA	W	L	H/9	HR/9	BB/9	K/9	KW	PERA	STUFF
2000	Vermont	NYP	42.0	50	33	9	19	18	7.07	1	4	10.7	1.9	4.1	3.9	0.5	4.11	-25
2001	Jupiter	Fla	52.3	53	25	3	22	25	4.30	3	3	9.1	0.5	3.8	4.3	0.6	2.75	-17

Here is a cult figure just waiting to happen. Chosen in the 44th round out of Lewis & Clark State, Ferrari is a 5′9″ gunslinger who unleashes his bullets from an unorthodox herky-jerky delivery with a permanently bent south paw. His fastball/slider mix seems broader because of his ability to changes speeds on the slider. The Expos love his makeup, and his reputation only grew with his leading the AFL in saves. Ferrari could move quickly into a lefty-killing role out of the bullpen.

Eric Good Throws L Age 22

YEAR	TEAM	LGE	IP	H	ER	HR	BB	K	ERA	W	L	H/9	HR/9	BB/9	K/9	KW	PERA	STUFF
1999	Vermont	NYP	72.0	80	48	8	40	28	6.00	3	5	10.0	1.0	5.0	3.5	0.3	8.97	-12
2000	CapeFear	SAL	35.3	37	18	2	15	17	4.58	2	2	9.4	0.5	3.8	4.3	0.6	5.25	1
2001	Jupiter	Fla	107.3	116	54	10	29	44	4.53	6	6	9.7	0.8	2.4	3.7	0.8	4.87	0

Eric Good is part of a deep crop of left-handers in the lower reaches of the Expos' system. Elbow problems that forced him to miss most of 2000 resurfaced to a lesser degree last year, causing his workload to be curtailed. To keep things simple, the Expos limit almost all of their minor-league hurlers to three pitches. Good's weapons of choice are a plus fastball, a change-up, and a hard curveball—which resembles a slider—as his out pitch.

Hideki Irabu Throws R Age 33

YEAR	TEAM	LGE	IP	H	ER	HR	BB	K	ERA	W	L	H/9	HR/9	BB/9	K/9	KW	PERA	STUFF
1999	NY Yanks	AL	175.0	173	82	23	38	132	4.22	10	9	8.9	1.2	2.0	6.8	1.7	4.57	15
2000	Montreal	NL	61.0	63	30	8	12	37	4.43	4	3	9.3	1.2	1.8	5.5	1.5	6.75	3
2001	Montreal	NL	17.7	17	8	3	3	14	4.08	1	1	8.7	1.5	1.5	7.1	2.3	4.68	17
2001	Ottawa	Int	22.3	23	12	3	8	14	4.84	1	1	9.3	1.2	3.2	5.6	0.9	6.19	-3

During Prohibition, Pete Alexander was rumored to be drunk while pitching in Game Seven of the 1926 World Series. His legendary performance earned a sympathetic portrayal by Ronald Reagan in the movie *The Winning Team*. Seventy-five years later, with alcohol as easy to buy as Tic Tacs, Hideki Irabu drank himself into a stupor before a Triple-A rehab start and had to be hospitalized. For his performance, he was suspended by the Expos and subsequently released. The one-time "Nolan Ryan of Japan" landed in Texas over the winter, but more importantly, does this mean Keanu Reeves could someday inhabit the White House?

Josh Karp Throws R Age 22

The Expos continued their arms buildup last June, using their top draft choice on a right-handed starter for the third straight year. Karp's build and stuff are similar to that of last year's overall number-one pick, Mark Prior, but Karp's work habits and mental makeup are light-years behind. The Expos wisely refused to offer him a major-league contract, leading to a last-minute signing and a delayed entry to the pros. Karp will debut at high-A Jupiter, which should prove a challenge.

Cliff Lee Throws L Age 23

YEAR	TEAM	LGE	IP	H	ER	HR	BB	K	ERA	W	L	H/9	HR/9	BB/9	K/9	KW	PERA	STUFF
2000	CapeFear	SAL	48.3	45	32	2	46	33	5.96	2	3	8.4	0.4	8.6	6.1	0.4	11.00	-10
2001	Jupiter	Fla	99.3	117	97	33	54	77	8.79	2	9	10.6	3.0	4.9	7.0	0.7	5.13	-3

The Expos want their mound prospects to induce contact early in the count so that they learn to trust their stuff. Even with that instruction, Lee posted the best strikeout rate of any starter in the Florida State League, showing how tough he is to hit. Lee has the highest ceiling of any lefty in the Expos' system; consistent success is just a matter of repeating his delivery.

Graeme Lloyd Throws L Age 35

YEAR	TEAM	LGE	IP	H	ER	HR	BB	K	ERA	W	L	H/9	HR/9	BB/9	K/9	KW	PERA	STUFF
1999	Toronto	AL	71.3	73	37	10	19	47	4.67	4	4	9.2	1.3	2.4	5.9	1.2	3.78	-4
2001	Montreal	NL	68.3	70	31	5	19	35	4.08	4	4	9.2	0.7	2.5	4.6	0.9	4.70	-10

Lloyd returned from an incredibly difficult 2000 to finish second in the NL in appearances. A year further removed from both the physical and emotional trauma, he should improve on last season's mediocre numbers. Though the Expos can pencil in up to 70 workmanlike innings from Lloyd, they still would have been better served to spend the $9 million they gave him as a free agent on something they really needed, like an intelligent marketing plan, or a new mascot.

Luke Lockwood Throws L Age 20

YEAR	TEAM	LGE	IP	H	ER	HR	BB	K	ERA	W	L	H/9	HR/9	BB/9	K/9	KW	PERA	STUFF
2000	CapeFear	SAL	47.7	55	35	7	26	17	6.61	2	3	10.4	1.3	4.9	3.2	0.3	8.40	-10
2001	Clinton	Mid	161.0	176	94	17	65	65	5.25	8	10	9.8	1.0	3.6	3.6	0.5	5.45	1

When fellow portsider Josh Girdley was shut down with a bum shoulder, Lockwood emerged as the ace of the Clinton staff. Victimized by poor defense (29 unearned runs in 26 starts) and worse run support, Lockwood finished with a deceptive 5-10 record. None of his offerings are much above average, but he locates his pitches well, knows how to set up hitters, and should add velocity as he fills out. In Lockwood and Rich Rundles, the Expos have two classic projectable left-handers.

Troy Mattes Throws R Age 26

YEAR	TEAM	LGE	IP	H	ER	HR	BB	K	ERA	W	L	H/9	HR/9	BB/9	K/9	KW	PERA	STUFF
1999	Jupiter	Fla	24.0	30	19	5	10	7	7.13	1	2	11.3	1.9	3.8	2.6	0.3	5.95	-28
1999	Harrisbg	Eas	99.0	116	71	18	40	39	6.45	4	7	10.5	1.6	3.6	3.5	0.5	7.01	-17
2000	Harrisbg	Eas	167.7	203	135	38	67	70	7.25	5	14	10.9	2.0	3.6	3.8	0.5	5.83	-19
2001	Ottawa	Int	82.0	80	41	4	42	48	4.50	5	4	8.8	0.4	4.6	5.3	0.6	5.31	-4
2001	Montreal	NL	43.3	49	30	8	19	21	6.23	2	3	10.2	1.7	3.9	4.4	0.6	6.37	-11

(Troy Mattes *continued*)

Injuries and ineffectiveness combined to create a season-long audition for the final two spots in the Expos' rotation. Mattes was one of many soft-tossing Ottawa hurlers who attended the extended casting call at Olympic Stadium. Like the others, Mattes left Montreal a month later without winning the role, but at least he's still on the 40-man roster and can try out again in the future.

Guillermo Mota Throws R Age 28

YEAR	TEAM	LGE	IP	H	ER	HR	BB	K	ERA	W	L	H/9	HR/9	BB/9	K/9	KW	PERA	STUFF
1999	Montreal	NL	55.0	58	29	5	21	24	4.75	3	3	9.5	0.8	3.4	3.9	0.6	3.55	-16
2000	Ottawa	Int	59.3	63	37	5	34	26	5.61	3	4	9.6	0.8	5.2	3.9	0.4	2.65	-25
2000	Montreal	NL	30.0	29	14	3	10	21	4.20	2	1	8.7	0.9	3.0	6.3	1.0	5.75	-4
2001	Montreal	NL	47.0	52	29	8	16	25	5.55	2	3	10.0	1.5	3.1	4.8	0.8	5.24	-17

Mota was squarely in the running for the soon-to-be vacant closer's job before rotator-cuff tendinitis struck in early July. He threw less than ten innings in the final three months, yet nearly doubled what had been a tidy 2.70 ERA. The Expos believe that a restful winter will take care of his ailing shoulder. Mota still has good command of only one pitch, but it's flaming high-90s gas and will earn him some save opportunities this season.

Bobby Munoz Throws R Age 34

YEAR	TEAM	LGE	IP	H	ER	HR	BB	K	ERA	W	L	H/9	HR/9	BB/9	K/9	KW	PERA	STUFF
1999	Durham	Int	56.3	57	34	6	33	36	5.43	2	4	9.1	1.0	5.3	5.8	0.5	6.15	-23
2000	Louisvil	Int	83.7	86	56	8	61	48	6.02	3	6	9.3	0.9	6.6	5.2	0.4	6.65	-23
2001	Ottawa	Int	106.7	112	58	7	50	45	4.89	5	7	9.5	0.6	4.2	3.8	0.4	4.91	-11
2001	Montreal	NL	42.0	47	26	5	19	17	5.57	2	3	10.1	1.1	4.1	3.6	0.4	5.17	-19

The one basic rule of shopping at yard sales is to avoid large, dirt-cheap items with moving mechanical parts because they either don't work properly or they're on the verge of breaking down. The Expos' decision to sign Big Bobby Munoz to a minor-league contract shows this tenet is applicable in the baseball world, as well.

Tomokazu Ohka Throws R Age 26

YEAR	TEAM	LGE	IP	H	ER	HR	BB	K	ERA	W	L	H/9	HR/9	BB/9	K/9	KW	PERA	STUFF
1999	Trenton	Eas	68.3	78	49	14	26	36	6.45	3	5	10.3	1.8	3.4	4.7	0.7	3.96	-3
1999	Pawtuckt	Int	68.3	64	25	5	10	51	3.29	5	3	8.4	0.7	1.3	6.7	2.5	2.10	27
2000	Pawtuckt	Int	124.3	137	68	19	23	63	4.92	6	8	9.9	1.4	1.7	4.6	1.4	3.83	3
2000	Boston	AL	70.3	71	33	6	21	40	4.22	4	4	9.1	0.8	2.7	5.1	1.0	2.68	8
2001	Pawtuckt	Int	44.7	50	27	7	11	22	5.44	2	3	10.1	1.4	2.2	4.4	1.0	9.47	-14
2001	Boston	AL	57.3	58	29	6	18	35	4.55	3	3	9.1	0.9	2.8	5.5	1.0	6.19	0
2001	Montreal	NL	54.0	59	27	7	9	25	4.50	3	3	9.8	1.2	1.5	4.2	1.4	4.76	0

It's hard to not be over-hyped when you go 15-0 in Triple-A one year and throw a perfect game the next. Still, Ohka's star has fallen faster than that of David Caruso. In four months, he went from the Red Sox' second-best starter to trade filler for two months of Ugueth Urbina. Ohka has never been either that good or that bad. What he will be is a reliable fixture in the back end of the Expos' rotation, starting this year.

Carl Pavano Throws R Age 26

YEAR	TEAM	LGE	IP	H	ER	HR	BB	K	ERA	W	L	H/9	HR/9	BB/9	K/9	KW	PERA	STUFF
1999	Montreal	NL	109.0	108	46	7	29	63	3.80	7	5	8.9	0.6	2.4	5.2	1.1	5.19	10
2000	Montreal	NL	96.3	96	43	7	28	57	4.02	6	5	9.0	0.7	2.6	5.3	1.0	3.38	12
2001	Ottawa	Int	26.7	31	19	6	6	13	6.41	1	2	10.5	2.0	2.0	4.4	1.1	5.40	-11
2001	Montreal	NL	45.3	47	24	6	14	29	4.76	2	3	9.3	1.2	2.8	5.8	1.0	6.71	2

Pavano's medical history reads like a script from *ER* minus the incestuous frolicking by an ethnically diverse cast. Although he managed eight late-season starts, he hasn't thrown without a burning sensation in his elbow in at least five years. It would be nice to see what he could do if he were able to take the mound 30 times this season, but that's little more than wishcasting.

Britt Reames Throws R Age 28

YEAR	TEAM	LGE	IP	H	ER	HR	BB	K	ERA	W	L	H/9	HR/9	BB/9	K/9	KW	PERA	STUFF
1999	Potomac	Car	35.3	41	30	5	28	10	7.64	1	3	10.4	1.3	7.1	2.5	0.2	7.77	-53
2000	Arkansas	Tex	41.0	45	29	7	21	23	6.37	2	3	9.9	1.5	4.6	5.0	0.5	8.37	-23
2000	Memphis	PCL	73.0	65	26	3	21	55	3.21	5	3	8.0	0.4	2.6	6.8	1.3	2.78	18
2000	St Louis	NL	38.7	37	20	4	19	28	4.66	2	2	8.6	0.9	4.4	6.5	0.7	3.39	7
2001	Montreal	NL	93.7	94	55	13	43	69	5.28	4	6	9.0	1.2	4.1	6.6	0.8	6.22	-5
2001	Ottawa	Int	52.0	55	28	6	17	26	4.85	3	3	9.5	1.0	2.9	4.5	0.8	5.11	-4

Getting Britt Reames for Dustin Hermanson seemed a nice bit of larceny until Reames lost his command going through customs. It led to some jack-tastic early-season results and a curative trip to Ottawa, where he recovered his curveball. Reames threw well out of the bullpen after returning, and the plan seems to be to leave him there. That would be peachy but for the fact the Expos lack starting pitching depth, and Reames is the best immediate option to fill the void.

Scott Stewart Throws L Age 26

YEAR	TEAM	LGE	IP	H	ER	HR	BB	K	ERA	W	L	H/9	HR/9	BB/9	K/9	KW	PERA	STUFF
1999	Norfolk	Int	104.3	103	49	10	34	69	4.23	6	6	8.9	0.9	2.9	6.0	1.0	4.70	3
2000	Norfolk	Int	76.3	73	29	4	18	46	3.42	5	3	8.6	0.5	2.1	5.4	1.3	4.35	-1
2001	Montreal	NL	45.3	44	20	4	12	31	3.97	3	2	8.7	0.8	2.4	6.2	1.3	3.64	0

Stewart signed a minor-league contract with the Expos to escape the logjam of southpaws ahead of him in the Mets' system. A non-roster invitee to spring training, he proceeded to win a situational job thanks to his ability to locate three pitches in the strike zone. Though Stewart's stuff is mediocre, he doesn't resort to trickery, instead just chucking and ducking. Sometimes his simple approach works, sometimes it doesn't.

Scott Strickland Throws R Age 26

YEAR	TEAM	LGE	IP	H	ER	HR	BB	K	ERA	W	L	H/9	HR/9	BB/9	K/9	KW	PERA	STUFF
1999	Jupiter	Fla	25.3	24	10	2	5	20	3.55	2	1	8.5	0.7	1.8	7.1	2.0	5.62	5
1999	Harrisbg	Eas	29.3	26	11	1	10	24	3.38	2	1	8.0	0.3	3.1	7.4	1.2	2.81	13
1999	Ottawa	Int	28.7	22	8	0	10	27	2.51	2	1	6.9	0.0	3.1	8.5	1.4	1.52	24
1999	Montreal	NL	18.0	16	10	3	9	21	5.00	1	1	8.0	1.5	4.5	10.5	1.2	4.55	19
2000	Montreal	NL	47.7	41	16	3	13	43	3.02	3	2	7.7	0.6	2.5	8.1	1.7	3.08	16
2001	Montreal	NL	77.0	70	37	8	37	68	4.32	5	4	8.2	0.9	4.3	7.9	0.9	3.85	4

When Montreal dealt free-agent-to-be Ugueth Urbina at the trading deadline, Strickland inherited what few save situations the team saw the rest of the way. He gave ownership exactly what it wanted—comparable performance at a rock-bottom price. That could change this year if opponents look at the numbers, as Strickland still sports a huge platoon split, and teams are apt to pinch-hit in their final at-bat.

Anthony Telford Throws R Age 36

YEAR	TEAM	LGE	IP	H	ER	HR	BB	K	ERA	W	L	H/9	HR/9	BB/9	K/9	KW	PERA	STUFF
1999	Montreal	NL	103.3	97	39	3	32	62	3.40	7	4	8.4	0.3	2.8	5.4	1.0	4.43	-2
2000	Montreal	NL	79.7	77	35	9	19	60	3.95	5	4	8.7	1.0	2.1	6.8	1.6	3.98	4
2001	Montreal	NL	8.3	10	7	2	4	4	7.56	0	1	10.8	2.2	4.3	4.3	0.5	14.89	-43
2001	Ottawa	Int	76.3	81	42	10	22	42	4.95	4	4	9.6	1.2	2.6	5.0	1.0	6.36	-15

Overall, power pitchers have longer careers than soft tossers because they can adjust the way they work to cover for a drop in velocity. Junk-baller Telford's career was approaching its expiration date even before he had arthroscopic shoulder surgery at the end of 2000. Telford had absolutely nothing when he returned last spring, his fastball topping out in the low 80s. Four months in single-decked stadiums only verified that he's done.

Mike Thurman Throws R Age 28

YEAR	TEAM	LGE	IP	H	ER	HR	BB	K	ERA	W	L	H/9	HR/9	BB/9	K/9	KW	PERA	STUFF
1999	Montreal	NL	145.0	152	75	16	44	77	4.66	8	8	9.4	1.0	2.7	4.8	0.9	4.69	0
2000	Ottawa	Int	18.0	20	11	1	10	6	5.50	1	1	10.0	0.5	5.0	3.0	0.3	8.96	-30
2000	Montreal	NL	95.0	99	50	8	38	46	4.74	5	6	9.4	0.8	3.6	4.4	0.6	6.41	-5
2001	Montreal	NL	146.0	155	79	18	45	77	4.87	7	9	9.6	1.1	2.8	4.7	0.9	5.32	-1

(Mike Thurman *continued*)

Thurman claims that the elbow tendinitis that plagued him in 2000 is a thing of the past and that he threw pain-free last year. While his peripheral numbers don't inspire confidence, they do support his assertion. That means Thurman is back to being a sinkerballer with marginal stuff, operating with a very thin margin for error. If he can further tighten his already taut control, he could be a league-average starter; any loosening and he's a Lynx.

T.J. Tucker **Throws R** **Age 23**

YEAR	TEAM	LGE	IP	H	ER	HR	BB	K	ERA	W	L	H/9	HR/9	BB/9	K/9	KW	PERA	STUFF
1999	Jupiter	Fla	39.3	40	23	4	19	24	5.26	2	2	9.2	0.9	4.3	5.5	0.6	1.85	15
1999	Harrisbg	Eas	114.0	124	68	17	38	60	5.37	5	8	9.8	1.3	3.0	4.7	0.8	4.63	10
2000	Harrisbg	Eas	39.7	51	39	12	18	17	8.85	1	3	11.6	2.7	4.1	3.9	0.5	4.17	-11
2001	Harrisbg	Eas	78.3	90	62	14	47	37	7.12	3	6	10.3	1.6	5.4	4.3	0.4	4.89	-8
2001	Ottawa	Int	78.7	86	55	14	37	48	6.29	3	6	9.8	1.6	4.2	5.5	0.6	5.09	4

The aborted comeback of "El Sid" along with the retirements of Alex Fernandez and Tony Gwynn have left the ranks of the horizontally gifted a little . . . uh . . . thin. Large-boned T.J. Tucker could help fill the breach, though he will take his improving three-pitch arsenal and gopher-ball fetish back to Ottawa to start the season. Not to drone on about Tucker's lack of conditioning, but how often does a team feel compelled to note that a player "worked out every day over the off-season" in its media guide?

Javier Vazquez **Throws R** **Age 26**

YEAR	TEAM	LGE	IP	H	ER	HR	BB	K	ERA	W	L	H/9	HR/9	BB/9	K/9	KW	PERA	STUFF
1999	Montreal	NL	156.0	158	77	19	44	102	4.44	9	8	9.1	1.1	2.5	5.9	1.2	5.18	12
1999	Ottawa	Int	44.3	44	25	7	15	37	5.08	2	3	8.9	1.4	3.0	7.5	1.2	4.75	19
2000	Montreal	NL	232.0	220	94	21	50	174	3.65	16	10	8.5	0.8	1.9	6.8	1.7	3.92	22
2001	Montreal	NL	213.0	200	83	20	39	167	3.51	15	9	8.5	0.8	1.6	7.1	2.1	3.57	23

Not many people have witnessed it, but Vazquez has become an absolute buzz saw on the mound, combining Curt Schilling's power with Greg Maddux's command and ability to change speeds. An inconsistent first half last season led to Vazquez ranking as the third flakiest starter in the majors according to Support-Neutral measures; however, over his final nine starts, he was 7-1 with a 0.90 ERA in 70 innings. He could win the Internet Baseball Awards Cy Young as soon as this November, but he won't be collecting any real hardware until the Expos field an offense that is consistently able to put a "W" next to Vazquez's name in the box score.

Justin Wayne **Throws R** **Age 23**

YEAR	TEAM	LGE	IP	H	ER	HR	BB	K	ERA	W	L	H/9	HR/9	BB/9	K/9	KW	PERA	STUFF
2000	Jupiter	Fla	26.0	29	19	5	13	16	6.58	1	2	10.0	1.7	4.5	5.5	0.6	9.97	-4
2001	Jupiter	Fla	40.3	38	14	0	11	21	3.12	3	1	8.5	0.0	2.5	4.7	1.0	5.02	9
2001	Harrisbg	Eas	91.7	93	47	6	43	46	4.61	5	5	9.1	0.6	4.2	4.5	0.5	3.19	5

Due to the high risk of injury, we're fond of saying that there is no such thing as a pitching prospect. Wayne is about as close as you'll find. His average stuff won't allow him to emerge as an ace, but he has superb command of four pitches. You can largely ignore his so-so walk rates, which are skewed by a steadfast refusal to give in to hitters (he allowed only four home runs all season). There is a good chance that Wayne will start the year in Ottawa, and a better one that he'll finish it in Montreal.

Masato Yoshii **Throws R** **Age 37**

YEAR	TEAM	LGE	IP	H	ER	HR	BB	K	ERA	W	L	H/9	HR/9	BB/9	K/9	KW	PERA	STUFF
1999	NY Mets	NL	171.3	184	95	24	49	95	4.99	9	10	9.7	1.3	2.6	5.0	1.0	4.23	2
2000	Colorado	NL	173.3	194	100	25	44	78	5.19	8	11	10.1	1.3	2.3	4.1	0.9	4.32	-2
2001	Montreal	NL	109.3	121	60	15	23	51	4.94	5	7	10.0	1.2	1.9	4.2	1.1	5.00	-9

Yoshii balked at the prospect of working in relief, earning a one-way ticket out of the Rockies' spring complex. With teams paring down rosters, he picked a poor time to grouse about his role, especially following minor elbow surgery and a typically gruesome Coors Field hazing. Two weeks into the season, the Expos pulled Yoshii from the breadline and, surprise, plopped him in the bullpen. While he has a pesky tendency to hang sliders, Yoshii adjusts his approach to whatever is working and can help the team as a swing man.

New York Mets

This is the seventh edition of *Baseball Prospectus*, so by now, we pretty much have the process down. Clay Davenport does the Translations in October, we write the book throughout October and November, edit it in December, lay it out in January, and take e-mails from Canadians who are having trouble getting their copy in February and March.

Mets Prospectus

2001 record: 82–80; Third place, NL East

Pythagenport W/L: 73–89

Runs scored: 642 (16th in NL)

Runs allowed: 713 (5th in NL)

Team EqA: .252 (14th in NL)

2001 batters age: 30.2 (fifth-oldest in NL)

2001 pitchers age: 30.8 (third-oldest in NL)

Ballpark: Shea Stadium; good pitchers' park; Park Factor of .945

2001: The numbers don't reflect just how successful their season really was, but millions of New Yorkers know.

2002: After a December to remember, the Mets will be better this year; how much better, given the holes they still have, is the question.

December is the really busy time, as we update as much as 70% of the book to reflect off-season player movement. The late end to the 2001 season, and the subsequent slow start of postseason activity, made this year's book a unique challenge. However, no team in the history of this project has ever caused us more headaches than the New York Mets did this year. They forced us to rewrite this chapter from scratch in early 2002, because beginning on the second weekend of December, the Mets spent three weeks revamping their team, addressing their severe lineup problems and trying to assemble an offense that would enable them to make a run at the declining Braves in 2002.

The 2001 Mets were a bad offensive team. Yes, they provided some late-season thrills with their unexpected September run at the division title. They can be proud of their role in buoying New York City's spirit in the wake of September 11. However, the dramatic last six weeks of the season didn't erase the stench of the Mets' earlier failures.

The Mets finished last in the major leagues in runs scored, and they really were that bad. They finished next-to-last in the National League in batting average, last in total bases, last in slugging average, last in triples, next-to-last in home runs, and last in isolated power. For good measure, they even finished tied for last in the league in sacrifice flies. The offense fell into this state because the player-development system hadn't produced any contributors, while a series of free agents contributed for just a year or two before age made their presence in the lineup a burden.

The two players who best fit this latter category, Todd Zeile and Robin Ventura, were at the center of the Mets' problems in 2001. Despite finishing last in the league in runs scored, the Mets were third in the league in runners left on base, behind only the Diamondbacks and Giants, two above-average offensive teams. Normally, teams with good offenses are near the top of the league in men left on base because the number of runners left on base is directly related to having runners on base, which is the key to a good offense. Generally, the more men a team has on base, the more runs they score.

The 2001 Mets stand out as an exception to this rule. They scored 33.0% of their base runners. Since 1993, only three teams have scored a lower percentage of their base runners—two expansion teams (the 1993 Marlins, who scored 30.8% of their base runners, and the 1998 Devil Rays, who scored 32.7% of their base runners), along with the 1996 Phillies, who plated 32.9% of their base runners. The Mets had a lineup full of slow players with limited power, guys like Zeile and Ventura who were above average at getting on base (each posted a .359 OBP) and lousy at moving runners around (Zeile slugged .373, Ventura .419).

By the end of the year, General Manager Steve Phillips had seen enough; he said at season's end that his priorities for the off-season were "offense, offense, and offense." Phillips also declared that he had no more of a budget to play with than he had had for the 2001 team, which made it seem like he had set out an almost impossible task for himself: improving the offense without adding to his expenses.

Phillips was undaunted. He opened the trade season by swapping Ventura for David Justice of the Yankees, then sending Justice to the Athletics for Mark Guthrie. The two trades will save the Mets about $5 million in 2002. Phillips then chewed Indians GM Mark Shapiro's ear until the two worked out a deal in which the Mets acquired superstar Roberto Alomar for Matt Lawton, Billy Traber, Alex Escobar, and Jerrod Riggan. Then Phillips signed former Met Roger Cedeno to a reasonable four-year, $18-million contract. With two moves, the Mets had transformed the top of their order.

The Mets then sent Desi Relaford and Tsuyoshi Shinjo to the Giants for Shawn Estes, giving the team some added depth in the starting-pitching department. Given that flexibility, the Mets subsequently traded Kevin Appier to the Angels for slugger Mo Vaughn, nominally giving the Mets the left-handed hitting power threat their offense needed. The last piece in the puzzle, free-agent outfielder Juan Gonzalez, was never placed; after a long courtship, Gonzalez signed with the Rangers. The end result of all this activity is presented in Table 1.

Table 1. Transmogrifying the Mets

December 1, 2001		January 1, 2002	
C:	Mike Piazza	C:	Mike Piazza
1B:	Todd Zeile	1B:	Mo Vaughn
2B:	Edgardo Alfonzo	2B:	Roberto Alomar
SS:	Rey Ordonez	SS:	Rey Ordonez
3B:	Robin Ventura	3B:	Edgardo Alfonzo
LF:	Benny Agbayani	LF:	Benny Agbayani
CF:	Jay Payton	CF:	Jay Payton
RF:	Matt Lawton	RF:	Roger Cedeno

None of the Mets' moves translates to an automatic division title. Some of them are high-risk, and, as you can see, all of the activity still leaves the Mets with Rey Ordonez and Jay Payton in the starting lineup. Mo Vaughn has been hampered by injuries ever since he left the Red Sox; even if he's completely healthy, he'll probably be the worst defensive first baseman in Mets history. He's also not the type of player who ages well. Roger Cedeno, meanwhile, the Mets' projected leadoff hitter, lost much of his plate discipline in 2001 and finished with just a .337 on-base percentage. The Mets obviously hope that he will return to his 1999-2000 form so that he can be an important force at the top of the lineup.

The payroll-shaving maneuvers Phillips executed were for naught because the team didn't get Gonzalez or any other power-hitting outfielder. The new lineup is an improvement over the old one; it's also not much better than league average, and it contains the same two out machines with whom the Mets opened the off-season: Jay Payton and Rey Ordonez. They also have a $6-million pinch hitter with no trade value in Todd Zeile.

The Mets could kill two birds with one stone by using Zeile at third base and Alfonzo at shortstop, assigning Ordonez to his primary position, defensive replacement. It's a high-risk idea: Zeile hasn't played third base since 1999, while Alfonzo hasn't played shortstop since '98, although he was a good one in the minor leagues. Keep in mind, this is the team that used Kevin Mitchell at shortstop on its way to a world championship, being managed by a man—Bobby Valentine—who once played Kevin Reimer alongside Pete Incaviglia in the outfield. They at least have to consider it, perhaps when fly-ball pitchers such as Bruce Chen and Steve Trachsel are starting.

Phillips sacrificed some pitching to make all this happen. Shawn Estes is nowhere near the pitcher Kevin Appier is; his ERAs away from Pac Bell Park the last two years have been 5.19 and 5.25. With the loss of Appier, and without the great two-thirds of a season Rick Reed provided, it's unlikely that the rotation will be quite as solid as it was in 2001.

Whether the revamping of the Mets ends in a divisional title or not, there's little question that Phillips chose the right direction. The Mets have a barren farm system, with their two best prospects prior to the trades an injury-prone outfielder and a pitcher with one season of professional experience and a serious question about the condition of his elbow. Trading away veteran talent for good prospects would have been nearly impossible, because no team was going to trade young talent for Robin Ventura or Todd Zeile. The Mets' best player is a 33-year-old catcher. They have no good regulars under 30. Their pitching staff is younger than their lineup, but not by much. Given the hand Phillips was dealt, it was worth it to try and squeeze one more run out of the Piazza Mets.

Was it enough? Mets fans are optimistic, but they're still one player short of having a good lineup. Additionally, the Mets are relying heavily on a shaky core. Alomar was one of the best players in baseball last year, but he's 34 and plays a physically demanding position. Piazza is 33, and while his performance is still Hall of Fame-caliber, it's a rare catcher who sustains his offense at that age. Vaughn wasn't very good in the first two years of his Angels' contract, then he missed all of 2001 to a biceps injury. He'll be better than Zeile, but Wilton projects a .262/.348/.475 line, which doesn't push the Mets towards October baseball.

The Mets' 2001 draft was recognized by *Baseball America* as one of the year's top five drafts. The farm system is definitely starting to assemble pitching talent at its lower levels. But it's going to take a while to rebuild the talent base of the franchise. They do have to resist trading their best remaining prospects, Jose Reyes and Aaron Heilman. Right now, though, the Mets are better off waiting to rebuild until there is something with which to do so. Their best bet is to take advantage of the presence in their lineup of the greatest hitting catcher of all time while he still is that. Steve Phillips has done the best job he could of reshaping the team enough to keep its window of opportunity open just a year or two longer.

HITTERS (BA: .270, OBP: .340, SLG: .440, EqA: .260)

Benny Agbayani LF Bats R Age 30

YEAR	TEAM	LGE	AB	H	DB	TP	HR	BB	SO	R	RBI	SB	CS	OUT	BA	OBP	SLG	EQA	EQR	DEFENSE
1999	Norfolk	Int	101	33	7	0	7	13	18	17	25	4	3	71	.327	.411	.604	.319	20	18-CF 0
1999	NY Mets	NL	278	80	18	3	14	29	56	41	40	5	4	202	.288	.361	.525	.286	44	65-OF -2
2000	NY Mets	NL	354	103	21	1	15	50	62	58	58	4	5	256	.291	.388	.483	.288	57	83-LF -2
2001	NY Mets	NL	299	88	17	2	6	35	62	30	29	4	5	216	.294	.375	.425	.269	40	67-LF -6
2002	*Colorado*	*NL*	*355*	*116*	*23*	*3*	*14*	*48*	*70*	*54*	*55*	*8*	*6*	*245*	*.327*	*.407*	*.527*	*.279*	*50*	

A variety of injuries made Agbayani almost an invisible man in 2001. When he actually was in the lineup, his lack of power was a major disappointment, and his defense has never exactly been sparkling. With all that, he did post a .269 EqA. "Hawaiian Punch," by the way, is one of the five best nicknames in baseball. Playing every day in Coors Field, he's going to put up a season that would make Fonzie Bichette blush.

Edgardo Alfonzo 2B Bats R Age 28

YEAR	TEAM	LGE	AB	H	DB	TP	HR	BB	SO	R	RBI	SB	CS	OUT	BA	OBP	SLG	EQA	EQR	DEFENSE
1999	NY Mets	NL	633	194	33	2	30	77	79	122	107	8	2	441	.306	.384	.507	.295	104	157-2B -4
2000	NY Mets	NL	551	180	39	2	26	88	64	109	92	3	2	373	.327	.423	.546	.319	107	142-2B -3
2001	NY Mets	NL	461	120	20	0	19	49	53	68	53	5	0	341	.260	.336	.427	.257	57	117-2B -3
2002	*NY Mets*	*NL*	*526*	*151*	*26*	*1*	*26*	*81*	*66*	*99*	*83*	*6*	*1*	*376*	*.287*	*.382*	*.489*	*.298*	*91*	

Alfonzo had established himself as a star in 1999 and 2000, but that Alfonzo never showed up in 2001. He suffered from back problems and appeared to be out of shape and tired. The words "Carlos Baerga" were heard in whispers, in reference to another star second baseman who fell off a cliff at age 27. Alfonzo devoted himself to a totally different regimen this off-season, and it's reasonable to expect a significant recovery in 2002. It's hard to believe he'll ever be the same player he was in '99 and '00. He's moving to third base to accommodate Alomar.

Chris Basak SS Bats R Age 24

YEAR	TEAM	LGE	AB	H	DB	TP	HR	BB	SO	R	RBI	SB	CS	OUT	BA	OBP	SLG	EQA	EQR	DEFENSE
2000	Pittsfld	NYP	259	69	11	2	1	16	42	27	11	13	8	198	.266	.312	.336	.222	23	57-SS -4
2001	St Lucie	Fla	485	98	17	2	4	32	134	53	35	16	7	394	.202	.255	.270	.186	29	119-SS -6
2001	Binghmtn	Eas	43	13	4	1	1	3	10	9	6	1	0	30	.302	.363	.512	.290	7	10-SS 4
2002	*NY Mets*	*NL*	*510*	*122*	*21*	*4*	*7*	*46*	*137*	*58*	*40*	*21*	*10*	*398*	*.239*	*.302*	*.337*	*.225*	*48*	

Basak looked like a top prospect after a promising year for Pittsfield in 2000. Then his offense evaporated at St. Lucie. Nevertheless, the Mets think highly of his glove work, promoting him to Binghamton late in the season despite his problems at the plate. Defense alone won't take Basak much further, and he's pretty old for big steps forward as a hitter.

Craig Brazell 1B Bats L Age 22

YEAR	TEAM	LGE	AB	H	DB	TP	HR	BB	SO	R	RBI	SB	CS	OUT	BA	OBP	SLG	EQA	EQR	DEFENSE
1999	Kingsprt	App	215	54	9	0	3	1	38	13	18	2	2	163	.251	.203	.335	.199	14	29-1B 0
2000	Columbia	SAL	409	77	12	0	8	9	88	24	39	1	2	334	.188	.212	.276	.165	19	79-1B -11
2001	Columbia	SAL	339	82	18	2	12	12	79	38	46	0	2	259	.242	.272	.413	.222	30	56-1B -3
2002	*NY Mets*	*NL*	*384*	*97*	*16*	*1*	*12*	*20*	*92*	*32*	*45*	*2*	*2*	*289*	*.253*	*.290*	*.393*	*.231*	*37*	

Brazell impressed the Mets with a strong show of power in his second year for Capital City, hitting 19 home runs and 25 doubles in just 83 games. A minor knee injury cut short his season but is not expected to affect him in 2002. The more pressing problem is his plate discipline, which borders on the ridiculous: just 12 unintentional walks in 356 plate appearances.

Jay Caligiuri 1B Bats R Age 22

YEAR	TEAM	LGE	AB	H	DB	TP	HR	BB	SO	R	RBI	SB	CS	OUT	BA	OBP	SLG	EQA	EQR	DEFENSE
2001	Brooklyn	NYP	245	57	9	1	4	17	37	25	21	2	1	189	.233	.289	.327	.210	19	50-1B 1
2002	*NY Mets*	*NL*	*270*	*66*	*8*	*1*	*6*	*24*	*44*	*27*	*26*	*3*	*1*	*205*	*.244*	*.306*	*.348*	*.228*	*25*	

(Jay Caligiuri *continued*)

The Mets' 13th-round pick in last year's draft isn't regarded as much of a prospect, but he had a terrific season with the bat. A third baseman in college, he played mostly first base for the Cyclones and is expected to stay there henceforth. Caligiuri is far more disciplined than the average hitter his age, and given the Mets' dearth of hitters at upper levels, will be given the opportunity to move up quickly through the system.

Enrique Cruz 3B/SS Bats R Age 20

YEAR	TEAM	LGE	AB	H	DB	TP	HR	BB	SO	R	RBI	SB	CS	OUT	BA	OBP	SLG	EQA	EQR	DEFENSE
2000	Kingsprt	App	229	40	7	0	5	14	67	18	20	7	4	193	.175	.225	.271	.173	12	39-3B 3 19-SS -1
2000	Columbia	SAL	163	23	4	0	2	18	47	13	9	0	2	142	.141	.228	.202	.155	7	42-SS -20
2001	Columbia	SAL	460	93	18	1	6	44	113	43	43	15	5	372	.202	.275	.285	.199	33	102-3B -8 22-SS -4
2002	*NY Mets*	*NL*	*426*	*91*	*16*	*1*	*8*	*49*	*119*	*49*	*38*	*21*	*6*	*341*	*.214*	*.295*	*.312*	*.219*	*38*	

Cruz is a toolsy third baseman who has held his own in the lower rungs of the Mets system. His plate discipline is better than average for his age, and scouts are impressed by his athleticism. He's split time so far, but he will be a third baseman from here on out. Cruz is one of the few high-upside prospects in this system.

Alex Escobar CF Bats R Age 23

YEAR	TEAM	LGE	AB	H	DB	TP	HR	BB	SO	R	RBI	SB	CS	OUT	BA	OBP	SLG	EQA	EQR	DEFENSE
2000	Binghmtn	Eas	439	109	18	4	14	44	117	60	49	16	4	334	.248	.322	.403	.247	51	119-CF 0
2001	Norfolk	Int	403	105	20	3	12	35	135	54	50	15	3	301	.261	.323	.414	.250	47	104-CF 1
2001	NY Mets	NL	50	11	1	0	3	3	16	3	8	1	0	39	.220	.264	.420	.227	5	13-CF -1
2002	*Clevelnd*	*AL*	*428*	*119*	*20*	*3*	*17*	*45*	*140*	*64*	*71*	*21*	*4*	*313*	*.278*	*.347*	*.458*	*.271*	*60*	

Escobar's debut at the big-league level—in fact, his whole season—was a bust. He showed occasional flashes of the tools that excite scouts, but his strike-zone judgment completely fell apart, and the results weren't pretty. He's still a good prospect, it's just time to remove the "potential superstar" label. Milton Bradley is a much better player right now, so Escobar faces an uphill battle in Cleveland.

Lenny Harris PH Bats L Age 37

YEAR	TEAM	LGE	AB	H	DB	TP	HR	BB	SO	R	RBI	SB	CS	OUT	BA	OBP	SLG	EQA	EQR	DEFENSE
1999	Colorado	NL	155	41	10	0	0	4	6	13	11	1	1	115	.265	.283	.329	.205	11	20-2B -7
1999	Arizona	NL	29	11	0	0	1	0	1	2	6	1	0	18	.379	.379	.483	.292	4	
2000	Arizona	NL	86	16	1	1	1	2	5	9	12	5	0	70	.186	.205	.256	.169	4	17-3B -2
2000	NY Mets	NL	140	43	7	3	3	15	16	22	13	8	1	98	.307	.374	.464	.287	22	16-3B -4
2001	NY Mets	NL	136	33	5	1	0	7	8	13	10	3	2	105	.243	.280	.294	.197	9	
2002	*Milwauke*	*NL*	*200*	*45*	*7*	*2*	*2*	*15*	*15*	*20*	*16*	*7*	*2*	*157*	*.225*	*.279*	*.310*	*.202*	*14*	

Among the many record chases in 2001, none was more pointless or boring than Harris's annoying and ultimately successful run at Manny Mota's all-time pinch-hit record. Harris clearly can't play any position anymore, and his bat looks like it's run out of hits, so the Mets should cut bait on Harris's veteran presence even if it means eating his 2002 contract.

Justin Huber C Bats R Age 19

YEAR	TEAM	LGE	AB	H	DB	TP	HR	BB	SO	R	RBI	SB	CS	OUT	BA	OBP	SLG	EQA	EQR	DEFENSE
2001	Kingsprt	App	165	36	7	0	4	10	46	13	17	1	1	130	.218	.278	.333	.207	13	46-C -8
2002	*NY Mets*	*NL*	*246*	*59*	*5*	*0*	*7*	*20*	*78*	*23*	*26*	*0*	*0*	*187*	*.240*	*.297*	*.346*	*.221*	*22*	

Huber hopes to be the second Australian catcher to make the major leagues, after David Nilsson. He started playing ball at a very young age for the Upwey-Ferntree Gully Baseball Club. (That's just fun to say.) His offense in short-season ball impressed the brass enough for him to be recognized by the organization as Kingsport's best player.

Mark Johnson 1B Bats L Age 34

YEAR	TEAM	LGE	AB	H	DB	TP	HR	BB	SO	R	RBI	SB	CS	OUT	BA	OBP	SLG	EQA	EQR	DEFENSE
1999	Hanshin	JpC	375	95	22	1	20	49	75	52	66	1	1	281	.253	.344	.477	.270	53	
2000	Norfolk	Int	320	82	17	1	16	58	53	44	53	11	2	240	.256	.377	.466	.286	52	37-1B 1 33-RF -3
2001	Norfolk	Int	156	47	10	0	9	21	19	26	25	2	1	110	.301	.389	.538	.302	28	40-1B 8
2001	NY Mets	NL	119	32	7	1	6	16	26	18	24	0	2	89	.269	.356	.496	.274	17	13-1B -2
2002	*NY Mets*	*NL*	*303*	*70*	*13*	*1*	*12*	*50*	*48*	*28*	*31*	*5*	*2*	*235*	*.231*	*.340*	*.399*	*.259*	*40*	

Johnson remains a solid bat off the bench who has no real position on the field. He provides enough potential pop to be worth a roster spot, especially for an AL team with a right-leaning lineup. The Mets' pickup of Mo Vaughn shuffles Todd Zeile to the bench and leaves them with no room for Johnson, so he'll be back at Norfolk.

Matt Lawton RF Bats L Age 30

YEAR	TEAM	LGE	AB	H	DB	TP	HR	BB	SO	R	RBI	SB	CS	OUT	BA	OBP	SLG	EQA	EQR	DEFENSE
1999	Minnesot	AL	401	106	13	0	9	53	37	55	53	25	4	299	.264	.358	.364	.258	50	95-RF -3
2000	Minnesot	AL	550	169	41	2	14	83	66	70	88	23	8	389	.307	.405	.465	.296	93	134-RF -10
2001	Minnesot	AL	375	113	19	0	13	64	40	72	53	17	7	260	.301	.400	.450	.294	63	85-RF -6
2001	NY Mets	NL	185	50	13	1	3	21	29	26	14	10	2	137	.270	.364	.400	.267	25	46-RF 0
2002	*Clevelnd*	*AL*	*499*	*146*	*27*	*1*	*14*	*82*	*58*	*77*	*73*	*24*	*8*	*360*	*.293*	*.392*	*.435*	*.284*	*77*	

The Rick Reed-for-Matt Lawton trade hurt both teams, because both Reed and Lawton are players who took extra advantage of their home parks. Lawton is at least a genuine everyday outfielder, which is more than you can say about the rest of the Mets' outfielders in 2001. Traded to Cleveland in the Alomar deal, Lawton subsequently signed a four-year deal and will play right field for the Tribe during their decline.

Joe McEwing UT Bats R Age 29

YEAR	TEAM	LGE	AB	H	DB	TP	HR	BB	SO	R	RBI	SB	CS	OUT	BA	OBP	SLG	EQA	EQR	DEFENSE	
1999	St Louis	NL	515	140	28	4	9	35	81	63	42	6	4	379	.272	.325	.394	.242	54	82-2B 0	52-OF -1
2000	Norfolk	Int	172	42	9	1	5	14	33	25	16	6	3	133	.244	.301	.395	.233	18	16-CF 0	11-3B 1
2000	NY Mets	NL	155	36	14	1	2	3	27	20	19	3	1	120	.232	.251	.374	.208	12	20-LF 1	
2001	NY Mets	NL	286	87	20	3	8	15	48	44	32	8	5	204	.304	.355	.479	.274	40	39-LF 0	17-3B 1
2002	*NY Mets*	*NL*	*421*	*116*	*29*	*3*	*12*	*33*	*77*	*63*	*44*	*11*	*5*	*310*	*.276*	*.328*	*.444*	*.264*	*55*		

After a poor 2000, McEwing reestablished himself as a major-league utility player in 2001. His flexibility and hustle will help him maintain a spot on the roster in 2002. His playing time will be determined by the health of better players.

Rey Ordonez SS Bats R Age 31

YEAR	TEAM	LGE	AB	H	DB	TP	HR	BB	SO	R	RBI	SB	CS	OUT	BA	OBP	SLG	EQA	EQR	DEFENSE
1999	NY Mets	NL	525	138	26	2	1	42	55	49	59	7	4	391	.263	.319	.326	.222	46	147-SS 11
2000	NY Mets	NL	135	27	5	0	0	15	15	10	9	0	0	108	.200	.280	.237	.185	8	40-SS -4
2001	NY Mets	NL	465	123	27	4	3	32	36	34	47	3	2	344	.265	.313	.359	.228	42	136-SS 7
2002	*NY Mets*	*NL*	*443*	*113*	*21*	*2*	*4*	*46*	*42*	*43*	*49*	*5*	*2*	*332*	*.255*	*.325*	*.339*	*.234*	*44*	

Ordonez slugged .336 in 2001 and finished eighth in the National League in intentional walks. Everyone else in the top ten slugged at least .566. While St. Rey made some limited offensive strides, it's safe to say he doesn't belong in that company. He's still a poor, undisciplined hitter and an above-average, acrobatic fielder. The Mets tried desperately to dump Ordonez's salary in late 2001, but no one took the bait. It's apparent that the league has recognized that Ordonez is not the second coming of Ozzie Smith; Ordonez didn't even win a Gold Glove in 2001.

Jay Payton CF Bats R Age 29

YEAR	TEAM	LGE	AB	H	DB	TP	HR	BB	SO	R	RBI	SB	CS	OUT	BA	OBP	SLG	EQA	EQR	DEFENSE
1999	Norfolk	Int	143	52	9	2	7	9	12	22	28	2	2	93	.364	.404	.601	.320	27	33-LF -1
2000	NY Mets	NL	494	145	20	1	18	24	55	61	61	4	12	361	.294	.330	.447	.250	56	128-CF 2
2001	NY Mets	NL	364	99	16	1	9	16	44	47	37	4	3	268	.272	.310	.396	.235	36	96-CF 1
2002	*NY Mets*	*NL*	*414*	*116*	*22*	*1*	*13*	*28*	*51*	*51*	*51*	*6*	*7*	*305*	*.280*	*.326*	*.432*	*.256*	*50*	

Payton is running out of chances. Injuries wiped out almost half of his 2001 season, and his play the rest of the year was a disappointment after a somewhat promising rookie season. Poor pitch selection is his biggest problem at the plate; he's constantly swinging at pitches that he can hit but can't drive. His hold on a job is tenuous, as the Mets will use Roger Cedeno in center field if they acquire a corner outfielder.

Timoniel Perez — RF — Bats L — Age 25

YEAR	TEAM	LGE	AB	H	DB	TP	HR	BB	SO	R	RBI	SB	CS	OUT	BA	OBP	SLG	EQA	EQR	DEFENSE
1999	Hiroshim	JpC	23	4	0	0	0	3	3	2	2	0	0	19	.174	.269	.174	.166	1	
2000	Norfolk	Int	292	98	15	4	6	12	25	40	32	10	6	200	.336	.367	.476	.278	41	70-CF 8
2000	NY Mets	NL	50	15	4	1	1	2	5	11	3	1	1	36	.300	.338	.480	.265	6	13-OF 1
2001	Norfolk	Int	195	67	7	2	6	13	17	35	18	13	2	130	.344	.389	.492	.299	32	46-OF -2
2001	NY Mets	NL	241	64	11	1	5	11	21	28	23	1	6	183	.266	.302	.382	.222	21	60-RF 3
2002	*NY Mets*	*NL*	*409*	*126*	*16*	*4*	*10*	*34*	*36*	*49*	*50*	*12*	*4*	*287*	*.308*	*.361*	*.440*	*.278*	*58*	

The late-season wonder child of 2000 came crashing back to earth with a huge splat in 2001. He simply wasn't ready for the majors offensively, and it showed. Perez has the potential to be a good fourth outfielder, especially for a team playing Benny Agbayani in left field, but he may need a bit more time in the minor leagues.

Jason Phillips — C — Bats R — Age 25

YEAR	TEAM	LGE	AB	H	DB	TP	HR	BB	SO	R	RBI	SB	CS	OUT	BA	OBP	SLG	EQA	EQR	DEFENSE
1999	St Lucie	Fla	285	60	9	1	7	17	32	27	34	0	1	226	.211	.264	.323	.198	20	67-C -4
1999	Binghmtn	Eas	142	28	5	0	5	9	20	10	17	0	0	114	.197	.253	.338	.199	10	38-C -1
2000	St Lucie	Fla	300	68	10	0	7	17	21	40	31	1	1	233	.227	.277	.330	.206	22	72-C 3
2000	Binghmtn	Eas	97	32	3	0	0	5	9	12	10	0	0	65	.330	.370	.361	.252	10	24-C -1
2001	Binghmtn	Eas	320	80	12	0	10	27	24	35	46	0	1	241	.250	.314	.381	.233	32	82-C -2
2001	Norfolk	Int	67	20	1	0	2	7	7	8	13	0	0	47	.299	.365	.403	.262	8	15-C 1
2002	*NY Mets*	*NL*	*407*	*105*	*10*	*0*	*13*	*34*	*44*	*47*	*55*	*0*	*1*	*303*	*.258*	*.315*	*.378*	*.239*	*42*	

Like Vance Wilson, Phillips is viewed primarily as a defensive catcher, thanks in part to an extraordinarily quick release. The Mets were encouraged by Phillips's offensive growth in 2001 and see him as part of the team's future. Keep in mind that by blocking off both infield corners this winter, the Mets effectively locked Piazza in at catcher for the next few years, blocking their catcher prospects.

Mike Piazza — C — Bats R — Age 33

YEAR	TEAM	LGE	AB	H	DB	TP	HR	BB	SO	R	RBI	SB	CS	OUT	BA	OBP	SLG	EQA	EQR	DEFENSE
1999	NY Mets	NL	538	164	21	0	42	45	65	100	120	2	2	376	.305	.360	.578	.299	92	129-C -7
2000	NY Mets	NL	488	161	24	0	39	52	63	90	111	4	2	329	.330	.397	.619	.323	97	119-C -8
2001	NY Mets	NL	509	161	27	0	39	64	74	86	100	0	2	350	.316	.394	.599	.316	99	125-C -12
2002	*NY Mets*	*NL*	*514*	*147*	*20*	*0*	*36*	*64*	*76*	*89*	*102*	*3*	*2*	*369*	*.286*	*.365*	*.535*	*.299*	*90*	

The astonishing thing about Piazza is not that he's the greatest hitting catcher of all time, which is pretty clear, but the distance between him and everybody else. His career Equivalent Average is .325; no 20th-century catcher finished his career behind the plate with an EqA higher than .310. The acquisitions of Mo Vaughn and Roberto Alomar (the latter moving Alfonzo to third base) effectively end speculation that Piazza will move out from behind the dish; there's nowhere for him to go.

Desi Relaford — IF — Bats B — Age 28

YEAR	TEAM	LGE	AB	H	DB	TP	HR	BB	SO	R	RBI	SB	CS	OUT	BA	OBP	SLG	EQA	EQR	DEFENSE	
1999	Philadel	NL	212	51	11	2	1	16	31	30	25	3	3	164	.241	.312	.325	.218	18	63-SS 1	
2000	Philadel	NL	254	56	11	3	3	44	41	28	28	5	0	198	.220	.353	.323	.243	29	78-SS -12	
2000	San Dieg	NL	160	35	2	0	2	25	24	26	16	8	0	125	.219	.334	.269	.227	15	42-SS 1	
2001	NY Mets	NL	304	98	20	0	11	26	55	45	40	14	5	211	.322	.383	.497	.293	49	44-2B -5	17-SS -1
2002	*San Fran*	*NL*	*385*	*100*	*20*	*2*	*9*	*49*	*71*	*66*	*55*	*15*	*4*	*289*	*.260*	*.343*	*.392*	*.264*	*52*		

Relaford's offense in 2001 was a surprise to just about everyone. He was far more aggressive at the plate, and that approach paid off as he hit with far more authority than he had in previous major-league seasons. Defensively, Relaford is acceptable at second base and third base, but definitely subpar at shortstop. Traded to the Giants, he should get a lot of the playing time at third base and will outhit that projection.

Jose Reyes — SS — Bats B — Age 19

YEAR	TEAM	LGE	AB	H	DB	TP	HR	BB	SO	R	RBI	SB	CS	OUT	BA	OBP	SLG	EQA	EQR	DEFENSE
2000	Kingsprt	App	137	23	3	1	0	11	44	11	4	3	2	116	.168	.235	.204	.160	6	33-SS 1
2001	Columbia	SAL	417	101	20	7	4	14	75	50	33	14	7	323	.242	.268	.353	.209	32	107-SS -2
2002	*NY Mets*	*NL*	*422*	*102*	*20*	*7*	*4*	*26*	*91*	*51*	*34*	*20*	*9*	*329*	*.242*	*.286*	*.351*	*.222*	*38*	

The most exciting prospect in the Mets system, Reyes was rated the top defensive shortstop in the South Atlantic League by *Baseball America*, and Mets officials favorably compare his defensive tools to those of Rey Ordonez. Offensively, the pop he displayed at such a young age is very promising. Because he is so young, the Mets plan to move him up slowly.

Tsuyoshi Shinjo — OF — Bats R — Age 30

YEAR	TEAM	LGE	AB	H	DB	TP	HR	BB	SO	R	RBI	SB	CS	OUT	BA	OBP	SLG	EQA	EQR	DEFENSE
1999	Hanshin	JpC	468	119	22	8	13	22	69	54	57	8	2	351	.254	.301	.419	.240	49	
2000	Hanshin	JpC	513	145	26	1	28	33	85	76	89	15	5	373	.283	.327	.501	.270	71	
2001	NY Mets	NL	404	116	23	1	11	23	59	49	60	4	5	293	.287	.334	.431	.252	47	109-OF 9
2002	*San Fran*	*NL*	*471*	*116*	*19*	*3*	*15*	*37*	*86*	*54*	*57*	*10*	*6*	*361*	*.246*	*.301*	*.395*	*.241*	*52*	

The Mets gambled that Shinjo would be more effective against American pitching than Japanese pitching, and it appears that they were right. All the team won, however, was yet another solid fourth outfielder. As impressive a defensive player as Shinjo turned out to be, he simply is not productive enough offensively to play every day.

Earl Snyder — 1B/3B — Bats R — Age 26

YEAR	TEAM	LGE	AB	H	DB	TP	HR	BB	SO	R	RBI	SB	CS	OUT	BA	OBP	SLG	EQA	EQR	DEFENSE
1999	Columbia	SAL	501	105	18	2	17	39	124	51	60	1	1	397	.210	.268	.355	.209	40	122-1B 6
2000	St Lucie	Fla	523	122	19	0	21	42	141	62	65	2	3	404	.233	.295	.390	.228	50	120-1B -5
2001	Binghmtn	Eas	412	99	26	2	15	50	108	58	59	3	1	314	.240	.326	.422	.250	49	83-1B -6 14-3B 0
2002	*Clevelnd*	*AL*	*451*	*118*	*23*	*1*	*20*	*58*	*122*	*63*	*67*	*2*	*2*	*335*	*.262*	*.346*	*.450*	*.263*	*60*	

It's a sign of a lousy system when the organizational Player of the Year ends up as an afterthought in a seven-player trade. Snyder was the player to be named in the Alomar deal. He's never impressed anyone defensively at first base, though he did manage to play a little third last year without hurting anyone. His opportunity will come next year, as both Travis Fryman and Jim Thome can leave Cleveland after this season.

Rob Stratton — RF — Bats R — Age 24

YEAR	TEAM	LGE	AB	H	DB	TP	HR	BB	SO	R	RBI	SB	CS	OUT	BA	OBP	SLG	EQA	EQR	DEFENSE
1999	Columbia	SAL	331	70	12	1	13	35	118	39	37	3	1	262	.211	.291	.372	.224	31	44-RF -8
2000	St Lucie	Fla	392	76	12	2	21	44	199	45	57	2	3	319	.194	.282	.395	.224	38	94-RF -8
2001	Binghmtn	Eas	488	105	21	1	22	47	196	58	65	6	3	386	.215	.290	.398	.229	49	108-RF -4
2002	*NY Mets*	*NL*	*450*	*97*	*16*	*1*	*24*	*50*	*206*	*57*	*61*	*5*	*3*	*356*	*.216*	*.294*	*.416*	*.241*	*51*	

Would you believe Russ Branyan Lite? Stratton has been slowly moving up the ladder while maintaining his reputation of having the most power of anyone in the organization. His offensive skill set is "swing hard," and he hasn't been able to establish much of a defensive reputation, so he's not going to advance much further. By the way, that's not just a DT thing: Stratton really did strike out 201 times at Binghamton last year.

Jorge Toca — 1B — Bats R — Age 31

YEAR	TEAM	LGE	AB	H	DB	TP	HR	BB	SO	R	RBI	SB	CS	OUT	BA	OBP	SLG	EQA	EQR	DEFENSE
1999	Binghmtn	Eas	279	72	10	1	15	23	43	46	48	3	3	210	.258	.321	.462	.255	35	49-LF 1 19-1B -1
1999	Norfolk	Int	175	54	10	1	4	4	22	21	23	0	2	123	.309	.327	.446	.251	19	44-1B 3
2000	Norfolk	Int	455	118	21	2	11	12	71	52	62	7	7	344	.259	.283	.387	.220	39	77-1B -10 18-LF -6
2001	Norfolk	Int	411	107	12	1	11	24	58	52	49	10	2	306	.260	.306	.375	.232	40	57-1B 3 40-LF -2
2001	NY Mets	NL	17	4	0	0	0	0	7	2	1	0	0	13	.235	.235	.235	.160	1	
2002	*NY Mets*	*NL*	*403*	*103*	*14*	*1*	*11*	*27*	*66*	*52*	*51*	*5*	*1*	*301*	*.256*	*.302*	*.377*	*.235*	*40*	

In his two seasons at Norfolk, Toca has demonstrated that he's not going to hit for average or significant power. His skills are limited enough that he's unlikely to ever earn any kind of major-league role. We've seen a handful of good Cuban pitchers so far, but the best hitter to come over is Rey Ordonez. Scary.

Jorge Velandia SS Bats R Age 27

YEAR	TEAM	LGE	AB	H	DB	TP	HR	BB	SO	R	RBI	SB	CS	OUT	BA	OBP	SLG	EQA	EQR	DEFENSE
1999	Oakland	AL	48	10	1	0	0	2	11	4	2	2	0	38	.208	.253	.229	.179	3	16-2B 3
2000	Sacramen	PCL	301	76	16	1	8	26	50	45	45	3	2	227	.252	.320	.392	.239	32	81-SS 14
2000	Oakland	AL	24	3	2	0	0	0	5	1	2	0	0	21	.125	.161	.208	.128	1	
2001	Norfolk	Int	263	64	14	0	7	16	43	24	38	8	4	203	.243	.295	.376	.226	25	61-SS 12
2002	*NY Mets*	*NL*	*312*	*73*	*13*	*1*	*8*	*28*	*56*	*37*	*31*	*8*	*3*	*242*	*.234*	*.297*	*.359*	*.229*	*30*	

Velandia is a slick-fielding shortstop with no significant offensive ability—Rey Ordonez without the panache. There are a few guys like this around—the Reds' Juan Castro, the Pirates' Jack Wilson—who would have made perfectly acceptable shortstops in 1974. The demands of the up-the-middle positions have changed dramatically in the past 25 years, one of the biggest factors in making our current era a high-scoring one.

Robin Ventura 3B Bats L Age 34

YEAR	TEAM	LGE	AB	H	DB	TP	HR	BB	SO	R	RBI	SB	CS	OUT	BA	OBP	SLG	EQA	EQR	DEFENSE
1999	NY Mets	NL	593	180	32	0	35	67	101	88	118	1	1	414	.304	.377	.535	.297	99	151-3B 16
2000	NY Mets	NL	475	113	22	1	25	69	83	61	83	3	5	367	.238	.337	.446	.258	62	120-3B 12
2001	NY Mets	NL	461	118	17	0	24	86	86	75	67	2	5	348	.256	.374	.449	.275	69	127-3B 13
2002	*NY Yanks*	*AL*	*494*	*123*	*17*	*0*	*27*	*83*	*94*	*68*	*83*	*2*	*4*	*375*	*.249*	*.357*	*.447*	*.274*	*74*	

Ventura has had the misfortune to play during a pretty good period for third baseman, and in lousy hitters' parks. He's been a hell of a player, consistent as sunrise on both sides of the ball, and even now a terrific defender. It wouldn't be a surprise to see him have another 1999 season, particularly in the power department.

Ty Wigginton IF Bats R Age 24

YEAR	TEAM	LGE	AB	H	DB	TP	HR	BB	SO	R	RBI	SB	CS	OUT	BA	OBP	SLG	EQA	EQR	DEFENSE	
1999	St Lucie	Fla	462	108	16	2	16	41	92	49	48	5	7	361	.234	.299	.381	.226	44	118-2B -15	
2000	Binghmtn	Eas	452	111	21	2	16	16	110	50	56	3	4	345	.246	.273	.407	.222	40	65-2B -10	45-3B -2
2001	Binghmtn	Eas	29	7	2	0	0	4	5	4	1	1	0	22	.241	.333	.310	.233	3		
2001	Norfolk	Int	264	64	7	0	8	27	61	28	24	3	3	203	.242	.316	.360	.229	25	34-3B -9	21-2B -2
2002	*NY Mets*	*NL*	*416*	*107*	*16*	*1*	*15*	*43*	*102*	*49*	*46*	*6*	*5*	*314*	*.257*	*.327*	*.409*	*.252*	*50*		

There's bad strike-zone judgment, and then there's Ty Wigginton. Wigginton swings at pitches over his head and at pitches that bounce several times before they hit home plate. Someday he's going to swing at a pitch thrown behind him. The Mets like the pop in his bat and had hoped to mold him into a utility infielder, but his defense at both second base and third base hasn't been good. The expiration date on his prospect status is approaching.

Vance Wilson C Bats R Age 29

YEAR	TEAM	LGE	AB	H	DB	TP	HR	BB	SO	R	RBI	SB	CS	OUT	BA	OBP	SLG	EQA	EQR	DEFENSE
1999	Norfolk	Int	53	13	1	0	3	3	8	8	4	1	0	40	.245	.295	.434	.243	6	14-C 0
2000	Norfolk	Int	402	100	16	1	16	19	64	42	55	9	5	307	.249	.298	.413	.236	41	99-C -2
2001	Norfolk	Int	230	56	10	0	7	12	31	23	31	0	1	175	.243	.298	.378	.225	21	64-C 0
2001	NY Mets	NL	58	19	3	0	0	1	14	3	7	0	1	40	.328	.356	.379	.244	6	17-C 2
2002	*NY Mets*	*NL*	*337*	*87*	*16*	*1*	*11*	*22*	*58*	*42*	*31*	*5*	*3*	*253*	*.258*	*.304*	*.409*	*.243*	*37*	

The big winner in the Todd Pratt trade was Wilson, who inherited the backup-catcher job after the Mets dumped the guy acquired for Pratt, Gary Bennett. He's a good glove man, exactly what the team needs backing up Piazza.

Todd Zeile 1B Bats R Age 36

YEAR	TEAM	LGE	AB	H	DB	TP	HR	BB	SO	R	RBI	SB	CS	OUT	BA	OBP	SLG	EQA	EQR	DEFENSE
1999	Texas	AL	581	173	36	2	26	50	83	78	95	1	2	410	.298	.357	.501	.280	85	149-3B -5
2000	NY Mets	NL	551	151	35	3	23	67	78	67	78	3	4	404	.274	.355	.474	.273	78	142-1B 6
2001	NY Mets	NL	537	153	25	1	11	70	87	70	67	1	0	384	.285	.372	.397	.264	69	143-1B 11
2002	*Colorado*	*NL*	*508*	*152*	*29*	*3*	*18*	*74*	*81*	*69*	*74*	*2*	*3*	*359*	*.299*	*.388*	*.474*	*.262*	*63*	

Zeile's total lack of power in 2001 was reportedly due to an elbow injury he suffered early in the season. The acquisition of Mo Vaughn takes away his job, and given that he has no trade value, he's reduced to a backup first baseman. Traded to the Rockies, he'll get to return to third base, where he'll be an adequate offensive replacement for Jeff Cirillo.

PITCHERS (ERA: 4.50, H/9: 9.0, HR/9: 1.0, BB/9: 3.0, K/9: 6.0, KW: 2.0, PERA: 4.50)

Kevin Appier — Throws R — Age 34

YEAR	TEAM	LGE	IP	H	ER	HR	BB	K	ERA	W	L	H/9	HR/9	BB/9	K/9	KW	PERA	STUFF
1999	KansasCy	AL	144.0	151	73	15	43	77	4.56	8	8	9.4	0.9	2.7	4.8	0.9	4.21	4
1999	Oakland	AL	72.3	71	36	8	28	52	4.48	4	4	8.8	1.0	3.5	6.5	0.9	5.71	8
2000	Oakland	AL	199.7	200	105	20	83	128	4.73	10	12	9.0	0.9	3.7	5.8	0.8	4.36	6
2001	NY Mets	NL	194.3	189	89	19	67	138	4.12	12	10	8.8	0.9	2.8	6.4	1.2	4.07	15

Appier gave the Mets his best season in years, continuing his surprising post-surgery improvement. Nothing he can possibly do, however, will justify the four-year, $34-million contract the Mets handed him last off-season. Traded for Mo Vaughn, he gives the Angels another six-inning, mid-rotation pitcher.

Armando Benitez — Throws R — Age 29

YEAR	TEAM	LGE	IP	H	ER	HR	BB	K	ERA	W	L	H/9	HR/9	BB/9	K/9	KW	PERA	STUFF
1999	NY Mets	NL	76.3	47	21	4	34	115	2.48	6	2	5.5	0.5	4.0	13.6	1.7	1.87	46
2000	NY Mets	NL	71.3	55	30	9	31	94	3.79	5	3	6.9	1.1	3.9	11.9	1.5	2.72	29
2001	NY Mets	NL	72.0	64	39	11	36	75	4.88	4	4	8.0	1.4	4.5	9.4	1.0	3.96	9

Mets fans have loudly declared that they want Benitez gone, but there's no better option available. Would they prefer Byung-Hyun Kim? Benitez clearly did not have a great season, and the trends in his numbers are all negative. It's also true that because the rest of the Mets bullpen was such a disaster, Bobby Valentine was forced to go to Benitez on days that Benitez shouldn't have been asked to pitch.

Corey Brittan — Throws R — Age 27

YEAR	TEAM	LGE	IP	H	ER	HR	BB	K	ERA	W	L	H/9	HR/9	BB/9	K/9	KW	PERA	STUFF
1999	Binghmtn	Eas	88.7	96	47	9	26	37	4.77	5	5	9.7	0.9	2.6	3.8	0.7	4.22	-19
2000	Binghmtn	Eas	73.7	75	35	2	35	30	4.28	4	4	9.2	0.2	4.3	3.7	0.4	4.19	-25
2001	Norfolk	Int	82.0	88	44	6	33	31	4.83	4	5	9.7	0.7	3.6	3.4	0.5	3.16	-23

Brittan pitched well as a setup man for the Tides in 2001, just as he had in Binghamton the year before. He's made it a long way for a 56th-round draft pick and might get a spring-training invitation one of these years. If his stuff was really major-league quality, he wouldn't be a minor league setup man.

Bruce Chen — Throws L — Age 25

YEAR	TEAM	LGE	IP	H	ER	HR	BB	K	ERA	W	L	H/9	HR/9	BB/9	K/9	KW	PERA	STUFF
1999	Atlanta	NL	47.7	49	33	10	23	41	6.23	2	3	9.3	1.9	4.3	7.7	0.9	5.22	7
1999	Richmond	Int	79.7	74	37	11	25	73	4.18	5	4	8.4	1.2	2.8	8.2	1.5	3.84	30
2000	Atlanta	NL	39.3	38	19	4	16	28	4.35	2	2	8.7	0.9	3.7	6.4	0.9	3.13	3
2000	Philadel	NL	92.3	91	44	12	22	71	4.29	5	5	8.9	1.2	2.1	6.9	1.6	3.33	22
2001	Philadel	NL	83.7	87	52	16	28	64	5.59	4	5	9.4	1.7	3.0	6.9	1.1	5.47	9
2001	Scran-WB	Int	17.3	19	10	3	6	10	5.19	1	1	9.9	1.6	3.1	5.2	0.8	4.66	0
2001	NY Mets	NL	56.0	58	35	9	25	38	5.63	2	4	9.3	1.4	4.0	6.1	0.8	5.85	2

Taking a chance on Chen was one of the smartest moves the Mets have made in years. Ditching Dennis Cook and Turk Wendell in the process was just gravy. It's certainly questionable, however, whether the Mets can turn Bruce Chen into the pitcher they think he should be. It's hard to tell whether the whispers about Chen's work habits have validity or are just plain old impatience. Rumors persist that he'll be traded to the Padres.

Mark Corey — Throws R — Age 27

YEAR	TEAM	LGE	IP	H	ER	HR	BB	K	ERA	W	L	H/9	HR/9	BB/9	K/9	KW	PERA	STUFF
1999	Binghmtn	Eas	157.0	181	115	28	73	69	6.59	5	12	10.4	1.6	4.2	4.0	0.5	7.40	-21
2000	Binghmtn	Eas	23.7	23	11	0	14	12	4.18	2	1	8.7	0.0	5.3	4.6	0.4	2.16	-17
2000	Norfolk	Int	66.0	78	55	15	32	32	7.50	2	5	10.6	2.0	4.4	4.4	0.5	8.66	-35
2001	Binghmtn	Eas	33.7	29	15	2	18	28	4.01	2	2	7.8	0.5	4.8	7.5	0.8	3.40	-6
2001	Norfolk	Int	35.0	31	19	1	28	29	4.89	2	2	8.0	0.3	7.2	7.5	0.5	2.24	-10

(Mark Corey *continued*)
Corey was the Mets' Minor League Pitcher of the Year in 2001, a fact that says more about the organization than about Corey. He did show marked improvement last year, increasing his velocity—his fastball was clocked as high as 96 mph—and saving 27 games for Binghamton and Norfolk. The exodus of Mets relievers gives him a real chance in 2002.

John Franco **Throws L** **Age 41**

YEAR	TEAM	LGE	IP	H	ER	HR	BB	K	ERA	W	L	H/9	HR/9	BB/9	K/9	KW	PERA	STUFF
1999	NY Mets	NL	43.0	36	14	1	16	37	2.93	4	1	7.5	0.2	3.3	7.7	1.2	2.94	12
2000	NY Mets	NL	55.3	50	25	5	21	50	4.07	3	3	8.1	0.8	3.4	8.1	1.2	3.71	8
2001	NY Mets	NL	52.3	52	27	7	17	40	4.64	3	3	8.9	1.2	2.9	6.9	1.2	4.43	-1

It will be a long time before anybody forgets the meatball Franco threw to Brian Jordan the last week of the season. Franco is still a decent relief pitcher, but the Mets didn't spend $10 million on him last winter just for his baseball skills. In his decade with the Mets, Franco has achieved a stronger connection to the New York community than any player in recent history. This connection was crystallized after the events of September 11, when Franco led the efforts of the Mets to honor the police and firefighters who died in the terrorist attack.

Dicky Gonzalez **Throws R** **Age 23**

YEAR	TEAM	LGE	IP	H	ER	HR	BB	K	ERA	W	L	H/9	HR/9	BB/9	K/9	KW	PERA	STUFF
1999	St Lucie	Fla	166.0	176	87	23	36	96	4.72	9	9	9.5	1.2	2.0	5.2	1.3	4.31	15
2000	Binghmtn	Eas	144.7	150	79	23	38	100	4.91	7	9	9.3	1.4	2.4	6.2	1.3	4.80	17
2001	Norfolk	Int	95.3	101	50	13	23	54	4.72	5	6	9.5	1.2	2.2	5.1	1.2	3.79	11
2001	NY Mets	NL	59.3	62	26	4	15	25	3.94	4	3	9.4	0.6	2.3	3.8	0.8	5.28	-3

In 2001, Gonzalez finally forced the organization to take him seriously. He's the type of pitcher who is often ignored by scouts because he doesn't throw that hard—his best fastballs peak at 90 mph—and he doesn't have great stuff. What has carried Gonzalez through the system is his top-notch command. He's definitely a major-league pitcher at this point, but he may end up in the bullpen because he often seems to need a lot of pitches to put batters away.

Aaron Heilman **Throws R** **Age 23**

YEAR	TEAM	LGE	IP	H	ER	HR	BB	K	ERA	W	L	H/9	HR/9	BB/9	K/9	KW	PERA	STUFF
2001	St Lucie	Fla	37.0	33	14	0	15	23	3.41	3	1	8.0	0.0	3.6	5.6	0.8	3.57	14

The Mets' first-round pick in 2001 out of Notre Dame, Heilman had no problem dominating the Florida State League with an excellent fastball with strong downward movement and solid breaking stuff. If all goes as planned in the spring, Heilmann will start 2002 in Binghamton and could be one of the first 2002 draft picks to land in the majors. Warning: he was worked hard in the shadow of the golden dome.

Bobby M. Jones **Throws L** **Age 30**

YEAR	TEAM	LGE	IP	H	ER	HR	BB	K	ERA	W	L	H/9	HR/9	BB/9	K/9	KW	PERA	STUFF
1999	Colorado	NL	116.0	127	84	20	64	67	6.52	4	9	9.9	1.6	5.0	5.2	0.5	5.34	-14
2000	Norfolk	Int	130.7	139	82	18	63	75	5.65	6	9	9.6	1.2	4.3	5.2	0.6	5.25	-8
2000	NY Mets	NL	21.7	20	11	2	12	18	4.57	1	1	8.3	0.8	5.0	7.5	0.8	4.37	1
2001	St Lucie	Fla	9.0	9	4	0	6	5	4.00	1	0	9.0	0.0	6.0	5.0	0.4	3.01	-19
2001	Binghmtn	Eas	4.0	3	1	0	0	3	2.25	0	0	6.8	0.0	0.0	6.8	-1.0	0.00	21

He's the lesser of the Bobby Joneses, though the "premium" Bobby Jones didn't fare so well in 2001, either. Jones's 2001 was more or less wiped out by rotator-cuff tendinitis and other assorted injuries. He's a free agent who will probably have a hard time getting back to the major leagues.

Robert Keppel **Throws R** **Age 20**

YEAR	TEAM	LGE	IP	H	ER	HR	BB	K	ERA	W	L	H/9	HR/9	BB/9	K/9	KW	PERA	STUFF
2000	Kingsprt	App	30.0	32	19	3	17	13	5.70	1	2	9.6	0.9	5.1	3.9	0.4	9.64	-12
2001	Columbia	SAL	122.0	136	68	14	35	44	5.02	6	8	10.0	1.0	2.6	3.2	0.6	6.16	-4

A supplementary first-round pick in the 2000 draft, Keppel held his own as one of the youngest pitchers in the South Atlantic League in 2001. He already has good command of a low-90s fastball and a slider and hasn't done anything to make the Mets change their mind about him. The Mets expect to advance him one level every year, so he'll likely start for St. Lucie in 2002.

Al Leiter — Throws L — Age 36

YEAR	TEAM	LGE	IP	H	ER	HR	BB	K	ERA	W	L	H/9	HR/9	BB/9	K/9	KW	PERA	STUFF
1999	NY Mets	NL	216.3	210	100	18	78	146	4.16	13	11	8.7	0.7	3.2	6.1	0.9	4.30	11
2000	NY Mets	NL	207.7	187	83	17	63	178	3.60	14	9	8.1	0.7	2.7	7.7	1.4	3.48	24
2001	NY Mets	NL	179.0	177	77	16	41	114	3.87	11	9	8.9	0.8	2.1	5.7	1.4	4.08	13

With Rick Reed gone, Leiter is clearly the ace of the Mets, though he probably fits the profile of a #2 starter better. His health has held up surprisingly well, but given his injury history and his age, it's hard to guess what kind of market there will be for him if he goes the free-agent route after the 2002 season.

Nicholas Maness — Throws R — Age 23

YEAR	TEAM	LGE	IP	H	ER	HR	BB	K	ERA	W	L	H/9	HR/9	BB/9	K/9	KW	PERA	STUFF
1999	Columbia	SAL	103.3	115	83	16	77	51	7.23	3	8	10.0	1.4	6.7	4.4	0.3	8.32	-12
2000	St Lucie	Fla	135.0	156	118	33	81	81	7.87	4	11	10.4	2.2	5.4	5.4	0.5	4.53	-3
2001	Binghmtn	Eas	148.0	160	98	18	83	70	5.96	6	10	9.7	1.1	5.0	4.3	0.4	6.66	-9

Maness was a top prospect after the 2000 season, but his stock fell drastically in 2001. His fastball lost almost five mph, and his control seemed to disappear completely at times. In retrospect, Maness's 2000 season received more respect than it deserved; he has to be considered a long shot at this point.

Neal Musser — Throws L — Age 21

YEAR	TEAM	LGE	IP	H	ER	HR	BB	K	ERA	W	L	H/9	HR/9	BB/9	K/9	KW	PERA	STUFF
2000	Kingsprt	App	33.7	38	17	3	8	9	4.54	2	2	10.2	0.8	2.1	2.4	0.6	3.70	-5
2001	Columbia	SAL	94.7	96	42	7	25	50	3.99	6	5	9.1	0.7	2.4	4.8	1.0	5.28	11
2001	St Lucie	Fla	46.0	48	26	5	21	25	5.09	2	3	9.4	1.0	4.1	4.9	0.6	6.26	3

Musser finally got his professional career going last year after being limited to just 65 innings the previous two seasons. He's similar to, but not as advanced as, Billy Traber, a big guy who relies more on control and command than on great stuff. How he handles the jump to Double-A will reveal a great deal.

C.J. Nitkowski — Throws L — Age 29

YEAR	TEAM	LGE	IP	H	ER	HR	BB	K	ERA	W	L	H/9	HR/9	BB/9	K/9	KW	PERA	STUFF
1999	Detroit	AL	79.0	75	42	10	38	65	4.78	4	5	8.5	1.1	4.3	7.4	0.9	4.06	0
2000	Detroit	AL	116.0	113	55	11	40	80	4.27	7	6	8.8	0.9	3.1	6.2	1.0	5.50	-2
2001	Detroit	AL	47.7	47	30	6	30	36	5.66	2	3	8.9	1.1	5.7	6.8	0.6	5.54	-12

The Mets acquired Nitkowski in early September, but he didn't get much chance to audition as a result of the Mets' sudden appearance in the pennant race. He's in Astros' camp and is the top candidate for the lefty-specialist role. Nitkowski vs. Tigers Fans in an online forum last year was priceless.

Ross Peeples — Throws L — Age 22

YEAR	TEAM	LGE	IP	H	ER	HR	BB	K	ERA	W	L	H/9	HR/9	BB/9	K/9	KW	PERA	STUFF
2000	Kingsprt	App	29.7	32	17	3	13	13	5.16	1	2	9.7	0.9	3.9	3.9	0.5	6.15	-14
2001	Brooklyn	NYP	77.7	79	40	3	41	34	4.64	4	5	9.2	0.3	4.8	3.9	0.4	3.16	-1

The first year of the Brooklyn Cyclones was a remarkable success both on and off the field, and Peeples was one of its biggest stars. He added a slider and a change-up to his previous fastball/curveball repertoire, and his sharp command of those pitches baffled his opponents.

Jerrod Riggan — Throws R — Age 28

YEAR	TEAM	LGE	IP	H	ER	HR	BB	K	ERA	W	L	H/9	HR/9	BB/9	K/9	KW	PERA	STUFF
1999	St Lucie	Fla	71.7	79	48	10	35	36	6.03	3	5	9.9	1.3	4.4	4.5	0.5	6.10	-35
2000	Binghmtn	Eas	62.3	56	25	4	22	49	3.61	4	3	8.1	0.6	3.2	7.1	1.1	1.54	0
2001	Norfolk	Int	31.0	32	16	6	5	25	4.65	1	2	9.3	1.7	1.5	7.3	2.5	2.54	0
2001	NY Mets	NL	45.0	43	23	4	21	33	4.60	2	3	8.6	0.8	4.2	6.6	0.8	3.76	-2

When the Mets veteran relief corps imploded, Riggan was given a chance to play a major role in the bullpen and excelled. Dealt to the Indians in the Alomar deal, he's going to have trouble landing a job in what is a bullpen loaded with live arms. He needs a break, such as Danys Baez going to the rotation or Paul Shuey getting injured. On second thought, he's in great shape.

Grant Roberts Throws R Age 24

YEAR	TEAM	LGE	IP	H	ER	HR	BB	K	ERA	W	L	H/9	HR/9	BB/9	K/9	KW	PERA	STUFF
1999	Binghmtn	Eas	133.0	139	70	12	49	66	4.74	7	8	9.4	0.8	3.3	4.5	0.7	5.81	4
1999	Norfolk	Int	30.7	27	11	1	10	24	3.23	2	1	7.9	0.3	2.9	7.0	1.2	4.57	27
2000	Norfolk	Int	161.0	154	69	7	61	97	3.86	10	8	8.6	0.4	3.4	5.4	0.8	4.00	15
2001	Norfolk	Int	72.0	71	32	5	21	42	4.00	4	4	8.9	0.6	2.6	5.3	1.0	5.83	-1
2001	NY Mets	NL	25.7	22	9	2	7	23	3.16	2	1	7.7	0.7	2.5	8.1	1.6	3.99	18

The Mets have always loved his stuff, but Roberts has been unable to translate it into success. Like Corey, Roberts benefits from the openings created in the bullpen this winter. With as many as four left-handed starters, the Mets will have to have a couple of right-handed long men around. Roberts should get established in that role, then move into the rotation in 2003. Things look very good for him.

Glendon Rusch Throws L Age 27

YEAR	TEAM	LGE	IP	H	ER	HR	BB	K	ERA	W	L	H/9	HR/9	BB/9	K/9	KW	PERA	STUFF
1999	Omaha	PCL	123.7	124	57	11	36	74	4.15	8	6	9.0	0.8	2.6	5.4	1.0	5.11	7
2000	NY Mets	NL	197.0	189	77	16	36	140	3.52	14	8	8.6	0.7	1.6	6.4	1.9	4.11	19
2001	NY Mets	NL	183.7	182	82	20	38	125	4.02	11	9	8.9	1.0	1.9	6.1	1.6	5.33	12

The Mets' great pitching find of 2000 had a very rough 2001, as he was pounded for almost 11 hits per nine innings pitched. Still, his control remained excellent, and there's every reason to think he'll continue to be a solid back-of-the-rotation starter for a number of years, with the potential to have a couple of All-Star seasons. He'd look a lot better on a team not playing Benny Agbayani and Roger Cedeno in the outfield.

Jae Weong Seo Throws R Age 25

YEAR	TEAM	LGE	IP	H	ER	HR	BB	K	ERA	W	L	H/9	HR/9	BB/9	K/9	KW	PERA	STUFF
1999	St Lucie	Fla	13.7	12	4	0	3	9	2.63	1	1	7.9	0.0	2.0	5.9	1.5	2.34	21
2001	St Lucie	Fla	23.3	29	19	6	8	10	7.33	1	2	11.2	2.3	3.1	3.9	0.6	6.34	-31
2001	Binghmtn	Eas	56.0	58	27	5	16	27	4.34	3	3	9.3	0.8	2.6	4.3	0.8	2.66	-1
2001	Norfolk	Int	48.0	53	24	5	7	18	4.50	3	2	9.9	0.9	1.3	3.4	1.3	4.12	-2

After missing almost two years as a result of Tommy John surgery, Seo made an impressive comeback at the top three levels of the Mets minor-league system in 2001. His velocity wasn't as good as it was before the surgery, but Seo demonstrated strong command of a 90-mph fastball, a deceptive change-up, and a curveball. Even though Seo is polished enough to pitch in the major leagues now, the Mets will likely let him build up his arm strength in the minors for much of the 2002 season, especially after tendinitis kept him out of the Arizona Fall League.

Pat Strange Throws R Age 21

YEAR	TEAM	LGE	IP	H	ER	HR	BB	K	ERA	W	L	H/9	HR/9	BB/9	K/9	KW	PERA	STUFF
1999	Columbia	SAL	152.3	160	67	8	39	58	3.96	10	7	9.5	0.5	2.3	3.4	0.7	4.46	5
2000	St Lucie	Fla	86.7	89	48	9	38	50	4.98	4	6	9.2	0.9	3.9	5.2	0.7	6.19	6
2000	Binghmtn	Eas	58.0	59	32	3	32	26	4.97	3	3	9.2	0.5	5.0	4.0	0.4	5.13	2
2001	Binghmtn	Eas	154.0	175	105	25	66	70	6.14	6	11	10.2	1.5	3.9	4.1	0.5	6.21	0

Strange has been the most hyped Mets pitcher in the system this side of Grant Roberts, but his 2001 did not enhance his reputation. While he has some impressive pitches and good control, his strikeout rate is too low to inspire confidence. Strange will be just 21 this year, and the Mets are optimistic about getting his mechanics straightened out and turning him into a complete pitcher in the long run.

Billy Traber Throws L Age 22

YEAR	TEAM	LGE	IP	H	ER	HR	BB	K	ERA	W	L	H/9	HR/9	BB/9	K/9	KW	PERA	STUFF
2001	St Lucie	Fla	99.7	100	41	5	26	49	3.70	7	4	9.0	0.5	2.3	4.4	0.9	4.22	9
2001	Binghmtn	Eas	45.0	46	24	6	17	30	4.80	2	3	9.2	1.2	3.4	6.0	0.9	5.93	12

After the Mets drafted Traber as their first pick in the 2000 draft, they discovered a frayed tendon in his elbow that cost him most of his bonus money. Whatever was or is wrong with his elbow, however, did not significantly hinder him on the mound last season. While the left-hander does not have a dominating fastball, he showed good command of four pitches in 2001. The Indians liked him enough to get him in the Alomar deal.

Steve Trachsel — Throws R — Age 31

YEAR	TEAM	LGE	IP	H	ER	HR	BB	K	ERA	W	L	H/9	HR/9	BB/9	K/9	KW	PERA	STUFF
1999	ChiCubs	NL	211.7	220	111	30	54	134	4.72	11	13	9.4	1.3	2.3	5.7	1.2	5.27	7
2000	TampaBay	AL	144.7	150	70	14	40	77	4.35	8	8	9.3	0.9	2.5	4.8	1.0	4.16	5
2000	Toronto	AL	65.0	71	37	8	20	32	5.12	3	4	9.8	1.1	2.8	4.4	0.8	4.65	-1
2001	NY Mets	NL	165.3	169	86	25	42	116	4.68	9	9	9.2	1.4	2.3	6.3	1.4	4.80	11
2001	Norfolk	Int	18.0	17	7	0	8	8	3.50	1	1	8.5	0.0	4.0	4.0	0.5	3.65	-1

A disastrous first half in which he posted a 6.72 ERA earned Trachsel a few weeks at Norfolk. He pitched brilliantly for the remainder of the season. Trachsel has always been unpredictable—who else could lead the Devil Rays to successive 1-0 victories over Pedro Martinez and Roger Clemens?—but his transformation into Cy Young in the second half was just plain incomprehensible. Expect more league-average innings in 2002.

Tyler Walker — Throws R — Age 26

YEAR	TEAM	LGE	IP	H	ER	HR	BB	K	ERA	W	L	H/9	HR/9	BB/9	K/9	KW	PERA	STUFF
1999	St Lucie	Fla	74.3	85	58	14	40	38	7.02	2	6	10.3	1.7	4.8	4.6	0.5	4.84	-13
1999	Binghmtn	Eas	69.0	80	55	16	34	40	7.17	2	6	10.4	2.1	4.4	5.2	0.6	7.06	-11
2000	Binghmtn	Eas	114.7	110	58	6	65	71	4.55	6	7	8.6	0.5	5.1	5.6	0.5	3.79	0
2000	Norfolk	Int	28.0	27	10	0	9	14	3.21	2	1	8.7	0.0	2.9	4.5	0.8	2.60	8
2001	St Lucie	Fla	17.0	17	6	0	4	6	3.18	1	1	9.0	0.0	2.1	3.2	0.8	13.01	-21
2001	Binghmtn	Eas	18.7	20	16	2	19	7	7.71	1	1	9.6	1.0	9.2	3.4	0.2	1.07	-34
2001	Norfolk	Int	37.3	44	29	10	10	24	6.99	1	3	10.6	2.4	2.4	5.8	1.2	5.53	-11

After a terrific 2000, Walker had a tough time coming back from off-season shoulder surgery. He was originally a catcher, and his 225-pound body (that after shedding 30 pounds during the 2000–01 off-season thanks to classes in diet management) still looks like a catcher's. He started to get his command back late in the season in Norfolk, but he obviously has much more to prove in the minors in 2002. He doesn't really have any well-developed pitches beyond a fastball and a curveball, so if he establishes himself in the majors it'll likely be as a reliever.

Donne Wall — Throws R — Age 34

YEAR	TEAM	LGE	IP	H	ER	HR	BB	K	ERA	W	L	H/9	HR/9	BB/9	K/9	KW	PERA	STUFF
1999	San Dieg	NL	67.3	69	37	11	19	48	4.95	3	4	9.2	1.5	2.5	6.4	1.3	3.92	-2
2000	San Dieg	NL	49.3	50	24	4	17	26	4.38	3	2	9.1	0.7	3.1	4.7	0.8	3.31	-9
2001	NY Mets	NL	42.3	46	26	7	15	25	5.53	2	3	9.8	1.5	3.2	5.3	0.8	5.31	-13

The most inexplicable Mets move in recent years was the trade of Bubba Trammell for Wall. The Mets traded away their only power-hitting outfielder for yet another soft-tossing middle reliever, one who just happened to be coming off of rotator-cuff surgery. Wall was pounded in the first half and was quickly relegated to a mop-up role for the rest of the season. Outrighted after the season, and a free agent as of mid-January.

Rick White — Throws R — Age 33

YEAR	TEAM	LGE	IP	H	ER	HR	BB	K	ERA	W	L	H/9	HR/9	BB/9	K/9	KW	PERA	STUFF
1999	TampaBay	AL	118.0	111	46	7	32	80	3.51	8	5	8.5	0.5	2.4	6.1	1.3	3.98	3
2000	TampaBay	AL	69.0	67	31	6	21	47	4.04	4	4	8.7	0.8	2.7	6.1	1.1	3.17	1
2000	NY Mets	NL	28.3	27	12	2	10	18	3.81	2	1	8.6	0.6	3.2	5.7	0.9	4.26	-3
2001	NY Mets	NL	67.7	68	30	6	15	41	3.99	4	4	9.0	0.8	2.0	5.5	1.4	5.15	-3

White was worked extremely hard in 1999 and 2000, and the Mets would have probably worked him just as hard last year if he hadn't made several trips to the disabled list. After Wendell was traded, White was used more in the traditional setup role. He signed a one-year deal with the Rockies and should replace Jay Powell as Jose Jimenez's setup man.

Philadelphia Phillies

One of Major League Baseball's notable problems of late is its lack of respect for the Law of Unintended Consequences. Since the game's stewards tend to run baseball by the seat of their pants, they can get slapped around pretty badly, because none of their fixes are designed well.

Examples litter the game. MLB wanted to slow salary growth and better distribute its revenues, so it created a system that incentivized the kind of tanking we've seen in Minnesota and Montreal. MLB wanted more mallparks so teams could raise ticket prices, and the result was resentment among fans as prices for the best seats doubled and tripled, with those seats primarily being sold to businesses with the ability to write off the cost. MLB created an extra tier of playoffs and ended up rendering some really good division races meaningless (NL West, 1996; NL East, 1999; NL Central, 2001).

That last one—the switch to a six-division format with expanded playoffs—had some obvious, immediate effects. Suddenly more teams were in contention later in the season. More teams considered themselves contenders at the July 31 trade deadline, improving the balance between buyers and sellers in the souk that plays out in the last few days of July.

The Law of Unintended Consequences took over from there. In the current format, the best team is even less likely to win the World Series than it was before, faced with yet another short series between the regular season and a championship. Nearly any rational analysis of the 2001 season had the Mariners or the A's as the best team, and neither even reached the Fall Classic. In this setup, a team is given greater opportunity to delude itself into thinking that it's good on the basis of its standing in its division, rather than on its record. Some teams may recognize their weaknesses but choose to stretch for the lottery ticket, having learned from the 2000 Yankees that a flawed team can still succeed in the playoffs if it can just get there. Others begin to drink their own Kool-Aid and believe that their near-contention status means that they're just a player or two away from postseason glory. The false promise provided by the lowered bar of success—the wild card—can warp an organization's decision-making.

The Phillies, an average team with some good core talent and weak competition, face this problem. They pushed the Braves to their 160th game last year, the hardest the Braves have had to work to make the playoffs since 1993. The Phils fell far enough behind in late August that most fans and pundits wrote them off as one of 2001's many first-half wonders (cf. the Cubs, the Twins), handing the Braves the division title with five or six weeks to go. But those pesky Phils stormed back into the race and closed within a game with five to play, including the next two against Atlanta. All in all, it was a great season.

Phillies Prospectus

2001 record: 86–76; Second place, NL East

Pythagenport W/L: 84–78

Runs scored: 746 (ninth in NL)

Runs allowed: 719 (sixth in NL)

Team EqA: .259 (tenth in NL)

2001 batters age: 26.5 (youngest in NL)

2001 pitchers age: 28.2 (tied for seventh-youngest in NL)

Ballpark: Veterans Stadium; neutral park; Park Factor of 1.002

2001: Surprise season led by good lineup core and pitching fell short, in large part due to massive OBP issues at the top of the lineup.

2002: Essentially the same cast returns, so the Phillies should hover at .500 or a little above, just shy of contention.

Or was it? The Phillies finished with the seventh-best record in the National League, just five wins over the break-even mark of 81. They won 13 of 15 in late May... and were just 73-74 outside of that stretch. They outscored their opponents by just 27 runs, or about a run a week over the course of a whole season. They burned through most of their Opening Day rotation and had dismal production yet again from some of their would-be anchor players. They made a rash deadline deal that cost them two good starting pitching prospects and a boatload of cash. And they likely raised expectations among fans and the local media that the team will be a contender in 2002. It isn't, not unless General Manager Ed Wade makes some substantial changes.

The Phillies came into 2001 with little fanfare. Wade had earned ridicule from analyst quarters during the off-season by spending a mint on three mediocre relief pitchers, moves that ignored the substantial problems with the team's offense as well as the dubious history of expensive free-agent middle relievers. He even collected the whole set of Brian Hunters, perhaps to make the weak starters in center field and at first base look better by comparison. Then he hired Larry Bowa, who hadn't managed a major-league team since a disastrous stint as the manager in San Diego in the late 1980s.

Expectations were low among analysts for a different reason: the wrath of Francona. Terry Francona's swan song as the Phillies'—and, one would hope, a major-league—manager had him doing his best Jim Leyland impersonation. He treated Randy Wolf, the best pitching prospect the organization had produced in ages, as if he was merely an android pulled from the closet every fifth day. He rode Curt Schilling hard in 2000 after the pitcher's return from surgery in December 1999, resulting in a less-effective Schilling for the first half of 2000. He worked the suddenly solid Robert Person too hard and watched Person's ERA rise by three-fourths of a run. And he tore through the Phils' mediocre bullpen. The expected aftereffects of Francona's irresponsible management cast a shadow over any hopes that the Phils would otherwise improve in 2001.

The Phillies did enjoy some major on-field successes. Jimmy Rollins had what might have been a Rookie of the Year campaign in some seasons; while his performance wasn't as good as his rotisserie stats might imply, he provided a salve to the perennial open sore that had been the Phillies' shortstop position. The bullpen, a problem area in 2000, was significantly better due to the addition of, yes, Jose Mesa and the midseason pickup of Jose Santiago. Omar Daal recovered from a horrific 2000 to be a league-average starter, and rookie Brandon Duckworth had a very good half-season debut.

New pitching coach Vern Ruhle contributed to the success of the pitching staff. The architect of some good, inexpensive pitching staffs in Houston, Ruhle was made the scapegoat for the Astros' horrible start in 2000, even though he bore little, if any, responsibility for it. Ruhle seems to do especially well with young pitchers, and he always emphasizes the need to throw strikes, two traits that proved especially valuable to the Phils in 2001, when a number of rookie pitchers passed through Philadelphia.

These high points helped overshadow the complete collapses of two players that the Phils expected to be major contributors to the team in 2001. Doug Glanville, always a bit of a risk in the leadoff spot because his OBPs depended heavily on his ability to hit singles, didn't hit at all in 2001. Glanville's collapse, combined with Rollins's mediocre walk total in the #2 hole, meant the bases were empty far too often for Scott Rolen and Bobby Abreu. While Randy Wolf didn't break down as a result of the overuse he endured in 1999 and 2000, he was ineffective and was bounced from the starting rotation in July. Adding to the problem was the inconsistency of Bruce Chen, the disappointing seasons by Pat Burrell and Travis Lee, and a season-ending injury to Mike Lieberthal in May.

But while staying in the playoff race until the season's final three games clearly exceeded fans' expectations, the Phils' contending status was largely a function of being in the majors' weakest division, a five-team contest in which no team showed any real interest in finishing first. The Expos were an embarrassment, as usual. The Mets turned back into pumpkins, and despite their year-end push for respectability, were outscored by their opponents by a sizable margin. The Braves did everything they could to sabotage their own offense, and they spent the year without their #3 starter, John Smoltz. Only the Marlins showed any real promise among the Phils' opponents, but they lacked the offense to sustain an early flirtation with contention. The unbalanced schedule and the weak division meant that the Phillies' success within the division bore little relation to success in any sort of absolute sense.

Phillies fans can take some solace in the fact that their team finished above the break-even mark despite having so many players who played below expectations, particularly since one likely culprit has been relieved of his duties.

The Phillies made a quixotic decision in hiring Richie Hebner as their hitting coach for the 2001 season. Hebner had presided over the destruction of a number of the Pirates' top hitting prospects during his tenure as Triple-A Nashville's hitting coach in 1999–2000. Hebner preaches what he played, with no emphasis whatsoever on patience, drawing walks, or pitch selection; he teaches players to be aggressive and make contact, a philosophy that turned Chad Hermansen into a .220/.280/.340 hitter in the Pacific Coast League. Hebner brought the same philosophy to Philly. The early struggles of Pat Burrell and later struggles of Travis Lee can hardly be considered a coincidence.

Then there's Dallas Green, the baseball equivalent of genital warts: he lies dormant for periods, but never really goes away, flaring up periodically, often at incredibly opportune times. Almost completely out of the headlines for years, Green opened his mouth last summer and proceeded to alienate one of the team's two top stars.

Scott Rolen has widely been perceived as an enigma, to put it mildly. After deservedly winning the Rookie of the Year Award, Rolen hasn't continued the march toward stardom that most observers expected. The stagnation in Rolen's offensive production has often been blamed on the hard surface at Veterans Stadium and its effect on Rolen's knees and cranky back—a reasonable explanation for Rolen's lack of growth at the plate.

In August, Dallas Green decided that he should serve as judge, jury, and executioner. Ignoring the possible health-related explanation for Rolen's struggles, as well as the team's remarkable performance to that point, Green lashed out at Rolen via the least professional channel available—the media. He questioned Rolen's manhood. He questioned Rolen's leadership skills. He blamed Rolen for whatever ailed the Phils. He blamed Rolen for green-lighting *Bob Patterson*. He said Rolen designed Palm Beach County's butterfly ballot. And so on.

The Phillies have done a reasonable job of excising the elements of the organization that led to its ten-year walk in the wilderness after its 1983 pennant, but the reappearance of Dallas Green in a patronage position is a mistake. Green has left a trail of destruction wherever he's worked. He presided over the shredding of the arms of Paul Wilson, Jason Isringhausen, and Bill Pulsipher, effectively ending Pulsipher's career and derailing Wilson's and Izzy's for three years apiece. He has no contribution to make to a major-league organization. While Green has revealed his presence, the real danger is that the diseased thinking he represents may have spread to other parts of the organization. The presence of such diseased thinking could make Ed Wade's job significantly more difficult.

The Phillies do sit in a promising position. They topped the .500 mark despite having more players underachieve than overachieve. They have an improving farm system projected to contribute a number of players to the major-league roster over the next couple of years. They've already eliminated one of the staffers responsible for some of last year's disappointments. If they can just patch up the soured relationship with their embattled star and eliminate the hardliners still hanging on in their organization, they'll be a force to reckon with in the East for the next few years.

HITTERS (BA: .270, OBP: .340, SLG: .440, EqA: .260)

Bobby Abreu RF Bats L Age 28

YEAR	TEAM	LGE	AB	H	DB	TP	HR	BB	SO	R	RBI	SB	CS	OUT	BA	OBP	SLG	EQA	EQR	DEFENSE
1999	Philadel	NL	544	178	35	10	20	101	105	112	86	22	9	375	.327	.435	.539	.323	111	133-RF -8
2000	Philadel	NL	576	177	42	9	24	92	106	98	73	26	8	407	.307	.403	.536	.310	109	151-RF 4
2001	Philadel	NL	589	173	47	4	31	102	116	120	110	35	14	430	.294	.399	.545	.308	113	150-RF -3
2002	*Philadel*	*NL*	*524*	*164*	*38*	*7*	*28*	*105*	*107*	*115*	*88*	*35*	*10*	*370*	*.313*	*.428*	*.573*	*.327*	*113*	

Just about the perfect ballplayer, Abreu brings every hitting skill that really matters—power, average, and plate discipline—to the plate, making him a near lock for a .400 OBP. He has good speed and runs the bases well. He's an above-average outfielder. And the Phillies, God love 'em, waited too long to sign him to a long-term deal. Abreu will be expensive and will probably still be among the best investments in baseball.

Marlon Anderson 2B Bats L Age 28

YEAR	TEAM	LGE	AB	H	DB	TP	HR	BB	SO	R	RBI	SB	CS	OUT	BA	OBP	SLG	EQA	EQR	DEFENSE
1999	Philadel	NL	454	114	26	4	5	18	56	46	51	11	2	342	.251	.283	.359	.218	38	99-2B 2
2000	Scran-WB	Int	402	118	17	6	8	32	42	51	47	19	9	293	.294	.352	.425	.262	51	93-2B -1
2000	Philadel	NL	163	37	7	1	1	10	20	9	14	2	2	128	.227	.272	.301	.195	11	40-2B 3
2001	Philadel	NL	523	158	31	2	11	32	63	72	62	8	5	370	.302	.344	.432	.259	63	134-2B 11
2002	*Philadel*	*NL*	*495*	*148*	*29*	*4*	*11*	*40*	*62*	*63*	*66*	*13*	*6*	*353*	*.299*	*.351*	*.440*	*.264*	*63*	

Anderson didn't belong in the majors in '99, and his exile to Triple-A for most of 2000 seems to have helped. He tightened his pitch selection slightly and added strength, resulting in a season that didn't give the Phillies another black hole in their lineup. On the other hand, Anderson was below average with the stick for a second baseman and rarely walks, making him someone the Phils should look to upgrade for 2002.

Pat Burrell LF Bats L Age 25

YEAR	TEAM	LGE	AB	H	DB	TP	HR	BB	SO	R	RBI	SB	CS	OUT	BA	OBP	SLG	EQA	EQR	DEFENSE
1999	Reading	Eas	422	119	21	4	21	60	103	66	64	2	2	305	.282	.371	.500	.286	67	81-1B -9 27-LF -1
2000	Scran-WB	Int	146	41	13	1	4	28	35	29	23	1	1	106	.281	.397	.466	.290	24	29-LF 1
2000	Philadel	NL	409	104	25	1	18	58	128	55	75	0	0	305	.254	.348	.452	.267	56	58-1B -3 42-LF -1
2001	Philadel	NL	540	144	31	2	27	67	137	73	91	2	1	397	.267	.352	.481	.275	79	132-LF -4
2002	*Philadel*	*NL*	*503*	*149*	*33*	*2*	*23*	*77*	*143*	*81*	*84*	*3*	*1*	*355*	*.296*	*.390*	*.507*	*.296*	*85*	

Burrell was simply not the same hitter in 2001 that he had been in previous years. Two things changed: Burrell started the year with a guaranteed major-league job, and his hitting coach was the General Sherman of slash-and-burn hitting coaches, Richie Hebner, who believes that you can't reach first base if you don't swing the bat. Burrell suffered most in April and May, and his subsequent improvement still didn't reveal the patient hitter he was before. Hebner's gone, so cross your fingers.

Marlon Byrd CF Bats R Age 24

YEAR	TEAM	LGE	AB	H	DB	TP	HR	BB	SO	R	RBI	SB	CS	OUT	BA	OBP	SLG	EQA	EQR	DEFENSE
1999	Batavia	NYP	250	54	4	2	8	18	78	24	27	3	1	197	.216	.274	.344	.210	20	44-LF -2
2000	Piedmont	SAL	527	126	20	7	12	34	118	68	59	19	5	406	.239	.290	.372	.226	49	103-LF 2
2001	Reading	Eas	523	147	19	5	23	47	90	91	74	21	4	380	.281	.347	.468	.274	75	134-CF 2
2002	*Philadel*	*NL*	*482*	*138*	*20*	*6*	*20*	*47*	*103*	*74*	*70*	*19*	*5*	*349*	*.286*	*.350*	*.477*	*.275*	*69*	

Free Byrd? It's pretty clear that Byrd could outproduce the Phils' current center fielder, Doug Glanville, right now, but the Phils have indicated that they want him to spend a year in Triple-A. Byrd's game has no real holes; he has excellent power, is selective at the plate, and has made himself a superior defender in center field after scouts pegged him as a left fielder. Byrd has worked his way back from a horrible leg injury he suffered in college, in which most of the muscles in his right calf died, so it would appear that those who underestimate Byrd are taking a risk. The Phillies need his offense and his exciting skills in the lineup every day.

Felipe Crespo UT Bats B Age 29

YEAR	TEAM	LGE	AB	H	DB	TP	HR	BB	SO	R	RBI	SB	CS	OUT	BA	OBP	SLG	EQA	EQR	DEFENSE	
1999	Fresno	PCL	376	108	21	4	18	65	67	75	62	13	6	274	.287	.399	.508	.300	68	66-1B 5	23-OF -3
2000	San Fran	NL	133	40	6	1	4	9	21	17	29	3	2	95	.301	.361	.451	.270	18	15-LF -3	
2001	San Fran	NL	67	15	0	0	5	6	22	9	12	1	1	53	.224	.302	.448	.244	8	12-1B -4	
2001	Philadel	NL	41	7	4	1	0	4	7	2	5	0	0	34	.171	.244	.317	.191	3		
2002	*Philadel*	*NL*	*319*	*87*	*16*	*4*	*15*	*48*	*73*	*53*	*58*	*7*	*5*	*237*	*.273*	*.368*	*.489*	*.281*	*49*		

The Phillies got Crespo in exchange for broken-down reliever Wayne Gomes in what seemed like a minor steal at the time, since Gomes looked like a man headed to see Dr. James Andrews. Crespo has a little pop and has shown the ability to draw a walk in the past, although he has lost some of that skill as he's struggled to stay in the majors. At the minimum salary, Crespo is worth a roster spot as a switch-hitter who can cover at five positions.

Andy Dominique C/1B Bats R Age 26

YEAR	TEAM	LGE	AB	H	DB	TP	HR	BB	SO	R	RBI	SB	CS	OUT	BA	OBP	SLG	EQA	EQR	DEFENSE	
1999	Clearwtr	Fla	494	102	22	2	11	51	95	56	62	2	2	394	.206	.287	.326	.210	40	45-C -9	34-1B -4
2000	Reading	Eas	332	72	16	0	13	26	58	37	40	0	1	261	.217	.283	.383	.221	30	52-C -11	28-1B 0
2001	Reading	Eas	269	67	9	0	11	33	44	38	42	2	1	203	.249	.332	.405	.249	31	51-C -2	10-1B 0
2001	Scran-WB	Int	137	24	4	0	4	11	31	16	20	0	0	113	.175	.240	.292	.182	8	34-1B -3	
2002	*Philadel*	*NL*	*425*	*102*	*20*	*1*	*15*	*49*	*84*	*56*	*64*	*1*	*1*	*324*	*.240*	*.319*	*.398*	*.239*	*45*		

Dominique started the year at Reading again and improved his performance significantly. We'd note that he's a league repeater, but Clay Davenport's recent research indicates that factor may not be significant (see page 467). Promoted to Triple-A, Dominique's bat looked slower than Tino Martinez running through cold molasses, casting doubt on his prospect status. More interesting to us, however, is the way he was used: the Phillies moved him to first base, where his bat is about as valuable as a used Furby, so they could play The Walbeck and non-prospect Jeremy Salazar behind the plate. If Dominique isn't worth playing behind the plate, then cut him and promote Nate Espy instead.

Nate Espy 1B Bats R Age 24

YEAR	TEAM	LGE	AB	H	DB	TP	HR	BB	SO	R	RBI	SB	CS	OUT	BA	OBP	SLG	EQA	EQR	DEFENSE
1999	Piedmont	SAL	309	62	13	1	7	34	59	26	25	1	1	248	.201	.281	.317	.206	24	74-1B -1
2000	Piedmont	SAL	476	112	20	1	14	71	112	62	54	3	0	364	.235	.337	.370	.244	53	128-1B 4
2001	Clearwtr	Fla	486	112	21	1	10	64	96	57	49	3	1	375	.230	.323	.340	.230	47	124-1B -7
2002	*Philadel*	*NL*	*448*	*115*	*21*	*1*	*12*	*63*	*100*	*51*	*46*	*4*	*1*	*334*	*.257*	*.348*	*.388*	*.251*	*53*	

Speak of the devil. Espy is a baseball rat who has produced well since turning pro as a 19-year-old high-school draftee. He has good power and draws tons of walks, but the organization believes that Espy is "blocked" by other prospects ahead of him. What do we think of that? Well, none of the first basemen the Phils played at Double- and Triple-A are in this chapter. Espy belonged at Double-A last year, and if the Phils are serious about building from the farm system, they'll push him hard this season.

Johnny Estrada C Bats R Age 26

YEAR	TEAM	LGE	AB	H	DB	TP	HR	BB	SO	R	RBI	SB	CS	OUT	BA	OBP	SLG	EQA	EQR	DEFENSE
1999	Clearwtr	Fla	344	76	8	0	8	10	29	26	36	1	0	268	.221	.245	.314	.188	21	70-C -4
2000	Reading	Eas	357	94	10	0	12	5	21	34	33	1	0	263	.263	.278	.392	.221	30	85-C 1
2001	Scran-WB	Int	132	37	13	0	0	6	6	13	15	0	0	95	.280	.315	.379	.233	12	30-C 2
2001	Philadel	NL	299	72	10	0	10	14	27	26	40	0	0	227	.241	.282	.375	.219	25	79-C 1
2002	*Philadel*	*NL*	*411*	*106*	*15*	*0*	*14*	*22*	*32*	*41*	*51*	*1*	*0*	*305*	*.258*	*.296*	*.397*	*.228*	*38*	

Estrada really needed at least a year of Triple-A before being thrown into the major-league fire, but he got only a few weeks before his promotion after Mike Lieberthal blew out his knee. The Phils decided to make Estrada their starter, a decision we might have applauded had Estrada drawn more than ten walks in 2000. Barring a late-career spike in his production, Estrada is probably maxed out as a #2 catcher.

P.J. Forbes UT Bats R Age 34

YEAR	TEAM	LGE	AB	H	DB	TP	HR	BB	SO	R	RBI	SB	CS	OUT	BA	OBP	SLG	EQA	EQR	DEFENSE
1999	Oklahoma	PCL	67	7	1	0	0	4	11	3	2	0	0	60	.104	.163	.119	.106	1	16-2B 0
1999	Rochestr	Int	349	86	12	2	0	20	38	41	16	4	0	263	.246	.292	.292	.204	25	40-3B 3 35-2B 6
2000	Scran-WB	Int	338	91	21	1	2	25	28	48	30	6	2	249	.269	.325	.355	.234	33	58-LF -2 23-3B 6
2001	Scran-WB	Int	524	156	27	2	5	47	67	79	59	4	0	368	.298	.358	.385	.255	61	89-2B 6 22-SS 4
2002	*Philadel*	*NL*	*485*	*125*	*24*	*2*	*4*	*48*	*61*	*72*	*36*	*7*	*1*	*361*	*.258*	*.325*	*.340*	*.228*	*45*	

The Phillies' mismanagement of their 40-man roster in 2001 was a major reason why they didn't overtake the anemic Braves. How many spots did this team waste? Rob Ducey was on the roster for more than two months. Turner Ward had two stints with the team before he was kicked off the 40-man roster. David Newhan appeared in a few April games. In September, Forbes, Nick Punto, and Tomas Perez all appeared in the majors. Perez, Punto, Reggie Taylor, and Felipe Crespo were all protected from the Rule 5 draft. Spots on the 40-man roster are not free, and using them on these guys isn't prudent.

Doug Glanville CF Bats R Age 31

YEAR	TEAM	LGE	AB	H	DB	TP	HR	BB	SO	R	RBI	SB	CS	OUT	BA	OBP	SLG	EQA	EQR	DEFENSE
1999	Philadel	NL	628	202	39	5	11	41	76	97	68	29	2	428	.322	.369	.452	.282	90	148-CF 7
2000	Philadel	NL	641	174	28	5	8	22	70	84	49	28	8	475	.271	.297	.368	.228	59	149-CF 2
2001	Philadel	NL	635	172	26	3	14	17	77	77	56	28	6	469	.271	.293	.387	.232	60	150-CF 16
2002	*Philadel*	*NL*	*573*	*169*	*30*	*3*	*12*	*31*	*72*	*83*	*56*	*25*	*6*	*410*	*.295*	*.331*	*.421*	*.254*	*67*	

The Phillies had to know this could happen. Glanville had posted average or slightly above-average OBPs for years by hitting for high batting averages without drawing walks. With batting average now recognized as a statistic subject to considerable variability, Glanville's 2001 collapse seems completely predictable in hindsight. Glanville is, at best, a #8 hitter with a good glove, and he would be better cast as a fourth outfielder.

Brian Hunter OOF! Bats R Age 31

YEAR	TEAM	LGE	AB	H	DB	TP	HR	BB	SO	R	RBI	SB	CS	OUT	BA	OBP	SLG	EQA	EQR	DEFENSE
1999	Detroit	AL	55	13	3	1	0	4	10	8	2	0	3	45	.236	.299	.327	.200	4	18-CF 2
1999	Seattle	AL	482	116	13	5	4	28	70	70	33	43	5	371	.241	.284	.313	.219	41	118-LF 6
2000	Colorado	NL	195	46	3	1	1	18	28	30	11	12	3	152	.236	.303	.277	.212	16	49-OF 0
2000	Cincnnti	NL	40	9	0	0	0	6	8	10	1	5	0	31	.225	.326	.225	.227	4	12-CF 2
2001	Philadel	NL	145	41	2	0	3	16	21	23	17	15	3	107	.283	.354	.359	.258	18	35-OF 0
2002	*Houston*	*NL*	*422*	*110*	*10*	*2*	*6*	*44*	*69*	*75*	*31*	*39*	*7*	*319*	*.261*	*.330*	*.336*	*.236*	*43*	

Hunter is an absolute waste of a 40-man roster spot, one the Phillies could have used to recall Rigo Beltran during their summer pitching shortage. Hunter has settled into a role as a good pinch runner, a luxury teams might be able to afford if MLB moves to 30-man active rosters. Sometimes, a bad decision is about more than money; it's about the misuse of a precious spot on the 25- or 40-man roster. The Astros gave Hunter a two-year, $1.8-million contract to be their fourth outfielder.

Kevin Jordan — IF — Bats R — Age 32

YEAR	TEAM	LGE	AB	H	DB	TP	HR	BB	SO	R	RBI	SB	CS	OUT	BA	OBP	SLG	EQA	EQR	DEFENSE
1999	Philadel	NL	348	98	17	3	4	20	31	35	48	0	0	250	.282	.331	.382	.241	36	46-3B 3 23-2B 3
2000	Philadel	NL	340	74	16	2	5	12	38	29	35	0	1	267	.218	.246	.321	.190	21	36-2B 1 34-3B 2
2001	Philadel	NL	113	28	2	0	2	14	18	9	14	0	0	85	.248	.331	.319	.227	10	
2002	*Philadel*	*NL*	*301*	*73*	*14*	*2*	*5*	*25*	*40*	*29*	*30*	*0*	*0*	*220*	*.243*	*.301*	*.352*	*.217*	*25*	

The inertia that plagues nearly every baseball organization—the devil you know is better than the one on waivers—has Kevin Jordan entering his eighth season in the City of Brotherly Love. At this point, he'd have to give up a homer to Joe Carter or restart MOVE to be forced out of the organization. The Phils' inability to develop a better utility infielder speaks to their horrible draft record in the last five years.

Travis Lee — 1B — Bats L — Age 27

YEAR	TEAM	LGE	AB	H	DB	TP	HR	BB	SO	R	RBI	SB	CS	OUT	BA	OBP	SLG	EQA	EQR	DEFENSE
1999	Arizona	NL	375	87	15	2	9	54	46	54	47	15	3	291	.232	.329	.355	.240	41	97-1B 5
2000	Arizona	NL	225	51	10	0	9	22	42	33	39	5	1	175	.227	.296	.391	.232	23	47-RF 4 15-1B -2
2000	Philadel	NL	180	42	11	1	1	38	30	19	13	3	0	138	.233	.372	.322	.252	22	43-1B 6
2001	Philadel	NL	556	149	35	2	20	68	92	78	92	3	4	411	.268	.351	.446	.265	74	153-1B -3
2002	*Philadel*	*NL*	*478*	*126*	*27*	*2*	*15*	*66*	*84*	*71*	*71*	*7*	*3*	*355*	*.264*	*.353*	*.423*	*.261*	*62*	

Lee resuscitated his career in the first half, then disappeared, hitting just two home runs between the All-Star break and September 23. Lee's career is one of bizarre splits and disappearing production that correlates with his control of the strike zone; his walk rate dropped badly in the second half as he lost the selectivity that served him so well in the first half. It could have been a case of Hebneritis. Because of his athleticism, Lee really belongs in left field.

Mike Lieberthal — C — Bats R — Age 30

YEAR	TEAM	LGE	AB	H	DB	TP	HR	BB	SO	R	RBI	SB	CS	OUT	BA	OBP	SLG	EQA	EQR	DEFENSE
1999	Philadel	NL	511	151	28	1	32	37	80	81	91	0	0	360	.295	.356	.542	.290	81	134-C 5
2000	Philadel	NL	391	108	22	0	17	34	49	52	69	2	0	283	.276	.342	.463	.267	52	102-C 6
2001	Philadel	NL	121	29	6	0	3	12	18	22	12	0	0	92	.240	.320	.364	.233	12	33-C 1
2002	*Philadel*	*NL*	*395*	*114*	*17*	*0*	*21*	*40*	*60*	*62*	*65*	*1*	*0*	*281*	*.289*	*.354*	*.491*	*.278*	*57*	

Lieberthal's season ended in April with a torn ACL, prompting all sorts of pronouncements that the Phillies' season was over. It obviously wasn't, proving once again that a good player is still only worth a few games on the margin. With Lieberthal expected to be healthy again in 2002 and Marlon Byrd just about ready, the Phils have a chance to sport a lineup without a major hole in it, which would go a long way towards bringing the NL East title to Philadelphia.

Anderson Machado — SS — Bats B — Age 21

YEAR	TEAM	LGE	AB	H	DB	TP	HR	BB	SO	R	RBI	SB	CS	OUT	BA	OBP	SLG	EQA	EQR	DEFENSE
1999	Piedmont	SAL	62	11	4	1	0	5	21	5	5	1	1	52	.177	.244	.274	.179	4	18-SS -1
2000	Clearwtr	Fla	425	83	17	4	1	39	114	38	24	17	11	353	.195	.263	.261	.186	26	117-SS -7
2001	Clearwtr	Fla	278	60	4	5	5	22	71	35	26	12	6	224	.216	.278	.320	.207	22	82-SS 0
2001	Reading	Eas	103	14	1	0	1	11	24	12	7	4	1	90	.136	.219	.175	.153	4	30-SS 1
2002	*Philadel*	*NL*	*404*	*94*	*13*	*4*	*7*	*45*	*113*	*47*	*39*	*23*	*10*	*320*	*.233*	*.310*	*.337*	*.223*	*37*	

Overhyped defensive prospects rarely turn out well, and while it's very early, Machado doesn't look so hot right now. He did make progress this year with the leather, making just 25 errors versus 44 in 2000. However, he managed only a .207 EqA as a single-A repeater, then managed a lusty 435 OPS in Double-A. This is the wrong organization in which to be a skills-deficient tools prospect.

Jason Michaels — CF/LF — Bats R — Age 26

YEAR	TEAM	LGE	AB	H	DB	TP	HR	BB	SO	R	RBI	SB	CS	OUT	BA	OBP	SLG	EQA	EQR	DEFENSE
1999	Clearwtr	Fla	456	109	25	3	10	50	116	65	42	5	4	351	.239	.316	.373	.233	46	90-CF 11
2000	Reading	Eas	440	115	26	2	9	20	90	58	57	5	3	328	.261	.296	.391	.228	41	111-CF 0
2001	Scran-WB	Int	425	109	18	2	17	36	117	57	67	9	3	319	.256	.322	.428	.251	50	100-LF -3
2002	*Philadel*	*NL*	*419*	*112*	*21*	*2*	*14*	*39*	*114*	*64*	*53*	*8*	*3*	*310*	*.267*	*.330*	*.427*	*.252*	*50*	

(Jason Michaels *continued*)

Michaels should crack the 25-man roster this year as a fourth outfielder, based largely on his athleticism and his strong defensive abilities. He does some good things on the baseball field, but his plate discipline has deteriorated as he's advanced through the minors, to the point that good major-league pitchers will eat him alive. Fourth outfielders need to be effective pinch hitters as well, and Michaels isn't yet.

Kevin Orie 3B Bats R Age 29

YEAR	TEAM	LGE	AB	H	DB	TP	HR	BB	SO	R	RBI	SB	CS	OUT	BA	OBP	SLG	EQA	EQR	DEFENSE
1999	Calgary	PCL	69	18	4	0	3	11	6	7	6	0	0	51	.261	.368	.449	.275	10	19-3B -5
1999	Florida	NL	242	62	11	0	8	19	40	25	29	1	0	180	.256	.318	.401	.241	26	64-3B 1
2000	Omaha	PCL	174	44	11	1	4	23	23	24	18	2	2	132	.253	.352	.397	.254	21	54-3B -3
2000	Columbus	Int	150	41	9	0	5	10	27	17	18	1	0	109	.273	.329	.433	.254	18	38-3B 0
2001	Scran-WB	Int	523	148	29	2	14	73	58	76	44	9	5	380	.283	.377	.426	.273	74	133-3B -4
2002	*ChiCubs*	*NL*	*479*	*133*	*25*	*1*	*17*	*76*	*63*	*65*	*56*	*8*	*3*	*349*	*.278*	*.377*	*.441*	*.280*	*72*	

Orie's fatal attraction to the disabled list has prevented him from getting the major-league job he deserves; at least a half-dozen major-league teams had inferior starters at third base in 2001, and no team had a better backup. Orie doesn't have the power typical for a third baseman, but he has superb control of the strike zone and is an excellent defender. His agent was remiss in allowing him to sign with the Phils last off-season, given all the teams with bigger holes at the hot corner.

Jorge Padilla RF Bats R Age 22

YEAR	TEAM	LGE	AB	H	DB	TP	HR	BB	SO	R	RBI	SB	CS	OUT	BA	OBP	SLG	EQA	EQR	DEFENSE
1999	Batavia	NYP	244	45	7	0	2	14	88	19	18	1	1	200	.184	.236	.238	.166	11	56-RF 1
1999	Piedmont	SAL	169	28	8	0	2	4	47	9	11	0	0	141	.166	.193	.249	.151	6	42-RF -1
2000	Piedmont	SAL	419	99	17	4	8	17	95	43	43	3	3	323	.236	.267	.353	.207	31	94-RF 2
2001	Clearwtr	Fla	366	80	8	1	13	28	78	45	47	13	5	290	.219	.280	.352	.217	32	92-RF -3
2002	*Philadel*	*NL*	*432*	*103*	*18*	*2*	*12*	*35*	*108*	*52*	*50*	*12*	*5*	*334*	*.238*	*.296*	*.373*	*.223*	*39*	

Padilla has excellent power and the proverbial five tools, and in 2001 he showed his first flashes of the Seven Skills. He posted the best walk rate and strikeout-to-walk ratio of his career, while becoming less of a mistake hitter. That said, he has a long way to go at the plate; the jump to Double-A will tell us a lot about whether he'll ever hit major-league pitching.

Tomas Perez SS/2B Bats B Age 28

YEAR	TEAM	LGE	AB	H	DB	TP	HR	BB	SO	R	RBI	SB	CS	OUT	BA	OBP	SLG	EQA	EQR	DEFENSE
1999	Edmonton	PCL	291	65	13	1	3	16	39	24	30	2	1	227	.223	.267	.306	.196	19	71-SS 0 11-2B 3
2000	Scran-WB	Int	281	80	15	2	9	13	47	41	50	3	1	202	.285	.320	.448	.254	33	55-3B -1 14-SS 2
2000	Philadel	NL	141	31	6	1	1	9	28	16	12	1	1	111	.220	.267	.298	.193	9	41-SS -6
2001	Philadel	NL	135	42	7	1	3	7	19	11	19	0	1	94	.311	.352	.444	.263	17	18-2B 1
2002	*Philadel*	*NL*	*353*	*96*	*19*	*2*	*7*	*27*	*60*	*39*	*48*	*3*	*2*	*259*	*.272*	*.324*	*.397*	*.240*	*37*	

Perez came into 2001 a career .232 hitter, but the same inertia that keeps Kevin Jordan in Philly kept Perez around anyway. He hit .304 last year in 135 at-bats, a raging fluke that might prolong his tenure in Philadelphia unless somebody has the cojones to scream "sample size" in a personnel meeting. Perez plays several positions poorly and doesn't hit, which is all the excuse the Phils should need to raise their voices.

Todd Pratt C Bats R Age 35

YEAR	TEAM	LGE	AB	H	DB	TP	HR	BB	SO	R	RBI	SB	CS	OUT	BA	OBP	SLG	EQA	EQR	DEFENSE
1999	NY Mets	NL	141	42	4	0	3	13	30	18	20	2	0	99	.298	.369	.390	.263	18	35-C 0
2000	NY Mets	NL	162	46	7	0	8	20	28	33	25	0	0	116	.284	.378	.475	.285	25	44-C 2
2001	NY Mets	NL	81	15	3	0	3	14	31	6	5	1	0	66	.185	.316	.333	.229	8	21-C -3
2001	Philadel	NL	93	20	3	0	2	19	21	12	7	0	0	73	.215	.353	.312	.238	10	27-C -1
2002	*Philadel*	*NL*	*182*	*43*	*5*	*0*	*6*	*30*	*49*	*26*	*23*	*1*	*0*	*139*	*.236*	*.344*	*.363*	*.244*	*20*	

Pratt's chance to be a starter has long passed him by, and he picked the wrong season to start slowly, since there were plenty of at-bats available to him once he was traded to Philadelphia. He turns 35 in February, meaning that the decline in 2001 could very well signal the end of the line. With Lieberthal healthy and Estrada capable of backing him up, Pratt will be superfluous.

Scott Rolen — 3B — Bats R — Age 27

YEAR	TEAM	LGE	AB	H	DB	TP	HR	BB	SO	R	RBI	SB	CS	OUT	BA	OBP	SLG	EQA	EQR	DEFENSE
1999	Philadel	NL	421	111	23	1	27	62	105	71	73	10	2	312	.264	.362	.515	.288	70	112-3B 10
2000	Philadel	NL	485	142	32	5	26	44	91	85	84	7	1	344	.293	.357	.540	.291	79	125-3B 13
2001	Philadel	NL	555	166	35	1	27	71	108	98	111	16	5	394	.299	.388	.512	.298	96	146-3B 23
2002	*Philadel*	*NL*	*493*	*146*	*31*	*2*	*26*	*76*	*105*	*90*	*86*	*17*	*3*	*350*	*.296*	*.390*	*.525*	*.303*	*88*	

The Phillies seem to be frustrated with Rolen because he hasn't turned into the next Mike Schmidt. Rolen's career path is certainly unusual: great rookie year, superb sophomore year, then a plateau just between the two levels. Rolen remains a very good player, ranking fourth among NL third basemen in EqA last year, and at 26, he has the time and the skills to turn into a great one. Be patient.

Jimmy Rollins — SS — Bats B — Age 23

YEAR	TEAM	LGE	AB	H	DB	TP	HR	BB	SO	R	RBI	SB	CS	OUT	BA	OBP	SLG	EQA	EQR	DEFENSE
1999	Reading	Eas	536	127	18	5	9	36	47	64	43	15	9	418	.237	.286	.340	.213	44	132-SS -3
2000	Scran-WB	Int	476	126	26	9	12	41	54	61	62	19	6	356	.265	.325	.433	.255	58	129-SS 4
2000	Philadel	NL	53	17	0	1	0	2	6	5	5	3	0	36	.321	.345	.358	.251	6	12-SS -2
2001	Philadel	NL	657	186	31	11	14	45	92	100	55	46	8	479	.283	.331	.428	.261	83	156-SS -6
2002	*Philadel*	*NL*	*572*	*176*	*27*	*10*	*14*	*52*	*77*	*94*	*64*	*38*	*9*	*405*	*.308*	*.365*	*.463*	*.281*	*85*	

Rollins's season probably would have won him the Rookie of the Year Award in most years, even if on the whole it wasn't as valuable as most people believed. His walk rate is barely adequate, and he's not a .300 hitter. On the other hand, he's at an age when even a good prospect is typically in the high minors, and he plays a position at which some offensive holes can be forgiven. A real hitting coach could make a big difference to a guy like Rollins.

Reggie Taylor — CF — Bats L — Age 25

YEAR	TEAM	LGE	AB	H	DB	TP	HR	BB	SO	R	RBI	SB	CS	OUT	BA	OBP	SLG	EQA	EQR	DEFENSE
1999	Reading	Eas	527	122	16	6	12	9	79	57	46	23	15	420	.231	.247	.353	.200	38	122-CF -2
2000	Scran-WB	Int	426	113	8	6	15	15	85	53	38	18	11	324	.265	.293	.418	.234	43	98-CF 4
2001	Scran-WB	Int	469	119	21	7	7	25	87	54	47	25	13	363	.254	.294	.373	.225	44	108-CF -1
2002	*Philadel*	*NL*	*448*	*117*	*15*	*7*	*11*	*27*	*90*	*60*	*43*	*25*	*13*	*343*	*.261*	*.303*	*.400*	*.234*	*45*	

Tools goof who can't stay healthy. The Phils really need to give up on this guy; they've been pushing him through their system since 1996 despite a lack of tangible progress. If they're looking for a fourth outfielder, the organization is awash in potential candidates, such as Eric Valent and Jason Michaels. Taylor appears to be beyond any redemption via instruction, so unless the Herb Washington role is coming back into vogue, he's a bad use of instruction time.

Chase Utley — 2B — Bats L — Age 23

YEAR	TEAM	LGE	AB	H	DB	TP	HR	BB	SO	R	RBI	SB	CS	OUT	BA	OBP	SLG	EQA	EQR	DEFENSE
2000	Batavia	NYP	158	35	9	0	2	11	27	14	13	2	2	125	.222	.276	.316	.201	11	34-2B 1
2001	Clearwtr	Fla	474	102	18	1	13	25	94	48	42	10	5	377	.215	.263	.340	.204	35	114-2B -9
2002	*Philadel*	*NL*	*430*	*107*	*20*	*1*	*14*	*34*	*90*	*51*	*50*	*12*	*6*	*329*	*.249*	*.304*	*.398*	*.233*	*43*	

Utley has been in the pros for a year and a half since the Phillies drafted him in the first round in 2000, and he has yet to show that he'll hit in the higher levels of the minors. He hasn't hit for average, and he isn't selective at the plate. He's also having enough trouble in the field to make a position move a possibility, although his bat is best suited to second base. On the plus side, he has very good power, so he could improve if he gets some strike-zone instruction.

Eric Valent — RF — Bats L — Age 25

YEAR	TEAM	LGE	AB	H	DB	TP	HR	BB	SO	R	RBI	SB	CS	OUT	BA	OBP	SLG	EQA	EQR	DEFENSE
1999	Clearwtr	Fla	524	121	24	4	15	42	124	65	69	3	2	405	.231	.291	.378	.224	48	129-RF -5
2000	Reading	Eas	478	110	17	3	19	55	92	66	68	1	2	370	.230	.313	.397	.238	51	122-RF 0
2001	Scran-WB	Int	457	122	24	2	21	47	97	64	75	0	1	336	.267	.342	.466	.266	62	87-RF 0 24-1B 0
2001	Philadel	NL	41	5	2	0	0	4	9	3	1	0	0	36	.122	.213	.171	.143	1	
2002	*Philadel*	*NL*	*458*	*119*	*26*	*2*	*19*	*56*	*103*	*70*	*73*	*1*	*1*	*340*	*.260*	*.340*	*.450*	*.261*	*59*	

(Eric Valent *continued*)

Valent's prospect status took a hit this year as hc saw his plate discipline take a dive in Triple-A. His power increased dramatically—he led the Red Barons in home runs, RBI, and slugging average—while his previously excellent walk rate dropped to merely adequate, as he found Triple-A pitchers tougher to handle. Valent could be a good fourth outfielder, but he needs to recapture the skills he showed in Double-A. He's definite trade bait.

PITCHERS (ERA: 4.50, H/9: 9.0, HR/9: 1.0, BB/9: 3.0, K/9: 6.0, KW: 2.0, PERA: 4.50)

Miguel Asencio — Throws R — Age 21

YEAR	TEAM	LGE	IP	H	ER	HR	BB	K	ERA	W	L	H/9	HR/9	BB/9	K/9	KW	PERA	STUFF
2001	Clearwtr	Fla	148.3	156	91	16	79	77	5.52	6	10	9.5	1.0	4.8	4.7	0.5	4.50	3

The Phils are high on Asencio, with good reason: At age 19, he already has three major-league quality pitches: a hard fastball with good movement, a good curve, and a sharp slider. Asencio has two drawbacks so far, but only one is within his power to fix. Asencio's control needs improvement, something that will likely come with age. Asencio's workload, however, needs more improvement; if the Phils keep pushing him eight to nine innings, they'll be lucky if he can go two innings by the time he reaches the majors.

Brad Baisley — Throws R — Age 22

YEAR	TEAM	LGE	IP	H	ER	HR	BB	K	ERA	W	L	H/9	HR/9	BB/9	K/9	KW	PERA	STUFF
1999	Piedmont	SAL	141.3	150	82	10	75	56	5.22	7	9	9.6	0.6	4.8	3.6	0.4	4.65	0
2000	Clearwtr	Fla	87.7	106	74	21	40	39	7.60	3	7	10.9	2.2	4.1	4.0	0.5	5.77	-6
2001	Clearwtr	Fla	62.3	70	38	9	20	27	5.49	3	4	10.1	1.3	2.9	3.9	0.7	5.43	-1
2001	Reading	Eas	62.7	83	60	20	18	24	8.62	1	6	11.9	2.9	2.6	3.4	0.7	8.99	-17

Baisley should be a top pitching prospect. He's big, throws hard, has decent control, and knows what he's doing on the mound. The problem is that he can't stay healthy; since facing more than 600 batters at age 19 in his first pro season, he has pitched just 215 innings in two years, missing time with a variety of elbow problems. You have to expect to hear about a visit to Dr. Andrews at some point, although Baisley is at least young enough to recover from that kind of surgery.

Rigo Beltran — Throws L — Age 32

YEAR	TEAM	LGE	IP	H	ER	HR	BB	K	ERA	W	L	H/9	HR/9	BB/9	K/9	KW	PERA	STUFF
1999	Norfolk	Int	22.0	19	10	1	13	19	4.09	1	1	7.8	0.4	5.3	7.8	0.7	2.16	-2
1999	NY Mets	NL	32.0	29	15	5	10	32	4.22	2	2	8.2	1.4	2.8	9.0	1.6	4.14	13
1999	Colorado	NL	14.0	12	7	2	6	14	4.50	1	1	7.7	1.3	3.9	9.0	1.2	5.40	7
2000	ColSprin	PCL	126.0	137	86	19	67	68	6.14	5	9	9.8	1.4	4.8	4.9	0.5	5.72	-17
2001	Scran-WB	Int	109.3	110	65	15	52	77	5.35	5	7	9.1	1.2	4.3	6.3	0.7	4.08	-9

Beltran's career may have been ruined by his brief stint in Colorado, which gave many GMs the wrong impression about his abilities. Beltran is very tough on right-handed hitters, largely because of his major-league screwball. He posted the second-best ERA in Scranton history last year, working his way into the rotation over the course of the season, but didn't get the call to the majors because the Phils couldn't (read: wouldn't) clear a spot on the 40-man roster for him. That type of bureaucratic thinking costs teams games. Beltran signed with the Red Sox and should be in the mix for their fifth-starter spot this spring.

Ricky Bottalico — Throws R — Age 32

YEAR	TEAM	LGE	IP	H	ER	HR	BB	K	ERA	W	L	H/9	HR/9	BB/9	K/9	KW	PERA	STUFF
1999	St Louis	NL	78.0	74	41	7	41	59	4.73	4	5	8.5	0.8	4.7	6.8	0.7	5.03	-5
2000	KansasCy	AL	72.0	71	42	10	34	55	5.25	3	5	8.9	1.3	4.3	6.9	0.8	3.93	-4
2001	Philadel	NL	62.0	63	35	9	22	46	5.08	3	4	9.1	1.3	3.2	6.7	1.0	4.12	-3

Bottalico provided the worst return on the three major relief investments Ed Wade made last off-season, which was as much due to injury as to his performance on the mound. When he was healthy, Bottalico was a quality middle reliever: not a guy to whom you should pay millions of dollars, but an asset in the bullpen if his price is reasonable.

Dave Coggin Throws R Age 25

YEAR	TEAM	LGE	IP	H	ER	HR	BB	K	ERA	W	L	H/9	HR/9	BB/9	K/9	KW	PERA	STUFF
1999	Reading	Eas	43.0	55	40	11	20	15	8.37	1	4	11.5	2.3	4.2	3.1	0.4	8.70	-26
2000	Clearwtr	Fla	31.7	33	19	3	17	15	5.40	2	2	9.4	0.9	4.8	4.3	0.4	4.03	-8
2000	Reading	Eas	43.0	50	31	9	14	21	6.49	2	3	10.5	1.9	2.9	4.4	0.8	6.06	-6
2000	Scran-WB	Int	43.7	44	26	2	32	23	5.36	2	3	9.1	0.4	6.6	4.7	0.4	5.73	-7
2000	Philadel	NL	29.3	30	13	2	10	15	3.99	2	1	9.2	0.6	3.1	4.6	0.8	5.97	2
2001	Scran-WB	Int	95.3	102	51	8	36	39	4.81	5	6	9.6	0.8	3.4	3.7	0.5	4.03	-3
2001	Philadel	NL	92.7	93	44	6	35	50	4.27	5	5	9.0	0.6	3.4	4.9	0.7	4.31	4

Coggin recovered from three years of injuries to plant himself firmly in the Phils' 2001 rotation. His stuff is only average or slightly above, but he has four pitches and succeeds by mixing them. That's a recipe for a long adjustment period to the majors, unfortunately, so while Coggin should eventually be a good mid-rotation starter, the Phils will probably end up dealing him if they stay in contention in 2002.

Dennis Cook Throws L Age 39

YEAR	TEAM	LGE	IP	H	ER	HR	BB	K	ERA	W	L	H/9	HR/9	BB/9	K/9	KW	PERA	STUFF
1999	NY Mets	NL	61.3	57	33	10	23	61	4.84	3	4	8.4	1.5	3.4	9.0	1.3	3.67	9
2000	NY Mets	NL	61.3	60	32	7	26	47	4.70	3	4	8.8	1.0	3.8	6.9	0.9	5.11	-3
2001	NY Mets	NL	33.0	32	17	5	9	27	4.64	2	2	8.7	1.4	2.5	7.4	1.5	4.72	1
2001	Philadel	NL	10.3	12	7	2	4	3	6.10	0	1	10.5	1.7	3.5	2.6	0.4	5.51	-35

You would think that overpaying for Rheal Cormier would have made the Phillies gun-shy about doing the same for another left-handed reliever, but overpay they did in a July deal they may regret for ten years. Cook, about a year removed from effectiveness, came over with Turk Wendell for top pitching prospect Bruce Chen and outstanding left-handed prospect Adam Walker. Walker probably could have done what Cook did for two months, at much lower cost.

Rheal Cormier Throws L Age 35

YEAR	TEAM	LGE	IP	H	ER	HR	BB	K	ERA	W	L	H/9	HR/9	BB/9	K/9	KW	PERA	STUFF
1999	Boston	AL	64.3	62	25	3	15	39	3.50	4	3	8.7	0.4	2.1	5.5	1.3	4.07	0
2000	Boston	AL	71.0	71	30	6	14	43	3.80	5	3	9.0	0.8	1.8	5.5	1.5	4.34	-2
2001	Philadel	NL	49.0	49	23	4	15	30	4.22	3	2	9.0	0.7	2.8	5.5	1.0	4.51	-6

Cormier wasn't the outright disaster that Bottalico was, but he hardly provided a good return on investment for the Phils. He wasn't especially effective against left-handed batters, and he has never been durable enough to be anything more than a specialist. Good left-handers should cost a little more than good right-handed relievers, but not this much. The Phillies need to focus on using their money to fill more critical spots on the roster.

Omar Daal Throws R Age 30

YEAR	TEAM	LGE	IP	H	ER	HR	BB	K	ERA	W	L	H/9	HR/9	BB/9	K/9	KW	PERA	STUFF
1999	Arizona	NL	210.7	209	99	19	66	133	4.23	12	11	8.9	0.8	2.8	5.7	1.0	3.46	11
2000	Arizona	NL	102.0	116	64	15	35	40	5.65	4	7	10.2	1.3	3.1	3.5	0.6	7.39	-15
2000	Philadel	NL	74.3	76	38	8	25	45	4.60	4	4	9.2	1.0	3.0	5.4	0.9	4.54	6
2001	Philadel	NL	178.0	193	97	22	50	86	4.90	9	11	9.8	1.1	2.5	4.3	0.9	4.79	0

Daal came some of the way back in 2001, although not to the extent that his improved won-lost record would indicate. Daal actually ranked slightly below average in his Support-Neutral performance, and he remained maddeningly inconsistent from start to start. Daal's numbers will get a superficial boost with his move to Los Angeles in 2002. The Dodgers will need him to recapture his '98–'99 form to help them in a tough division.

Brandon Duckworth Throws R Age 26

YEAR	TEAM	LGE	IP	H	ER	HR	BB	K	ERA	W	L	H/9	HR/9	BB/9	K/9	KW	PERA	STUFF
1999	Clearwtr	Fla	136.0	164	109	31	55	60	7.21	4	11	10.9	2.1	3.6	4.0	0.5	7.71	-23
2000	Reading	Eas	160.3	173	109	33	62	115	6.12	6	12	9.7	1.9	3.5	6.5	0.9	4.88	0
2001	Scran-WB	Int	141.7	144	77	21	46	102	4.89	7	9	9.1	1.3	2.9	6.5	1.1	3.70	6
2001	Philadel	NL	63.3	62	27	2	26	32	3.84	4	3	8.8	0.3	3.7	4.5	0.6	3.74	4

(Brandon Duckworth *continued*)

Hold your horses. Duckworth did have an outstanding half-season debut, with a superb ERA and eight quality starts in 11 trips to the hill. His peripherals didn't support the ERA; Duckworth allowed just two home runs in 69 innings, an unbelievably low rate and one unlikely to be maintained. He'll have to keep more men off the bases as the home runs inevitably come. While Duckworth still projects to be an All-Star pitcher, he has some developing to do in 2002.

Nelson Figueroa Throws R Age 28

YEAR	TEAM	LGE	IP	H	ER	HR	BB	K	ERA	W	L	H/9	HR/9	BB/9	K/9	KW	PERA	STUFF
1999	Tucson	PCL	127.7	137	77	19	48	71	5.43	6	8	9.7	1.3	3.4	5.0	0.7	4.06	-7
2000	Tucson	PCL	109.3	115	55	12	30	56	4.53	6	6	9.5	1.0	2.5	4.6	0.9	3.26	0
2000	Arizona	NL	15.3	19	12	4	4	6	7.04	1	1	11.2	2.3	2.3	3.5	0.8	6.68	-18
2000	Scran-WB	Int	48.3	58	37	13	12	26	6.89	1	4	10.8	2.4	2.2	4.8	1.1	6.13	-13
2001	Scran-WB	Int	84.3	86	41	9	23	50	4.38	5	4	9.2	1.0	2.5	5.3	1.1	4.46	3
2001	Philadel	NL	87.3	88	43	7	33	49	4.43	5	5	9.1	0.7	3.4	5.0	0.7	4.00	1

A right-handed finesse pitcher with good control is lucky to get one chance in the majors; if he screws it up, he'll become intimately familiar with the best late-night dining Pawtucket and Des Moines have to offer. Figueroa got his one chance with the Phils this year and he capitalized, providing above-average work in 13 starts, including six quality starts. There's no real upside here, so as the young guns advance, Figueroa should settle into a swing role.

Geoff Geary Throws R Age 25

YEAR	TEAM	LGE	IP	H	ER	HR	BB	K	ERA	W	L	H/9	HR/9	BB/9	K/9	KW	PERA	STUFF
1999	Clearwtr	Fla	144.7	170	94	24	39	50	5.85	6	10	10.6	1.5	2.4	3.1	0.6	6.19	-10
2000	Reading	Eas	131.0	147	81	27	24	78	5.56	6	9	10.1	1.9	1.6	5.4	1.6	5.41	4
2001	Reading	Eas	105.7	124	76	23	30	51	6.47	4	8	10.6	2.0	2.6	4.3	0.9	5.41	-18
2001	Scran-WB	Int	25.7	26	12	3	7	16	4.21	2	1	9.1	1.1	2.5	5.6	1.1	8.42	-5

Geary is a small right-hander who zipped up the Phillies' chain quickly until hitting the Triple-A wall last year. He runs his fastball into the low 90s and relies heavily on a late-breaking slider that has allowed him to remain in and around the strike zone without too much risk. His stuff is good enough for the majors, but he'll need the serious instruction Vern Ruhle provided to his pitchers in Houston. Bringing him into the Phillies' bullpen as soon as he handles Triple-A might be the best development route.

Jose Mesa Throws R Age 36

YEAR	TEAM	LGE	IP	H	ER	HR	BB	K	ERA	W	L	H/9	HR/9	BB/9	K/9	KW	PERA	STUFF
1999	Seattle	AL	72.7	77	44	10	33	42	5.45	3	5	9.5	1.2	4.1	5.2	0.6	4.62	-15
2000	Seattle	AL	86.7	77	40	10	34	83	4.15	5	5	8.0	1.0	3.5	8.6	1.2	4.82	9
2001	Philadel	NL	67.3	62	25	3	18	47	3.34	5	2	8.3	0.4	2.4	6.3	1.3	3.34	4

The gamble worked, sort of. Mesa had his most effective season since he cost the Indians the 1997 World Series, and he was the Phils' top reliever last year. On the other hand, he showed plenty of signs that the Jose Mesa who ignited rallies around the majors the previous three years is still there. While Mesa wasn't the disaster many analysts, including ours, predicted, his cost exceeded his value, a situation that will only get worse as his contract progresses.

Brett Myers Throws R Age 21

YEAR	TEAM	LGE	IP	H	ER	HR	BB	K	ERA	W	L	H/9	HR/9	BB/9	K/9	KW	PERA	STUFF
2000	Piedmont	SAL	173.7	188	106	17	88	73	5.49	8	11	9.7	0.9	4.6	3.8	0.4	5.50	0
2001	Reading	Eas	152.3	172	106	31	55	85	6.26	6	11	10.2	1.8	3.2	5.0	0.8	5.10	8

The current jewel of the Phillies' farm system, Myers elicits comparisons to a young Curt Schilling with his attitude and his stuff, including a nasty curve and a very strong fastball. The Phils switched him from a four-seam fastball to a two-seamer last year, which helped him get more ground balls and reduce the number of pitches he'd have to throw each inning. Standard pitching-prospect caveats apply, but right now, Myers is right on track.

Doug Nickle Throws R Age 27

YEAR	TEAM	LGE	IP	H	ER	HR	BB	K	ERA	W	L	H/9	HR/9	BB/9	K/9	KW	PERA	STUFF
1999	Clearwtr	Fla	70.0	68	33	3	34	38	4.24	4	4	8.7	0.4	4.4	4.9	0.6	4.65	-22
2000	Reading	Eas	71.7	77	40	8	27	36	5.02	4	4	9.7	1.0	3.4	4.5	0.7	3.87	-22
2001	Scran-WB	Int	80.7	80	42	3	47	41	4.69	4	5	8.9	0.3	5.2	4.6	0.4	2.62	-18

Beware the moniker "Closer of the Future," for it is thrown around with great abandon. Nickle, the bounty brought in when the Phillies dumped the Gregg Jefferies problem on the Angels, looks like he might be a middle reliever, which makes him about as valuable as a hundred or so other pitchers kicking around the high minors. He has a shot to be a good setup guy; barring a major step up in performance, that's about it.

Franklin Nunez Throws R Age 25

YEAR	TEAM	LGE	IP	H	ER	HR	BB	K	ERA	W	L	H/9	HR/9	BB/9	K/9	KW	PERA	STUFF
1999	Piedmont	SAL	76.7	79	44	8	35	43	5.17	4	5	9.3	0.9	4.1	5.0	0.6	6.47	0
2000	Clearwtr	Fla	112.3	121	76	10	76	47	6.09	4	8	9.7	0.8	6.1	3.8	0.3	5.95	-21
2001	Reading	Eas	109.3	115	77	15	73	65	6.34	4	8	9.5	1.2	6.0	5.4	0.4	7.82	-27

Nunez's fastball should be measured in BTUs, but problems with his command hindered his development, not to mention his ability to record outs, until last year. The Phils moved him to the rotation in 2001 to allow their coaches to establish a regular schedule for his instructional sessions, and that appears to have helped, especially with his curve. He's still ticketed for the pen, but until he proves he can't start, they should keep trying.

Eddie Oropesa Throws L Age 30

YEAR	TEAM	LGE	IP	H	ER	HR	BB	K	ERA	W	L	H/9	HR/9	BB/9	K/9	KW	PERA	STUFF
1999	Fresno	PCL	102.0	119	80	18	57	41	7.06	3	8	10.5	1.6	5.0	3.6	0.4	6.22	-29
2000	Shrevprt	Tex	75.0	79	52	11	47	45	6.24	3	5	9.5	1.3	5.6	5.4	0.5	5.96	-33
2001	Scran-WB	Int	15.0	16	8	1	5	7	4.80	1	1	9.6	0.6	3.0	4.2	0.7	3.86	-18
2001	Philadel	NL	18.0	17	11	1	15	12	5.50	1	1	8.5	0.5	7.5	6.0	0.4	4.69	-18

This is how you find left-handed relievers. Oropesa, an early Cuban defector without the marketing hype that usually accompanies such players, bounced around the minors for seven years, posting an ERA over 4.00 just once (during a stint as a starter) but getting just one shot above Double-A. Oropesa was nothing more than an average reliever for the Phils; then again, he didn't cost the team any prospects or serious money, either. He signed a minor-league deal with the Diamondbacks in November.

Vicente Padilla Throws R Age 24

YEAR	TEAM	LGE	IP	H	ER	HR	BB	K	ERA	W	L	H/9	HR/9	BB/9	K/9	KW	PERA	STUFF
1999	Tucson	PCL	97.7	101	43	6	25	44	3.96	6	5	9.3	0.6	2.3	4.1	0.9	3.92	6
1999	Arizona	NL	3.7	5	4	1	3	0	9.82	0	0	12.3	2.5	7.4	0.0	0.0	14.96	-74
2000	Tucson	PCL	20.0	18	9	2	8	18	4.05	1	1	8.1	0.9	3.6	8.1	1.1	3.88	16
2000	Arizona	NL	36.0	31	10	0	8	27	2.50	3	1	7.8	0.0	2.0	6.8	1.7	2.30	17
2000	Philadel	NL	33.3	34	17	3	15	19	4.59	2	2	9.2	0.8	4.1	5.1	0.6	6.12	-9
2001	Scran-WB	Int	78.0	78	35	10	12	58	4.04	5	4	9.0	1.2	1.4	6.7	2.4	3.07	20
2001	Philadel	NL	34.3	31	12	1	11	23	3.15	3	1	8.1	0.3	2.9	6.0	1.0	4.71	4

Vern Ruhle has a very good track record with pitching projects, but even the best pitching coaches aren't perfect. Padilla has a good arm and no idea what to do with it. He's also burdened with the Closer of the Future tag, but he pitched well as a starter in Scranton after his demotion. Padilla has to have something to complement his fastball, because he can't just blow it by hitters; until he develops something, he's Triple-A material.

Robert Person Throws R Age 33

YEAR	TEAM	LGE	IP	H	ER	HR	BB	K	ERA	W	L	H/9	HR/9	BB/9	K/9	KW	PERA	STUFF
1999	Toronto	AL	11.0	9	8	1	13	12	6.55	0	1	7.4	0.8	10.6	9.8	0.5	8.24	-11
1999	Philadel	NL	137.7	135	79	21	59	114	5.16	6	9	8.8	1.4	3.9	7.5	1.0	4.28	8
2000	Philadel	NL	173.0	154	75	11	78	146	3.90	11	8	8.0	0.6	4.1	7.6	0.9	3.40	20
2001	Philadel	NL	193.7	194	108	29	72	147	5.02	10	12	9.0	1.3	3.3	6.8	1.0	4.40	11

(Robert Person *continued*)
The Phils' most valuable starting pitcher was nearly relegated to a career as a closer, which, despite everything you may have read, is nowhere near as valuable to a team as a 200-inning starter. The Blue Jays tried to force Person into the closer role, but he was so horrible that they ended up dealing him for Paul Spoljaric, who is now out of baseball. Give the Phils credit for using Person correctly, and give Person credit for overcoming the way he was mishandled.

Cliff Politte **Throws R** **Age 28**

YEAR	TEAM	LGE	IP	H	ER	HR	BB	K	ERA	W	L	H/9	HR/9	BB/9	K/9	KW	PERA	STUFF
1999	Reading	Eas	108.3	122	73	20	39	58	6.06	4	8	10.1	1.7	3.2	4.8	0.7	4.79	-22
1999	Philadel	NL	18.3	18	11	2	13	14	5.40	1	1	8.8	1.0	6.4	6.9	0.5	6.43	-12
2000	Scran-WB	Int	110.7	107	55	11	45	79	4.47	6	6	8.7	0.9	3.7	6.4	0.9	4.37	3
2000	Philadel	NL	59.0	58	30	7	22	44	4.58	3	4	8.8	1.1	3.4	6.7	1.0	3.28	11
2001	Clearwtr	Fla	11.0	10	4	0	4	8	3.27	1	0	8.2	0.0	3.3	6.5	1.0	5.02	-6
2001	Philadel	NL	25.0	23	10	2	7	18	3.60	2	1	8.3	0.7	2.5	6.5	1.3	2.74	4

Politte shares the same tortured history of many Phillies, with a long record of freak injuries interrupting periods of effectiveness. He throws hard, has good control, and his arm is in good shape. Nelson Figueroa's spot can be had in 2002, so Politte probably won't spend the whole season in the bullpen if he can stay off of the DL.

Jose Santiago **Throws R** **Age 27**

YEAR	TEAM	LGE	IP	H	ER	HR	BB	K	ERA	W	L	H/9	HR/9	BB/9	K/9	KW	PERA	STUFF
1999	KansasCy	AL	46.0	53	27	6	12	15	5.28	2	3	10.4	1.2	2.3	2.9	0.6	3.54	-19
2000	KansasCy	AL	70.7	70	32	6	21	44	4.08	4	4	8.9	0.8	2.7	5.6	1.0	3.42	-1
2000	Omaha	PCL	17.3	19	9	3	3	10	4.67	1	1	9.9	1.6	1.6	5.2	1.7	4.02	-12
2001	KansasCy	AL	32.3	33	14	2	9	14	3.90	2	2	9.2	0.6	2.5	3.9	0.8	5.87	-13
2001	Philadel	NL	60.0	63	24	3	12	23	3.60	4	3	9.5	0.4	1.8	3.5	1.0	3.57	-11

Let's consider the lesson here. The Phils spent more than $10 million in first-year salaries alone to acquire three journeyman relief pitchers of no distinction. One pitched well, one was mediocre, and one was awful. The Phils acquired another reliever (Santiago) in a June trade for the ineffective Paul Byrd, paying Santiago less than $1 million for his time, and he was the team's second-most effective reliever last season. Isn't it obvious?

Carlos Silva **Throws R** **Age 23**

YEAR	TEAM	LGE	IP	H	ER	HR	BB	K	ERA	W	L	H/9	HR/9	BB/9	K/9	KW	PERA	STUFF
1999	Piedmont	SAL	168.0	185	88	12	56	51	4.71	9	10	9.9	0.6	3.0	2.7	0.5	5.90	-3
2000	Clearwtr	Fla	188.3	211	90	16	31	54	4.30	11	10	10.1	0.8	1.5	2.6	0.9	6.14	-3
2001	Reading	Eas	178.3	208	108	29	34	66	5.45	8	12	10.5	1.5	1.7	3.3	1.0	5.29	-2

The knock on Silva has always been that he doesn't get the strikeouts a pitcher with his fastball should get, largely because his off-speed stuff isn't very good. He's also somewhat homer-prone. Silva induces ground balls and has excellent control, so he keeps moving up the ladder. He'll likely hit the wall in Triple-A, at which point he'll end up in the relief role for which his stuff is best suited. If he keeps the ball down more consistently, he'll be decent.

Robinson Tejeda **Throws R** **Age 20**

YEAR	TEAM	LGE	IP	H	ER	HR	BB	K	ERA	W	L	H/9	HR/9	BB/9	K/9	KW	PERA	STUFF
2001	Lakewood	SAL	144.3	160	107	25	82	78	6.67	5	11	10.0	1.6	5.1	4.9	0.5	7.60	0

A name to remember. Tejeda had an excellent year in his full-season debut, showing why the Phils are excited about him as a long-term prospect. He already brings his fastball up to 90-plus and is willing to throw it inside. He also showed greatly improved composure as the season progressed. The concern with Tejeda and particularly his teammate Taylor Buchholz is workload, as the Phils have a dismal track record with very young pitchers.

Amaury Telemaco Throws R Age 28

YEAR	TEAM	LGE	IP	H	ER	HR	BB	K	ERA	W	L	H/9	HR/9	BB/9	K/9	KW	PERA	STUFF
1999	Tucson	PCL	19.0	19	9	1	7	11	4.26	1	1	9.0	0.5	3.3	5.2	0.8	5.48	-14
1999	Philadel	NL	47.0	47	26	7	17	37	4.98	2	3	9.0	1.3	3.3	7.1	1.1	5.02	-2
2000	Philadel	NL	24.3	26	17	5	12	20	6.29	1	2	9.6	1.8	4.4	7.4	0.8	7.30	-8
2000	Scran-WB	Int	120.0	133	79	21	46	66	5.93	5	8	10.0	1.6	3.5	4.9	0.7	5.33	-9
2001	Philadel	NL	85.0	92	51	13	29	47	5.40	4	5	9.7	1.4	3.1	5.0	0.8	5.88	-8
2001	Scran-WB	Int	26.0	29	18	6	8	17	6.23	1	2	10.0	2.1	2.8	5.9	1.1	5.26	-5

Telemaco has the unfortunate habit of getting hurt whenever he gets an extended opportunity in the majors. Telemaco started the year in the bullpen, pitched well, jumped into the rotation, pitched well at times, then lost it, ending up on Scranton's disabled list with a sore shoulder that ended his season and required surgery. When healthy, Telemaco is a good fifth starter with upside, but even prospects run out of chances if they can't pitch full seasons.

Evan Thomas Throws R Age 28

YEAR	TEAM	LGE	IP	H	ER	HR	BB	K	ERA	W	L	H/9	HR/9	BB/9	K/9	KW	PERA	STUFF
1999	Reading	Eas	128.7	130	69	12	59	76	4.83	7	7	9.1	0.8	4.1	5.3	0.6	4.83	-13
2000	Scran-WB	Int	169.0	181	97	24	54	95	5.17	8	11	9.6	1.3	2.9	5.1	0.9	4.48	-2
2001	Scran-WB	Int	106.0	123	78	21	46	50	6.62	4	8	10.4	1.8	3.9	4.2	0.5	7.72	-22

A short right-hander who pitched well in his first Triple-A exposure in 2000, Thomas was a victim of the Phils' spring starting-pitching surplus, and then a pair of ankle injuries wrecked his season, injuries which may have caused the shoulder discomfort that shut him down for good. If he doesn't leave his velocity on the operating table, he could be a good fifth starter/swing man for the minimum salary, with substantial upside.

Turk Wendell Throws R Age 35

YEAR	TEAM	LGE	IP	H	ER	HR	BB	K	ERA	W	L	H/9	HR/9	BB/9	K/9	KW	PERA	STUFF
1999	NY Mets	NL	86.7	81	40	9	31	69	4.15	5	5	8.4	0.9	3.2	7.2	1.1	3.10	4
2000	NY Mets	NL	79.0	74	39	8	34	65	4.44	5	4	8.4	0.9	3.9	7.4	1.0	3.75	2
2001	NY Mets	NL	46.7	48	28	7	20	33	5.40	2	3	9.3	1.3	3.9	6.4	0.8	4.23	-7
2001	Philadel	NL	16.3	18	13	3	11	12	7.16	1	1	9.9	1.7	6.1	6.6	0.5	7.37	-22

Philadelphia is the powder keg of baseball, and Turk Wendell is quite clearly a match. Wendell's candor and superstitions play well when he plays well, but he was simply horrible after he came over from the Mets in a highly questionable deal. If Bruce Chen becomes the pitcher we expect him to be, Wendell will be even more reviled in Philly. If Adam Walker develops, too, Wendell might want to call Mitch Williams for advice on joining the Ex-Phillie Protection Program.

Randy Wolf Throws L Age 25

YEAR	TEAM	LGE	IP	H	ER	HR	BB	K	ERA	W	L	H/9	HR/9	BB/9	K/9	KW	PERA	STUFF
1999	Scran-WB	Int	78.0	76	38	9	28	58	4.38	5	4	8.8	1.0	3.2	6.7	1.0	4.11	20
1999	Philadel	NL	125.3	122	71	18	56	104	5.10	6	8	8.8	1.3	4.0	7.5	0.9	5.21	17
2000	Philadel	NL	210.7	209	102	22	68	142	4.36	12	11	8.9	0.9	2.9	6.1	1.0	4.18	14
2001	Philadel	NL	157.7	146	65	13	46	122	3.71	11	7	8.3	0.7	2.6	7.0	1.3	4.04	20

As badly as Wolf was abused in 2000 and in the early going of 2001, he seemed to recover his arm strength during his demotion to the bullpen, returning to post a 2.19 ERA and allow just 62 base runners in 70 innings over ten post-break starts. On talent alone, Wolf is among the NL's best young pitchers; by the end of 2002, he'll either be a Cy Young contender or he'll have a torn labrum.

Pittsburgh Pirates

The Pirates came into the 2001 season full of misplaced hope. They had a new manager, a projected Cy Young Award winner at the head of their rotation, two bona fide All-Stars in their lineup, and two new free-agent signings. Their new home, PNC Park, may be the best of the new breed of ballparks, and it earned rave reviews from observers before the first game was ever played there.

The team had threatened to leave Pittsburgh if the local and state governments didn't cough up money for a new ballpark. When the voters of Allegheny County resoundingly defeated a tax increase designed solely to fund new baseball and football stadiums, the Pirates and Steelers drew up a play now called the Immaculate Deception, in which funding was pushed through the state legislature in a last-minute maneuver that sidestepped public comment and debate. The outcry over this maneuver was deflected by the refrain that once the Pirates had their new stadium, they'd be able to compete with the big boys of the major leagues.

Pirates Prospectus

2001 record: 62–100; Sixth place, NL Central

Pythagenport W/L: 61–101

Runs scored: 657 (15th in NL)

Runs allowed: 858 (15th in NL)

Team EqA: .244 (16th in NL)

2001 batters age: 27.7 (third-youngest in NL)

2001 pitchers age: 26.8 (tied for third-youngest in NL)

Ballpark: PNC Park; neutral park, Park Factor of .997

2001: The new park is beautiful. The team that played in it belonged in Three Rivers. Or one of them, anyway.

2002: They're still working their way through the roster's dead weight. 75 wins would be a good year.

Whatever the politics behind its funding, PNC Park's opening represented a complete break with the antiseptic environment of Three Rivers Stadium. It's just a shame that the Pirates waited until the park opened to break with GM Cam Bonifay and his lengthy record of failure. Bonifay's delayed departure contributed to a 100-loss season that was as ugly as the ballpark is beautiful.

Cy Young candidate Kris Benson started the season on the shelf before having Tommy John surgery that will probably keep him out for the start of the 2002 season. The free agents, Derek Bell and Terry Mulholland, both performed as they had in the 2000 season, which is to say horribly. New manager Lloyd McClendon produced more memorable quotes than memorable wins as the Bucs lost 100 games, tying for the worst record in baseball and marking just the second time since 1954 that the Pirates have lost at least 100 games. As a result, PNC Park wasn't even 90% full for 18 of the Pirates' last 21 games, despite its status as the smallest-capacity ballpark in the majors.

The silver lining in all of this is that the architect of the Pirates' anti-juggernaut, Cam Bonifay, was relieved of his duties in June. It is astounding that owner Kevin McClatchy didn't fire Bonifay sooner, as the Bucs have suffered seven straight losing seasons, including two 93-loss campaigns in the last three years. While it's disappointing that McClatchy didn't make the move right after the 2000 season—which would have prevented Bonifay from signing Bell and Mulholland, continuing to mess with Warren Morris, and nearly derailing Aramis Ramirez for the fourth straight season—the closing of the Cam Bonifay chapter in Pittsburgh was a necessary step for the team to move forward.

Bonifay's lengthy reign of error was not without its high points. He regularly abused former Indians GM John Hart in the way that the A's Billy Beane has abused the Royals' Allard Baird. Bonifay sent talented but fragile reliever Ricardo Rincon to the Tribe for a reserve outfielder named Brian Giles, then Bonifay escaped the ludicrous contract he gave Wil Cordero by dumping it on Hart in exchange for Enrique Wilson and Alex Ramirez. He even managed to extract prospects from other teams after 1996, when every expensive Pirate was traded, most notably in the deal that sent Orlando Merced, Carlos Garcia, and Dan Plesac to Toronto for six players, two of whom (Abraham Nunez and Craig Wilson) will be on the Pirates' Opening Day roster this year.

Bonifay and his now-departed Director of Player Personnel Paul Tinnell also made good use of the tools that are crucial to every low-revenue baseball team. They signed minor-league free agents, including Todd Ritchie, Josias Manzanillo, and Ivan Cruz. They used the Rule 5 draft to grab Emil Brown, Scott Sauerbeck, Brian Smith, and the ill-fated Javier Martinez. They set up a relationship with the Mexico City Red Devils that netted them Rincon and Francisco Cordova. And Bonifay gained cost certainty by locking up many of his talented young players to multiyear contracts, including the deals that kept Jason Kendall and Jason Schmidt in Pittsburgh as they went through what ordinarily would have been expensive arbitration years.

It was Bonifay's work in these areas that helped him assemble the ragtag 1997 squad that came as close as any Bonifay team to making the playoffs or to reaching the .500 mark. Kevin Young, brought back to the organization as a minor-league free agent, posted an 867 OPS. Joe Randa, obtained in the Jay Bell/Jeff King dump, came in at 817. Rich Loiselle, acquired in a deadline deal the year before for Danny Darwin, saved 29 games and was the team's best right-handed reliever. Throw in a couple of developing youngsters and a no-name pitching staff built largely through the farm system, and you have The $9-Million Team That Could.

It all unraveled for Bonifay and the Pirates after the 1998 season, when owner Kevin McClatchy, no doubt pleased at the increased support fans had shown for the Pirates in '97 and '98 (up until their September collapse), loosened the purse strings so his GM could pursue free agents. Bonifay increased the payroll without improving the team, and at the same time he couldn't distinguish between fluke successes such as Kevin Young and bona fide talents such as Jon Lieber. Young received a four-year, $24-million extension that likely would have more than satisfied Lieber, who at the time had just two full seasons as a starting pitcher under his belt. With that much money committed to Young, Lieber had to go, so he was traded to Chicago for Brant Brown. Brown is now out of baseball entirely, while Lieber has become one of the game's true workhorses.

At the same time, the decisions made easy by the team's once-strained financial situation became harder when more expensive options cluttered the picture. Aramis Ramirez hit .300 with 34 homers in 2001, so why hadn't he been given an opportunity to play every day in 2000? Are we to believe that he wasn't ready? Pat Meares, non-tendered by the Twins in 1999, was brought in to play shortstop, then signed to an absurd contract extension. Could Abraham Nunez have been any worse than Meares?

The Derek Bell signing was probably the straw that broke Cam Bonifay's career, though. Bell's two-year, $9.5-million contract was the object of wide derision in the industry and in the press. Like Wil Cordero the year before, Bell got big money from the Pirates despite not receiving contract offers of comparable length or money from any other team—and no wonder. Aside from a freak April in 2000, when he hit over .400 with no more walks or power than usual, Bell had hit just .237/.315/.369 over the previous two seasons—unacceptable at any position and particularly obscene for a mediocre right fielder.

On June 11, Bonifay was let go and replaced by Dave Littlefield, who had studied with one of the game's yogi GMs, Florida's Dave Dombrowski. Littlefield has come in with a mandate and a vision, both of which will be necessary for him to succeed given the difficult straits in which the Pirates find themselves.

The Pirates currently have very little to work with on their 40-man roster. Of the 39 players left after the team made its first cuts in October, only 16 might be considered worthwhile uses of their roster slots: Jimmy Anderson, Bronson Arroyo, Joe Beimel, Kris Benson, Damaso Marte, Tony McKnight, Todd Ritchie, Ryan Vogelsong, Dave Williams, Humberto Cota, Jason Kendall, Jack Wilson, Craig Wilson, Warren Morris, Aramis Ramirez, and Brian Giles. That gives the team one outfielder and just six other hitters on the 40-man roster. While the farm system will provide a few new names to add to that list, it's too barren to fill even half of those 24 open slots.

This rough analysis highlights one problem that Littlefield must address: the Pirates' failure to develop skilled hitters. The Pirates haven't done a poor job in drafting, but they have mixed a tools-oriented draft approach with a skills-deficient development approach. Pirates prospects are not taught the strike zone, nor are they taught pitch recognition. Meanwhile, reports of players with poor work ethics are rampant, particularly among the system's top prospects. Chad Hermansen is the most glaring example of a gifted hitter who has not been taught the skills he needs to play in the majors, but Emil Brown, Freddy Garcia, Ron Wright, T.J. Staton, and apparently now J.J. Davis are all hitters who either didn't receive needed instruction or whose poor work habits were tolerated—or both. J.R. House is stagnating; Aron Weston's career is in jeopardy from injuries and impotence at the plate; Tony Alvarez looks like a new version of Tony Womack.

Littlefield has already demonstrated that he has a vision. As long as it's a decent one, he's way ahead of the GMs at drifting franchises such as the Devil Rays and Royals. He speaks of the need for efficiency in allocating the funds in the roster budget, and he identfied the long-term deals given to Young, Meares, and Bell as inefficient: the deals were not bad because they didn't work out, but bad because the salaries were disproportionate to the expected value of the players' performances. Those three albatrosses hang around Littlefield's neck, but with the money already spent and no face to save because they weren't his deals, he should be willing to cut all three this winter to make room on the 40-man roster. Doing so would free up playing time for players such as Jack Wilson, Craig Wilson, and Rico Washington, important parts of the Pirates' future.

Littlefield's other main developmental focus is on building with pitching, a model more or less successfully used by the White Sox and by Littlefield's former employers in the Everglades. The Pirates have a good stable of finesse pitchers in the low minors, but between injuries and the Double-A wall, the survival rate of such prospects is slim. Focusing on pitchers to the partial exclusion of hitter development is a high-risk, moderate-reward strategy; even the organizations best at pitcher development see injury problems among their pitchers, and the downside is enormous.

Another good sign for the Pirates under Littlefield is that he has been given the authority to clean house. Gone are Tinnell, Assistant GM John Sirignano, Director of Scouting Mickey White, roving infield instructor Bobby Meacham, and a host of other people from their baseball operations, some with significant tenure. There is, sadly, little room for sentiment when an organization has such a long track record of failure.

Turning this moribund franchise into even a modest contender will be a difficult task for Littlefield and his staff, but it can be made significantly easier with some early, bold strokes of the pen (or, in the cases of Young, Meares, and Bell, of the Liquid Paper brush). Littlefield's first moves have given Pirates fans a glimmer of hope; come the fall of 2003, we could be talking about the first meaningful September games in PNC Park.

HITTERS (BA: .270, OBP: .340, SLG: .440, EqA: .260)

Tony Alvarez LF Bats R Age 23

YEAR	TEAM	LGE	AB	H	DB	TP	HR	BB	SO	R	RBI	SB	CS	OUT	BA	OBP	SLG	EQA	EQR	DEFENSE
1999	Willmspt	NYP	202	49	9	0	5	13	40	24	28	14	6	159	.243	.307	.361	.231	20	33-3B -4
2000	Hickory	SAL	451	101	18	2	10	26	99	46	49	22	14	364	.224	.275	.339	.209	36	101-LF 0
2001	Lynchbrg	Car	96	27	2	0	2	6	11	8	9	4	2	71	.281	.324	.365	.235	9	18-LF -4
2001	Altoona	Eas	259	73	13	1	5	10	29	30	22	12	7	194	.282	.318	.398	.239	27	62-LF -2
2002	*Pittsbrg*	*NL*	*421*	*113*	*17*	*1*	*11*	*31*	*72*	*51*	*57*	*23*	*13*	*322*	*.268*	*.319*	*.392*	*.240*	*45*	

Exciting does not mean useful. Alvarez's talents are undeniable; he's fast, with a good slashing stroke at the plate, and he plays extremely hard. The Pirates have long been unable to convert toolsy prospects such as Alvarez into actual baseball players, resulting in seasons like Alvarez's 2001, in which he posted a composite OPS of 826, despite drawing just 16 walks in 370 plate appearances. Fixing him should be a top priority for the new Pirates front office.

Derek Bell RF Bats R Age 33

YEAR	TEAM	LGE	AB	H	DB	TP	HR	BB	SO	R	RBI	SB	CS	OUT	BA	OBP	SLG	EQA	EQR	DEFENSE
1999	Houston	NL	513	122	15	0	15	44	119	59	66	16	6	397	.238	.303	.355	.226	48	113-RF -13
2000	NY Mets	NL	553	150	28	1	20	58	115	87	69	8	4	407	.271	.346	.434	.261	71	127-RF -4
2001	Pittsbrg	NL	157	29	4	0	5	24	32	15	14	0	2	130	.185	.293	.306	.206	13	40-RF 0
2001	Nashvill	PCL	68	10	2	0	1	9	17	10	8	0	0	58	.147	.253	.221	.172	4	
2002	*Pittsbrg*	*NL*	*451*	*106*	*13*	*0*	*18*	*62*	*105*	*63*	*62*	*10*	*5*	*350*	*.235*	*.327*	*.384*	*.244*	*51*	

Talk about an organizational breakdown. Did no one in the Pittsburgh front office realize that this was a horrible signing? Perhaps Cam Bonifay didn't. But clearly John Sirignano didn't, and Paul Tinnell didn't and . . . well, that's why all three men are gone. Bell is a horrific waste of a roster spot, an offensive cipher, a defensive liability, a clubhouse cancer, and a fashion nightmare. This cost should be sunk in the Allegheny.

Josh Bonifay 2B Bats R Age 23

YEAR	TEAM	LGE	AB	H	DB	TP	HR	BB	SO	R	RBI	SB	CS	OUT	BA	OBP	SLG	EQA	EQR	DEFENSE
1999	Willmspt	NYP	208	40	5	1	3	15	61	28	10	1	1	169	.192	.249	.269	.180	12	37-2B -6
2000	Hickory	SAL	388	84	10	1	10	33	111	43	40	5	4	307	.216	.280	.325	.207	30	95-2B -11
2001	Hickory	SAL	67	16	1	0	2	4	16	7	7	1	2	53	.239	.286	.343	.207	5	
2001	Lynchbrg	Car	332	82	11	0	11	22	87	35	32	3	2	252	.247	.297	.380	.226	31	50-LF -4 11-2B -1
2002	*Pittsbrg*	*NL*	*378*	*96*	*12*	*1*	*13*	*36*	*109*	*63*	*36*	*6*	*4*	*287*	*.254*	*.319*	*.394*	*.240*	*41*	

Josh Bonifay has at least proven that he has the bat to be in professional baseball, unlike, say, Woody Woodward's son. The problem is that he is positionless, brutal at second base, and lacking the arm or the bat to play the outfield, so it's not clear how he could fit on a major-league roster. With Cam gone, the Pirates should free up some roster space and cut Josh loose.

Adrian Brown — CF — Bats B — Age 28

YEAR	TEAM	LGE	AB	H	DB	TP	HR	BB	SO	R	RBI	SB	CS	OUT	BA	OBP	SLG	EQA	EQR	DEFENSE
1999	Pittsbrg	NL	226	60	5	2	4	30	36	33	16	4	3	169	.265	.354	.358	.246	25	56-RF -3
1999	Nashvill	PCL	55	16	1	1	0	10	7	8	3	5	1	40	.291	.400	.345	.275	8	16-LF 0
2000	Pittsbrg	NL	309	96	18	3	4	25	31	62	27	12	1	214	.311	.362	.427	.272	41	75-CF -2
2001	Pittsbrg	NL	31	6	0	0	1	3	3	3	2	2	1	26	.194	.265	.290	.197	2	
2001	Altoona	Eas	31	9	0	1	0	1	7	6	1	1	1	23	.290	.313	.355	.222	3	
2002	*Pittsbrg*	*NL*	*287*	*80*	*13*	*3*	*4*	*37*	*40*	*50*	*22*	*12*	*2*	*209*	*.279*	*.361*	*.387*	*.264*	*37*	

Brown may have missed his chance. He started the season projected as the center fielder, but a bum shoulder affected his swing, and he ended up playing in just eight games before undergoing surgery that ended his season. Brown is helped by the Bucs not having a decent center fielder in the high minors, although they could continue to play Brian Giles in center and tap into their reserve of corner outfielders. As a fourth outfielder, Brown is recommended.

Humberto Cota — C — Bats R — Age 23

YEAR	TEAM	LGE	AB	H	DB	TP	HR	BB	SO	R	RBI	SB	CS	OUT	BA	OBP	SLG	EQA	EQR	DEFENSE
1999	Charl-SC	SAL	342	75	13	1	6	15	54	30	41	0	1	268	.219	.254	.316	.192	22	61-C -11
1999	Hickory	SAL	139	29	9	1	1	15	21	19	13	1	1	111	.209	.286	.309	.205	11	29-C -1
2000	Altoona	Eas	435	105	14	1	8	14	82	41	36	4	3	333	.241	.268	.333	.202	31	90-C -23
2001	Nashvill	PCL	376	104	19	1	12	23	67	52	61	6	2	274	.277	.327	.428	.252	44	85-C -7
2002	*Pittsbrg*	*NL*	*478*	*124*	*21*	*2*	*13*	*37*	*93*	*60*	*63*	*7*	*3*	*357*	*.259*	*.313*	*.393*	*.238*	*49*	

Cota returned from an injury-marred 2000 season to post his best numbers yet, boosted by health and the Pacific Coast League. He showed good pop at the plate and, most importantly, his best glove work as a pro, including some quality plate-blocking to go with his strong throwing arm. That said, he doesn't walk much, so he could use another half-season in Triple-A before becoming Jason Kendall's backup.

J.J. Davis — LF — Bats R — Age 23

YEAR	TEAM	LGE	AB	H	DB	TP	HR	BB	SO	R	RBI	SB	CS	OUT	BA	OBP	SLG	EQA	EQR	DEFENSE
1999	Hickory	SAL	329	68	14	1	12	32	105	39	41	1	3	264	.207	.280	.365	.215	28	45-RF -6
2000	Lynchbrg	Car	496	102	19	1	17	36	173	59	57	5	3	397	.206	.262	.351	.206	38	119-RF -13
2001	Altoona	Eas	234	53	12	2	3	20	77	20	22	2	3	184	.226	.291	.333	.211	19	57-RF -2
2002	*Pittsbrg*	*NL*	*431*	*104*	*22*	*2*	*14*	*49*	*155*	*57*	*55*	*6*	*5*	*332*	*.241*	*.319*	*.399*	*.242*	*48*	

The Pirates' top draft pick from '97 continued his descent into prospect oblivion, this time by announcing (and showing) that he doesn't enjoy hitting or playing the outfield any more and wants to return to pitching. The Pirates haven't decided if they want to move him to the mound; given that he has yet to have a good offensive season in the minors, there's little to be lost if they do.

Brian Giles — LF/CF — Bats L — Age 31

YEAR	TEAM	LGE	AB	H	DB	TP	HR	BB	SO	R	RBI	SB	CS	OUT	BA	OBP	SLG	EQA	EQR	DEFENSE
1999	Pittsbrg	NL	520	161	32	3	38	88	74	106	107	5	2	361	.310	.412	.602	.325	109	138-CF -3
2000	Pittsbrg	NL	560	174	38	6	34	106	63	108	115	6	0	386	.311	.426	.582	.329	120	153-OF 2
2001	Pittsbrg	NL	578	184	38	8	37	86	57	120	97	13	6	400	.318	.409	.604	.324	119	160-LF -10
2002	*Pittsbrg*	*NL*	*558*	*173*	*35*	*6*	*34*	*99*	*64*	*110*	*106*	*9*	*3*	*388*	*.310*	*.414*	*.577*	*.324*	*116*	

It was a slight off-year for the Pirates' offensive anchor, but a return to form by Kendall and another step up by Aramis Ramirez should boost Giles's counting stats in '02. Giles is the anti-Pirate: patient, deliberate, powerful, good. Now that John Hart is the GM in Texas, Littlefield should put his new office number in the first speed-dial slot on his phone. Joe Beimel might fetch the Pirates another star.

Kevin Haverbusch LF Bats R Age 26

YEAR	TEAM	LGE	AB	H	DB	TP	HR	BB	SO	R	RBI	SB	CS	OUT	BA	OBP	SLG	EQA	EQR	DEFENSE
1999	Altoona	Eas	335	88	18	1	12	7	60	47	48	4	3	250	.263	.300	.430	.239	35	79-3B -20
2000	Altoona	Eas	143	36	3	0	5	8	15	19	17	1	1	108	.252	.297	.378	.225	13	30-3B -10
2001	Altoona	Eas	155	37	9	1	2	6	22	16	17	1	1	119	.239	.272	.348	.207	12	22-2B -2
2001	Nashvill	PCL	146	45	6	1	6	4	31	20	25	3	1	102	.308	.344	.486	.273	20	20-LF -1
2002	*Pittsbrg*	*NL*	*294*	*81*	*13*	*2*	*10*	*15*	*53*	*43*	*40*	*6*	*2*	*215*	*.276*	*.311*	*.435*	*.249*	*33*	

Haverbusch is an extreme example of the type of hitter Cam Bonifay drafted, sort of like the sauce you'd get if you pan-seared J.J. Davis and deglazed the pan with Alex Hernandez. He has a quick bat and no other baseball abilities of note. He's drawn 67 walks in five years in the minors, and his arm is so erratic that he's been moved to left field. Sometimes, those brown bits at the bottom of the pan just aren't worth saving.

Chad Hermansen CF Bats R Age 24

YEAR	TEAM	LGE	AB	H	DB	TP	HR	BB	SO	R	RBI	SB	CS	OUT	BA	OBP	SLG	EQA	EQR	DEFENSE
1999	Nashvill	PCL	491	120	22	1	26	29	109	70	75	15	8	379	.244	.290	.452	.242	55	117-CF 2
1999	Pittsbrg	NL	60	14	2	0	1	6	18	5	3	2	2	48	.233	.313	.317	.216	5	14-OF -1
2000	Pittsbrg	NL	109	20	4	1	2	5	34	12	8	0	0	89	.183	.219	.294	.173	6	23-CF -3
2000	Nashvill	PCL	295	62	9	1	10	19	86	38	31	12	3	236	.210	.273	.349	.215	25	74-OF -2
2001	Nashvill	PCL	447	102	21	4	14	38	140	64	53	18	5	350	.228	.293	.387	.232	45	115-OF 2
2001	Pittsbrg	NL	55	10	1	0	2	1	15	5	5	0	1	46	.182	.196	.309	.163	2	14-RF 1
2002	*Pittsbrg*	*NL*	*530*	*129*	*22*	*3*	*22*	*49*	*167*	*80*	*69*	*22*	*6*	*406*	*.243*	*.307*	*.421*	*.247*	*62*	

He's still operating on the same code: If (strike=true) (Swing[ball];) Else (Swing Anyway[ball];). Until Hermansen is taught to identify a breaking ball, he's not going to develop at all as a hitter. He's a great defensive center fielder with good tools. Out of options, he has to make the 25-man roster or hit the road, but learning in the majors will be difficult for a player who hasn't mastered Triple-A. If the A's grab him, he'll be an All-Star in two years.

Alex Hernandez 1B Bats L Age 25

YEAR	TEAM	LGE	AB	H	DB	TP	HR	BB	SO	R	RBI	SB	CS	OUT	BA	OBP	SLG	EQA	EQR	DEFENSE
1999	Altoona	Eas	485	112	24	2	12	40	110	64	50	7	5	378	.231	.291	.363	.220	43	103-RF -5
2000	Altoona	Eas	202	61	12	1	4	9	43	24	27	1	1	142	.302	.332	.431	.252	23	39-CF -3
2000	Nashvill	PCL	275	70	16	1	7	7	58	24	29	4	2	207	.255	.275	.396	.221	24	43-1B -2 23-RF 0
2000	Pittsbrg	NL	60	12	2	0	1	0	12	4	5	1	1	49	.200	.200	.283	.161	3	12-1B -2
2001	Nashvill	PCL	340	92	12	1	7	13	59	39	31	3	3	251	.271	.303	.374	.225	30	46-1B -7 34-RF -2
2002	*Cincnnti*	*NL*	*481*	*133*	*22*	*2*	*13*	*33*	*101*	*62*	*54*	*6*	*3*	*351*	*.277*	*.323*	*.412*	*.245*	*52*	

Hernandez was outrighted off the 40-man roster in October, in a sure sign that things will be different under Dave Littlefield. The Pirates gave him plenty of chances, but despite good tools, he hasn't shown any inclination to work on developing skills, of which he has none. Haverbusch and Davis should view Hernandez's release as fair warning that they need to get their acts together. Hernandez signed a minor-league deal with the Reds in October.

J.R. House C Bats R Age 22

YEAR	TEAM	LGE	AB	H	DB	TP	HR	BB	SO	R	RBI	SB	CS	OUT	BA	OBP	SLG	EQA	EQR	DEFENSE
1999	Willmspt	NYP	103	22	3	0	1	5	23	8	8	0	0	81	.214	.250	.272	.179	5	14-C -1
2000	Hickory	SAL	430	113	16	1	15	31	97	54	55	0	1	318	.263	.316	.409	.241	45	77-C -15
2001	Altoona	Eas	437	104	20	1	10	35	100	48	50	1	1	334	.238	.299	.357	.222	39	88-C -14 11-1B -1
2002	*Pittsbrg*	*NL*	*412*	*115*	*17*	*1*	*14*	*37*	*101*	*52*	*54*	*1*	*1*	*298*	*.279*	*.339*	*.427*	*.258*	*50*	

In the midst of his worst season as a pro baseball player, the golden boy decided not to play football at West Virginia after all. Part of the problem was the jump from low-A ball to a Double-A park and league that are very pitcher-friendly, but the evaporation of his plate discipline is a concern. On the plus side, his plate-blocking improved significantly, and it's possible that the Pirates might break a long stretch of failing to develop a good defensive catcher.

Adam Hyzdu RF Bats R Age 30

YEAR	TEAM	LGE	AB	H	DB	TP	HR	BB	SO	R	RBI	SB	CS	OUT	BA	OBP	SLG	EQA	EQR	DEFENSE			
1999	Pawtuckt	Int	35	8	0	0	1	3	12	4	5	0	0	27	.229	.289	.314	.207	3				
1999	Altoona	Eas	352	99	22	1	19	29	62	52	59	5	3	256	.281	.339	.511	.275	51	58-LF	-5	18-1B	-1
1999	Nashvill	PCL	44	10	1	0	4	3	10	5	10	0	0	34	.227	.277	.523	.253	5	12-RF	2		
2000	Altoona	Eas	531	138	27	1	20	75	105	78	83	2	5	390	.260	.350	.473	.272	77	135-OF	-3		
2000	Pittsbrg	NL	18	7	1	0	1	0	4	2	4	0	0	11	.389	.389	.611	.320	3				
2001	Nashvill	PCL	260	69	16	1	9	16	62	33	32	1	2	193	.265	.308	.438	.244	28	58-RF	7		
2001	Pittsbrg	NL	72	16	1	0	5	4	15	7	9	0	1	57	.222	.270	.444	.228	7	14-RF	-1		
2002	*Pittsbrg*	*NL*	*467*	*127*	*22*	*1*	*24*	*52*	*107*	*66*	*73*	*2*	*3*	*343*	*.272*	*.345*	*.478*	*.272*	*66*				

Hyzdu didn't really do enough in his first extended big-league opportunity to give himself a shot at a significant pension, although his five home runs may get him a return engagement with the Pirates anyway. One would hope that some major-league teams noticed that Hyzdu wasn't overmatched by major-league pitchers. Still, Hyzdu is more of a Quadruple-A hitter; then again, so is Derek Bell, and you see what that got him.

Jason Kendall C/LF Bats R Age 28

YEAR	TEAM	LGE	AB	H	DB	TP	HR	BB	SO	R	RBI	SB	CS	OUT	BA	OBP	SLG	EQA	EQR	DEFENSE			
1999	Pittsbrg	NL	280	92	20	3	8	34	30	58	39	19	3	191	.329	.423	.507	.317	54	74-C	7		
2000	Pittsbrg	NL	581	182	32	5	14	71	72	106	54	20	12	411	.313	.400	.458	.289	92	145-C	-1		
2001	Pittsbrg	NL	608	169	23	2	10	41	41	87	55	13	14	453	.278	.339	.372	.239	63	125-C	-5	26-LF	-5
2002	*Pittsbrg*	*NL*	*564*	*166*	*28*	*3*	*14*	*57*	*53*	*94*	*61*	*22*	*12*	*410*	*.294*	*.359*	*.429*	*.267*	*76*				

Kendall played the whole year with a bum thumb and easily had his worst year in the majors. He had surgery to correct the problem in October and should be fine for spring training. This was his age 27 year, so don't be surprised if he rebounds and has a performance spike all at once. The left-field experiment is over.

Rob Mackowiak UT Bats L Age 26

YEAR	TEAM	LGE	AB	H	DB	TP	HR	BB	SO	R	RBI	SB	CS	OUT	BA	OBP	SLG	EQA	EQR	DEFENSE			
1999	Lynchbrg	Car	266	67	6	2	6	12	57	38	21	5	3	202	.252	.292	.357	.219	23	58-2B	-2		
1999	Altoona	Eas	197	47	12	2	3	5	34	18	22	0	1	151	.239	.272	.365	.210	15	52-2B	-3		
2000	Altoona	Eas	532	144	28	2	13	15	99	68	70	12	4	392	.271	.297	.404	.234	52	69-2B	-4	33-RF	-3
2001	Nashvill	PCL	118	29	2	0	4	6	35	12	12	1	1	90	.246	.282	.364	.215	10	13-RF	-1	10-2B	0
2001	Pittsbrg	NL	215	60	15	2	4	14	44	31	22	4	3	158	.279	.330	.423	.250	25	35-RF	1	17-2B	-1
2002	*Pittsbrg*	*NL*	*440*	*120*	*23*	*2*	*12*	*27*	*101*	*61*	*51*	*8*	*5*	*325*	*.273*	*.315*	*.416*	*.244*	*48*				

The Pirates' inability to tell the difference between Mackowiak and a real baseball player is very disturbing. Lloyd McClendon's willingness to play him in the outfield is terrifying, especially since Mackowiak isn't an asset defensively, either. He gets the uniform dirty, low walk totals be damned. Rico Washington deserves this roster spot, and Tony Alvarez has some claim to it as well.

Gary Matthews CF Bats B Age 27

YEAR	TEAM	LGE	AB	H	DB	TP	HR	BB	SO	R	RBI	SB	CS	OUT	BA	OBP	SLG	EQA	EQR	DEFENSE	
1999	LasVegas	PCL	415	90	18	2	7	49	95	43	39	12	5	330	.217	.307	.320	.220	37	120-CF	-3
1999	San Dieg	NL	36	8	0	0	0	9	8	4	4	2	0	28	.222	.378	.222	.239	4	10-RF	0
2000	Iowa	PCL	211	47	9	2	5	14	40	22	18	4	1	165	.223	.271	.355	.212	17	57-CF	-2
2000	ChiCubs	NL	159	30	2	2	4	13	26	24	14	3	0	129	.189	.254	.302	.194	11	39-LF	1
2001	ChiCubs	NL	259	59	9	2	9	37	47	43	31	5	3	203	.228	.326	.382	.241	29	77-CF	-5
2001	Pittsbrg	NL	147	37	6	1	5	22	38	23	14	3	2	112	.252	.349	.408	.256	19	42-CF	-1
2002	*NY Mets*	*NL*	*425*	*101*	*17*	*3*	*12*	*56*	*94*	*57*	*47*	*12*	*3*	*327*	*.238*	*.326*	*.376*	*.249*	*50*		

You know you're old when the children of the guys you rooted for as a child are now major leaguers. (You're Jeff Bower old when their grandchildren are retiring.) Matthews only got to play because the Pirates outfield was hit by injuries, and he just had his age-27 peak; if you missed it, you can be forgiven. *Mama's Family* was probably on TBS or something. Matthews was sold to the Mets and projects as their fourth outfielder, and he could work his way into a platoon with Jay Payton or Benny Agbayani.

Nathan McLouth CF Bats L Age 20

YEAR	TEAM	LGE	AB	H	DB	TP	HR	BB	SO	R	RBI	SB	CS	OUT	BA	OBP	SLG	EQA	EQR	DEFENSE
2001	Hickory	SAL	368	83	16	2	8	32	57	42	37	9	4	289	.226	.293	.345	.218	32	93-CF -8
2002	*Pittsbrg*	*NL*	*401*	*96*	*15*	*2*	*10*	*48*	*66*	*50*	*42*	*16*	*4*	*309*	*.239*	*.321*	*.362*	*.238*	*43*	

McLouth and Rule 5 refugee Yurendell Decaster were the only hitting prospects of any merit to see time at Hickory this year, and neither projects as a starter at this point. McLouth played a good center field in his first year at the position and led the Crawdads in OBP in his first pro season. The Pirates bought him away from a baseball scholarship at Michigan, so he'll get extra chances.

Pat Meares 2B/SS Bats R Age 33

YEAR	TEAM	LGE	AB	H	DB	TP	HR	BB	SO	R	RBI	SB	CS	OUT	BA	OBP	SLG	EQA	EQR	DEFENSE
1999	Pittsbrg	NL	91	28	3	0	0	8	19	14	6	0	0	63	.308	.376	.341	.251	10	19-SS 0
2000	Pittsbrg	NL	465	112	21	2	13	30	83	53	45	1	0	353	.241	.297	.378	.227	43	119-SS -3
2001	Pittsbrg	NL	271	61	12	1	4	9	38	29	26	0	2	212	.225	.254	.321	.191	17	69-2B 0
2002	*Pittsbrg*	*NL*	*391*	*90*	*15*	*1*	*10*	*29*	*68*	*57*	*33*	*1*	*1*	*302*	*.230*	*.283*	*.350*	*.211*	*31*	

If Meares didn't have that four-year contract, he'd have been lucky to be on the Pirates' roster in 2001, let alone in the mix for a starting role. Meares has hit .238/.293/.352 since joining the Pirates, which is Rey Ordonez territory. The middle infield will be one of Dave Littlefield's best chances to make a clean break with the recent past, and sending Meares up the Monongahela should be on his to-do list.

Dan Meier RF/1B Bats L Age 24

YEAR	TEAM	LGE	AB	H	DB	TP	HR	BB	SO	R	RBI	SB	CS	OUT	BA	OBP	SLG	EQA	EQR	DEFENSE
1999	High Des	Cal	411	80	16	2	14	48	140	51	48	0	0	331	.195	.285	.345	.215	35	95-1B 2
2000	High Des	Cal	30	6	1	0	1	5	8	4	2	0	0	24	.200	.314	.333	.225	3	
2000	El Paso	Tex	62	10	1	1	1	1	25	5	4	0	1	53	.161	.175	.258	.142	2	14-1B 1
2000	Lynchbrg	Car	207	52	6	1	11	21	47	34	29	1	1	156	.251	.330	.449	.257	26	33-1B 0
2001	Lynchbrg	Car	76	18	3	0	3	8	21	9	10	1	1	59	.237	.310	.395	.234	8	
2001	Altoona	Eas	325	77	13	3	11	40	78	40	34	1	1	249	.237	.324	.397	.243	36	47-RF -4 27-1B 0
2002	*Pittsbrg*	*NL*	*434*	*106*	*18*	*3*	*18*	*54*	*124*	*64*	*57*	*1*	*1*	*329*	*.244*	*.328*	*.424*	*.253*	*53*	

The Pirates gave Meier what arguably would have been his last chance as a pro in 2000, and he's managed to make himself into a viable fifth-outfielder/pinch-hitter candidate for a major-league team. He showed good power in a tough power park, draws plenty of walks, and is an adequate right fielder. The old Pirates might have signed a free agent to fill that role; the new Pirates could just put Meier into it by midyear.

Warren Morris 2B Bats L Age 28

YEAR	TEAM	LGE	AB	H	DB	TP	HR	BB	SO	R	RBI	SB	CS	OUT	BA	OBP	SLG	EQA	EQR	DEFENSE
1999	Pittsbrg	NL	512	144	20	3	15	52	81	63	69	2	7	375	.281	.350	.420	.255	62	136-2B -7
2000	Pittsbrg	NL	531	135	31	2	3	58	72	65	41	6	10	406	.254	.330	.337	.227	50	130-2B -4
2001	Nashvill	PCL	222	62	15	1	4	11	19	23	33	3	3	163	.279	.317	.410	.240	23	46-2B -1
2001	Pittsbrg	NL	103	22	3	0	3	3	8	6	12	2	3	84	.214	.247	.330	.190	7	22-2B -1
2002	*Pittsbrg*	*NL*	*473*	*124*	*22*	*2*	*9*	*52*	*59*	*56*	*52*	*8*	*9*	*358*	*.262*	*.335*	*.374*	*.240*	*51*	

He needs a change of scenery or, better yet, a change of manager. Morris no longer even remotely resembles the hitter he was in '99; his 2000 numbers weren't a complete disaster, but the loss of his job plus the Pirates' questionable hitting instruction now have Morris swinging at everything, often for the fences, in the hopes that a hot week will make him McClendon's new best friend. When your players are pressing to endear themselves to your fickle manager, getting rid of the players is not the answer.

Abraham Nunez SS Bats B Age 26

YEAR	TEAM	LGE	AB	H	DB	TP	HR	BB	SO	R	RBI	SB	CS	OUT	BA	OBP	SLG	EQA	EQR	DEFENSE
1999	Nashvill	PCL	57	16	0	0	0	4	7	10	2	1	0	41	.281	.328	.281	.217	4	15-SS -3
1999	Pittsbrg	NL	260	57	8	0	0	25	50	24	16	8	1	204	.219	.290	.250	.197	18	55-SS -5 13-2B 2
2000	Nashvill	PCL	351	90	9	1	3	28	44	40	24	15	4	265	.256	.313	.313	.221	31	78-SS 0
2000	Pittsbrg	NL	92	21	1	0	1	6	13	10	8	0	0	71	.228	.276	.272	.190	6	18-SS -2
2001	Pittsbrg	NL	302	83	12	4	1	26	45	31	22	8	2	221	.275	.334	.351	.238	30	39-2B -5 37-SS 4
2002	*Pittsbrg*	*NL*	*376*	*101*	*12*	*2*	*3*	*37*	*59*	*49*	*29*	*16*	*3*	*278*	*.269*	*.334*	*.335*	*.238*	*38*	

Nunez came to the Pirates in the same salary dump that brought in Craig Wilson, and since little of value was surrendered, you can already say the Bucs got a good deal. Nunez was expected to be more than he's been to date: a guy who draws a few walks, plays inconsistently good defense, and has no power. Nunez can sting the ball into the gaps, so a little more patience might make him a major-league ballplayer.

Keith Osik C Bats R Age 33

YEAR	TEAM	LGE	AB	H	DB	TP	HR	BB	SO	R	RBI	SB	CS	OUT	BA	OBP	SLG	EQA	EQR	DEFENSE
1999	Nashvill	PCL	11	1	0	0	0	0	1	0	0	0	0	10	.091	.144	.091	.088	0	
1999	Pittsbrg	NL	168	31	3	1	2	9	28	12	12	0	0	137	.185	.230	.250	.167	8	42-C 2
2000	Pittsbrg	NL	124	36	6	1	4	12	10	11	21	3	0	88	.290	.373	.452	.281	18	18-C -1 10-3B -3
2001	Pittsbrg	NL	120	26	2	0	3	13	20	9	15	1	0	94	.217	.305	.308	.215	10	30-C -1
2002	*Pittsbrg*	*NL*	*157*	*35*	*4*	*1*	*5*	*19*	*24*	*15*	*19*	*3*	*0*	*122*	*.223*	*.307*	*.357*	*.230*	*15*	

A few years ago, Cam Bonifay needed a backup catcher for emerging star Jason Kendall. He went down to the five-and-dime—usually the best place to get a backup catcher—stuck a nickel in a vending machine, and out came Osik. That vending-machine backup catcher is kind of worn, and he's getting in the way of actual prospects, so it's time to get rid of him. If the prospects don't work out, there's always another nickel.

Aramis Ramirez 3B Bats R Age 24

YEAR	TEAM	LGE	AB	H	DB	TP	HR	BB	SO	R	RBI	SB	CS	OUT	BA	OBP	SLG	EQA	EQR	DEFENSE
1999	Nashvill	PCL	455	133	23	1	18	61	51	72	58	4	2	324	.292	.383	.466	.285	70	122-3B -15
1999	Pittsbrg	NL	56	10	1	1	0	6	8	2	6	0	0	46	.179	.258	.232	.175	3	16-3B -4
2000	Pittsbrg	NL	256	65	15	2	6	7	33	19	34	0	0	191	.254	.286	.398	.226	23	56-3B -7
2000	Nashvill	PCL	166	54	10	1	4	8	25	22	21	1	1	113	.325	.367	.470	.277	23	42-3B -4
2001	Pittsbrg	NL	605	188	34	0	37	37	85	86	117	5	4	421	.311	.357	.550	.291	96	155-3B -6
2002	*Pittsbrg*	*NL*	*530*	*167*	*27*	*2*	*26*	*49*	*77*	*77*	*86*	*6*	*3*	*366*	*.315*	*.373*	*.521*	*.295*	*86*	

They finally had no choice but to let him play, probably because Ed Sprague's agent doesn't have call waiting. Ramirez's season offered just a taste of his skills; he drew far more walks in the minors, so if the Pirates haven't ruined his batting eye, he could be the second-best third baseman in the league very shortly. And he's just 24 years old. Littlefield's first long-term contract discussion should be with Ramirez's agent; let's hope he does have call waiting.

Julian "Tike" Redman OF Bats L Age 25

YEAR	TEAM	LGE	AB	H	DB	TP	HR	BB	SO	R	RBI	SB	CS	OUT	BA	OBP	SLG	EQA	EQR	DEFENSE
1999	Altoona	Eas	542	132	19	8	3	38	52	68	49	18	11	421	.244	.295	.325	.213	44	133-CF 1
2000	Nashvill	PCL	506	121	23	7	4	23	71	49	40	17	14	399	.239	.275	.336	.205	38	119-CF -5
2001	Nashvill	PCL	396	110	18	8	2	23	34	45	35	17	6	292	.278	.322	.379	.239	41	94-CF 5
2001	Pittsbrg	NL	125	29	4	1	1	4	21	8	5	3	5	101	.232	.256	.304	.184	7	35-CF 6
2002	*Pittsbrg*	*NL*	*478*	*130*	*19*	*7*	*5*	*37*	*60*	*64*	*45*	*21*	*11*	*359*	*.272*	*.324*	*.372*	*.238*	*50*	

He's running out of chances, especially in the New Era of Accountability. Redman is fast, but like Haverbusch's swing, speed alone won't get you out of Triple-A. He might be useful if he drew 100 walks a year instead of 100 walks a decade. If the Pirates are looking for another outfielder from their system, Ryan Radmanovich (who drew 70 walks on the season, 22 more than any other Sounds hitter) would be a better choice.

Armando Rios RF Bats L Age 30

YEAR	TEAM	LGE	AB	H	DB	TP	HR	BB	SO	R	RBI	SB	CS	OUT	BA	OBP	SLG	EQA	EQR	DEFENSE	
1999	Fresno	PCL	107	26	3	0	3	9	20	18	16	2	1	82	.243	.318	.355	.230	10	18-OF -1	
1999	San Fran	NL	151	49	6	0	8	23	32	31	28	6	4	106	.325	.417	.523	.308	28	38-RF 2	
2000	San Fran	NL	237	66	14	5	11	28	39	39	51	3	2	173	.278	.355	.519	.283	37	58-RF 2	
2001	San Fran	NL	320	89	17	3	15	33	62	41	52	3	2	233	.278	.346	.491	.274	46	78-RF 7	
2002	*Pittsbrg*	*NL*	*297*	*84*	*16*	*3*	*13*	*36*	*60*	*52*	*54*	*6*	*3*	*216*	*.283*	*.360*	*.488*	*.282*	*46*		

One can only wish Littlefield better karma in future trades, as Rios blew out his ACL in his second game with the Pirates. Rios is often viewed as an up-and-coming hitter, but he's already 30 years old and not likely to get much better. His combination of a little patience and 20-homer pop will be neat until he gets expensive, which will happen in 2003. Disregard that projection; Rios will miss most, if not all, of 2002.

Rico Washington 3B/C Bats L Age 24

YEAR	TEAM	LGE	AB	H	DB	TP	HR	BB	SO	R	RBI	SB	CS	OUT	BA	OBP	SLG	EQA	EQR	DEFENSE	
1999	Hickory	SAL	300	80	10	1	8	35	48	48	32	2	1	221	.267	.350	.387	.252	35	54-C -19	
1999	Lynchbrg	Car	211	50	4	0	6	21	45	23	23	2	1	162	.237	.312	.341	.225	19	31-3B 0	13-C -3
2000	Altoona	Eas	515	121	21	4	8	42	76	63	48	3	6	400	.235	.296	.338	.214	42	73-3B -2	61-2B -10
2001	Altoona	Eas	299	82	10	0	5	20	48	28	27	4	3	221	.274	.326	.358	.232	29	49-3B 0	21-2B -7
2002	*Pittsbrg*	*NL*	*460*	*124*	*16*	*2*	*12*	*47*	*79*	*65*	*51*	*7*	*6*	*342*	*.270*	*.337*	*.391*	*.247*	*52*		

Washington is a solid prospect who got off to a great start in 2001, leading the Eastern League in batting average until he suffered a Nick Johnson-esque hand injury in late May that cost him more than 60 games. Washington is adequate defensively at second base and catcher and can play third base and left field if needed; add Washington to Craig Wilson, mix, and you can trade Keith Osik to the Royals.

Craig Wilson 1B/C Bats R Age 25

YEAR	TEAM	LGE	AB	H	DB	TP	HR	BB	SO	R	RBI	SB	CS	OUT	BA	OBP	SLG	EQA	EQR	DEFENSE	
1999	Altoona	Eas	370	91	19	2	16	29	104	48	54	1	2	281	.246	.319	.438	.249	44	33-C -10	13-1B -4
2000	Nashvill	PCL	396	104	20	1	28	35	117	67	67	1	1	293	.263	.350	.530	.284	63	66-C -5	28-1B 0
2001	Nashvill	PCL	45	12	1	1	1	2	13	3	3	0	0	33	.267	.307	.400	.235	4		
2001	Pittsbrg	NL	158	51	3	1	13	15	45	28	32	3	1	108	.323	.400	.601	.320	31	18-1B 0	10-RF -1
2002	*Pittsbrg*	*NL*	*360*	*105*	*16*	*2*	*22*	*38*	*112*	*58*	*63*	*3*	*1*	*256*	*.292*	*.359*	*.531*	*.291*	*59*		

He can hit a little; only Brian Giles had a higher OPS among Pirates hitters in 2001. Wilson's not useless in the field, although McClendon has yet to really realize it. Wilson should be the team's regular first baseman and backup catcher. He'll never be more than a Three True Outcomes hitter, but so what? If he plays every day, he'll crush 30 homers and be the team's best-hitting first baseman of the last 20 years.

Jack Wilson SS Bats R Age 24

YEAR	TEAM	LGE	AB	H	DB	TP	HR	BB	SO	R	RBI	SB	CS	OUT	BA	OBP	SLG	EQA	EQR	DEFENSE
1999	Peoria	Mid	251	67	15	2	2	7	25	29	17	5	3	187	.267	.289	.367	.219	21	64-SS -10
1999	Potomac	Car	261	65	6	1	2	12	31	33	13	4	3	199	.249	.283	.303	.200	18	63-SS -1
2000	Potomac	Car	48	11	0	1	1	4	10	5	4	1	2	39	.229	.288	.333	.205	4	13-SS -1
2000	Altoona	Eas	142	32	8	1	1	11	18	15	13	1	2	112	.225	.286	.317	.204	11	29-SS 0
2000	Arkansas	Tex	345	88	19	5	5	24	59	51	25	1	2	259	.255	.309	.383	.231	33	88-SS 6
2001	Pittsbrg	NL	391	92	18	1	3	14	59	47	26	1	3	302	.235	.263	.309	.192	25	97-SS 2
2001	Nashvill	PCL	103	35	4	1	1	8	12	17	6	2	2	70	.340	.394	.427	.277	14	23-SS 3
2002	*Pittsbrg*	*NL*	*492*	*133*	*25*	*3*	*6*	*34*	*76*	*69*	*35*	*6*	*5*	*363*	*.270*	*.317*	*.370*	*.232*	*47*	

He didn't belong in the majors the first time, and despite a hot month after he returned from Triple-A, it's debatable whether rushing him back was the right move. Wilson has the glove to be a great major-league shortstop, and while his bat has promise, it doesn't promise to hit the ball much in the near future. Wilson's outlook would improve dramatically if he gained some patience; maybe they should handcuff him to Brian Giles for three months.

Kevin Young 1B Bats R Age 33

YEAR	TEAM	LGE	AB	H	DB	TP	HR	BB	SO	R	RBI	SB	CS	OUT	BA	OBP	SLG	EQA	EQR	DEFENSE
1999	Pittsbrg	NL	584	170	40	5	26	68	115	98	99	18	10	424	.291	.376	.510	.290	96	153-1B -6
2000	Pittsbrg	NL	500	129	21	1	21	25	88	74	86	8	3	374	.258	.303	.430	.242	54	119-1B -16
2001	Pittsbrg	NL	450	109	25	0	17	40	101	54	69	15	11	352	.242	.316	.411	.241	50	119-1B 4
2002	*Pittsbrg*	*NL*	*542*	*133*	*26*	*2*	*22*	*54*	*120*	*78*	*82*	*16*	*10*	*419*	*.245*	*.314*	*.423*	*.240*	*63*	

The heart and soul of this dysfunctional franchise. Young had one superficially good year, one actually good year, and got a four-year contract that was dumped on the coffin of Cam Bonifay's career with those of Meares and Bell. Young has two more years on his contract, $8 million owed to him, and no value to anyone because he's a no-power, never-walkin', error-makin' first baseman. Oops.

Walter Young 1B Bats L Age 22

YEAR	TEAM	LGE	AB	H	DB	TP	HR	BB	SO	R	RBI	SB	CS	OUT	BA	OBP	SLG	EQA	EQR	DEFENSE
2000	Willmspt	NYP	93	14	1	0	2	0	30	3	8	0	0	79	.151	.154	.226	.128	2	18-1B -5
2001	Willmspt	NYP	239	53	4	0	9	13	51	27	29	1	1	187	.222	.268	.351	.207	18	44-1B -3
2002	*Pittsbrg*	*NL*	*254*	*62*	*6*	*0*	*10*	*18*	*63*	*24*	*32*	*1*	*1*	*193*	*.244*	*.294*	*.386*	*.226*	*24*	

A giant among the twerps of the New York-Penn League, Young turned down a football scholarship at LSU. Three years into his baseball career, he still hasn't played in a full-season league. He showed some growth as a hitter in 2001, doubling his walk rate to a still-low once per 13.5 plate appearances and tying for the league lead in homers. He continues to have trouble with breaking pitches and needs to control his weight. A project.

PITCHERS (ERA: 4.50, H/9: 9.0, HR/9: 1.0, BB/9: 3.0, K/9: 6.0, KW: 2.0, PERA: 4.50)

Carlos Alvarado Throws R Age 24

YEAR	TEAM	LGE	IP	H	ER	HR	BB	K	ERA	W	L	H/9	HR/9	BB/9	K/9	KW	PERA	STUFF
1999	Lynchbrg	Car	91.3	96	54	8	50	44	5.32	4	6	9.5	0.8	4.9	4.3	0.4	6.24	-6
2000	Lynchbrg	Car	49.7	53	31	4	29	21	5.62	2	4	9.6	0.7	5.3	3.8	0.4	7.05	-19
2000	Altoona	Eas	31.3	32	20	4	19	20	5.74	1	2	9.2	1.1	5.5	5.7	0.5	5.70	-10
2001	Lynchbrg	Car	10.3	10	7	0	11	4	6.10	0	1	8.7	0.0	9.6	3.5	0.2	6.28	-38
2001	Altoona	Eas	80.7	84	48	9	38	46	5.36	4	5	9.4	1.0	4.2	5.1	0.6	6.91	-11

Sleeper. Alvarado had an undistinguished career as a starter through mid-2000 and scuffled as a reliever in Altoona after that. In the spring of 2001, he showed up with a better curve and a much better change-up, did well as a reliever, then was Altoona's best starter in the second half of the year. He's a six-year free agent and could be a great middle reliever for someone in 2002.

Jimmy Anderson Throws L Age 26

YEAR	TEAM	LGE	IP	H	ER	HR	BB	K	ERA	W	L	H/9	HR/9	BB/9	K/9	KW	PERA	STUFF
1999	Nashvill	PCL	141.3	140	58	5	42	70	3.69	10	6	8.9	0.3	2.7	4.5	0.8	4.37	8
1999	Pittsbrg	NL	28.0	30	15	2	13	12	4.82	1	2	9.6	0.6	4.2	3.9	0.5	4.17	-13
2000	Pittsbrg	NL	150.7	159	74	12	48	65	4.42	9	8	9.5	0.7	2.9	3.9	0.7	5.33	-2
2001	Pittsbrg	NL	200.7	215	102	13	74	72	4.57	11	11	9.6	0.6	3.3	3.2	0.5	5.34	-6

Credit where it's due: the Pirates have stuck with Anderson well beyond any reasonable analysis of his performance dictated, and their persistence has paid off. Anderson lives by keeping the ball down, inducing ground ball after ground ball. That's not a good strategy with the Bucs' current infield, but there's a hint of a young Jamie Moyer here, and the defense has to improve eventually.

Bronson Arroyo Throws R Age 25

YEAR	TEAM	LGE	IP	H	ER	HR	BB	K	ERA	W	L	H/9	HR/9	BB/9	K/9	KW	PERA	STUFF
1999	Altoona	Eas	154.7	172	97	22	58	70	5.64	7	10	10.0	1.3	3.4	4.1	0.6	5.15	-1
1999	Nashvill	PCL	15.7	16	9	1	10	8	5.17	1	1	9.2	0.6	5.7	4.6	0.4	10.07	-10
2000	Nashvill	PCL	86.7	92	43	9	24	42	4.47	5	5	9.6	0.9	2.5	4.4	0.9	4.38	4
2000	Pittsbrg	NL	76.3	79	42	9	30	44	4.95	4	4	9.3	1.1	3.5	5.2	0.7	6.94	-4
2001	Nashvill	PCL	64.3	68	33	7	18	34	4.62	3	4	9.5	1.0	2.5	4.8	0.9	4.91	3
2001	Pittsbrg	NL	84.7	95	51	10	30	31	5.42	4	5	10.1	1.1	3.2	3.3	0.5	5.47	-15

The Pirates tend to promote pitchers because they've "completed" Triple-A, not because they've earned it—sort of like your average inner-city public school, or Harvard. Arroyo was not ready for a starting role in the majors, and despite having four pitches, he doesn't have the command that gives you confidence he ever will be. He did well in relief this year; that should be his role for at least another full season.

Joe Beimel Throws L Age 25

YEAR	TEAM	LGE	IP	H	ER	HR	BB	K	ERA	W	L	H/9	HR/9	BB/9	K/9	KW	PERA	STUFF
1999	Hickory	SAL	131.7	157	102	25	61	50	6.97	4	11	10.7	1.7	4.2	3.4	0.4	7.88	-22
2000	Lynchbrg	Car	116.7	132	76	15	55	43	5.86	5	8	10.2	1.2	4.2	3.3	0.4	5.10	-14
2000	Altoona	Eas	62.0	78	53	15	23	20	7.69	2	5	11.3	2.2	3.3	2.9	0.4	6.90	-21
2001	Pittsbrg	NL	112.7	121	62	10	44	47	4.95	6	7	9.7	0.8	3.5	3.8	0.5	5.59	-14

Beimel had barely pitched above A ball before 2001, getting shelled in a handful of Double-A appearances in 2000. He's a local boy who went to Duquesne, which may have helped him get to the majors, where he survived and became the most effective reliever the Pirates had at 8.4 ARP. He's not the extreme lefty-killer that would make him an ideal specialist, but he could develop into Steve Kline with more experience.

Kris Benson Throws R Age 27

YEAR	TEAM	LGE	IP	H	ER	HR	BB	K	ERA	W	L	H/9	HR/9	BB/9	K/9	KW	PERA	STUFF
1998	Nashvill	PCL	156.3	170	100	29	51	100	5.76	6	11	9.8	1.7	2.9	5.8	1.0	5.81	2
1999	Pittsbrg	NL	197.0	192	90	15	69	125	4.11	12	10	8.8	0.7	3.2	5.7	0.9	4.35	10
2000	Pittsbrg	NL	220.3	211	100	21	71	164	4.08	13	11	8.6	0.9	2.9	6.7	1.2	3.90	15

One of four Tommy John surgery patients in the Pirates' organization this year, Benson signed a four-year contract just in time to miss the first year and a half or so. Considered a Cy Young Award candidate before the injury, Benson probably won't return to that form until mid-2003 or so, which should give the Pirates enough time to realize that they should have shut him down entirely when he first came up lame in August of 2000.

Brady Borner Throws L Age 23

YEAR	TEAM	LGE	IP	H	ER	HR	BB	K	ERA	W	L	H/9	HR/9	BB/9	K/9	KW	PERA	STUFF
2001	Willmspt	NYP	10.0	13	9	3	1	6	8.10	0	1	11.7	2.7	0.9	5.4	3.0	1.16	0
2001	Hickory	SAL	54.0	63	39	12	18	28	6.50	2	4	10.5	2.0	3.0	4.7	0.8	4.17	-1

Sean Burnett got the press, but the Crawdads had a number of pitchers who posted gaudy pitching lines in 2001. Jeff Sharber, drafted in 2001, had a 1.99 ERA in seven starts. Chris Young, a third-round pick in 2000, posted good peripherals when he wasn't attending classes at Princeton. Patrick O'Brien's numbers were close to Young's when he wasn't attending classes at Notre Dame.

Brady Borner, however, got noticed for having perhaps the best stuff of the group, even though he was picked in just the 31st round in 2001. He's a short left-hander with three plus pitches, including a fastball with good movement, and he wasn't worked hard at Wayne State College. Pitchers drafted this low are a crapshoot; if the Pirates get two major leaguers out of this group, they should consider themselves lucky.

Bobby Bradley Throws R Age 21

YEAR	TEAM	LGE	IP	H	ER	HR	BB	K	ERA	W	L	H/9	HR/9	BB/9	K/9	KW	PERA	STUFF
2000	Hickory	SAL	81.0	76	36	7	27	61	4.00	5	4	8.4	0.8	3.0	6.8	1.1	4.59	27
2001	Lynchbrg	Car	48.0	51	32	7	27	27	6.00	2	3	9.6	1.3	5.1	5.1	0.5	5.74	2

Developing pitching is about quantity and quality, because even when you take care of a pitcher's arm, it can break down. Bradley missed almost the entire 2001 season with elbow trouble and ended up having Tommy John surgery in October. He should be back on the field in March of 2003, but he's going to have to improve his work ethic to get back in shape and recapture his mind-blowing curve.

Sean Burnett Throws L Age 19

YEAR	TEAM	LGE	IP	H	ER	HR	BB	K	ERA	W	L	H/9	HR/9	BB/9	K/9	KW	PERA	STUFF
2001	Hickory	SAL	160.3	182	00	25	47	00	5.50	7	11	10.2	1.4	2.6	3.8	0.7	5.15	4

Before you start thinking about a rotation of Benson, Bradley, and Burnett in 2004, take a deep breath. Burnett's stuff didn't impress the scouts that much, and he gave up more than a hit an inning with an unimpressive strikeout rate. His change-up is wicked, but his fastball is just good, and he needs to develop a better breaking pitch. For a #1 pick (#19 overall in 2000), you'd like to see more than that at this level.

Adrian Burnside Throws L Age 25

YEAR	TEAM	LGE	IP	H	ER	HR	BB	K	ERA	W	L	H/9	HR/9	BB/9	K/9	KW	PERA	STUFF
1999	San Bern	Cal	131.7	135	74	13	63	74	5.06	7	8	9.2	0.9	4.3	5.1	0.6	5.40	0
2000	SanAnton	Tex	88.7	90	57	10	57	55	5.79	4	6	9.1	1.0	5.8	5.6	0.5	4.79	-2
2001	Jacksnvl	Sou	60.0	65	44	10	37	38	6.60	2	5	9.8	1.5	5.0	5.7	0.5	3.30	-11
2001	Altoona	Eas	31.0	33	23	5	20	19	6.68	1	2	9.6	1.5	5.8	5.5	0.5	6.27	-15

Acquired from the Dodgers in the outrageously funny Terry Mulholland trade (watch for the UPN sitcom version, coming next fall), Burnside is seen by the Pirates as a relief candidate, although his stuff should eventually get him into the rotation. He throws in the low to mid 90s and has a good breaking pitch and developing change-up. Mulholland's gotten by on less for years.

Francisco Cordova Throws R Age 30

YEAR	TEAM	LGE	IP	H	ER	HR	BB	K	ERA	W	L	H/9	HR/9	BB/9	K/9	KW	PERA	STUFF
1999	Pittsbrg	NL	163.0	168	79	15	49	88	4.36	9	9	9.3	0.8	2.7	4.9	0.9	4.21	5
2000	Pittsbrg	NL	99.0	101	50	11	31	59	4.55	6	6	9.2	1.0	2.8	5.4	1.0	5.41	3

Cordova is the most effective of the always-hurt holdovers from the '97-'98 glory days, such as they were. Rich Loiselle can't throw strikes any more and was cut loose, and Jose Silva became a walking malpractice suit and is now with the Reds. Cordova blew his elbow out entirely last spring, which could be good news if it allows him a year or two of health once he returns. Cordova would make a great minor-league contract gamble for a cagey team.

Mike Fetters Throws R Age 37

YEAR	TEAM	LGE	IP	H	ER	HR	BB	K	ERA	W	L	H/9	HR/9	BB/9	K/9	KW	PERA	STUFF
1999	Baltimor	AL	32.3	33	21	4	18	22	5.85	1	3	9.2	1.1	5.0	6.1	0.6	5.91	-14
2000	LosAngls	NL	46.7	46	26	6	21	36	5.01	2	3	8.9	1.2	4.1	6.9	0.9	3.15	-2
2001	LosAngls	NL	29.3	31	19	5	12	21	5.83	1	2	9.5	1.5	3.7	6.4	0.9	7.37	-13
2001	Pittsbrg	NL	16.7	16	10	1	12	9	5.40	1	1	8.6	0.5	6.5	4.9	0.4	4.55	-21

The booby prize for sending off Terry Mulholland, Fetters was horribly ineffective for the Pirates despite his eight-for-nine performance in save opportunities, walking 13 men in 17 1/3 innings. He's had just one healthy season in his last four, and he clearly doesn't have Jenny Craig's number in his Palm Pilot. Fetters is signed for about $2 million for 2002; with Josias Manzanillo showing more competence both overall and as a closer, Fetters should be trade bait.

Joshua Higgins Throws R Age 23

YEAR	TEAM	LGE	IP	H	ER	HR	BB	K	ERA	W	L	H/9	HR/9	BB/9	K/9	KW	PERA	STUFF
2000	Willmspt	NYP	32.7	34	17	4	10	20	4.68	2	2	9.4	1.1	2.8	5.5	1.0	2.73	-1
2001	Hickory	SAL	56.7	59	29	7	16	35	4.61	3	3	9.4	1.1	2.5	5.6	1.1	3.38	-5

Higgins is a minor-league closer, which ordinarily would give him about as much chance of reaching the majors as Gary Huckabay has of seeing his feet without a mirror. Higgins has something else up, er, at the end of his sleeve: two fingers on his pitching hand are more than an inch longer than they should be, so his change-up moves like a spitball, making him nearly unhittable, at least in the Sally League. He's someone to watch.

Mike Lincoln Throws R Age 27

YEAR	TEAM	LGE	IP	H	ER	HR	BB	K	ERA	W	L	H/9	HR/9	BB/9	K/9	KW	PERA	STUFF
1999	SaltLake	PCL	63.0	74	46	13	23	28	6.57	2	5	10.6	1.9	3.3	4.0	0.6	7.08	-13
1999	Minnesot	AL	81.7	92	46	9	22	27	5.07	4	5	10.1	1.0	2.4	3.0	0.6	5.73	-12
2000	SaltLake	PCL	73.3	79	34	5	17	26	4.17	4	4	9.7	0.6	2.1	3.2	0.8	4.07	-4
2000	Minnesot	AL	23.3	30	25	8	11	15	9.64	1	2	11.6	3.1	4.2	5.8	0.7	8.72	-28
2001	Nashvill	PCL	88.7	97	54	13	32	45	5.48	4	6	9.8	1.3	3.2	4.6	0.7	4.69	-10
2001	Pittsbrg	NL	37.0	37	16	3	10	19	3.89	2	2	9.0	0.7	2.4	4.6	0.9	3.55	-7

A soft tosser signed as a six-year minor-league free agent (à la Todd Ritchie), Lincoln thrived on a move to the bullpen in Triple-A. He pitched extremely well for the Pirates in relief until he strained his hip, after which he was a punching bag. Lincoln throws strikes and keeps the ball down when he's 100%, but he is probably maxed out as a good middle reliever.

Josias Manzanillo Throws R Age 34

YEAR	TEAM	LGE	IP	H	ER	HR	BB	K	ERA	W	L	H/9	HR/9	BB/9	K/9	KW	PERA	STUFF
1999	NY Mets	NL	19.3	18	10	5	3	23	4.66	1	1	8.4	2.3	1.4	10.7	3.8	5.49	21
2000	Nashvill	PCL	23.3	20	7	0	6	16	2.70	2	1	7.7	0.0	2.3	6.2	1.3	3.50	2
2000	Pittsbrg	NL	57.0	57	31	5	26	35	4.89	3	3	9.0	0.8	4.1	5.5	0.7	3.20	-7
2001	Pittsbrg	NL	75.0	64	26	3	23	64	3.12	5	3	7.7	0.4	2.8	7.7	1.4	3.59	12

Not only did Manzanillo not turn into a pumpkin, he improved his performance across the board, finally pitching the way he did in '94 for the Mets and in Triple-A ever since. His 1999 elbow surgery brought new life to his late-breaking slider, and he kept it down all year, holding right-handed hitters to a .251 slugging percentage. He should open 2002 as the closer if the Pirates can re-sign him, and he is more proof that spending money on relievers is dumb.

Damaso Marte Throws L Age 27

YEAR	TEAM	LGE	IP	H	ER	HR	BB	K	ERA	W	L	H/9	HR/9	BB/9	K/9	KW	PERA	STUFF
1999	Tacoma	PCL	73.7	83	59	15	43	43	7.21	2	6	10.1	1.8	5.3	5.3	0.5	5.54	-22
2001	Norwich	Eas	34.0	36	20	5	10	20	5.29	2	2	9.5	1.3	2.6	5.3	1.0	6.13	-21
2001	Pittsbrg	NL	35.3	33	16	4	11	31	4.08	2	2	8.4	1.0	2.8	7.9	1.4	5.18	8

Failed starting pitching prospects often make very good middle relievers; Marte meets part one and is most of the way to part two. He throws hard, but he never had the command to succeed as a starter above A ball. A little experience might help him be a contributor: he held hitters to .231/.294/.346 with the bases empty but was smacked to the tune of .276/.353/.569 with men on base.

Tony McKnight Throws R Age 25

YEAR	TEAM	LGE	IP	H	ER	HR	BB	K	ERA	W	L	H/9	HR/9	BB/9	K/9	KW	PERA	STUFF
1999	Jackson	Tex	153.7	165	88	22	48	85	5.15	7	10	9.7	1.3	2.8	5.0	0.9	3.82	7
2000	Round Ro	Tex	33.0	38	22	6	10	16	6.00	1	3	10.4	1.6	2.7	4.4	0.8	6.34	-7
2000	New Orln	PCL	120.0	131	63	13	34	51	4.72	6	7	9.8	1.0	2.6	3.8	0.8	5.36	0
2000	Houston	NL	35.3	36	16	3	7	20	4.08	2	2	9.2	0.8	1.8	5.1	1.4	4.19	12
2001	New Orln	PCL	92.7	102	53	12	28	42	5.15	4	6	9.9	1.2	2.7	4.1	0.8	6.48	-7
2001	Houston	NL	17.3	20	11	3	3	8	5.71	1	1	10.4	1.6	1.6	4.2	1.3	3.74	1
2001	Pittsbrg	NL	68.3	80	46	13	19	29	6.06	3	5	10.5	1.7	2.5	3.8	0.8	5.68	-7

While getting McKnight from Houston for Mike Williams was a heist, McKnight didn't belong in the majors, much less in the Pirates rotation, after getting knocked around Triple-A for the first four months of the year. McKnight runs it into the low 90s with a pretty good curve, but he has been hurt so often that he doesn't have the experience at high levels that you'd like to see. A spot in the Pirates' bullpen should be his ceiling for 2002.

Omar Olivares — Throws R — Age 34

YEAR	TEAM	LGE	IP	H	ER	HR	BB	K	ERA	W	L	H/9	HR/9	BB/9	K/9	KW	PERA	STUFF
1999	Anaheim	AL	131.7	141	65	10	41	49	4.44	8	7	9.6	0.7	2.8	3.3	0.6	3.59	-2
1999	Oakland	AL	76.7	81	40	7	27	36	4.70	4	5	9.5	0.8	3.2	4.2	0.7	4.52	0
2000	Oakland	AL	115.7	120	60	9	49	56	4.67	6	7	9.3	0.7	3.8	4.4	0.6	6.22	-5
2001	Pittsbrg	NL	107.0	116	63	15	38	55	5.30	5	7	9.8	1.3	3.2	4.6	0.7	7.08	-15

Done as a Pirate and, one would assume, as a major-league pitcher. Olivares doesn't have the movement on his fastball to survive any loss of command, meaning that PNC Park bleacher creatures had a pretty good time when Olivares was on the mound. The Pirates have other arms to evaluate, and there are plenty of better starting-pitching options at Triple-A for other teams to consider.

Justin Reid — Throws R — Age 25

YEAR	TEAM	LGE	IP	H	ER	HR	BB	K	ERA	W	L	H/9	HR/9	BB/9	K/9	KW	PERA	STUFF
1999	Willmspt	NYP	64.3	73	47	11	32	31	6.58	2	5	10.2	1.5	4.5	4.3	0.5	8.88	-19
2000	Hickory	SAL	162.0	187	110	33	43	81	6.11	6	12	10.4	1.8	2.4	4.5	0.9	6.66	-8
2001	Lynchbrg	Car	53.0	63	35	11	10	23	5.94	2	4	10.7	1.9	1.7	3.9	1.1	4.01	-10
2001	Altoona	Eas	107.3	116	49	9	20	41	4.11	7	5	9.7	0.8	1.7	3.4	1.0	4.67	-1

Reid, like most Pirates pitching prospects, doesn't have blazing stuff, and he gets the obligatory Greg Maddux comparison because he's a smart pitcher who paints the corners. He has a reputation as a very quick study and relies on his control and planning to get out hitters. His strikeout rate deteriorated when he reached Double-A this year, and he has a short window of opportunity to make it in Pittsburgh before the next wave of prospects arrives.

Todd Ritchie — Throws R — Age 30

YEAR	TEAM	LGE	IP	H	ER	HR	BB	K	ERA	W	L	H/9	HR/9	BB/9	K/9	KW	PERA	STUFF
1999	Pittsbrg	NL	173.0	177	80	16	45	96	4.16	10	9	9.2	0.8	2.3	5.0	1.1	3.72	8
2000	Pittsbrg	NL	193.0	202	94	23	42	110	4.38	11	10	9.4	1.1	2.0	5.1	1.3	4.84	7
2001	Pittsbrg	NL	197.7	208	95	20	47	100	4.33	11	11	9.5	0.9	2.1	4.6	1.1	5.09	3

Occasionally unhittable, Ritchie became the staff's erstwhile ace, pretty cool for someone picked up as a minor-league free agent in early 1999. More cool: Littlefield turned him into Kip Wells, Josh Fogg, and Sean Lowe. Ritchie will be the White Sox' #2 starter, providing bulk innings but little upside. Still think won-lost records mean something? Ritchie's first half: 5-9, 4.07 ERA. Ritchie's second half: 6-6, 4.97 ERA.

Scott Sauerbeck — Throws L — Age 30

YEAR	TEAM	LGE	IP	H	ER	HR	BB	K	ERA	W	L	H/9	HR/9	BB/9	K/9	KW	PERA	STUFF
1999	Pittsbrg	NL	65.7	62	33	6	32	50	4.52	3	4	8.5	0.8	4.4	6.9	0.8	2.29	0
2000	Pittsbrg	NL	80.3	67	36	4	50	74	4.03	5	4	7.5	0.4	5.6	8.3	0.7	3.88	5
2001	Pittsbrg	NL	64.0	52	27	3	36	64	3.80	4	3	7.3	0.4	5.1	9.0	0.9	5.85	8

Sauerbeck's multiyear deal serves as an example of all that was wrong with Bonifay's philosophy, which included 1) locking all players up to long-term deals, regardless of their quality; 2) assuming that what worked once (using the Rule 5 draft to grab a useful reliever) won't work again; and 3) looking at superficial stats instead of meaningful ones. Sauerbeck's fastball couldn't outrun traffic on the Fort Pitt Bridge during rush hour; he's just in the way.

Brian Smith — Throws R — Age 29

YEAR	TEAM	LGE	IP	H	ER	HR	BB	K	ERA	W	L	H/9	HR/9	BB/9	K/9	KW	PERA	STUFF
1999	Knoxvill	Sou	36.0	42	22	7	7	16	5.50	2	2	10.5	1.8	1.8	4.0	1.1	7.77	-31
1999	Syracuse	Int	46.3	49	33	8	26	33	6.41	2	3	9.5	1.6	5.1	6.4	0.6	4.42	-20
2000	Altoona	Eas	25.0	23	9	0	10	14	3.24	2	1	8.3	0.0	3.6	5.0	0.7	2.82	-10
2001	Nashvill	PCL	37.3	41	22	6	9	21	5.30	2	2	9.9	1.4	2.2	5.1	1.2	6.23	-20

Smith has a good arm that hasn't been healthy much since the Pirates picked him in the 1999 Rule 5 draft. He was healthy enough in the last half of 2001 to have a good run as Nashville's closer. He locates the ball well and throws strikes, but he still leaves too much over the plate to be truly effective. That said, he's a small adjustment away from joining the Pirates' bullpen and should ride the Nashville Shuttle this year.

John Van Benschoten DH Bats R Age 22

YEAR	TEAM	LGE	AB	H	DB	TP	HR	BB	SO	R	RBI	SB	CS	OUT	BA	OBP	SLG	EQA	EQR	DEFENSE
2001	Willmspt	NYP	78	14	4	0	0	4	27	6	6	1	1	65	.179	.227	.231	.160	3	
2002	*Pittsbrg*	*NL*	*125*	*27*	*5*	*0*	*0*	*9*	*47*	*11*	*8*	*5*	*2*	*100*	*.216*	*.269*	*.256*	*.177*	*7*	

John Van Benschoten Throws R Age 22

YEAR	TEAM	LGE	IP	H	ER	HR	BB	K	ERA	W	L	H/9	HR/9	BB/9	K/9	KW	PERA	STUFF
2001	Willmspt	NYP	25.7	26	12	0	14	10	4.21	2	1	9.1	0.0	4.9	3.5	0.4	6.04	-14

Van Benschoten scored an eight on the scouts' two-to-eight scale for rating power hitters, so the Pirates, having learned nothing from the Clint Johnston and J.J. Davis fiascoes, decided to make him a pitcher. He struggled badly in his first mound appearances, then improved as the season went on, impressing scouts with a fastball that tails away in the zone and a great hard-breaking slider. He also DH'd in 32 games, but not enough to find a groove at the plate. So here's a question for the new regime: given that these moves haven't worked out so far, why not let Van Benschoten serve as the DH in every game until it's evident that he has a career as a pitcher?

Ryan Vogelsong Throws R Age 24

YEAR	TEAM	LGE	IP	H	ER	HR	BB	K	ERA	W	L	H/9	HR/9	BB/9	K/9	KW	PERA	STUFF
1999	San Jose	Cal	64.0	59	31	5	30	51	4.36	4	3	8.3	0.7	4.2	7.2	0.9	3.85	21
1999	Shrevprt	Tex	30.0	38	32	10	16	17	9.60	1	2	11.4	3.0	4.8	5.1	0.5	9.04	-14
2000	Shrevprt	Tex	155.3	162	94	23	68	102	5.45	7	10	9.4	1.3	3.9	5.9	0.8	5.37	7
2001	Fresno	PCL	52.0	51	27	6	20	38	4.67	3	3	8.8	1.0	3.5	6.6	0.9	2.67	16
2001	San Fran	NL	27.0	30	19	4	13	14	6.33	1	2	10.0	1.3	4.3	4.7	0.5	7.10	-17
2001	Nashvill	PCL	30.7	28	16	2	17	24	4.70	1	2	8.2	0.6	5.0	7.0	0.7	4.63	13
2001	Pittsbrg	NL	7.0	7	5	1	5	6	6.43	0	1	9.0	1.3	6.4	7.7	0.6	14.91	-10

His injury hurt the Pirates more than Rios's did. Both players hurt themselves in their second appearance with the Pirates, but Rios's injury was milder, and he was the less important of the two players acquired in the Schmidt deal. Vogelsong boasts the combination of stuff (good fastball, plus curve) and smarts that the Pirates haven't been able to develop in their own pitchers. Tommy John surgery has him out for all of 2002; he probably won't be worth a look until 2004.

Dave Williams Throws L Age 23

YEAR	TEAM	LGE	IP	H	ER	HR	BB	K	ERA	W	L	H/9	HR/9	BB/9	K/9	KW	PERA	STUFF
1999	Willmspt	NYP	43.0	46	24	5	15	22	5.02	2	3	9.6	1.0	3.1	4.6	0.7	4.82	8
1999	Hickory	SAL	54.0	63	36	10	15	24	6.00	2	4	10.5	1.7	2.5	4.0	0.8	4.53	2
2000	Hickory	SAL	163.0	182	110	34	50	100	6.07	6	12	10.0	1.9	2.8	5.5	1.0	4.75	8
2000	Lynchbrg	Car	12.0	16	12	4	3	5	9.00	0	1	12.0	3.0	2.3	3.8	0.8	8.09	-15
2001	Altoona	Eas	53.0	63	39	12	15	26	6.62	2	4	10.7	2.0	2.5	4.4	0.9	3.47	0
2001	Pittsbrg	NL	103.0	113	62	13	40	46	5.42	4	7	9.9	1.1	3.5	4.0	0.6	4.16	-2

He led the minors in strikeouts in 2000, and, despite modest stuff, Williams still hasn't had a full-year ERA above 4.00. He has great command of all of his pitches, throws strikes, and keeps his composure under pressure—such as, for example, the pressure of being rushed to the majors just a season removed from the Sally League. Despite his inexperience, he had the best Support-Neutral winning percentage among Pirates' starters in 2001. Given time, he's going to be a very good one.

St. Louis Cardinals

Bill James wrote a number of really cool articles on the minor leagues. One of his recurring themes was that there's some sort of ongoing confidence game being played against the patrons of minor-league baseball, in that they're not really seeing the best baseball games possible, but rather they're paying to watch exercises in player development for an entirely different league. The minor-league system of the Cardinals has become the very symbol of this syndrome. The Cardinals' affiliates had a grand total of zero winning records in 2001, and not a single Cardinals farm club made its league's playoffs—the third time in five years the Cardinals could make that dubious claim.

Nevertheless, the Cardinals farm system, despite stacking up losses like Anthony Young going through a rough patch, was the best in baseball in 2001. By what measure? By the number of kick-ass-and-take-names rookies who stomped through the NL like Gulliver through Lilliput. That number is either 1 or 1.5, depending on how one rates Bud Smith's initial pass through the league.

Albert Pujols jumped straight from the Carolina League to the bigs and had an offensive season that wouldn't have been out of place in the middle of Albert Belle's peak. Defensively, he was both effective and versatile, playing third base well and filling in competently at first base and in the outfield as necessitated by injuries to Mark McGwire, Ray Lankford, and J.D. Drew. A year ago, almost no one had heard of Pujols; by November, he was as serious an MVP candidate as one could be while playing in the same league as Barry Bonds.

Bud Smith pitched great at Memphis and got the call to the big club in July. He showed flashes of brilliance, posting a 3.83 ERA during the regular season—including a no-hitter against the Padres—and pitching well in his one Division Series start. If a farm system can produce an above-average starter and a runaway Rookie of the Year, it's a great farm system for the time being, no matter how badly the teams within it performed in their respective leagues. It may not be a great deal for the fans of those affiliates, but it was a great deal for the Cardinals in 2001.

Cardinals Prospectus

2001 record: 93–69; Second place, NL Central; NL wild card, Lost to Diamondbacks in Division Series, 3–2

Pythagenport W/L: 94–68

Runs scored: 814 (fourth in NL)

Runs allowed: 684 (third in NL)

Team EqA: .268 (tied for second in NL)

2001 batters age: 28.7 (seventh-youngest in NL)

2001 pitchers age: 29.1 (sixth-oldest in NL)

Ballpark: Busch Stadium; neutral park; Park Factor of 1.000

2001: The end of the McGwire Era saw a division title and the emergence of a potential heir to the throne.

2002: They're pretty old, and didn't improve themselves in the offseason, making some bad signings. A hard team to project.

The Cardinals' player-development philosophy has been very successful, and it's a little different from that of most organizations. Where many clubs mitigate their risk through a portfolio of key players, the Cardinals have focused on individuals who have a low risk of failure and have dedicated a lot of resources to those players. Pujols, Smith, Drew, and Rick Ankiel are all examples of the kind of success possible under this strategy. And because truly great players are considerably more scarce than good players, this strategy can yield a tremendous payoff, part of which the Cardinals reaped in 2001, and part of which they will reap in the future.

Having coughed up Pujols and Smith, the Cardinals' farm system is now a pretty much bare cupboard, a situation that is of less concern for them than it would be for other clubs. There's already a lot of young talent on the big club, and the next Grade-A prospect for the Cardinals is probably playing college ball somewhere, waiting to be snatched up in the first-year-player draft in June.

The Cardinals' player-development system has been a big advantage for them over the last three seasons, but that's about to change. See, the Cardinals have the misfortune of playing in the NL Central, which is poised to enter a renaissance period, having the lion's share of the game's potential impact players over the next few seasons. The Cubs have a farm system that includes Juan Cruz, Mark Prior, Carlos Zambrano, Bobby Hill, Alleged Human Ben Christensen, and Hee Choi. At least one or two of those guys are going to make the Cubs a lot better ball club. The Astros' farm system has cranked out a number of quality arms in just the last 18 months, with Roy Oswalt, Tim Redding, Carlos Hernandez, and Wade Miller joining the big club, alongside a young hitting nucleus that's nearly as good as any team's. In Cincinnati,

Adam Dunn was almost as impressive as Pujols in a late-season call-up, and Austin Kearns, who was virtually identical to Dunn in 2000, isn't far behind him. Hell, things even look somewhat brighter in Pittsburgh, where Cam Bonifay was run out of town just before his master plan was completed. Barring realignment, or a run of colossally stupid moves, the NL Central is going to be one of the toughest divisions in baseball for the next two to three years.

So what should Cardinals GM Walt Jocketty do?

He should probably do something dangerous: stand pat, and make a couple of fairly easy tweaks. The Cardinals are in pretty good shape going into the 2002 season. The up-the-middle backbone is strong in fair territory, with Fernando Vina, Jim Edmonds, and Edgar Renteria supporting a crater of Mike DiFelice and Mike Matheny behind the plate. At the corners, Pujols and Drew are among the best players in the league at third base and right field. Tino Martinez, signed to replace Mark McGwire, will be average or below at first base, leaving only left field to be filled.

The Redbirds' rotation starts off with Darryl Kile, Matt Morris, and Bud Smith, which is absolutely a championship-caliber front of the rotation. The #4 spot may end up being filled by the last gasp of Andy Benes or, if the Cardinals are feeling risky, Rick Ankiel, but that's not likely to happen until at least partway through the season. The bullpen is fairly well set from the left side, with Steve Kline and Mike Matthews. On the right side, there are a number of internal options, such as Dave Veres, if his finger is healthy. Mike Timlin and the newly acquired Jason Isringhausen can get the club through the end of the game. Jocketty has done a good job of putting together a situation that he can't really screw up—he just needs people to be healthy and perform at a level commensurate with reasonable expectations. Meanwhile, he has to fill out the back of the rotation and left field.

The Cardinals roster won't reflect just the work of Walt Jocketty, but also the well-chronicled preferences of media-approved genius Tony LaRussa. LaRussa loves positional flexibility in his bench players and semi-regulars, and he always finds roster space and playing time for people such as Scott Hemond, Mike Gallego, and Craig Paquette, often at the expense of superior offensive players. Finding and using these guys usually isn't enough for LaRussa; he also likes to train people for the role, be they as old as Shawon Dunston or as young as Albert Pujols. There's nothing wrong with wanting maximum flexibility, but LaRussa can, from time to time, value flexibility above productivity. In an improving division, that may be an unaffordable luxury.

LaRussa's genius status is amazingly durable, even more so than his Sean Young *Bladerunner* hairdo. After riding Alan Benes and Matt Morris hard, then watching them undergo a series of major injuries and surgeries, LaRussa returned to leaning pretty heavily on Morris again in 2001. The Cardinals aren't going to have an extra quality starting pitcher lying around, so Duncan and LaRussa will have to be pretty careful in 2002.

Tactically, LaRussa was one of the unluckiest managers ever in the NL Division Series, out-managing Bob Brenly (see also G. Gordon Liddy's *Beating Up Quadriplegics*, Muntz Press) to have his lights-out lefty killer, Steve Kline, facing Tony Womack, one of the weakest left-handed hitters in baseball. Still, this is baseball, strange things happen, and the Cardinals went home. Of course, things broke the Diamondbacks' way throughout the Division Series, and LaRussa did catch some editorial flak, some of which was deserved, and some of which wasn't. For example, more than one observer (OK, everyone who saw it) had no idea why LaRussa sent Matt Morris and Mike Matheny to the plate to hit for themselves late in Game Five against Curt Schilling. Others wanted LaRussa summarily executed for allowing a clearly tired Mike Matthews to pitch to any right-handed hitter in the postseason.

But no manager nails every move, and those of us observing from the outside don't often have perfect information. LaRussa gets caught up more in certain strategies than is probably optimal, but he keeps the players motivated, and he has a relationship with Dave Duncan that allows him to get some very good performances from his pitchers over the course of a season. He's well respected by his peers and his players, and there's no reason to think he'll make the kind of drastic mistakes that would torpedo the Cardinals' chances in 2002.

The building dynamic in the NL Central is going to make for some really amazing baseball. The Cardinals have a blend of great young talent, a management team with a good track record of finding and rehabbing veterans, and quality players such as Vina and Edmonds at the tail end of their primes. The Cards are being pursued by organizations with some of the best young talent they've ever had, and everyone is seeking a balance that will allow the big club to get the best production possible from some very exotic mixes of young monsters and aging veterans. The team that ends up on top could well be the team that figures out how to pick up affordable and effective role players to fill the gaps that will inevitably open up due to injuries and unpredictable development paths. So in a division that will be dominated by players such as J.D. Drew, Albert Pujols, Bud Smith, Sammy Sosa, Mark Prior, Kerry Wood, Lance Berkman, Tim Redding, Roy Oswalt, and Daryle Ward, the difference could well be players such as Billy McMillon, Ben Weber, Mark Sweeney, or Steve Kline.

There's high drama potential in St. Louis in 2002. A lot of things could happen, and most of them will make good copy. They could bring Ankiel back, he could be fine, and the Cardinals could cruise, Mariners-style, to an easy crown. J.D. Drew could be healthy all year, post a season that looks something like .320/.420/.650, and still be just the second- or third-best outfielder in the division. On the other hand, Edmonds and Drew could both miss large parts of the year due to injury, allowing Kerry Robinson, Eli Marrero, and Mike DiFelice to drag down the offense, creating an opportunity for the Astros and Cubs.

The best possible scenario is that we'll see the Cardinals, Cubs, and Astros all develop their youth, stay healthy, and play well, leading to what could be a historic series of pennant races over the next several years. The Cardinals are well positioned to do their part; if Duncan and LaRussa can keep the rotation healthy and spot the relief well, they won't be able to put a bad enough offense on the field to keep the Cardinals out of the postseason, even with both Mike Matheny and Mike DiFelice on the roster.

HITTERS (BA: .270, OBP: .340, SLG: .440, EqA: .260)

Bobby Bonilla PH Bats B Age 39

YEAR	TEAM	LGE	AB	H	DB	TP	HR	BB	SO	R	RBI	SB	CS	OUT	BA	OBP	SLG	EQA	EQR	DEFENSE
1999	NY Mets	NL	120	20	5	0	4	18	15	12	17	0	1	101	.167	.280	.308	.203	9	22-RF -1
2000	Atlanta	NL	241	62	13	3	5	33	47	23	27	0	0	179	.257	.349	.398	.254	29	43-LF -13
2001	St Louis	NL	175	39	5	0	6	22	45	18	23	1	1	137	.223	.312	.354	.227	17	27-1B -4
2002	*St Louis*	*NL*	*216*	*40*	*8*	*1*	*5*	*31*	*51*	*19*	*24*	*0*	*1*	*177*	*.185*	*.287*	*.301*	*.198*	*16*	

Barring a return to a front office run by Al Harazin, Bonilla's career is probably over. Bonilla can't play the outfield any more, and he's not even really acceptable at first base. That means either DH duty, or work as a pure pinch hitter, not enough to warrant a roster spot when most clubs are intent on carrying 19 or 20 pitchers on their 25-man roster. Bonilla has had a solid career, during which he was both overrated and underrated at various times. In his prime, he was a .290/.375/.500 hitter in an era of lower offense.

Miguel Cairo 2B/3B Bats R Age 28

YEAR	TEAM	LGE	AB	H	DB	TP	HR	BB	SO	R	RBI	SB	CS	OUT	BA	OBP	SLG	EQA	EQR	DEFENSE
1999	TampaBay	AL	463	142	18	5	3	19	40	60	35	21	7	328	.307	.342	.387	.250	51	112-2B 4
2000	TampaBay	AL	373	100	20	2	1	25	30	48	33	28	8	281	.268	.318	.340	.233	37	99-2B 0
2001	Iowa		PCL	122	33	7	1	2	8	10	19	11	3	3	92	.270	.319	.393	.236	1226-2B -4
2001	ChiCubs	NL	124	37	4	1	2	15	18	21	9	2	1	88	.298	.374	.395	.264	16	22-3B -3
2001	St Louis	NL	33	11	3	0	2	2	2	5	8	0	0	22	.333	.371	.606	.310	6	
2002	*St Louis*	*NL*	*420*	*125*	*19*	*3*	*6*	*33*	*43*	*61*	*38*	*20*	*6*	*301*	*.298*	*.349*	*.400*	*.259*	*51*	

Cairo represents another type of player that Tony LaRussa likes. He can play second base very well, third base slightly less so, he puts the ball in play, and he can run a little. The Cardinals are collecting these guys like they're expecting a rule change that will force defenders to switch positions for each batter. Cairo has more name value than some of the others, so he might be moved or end up somewhere else in February.

Stubby Clapp 2B/OF Bats L Age 29

YEAR	TEAM	LGE	AB	H	DB	TP	HR	BB	SO	R	RBI	SB	CS	OUT	BA	OBP	SLG	EQA	EQR	DEFENSE
1999	Memphis	PCL	390	89	23	1	11	45	88	57	48	5	5	306	.228	.311	.377	.231	39	57-2B -3 31-LF -1
2000	Memphis	PCL	508	130	26	6	1	65	85	73	43	7	4	382	.256	.345	.337	.238	53	127-2B -5
2001	Memphis	PCL	301	84	14	5	4	39	42	42	28	7	3	220	.279	.363	.399	.261	38	82-2B 4
2001	St Louis	NL	25	5	3	0	0	1	6	1	1	0	0	20	.200	.231	.320	.184	1	
2002	*St Louis*	*NL*	*458*	*120*	*25*	*6*	*9*	*60*	*81*	*74*	*52*	*11*	*4*	*342*	*.262*	*.347*	*.402*	*.257*	*57*	

Clapp is a little guy who is versatile defensively. He can play most positions to some extent, won't kill you in the middle infield, and has a comparable skill set to Craig Grebeck, Frank Menechino, and Chris Snopek, with a little bit of power and a good batting eye. Clapp will likely be fighting for a 25th-man spot for the next couple of years. As a backup and left-handed pinch hitter who won't destroy your offense if pressed into service for a week, he's a good guy to have.

Covelli Crisp OF Bats B Age 22

YEAR	TEAM	LGE	AB	H	DB	TP	HR	BB	SO	R	RBI	SB	CS	OUT	BA	OBP	SLG	EQA	EQR	DEFENSE
1999	JohnsnCy	App	234	39	4	2	1	24	46	24	10	9	4	199	.167	.246	.214	.171	12	60-2B -16
2000	New Jrsy	NYP	139	28	3	0	0	6	26	10	10	11	3	114	.201	.237	.223	.173	7	29-LF -1
2000	Peoria	Mid	102	23	6	0	0	11	17	10	5	4	2	81	.225	.301	.284	.208	8	22-LF 1
2001	Potomac	Car	549	138	16	2	10	44	64	65	37	24	13	424	.251	.307	.342	.223	50	134-LF -3
2002	*St Louis*	*NL*	*485*	*123*	*16*	*2*	*8*	*45*	*70*	*63*	*38*	*27*	*11*	*373*	*.254*	*.317*	*.344*	*.230*	*47*	

How can you not root for someone with that name? Crisp was tabbed the best hitting prospect in the Carolina League in 2001 by *Baseball America*, and he was the Cardinals' Minor League Player of the Year. He's a natural left-handed hitter whom the Cardinals are teaching to switch-hit. Crisp has been noted for his confidence and aggressiveness. If he's going to make it to St. Louis as an outfielder, it's time to get it in gear immediately. For a 21-year-old, a .306 batting average in the Carolina League is good, not great.

J.D. Drew OF Bats L Age 26

YEAR	TEAM	LGE	AB	H	DB	TP	HR	BB	SO	R	RBI	SB	CS	OUT	BA	OBP	SLG	EQA	EQR	DEFENSE
1999	St Louis	NL	369	89	17	5	13	46	71	69	37	16	3	283	.241	.335	.420	.258	48	95-CF 0
1999	Memphis	PCL	86	23	2	1	2	6	18	8	12	5	1	64	.267	.325	.384	.246	10	22-CF 0
2000	St Louis	NL	408	117	18	2	17	61	91	69	53	15	9	300	.287	.386	.466	.285	65	109-RF 0
2001	St Louis	NL	376	125	18	6	27	54	64	83	75	13	3	254	.332	.420	.628	.335	83	102-RF -4
2002	*St Louis*	*NL*	*397*	*120*	*21*	*4*	*23*	*68*	*79*	*86*	*61*	*20*	*6*	*283*	*.302*	*.404*	*.549*	*.314*	*78*	

Lower back sprain, bruised chest, wrenched ankle, strep throat, broken hand. No, it's not Les Nessman's winter itinerary, it's a brief overview of J.D.'s 2001 Medical Mystery Tour. When Drew was in the lineup, he was in a very select group of performers in a cluster behind Barry Bonds, and every bit as good as advertised. Hopefully, he won't take the Fred Lynn career path into several immovable objects. If he can find his way to 650 plate appearances, he'll be a good bet for the NL MVP Award.

Chris Duncan 1B Bats L Age 21

YEAR	TEAM	LGE	AB	H	DB	TP	HR	BB	SO	R	RBI	SB	CS	OUT	BA	OBP	SLG	EQA	EQR	DEFENSE
1999	JohnsnCy	App	204	28	4	0	3	13	70	11	15	1	1	177	.137	.190	.201	.140	6	52-1B -1
2000	Peoria	Mid	462	97	16	0	9	21	123	37	41	0	1	366	.210	.248	.303	.187	28	85-1B -19
2001	Peoria	Mid	306	74	14	1	9	27	60	30	38	7	3	235	.242	.306	.382	.233	31	78-1B -13
2001	Potomac	Car	171	27	3	0	3	9	47	10	13	3	3	147	.158	.202	.228	.151	6	47-1B -2
2002	*St Louis*	*NL*	*445*	*107*	*19*	*1*	*15*	*39*	*118*	*45*	*60*	*7*	*5*	*343*	*.240*	*.302*	*.389*	*.230*	*44*	

I . . . am . . . IRONGLOVE! Duncan's power is more than just intriguing; he puts on a major show in batting practice and has blasted some memorable shots in the Midwest and Carolina leagues. He's still learning some semblance of bat control and strike-zone judgment, and he is young enough that he has time to develop those skills. His glove work is just shy of terrifying. The Cardinals aren't really worried yet about his ability to pick up balls in the dirt or make throws around the diamond; they're more focused right now on getting him to field three-hoppers hit right at him and to catch routine throws from around the infield. He has a lot of battles to fight before he gets a shot at the bigs; he's worth the time the organization is investing in him.

Jim Edmonds CF Bats L Age 32

YEAR	TEAM	LGE	AB	H	DB	TP	HR	BB	SO	R	RBI	SB	CS	OUT	BA	OBP	SLG	EQA	EQR	DEFENSE
1999	Anaheim	AL	202	52	18	2	5	26	40	34	22	5	4	154	.257	.342	.441	.259	26	42-CF 5
2000	St Louis	NL	526	153	21	0	42	95	153	124	102	9	3	376	.291	.404	.570	.316	105	141-CF 4
2001	St Louis	NL	501	157	33	1	32	90	115	97	113	5	5	349	.313	.421	.575	.322	102	136-CF 2
2002	*St Louis*	*NL*	*470*	*139*	*27*	*1*	*33*	*84*	*124*	*100*	*84*	*8*	*5*	*336*	*.296*	*.403*	*.568*	*.315*	*93*	

An above-average but overrated defensive center fielder. Edmonds has developed into one of the best hitters in the league, with improved patience and a much better ability to drive the ball hard to the opposite field. In the 2001 Cardinals outfield, he was The Healthy One, playing 150 games and lighting up the NL in the second half. Edmonds has made himself into a truly top-tier ballplayer; he's still not particularly dangerous against left-handers, but he slaughters righties. If he's healthy, he may be both a legitimate MVP candidate and the second-best outfielder on his own team.

Troy Farnsworth   3B/1B   Bats R   Age 26

YEAR	TEAM	LGE	AB	H	DB	TP	HR	BB	SO	R	RBI	SB	CS	OUT	BA	OBP	SLG	EQA	EQR	DEFENSE
1999	Peoria	Mid	509	102	22	1	13	33	135	50	48	1	1	408	.200	.257	.324	.197	35	81-3B -1 41-1B -8
2000	Potomac	Car	523	108	16	2	18	29	135	52	80	4	2	417	.207	.255	.348	.203	38	61-1B 0 40-3B 2
2001	New Havn	Eas	429	92	16	1	15	27	101	42	60	3	5	342	.214	.274	.361	.211	35	92-3B -3 22-1B -1
2002	*St Louis*	*NL*	*449*	*104*	*18*	*1*	*16*	*35*	*120*	*52*	*59*	*4*	*3*	*340*	*.232*	*.287*	*.383*	*.222*	*41*	

Farnsworth is not even really a tweener. Despite getting some play in the press, he was 25 in Double A, didn't hit for much average, showed bad strike-zone judgment, and wasn't impressive defensively. If he wants to have a shot at a major-league career, he needs to have a lights-out 200 at-bats to start the 2002 season, then sit down in front of Adobe Photoshop with photos of Walt Jocketty, a petting zoo, the Absolut vodka logo, and Phyllis Schlafly.

John Gall   1B/3B   Bats R   Age 24

YEAR	TEAM	LGE	AB	H	DB	TP	HR	BB	SO	R	RBI	SB	CS	OUT	BA	OBP	SLG	EQA	EQR	DEFENSE
2000	New Jrsy	NYP	269	50	3	0	3	14	43	17	19	7	3	222	.186	.227	.230	.164	12	58-1B -1 12-3B 0
2001	Peoria	Mid	209	50	12	0	4	12	20	19	31	0	2	161	.239	.286	.354	.212	17	44-1B -4
2001	Potomac	Car	329	87	12	0	6	20	40	37	28	4	4	246	.264	.309	.356	.224	29	43-1B 0 27-3B -3
2002	*St Louis*	*NL*	*516*	*135*	*16*	*0*	*12*	*42*	*68*	*54*	*56*	*9*	*7*	*388*	*.262*	*.317*	*.362*	*.229*	*49*	

The organization is somewhat high on Gall, which is more of a comment on the state of the Cardinals' system than it is on Gall. He's a tweener from the Stanford program with some doubles power that could develop into legitimate pop. He controls the strike zone and makes contact fairly well. Scouts expect him to break out the power stick starting this year after making the adjustment from aluminum bats. The scouting reports on Gall are considerably better than his performance; we'll have to see which set of information is closer to reality.

Chris Haas   3B/1B   Bats L   Age 25

YEAR	TEAM	LGE	AB	H	DB	TP	HR	BB	SO	R	RBI	SB	CS	OUT	BA	OBP	SLG	EQA	EQR	DEFENSE
1999	Memphis	PCL	395	80	17	1	14	57	142	50	56	3	3	318	.203	.305	.357	.226	38	76-3B 5 29-1B -1
2000	Arkansas	Tex	294	70	12	0	14	28	84	40	43	0	1	225	.238	.309	.422	.241	32	61-3B 2 14-1B -3
2001	WestTenn	Sou	430	95	15	3	20	52	148	56	58	1	1	336	.221	.307	.409	.239	47	97-1B -5 13-3B -3
2002	*St Louis*	*NL*	*385*	*97*	*17*	*2*	*18*	*50*	*136*	*56*	*63*	*1*	*1*	*289*	*.252*	*.338*	*.447*	*.262*	*51*	

If you go from Triple-A to Double-A in two years, there's usually something in your career that you'd like to change. In the case of Haas, it's the elbow troubles that have prevented him from developing as a hitter. After a year in the Cubs' system, he's returned to the Cardinals as a minor-league free agent and will spend the season trying to get back some of his lost bat speed. Haas is still young enough to have a major-league career, if he can rebuild and consolidate his skills.

Carlos Hernandez   C   Bats R   Age 35

YEAR	TEAM	LGE	AB	H	DB	TP	HR	BB	SO	R	RBI	SB	CS	OUT	BA	OBP	SLG	EQA	EQR	DEFENSE
2000	San Dieg	NL	194	51	6	0	4	14	24	16	27	1	3	146	.263	.321	.356	.227	18	50-C 0
2000	St Louis	NL	51	14	3	0	1	5	8	7	9	1	0	37	.275	.349	.392	.256	6	14-C -3
2002	*Colorado*	*NL*	*205*	*59*	*6*	*0*	*6*	*21*	*27*	*21*	*28*	*3*	*3*	*149*	*.288*	*.354*	*.405*	*.229*	*19*	

He attempted to be ready to play in time for the end of the season, but he hit approximately like Mike Matheny. Hernandez's back problems are going to recur; he'll have to have a nice convergence of health, opportunity, and quick success in order to extend his career much further.

Tim Lemon   OF   Bats R   Age 21

YEAR	TEAM	LGE	AB	H	DB	TP	HR	BB	SO	R	RBI	SB	CS	OUT	BA	OBP	SLG	EQA	EQR	DEFENSE
1999	New Jrsy	NYP	250	38	4	1	3	13	69	14	18	5	9	221	.152	.201	.212	.144	9	66-CF -6
2000	Peoria	Mid	474	90	19	3	8	6	116	44	36	12	7	391	.190	.204	.293	.169	23	115-CF -7
2001	Peoria	Mid	489	90	23	2	10	20	181	41	41	16	6	405	.184	.220	.301	.180	28	114-RF -14
2002	*St Louis*	*NL*	*455*	*102*	*21*	*2*	*13*	*26*	*159*	*52*	*52*	*20*	*9*	*362*	*.224*	*.266*	*.365*	*.211*	*37*	

If you're asked to repeat a level and improve your plate discipine, is it a good thing to show some improvement and still end up with a strikeout-to-walk ratio of 165-to-27? Lemon is an extreme hacker with some very raw physical tools: he can run, throw, and hit for power. There's still a lot of tuning to do, though. If he wants to be part of the Cardinals' plans, he needs to step up in a hurry, both at the plate and in the field.

Lou Lucca 3B Bats R Age 31

YEAR	TEAM	LGE	AB	H	DB	TP	HR	BB	SO	R	RBI	SB	CS	OUT	BA	OBP	SLG	EQA	EQR	DEFENSE
1999	Scran-WB	Int	534	136	30	2	10	15	88	52	58	3	5	403	.255	.284	.375	.217	44	134-3B 11
2000	Memphis	PCL	463	123	27	1	13	23	59	58	57	5	3	343	.266	.310	.413	.240	48	109-3B 8
2001	Memphis	PCL	478	118	26	1	8	26	61	51	56	2	2	362	.247	.295	.356	.219	41	97-3B 8 17-2B -2
2002	*Cincnnti*	*NL*	*450*	*119*	*24*	*1*	*11*	*34*	*64*	*53*	*55*	*4*	*3*	*334*	*.264*	*.316*	*.396*	*.237*	*46*	

Lucca is a minor-league edition of Billy Cox in a league where no Roger Kahns are lurking to sing his praises. Lucca can pick it at third base, and he has some sock. Teams with an old slugger or a developing left-handed hitter who might need a defensive replacement and spot starter against Randy Johnson could use a guy like this. Realistically, he's doomed to be a Triple-A lifer.

T.J. Maier 2B Bats R Age 27

YEAR	TEAM	LGE	AB	H	DB	TP	HR	BB	SO	R	RBI	SB	CS	OUT	BA	OBP	SLG	EQA	EQR	DEFENSE
1999	Potomac	Car	364	80	5	0	4	40	61	39	30	7	5	289	.220	.300	.266	.201	26	56-3B 4 20-2B -3
2000	Arkansas	Tex	367	93	14	2	5	34	42	45	31	8	5	279	.253	.323	.343	.229	35	91-2B 6
2001	New Havn	Eas	265	68	19	1	3	34	56	41	30	6	3	200	.257	.349	.370	.248	31	72-2B 9
2002	*St Louis*	*NL*	*327*	*85*	*15*	*1*	*5*	*40*	*60*	*48*	*35*	*10*	*5*	*247*	*.260*	*.341*	*.358*	*.242*	*36*	

Maier's one of the two or three best defensive second basemen in all of organized baseball. His hands are Bill Mazeroski quick, his footwork solid and agile. Unfortunately for him, he's in an organization with a bunch of guys who are pretty darn good around the bag, most of whom can play other positions. 2001 was the first time Maier had really shown much with the bat, hitting .282 with good plate discipline in a tough hitters' environment. He will likely start the season in Triple-A and will have to light it up early and often to grab some attention. Maier is a good enough player to get a major-league job somewhere along the way, preferably behind a ground-ball staff.

Eli Marrero C Bats R Age 28

YEAR	TEAM	LGE	AB	H	DB	TP	HR	BB	SO	R	RBI	SB	CS	OUT	BA	OBP	SLG	EQA	EQR	DEFENSE
1999	St Louis	NL	319	62	13	1	6	14	52	30	33	9	2	259	.194	.230	.298	.183	19	74-C 7
2000	St Louis	NL	103	23	4	1	5	7	15	20	17	4	0	80	.223	.290	.427	.243	12	27-C 4
2001	St Louis	NL	204	56	12	3	6	13	31	38	24	6	3	151	.275	.318	.451	.253	24	49-C -1
2002	*St Louis*	*NL*	*272*	*66*	*14*	*2*	*9*	*21*	*45*	*41*	*37*	*9*	*2*	*208*	*.243*	*.297*	*.408*	*.238*	*29*	

With the signing of Mike DiFelice, there's speculation that LaRussa will now be free to use Marrero at first base and in the outfield corners even more than he did last year. Past comparisons we've made to Sandy Alomar look pretty weak when Marrero is getting shunted into the Scott Hemond role. Then again, this is the Cardinals, where position flexibility is more than just a good idea—it's a way of life.

Mike Matheny C Bats R Age 31

YEAR	TEAM	LGE	AB	H	DB	TP	HR	BB	SO	R	RBI	SB	CS	OUT	BA	OBP	SLG	EQA	EQR	DEFENSE
1999	Toronto	AL	162	36	4	0	4	11	33	16	17	0	0	126	.222	.275	.321	.203	12	52-C 1
2000	St Louis	NL	420	109	22	1	6	26	88	42	45	0	0	311	.260	.308	.360	.226	38	115-C 16
2001	St Louis	NL	382	88	8	1	8	26	64	41	45	0	1	295	.230	.285	.319	.206	28	112-C 8
2002	*St Louis*	*NL*	*344*	*80*	*8*	*0*	*8*	*31*	*69*	*34*	*36*	*0*	*0*	*264*	*.233*	*.296*	*.326*	*.209*	*26*	

Collect all the MLB-Approved Catch-and-Throw Guys®! The Cardinals, deciding to buy high and sell low, signed Matheny to a three-year extension at the start of the 2001 season, so he's going to be in the shadow of Eliot Hall through 2004. Matheny isn't much of a hitter and has been kind of erratic at throwing out base stealers. Pitchers like working with him, though, so he'll be consuming outs for the Redbirds until the end of the first Bush administration. Or is it the second?

Keith McDonald C Bats R Age 29

YEAR	TEAM	LGE	AB	H	DB	TP	HR	BB	SO	R	RBI	SB	CS	OUT	BA	OBP	SLG	EQA	EQR	DEFENSE
1999	Arkansas	Tex	164	44	3	0	3	11	36	16	12	1	0	120	.268	.322	.341	.228	15	38-C -5
1999	Memphis	PCL	112	30	5	0	4	17	23	16	21	1	0	82	.268	.364	.420	.268	15	23-C 0
2000	Memphis	PCL	267	66	8	0	6	22	57	28	26	0	2	203	.247	.310	.345	.221	23	71-C 0
2001	Memphis	PCL	333	81	17	1	10	23	54	37	36	1	0	252	.243	.295	.390	.229	32	88-C -5
2002	*St Louis*	*NL*	*298*	*76*	*13*	*1*	*10*	*31*	*59*	*37*	*37*	*1*	*1*	*223*	*.255*	*.325*	*.406*	*.246*	*33*	

Should 27-man rosters come about, Tony LaRussa is the one manager who will find a way to carry four catchers. Barring that, McDonald is probably screwed by the acquisition of DiFelice. Considering the Cardinals are already burning a roster spot on a defensive replacement such as Matheny, they'd be better off carrying McDonald for his slightly better bat. DiFelice has more big-league experience, and he's over 30, and those things matter to the Cardinals.

Mark McGwire 1B Bats R Age 38

YEAR	TEAM	LGE	AB	H	DB	TP	HR	BB	SO	R	RBI	SB	CS	OUT	BA	OBP	SLG	EQA	EQR	DEFENSE	
1999	St Louis	NL	520	142	24	1	62	126	130	116	135	0	0	378	.273	.417	.081	.340	128	140-1B	-7
2000	St Louis	NL	230	71	9	0	30	72	72	50	67	1	0	165	.301	.475	.720	.371	60	66 1B	5
2001	St Louis	NL	300	59	9	0	28	54	100	51	64	0	0	241	.197	.324	.507	.269	45	78-1B	-2
2002	*St Louis*	*NL*	*449*	*98*	*19*	*0*	*46*	*108*	*148*	*88*	*100*	*0*	*0*	*351*	*.218*	*.370*	*.568*	*.301*	*87*		

Usually, we don't profile retirees or run projections for them, but dammit, Big Red was still valuable. His doctors seem to think he was physically able to play, but at the end, McGwire just didn't feel he could do it. A Mark McGwire at-bat was one of those "worth the price of admission" things that people say don't exist in the game these days. Like all baseball fans, we say thank you to McGwire for the class he demonstrated in 1998, as well as for blasts like the one off Randy Johnson in 1997. No one did a better job of taking our collective breath away.

Chris Morris CF Bats R Age 22

YEAR	TEAM	LGE	AB	H	DB	TP	HR	BB	SO	R	RBI	SB	CS	OUT	BA	OBP	SLG	EQA	EQR	DEFENSE	
2000	New Jrsy	NYP	198	31	1	1	0	33	56	19	12	18	9	175	.157	.281	.172	.182	12	52-CF	-2
2001	Peoria	Mid	501	122	10	5	2	62	111	55	29	54	20	398	.244	.327	.295	.229	50	132-CF	-1
2002	*St Louis*	*NL*	*481*	*119*	*11*	*4*	*3*	*76*	*120*	*66*	*41*	*57*	*17*	*379*	*.247*	*.350*	*.306*	*.244*	*56*		

A good rule of thumb: if a guy's stolen bases, triples, and walks total more than 200, he's an interesting player. Morris led the minors in steals with 111, against only 24 caught stealing and one GIDP. He also hit .294 in the Midwest League at age 21 and drew upwards of 80 walks in 134 games. He's described as "raw" defensively, with an arm that may be stretched in center field. Even with those weaknesses, Morris has a mix of skills that could make him a very valuable player. If he can learn a little technique in the outfield and develop his hitting to where he could hit, say, .280 in the majors with 70-80 walks and 70-80 stolen bases, well, he'll be a multimillionaire, and possibly part of a championship team.

Bill Ortega RF Bats R Age 26

YEAR	TEAM	LGE	AB	H	DB	TP	HR	BB	SO	R	RBI	SB	CS	OUT	BA	OBP	SLG	EQA	EQR	DEFENSE	
1999	Potomac	Car	429	109	23	2	7	25	69	51	52	4	4	324	.254	.298	.366	.222	38	109-RF	7
1999	Arkansas	Tex	69	22	5	0	2	8	9	8	8	0	0	47	.319	.390	.478	.290	11	20-RF	1
2000	Arkansas	Tex	332	93	16	3	9	18	42	40	44	1	3	242	.280	.322	.428	.246	36	82-RF	-6
2001	Memphis	PCL	495	131	23	3	5	38	67	48	53	5	5	369	.265	.321	.354	.229	46	116-RF	-7
2002	*St Louis*	*NL*	*437*	*119*	*21*	*3*	*9*	*40*	*64*	*54*	*53*	*6*	*5*	*322*	*.272*	*.333*	*.396*	*.246*	*48*		

Ortega is the MLBPA's worst nightmare. He's good enough to replace a lot of guys in the majors making millions of bucks a year. His defensive reputation is considerable, despite the poor fielding numbers shown above. He'll go into camp as a dark-horse candidate for an OF spot. Like most of the hitters in the Arizona Fall League last year, Ortega beat the crap out of the ball for six weeks, posting a .387/.482/.559 campaign in Phoenix.

Craig Paquette 1B/3B/LF Bats R Age 33

YEAR	TEAM	LGE	AB	H	DB	TP	HR	BB	SO	R	RBI	SB	CS	OUT	BA	OBP	SLG	EQA	EQR	DEFENSE			
1999	Norfolk	Int	282	72	18	2	13	7	44	34	44	2	0	210	.255	.279	.472	.243	31	36-3B	0	19-RF	2
1999	St Louis	NL	158	45	6	0	10	4	35	21	35	1	0	113	.285	.302	.513	.263	20	19-RF	-1		
2000	St Louis	NL	387	94	23	2	15	21	76	45	58	4	3	296	.243	.285	.429	.233	39	60-3B	-6	17-LF	-1
2001	St Louis	NL	341	100	14	0	16	16	57	48	66	3	1	242	.293	.332	.475	.265	44	39-LF	0	22-3B	-3
2002	*Detroit*	*AL*	*410*	*104*	*19*	*1*	*18*	*23*	*77*	*49*	*64*	*5*	*1*	*307*	*.254*	*.293*	*.437*	*.246*	*46*				

As his defensive usefulness has declined, he's become a better hitter. In 2001, Paquette probably had his best season with the bat, but you still don't want him out there chewing up outs for more than a couple of hundred at-bats. He can play a corner-outfield or corner-infield spot pretty well, and he has a pretty dramatic reverse platoon split. The Tigers, who already have a few guys like this, signed Paquette.

Placido Polanco IF Bats R Age 26

YEAR	TEAM	LGE	AB	H	DB	TP	HR	BB	SO	R	RBI	SB	CS	OUT	BA	OBP	SLG	EQA	EQR	DEFENSE			
1999	Memphis	PCL	118	29	2	1	0	3	10	14	8	2	0	89	.246	.269	.280	.191	7	19-2B	6		
1999	St Louis	NL	221	61	8	3	1	12	22	23	18	1	3	163	.276	.313	.353	.222	19	45-2B	-1		
2000	St Louis	NL	325	102	11	3	5	11	24	48	37	4	4	227	.314	.338	.412	.249	35	37-2B	4	27-3B	1
2001	St Louis	NL	565	180	27	4	3	22	36	91	39	12	3	388	.319	.349	.396	.254	63	87-3B	13	34-SS	5
2002	*St Louis*	*NL*	*476*	*147*	*20*	*4*	*5*	*30*	*35*	*73*	*44*	*11*	*4*	*333*	*.309*	*.350*	*.399*	*.256*	*55*				

Polanco is a great defensive utility guy. His technique is excellent at three infield positions, which makes him a very valuable spare part. He's stretched to help a club beyond that role. He needs to hit .300 to have any semblance of offensive value, and he might well continue to do that. At the plate, he's a traditional slap hitter who puts the ball in play and runs. Polanco dropped more than 50 points of batting average from the first half to the second half last year. If things work out for him, he can have a peak in which he helps a club as a middle infielder. More likely is that he'll have a nice career as a defensive fill-in and bat off the bench.

Albert Pujols 3B/OF Bats R Age 22

YEAR	TEAM	LGE	AB	H	DB	TP	HR	BB	SO	R	RBI	SB	CS	OUT	BA	OBP	SLG	EQA	EQR	DEFENSE			
2000	Peoria	Mid	406	105	23	3	12	23	41	44	53	1	2	304	.259	.302	.419	.237	41	104-3B	10		
2000	Potomac	Car	83	20	4	1	2	4	8	9	7	1	1	64	.241	.276	.386	.218	7	20-3B	5		
2001	St Louis	NL	591	201	49	4	37	66	79	116	132	1	3	393	.340	.413	.624	.329	122	70-OF	-2	54-3B	1
2002	*St Louis*	*NL*	*535*	*177*	*43*	*4*	*29*	*60*	*71*	*90*	*98*	*2*	*2*	*360*	*.331*	*.398*	*.589*	*.318*	*103*				

He's older than advertised, by at least three years according to some estimates. It was apparently a not-so-open secret in his college program, but the party line is that he "graduated early" from high school in the Dominican Republic. From a practical standpoint, who really cares? His age is most germane to issues such as his likely career totals, not whether he can help the Cardinals. Pujols can mash the ball and will continue to do so into the foreseeable future. If he plays third base, he'll be the best third baseman in the National League in 2002.

Edgar Renteria SS Bats R Age 26

YEAR	TEAM	LGE	AB	H	DB	TP	HR	BB	SO	R	RBI	SB	CS	OUT	BA	OBP	SLG	EQA	EQR	DEFENSE	
1999	St Louis	NL	587	160	34	2	12	46	76	88	60	32	8	435	.273	.328	.399	.250	68	144-SS	-16
2000	St Louis	NL	565	154	26	1	17	55	71	88	72	19	14	425	.273	.338	.412	.250	67	142-SS	-1
2001	St Louis	NL	494	133	21	3	10	37	62	57	59	17	4	365	.269	.323	.385	.242	53	128-SS	-1
2002	*St Louis*	*NL*	*500*	*142*	*26*	*2*	*15*	*53*	*68*	*81*	*61*	*23*	*8*	*366*	*.284*	*.353*	*.434*	*.268*	*68*		

When we compared him to Edgardo Alfonzo, it was because we thought Renteria would get better, not because Alfonzo would get worse. Renteria stumbled through a wretched first half, looking completely lost at the plate with a newly elongated swing and no apparent approach. After the All-Star break, he tightened up his stroke and hit fairly well, posting a .283/.341/.413. He's still young and has a couple of years to avoid the dreaded Alex Gonzalez career path—or the even worse Brent Gates career path.

Kerry Robinson OF Bats L Age 28

YEAR	TEAM	LGE	AB	H	DB	TP	HR	BB	SO	R	RBI	SB	CS	OUT	BA	OBP	SLG	EQA	EQR	DEFENSE	
1999	Tacoma	PCL	331	98	13	6	1	12	40	43	28	24	6	239	.296	.321	.381	.243	35	68-LF	-3
1999	Indianap	Int	129	32	3	1	1	2	11	18	11	10	4	101	.248	.264	.310	.201	9	33-CF	2
2000	Columbus	Int	440	132	16	6	1	33	39	62	28	29	15	323	.300	.351	.370	.248	49	105-CF	-6
2001	St Louis	NL	186	54	7	1	1	12	17	36	15	11	2	134	.290	.338	.355	.245	20	48-LF	1
2002	*St Louis*	*NL*	*374*	*112*	*15*	*4*	*3*	*27*	*42*	*62*	*31*	*17*	*6*	*268*	*.299*	*.347*	*.385*	*.253*	*43*		

He's what Whitey Herzog would call "a jackrabbit." Robinson takes a very strange hack at the ball and runs like crazy, resulting in a large number of grounders and high chops that he can beat out for singles. He's actually pretty quick getting the bat through the hitting zone, and he could help a few major-league clubs as a pinch hitter/defensive replacement. There are rumors that the Cardinals will include Robinson as part of a platoon in left field; there's no way the Cardinals braintrust will let that happen.

Luis Saturria OF Bats R Age 25

YEAR	TEAM	LGE	AB	H	DB	TP	HR	BB	SO	R	RBI	SB	CS	OUT	BA	OBP	SLG	EQA	EQR	DEFENSE
1999	Arkansas	Tex	486	103	25	2	12	27	139	50	45	10	6	389	.212	.258	.346	.203	36	137-RF -4
2000	Arkansas	Tex	481	115	20	6	16	30	124	58	54	11	7	373	.239	.289	.405	.229	47	127-CF 12
2001	Memphis	PCL	413	86	14	4	11	30	104	55	41	6	7	334	.208	.268	.341	.204	32	115-CF 17
2002	*St Louis*	*NL*	*434*	*105*	*21*	*4*	*14*	*36*	*121*	*56*	*48*	*8*	*3*	*332*	*.242*	*.300*	*.406*	*.238*	*45*	

Four years ago, Saturria took huge hacks at 75–85% of the pitches thrown near him. Nothing has changed. He hasn't shown any development as a hitter and is kind of stuck in the Tony Armas/Ron Kittle offensive mode, but without the refined bat control of either. We haven't actually seen him leave his shoes during a swing, but we're pretty sure it's happened. Saturria's defensive reputation does not match the data we have for him. If he's really as good as the numbers indicate, he might be good enough for the majors a year or two down the road. Until he improves his plate discipline by about 30%, it's Triple-A time.

Esix Snead CF Bats B Age 26

YEAR	TEAM	LGE	AB	H	DB	TP	HR	BB	SO	R	RBI	SB	CS	OUT	BA	OBP	SLG	EQA	EQR	DEFENSE
1999	Peoria	Mid	188	30	7	0	1	23	46	20	11	14	6	164	.160	.255	.213	.179	11	59-CF 5
1999	Potomac	Car	257	42	9	3	0	22	57	25	11	18	8	223	.163	.235	.222	.172	14	67-CF 6
2000	Potomac	Car	509	106	13	2	1	52	99	54	27	56	27	429	.208	.286	.248	.199	38	132-CF 2
2001	New Havn	Eas	531	114	21	4	1	40	112	59	30	43	16	433	.215	.278	.275	.202	40	132-CF 10
2002	*NY Mets*	*NL*	*456*	*96*	*11*	*3*	*3*	*51*	*103*	*56*	*27*	*53*	*24*	*383*	*.211*	*.290*	*.268*	*.208*	*38*	

The Cardinals called him the best student in the organization. He'd also probably be the best baseball player for Vince Caiazza's Madison High School Knights in Brooklyn. Actually, sadly, possibly not. Snead has one offensive skill: running really fast. He's not the muscle-bound basher that someone like Brian L. Hunter is, so he'll have to work on that in the minors for a little longer. Defensively, he's a legit center fielder. If he can hit .275, he could have Hunter's career. Taken by the Mets in the Rule 5 draft.

Chris Snopek IF Bats R Age 31

YEAR	TEAM	LGE	AB	H	DB	TP	HR	BB	SO	R	RBI	SB	CS	OUT	BA	OBP	SLG	EQA	EQR	DEFENSE	
1999	Indianap	Int	381	99	22	2	8	34	48	54	53	12	5	287	.260	.325	.391	.243	42	34-3B 0	26-SS 5
2000	Tacoma	PCL	394	110	21	1	12	35	39	63	39	9	5	289	.279	.343	.429	.258	49	48-SS -6	20-2B -2
2001	Iowa	PCL	468	118	20	0	14	30	61	55	49	6	4	354	.252	.299	.385	.228	44	63-SS 0	38-3B -4
2002	*St Louis*	*NL*	*436*	*117*	*21*	*1*	*15*	*42*	*58*	*64*	*56*	*11*	*4*	*323*	*.268*	*.333*	*.424*	*.256*	*53*		

He's been signed to a minor-league contract, and now that McGwire is out of the picture, he might get a shot to be a utility infielder. Snopek has been undervalued for most of his career. He can play defense pretty well in the middle infield, hit for a moderate average and some power, and will take a walk. He's an insurance policy to have around in case something happens to Vina, Pujols, or Renteria. Of course, he's not Tony LaRussa Approved, so he'll be behind Polanco if he even makes the squad.

Fernando Vina 2B Bats L Age 33

YEAR	TEAM	LGE	AB	H	DB	TP	HR	BB	SO	R	RBI	SB	CS	OUT	BA	OBP	SLG	EQA	EQR	DEFENSE
1999	Milwauke	NL	155	41	4	0	2	12	6	16	16	4	2	116	.265	.333	.329	.230	15	36-2B 3
2000	St Louis	NL	490	146	25	5	4	29	33	77	29	9	8	352	.298	.367	.394	.258	60	118-2B 15
2001	St Louis	NL	632	199	31	8	9	29	30	98	58	17	7	440	.315	.361	.432	.267	81	147-2B 3
2002	*St Louis*	*NL*	*522*	*146*	*25*	*5*	*8*	*41*	*30*	*74*	*51*	*14*	*7*	*383*	*.280*	*.332*	*.393*	*.246*	*57*	

Vina is an outstanding defensive second baseman who does almost everything pretty well. He's a great bunter to both sides of the mound, he augments a low walk total with a few HBPs, and he turns a lot of easy doubles into triples. Vina is a hustle player with some legitimate skills, and it wouldn't be surprising to see him start turning a few of those doubles into home runs. He will outperform the forecast above and could blossom into a 15-homer guy.

PITCHERS (ERA: 4.50, H/9: 9.0, HR/9: 1.0, BB/9: 3.0, K/9: 6.0, KW: 2.0, PERA: 4.50)

Rick Ankiel Throws L Age 22

YEAR	TEAM	LGE	IP	H	ER	HR	BB	K	ERA	W	L	H/9	HR/9	BB/9	K/9	KW	PERA	STUFF
1999	Arkansas	Tex	46.7	36	16	3	18	54	3.09	3	2	6.9	0.6	3.5	10.4	1.5	1.23	57
1999	Memphis	PCL	89.3	75	41	8	48	90	4.13	5	5	7.6	0.8	4.8	9.1	0.9	3.59	37
1999	St Louis	NL	33.3	27	11	2	12	35	2.97	3	1	7.3	0.5	3.2	9.5	1.5	2.98	38
2000	St Louis	NL	173.0	151	79	19	74	172	4.11	10	9	7.9	1.0	3.8	8.9	1.2	3.71	36
2001	St Louis	NL	23.3	24	23	6	22	22	8.87	1	2	9.3	2.3	8.5	8.5	0.5	7.81	0
2001	JohnsnCy	App	81.7	72	29	2	27	62	3.20	6	3	7.9	0.2	3.0	6.8	1.1	2.95	28

Rick Ankiel DH Bats L Age 22

YEAR	TEAM	LGE	AB	H	DB	TP	HR	BB	SO	R	RBI	SB	CS	OUT	BA	OBP	SLG	EQA	EQR
2001	JohnsnCy	App	108	21	3	0	5	7	28	11	17	0	0	87	.194	.247	.361	.202	8
2002	*St Louis*	*NL*	*150*	*34*	*5*	*0*	*6*	*13*	*42*	*16*	*19*	*0*	*0*	*116*	*.227*	*.288*	*.380*	*.222*	*13*

After his brutal April in the bigs, Ankiel pitched well at Johnson City. He seemed to relax a bit and by all accounts was enjoying playing the game, both on the mound and in the batter's box. Everyone knows he has the physical skills to pitch, but there is no road map back from where he's gone. Until he's on a major-league mound, pitching in a high-pressure situation in front of a hostile crowd after facing countless questions from the press about his confidence, no one knows what's going to happen. Ankiel is young enough that he'll get ten years and countless chances to try to come back, probably in a variety of roles. We're rooting for him, but we have no idea what's going to happen. Well, we know he'll likely outhit Doug Glanville. Beyond that, anyone who tells you they know how Ankiel will do once he returns is either an idiot, lying, or both. You have to root for him, though.

Alan Benes Throws R Age 30

YEAR	TEAM	LGE	IP	H	ER	HR	BB	K	ERA	W	L	H/9	HR/9	BB/9	K/9	KW	PERA	STUFF
2000	Memphis	PCL	39.3	48	36	10	22	19	8.24	1	3	11.0	2.3	5.0	4.3	0.4	8.21	-35
2000	St Louis	NL	47.7	52	29	6	19	23	5.48	2	3	9.8	1.1	3.6	4.3	0.6	5.83	-18
2001	Memphis	PCL	143.7	158	89	17	65	61	5.58	6	10	9.9	1.1	4.1	3.8	0.5	5.64	-15
2001	St Louis	NL	13.0	16	15	4	11	8	10.38	0	1	11.1	2.8	7.6	5.5	0.4	7.28	-40

There's nothing here to indicate that Alan is going to be effective in any role any time soon. His velocity and movement have vanished, his command is gone, and he needs to rebuild his motion and career from the ground up. He'll likely end up as a rotation filler for some Triple-A club, and he will have to get lucky to get another shot in the bigs.

Andy Benes Throws R Age 34

YEAR	TEAM	LGE	IP	H	ER	HR	BB	K	ERA	W	L	H/9	HR/9	BB/9	K/9	KW	PERA	STUFF
1999	Arizona	NL	202.3	214	119	31	69	127	5.29	9	13	9.5	1.4	3.1	5.6	0.9	4.77	4
2000	St Louis	NL	169.3	174	95	27	56	122	5.05	8	11	9.2	1.4	3.0	6.5	1.1	4.65	8
2001	St Louis	NL	103.0	119	88	26	55	63	7.69	3	8	10.4	2.3	4.8	5.5	0.6	7.65	-19

Andy Benes was once an outstanding starting pitcher. He was consistent, nasty, and dependable, year in and year out. At this point, he looks positively horrid. His effective velocity is gone, but he still pitches as if his fastball was good enough to blow people away. The result is pretty predictable—complete and utter poundings on a regular basis. He may yet learn how to pitch with lesser stuff than he had at 25; if he doesn't, he'll be out of baseball in 18 months. His few quality starts (six) came against the Rockies at home, the Pirates, Phillies, White Sox, and the Reds twice. The games against the Reds and the Sox did not include Ken Griffey or Frank Thomas, respectively. He could bounce back, but it might be as a reliever in the second half.

B.R. Cook Throws R Age 24

YEAR	TEAM	LGE	IP	H	ER	HR	BB	K	ERA	W	L	H/9	HR/9	BB/9	K/9	KW	PERA	STUFF
1999	New Jrsy	NYP	44.0	48	28	5	21	20	5.73	2	3	9.8	1.0	4.3	4.1	0.5	5.72	-6
2000	Peoria	Mid	94.3	108	77	18	60	46	7.35	3	7	10.3	1.7	5.7	4.4	0.4	8.70	-18
2000	Potomac	Car	42.7	50	36	7	31	13	7.59	1	4	10.5	1.5	6.5	2.7	0.2	8.63	-30
2001	Potomac	Car	46.0	51	27	5	18	18	5.28	2	3	10.0	1.0	3.5	3.5	0.5	5.58	-10
2001	New Havn	Eas	117.3	131	76	17	49	53	5.83	5	8	10.0	1.3	3.8	4.1	0.5	6.73	-8

Cook is your garden-variety pitching prospect. That is, he's a long shot. He has a middling fastball and slider, and he's working to develop the rest of his repertoire. A 3.99 ERA and middle-of-the-pack strikeout rate in the Eastern League isn't anything special. Cook's best chance to make the majors is probably as a swing man or relief specialist. If he can improve his control about one walk per nine innings, he has a shot. He's likely to be pasted around in Triple-A until he learns to make the necessary adjustments.

Mike Crudale Throws R Age 25

YEAR	TEAM	LGE	IP	H	ER	HR	BB	K	ERA	W	L	H/9	HR/9	BB/9	K/9	KW	PERA	STUFF
1999	JohnsnCy	App	33.0	34	19	2	19	15	5.10	2	2	9.3	0.5	5.2	4.1	0.4	4.94	-22
2000	Peoria	Mid	48.3	52	28	5	20	23	5.21	2	3	9.7	0.9	3.7	4.3	0.6	4.68	-22
2000	Potomac	Car	26.3	32	24	7	14	15	8.20	1	2	10.9	2.4	4.8	5.1	0.5	8.45	-38
2001	New Havn	Eas	79.3	83	48	12	32	50	5.45	4	5	9.4	1.4	3.6	5.7	0.8	6.83	-20

Yes, he had good control. Yes, he struck out more than a guy per inning. But he was 24 years old in a great situation for a pitcher to succeed. Crudale has a plus fastball, but it's somewhat flat, and he needs to develop his secondary pitches to have a reasonable shot at a career. Either that, or get traded to Texas.

Luther Hackman Throws R Age 27

YEAR	TEAM	LGE	IP	H	ER	HR	BB	K	ERA	W	L	H/9	HR/9	BB/9	K/9	KW	PERA	STUFF
1999	Carolina	Sou	60.3	63	37	7	32	31	5.52	3	4	9.4	1.0	4.8	4.6	0.5	5.80	-11
1999	ColSprin	PCL	104.7	102	52	7	47	64	4.47	6	6	8.8	0.6	4.0	5.5	0.7	3.77	6
1999	Colorado	NL	18.0	21	16	4	10	9	8.00	0	2	10.5	2.0	5.0	4.5	0.4	7.83	-25
2000	Memphis	PCL	121.3	136	71	15	38	47	5.27	5	8	10.1	1.1	2.8	3.5	0.6	6.18	-13
2001	Memphis	PCL	21.3	24	10	3	1	8	4.22	1	1	10.1	1.3	0.4	3.4	4.0	3.48	-16
2001	St Louis	NL	31.3	35	21	6	13	19	6.03	1	2	10.1	1.7	3.7	5.5	0.7	4.50	-16

Hackman will fight to have a career as a two-pitch guy out of the bullpen, battling for the 11th or 12th spot on the staff for the next couple of years. The bone-spur problem he had in 2000 appears to be a thing of the past. His velocity increased slightly towards the end of the season, an encouraging sign.

Dustin Hermanson Throws R Age 29

YEAR	TEAM	LGE	IP	H	ER	HR	BB	K	ERA	W	L	H/9	HR/9	BB/9	K/9	KW	PERA	STUFF
1999	Montreal	NL	221.3	222	98	19	58	131	3.98	14	11	9.0	0.8	2.4	5.3	1.1	4.16	10
2000	Montreal	NL	203.0	223	112	23	62	84	4.97	10	13	9.9	1.0	2.7	3.7	0.7	5.31	-7
2001	St Louis	NL	181.3	198	113	29	65	99	5.61	8	12	9.8	1.4	3.2	4.9	0.8	4.92	-1

Still maddening after all these years. His stuff can vary a huge amount from start to start, and even when it's on, Hermanson will occasionally find a way to let hitters off the hook. His workload in 1999 might simply have been too much. The dramatic drop in his strikeout rate didn't do much to inspire confidence going into the 2001 season, and there's nothing he showed in 2001 that makes one think that all his promise will finally be realized. Still, he's a middle-of-the-rotation guy who can give you 30–34 starts, and even with that brutal ERA, he did make 19 quality starts in 2001. Traded to the Red Sox, Hermanson will be their #3 starter.

Chad Hutchinson Throws R Age 25

YEAR	TEAM	LGE	IP	H	ER	HR	BB	K	ERA	W	L	H/9	HR/9	BB/9	K/9	KW	PERA	STUFF
1999	Arkansas	Tex	141.3	138	90	17	93	108	5.73	6	10	8.8	1.1	5.9	6.9	0.6	5.65	8
2000	Arkansas	Tex	48.0	43	22	2	28	36	4.13	3	2	8.1	0.4	5.3	6.8	0.6	4.60	7
2001	Memphis	PCL	99.7	94	83	10	123	76	7.49	3	8	8.5	0.9	11.1	6.9	0.3	9.69	-27

He of the nasty slider and potential football career. Hutchinson continued to battle his command problems in 2001, walking 104 batters and throwing 17 wild pitches in 98 innings. There's no doubt about Hutchinson's ability to throw great pitches. Sometimes, everything comes together and a guy like this will turn into a nasty closer. More often, things gradually improve, but never enough to make him an effective major-league pitcher.

Mike James Throws R Age 34

YEAR	TEAM	LGE	IP	H	ER	HR	BB	K	ERA	W	L	H/9	HR/9	BB/9	K/9	KW	PERA	STUFF
2000	St Louis	NL	49.0	49	26	6	20	36	4.78	2	3	9.0	1.1	3.7	6.6	0.9	3.48	-3
2001	St Louis	NL	37.7	39	21	4	15	21	5.02	2	2	9.3	1.0	3.6	5.0	0.7	5.63	-14

(Mike James *continued*)
He fought his way back to credibility, only to have the dreaded "sore shoulder" that naturally ended up being the scarier "rotator-cuff inflammation." James missed a couple of months and wasn't 100% when he came back. If he can get fully healthy, he can help a club as a setup man, but "fully healthy" may be out of reach. For the record, when you hear "sore shoulder," and things don't get better inside a few days, just conjure a mental picture of what the drumstick areas on your family's Thanksgiving turkey look like about two hours after the meal is over.

Jimmy Journell Throws R Age 24

YEAR	TEAM	LGE	IP	H	ER	HR	BB	K	ERA	W	L	H/9	HR/9	BB/9	K/9	KW	PERA	STUFF
2000	New Jrsy	NYP	28.3	25	18	0	31	19	5.72	1	2	7.9	0.0	9.8	6.0	0.3	5.50	-17
2001	Potomac	Car	144.0	154	90	20	64	80	5.63	6	10	9.6	1.3	4.0	5.0	0.6	5.02	-4

Journell had an outstanding bounce-back from Tommy John surgery. While he was initially projected to be a reliever, the decision to use him as a starter to get him innings turned into an exploration to see if he should just be a starter after all. He throws hard, as you'd expect, and made unexpected progress with his slider. The Cardinals have changed his delivery from the sidearm motion he used at Illinois to three-quarters. It's going to take at least another year or two to consolidate all these lessons, changes, and continued rehabilitation.

Darryl Kile Throws R Age 33

YEAR	TEAM	LGE	IP	H	ER	HR	BB	K	ERA	W	L	H/9	HR/9	BB/9	K/9	KW	PERA	STUFF
1999	Colorado	NL	198.3	214	126	27	91	104	5.72	8	14	9.7	1.2	4.1	4.7	0.6	5.19	-4
2000	St Louis	NL	231.7	229	106	29	48	171	4.12	14	12	8.9	1.1	1.9	6.6	1.8	3.81	18
2001	St Louis	NL	221.0	216	96	19	58	144	3.91	14	11	8.8	0.8	2.4	5.9	1.2	3.26	14

Kile had 25 combined quality starts and blown quality starts in 34 starts overall. The four blown quality starts were tied for second in the league with Mike Hampton behind Livan Hernandez's eye-popping eight. For the rest of his life, Kile will probably be getting phone calls from pitchers considering signing with the Rockies. He still has that amazing curveball, combined with a plus fastball and good command of the strike zone. He's an underrated pitcher, both in terms of his effectiveness and how much fun he is to watch. Brian Jordan is already starting to bail out against a curveball that Kile's going to throw him in early May.

Steve Kline Throws L Age 29

YEAR	TEAM	LGE	IP	H	ER	HR	BB	K	ERA	W	L	H/9	HR/9	BB/9	K/9	KW	PERA	STUFF
1999	Montreal	NL	68.7	62	32	7	28	62	4.19	4	4	8.1	0.9	3.7	8.1	1.1	3.76	6
2000	Montreal	NL	85.7	83	37	7	22	57	3.89	6	4	8.7	0.7	2.3	6.0	1.3	3.59	0
2001	St Louis	NL	67.7	63	28	3	26	43	3.72	5	3	8.4	0.4	3.5	5.7	0.8	1.90	-1

Kline appeared in 89 games, averaging less than an inning per appearance. The very prototype of the left-handed specialist, Kline shut down lefties more effectively than Roy Cohn on a Frappuccino bender. Left-handed batters rung up a whopping zero extra-base hits against him, hitting a lusty .149. There's no reason to think that his role will change dramatically, or that he'll have a sudden dropoff in effectiveness.

Jeremy Lambert Throws R Age 23

YEAR	TEAM	LGE	IP	H	ER	HR	BB	K	ERA	W	L	H/9	HR/9	BB/9	K/9	KW	PERA	STUFF
1999	Peoria	Mid	36.3	46	42	11	30	16	10.40	1	3	11.4	2.7	7.4	4.0	0.3	11.58	-40
2000	Potomac	Car	29.7	30	13	2	8	17	3.94	2	1	9.1	0.6	2.4	5.2	1.1	6.70	-2
2000	Arkansas	Tex	48.3	40	20	2	28	44	3.72	3	2	7.4	0.4	5.2	8.2	0.8	5.80	13
2001	New Havn	Eas	33.7	33	23	6	22	32	6.15	1	3	8.8	1.6	5.9	8.6	0.7	5.91	1
2001	Memphis	PCL	28.3	30	20	8	9	28	6.35	1	2	9.5	2.5	2.9	8.9	1.6	4.56	11

Lambert struck out 13 guys per nine innings in New Haven and made the transition to Triple-A gracefully, to say the least, fanning 39 in 30 innings with other good peripherals to go along with it. He has a major-league-average fastball and a plus slider, thrown from a compact delivery. Minor-league closers are fraught with risk, but Lambert did nothing in 2001 but demonstrate that he deserves a shot in the bigs.

Scotty Layfield — Throws R — Age 25

YEAR	TEAM	LGE	IP	H	ER	HR	BB	K	ERA	W	L	H/9	HR/9	BB/9	K/9	KW	PERA	STUFF
1999	New Jrsy	NYP	31.0	40	37	9	29	12	10.74	0	3	11.6	2.6	8.4	3.5	0.2	6.48	-51
2000	Peoria	Mid	56.3	65	54	11	50	25	8.63	1	5	10.4	1.8	8.0	4.0	0.3	11.83	-57
2001	Potomac	Car	51.0	49	26	3	30	31	4.59	3	3	8.6	0.5	5.3	5.5	0.5	3.69	-22

He got a late start as a pitcher, having only begun pitching seriously in college. Layfield has an above-average fastball and slider, and his likely future is out of the bullpen. Still learning the craft, he is expected to clean up his mechanics and add another mph or two. He could be a real sleeper as a bullpen guy late in the season. Normal minor-league-closer caveats apply.

T.J. Mathews — Throws R — Age 32

YEAR	TEAM	LGE	IP	H	ER	HR	BB	K	ERA	W	L	H/9	HR/9	BB/9	K/9	KW	PERA	STUFF
1999	Oakland	AL	56.3	56	29	8	17	42	4.63	3	3	8.9	1.3	2.7	6.7	1.2	3.72	0
2000	Oakland	AL	63.7	66	35	9	20	42	4.95	3	4	9.3	1.3	2.8	5.9	1.0	5.23	-7
2001	Oakland	AL	25.0	24	12	2	10	18	4.32	2	1	8.6	0.7	3.6	6.5	0.9	5.16	-2
2001	Memphis	PCL	15.7	14	4	0	1	9	2.30	2	0	8.0	0.0	0.6	5.2	4.5	3.01	2
2001	St Louis	NL	13.0	14	6	2	1	8	4.15	1	0	9.7	1.4	0.7	5.5	4.0	3.64	0

Mathews looked like he would be a solid bullpen guy for the A's when they got him in The Trade, but he has been consistently disappointing. His peripheral ERAs still look good, and his pitches have the same nice motion they did before 1999. He just keeps leaving fat pitches in the zone. It wouldn't be a surprise to see him rebound and be a solid contributor again. It also wouldn't be a surprise to see him go through four or five teams before that happens. The Astros get first crack at turning him around.

Mike Matthews — Throws L — Age 28

YEAR	TEAM	LGE	IP	H	ER	HR	BB	K	ERA	W	L	H/9	HR/9	BB/9	K/9	KW	PERA	STUFF
1999	Akron	Eas	25.3	39	40	12	18	6	14.21	0	3	13.9	4.3	6.4	2.1	0.2	14.10	-86
1999	Buffalo	Int	21.7	24	19	4	19	11	7.89	0	2	10.0	1.7	7.9	4.6	0.3	8.20	-51
2000	Memphis	PCL	48.0	47	31	6	34	36	5.81	2	3	8.8	1.1	6.4	6.8	0.5	3.80	-4
2000	St Louis	NL	10.7	11	8	2	8	7	6.75	0	1	9.3	1.7	6.8	5.9	0.4	10.40	-32
2001	St Louis	NL	82.3	81	42	9	30	58	4.59	4	5	8.9	1.0	3.3	6.3	1.0	3.21	0

Thanks to surprise visits from Mr. Injury, the Cardinals called upon Matthews to spend time in both the rotation and the bullpen. He responded fairly well, pitching like a league-average starter while in the rotation and being absolutely dominant out of the pen. As great as Kline was, Matthews was even better, with a 1.08 ERA in 41 relief innings. This is the kind of quiet surprise year that can (and did) push a team towards the postseason. As great he was in 2001, his numbers were out of line with his previous performance. If the improvement is real, chalk up another Rick Honeycutt for Dave Duncan. If Matthews were a Latino, people would probably question his age. He was only 27 this year but is a dead ringer for J.K. Simmons, who is considerably older.

Matt Morris — Throws R — Age 27

YEAR	TEAM	LGE	IP	H	ER	HR	BB	K	ERA	W	L	H/9	HR/9	BB/9	K/9	KW	PERA	STUFF
2000	Memphis	PCL	15.7	18	11	3	6	6	6.32	1	1	10.3	1.7	3.4	3.4	0.5	9.21	-28
2000	St Louis	NL	54.0	53	22	3	14	30	3.67	4	2	8.8	0.5	2.3	5.0	1.1	3.37	-1
2001	St Louis	NL	213.7	199	77	11	48	149	3.24	16	8	8.4	0.5	2.0	6.3	1.6	3.55	20

Morris is an excellent #1 starter whose workload causes some Cardinals fans to suffer pretty brutal night sweats. He has great stuff, and even Greg Maddux has praised his "pitching intelligence." Many people have openly questioned LaRussa and Duncan's handling of Morris. Just as the critics crawled out of the woodwork when Rick Ankiel's workload got a little high in 2000, the end of the 2001 campaign brought out a lot of amateur orthopedists. Morris didn't show any performance decay in the second half, and Duncan/LaRussa did keep his pitch counts down. If he's healthy, he's as good a Cy Young bet as anyone not named Johnson. He signed a three-year, $27-million deal with the Cardinals that certainly appears to be a bargain for the team.

Chris Narveson — Throws L — Age 20

YEAR	TEAM	LGE	IP	H	ER	HR	BB	K	ERA	W	L	H/9	HR/9	BB/9	K/9	KW	PERA	STUFF
2000	JohnsnCy	App	53.3	68	60	18	33	28	10.13	1	5	11.5	3.0	5.6	4.7	0.4	7.16	-11
2001	Peoria	Mid	46.3	48	25	7	15	30	4.86	2	3	9.3	1.4	2.9	5.8	1.0	3.38	19
2001	Potomac	Car	62.7	69	36	9	17	31	5.17	3	4	9.9	1.3	2.4	4.5	0.9	4.10	10

(Chris Narveson *continued*)

Narveson is probably thc best-regardcd pitching prospect in the organization. His fastball is above average, reaching 94 mph, averaging 91 mph, with well-above-average movement. He has a full four-pitch repertoire, solid mechanics, and has earned the coveted "poised" label. He's also torn his elbow and was shut down in July. If he's healthy, he's going to be a very good prospect.

Josh Pearce Throws R Age 24

YEAR	TEAM	LGE	IP	H	ER	HR	BB	K	ERA	W	L	H/9	HR/9	BB/9	K/9	KW	PERA	STUFF
1999	New Jrsy	NYP	75.3	94	67	22	27	37	8.00	2	6	11.2	2.6	3.2	4.4	0.7	7.72	-10
2000	Potomac	Car	63.0	74	39	11	11	24	5.57	3	4	10.6	1.6	1.6	3.4	1.1	4.70	-3
2000	Arkansas	Tex	99.3	117	71	20	35	44	6.43	4	7	10.6	1.8	3.2	4.0	0.6	7.06	-8
2001	New Havn	Eas	112.7	123	71	17	45	61	5.67	5	8	9.8	1.4	3.6	4.9	0.7	5.75	-1
2001	Memphis	PCL	66.7	79	43	13	14	26	5.81	3	4	10.7	1.8	1.9	3.5	0.9	6.16	-6

Pearce has posted good numbers, works off a good curveball, and yet, we see only a ticking time bomb. He threw nearly 300 innings at the age of 20 in four leagues, so despite the shiny peripherals, he's probably going to hit the injury nexus like so much *musca domestica*. Pearce is a control prospect, and if he does manage to stay healthy, he still needs to eliminate the long ball.

Bud Smith Throws L Age 22

YEAR	TEAM	LGE	IP	H	ER	HR	BB	K	ERA	W	L	H/9	HR/9	BB/9	K/9	KW	PERA	STUFF
1999	Peoria	Mid	54.3	58	32	8	18	34	5.30	3	3	9.6	1.3	3.0	5.6	0.9	4.09	17
1999	Potomac	Car	103.0	101	43	4	35	54	3.76	6	5	8.8	0.3	3.1	4.7	0.8	5.05	13
2000	Arkansas	Tex	107.3	103	43	8	27	71	3.61	7	5	8.6	0.7	2.3	6.0	1.3	2.97	26
2000	Memphis	PCL	50.7	53	25	5	14	27	4.44	3	3	9.4	0.9	2.5	4.8	1.0	4.08	13
2001	Memphis	PCL	109.0	110	48	7	32	56	3.96	7	5	9.1	0.6	2.6	4.6	0.9	3.51	12
2001	St Louis	NL	79.0	83	41	10	21	47	4.67	4	5	9.5	1.1	2.4	5.4	1.1	4.21	11

Smith was highly touted in high school, where he broke some of Nomar Garciaparra's hitting records. Smith blazed through the Cardinals system, showing tremendous command of a slightly below-average fastball along with great off-speed and breaking stuff. He has terrific control, changes speeds well, and moves the ball around the strike zone like a 15-year veteran. He wasn't consistently dominating, in that he had only eight quality starts in 14 outings, but considering how he was introduced to the big leagues, that's nitpicking.

There is a tendency among analysts to characterize weaknesses as strengths when they like a player. If a guy doesn't have a great fastball, he's compared to Greg Maddux. No control? Hey, Randy Johnson didn't have control when he first came up. Smith looks like an amazing pitcher, and he may have some rough spots in terms of making the adjustments as he goes through the league a second time, but there's nothing in his record that portends anything except great success.

Gene Stechschulte Throws R Age 28

YEAR	TEAM	LGE	IP	H	ER	HR	BB	K	ERA	W	L	H/9	HR/9	BB/9	K/9	KW	PERA	STUFF
1999	Arkansas	Tex	42.0	45	31	7	26	25	6.64	2	3	9.6	1.5	5.6	5.4	0.5	7.29	-38
2000	Memphis	PCL	45.3	47	26	6	19	26	5.16	2	3	9.3	1.2	3.8	5.2	0.7	2.84	-18
2000	St Louis	NL	24.3	29	21	5	14	11	7.77	1	2	10.7	1.8	5.2	4.1	0.4	6.96	-34
2001	St Louis	NL	67.0	70	38	9	27	41	5.10	3	4	9.4	1.2	3.6	5.5	0.8	4.46	-11

He performed pretty well as a depth right-hander out of the bullpen. Stechschulte's strikeout rate isn't overwhelming, and he does give up a lot of long balls. He's going to have to demonstrate that he can be reliable for at least another 100 innings or so and learn to keep the ball down. LaRussa can have a very long memory when it comes to late-game home runs.

Garrett Stephenson Throws R Age 30

YEAR	TEAM	LGE	IP	H	ER	HR	BB	K	ERA	W	L	H/9	HR/9	BB/9	K/9	KW	PERA	STUFF
1999	Memphis	PCL	24.7	26	13	2	8	13	4.74	1	2	9.5	0.7	2.9	4.7	0.8	3.39	1
1999	St Louis	NL	87.0	89	44	10	24	53	4.55	5	5	9.2	1.0	2.5	5.5	1.1	4.13	4
2000	St Louis	NL	201.7	216	109	27	52	109	4.86	10	12	9.6	1.2	2.3	4.9	1.0	4.26	4

He probably doesn't enter into the Cardinals' plans in 2002. Stephenson's elbow rehabilitation still has a ways to go, and he'll have an opportunity to work his way back to health with an extended rehab stint in the minors. He won't be at full strength until at least the end of the 2002 season.

Nick Stocks **Throws R** **Age 23**

YEAR	TEAM	LGE	IP	H	ER	HR	BB	K	ERA	W	L	H/9	HR/9	BB/9	K/9	KW	PERA	STUFF
2000	Peoria	Mid	148.0	153	73	10	58	68	4.44	8	8	9.3	0.6	3.5	4.1	0.6	7.26	1
2001	New Havn	Eas	82.0	93	61	15	42	41	6.70	3	6	10.2	1.6	4.6	4.5	0.5	7.31	10

The Cardinals love his competitiveness on the mound almost as much as they love his mid-90s fastball. Back injuries hounded Stocks for most of the 2001 season; he'll spend the year trying to tighten up his mechanics in Double-A, unless he has that Control Moment of Epiphany.

Mike Timlin **Throws R** **Age 36**

YEAR	TEAM	LGE	IP	H	ER	HR	BB	K	ERA	W	L	H/9	HR/9	BB/9	K/9	KW	PERA	STUFF
1999	Baltimor	AL	61.3	59	30	8	19	50	4.40	4	3	8.7	1.2	2.8	7.3	1.3	3.79	3
2000	Baltimor	AL	36.0	36	20	5	12	26	5.00	2	2	9.0	1.3	3.0	6.5	1.1	4.94	-4
2000	St Louis	NL	31.0	28	15	2	16	23	4.35	2	1	8.1	0.6	4.6	6.7	0.7	3.01	-1
2001	St Louis	NL	71.3	72	31	5	17	38	3.91	5	3	9.1	0.6	2.1	4.8	1.1	4.30	-6

Timlin has good stuff, knows how to use it, and will likely be in a role in 2002 similar to the one he's filled for years. One thing that's worrisome is his strikeout rate, which took a pretty notable drop. He gave up nearly a third of his runs for the entire season in a one-week stretch against the Cubs and Padres at the end of August.

Dave Veres **Throws R** **Age 35**

YEAR	TEAM	LGE	IP	H	ER	HR	BB	K	ERA	W	L	H/9	HR/9	BB/9	K/9	KW	PERA	STUFF
1999	Colorado	NL	81.3	80	44	12	31	64	4.87	4	5	8.9	1.3	3.4	7.1	1.0	3.94	-1
2000	St Louis	NL	75.7	69	29	5	21	60	3.45	5	3	8.2	0.6	2.5	7.1	1.4	2.79	9
2001	St Louis	NL	61.3	62	36	10	25	49	5.28	3	4	9.1	1.5	3.7	7.2	1.0	3.94	-2

Veres had one of those lingering injuries that doesn't get as much attention as it should. His index finger was problematic for a large part of the season, which prevented him from effectively using his splitter. In such circumstances, the loss isn't just the pitch in question—it's the lost threat of that pitch, leading to decreased effectiveness of all your other pitches. Veres is a good bet to rebound some in 2002, although it may be in a new role with a new team.

Blake Williams **Throws R** **Age 23**

YEAR	TEAM	LGE	IP	H	ER	HR	BB	K	ERA	W	L	H/9	HR/9	BB/9	K/9	KW	PERA	STUFF
2000	New Jrsy	NYP	26.0	29	18	4	11	12	6.23	1	2	10.0	1.4	3.8	4.2	0.5	3.48	-4
2001	Potomac	Car	97.0	119	88	28	42	51	8.16	3	8	11.0	2.6	3.9	4.7	0.6	5.19	-9

A first-rounder drafted out of Southwest Texas State in 2000, Williams throws in the low 90s with a mid-80s slurve. In July, he complained of a twinge in the elbow. You know the way the story goes from there, from "sprained elbow" to "Tommy John surgery." Williams will be out of action until at least the beginning of the 2003 season. He wasn't the only Cardinals prospect to face the knife; Chance Caple blew out his elbow, too. It was a bad year for Cardinals' pitching suspects.

Woody Williams **Throws R** **Age 35**

YEAR	TEAM	LGE	IP	H	ER	HR	BB	K	ERA	W	L	H/9	HR/9	BB/9	K/9	KW	PERA	STUFF
1999	San Dieg	NL	208.3	223	119	32	61	123	5.14	10	13	9.6	1.4	2.6	5.3	1.0	4.52	4
2000	San Dieg	NL	164.3	171	86	21	44	99	4.71	9	9	9.4	1.2	2.4	5.4	1.1	3.92	8
2001	San Dieg	NL	142.7	157	84	25	33	82	5.30	7	9	9.9	1.6	2.1	5.2	1.2	5.80	2
2001	St Louis	NL	66.7	66	30	6	17	42	4.05	4	3	8.9	0.8	2.3	5.7	1.2	2.62	14

Sometimes, a change of scenery can do a world of good. Williams is a junk-balling lefty from the right side, offering up well-placed fastballs with below-average velocity. He changes pace fairly well and throws all of his pitches with the same motion. If hitters can lay off the pitches that drop out of the strike zone, they can kill him. If the umpire is giving him the bonus corner six inches off the plate, it's going to be a long day for batters. For the Cardinals, Williams had eight quality starts in 11, almost as many as he had with the Padres (ten in 23).

San Diego Padres

They're a small-market team on the West Coast with a bright future. They value the base on balls and led the majors in walks in 2001. The major-league roster is very young and boasts power at the corners and a few pitchers who have a good shot at being among the league's best. The minor-league system, a weakness not too long ago, is brimming with talent. The front office routinely fleeces other organizations in trades and rarely makes a mistake. Despite a low payroll, they should be considered one of the favorites to win the West in 2002.

Padres Prospectus

2001 record: 79–83; Fourth place, NL West
Pythagenport W/L: 79–83
Runs scored: 789 (sixth in NL)
Runs allowed: 812 (12th in NL)
Team EqA: .265 (tied for sixth in NL)
2001 batters age: 28.9 (eighth-youngest in NL)
2001 pitchers age: 28.4 (eighth-oldest in NL)
Ballpark: Qualcomm Stadium; excellent pitchers' park; Park Factor of .934
2001: Puttered through an unimpressive year as Kevin Towers kept assembling pieces.
2002: The game's sleeper team. A division title is within reach, and they're going to get much, much better.

Yes, we're enthusiastic about the Oakland Athletics, but that's not the team we're describing here. Since losing the World Series in 1998, the San Diego Padres have been in transition from an old, last-gasp pennant contender that couldn't compete in the free-agent market to a youthful, talented club, and the metamorphosis is nearly complete. General Manager Kevin Towers and company have orchestrated the turnaround, and the San Diego fans will reap the reward for years to come.

The Padres nearly started 2001 with what appeared to be a huge misstep, as third baseman and two-time team MVP Phil Nevin was almost traded to the Brewers for outfielder Jeromy Burnitz. Apparently, the deal was done, but Burnitz, a San Diego native, wouldn't agree to the San Diego discount: a contract extension worth about $6 million a year. Burnitz is a fine player, but Nevin was signed at less than half that through 2003, outhit Burnitz by a large margin in 2000, is nearly two years younger, and should be worth more. Luckily for the Friars, Nevin remained in the fold, and he had his finest season in 2001, setting career highs in batting average, home runs, and walks.

Saved from itself, the Padres front office did an excellent job all year of cutting deadwood and filling holes in the squad. They traded middle reliever Donne Wall to the Mets for outfielder Bubba Trammell, whose availability on a Mets team with serious outfield problems remains inexplicable. During spring training, enigmatic starter Matt Clement and below-average starting outfielder Eric Owens were packaged and sent to the Marlins for right fielder Mark Kotsay and infielder Cesar Crespo. That trade helped soften the impact of finally cutting bait with Ruben Rivera, a physically gifted outfielder whose short attention span and love of the nightlife frustrated the organization. Before these deals, the Padres were looking at an outfield of Owens, Rivera, and Mike Darr, which would have been pathetic. Afterwards, the Padres had Darr, Kotsay, and Trammell, a big improvement, even without taking into account Kotsay's development and successful transition to center field in 2001.

In an effort to upgrade from Chris Gomez at shortstop, the Padres traded for Brewers minor-leaguer Santiago Perez and grabbed Donaldo Mendez from the Astros in the Rule 5 draft. After getting varying degrees of miserable performance from all three players, Towers was able to flip suddenly dominant setup man Jay Witasick to the Yankees for D'Angelo Jimenez.

This trade, the highlight of a great year for General Manager Kevin Towers, completed a chain in which the Padres had traded Brian Meadows, one of the worst starting pitchers in the majors, to the Royals for Witasick, a hard thrower who had struggled as a starter. After giving him a few starts, the Padres converted Witasick to relief, and he spent the first two months of the 2001 season sitting people down. With Witasick at his peak value, the Padres swapped him even-up for the best shortstop prospect in the high minors. Meanwhile, Allard Baird banished Meadows to the minors and solved his shortstop problem by dealing his best outfielder for Neifi Perez, who can't hit at sea level and is on the brink of becoming expensive. The Padres and the Royals are both small-market teams, but the Padres aren't slitting their wrists about it. In San Diego, Jimenez was immediately handed the shortstop job and was an improvement on his predecessors, despite his erratic glove work.

At the trade deadline, the Padres managed to get something for imminent free agent Sterling Hitchcock, trading him to the Yankees for a couple of Grade-C prospects. In early August, Woody Williams was traded to the St. Louis Cardinals for Ray Lankford.

Audience participation time: when is the last time Kevin Towers made an obviously bad trade? We've talked this over, and there's not really a consensus. If you were mean-spirited, you could count Williams-for-Lankford as a bad deal, but at the time it sure didn't look that way. It's not clear what got into Williams after his arrival in St. Louis, but if you predicted he'd somehow unlock the secret to cutting his ERA from 4.97 to 2.28 on the flight into Lambert International, you probably won your fantasy league. Regardless, this was another example of dealing from strength to fix a problem; again, the Padres leveraged their organizational pitching depth to unload an ineffective, pricey starter. At worst, the Padres got a platoon partner for Trammell; at best, they got a full-time starter in the outfield who would send Darr and Rickey Henderson to the bench.

Towers was able to make these moves because the Padres have revitalized their minor-league system, drafting aggressively and developing the talent in house. Control freak Brian Lawrence got his hands on a major-league rotation slot last summer and doesn't look like he'll give it up anytime soon. Former Red Sox property Dennis Tankersley was a buzzsaw, ripping through the California and Southern leagues. A year after being sent through waivers, Jason Middlebrook was productive in Portland and with the Padres. Jake Peavy pitched very well at Lake Elsinore and Mobile. Junior Herndon and Wascar Serrano made their major-league debuts, though they both need some more time in Triple-A and have more value as trade bait than as rotation candidates.

Several pitchers at lower levels had outstanding seasons; in fact, a Padres affiliate was named *Baseball America*'s Minor League Organization of the Year for the second time in four seasons. This time, it was the Lake Elsinore Storm, a team that boasted a star-studded pitching staff and a 91-49 record. Even Brett Jodie, one of the borderline prospects acquired in the Hitchcock trade, had a useful season. With this much depth behind current starters Brian Tollberg, Bobby Jones, and Kevin Jarvis, the makings of a good rotation are here.

That's not to say everything went according to plan in 2001. As the Padres unexpectedly stuck close to the pack in the first half, and as the bullpen hit a rough spot with Tom Davey hurting and Kevin Walker out for the season, Manager Bruce Bochy rode his starters hard. That worked out all right for Williams, but the Padres didn't get so lucky with young starter Adam Eaton, who was lost for the season on July 6. He'll be out most or all of 2002 as well, recovering from Tommy John surgery. Bochy is generally careful with his younger starters, so hopefully the experience with Eaton will reinforce that behavior with the young blood coming up through the system.

The Padres have the organizational depth to deal with the loss of Eaton, and their aggressive scouting and drafting strategies are to thank for that. The team has shown it isn't afraid to draft players who present signability problems and do what it takes to get them signed. They acquired Xavier Nady, possibly the top college hitter in 2000's draft, by doing just that. Rather than being scared off by agent Scott Boras's demands, the Padres scouted Nady carefully, made their decision about what he was worth, and picked up first-round talent with a second-round pick. In 2001, the Padres were the third team to draft University of San Francisco slugger Taggert Bozied, but the first to get a deal done with him, signing him in November. With a second-round pick, the team also drafted pitcher Matt Harrington, the consensus class of the 2000 draft who couldn't come to an agreement with the Rockies. If the Padres can sign Harrington—something that looks unlikely as we go to press—they will have vultured another top pitcher to add to their collection.

Nevin, top prospect Sean Burroughs, Nady, Bozied, and 2001 first-round selection Jake Gautreau are all third basemen, and only one of them can play that position for the Padres. Rather than attacking the problem by wondering why they drafted all of these guys in the first place and trading them for pennies on the dollar, the team has done something we'd like to see more often: they're trying them out at different positions. Nevin will move to first base in 2002, which isn't exactly a controversial decision. The team has already tried Gautreau at second base, and Nady is supposed to give the position a shot once he's recovered from off-season elbow surgery. This qualifies as a creative solution in an industry that often behaves as if the last new idea it liked was the steam engine. Instead of waiting for a Jeff Kent-style offensive second baseman to fall into its laps, the organization is working to develop one of its own; if it doesn't work, no harm, no foul, move the guy back to third base and try something else. If it does work, well, putting Kent in the middle of a team's lineup can make them tougher on opposing pitchers than Lizzie Grubman is on a street full of clubgoers.

In 2002, the infusion of talent and the work of hitting coach Duane Espy will give the club a shot in the arm when it comes to avoiding outs. The 2001 squad collected a club-record and league-high 678 bases on balls, and full seasons from Jimenez and Burroughs give the Padres the foundation for a similar showing this year. The 2001 Padres ranked in the middle of the pack in Equivalent Average, and they have the personnel to improve on that. The pitching staff will make or break the team this year. If the Padres get some league-average innings from Middlebrook, Herndon, Peavy, or Serrano, they'll contend for the division title with a payroll just above $30 million.

Padres fans got more good news in late November, when the San Diego city council passed a revised plan to cover San Diego's share of the new ballpark's funding. Both the city and the Padres are now moving forward with their bond issues, and the ballpark is back on track, although the legal challenges persist. The plan is for the team to move into its new bayfront digs for the 2004 season, and Padres management has already noted that the team's payroll could be doubled with the opening of the new park.

Changes are coming to major-league baseball, and better ones than half-baked contraction schemes or crusades to make games shorter. Owners will begin holding their management teams accountable for years of continued mediocrity. Organizations will start to preach fundamentals, such as control of the strike zone, at the expense of drilling on bunts and squeeze plays. Teams will make fewer mistakes in talent evaluation, acquisition, and retention, and they will commit to building from within. General managers will be hired based on their qualifications to assemble a team and execute a plan in this new era, and not because their dad was a GM for 23 years. Until then, the Padres have the edge on the competition, which will negate their small-market status and then some.

HITTERS (BA: .270, OBP: .340, SLG: .440, EqA: .260)

Alex Arias IF Bats R Age 34

YEAR	TEAM	LGE	AB	H	DB	TP	HR	BB	SO	R	RBI	SB	CS	OUT	BA	OBP	SLG	EQA	EQR	DEFENSE
1999	Philadel	NL	347	103	20	1	4	32	29	42	45	2	2	246	.297	.363	.395	.258	41	81-SS -3
2000	Philadel	NL	156	29	6	0	3	14	26	16	15	1	0	127	.186	.264	.282	.192	10	31-SS 2
2001	San Dieg	NL	138	34	6	0	3	17	19	20	13	1	0	104	.246	.332	.355	.238	14	11-1B 0
2002	*Seattle*	*AL*	*279*	*61*	*11*	*0*	*6*	*29*	*38*	*31*	*30*	*2*	*1*	*219*	*.219*	*.292*	*.323*	*.216*	*24*	

Signed to a two-year deal to stabilize the bench defensively, Arias didn't do much hitting but was reliable with the glove wherever Bochy put him in 2001. Arias plays legitimate defense anywhere in the infield and allows the Padres to carry bats on the rest of the bench. Traded to the Mariners in the Ben Davis deal.

Emil Brown CF Bats R Age 27

YEAR	TEAM	LGE	AB	H	DB	TP	HR	BB	SO	R	RBI	SB	CS	OUT	BA	OBP	SLG	EQA	EQR	DEFENSE
1999	Nashvill	PCL	424	117	16	5	14	30	73	77	47	12	4	311	.276	.331	.436	.257	52	103-RF -12
2000	Nashvill	PCL	237	69	15	1	5	32	43	34	21	19	4	172	.291	.386	.426	.284	37	65-RF -1
2000	Pittsbrg	NL	120	26	3	0	4	9	31	13	17	3	1	95	.217	.286	.342	.216	10	29-OF 0
2001	Pittsbrg	NL	123	26	4	1	3	15	36	19	13	10	4	101	.211	.305	.333	.226	12	35-CF 1
2001	Portland	PCL	78	23	6	1	3	6	15	8	7	3	1	56	.295	.355	.513	.285	12	19-CF 0
2002	*San Dieg*	*NL*	*375*	*94*	*19*	*3*	*11*	*43*	*91*	*63*	*38*	*14*	*3*	*284*	*.251*	*.328*	*.405*	*.261*	*50*	

Brown is better than some starting major-league outfielders, but never established himself in Pittsburgh. Nabbed from the Pirates in July for two non-prospects, he found himself lost in the deep Padres outfield and spent the rest of the season in Portland. He has the skill set to be a great fourth outfielder, and with Ryan Klesko manning right field this year, could be a valuable player to the Padres.

Sean Burroughs 3B Bats R Age 21

YEAR	TEAM	LGE	AB	H	DB	TP	HR	BB	SO	R	RBI	SB	CS	OUT	BA	OBP	SLG	EQA	EQR	DEFENSE
1999	Ft Wayne	Mid	433	118	23	1	3	49	64	42	49	8	8	323	.273	.355	.351	.243	47	115-3B -9
2000	Mobile	Sou	407	106	26	3	2	45	45	42	35	4	5	306	.260	.336	.354	.236	41	106-3B -6
2001	Portland	PCL	395	118	23	1	8	34	49	52	48	8	2	279	.299	.358	.423	.265	51	96-3B 7
2002	*San Dieg*	*NL*	*424*	*125*	*30*	*2*	*7*	*52*	*57*	*53*	*54*	*12*	*5*	*304*	*.295*	*.372*	*.425*	*.282*	*64*	

This is why the Padres are moving their best player to first base. The Padres wanted to try Burroughs at second base in the instructional league, but a deep shoulder bruise nixed that idea. As expected, Burroughs's power is coming around. He's worked hard on his defense over the last couple of years and is now regarded as a plus at third base. Burroughs is the early-line favorite for the NL Rookie of the Year Award.

Mike Colangelo OF Bats R Age 25

YEAR	TEAM	LGE	AB	H	DB	TP	HR	BB	SO	R	RBI	SB	CS	OUT	BA	OBP	SLG	EQA	EQR	DEFENSE
1999	Erie	Eas	109	31	8	2	1	10	22	19	10	2	2	80	.284	.357	.422	.260	14	24-RF -6
1999	Edmonton	PCL	102	32	5	1	0	11	16	10	7	1	1	71	.314	.388	.382	.265	13	22-LF -4
2001	Portland	PCL	182	44	8	1	3	28	40	23	20	4	2	140	.242	.355	.346	.246	21	53-LF 3
2001	San Dieg	NL	92	24	3	3	2	8	25	11	8	0	0	68	.261	.325	.424	.249	11	22-LF -1
2002	*Oakland*	*AL*	*290*	*79*	*13*	*4*	*6*	*38*	*70*	*40*	*26*	*0*	*0*	*211*	*.272*	*.357*	*.407*	*.267*	*39*	

Colangelo is a good enough fly chaser to spot start in center field, and he has usually been more patient than he was last year. A compact swing and some speed on the bases round out the package. He's been claimed on waivers by the A's and is expected to compete with Eric Byrnes for an extra outfielder slot. It wouldn't be a bad idea for the A's to let Colangelo play center field, moving Terrence Long to left field where he belongs.

Cesar Crespo UT Bats B Age 23

YEAR	TEAM	LGE	AB	H	DB	TP	HR	BB	SO	R	RBI	SB	CS	OUT	BA	OBP	SLG	EQA	EQR	DEFENSE
1999	Brevard	Fla	438	104	15	1	5	46	97	46	29	12	5	339	.237	.311	.311	.218	38	97-2B -13
2000	Portland	Eas	491	111	17	3	9	60	122	74	47	28	12	391	.226	.312	.328	.225	47	114-CF -7 16-2B -2
2001	Portland	PCL	275	67	15	2	7	36	60	40	25	20	3	211	.244	.333	.389	.254	34	32-2B 1 21-RF 1
2001	San Dieg	NL	155	36	5	0	5	24	42	29	14	6	2	121	.232	.335	.361	.243	18	27-2B -6 13-CF 0
2002	*San Dieg*	*NL*	*480*	*111*	*20*	*2*	*11*	*64*	*124*	*71*	*42*	*28*	*7*	*376*	*.231*	*.322*	*.350*	*.247*	*57*	

A pretty fair prospect picked up in the Mark Kotsay deal, Crespo split the season between Portland and San Diego and played well all around the diamond. He's never going to be a great hitter, but with his eye and speed he could have an above-average peak at second base or be a great utility player. He'd benefit from playing every day at Portland in 2002.

Mike Darr OF Bats L Age 26

YEAR	TEAM	LGE	AB	H	DB	TP	HR	BB	SO	R	RBI	SB	CS	OUT	BA	OBP	SLG	EQA	EQR	DEFENSE
1999	LasVegas	PCL	375	95	19	0	10	42	94	43	48	8	2	282	.253	.333	.384	.246	42	95-RF -2
2000	LasVegas	PCL	358	108	19	4	7	33	53	60	48	9	4	254	.302	.363	.436	.269	48	89-CF 0
2000	San Dieg	NL	209	58	16	4	1	20	41	22	30	9	1	152	.278	.341	.407	.258	26	54-RF 6
2001	San Dieg	NL	293	87	15	1	2	37	61	39	37	6	2	208	.297	.377	.375	.262	37	77-RF 5
2002	*San Dieg*	*NL*	*455*	*124*	*25*	*3*	*7*	*56*	*101*	*58*	*55*	*12*	*4*	*335*	*.273*	*.352*	*.387*	*.265*	*61*	

His chances of sticking with San Diego look pretty poor. With Klesko moving to right field, there's no place for Darr to start. Darr is a plus defensive corner outfielder who should hit for more power than he did in 2001, so someone ought to be interested in him.

Ben Davis C Bats B Age 25

YEAR	TEAM	LGE	AB	H	DB	TP	HR	BB	SO	R	RBI	SB	CS	OUT	BA	OBP	SLG	EQA	EQR	DEFENSE
1999	LasVegas	PCL	196	52	14	1	5	20	38	20	32	3	1	145	.265	.337	.423	.256	24	58-C -2
1999	San Dieg	NL	269	68	16	1	5	22	65	30	30	2	1	202	.253	.309	.375	.231	26	69-C 0
2000	LasVegas	PCL	219	51	11	1	6	30	42	29	30	4	2	170	.233	.327	.374	.240	24	59-C -5
2000	San Dieg	NL	132	31	4	0	4	12	32	12	15	1	1	102	.235	.299	.356	.221	12	34-C -1
2001	San Dieg	NL	453	117	14	0	14	64	95	59	63	4	4	340	.258	.354	.382	.251	54	120-C 2
2002	*Seattle*	*AL*	*412*	*107*	*17*	*1*	*15*	*56*	*92*	*51*	*61*	*5*	*3*	*308*	*.260*	*.348*	*.415*	*.268*	*57*	

Prior to the All-Star break, Davis was the best catcher in the National League. Not even Miss Cleo could have predicted that. As the season progressed, he wore down and so did his production; Davis is a large man, especially for a catcher, and his endurance is something to keep an eye on. He's been traded to the Mariners, for whom he'll be the everyday catcher.

Kory DeHaan CF Bats L Age 25

YEAR	TEAM	LGE	AB	H	DB	TP	HR	BB	SO	R	RBI	SB	CS	OUT	BA	OBP	SLG	EQA	EQR	DEFENSE
1999	Lynchbrg	Car	301	81	13	3	6	25	63	38	29	17	7	227	.269	.329	.392	.246	34	75-CF -4
1999	Altoona	Eas	193	47	14	1	2	7	46	21	19	8	4	150	.244	.274	.358	.213	16	45-OF -3
2000	San Dieg	NL	105	23	5	0	3	3	36	19	14	4	2	84	.219	.241	.352	.199	7	24-RF 1
2001	Mobile	Sou	163	42	9	1	3	17	26	24	19	8	3	124	.258	.332	.380	.245	18	40-RF -1
2001	Portland	PCL	304	71	7	4	6	19	64	30	24	11	8	240	.234	.282	.342	.211	25	80-CF 10
2002	*San Dieg*	*NL*	*412*	*102*	*17*	*3*	*8*	*36*	*95*	*59*	*40*	*22*	*10*	*320*	*.248*	*.308*	*.362*	*.239*	*45*	

DeHaan is still scrapping to consolidate the gains he made in 1999 at Lynchburg, before he blew an entire season getting spotty playing time with the Padres as a Rule 5 draftee. His left-handed stick and foot speed will give him more opportunities to excel, just not with the Padres, who have many better outfielders in the organization.

Kevin Eberwein 1B/3B Bats R Age 25

YEAR	TEAM	LGE	AB	H	DB	TP	HR	BB	SO	R	RBI	SB	CS	OUT	BA	OBP	SLG	EQA	EQR	DEFENSE
1999	R Cucmng	Cal	417	86	21	2	12	27	141	45	42	4	3	334	.206	.264	.353	.207	32	91-3B 0
2000	Mobile	Sou	385	94	13	1	16	33	76	51	59	1	1	292	.244	.306	.408	.237	40	91-1B -5
2001	Lk Elsin	Cal	31	8	1	0	2	5	6	4	3	0	0	23	.258	.369	.484	.283	5	
2001	Portland	PCL	94	23	7	1	2	10	20	14	9	0	2	73	.245	.326	.404	.239	10	13-1B -1 11-3B 0
2002	*San Dieg*	*NL*	*355*	*85*	*16*	*2*	*15*	*37*	*92*	*49*	*45*	*3*	*2*	*272*	*.239*	*.311*	*.423*	*.254*	*44*	

A neat before-and-after snapshot of the Padres minor-league system: three years ago, Eberwein and Pete "Hackmaster Flash" Tucci were the top hitters in the organization. Eberwein can handle either outfield corner and has pop, but he's obviously going to have a problem breaking through with the Padres. His best chance to get major-league playing time is to choose his next employer wisely.

Vince Faison LF Bats R Age 21

YEAR	TEAM	LGE	AB	H	DB	TP	HR	BB	SO	R	RBI	SB	CS	OUT	BA	OBP	SLG	EQA	EQR	DEFENSE
2000	Ft Wayne	Mid	467	87	16	1	9	13	176	45	27	10	3	383	.186	.212	.283	.171	23	114-CF -12
2001	Ft Wayne	Mid	145	24	2	0	1	13	38	9	6	5	2	123	.166	.240	.200	.164	7	39-CF -3
2001	Lk Elsin	Cal	280	54	9	2	5	18	90	19	25	6	5	231	.193	.244	.293	.184	17	71-LF -12
2002	*San Dieg*	*NL*	*455*	*97*	*14*	*2*	*12*	*35*	*163*	*60*	*24*	*16*	*8*	*366*	*.213*	*.269*	*.332*	*.211*	*38*	

Faison was a lesser light on a stacked Lake Elsinore squad; hitting .233 in A ball won't get you promoted, regardless of your status as a former first-round pick. A tools draftee, Faison is great athlete who has problems with virtually every phase of the game and is in danger of falling off the radar.

Jake Gautreau 3B Bats L Age 22

YEAR	TEAM	LGE	AB	H	DB	TP	HR	BB	SO	R	RBI	SB	CS	OUT	BA	OBP	SLG	EQA	EQR	DEFENSE
2001	Eugene	Nwn	184	42	8	0	5	15	52	17	22	0	1	143	.228	.292	.353	.217	16	43-3B 2
2002	*San Dieg*	*NL*	*224*	*53*	*6*	*0*	*7*	*23*	*69*	*23*	*25*	*1*	*1*	*172*	*.237*	*.308*	*.357*	*.234*	*23*	

Gautreau, the Padres' #1 pick last year, was one of the top hitters in the 2001 draft. He was a third baseman in college, but given the organization's ridiculous depth at that position, he played second base in instructional league, with reportedly good results. He'll start 2002 at Lake Elsinore.

Wiki Gonzalez C Bats R Age 28

YEAR	TEAM	LGE	AB	H	DB	TP	HR	BB	SO	R	RBI	SB	CS	OUT	BA	OBP	SLG	EQA	EQR	DEFENSE
1999	Mobile	Sou	226	65	12	1	8	21	28	29	35	0	0	161	.288	.359	.456	.272	31	51-C 6
1999	LasVegas	PCL	90	22	3	0	5	4	9	10	9	0	0	68	.244	.292	.444	.240	10	23-C -4
1999	San Dieg	NL	84	22	3	1	3	0	7	7	12	0	0	62	.262	.270	.429	.227	8	17-C 4
2000	San Dieg	NL	289	71	16	1	5	26	28	25	30	1	2	220	.246	.314	.360	.228	27	76-C 1
2001	San Dieg	NL	162	48	7	0	8	10	24	17	28	2	0	114	.296	.349	.488	.277	23	37-C 0
2002	*San Dieg*	*NL*	*323*	*84*	*16*	*1*	*11*	*34*	*44*	*35*	*41*	*1*	*1*	*240*	*.260*	*.331*	*.418*	*.261*	*42*	

It wasn't a bad year for Padres catchers. Davis had a breakout season, and Gonzalez busted through with good power and better defense backing him up. With the trade of Davis, Gonzalez will get the lion's share of playing time in 2002. Look for him to be above average for the position and do a great job controlling the running game.

Tony Gwynn RF Bats L Age 42

YEAR	TEAM	LGE	AB	H	DB	TP	HR	BB	SO	R	RBI	SB	CS	OUT	BA	OBP	SLG	EQA	EQR	DEFENSE
1999	San Dieg	NL	417	144	18	0	14	24	13	58	64	6	2	275	.345	.384	.489	.291	63	82-RF -7
2000	San Dieg	NL	129	43	9	0	2	8	4	17	18	0	1	87	.333	.376	.450	.275	17	20-RF -3
2001	San Dieg	NL	103	35	10	1	1	10	8	8	18	1	0	68	.340	.398	.485	.297	16	13-RF -3

And so it ends for the Mighty Gwynn, who announced his retirement in June and is shaping the future of the San Diego State baseball program as you read this. Gwynn's last two seasons read like a major-league trainer's horror story. His broken-down body never did nullify the famous swing, though, even when he was reduced to pinch-hitting. He personifies the team in many a San Diegan's mind, and what he gave up in cash to stay with the Padres for his entire career is given back a hundred-fold in respect and admiration by the fans.

Rickey Henderson LF Bats R Age 43

YEAR	TEAM	LGE	AB	H	DB	TP	HR	BB	SO	R	RBI	SB	CS	OUT	BA	OBP	SLG	EQA	EQR	DEFENSE
1999	NY Mets	NL	441	138	21	0	15	77	76	84	41	32	15	318	.313	.417	.463	.298	77	98-LF -5
2000	NY Mets	NL	97	21	2	0	0	24	18	17	3	5	2	78	.216	.381	.237	.238	11	22-LF -4
2000	Seattle	AL	324	84	13	2	5	59	48	59	31	33	10	250	.259	.377	.358	.265	45	83-LF 1
2001	San Dieg	NL	384	96	18	3	9	79	71	75	46	25	7	295	.250	.381	.383	.271	56	90-LF -6
2002	*San Dieg*	*NL*	*403*	*81*	*16*	*2*	*6*	*77*	*77*	*63*	*26*	*27*	*11*	*333*	*.201*	*.329*	*.295*	*.236*	*45*	

Henderson signed late in spring training after the team finally rid itself of Ruben Rivera. He played more than expected and reached several career milestones, to the delight of Padres fans. Henderson wants to keep playing; despite his on-base skills, he's not a great option for the Padres, who have extra outfielders hanging from the rafters. He'll have to go somewhere else to play.

Damian Jackson 2B Bats R Age 28

YEAR	TEAM	LGE	AB	H	DB	TP	HR	BB	SO	R	RBI	SB	CS	OUT	BA	OBP	SLG	EQA	EQR	DEFENSE
1999	San Dieg	NL	393	91	20	2	10	49	97	55	39	30	10	312	.232	.321	.369	.241	45	92-SS -8 16-2B 1
2000	San Dieg	NL	478	128	29	6	6	56	99	69	37	27	6	356	.268	.348	.391	.258	60	83-SS 4 33-2B 3
2001	San Dieg	NL	446	118	24	6	4	42	109	73	41	24	6	333	.265	.335	.373	.247	50	114-2B 4
2002	*San Dieg*	*NL*	*421*	*105*	*25*	*5*	*8*	*55*	*106*	*65*	*40*	*29*	*6*	*322*	*.249*	*.336*	*.390*	*.265*	*58*	

It was another disappointing season for Jackson, who was dropped from leadoff to the bottom of the order as the Padres jelled. Jackson is a good second baseman with especially impressive range, a great base stealer, and has some theoretical on-base skills that he needs to turn into reality to have a career. He re-signed with the team for 2002 and is expected to back up the next guy at second base, now that Ramon Vazquez is on board to play shortstop.

D'Angelo Jimenez SS Bats B Age 24

YEAR	TEAM	LGE	AB	H	DB	TP	HR	BB	SO	R	RBI	SB	CS	OUT	BA	OBP	SLG	EQA	EQR	DEFENSE
1999	Columbus	Int	525	158	27	4	13	48	70	79	72	19	12	379	.301	.360	.442	.267	70	116-SS -5
2001	Columbus	Int	218	55	10	1	5	23	29	33	18	4	5	168	.252	.326	.376	.235	22	30-2B -3 13-SS 4
2001	San Dieg	NL	312	93	13	0	6	37	58	48	38	2	3	222	.298	.372	.397	.262	39	85-SS -3
2002	*San Dieg*	*NL*	*499*	*141*	*21*	*2*	*13*	*67*	*87*	*79*	*56*	*13*	*9*	*367*	*.283*	*.367*	*.411*	*.275*	*73*	

A so-so defensive player, Jimenez is already a legitimate major-league leadoff hitter. The Padres were concerned enough about his defense at shortstop to pick up Ramon Vazquez from the Mariners, and will move Jimenez to second base. This decreases his value and increases the risk that he'll get injured, so his future isn't as bright as it looked late last year. He should still be a valuable player.

Ben Johnson RF Bats R Age 21

YEAR	TEAM	LGE	AB	H	DB	TP	HR	BB	SO	R	RBI	SB	CS	OUT	BA	OBP	SLG	EQA	EQR	DEFENSE
1999	JohnsnCy	App	202	42	6	0	4	15	64	16	21	4	3	163	.208	.268	.297	.195	14	51-RF -1
2000	Ft Wayne	Mid	112	19	5	1	2	3	28	8	8	0	2	95	.170	.200	.286	.160	5	29-RF 2
2000	Peoria	Mid	345	69	13	1	10	35	86	40	31	9	4	280	.200	.278	.330	.210	28	86-RF -6
2001	Lk Elsin	Cal	514	119	29	3	9	40	135	58	45	12	5	400	.232	.294	.352	.220	46	129-RF -12
2002	*San Dieg*	*NL*	*502*	*118*	*25*	*2*	*14*	*47*	*143*	*58*	*60*	*18*	*9*	*393*	*.235*	*.301*	*.376*	*.239*	*55*	

(Ben Johnson *continued*)
Johnson is a raw talent who, unlike most toolsy players, doesn't mind taking a walk. Of course, he doesn't mind striking out, either. He has the wheels to be a very good center fielder and base stealer as he matures and his technique improves, and he will need to do both to upgrade his prospect status. He'll start the season with Mobile.

Ryan Klesko 1B Bats L Age 31

YEAR	TEAM	LGE	AB	H	DB	TP	HR	BB	SO	R	RBI	SB	CS	OUT	BA	OBP	SLG	EQA	EQR	DEFENSE
1999	Atlanta	NL	405	120	27	2	21	48	64	54	76	4	2	287	.296	.374	.528	.294	67	58-1B -7 36-LF -3
2000	San Dieg	NL	503	147	35	2	27	85	74	89	92	22	7	364	.292	.395	.531	.305	93	123-1B -1
2001	San Dieg	NL	545	166	38	6	31	86	75	112	119	23	4	383	.305	.402	.567	.317	108	140-1B -12
2002	*San Dieg*	*NL*	*484*	*141*	*33*	*3*	*24*	*78*	*75*	*79*	*88*	*21*	*4*	*347*	*.291*	*.390*	*.521*	*.315*	*96*	

Klesko started last season looking like Baby Giambi with speed. He's done great things with his plate discipline and become one of the most dangerous hitters in baseball. Another second-half slump knocked his numbers down, and he still can't hit lefties, but he's the engine that makes the Padres offense go and is still improving.

The Padres are moving Klesko to right field, and not a moment too soon. In 2001, Klesko was to defense what Carrot Top is to comedy. He's one of the worst-fielding first basemen at the major-league level, whose consistently poor positioning coupled with his lack of success at digging out bad throws made every routine play an adventure. He has fair quickness and range around the bag, but the fundamentals are just not there. With the move, throwing errors on the part of Padres infielders will mysteriously plummet.

Graham Koonce 1B Bats L Age 27

YEAR	TEAM	LGE	AB	H	DB	TP	HR	BB	SO	R	RBI	SB	CS	OUT	BA	OBP	SLG	EQA	EQR	DEFENSE
1999	R Cucmng	Cal	475	107	10	1	13	52	111	50	50	2	1	369	.225	.309	.333	.221	42	126-1B -11
2000	R Cucmng	Cal	486	116	25	2	14	73	106	65	59	0	0	370	.239	.340	.385	.248	56	132-1B 2
2001	Mobile	Sou	334	77	11	0	12	73	81	45	40	0	0	257	.231	.372	.371	.260	44	50-1B -3 22-LF -4
2002	*San Dieg*	*NL*	*433*	*101*	*16*	*1*	*14*	*73*	*110*	*55*	*50*	*0*	*0*	*332*	*.233*	*.344*	*.372*	*.257*	*56*	

He's obviously too old to have much of a major-league career, and he's putting up his numbers in the Southern League against younger competition, but Koonce personifies the trend towards A's-style plate discipline throughout the chain. In 1999, Koonce's career was all but over after a mediocre season. Now, he's a borderline bench player and may still have another couple of years' improvement in him.

Mark Kotsay CF Bats L Age 26

YEAR	TEAM	LGE	AB	H	DB	TP	HR	BB	SO	R	RBI	SB	CS	OUT	BA	OBP	SLG	EQA	EQR	DEFENSE
1999	Florida	NL	499	136	24	8	9	23	46	57	49	6	6	369	.273	.305	.407	.234	49	105-RF 9 13-1B 0
2000	Florida	NL	536	161	33	4	12	35	42	86	55	18	9	384	.300	.343	.444	.262	67	130-RF 7
2001	San Dieg	NL	411	129	27	1	12	46	49	72	64	14	5	287	.314	.385	.472	.288	64	110-CF 1
2002	*San Dieg*	*NL*	*485*	*141*	*25*	*4*	*15*	*47*	*54*	*74*	*55*	*16*	*8*	*352*	*.291*	*.353*	*.452*	*.280*	*73*	

Taking a bad pitch has additional advantages besides the occasional free base; looking for the better pitch to hit should result in better contact, as it did for Kotsay in 2001. He was stolen from the Marlins in a preseason trade, and other than a sprained hand and a strained hammy, all signs were positive in San Diego. Look for more improvement in 2002, both offensively and in the field.

Ray Lankford LF Bats L Age 35

YEAR	TEAM	LGE	AB	H	DB	TP	HR	BB	SO	R	RBI	SB	CS	OUT	BA	OBP	SLG	EQA	EQR	DEFENSE
1999	St Louis	NL	423	128	28	1	16	43	102	74	60	12	4	299	.303	.371	.487	.285	65	102-LF 3
2000	St Louis	NL	394	98	16	3	25	64	136	70	61	4	6	302	.249	.359	.495	.277	61	97-LF -6
2001	St Louis	NL	265	65	20	3	15	42	89	40	40	4	2	202	.245	.352	.513	.281	42	72-LF 0
2001	San Dieg	NL	127	39	12	1	4	17	34	22	20	6	0	88	.307	.395	.512	.307	23	30-LF -2
2002	*San Dieg*	*NL*	*387*	*94*	*21*	*3*	*17*	*60*	*131*	*65*	*52*	*9*	*4*	*297*	*.243*	*.345*	*.444*	*.275*	*59*	

The classy Cardinal was acquired in a post-deadline deal for Woody Williams after a soap opera finish to his St. Louis career. He's a big-league talent whose days of starting every game may be behind him due to lower-body problems and the reappearance of a massive platoon split. A Ray Lankford/Bubba Trammell platoon in left field will be very good.

Dave Magadan PH/3B Bats L Age 39

YEAR	TEAM	LGE	AB	H	DB	TP	HR	BB	SO	R	RBI	SB	CS	OUT	BA	OBP	SLG	EQA	EQR	DEFENSE
1999	San Dieg	NL	251	71	13	1	2	43	33	21	30	1	3	183	.283	.388	.367	.261	32	36-3B 1 24-1B -1
2000	San Dieg	NL	134	38	4	0	3	31	21	13	22	0	0	96	.284	.418	.381	.283	21	18-3B -1
2001	San Dieg	NL	129	35	4	0	2	12	17	12	14	0	0	94	.271	.337	.349	.236	13	17-3B -4

Magadan's offense obviously suffered, and he also lost a lot of his defensive value in 2001; he made several costly muffs, and his arm looked worse than ever. After enduring his first bad year in a Padres uniform and his first season with more strikeouts than walks, Magadan retired to become the Padres' minor-league hitting coordinator.

Donaldo Mendez SS Bats R Age 24

YEAR	TEAM	LGE	AB	H	DB	TP	HR	BB	SO	R	RBI	SB	CS	OUT	BA	OBP	SLG	EQA	EQR	DEFENSE
1999	Auburn	NYP	87	15	2	0	0	0	26	4	7	3	3	75	.172	.186	.195	.134	2	21-SS -8
2000	Michigan	Mid	378	85	6	0	4	19	75	41	39	19	8	300	.225	.273	.272	.195	25	100-SS 9
2001	San Dieg	NL	119	22	4	1	1	4	31	13	6	1	2	99	.185	.226	.261	.165	6	33-SS -7
2002	*San Dieg*	*NL*	*334*	*69*	*6*	*1*	*4*	*20*	*83*	*34*	*35*	*14*	*5*	*270*	*.207*	*.251*	*.266*	*.182*	*19*	

Handed the starting shortstop job in April, Mendez had a case of nerves that made every throw to first base a nail-biter. An injured knee landed him on the DL in June, after which he didn't see another at bat. The organization is high on him, but with a young, inexpensive middle infield in place, it's hard to see where his opportunity lies.

Xavier Nady 1B Bats R Age 23

YEAR	TEAM	LGE	AB	H	DB	TP	HR	BB	SO	R	RBI	SB	CS	OUT	BA	OBP	SLG	EQA	EQR	DEFENSE
2001	Lk Elsin	Cal	539	134	22	1	20	47	104	71	70	4	0	405	.249	.314	.404	.242	58	107-1B 3
2002	*San Dieg*	*NL*	*457*	*117*	*19*	*1*	*21*	*46*	*95*	*61*	*64*	*5*	*0*	*340*	*.256*	*.324*	*.440*	*.266*	*62*	

The Cal League MVP's season was shut down early as he underwent surgery to rebuild his right elbow. He should be swinging the bat in time for the 2002 season but won't play the field until midseason at the earliest. With their plethora of talent at the corners, the Padres want to try Nady at second base. If he can handle the position, he'll give the Padres their very own Jeff Kent.

Phil Nevin 3B Bats R Age 31

YEAR	TEAM	LGE	AB	H	DB	TP	HR	BB	SO	R	RBI	SB	CS	OUT	BA	OBP	SLG	EQA	EQR	DEFENSE
1999	San Dieg	NL	388	107	22	0	27	47	76	53	86	1	0	281	.276	.355	.541	.290	64	58-3B 9 24-C -1
2000	San Dieg	NL	547	170	30	1	34	53	111	88	108	2	0	377	.311	.375	.556	.302	94	136-3B -13
2001	San Dieg	NL	553	179	29	0	44	69	125	103	134	4	4	378	.324	.402	.615	.322	111	137-3B -1
2002	*San Dieg*	*NL*	*491*	*143*	*22*	*0*	*33*	*64*	*116*	*72*	*101*	*3*	*2*	*350*	*.291*	*.373*	*.538*	*.307*	*92*	

Even though Nevin was the subject of many a trade rumor in 2001, the uncertainty didn't keep him from having a monster season. He's moving to first base in 2002 and should handle the position fine. At third base, his arm is strong but scattershot; his glove is otherwise unfairly maligned. Nevin never gets cheated, which keeps his walk rate lower than Klesko's despite the respect the league affords him. He signed a $34-million contract extension through 2006—a bargain for a hitter of Nevin's caliber.

Jeremy Owens CF Bats R Age 25

YEAR	TEAM	LGE	AB	H	DB	TP	HR	BB	SO	R	RBI	SB	CS	OUT	BA	OBP	SLG	EQA	EQR	DEFENSE
1999	Ft Wayne	Mid	522	118	20	6	7	39	167	67	42	32	11	414	.226	.285	.328	.215	45	128-CF -1
2000	R Cucmng	Cal	579	127	23	5	13	37	185	64	41	25	8	460	.219	.269	.344	.211	47	138-CF 16
2001	Mobile	Sou	405	78	19	4	6	43	146	38	22	22	9	336	.193	.272	.304	.204	32	106-CF 5
2001	Lk Elsin	Cal	92	15	1	1	2	6	37	6	6	2	1	78	.163	.218	.261	.168	4	13-CF 6
2002	*San Dieg*	*NL*	*527*	*113*	*18*	*5*	*13*	*52*	*198*	*67*	*42*	*33*	*12*	*426*	*.214*	*.285*	*.342*	*.227*	*52*	

Owens, a highly touted prospect just two years ago, started the season in Mobile before being demoted to Lake Elsinore to work on making contact. He's a great defensive center fielder whose bat isn't developing, so a sea change is necessary for him to have a career.

Santiago Perez SS/OF Bats B Age 26

YEAR	TEAM	LGE	AB	H	DB	TP	HR	BB	SO	R	RBI	SB	CS	OUT	BA	OBP	SLG	EQA	EQR	DEFENSE
1999	Louisvil	Int	407	100	21	7	6	24	88	47	32	16	4	311	.246	.290	.376	.227	38	94-SS -21
2000	Indianap	Int	410	106	25	5	5	37	94	65	30	24	7	311	.259	.321	.380	.242	45	100-SS -15
2000	Milwauke	NL	52	9	1	0	0	8	8	7	2	4	0	43	.173	.293	.192	.198	4	14-SS -2
2001	Portland	PCL	184	47	8	0	5	14	54	27	10	16	3	140	.255	.313	.380	.244	21	36-CF 0
2001	San Dieg	NL	82	18	1	0	0	15	25	14	4	5	1	65	.220	.340	.232	.220	7	16-OF -1
2002	*Texas*	*AL*	*423*	*114*	*24*	*4*	*9*	*51*	*112*	*66*	*33*	*27*	*5*	*314*	*.270*	*.348*	*.409*	*.261*	*54*	

Perez, a boot-tastic defender in the minors, was supposed to be in the mix for the wide-open shortstop job before the season started. He played all over the field before being designated for assignment in July. He's not a terrible utility player, but the big-league roster is crowded for 2002, and Cesar Crespo already has Perez's job.

Kevin Reese RF Bats L Age 24

YEAR	TEAM	LGE	AB	H	DB	TP	HR	BB	SO	R	RBI	SB	CS	OUT	BA	OBP	SLG	EQA	EQR	DEFENSE
2000	IdahoFls	Pio	199	47	9	1	1	23	36	23	17	4	2	154	.236	.318	.307	.220	17	41-RF -6
2001	Ft Wayne	Mid	472	122	23	3	9	40	68	57	48	14	7	357	.258	.319	.377	.236	48	121-RF -1
2002	*San Dieg*	*NL*	*422*	*109*	*23*	*2*	*9*	*44*	*69*	*57*	*47*	*17*	*7*	*321*	*.258*	*.328*	*.386*	*.254*	*52*	

A local college prospect drafted in the 27th round in 2000, Reese showed an improved power stroke at Fort Wayne and was a Midwest League All-Star. Major-league teams should move fundamentally advanced prospects such as Reese through the chain quickly, especially considering that these guys are usually old for their leagues.

Bubba Trammell OF Bats R Age 30

YEAR	TEAM	LGE	AB	H	DB	TP	HR	BB	SO	R	RBI	SB	CS	OUT	BA	OBP	SLG	EQA	EQR	DEFENSE
1999	Durham	Int	186	47	7	0	7	12	34	21	26	0	0	139	.253	.298	.403	.232	18	43-LF -3
1999	TampaBay	AL	280	84	15	1	16	40	33	48	39	0	2	198	.300	.389	.532	.299	48	73-LF 0
2000	TampaBay	AL	187	53	10	2	8	19	26	18	33	3	0	134	.283	.356	.487	.280	28	39-LF -5
2000	NY Mets	NL	57	14	2	0	3	7	17	9	12	1	0	43	.246	.328	.439	.258	7	13-RF -1
2001	San Dieg	NL	495	138	22	3	26	46	66	71	97	2	2	359	.279	.344	.493	.273	70	118-RF 1
2002	*San Dieg*	*NL*	*419*	*112*	*19*	*2*	*21*	*52*	*64*	*58*	*66*	*3*	*1*	*308*	*.267*	*.348*	*.473*	*.283*	*66*	

Trammell looked like he would be scrapping for playing time yet again before Gwynn went down with injuries. He never looked back, turning in a fair year for the Padres and inking a three-year deal at the end of the season. His performance was somewhat disappointing, and he should hit better this year. He may be the Mets' best outfielder by the time you read this.

PITCHERS (ERA: 4.50, H/9: 9.0, HR/9: 1.0, BB/9: 3.0, K/9: 6.0, KW: 2.0, PERA: 4.50)

Mike Bynum Throws L Age 24

YEAR	TEAM	LGE	IP	H	ER	HR	BB	K	ERA	W	L	H/9	HR/9	BB/9	K/9	KW	PERA	STUFF
1999	R Cucmng	Cal	39.0	36	14	2	9	26	3.23	3	1	8.3	0.5	2.1	6.0	1.4	4.38	20
2000	R Cucmng	Cal	122.3	120	60	8	53	73	4.41	7	7	8.8	0.6	3.9	5.4	0.7	4.73	8
2000	Mobile	Sou	33.3	35	20	4	16	18	5.40	2	2	9.5	1.1	4.3	4.9	0.6	4.09	2
2001	Mobile	Sou	80.7	99	74	22	40	42	8.26	2	7	11.0	2.5	4.5	4.7	0.5	7.49	-18

Knee problems caused Bynum to miss all of June and ended his season in August. He'll have a repeat engagement—probably a short one, if he's back to his usual self—in 2002. Bynum throws a slider with a grip the organization calls "the Lobster," a pitch that is devastating when he's locating it well. The merchandising possibilities in San Diego, a coastal city that likes its shellfish, are plentiful.

Eric Cyr Throws L Age 23

YEAR	TEAM	LGE	IP	H	ER	HR	BB	K	ERA	W	L	H/9	HR/9	BB/9	K/9	KW	PERA	STUFF
2000	Ft Wayne	Mid	31.7	34	22	5	17	18	6.25	1	3	9.7	1.4	4.8	5.1	0.5	6.82	-8
2001	Lk Elsin	Cal	97.7	87	34	2	30	69	3.13	7	4	8.0	0.2	2.8	6.4	1.1	3.28	18

In Cyr's first season in the California League, he blew away the opposition on his way to an All-Star spot. He sports a nasty fastball/curve combination, works the corners well, and had a strong showing in the Arizona Fall League. He'll move to Mobile in 2002, while trying to put an ugly off-season—he spent a month in jail after pleading guilty to a misdemeanor—behind him.

Tom Davey Throws R Age 28

YEAR	TEAM	LGE	IP	H	ER	HR	BB	K	ERA	W	L	H/9	HR/9	BB/9	K/9	KW	PERA	STUFF
1999	Syracuse	Int	33.3	34	18	1	20	14	4.86	2	2	9.2	0.3	5.4	3.8	0.3	4.14	-12
1999	Toronto	AL	45.0	40	21	4	22	42	4.20	3	2	8.0	0.8	4.4	8.4	1.0	4.81	7
1999	Seattle	AL	22.3	19	9	0	12	17	3.63	1	1	7.7	0.0	4.8	6.9	0.7	4.68	1
2000	Tacoma	PCL	96.3	103	59	14	40	55	5.51	4	7	9.6	1.3	3.7	5.1	0.7	6.61	-18
2000	LasVegas	PCL	19.7	18	7	0	7	12	3.20	1	1	8.2	0.0	3.2	5.5	0.9	7.52	-11
2000	San Dieg	NL	12.7	13	4	0	2	5	2.84	1	0	9.2	0.0	1.4	3.6	1.3	0.70	-2
2001	San Dieg	NL	38.7	35	17	3	15	30	3.96	2	2	8.1	0.7	3.5	7.0	1.0	5.53	0

Davey turned in a surprisingly solid half-season of work before suffering a shoulder strain. He hit the DL in late July and never returned, eventually undergoing surgery. He isn't likely to be ready to pitch by the start of the season, and as with all pitchers coming off shoulder surgery, he'll need to be watched closely.

Adam Eaton Throws R Age 24

YEAR	TEAM	LGE	IP	H	ER	HR	BB	K	ERA	W	L	H/9	HR/9	BB/9	K/9	KW	PERA	STUFF
1999	Clearwtr	Fla	73.0	75	36	4	29	34	4.44	4	4	9.2	0.5	3.6	4.2	0.6	6.07	0
1999	Reading	Eas	72.3	77	46	13	28	47	5.72	3	5	9.6	1.6	3.5	5.8	0.8	3.85	12
1999	Scran-WB	Int	20.0	21	9	1	6	8	4.05	1	1	9.5	0.4	2.7	3.6	0.7	4.20	5
2000	Mobile	Sou	55.7	54	26	5	18	39	4.20	3	3	8.7	0.8	2.9	6.3	1.1	4.07	17
2000	San Dieg	NL	136.3	138	69	13	50	80	4.56	7	8	9.1	0.9	3.3	5.3	0.8	4.15	10
2001	San Dieg	NL	110.7	111	61	18	36	88	4.96	5	7	9.0	1.5	2.9	7.2	1.2	4.99	17

Slag-u-licious! As the Padres climbed into contention in May, Eaton rebounded from his early Colorado-assisted funk to pitch very well. Bruce Bochy rode him way too hard; despite starting only 17 games, Eaton's Stress score of 48 ended up being the fifth-highest score in the majors for 2001. After a four-start stretch in which he averaged nearly 120 pitches an outing, he was shut down for the season with a ligament strain. He underwent Tommy John surgery and will miss the entire season. This is probably the worst thing Bochy, who hasn't made a ton of mistakes, has done as a manager.

Jeremy Fikac Throws R Age 27

YEAR	TEAM	LGE	IP	H	ER	HR	BB	K	ERA	W	L	H/9	HR/9	BB/9	K/9	KW	PERA	STUFF
1999	R Cucmng	Cal	86.0	99	71	15	58	37	7.43	3	7	10.4	1.6	6.1	3.9	0.3	7.11	-46
2000	R Cucmng	Cal	70.0	66	32	5	29	49	4.11	4	4	8.5	0.6	3.7	6.3	0.8	3.23	-13
2001	Mobile	Sou	65.0	64	32	5	26	40	4.43	4	3	8.9	0.7	3.6	5.5	0.8	3.13	-14
2001	San Dieg	NL	22.7	22	9	2	4	15	3.57	2	1	8.7	0.8	1.6	6.0	1.9	2.18	4

Fikac turned up the heat in 2000 and carried it over to 2001 as he ended the season with respectable numbers in the majors. While he still doesn't tickle the radar gun, Fikac knows how to pitch and will be a member of the pen in 2002. Factoid: now that Gwynn has retired, Fikac has been in the Padres organization longer than anyone else.

Matt Harrington Throws R Age 20

YEAR	TEAM	LGE	IP	H	ER	HR	BB	K	ERA	W	L	H/9	HR/9	BB/9	K/9	KW	PERA	STUFF
2001	StPaul	Nth	19.0	21	22	4	27	11	10.42	0	2	9.9	1.9	12.8	5.2	0.2	11.36	-38

Agent Tommy Tanzer's hardline campaign for a $4.95-million signing bonus may have screwed up Harrington's career irreparably. As the Rockies' first-round pick and the consensus top prep pitcher in the 2000 draft, Harrington walked away from Colorado's best offer—$1.25 million below his demands—on Tanzer's advice. Pitching in limited action in the Northern League against advanced competition, Harrington looked awful, and the Padres selected him with the 58th pick in the 2001 draft. Three things are sure: if he signs, he won't get $3.7 million; whatever happens with the contract, he's lost a year of development; and if Tanzer truly believes this is a positive outcome, he's a moron. Harrington will probably be back in the 2002 draft.

Junior Herndon Throws R Age 23

YEAR	TEAM	LGE	IP	H	ER	HR	BB	K	ERA	W	L	H/9	HR/9	BB/9	K/9	KW	PERA	STUFF
1999	Mobile	Sou	159.3	194	122	35	53	61	6.89	5	13	11.0	2.0	3.0	3.4	0.6	5.81	-3
2000	LasVegas	PCL	138.0	150	83	15	62	60	5.41	6	9	9.8	1.0	4.0	3.9	0.5	5.37	-3
2001	Portland	PCL	113.0	137	84	21	44	33	6.69	4	9	10.9	1.7	3.5	2.6	0.4	6.21	-15
2001	San Dieg	NL	42.3	49	28	4	22	11	5.95	2	3	10.4	0.9	4.7	2.3	0.3	7.61	-25

Herndon made his major-league debut in 2001 and wasn't all that effective. His ratios are really worrisome; starters who are successful in the majors while striking out a batter every three innings are a rare breed. Herndon has a shot at a rotation spot in 2002, but he's towards the back of a large group of candidates, all of whom are about to be passed by the real good prospects.

Trevor Hoffman Throws R Age 34

YEAR	TEAM	LGE	IP	H	ER	HR	BB	K	ERA	W	L	H/9	HR/9	BB/9	K/9	KW	PERA	STUFF
1999	San Dieg	NL	66.0	55	21	5	13	66	2.86	5	2	7.5	0.7	1.8	9.0	2.5	3.04	22
2000	San Dieg	NL	73.3	62	23	6	9	76	2.82	6	2	7.6	0.7	1.1	9.3	4.2	3.57	25
2001	San Dieg	NL	56.0	53	29	9	19	51	4.66	3	3	8.5	1.4	3.1	8.2	1.3	3.96	6

Hoffman has begun the long slide downhill; he's slowly losing velocity and effectiveness, and, despite the saves, he was barely above average last year as measured by Adjusted Runs Prevented. Hoffman has enough off-speed stuff to stick around for quite a while. His usage patterns and Qualcomm Stadium will mask much of the decline.

Ben Howard Throws R Age 23

YEAR	TEAM	LGE	IP	H	ER	HR	BB	K	ERA	W	L	H/9	HR/9	BB/9	K/9	KW	PERA	STUFF
1999	Ft Wayne	Mid	135.7	162	148	36	124	75	9.82	3	12	10.7	2.4	8.2	5.0	0.3	7.70	-16
2000	R Cucmng	Cal	105.0	103	89	16	110	88	7.63	3	9	8.8	1.4	9.4	7.5	0.4	8.44	-8
2001	Lk Elsin	Cal	100.3	101	50	8	41	56	4.49	6	5	9.1	0.7	3.7	5.0	0.7	4.29	5
2001	Mobile	Sou	26.0	27	19	5	16	18	6.58	1	2	9.3	1.7	5.5	6.2	0.6	3.43	0

Howard started the season with the Storm and pitched very well, putting up a 2.83 ERA with better than a three-to-one strikeout-to-walk ratio and starting the league's All-Star game. He'll begin 2002 in the Mobile rotation, where his control will be watched very closely; as you can see, he often struggles to find the strike zone.

Kevin Jarvis Throws R Age 32

YEAR	TEAM	LGE	IP	H	ER	HR	BB	K	ERA	W	L	H/9	HR/9	BB/9	K/9	KW	PERA	STUFF
1999	Vancouvr	PCL	102.3	118	67	18	30	43	5.89	4	7	10.4	1.6	2.6	3.8	0.7	4.84	-12
2000	ColSprin	PCL	33.7	35	16	1	14	13	4.28	2	2	9.4	0.3	3.7	3.5	0.5	1.29	-3
2000	Colorado	NL	118.3	135	73	21	27	53	5.55	5	8	10.3	1.6	2.1	4.0	1.0	4.66	-7
2001	San Dieg	NL	180.3	198	108	33	44	107	5.39	8	12	9.9	1.6	2.2	5.3	1.2	5.29	2

Despite being a long shot to make the team, Jarvis got the chance to start with the Padres and ended up leading the staff in wins. At his best, he's an innings-munching #4 starter with a taterrific streak. The three-year contract the Padres gave him was one of the stranger deals of the winter; he's not a good bet to repeat even the mild success of 2001.

Brett Jodie Throws R Age 25

YEAR	TEAM	LGE	IP	H	ER	HR	BB	K	ERA	W	L	H/9	HR/9	BB/9	K/9	KW	PERA	STUFF
1999	Greensbr	SAL	120.3	139	74	21	25	52	5.53	5	8	10.4	1.6	1.9	3.9	1.0	6.28	-7
2000	Tampa	Fla	143.3	148	65	11	39	71	4.08	9	7	9.3	0.7	2.4	4.5	0.9	4.93	1
2000	Norwich	Eas	17.7	23	17	6	5	6	8.66	0	2	11.7	3.1	2.5	3.1	0.6	4.44	-20
2001	Columbus	Int	118.3	131	62	12	29	44	4.72	6	7	10.0	0.9	2.2	3.3	0.8	4.18	-2
2001	Portland	PCL	29.0	36	26	8	9	13	8.07	1	2	11.2	2.5	2.8	4.0	0.7	5.50	-14
2001	San Dieg	NL	20.0	25	20	6	11	10	9.00	0	2	11.3	2.7	5.0	4.5	0.5	4.92	-25

Jodie was acquired in the Sterling Hitchcock salary dump at the deadline. He's not a great prospect, although he should at least hold his own at Portland. He'll be at the back of the line for a starting job in San Diego, chatting with Junior Herndon. Reclaimed on waiver by the Yankees.

Bobby J. Jones Throws R Age 32

YEAR	TEAM	LGE	IP	H	ER	HR	BB	K	ERA	W	L	H/9	HR/9	BB/9	K/9	KW	PERA	STUFF
1999	NY Mets	NL	62.3	64	23	3	9	28	3.32	5	2	9.2	0.4	1.3	4.0	1.6	5.34	3
2000	Norfolk	Int	24.7	30	19	7	4	14	6.93	1	2	10.9	2.6	1.5	5.1	1.8	6.27	-10
2000	NY Mets	NL	157.0	173	90	23	40	76	5.16	7	10	9.9	1.3	2.3	4.4	0.9	5.01	-1
2001	San Dieg	NL	195.3	221	113	33	34	91	5.21	9	13	10.2	1.5	1.6	4.2	1.3	6.71	-3

Jones waited the market into oblivion last off-season, a move that allowed the Padres to sign him in February at a dirt-cheap price. He flashed his usual great control, but hitters were all over his 85-mph fastball and slugged .495 against him. The Padres picked up his 2002 option and added one for 2003, so he'll be back.

Brian Lawrence Throws R Age 26

YEAR	TEAM	LGE	IP	H	ER	HR	BB	K	ERA	W	L	H/9	HR/9	BB/9	K/9	KW	PERA	STUFF
1999	R Cucmng	Cal	179.0	183	75	12	37	88	3.77	12	8	9.2	0.6	1.9	4.4	1.2	4.58	5
2000	Mobile	Sou	121.3	124	57	12	32	70	4.23	7	6	9.2	0.9	2.4	5.2	1.1	4.13	5
2000	LasVegas	PCL	47.7	48	22	7	7	36	4.15	3	2	9.1	1.3	1.3	6.8	2.6	2.33	21
2001	Portland	PCL	44.3	44	24	4	22	27	4.87	2	3	8.9	0.8	4.5	5.5	0.6	5.52	-7
2001	San Dieg	NL	109.0	108	48	9	30	68	3.96	7	5	8.9	0.7	2.5	5.6	1.1	4.41	6

Lawrence shuttled between the minors and the Padres until Sterling Hitchcock was moved at the deadline. Handed a rotation spot, he rattled off eight quality starts in 12 outings down the stretch. For a pitcher with a pedestrian fastball, his strikeout numbers are good, thanks to great control. Pick Lawrence up if you can for 2002; he's on track for a heck of a season.

David Lee Throws R Age 29

YEAR	TEAM	LGE	IP	H	ER	HR	BB	K	ERA	W	L	H/9	HR/9	BB/9	K/9	KW	PERA	STUFF
1999	Colorado	NL	48.7	46	24	3	24	34	4.44	3	2	8.5	0.6	4.4	6.3	0.7	2.83	-2
2000	Colorado	NL	6.7	8	8	2	5	5	10.80	0	1	10.8	2.7	6.8	6.8	0.5	10.20	-36
2000	ColSprin	PCL	48.0	54	41	11	30	31	7.69	1	4	10.1	2.1	5.6	5.8	0.5	6.61	-36
2001	Portland	PCL	10.7	9	4	0	6	9	3.38	1	0	7.6	0.0	5.1	7.6	0.8	0.94	3
2001	San Dieg	NL	48.3	48	27	5	24	34	5.03	2	3	8.9	0.9	4.5	6.3	0.7	3.92	-6

It's tough to believe that this is the same guy who was the Rockies closer for about ten minutes in 2000. Lee was acquired from the Yankees for Carlos Almanzar before the season started and unexpectedly saw a lot of major-league action. He cooks with gas, works cheap, and can help a team from the bullpen.

Carlton Loewer Throws R Age 28

YEAR	TEAM	LGE	IP	H	ER	HR	BB	K	ERA	W	L	H/9	HR/9	BB/9	K/9	KW	PERA	STUFF
1999	Philadel	NL	92.3	97	44	8	22	43	4.29	5	5	9.5	0.8	2.1	4.2	1.0	4.90	-2
2001	Lk Elsin	Cal	10.3	10	5	0	6	6	4.35	1	0	8.7	0.0	5.2	5.2	0.5	8.59	-22
2001	Portland	PCL	84.0	90	42	9	19	40	4.50	5	4	9.6	1.0	2.0	4.3	1.1	5.84	-3

His surgically repaired shoulder still isn't right, but Loewer is the kind of pitcher worth taking a chance on. He was pretty good not too long ago, he's still rehabbing and working to return to form, he's young, and he's inexpensive. Depending on him to take the ball 30 times is a bad idea; signing him to round out the Triple-A rotation with the option of promoting him if he does well is a good one.

David Lundquist Throws R Age 29

YEAR	TEAM	LGE	IP	H	ER	HR	BB	K	ERA	W	L	H/9	HR/9	BB/9	K/9	KW	PERA	STUFF
1999	ChiSox	AL	24.0	23	12	3	10	18	4.50	2	1	8.6	1.1	3.8	6.8	0.9	7.27	-6
2001	Portland	PCL	62.3	63	34	8	26	42	4.91	3	4	9.1	1.2	3.8	6.1	0.8	4.44	-15
2001	San Dieg	NL	19.7	18	7	1	6	15	3.20	1	1	8.2	0.5	2.7	6.9	1.3	6.30	3

After breaking into the big leagues with the White Sox in 1999, Lundquist tore up his elbow and subsequently was picked up and designated for assignment by Kansas City. There's no greater insult to a reliever than to be waived by the Royals. Lundquist did some good work in Portland and could help the Padres bullpen in 2002.

Chuck McElroy Throws L Age 34

YEAR	TEAM	LGE	IP	H	ER	HR	BB	K	ERA	W	L	H/9	HR/9	BB/9	K/9	KW	PERA	STUFF
1999	Colorado	NL	43.0	44	29	7	23	33	6.07	2	3	9.2	1.5	4.8	6.9	0.7	4.70	-9
1999	NY Mets	NL	13.3	13	6	0	7	6	4.05	1	0	8.8	0.0	4.7	4.1	0.4	3.22	-15
2000	Baltimor	AL	64.7	60	30	5	28	50	4.18	4	3	8.4	0.7	3.9	7.0	0.9	4.47	1
2001	Baltimor	AL	45.3	51	34	7	27	21	6.75	2	3	10.1	1.4	5.4	4.2	0.4	5.50	-24
2001	San Dieg	NL	30.3	32	21	5	16	20	6.23	1	2	9.5	1.5	4.7	5.9	0.6	7.72	-19

McElroy started the season as the Orioles' fifth starter and ended it with some garbage time in the Padres bullpen. He hasn't been consistently effective since 1998; a team scrapping for relief pitchers might take a chance on him, but I don't think it'll be the Padres. He's never had much of a platoon split, and he needs to find a team willing to use him for two innings at a time, instead of two batters.

Jason Middlebrook Throws R Age 27

YEAR	TEAM	LGE	IP	H	ER	HR	BB	K	ERA	W	L	H/9	HR/9	BB/9	K/9	KW	PERA	STUFF
1999	Mobile	Sou	64.7	80	57	15	34	24	7.93	2	5	11.1	2.1	4.7	3.3	0.4	10.32	-37
2000	Mobile	Sou	117.3	149	113	31	62	43	8.67	3	10	11.4	2.4	4.8	3.3	0.3	10.11	-45
2001	Mobile	Sou	48.7	47	18	2	12	27	3.33	3	2	8.7	0.4	2.2	5.0	1.1	2.55	6
2001	Portland	PCL	88.0	91	43	6	29	42	4.40	5	5	9.3	0.6	3.0	4.3	0.7	4.25	-1
2001	San Dieg	NL	17.0	22	17	5	9	8	9.00	0	2	11.6	2.6	4.8	4.2	0.4	5.44	-24

In 2000, Middlebrook was an organizational hot potato, hopping back and forth between the Padres and Mets. In 2001, he finally developed some semblance of control of his wicked curve and began to repay the investment the Padres have made in him. He'll be a serious competitor for a rotation slot at some point in 2002.

Rodney Myers Throws R Age 33

YEAR	TEAM	LGE	IP	H	ER	HR	BB	K	ERA	W	L	H/9	HR/9	BB/9	K/9	KW	PERA	STUFF
1999	Iowa	PCL	30.3	32	18	4	13	16	5.34	1	2	9.5	1.2	3.9	4.7	0.6	5.73	-24
1999	ChiCubs	NL	65.3	70	37	9	21	37	5.10	3	4	9.6	1.2	2.9	5.1	0.9	4.35	-10
2001	Portland	PCL	14.3	14	8	1	6	9	5.02	1	1	8.8	0.6	3.8	5.7	0.8	3.77	-11
2001	San Dieg	NL	46.3	49	26	5	18	23	5.05	2	3	9.5	1.0	3.5	4.5	0.6	6.26	-17

Myers managed to work his way into the Padres pen in 2001 following an ugly torn patellar tendon that wiped out his 2000 season. Having done so, he pitched like the thoroughly replaceable commodity he is. Someone might be interested in his services in 2002; heck, they might even want him to do some pitching.

Jose Nunez Throws L Age 23

YEAR	TEAM	LGE	IP	H	ER	HR	BB	K	ERA	W	L	H/9	HR/9	BB/9	K/9	KW	PERA	STUFF
1999	Kingsprt	App	70.3	84	50	14	19	27	6.40	3	5	10.7	1.8	2.4	3.5	0.7	5.75	-5
2000	Columbia	SAL	93.0	99	54	15	29	58	5.23	4	6	9.6	1.5	2.8	5.6	1.0	4.60	0
2001	LosAngls	NL	8.7	10	9	4	4	9	9.35	0	1	10.4	4.2	4.2	9.3	1.1	19.54	-17
2001	San Dieg	NL	50.7	45	20	3	18	39	3.55	4	2	8.0	0.5	3.2	6.9	1.1	3.70	9

Nunez, a Rule 5 draftee, appeared clueless in the early going for the Dodgers and got himself waived and picked up by the Padres. It looked like the Pads were crazy to burn a roster spot on him at the time; after a 1.24 ERA and a strikeout per inning in the second half of the season, it looked like a pretty good move. For his sake, let's hope he doesn't get shoehorned into a middle-relief or specialist role, because he has the arm to do more.

Jimmy Osting Throws L Age 25

YEAR	TEAM	LGE	IP	H	ER	HR	BB	K	ERA	W	L	H/9	HR/9	BB/9	K/9	KW	PERA	STUFF
1999	Macon	SAL	141.0	164	96	27	42	65	6.13	6	10	10.5	1.7	2.7	4.1	0.8	4.38	-4
2000	Myrtle B	Car	24.0	24	9	0	6	9	3.38	2	1	9.0	0.0	2.3	3.4	0.8	5.13	0
2000	Greenvil	Sou	69.3	77	46	11	31	33	5.97	3	5	10.0	1.4	4.0	4.3	0.5	4.71	-6
2000	Reading	Eas	56.7	58	29	2	29	22	4.61	3	3	9.2	0.3	4.6	3.5	0.4	3.18	-4
2001	Mobile	Sou	91.3	100	61	10	52	39	6.01	4	6	9.9	1.0	5.1	3.8	0.4	5.42	10
2001	Portland	PCL	27.7	34	22	6	12	10	7.16	1	2	11.1	2.0	3.9	3.3	0.4	11.12	-29

He did the waiver-wire boogie in 2001, jumping from the Phillies to the Rockies to the Padres in a matter of weeks. Osting is a talented pitcher who isn't ready for prime time yet, and a team with a free roster slot should have grabbed him and stashed him in the minors. The Padres got to him first, then designated him for assignment in September, allowing the Brewers to snap him up.

Jacob Peavy Throws R Age 21

YEAR	TEAM	LGE	IP	H	ER	HR	BB	K	ERA	W	L	H/9	HR/9	BB/9	K/9	KW	PERA	STUFF
2000	Ft Wayne	Mid	131.0	128	70	14	59	94	4.81	7	8	8.8	1.0	4.1	6.5	0.8	5.65	17
2001	Lk Elsin	Cal	102.0	97	50	11	40	79	4.41	6	5	8.6	1.0	3.5	7.0	1.0	4.41	23
2001	Mobile	Sou	26.3	24	15	5	13	28	5.13	1	2	8.2	1.7	4.4	9.6	1.1	3.27	40

Peavy earned a midseason promotion from Lake Elsinore to Mobile, which is where he'll start next season. With Cyr, Howard, and Peavy anchoring the rotation, the Baybears are going to be hell on the Southern League's hitters. Peavy might have the best raw stuff of any Padres pitching prospect, and he knows what to do with it, striking out a ton of batters. He and Dennis Tankersley are #1 and #1A on the Padres' prospect list.

Mark Phillips Throws L Age 20

YEAR	TEAM	LGE	IP	H	ER	HR	BB	K	ERA	W	L	H/9	HR/9	BB/9	K/9	KW	PERA	STUFF
2000	IdahoFls	Pio	37.0	40	27	5	27	19	6.57	1	3	9.7	1.2	6.6	4.6	0.4	8.38	-9
2001	Eugene	Nwn	20.3	22	14	3	13	9	6.20	1	1	9.7	1.3	5.8	4.0	0.3	5.91	-5
2001	Ft Wayne	Mid	28.3	29	17	2	18	15	5.40	1	2	9.2	0.6	5.7	4.8	0.4	4.27	7
2001	Lk Elsin	Cal	27.3	24	12	0	17	19	3.95	2	1	7.9	0.0	5.6	6.3	0.6	3.24	21

Phillips, the Padres' top pick in 2000, moved through three levels in 2001, ending his season with five solid starts at Lake Elsinore, where he'll anchor the Storm's staff in 2001. He has a very good fastball, especially for a 20-year-old left-hander, and a plus curve; like many hot prep pitchers, his control isn't where it needs to be for him to have continued success.

Wascar Serrano Throws R Age 24

YEAR	TEAM	LGE	IP	H	ER	HR	BB	K	ERA	W	L	H/9	HR/9	BB/9	K/9	KW	PERA	STUFF
1999	R Cucmng	Cal	127.7	134	73	18	47	77	5.15	6	8	9.4	1.3	3.3	5.4	0.8	4.33	10
1999	Mobile	Sou	43.0	49	29	7	17	20	6.07	2	3	10.3	1.5	3.6	4.2	0.6	6.30	-1
2000	Mobile	Sou	107.3	114	69	20	43	75	5.79	5	7	9.6	1.7	3.6	6.3	0.9	4.34	9
2001	Portland	PCL	93.0	98	54	11	40	52	5.23	4	6	9.5	1.1	3.9	5.0	0.6	5.36	-5
2001	San Dieg	NL	48.3	50	27	6	19	31	5.03	2	3	9.3	1.1	3.5	5.8	0.8	7.57	-5

Serrano was slated for a season in Portland but ended up shuttling to and from San Diego when a fill-in was needed. While he wasn't impressive, having to learn a new role—relief—at the major-league level was a factor. Rather than have another year to sharpen his control with the Beavers in 2002, he was packaged to the Mariners.

Dennis Tankersley **Throws R** **Age 23**

YEAR	TEAM	LGE	IP	H	ER	HR	BB	K	ERA	W	L	H/9	HR/9	BB/9	K/9	KW	PERA	STUFF
2000	Augusta	SAL	75.3	81	50	10	41	39	5.97	3	5	9.7	1.2	4.9	4.7	0.5	7.01	-6
2000	Ft Wayne	Mid	62.7	65	41	12	28	50	5.89	3	4	9.3	1.7	4.0	7.2	0.9	4.67	15
2001	Lk Elsin	Cal	49.0	44	18	2	15	36	3.31	3	2	8.1	0.4	2.8	6.6	1.2	1.13	25
2001	Mobile	Sou	63.7	61	34	9	26	56	4.81	3	4	8.6	1.3	3.7	7.9	1.1	3.78	22
2001	Portland	PCL	14.7	15	10	2	9	11	6.14	1	1	9.2	1.2	5.5	6.8	0.6	9.10	3

The Tank ripped through two levels of competition before he was shut down with a tired arm at Portland; a precautionary MRI was negative. He firmly established himself as one of the best pitching prospects in baseball, making it all the more ridiculous that he was acquired for Ed Freakin' Sprague. He'll be in competition for a rotation slot later in the season.

Brian Tollberg **Throws R** **Age 29**

YEAR	TEAM	LGE	IP	H	ER	HR	BB	K	ERA	W	L	H/9	HR/9	BB/9	K/9	KW	PERA	STUFF
1999	LasVegas	PCL	30.7	33	15	4	7	15	4.40	2	1	9.7	1.2	2.1	4.4	1.1	5.18	-2
2000	LasVegas	PCL	76.0	77	31	7	12	43	3.67	5	3	9.1	0.8	1.4	5.1	1.8	3.33	8
2000	San Dieg	NL	121.0	125	57	12	29	68	4.24	7	6	9.3	0.9	2.2	5.1	1.2	4.37	7
2001	San Dieg	NL	115.0	123	56	13	22	57	4.38	7	6	9.6	1.0	1.7	4.5	1.3	4.72	4

Tollberg's sophomore season was interrupted by a fractured finger in early May, an injury that caused him to miss more than two months. When he did pitch, he did a good job working the strike zone and showed no ill effects from his career-high 197 IP in 2000. With Eaton out, Tollberg will be even more critical to the rotation in 2002.

J.J. Trujillo **Throws R** **Age 26**

YEAR	TEAM	LGE	IP	H	ER	HR	BB	K	ERA	W	L	H/9	HR/9	BB/9	K/9	KW	PERA	STUFF
2000	Ft Wayne	Mid	66.3	70	42	9	34	40	5.70	3	4	9.5	1.2	4.6	5.4	0.6	3.25	-26
2001	Lk Elsin	Cal	27.3	28	18	2	19	14	5.93	1	2	9.2	0.7	6.3	4.6	0.4	3.35	-34
2001	Mobile	Sou	49.0	49	24	2	26	24	4.41	3	2	9.0	0.4	4.8	4.4	0.5	5.28	-26

Very few minor-league closers have become factors in the major leagues, but given the wide-open nature of the Padres' bullpen going into 2002, Trujillo could work himself into the picture with a hot start. He's a submariner who keeps hitters off their game despite not posting great strikeout numbers.

Kevin Walker **Throws L** **Age 25**

YEAR	TEAM	LGE	IP	H	ER	HR	BB	K	ERA	W	L	H/9	HR/9	BB/9	K/9	KW	PERA	STUFF
1999	R Cucmng	Cal	38.3	40	23	4	22	20	5.40	2	2	9.4	0.9	5.2	4.7	0.5	5.01	-18
2000	San Dieg	NL	64.3	59	30	5	31	50	4.20	4	3	8.3	0.7	4.3	7.0	0.8	4.67	2
2001	San Dieg	NL	11.0	7	4	0	7	14	3.27	1	0	5.7	0.0	5.7	11.5	1.0	3.18	29

The Padres' best left-hander out of the pen, Walker managed just 12 innings before hitting the disabled list with tendinitis. He later learned that Tommy John surgery would keep him out until at least the 2002 All-Star break. In his absence, no one has gotten Bochy's attention, so Walker will be welcomed back enthusiastically.

San Francisco Giants

Barry Bonds.

Barry #!$@%! Bonds.

Any story about the 2001 San Francisco Giants begins and ends with Barry Bonds. Bonds had the greatest season anyone reading this has ever or will ever witness, a performance comparable to only the best seasons of the greatest player in the game's history, Babe Ruth. He shattered the records for home runs, walks, and slugging percentage, and set an assortment of other marks, conventional and sabermetric.

Yet even with what may have been the greatest season ever, and with one of the top ten seasons ever by a shortstop (Rich Aurilia), and with a great second baseman in the middle of his peak (Jeff Kent), the Giants weren't able to make the playoffs. They stayed in the race deep into September, falling short on the last Friday of the regular season, on the same night Bonds broke Mark McGwire's home-run record.

How does that happen? Well, the Giants' pitching staff wasn't effective. The team allowed 748 runs, ninth-highest in the NL, despite playing in a very good pitchers' park. A below-average rotation cost the team about a win, and was backed up by a collection of relievers who lived to allow inherited runs. According to Michael Wolverton's analysis, the Giants' relief corps cost the team a full win over the course of the season by their performance in allowing runners inherited from the starters to score. That was the worst figure in baseball. Overall, the Giants' bullpen ranked 13th in the National League in Adjusted Runs Prevented, costing the Giants 26 runs, or more than two wins, as compared to an average bullpen.

The offense was good, as any offense with a guy tying the OPS record will be; the Giants led the NL in Equivalent Average and Equivalent Runs. Still, they ranked just fifth in the NL in runs scored, and the gap between their expected run total and their actual run total, 64 runs, was the largest underperformance in the league. In fact, it was larger than the underperformance of the next two worst teams combined.

How does that happen? Well, poor performance with runners in scoring position is one reason. Overall, the Giants outhit the league. But while the National League hit .264 with a .422 slugging average with RISP, the Giants batted just .252 with a .409 slugging average. Over nearly 1,400 at-bats, that adds up.

Giants Prospectus

2001 record: 90–72; Second place, NL West

Pythagenport W/L: 86–76

Runs scored: 799 (fifth in NL)

Runs allowed: 748 (ninth in NL)

Team EqA: .283 (first in NL)

2001 batters age: 31.8 (second-oldest in NL)

2001 pitchers age: 28.8 (seventh-oldest in NL)

Ballpark: Pac Bell Park; excellent pitchers' park; Park Factor of .920

2001: When the greatest season ever can't get you into the playoffs, it's a sign that the rest of the team needs work.

2002: They kept Barry Bonds, but fixed no problems in the offseason. It's hard to see them matching 2001's record.

While Bonds's excellent plate discipline is one of the things that makes him great, he walked 71 times with runners in scoring position and had just 89 at-bats with RISP (he hit a ridiculous .382 with a .944 slugging percentage in those situations). That's not a lot of opportunities for a team's best player. By comparison, Luis Gonzalez and Sammy Sosa also batted third for their teams and had phenomenal seasons. Gonzalez had 136 at-bats and 41 walks with RISP, while Sosa had 139 at-bats and 63 walks. Other #3 hitters got well over 100 at-bats with RISP, such as Jeff Bagwell (150), Ryan Klesko (135), and Chipper Jones (113).

The Giants' RISP chances were distributed differently than most other teams because of Bonds's patience and the willingness of opposing teams to pitch him differently. As a result, the Giants' best player got fewer RISP at-bats than comparable players on other teams, which contributed to the underperformance of San Francisco's offense. Jeff Kent, who hit .343 and slugged .624 with RISP in winning the MVP in 2000, hit .268 and slugged .482 with RISP in 2001. Behind Kent, the Giants had nothing for most of the season, although Andres Galarraga hit well after his arrival.

The Giants had a dysfunctional lineup. For much of the season, it was basically the three core players and nothing else. In the second half, they began to get some offense from center field, right field, and an effective first-base platoon, but that still left two positions at which they were getting replacement-level offense. Benito Santiago's .239 EqA, weighted down by a .295 OBP, was a major problem. At third base, utility man Ramon Martinez had the job dropped in his lap after Russ Davis and Pedro Feliz kicked it, and he was horrible as a regular.

The Giants were in some ways reminiscent of the Mariners of the mid-to-late 1990s. Those teams had three of the best players in baseball in Ken Griffey Jr., Alex Rodriguez, and Randy Johnson, as well as second-tier stars such as Edgar Martinez and Jay Buhner. They were hamstrung by gaping holes in the bullpen and at three or four positions every year, though, and while they made the postseason a couple of times, they never achieved what they should have with that talent core.

Unlike the Mariners, who broke up that core over a period of 15 months, the Giants will sally forth with their team intact. Despite Bonds's having his year for the ages, he wasn't able to find what he wanted on the open market. With the situation for free agents, even great ones, looking bleak, Bonds elected to stay with the Giants. In January, he signed a $90-million contract, running for four, five, or 15 years, depending on your viewpoint. Regardless, keeping Bonds sets the course for the team for the next five seasons.

Certainly, the Giants can afford to write the checks. While they'll be paying down the debt on privately-funded Pac Bell Park for some time, the park generates a massive amount of revenue from a variety of sources. The Giants grossed $170 million last year, fifth in MLB; even with debt service, they can support a payroll well into the $60-$70 million range, more than enough to finance a contending team. Money should not be an issue for a while.

In the long term, Peter Magowan is going to reap some amazing profits with this team. The park will eventually be paid off, and as the Dodgers have shown, owning your own ballpark is a license to print money. The Giants' plan hasn't yet taken hold elsewhere, in part because of the greed of MLB owners—they want taxpayer dollars—and in part because of fear of carrying a large debt load. Once Pac Bell Park's debt is paid, the Giants will routinely be among the game's most profitable teams, and the Giants' franchise value will shoot through the roof.

Pac Bell Park isn't a burden: it's a long-term investment that will cause appreciation of the primary asset, the ball club. The capital sunk into the park is the kind of money businessmen—that's what the owners are, businessmen—spend every day in the hopes of bringing back more money.

With a new stadium to fill, the Giants will have to continue their course of patch-and-tape. They've signed Bonds to the huge contract, and you can't go through a rebuilding process with that kind of player on your team. They will continue to draft low, and if this year is any indication, will stock up on as many college arms as they can. It's not the worst strategy, but it doesn't address the glaring need for impact hitters throughout the organization. The Giants' top hitting prospects are mostly corner outfielders or first basemen who, if everything breaks right, are going to hit right around average for their positions, guys like Tony Torcato and Sean McGowan. They also have a bunch of third-base suspects who don't walk and/or can't stay healthy. They will eventually need to shift gears and draft some high-school position players who can take over for Rich Aurilia and Jeff Kent someday, as well as fill the ever present holes in center field and behind the plate.

The benefit to taking college pitchers is that they ripen as trade bait pretty quickly. With a veteran staff entrenched in Pac Bell Park, Brian Sabean is going to look to the player-development staff for fodder, not replacements. If the farm system can churn out a few attractive arms every July, Sabean can use them to patch the holes he always seems to have and keep the Giants in one more pennant race. Pitchers Jesse Foppert and Brad Hennessey, high picks last June, could be in other organizations come July as the Giants come to realize their scars at third base and catcher are cancelling out the greatness of their core players.

This isn't how we would recommend running a team in the long term. When Bonds finally does retire, the Giants are almost certain to go through an extended down cycle. Bonds is part of a very old core on this team—it's possible that no Opening Day starter will be under the age of 30—and when that core loses it, the Giants are going down hard.

However, different situations require different solutions. Brian Sabean has correctly ascertained where the Giants are in the success cycle, and he is maximizing their opportunities as best he can. He could do a better job of identifying the right players to fill holes—signing out machines such as Benito Santiago and Russ Davis does more harm than good—but he has a plan, and executing a mediocre plan is better than having no plan at all.

HITTERS (BA: .270, OBP: .340, SLG: .440, EqA: .260)

Rich Aurilia SS Bats R Age 30

YEAR	TEAM	LGE	AB	H	DB	TP	HR	BB	SO	R	RBI	SB	CS	OUT	BA	OBP	SLG	EQA	EQR	DEFENSE
1999	San Fran	NL	564	162	22	0	24	36	66	68	79	1	3	405	.287	.335	.454	.259	69	141-SS 3
2000	San Fran	NL	518	145	25	2	21	47	83	68	79	1	2	375	.280	.340	.458	.263	66	136-SS 10
2001	San Fran	NL	645	222	38	5	39	45	70	123	103	1	3	426	.344	.387	.600	.314	118	146-SS 8
2002	*San Fran*	*NL*	*592*	*174*	*28*	*3*	*27*	*54*	*79*	*83*	*89*	*2*	*3*	*421*	*.294*	*.353*	*.488*	*.286*	*92*	

Three factors contributed to his awesome season: he cut his strikeout rate, he stayed healthy, and he got bigger, adding distance to the many fly balls he hits. Overall, it was one of the best shortstop seasons in history, lost behind a better one in Texas and The Greatest Season Ever. Even regressing to the mean this year, he'll be the best shortstop in the league. Underrated defender.

Marvin Benard CF Bats L Age 31

YEAR	TEAM	LGE	AB	H	DB	TP	HR	BB	SO	R	RBI	SB	CS	OUT	BA	OBP	SLG	EQA	EQR	DEFENSE
1999	San Fran	NL	568	166	35	5	17	48	90	98	62	23	14	416	.292	.354	.461	.269	78	136-CF -3
2000	San Fran	NL	570	157	27	6	13	55	89	102	56	21	8	420	.275	.345	.412	.257	71	141-CF -1
2001	San Fran	NL	397	115	21	2	16	27	56	76	48	10	5	287	.290	.340	.474	.268	53	91-CF -4
2002	*San Fran*	*NL*	*517*	*139*	*22*	*4*	*15*	*53*	*84*	*87*	*52*	*15*	*8*	*386*	*.269*	*.337*	*.414*	*.262*	*68*	

You have to chalk this one up to Dusty Baker. He could have buried Benard, who was hitting .196/.269/.296 on June 3. While Baker gave some of Benard's playing time to Calvin Murray, he never gave up on his nominal starter. Benard began wearing contacts in June and bounced back to hit .331/.370/.556 after the All-Star break. That said, he's a tweener, not good enough with the bat to help in the corners, and lacking the range to play a good center field, especially in Pac Bell Park. Tsuyoshi Shinjo could take some of his innings this year.

Julian Benavidez 3B Bats R Age 20

YEAR	TEAM	LGE	AB	H	DB	TP	HR	BB	SO	R	RBI	SB	CS	OUT	BA	OBP	SLG	EQA	EQR	DEFENSE
2001	Salem OR	Nwn	193	44	8	0	5	16	59	22	21	1	1	150	.228	.288	.347	.215	16	47-3B 0
2002	*San Fran*	*NL*	*260*	*63*	*6*	*0*	*9*	*23*	*86*	*27*	*30*	*1*	*1*	*198*	*.242*	*.304*	*.369*	*.235*	*26*	

Benavidez, a third-round pick in the 2001 draft, impressed in his professional debut by showing good power and patience for a 19-year-old. The Giants have virtually no high-upside position players, so look for them to push Benavidez to the Cal League in 2002. Caution: being a third-base prospect in the Giants' organization can be hazardous to your career.

Barry Bonds LF Bats L Age 37

YEAR	TEAM	LGE	AB	H	DB	TP	HR	BB	SO	R	RBI	SB	CS	OUT	BA	OBP	SLG	EQA	EQR	DEFENSE
1999	San Fran	NL	358	95	19	2	35	69	57	90	80	13	2	265	.265	.388	.623	.321	77	92-LF -1
2000	San Fran	NL	489	155	30	4	51	112	71	132	106	11	3	337	.317	.447	.708	.359	130	125-LF 3
2001	San Fran	NL	488	174	38	2	78	176	79	141	149	13	3	317	.357	.532	.922	.429	191	131-LF -7
2002	*San Fran*	*NL*	*447*	*115*	*31*	*2*	*51*	*136*	*76*	*126*	*105*	*13*	*3*	*335*	*.257*	*.431*	*.678*	*.357*	*127*	

The sudden end to Mark McGwire's career serves as a lesson about making predictions about the future of old ballplayers, so let's just say Bonds has a reasonable chance to retire holding two or three of the game's most revered records, as well as a place alongside his godfather as one of the SMALL_NUMBER greatest to ever play the game. The five-year, $90-million contract he signed in January should mean he retires a Giant.

Eric Davis RF Bats R Age 40

YEAR	TEAM	LGE	AB	H	DB	TP	HR	BB	SO	R	RBI	SB	CS	OUT	BA	OBP	SLG	EQA	EQR	DEFENSE
1999	St Louis	NL	191	48	8	2	5	28	45	26	28	4	4	147	.251	.350	.393	.251	23	44-RF 0
2000	St Louis	NL	255	76	11	0	7	32	55	36	39	1	1	180	.298	.378	.424	.272	35	58-RF -5
2001	San Fran	NL	158	36	9	3	4	12	32	19	24	1	1	123	.228	.286	.399	.226	15	33-RF -1

One of the great moments of last season was the ovation Davis received at the end of his last game in Cincinnati. He had two different careers with the Reds, the first in the mid-1980s as one of the most exciting players ever—if only for two years—the second ten years later as a prodigal son making a comeback from assorted injuries. He was one of those "worth the price of admission" ballplayers who, like Pete Reiser and Fred Lynn, probably curtailed his success by pushing his body past its limits. He will be missed.

Russ Davis 3B Bats R Age 32

YEAR	TEAM	LGE	AB	H	DB	TP	HR	BB	SO	R	RBI	SB	CS	OUT	BA	OBP	SLG	EQA	EQR	DEFENSE
1999	Seattle	AL	430	109	18	1	22	28	98	55	58	3	3	324	.253	.306	.453	.247	49	111-3B -2
2000	San Fran	NL	183	49	4	0	10	7	27	27	25	0	3	137	.268	.301	.454	.241	20	26-3B -3
2001	San Fran	NL	169	47	15	1	7	16	42	17	18	1	0	122	.278	.343	.503	.277	25	38-3B -5
2002	*San Fran*	*NL*	*343*	*84*	*17*	*1*	*18*	*29*	*80*	*47*	*45*	*3*	*2*	*261*	*.245*	*.304*	*.458*	*.259*	*44*	

During the off-season, many people began taking the MLBPA to task for the perception that it doesn't care about the rank and file. It's a disingenuous argument in that its supporters appear to care less about the interests of baseball players and more about the union's refusal to accept a salary cap in exchange for things that *might* impact players further down the pay scale.

One thing the Players Association does need to address, however, is the lack of a decent family-leave provision within the game. Russ Davis lost his father earlier this year, and when it affected his play, the team had no recourse other than releasing him or playing short one player. The Yankees went through a similar situation as Bernie Williams missed a large chunk of time tending to, and eventually mourning, his father. Two other players, Preston Wilson and Mark Gardner, were already on the DL when personal problems arose, enabling them to deal with the problems at their own pace.

You would think a team could use the disabled list for this type of thing, but when the Yankees tried to disable Williams, they were told they could not do so. The MLBPA has to work towards a rule that allows players to be granted time off to be with their families without it negatively impacting the team.

Shawon Dunston UT Bats R Age 39

YEAR	TEAM	LGE	AB	H	DB	TP	HR	BB	SO	R	RBI	SB	CS	OUT	BA	OBP	SLG	EQA	EQR	DEFENSE
1999	NY Mets	NL	93	32	5	1	0	0	15	12	15	4	1	62	.344	.358	.419	.265	11	21-CF 0
1999	St Louis	NL	151	46	5	2	5	0	21	22	24	5	3	108	.305	.318	.464	.255	18	17-OF 0
2000	St Louis	NL	218	54	11	2	12	3	43	27	41	3	1	165	.248	.267	.482	.240	23	39-LF 1
2001	San Fran	NL	188	56	13	3	9	1	27	28	26	3	1	133	.298	.307	.543	.272	26	37-OF -2
2002	*San Fran*	*NL*	*225*	*53*	*12*	*3*	*8*	*6*	*40*	*29*	*34*	*5*	*2*	*174*	*.236*	*.255*	*.422*	*.230*	*22*	

Dunston has always been a hacker, but his last few seasons are redefining the term. He has five straight seasons of single-digit walk totals, adding up to 24 free passes in 1,411 trips to the plate. He doesn't play the infield any more, and as an extra outfielder, he's not worth the roster spot.

Pedro Feliz 3B Bats R Age 25

YEAR	TEAM	LGE	AB	H	DB	TP	HR	BB	SO	R	RBI	SB	CS	OUT	BA	OBP	SLG	EQA	EQR	DEFENSE
1999	Shrevprt	Tex	492	109	19	3	11	13	93	41	58	3	1	384	.222	.244	.339	.195	32	128-3B 9
2000	Fresno	PCL	495	131	26	1	27	20	91	65	78	1	1	365	.265	.295	.485	.251	58	121-3B 5
2001	San Fran	NL	222	55	12	1	7	9	42	26	24	2	1	168	.248	.282	.405	.227	21	57-3B -12
2002	*San Fran*	*NL*	*411*	*102*	*20*	*2*	*17*	*24*	*84*	*48*	*60*	*3*	*1*	*310*	*.248*	*.290*	*.431*	*.246*	*47*	

Big power numbers in the Pacific Coast League convinced the Giants that Feliz, a Jim Presley hit-alike, was ready to take over at third base. He was awful, ceding much of his playing time to Ramon Martinez in the second half. Desi Relaford should push Feliz into a platoon this year, a role in which he can succeed (1085 OPS against lefties last year, .300 with good power against them in Triple-A in 2000).

Andres Galarraga 1B Bats R Age 41

YEAR	TEAM	LGE	AB	H	DB	TP	HR	BB	SO	R	RBI	SB	CS	OUT	BA	OBP	SLG	EQA	EQR	DEFENSE
1998	Atlanta	NL	565	176	22	1	49	62	134	108	126	7	6	395	.312	.402	.614	.321	116	145-1B -13
2000	Atlanta	NL	498	150	23	1	28	29	116	65	96	3	5	353	.301	.358	.520	.283	75	121-1B -8
2001	Texas	AL	243	60	11	0	13	19	59	34	37	1	0	183	.247	.319	.453	.255	30	24-1B -1
2001	San Fran	NL	158	49	15	1	7	12	42	19	37	0	3	112	.310	.367	.551	.290	25	34-1B -7
2002	*San Fran*	*NL*	*409*	*92*	*19*	*1*	*16*	*37*	*108*	*46*	*54*	*2*	*4*	*321*	*.225*	*.289*	*.394*	*.233*	*42*	

Like Eric Davis, Galarraga has had a distinctly non-standard career path, featuring two distinct comebacks, including one from cancer. He wasn't a savior for the Giants, just a guy better than J.T. Snow whose RBI numbers looked as good as you'd expect from someone hitting behind Barry Bonds. He's one of the many mid-level and below free agents still unemployed as we go to press.

Edwards Guzman — C — Bats L — Age 25

YEAR	TEAM	LGE	AB	H	DB	TP	HR	BB	SO	R	RBI	SB	CS	OUT	BA	OBP	SLG	EQA	EQR	DEFENSE	
1999	Fresno	PCL	351	83	5	0	7	14	46	37	38	5	4	272	.236	.270	.311	.197	23	54-3B 1	29-C -7
2000	Fresno	PCL	415	102	18	1	5	10	42	40	39	1	3	316	.246	.270	.330	.200	28	32-2B -4	29-C -3
2001	Fresno	PCL	70	22	3	1	0	4	3	10	8	0	1	49	.314	.351	.386	.245	7	11-C -3	
2001	San Fran	NL	116	31	3	0	4	5	14	8	8	0	0	85	.267	.298	.397	.230	11	14-C 1	
2002	*San Fran*	*NL*	*355*	*92*	*14*	*1*	*8*	*21*	*41*	*43*	*41*	*3*	*3*	*266*	*.259*	*.301*	*.372*	*.232*	*35*		

Guzman is about as valuable as a player with his limited hitting ability can be. A converted infielder now nominally a backup catcher, he can play six positions, run for the slower guys on the roster, and slap singles as an extra lefty bat on the bench. A guy like this is valuable for a team carrying 11 pitchers, mandatory for a team carrying 12. He's better than Benito Santiago, although it's not like he'd help much as a starter.

Jeff Kent — 2B — Bats R — Age 34

YEAR	TEAM	LGE	AB	H	DB	TP	HR	BB	SO	R	RBI	SB	CS	OUT	BA	OBP	SLG	EQA	EQR	DEFENSE	
1999	San Fran	NL	516	151	36	2	25	55	104	85	99	11	6	371	.293	.366	.516	.288	82	125-2B -6	
2000	San Fran	NL	598	205	43	6	35	83	98	115	125	11	10	402	.343	.430	.610	.331	127	141-2B 6	
2001	San Fran	NL	616	197	53	6	23	62	81	90	113	7	6	425	.320	.390	.537	.301	106	132-2B 8	23-1B -1
2002	*San Fran*	*NL*	*540*	*159*	*37*	*4*	*21*	*69*	*88*	*80*	*94*	*10*	*8*	*389*	*.294*	*.374*	*.494*	*.298*	*93*		

His season looked like a disappointment because of the expectations set by his MVP campaign and a decline in his performance with men on base. Kent did poorly in at-bats preceded by intentional walks to Barry Bonds, aggravating the perception that he was having a bad year. In reality, he was the best second baseman in the league by a large margin. He's never mentioned in Hall of Fame discussions, but he's had a better career than some HOF second basemen, and he's had Joe Gordon as his best age-based comparison for four years now.

Ramon Martinez — IF — Bats R — Age 29

YEAR	TEAM	LGE	AB	H	DB	TP	HR	BB	SO	R	RBI	SB	CS	OUT	BA	OBP	SLG	EQA	EQR	DEFENSE	
1999	Fresno	PCL	111	31	7	1	1	9	16	10	13	1	0	80	.279	.333	.387	.245	12	22-SS -1	
1999	San Fran	NL	145	38	4	0	6	13	18	21	19	1	2	109	.262	.323	.414	.243	16	22-2B 3	
2000	San Fran	NL	192	60	14	2	6	13	20	31	25	3	2	134	.313	.359	.500	.281	28	26-SS 2	18-2B -3
2001	San Fran	NL	396	109	20	4	5	36	44	53	41	1	2	289	.275	.342	.384	.245	43	62-3B 1	29-2B 6
2002	*San Fran*	*NL*	*337*	*89*	*17*	*2*	*8*	*36*	*41*	*44*	*38*	*3*	*2*	*250*	*.264*	*.335*	*.398*	*.257*	*42*		

The trade of Bill Mueller might have cost the Giants the division last year, because their third-base situation was a hole all season long. Russ Davis didn't hit, Pedro Feliz was worse, and Ramon Martinez, a passable solution in the early summer, wore down badly in an everyday role. He hit .153/.189/.224 in 85 August at-bats. As a utility infielder who can field all three spots, Martinez is an asset.

Sean McGowan — LF/1B — Bats R — Age 25

YEAR	TEAM	LGE	AB	H	DB	TP	HR	BB	SO	R	RBI	SB	CS	OUT	BA	OBP	SLG	EQA	EQR	DEFENSE	
1999	Salem OR	Nwn	252	59	8	1	7	8	65	20	28	1	1	194	.234	.259	.357	.204	18	32-1B 0	
2000	San Jose	Cal	461	126	23	1	10	24	72	42	71	2	2	337	.273	.313	.393	.235	45	101-1B -8	
2000	Shrevprt	Tex	68	20	4	0	0	0	8	4	9	0	0	48	.294	.294	.353	.216	5	17-1B 0	
2001	Shrevprt	Tex	125	33	3	0	3	4	19	9	13	0	1	93	.264	.287	.360	.214	10	13-1B -1	
2001	Fresno	PCL	384	96	25	1	11	21	86	48	51	1	0	288	.250	.291	.406	.231	37	49-LF -8	34-1B -1
2002	*San Fran*	*NL*	*460*	*123*	*20*	*1*	*13*	*30*	*97*	*45*	*61*	*1*	*1*	*338*	*.267*	*.312*	*.400*	*.246*	*51*		

If you've been paying attention, you've noticed a distinct lack of minor leaguers in this chapter. The Giants' farm system looks roughly like Kansas City in the last scene of *The Day After.* McGowan is a slightly better version of Pedro Feliz, without the ability to play third base or, for that matter, any position other than first base. He'll rack up some good numbers in Fresno and garner some bench time in 2002.

Damon Minor 1B Bats L Age 28

YEAR	TEAM	LGE	AB	H	DB	TP	HR	BB	SO	R	RBI	SB	CS	OUT	BA	OBP	SLG	EQA	EQR	DEFENSE
1999	Shrevprt	Tex	481	114	26	2	16	63	119	60	61	1	0	367	.237	.332	.399	.248	56	129-1B 9
2000	Fresno	PCL	475	120	17	1	25	70	94	64	78	0	0	355	.253	.349	.451	.267	65	129-1B -14
2001	Fresno	PCL	399	107	16	2	19	39	75	59	55	1	1	293	.268	.338	.461	.264	52	101-1B -7
2001	San Fran	NL	45	8	2	0	0	3	7	4	4	0	0	37	.178	.229	.222	.159	2	10-1B -1
2002	*San Fran*	*NL*	*430*	*109*	*20*	*2*	*19*	*61*	*92*	*58*	*62*	*1*	*0*	*321*	*.253*	*.346*	*.442*	*.274*	*63*	

Guys like Damon Minor don't catch many breaks, and they need to take advantage when those breaks come along. Minor didn't, hitting an empty .273 during a J.T. Snow trip to the disabled list. Snow returned, Galarraga arrived, and Minor was forgotten. He doesn't fit the Giants well, although he'd make a good backup for someone like Mike Sweeney or Richie Sexson.

Calvin Murray CF Bats R Age 30

YEAR	TEAM	LGE	AB	H	DB	TP	HR	BB	SO	R	RBI	SB	CS	OUT	BA	OBP	SLG	EQA	EQR	DEFENSE
1999	Fresno	PCL	534	155	26	5	17	41	81	92	54	31	11	390	.290	.343	.453	.267	72	129-CF 0
2000	San Fran	NL	197	50	13	1	2	27	30	36	22	9	3	150	.254	.351	.360	.250	23	56-CF 0
2001	Fresno	PCL	136	30	5	1	3	11	30	14	9	2	2	108	.221	.282	.338	.209	11	34-CF 4
2001	San Fran	NL	330	89	16	2	6	31	48	59	27	8	8	249	.270	.337	.385	.242	36	86-CF 3
2002	*San Fran*	*NL*	*451*	*114*	*22*	*3*	*10*	*52*	*79*	*74*	*44*	*20*	*11*	*348*	*.253*	*.330*	*.381*	*.252*	*55*	

Murray actually became the starting center fielder in June, as Marvin Benard worked through his slump. On a six-game road swing through San Diego and St. Louis, he hit .452 with four home runs, bumping his OPS nearly 200 points. Outside of that week, Murray hit .224 with two bombs. While he didn't keep the center-field job, he also didn't get demoted once Benard started hitting, and he is now an "established" major leaguer. One hot week can change a man's life; in this case, it's worth millions of dollars in salary and pension to Murray.

Lance Niekro 3B Bats R Age 23

YEAR	TEAM	LGE	AB	H	DB	TP	HR	BB	SO	R	RBI	SB	CS	OUT	BA	OBP	SLG	EQA	EQR	DEFENSE
2000	Salem OR	Nwn	197	52	7	2	4	4	27	17	25	1	0	145	.264	.284	.381	.221	17	29-3B -1
2001	San Jose	Cal	164	40	6	0	3	2	13	13	26	2	2	126	.244	.253	.335	.195	11	32-3B 1
2002	*San Fran*	*NL*	*231*	*59*	*9*	*1*	*6*	*9*	*26*	*22*	*28*	*3*	*2*	*174*	*.255*	*.283*	*.381*	*.228*	*22*	

If Niekro's name was John Smith or something, he probably wouldn't be in the book. Well, given this organization, he might; hell, Robby Thompson almost got an entry. Niekro has a bum right shoulder that cost him most of the 2001 season. In the eight weeks he did play, he walked four times. He can't be taken seriously as a prospect until at least one of those problems is solved.

An organizational issue: Giants' affiliates finished last in the PCL, last in the Texas League, and seventh (out of ten teams) in the California League in walks drawn. Almost all of their nominal prospects have plate-discipline problems. There's hope at lower levels: their affiliates in the South Atlantic and Northwest leagues finished first and second in walks drawn.

Cody Ransom SS Bats R Age 26

YEAR	TEAM	LGE	AB	H	DB	TP	HR	BB	SO	R	RBI	SB	CS	OUT	BA	OBP	SLG	EQA	EQR	DEFENSE
1999	Bakrsfld	Cal	356	75	8	3	8	37	109	44	29	8	4	285	.211	.292	.317	.212	29	99-SS -2
1999	Shrevprt	Tex	42	5	0	0	2	3	23	5	4	0	0	37	.119	.190	.262	.156	2	12-SS 3
2000	Shrevprt	Tex	465	83	18	1	6	26	142	45	36	6	2	384	.178	.222	.260	.169	22	128-SS -18
2001	Fresno	PCL	463	97	16	4	18	40	124	61	60	14	2	368	.210	.272	.378	.221	42	132-SS -3
2002	*San Fran*	*NL*	*411*	*85*	*15*	*3*	*13*	*45*	*129*	*57*	*41*	*10*	*2*	*328*	*.207*	*.285*	*.353*	*.226*	*40*	

It's hard to know what to make of Ransom. He has an excellent defensive reputation, good enough to get him into last year's Futures Game. His raw defensive numbers are very good, but they don't translate well, as you see above. At the plate, he hits like Jose Hernandez: lots of strikeouts, few walks, decent power. If his defense is all that, he can have a career. There's considerable speculation that Ransom will push Aurilia to third base by 2003, which would be an awful waste of Aurilia.

Benito Santiago C Bats R Age 37

YEAR	TEAM	LGE	AB	H	DB	TP	HR	BB	SO	R	RBI	SB	CS	OUT	BA	OBP	SLG	EQA	EQR	DEFENSE
1999	ChiCubs	NL	351	86	18	3	7	28	66	27	34	1	1	266	.245	.304	.373	.228	33	91-C 4
2000	Cincnnti	NL	253	65	9	1	8	16	41	21	42	2	2	190	.257	.303	.395	.232	25	67-C 3
2001	San Fran	NL	482	136	29	4	6	21	66	43	48	5	4	350	.282	.314	.396	.236	48	121-C 2
2002	*San Fran*	*NL*	*397*	*88*	*21*	*3*	*6*	*30*	*63*	*30*	*38*	*4*	*3*	*312*	*.222*	*.276*	*.335*	*.211*	*32*	

Dusty Baker's preference for veterans has worked when he's been able to get good years out of aging players like Ellis Burks. The downside is Benito Santiago, who parlayed a hot start into the most playing time he'd had in five years and a contract extension. After May, though, he just killed the Giants, with an OBP under .270. The Giants desperately need a real catcher.

J.T. Snow 1B Bats L Age 34

YEAR	TEAM	LGE	AB	H	DB	TP	HR	BB	SO	R	RBI	SB	CS	OUT	BA	OBP	SLG	EQA	EQR	DEFENSE
1999	San Fran	NL	576	160	26	2	25	79	112	94	96	0	4	420	.278	.370	.460	.275	84	148-1B 10
2000	San Fran	NL	545	159	34	2	20	60	118	83	96	1	3	389	.292	.372	.472	.280	80	143-1B 3
2001	San Fran	NL	289	77	12	1	9	54	69	46	37	0	0	212	.266	.387	.408	.275	42	77-1B 2
2002	*San Fran*	*NL*	*498*	*125*	*25*	*2*	*17*	*83*	*122*	*77*	*71*	*0*	*2*	*375*	*.251*	*.358*	*.412*	*.271*	*72*	

Snow missed much of the first half with rib and groin injuries, and he was awful when he did play. After a trip to the DL, he returned to bat .306/.403/.446 in the second half, combining with Galarraga to make first base a strong suit for the Giants. While Snow has been a target of ours over the years, we have to note that he's been a pretty good player for the past three seasons, and that Clay Davenport's system rates his defense as consistently above average. The Giants have bigger problems.

Tony Torcato LF Bats L Age 22

YEAR	TEAM	LGE	AB	H	DB	TP	HR	BB	SO	R	RBI	SB	CS	OUT	BA	OBP	SLG	EQA	EQR	DEFENSE
1999	Bakrsfld	Cal	418	95	11	0	5	18	68	32	39	1	1	324	.227	.262	.289	.188	25	79-3B -9
2000	San Jose	Cal	495	135	27	1	6	21	63	53	59	9	3	363	.273	.306	.368	.228	45	104-3B -14
2001	San Jose	Cal	261	74	17	1	1	13	38	28	33	5	2	189	.284	.322	.368	.234	25	13-LF -1
2001	Shrevprt	Tex	148	38	7	1	1	7	15	11	19	0	1	111	.257	.299	.338	.214	12	36-LF 2
2001	Fresno	PCL	146	40	8	1	1	3	18	17	7	0	1	107	.274	.289	.363	.215	11	34-LF 2
2002	*San Fran*	*NL*	*543*	*151*	*28*	*2*	*8*	*35*	*77*	*60*	*66*	*4*	*2*	*394*	*.278*	*.322*	*.381*	*.246*	*59*	

After a few years as a lousy third baseman, Torcato quickly became an adequate left fielder. He'll have to move again this year, now that Bonds is in the fold through 2005. More importantly, he'll have to add some meat to his high-average, gap-hitting style. He had just 22 unintentional walks and five home runs last season, unacceptable numbers for a corner outfielder. He'll make a cameo in San Francisco this year and be the frontrunner for the right-field job in 2003. There's a 15% chance he becomes Bobby Higginson.

Yorvit Torrealba C Bats R Age 23

YEAR	TEAM	LGE	AB	H	DB	TP	HR	BB	SO	R	RBI	SB	CS	OUT	BA	OBP	SLG	EQA	EQR	DEFENSE
1999	San Jose	Cal	73	19	0	0	2	3	15	6	10	0	0	54	.260	.294	.342	.215	6	19-C -4
1999	Shrevprt	Tex	217	46	8	1	3	7	35	20	14	0	1	172	.212	.241	.300	.182	12	49-C -3
1999	Fresno	PCL	62	14	0	0	2	3	10	7	8	0	1	49	.226	.277	.323	.199	4	17-C -2
2000	Shrevprt	Tex	400	100	18	1	3	22	55	39	24	1	2	302	.250	.295	.322	.210	30	104-C -5
2001	Fresno	PCL	387	92	19	2	6	18	59	46	28	2	2	297	.238	.276	.344	.208	29	106-C -2
2002	*San Fran*	*NL*	*390*	*102*	*19*	*2*	*7*	*26*	*63*	*48*	*35*	*2*	*2*	*290*	*.262*	*.308*	*.374*	*.237*	*40*	

What were the odds of two catchers named "Torrealba" making their major-league debuts in the same week? Yorvit and Steve (with the Braves) turned the trick last September. This Torrealba is a glove man who could hit an empty .275 in the majors; that sucks, until you realize he would be both better and cheaper than Benito Santiago. John Flaherty looked about like this in 1994, so don't be surprised to see Torrealba as a staple of Hacking Mass lineups for years to come.

Carlos Valderrama CF Bats R Age 24

YEAR	TEAM	LGE	AB	H	DB	TP	HR	BB	SO	R	RBI	SB	CS	OUT	BA	OBP	SLG	EQA	EQR	DEFENSE
1999	Salem OR	Nwn	133	28	3	0	1	5	40	13	9	7	2	107	.211	.239	.256	.178	7	33-RF 1
1999	San Jose	Cal	90	19	1	0	0	2	19	7	8	4	2	73	.211	.228	.222	.161	4	21-RF 0
2000	Bakrsfld	Cal	437	113	17	2	10	21	97	48	52	24	7	331	.259	.296	.375	.230	42	107-LF -3
2001	Shrevprt	Tex	161	42	10	1	1	15	29	22	8	7	4	123	.261	.324	.354	.232	16	38-CF -1
2002	*San Fran*	*NL*	*386*	*99*	*18*	*2*	*7*	*31*	*89*	*52*	*42*	*23*	*7*	*294*	*.256*	*.312*	*.368*	*.245*	*43*	

He's not the same guy with the blond Afro who kicks balls for a living. This Valderrama is a slap-and-dash center-field prospect with a near-perfect skill set for a fourth outfielder. He caught the shoulder injuries that were going around the Giants' system, missing the last three months of the season. He'll eventually make a run at Calvin Murray's job.

John Vander Wal RF Bats L Age 36

YEAR	TEAM	LGE	AB	H	DB	TP	HR	BB	SO	R	RBI	SB	CS	OUT	BA	OBP	SLG	EQA	EQR	DEFENSE	
1999	San Dieg	NL	249	70	14	0	8	35	55	26	42	2	1	180	.281	.374	.434	.274	35	38-LF 1	19-1B -3
2000	Pittsbrg	NL	385	114	23	0	25	67	84	71	90	11	2	273	.296	.403	.551	.313	75	70-RF -4	27-1B -3
2001	Pittsbrg	NL	314	90	23	3	11	40	71	40	51	7	4	228	.287	.369	.484	.282	48	61-RF -7	12-1B -2
2001	San Fran	NL	141	39	7	1	3	26	32	21	22	1	2	104	.277	.389	.404	.271	20	33-RF 3	
2002	*NY Yanks*	*AL*	*396*	*103*	*24*	*2*	*15*	*72*	*93*	*52*	*68*	*8*	*4*	*297*	*.260*	*.374*	*.444*	*.283*	*63*		

Life is funny. Three years ago, Vander Wal couldn't get any playing time despite showing some good offensive skills. He backed into a job in Pittsburgh, signed a two-year deal, then found himself desired by teams in pennant races and others coming off World Series appearances, despite being basically the same player he'd been when he was unwanted. He'll play as much or as little as the health of Rondell White and Nick Johnson allows.

PITCHERS (ERA: 4.50, H/9: 9.0, HR/9: 1.0, BB/9: 3.0, K/9: 6.0, KW: 2.0, PERA: 4.50)

Kurt Ainsworth Throws R Age 23

YEAR	TEAM	LGE	IP	H	ER	HR	BB	K	ERA	W	L	H/9	HR/9	BB/9	K/9	KW	PERA	STUFF
1999	Salem OR	Nwn	44.3	40	19	2	20	34	3.86	3	2	8.1	0.4	4.1	6.9	0.9	3.99	21
2000	Shrevprt	Tex	153.3	159	86	18	62	90	5.05	8	9	9.3	1.1	3.6	5.3	0.7	4.32	9
2001	Fresno	PCL	146.0	148	87	23	61	112	5.36	7	9	9.1	1.4	3.8	6.9	0.9	5.26	15

After some terrible beatings in April, Ainsworth settled down to pitch very well the rest of the season. He's a four-pitch pitcher who gets into the low 90s with his fastball, and he should slide into the Giants' fifth-starter slot this season. The Giants' good infield defense will help him tremendously.

Luke Anderson Throws R Age 24

YEAR	TEAM	LGE	IP	H	ER	HR	BB	K	ERA	W	L	H/9	HR/9	BB/9	K/9	KW	PERA	STUFF
2000	Salem OR	Nwn	29.3	28	14	3	12	25	4.30	2	1	8.6	0.9	3.7	7.7	1.0	2.09	7
2001	San Jose	Cal	64.3	68	34	8	18	37	4.76	3	4	9.5	1.1	2.5	5.2	1.0	4.31	-13

Anderson is a closer prospect who saved 30 games while relying on a very good splitter. He made an assortment of league and level All-Star teams, while not showing up on many prospect lists. With Jackson Markert, the Sally League's top closer, coming up hard behind him, Anderson's prospect peak may have passed. Darwin would have loved player development.

Brian Boehringer Throws R Age 32

YEAR	TEAM	LGE	IP	H	ER	HR	BB	K	ERA	W	L	H/9	HR/9	BB/9	K/9	KW	PERA	STUFF
1999	San Dieg	NL	96.0	97	47	10	29	58	4.41	6	5	9.1	0.9	2.7	5.4	1.0	3.58	0
2000	San Dieg	NL	15.7	19	13	4	8	8	7.47	1	1	10.9	2.3	4.6	4.6	0.5	8.50	-30
2001	NY Yanks	AL	36.3	32	14	3	11	31	3.47	3	1	7.9	0.7	2.7	7.7	1.4	3.64	11
2001	San Fran	NL	32.7	32	18	4	15	22	4.96	2	2	8.8	1.1	4.1	6.1	0.7	5.66	-10

Boehringer tried to pitch through a groin injury in early June and was alternately unavailable and terrible. The Yankees should simply have placed him on the disabled list, but they were thin in the bullpen and trying to make things work. They eventually dumped him on the Giants for Bobby Estalella. He's a serviceable low-leverage reliever and another mid-January free agent.

Boof Bonser   Throws R   Age 20

YEAR	TEAM	LGE	IP	H	ER	HR	BB	K	ERA	W	L	H/9	HR/9	BB/9	K/9	KW	PERA	STUFF
2000	Salem OR	Nwn	30.0	33	31	6	34	19	9.30	1	2	9.9	1.8	10.2	5.7	0.3	8.68	-15
2001	Hagerstn	SAL	126.7	126	83	16	86	91	5.90	5	9	9.0	1.1	6.1	6.5	0.5	3.85	12

Bonser has flown up prospect lists based on his good performance at Hagerstown. While he had a good year, both statistically and by scouting measures, there are serious concerns here. Bonser is already 6′4″ and 230 pounds, and he probably has some growth left in him, so weight is going to be a concern. Additionally, he has to make a two-level jump this season, and the change in pitching environments will be dramatic. Finally, he's yet to make it through the injury nexus. The chances of Bonser looking as good in eight months as he does right now are slim. If he can get to the majors, the Giants are the team for him: Russ Ortiz and Livan Hernandez are carrying on the Rick Reuschel tradition.

Jason Christiansen   Throws L   Age 32

YEAR	TEAM	LGE	IP	H	ER	HR	BB	K	ERA	W	L	H/9	HR/9	BB/9	K/9	KW	PERA	STUFF
1999	Pittsbrg	NL	36.3	31	16	2	18	32	3.96	2	2	7.7	0.5	4.5	7.9	0.9	3.67	6
2000	Pittsbrg	NL	37.7	31	16	2	21	36	3.82	2	2	7.4	0.5	5.0	8.6	0.9	4.72	7
2000	St Louis	NL	11.3	10	4	1	2	11	3.18	1	0	7.9	0.8	1.6	8.7	2.8	5.69	15
2001	St Louis	NL	17.7	18	12	3	9	15	6.11	1	1	9.2	1.5	4.6	7.6	0.8	4.62	-6
2001	San Fran	NL	15.7	15	6	1	4	10	3.45	1	1	8.6	0.6	2.3	5.7	1.3	1.71	1

One reason the Giants have so few prospects in this chapter is that they made a bunch of trades at last July's deadline, dealing their B prospects for guys like Christiansen. He's miscast as a spot lefty, with a history of effectiveness against right-handed batters. Balanced against that is his inability to stay healthy for consecutive weeks. The Giants signed him to a three-year deal after the season. Hey, don't look at us.

Robbie Crabtree   Throws R   Age 29

YEAR	TEAM	LGE	IP	H	ER	HR	BB	K	ERA	W	L	H/9	HR/9	BB/9	K/9	KW	PERA	STUFF
1999	Shrevprt	Tex	62.0	59	27	3	23	40	3.92	4	3	8.6	0.4	3.3	5.8	0.9	3.99	-9
1999	Fresno	PCL	36.3	34	15	2	12	27	3.72	2	2	8.4	0.5	3.0	6.7	1.1	6.16	-4
2000	Fresno	PCL	130.0	128	56	10	33	83	3.88	8	6	8.9	0.7	2.3	5.7	1.3	4.76	-5
2001	Fresno	PCL	113.3	119	63	13	43	62	5.00	6	7	9.5	1.0	3.4	4.9	0.7	4.75	-18

It would be interesting to research usage patterns in the minor leagues. Crabtree has thrown 127 2/3 and 114 2/3 innings in relief for Fresno the past two seasons, far more than any major-league reliever has thrown, making 63 appearances each season. We've stumped for him to get a job with the Giants for years, because he can pitch. He'll eventually land in the majors and surprise people.

Felix Diaz   Throws R   Age 20

YEAR	TEAM	LGE	IP	H	ER	HR	BB	K	ERA	W	L	H/9	HR/9	BB/9	K/9	KW	PERA	STUFF
2001	Hagerstn	SAL	51.0	56	35	9	23	29	6.18	2	4	9.9	1.6	4.1	5.1	0.6	6.73	-2

Rangy, hard-throwing prospect doomed to be compared to Pedro Martinez. Diaz missed about half the season with arm soreness before wowing people in the Arizona Fall League: 21 strikeouts and seven walks in 15 innings. Scouts love him; scouts love all pitchers before they undergo general anesthesia for the first time.

Shawn Estes   Throws L   Age 29

YEAR	TEAM	LGE	IP	H	ER	HR	BB	K	ERA	W	L	H/9	HR/9	BB/9	K/9	KW	PERA	STUFF
1999	San Fran	NL	208.7	204	108	20	94	143	4.66	11	12	8.8	0.9	4.1	6.2	0.8	5.17	7
2000	San Fran	NL	196.3	188	91	10	89	121	4.17	12	10	8.6	0.5	4.1	5.5	0.7	4.63	7
2001	San Fran	NL	151.7	150	75	10	69	88	4.45	9	8	8.9	0.6	4.1	5.2	0.6	4.76	3

His strikeout rate has deteriorated to the point that his ability to stay in a rotation will come into question. He simply hasn't been the same since his excellent 1997 season, managing 200 innings just once since then. He's never missed a year, just been battling nagging injuries on a constant basis. Shea Stadium will help him; a year off might help more.

Jesse Foppert — Throws R — Age 21

YEAR	TEAM	LGE	IP	H	ER	HR	BB	K	ERA	W	L	H/9	HR/9	BB/9	K/9	KW	PERA	STUFF
2001	Salem OR	Nwn	60.3	71	56	18	33	42	8.35	2	5	10.6	2.7	4.9	6.3	0.6	3.11	4

Sometimes a hometown selection ends up as more. The Giants took Foppert, a USF product, in the second round of last year's draft. He might have been overqualified for the Northwest League, with a four-pitch assortment and good command. They should push him to Double-A quickly and let him get used to better competition.

Aaron Fultz — Throws L — Age 28

YEAR	TEAM	LGE	IP	H	ER	HR	BB	K	ERA	W	L	H/9	HR/9	BB/9	K/9	KW	PERA	STUFF
1999	Fresno	PCL	135.7	155	114	38	60	101	7.56	4	11	10.3	2.5	4.0	6.7	0.8	5.83	-18
2000	San Fran	NL	70.7	67	33	7	23	55	4.20	4	4	8.5	0.9	2.9	7.0	1.2	4.88	2
2001	San Fran	NL	69.3	67	32	8	19	54	4.15	4	4	8.7	1.0	2.5	7.0	1.4	5.47	1

Unlike many pitchers who are shoehorned into the job, Fultz is a situational lefty who actually is suited for the role. He's not real effective against right-handed batters, is effective pitching back-to-back days, and tires pretty quickly.

Mark Gardner — Throws R — Age 40

YEAR	TEAM	LGE	IP	H	ER	HR	BB	K	ERA	W	L	H/9	HR/9	BB/9	K/9	KW	PERA	STUFF
1999	San Fran	NL	137.3	153	91	26	48	77	5.96	5	10	10.0	1.7	3.1	5.0	0.8	6.43	-7
2000	San Fran	NL	151.3	157	70	15	35	82	4.16	9	8	9.3	0.9	2.1	4.9	1.2	4.30	4
2001	San Fran	NL	85.3	97	57	15	30	43	6.01	3	6	10.2	1.6	3.2	4.5	0.7	6.03	-12

After a surprisingly good 2000, in which he improved his command and had some good luck, Gardner reverted to form last season. He's not a bad last man on the staff for a team like the Giants, who have pitchers prone to the occasional disaster start and to DL trips. His career could well be over.

Wayne Gomes — Throws R — Age 29

YEAR	TEAM	LGE	IP	H	ER	HR	BB	K	ERA	W	L	H/9	HR/9	BB/9	K/9	KW	PERA	STUFF
1999	Philadel	NL	75.0	71	40	5	47	52	4.80	4	4	8.5	0.6	5.6	6.2	0.6	4.18	-9
2000	Philadel	NL	74.3	74	35	5	29	44	4.24	4	4	9.0	0.6	3.5	5.3	0.8	4.48	-7
2001	Philadel	NL	47.3	47	23	3	20	28	4.37	3	2	8.9	0.6	3.8	5.3	0.7	4.27	-8
2001	San Fran	NL	16.3	16	9	3	6	14	4.96	1	1	8.8	1.7	3.3	7.7	1.2	9.06	-5

Did the Phillies trade damaged goods? Gomes was sent to the Giants for utility man Felipe Crespo, having been scored upon in three of his last four outings. He got knocked around with the Giants, then went on the DL with patellar tendinitis (the injury that ended Mark McGwire's career). No complaints were filed, but that's awfully coincidental. Gomes was non-tendered and is a free agent.

Brad Hennessey — Throws R — Age 22

YEAR	TEAM	LGE	IP	H	ER	HR	BB	K	ERA	W	L	H/9	HR/9	BB/9	K/9	KW	PERA	STUFF
2001	Salem OR	Nwn	32.7	36	19	3	16	11	5.23	2	2	9.9	0.8	4.4	3.0	0.3	3.21	-13

Generally, a college pitcher selected in the first round has no business going to the Northwest League. The Giants sent two guys who fit that description to the lowest rung on their ladder. Hennessey, drafted at #21 out of Youngstown State, wasn't as impressive as Foppert was. He'll open 2002 in San Jose, trying to add something to his fastball/slider combination.

We've covered three guys who played for Salem-Keizer last year. That's a lot of Northwest League players for any chapter, and indicative of how little talent the Giants have at the upper levels of their system.

Livan Hernandez — Throws R — Age 27

YEAR	TEAM	LGE	IP	H	ER	HR	BB	K	ERA	W	L	H/9	HR/9	BB/9	K/9	KW	PERA	STUFF
1999	Florida	NL	143.7	147	73	16	46	87	4.57	8	8	9.2	1.0	2.9	5.5	0.9	4.90	7
1999	San Fran	NL	65.3	64	29	6	18	42	3.99	4	3	8.8	0.8	2.5	5.8	1.2	4.36	13
2000	San Fran	NL	247.3	247	108	20	60	147	3.93	15	12	9.0	0.7	2.2	5.3	1.2	4.23	11
2001	San Fran	NL	225.7	237	116	21	76	111	4.63	12	13	9.5	0.8	3.0	4.4	0.7	6.12	-1

Hernandez's improved control helped him post perhaps his best season in 2000. It wasn't as good in 2001, and his strikeout rate declined even further, although he stayed in the rotation and threw his usual 200-odd innings. We've been predicting doom for so long it's almost cliché to do so again, but the signs of collapse are evident.

Ryan Jensen — Throws R — Age 26

YEAR	TEAM	LGE	IP	H	ER	HR	BB	K	ERA	W	L	H/9	HR/9	BB/9	K/9	KW	PERA	STUFF
1999	Fresno	PCL	160.3	158	86	18	70	114	4.83	8	10	8.9	1.0	3.9	6.4	0.8	5.00	11
2000	Fresno	PCL	143.7	152	90	22	62	88	5.64	6	10	9.5	1.4	3.9	5.5	0.7	6.56	-4
2001	Fresno	PCL	102.3	107	60	13	43	60	5.28	5	6	9.4	1.1	3.8	5.3	0.7	3.94	-5
2001	San Fran	NL	40.7	43	25	4	22	21	5.53	2	3	9.5	0.9	4.9	4.6	0.5	4.82	-10

Jensen, frighteningly familiar with the raisin capital of California, pitched well in seven starts for the Giants, mostly as an injury replacement. His numbers were dragged down by three relief outings. Relieving can be a hard adjustment for a starter, and Jensen hadn't relieved since 1998 and has done it just three times. There's no room at this inn, but if he can get to another organization, he can be a decent innings-muncher.

Robb Nen — Throws R — Age 32

YEAR	TEAM	LGE	IP	H	ER	HR	BB	K	ERA	W	L	H/9	HR/9	BB/9	K/9	KW	PERA	STUFF
1999	San Fran	NL	77.0	69	32	8	23	69	3.74	5	4	8.1	0.9	2.7	8.1	1.5	4.32	9
2000	San Fran	NL	64.0	46	17	4	16	82	2.39	5	2	6.5	0.6	2.3	11.5	2.6	2.02	38
2001	San Fran	NL	74.0	61	25	5	20	75	3.04	5	3	7.4	0.6	2.4	9.1	1.9	3.50	20

The Yankees get all the publicity for making games seven innings long, but the last two seasons, Felix Rodriguez and Robb Nen have been just as nasty a tandem as Mariano Rivera and the Riverettes. Nen occasionally is pushed too hard by Dusty Baker; it's a self-correcting mechanism, though. Baker goes to the well once too often, Nen coughs up an important homer, Baker backs off. Nen has passed Trevor Hoffman as the best closer in the league.

Russ Ortiz — Throws R — Age 28

YEAR	TEAM	LGE	IP	H	ER	HR	BB	K	ERA	W	L	H/9	HR/9	BB/9	K/9	KW	PERA	STUFF
1999	San Fran	NL	206.3	203	103	23	105	148	4.05	10	13	8.9	1.0	4.6	6.5	.7	4.49	7
2000	San Fran	NL	198.0	196	100	26	92	148	4.73	10	12	8.9	1.2	4.2	6.7	.8	4.55	7
2001	San Fran	NL	205.7	195	80	12	81	136	3.55	13	10	8.5	.5	3.5	6.0	.8	3.50	11

A big guy who just looks like a workhorse, Ortiz improved his control last season and made fewer mistakes, leading to his best season as a Giant. He didn't exceed 121 pitches all season, thanks to a better job of throwing strikes and the presence of some great relievers. Ortiz could shave a bit more off of his walk rate and move to the fringes of the Cy Young Award race.

Felix Rodriguez — Throws R — Age 29

YEAR	TEAM	LGE	IP	H	ER	HR	BB	K	ERA	W	L	H/9	HR/9	BB/9	K/9	KW	PERA	STUFF
1999	San Fran	NL	68.3	65	27	6	24	50	3.72	4	4	8.6	.8	3.2	6.6	1.0	3.56	1
2000	San Fran	NL	82.7	67	27	5	35	84	2.81	6	3	7.3	.5	3.8	9.1	1.2	2.94	17
2001	San Fran	NL	74.3	61	23	4	24	73	1.72	5	3	7.4	.5	2.9	8.8	1.5	2.78	19

Wow, does he ever throw hard. Watching him is fun, because you're genuinely surprised when a hitter makes contact, much less does something positive. He'll sustain this for another season before moving on to close somewhere and then blowing out his arm. People who insist baseball is boring, or that all the games look the same, clearly aren't paying attention. Isn't it at all fascinating that players can succeed with such completely disparate skill sets as Rodriguez and...

Kirk Rueter — Throws L — Age 31

YEAR	TEAM	LGE	IP	H	ER	HR	BB	K	ERA	W	L	H/9	HR/9	BB/9	K/9	KW	PERA	STUFF
1999	San Fran	NL	190.7	212	108	27	46	85	5.10	9	12	10.0	1.3	2.2	4.0	0.9	5.54	-4
2000	San Fran	NL	186.0	210	104	21	51	63	5.03	9	12	10.2	1.0	2.5	3.0	0.6	4.45	-7
2001	San Fran	NL	185.7	209	108	22	59	67	5.24	9	12	10.1	1.1	2.9	3.2	0.6	5.22	-9

...who couldn't break a champagne bottle on the hull of a ship. Rueter has maintained a rotation spot for five years without ever striking out more than 115 batters. Rueter is effective from the stretch, completely shutting down the running game (three steals in 12 attempts) and the batters (OPS 140 points lower with runners on base).

Jason Schmidt Throws R Age 29

YEAR	TEAM	LGE	IP	H	ER	HR	BB	K	ERA	W	L	H/9	HR/9	BB/9	K/9	KW	PERA	STUFF
1999	Pittsbrg	NL	216.7	219	107	22	71	133	4.44	12	12	9.1	0.9	2.9	5.5	0.9	4.21	8
2000	Pittsbrg	NL	67.0	65	34	5	34	45	4.57	3	4	8.7	0.7	4.6	6.0	0.7	5.54	4
2001	Pittsbrg	NL	81.3	79	39	9	25	62	4.32	5	4	8.7	1.0	2.8	6.9	1.2	4.90	15
2001	San Fran	NL	64.3	55	25	2	30	52	3.50	4	3	7.7	0.3	4.2	7.3	0.9	4.25	19

Early in 2002, two BP staffers were talking about the free-agent market, and one made the comment that the Darren Dreifort contract would be the last of its kind, an eight-figure deal for significant years to a pitcher of questionable achievement. That may be so, but the Jason Schmidt contract certainly fits the category. Did anyone have him pegged for a four-year, $32-million contract at the All-Star break? He was traded, had two good months in a great pitchers' park, and presto change-o, he's a rich man. As long as teams pay through the nose for pitchers based on a few months' of health and effectiveness, the market is always going to skew upward. Schmidt's ticking can be heard in wine country.

Jeff Urban Throws L Age 25

YEAR	TEAM	LGE	IP	H	ER	HR	BB	K	ERA	W	L	H/9	HR/9	BB/9	K/9	KW	PERA	STUFF
1999	San Jose	Cal	81.0	86	45	13	21	51	5.00	4	5	9.6	1.4	2.3	5.7	1.2	5.42	7
1999	Shrevprt	Tex	77.3	85	45	12	21	39	5.24	4	5	9.9	1.4	2.4	4.5	0.9	7.93	-3
2001	Shrevprt	Tex	159.0	184	104	29	42	71	5.89	7	11	10.4	1.6	2.4	4.0	0.8	6.49	-11

Two years ago, Urban was one of the Giants' top pitching prospects. He missed 2000 with a torn labrum but didn't have much velocity to lose, so he worked on command and location in 2001. The results were essentially no different than before the injury; he needs to sharpen his control to make the majors as part of the Tommy John class of pitcher. (The style, not the surgery.)

Jerome Williams Throws R Age 20

YEAR	TEAM	LGE	IP	H	ER	HR	BB	K	ERA	W	L	H/9	HR/9	BB/9	K/9	KW	PERA	STUFF
1999	Salem OR	Nwn	36.0	36	16	2	12	18	4.00	2	2	9.0	0.5	3.0	4.5	0.8	3.48	12
2000	San Jose	Cal	117.3	121	64	12	48	68	4.91	6	7	9.3	0.9	3.7	5.2	0.7	4.56	13
2001	Shrevprt	Tex	123.7	142	83	23	40	57	6.04	5	9	10.3	1.7	2.9	4.1	0.7	5.62	2

Somewhere, a scout drools. Williams is the top prospect in the organization, even better than Olympian Kurt Ainsworth. He already throws four pitches, including a low-90s fastball and a slider that improved considerably last year. For various reasons, including the death of his mother early in 2001, Williams hasn't been worked hard at a young age. Just 20, he'll open the year at Triple-A in a very unfriendly environment; if he struggles, it's not necessarily a bad thing, nor unexpected. The Mets' Benny Agbayani is "Hawaiian Punch"; can Williams, from Honolulu, be "Hawaiian Punchout"?

Tim Worrell Throws R Age 34

YEAR	TEAM	LGE	IP	H	ER	HR	BB	K	ERA	W	L	H/9	HR/9	BB/9	K/9	KW	PERA	STUFF
1999	Oakland	AL	72.3	64	30	5	28	61	3.73	5	3	8.0	0.6	3.5	7.6	1.1	4.30	7
2000	Baltimor	AL	8.0	10	8	3	4	5	9.00	0	1	11.3	3.4	4.5	5.6	0.6	6.46	-30
2000	ChiCubs	NL	63.0	61	29	6	20	46	4.14	4	3	8.7	0.9	2.9	6.6	1.1	2.66	2
2001	San Fran	NL	75.0	70	32	4	30	51	3.84	5	3	8.4	0.5	3.6	6.1	0.9	4.09	-1

Worrell is a quality setup man who, because of the Giants' depth in the bullpen, gets used in middle relief. As good as Worrell was last year, trading Bill Mueller for him without having a real backup in place was a poor decision. Worrell is in a park that minimizes his problems with the long ball, and he should provide 70 good innings this year.

Chad Zerbe Throws L Age 30

YEAR	TEAM	LGE	IP	H	ER	HR	BB	K	ERA	W	L	H/9	HR/9	BB/9	K/9	KW	PERA	STUFF
1999	Bakrsfld	Cal	125.3	137	65	9	44	40	4.67	7	7	9.8	0.6	3.2	2.9	0.5	6.26	-16
1999	Shrevprt	Tex	38.3	44	22	3	13	10	5.17	2	2	10.3	0.7	3.1	2.3	0.4	3.79	-15
2000	Shrevprt	Tex	39.0	39	16	2	10	20	3.69	2	2	9.0	0.5	2.3	4.6	1.0	3.40	-1
2000	Fresno	PCL	84.0	91	40	7	18	29	4.29	5	4	9.8	0.8	1.9	3.1	0.8	5.14	-10
2001	Fresno	PCL	25.3	27	15	2	11	11	5.33	1	2	9.6	0.7	3.9	3.9	0.5	4.99	-25
2001	San Fran	NL	37.7	39	17	3	9	18	4.06	2	2	9.3	0.7	2.2	4.3	1.0	5.23	-10

The signing of Jason Christiansen eliminates Zerbe's probable role in bullpen. He's been a starter in the past and would best fit a long-relief/spot-starter role. He doesn't throw hard at all, he just gets guys out by changing speeds and throwing strikes.

Understanding and Measuring Replacement Level

by Keith Woolner

> The best way to find something you have lost is to buy a replacement.
> — Ann Landers

When analyzing the performance of baseball players, it's important to consider the context in which they play. Statistics compiled in a high-offense era like the 1930s are worth less than they appear to be, because runs were abundant then. Similarly, runs are worth more when they are scarce, such as in the dead-ball era, or the high-strike, high-mound era of the 1960s. For years, baseball analysts have compensated for the varying contexts by comparing players to the league offensive level. *Total Baseball*'s Linear Weights and Bill James's Offensive Winning Percentage are two examples of metrics that use the league's average batting performance as their baseline.

However, in recent years, comparing a player's performance to the performance that could be obtained from a readily available bench player or a fringe major-leaguer has gained wider acceptance because this method better reflects the talent distribution in the major leagues. This benchmark, dubbed "replacement level," is an important concept because the usual methods of measuring player value against a league or positional average betray us in ascertaining the true contribution of a player.

Baseball is a zero-sum game in which one team wins at the expense of another. Winning a game occurs by scoring more runs than the opposition, and a team's success in producing wins is dependent upon its ability to produce more runs than its opponents.

At the highest level of competition, the major leagues, there are a finite number of teams and roster spots per team, thus capping the total number of jobs available at any one time. If there is a population of employable players substantially larger than the total number of jobs to fill, and if the skill levels of those players can be estimated by employers beforehand, then rational employers (teams) will be able to be selective in choosing which players to employ. In fact, the very worst players in the population will never get hired, because someone better can always be found to do the job.

From the team's perspective, there will be some threshold of performance below which they will never have to employ a player. If there are T teams, R roster spots per team, and N total jobs, where $N = T \times R$, then this threshold of performance will be approximately the level of the $N+1$th best player available, subject to other complicating factors that will be discussed later. No team will have to settle for a player much worse in performance than that, because they can always hire the best unemployed player to fill the gap. Every team is capable of having players who perform at this level.

If a player of a certain level of performance is readily available to all teams with little expenditure of resources, no competitive advantage is conferred on a team that plays him. Instead, that level of performance constitutes the minimum level necessary to appear on a major-league team. If value in baseball is driven by maximizing wins (or almost equivalently, maximizing the likelihood of reaching the postseason and then winning the World Series), then this freely available resource is the zero point in value. Teams win more often than others only if they field better talent than that which is freely available. We'll refer to this level of performance that is available to all teams as the "replacement level," since any team could, if it suddenly had a gap to fill on its roster, acquire a player of this value to replace the loss.

Furthermore, the performance of every other player will be equal to or better than that of the Nth player; thus the average level of performance across all employed players will be greater than the replacement level.

Any competitive advantage a team has must translate to better on-field performance. A commodity that is easily available to all teams at minimal cost confers no competitive advantage and therefore is of minimal value. Baseball value comes from scarcity. Since average players, by definition, perform at a level at which there is more than a trivial number of players both better and worse than them, they cannot represent the freely available talent level, assuming rational decision makers.

The Problems With Average-Based Metrics

Measures that use average production as a reference point, such as *Total Baseball*'s Total Player Rating (TPR), incorrectly estimate the contribution of average players by improperly crediting the value of playing time at an average level of production. Let's look at an example that illustrates where an average-value analysis fails. Compare two players on otherwise identical teams, as shown in Table 1.

(Throughout this analysis, we'll be using Equivalent Average [EqA] as the metric for offensive performance, because it aggregates all major aspects of the offense into a single measure. Using a single number to represent performance simplifies the explanation. However, the principles discussed here can easily be extended to any valuation system the reader may desire.)

Table 1. Historical Talent Distribution

Name	PA	EqA
Joe Average	600	.260
Flash Fragile	100	.320

Joe Average is a steady but unspectacular performer, producing at exactly the league average. Flash Fragile hits like an MVP when he's in the lineup but is rarely healthy enough to play.

Assume that 600 plate appearances are needed from each position to complete a season. Joe can play the entire season for his team. Flash, on the other hand, accounts for just 16.7% of the plate appearances needed from his position. How will his team fill the rest of that playing time?

Suppose Flash's team did not know about his durability problems at the start of the season. If they expected him to play all or most of the season, they would not have expended considerable resources on acquiring another player at the same position. Flash's team may be forced to play a utility bench player, find some journeyman, or perhaps call up a player from Triple-A to fill the gap. That's the best the team can do without sacrificing more resources (including future value in the form of prospects) to fill Flash's lost playing time.

Suppose that the team has Bill Backup on the bench and makes him the starter when Flash gets hurt. Bill is likely a fringe player drawing a modest salary. If he were a significantly better player, he would likely have a starting job somewhere else.

Based on Bill's history, and assuming he is a typical backup player, we may expect a .230 EqA from him while filling in for Flash. The two teams then get the production shown in Table 2 from the positions Joe, Flash, and Bill play.

Table 2.

Name	PA	EqA
Joe Average	600	.260
Flash Fragile	100	.320
Bill Backup	500	.230
Total	600	.245

Joe's team is in better shape because they get a .260 EqA out of his spot in the lineup, whereas Flash and Bill's team manages just a .245 EqA because of Flash's inability to stay in the lineup, coupled with Bill's overall offensive weakness.

Over the course of the season, Joe's performance exceeds the combined contributions of Flash and Bill. We've established above that Bill's contribution is zero, as he is providing just replacement-level value. Thus, Joe's value must exceed Flash's. Yet compared to league average, Flash will be measured as the more valuable player. Thus, comparison to average does not completely capture what we think of as value.

Now, it's not strictly true that all bench players are helpless with the bat, nor do they all make the minimum salary. Players have roles beyond being the "vice-shortstop," whose job it is to inquire daily as to the health of the starting shortstop. Players will also be called upon to pinch-hit or pinch-run, to participate in double switches, to take the field as late-inning defensive replacements, and to give the regular starters an occasional rest even when they are not injured. Teams invest more than the minimum resources in bench players because of their extra utility. Reality is more complex than the simplified example being presented here, where we are limiting the discussion to the role of replacing an unavailable starting player.

Replacement Level Theory

If the talent distribution in baseball is similar to the distribution of most other things and follows a bell curve, why aren't players that are approximately average in skill more prevalent than both those well above average and those well below average, as in Figure 1?

The actual performance of players throughout baseball history does not match a bell-curve shape. There have been far more mediocre or outright bad players than outstanding hitters as shown in Table 3.

It still appears as if there's a bell-like curve, albeit a skewed one, because the middle two groups are higher than the tails.

The talent distribution in baseball is such that there are very few superstar-level players, a somewhat larger number of average ones, and a practically unlimited number of scrubs. This is usually represented as the tail end of a bell curve or normal distribution (see Figure 2), with the vast

Figure 1. Distribution of baseball talent (if normally distributed around major league average EqA)

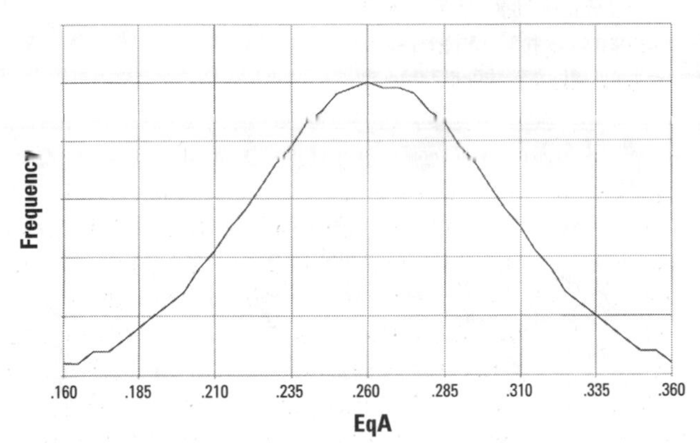

Table 3. Historical talent distribution

Player EqA in a season, 1901–2000	Percentage of players (min: 10 AB)	Expected from normal distribution
< .200	27.8%	6.5%
.200–.260	38.6%	43.5%
.260–320	30.3 %	43.5%
.320+	3.3%	6.5%

Figure 2. Distribution of baseball talent (tail end of normal distribution)

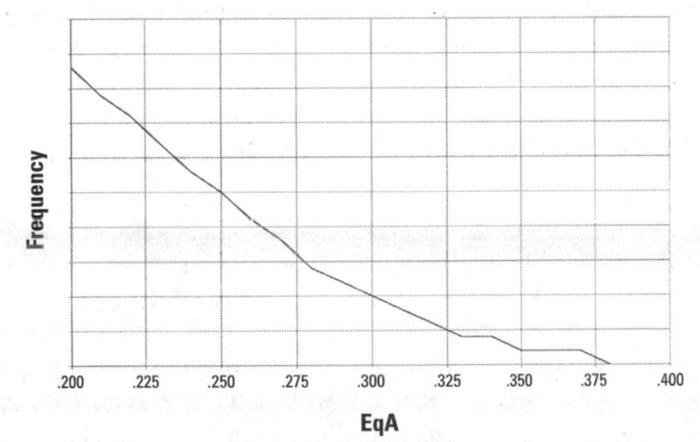

majority of the overall population already weeded out prior to reaching MLB.

Playing time is weighted heavily towards the players at the right side of the tail, so the apparent league average ends up being higher than the median would be.

We wrote a computer simulation to explore how several factors interact in altering replacement level. The model generates a pool of potential players in which each player has a randomly determined talent level. Each team in the league selects the best available player to fill a roster slot in turn until all the slots on the team are filled. Within the simulation, we can specify how many players are in the talent pool, what their mean talent level is, the distribution of talent (the standard deviation in ability), the number of teams in the league, and the number of players each team selects.

For the purposes of the simulation, we used EqA as the player talent metric, rating all players on that scale. The major-league average EqA is .260, and the scale is calibrated to resemble the familiar range of batting average. However, the specific measure and the units in which it's expressed are not important to the results of the simulation; any measure of performance would be suitable.

We used a league of 30 teams, each selecting one player at each position from a pool of 10,000 potential players (the talent pool here would assume the majors, minors, college ball, and top high-school players). The mean ability of the pool is a .100 EqA, with a standard deviation of 60 points of EqA (i.e., two-thirds of players will fall between a .040 EqA and a .160 EqA). This scenario may not exactly represent the way the major leagues operate, but it shares enough characteristics to make the demonstration of certain relevant points worthwhile.

To determine replacement level, the simulation looks at the best remaining players once the teams have drafted, selecting one player per team as the marginal player pool. The median talent level of the marginal player pool is considered to be replacement level. For each run of the simulation, it reports the average starting player level and the average replacement level.

In the first simulation, we assumed perfect information: every team knows exactly how each player will perform, and they select the best player available with every pick. Table 4 shows the results of one such run of the simulation.

Table 4.

Simulation Rules:

Population = 10000
Talent: mean = .100, std dev = .060
30 teams selecting one player each

Results:

Best starting player:	.324 EqA
Worst starting player:	.266 EqA
Median starting player:	.284 EqA
Median replacement player:	.258 EqA

One important distinction to draw when assessing replacement level is the role that information (or lack of it) plays. Uncertainty, as discussed here, means that a player's true level of ability cannot be determined precisely. Our best guess could be higher or lower than the player's true level of ability. The less information we have, the greater the uncertainty, and the wider the potential range of error.

Information in baseball comes primarily from 1) scouting reports, 2) the assessment of managers and coaches (for players within an MLB organization), and 3) the statistical record of a player's performance. The quality of these assessments will determine how accurately management can determine player ability. The quality of information available throughout the league has an impact on the decision process that affects what the expected replacement-level performance will be.

We can alter the quality of information available by introducing some uncertainty, or error, into what a player's perceived value is. For example, a player with an actual EqA of .250 may be "perceived" by the teams at the time of the draft as having an EqA of .260, and he may be selected ahead of a player with a true EqA of .255, who may be perceived as a .245 EqA player. The effect of introducing uncertainty or less-than-perfect information is something we can examine.

In the next run of the simulation, each player's ability is only known to within plus or minus 25 points of EqA, with any value within that range equally likely (uniform distribution). There is no bias towards overrating or underrating each player—either is equally likely. Each team can still see roughly how good a player is, but instead of seeing player ability with the sharp focus of complete accuracy, the view is "blurred" to some degree (see Table 5).

Table 5.

Simulation Rules:

Population = 10000
Uncertainty = +/− .025 EqA
Ability: mean = .100, std dev = .060
30 teams selecting one player each

Results:

	Expected EqA (observed at draft time)	Actual EqA
Best starting player:	.354	.330
Worst starting player:	.265	.246
Median starting player:	.280	.265
Median replacement player:	.259	.250

Notice the gap between the performance that was expected when the players were drafted and the subsequent actual performance.

Increasing the uncertainty level results in even more dramatic disconnects between the expected and actual performance levels. In the next simulation run shown in Table 6, the level of uncertainty is increased to plus or minus .075 EqA.

Imperfect information causes a bias toward picking players who are playing "over their heads" or who otherwise appear to be better than they are, even if the cause of the uncertainty itself does not tend to skew high or low. We have no reason to expect that any given player's rating is biased higher or lower than his true level of play, but because teams select the highest observed talent level, the percentage of players selected is skewed towards those who will be "overrated." Increasing the unreliability further increases the gap between the expected performance and the actual performance. Thus, the "expected" performance of the player with the highest available expected EqA is almost certainly higher than what the team will get in general as replacement level!

Table 6.

Simulation Rules:

Population = 10000
Uncertainty = +/− .075 EqA
Ability: mean = .100, std dev = .060
30 teams selecting one player each

Results:

	Expected EqA (observed at draft time)	Actual EqA
Best starting player:	.388	.324
Worst starting player:	.302	.234
Median starting player:	.327	.270
Median replacement player:	.291	.240

We have not yet explicitly dealt with the economic aspects of replacement level, yet these aspects are essential to the concept. When we discuss the acquisition of a replacement-level player, we expect the organization to expend a minimum of resources to acquire him. When we say "resources," we usually think of the financial costs, but any limited resource the organization expends to acquire a player figures into the overall cost of the acquisition. Money, in the form of the player's salary and/or purchase price, is the most obvious example. The attention a GM, field manager, or other staff has to invest in identifying the replacement player has an opportunity cost, if there are other matters of higher importance at hand. The time it may take a replacement to arrive, if one is not immediately available, may mean the team plays a game or two with a 24-man roster. If the desired player is on another team, and the GM needs to call in a favor, that could use up a tiny bit of leverage that would have served the team better at some other time.

In most cases, the primary costs will be player salary and acquisition/transaction costs, if the player is not on the major-league roster or is in another organization.

The replacement pool for an N-team league does not begin with the N+1th best player. At any moment, a certain percentage of starting players will be injured. If the position is particularly physically demanding, such as catcher or second base, there may be more injuries at any given time than there would be at a less stressful position. Because we are concerned with what's available to a team that has a player injured at the moment, we need to consider that not all potential replacements will be available. This assumes we're not looking at the first player ever to be injured (whose team would thus have first choice of all replacements). A further implication is that improvements in medical procedures or new treatments for injuries (such as Tommy John surgery) can influence replacement level.

So far, we have implicitly assumed that the team that loses a player will directly replace all of his playing time with the acquired replacement, an overly simplistic assumption. Since there are more roster spots than positions, teams have the opportunity to acquire replacements prior to actually needing them. Thus when a starting player is lost, his playing time doesn't typically go to the player signed or called up to fill the roster spot, but to a bench player already on the roster. The replacement player gets some smaller portion of playing time, such as when the bench player (now starting) is rested. The replacement player need not even play the same position as the injured player—the team could opt to call up another relief pitcher or a player who can help elsewhere on the field.

We've identified several key aspects of replacement level:

- Replacement level is an *expected* level of performance at the time a decision is made.
- Replacement level can be *positionally dependent.*
- Replacement level requires a *minimal allocation of resources.*
- Replacement level is a function of the *number of starting jobs.*
- Replacement level is a function of the *size of the talent pool.*
- Replacement level is only applicable at the *far right tail of the talent bell curve.*
- Replacement level is a function of *injury rate.*
- Replacement level is dependent on the *availability and accuracy of player information.*

Using these concepts, we can define replacement level as follows:

Replacement level is the expected level of performance a major-league team will receive from one or more of the best available players who substitute for a suddenly unavailable starting player at the same position, and who can be obtained with minimal expenditure of team resources.

Replacement Level in Practice

In acknowledging the complicating effect that uncertain information has on the assessment of replacement value, and to capture the actual quality of decision making that occurs in major-league baseball, we propose using the actual performance of major-league players who were not the primary starter for their teams to establish the replacement level.

Why, if replacement-level talent is freely available, do we see players performing below it? There are several possibilities:

- **Improper evaluation/bad information.** As we've seen, poor information can lead to inaccurate assessments of a player's true value.
- **Suboptimal decision making.** The team may continue to play a highly compensated player, even if his performance drops to unacceptable levels. To do so ignores the principle of sunk costs, but it can, and does, happen.
- **Strategic reasons other than short-term win maximization.** Playing a promising prospect in the majors, even if he's overmatched for a while, may be a good player-development strategy. If the team is not in contention, the long-term benefits of developing the player may outweigh the short-term, sub-replacement-level performance.
- **Injury.** A player normally able to perform above replacement level may play poorly while hurt or while recovering.
- **Alternate beliefs about replacement level.** Management may believe that the best available replacements are significantly worse than they actually are, leading to the overrating of low-level talent already on hand.
- **Defensive performance**. Throughout much of this discussion, we are concerning ourselves only with offense. A player's total value includes defensive play (and, if you are inclined, intangibles). An exceptional defender may be a below-replacement-level hitter and still have a positive impact on the team's chances. Ozzie Smith in his early years is a good example of a seemingly below-replacement-level player whose glove added enough value to warrant him keeping his job.
- **Sample size/statistical noise.** A sabermetrician's favorite "excuse." Given a handful of plate appearances, a variance in observed performance around a true level of ability is enormous.

As we've seen, population size and information quality can affect replacement level. There's reason to believe that different eras in baseball history have had significant differences in these key areas. Therefore, it is possible that replacement level would need to be determined separately for each identifiable epoch of baseball history.

Perhaps the most obvious changes have been in the available population pool, which has been positively impacted by the increase in the U.S. population in the past 125 years, integration in the 1947-1960 period, international development efforts (especially in Latin America), and the arrival of Asian league players. Improvements in training, nutrition, and surgery have extended the useful life of many players. The increasing attractiveness of the financial rewards of a baseball career relative to other options, including other major sports, may draw more potential players into the development pool.

Informational improvements include more investment in scouting, standardization of player evaluation, technological tools such as radar guns, creation of player databases, enhanced medical and biomechanical assessments, and the like.

Offensive skill is only part of the equation. A player is also selected for his defensive skills, and, in particular, a certain level of aptitude is necessary for a player to be considered for the harder defensive positions (e.g. catcher, shortstop, center field, and second base). The necessity of requiring a minimum threshold of defensive ability while maximizing the offensive contribution has interesting effects.

In addition, playing a difficult position, such as catcher, over many years can have debilitating effects, such as knee damage that robs a player of his speed and damages his offensive skills. Because such effects are common to all players who play that position, the effect would be to drive down the overall offensive level, and thus the replacement level, of that position.

Again, we turn to the simulated approach. We continued to generate EqA for each of 10,000 players with an average of .100 and a deviation of .060. In addition, we generated a randomly determined defensive ability, on a scale of 1 to 10, normally distributed around a mean of 5 with a deviation of 2. We then set a minimum defensive criterion (e.g., a player has to have a defensive rating of 6 to qualify) and looked at what the resulting starting and replacement averages are (shown in Table 7). Note that we're using the same simulated block of players in each case.

The largest impact of defensive qualifications on average starter or replacement performance occurs when the minimum threshold is at or above the average defensive level. At lower levels, there are relatively few players who fail to meet the qualifications, and thus the talent pool remains close to the overall size. As you eliminate a larger percentage for failing to make the minimum defensive threshold, the talent pool shrinks, driving down the average level of offensive performance you can expect from the position.

We will investigate several possibilities for replacement-level metrics, ideally seeking one that is relatively consistent across baseball history. In order to do so, we need to separate the players in any given season into starters and replacements so that their composite performance can be analyzed.

For the purposes of this study, we have used Sean Lahman's baseball database (available for free download at *http://www.baseball1.com*). For every player, we identified his primary position as the position listed first in the Lahman data. For each team season, we identified the starter as the player with the most plate appearances among all players on the team with that primary position. The Lahman data does not separate the three positions for outfielders, so we simply took the three outfielders with the most plate appearances as the starters. Designated hitters were used in American League seasons from 1973 onward. All years from 1893 through 1998—the latest year for which the Lahman data has positional information—were used.

Replacements are simply defined as all players in a season who are not starters. We took the position at which the player most often appeared (according to the Lahman database) and used that as his primary position. Players were grouped by primary position to obtain and measure the replacement pool for that position.

In Figures 3–6, the data points represent a 10-year moving average of starter, replacement, and league offense. We used 10-year averages because the single-year data points varied widely from season to season, making the discernment of overall trends difficult through the statistical noise.

As seen in Figure 3, in the past 25 years the gap between the best and worst offensive positions seems to be narrowing. The performance of backup shortstops is rising closer to league average, while backup first basemen and outfielders have declined (though less dramatically). Backup first basemen start the century with no more offensive prowess than players at most other positions; it is the backup outfielders who are the strongest offensively. Replacement second basemen peak offensively in the teens, then drop dramatically as the game becomes more high scoring. Integration doesn't seem to have affected backups consistently. The 1950s and 1960s see sharp rises from backup shortstops and first basemen, but flat performance or slight declines in the outfield and at third base. The backup shortstops of the late 1970s and early 1980s were, collectively, the worst performers of

Table 7.

Fielding threshold	Average EqA of starters	Average EqA of replacements
1	.284	.259
2	.283	.258
3	.283	.258
4	.283	.257
5	.278	.253
6	.260	.237
7	.250	.228
8	.228	.204
9	.195	.159
10	.145	.100

Figure 3. Backup performance as a percentage of league average

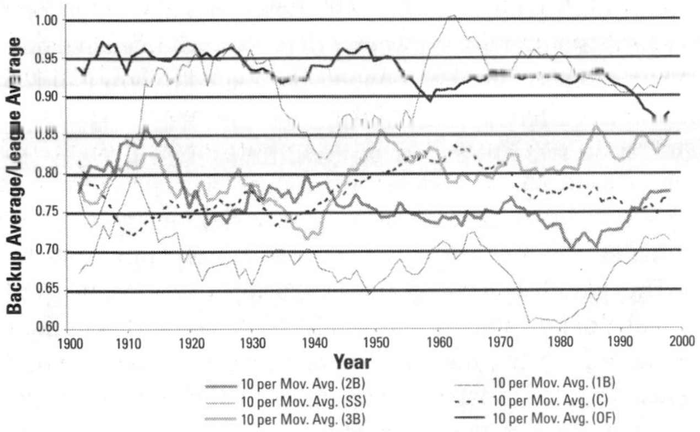

Figure 5. Difference between starters and backups as a percentage of league average

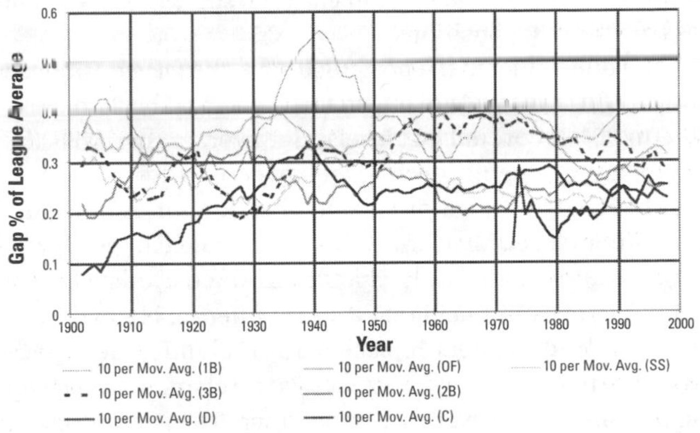

Figure 4. Difference in performance between starters and backups by position

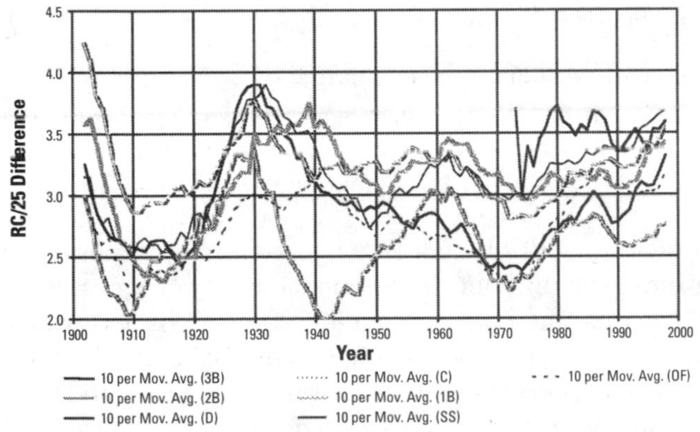

Figure 6. Backup performance as a percentage of positional average

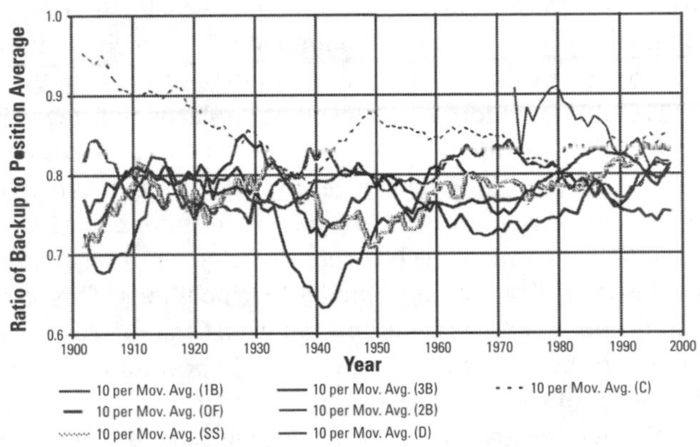

the entire century, relative to league average. Perhaps part of why the great shortstops of today seem so outstanding is that we're coming off of a couple of decades in which finding a decent stick off the bench at shortstop was nearly impossible.

In Figure 4, we compare starters and backups directly. There seems to be some correlation with offensive level, given the peak around 1930 and the rise since 1970. Overall, we are still looking at a variance of 2.00 runs created per 25 outs (RC/25) depending on position and era.

In Figure 5, the difference between the RC/25 for starters and the RC/25 for replacements is compared to the league average for each position. The most notable features are the spike at first base around 1940 (indicating a large gap between starting and replacement first basemen) and the small gap between catchers at the turn of the century. There is a fair amount of fluctuation here, although narrower than we've seen in previous examples.

The range in Figure 6 is even narrower compared to the other charts; since 1960, every established position posts ten-year averages within 80%, plus or minus 8%, a gap that narrows slightly more over the past couple of decades.

Two major deviations from this range exist in the pre-1960 era. Catcher backups start the century nearly equal to regular catchers on offense, with a long gradual decline before rebounding and stabilizing starting around 1940. The other exception is backup first basemen, who experience a large decline in the '30s and '40s relative to starting first basemen and who, even in the 1900s, 1950s, and 1990s, had substantially lower EqA than replacements at other positions relative to the standards of the position. Across all of the years tracked, backup first basemen were slightly lower than positional average, and backup catchers slightly higher than was true for most positions.

The one outlier in the post-1960 era is the DH, introduced in 1973, which for most of the first ten years had backup levels close to 90% of overall DH levels. However, in the 1980s the backup level generally declined relative to starters.

This chart shows a promising direction for establishing replacement level. Measuring it as a percentage of positional average captures not only changes in offensive levels, but also differences in positional average offense. Higher levels of offense lead to larger replacement-level differences, thus backup catchers are closer to average catchers than backup first basemen are to average first basemen. The gaps are larger (in absolute terms) in the 1990s than they were in the 1960s.

As a sanity check, it's worthwhile to compare these conclusions to some prior work on replacement level. Bill James's concept of a replacement level 1.00 RC/25 below average coincides with our results as well, since a league with a 5.00 RC/25 would have replacement level set at 4.00 RC/25. My prior work on Value Over Replacement Level (VORP) used a replacement-level delta of 70 points of OPS, which is in the same range.

This information indicates that replacement level is positionally dependent. A good estimate is that replacement level is 80% of positional average, with 85% for catchers and 75% for first basemen. This can mean a difference of half a run in RC/25 between first basemen and catchers, or a quarter of a run when compared to most other positions. This may only amount to a handful of runs per year. Over the course of a career, the positional differences could add up to several wins worth of value.

The designated hitter is a special case to consider, because he has no defensive responsibilities or other duties that detract from his primary offensive role. Yet in many years, first basemen or corner outfielders may outhit designated hitters as a group. Replacement-level theory would dictate that DHs would have a replacement level at least as high as any other position, because any replacement-level first baseman could DH as well.

However, in practice there are ways the DH slot is used other than to play the very best available offensive player. The DH slot is often used as a way to ease injured players back into the lineup, or as a partial day off for regulars, giving them a break from the rigors of fielding while keeping their bats in the lineup. These players may not provide optimal production in the games at DH, but the long-term value of the tactic outweighs the short-term cost.

Also, in the historical data, there appears to be a period of adjustment as managers learned how to best utilize the new lineup flexibility the DH allowed. It took several seasons for roster decisions and player-development plans to fully exploit the offensive potential of the DH position.

One of the assumptions underlying replacement level is that there is a tradeoff between offensive and defensive performance. If a skill were completely unrelated to how a player is selected for his job, then we'd expect a more or less random distribution of that skill. This is important in the case of pitchers, whose defensive responsibilities so overwhelm any offensive contribution that it's unclear if offensive production has any bearing on a pitcher's chances of retaining a job.

This can best be seen by comparing the offensive performance of "regular" pitchers and "replacement" pitchers. For example, using the 2001 data, and taking the group of pitchers with the most plate appearances such that they total 80% of all pitcher PAs, regular pitchers hit .143/.164/.176, while backups hit .144/.178/.185. If anything, the pitchers who come to the plate most often are worse hitters than the rest of the pool.

A quick and dirty formula for estimating how many points of AVG, OBP, and SLG to subtract from positional average to get backup average is:

$$\text{RepLvl Points} = (R)^{1/3} \times P,$$

where R = RC/25 for the position

and P = .019 for positions having a 80% replacement level
.014 for positions having a 85% replacement level
.025 for positions having a 75% replacement level

For an outfielder (an 80% replacement-level position), take the cube root of the positional average (expressed as RC/25), and multiply by 19 points. Thus a position with a 6.00 RC/25 would have a replacement level that lies about 34.5 points below the positional average AVG, OBP, and SLG.

Next, we turn our attention to determining replacement levels for pitching. There are, broadly speaking, two different "positions" for pitchers—starters and relievers. Though they seem to perform the same function, the specific requirements for starters and relievers are slightly different. Starting pitchers must have the endurance to pitch six or more innings on regular rest, while relief pitchers do not need the same stamina but must be conditioned to return on shorter, longer, or otherwise sporadic rest.

This parallels the situation with position players, who need two sets of skills—offensive and defensive—to effectively hold a job. With pitching, both effectiveness and endurance are needed to hold a starting job, whereas the lower requirements for endurance among relief pitchers should mean that the effectiveness of relievers is higher as a group. In terms of having their effectiveness measured, starting pitchers also have the disadvantage of often being called upon to pitch until they tire, a state that is usually characterized by the pitcher allowing batters to reach base or score (i.e. a drop in effectiveness). Relievers may not be called upon to test the limits of their stamina in quite the same way, and thus their performances do not include their tiring phase as often as do the performances of starting pitchers.

To determine the replacement-level breakpoint for starting pitchers, we'll initially stick with the modern period that is most familiar to us. The five-man rotation has been established for some time, so we'll treat each spot in the rotation as a "position" comparable to how we treated position players in the previous section.

Removing the five pitchers on each team who accumulated the most starts in each season, and totaling the performance of the rest of the starters (ignoring any relief appearances) yields the following results in Table 8.

The top five pitchers with the most starts on each team account for between 78% and 84% of all starts in most years (they exceeded 85% in the strike years of 1981 and 1994). This means that a typical team dips into the replacement pool for about 30 starts a year—nearly the equivalent of a full-time starter. Regressing the observed replacement-level RA against the RA for the entire season yields the following approximation:

$$\text{Replacement Level RA} = 1.37 \times \text{League RA} - 0.66$$

Table 8. Starting Pitchers

YEAR	GS	GS TOP5	RA	START RA	REPL RA
1978	4204	3565	4.16	4.03	5.00
1979	4196	3468	4.55	4.40	5.43
1980	4210	3507	4.42	4.27	5.32
1981	2788	2404	4.10	4.02	4.70
1982	4214	3528	4.50	4.35	5.37
1983	4218	3498	4.46	4.31	5.34
1984	4210	3553	4.43	4.24	5.72
1985	4206	3517	4.41	4.22	5.58
1986	4206	3480	4.53	4.38	5.35
1987	4210	3427	4.88	4.71	5.73
1988	4200	3511	4.22	4.08	5.13
1989	4212	3395	4.30	4.10	5.24
1990	4210	3419	4.40	4.24	5.20
1991	4208	3386	4.42	4.20	5.55
1992	4212	3408	4.24	4.04	5.25
1993	4538	3679	4.69	4.48	5.75
1994	3200	2728	4.99	4.76	6.62
1995	4034	3171	4.98	4.72	6.14
1996	4534	3658	5.19	4.93	6.51
1997	4532	3632	4.87	4.57	6.34
1998	4864	3990	4.95	4.76	5.99
1999	4856	3997	5.26	5.04	6.48
2000	4858	3831	5.28	5.06	6.26
2001	4858	3915	4.98	4.81	5.79

Next, we attempted to compare this metric against historical data using the baseball1.com database. For pitchers who only started, this is fairly easy. For pitchers who both started and relieved—as is typical for the replacement pitchers we're considering—this data set presents some challenges, as it does not distinguish between starting and relief performance. To estimate the splits from the pitchers' total line, we used the performance of pitchers from 1978–2000 who both started (at least five games) and relieved (at least 15 games). We found that the average starting performance was 3.33 times as long as the average relief performance (in innings), and the average RA was 20% higher in starting appearances than in relief appearances. We assumed that similar proportions hold true for prior years (an assumption that may or may not be validated once more game data from earlier eras becomes available) and estimated splits for each pitcher based on their appearances, games started, innings pitched, and ERA.

As it turns out, in every season since 1904, the top five starting pitchers per team reached 80% of team starts (comparable to the coverage five pitchers give in the 1978-2001 time frame). The distribution in starts across the five pitchers varies, with the top three pitchers on any given team getting a larger fraction of the 80% than the #4 and/or #5 pitchers. Consequently we've used a five-man depth of rotation for the entire data set, even in the early eras we think of as the eras of the four man or three-man rotations. For those desiring greater granularity in replacement-level depth by era, 1893-1904 would use four pitchers per team, 1884-1892 would use two pitchers per team, and teams in 1883 and earlier essentially used one pitcher for 80% of their starts (see Figure 7).

The formula returns slightly higher levels than our estimated replacement level. However, since the formula was derived from more precise data on starters, and since the results are still generally in the right region with our estimated

Figure 7. Replacement level ERA formula for starters

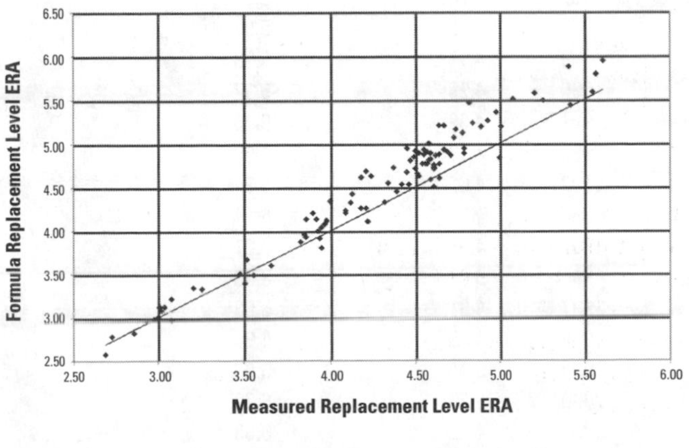

replacement levels for other eras, we'll continue to use it to estimate starting-pitcher replacement level in general. In other words, we're more confident in the formula for estimating replacement level than in the formulas used in the approximation of replacement level in the historical data set.

We could easily assume that replacement level for relievers is the same as for starters (and indeed, in my prior VORP work, we did exactly that). However, for reasons we outlined earlier, the combination and thresholds of skills required for relief pitching are different enough to warrant treating it as another position, so let's extend the analysis to relief pitchers as a separate group.

To determine replacement level for relief pitchers, we adopted the same threshold that we observed with starting pitchers—the 80% playing-time coverage for regulars. Removing the pitchers with the most relief innings until 80% of all the league relief innings have been accounted for, and computing the aggregate performance of relievers across the remaining 20% of relief innings yields Table 9.

Overall, replacement relief pitchers do a little better than replacement starting pitchers—about two tenths of a run—although there are some seasons (including 2000 and 2001) in which replacement starters have a bit of an edge. This is consistent with the endurance limitation on both the available pool of relief pitchers and the degradation of performance as a pitcher tires. The pool of potential relievers is greater because pitchers with lower endurance are not automatically eliminated (see Figure 8).

Table 9. Relief Pitchers

Year	League RA	Reliever Replacement RA
1978	4.14	4.61
1979	4.49	5.14
1980	4.29	5.28
1981	4.00	4.48
1982	4.30	4.63
1983	4.33	4.88
1984	4.28	4.62
1985	4.35	5.30
1986	4.43	5.34
1987	4.76	5.55
1988	4.15	5.01
1989	4.15	5.23
1990	4.29	5.37
1991	4.32	5.30
1992	4.13	4.69
1993	4.63	5.94
1994	4.96	6.24
1995	4.88	6.01
1996	5.07	6.33
1997	4.81	5.98
1998	4.83	5.94
1999	5.14	6.50
2000	5.20	6.73
2001	4.82	6.83

Figure 8. Replacement Reliever RA vs. League RA

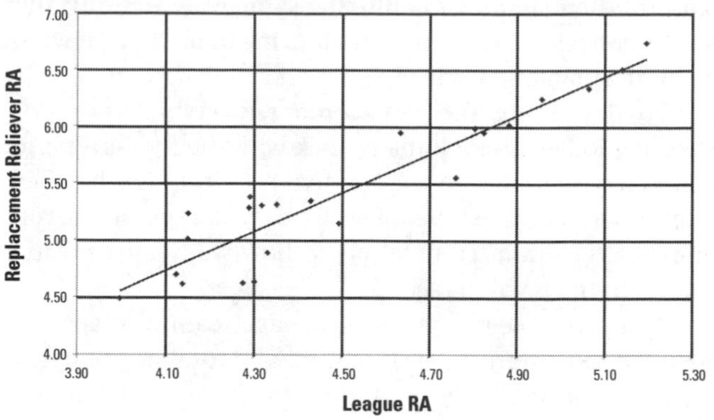

Regressing the RA of replacement relief pitchers against league RA yields the following formula (and an R^2 value of .0.878):

$$\text{RepLvlReliefRA} = 1.70 \times \text{LgRA} + 2.27$$

Replacement Level and Value Assessments

Replacement level sets the "zero" level of value much lower than average-level-based metrics do. The effects of this are:

- Players who are above replacement level but below average will be recognized as having made a positive contribution to their teams.
- For two players who are both league average, the one with more playing time will be credited as having more value.
- Players who are below average but above replacement level will not be penalized (by having greater negative value) for having more playing time.
- For two players above average and with comparable playing time, the relative value of one versus the other will not change significantly, although the absolute measurement of value will be changed (since value is measured above replacement rather than above average).
- Generally speaking, the positive value of playing time will be more correctly recognized using a replacement-level metric.
- Value measurements will more closely approximate the tradeoffs that team management faces in making roster decisions.

In comparison to VORP, my previous work on replacement level, the new system for determining replacement level has only a small effect on position players. The benchmark we had been using for replacement level, 70 points of OPS below positional average, was developed using the high-offense era of the 1990s, and thus our new formula matches it fairly well.

For lower-offense eras, replacement level will not be as far below average. For catchers, replacement level will be closer to the catcher average, making catchers such as Mike Piazza slightly less valuable than under the old system. For first basemen and DHs, replacement level is slightly lower than before, so Jason Giambi and his ilk will be rated slightly higher.

For pitchers, the largest changes will be for relievers, who will be held to a slightly higher standard than VORP had done previously (+1.00 above league RA, regardless of league offensive level). Starting pitchers will thus be rated as relatively more valuable, even beyond what the additional weight of their innings contributed.

Full VORP ratings, revised to include the new findings presented in this article, will be published on the *Baseball Prospectus* Web site.

Replacement level is an important concept in understanding the economics of the game and in particular why unremarkable talent has been overvalued.

To use a simple example, let's ignore the metrics of RC/25, VORP, and the like, and use an easy counting stat—home runs. Suppose a top home-run hitter, one who can club 50 homers a season, is worth $20 million a year in the open market in the year 2001. Without a concept of replacement level, a team's decision maker might assume that a 25-homer hitter is worth half that amount, or $10 million per year.

We now know from our replacement-level analysis that a replacement-level first baseman is capable of hitting around .240/.325/.445, roughly comparable to the unadjusted performances of Greg Vaughn, Ben Petrick, David Justice, or the Texas Rangers performances of Ken Caminiti and Andres Galarraga, who collectively hit about 18-20 home runs in a full season. We'll use 18 HR/season as replacement level, which by definition is minimal cost. (Even though these players were not minimal cost, they certainly didn't earn their salaries with these performances.) Using $500,000 as replacement-level cost (including a minimal player salary plus some overhead), the 50-homer player sets a price of about $600,000 per home run above replacement level. This means the 25-homer player is worth about $4.2 million; the original $10-million guess overestimated his value by 134%! It's easy to see from this kind of analysis that the middle of the market is where the greatest discrepancies between actual value and player salaries are occurring.

Though we've tried to be as comprehensive as possible within the space provided, there are still several topics that can be investigated which may impact our understanding of replacement level. These include:

- **Direct measurement of interpositional defensive difficulty and/or skill scarcity.** Using differences in positional offense levels is a proxy for estimating the defensive difficulty of the position, or the scarcity of the skill set required to play the position. A more direct method of comparing positions, perhaps through comparison of defensive performance of players who play multiple positions, or who switch positions in consecutive seasons, may help validate or refute the conclusions of current methods.
- **Effect of general athleticism on positional average at related positions.** There are sets of positions that require generally similar skills. The corner-outfield positions and the middle infield are two such possible sets. First base and DH may be similar in requiring the lowest levels of defensive skill. When looking at players capable of playing both positions within a set, there may be a tendency for the better overall athlete to play the harder position and, as such, cause the observer to underestimate or even reverse the difficulty differences between the two positions. Though we have discussed offensive and defensive skills as being completely separate, there is some overlap. Skills such as hand-eye coordination and arm strength are useful on both sides of the ball. This creates a small-scale positive correlation between offensive and defensive skills in the range where similar skill sets are required for different positions.
- **Separation of outfield replacement level.** Further refinement of positional data could allow us to verify that left fielders, center fielders, and right fielders all individually follow the 80% rule.
- **Further investigation into the replacement level of the designated hitter.** If it can be shown that healthy players actually suffer with the bat when playing DH rather than playing the field, then the DH positional average and replacement level should be adjusted accordingly.
- **Adjusting projections to account for the overachiever bias.** As we've seen, imperfect information, even if unbiased, creates a tendency to select players who appear to be better than they actually are. Since the selection process focuses on players from the extreme right side of the distribution of talent, at any given apparent skill level, there will be more overachievers represented than underachievers. It's unclear, at this point, how to reconcile this bias with current projection systems, which may or may not incorporate a regression to the overall population mean.
- **Additional study of replacement levels during the early eras of baseball.** As you go back further in time, the environment in which players were identified and developed resembles the modern game less and less. In particular, the size of the talent pool and the quality

of information were dramatically inferior a century ago. The impact of having multiple leagues of varying stability and an independent minor-league system also impacted the availability, and perhaps the willingness, of players to play for a self-declared "major league." The interaction of all these factors makes the replacement-level system presented here potentially less relevant for the early years of the game.

- **Minor-league replacement level.** There's a real question as to whether replacement level has any relevance at the minor-league level. Implicit in the analysis presented here is that the selecting team can sign any available player it wants. If that's true, then the minor-league team could sign a player of major-league replacement level. However, the minor leagues are primarily developmental leagues that weed out those incapable of contributing at the major-league level. This would mean that replacement level would be higher than minor-league average, which is counterintuitive. The existing model doesn't consider the possibility that the player may not wish to sign with the selecting team, which is certainly the case for a major-league replacement-level player pursued by, say, a high-A minor-league team. It might be possible to develop some way to exclude some upper portion of the available population when determining minor-league replacement level, but it's an open question as to whether there's even any value in the concept of minor-league replacement level.
- **Replacement level analysis for alternate top-level leagues.** Unlike the minor leagues, which are an intermediate step on the way to the majors, there are leagues such as the Japanese leagues and, in the past, the Negro leagues, which represent the top level of competition for their own population of players. Replacement level for these leagues would need to be determined separately, as the interplay between league offensive level, the size of the population pool, the talent distribution, quality of information, and even differences in league rules and playing conditions means the major-league replacement level is largely irrelevant.
- **Better analysis of financial costs of player development, scouting, and acquisition.** Replacement level is as much an economic concept as a performance concept. Very little work has been done in measuring the true cost of scouting information, player-development systems, and transaction fees. Equating the opportunity costs of making a low-level trade, promoting a Triple-A player, or signing a journeyman free agent may not be well grounded in the fiscal realities of operating a major-league club.
- **Defensive replacement level.** Other than assuming a certain minimum competence to play a position, this analysis has largely ignored variations in defensive performance. Implicitly, we've been assuming that all potential replacement-level players are average defensively (or at least, that they do not differ significantly from each other). Clearly, this is not the case, although it reflects a common (but as yet unproven) belief that good glove men are easier to come by than good hitters. A player both at replacement level on offense and defense may, in fact, be below the "aggregate" replacement level, if decent defenders at offensive replacement level are available. But the interplay between offensive replacement level and a potential "defensive" replacement level is not immediately clear.

Conclusion

Replacement level is an important concept in correctly measuring the value of a baseball player, as it reflects the distribution of readily available talent. Both position and offensive environment affect replacement level, as do more theoretical factors such as quality of information and size of the talent pool. Using replacement level allows for a more accurate valuation of playing time and can have a huge economic impact in avoiding gross overpayment for middle-tier performance. If the fundamental concepts of replacement level were better understood in major-league front offices, even if this particular measurement system were not used, teams would be able to better allocate their payroll dollars and avoid some of the albatross contracts they have hung around their own necks.

Doing It Over

by Clay Davenport

You can count on it every year. A player—let's call him Marcus Thames—will have a breakout year in the minors. And in this book, in John Sickels's book, in *Baseball America,* on the Internet, people will dismiss his breakthrough because—horrors!—he had played in the same league the previous season.

Well, baseball isn't grade school, where repeating a grade means you get the exact same material as the year before, and sometimes the exact same tests. Even if you didn't face a new set of pitchers, they wouldn't throw the same pitches in the same situations, unless you're as dumb as a Hollywood blonde waiting tables at Hooters and you keep chasing pitches. Repeating a league is nothing more than a chance to keep playing without having the odds further stacked against you. Improvements are real, and, except at the lowest levels, there should be no stigma attached to such breakthroughs.

That's not to say that it is a good thing to repeat a league; it isn't. A player who repeats a league is two to three times more likely to be out of baseball within the next two years than a player who advances. He is more likely to be an older player, and age is key for prospects, regardless of level. If the player improves a lot, that probably means he had a bad year a year ago, and that creates the dilemma of figuring out whether his real ability is the good year, the bad year, or some ugly middle ground. However, if you are looking at a 23-year-old with a translated EqA of .237 last year and .217 the year before that, whether the most recent performance was in the same league or a higher league makes absolutely no difference in evaluating his prospect status.

I think part of the reason everyone believes repeating a league is significant is because they look at the basic stats. One of the qualities that sets apart ballplayers who make the majors from those who don't is the ability to learn, to improve, to be a growth stock. Our assumptions about "player growth" leading to a peak around age 27 are based almost entirely on the players who do grow and make it, playing at age 27 while their less learning-abled counterparts who matched them at 20 are in their third year at UPS. Those who make it "grow" their EqA by an average of 3% or so a year during their early 20s—call it six or seven points. Few do so gradually, though; many players do three or four years of growing all at once, so jumps of 30 points are far from a rare occurrence.

Most of the time, the impact of a 30-point EqA jump is disguised. Each level in the minors is worth about 15 points of EqA. Someone who moves up a level and doesn't improve at all looks like he did considerably worse; what looks like a modest improvement is really a strong one, because even when we know better, we don't factor in the league difference strongly enough. A player who has a 30-point jump while repeating a league, though—there's nothing to hide the improvement. We see the whole 30 points, instead of only 15, and we write it off as unrealistic.

Let's look at some numbers. For all players who played at the same level in consecutive seasons in the 1990s, I've listed the ratio of their EqAs in the two years in Table 1. Figures above 1.00 mean that, as a group, they got better, while those less than 1.00 mean they got worse. In Table 2 I list the same, but for players who advanced one level. "Normal growth" should show up as 1.030 or thereabouts, with any repeat effect showing in higher numbers.

Table 1. Repeaters (EqA Year 2 / EqA Year 1)

	MJ	AAA	AA	hiA	midA	short
19				1.031	1.070	1.055
20			1.054	1.043	1.065	1.075
21	1.035	.976	1.031	1.042	1.031	1.030
22	1.001	1.026	1.039	1.035	1.035	1.028
23	1.025	1.007	1.026	1.030	1.003	
24	.994	1.010	1.016	1.029		
25	1.014	1.002	1.000	.995		

Ratios tend to decline from right to left and from top to bottom. Improvement, from growth or repeat effects, becomes less noticeable with increasing age and league. The effect at the major-league and Triple-A levels appears to be totally non-existent. The effect at Double-A and high-A (Florida State, California, Carolina leagues) is consistent with "normal growth," with a sharp decline apparent at age 25. A similar sharp decline shows up in the middle-A (Midwest and South Atlantic) leagues at age 23, and in Triple-A at age 27 (.991 at 26, .959 at 27).

Major-leaguers are all repeaters, of course, with nowhere to advance until the big-market teams form a separate league. Here, notice that the advancers lose more of their EqA, relative to league average, moving from Triple-A to the majors than in any other jump, contradicting some who claim that Double-A to Triple-A is the toughest transition.

Table 2. Advancers (EqA Year 2/ EqA Year 1)

	MJ	AAA	AA	hiA	midA	short
19				.984	.996	.970
20			.968	.957	.973	.968
21		.858	.942	.948	.972	.974
22		.866	.942	.940	.956	.979
23		.873	.941	.947	.941	.961
24		.848	.922	.942	.942	
25		.870	.904	.897		

There's a similar, though less pronounced, pattern of declines from right to left and top to bottom. The same dropoffs at Double-A, high-A, and middle-A that we saw in the first table appear again. Players who advance a league show the same growth pattern as those who do not; the growth is simply masked by the 7–15 points lost in the move to a higher league.

Incidentally, these dropoffs are the basis for the age adjustment I build into the DTs, downgrading players who are unusually old for their league; the old guys really don't perform at higher levels as well as you would expect.

For entire groups of players, there is little or no extra benefit to repeating a league, except at the lowest levels. That conclusion is only for one year; is it possible that the year spent repeating a level hurts the player in the next few years?

If anything, the opposite is true, as shown in Table 3.

In each case, the first row is the players who repeated the league in years 1 and 2, along with what they did in the next two years, while the second row is the same information for players who advanced. Every time, the advancers start out 12 to 19 points ahead of the repeaters, but everywhere except Triple-A, the gap narrows over the next four years. It never closes—the initial advantage holds out till the end. A lot of this could be selection bias; the repeat-players group is presumably losing its worst-performing players at a rate two to three times higher than the advancers group... but at least among the survivors, those who repeated a league below Triple-A improve more over the next few years than those who advanced.

So on average, the repeating players don't fare any worse. Surely, though, those who show really large gains—and those are the ones who concern us—don't hold their value as well as those who moved up. Or do they?

Let's look at the data again in Table 4, this time selecting only players who gained at least 20 points of EqA in their second year.

Players from the Midwest and Sally leagues always held their second-year gains, at least as a group; they did not fall back to their old levels, whether they advanced or repeated. The players who were promoted at age 20 or earlier gained ground on their repeating comrades, as they were about 12 points better in year 1 and about 20 points better by year 4. That trend reversed among older players, as those who repeated made up most of the ground separating them from advancing players of comparable age. There is certainly no evidence that the promoted players showed any greater value after year 4 than they did in year 1.

Table 5 is the same table, for the high-A leagues.

Again, all of the scores for years 3 and 4 are much closer to year 2 than to year 1—the players held their gains. The importance of age is easy to see, as the 21-and-younger groups continued to improve in years 3 and 4, while the 22-and-older groups stagnated. Any differences in growth seen here favor those who repeated, as they end up closer to the advancers in year 4 than they were in year 1, but only by a little. I have to stick with the null hypothesis: there is no significant difference in their tendencies over the four-year period. All the advantages for the second group were present at the start.

Table 6 presents the Double-A players.

Double-A is even more favorable to those who stayed behind.

I have to say that the bias against players who repeat a league is an overreaction to seeing statistics in the nude, unclothed by a change in league difficulty. Repeaters do

Table 3.

League repeated	EqA1	EqA2	EqA3	EqA4	Delta	Washout
International	243	248	248	246	3	24
	255	259	259	262	9	10
Pacific Coast	240	241	243	242	2	24
	251	256	256	259	8	10
Eastern	215	226	230	233	18	41
	233	239	245	248	15	19
Southern	214	226	232	232	18	38
	230	239	240	245	15	13
Texas	211	223	229	230	19	32
	230	235	239	242	12	14
Carolina	198	212	219	224	26	37
	213	222	231	234	21	22
California	196	211	219	226	30	39
	213	223	228	233	20	24
Florida State	196	207	214	222	26	39
	212	221	230	236	24	21
Midwest	186	200	209	215	29	39
	198	208	218	224	26	31
South Atlantic	180	195	207	215	35	44
	194	206	216	225	30	25

Table 4.

		Repeating				Moving Up One Level			
		Yr1	Yr2	Yr3	Yr4	Yr1	Yr2	Yr3	Yr4
mid-A	19−	169	201	209	214	185	219	222	235
	20	176	205	206	208	183	218	217	225
	21	178	213	211	222	100	220	224	225
	22+	179	217	221	220	192	223	220	225

Table 5.

		Repeating				Moving Up One Level			
		Yr1	Yr2	Yr3	Yr4	Yr1	Yr2	Yr3	Yr4
high-A	20−	180	216	222	223	205	240	242	250
	21	188	221	219	236	204	238	235	247
	22	187	223	222	220	205	236	236	234
	23+	191	225	222	226	204	239	227	231

Table 6.

		Repeating				Moving Up One Level			
		Yr1	Yr2	Yr3	Yr4	Yr1	Yr2	Yr3	Yr4
Double-A	21−	196	235	237	232	219	256	247	251
	22	197	238	232	237	218	256	250	257
	23	203	240	236	237	222	262	246	248
	24+	211	244	239	237	219	253	243	239

worse than players the same age who were promoted because the ones who were promoted were better to start with; once you take that into consideration, there's nothing to suggest that the repeaters were harmed by the experience of repeating a level; if anything, the data suggests that they benefited slightly.

So what can we expect for Marcus Thames? He would count in this study as a 23-year-old Double-A repeater, who went from a .213 EqA to .287. Few players have posted a jump like that; of the ten players of his age and level who were grossly similar (EqA rise of 50+ points, to at least .250), four clearly had fluke seasons, as they all returned to their previous level and never hit so well again (two of them, it should be added, had their great year in a half-season of work). Doug Mientkiewicz dropped like a stone the year after being promoted to the majors, but he has since rebounded. Another, Kevin Koslofski, lost about half of his EqA gain and had a brief major-league career. The other four stayed within ten points of their year 2 EqA: Brian Daubach and Angel Echevarria made the show, while Mark Merchant and Aaron Guiel have not.

I'll fall back on my one-third rule, which says that a player who makes such a large jump in EqA will tend to give a third of it back. Thames will hit around .260, and could make the majors in midseason as a fourth outfielder.

The Problem with "Peak"

by Michael Wolverton

Let's talk about greatness. The consensus view among analysts is that there are two equally legitimate criteria for determining how great a player was: career value and peak value. Bill James made this distinction explicit in his 1985 *Historical Baseball Abstract,* and the rest of the baseball-analysis world has widely accepted this either/or nature of greatness.

The idea behind career value is clear enough: how much did the player contribute to his teams over the course of his career? Plenty of baseball analysts have taken on this question, and many have come up with satisfactory methods for quantifying career value.

The idea behind peak value is also pretty clear: how good was the player at his best? But when people started to dig deeper and tried to come up with metrics to quantify this notion of peak, it became clear that it was a very difficult task. When exactly is a player "at his best?" How can you measure how valuable a player is (to use James's words) "at some moment in his career"? James never attempted to offer a concrete, quantifiable metric for peak—yet another indication that he is much wiser than the rest of us. Many of the concrete peak metrics that have been proposed since then have serious problems.

The first of these problems is arbitrary thresholds. Most peak metrics tend to be something like "best N years of the player's career," where N is completely arbitrary. Metrics like this end up rewarding players who have exactly N good years, in effect penalizing players who have N + 1 or more good years. Even worse, some fans of short-career players have advocated peak metrics that coincidentally happen to cast their guy in the best possible light. Fans of Sandy Koufax have asserted that a player's peak should be his best four consecutive years, which of course would rank Koufax among the top two or three pitchers of all time. A fan of Dale Murphy gerrymandered a peak metric—best five seasons, without the "consecutive" qualifier—that placed Murphy adjacent to Hall of Famers in his lists. The Murphy fan could respond to objections with "five is just as good as any other N." It's hard to argue with that, but why have an N at all?

The second problem is what I call arbitrary partitioning. A characteristic of most peak metrics is that they systematically ignore large chunks of a player's career. I look at it this way. Peak is a way of partitioning a player's career: there are his best years, and there's everything else. But there are plenty of other ways of partitioning a career. We could break a hitter's career into his stolen-base contribution and everything else. For a starting pitcher we could separate his shutouts from his non-shutout starts. None of those ways of partitioning is any better than the other—they're all arbitrary. A player's base-stealing and shutouts are certainly meaningful contributors to winning, just as a player's peak years are.

I can't prove that a great peak by itself doesn't make a player great, any more than I can prove that great stolen-base or shutout totals by themselves don't make a player great. Of course, someone who said he was primarily interested in stolen-base totals or pitcher shutouts in evaluating player greatness would be ignored. Yet that same community doesn't think twice about analysts who say they are primarily interested in using a handful of peak seasons to evaluate player greatness. When determining a player's greatness, stolen bases, shutouts, and peak seasons should be considered in the context of everything else the player did.

Winning Pennants

The assumption that underlies my argument is that a player is great to the extent he helps his teams win. Most researchers attempt to quantify player value in terms of how many games they helped their teams win. There are any number of statistics that measure a player's value in added wins, and in the rest of the essay I'll refer to an N-win player, meaning a player who rates as having contributed N wins above average or replacement level according to one of these methods.

Wins, though, are just a means to an end. A player's goal during the regular season is to help his team get into the playoffs, i.e., to help his team win pennants. It's possible that players with different career profiles—high-peak or low-peak—will contribute differently toward their teams' pennant chances, even if their win contributions are equal. If so, quantifying that difference would provide an alternative to arbitrary peak metrics. It would allow us to attach a non-arbitrary value to a player's peak—the difference that career shape makes in expected pennants for his teams–and incorporate that difference in his career value.

James himself raised exactly this question in his 1994 book *The Politics of Glory.* In the context of comparing high-peak Don Drysdale to low-peak Milt Pappas, James hypothesized that players worth the same number of career wins but with different career shapes have different impacts on the number of pennants their teams win. For example, a player like Drysdale might be expected to produce more pennants than a player like Pappas, even though the two had nearly identical career win/loss records.

James ran a series of computer simulations to test his theory. He constructed two hypothetical pitchers who had equal value measured in career wins, with one having a higher peak than the other. He then added each pitcher to a league-average team, simulated a large number of seasons, and recorded how often each team made the playoffs. What he found is that the average team with the high-peak pitcher added made the playoffs more often than the average team with the low-peak pitcher. The difference in pennants seemed small—under the simulation based on the most realistic assumptions, the high-peak player produced 23 extra pennants in 10,000 seasons—but James concluded it was still large enough to suggest that there is a measurable difference between the values of high-peak and low-peak careers.

One of the questions left unanswered in *The Politics of Glory* is why. Why would a high-peak player contribute more expected pennants to his team than a low-peak player, assuming the number of career wins they contributed is the same? Sure, the high-peak player's best seasons would produce more wins for his team than the low-peak player's best seasons, and therefore the high-peak player's teams would reach the playoffs more often in those seasons. But the high-peak player's worst seasons would see his team reach the playoffs correspondingly less often than the low-peak player's. All things being equal, we might expect these two effects to cancel each other out.

So is there a pennant-producing benefit to a high peak, or was it just a quirk of James's simulation? I've concluded the benefit is real, and the reason lies partly in the way team wins are distributed. Team wins are distributed like a bell curve, also known as a normal distribution. Figure 1 shows the distribution of team regular season winning percentage since 1900 plotted against a theoretical normal distribution; you can see how good the fit is. Most teams finish the regular season around .500, fewer finish around .600 or .400, and still fewer around .700 or .300.

If you add a player with positive value to a random team, he can be expected to add wins to that team, and therefore make them more likely to win a pennant. What we want to know is for what percentage of those random teams will the player's contribution make the difference between winning a pennant and not winning one? That's essentially what James's study was measuring. (James actually added the player to an average team—a team with the ability to win 50% of its games—rather than a random team. But randomness in that team's performance in James's simulation would also produce a normal distribution for its actual win totals, albeit a different normal distribution from the one in Figure 1.)

Figure 1. Distribution of team winning percentage since 1900

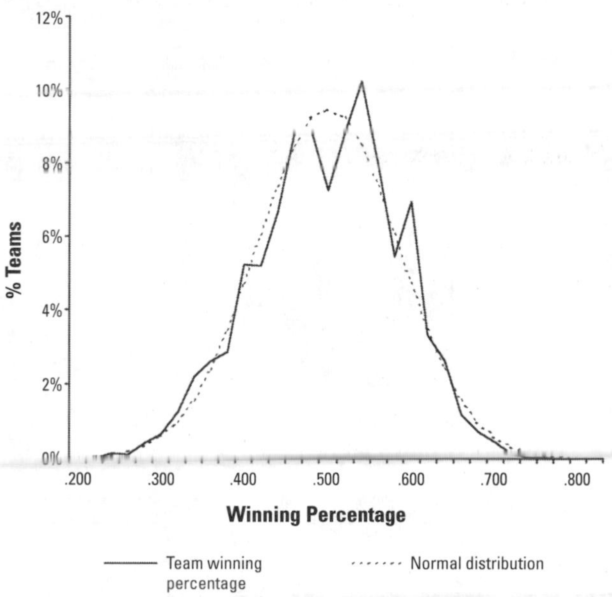

Here's the key idea: because of the bell curve, a player with a great season will take disproportionately more teams to the playoffs than a player with a good season. This is easy to see with an example, shown in Figure 2. This figure shows the far right side of the team win distribution of Figure 1. Imagine for a minute that a team wins a pennant if they win 95 games or more. A good player who contributes an extra five wins will take teams that would win 90 to 94 games without him into the playoffs. This is represented by the darkly-shaded area under the graph. A great player who contributes an extra 10 wins would take those same 90-94 win teams into the playoffs, plus teams that would win 85 to 89 games, shown by the lightly-shaded area under the graph. The key is that, because of the bell curve, there are more of the 85-89 win teams than there are of the 90-94 win teams. So a ten-win individual season is worth more than two five-win seasons.

Of course, teams don't automatically win a pennant with 95 wins. In fact, the win total for pennant winners also follows a normal distribution, so that's what we'll use in our model below.

Figure 2. A 10-win season is worth more than twice as many pennants as a 5-win season

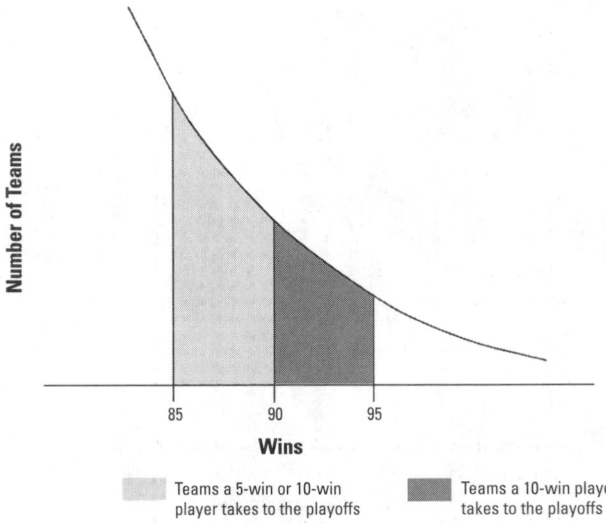

Calculating Pennants Added

We know from James's simulations that a high-peak player can, in theory, produce more pennants than a low-peak player. What we still need to find out is whether the effect makes a difference in practice. That is, do real major-league players show a noticeable difference in their effect on team pennants because of the caliber of their peak? We obviously can't use a simulation like James's on each of the 15,000 or so players in major-league history, even if we trusted the program to simulate seasons accurately. Instead, we need a simple formula for calculating a player's value in pennants that anyone with access to a spreadsheet can use.

Given that a player contributes w wins during a season, how often will a random team with those added w wins win a pennant? In other words, we want to know the probability that

$$w \geq P - R$$

where P is the number of wins it takes to win the pennant, and R is the number of wins of a random team. Here, P and R are not single values but are random variables that are defined by a probability distribution, in this case the bell-curve (normal) distribution.

To deal with differing lengths of seasons over the years, we'll make the model a little bit more complicated, rewriting the above inequality as:

$$w \geq g\,(P_{pct} - R_{pct})$$

where g is the average number of games played during the season in question, P_{pct} is the winning percentage it takes to win a pennant, and R_{pct} is the winning percentage of a random team. As with P and R, P_{pct} and R_{pct} are normally distributed random variables (we assume that these two variables are independent, and we'll leave the number-crunching without that assumption for future work). By adding the season length into the model, we recognize that a shorter season—154-game seasons or strike seasons—inflates the pennant value of a w-win year from a player.

The solution to problems like this is the cumulative normal distribution function. There is a closed-form formula for this function, but it's fairly ugly and it's not really the point of this article. Fortunately, we don't need to know the closed form, because Microsoft Excel and other software have it built in. So I'll write the function here in pretty much the same format you'd use to get Excel to calculate it. The probability of a random team plus a w-win player winning a pennant is:

$$\text{Pennants}(w) = \text{Normdist}\left\{w, g\left[E(P_{pct}) - E(R_{pct})\right]\right\}, g\sqrt{\text{stdev}(P_{pct})^2 + \text{sdev}(R_{pct})^2}$$

(To use the NORMDIST function in Excel, you have to add a fourth argument: TRUE.)

where

- g is the average number of games played during the season in question.
- $E(P_{pct})$ is the expected (average) winning percentage of a pennant-winner. Since 1900, the average first-place winning percentage has been .612, so that's the number we'll use.
- $E(R_{pct})$ is the expected winning percentage of all teams (.500, of course).
- $\text{stdev}(P_{pct})$ is the standard deviation of first-place winning percentages (since 1900, it's 0.045)
- $\text{stdev}(R_{pct})$ is the standard deviation of all team winning percentages (since 1900, it's 0.084)

The last step in calculating the player's value in expected pennants added is to subtract the probability that his team would have made the playoffs without him:

$$\text{Pennants Added}(w) = \text{Pennants}(w) - \text{Pennants}(0)$$

Figure 3 shows how a player's value in wins translates to value in pennants using this formula. You can see that there's a slight upward curve in the graph, and that's what makes the high-peak player more valuable than a low-peak player. The curve looks slight, but it's enough to make a difference in many cases. For example, one ten-win season is worth 15% more in pennant value than two five-win seasons, and 30% more than five two-win seasons.

Figure 3. Mapping between added wins and added pennants

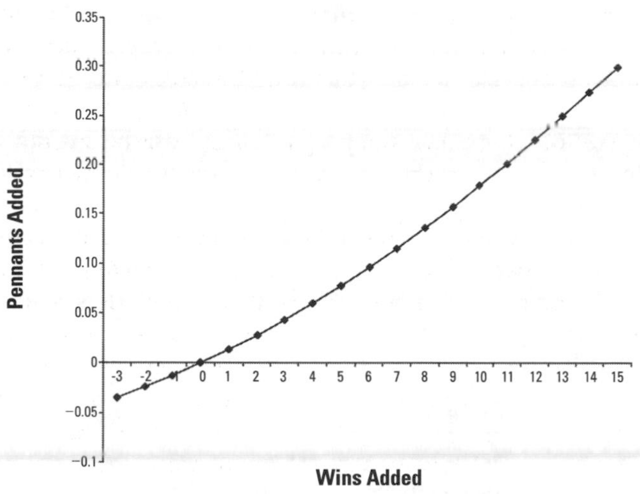

The Greatest Career and Peak Players

We designed this metric to evaluate real players according to their contribution to team pennants. We calculated player value in Wins Added by using modified versions of Pete Palmer's statistics: Adjusted Batting Wins for hitters and Adjusted Pitching Wins for pitchers. In both cases, the win total was based on a comparison to a replacement-level player. A replacement-level hitter was defined to be one who contributes 20% fewer runs than a league-average hitter, while a replacement-level pitcher was defined as one who allowed 20% more runs than an average pitcher. We then used the resulting Wins Added number to compute Pennants Added, as defined above.

Table 1 lists the top 20 hitters since the first year of the modern World Series by Pennants Added. Only players whose careers began in 1903 or later were considered, so for example, Honus Wagner was ineligible for this list. These numbers reflect the players' hitting performance only; fielding and baserunning are ignored, and there is no adjustment for difficulty of the position(s) the player played.

If you put Babe Ruth on random teams for each of his 22 seasons in the majors, those teams could be expected to reach the postseason 3.55 times more than they would have without him. When you think about it, that's an amazing number: one player worth three-and-a-half pennants by himself. Most players never make it to three postseasons, let alone account for that many just on their own performance.

I included the Wins Added column in the table so you can see how much difference the pennants calculation makes in the ranking of real players. High-peak players like Lou Gehrig and Rogers Hornsby rank a few places higher in Pennants Added than they do in Wins Added, while lower-peak players like Carl Yastrzemski and Frank Robinson fall a few places. Or take Willie Stargell and Frank Thomas the Latter (not shown in the table). The two have identical Wins Added totals of 83, and they rank 33rd and 34th all-time by that measure. When rated by Pennants added, the high-peak Thomas moves up to 22nd all-time, while the low-peak Stargell drops to 40th, with 17 players separating the two.

On the other hand, there are no cases, in the top 20 list or outside of it, where Pennants Added makes such a huge difference that it would radically, qualitatively change our perception of the player. There are no examples of players with mediocre career Wins Added totals who turn up elite Pennants Added totals because of a few great seasons. In this way, my results jibe with the most realistic of James's simulations: the extra pennants produced by a high-peak player can be meaningful, but not overwhelming.

Table 1.

Player	Wins Added	Pennants Added
Babe Ruth	179	3.55
Ted Williams	153	2.89
Ty Cobb	147	2.66
Stan Musial	147	2.66
Lou Gehrig	136	2.63
Hank Aaron	148	2.52
Willie Mays	137	2.36
Rogers Hornsby	122	2.28
Barry Bonds	123	2.25
Mickey Mantle	126	2.24
Tris Speaker	124	2.22
Mel Ott	122	2.17
Jimmie Foxx	116	2.14
Frank Robinson	123	2.06
Eddie Collins	102	1.75
Mike Schmidt	98	1.67
Eddie Mathews	95	1.63
Carl Yastrzemski	102	1.62
Rickey Henderson	99	1.61
Harry Heilmann	87	1.54

Table 2 lists the top 20 pitchers by Pennants Added. Again, only careers that began in 1903 or later or considered, so Cy Young and Christy Mathewson don't appear.

As with the hitters, some high-peak pitchers move up a few spots in the rankings when measured in Pennants

Table 2.

Pitcher	Wins Added	Pennants Added
Walter Johnson	150	2.90
Pete Alexander	125	2.28
Lefty Grove	111	2.03
Roger Clemens	105	1.77
Tom Seaver	105	1.76
Warren Spahn	99	1.69
Greg Maddux	90	1.60
Bert Blyleven	92	1.50
Carl Hubbell	83	1.46
Gaylord Perry	89	1.44
Steve Carlton	85	1.42
Robin Roberts	82	1.40
Bob Feller	79	1.40
Bob Gibson	83	1.37
Jim Palmer	83	1.37
Ed Walsh	71	1.34
Phil Niekro	84	1.33
Nolan Ryan	79	1.26
Ferguson Jenkins	79	1.25
Don Sutton	80	1.24

Added, such as Carl Hubbell, Bob Feller, and especially Ed Walsh, while some low-peak pitchers move down, notably Phil Niekro and Don Sutton. Consider two pitchers outside the top 20, Stan Coveleski and Tommy John. The two are nearly identical in Wins Added, ranking 27th and 29th with 66 and 65 wins, respectively. But Coveleski, with a short career full of excellent seasons, fares far better in Pennants Added, ranking 22nd compared to John's 39th.

So far, we've used this method to incorporate the extra pennant benefit of a high peak into a player's career value. Can we also use it to measure a player's peak in isolation? Yes, at least for one possible interpretation of "peak." By looking at the difference between the two measures listed above—career Pennants Added minus career Wins Added—we are left with just the extra pennant benefit of the peak. Of course, we can't directly subtract wins from pennants, so we'll normalize the Wins Added total by multiplying by the historical pennants/wins ratio:

$$\text{Peak} = \text{Pennants Added} - \text{Wins Added}\,\frac{\text{Pennants Added}}{\text{Wins Added}}$$

where ΣPennants Added is the sum of all Pennants Added totals for all players in history, and ΣWins Added is the sum of all Wins Added totals for all players in history.

This measure is based on a slightly different meaning of the concept of peak than the one most commonly used. While most peak metrics try to measure how valuable a player was at his best, this one measures how much extra value the player gave his teams by concentrating his best performance into individual seasons.

As I argued at the beginning, I don't believe that any measure of peak, including this one, should be used to assess player greatness by itself. But if I didn't convince you and you're still a big believer in peak value, at least this measure doesn't have the shortcomings that I noted in other peak measures: there are no arbitrary thresholds in the formula, and this measure of peak does not ignore any part of the player's career.

In Table 3, you'll find the 20 best peaks for hitters by this measure.

Table 3.

Player	Peak
Babe Ruth	0.69
Lou Gehrig	0.45
Ted Williams	0.44
Rogers Hornsby	0.33
Stan Musial	0.30
Ty Cobb	0.30
Barry Bonds	0.28
Jimmie Foxx	0.28
Tris Speaker	0.23
Mickey Mantle	0.22
Frank Thomas	0.22
Mel Ott	0.21
Willie Mays	0.17
Jeff Bagwell	0.17
Hank Aaron	0.16
Harry Heilmann	0.15
Joe DiMaggio	0.14
Hank Greenberg	0.14
Joe Jackson	0.12
Johnny Mize	0.12

There's a lot of overlap between this list and the all-time career hitters list, and for good reason. If a player has built up great career totals, it serves to reason that he had some great seasons along the way. It would be difficult to accumulate impressive career numbers without having some great seasons. So there's no surprise that the top 13 career hitters all fall within the top 15 on the Peak list.

There are exceptions. Frank Robinson, Carl Yastrzemski, and Rickey Henderson all make the career top 20 with relatively low peaks. (This is considering Henderson's hitting only; his contribution on the base paths isn't being measured here.) In fact, Yastrzemski's peak rates as slightly negative by this measure. Other all-time great career hitters with peaks that rate near zero are Pete Rose, Willie McCovey, Al Kaline, Joe Morgan, and Reggie Jackson.

Table 4 has the peak list for pitchers.

Table 4.

Pitcher	Peak
Walter Johnson	0.53
Pete Alexander	0.31
Lefty Grove	0.28
Ed Walsh	0.23
Greg Maddux	0.18
Stan Coveleski	0.18
Bob Feller	0.16
Carl Hubbell	0.16
Eddie Cicotte	0.13
Roger Clemens	0.12
Warren Spahn	0.12
Hippo Vaughn	0.12
Hal Newhouser	0.12
Dazzy Vance	0.12
Randy Johnson	0.11
Babe Adams	0.11
Robin Roberts	0.11
Wilbur Cooper	0.10
Tom Seaver	0.10
Carl Mays	0.10

There's a much greater difference between the career and peak lists with pitchers than with hitters. Lots of new names show up on this list, some we might expect—Eddie Cicotte, Dazzy Vance, Randy Johnson—and some we might not: Hippo Vaughn, Babe Adams, Wilbur Cooper.

Where is "Mr. Peak"? Sandy Koufax's peak rates 42nd all time by this measure, behind Dizzy Dean, Pedro Martinez, Mike Mussina, Bob Gibson, and many others. There are several factors contributing to this seemingly low ranking for Koufax, but one of the main ones is that this metric doesn't ignore seasons. Koufax essentially had four seasons that contributed to his Peak rating. Other elite pitchers who finished ahead of Koufax had more than four seasons that were good enough to get them on the upper end of Figure 3's curve. Because this Peak metric attaches value to those extra seasons of greatness by Gibson, et al., it rates some of these other pitchers as having comparable or superior peaks to Koufax.

There are plenty of issues not addressed here. Should the model account for the fact that four times as many teams make the playoffs today as in the 1950s? Should the diminished importance of the regular season today cause us to attach more weight to postseason performance in player evaluations? Clearly there is a lot of work left to do, but I hope this essay has given a new perspective on the notion of peak, and presented some new tools that will help in our ongoing effort to measure players' careers.

Graying the Game

by Clay Davenport

The last few years have been a testament to the ability of older players. Barry Bonds's assault on the record books last season came on the heels of recent accomplishments of Mark McGwire, Edgar Martinez, Randy Johnson, Roger Clemens—great players all thriving far past the "peak" age of 27. Is this is an isolated occurrence, or a new reality for analysts to ponder?

Well, it's clear that we are in a highly anomalous time. If we define "older players" as those 32 and above, and "young players" as those 24 and under, and chart out the proportion of plate appearances that went to each, we see this in Firgure 1.

The chart splits into roughly six eras, to my eye:

- The early days, from 1871 up to 1905 or so. Young players dominated the game in the beginning, and old-timers hardly existed. Initially, that was because without a professional league, all the men who would have been 30-year-old players needed to make a living, and had gone off and gotten married and had kids and become respectable citizens.

  Another reason is that salaries were relatively more than they were later in baseball history, and the Gilded Age offered a young, ambitious man numerous business opportunities for advancement, as exemplified by Al Spalding. A third reason was that the primitive equipment and medical knowledge contributed to injuries and lengthened the odds of coming back from them. However, the proportion of younger players diminished more or less continuously, and after the first ten years the proportion of older players started rising consistently. The contraction of 1900 favored veterans, and they pulled ahead of the kids for eight years.

Figure 1. Young versus old

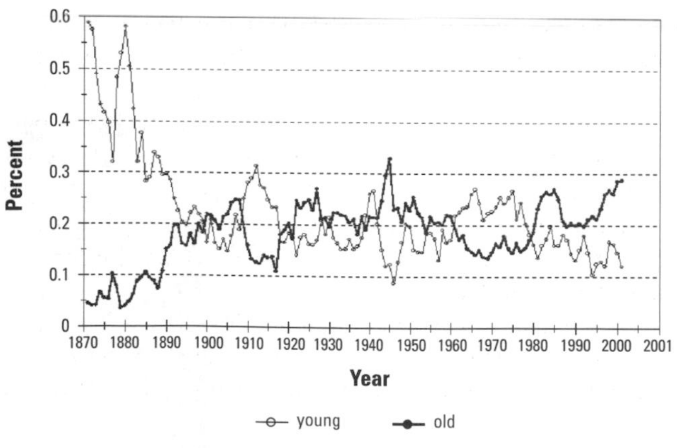

- About 1905, the historical trend towards older players suddenly reversed. By 1912, young players made up more than 30% of major-league appearances, the first time they had done that in 25 years, and the last time ever. The running game became paramount, to a much greater degree than it had been in the 1800s. The proportion of young players quickly fell; it looks as if the trends from 1905–25 are entirely driven by the Ty Cobb/Tris Speaker/Eddie Collins class of 1905: they endured, while all other ages rotated out in turn.
- Starting in 1918, the older players moved back into the lead, and held it with very short breaks until 1960. The stolen base fell by the wayside and home runs emerged to take their place.
- World War II fell right in the middle of this long period. Young players were drafted or volunteered, leaving the game to men who, due to age or other infirmity, were exempt from the draft. When the soldiers returned, they pretty much had to be given their jobs back. The result was that older players were never so common as they were in 1945, and young players were never so rare as they were in 1946.

  The effects were larger than just the war years. It looked for all the world like a new age of youth was sweeping into baseball in 1939–41; their numbers climbed sharply until the draft stopped that trend cold. That cut-off went all the way down through the minors, breaking the majors' talent-supply system and perhaps hastening the raids on the Negro leagues. The budding youth revolution fizzled, and the old guys ruled a game ever more dependent on the walk and the home run through the 1950s.
- Expansion, in 1961, provided the kids the wedge they needed to move back into the lead. The stolen base once again became an important part of team offense. Young players would hold that lead for 20 years; demographics—they were the children of the Baby Boom—probably had a role in keeping a large supply of young players coming.
- The recent era. The proportion of young players has been slipping steadily since 1975, while the number of older players has risen, until each has reached levels

only seen during World War II. Older players have outnumbered young players ever since 1980, the longest continuous stretch in history, and the gap has actually widened in recent years. The Baby Bust generation came of age during this period, although that effect should be diminishing. It is also the era of free agency; salaries now increase so much over the length of a career that by the end of it journeymen earn what had been star or superstar money when it started. Meanwhile, as it did during the 1950s, the game has changed to put greater emphasis on what Bill James called old players' skills—home runs and walks. Declining numbers of balls in play has led to a de-emphasis of defense, another boon to the codgers.

I don't know whether the change in the game now is a result of the older players or a cause of it, but a continued emphasis on these old players' skills will keep young players bottled up in the minors until they are old enough to develop those skills themselves. Perhaps the Orioles are the future of the game.

Older players being more common than ever before has some role in the performances we've seen in recent years, simply by providing older players with more opportunities to succeed than they ever had before.

What else is happening? The classic study by Bill James defined the peak age as 27; is that still the case? Has the career path changed?

As Figure 2 shows, my choice of indices ("most Equivalent Runs," "best Equivalent Average with at least 200 plate appearances," "most Equivalent Runs above replacement value") all gave the same answer: a definite "yes, but..." *Yes,* the peak is still clearly right around 27, *but,* there are a lot more cases of 31- and 32-year-old peaks than we would have expected from history. The peak is a little broader than before, and the added breadth is all on the back side.

A similar pattern emerges from a more involved study I conducted, using cohorts. A cohort, in statistical terms, is a group of people born at roughly the same time, whose aging patterns can be studied. I defined the members to be every man who played in the majors since 1900, five years apart for each starting age between 20 and 35. My first cohort, then is every 20-year-old from 1900 who also played in 1905, every 20-year-old in 1901 who played in 1906, and so on through to every 20-year-old in 1996 who also played in 2001. That is 97 separate cohorts. I also had 97 cohorts for 21-year-olds, and 97 for age 23, through to age 35.

To compare players accurately with themselves five years later, you have to ensure that each member of the group carries the same weight in each sample; you don't want to see the group EqA increase because Barry Bonds's share of the plate appearances grew from 10% to 30%. I prorate each player to the least number of plate appearances he had in the two years. If Geronimo Berroa had 609 PAs in 1995, and 35 PAs in 2000, he counts for just 35 PAs in both years.

Figure 2. Peak EqR by age

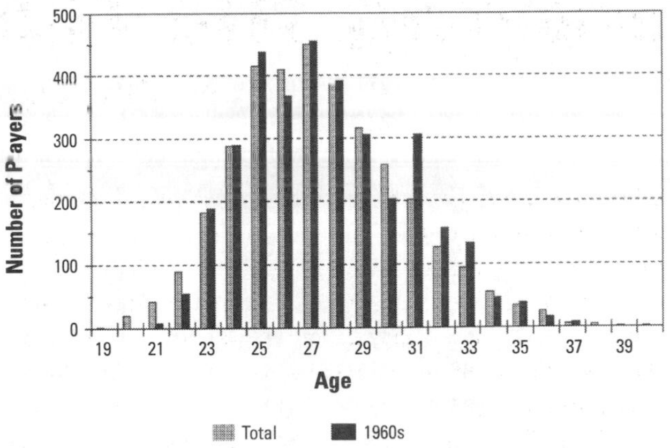

On the left-hand side of Table 1, I've averaged together all of the cohorts for a given age from 1900–96; the right side of the table only averages the last five cohorts, those starting in 1992 through 1996.

PA Ratio is the total number of plate appearances, unadjusted for cohort balance, between the fifth year and the first year. EqA1 is the group EqA in the first year, EqA5 the same in the fifth year, and Delta is simply the differences in the EqAs.

The first thing to notice is that the PA ratios decline almost continuously with age in both sets, but the ratios recently are offset by a year. That is, the recent age-26 PA Ratio is closer to the historic age-25 PA Ratio than the historic age-26 ratio. Historically speaking, players lost 50% of their plate appearances between age 28 and 33; recently, though, it takes until 30–35 to lose half the PAs.

The next thing to notice is that the delta EQAs are not very different for the two groups at most ages. The differences we see are at the ends, when the sample sizes get smaller, and, once again, a smaller than expected drop for the recent cohorts from their early 30s. Barry Bonds, by himself, explains the difference between the recent 31-to-36 cohorts and those of all time: his 2001 performance was worth five points of EqA to the "after" group.

My best explanation for this data is that the aging pattern has shifted slightly older. The primary peak still comes around age 27, but that age 27 peak has always been a little broad. It looks as if it has gotten broader; where before there was a steep dropoff at age 29, now we don't see the dropoff really kick in until 32.

As to reasons why, one might be the style of play. Aging patterns interact with the style of play; an era like the current one, with its emphasis on the home run, is going to be much

Table 1:

Age	PA Ratio	EqA1	EqA5	Delta	PA Ratio	EqA1	EqA5	Delta
20	13.43	261	281	+20	32.07	288	294	+6
21	5.57	263	276	+13	18.56	245	290	+45
22	2.93	265	277	+12	6.10	265	277	+12
23	1.81	268	274	+6	2.58	266	270	+4
24	1.23	271	275	+4	1.44	271	283	+12
25	.92	272	272	0	1.09	271	274	+3
26	.72	274	272	-2	.90	279	277	-2
27	.59	278	272	-6	.73	281	275	-6
28	.50	278	272	-6	.70	284	276	-8
29	.42	280	273	-7	.61	284	278	-6
30	.34	282	271	-11	.52	282	278	-4
31	.28	286	272	-14	.33	295	286	-9
32	.22	285	272	-13	.29	297	281	-16
33	.18	285	268	-17	.26	291	279	-12
34	.14	289	268	-21	.22	299	275	-24
35	.12	289	270	-19	.26	288	267	-21
36	.10	286	267	-19	.14	311	269	-42

more enabling to an older player than a speed-centered game is. Why? Home-run hitting, restricted to players who hit at least 20, peaks a little later than the average for EqR, occurring in a broad 26-to-32 peak instead of a 25-to-29 peak. It would be natural for the peak to shift a little in an era that favors older skills, just as it would shift younger in an era that favored youthful skills. A rule change that opened up stolen bases a little—by restricting pickoff throws to first base, say—would probably bring more young players into the game to take advantage.

I think there is little question that players in modern times do recognize that their bodies are an enormously valuable asset, more so than players of the past did. A large part of that is simply that there is so much more money involved than ever before. Weight training, continuous off-season training, far more attention paid to diet, far less attention paid to alcohol... I'm pretty sure that all of these contribute to players reaching a higher athletic skill level than ever before, and help to keep them at that level for a slightly longer period of time. I don't think that's really the issue, though, because the 23-year-olds who would be pushing them out of the way also have those advantages over the 23-year-olds of the past, and I don't know that the number of players who genuinely sabotaged themselves with liquor is enough to make up the difference.

It is also possible that modern medicine has a hand in the change. It is an irony, although not entirely unexpected, that our era, ridiculed by old-timers for its extensive disabled lists, should have so many more players coming back from injuries to play extra years.

Could it be, and I know this will be heresy to old-timers, that the skill level involved is now so much higher that it takes longer to learn? That would keep players in the minor leagues for a longer time. The average skill level has generally increased over time, as Dick Cramer showed in a *Baseball Research Journal* article in the 1970s, but I did not see any great increase in the 1990s, and there actually appears to have been a small downtick in 2001.

Is it the money? When a team guarantees a player's contract for two or three years, it is tough for them to accept that the money is gone and that they might be better off moving the player to the bench, or to the waiver wire, if he becomes unproductive. On the other hand, front offices looking to cut costs have a powerful incentive to favor young, cheap players over expensive, aging veterans, which they are not doing. The money cuts another way, though; the current rules on arbitration and free agency mean that a clock starts ticking as soon as a player is brought up, so there are advantages to keeping a player out of the majors until he is ready to contribute at a higher level. Training at the major league level gets frighteningly expensive when it costs you an extra year of Adam Dunn.

Looking back at Figure 1, you can see that the age patterns have had abrupt changes in direction several times. I think it is likely that another such change will occur in the next few years, although I have absolutely no factual basis for that belief; it is just that, in a historical sense, it is time for a change.

Fairness in Scheduling

by Jeff Hildebrand

Major League Baseball moved to a three-divisions-per-league alignment in 1994, adding an extra tier of playoffs and a wild-card qualifier. One of the arguments advanced in favor of the format was that it would guarantee that the two best teams in each league would make the playoffs. This argument played well in San Francisco, where the Giants had just won 103 games in finishing second to the Atlanta Braves in the NL West, missing the playoffs. While an argument can be made that the sacrifice of pennant races between great teams is too high a price to pay, ensuring that the second-best team in the league makes the postseason is one of the more defensible arguments in favor of the wild card. Or at least it would be if it were true. Unfortunately, it has never been completely true, and recent changes to the schedule have caused some to suggest that it may be even less true now.

The problem lies in the question of how you define the concept of the "best" teams. It is certainly true that the teams with the two best records in each league will make the post-season, but those teams may not be the two best in the league. Luck has always played some factor in the final standings each year, no matter what the schedule or playoff format has been. A team that winds up facing Randy Johnson and Greg Maddux four times each over the course of the season will be at a disadvantage compared to a team that only has to face those pitchers once or twice. Bad bounces may very well even out in the long run, but "the long run" is substantially longer than one baseball season. These small variations can easily cause a swing of several games, and mean a stronger team could find itself left out of the playoffs even with the wild-card format.

Over the past six years a series of changes to the schedule, culminating with the shift to the unbalanced schedule in 2001, increase the potential disconnect between a team's quality and its record. The Cardinals won the wild card by a relatively slim three-game margin over the Giants. They played 51 games against the Brewers, Pirates, and Reds, three of the worst teams in the league. The Giants played those teams just 21 times, and had only one relative patsy in their division, the Rockies. While the issue of luck makes it impossible to say for sure in any one individual case, it is certainly within the realm of possibility that the team which was the original poster child for including a wild card got left out in the cold again, this time thanks to the schedule.

The Ever-Changing Schedule

With this in mind, it makes sense to see how much effect the schedule can have on whether the strongest teams make the playoffs. To be fair, teams competing for the same playoff berths should face the same opponents the same number of times. Up until 1993, this was the case, with every team having the same number of games against teams in their own division and against teams in other divisions. Since then, the game has slowly backed away from this principle until completely abandoning it last year. With the switch to three divisions and the wild card in 1995, a tiny amount of imbalance crept in simply because the math did not work with a 162-game season. However, the effects were minimal, the difference between playing 12 games or 13 games against a given opponent. In the five seasons between 1997 and 2001, baseball used four different schedules and the imbalances got worse with each change in schedule.

1997 saw the introduction of interleague play, so teams in different divisions faced different opponents, yet still competed for the same wild-card spot. The 1998 expansion that added two NL teams made scheduling interleague play substantially more difficult and led to oddities such as teams in the same division playing different numbers of interleague games. An extra series of interleague games was added in 2000, increasing the variation of schedules for teams within a single division. Finally, the unbalanced schedule was introduced in 2001. It served its purpose in the sense of allowing for more dramatic tension towards the end of the season, with both the NL East and NL Central featuring late-season head-to-head matchups between the teams competing for the division title. While this is certainly good for raising the level of attention paid to baseball in the regular season, it also provides a loophole for weaker teams to make the playoffs. The wild card was supposed to help the good team that by bad luck just happened to fall into a strong division. With the unbalanced schedule, that team now faces a much tougher road than their competition in weaker divisions.

Designing a Simulation

It is impossible to use the few seasons' worth of results we have to determine whether the choice of schedule affects which teams make the playoffs. With only one or two seasons under each schedule, there is nothing resembling a large-enough sample to reach conclusions. Instead, we devised a simulation to study the question.

For each simulated season, the first step was to generate a strength quantity for each team. These numbers were based on existing data for runs scored by a team in a season, and roughly follow a normal distribution with a mean of 709.2 and a standard deviation of 90.6. The team strengths were chosen to have the same distribution. These team strengths are then used to generate a table of probabilities listing the odds of each team beating any other team. This is done by using a variant on Bill James's Pythagorean formula, with the probability of team A beating team B while playing at home given by

$$\frac{(\text{Strength A})^2}{(\text{Strength A})^2 + (\text{Strength B})^2} + .03$$

The .03 at the end comes from the fact that the home team has won about 53% of all games over the past few years.

Once this table of probabilities was generated, a "season" was played by generating uniformly distributed random numbers between 0 and 1. If the number was less than the probability of team A beating team B, then team A was credited with a win and team B with a loss. If the number was higher than the probability, the win went to team B instead. Once a complete season was played, the records of each team were recorded along with a ranking of their strength within the league.

Simulating the season this way preserves some of the luck that occurs during the course of a season, providing insight into what might happen, but at the same time potentially obscuring the scheduling effects. Therefore, expected values were also computed for each team's record. The expected number of wins for a team is the number of wins it would get if all probabilities held exactly true, i.e., if the probability of beating another team is .6, then the team is assumed to win exactly 60% of the games against the other team. Under a perfectly balanced schedule, using expected values for the record would guarantee that the strongest team always won its division and that if the second strongest team was in the same division it would get the wild card. We can interpret the results from the expected values to tell us who the favorites are in a given season.

Testing the Schedules

Using this process, 1,000 seasons were simulated for several different schedules and playoff formats. For each season new team strengths (and therefore probabilities of winning games) were computed. As a baseline case the essentially balanced schedule of 1995-96 was used and the results are pretty much as expected. First consider the outcomes of the simulated seasons in Table 1.

Table 1.

Team Strength Rank	1	2	3	4	5	6	7	8	9	10	11	12	13	14
Playoff Appearances	1771	1524	1248	940	776	573	398	317	198	133	67	33	15	7

We can see there was considerable variation among the strength of the teams that made it to the playoffs, but primarily the stronger teams made them. The top-ranked team in each league advanced 1,771 out of 2,000 possible times. That may seem somewhat low, but essentially it means that once every five seasons the strongest team ran into bad luck and finished off the pace. Also startling is the few times that the worst-ranked team somehow made it into the playoffs, but keep in mind that this represents seven times over 1,000 seasons, roughly equivalent to once every 140 seasons and usually occurs because the team happened to fall into an extremely weak division and had a run of luck. Given some of the weak teams that have snuck into the playoffs over the past 30 years in similar circumstances (such as the 1973 Mets, the 1987 Twins, or whichever team would have won the 1994 AL West) it seems less ridiculous that the weakest team in a league might just get lucky and sneak in.

Now consider the results in Table 2 using the expected values for the 1995-96 schedule.

Table 2.

Team Strength Rank	1	2	3	4	5	6	7	8	9	10	11
Playoff Appearances	2000	1996	1853	1181	452	267	140	65	35	10	1

Even using the expected values we see that we aren't absolutely guaranteed of having the best two teams making the playoffs: there's a miss once every 250 seasons. These are all due to the very small variations from a completely balanced schedule that were present. If the three strongest teams were all in one division and if the second and third strongest were of very similar strength, those one-game differences in the schedule could make the difference in determining who went to the playoffs. At the other end, the teams in the lowest half of either league only made the playoffs about once every 10 seasons, due entirely to the distribution of teams among the divisions. The 11th-ranked team only snuck in because in one season the four worst teams in the league comprised one of the West divisions.

One additional, and not at all surprising, result was found. The teams in five-team divisions made the playoffs less often than teams in four-team divisions. Using the simulated seasons, the teams in the five-team divisions made the playoffs an average of 276 times while the teams in the four-team divisions made it an average of 310 times. This pattern repeated itself for every schedule format tested; the larger the division, the less often a team would make the playoffs. During the 2000 season there was talk of realigning the American League to a 4-6-4 format, but that was scrapped due to complaints from the teams who would have been in the six-team AL Central. Their concerns were very clearly valid.

Now let's consider the results in Table 3 we get by using the schedule of 2001, again playing 1,000 seasons.

Table 3.

Team Strength Rank	1	2	3	4	5	6	7	8	9	10	11	12	13	14	15	16
Playoff Appearances	1747	1492	1214	982	798	556	405	290	201	136	92	41	32	9	4	1

The differences between this and the 1995 schedule are not particularly large. The three strongest teams made it to the playoffs less often, by about 30 times each. On the other hand if we look at the average strength rank of the teams who made the playoffs, we find for the 1995-96 schedule it is 3.69, while for the current schedule it is 3.76. This is a drop, but hardly a huge one. The data in Table 4 for the expected values show a similar result.

Table 4.

Team Strength Rank	1	2	3	4	5	6	7	8	9	10	11	12
Playoff Appearances	2000	1969	1734	1149	556	288	148	100	39	14	2	1

While the top-ranked team still always made the playoffs, the next three strongest teams all had dropoffs in the number of times they would be expected to make the playoffs. Still the change in average playoff rank is not particularly severe, falling from 2.76 to 2.83.

Furthermore, since there are several factors which have changed between 1995 and 2001, it would be premature to blame this change solely on the unbalanced schedule. The effects of interleague play and the addition of two more teams cannot be discounted. To examine these, simulations using the 1997 and 1998 schedules will be useful.

Table 5 shows the results of 1,000 simulated seasons using the 1997 schedule.

Table 5.

Team Strength Rank	1	2	3	4	5	6	7	8	9	10	11	12	13	14
Playoff Appearances	1731	1524	1223	989	772	538	404	310	232	136	73	43	23	2

Table 6 shows the results using expected values from those seasons.

Table 6.

Team Strength Rank	1	2	3	4	5	6	7	8	9	10	11
Playoff Appearances	2000	1998	1821	1202	488	224	131	89	33	14	0

Table 7 shows the results of 1,000 simulated seasons using the 1998 schedule.

Table 7.

Team Strength Rank	1	2	3	4	5	6	7	8	9	10	11	12	13	14	15	16
Playoff Appearances	1762	1477	1224	966	719	597	428	313	189	151	80	53	18	16	5	2

Table 8 shows the results using expected values from those seasons.

Table 8.

Team Strength Rank	1	2	3	4	5	6	7	8	9	10	11	12
Playoff Appearances	2000	1995	1829	1179	471	264	150	61	37	10	3	1

We can summarize the results in Table 9, looking at the average strength of the playoff teams as well as how close we come to the desired goal of having the four strongest teams make the playoffs.

Table 9.

Schedule	Simulation Average Rank	Simulation % Top 4 Teams	Expected Value Average Rank	Expected Value % Top 4 Teams
1995	3.69	68.5%	2.76	87.9%
1997	3.74	68.3%	2.76	87.8%
1998	3.78	67.9%	2.77	87.5%
2001	3.76	67.9%	2.83	85.7%

In a world in which the four strongest teams made the playoffs, we would have an average rank of 2.5 and a percentage of 100%. Therefore while the unbalanced schedule of 2001 appears to have an impact on the results found using the expected values, this impact is dwarfed by two other factors.

First is the effect of dividing the league into divisions. If the teams were to play a perfectly balanced schedule with no interleague play, and if the four best records made the playoffs regardless of their division, then at least in terms of expected value we could be sure that the top four teams always made the playoffs. Even using the slightly unbalanced schedule of 1995, if the playoff teams were just the four teams with the best records, then the top four teams would be expected to make the playoffs more than 99% of the time, with the top three always making it, and the fifth-strongest team sometimes eking past the fourth-strongest in cases where the team strengths are so close to equal as to make the difference essentially meaningless. The 11% drop in how often the top four teams make the playoffs that is caused by the split into divisions is much larger than the 2% drop caused by the unbalanced schedule. Put another way, if Giants fans want to complain about their bad luck, their real bad luck was that in 2001, just like in 1993, they happened to be in the wrong division: in both years, their record would have been enough to win the NL East.

Even more than the division structure, however, it is basic variation—also known as "luck"—which plays the largest role in determining whether the best teams make the playoffs. We can see the influence of luck by comparing the results using expected values with those in which each game was simulated; the results using the 1998 and 2001 schedules are particularly illuminating.

Using the expected values, the unbalanced schedule caused the average rank of a playoff team to rise and the percentage of four strongest teams making the playoffs to drop. In our particular simulation of the seasons, the reverse happened. Indeed, the percentages of seasons in which the playoff teams were decided by a tie-breaking playoff game (built into the simulations) is far larger than the differences in percentages between the various schedules. If the unbalanced schedule does change things, the effects are so small as to be statistically insignificant.

A Better Mousetrap

Given what we've learned from these simulations, we can propose alternatives that address the few problems that have emerged. The most consistent problem we found was that teams in smaller divisions made the playoffs more often than teams in large divisions. Any optimal scenario should have the same number of teams in each division. With 30 teams, this would require an odd number of teams in each league, a cure much worse than the disease.

With that in mind, all of our proposed schedules are long-term plans predicated on two 16-team leagues. The popular notion that the game's expansions have diluted the game is false: there is more than enough high-caliber baseball talent available to support an additional two teams, and the expansion would solve an assortment of scheduling issues. We'll also concede that there is no going back to the days of only four playoff teams; for good or for ill, the extra round of playoffs generates revenue, so it is here to stay.

One possible scenario with 32 teams is to eliminate the wild card altogether and simply go with four divisions per league of four teams each. While four-team divisions are regarded with suspicion by many people (and rightly so, as we'll see) this structure does lend itself to a very nice schedule. If interleague play is dropped, then a team could play 18 games against the other teams in its division and nine games against each of the teams in the other divisions. From the perspective of making the scheduler's life easier, this format would be far and away the best option. Unfortunately, it does not do the job of making sure the best teams make the playoffs, as we can see in Table 10 from the results of our simulation.

Table 10.

Team Strength Rank	1	2	3	4	5	6	7	8	9	10	11	12	13	14	15	16
Playoff Appearances	1582	1302	1062	905	741	605	482	393	296	225	175	114	54	38	19	7

Without the wild card, the distribution of the strongest teams is a huge factor in who makes the playoffs. As a result, we see a lot more mediocre teams advancing. The average ranking of the playoff teams is a startling 4.34 and the percentage of playoff spots going to the four strongest teams is down to 60.6%. The figures in Table 11 computed using expected value do not speak well for this format, either.

Table 11.

Team Strength Rank	1	2	3	4	5	6	7	8	9	10	11	12	13
Playoff Appearances	2000	1600	1240	999	736	534	346	245	160	90	33	14	3

The average rank of playoff teams here is 3.39, with just 73% of playoff berths expected to go to teams in the top four. Indeed, under this format we could expect three playoff teams every decade from the weaker half of the league. Last year, I wrote an article for the *Baseball Prospectus* Web site (*http://www.baseballprospectus.com/news/20010108hildebrand.html*) describing how this schedule would be very easy to set up and how it made logistical sense. Several astute readers asked about what such a schedule would do to the quality of teams making the playoffs, questions that led to this article. It's now clear that the logistical advantages aside, this would be a disastrous move for baseball. (The more cynical readers can now start a pool as to how long it will be before this proposal is being seriously considered by ownership.)

A different approach would be to go back to two divisions in each league, now with eight teams in each, and including two wild card teams from each league. The two wild cards can be the second place team in each division, or the two non-division-winners with the best records. Both options will be considered. Without interleague play, the sanest unbalanced schedule would involve a team playing each team within their division 14 times and each team in the other division eight times. This is roughly the same proportion of intradivision games to interdivision games that worked so well for many years with a National League of two six-team divisions.

First, consider the case in which the playoff teams are simply the top two teams in each division. This plan does not fare too well (see Table 12).

Table 12.

Team Strength Rank	1	2	3	4	5	6	7	8	9	10	11	12	13	14	15	16
Playoff Appearances	1000	1400	1171	000	770	[illegible]	[illegible]	[illegible]	[illegible]	[illegible]	00	[illegible]	10	[illegible]	[illegible]	1

Just 65.8% of the playoff berths go to the four strongest teams, lower than in any of the schedules that have been tested so far. This is almost entirely due to the reduced number of times that the strongest team makes the playoffs. Since that team has nowhere to go but down, the key factor in whether they make the playoffs is the strength of their competitors. Under the three-division, one-wild card format, even if the strongest team was passed in its division, it would still be the most likely candidate for the wild card, so in both scenarios they would likely have two playoff spots in their division. However, with only two divisions, the odds of their division being loaded (for example, with three of the four strongest teams) rises considerably. Because the stronger teams need less luck to pass the strongest team, it is much more likely that two teams will do so. The results in Table 13 for the expected values point out a related problem.

Table 13.

Team Strength Rank	1	2	3	4	5	6	7	8	9	10
Playoff Appearances	2000	2000	1602	1134	656	383	145	61	13	6

Here, just 84.2% of the playoff spots go to the top four teams, again due to strong teams being concentrated in a single division; in this case, however, it's the third- and fourth-strongest teams which get bumped, because they're more likely to have too many strong teams in their own division. On the other hand the teams in the weaker half of the league are not the beneficiaries, with those teams expected to make the playoffs only once every 50 seasons, hardly a common occurrence.

Finally, we consider the two-division set-up in which both wild-card teams can come from the same division, and with this we finally have a reasonable candidate. The results of our simulations produce the following playoff teams in Table 14.

Table 14.

Team Strength Rank	1	2	3	4	5	6	7	8	9	10	11	12	13	14	15	16
Playoff Appearances	1767	1551	1248	967	771	517	400	302	179	135	73	49	25	12	4	0

The percentage of top four strongest teams in the playoffs and average rank of the playoff teams, 69.2% and 3.69, is comparable to or slightly better than the original 1995 balanced schedule, especially considering that there are two more teams in each league. However, the problem of different-sized divisions giving teams different chances of making the playoffs has been eliminated. If the playoff berths were evenly distributed among all teams, we would expect each team to make 250 postseason appearances. The simulations using that structure followed that very closely, with 27 of the 32 teams falling between 240 and 260 playoff berths. The spread between the largest number of appearances (276) and the smallest (233) is actually one less than the difference seen between the average of the five-team divisions and the four-team division using the 1995 schedule. The benefits of this format are also clear when examining the expected values in Table 15.

Table 15.

Team Strength Rank	1	2	3	4	5	6	7	8	9
Playoff Appearances	2000	2000	1970	1657	274	76	17	5	1

Here the average rank of the playoff teams is 2.57, very close to the optimal 2.5 value, while 95.3% of the playoff berths are expected to go to the four strongest teams. It takes a very peculiar set of circumstances for a team in the weaker half of the league to be a favorite for a playoff berth, which is clearly how it should be. Short of lumping everyone together in one division with a balanced schedule and taking the best records, this is likely the best possible outcome.

There are some problems with the current playoff structure in baseball. While the unbalanced schedule does not help matters, it is also not the biggest problem with the format, and it is not the worst possible option. It is the unbalanced divisions, not the unbalanced schedule, that poses the biggest problem, so if changes are to be made, that is clearly a reasonable place to start.

Acknowledgments

I'd like to thank John "Rowan" Littell of Earlham College and Will Quale for their help turning my algorithms into usable computer code for this project.

Top 40 Prospects

by Rany Jazayerli

Baseball runs in cycles. Pitchers dominate one era, hitters the next. Cookie-cutter stadiums are built by one generation, and torn down by the next as retro-ballparks go up in their place. Artificial turf is everywhere in the 1970s, and being ripped out like it was covered in anthrax 20 years later.

The same holds true for baseball talent. In the late 1980s, *Sports Illustrated* published an article lamenting the decline and fall of the catching position. Within five years, two of the ten greatest catchers of all time were firmly entrenched behind the plate, and the 1993 season was widely considered to be the best ever for catchers. Today, you hear front-office types whining about how there's no talent at third base, even as there is more talent at third base in the minors than at any other position.

Minor-league talent is also cyclical. One year, farm systems are bursting with fruit ripe for the plucking, and the next, the wells are dry. Last year, we lamented what a terrible season 2000 had been for minor-league prospects, and how nearly half of the preseason's top prospects had suffered precipitous declines. So naturally, the 2001 rookie crop was the best in a generation, in star quality if not in depth. Ichiro Suzuki was named the American League's Most Valuable Player, and he wasn't even the best rookie in baseball. Albert Pujols had perhaps the best rookie season in National League history.

Even the lesser lights produced historic performances. C.C. Sabathia, who had never pitched above Double-A before 2001, became the youngest left-hander to win 17 games in a season since Babe Ruth in 1915. Roy Oswalt became the first rookie (and the youngest pitcher) ever to throw 100 innings with a strikeout-to-walk ratio of six-to-one or higher. Jimmy Rollins led the National League in steals; he and Ichiro became the first pair of rookies ever to lead their respective leagues in stolen bases. Rollins also hit 14 home runs, and he didn't even have the best power/speed combination among rookie middle infielders. Alfonso Soriano hit 18 homers and stole 43 bases, becoming the first rookie middle infielder ever to hit more than 15 homers and steal more than 30 bases.

Adam Dunn may have a better future than all of them.

While this year's rookie crop will be hard-pressed to match its predecessor's performance, it matches up favorably in terms of talent. The 2002 group will get an immediate leg up if it can get any kind of production from this year's #1 prospect. Any production at all. A good week. A two-hit game. A well-struck foul ball.

See, in 2001, for the second year in a row, our #1 prospect failed to so much as suit up for a game. The *Baseball Prospectus* jinx is in danger of reaching *Sports Illustrated* levels, which is unwelcome news to the unfortunate young man doomed to follow the same path as Nick Johnson and Ryan Anderson before him.

It is, therefore, our unhappy duty to report that—unless Tom Hicks's check arrives before you read this—the *Baseball Prospectus* 2002 Prospect of the Year is . . . Hank Blalock.

1. Hank Blalock 3B Texas Rangers Age 21

	AVG	OBP	SLG	EqA	Defense
2000	.237	.296	.325	.215	3B: 0
2001	.289	.355	.463	.273	3B: +9

The Blalock story starts with minor-league guru John Sickels. Sickels, who is well known to most of you as the author of the *STATS Inc. Minor League Handbook*, is very conservative when it comes to evaluating prospects. This can be aggravating when you want a strong, opinionated statement about a particular player, but given the inherent unpredictability of young men, it's also a sign of wisdom. Plus, it means that when Sickels displays enthusiasm about a player, you take notice.

That was the case with his comments on Hank Blalock in the 2000 *Handbook*. Sickels wrote ". . . I could see Blalock developing into a George Brett-type hitter. Yes, I know what I'm saying . . . I have a great feeling about this one." That would be high praise for any prospect; for a player just drafted out of high school, who had spent the season in rookie ball, it was almost unprecedented.

It was also uncannily prescient. As a 19-year-old, Blalock hit .299 in a full-season league, with 31 steals and more walks than strikeouts. That was just a precursor to last season, in which he hit .380 in A ball, .327 in Double-A, smoked 60 extra-base hits, drew 65 walks, and played great defense at third base. The George Brett comparisons are almost inescapable. Like Brett, Blalock uses the whole field, hitting the ball into the gaps, in the corner, and over the fence. Brett hit for the cycle twice in his career; Blalock hit for the cycle *twice in three days* after he was promoted to Double-A, an accomplishment without equal in professional baseball. He then headed to the Arizona Fall League, where he led the circuit with 11 home runs and an AFL-record .715 slugging average.

Plus, isn't "Hank Blalock" a name that just drips baseball? Like the Victoria's Secret model named Laetitia, his name seems to call out his destiny.

2. Josh Beckett RHP Florida Marlins Age 22

	H/9	BB/9	K/9	ERA	PERA
2000	9.6	2.7	5.6	5.30	3.68
2001	7.7	3.0	8.7	3.70	2.57

Okay, so maybe he did deserve to be on our Top 40 list last year. You all should know the Josh Beckett Story by now. The first prep right-hander to be selected as high as #2 overall since the 1970s, Beckett was babied by the Marlins in 2000 as he worked his way through some tendinitis. Last year, the gloves came off: Beckett punched out 203 batters in 140 innings, allowing just 82 hits and 34 walks between A ball and Double-A. He was so intimidated by major-league hitters that he posted a 1.50 ERA in four September starts, allowing just 14 hits in 24 innings. His fastball and curveball both rank among the two or three best in the minor leagues, and his change-up has been impressive on those rare occasions that he actually uses it. He can thank Ryan Anderson for our decision to not call him the #1 prospect in the game, but he's the best pitching prospect baseball has seen in years—better than Anderson, better than Rick Ankiel, better than Kerry Wood. Even his age is a positive; Beckett turns 22 in May, which means he might be a little more ready to withstand the rigors of being a major-league ace. If he stays healthy, he's not just a Rookie of the Year candidate, but a legitimate Cy Young Award threat.

3. Sean Burroughs 3B San Diego Padres Age 21

	AVG	OBP	SLG	EqA	Defense
2000	.263	.339	.356	.237	3B: –9
2001	.299	.358	.420	.265	3B: +12

Burroughs has now ranked fourth, second, and third on our list the last three years, which certainly gives him a leg up on the highly coveted "BP Prospect of the Decade" honors. He did nothing to hurt his standing last year; despite missing a month of the season with minor knee surgery, he began to show the power that has long been expected of him, hitting nine homers (more than doubling his career total) and recording an isolated power of .145, while remaining among the youngest players at his classification. With Burroughs, Phil Nevin, Xavier Nady, Jake Gautreau, and Taggert Bozied, the Padres have the most potential depth at one position that I've ever seen. It doesn't really matter; Burroughs is going to be their starter for as long as he wants to be, and everyone else is just going to have to either learn another position, or learn another team's signs.

4. Nick Johnson 1B New York Yankees Age 23

	AVG	OBP	SLG	EqA	Defense
1999	.300	.452	.459	.314	1B: –3
2001	.253	.392	.446	.287	1B: –8

The bad news: Johnson's OBP dropped more than a hundred points where it stood before his hand injury. The good news: it was still .407. Johnson shook off the effects of a missed season about as well as could be expected. His power didn't slip at all; the decline in his performance can be blamed almost entirely on the 89-point drop in his batting average, a figure that can vary dramatically. Players with hand injuries usually don't return to 100% until the second season following the injury; with very little pressure on him at the bottom of the Yankees' lineup, Johnson could post the highest OBP by a rookie since Ted Williams clocked in at .436 in 1939.

5. Wilson Betemit SS/3B Atlanta Braves Age 20

	AVG	OBP	SLG	EqA	Defense
2000	.238	.283	.321	.204	SS: –43
2001	.267	.308	.390	.236	SS: –10

Betemit first made news when it was revealed that, like Adrian Beltre, he had been signed before his 16th birthday. The Braves were able to settle his lawsuit without losing his rights, which was most fortuitous for them. Playing all of 2001 as a teenager, Betemit got better throughout the season, hitting an impressive .355 in Double-A. Rafael Furcal's presence likely means that Betemit, a natural but raw shortstop, will move to third base. Betemit is not ready for the majors just yet, and while Furcal handled the same jump with surprising ease, the signing of Vinny Castilla means the Braves will give Betemit at least another year to consolidate his gains. Those who want to write the epitaph to the Braves' dynasty ought to remember that they control the rights to both Joneses, Betemit, Furcal, and Marcus Giles through at least the 2005 season.

6. Carlos Pena 1B Oakland Athletics Age 24

	AVG	OBP	SLG	EqA	Defense
2000	.254	.351	.427	.264	1B: –18
2001	.267	.373	.497	.290	1B: +5

Pena's raw numbers in 2001 were almost identical to his from the year before, which hides the improvement he made during the season. After hitting just .230 with nine homers through July 1, Pena hit .339 with 14 homers the rest of the way, then posted an 861 OPS with the Rangers in September. He gets high marks for his defense, his baseball instincts, and his work ethic. Pena is a little old for a top prospect, but he's clearly ready to step into a major-league lineup. Stealing

Pena from the Rangers is going to go down as one of Billy Beane's best moves yet.

7. Joe Borchard CF Chicago White Sox Age 23

	AVG	OBP	SLG	EqA	Defense
2000	.245	.321	.377	.237	RF: 0
2001	.266	.339	.435	.258	CF: –2

Signed for $5.3 million, a record bonus for a drafted player, Borchard showed that the athleticism he'd displayed as Stanford's quarterback could be translated into baseball skills. He showed excellent power in his first full season; some scouts say he has the most power potential of any player since Mark McGwire. His high strikeout total (158) worries some, but we actually see that as a positive: research done by Clay Davenport shows that high strikeout totals can be a *positive* sign for minor-league hitters, presumably because those hitters have an easily identiable flaw that they can correct. Borchard is only an adequate defender in center field, but with Carlos Lee and Magglio Ordonez manning the corners, the White Sox have no plans to move him. He's probably not going to burst on the scene this year; by 2003, he should be a perennial 30-homer threat.

8. Juan Cruz RHP Chicago Cubs Age 21

	H/9	BB/9	K/9	ERA	PERA
2000	9.5	6.0	6.5	5.81	6.94
2001	8.5	4.4	6.6	4.89	4.50

The slender Dominican continued to show the electric fastball that propelled him on to the prospect scene a year ago. His minor-league performance in 2001, while excellent, did not distinguish him from the non-Beckett crowd. What did was his reaction to being thrown into the Cubs' rotation late in the year; in eight starts, Cruz posted a 3.22 ERA while showing better control than he had in the minors. He has a good health record, he hasn't been abused, there's an opening for him in Chicago, and he has already shown he isn't intimidated by major-league hitters.

9. Marlon Byrd CF Philadelphia Phillies Age 24

	AVG	OBP	SLG	EqA	Defense
2000	.239	.290	.374	.226	LF: +3
2001	.279	.346	.465	.272	CF: +2

A year ago, we came under some scrutiny for handing our #9 spot to another up-the-middle Phillies prospect, Jimmy Rollins, who didn't make the top 30 in any other publication. Byrd hit .316, he has a solid grasp of the strike zone, and he was nearly a 30/30 man last year, missing by just two home runs. His most impressive tool, though, may be his work ethic. A freak injury in college cut off the circulation to one of his legs and required surgery to remove dead muscle tissue. Instead of ending his career, the injury spurred Byrd into becoming a fitness freak, and he now packs 225 pounds of muscle on a body that's generously listed as 6′0″. How quickly he emerges as a force in the Phillies' outfield depends on how soon the Phillies realize that Doug Glanville and his .285 OBP belong on the bench.

10. Mark Teixeira 3B Texas Rangers Age 22

No Professional Record

He's light on pro experience—he has none—but heavy on everything else. Teixeira was on his way to one of the most impressive collegiate careers ever when he tore up his ankle early in his junior season. It's a testimony to how well regarded he was that, despite missing half the season and showing decreased range afield in his return, Teixeira was still the first college hitter drafted in 2001. He's a switch-hitter with power and plate discipline from both sides of the plate, hitting "only" .419 last season after hitting .427/.549/.772 in 2000 and becoming just the second sophomore ever to win *Baseball America*'s Collegiate Player of the Year award. Before the injury he was considered an above-average third baseman, and eventually he'll do battle with Blalock for the right to man the hot corner in Arlington. With two infielders among the Top 10, and Alex Rodriguez manning shortstop into the next decade, the Rangers have a chance to put together one of the best infields of all time.

11. Dennis Tankersley RHP San Diego Padres Age 23

	H/9	BB/9	K/9	ERA	PERA
2000	9.5	4.5	5.8	5.94	6.31
2001	8.5	3.5	7.3	2.97	4.61

and

12. Jacob Peavy RHP San Diego Padres Age 21

	H/9	BB/9	K/9	ERA	PERA
2000	8.8	4.1	6.5	5.65	5.10
2001	8.5	3.7	7.5	4.17	4.82

Flip a coin, throw a dart, spin a bottle. If you want to decide which of these two is going to have the better future, you're as likely to pick correctly as we are. For now, The Tank is our pick, as much because the Red Sox dumped him for Ed Sprague as because his fastball suddenly moved into the Kevin Brown class after the trade. Tankersley was actually more impressive than Josh Beckett was in A ball (0.52 ERA, 29 hits in 52 innings), and continued to pitch extremely well in the high minors. Peavy's fastball doesn't have the movement of Tankersley's, but it may have more velocity, and he supplements it with a nice slider and change-up. Peavy struck out 44 batters in 28 innings after reaching Double-A, and is more than two years younger than Tankersley.

Trying to decide between the two is like trying to decide whether Mena Suvari or Rachel Weisz holds the Hollywood record for "most widely-spaced eyes": interesting, but ultimately pointless. They're both Padres' farmhands, and they're the two biggest reasons why the Padres have the most underrated farm system in baseball.

13. Austin Kearns OF Cincinnati Reds Age 22

	AVG	OBP	SLG	EqA	Defense
2000	.240	.325	.403	.245	RF: –10
2001	.238	.314	.371	.232	RF: –16

A year ago, he and Adam Dunn were joined at the hip, or at least in our rankings. While Dunn went on to swat 51 homers, Kearns tore a ligament in his hand early in the season and struggled all summer. He finally got healthy late in the year, lifting his overall EqA in Double-A closer to his 2000 performance, then got medieval on the AFL, hitting .371/.460/.578 in 33 games, which translates to a .301 EqA. Kearns is why the Reds have gotten rid of seemingly every outfielder not named Dunn or Ken Griffey (Michael Tucker, Ruben Rivera, Alex Ochoa, Dmitri Young). With two-thirds of a superstar outfield already in place, there is an incredibly high possibility—maybe as high as 50%—that the Reds' outfield, circa 2004, will rank as one of the greatest of all time.

14. Mark Prior RHP Chicago Cubs Age 21

No Professional Record

It's even harder to slot Prior than it was to rank Teixeira; not only has Prior yet to make his professional debut, he's a pitcher. He deserves to be here anyway, because he had the greatest season ever by a collegiate pitcher. Prior went 14-1, 1.50, with 91 hits allowed in 132 innings and a sublime 189-to-17 strikeout-to-walk ratio. He was so dominant, in fact, that despite throwing a number of complete games, he faced so few hitters that his pitch counts were reasonable for a college pitcher; he never threw more than 133 pitches, and exceeded 125 pitches just three times. It would be a mild upset if he wasn't in the Cubs' rotation by September, and if he wasn't on the All-Star team by 2004.

15. Brandon Phillips SS Montreal Expos Age 21

	AVG	OBP	SLG	EqA	Defense
2000	.192	.236	.287	.180	SS: –21
2001	.260	.315	.381	.241	SS: –7

Phillips is the kind of guy the Expos used to develop in droves: a young, multi-talented player at an up-the-middle position. He's a fine-fielding shortstop who has across-the-board tools: 31 doubles, 11 homers, 50 walks, and 30 steals adorn his .292 average. Best of all, he doesn't turn 21 until late June; he became the first Expo to reach Double-A before turning 20 since Ugueth Urbina did so in 1993. He hit .344 in the AFL and was named the #3 prospect in the league. Phillips is a good candidate to be Northern Virginia's first Rookie of the Year in 2003.

16. Adrian Gonzalez 1B Florida Marlins Age 20

	AVG	OBP	SLG	EqA	Defense
2000	.226	.314	.290	.213	N/A
2001	.241	.299	.356	.221	1B: +15

Widely derided as a signability pick after he was selected first overall in the 2000 draft, Gonzalez has proven that he deserved the top spot on merit. He's an extremely polished hitter for his age, and his defensive numbers match his reputation as an outstanding fielder. People have compared him to a cross between Mark Grace and Rafael Palmeiro, which is a hard hybrid to imagine. Given his line-drive swing, moderate power, and great defense, I think the most accurate and evocative comparison is to Keith Hernandez. He's the early favorite for 2004 Rookie of the Year honors.

17. Angel Berroa SS Kansas City Royals Age 22

	AVG	OBP	SLG	EqA	Defense
2000	.229	.261	.343	.201	SS: –41
2001	.265	.295	.406	.240	SS: –5

The Johnny Damon trade wasn't all bad for the Royals. While the primary target of Allard Baird's desire was about as useful as you'd expect a 36-year-old closer for a last place team to be, the secondary swap of players—Mark Ellis for Berroa—ranks as the best move of Baird's career. Berroa is a natural shortstop who went a long way towards converting his tools into skills last season. After making 54 errors in 2000, he made just 30 last season, and his power continued to develop, as he smoked 60 extra-base hits despite spending two months in one of the toughest hitters' parks in baseball. His plate discipline was abysmal to start the season, but the Royals made a concerted effort to teach him the strike zone, and Berroa drew half of his 26 walks in the final five weeks of the season. (He must understand the importance of getting on base, as he led organized baseball with 36 hit-by-pitches.) His impressive two-week audition in September is why Neifi Perez has suddenly worn out his welcome in K.C. Berroa has a chance to be the greatest shortstop in franchise history; he's already the greatest shortstop prospect the Royals have ever had.

18. Michael Cuddyer 3B/1B/OF Minnesota Twins Age 23

	AVG	OBP	SLG	EqA	Defense
2000	.238	.307	.351	.223	3B: –25
2001	.269	.340	.457	.265	3B: –6 1B: –21

It's become painfully obvious that Cuddyer's future is not at third base, but his leap forward with the bat last year has made his defensive inadequacies much more tolerable. After hitting just six home runs in 2000, Cuddyer hit 30 last season, and totaled 69 extra-base hits, more than any other player in our Top 40. His power explosion has the Twins thinking that he could plug their hole in right field; freed of the responsibility of playing a position that stretches his abilities, Cuddyer could break out with a big year.

19. Chris Snelling OF Seattle Mariners Age 20

	AVG	OBP	SLG	EqA	Defense
2000	.246	.310	.369	.228	CF: –17
2001	.277	.339	.389	.246	LF: –2

Snelling is constantly compared to Lenny Dykstra, as much for his size (5′9″) and gung-ho style of play as for his ability. This is one of those times where the comparison actually doesn't do justice to the prospect. Snelling is a five-tool talent of the highest order, winning the Cal League batting title, whacking 46 extra-base hits, and playing the hell out of the outfield, all while still in his teens. He does it with a flair and attitude you wouldn't expect from a native of the relatively virgin baseball territory of Australia. He's a good bet to surpass Dave Nilsson as the best position player ever from his home country. He ranks this low because he still has no experience in the high minors, but if there's one player on this list who gives off Albert Pujols-like "he could be special" vibes, it's Snelling.

20. Jack Cust "OF" Colorado Rockies Age 23

	AVG	OBP	SLG	EqA	Defense
2000	.227	.356	.383	.253	LF: –17
2001	.237	.371	.427	.272	RF: –22

How great a hitters' environment is Denver? Cust jumped seven spots on our list by virtue of being traded to the Rockies in January. If you've longed for the days when Greg Luzinski and Lonnie Smith put a thrill into the mundane act of catching a routine fly ball, then you're going to find Cust a treat. He is, unquestionably, the worst defensive player ever to appear in our Top 40, costing his teams an amazing 47 runs the last three years despite being hidden in left field. In fairness to Cust, he's a native of first base, forced to emigrate because of players like Erubiel Durazo and Mark Grace. He could play left field for the Rockies, or be traded to an American League team to play his natural position, DH. Either way, his future is a lot brighter than it was in December.

21. Nick Neugebauer RHP Milwaukee Brewers Age 21

	H/9	BB/9	K/9	ERA	PERA
2000	7.6	9.9	7.9	6.02	5.94
2001	7.9	4.8	8.2	4.55	4.52

On pure ability, Neugebauer deserves to rank about ten spots higher; he was clearly the second-best pitcher in the minors last season, better than the competition by nearly the same degree that Beckett was better than him. But Neugebauer's 2001 season was ended by surgery to repair a tear of his labrum and partial tear of his rotator cuff, and while the Brewers are saying he'll be ready for spring training, consider the source. This is the same organization that can't keep Jeff D'Amico healthy for consecutive weeks, and for that matter, it's the same organization that spawned Bud Selig and his Amazing Prophecies of Doom™. If he's healthy, Neugebauer is probably the closest thing to Nolan Ryan in baseball today. Just keep in mind that Nolan Ryan didn't become *Nolan Ryan* until he turned 25.

22. Juan Rivera OF New York Yankees Age 23

	AVG	OBP	SLG	EqA	Defense
2000	.233	.280	.361	.215	RF: –6
2001	.295	.333	.493	.266	RF: +1

A talented bad-ball hitter who broke through in a big way in 2001, Rivera is less likely to be starting in Yankee Stadium this year than he is to be packaged in the Yankees' next big mid-season trade that puts them over the top. WARNING: The following statement is not based on evidence. Looking at Juan's performance, I can't help but think of another Yankees' phenom named Rivera, known to his friends as "Ruben." You've been warned.

23. Carlos Hernandez LHP Houston Astros Age 22

	H/9	BB/9	K/9	ERA	PERA
2000	9.7	5.9	5.6	6.00	7.34
2001	8.5	5.1	7.5	4.29	5.49

The latest product of the Astros' amazing Venezuelan pipeline, Hernandez vaulted over a half-dozen other pitching prospects in the system, breezing through hitters in Double-A despite skipping a level, and finished the season with three tremendous starts (1.02 ERA) for the Astros. Like Roy Oswalt, Tim Redding, and just about every other pitcher in the Astros' system, the 5′10″ Hernandez is a tribute to the organization's willingness to accept short pitchers on their merits. Alas, Hernandez fell victim to the young starters' curse, injuring his rotator cuff—albeit while diving back into a base, not while pitching. He rehabbed vigorously over the offseason, and the Astros are confident that he will be ready for spring training without requiring surgery. Unlike the Brewers, the Astros have the credentials to back up their claim. If he's healthy, he could win 15 games this season. Of course, the same could be said for...

24. Ryan Anderson LHP Seattle Mariners Age 22

	H/9	BB/9	K/9	ERA	PERA
2000	7.3	4.4	10.0	4.56	4.13

... who still hasn't forgiven us for naming him our #1 prospect a year ago. Anderson missed the whole season following surgery to repair a torn labrum; while the labrum isn't generally considered part of the rotator cuff when discussed in baseball terms, it essentially represents the lining of the cuff, and an injury to it is nearly as serious. Fortunately, Anderson has matured tremendously since having a bad-boy reputation in his teens, and took his rehab seriously enough that a full recovery is certainly possible. He's unlikely to be at 100% this season, and the Mariners have the depth to keep him in Tacoma for as long as it takes for him to regain his form. By 2003, the Space Needle should finally be standing tall in Seattle.

25. Josh Phelps C Toronto Blue Jays Age 24

	AVG	OBP	SLG	EqA	Defense
2000	.228	.273	.426	.234	C: –30
2001	.251	.336	.431	.260	C: –24

Try as they might, the Blue Jays can't ignore Phelps as a prospect. His defense behind the plate is charitably described as "raw," but he has shown major-league power since 1999, and last year he learned to dominate the strike zone as well, adding 80 walks and 17 HBPs to his 31 homers and 36 doubles. Besides, Darrin Fletcher isn't exactly Jim Sundberg. The hiring of J.P. Ricciardi bodes well for Phelps's chances to be evaluated on his merits, not on how well he fits the prototype of a backstop. His long-term future as a catcher looks good, as fellow catching prospect Jayson Werth appears headed for a position change.

26. Orlando Hudson 2B Toronto Blue Jays Age 24

	AVG	OBP	SLG	EqA	Defense
2000	.229	.285	.315	.206	3B: +10
2001	.281	.351	.432	.266	2B: +21

Lately, the Blue Jays have become a factory for middle-infield prospects; having packaged Mike Young and Brent Abernathy to other teams, they quickly churned out Felipe Lopez and Cesar Izturis, both of whom were in the Jays' lineup by August. Orlando Hudson is right behind them, as he broke out in his first full year in Double-A, hitting over .300 from both sides of the plate while making the transition from third base to second base so effortlessly that his defensive numbers from last season are the most impressive of any Top 40 prospect. He then hit .423 in a brief AFL audition before heading off to represent Team USA in international competition. Hudson's stock has risen since Ricciardi took over as general manager: the trades of Izturis and Alex Gonzalez mean that Hudson needs only to beat out Homer Bush for the Jays' second-base job.

27. John Stephens RHP Baltimore Orioles Age 22

	H/9	BB/9	K/9	ERA	PERA
2000	9.1	1.8	5.3	4.48	4.11
2001	8.8	2.4	6.5	3.63	4.40

While nobody takes Stephens seriously, there is no more fascinating prospect on this list. His minor-league numbers look like those of Greg Maddux, but on the mound his stuff looks like Greg Gumbel's. He has had to prove himself at every level, and has succeeded: he led the minors with 217 strikeouts in low-A ball in 1999; he posted a 121-to-22 strikeout-to-walk ratio in high-A ball in 2000; and last year, making a treacherous climb for a finesse pitcher, he had the best performance of his career, going 11-4, 1.84 in Double-A, with 95 hits in 132 innings with 130 strikeouts and 21 walks. In nine starts in Triple-A, he posted a career-high 4.03 ERA, but still struck out 61 batters in 58 innings.

So why does he get no respect? His fastball, which was borderline average when he became a pro, fell into the upper 70s after he suffered a neck injury three years ago. Somehow, with good command and a great curveball, he learned to compensate, and his fastball has slowly crept back up into the low 80s, giving him all the advantage he needed to take on the high minors. While there have been left-handers who have survived with this kind of velocity—think John Tudor, late in his career—I cannot think of a single right-handed pitcher who was able to pitch well with this limited a fastball without resorting to a sidearm delivery. Stephens deserves the opportunity to be the first, and the Orioles' success with Josh Towers, a similar, if less extreme, pitcher, gives us hope that Stephens will get it.

28. Rafael Soriano RHP Seattle Mariners Age 22

	H/9	BB/9	K/9	ERA	PERA
2000	9.4	4.3	4.0	4.12	5.01
2001	9.0	4.6	6.4	3.78	5.54

Converted from the outfield to the mound just three years ago, Soriano has shot through the minors with a devastating fastball/slider combination. The all-around improvement in his performance from 2000 to 2001 is a testament to how quickly he has picked up the craft of pitching. His two-pitch repertoire, and the Mariners' incredible stable of starting pitchers, suggests that he could make his initial impact as a reliever. As converted position players go, he has a chance to be the most impressive success story since Trevor Hoffman.

29. Justin Morneau 1B Minnesota Twins Age 21

	AVG	OBP	SLG	EqA	Defense
2000	.130	.167	.217	.133	N/A
2001	.258	.312	.381	.238	1B: –6

The Twins already knew Morneau could hit—he batted .402 in his second go 'round in rookie ball—and so, concerned about his defense and propensity for injury behind the plate, they allowed him to shed the tools of ignorance and concentrate on what he does best. Morneau posted a 1017 OPS in the Midwest League and was quickly moved up the chain. He's no Doug Mientkiewicz with the glove; what's more important is that in about two years, they'll be saying that Mientkiewicz is no Justin Morneau with the bat.

30. Ty Howington LHP Cincinnati Reds Age 21

	H/9	BB/9	K/9	ERA	PERA
2000	9.7	6.0	4.2	7.66	6.58
2001	8.7	5.0	6.1	4.33	5.19

Bone spurs are supposed to slow a pitcher down, but nobody told Ty Howington, who came back from minor surgery in May (not to mention an inauspicious debut in 2000) to dominate three minor league levels, punctuating his season with seven solid starts in Double-A. His physique (a lanky 6′4″) and pedigree (a former first-round pick) augurs well, and the Reds' beleaguered rotation means he will be given every opportunity to advance as fast as his performance dictates. He's high-risk, although no more high-risk than any other young pitcher, as the two lefties ahead of him on this list can attest.

31. Morgan Ensberg 3B Houston Astros Age 26

	AVG	OBP	SLG	EqA	Defense
2000	.256	.353	.438	.262	3B: +8
2001	.291	.375	.531	.294	3B: +11

By far the oldest player on this list, Ensberg nevertheless is a worthy member of the Top 40, both because of his polish (his .294 EqA in 2001 is the highest of any player on the list) and opportunity: with Vinny Castilla departing Houston, the Astros have an immediate opening available for Ensberg, whose right-handed power plays perfectly in Bankrupt Energy Company Field. His performance last season was all the more remarkable given that he missed two months with a broken bone in his hand. If he wins the starting job in spring training, he's probably the #2 choice behind Beckett for the NL Rookie of the Year.

32. Corwin Malone LHP Chicago White Sox Age 21

	H/9	BB/9	K/9	ERA	PERA
2000	9.3	8.4	5.9	8.35	7.59
2001	8.8	5.0	5.4	3.53	5.09

No one on this list emerged from greater obscurity than Malone, who was a middle reliever with a 4.90 ERA in low-A ball the year before. In 2001, he learned to get his curveball over for strikes, and emerged as the best White Sox pitcher in a farm system ravaged by injuries. Malone still needs another season's worth of experience against hitters in the high minors, but those same injuries are likely to give him a shot with the big club sooner rather than later.

33. Alex Escobar CF Cleveland Indians Age 23

	AVG	OBP	SLG	EqA	Defense
2000	.246	.320	.401	.246	CF: 0
2001	.253	.311	.411	.245	CF: 0

Escobar was widely viewed as a big disappointment in 2001, as his strikeout-to-walk ratio deteriorated and he hit just .267 with 12 homers in Triple-A. However, Norfolk is a tough park for hitters, and his overall EqA was virtually identical to what it was in 2000. He also managed to stay healthy for the second consecutive year, a good sign for a player who until recently was as fragile as Mariah Carey's psyche. While the Andruw Jones comparisons are a little dated, the Ruben Rivera whispers are a little premature. Given the build-up that he'd been given in New York, being traded to the Indians—a team that has enough outfield depth to work him into the lineup slowly—is probably the best thing for him.

34. Kenny Baugh RHP Detroit Tigers Age 23

	H/9	BB/9	K/9	ERA	PERA
2001	9.0	3.2	5.9	5.50	5.01

The Tigers' #1 draft pick in 2001 will probably be the first member of his draft class to reach the majors, ahead of even Teixeira and Prior. Four years of college training allowed him to power his way through Double-A before he was shut down as a precaution, suffering from a tired arm. The abuse his arm took—he was the most-overworked collegiate pitcher in 2001 by a country mile—is the main reason to be conservative about his outlook. If he's healthy, he'll be in the Tigers' rotation by May. Comerica Park gives him a leg up on success.

35. Jason Lane LF Houston Astros Age 25

	AVG	OBP	SLG	EqA	Defense
2000	.237	.294	.374	.225	LF: –7
2001	.279	.352	.501	.280	LF: –2

Drafted out of collegiate powerhouse USC, Lane slipped to the sixth round because all he does is hit. As if that's such a bad thing . . . the Astros took flak for using the same philosophy to draft Lance Berkman in the first round, and look how that's turned out. Lane is a tremendous offensive force and an adequate left fielder. Moises Alou's departure gives Lane an excellent opportunity to win a job as Daryle Ward's platoon partner in left field. He loses points for being silly enough to bat right-handed despite throwing left-handed, particularly for a team that's already skewed more to the right than Bill O'Reilly.

36. Ken Harvey 1B Kansas City Royals Age 24

	AVG	OBP	SLG	EqA	Defense
2000	.284	.332	.391	.242	1B: –18
2001	.297	.334	.437	.261	1B: +4

See above. Harvey was a fifth-round pick out of Nebraska because he was a "one-tool" player, never mind that he used that one tool to lead the NCAA in batting average his junior season. His career average in the minors is .359, and he has never batted lower than .335 as a pro. It's true that his other skills are less developed; he's never hit more than 15 homers (although his career slugging average is .536), he walked just 31 times last year, and he's not exactly a paragon of grace around the bag. With the Royals, the last point may be the most important. With Chuck Knoblauch and Michael Tucker occupying space in Kansas City this year, Harvey will probably spend the year in Triple-A, where he will work on hitting for power and keeping the weight off his chronically-injured toe.

37. Bobby Hill 2B Chicago Cubs Age 24

	AVG	OBP	SLG	EqA	Defense
2000	.242	.351	.352	.252	N/A
2001	.273	.351	.347	.246	2B: -6

The pride of the Atlantic League finally signed with the Cubs and headed straight to Double-A, where he showcased the same skills that were on display for the Newark Bears. He's a true switch-hitter who gets on base (.396 OBP) and can run, making him as well suited for the leadoff role as the man who the Cubs want him to replace, Eric Young, used to be. He missed half the regular season with a slow-healing groin injury; returning to action in the AFL, he hit .345 with a .442 OBP, confirming the Cubs' suspicions that, despite occasionally shaky defense, he's almost ready for the majors.

38. Nate Cornejo RHP Detroit Tigers Age 22

	H/9	BB/9	K/9	ERA	PERA
2000	9.8	4.4	4.3	6.03	6.20
2001	9.7	4.0	5.0	4.64	6.04

He's seven months younger than Baugh and has already finished with the minor leagues, but ranks this low because he spent the last six weeks of 2001 looking like the proverbial deer in the headlights. It may take him the better part of a year to recover from his shelling at the hands of major-league hitters. Long-term, his sinking fastball and impeccable health record should make him a durable innings-eater at worst. At best, well, the words "Kevin Brown" come to mind, and we're not referring to the catcher.

39. Esteban German 2B Oakland Athletics Age 23

	AVG	OBP	SLG	EqA	Defense
2000	.225	.291	.299	.216	2B: -26
2001	.270	.351	.359	.255	2B: -7

Two years after he first made our prospect list, German has regrouped from a lost season and regained his old promise. The walks (81) and steals (48) are still there, and whereas he used to swing a toothpick, he has now upgraded to at least a twig. After hitting just nine homers in three pro seasons, German hit 10 last season, along with 28 doubles and three triples. He did spend most of the season in Midland, where pop-ups can usually be hauled in at the warning track if the wind is blowing in. After hitting .373 in his first exposure to Triple-A, he's finally reached the point where he can be taken seriously as a prospect, rather than a statistical oddity. The A's need a new leadoff hitter, and only Frankie Menechino is in his way, which should make for a fascinating battle between a Frank and a German. Thank you, and remember to tip your waitress on the way out.

40. (tie) Carl Crawford OF Tampa Bay Devil Rays Age 20

	AVG	OBP	SLG	EqA	Defense
2000	.238	.265	.313	.201	RF: -14
2001	.247	.285	.311	.205	CF: 0

and

Josh Hamilton OF Tampa Bay Devil Rays Age 21

	AVG	OBP	SLG	EqA	Defense
2000	.234	.266	.349	.206	CF: -12
2001	.165	.209	.239	.165	CF: -15

After some columnists stumped for Hamilton to make the Devil Rays out of spring training, he hit just .180 in Double-A before back problems finally ended his season. The #1 overall pick in 1999 still has a world of talent, but bad backs have a habit of turning chronic. Meanwhile, his teammate Carl Crawford survived his own jump to Double-A at age 19; he hit just .274 with little power, while striking out less (102 to 90) and walking more (32 to 36) than he did in 2000, despite skipping a level. He's still far from being a finished product, but he has a chance to make good on those Kenny Lofton comparisons one day. When Lofton was 20, he was still playing college basketball at the University of Arizona.

Honorable Mention

Brandon Claussen, LHP, New York Yankees: Claussen, selected by the Yankees in 1998 as a draft-and-follow, flashed a mid-90s fastball and a wicked cutter on the way to leading the minor leagues with 220 strikeouts, even more than Josh Beckett had. His workload (187 innings) is a cause for concern, however. The Yankees have no need for him—he's not making $10 million a year, after all—but chances are he'll be a quality left-hander for some other team soon.

Mario Encarnacion, OF, Colorado Rockies: Just when it looked like Encarnacion had finally played himself off the prospect charts, he won the lottery and became a Rockie. He's a fine prospect in his own right; it's just in Colorado he has a chance to hit 40 homers a year (30 at home) and become the next overrated superstar, the second coming of Dante Bichette, albeit with better defense, and hopefully a better haircut.

Jimmy Gobble, LHP, Kansas City Royals: Gobble is cut from the same cloth as Chris George, a left-handed high-schooler drafted in the supplemental first round who enhances an upper-80s fastball with a quality change-up. Gobble may actually have better stuff than George, thanks to an excellent curveball. He surrendered barely a baserunner an inning as a 19-year-old pitching in high-A ball.

Drew Henson, 3B, New York Yankees: As much as this Wolverine alumnus might want him to fail at baseball so that he can go back to throwing a pigskin on Saturdays, it doesn't appear that Henson will allow that to happen. His 2001 season was ruined by a broken hand and some appalling plate discipline, but he found both health and patience in the AFL, hitting .314/.407/.570 and being named the league's #2 prospect. He's about a year away from honoring the terms of the six-year contract the Yankees gave him, one that may still prove to be a worthwhile investment.

Omar Infante, SS, Detroit Tigers: Infante's combination of age, average, and defensive ability merits an Honorable Mention despite his having little semblance of power or plate discipline. His two weaknesses figured to catch up to him on his promotion to Double-A, and instead he had his best season. If the Tigers give him another year or two to allow his bat to catch up with the rest of his skills, he has a chance to be a lot more than just the next Deivi Cruz.

Adam Johnson, RHP, Minnesota Twins: He was selected #2 overall because he fit the Twins' budget, but his performance since being drafted has taken the "sign" out of signability. The Twins' surprising emergence forced them to accelerate his timetable, with the usual results. He should be ready to join the Twins' rotation by mid-season, although they may be tempted to have him break camp in the bullpen. Hey, you would be tempted too if your closer was LaTroy Hawkins.

Kelly Johnson, SS, Atlanta Braves: A left-handed-hitting shortstop who hit .289 with 23 homers, 71 walks, and 25 steals, Johnson is coming off the best season by any 18-year-old in professional baseball. While his offensive ability is undeniable, he's likely to eventually move to third base, if not further down the defensive spectrum.

Casey Kotchman, 1B, Anaheim Angels: Kotchman ranks among the most polished high-school draftees ever: his dad is a coach with the Angels, he played high school in one of the most competitive areas of the country, and after going 20-for-37 (.541) in an abbreviated pro debut, he looks like an incredible steal with the 13th overall pick. Kotchman is a very similar player to Adrian Gonzalez, with the potential to be even better.

Joe Mauer, C, Minnesota Twins: High-school catchers are supposed to be among the worst gambles you can make in the first round. Then again, high-school catchers aren't supposed to hit .400 in their pro debut, with nearly twice as many walks as strikeouts. Mauer's defensive skills easily project to major-league caliber; if he continues to show as much with the bat as he did last year, the Twins may actually look smart for picking the hometown boy over Prior and Teixeira.

Corky Miller, C, Cincinnati Reds: A late-blooming catcher who hit just .233 a year ago, Miller posted OBPs above .400 and slugging averages above .500 at both Double-A and Triple-A, and he has a shotgun for an arm, throwing out six of 14 would-be base-stealers in his brief time with the Reds. He really ought to go by "Plunky"; he's been hit by 112 pitches in a minor-league career of just 350 games. Miller is quite capable of beating out Jason LaRue and Kelly Stinnett in a fair fight for the starting job this year.

Mario Ramos, LHP, Texas Rangers: Until he was traded to the Rangers for Carlos Pena, Ramos was the next big thing to enter the A's rotation. He has neither the first-round halo of Mark Mulder and Barry Zito nor the amazing sinker of Tim Hudson. He does, however, have terrific command of three pitches and an intellectual approach to the job that allowed him to post a 3.07 ERA in the hurlers' hell that is Midland, and a 3.14 ERA in the hangar at Sacramento. Ex-scouting director turned Rangers Assistant GM Grady Fuson is a big believer, and stepping into the Rangers rotation will give him a ton of run support.

Jamal Strong, OF, Seattle Mariners: The Esteban German of the outfield, Strong has quintessential leadoff skills, stealing 82 bases in 94 attempts while running up a .436 OBP. He doesn't make the Top 40 because it's not that impressive to see a 22-year-old beat up on the low minors, and because he has next to no power. If he can continue to get on base twice a game in Double-A, maybe the Mariners will start to think about moving Ichiro into the #2 hole.

Brad Wilkerson, OF, Montreal Expos: He knows the strike zone, and—unlike Peter Bergeron—he hasn't let the Expos beat that knowledge out of him. Wilkerson is unlikely to become a superstar, but he's a professional hitter who should be an above-average left fielder for many years to come.

Jerome Williams, RHP, San Francisco Giants: Frequently overlooked as a prospect in his own organization, Williams is the same age as Boof Bonser, and nearly as polished as Kurt Ainsworth. Boasting an easy-riding fastball with tremendous movement, Williams was an above-average starter in the Texas League at age 19. Dusty Baker's preference for veterans means that Williams will probably spend the year in Triple-A; he's an excellent candidate to be among the best pitching prospects in baseball a year from now.

Carlos Zambrano, RHP, Chicago Cubs: On paper, Zambrano is just a hair behind teammate Juan Cruz among the best pitching prospects in baseball. It's not an exaggeration to say that there's more dispute over Zambrano's listed birthdate (6/1/81) than over the birthdate of any other prospect in the game. If he's really 23 or 24, or even older, his performance is not nearly so impressive. He has a very high upside, but pitching prospects are hard enough to evaluate without throwing another variable into the equation.

Parks and Park Factors

"ParkFac" is the park factor used to compile the ratings for the 2001 season. When possible, it is the average of the 2001, 2000, and 1999 single-season park factors.

Leagues:

AL = American League	FSL = Florida State League	NL = National League	SAL = South Atlantic League
App = Appalachian League	Int = International League	Nwn = Northwest League	Sou = Southern League
Car = Carolina League	JpC = Japan Central League	NYP = New York-Penn League	Tex = Texas League
Cal = California League	JpP = Japan Pacific League	PCL = Pacific Coast League	
Eas = Eastern League	Mid = Midwest League	Pio = Pioneer League	

Team	Leag.	Level	ParkFac
Akron	Eas	AA	972
Altoona	Eas	AA	944
Anaheim	AL	Major	1029
Arizona	NL	Major	1014
Arkansas	Tex	AA	961
Ashevlle	SAL	Low A	1168
Atlanta	NL	Major	982
Auburn	NYP	Short-season A	1023
Augusta	SAL	Low A	976
Bakrsfld	Cal	High A	992
Baltimor	AL	Major	963
Batavia	NYP	Short-season A	1036
Beloit	Mid	Low A	1014
Billings	Pio	Rookie	992
Binghmtn	Eas	AA	1115
Birmnghm	Sou	AA	942
Bluefield	App	Rookie	1099
Boise	Nwn	Short-season A	1050
Boston	AL	Major	1023
Bowie	Eas	AA	989
Brevard	FSL	High A	954
Bristol	App	Rookie	1031
BrlngtnNC	App	Rookie	947
Brooklyn	NYP	Short-season A	1048
Buffalo	Int	AAA	1017
Burlingt	Mid	Low A	1050
Calgary	PCL	AAA	1148
Carolina	Sou	AA	1005
Casper	Pio	Rookie	1065
CedarRpd	Mid	Low A	979
Charl-SC	SAL	Low A	1002
Charl-WV	SAL	Low A	982
Charlott	FSL	High A	1006
Charlott	Int	AAA	1038
Chattang	Sou	AA	993
ChiCubs	NL	Major	984
ChiSox	AL	Major	1026
Chiba	JpP	Japan	1009
Chunichi	JpC	Japan	932
Cincnnti	NL	Major	994
Clearwtr	FSL	High A	1063
Clevelnd	AL	Major	1026
Clinton	Mid	Low A	1024
ColSprin	PCL	AAA	1126
Colorado	NL	Major	1265
Columbia	SAL	Low A	1025
Columbus	Int	AAA	972
Columbus	SAL	Low A	1052
Danville	App	Rookie	973
Dayton	Mid	Low A	1015
Daytona	FSL	High A	1028
Delmarva	SAL	Low A	939
Detroit	AL	Major	990
Dunedin	FSL	High A	1050
Durham	Int	AAA	975
Edmonton	PCL	AAA	1019
El Paso	Tex	AA	1142
Elizbthn	App	Rookie	975
Erie	Eas	AA	1067
Eugene	Nwn	Short-season A	1004
Everett	Nwn	Short-season A	1083
Florida	NL	Major	954
Frederck	Car	High A	1000
Fresno	PCL	AAA	1065
Ft Myers	FSL	High A	943
Ft Wayne	Mid	Low A	980
Fukuoka	JpP	Japan	970
GreatFls	Pio	Rookie	972
Greensbr	SAL	Low A	1019
Greenvil	Sou	AA	1087
Hagerstn	SAL	Low A	1050
Hanshin	JpC	Japan	969
Harrisbg	Eas	AA	1071
Hickory	SAL	Low A	1026
High Des	Cal	High A	1175
Hiroshim	JpC	Japan	1039
Houston	NL	Major	1060
HudsnVal	NYP	Short-season A	1035
Huntsvil	Sou	AA	1014
IdahoFls	Pio	Rookie	974
Indianap	Int	AAA	1031
Iowa	PCL	AAA	953
Jacksnvl	Sou	AA	1010
Jamestwn	NYP	Short-season A	1038
JohnsnCy	App	Rookie	1064
Jupiter	FSL	High A	954
KaneCnty	Mid	Low A	999
Kannapls	SAL	Low A	1010
KansasCy	AL	Major	1058
Kingsprt	App	Rookie	999
Kinston	Car	High A	992
Lakeland	FSL	High A	1052
Lakewood	SAL	Low A	874
Lancastr	Cal	High A	1164
Lansing	Mid	Low A	1064
LasVegas	PCL	AAA	1056
Lexingtn	SAL	Low A	1014
Lk Elsin	Cal	High A	952
LosAngls	NL	Major	938
Louisvil	Int	AAA	1028
Lowell	NYP	Short-season A	953
Lynchbrg	Car	High A	1079
Macon	SAL	Low A	1015
MahngVal	NYP	Short-season A	1042
Martnsvl	App	Rookie	920

Team	Leag.	Level	ParkFac
Med Hat	Pio	Rookie	999
Memphis	PCL	AAA	918
Michigan	Mid	Low A	1055
Midland	Tex	AA	1097
Milwauke	NL	Major	1001
Minnesot	AL	Major	1057
Missoula	Pio	Rookie	977
Mobile	Sou	AA	1002
Modesto	Cal	High A	995
Montreal	NL	Major	1027
Mudville	Cal	High A	916
Myrtle B	Car	High A	901
NY Mets	NL	Major	945
NY Yanks	AL	Major	982
Nashvill	PCL	AAA	938
New Brit	Eas	AA	1000
New Havn	Eas	AA	976
New Jrsy	NYP	Short-season A	932
New Orln	PCL	AAA	890
Nippon	JpP	Japan	1071
Norfolk	Int	AAA	978
Norwich	Eas	AA	962
Oakland	AL	Major	976
Ogden	Pio	Rookie	1027
Oklahoma	PCL	AAA	947
Omaha	PCL	AAA	983
Oneonta	NYP	Short-season A	999
Orix	JpP	Japan	1023
Orlando	Sou	AA	968
Osaka	JpP	Japan	974
Ottawa	Int	AAA	997
Pawtuckt	Int	AAA	1009
Peoria	Mid	Low A	969
Philadel	NL	Major	1002
Pittsbrg	NL	Major	997
Pittsfld	NYP	Short-season A	942
Portland	Eas	AA	1026
Portland	PCL	AAA	916
Potomac	Car	High A	1061
Princetn	App	Rookie	1010
Provo	Pio	Rookie	948
Pulaski	App	Rookie	1025
Quad Cit	Mid	Low A	1009
R Cucmng	Cal	High A	967
Reading	Eas	AA	1008
Richmond	Int	AAA	1008
Rochestr	Int	AAA	994
Round Ro	Tex	AA	951
Sacramen	PCL	AAA	976
Salem OR	Nwn	Short-season A	1064
Salem VA	Car	High A	1013
SaltLake	PCL	AAA	1092
SanAnton	Tex	AA	917
San Bern	Cal	High A	959
San Dieg	NL	Major	934
San Fran	NL	Major	919
San Jose	Cal	High A	942
Sarasota	FSL	High A	1000
Savannah	SAL	Low A	940
Scran-WB	Int	AAA	971
Seattle	AL	Major	932
Seibu	JpP	Japan	1001
Shrevprt	Tex	AA	974
Spokane	Nwn	Short-season A	1004
St Louis	NL	Major	1000
St Lucie	FSL	High A	1005
StatenIs	NYP	Short-season A	1000
Sth Bend	Mid	Low A	998
Syracuse	Int	AAA	1054
Tacoma	PCL	AAA	905
TampaBay	AL	Major	1003
Tampa	FSL	High A	962
Tennesse	Sou	AA	1074
Texas	AL	Major	1033
Toledo	Int	AAA	1012
Toronto	AL	Major	1038
Trenton	Eas	AA	968
Tri-City	Nwn	Short-season A	892
Tucson	PCL	AAA	1062
Tulsa	Tex	AA	1011
Utica	NYP	Short-season A	1017
Vancouvr	Nwn	Short-season A	903
Vermont	NYP	Short-season A	1011
Vero Bch	FSL	High A	1060
Visalia	Cal	High A	986
W Michgn	Mid	Low A	923
WestTenn	Sou	AA	967
Wichita	Tex	AA	1000
Willmspt	NYP	Short-season A	991
WilmngNC	SAL	Low A	922
Wilmngtn	Car	High A	985
Wisconsn	Mid	Low A	979
WnstnSlm	Car	High A	1013
Yakima	Nwn	Short-season A	949
Yakult	JpC	Japan	1018
Yokohama	JpC	Japan	1037
Yomiuri	JpC	Japan	1017

Index

The following is an alphabetical index of the players in *Baseball Prospectus 2002.* Davenport Translations for players not listed here can be found at *http://www.baseballprospectus.com.*

Biographies

Jeff Bower works as an engineer in the microelectronics group for a Northwest OEM and is the president of NW SABR. He lives in Seattle with his family of four and a small menagerie. Rapidly becoming known as the Randy Smith of house remodeling, he has made little progress in his ten-year plan, but his wife allows him to remain with the organization.

Clay Davenport is a meteorologist living in Bowie, Md.

Jeff Hildebrand is in his final year as a visiting assistant professor of mathematics at Allegheny College in western Pennsylvania. After ten years of having the Brewers and the Pirates as local teams, he's hoping to move somewhere where he can watch major-league baseball again.

Gary Huckabay lives in Clayton, California with his wife, Kathy; dogs, Annie and Odin; and cat, Simmon. He received his Masters of Business Administration from the UC Davis Graduate School of Management, and can often be found creating sawdust in his workshop.

Chris Kahrl is one of the founders of *Baseball Prospectus.* He's slowly coming to terms with living in a sports backwater, hundreds of miles from a major-league team, now that he lives near Washington, D.C. Having long ago accepted the relentless logic of the Punnett Square, he's not placing any panic-stricken calls to the Hair Club for Men.

Rany Jazayerli is a dermatology resident at Henry Ford Hospital, and can almost see Comerica Park from the 16th-floor clinic window. He's thinking about starting a family with his wife of four years, Belsam, and hopes the kids all turn out left-handed like their mom.

Keith Law has been a member of *Baseball Prospectus* since 1996, and has written on fantasy baseball for ESPN.com. He holds a Master's of Science in Industrial Administration from Carnegie Mellon University. Since contributing to this year's edition of the book, he's moved on to work with the Toronto Blue Jays.

Mat Olkin is a writer and copy editor for *Baseball Weekly.* He contributes to the *STATS Inc. Major League Scouting Notebook* and the *Fantasy Baseball Index,* and pens his own annual book, the *Baseball Examiner.* His father is a Red Sox fan; Mat thus learned at an early age the hazards of rooting for the Red Sox, and decided to pull for the Brewers instead.

Joe Sheehan is the managing editor of *Baseball Prospectus,* and a founding member of the group. He lives in Rosemead, California with his wife, Sophia. After seven years, he finds he has nothing interesting to say about himself in his book bio, most likely the result of spending too much time watching baseball.

Greg Spira has been a member of the Society for American Baseball Research and an author of baseball articles on the Internet for more than a decade. He has contributed work to baseball books such as *Baseball: The Biographical Encyclopedia* and was a co-editor of the seventh edition of *Total Baseball.* He is a graduate of Harvard College and currently lives in Kingston, New York.

Dave Pease works for a wireless communications company in sunny San Diego, where his plan to retire at 30 isn't looking too promising. He enjoys mp3s, racquetball, and mocking IKEA furniture. He was devastated when the Bums fired Kevin Malone.

Michael Wolverton has been writing about baseball since age 7, when he wrote a fan letter to Tony Oliva. He is still waiting for a reply. He works as a research scientist in the San Francisco Bay Area, where he lives with his wife, Cindy, and sons Scott, 5, and Mark, 2.

Keith Woolner survived the Internet implosion in Silicon Valley, where he is still gainfully employed in the software industry. He holds undergraduate degrees in Mathematics, Computer Science, and Management from M.I.T., and a Master's degree in Decision Analysis from Stanford University. Keith has found a truly marvelous proof showing how the Red Sox can win the World Series, but this bio is too narrow to contain it.

Derek Zumsteg is a Seattle-area baseball fan, writer, drinker, and does IT project management work. Author and University of Washington professor emeritus Roger Sale once told Derek, "you are the worst example of your generation." Derek's first screenplay was optioned during the 2001 season, but he still needs an agent.